"This is the book I wish I'd had when I was teaching Greek to university and seminary students. It beckons the new generation into a kind of intellectual maturity: understanding not only the New Testament but also the world in which it was birthed. That's what we need if we, today, are to relate the Scriptures to our world. This book is a gift that will keep on giving."

—**N. T. Wright**, former Bishop of Durham; University of St. Andrews (emeritus); Wycliffe Hall, Oxford

"For many students, the Greek New Testament and the Septuagint are as far as they venture in Greek studies, but the world beyond the Greek Bible is big. Enter Max Botner's wonderful resource, *Beyond the Greek New Testament*. Botner introduces a wide array of texts, beginning with the Septuagint and the Apostolic Fathers and continuing with the OT Pseudepigrapha, Philo, Josephus, and classical historians, philosophers, poets, and playwrights. Botner introduces each corpus and guides students through the necessary grammar and vocabulary. He makes a compelling case that going beyond the Greek New Testament is one of the best ways to gain proficiency and the motivation to continue one's Greek journey well beyond seminary studies. As I read this book, I felt the excitement that I had when I first started reading Greek texts, when I sensed a vast new world opening up before me. I wish that this book had been available then! It will certainly be a valuable resource now."

—**Dana M. Harris**, Trinity Evangelical Divinity School

"Botner's premise is that reading beyond the Greek New Testament equips you to read it more skillfully. This book provides an incredible spread of texts to do just that, with readings from the Septuagint, the Apostolic Fathers, Jewish and Greek historians, and Greek poets. Even more, Botner demonstrates his own skill by providing masterful introductions, notes, and glosses. Anyone who picks up this book will have an exceptional resource for improving their Greek. It should be a standard textbook for any advanced Greek class."

—**Elizabeth E. Shively**, St. Mary's College, University of St. Andrews

"I love this textbook! This is a phenomenal way to introduce students both to more advanced Greek readings and to significant ancient texts that are outside the Greek New Testament. Serious students will come away with increased facility to read Greek and with a wealth of insight about the ancient world."

—**Joshua W. Jipp**, Trinity Evangelical Divinity School

"With *Beyond the Greek New Testament*, Max Botner fills an important niche in Greek studies. He eases the way into secular Greek for those previously exposed primarily to New Testament Greek. With helpful introductions, notes, and vocabulary for a wide range of texts, both prose and poetry, chosen carefully for their relevance to students of New Testament Greek, Botner skillfully opens up the broader Greek world for an audience that will surely profit from learning about the social and linguistic environment in which the New Testament was composed."

—**J. S. Rundin**, University of California, Davis

Beyond the
GREEK
New Testament

Beyond the
GREEK
New Testament

ADVANCED READINGS
for Students of Biblical Studies

Max Botner

Baker Academic
a division of Baker Publishing Group
Grand Rapids, Michigan

© 2023 by Max Botner

Published by Baker Academic
a division of Baker Publishing Group
Grand Rapids, Michigan
www.bakeracademic.com

All rights reserved. No part of this publication may be reproduced, stored in a retrieval system, or transmitted in any form or by any means—for example, electronic, photocopy, recording—without the prior written permission of the publisher. The only exception is brief quotations in printed reviews.

Library of Congress Cataloging-in-Publication Data
Names: Botner, Max, 1985– author.
Title: Beyond the Greek New Testament : advanced readings for students of biblical studies / Max Botner.
Description: Grand Rapids, Michigan : Baker Academic, a division of Baker Publishing Group, [2023] | Includes bibliographical references.
Identifiers: LCCN 2022033475 | ISBN 9781540965028 (paperback) | ISBN 9781540966063 (casebound) | ISBN 9781493437931 (ebook) | ISBN 9781493437948 (pdf)
Subjects: LCSH: Bible. New Testament. Greek—Study and teaching. | Bible. New Testament. Greek—Criticism, interpretation, etc. | Greek language, Biblical—Study and teaching.
Classification: LCC BS2325 .B67 2023 | DDC 225.4/8—dc23/eng/20220930
LC record available at https://lccn.loc.gov/2022033475

Unless indicated otherwise, all translations are the author's own.

Scripture quotations labeled NRSV are from the New Revised Standard Version of the Bible, copyright © 1989 National Council of the Churches of Christ in the United States of America. Used by permission. All rights reserved.

Baker Publishing Group publications use paper produced from sustainable forestry practices and post-consumer waste whenever possible.

23   24   25   26   27   28   29   7   6   5   4   3   2   1

In Memoriam of Rex Stem
doctori optimo, viro summae virtutis

Contents

Acknowledgments xiii

Abbreviations xv

Introduction 1

Part 1 Reading the Septuagint 11

1.1 LXX Deuteronomy 13
    1.1.1 The Song of Moses: Deuteronomy 31:30–32:43 14

1.2 LXX Isaiah 22
    1.2.1 The Poem of the Suffering Servant: Isaiah 52:13–53:12 23

1.3 2 Maccabees 27
    1.3.1 The Martyrdom of a Jewish Mother and Her Seven Sons: 2 Maccabees 7 28

1.4 4 Maccabees 35
    1.4.1 The Martyrdom of Eleazar: 4 Maccabees 6 36

Part 2 Reading the Apostolic Fathers 41

2.1 1 Clement 43
    2.1.1 Exemplars of Faithful Obedience: 1 Clement 9.1–12.8 44

2.2 Ignatius of Antioch 49
    2.2.1 Warnings about False Teachers: *To the Ephesians* 7–9 50

2.3 Polycarp of Smyrna 53
    2.3.1 The Trial of Polycarp: Martyrdom of Polycarp 9.1–11.2 54

2.4 The Epistle of Barnabas 57
    2.4.1 Lessons from the Day of Atonement: Epistle of Barnabas 7 58

2.5 The Epistle to Diognetus 62
    2.5.1 A Case for Christian Distinctiveness: Epistle to Diognetus 5 63

Part 3 Reading Old Testament Pseudepigrapha 67

3.1 The Letter of Aristeas 69
    3.1.1 The Rationale of Jewish Law: Letter of Aristeas 128–143, 170–171 70
    3.1.2 The Translation of the Law: Letter of Aristeas 301–316 76

3.2 Joseph and Aseneth 81
    3.2.1 Joseph Prays for Aseneth's Conversion: Joseph and Aseneth 8:5–9 (4–11) 82
    3.2.2 Aseneth Partakes of the Heavenly Food: Joseph and Aseneth 15:1–10 (1–11); 15:13–16:16 (15:14–16:9) 85

3.3 Sibylline Oracles 90
    3.3.1 A King from the Sun and the Final Assault on the Temple: Sibylline Oracles 3:652–668, 702–723 91

3.4 The Sentences of Pseudo-Phocylides 95
    3.4.1 Admonition to Mercy: Pseudo-Phocylides 22–41 96

3.5 Fragments of Hellenistic Jewish Writers 99
    3.5.1 Theodotus the Poet 100

3.5.1.1 Jacob and the Shechemites—Fragment 4: Eusebius, *Praeparatio evangelica* 9.22.4–6   101

3.5.1.2 On Circumcision—Fragment 5: Eusebius, *Praeparatio evangelica* 9.22.7   103

3.5.2 Ezekiel the Tragedian   104

3.5.2.1 Moses on the Heavenly Throne—Fragments 6 and 7: Eusebius, *Praeparatio evangelica* 9.29.5–6   105

3.5.3 Aristobulus the Philosopher   108

3.5.3.1 Moses as the Font of All Wisdom—Fragment 3: Eusebius, *Praeparatio evangelica* 13.12.1–2   109

3.5.4 Eupolemus the Historian   111

3.5.4.1 Moses as the First Sage—Fragment 1: Eusebius, *Praeparatio evangelica* 9.25.4–26.1   112

Part 4 Reading Philo   113

4.1 Allegorical Commentary   115

4.1.1 The Heavenly Human and the Earthly Human, Part 1: *Allegorical Interpretation* 1.31–32   116

4.1.2 The Heavenly Human and the Earthly Human, Part 2: *Allegorical Interpretation* 1.33–42   118

4.1.3 The Call of Abraham: *Allegorical Interpretation* 3.83–84   123

4.2 Exposition of the Law   125

4.2.1 Prologue—Moses the Lawgiver: *On the Creation of the World* 1–6   126

4.2.2 The Image of God, Part 1: *On the Creation of the World* 69–71   129

4.2.3 The Image of God, Part 2: *On the Creation of the World* 72–76   132

4.2.4 The First Humans in the Garden, Part 1: *On the Creation of the World* 151–152   135

4.2.5 The First Humans in the Garden, Part 2: *On the Creation of the World* 153–156   138

4.2.6 The Faith of Abraham: *On the Life of Abraham* 262, 268–269, 273–276   142

4.2.7 The Cosmic Temple and the Jerusalem Temple: *On the Special Laws* 1.66–70   145

4.2.8 The Sacrificial System: *On the Special Laws* 1.194–197   148

4.3 Historical and Apologetic Works   150

4.3.1 The Mockery of King Agrippa: *Against Flaccus* 36–43   151

4.3.2 In Praise of Caesar Augustus: *On the Embassy to Gaius* 143–150   155

Part 5 Reading Josephus   159

5.1 *Jewish War*   161

5.1.1 Prologue, Part 1: *Jewish War* 1.1–6   162

5.1.2 Prologue, Part 2: *Jewish War* 1.7–16   165

5.1.3 The Philosophical Schools of Judaism, Part 1: *Jewish War* 2.119–123, 137–142   169

5.1.4 The Philosophical Schools of Judaism, Part 2: *Jewish War* 2.150–166   174

5.1.5 Another Jesus Predicts the Destruction of the Temple: *Jewish War* 6.300–309   180

5.2 *Jewish Antiquities*   183

5.2.1 The Moral Lesson of *Jewish Antiquities*: *Jewish Antiquities* 1.14–17   184

5.2.2 The Binding of Isaac: *Jewish Antiquities* 1.222–224, 228–236   186

5.2.3 The Departure of Moses: *Jewish Antiquities* 4.323–331   191

5.2.4 The Conversion of King Izates: *Jewish Antiquities* 20.38–48   194

5.3 *The Life*   197

5.3.1 Ancestry and Education: *The Life* 1–12   198

5.4 *Against Apion*   202

5.4.1 Jewish Virtue: *Against Apion* 2.190–198   203

Part 6 Reading Historians and Biographers 207

6.1 Herodotus 209
- 6.1.1 The Purpose of the Inquiry: *Histories* 1.1 210
- 6.1.2 Cyrus Captures Babylon: *Histories* 1.189–191 211
- 6.1.3 On the Origins of Circumcision: *Histories* 2.104 215

6.2 Thucydides 217
- 6.2.1 Prologue: *History of the Peloponnesian War* 1.1–3 218
- 6.2.2 Method for Reporting Speeches: *History of the Peloponnesian War* 1.22.1–4 220

6.3 Diodorus Siculus 223
- 6.3.1 Lawgivers from Egypt: *Library of History* 1.94.1–2 224
- 6.3.2 Anti-Jewish Propaganda: *Library of History* 34.1.1–5 227

6.4 Dio Cassius 230
- 6.4.1 How Octavian Received the Honorific *Augustus*: *Roman History* 53.16.4–8 231

6.5 Plutarch 234
- 6.5.1 The Biographer's Aim: *Alexander* 1.1–2.4 235
- 6.5.2 Alexander and the Prophet of Ammon: *Alexander* 27.3–6 239

6.6 Lucian 241
- 6.6.1 The Purpose of Biography: *Demonax* 2 242
- 6.6.2 The Lifestyle of Demonax: *Demonax* 5–7 243
- 6.6.3 Sayings of Demonax: *Demonax* 25, 40, 50 246

6.7 Philostratus 248
- 6.7.1 The Birth of Apollonius: *Life of Apollonius* 1.4–5 249
- 6.7.2 Apollonius the Exorcist: *Life of Apollonius* 4.20.1–3 252
- 6.7.3 Apollonius Raises the Dead: *Life of Apollonius* 4.45.1–2 255

Part 7 Reading Philosophers and Rhetoricians 257

7.1 Plato 259
- 7.1.1 Socrates's Prologue to His Defense: *Apology of Socrates* 17a–18a 260
- 7.1.2 Socrates's Resolution in the Face of Death: *Apology of Socrates* 29b–30c 263
- 7.1.3 The Act of Creation: *Timaeus* 29d–30c 266
- 7.1.4 Human Law as the Second-Best Option: *Laws* 874e–875d 269

7.2 Aristotle 272
- 7.2.1 On the Telos of the Human Function: *Nicomachean Ethics* 1097a26–1098a20 273
- 7.2.2 On Household Management: *Politics* 1253b1–32, 1254a9–24, 1254b3–24, 1260a8–33 278
- 7.2.3 On the Three Forms of Rhetoric: *Rhetoric* 1358a36–1358b32 284

7.3 Epictetus 287
- 7.3.1 How May Each Several Thing Be Done Acceptably to the Gods? *Discourses* 1.13.1–5 288
- 7.3.2 On Preconceptions: *Discourses* 1.22.1–4 290
- 7.3.3 That Although We Are Unable to Fulfill the Profession of a Human, We Adopt That of a Philosopher: *Discourses* 2.9.13–22 292
- 7.3.4 How Ought We Adjust Our Preconceptions to Individual Instances? *Discourses* 2.17.14–22 296
- 7.3.5 What Is the Distinctive Characteristic of Error? *Discourses* 2.26.1–5 298

7.4 Dio Chrysostom 300
- 7.4.1 On the Need for Repetition: *On Covetousness* 1–6 301
- 7.4.2 On Concord: *A Political Address in the Assembly* 14–16 305

7.5 Plutarch 308
- 7.5.1 On Balancing Rhetoric: *How to Tell a Flatterer from a Friend* 37 (*Mor.* 74d–e) 309

- 7.5.2 Advice to Bride and Groom: *Advice to Bride and Groom* 33–34 (*Mor.* 142e–f)   311
- 7.5.3 Attacking Barbarian Superstition: *On Superstition* 3, 8 (*Mor.* 165d–166a, 169c)   313

7.6 Diogenes Laertius   317
- 7.6.1 The Lifestyle of the Cynic: *Lives of Eminent Philosophers* 6.37–38   318
- 7.6.2 Stoic Theology: *Lives of Eminent Philosophers* 7.148–149   320
- 7.6.3 Stoic Cosmology: *Lives of Eminent Philosophers* 7.156   322
- 7.6.4 An Epicurean Perspective on Death: *Lives of Eminent Philosophers* 10.124–127   324

Part 8 Reading Poets and Playwrights   327

8.1 Homer   329
- 8.1.1 The Wrath of Achilles: *Iliad* 1.1–21   330
- 8.1.2 Achilles Slays Hector: *Iliad* 22.289–336   333

8.2 Hesiod   338
- 8.2.1 An Etiology of Sacrifice: *Theogony* 535–560   339
- 8.2.2 An Etiology of Woman: *Theogony* 561–616   342

8.3 Sophocles   347
- 8.3.1 Oedipus and Teiresias: *Oedipus the King* 300–315, 447–462   348
- 8.3.2 Antigone Defies Creon: *Antigone* 450–470   351

8.4 Euripides   353
- 8.4.1 Pentheus Interrogates Dionysus: *Bacchae* 434–518   354
- 8.4.2 The Sacrifice of Iphigenia: *Iphigeneia at Aulis* 1540–1562   360

Works Cited   363

Acknowledgments

The idea for the book began with a conversation that I had with my colleague Tim Gombis in the fall of 2020. Tim knew that I was set to launch an advanced Greek course in the spring of 2021 and was curious about which textbook I planned to use. I had to confess that I was somewhat at a loss. While there are seemingly endless resources available to Greek teachers and students, none achieve (or claim to achieve) what I was attempting to do with this course: to prepare students who had learned Greek through a New Testament Greek textbook to read *beyond* the New Testament—not only the Septuagint and Apostolic Fathers but also Philo, Josephus, historians, philosophers, and so forth. After listening to my ramblings for the better part of an hour (gracious human that he is), Tim encouraged me to create the book that I wished existed. Were it not for his encouragement, I would never have attempted such an endeavor.

I was extremely fortunate to have a talented group of students on which to test my material: Daryl Andresen, Jennifer McCormick-Bridgewater, Sean Miller, Ian Newberry, Ryan Olexa, Jennifer Reil, Kyle Rouse, and J. C. Schroeder. These students were kind enough not only to provide feedback on my notes and commentary but also to suggest additional features that they would like to see in the book. To the extent that this reader proves useful, this group deserves much of the credit.

Thanks are also due to my meticulous research assistant, Lydia Bindon, and to the incredible team at Baker Academic. I am especially grateful to Bryan Dyer for giving me the freedom to create the Greek reader that I wish had existed when I was a student.

Preparing this book was an opportunity to remember those who imparted to me a love of ancient languages. Here I would like to express my deepest gratitude to the professors of the Classics department at U. C. Davis, two of whom deserve special mention: John Rundin and the late Rex Stem. Both were artists in the classroom and remain the prime exemplars that I bring with me whenever I teach Greek and Latin. I have many fond memories of Rex; from his ability to memorize every student's name on the first day of class to his unchecked excitement at our first encounter with the double dative construction—his love of Latin was simply infectious. Above all, I will remember a man who was the consummate champion of his students, who continued to believe in me even when I could no longer believe in myself.

Finally, I wish to express my immeasurable gratitude to my partner, Jessica, and to our four children, Ava, Noah, Olivia, and Owen. They continue to remind me of what matters most in life. If ever there were a danger that I might take myself too seriously, these wonderful humans have put an end to it.

Abbreviations

General and Grammatical

§(§)	section(s)
abl.	ablative
absol.	absolute
acc.	accusative
act.	active
adv.	adverb, adverbial
alt.	altered, alternative
aor.	aorist
apud	in the works of, according to
art.	article, articular
Att.	Attic
attrib.	attributive
aug.	augment
BCE	before the Common Era
ca.	*circa*, about, approximately
CE	of the Common Era
cf.	*confer*, compare
chap(s).	chapter(s)
circ.	circumstantial
comp.	complement, complementary
compar.	comparative/comparison
constr.	construction
dat.	dative
decl.	declension
demon.	demonstrative
disc.	discourse
distrib.	distributive
e.g.	*exempli gratia*, for example
epex.	epexegetical
esp.	especially
etc.	*et cetera*, and the rest
euph.	euphemism
extens.	extension
fam.	family
fem.	feminine
fig.	figurative
frag.	fragment
fut.	future
gen.	genitive
Gk.	Greek
Hb.	Hebrew
i.e.	*id est*, that is
impers.	impersonal
impf.	imperfect
impv.	imperative
indecl.	indeclinable
indic.	indicative
indir.	indirect
inf.	infinitive
intrans.	intransitive
Ion.	Ionic
irreg.	irregular
Lat.	Latin
lit.	literally
l(l).	line(s)
LXX	Septuagint
masc.	masculine
metaph.	metaphorical
mid.	middle
MS(S)	manuscript(s)
MT	Masoretic Text
NB	*nota bene*, take careful note
neg.	negative
neut.	neuter
n(n).	note(s)
no.	number
nom.	nominative
obj.	object, objective
OG	Old Greek

opt.	optative	Song	Song of Songs
par(r).	parallel(s)	Isa.	Isaiah
partic.	particle	Jer.	Jeremiah
pass.	passive	Lam.	Lamentations
pers.	person	Ezek.	Ezekiel
pf.	perfect	Dan.	Daniel
pl.	plural	Hosea	Hosea
plpf.	pluperfect	Joel	Joel
pred.	predicate	Amos	Amos
prep.	preposition, prepositional	Obad.	Obadiah
pres.	present	Jon.	Jonah
pron.	pronoun	Mic.	Micah
ptc.	participle	Nah.	Nahum
quest(s).	questions	Hab.	Habakkuk
rel.	relative	Zeph.	Zephaniah
sg.	singular	Hag.	Haggai
subj.	subjunctive	Zech.	Zechariah
subst.	substantival	Mal.	Malachi
superl.	superlative		
supp.	supplement, supplementary		
temp.	temporal		
trans.	translation, translated by		
voc.	vocative		
v(v).	verse(s)		

Old Testament

Gen.	Genesis		
Exod.	Exodus		
Lev.	Leviticus		
Num.	Numbers		
Deut.	Deuteronomy		
Josh.	Joshua		
Judg.	Judges		
Ruth	Ruth		
1 Sam.	1 Samuel		
2 Sam.	2 Samuel		
1 Kings	1 Kings		
2 Kings	2 Kings		
1 Chron.	1 Chronicles		
2 Chron.	2 Chronicles		
Ezra	Ezra		
Neh.	Nehemiah		
Esther	Esther		
Job	Job		
Ps(s).	Psalm(s)		
Prov.	Proverbs		
Eccles.	Ecclesiastes		

New Testament

Matt.	Matthew
Mark	Mark
Luke	Luke
John	John
Acts	Acts
Rom.	Romans
1 Cor.	1 Corinthians
2 Cor.	2 Corinthians
Gal.	Galatians
Eph.	Ephesians
Phil.	Philippians
Col.	Colossians
1 Thess.	1 Thessalonians
2 Thess.	2 Thessalonians
1 Tim.	1 Timothy
2 Tim.	2 Timothy
Titus	Titus
Philem.	Philemon
Heb.	Hebrews
James	James
1 Pet.	1 Peter
2 Pet.	2 Peter
1 John	1 John
2 John	2 John
3 John	3 John
Jude	Jude
Rev.	Revelation

Old Testament Apocrypha

Bar.	Baruch
Jdt.	Judith
1–4 Macc.	1–4 Maccabees
Sir.	Sirach (Ecclesiasticus)
Tob.	Tobit
Wis.	Wisdom (of Solomon)

Old Testament Pseudepigrapha

2 Bar.	2 Baruch (Syriac Apocalypse)
1 En.	1 Enoch (Ethiopic Apocalypse)
3 En.	3 Enoch (Hebrew Apocalypse)
Ezek. Trag.	Ezekiel the Tragedian
4 Ezra	4 Ezra
Jos. Asen.	Joseph and Aseneth
Jub.	Jubilees
LAB	Liber antiquitatum biblicarum (Pseudo-Philo)
Let. Aris.	Letter of Aristeas
Ps.-Eup.	Pseudo-Eupolemus
Ps.-Phoc.	Pseudo-Phocylides
Pss. Sol.	Psalms of Solomon
Sib. Or.	Sibylline Oracles
T. Ab.	Testament of Abraham
T. Benj.	Testament of Benjamin
T. Dan	Testament of Dan
T. Jud.	Testament of Judah
T. Levi	Testament of Levi
T. Mos.	Testament of Moses

Qumran / Dead Sea Scrolls

1QIsa^a	Isaiah^a
1QM	War Scroll (Milḥamah)
1QS	Rule of the Community (Serek Hayaḥad)
1Q8 (1QIsa^b)	Isaiah^b
1Q28a (1QSa)	Rule of the Congregation (appendix a to 1QS)
4Q37 (4QDeut^j)	Deuteronomy^j
4Q44 (4QDeut^q)	Deuteronomy^q
4Q58 (4QIsa^d)	Isaiah^d
4Q141 (4QPhyl N)	Phylacteries N
4Q174 (4QFlor)	Florilegium, also Midrash on Eschatology^a (MidrEschat^a)
4Q226 (4QpsJub^b)	Pseudo-Jubilees^b
4Q246 (4QapocrDan ar)	Apocryphon of Daniel
4Q320 (4QCalDoc A)	Calendrical Document A
4Q321 (4QCalDoc B)	Calendrical Document B
4Q372 (4QapocrJoseph^b)	Aprocryphon of Joseph^b
4Q521 (4QMessAp)	Messianic Apocalypse
11Q19 (11QT)	Temple Scroll
CD	Damascus Document^a

Philo

Abr.	*De Abrahamo* (*On the Life of Abraham*)
Aet.	*De aeternitate mundi* (*On the Eternity of the World*)
Cher.	*De cherubim*
Conf.	*De confusione linguarum*
Contempl.	*De vita contemplativa* (*On the Contemplative Life*)
Decal.	*De decalogo* (*On the Decalogue*)
Det.	*Quod deterius potiori insidari soleat*
Ebr.	*De ebrietate*
Flacc.	*In Flaccum* (*Against Flaccus*)
Fug.	*De fuga et inventione*
Gig.	*De gigantibus*
Her.	*Quis rerum divinarum heres sit*
Hypoth.	*Hypothetica*
Ios.	*De Iosepho* (*On the Life of Joseph*)
Leg.	*Legum allegoriae* (*Allegorical Interpretation*)
Legat.	*Legatio ad Gaium* (*On the Embassy to Gaius*)
Migr.	*De migratione Abrahami* (*On the Migration of Abraham*)
Mos.	*De vita Mosis* (*On the Life of Moses*)
Mut.	*De mutatione nominum*
Opif.	*De opificio mundi* (*On the Creation of the World*)
Plant.	*De plantatione*
Praem.	*De praemiis et poenis* (*On Rewards and Punishments*)
Prob.	*Quod omnis probus liber sit* (*That Every Good Person Is Free*)
QG	*Quaestiones et solutiones in Genesin* (*Questions and Answers on Genesis*)
Sacr.	*De sacrificiis Abelis et Caini*
Sobr.	*De sobrietate*
Somn.	*De somniis*
Spec.	*De specialibus legibus* (*On the Special Laws*)
Virt.	*De virtutibus* (*On the Virtues*)

Josephus

A.J.	*Antiquitates judaicae* (*Jewish Antiquities*)
B.J.	*Bellum judaicum* (*Jewish War*)
C. Ap.	*Contra Apionem* (*Against Apion*)
Vita	*Vita* (*The Life*)

Targums

Frg. Tg.	Fragmentary Targum
Tg. Neof.	Targum Neofiti
Tg. Onq.	Targum Onqelos
Tg. Ps.-J.	Targum Pseudo-Jonathan

Rabbinic Works

b.	Babylonian Talmud
Git.	Gittin
Hag.	Hagigah
m.	Mishnah
Menah.	Menahot
Ned.	Nedarim
Pesah.	Pesahim
Pesiq. Rab.	Pesiqta Rabbati
Sukkah	Sukkah
y.	Jerusalem Talmud
Yevam.	Yevamot
Yoma	Yoma (= Kippurim)

Apostolic Fathers

Barn.	Epistle of Barnabas
1 Clem.	1 Clement
Did.	Didache
Diogn.	Epistle to Diognetus
Herm. Sim.	Shepherd of Hermas, Similitude(s)
Herm. Vis.	Shepherd of Hermas, Vision(s)
Ign. *Eph.*	Ignatius, *To the Ephesians*
Ign. *Magn.*	Ignatius, *To the Magnesians*
Ign. *Phld.*	Ignatius, *To the Philadelphians*
Ign. *Pol.*	Ignatius, *To Polycarp*
Ign. *Rom.*	Ignatius, *To the Romans*
Ign. *Smyrn.*	Ignatius, *To the Smyrnaeans*
Ign. *Trall.*	Ignatius, *To the Trallians*
Mart. Pol.	Martyrdom of Polycarp
Pol. *Phil.*	Polycarp, *To the Philippians*

New Testament Apocrypha and Pseudepigrapha

Gos. Pet.	Gospel of Peter
Gos. Thom.	Gospel of Thomas

Classical Authors

Aeschylus

Ag.	*Agamemnon*
Eum.	*Eumenides*
Pers.	*Persae* (*Persians*)

Aristophanes

Eq.	*Equites* (*Knights*)
Nub.	*Nubes* (*Clouds*)

Aristotle

Eth. eud.	*Ethica eudemia* (*Eudemian Ethics*)
Eth. nic.	*Ethica nicomachea* (*Nicomachean Ethics*)
Metaph.	*Metaphysica* (*Metaphysics*)
Pol.	*Politica* (*Politics*)
Rhet.	*Rhetorica* (*Rhetoric*)

Augustus

RG	*Res Gestae Divi Augusti* (*The Achievements of the Divine Augustus*)

Cicero

Dom.	*De domo suo*
Fat.	*De fato*
Leg.	*De legibus*
Nat. d.	*De natura deorum*
Rep.	*De republica*
Rhet. Her.	*Rhetorica ad Herennium*

Dio Cassius

Hist. rom.	*Historiae romanae* (*Roman History*)

Dio Chrysostom

Avar.	*De avaritia* (*Or.* 17) (*On Covetousness*)
Exil.	*De exilio* (*Or.* 13) (*On Banishment*)
In cont.	*In contione* (*Or.* 48) (*A Political Address in the Assembly*)
Or.	*Oratio*(*nes*)
1 Regn.	*De regno i* (*Or.* 1) (*On Kingship 1*)
2 Regn.	*De regno ii* (*Or.* 2) (*On Kingship 2*)

Diodorus Siculus
Bib. hist.   Bibliotheca historica (*Library of History*)

Diogenes Laertius
Vit. phil.   Vitae philosophorum (*Lives of Eminent Philosophers*)

Epictetus
Diatr.   Diatribai/Dissertationes (*Discourses*)
Ench.   Enchiridion (*Handbook*)

Epicurus
Men.   Epistula ad Menoeceum

Euripides
Bacch.   Bacchae
Hipp.   Hippolytus
Iph. aul.   Iphigenia aulidensis (*Iphigeneia at Aulis*)
Iph. taur.   Iphigenia taurica (*Iphigeneia at Tauris*)
Orest.   Orestes
Suppl.   Supplices (*Suppliants*)
Tro.   Troades (*Daughters of Troy*)

Galen
Hippoc. et Plat.   De placitis Hippocratis et Platonis (*On the Doctrines of Hippocrates and Plato*)

Herodotus
Hist.   Historiae (*Histories*)

Hesiod
Op.   Opera et dies (*Works and Days*)
Theog.   Theogonia (*Theogony*)

Homer
Il.   Ilias (*Iliad*)
Od.   Odyssea (*Odyssey*)

Horace
Sat.   Satirae (*Satires*)

Hyginus
Astr.   De astronomica

Isocrates
Demon.   Ad Demonicum (Or. 1) (*To Demonicus*)

Julian
Or.   Oratio(nes)

Juvenal
Sat.   Satirae (*Satires*)

Livy
Ab urbe cond.   Ab urbe condita

Lucian
Demon.   Demonax
Dial. d.   Dialogi deorum (*Dialogues of the Gods*)
Hist. cons.   Quomodo historia conscribenda sit (*How to Write History*)
Men.   Menippus (Necyomantia) (*Menippus, or Descent into Hades*)
Prom.   Prometheus

Maximus of Tyre
Disc.   Discourses

Menander
Mon.   Monostichoi

Ovid
Ars   Ars amatoria
Metam.   Metamorphoses

Pausanius
Descr.   Graeciae descriptio (*Description of Greece*)

Philostratus
Vit. Apoll.   Vita Apollonii (*Life of Apollonius*)
Vit. soph.   Vitae sophistarum

Plato
Alc. maj.   Alcibiades major (*Greater Alcibiades*)
Apol.   Apologia (*Apology of Socrates*)
Ep.   Epistulae (*Letters*)
Euthyphr.   Euthyphro
Gorg.   Gorgias

Leg.	Leges (Laws)	**Seneca**	
Phaedr.	Phaedrus	Clem.	De clementia
Pol.	Politicus (Statesman)	Ep.	Epistulae morales
Prot.	Protagoras		
Resp.	Respublica (Republic)	**Sophocles**	
Soph.	Sophista (Sophist)	Aj.	Ajax
Theaet.	Theaetetus	Ant.	Antigone
Tim.	Timaeus	Oed. tyr.	Oedipus tyrannus (Oedipus the King)

Pliny the Elder

Nat.   Naturalis historia (Natural History)

Suetonius

Aug.	Divus Augustus
Tib.	Tiberius

Pliny the Younger

Ep.   Epistulae

Tacitus

Ann.	Annales
Hist.	Historiae

Plutarch

Adul. amic.	Quomodo adulator ab amico internoscatur (How to Tell a Flatterer from a Friend)
Alex.	Alexander
Cic.	Cicero
Conj. praec.	Conjugalia praecepta (Advice to Bride and Groom)
Dion	Dion
Lyc.	Lycurgus
Mor.	Moralia (Moral Essays)
Num.	Numa
Per.	Pericles
Quaest. conv.	Quaestionum convivialium libri IX
Sol.	Solon
Superst.	De superstitione (On Superstition)
Them.	Themistocles

Thucydides

Hist. pel.   Historia belli peloponnesiaci (History of the Peloponnesian War)

Xenophon

Mem.   Memorabilia

Patristic Writings

Aristides

Apol.	Apologia
Or.	Oratione

Arrian

Anab.   Anabasis

Polybius

Hist.   Historiae (Histories)

Augustine

Civ.   De civitate Dei (The City of God)

Pseudo-Sallust

Ep.   Epistulae

Clement of Alexandria

Strom.   Stromateis (Miscellanies)

Quintilian

Inst.   Institutio oratoria (The Orator's Education)

Eusebius

Hist. eccl.	Historia ecclesiastica (Ecclesiastical History)
Praep. ev.	Praeparatio evangelica (Preparation for the Gospel)

Sallust

Bell. Cat.	Bellum Catilinae (Conspiracy of Catiline)
Hist.	Historiae

Hippolytus

Fr. Prov.	Fragmenta in Proverbia

Irenaeus

Epid.	Epideixis tou apostolikou kērygmatos (*Demonstration of the Apostolic Preaching*)
Haer.	Adversus haereses (*Against Heresies*)

Justin Martyr

1 Apol.	Apologia i (*First Apology*)
Dial.	Dialogus cum Tryphone (*Dialogue with Trypho*)

Melito

Pascha	De Pascha (*On Passover*)

Origen

Cels.	Contra Celsum (*Against Celsus*)
Comm. Jo.	Comentarii in evangelium Joannis
Hom. Lev.	Homiliae in Leviticum
Mart.	Exhortatio ad martyrium (*Exhortation to Martyrdom*)
Princ.	De principiis / Peri archōn (*First Principles*)

Tertullian

Apol.	Apologeticus (*Apology*)
Marc.	Adversus Marcionem (*Against Marcion*)
Scorp.	Scorpiace (*Antidote for the Scorpion's Sting*)

Other Early Christian Works

Acts Scill.	Acts of Scillitan Martyrs
Lyons	Letter of the Churches of Vienne and Lyons
Mart. Apoll.	Martyrdom of Apollonius
Mart. Carp.	Martyrdom of Carpus, Papylus, and Agathonike
Mart. Justin	Martyrdom of Justin
Passio	Passion of Perpetua and Felicitas

Secondary Resources

ANRW	*Aufstieg und Niedergang der römischen Welt: Geschichte und Kultur Roms im Spiegel der neueren Forschung*. Part 2, *Principat*. Edited by Hildegard Temporini and Wolfgang Haase. Berlin: de Gruyter, 1972–
APOT	*The Apocrypha and Pseudepigrapha of the Old Testament*. Edited by Robert H. Charles. 2 vols. Oxford: Clarendon, 1913.
AYBRL	Anchor Yale Bible Reference Library
BDAG	Danker, Frederick W., Walter Bauer, William F. Arndt, and F. Wilbur Gingrich. *Greek-English Lexicon of the New Testament and Other Early Christian Literature*. 3rd ed. Chicago: University of Chicago Press, 2000.
BDF	Blass, Friedrich, Albert Debrunner, and Robert W. Funk. *A Greek Grammar of the New Testament and Other Early Christian Literature*. Chicago: University of Chicago Press, 1961.
BJP	Brill Josephus Project
BZNW	Beihefte zur Zeitschrift für die neutestamentliche Wissenschaft
CEJL	Commentaries on Early Jewish Literature
CGCG	*The Cambridge Grammar of Classical Greek*. Edited by Evert van Emde Boas, Albert Rijksbaron, Luuk Huitink, and Mathieu de Bakker. Cambridge: Cambridge University Press, 2019.
CGL	*The Cambridge Greek Lexicon*. Edited by J. Diggle, B. L. Fraser, P. James, O. B. Simkin, A. A. Thompson, and S. J. Westripp. Cambridge: Cambridge University Press, 2021.
FGH	*Die Fragmente der griechischen Historiker*. Edited by Felix Jacoby. Leiden: Brill, 1954–64.
GELS	*A Greek-English Lexicon of the Septuagint*. Edited by Takamitsu Muraoka. Leuven: Peeters, 2009.
JSJ	*Journal for the Study of Judaism in the Persian, Hellenistic, and Roman Periods*
JSJSup	Journal for the Study of Judaism Supplement Series
JSP	*Journal for the Study of the Pseudepigrapha*
JSPSup	Journal for the Study of the Pseudepigrapha Supplement Series
LCL	Loeb Classical Library

LSJ	Liddell, Henry George, Robert Scott, and Henry Stuart Jones. *A Greek-English Lexicon*. 9th ed. with revised supplement. Oxford: Clarendon, 1996.	S	Smyth, Herbert Weir. *Greek Grammar*. Revised by Gordon M. Messing. Cambridge, MA: Harvard University Press, 1984.
MGS	Montanari, Franco, Madeleine Goh, and Chad Schroeder. *The Brill Dictionary of Ancient Greek*. Leiden: Brill, 2014.	SBLDS	Society of Biblical Literature Dissertation Series
		SC	Sources chrétiennes
		SCS	Septuagint and Cognate Studies
NETS	*A New English Translation of the Septuagint*. Edited by A. Pietersma and B. G. Wright. Oxford: Oxford University Press, 2007.	SSG	*A Syntax of Septuagint Greek*. Takamitsu Muraoka. Leuven: Peeters, 2016.
		SVF	*Stoicorum Veterum Fragmenta*. Hans Friedrich August von Arnim. 4 vols. Leipzig: Teubner, 1903–24.
NovTSup	Novum Testamentum Supplement Series	SVTP	Studia in Veteris Testamentari Pseudepigraphica
NTS	*New Testament Studies*	TrGF	*Tragicorum Graecorum Fragmenta*. Volume 1, *Didascaliae tragicae, Catalogi tragicorum et tragoediarum, Testimonia et fragmenta tragicorum minorum*. Edited by Bruno Snell. 2nd ed. Göttingen: Vandenhoeck & Ruprecht, 1981.
OGIS	*Orientis Graeci Inscriptiones Selectae*. Edited by Wilhelm Dittenberger. 2 vols. Leipzig: Hirzel, 1903–5.		
OTP	*Old Testament Pseudepigrapha*. Edited by James H. Charlesworth. 2 vols. New York: Doubleday, 1983, 1985.		
		WUNT	Wissenschaftliche Untersuchungen zum Neuen Testament
PACS	Philo of Alexandria Commentary Series		

Introduction

This reader is designed to address the specific needs and interests of students of biblical and religious studies. Many students—and scholars, for that matter—learn Greek at seminaries and divinity schools in courses devoted to preparing students to use language tools in sermon preparation. Students who wish to continue in their education, therefore, often find their language skills in need of remediation. While there is no shortage of resources targeted at those who want to "keep up" their Greek, the same cannot be said for those who want to progress toward reading ancient texts.[1] This reader aims to fill this lacuna by preparing students to read and enjoy the vast and diverse corpora of ancient Greek literature.

Before I introduce the features of the reader, however, I should take a moment to address a question that I often encounter in my role as a seminary professor: If the student's primary goal is to become a proficient reader of the Greek New Testament, why should she care to read beyond it? This question is personal. Like many of my readers, I learned Greek at a seminary (at an extension campus, one night per week). When I graduated, I had yet to read a single book of the Greek New Testament in its entirety. Fortunately, by some happy coincidence or act of providence, I stumbled into the Classics program at U. C. Davis. I still remember my professor's response when I asked him what to expect in the course on Euripides's *Bacchae*. "We're going to read the play," he said, clearly confused by my question. "The whole play!" I thought. "Is he crazy?!" But that is exactly what we did, and my experience with Greek has never been the same. To this day, I maintain that the best way to become a proficient reader of the Greek New Testament is to read beyond it.

Of course, the path toward proficiency in ancient Greek will look different for each person. There are no "masters," only more experienced travelers. My hope is that this reader will serve as a guidepost to fellow travelers—to the wayward, itinerant, and resolute alike.

Vocabulary, Grammar, and Discourse

A fundamental premise of this reader is that the best way to learn vocabulary and grammar is by reading as much Greek as possible. To ensure that readers do not constantly need to reference the lexica, I offer maximal help with vocabulary: all terms used fewer than thirty times in the New Testament are glossed. In addition, I provide notes on grammar that are keyed to standard reference works: Blass, Debrunner, and Funk's *A Greek Grammar*

---

1. The two exceptions are Decker 2007 and McLean 2014, both of which are excellent resources but are limited in scope.

of the New Testament and Other Early Christian Literature (BDF), Smyth's *Greek Grammar* (S), and *The Cambridge Grammar of Classical Greek* (CGCG). My notes focus on areas of grammar either that are not covered in New Testament Greek textbooks or with which, in my experience, students tend to struggle. These are as follows.

1. Participles

Participles are classified under three categories: supplementary, circumstantial, and attributive.

The **supplementary** participle functions as an *obligatory constituent* of the main verb; that is, it complements the following:

- verbs of direct sensory perception ("see," "hear," etc.), verbs that describe some phase of action ("begin," "continue," "stop," etc.), and verbs that signify "endure," "persist," "grow weary," and so on (cf. BDF §414; S §§2097–2105; CGCG §52.9). For example,
    - ὡς δ' ἐσεῖδεν Ἀγαμέμνων ἄναξ / ἐπὶ σφαγὰς **στείχουσαν** εἰς ἄλσος **κόρην** (Euripides, *Iph. aul.* 1547–1548)
    - When King Agamemnon looked upon **the girl entering** the grove for slaughter
    - ἐὰν διὰ τῶν αὐτῶν λόγων ἀκούητέ **μου ἀπολογουμένου**, δι' ὧνπερ εἴωθα λέγειν (Plato, *Apol.* 17c)
    - If you hear **me making my defense** with the same words with which I am accustomed to speak
        NB: The participle is in the genitive case because the verb involves direct auditory perception.
- verbs of knowledge ("know that," "hear that," "see that," etc.), verbs that demonstrate ("show that," "report that," etc.), and verbs that express an emotional state ("be pleased that,"

"be ashamed that," etc.)—that is, verbs that introduce *indirect discourse* (cf. BDF §416; S §§2106–2115; CGCG §52.10). For example,
    - ἔσται οὕτως, ὡς ἐλάλησας ἡμῖν. ὡς ἐὰν οὖν γνῷς **παραγινομένους ἡμᾶς** (1 Clem. 12.6)
    - It will be just as you said to us. So, when you learn **that we are approaching**
    - ἀπεδείκνυον δὲ καὶ **τοὺς προγόνους** αὐτῶν ὡς ἀσεβεῖς καὶ μισουμένους ὑπὸ τῶν θεῶν ἐξ ἁπάσης τῆς Αἰγύπτου **πεφυγαδευμένους** (Diodorus Siculus, *Bib. hist.* 34.1.1)
    - They point out, too, **that** their **ancestors**, on the grounds that they are impious and despised by the gods, **were banished** from all Egypt.

    NB: In Attic Greek, supplementary participles "specify that the action is actually realized or that the propositional content is true." This is in contrast to the use of infinitives, "which do not specify the actions they express as true" (CGCG §52.8; cf. S §2110). This distinction, however, does not seem to have been maintained as carefully in Hellenistic Greek (cf. BDF §416).

- verbs that express a certain way of being or acting: τυγχάνω ("happen"), λανθάνω ("escape the notice of"), and φθάνω ("anticipate," "be earlier than") (cf. S §2096; CGCG §52.11). For example,
    - "λανθάνεις," εἶπεν, "ὦ βασιλεῦ τὰ μέγιστα τοὺς νόμους καὶ δι' αὐτῶν τὸν θεὸν **ἀδικῶν**" (Josephus, *A.J.* 20.44)
    - "In your ignorance," he said, "O king, **you are guilty** of the greatest offence against the laws and thereby against God."

- εἴ μοι προέκειτο νῦν ὑπὲρ ὁμονοίας λέγειν, εἶπον ἂν πολλὰ καὶ περὶ τῶν ἀνθρωπίνων καὶ περὶ τῶν οὐρανίων παθημάτων, ὅτι τὰ θεῖα ταῦτα καὶ μεγάλα ὁμονοίας <u>τυγχάνει</u> **δεόμενα** καὶ φιλίας (Dio Chrysostom, *In cont.* 14)
- If my purpose now were to speak on behalf of concord, I would have much to say about both the human and celestial experiences—namely, that these divine and great things <u>happen</u> **to need** concord and friendship.

The **circumstantial** participle, by contrast, functions as a *satellite* (i.e., an optional constituent) of the main verbs. Its force "does not lie in the participle itself, but is derived from the context. Unless attended by some modifying adverb, the context often does not decide whether the participle has a temporal, a causal, a conditional, a concessive force, etc.; and some participles may be referred to more than one of the above classes" (S §2069). Moreover, as Runge (2010, 248) observes, "The preoccupation with classification for the sake of translation has done much to distract attention from understanding the discourse function of the Greek participle." This we may summarize as follows: broadly speaking, circumstantial participles that precede the verb serve as *frames* (i.e., they set the stage for the main action), while circumstantial participles that follow the verb *elaborate on* the main action in some way (249–68). So, for example,

διαστειλάμενος οὖν τὰ τῆς εὐσεβείας καὶ δικαιοσύνης πρῶτον ὁ νομοθέτης ἡμῶν, καὶ **διδάξας** ἕκαστα περὶ τούτων, . . . καὶ τὰς βλάβας **προδηλώσας** καὶ τὰς ὑπὸ τοῦ θεοῦ γινομένας ἐπιπομπὰς τοῖς αἰτίοις, . . . ταῦτ᾽ οὖν **ἐξεργαζόμενος** ἀκριβῶς καὶ πρόδηλα **θεὶς** <u>ἔδειξεν</u> ὅτι, κἂν ἐννοηθῇ τις κακίαν ἐπιτελεῖν, οὐκ ἂν λάθοι, μὴ ὅτι καὶ πράξας, διὰ πάσης τῆς νομοθεσίας τὸ τοῦ θεοῦ δυνατὸν *ἐνδεικνύμενος*. (Let. Aris. 131, 133)

Thus, at the outset, our lawgiver **giving express commandments** concerning piety and justice, and **giving instruction** on each of the various matters concerning these, . . . and **making clear** the harms and visitations sent by God upon the guilty, . . . thus **working out** these things accurately and **having made** them abundantly clear <u>demonstrated</u> that, even if someone should contemplate carrying out evil, he would not escape, let alone if he actually does the deed, *indicating* the power of God through the entire legislation.

In this instance, five participles (**bold**) frame the main verb ἔδειξεν, on which the subsequent participle (*italics*) elaborates.

When the subject of the circumstantial participle is not a constituent of the main clause, the participle is put in the genitive case; that is, as a **genitive absolute** (cf. BDF §423; S §2070; *CGCG* §52.32). For example,

τῶν δὲ παραχρῆμα **ἐκπυρωθέντων** τὸν γενόμενον αὐτῶν προήγορον <u>προσέταξεν</u> γλωσσοτομεῖν καὶ περισκυθίσαντας ἀκρωτηριάζειν **τῶν λοιπῶν ἀδελφῶν καὶ τῆς μητρὸς συνορώντων**. (2 Macc. 7:4)

When these had been immediately **heated**, <u>he ordered</u> (them) to cut out the tongue of the one who had become the spokesman and to scalp him and cut off his hands and feet **while the rest of the brothers and their mother looked on**.

When the participle cannot have a subject because the verb is impersonal, it is put in the accusative case—that is, as an **accusative absolute** (cf. BDF §424; S §2076; *CGCG* §52.33). For example,

ἀλλ᾽ ἐπεὶ θεοῦ τε βουλομένου σὸς πατὴρ ἐγενόμην καὶ πάλιν τούτῳ **δοκοῦν** ἀποτίθεμαί σε, φέρε γενναίως τὴν καθιέρωσιν· (Josephus, *A.J.* 1.229)

But, since God willed [gen. absol.] that I become your father and again **since it seems good** [acc. absol.] to him, I am resigning you, bear your dedication bravely.

The **attributive** participle (typically arthrous) modifies a noun, with which it agrees in case, number, and gender, and is placed in the attributive position (cf. BDF §412; S §2049; *CGCG* §52.46). For example,

ἡμεῖς μέν τοι **τῶν ἡψημένων** βρωμάτων παραθήσομεν, σὺ δὲ ὑποκρινόμενος τῶν ὑείων ἀπογεύεσθαι σώθητι (4 Macc. 6:15)

We (take note) will set before you some **cooked** food; save yourself by pretending to eat of the pig meat.

As with adjectives, attributive participles may be substantivized. For example,

καὶ **τὸν** μὲν **εἰπόντα** οὐδεὶς εἶδεν, τὴν δὲ φωνὴν τῶν ἡμετέρων **οἱ παρόντες** ἤκουσαν (Mart. Pol. 9.1)

And no one saw **the one who said** this, but **those** of ours **who were present** heard the voice.

Finally, note the predicate use of the participle in periphrastic constructions: εἰμί (or some other auxiliary verb) with an anarthrous participle. "The combined phrase is roughly equivalent to a finite form of the same verb (and in the same tense-aspect stem)" (*CGCG* §52.51). For example,

προστεταγμένον γὰρ **ἦν** αὐτῷ διὰ τοῦ βασιλέως (Let. Aris. 304)

For **it had been commanded** to him by the king

The periphrastic is equivalent to the pluperfect tense, which is used in narrative to supply background information. For example,

καὶ ποιήσω σε εἰς ἔθνος μέγα καὶ εὐλογήσω σε καὶ μεγαλυνῶ τὸ ὄνομά σου, καὶ **ἔσῃ εὐλογημένος** (1 Clem. 10.3)

I will make you into a great nation and I will bless you and enlarge your name, and **you will be blessed**.

The periphrastic is the equivalent to the future-perfect tense.

2. The Articular Infinitive

The neuter singular article is added to the infinitive to turn it into a noun phrase, which may function as a subject, object, attributive modifier, or verbal complement (cf. BDF §§398–410; S §§2025–2038; *CGCG* §§51.38–39). Some examples:

φησὶ δὲ **περὶ τοῦ δεῖν** περιτέμνεσθαι αὐτοὺς ὁ Ἰακώβ (Theodotus, frag. 4.6)

Now **about it being necessary** for them to be circumcised, Jacob says . . .

συνέθιζε δὲ **ἐν τῷ νομίζειν** μηδὲν πρὸς ἡμᾶς εἶναι τὸν θάνατον (Diogenes Laertius, *Vit. phil.* 10.124)

Accustom yourself **in thinking** that death is nothing to us.

When the infinitive has its own subject, it is placed in the accusative case. For example,

ἐκ τοῦ παρόντος **ἡμᾶς ζῆν** ἀπολύεις (2 Macc. 7:9)

You release us from our present **living**.

3. The Infinitive in Indirect Discourse

Indirect discourse involves reported speech, thought, and so on and takes either a ὅτι/ὡς-clause (i.e., ὅτι or ὡς with an indicative verb), an accusative-and-participle construction (examples of this use of the supplementary participle are provided above), or an accusative-and-infinitive construction (cf. BDF §§396–97; S §§2016–2024; *CGCG* §§51.19–27). Since the latter often proves a challenge for students, I think it prudent to review the basics.

- When the subject of the infinitive and the main verb are co-referential, the subject of the infinitive is not separately expressed. For example,
  - καὶ γὰρ ἔφησεν **ἀκηκοέναι** Θεοπόμπου (Let. Aris. 314)
  - And, in fact, he [Demetrius] said that **he heard** from Theopompus.

- In most cases, the subject of the infinitive differs from that of the main verb and is expressed in the accusative case. For example,
  - διὸ τὸν μὲν οὐράνιόν φησιν οὐ **πεπλάσθαι**, κατ' εἰκόνα δὲ **τετυπῶσθαι** θεοῦ, τὸν δὲ γήϊνον πλάσμα, ἀλλ' οὐ γέννημα, **εἶναι** τοῦ τεχνίτου (Philo, *Leg.* 1.31)
  - For this reason he says that the heavenly [human] **was** not **molded** but **stamped** after the image of God, while the earthly [human] **is** a molded work—not the offspring—of the artificer.

- The tense of the infinitive depends on the tense-aspect of the indicative that would have been used in direct discourse. For example,
  - Ἕκτορ, ἀτάρ που ἔφης Πατροκλῆ' ἐξεναρίζων / σῶς **ἔσσεσθ**' (Homer, *Il.* 22.331–332)
  - Hector, you thought, I reckon, that while you were spoiling Patroclus, **you would be** safe.

The future infinitive expresses action that is posterior to that of the main verb, ἔφης.

4. The Optative Mood

The optative mood is infrequent in the New Testament and is thus an area with which some readers may be unfamiliar. While its uses might initially seem complex (yes, there's more to the optative than Paul's μὴ γένοιτο), they are relatively straightforward once one grasps the principle: potential and cupitive (wish) optatives are used in main clauses, oblique optatives in subordinate clauses.

- The **potential** optative is used with ἄν to express something that might occur, to make a weaker assertion, to express a cautious command or request, or to make an emphatic negation (cf. BDF §385; S §§1824–1834; *CGCG* §34.13). For example,
  - τὸ σύνολον δὲ μάλιστά τις **ἄν** ἐκ ταύτης **μάθοι** τῆς ἱστορίας (Josephus, *A.J.* 1.14)
  - But, in general, anyone who **would learn** first and foremost from this history

- The **cupitive** optative (without ἄν) is used to express a wish and may be accompanied by εἴθε, εἰ, γάρ, or ὡς (cf. BDF §384; S §§1814–1819; *CGCG* §34.14). For example,
  - **εἴθε** δὲ μὴ **χρῄζοις** μήτ' ἔκνομα μήτε δικαίως (Ps.-Phoc. 33)
  - But **may you** never **need** it [the sword], neither unjustly nor justly.

- The **oblique** optative may be a substitute for other moods in subordinate clauses *when the main verb is in secondary sequence* (i.e., imperfect, aorist, or pluperfect) (cf. BDF §386; S §2619; *CGCG* §40.12). For example,

- προσαχθέντα οὖν αὐτὸν ἀνηρώτα ὁ ἀνθύπατος, εἰ αὐτὸς **εἴη** Πολύκαρπος (Mart. Pol. 9.2)
- When he was brought before him, the proconsul asked if he **was** Polycarp.
  The optative is used in place of the indicative in an indirect question.

- συνελάσαντες τὸν ἄθλιον ἄχρι τοῦ γυμνασίου καὶ στήσαντες μετέωρον, ἵνα **καθορῷτο** πρὸς πάντων, βύβλον μὲν εὐρύναντες ἀντὶ διαδήματος ἐπιτιθέασιν αὐτοῦ τῇ κεφαλῇ (Philo, *Flacc.* 37)
- They having driven the poor fellow as far as the gymnasium and having set him up on high, in order that **he might look down** toward all the people, having spread wide a sheet of byblus, set it upon his head in place of a diadem.
  The optative is used for the subjunctive in a purpose clause.

5. Verbal Adjectives Ending in -τέος, -τέα, or -τέον

Verbal adjectives (or gerundives) ending in -τέος, -τέα, or -τέον express passive necessity and may modify a noun with which they agree in gender, number, and case ("personal [passive] construction") or be used impersonally ("impersonal [active] construction," typically neuter singular -τέον, though sometimes neuter plural -τέα). The agent of the passive action is expressed in the dative case (cf. S §§2149–2152; *CGCG* §37.2-3).

- Impersonal (active) construction:
  - οὐ μὴν διὰ τοῦθ' **ἡσυχαστέον**, ἀλλ' ἕνεκα τοῦ θεοφιλοῦς καὶ ὑπὲρ δύναμιν **ἐπιτολμητέον** λέγειν (Philo, *Opif.* 4)
  - Yet, surely we should not for this reason pass this over in silence [lit., **a thing necessary (for us) to pass over in silence**], but for the sake of the god-beloved [Moses] we must dare [lit., **a thing necessary (for us) to dare**] to speak even beyond our ability.

- Personal (passive) construction:
  - τούτων δὲ **ληπτέος** ὅρος τις (Aristotle, *Eth. nic.* 1097b12–13)
  - A certain limit to these **must be assumed** [by us].

6. Subordinate-Clause Structures

Here I note subordinate-clause structures that do not occur (frequently) in the New Testament.

- **Fear clauses** complement verbs of fearing and are introduced by μή ("that") followed by a subjunctive (aorist or present for fear of possible future actions, present or perfect for fear of possible present actions) or an indicative (aorist or present for fear that something was or is occurring) (cf. S §§2221–2232; *CGCG* §§43.3–5). For example,

  - γέγραφε δ' αὐτὸν ἐν ταῖς ἱεραῖς βίβλοις τεθνεῶτα, δείσας **μὴ** δι' ὑπερβολὴν τῆς περὶ αὐτὸν ἀρετῆς πρὸς τὸ θεῖον αὐτὸν ἀναχωρῆσαι **τολμήσωσιν** εἰπεῖν (Josephus, *A.J.* 4.326)
  - But he has written of himself in the holy writings that he died, fearing **that**, on account of the preeminence of virtue that surrounds him, **they might dare** to say that he had returned to the deity.

- **Effort clauses** complement verbs of effort, caution, contriving, and so on and are introduced by ὅπως (or ὡς) followed by a future indicative (cf. S §§2209–19; *CGCG* §§44.2–5). For example,

- ὦ ἄριστε ἀνδρῶν . . . χρημάτων μὲν οὐκ αἰσχύνει ἐπιμελούμενος, **ὅπως σοι ἔσται** ὡς πλεῖστα, καὶ δόξης καὶ τιμῆς, φρονήσεως δὲ καὶ ἀληθείας καὶ τῆς ψυχῆς, **ὅπως** ὡς βελτίστη **ἔσται**, οὐκ ἐπιμελεῖ οὐδὲ φροντίζεις; (Plato, *Apol.* 29d–e)
  - Most excellent man, . . . are you not ashamed in your concern for possessions, **that** they **be** yours as much as possible, and for reputation and honor, when you neither care nor take thought for prudence, truth, and the soul, **that** they **be** as supreme as possible?

- A **future participle** (frequently with ὡς) is used to express purpose (cf. S §2086; *CGCG* §52.41). For example,
  - ἐπεὶ γὰρ εἰσῆλθεν **ἀσπασόμενος** αὐτὸν καὶ κατέλαβε τὸν Μωυσέος νόμον ἀναγινώσκοντα (Josephus, *A.J.* 20.44)
  - For, when he entered **to greet** him, and he found him reading the law of Moses . . .
  - προσποιηθῆναι δ᾽ αὐτῷ τὸν Ἑρμῆν δεδωκέναι τούτους, **ὡς** μεγάλων ἀγαθῶν αἰτίους **ἐσομένους** (Diodorus Siculus, *Bib. hist.* 1.94.1)
  - He [Mneves] claimed that Hermes had given these [laws] to him that **they might be** the cause of many good things.

- The optative mood is used in **fourth-class** ("future less vivid"), or **potential**, **conditions**: εἰ with optative in the protasis, ἄν with optative in the apodosis (cf. S §2329; *CGCG* §49.8). For example,
  - μᾶλλον δέ, **εἰ** πάντες τὸ αὐτὸ **φρονήσειαν**, **ἐκλιπεῖν ἂν** τὸ γένος τάχιστα (Josephus, *A.J.* 2.160)
  - Moreover, [they claim that] **if** all people **were to think** the same, then the human race **would** swiftly **come to an end**.
    The infinitive replaces the optative because of indirect discourse.
  - ἐπεὶ ταῦτα **εἴ** ποτέ τις ἀνθρώπων φύσει ἱκανός, θείᾳ μοίρᾳ γεννηθείς, παραλαβεῖν δυνατὸς **εἴη**, νόμων οὐδὲν **ἂν δέοιτο** τῶν ἀρξόντων ἑαυτοῦ (Plato, *Leg.* 875c)
  - Yet **if** ever there **should be** a man who is able and competent by nature, having been born of a divine lot, to assume such an office, **he would have** no need for laws to rule over him.

7. Particles

One of my favorite features of *CGCG* (and there are many!) is that the authors clearly describe the function of particles. The power of this approach is clear when one recognizes that function entails the various nuances and nomenclature that grammarians have traditionally identified (see, e.g., Runge 2010, 17–57). So, for example, rather than attempting to memorize various glosses for the postpositive particle γε (which is often best left untranslated), the student should learn that the particle "focuses attention on the word or phrase it follows (or sometimes the clause as a whole), and limits the applicability of the content of the utterance to *at least* or (*more*) *precisely* that specific element" (*CGCG* §59.53).

My notes focus on the function of particles and particle combinations that are less common (or unattested) in the New Testament. For additional information, readers should consult Smyth, *CGCG*, and Denniston's *The Greek Particles* (1966), which is still the most comprehensive resource on the subject.

What to Expect and Where to Begin

I have designed the reader so that students and independent learners can jump in wherever they see fit. The material is grouped into eight parts: (1) the Septuagint, (2) the Apostolic Fathers, (3) Old Testament Pseudepigrapha, (4) Philo, (5) Josephus, (6) historians and biographers, (7) philosophers and rhetoricians, and (8) poets and playwrights. Each part begins with a short introduction to help orient the reader to the material. Herein I note the Greek edition on which the text is based along with the English translation. In instances where these are the same, the heading reads "Text and Translation." In cases where the Greek edition does not include an English translation, or I believe there is a superior English translation, the heading "Text" is followed by the heading "Recommended Translation."[2] I also include references to Scripture that you may wish to consult alongside the reading(s). Most of these are found in the Protestant canon, but some are references to deuterocanonical or other early Jewish and Christian literature. Finally, I conclude each reading passage with notes. These are not intended to be comprehensive but merely aim to stimulate insight and conversation as well as to guide readers to some of the important secondary literature.

The material is not necessarily organized so that it moves from intermediate to advanced. Broadly speaking, most of the easier passages are found in parts 1 and 2 (and in some of part 3). The readings in parts 4–8 may prove more difficult, but for different reasons. For example, Attic and "Atticizing" writers use more ornate syntax than the writers of the New Testament, whereas epic poetry, while not grammatically complex, necessitates the study of morphology and meter. The primary reason for a reading to be determined "difficult," however, is a lack of familiarity with the author. Thus, the more time you spend with an author—whether Plato, Paul, or Plutarch—the more accustomed you will become to their vocabulary, style, and idiosyncrasies.

Where, then, should you begin? My suggestion is that you start with part 1 and work your way through the parts in order. This ensures that you encounter the full range of genres, styles, vocabulary, and so forth. If, however, you purchased the reader because you have a particular interest or goal—for example, you really want to read Philo—do not let the order of the parts hold you back. Ultimately, this book is merely a means to an end, and indeed nothing would make me happier than to hear that you have put it down so that you can take up the original works themselves.

Additional Resources

I did not create this reader with the intention that it would require the purchase of additional resources. There are, however, some resources that I would strongly encourage you to acquire at some point. First, I cannot recommend *CGCG* highly enough. Herein readers will find clear and up-to-date discussions of verbal tense and aspect, word order, and textual coherence, among other things, all of which are informed by recent insights in linguistics. The only downside to *CGCG* is that it does not always provide the amount of detail that is found in Smyth. Ideally, then, you should have both. That said, the most comprehensive grammars of Classical Greek remain Kühner and Gerth's *Ausführliche Grammatik der griechischen Sprache* and Schwyzer's *Griechische Grammatik*. (So, some incentive to learn German!)

There are, of course, numerous grammars of Hellenistic Greek and the various corpora that fall within its domain. I assume most readers are

---

2. Many of these texts and translations are available for free online. See, e.g., http://www.perseus.tufts.edu/hopper/collection?collection=Perseus:collection:Greco-Roman.

familiar with Daniel Wallace's *Greek Grammar Beyond the Basics*. I also recommend Heinrich von Siebenthal's *Ancient Greek Grammar for the Study of the New Testament*. For the Septuagint, the best resource is Muraoka's *A Syntax of Septuagint Greek*. Finally, readers may wish to note the following grammars on Greek papyri: Mayser's *Grammatik der griechischen Papyri aus der Ptolemäerzeit*, Palmer's *A Grammar of the Post-Ptolemaic Papyri*, and Gignac's *A Grammar of the Greek Papyri of the Roman and Byzantine Periods*.

As for lexica, BDAG remains the standard for biblical studies, and LSJ remains the standard for Classics. *The Brill Dictionary of Ancient Greek* (MGS), which stands in the tradition of LSJ, is also an excellent resource. (MGS often presents the data in a clearer and more accessible format than LSJ.) Finally, the recently released *Cambridge Greek Lexicon* (*CGL*) includes a fresh assessment of the source material and presents the data in a unique format. No doubt it will be an indispensable resource for years to come.

PART 1

Reading the Septuagint

The term "Septuagint" is used broadly to designate the Greek Jewish scriptures: a diverse body of literature comprised not only of translations and expansions of Hebrew and Aramaic texts but also of original Greek compositions.[1] According to the Letter of Aristeas (see §3.1 below), Ptolemy II Philadelphus (285–247 BCE) commissioned the Jerusalem high priest Eleazar to dispatch a group of seventy-two translators (six men from each of the twelve tribes) to translate the Pentateuch into Greek.[2] The raison d'être of the pseudepigraphal letter, which was probably composed a century or so after its purported date, is to establish the Greek Pentateuch (and by extension, other Greek scriptures) as sacred scripture. In other words, the Letter of Aristeas offers a post hoc justification for the practice of translating the Hebrew scriptures into Greek.

Manuscript evidence confirms that this practice must have begun no later than the mid-third century BCE. Yet the Septuagint is the product not of a translation committee but of a disparate group of translators who worked at various times and in various places. Moreover, the transmission histories of these books are complex; ongoing revisions, multiple recensions, and extensive cross-pollination among witnesses present serious obstacles to our reconstruction of an "original" text. Scholars use the term "Septuagint" (LXX), or "Old Greek" (OG), to designate the oldest *accessible* text (critically reconstructed) that may correspond to the text of an original translation.[3]

The select reading passages in this chapter are intended to reflect the diversity of Septuagint texts. The first two are translations of Hebrew texts (Deut. 32 and Isa. 53), while the latter two are Greek compositions (2 Macc. 7 and 4 Macc. 6).

---

1. The "canon" of the Septuagint is a modern convention, due in large measure to the success of Rahlfs's 1935 edition, now slightly revised as Rahlfs and Hanhart 2006.

2. The number of translators was subsequently abbreviated to seventy (cf. Josephus, *A.J.* 12.57). Jobes and Silva (2015, 23) note that the term "Septuagint" "first appears in Greek (*hoi hebdomēkota*, 'the seventy') in the mid-second century and thereafter only in Christian writers, such as Justin, Irenaeus, and Chrysostom. The term was most often used by these writers to refer in general to the entire Greek OT, without distinguishing its various revisions and forms."

3. For further study, see Jobes and Silva 2015; McLay 2003. For introductions to Septuagint books and select issues, see Aitken 2015; Kreuzer 2019; Salvesen and Law 2021. For the purposes of scholarship, you should use the volumes in the Göttingen series. In cases where these do not yet exist, it is acceptable to use Rahlfs and Hanhart 2006.

1.1

LXX Deuteronomy

The Greek translation of Deuteronomy occurred in the third or second century BCE in Alexandria, Egypt. The translator "demonstrates a pattern of strict adherence to Hebrew word order at the expense of standard Greek style, along with a tendency toward quantitative representation—one Greek word for one Hebrew word—as much as possible" (Peters 2019, 132–33). For example, the translator had a penchant for rendering the Hebrew conjunction כִּי (first position) with ὅτι rather than γάρ (Aejmelaeus 1982). Instances where the translator deviates from the Hebrew *Vorlage* tend to involve semantic leveling (the use of a single Greek term to render multiple Hebrew terms), semantic differentiation (the use of multiple Greek terms to render a single Hebrew term), or neologisms (the construction of a new Greek word to replicate the Hebrew syntax).

The Song of Moses (Deut. 32) is one of the iconic passages of the Hebrew Bible. Deuteronomy 28–32 furnished early Jewish writers with a basic pattern of Israel's story, a theological history that moves from covenant inauguration to covenant infidelity to punishment (covenant curses) to repentance and eschatological vindication (Nickelsburg 2006a). Thus we encounter references to the Song in an array of early Jewish texts and realia, including Tobit, Baruch, 2 Maccabees, the Dead Sea Scrolls (scrolls and *tefillin* 4Q141), Philo, Josephus, the Testament of Moses, and Pseudo-Philo, as well as in the New Testament, especially the letters of Paul (Lincicum 2010).

Text: Wevers 1977

Recommended Translation: *NETS* (http://ccat.sas.upenn.edu/nets/edition/05-deut-nets.pdf)

Supplemental Scripture: Bar. 4; 2 Macc. 7:6; Rom. 10:19; 1 Cor. 10:14–22; Heb. 1:6; Rev. 15:3

1.1.1

The Song of Moses

Deuteronomy 31:30–32:43

31:30Καὶ ἐλάλησεν Μωυσῆς εἰς τὰ ὦτα[1] πάσης ἐκκλησίας Ισραηλ τὰ ῥήματα τῆς ᾠδῆς[2] ταύτης ἕως εἰς τέλος.[3]
  32:1Πρόσεχε,[4] οὐρανέ, καὶ λαλήσω,
  καὶ ἀκουέτω ἡ γῆ ῥήματα ἐκ στόματός μου.
  2προσδοκάσθω[5] ὡς ὑετὸς[6] τὸ ἀπόφθεγμά[7] μου,
  καὶ καταβήτω ὡς δρόσος[8] τὰ ῥήματά μου,
  ὡσεὶ[9] ὄμβρος[10] ἐπ' ἄγρωστιν[11]
  καὶ ὡσεὶ νιφετὸς[12] ἐπὶ χόρτον.[13]
  3ὅτι ὄνομα κυρίου ἐκάλεσα·
  δότε μεγαλωσύνην[14] τῷ θεῷ ἡμῶν.
  4θεός,[15] ἀληθινὰ τὰ ἔργα αὐτοῦ,
  καὶ πᾶσαι αἱ ὁδοὶ αὐτοῦ κρίσις·[16]
  θεὸς πιστός,[17] καὶ οὐκ ἔστιν ἀδικία,[18]
  δίκαιος καὶ ὅσιος[19] κύριος.
  5ἡμάρτοσαν οὐκ αὐτῷ τέκνα μωμητά,[20]
  γενεὰ σκολιὰ[21] καὶ διεστραμμένη.[22]

1. οὖς, ὠτός, τό, *ear*.
2. ᾠδή, -ῆς, ἡ, *song*.
3. This verse is the superscription of the song, which Moses is said to have delivered ἕως εἰς τέλος, "right up to the end"—that is, in its entirety (cf. 32:44).
4. Pres. act. impv. 2 sg., προσέχω, *pay attention, give heed*.
5. Pres. mid. impv. 3 sg., προσδοκάω, *await*.
6. ὑετός, -οῦ, ὁ, *rain*.
7. ἀπόφθεγμα, -ατος, τό, *utterance*.
8. δρόσος, -ου, ἡ, *dew*.
9. Adv. (ὡς, εἰ), *as*.
10. ὄμβρος, -ου, ὁ, *shower, rainstorm*.
11. ἄγρωστις, -ιδος, ἡ, *Cynodon dactylon* (or "dog's tooth grass"; LSJ, 16).
12. νιφετός, -οῦ, ὁ, *snowfall*.
13. χόρτος, -ου, ὁ, *grass*.
14. μεγαλωσύνη, -ης, ἡ, *greatness, majesty*.
15. Nom. pendent (or absol.); i.e., the nominative is placed outside the clause (left dislocation). This is a common feature of Greek syntax (cf. S §§940–42; *CGCG* §60.34) and serves "to place the new entity in marked focus for the sake of emphasis or to create a frame of reference for the clause that follows" (Runge 2010, 291). Since the nominative pendent is common in Hebrew, where it is used to state the focus or topic of the sentence (cf. Williams 2007, §35), it occurs frequently in LXX texts (cf. *SSG* §84).
16. κρίσις, -εως, ἡ, *justice, uprightness*.
17. Nom. pendent. See n. 15.
18. The Greek is a faithful rendering of the Hebrew but reads somewhat awkwardly. Most MSS supply ἐν αὐτῷ as an explanatory gloss (Wevers 1995, 511).
19. ὅσιος, -α, -ον, *holy*.
20. μωμητός, -ή, -όν, *blameworthy*. The translator is attempting to make sense of ambiguities in the *Vorlage*. Read οὐκ αὐτῷ as modifying τέκνα (Wevers 1995, 511). Peters (*NETS*): "blemished children, not his, have sinned."
21. σκολιός, -ά, -όν, *crooked*.
22. Pf. pass. ptc. nom. fem. sg., διαστρέφω, (pass.) *be turned, perverted*; attrib.

⁶ταῦτα κυρίῳ ἀνταποδίδοτε²³ οὕτως,
λαὸς μωρὸς²⁴ καὶ οὐχὶ σοφός;²⁵
οὐκ αὐτὸς οὗτός σου πατὴρ ἐκτήσατό²⁶ σε
καὶ ἐποίησέν σε καὶ ἔκτισέν²⁷ σε;
⁷μνήσθητε²⁸ ἡμέρας αἰῶνος,²⁹
σύνετε³⁰ ἔτη³¹ γενεᾶς³² γενεῶν·
ἐπερώτησον³³ τὸν πατέρα σου, καὶ ἀναγγε-
    λεῖ³⁴ σοι,
τοὺς πρεσβυτέρους σου, καὶ ἐροῦσίν σοι.
⁸ὅτε διεμέριζεν³⁵ ὁ ὕψιστος³⁶ ἔθνη,
ὡς διέσπειρεν³⁷ υἱοὺς Αδάμ,
ἔστησεν ὅρια³⁸ ἐθνῶν
κατὰ ἀριθμὸν³⁹ υἱῶν⁴⁰ θεοῦ,
⁹καὶ ἐγενήθη μερὶς⁴¹ κυρίου λαὸς αὐτοῦ
    Ιακώβ,
σχοίνισμα⁴² κληρονομίας⁴³ αὐτοῦ Ισραήλ.
¹⁰αὐτάρκησεν⁴⁴ αὐτὸν ἐν γῇ ἐρήμῳ,
ἐν δίψει⁴⁵ καύματος⁴⁶ ἐν ἀνύδρῳ·⁴⁷
ἐκύκλωσεν⁴⁸ αὐτὸν καὶ ἐπαίδευσεν⁴⁹ αὐτὸν
καὶ διεφύλαξεν⁵⁰ αὐτὸν ὡς κόραν⁵¹
    ὀφθαλμοῦ,
¹¹ὡς ἀετὸς⁵² σκεπάσαι⁵³ νοσσιὰν⁵⁴ αὐτοῦ
καὶ⁵⁵ ἐπὶ τοῖς νεοσσοῖς⁵⁶ αὐτοῦ ἐπεπόθησεν,⁵⁷
διεὶς⁵⁸ τὰς πτέρυγας⁵⁹ αὐτοῦ ἐδέξατο αὐτοὺς
καὶ ἀνέλαβεν⁶⁰ αὐτοὺς ἐπὶ τῶν μεταφρένων⁶¹
    αὐτοῦ.
¹²κύριος μόνος ἦγεν αὐτούς,
καὶ οὐκ ἦν μετ' αὐτῶν θεὸς ἀλλότριος.⁶²
¹³ἀνεβίβασεν⁶³ αὐτοὺς ἐπὶ τὴν ἰσχὺν⁶⁴ τῆς
    γῆς,
ἐψώμισεν⁶⁵ αὐτοὺς γενήματα⁶⁶ ἀγρῶν.⁶⁷

23. Pres. act. indic. 2 pl., ἀνταποδίδωμι, *give back, repay, recompense*.
24. μωρός, -ά, -όν, *foolish*.
25. σοφός, -ή, -όν, *wise*.
26. Aor. mid. indic. 3 sg., κτάομαι, *obtain, acquire*.
27. Aor. act. indic. 3 sg., κτίζω, *create*.
28. Aor. pass. impv. 2 pl., μιμνῄσκομαι, *remember, recall*.
29. αἰών, -ῶνος, ὁ, (very remote past) *long ago*.
30. Aor. act. impv. 2 pl., συνίημι, *consider*.
31. ἔτος, -ους, τό, *year*.
32. γενεά, -ᾶς, ἡ, *generation*.
33. Aor. act. impv. 2 sg., ἐπερωτάω, *ask, inquire*.
34. Fut. act. indic. 3 sg., ἀναγγέλλω, *report, announce*.
35. Impf. act. indic. 3 sg., διαμερίζω, *divide*.
36. ὕψιστος, -η, -ον, (epithet) *Most High*.
37. Aor. act. indic. 3 sg., διασπείρω, *scatter*; modified by ὡς, which is best read as a compar. adv., though it could be read temporally (*SSG* §76d). For further discussion, see notes.
38. ὅριον, -ου, τό, *border, limit*.
39. ἀριθμός, -οῦ, ὁ, *number*.
40. Rahlfs and Hanhart 2006 reads ἀγγέλων. See notes for further discussion.
41. μερίς, -ίδος, ἡ, *part, portion*.
42. σχοίνισμα, -ατος, τό, *land-measure* (cf. LSJ, 1747.III).
43. κληρονομία, -ας, ἡ, *inheritance*.
44. Aor. act. indic. 3 sg., αὐταρκέω, from αὐτάρκης ("self-sufficient"). Thus Wevers (1995, 514): "to make self-sufficient." Muraoka: "to supply with necessities" (*GELS*, 103).
45. δίψος, -εως, τό, *thirst*.
46. καῦμα, -ατος, τό, *heat* (from the sun).
47. ἄνυδρος, -ον, *waterless*.
48. Aor. act. indic. 3 sg., κυκλόω, *encircle*.
49. Aor. act. indic. 3 sg., παιδεύω, *train, discipline*.
50. Aor. act. indic. 3 sg., διαφυλάσσω, *guard*.
51. κόρη, -ης, ἡ, *pupil*.
52. ἀετός, -οῦ, ὁ, *eagle*.
53. Aor. act. opt. 3 sg., σκεπάζω, *cover, shelter*; potential opt. in a clause of comparison (cf. *SSG* §29dc; typically with ἄν; S §2477; *CGCG* §49.22). For further discussion, see notes.
54. νοσσιά, -ᾶς, ἡ, *brood, nest*.
55. The translator apparently read only the first clause as constituting the subordinate clause of comparison (ὡς with aor. opt.). The main clause shifts to the aorist indicative with adverbial καί: "*As* an eagle would watch over . . . *so* he [the Lord] yearned" (cf. *NETS*). The subsequent lines (11c-d) expand on 11b.
56. νεοσσός, -οῦ, ὁ, *nestling*.
57. Aor. pass. indic. 3 sg., ἐπιποθέω, *have affection for*.
58. Aor. act. ptc. nom. masc. sg., διίημι, *spread*; circ.
59. πτέρυξ, -γος, ἡ, *wing*.
60. Aor. act. indic. 3 sg., ἀναλαμβάνω, *take up*.
61. μετάφρενον, -ου, τό, (always pl.) *back*.
62. ἀλλότριος, -α, -ον, *foreign*.
63. Aor. act. indic. 3 sg., ἀναβιβάζω, *bring up*.
64. ἰσχύς, -ύος, ἡ, *strength* (i.e., "the most fertile part of the land" [*GELS*, 345.e]).
65. Aor. act. indic. 3 sg., ψωμίζω, *feed*; with double acc. (cf. BDF §155; S §1628; *CGCG* §30.9).
66. γένημα, -ατος, τό, *produce*.
67. ἀγρός, -οῦ, ὁ, *field*.

ἐθήλασαν[68] μέλι[69] ἐκ πέτρας[70]
καὶ ἔλαιον[71] ἐκ στερεᾶς[72] πέτρας,
14βούτυρον[73] βοῶν[74] καὶ γάλα[75] προβάτων
μετὰ στέατος[76] ἀρνῶν[77] καὶ κριῶν,[78]
υἱῶν ταύρων[79] καὶ τράγων[80]
μετὰ στέατος νεφρῶν[81] πυροῦ,[82]
καὶ αἷμα σταφυλῆς[83] ἔπιον[84] οἶνον.[85]
15καὶ ἔφαγεν Ιακωβ καὶ ἐνεπλήσθη,[86]
καὶ ἀπελάκτισεν[87] ὁ ἠγαπημένος,
ἐλιπάνθη,[88] ἐπαχύνθη,[89] ἐπλατύνθη.[90]
καὶ ἐγκατέλιπεν[91] θεὸν τὸν ποιήσαντα αὐτόν,
καὶ ἀπέστη[92] ἀπὸ θεοῦ σωτῆρος[93] αὐτοῦ.
16παρώξυνάν[94] με ἐπ᾽ ἀλλοτρίοις,
ἐν βδελύγμασιν[95] αὐτῶν ἐξεπίκρανάν[96] με·
17ἔθυσαν[97] δαιμονίοις καὶ οὐ θεῷ,
θεοῖς, οἷς οὐκ ᾔδεισαν·

καινοὶ[98] πρόσφατοι[99] ἥκασιν,[100]
οὓς οὐκ ᾔδεισαν οἱ πατέρες αὐτῶν.
18θεὸν τὸν γεννήσαντά σε ἐγκατέλιπες
καὶ ἐπελάθου[101] θεοῦ τοῦ τρέφοντός[102] σε.
19καὶ εἶδεν κύριος καὶ ἐζήλωσεν,[103]
καὶ παρωξύνθη δι᾽ ὀργὴν υἱῶν αὐτοῦ καὶ
  θυγατέρων.[104]
20καὶ εἶπεν Ἀποστρέψω[105] τὸ πρόσωπόν μου
  ἀπ᾽ αὐτῶν,
καὶ δείξω τί ἔσται αὐτοῖς ἐπ᾽ ἐσχάτων·
ὅτι γενεὰ ἐξεστραμμένη[106] ἐστίν,
υἱοί,[107] οἷς[108] οὐκ ἔστιν πίστις ἐν αὐτοῖς.
21αὐτοὶ παρεζήλωσάν[109] με ἐπ᾽ οὐ θεῷ,
παρώργισάν[110] με ἐν τοῖς εἰδώλοις αὐτῶν·
κἀγὼ παραζηλώσω αὐτοὺς ἐπ᾽ οὐκ ἔθνει,
ἐπ᾽ ἔθνει ἀσυνέτῳ[111] παροργιῶ[112] αὐτούς.
22ὅτι πῦρ ἐκκέκαυται[113] ἐκ τοῦ θυμοῦ[114] μου,

68. Aor. act. indic. 3 pl., θηλάζω, *nurse*.
69. μέλι, -ιτος, τό, *honey*.
70. πέτρα, -ας, ἡ, *rock*.
71. ἔλαιον, -ου, τό, *olive oil*.
72. στερεός, -ά, -όν, *solid, strong*.
73. βούτυρον, -ου, τό, *butter*.
74. βοῦς, -οός, ὁ/ἡ, *cow*
75. γάλα, -ας, ἡ, *milk*.
76. στέαρ, -ατος, τό, *fat*.
77. ἀρνός, -οῦ, ὁ, *lamb*.
78. κριός, -οῦ, ὁ, *ram*.
79. ταῦρος, -ου, ὁ, *bull, ox*.
80. τράγος, -ου, ὁ, *goat*.
81. νεφρός, -οῦ, ὁ, *kidney*.
82. πυρός, -οῦ, ὁ, *wheat*.
83. σταφυλή, -ῆς, ἡ, *(bunch of) grapes*.
84. Aor. act. indic. 3 pl., πίνω, *drink*.
85. οἶνος, -ου, ὁ, *wine*; appositive to αἷμα σταφυλῆς (cf. SSG §33e).
86. Aor. pass. indic. 3 sg., ἐμπίμπλημι, (pass.) *be filled, sated*.
87. Aor. act. indic. 3 sg., ἀπολακτίζω, *kick*.
88. Aor. pass. indic. 3 sg., λιπαίνω, (pass.) *be fattened*.
89. Aor. pass. indic. 3 sg., παχύνω, (pass.) *grow fat, become big*.
90. Aor. pass. indic. 3 sg., πλατύνω, (pass.) *become wide*.
91. Aor. act. indic. 3 sg., ἐγκαταλείπω, *abandon, forsake*.
92. Aor. act. indic. 3 sg., ἀφίστημι, (intrans.) *move away from*.
93. σωτήρ, -ῆρος, ὁ, *savior, deliverer*.
94. Aor. act. indic. 3 pl., παροξύνω, *provoke*.
95. βδέλυγμα, -ατος, τό, *abomination*.
96. Aor. act. indic. 3 pl., ἐκπικραίνω, *embitter*.
97. Aor. act. indic. 3 pl., θύω, *sacrifice*.

98. καινός, -ή, -όν, *new*.
99. πρόσφατος, -ον, *recent*, (subst.) *recent ones*.
100. Pf. act. indic. 3 pl., ἥκω, *come*.
101. Aor. mid. indic. 2 sg., ἐπιλανθάνω, *forget*; with gen.
102. Pres. act. ptc. gen. masc. sg., τρέφω, *nourish*; attrib. (subst.).
103. Aor. act. indic. 3 sg., ζηλόω, *be jealous*.
104. θυγάτηρ, -ατρός, ἡ, *daughter*. Wevers (1995, 520) reads υἱῶν and θυγατέρων as objective: "on account of wrath *against* his sons and daughters." Alternatively, one could take them as subjective: "on account of the wrath of his sons and daughters" (NETS).
105. Fut. act. indic. 1 sg., ἀποστρέφω, *turn away*.
106. Pf. pass. ptc. nom. fem. sg., ἐκστρέφω, (pass.) *be twisted/put out of joint*; attrib.
107. Nom. pendent. See n. 15.
108. The fronted constituent (*casus pendens*) is resumed by a pronoun in the same case (οἷς . . . ἐν αὐτοῖς), the result of quantitative representation of the Hebrew syntax (cf. SSG §84b). Translated: "in whom there is no faith."
109. Aor. act. indic. 3 pl., παραζηλόω, *make jealous*; ἐπ᾽ οὐ θεῷ supplies the grounds.
110. Aor. act. indic. 3 pl., παροργίζω, *provoke to anger*.
111. ἀσύνετος, -ον, *without understanding*.
112. Fut. act. indic. 1 sg., παροργίζω.
113. Pf. pass. indic. 3 sg., ἐκκαίω, (pass.) *be ignited*.
114. θυμός, -οῦ, ὁ, *anger*.

καυθήσεται[115] ἕως[116] ᾅδου[117] κάτω,[118]
καταφάγεται[119] γῆν καὶ τὰ γενήματα αὐτῆς,
φλέξει[120] θεμέλια[121] ὀρέων.[122]
[23]συνάξω εἰς αὐτοὺς κακά,
καὶ τὰ βέλη[123] μου συντελέσω[124] εἰς αὐτούς.
[24]τηκόμενοι[125] λιμῷ[126] καὶ βρώσει[127] ὀρνέων,[128]
καὶ ὀπισθότονος[129] ἀνίατος·[130]
ὀδόντας[131] θηρίων ἀποστελῶ εἰς αὐτούς,
μετὰ θυμοῦ συρόντων[132] ἐπὶ γῆς.
[25]ἔξωθεν[133] ἀτεκνώσει[134] αὐτοὺς μάχαιρα,[135]
καὶ ἐκ τῶν ταμιείων[136] φόβος·
νεανίσκος[137] σὺν παρθένῳ,[138]
θηλάζων[139] μετὰ καθεστηκότος[140]
  πρεσβύτου.[141]

[26]εἶπα Διασπερῶ[142] αὐτούς,
παύσω[143] δὴ[144] ἐξ ἀνθρώπων τὸ μνημόσυνον[145]
  αὐτῶν·
[27]εἰ μὴ δι' ὀργὴν ἐχθρῶν, ἵνα μὴ
  μακροχρονίσωσιν,[146]
καὶ ἵνα μὴ συνεπιθῶνται[147] οἱ ὑπεναντίοι,[148]
μὴ εἴπωσιν[149] Ἡ χεὶρ ἡμῶν ἡ ὑψηλή,[150]
καὶ οὐχὶ κύριος ἐποίησεν ταῦτα πάντα.
[28]ὅτι ἔθνος ἀπολωλεκὸς[151] βουλήν[152] ἐστιν,
καὶ οὐκ ἔστιν ἐν αὐτοῖς ἐπιστήμη.[153]
[29]οὐκ ἐφρόνησαν[154] συνιέναι[155] ταῦτα·
καταδεξάσθωσαν[156] εἰς τὸν ἐπιόντα[157]
  χρόνον.
[30]πῶς διώξεται[158] εἰς χιλίους,[159]
καὶ δύο μετακινήσουσιν[160] μυριάδας,[161]

115. Fut. pass. indic. 3 sg., καίω, (intrans.) *burn*.
116. Prep. with gen., *up to, as far as*.
117. ᾅδης, -ου, ὁ, *Hades*.
118. Adv., *below*.
119. Fut. mid. indic. 3 sg., κατεσθίω, *devour*.
120. Fut. act. indic. 3 sg., φλέγω, *set on fire*.
121. θεμέλιον, -ου, τό, *foundation*.
122. ὄρος, -ους, τό, *mountain*.
123. βέλος, -ους, τό, *arrow*.
124. Fut. act. indic. 1 sg., συντελέω, *finish off, use up*.
125. Pres. pass. ptc. nom. masc. pl., τήκω, (pass.) *be wasted away*.
126. λιμός, -οῦ, ὁ, *famine*.
127. βρῶσις, -εως, ἡ, *eating*.
128. ὄρνεον, -ου, τό, *bird*.
129. ὀπισθότονος, -ου, ὁ, *opisthotony* (medical condition that curves the body backward).
130. ἀνίατος, -ον, *incurable*.
131. ὀδούς, -όντος, ὁ, *tooth*.
132. Pres. act. ptc. gen. masc. pl., σύρω, *to crawl*; attrib. (subst.); i.e., "creatures that drag/crawl."
133. Adv., *from outside*.
134. Fut. act. indic. 3 sg., ἀτεκνόω, *make barren*.
135. μάχαιρα, -ας, ἡ, *dagger*.
136. ταμιεῖον, -ου, τό, *small inner room*, (metaph.) one's inner being.
137. νεανίσκος, -ου, ὁ, *young man*.
138. παρθένος, -ου, ἡ, *virgin, maiden*.
139. Pres. act. ptc. nom. masc. sg., θηλάζω, *nurse*; attrib. (subst.).
140. Pf. act. ptc. gen. masc. sg., καθίστημι, (intrans.) *be, be established*; attrib. (subst.).
141. πρεσβύτης, -ου, ὁ, *old man*.

142. Fut. act. indic. 1 sg., διασπείρω, *scatter*.
143. Fut. act. indic. 1 sg., παύω, *make cease*. Wevers (1995, 254) reads it as a hortatory subjunctive.
144. Postpositive partic., *certainly, surely, indeed*: "indicates that the speaker considers (and invites the addressee to consider) the text segment or word (group) which it modifies as evident, clear, or precise" (*CGCG* §59.44).
145. μνημόσυνον, -ου, τό, *remembrance*.
146. Aor. act. subj. 3 pl., μακροχρονίζω, *last for a long time*; purpose clause (cf. BDF §369; S §2193; *CGCG* §45.3).
147. Aor. mid. subj. 3 pl., συνεπιτίθημι, (mid.) *join in attacking* (*GELS*, 655), though the sense is somewhat ambiguous: "so that their adversaries not collaborate" (*NETS*); "and let not their adversaries boast" (Dogniez and Harl 1992, 334).
148. ὑπεναντίος, -ου, ὁ, *opponent, adversary*.
149. Prohibitive (cf. BDF §364; S §1800; *CGCG* §34.7). Wevers (1995, 524) reads the verb as an extension of the purpose clause. For further discussion, see notes.
150. ὑψηλός, -ή, -όν, *lifted high, raised*.
151. Pf. act. ptc. nom. neut. sg., ἀπόλλυμι, *lose* (something); ἀπολωλεκὸς βουλήν, "at their wits' end" (*GELS*, 79.II.4).
152. βουλή, -ῆς, ἡ, *council*.
153. ἐπιστήμη, -ης, ἡ, *knowledge*.
154. Aor. act. indic. 3 pl., φρονέω, *be wise*.
155. Pres. act. inf. συνίημι, *understand*; result (cf. BDF §391; S §2011; *CGCG* §51.16).
156. Aor. mid. impv. 3 pl., καταδέχομαι, *accept*.
157. Pres. act. ptc. acc. masc. sg., ἔπειμι, *follow, come after*; attrib.
158. Fut. mid. indic. 3 sg., διώκω, *pursue*.
159. χίλιοι, -αι, -α, *a thousand*.
160. Fut. act. indic. 3 pl., μετακινέω, *remove*.
161. μυριάς, -άδος, ἡ, *myriad, ten thousand*.

εἰ μὴ ὁ θεὸς ἀπέδοτο¹⁶² αὐτούς,
καὶ κύριος παρέδωκεν¹⁶³ αὐτούς;
³¹ὅτι οὐκ ἔστιν¹⁶⁴ ὡς ὁ θεὸς ἡμῶν οἱ θεοὶ
  αὐτῶν·
οἱ δὲ ἐχθροὶ ἡμῶν ἀνόητοι.¹⁶⁵
³²ἐκ γὰρ ἀμπέλου¹⁶⁶ Σοδόμων ἡ ἄμπελος
  αὐτῶν,
καὶ ἡ κληματὶς¹⁶⁷ αὐτῶν ἐκ Γομόρρας·
ἡ σταφυλὴ αὐτῶν σταφυλὴ χολῆς,¹⁶⁸
βότρυς¹⁶⁹ πικρίας¹⁷⁰ αὐτοῖς·
³³θυμὸς δρακόντων¹⁷¹ ὁ οἶνος αὐτῶν,
καὶ θυμὸς ἀσπίδων¹⁷² ἀνίατος.¹⁷³
³⁴οὐκ ἰδοὺ ταῦτα συνῆκται¹⁷⁴ παρ' ἐμοί,
καὶ ἐσφράγισται¹⁷⁵ ἐν τοῖς θησαυροῖς¹⁷⁶ μου;
³⁵ἐν ἡμέρᾳ ἐκδικήσεως¹⁷⁷ ἀνταποδώσω,¹⁷⁸
ἐν καιρῷ, ὅταν σφαλῇ¹⁷⁹ ὁ πούς αὐτῶν·
ὅτι ἐγγὺς¹⁸⁰ ἡμέρα ἀπωλείας¹⁸¹ αὐτῶν,
καὶ πάρεστιν¹⁸² ἕτοιμα¹⁸³ ὑμῖν.

³⁶ὅτι κρινεῖ¹⁸⁴ κύριος τὸν λαὸν αὐτοῦ,
καὶ ἐπὶ τοῖς δούλοις αὐτοῦ παρακληθήσεται·¹⁸⁵
εἶδεν γὰρ παραλελυμένους¹⁸⁶ αὐτοὺς
καὶ ἐκλελοιπότας¹⁸⁷ ἐν ἐπαγωγῇ¹⁸⁸ καὶ
  παρειμένους.¹⁸⁹
³⁷καὶ εἶπεν κύριος Ποῦ εἰσιν οἱ θεοὶ αὐτῶν,
ἐφ' οἷς ἐπεποίθεισαν¹⁹⁰ ἐπ' αὐτοῖς,
³⁸ὧν τὸ στέαρ¹⁹¹ τῶν θυσιῶν¹⁹² αὐτῶν
  ἠσθίετε,
καὶ ἐπίνετε τὸν οἶνον τῶν σπονδῶν¹⁹³ αὐτῶν;
ἀναστήτωσαν¹⁹⁴ καὶ βοηθησάτωσαν¹⁹⁵ ὑμῖν,
καὶ γενηθήτωσαν ὑμῖν σκεπασταί.¹⁹⁶
³⁹ἴδετε ἴδετε ὅτι ἐγώ εἰμι,
καὶ οὐκ ἔστιν θεὸς πλὴν¹⁹⁷ ἐμοῦ·
ἐγὼ ἀποκτενῶ¹⁹⁸ καὶ ζῆν ποιήσω,
πατάξω¹⁹⁹ κἀγὼ ἰάσομαι,²⁰⁰
καὶ οὐκ ἔστιν ὃς ἐξελεῖται²⁰¹ ἐκ τῶν χειρῶν
  μου.
⁴⁰ὅτι ἀρῶ εἰς τὸν οὐρανὸν τὴν χεῖρά μου

---

162. Aor. mid. indic. 3 sg., ἀποδίδωμι, (mid.) *sell*.
163. Aor. act. indic. 3 sg., παραδίδωμι, *hand over*.
164. "A clause may start off with a verb in the singular, then followed by a close constituent in the plural" (*SSG* §77bk; cf. S §961).
165. ἀνόητος, -ον, *without understanding, foolish*.
166. ἄμπελος, -ου, ἡ, *vine*.
167. κληματίς, -ίδος, ἡ, *vine branch*.
168. χολή, -ῆς, ἡ, *gall*.
169. βότρυς, -υος, ὁ, *bunch/cluster* (of grapes).
170. πικρία, -ας, ἡ, *bitterness*.
171. δράκων, -οντος, ὁ, *dragon, serpent*.
172. ἀσπίς, -ίδος, ἡ, *asp*.
173. ἀνίατος, -ον, *incurable*.
174. Pf. pass. indic. 3 sg., συνάγω, (pass.) *be gathered*.
175. Pf. pass. indic. 3 sg., σφραγίζω, (pass.) *be sealed*.
176. θησαυρός, -οῦ, ὁ, *treasury*.
177. ἐκδίκησις, -εως, ἡ, *vengeance, retribution*.
178. Fut. act. indic. 1 sg., ἀνταποδίδωμι, *repay*.
179. Aor. pass. subj. 3 sg., σφάλλω, (pass.) *be tripped up, stumble*; fut. temp. clause (cf. BDF §382; S §2401; CGCG §40.9).
180. Adv., *near*.
181. ἀπωλεία, -ας, ἡ, *destruction*.
182. Pres. act. indic. 3 sg., πάρειμι, *be present*.
183. ἕτοιμος, -ον, *ready*, (subst. "that which is prepared"); cf. ταῦτα in v. 34.

184. Fut. act. indic. 3 sg., κρίνω, *judge*; here in the sense of *vindicate*.
185. Fut. pass. indic. 3 sg., παρακαλέω, (pass.) *be swayed, relent*.
186. Pf. pass. ptc. acc. masc. pl., παραλύω, (pass.) *be paralyzed*; supp. (εἶδεν).
187. Pf. act. ptc. acc. masc. pl., ἐκλείπω, *fail, lose strength*; supp. (εἶδεν).
188. ἐπαγωγή, -ῆς, ἡ, *attack*.
189. Pf. pass. ptc. acc. masc. pl., παρίημι, (pass.) *be weakened*; supp. (εἶδεν).
190. Plpf. act. indic. 3 pl., πείθω, *trust*; with dat., which is resumed by a pronoun (resumptive pron.) in the same case (ἐφ' οἷς . . . ἐπ' αὐτοῖς). Translated: "in whom they had put their trust." See n. 108.
191. στέαρ, -ατος, τό, *fat*.
192. θυσία, -ας, ἡ, *sacrifice*.
193. σπονδή, -ῆς, ἡ, *libation*.
194. Aor. act. impv. 3 pl., ἀνίστημι, *rise up*.
195. Aor. act. impv. 3 pl., βοηθέω, *help*; with dat.
196. σκεπαστής, -οῦ, ὁ, *protector*.
197. Prep. with gen., *except, besides, other than*.
198. Fut. act. indic. 1 sg., ἀποκτείνω, *kill*.
199. Fut. act. indic. 1 sg., πατάσσω, *strike*.
200. Fut. mid. indic. 1 sg., ἰάομαι, *heal*.
201. Fut. act. indic. 3 sg., ἐξαιρέω, *take away*.

καὶ ὀμοῦμαι²⁰² τῇ δεξιᾷ μου
καὶ ἐρῶ Ζῶ ἐγὼ εἰς τὸν αἰῶνα,
⁴¹ὅτι παροξυνῶ²⁰³ ὡς ἀστραπὴν²⁰⁴ τὴν μάχαιράν μου,
καὶ ἀνθέξεται²⁰⁵ κρίματος²⁰⁶ ἡ χείρ μου,
καὶ ἀνταποδώσω δίκην²⁰⁷ τοῖς ἐχθροῖς,
καὶ τοῖς μισοῦσίν²⁰⁸ με ἀνταποδώσω·
⁴²μεθύσω²⁰⁹ τὰ βέλη²¹⁰ μου ἀφ᾽ αἵματος,
καὶ ἡ μάχαιρά μου καταφάγεται²¹¹ κρέα,²¹²
ἀφ᾽ αἵματος τραυματιῶν²¹³ καὶ αἰχμαλωσίας,²¹⁴
ἀπὸ κεφαλῆς ἀρχόντων ἐχθρῶν.
⁴³εὐφράνθητε,²¹⁵ οὐρανοί, ἅμα²¹⁶ αὐτῷ,
καὶ προσκυνησάτωσαν²¹⁷ αὐτῷ πάντες υἱοὶ
  θεοῦ·
εὐφράνθητε, ἔθνη, μετὰ τοῦ λαοῦ αὐτοῦ,
καὶ ἐνισχυσάτωσαν²¹⁸ αὐτῷ πάντες ἄγγελοι
  θεοῦ·
ὅτι τὸ αἷμα τῶν υἱῶν αὐτοῦ ἐκδικεῖται,²¹⁹
καὶ ἐκδικήσει καὶ ἀνταποδώσει δίκην τοῖς
  ἐχθροῖς,
καὶ τοῖς μισοῦσιν ἀνταποδώσει,
καὶ ἐκκαθαριεῖ²²⁰ κύριος τὴν γῆν τοῦ λαοῦ
  αὐτοῦ.

202. Fut. mid. indic. 1 sg., ὄμνυμι, *swear* (an oath).
203. Fut. act. indic. 1 sg., παροξύνω, *sharpen*.
204. ἀστραπή, -ῆς, ἡ, *lightning*.
205. Fut. mid. indic. 3 sg., ἀντέχω, *hold fast, take hold of*; with gen.
206. κρίμα, -ατος, τό, *judgment*.
207. δίκη, -ης, ἡ, *justice*.
208. Pres. act. ptc. dat. masc. pl., μισέω, *hate*; attrib. (subst.).
209. Fut. act. indic. 1 sg., μεθύσκω, *make drunk*.
210. βέλος, -ους, τό, *arrow*.
211. Fut. mid. indic. 3 sg., κατεσθίω, *devour*.
212. κρέας, κρέως, τό, (pl. κρέα) *meat, flesh*.
213. τραυματίας, -ου, ὁ, *wounded person*.
214. αἰχμαλωσία, -ας, ἡ, *captives* (collective).
215. Aor. pass. impv. 2 pl., εὐφραίνω, (pass.) *rejoice, be glad*.
216. Prep. with dat., *togther with*.
217. Aor. act. impv. 3 pl., προσκυνέω, *do obeisance, worship*.
218. Aor. act. impv. 3 pl., ἐνισχύω, *be powerful, prevail*.
219. Pres. mid. indic. 3 sg., ἐκδικέω, *avenge*.
220. Fut. act. indic. 3 sg., ἐκκαθαρίζω, *purify*.

NOTES

32:4. θεός. The OG reads θεός where the MT reads צוּר ("Rock"), a poetic name for the deity (cf. vv. 15, 18, 30, 31; omitted in v. 37, on which see below). The most likely explanation is that the translator has substituted the referent for the image (e.g., Olofsson 1990; Dogniez and Harl 1992, 322). Peters argues, by contrast, that the evidence points in the opposite direction—namely, that the translator's *Vorlage* read אלהים and that צוּר is a creation of the Masoretes (2019, 137–38; full argument in Peters 2012).

32:8. ὅτε διεμέριζεν ὁ ὕψιστος ἔθνη, ὡς διέσπειρεν υἱοὺς Ἀδάμ. The lines are parallel in the MT (i.e., ב with the infinitive construct). The translator renders the first with ὅτε plus a finite verb and the second with ὡς plus a finite verb. The shift opens two interpretive possibilities. On the one hand, the translator may have intended ὡς to be read temporally and thus as an equivalent to ὅτε (*SSG* §76d). On the other hand, the shift might suggest that the translator read the second clause as a subordinate clause of comparison. The latter seems the more natural reading. Thus, "The Most High divided the gentiles *as* he scattered the sons of Adam" (*NETS*).

32:8. υἱῶν θεοῦ. Most manuscripts read ἀγγέλων instead of υἱῶν, but the latter is preserved in manuscript 848, whose *Vorlage* may be attested in 4Q37 (4QDeutʲ): בני אלוהים. Wevers (1995, 513) states, "The change to 'angels' was clearly a later attempt to avoid any notion of lesser deities in favor of God's messengers." The MT's בני ישראל ("sons of Israel") also attests to the desire to downplay the notion of the divine council, though it may reflect an alternative *Vorlage*, perhaps בני אלים or בני אל (Wevers 1978, 85).

32:15. θεοῦ σωτῆρος αὐτοῦ. The MT reads צוּר ישעתו ("the Rock of his salvation"). Incidentally, this is the only time in the LXX Pentateuch that God is called σωτήρ, "savior" (Wevers 1995, 518).

32:26. παύσω δὴ ἐξ ἀνθρώπων τὸ μνημόσυνον αὐτῶν. According to Wevers (1995, 524), the translator uses δή "to ensure the reading of παύσω as a hortatory subjunctive, reflecting the long form אשביתה 'let me put to rest.'" I am unsure how the particle ensures such a reading. The particle can be used to underscore a hortatory subjunctive (cf. Denniston 1966, 217), but it does not establish the mood of the verb. In the LXX examples Muraoka examines, the primary feature that distinguishes an aorist subjunctive first-person singular from a future indicative first-person singular is the presence of an accompanying imperative—for example, δεῦτε (*SSG* §29ba(i)).

32:27. μὴ εἴπωσιν. Wevers (1995, 524) interprets this as part of the purpose clause. His justification for doing so appears to be contingent on the observation that μὴ εἴπωσιν renders a negative purpose clause in the Hebrew *Vorlage* (פן־יאמרו). The shift in the syntax, however, suggests that μὴ εἴπωσιν is best taken as expressing prohibition (so *NETS*; *SSG* §29ba(ii)), though, admittedly, it is not entirely clear what the translator was attempting to do.

32:30. εἰ μὴ ὁ θεὸς ἀπέδοτο αὐτούς, καὶ κύριος παρέδωκεν αὐτούς. The MT reads צורם ("their Rock") where the OG reads ὁ θεός (see note on 32:4). It is unclear whether the referent of αὐτούς is Israel or Israel's enemies. If it is the former, as I take it, then the exception clause offers the only explanation for the success of Israel's enemies: God has handed over his people to their enemies for a time.

32:36. ὅτι κρινεῖ κύριος τὸν λαὸν αὐτοῦ, καὶ ἐπὶ τοῖς δούλοις αὐτοῦ παρακληθήσεται. The judgment envisaged must be the Lord's judgment *on behalf of* Israel—that is, vindication (cf. Ps. 134:14 LXX). The reason (γάρ) for the cessation of the divine wrath comes subsequently in verse 36c–d: the Lord has seen the oppression of his people. This line gets taken up by the Maccabean martyrs (cf. 2 Macc. 7:6, 34; see §1.3.1 below).

32:37. ἐφ' οἷς ἐπεποίθεισαν ἐπ' αὐτοῖς. The MT reads צור חסיו בו ("Rock, in whom they took refuge"). Once the translator made the decision to render צור with ἐφ' οἷς, it became necessary to pluralize the object of the preposition (בו; ἐπ' αὐτοῖς) as well.

32:43. The following chart compares the OG, the MT, and 4Q44 (4QDeutq).

	OG	MT	4Q44 (4QDeutq)
1	εὐφράνθητε, οὐρανοί, ἅμα αὐτῷ,		הרנינו שמים עמו
2	καὶ προσκυνησάτωσαν αὐτῷ πάντες υἱοὶ θεοῦ·		והשתחוו לו כל אלהים
3	εὐφράνθητε, ἔθνη, μετὰ τοῦ λαοῦ αὐτοῦ,	הרנינו גוים עמו	
4	καὶ ἐνισχυσάτωσαν αὐτῷ πάντες ἄγγελοι θεοῦ		
5	ὅτι τὸ αἷμα τῶν υἱῶν αὐτοῦ ἐκδικεῖται,	כי דם־עבדיו יקום	כי דם בניו יקום
6	καὶ ἐκδικήσει, καὶ ἀνταποδώσει δίκην τοῖς ἐχθροῖς·	ונקם ישיב לצריו	ונקם ישיב לצריו
7	καὶ τοῖς μισοῦσιν ἀνταποδώσει,		ולמשנאיו ישלם
8	καὶ ἐκκαθαριεῖ κύριος τὴν γῆν τοῦ λαοῦ αὐτοῦ.	וכפר אדמתו עמו	ויכפר אדמת עמו

Observations: The MT lacks hemistichs one, two, four, and seven. The text of 4Q44 (4QDeut^q) is much closer to the OG, where the two more or less agree at hemistichs one, two, five, six, seven, and eight. There are, however, some interesting differences. For instance, the line corresponding to καὶ προσκυνησάτωσαν αὐτῷ πάντες υἱοὶ θεοῦ in 4Q44 reads "and let all the *gods* [אלהים] worship him." The Greek translator thus avoids designating the lesser deities as "gods." Most LXX manuscripts, in turn, read ἄγγελοι instead of υἱοί, which parallels πάντες ἄγγελοι θεοῦ in line four (not attested in 4Q44). The OG and 4Q44 also agree against the MT on minor details. For example, both have, "for he [God] avenges / will avenge the blood of his *sons*" (ὅτι τὸ αἷμα τῶν υἱῶν αὐτοῦ ἐκδικεῖται // כי דם בניו יקום), whereas the MT has, "for he avenges / will avenge the blood of his *servants* [עבדיו]." Moreover, the final line in the OG, "and the Lord will cleanse the land of his people," reflects the reading attested in 4Q44 (except for κύριος). The MT, by contrast, reads וכפר אדמתו עמו, which is more difficult to interpret; perhaps, "he will make atonement for his land and people."

1.2

LXX Isaiah

The Greek translation of Isaiah occurred in the second century BCE in Egypt. The Old Greek is often classified as a "free" translation, as opposed to the "literal" (i.e., isomorphic) translations of, for example, the LXX Pentateuch. Scholars point to a variety of factors that might have informed the translator's technique, including concerns of Greek syntax, stylistic variation, assimilation to the immediate context, and the influence from other passages in OG Isaiah or other biblical books (Kooji 2019, 519; Ngunga and Schaper 2015, 461–62). In so doing, the translator sought to ensure that the message of Isaiah would capture the imaginations of diaspora Jews living in Ptolemaic Egypt (esp. Wagner 2013).

Isaiah's fourth servant poem (Isa. 52:13–53:12) is, of course, of great significance for Christian theology. Yet the identity of the Isaian servant is part of a larger and ongoing conversation in early Judaism about the identity of God's people (Lyons and Stromberg 2021). The Old Greek version is an essential witness to the complex (and in places, convoluted) message of the poem.

Text: Ziegler 1983
Recommended Translation: *NETS* (http://ccat.sas.upenn.edu/nets/edition/33-esaias-nets.pdf)
Supplemental Scripture: Dan. 12:1–4; Wis. 2:12–20; Acts 8:26–40; 1 Pet. 2:18–25

1.2.1

The Poem of the Suffering Servant

Isaiah 52:13–53:12

52:13Ἰδοὺ συνήσει¹ ὁ παῖς² μου καὶ ὑψωθήσεται³ καὶ δοξασθήσεται⁴ σφόδρα.⁵ **14**ὃν τρόπον⁶ ἐκστήσονται⁷ ἐπὶ σὲ πολλοί, οὕτως ἀδοξήσει⁸ ἀπὸ ἀνθρώπων τὸ εἶδός⁹ σου καὶ ἡ δόξα σου ἀπὸ τῶν ἀνθρώπων, **15**οὕτως θαυμάσονται¹⁰ ἔθνη πολλὰ ἐπ' αὐτῷ, καὶ συνέξουσιν¹¹ βασιλεῖς τὸ στόμα αὐτῶν· ὅτι οἷς οὐκ ἀνηγγέλη¹² περὶ αὐτοῦ, ὄψονται, καὶ οἳ οὐκ ἀκηκόασιν, συνήσουσιν. **53:1**κύριε, τίς ἐπίστευσεν τῇ ἀκοῇ¹³ ἡμῶν; καὶ ὁ βραχίων¹⁴ κυρίου τίνι ἀπεκαλύφθη;¹⁵ **2**ἀνέτειλε¹⁶ μὲν ἐναντίον¹⁷ αὐτοῦ ὡς παιδίον,¹⁸ ὡς ῥίζα¹⁹ ἐν γῇ διψώσῃ,²⁰ οὐκ ἔστιν εἶδος αὐτῷ οὐδὲ δόξα· καὶ εἴδομεν αὐτόν, καὶ οὐκ εἶχεν εἶδος οὐδὲ κάλλος.²¹ **3**ἀλλὰ τὸ εἶδος αὐτοῦ ἄτιμον²² ἐκλεῖπον²³ παρὰ πάντας ἀνθρώπους, ἄνθρωπος ἐν πληγῇ²⁴ ὢν καὶ εἰδὼς φέρειν²⁵ μαλακίαν,²⁶ ὅτι ἀπέστραπται²⁷ τὸ πρόσωπον αὐτοῦ, ἠτιμάσθη²⁸ καὶ

---

1. Fut. act. indic. 3 sg., συνίημι, *comprehend, understand*.
2. παῖς, παιδός, ὁ, a translation equivalent for עבד ("servant") in LXX Isaiah.
3. Fut. pass. indic. 3 sg., ὑψόω, (pass.) *be lifted up*.
4. Fut. pass. indic. 3 sg., δοξάζω, (pass.) *be glorified*.
5. Adv., *very much, greatly*.
6. ὃν τρόπον . . . οὕτως, *just as . . . so*. The correlative οὕτως comes in v. 15, after the parenthetical statement.
7. Fut. mid. indic. 3 pl., ἐξίστημι, *be astonished*.
8. Fut. act. indic. 3 sg., ἀδοξέω, *hold* (someone) *in low esteem*.
9. εἶδος, -ους, τό, *form*.
10. Fut. mid. indic. 3 pl., θαυμάζω, *marvel, wonder*.
11. Fut. act. indic. 3 pl., συνέχω, *hold fast, shut*.
12. Aor. pass. indic. 3 sg., ἀναγγέλλω, (pass.) *be announced*. The content of the impersonal subjunctive ("it was reported") is explicated by περὶ αὐτοῦ, and the recipient is expressed in the dative (cf. *SSG* §63d).
13. ἀκοή, -ῆς, ἡ, *report*; dat. comp. of ἐπίστευσεν.
14. βραχίων, -ονος, ὁ, *arm*; nom. pendent (cf. *SSG* §84; S §§940–42; *CGCG* §60.34).
15. Aor. pass. indic. 3 sg., ἀποκαλύπτω, (pass.) *be revealed*.
16. Aor. act. indic. 3 sg., ἀνατέλλω, *spring up, sprout*; emendation; for further discussion, see notes.
17. Prep. with gen., *before*.
18. παιδίον, -ου, τό, *young child*.
19. ῥίζα, -ης, ἡ, *root*.
20. Pres. act. ptc. dat. fem. sg., διψάω, *be thirsty*; attrib.
21. κάλλος, -ους, τό, *beauty*.
22. ἄτιμος, -ον, *without honor*.
23. Pres. act. ptc. nom. neut. sg., ἐκλείπω, *lose strength, fail*.
24. πληγή, -ῆς, ἡ, *blow*; ἐν πληγῇ εἰμί, *be struck down with misfortune* (BDAG, 825.3).
25. οἶδα takes a participle to express intellectual knowledge ("know that something is the case") or an infinitive to express practical knowledge ("knowing *how to bear* sickness"), as here (cf. S §2139; *CGCG* §51.8).
26. μαλακία, -ας, ἡ, *sickness, disease*.
27. Pf. pass. indic. 3 sg., ἀποστέφω, (intrans.) *be turned away*.
28. Aor. pass. indic. 3 sg., ἀτιμάζω, (pass.) *be dishonored*.

οὐκ ἐλογίσθη.²⁹ ⁴οὗτος τὰς ἁμαρτίας ἡμῶν φέρει καὶ περὶ ἡμῶν ὀδυνᾶται,³⁰ καὶ ἡμεῖς ἐλογισάμεθα αὐτὸν εἶναι ἐν πόνῳ³¹ καὶ ἐν πληγῇ καὶ ἐν κακώσει.³² ⁵αὐτὸς δὲ ἐτραυματίσθη³³ διὰ τὰς ἀνομίας³⁴ ἡμῶν καὶ μεμαλάκισται³⁵ διὰ τὰς ἁμαρτίας ἡμῶν· παιδεία³⁶ εἰρήνης ἡμῶν ἐπ' αὐτόν, τῷ μώλωπι³⁷ αὐτοῦ ἡμεῖς ἰάθημεν.³⁸ ⁶πάντες ὡς πρόβατα³⁹ ἐπλανήθημεν,⁴⁰ ἄνθρωπος⁴¹ τῇ ὁδῷ αὐτοῦ ἐπλανήθη· καὶ κύριος παρέδωκεν⁴² αὐτὸν ταῖς ἁμαρτίαις ἡμῶν. ⁷καὶ αὐτὸς διὰ τὸ κεκακῶσθαι⁴³ οὐκ ἀνοίγει⁴⁴ τὸ στόμα· ὡς⁴⁵ πρόβατον ἐπὶ σφαγὴν⁴⁶ ἤχθη καὶ ὡς ἀμνὸς⁴⁷ ἐναντίον⁴⁸ τοῦ κείροντος⁴⁹ αὐτὸν ἄφωνος⁵⁰ οὕτως οὐκ ἀνοίγει τὸ στόμα αὐτοῦ. ⁸ἐν τῇ ταπεινώσει⁵¹ ἡ κρίσις⁵² αὐτοῦ ἤρθη· τὴν γενεὰν⁵³ αὐτοῦ τίς διηγήσεται;⁵⁴ ὅτι αἴρεται ἀπὸ τῆς γῆς ἡ ζωὴ αὐτοῦ, ἀπὸ τῶν ἀνομιῶν τοῦ λαοῦ μου ἤχθη εἰς θάνατον. ⁹καὶ δώσω τοὺς πονηροὺς ἀντὶ⁵⁵ τῆς ταφῆς⁵⁶ αὐτοῦ καὶ τοὺς πλουσίους⁵⁷ ἀντὶ τοῦ θανάτου αὐτοῦ· ὅτι ἀνομίαν οὐκ ἐποίησεν, οὐδὲ εὑρέθη δόλος⁵⁸ ἐν τῷ στόματι αὐτοῦ. ¹⁰καὶ κύριος βούλεται καθαρίσαι⁵⁹ αὐτὸν τῆς πληγῆς· ἐὰν δῶτε περὶ ἁμαρτίας,⁶⁰ ἡ ψυχὴ ὑμῶν ὄψεται σπέρμα μακρόβιον·⁶¹ καὶ βούλεται κύριος ἀφελεῖν⁶² ¹¹ἀπὸ τοῦ πόνου τῆς ψυχῆς αὐτοῦ, δεῖξαι⁶³ αὐτῷ φῶς καὶ πλάσαι⁶⁴ τῇ συνέσει, δικαιῶσαι⁶⁵ δίκαιον εὖ⁶⁶ δουλεύοντα⁶⁷ πολλοῖς, καὶ τὰς ἁμαρτίας αὐτῶν αὐτὸς ἀνοίσει.⁶⁸ ¹²διὰ τοῦτο αὐτὸς κληρονομήσει⁶⁹ πολλοὺς καὶ τῶν ἰσχυρῶν⁷⁰ μεριεῖ⁷¹ σκῦλα,⁷² ἀνθ' ὧν⁷³ παρεδόθη εἰς θάνατον ἡ ψυχὴ αὐτοῦ, καὶ ἐν τοῖς ἀνόμοις ἐλογίσθη· καὶ αὐτὸς ἁμαρτίας πολλῶν ἀνήνεγκεν καὶ διὰ τὰς ἁμαρτίας αὐτῶν παρεδόθη.

29. Aor. pass. indic. 3 sg., λογίζομαι, (pass.) *be considered/regarded* (as something).
30. Pres. pass. indic. 3 sg., ὀδυνάω, *suffer pain*.
31. πόνος, -ου, ὁ, *toil, suffering, hardship*.
32. κάκωσις, -εως, ἡ, *mistreatment, oppression*.
33. Aor. pass. indic. 3 sg., τραυματίζω, *wounded*.
34. ἀνομία, -ας, ἡ, *lawlessness*.
35. Pf. mid. indic. 3 sg., μαλακίζω, *become weak/ill*.
36. παιδεία, -ας, ἡ, *discipline, punishment*.
37. μώλωψ, -ωπος, ὁ, *wound, stripe*; dat. of means.
38. Aor. pass. indic. 1 pl., ἰάομαι, (pass.) *be healed*.
39. πρόβατον, -ου, τό, *sheep*.
40. Aor. pass. indic. 1 pl., πλανάω, (intrans.) *go astray*.
41. Distributive; i.e., "(each) person" (cf. *SSG* §77bb).
42. Aor. act. indic. 3 sg., παραδίδωμι, *hand over*.
43. Pf. pass. inf., κακόω, *be afflicted*. διὰ τό with an infinitive expresses cause (cf. BDF §402; *CGCG* §51.40). Ekblad (1999, 227) argues it should be taken temporally—i.e., "during the oppression"—which is a possible but far less common use of the collocation.
44. Pres. act. indic. 3 sg., ἀνοίγω, *open*.
45. ὡς . . . ὡς . . . οὕτως, *as . . . as . . . so*.
46. σφαγή, -ῆς, ἡ, *slaughter*.
47. ἀμνός, -οῦ, ὁ, *lamb*.
48. Prep. with gen., *before, in front of*.
49. Pres. act. ptc. gen. masc. sg., κείρω, *shear*; attrib. (subst.).
50. ἄφωνος, -ον, *mute, silent*.
51. ταπείνωσις, -εως, ἡ, *humiliation, lowliness*.
52. κρίσις, -εως, ἡ, *judgment*.
53. γενεά, -ᾶς, ἡ, *generation*; variously translated, "generation" (*NETS*), "life-story" (*GELS*, 127.4), or "family history" (BDAG, 192.4). The word order reflects the Hebrew *casus pendens* (cf. *SSG* §84b). The placement of a noun outside of the clause serves a similar discourse function in Greek: i.e., thematic highlighting.

NOTES

52:14. ὃν τρόπον . . . οὕτως. The challenges with the Greek syntax are the same as its Hebrew *Vorlage*

54. Fut. mid. indic. 3 sg., διηγέομαι, *tell, describe*.
55. Prep. with gen., *for, in place of*.
56. ταφή, -ῆς, ἡ, *burial, grave*.
57. πλούσιος, -α, -ον, *wealthy, rich*.
58. δόλος, -ου, ὁ, *deceit*.
59. Aor. act. inf., καθαρίζω, *cleanse*; comp. of βούλεται.
60. The collocation περὶ ἁμαρτίας is the translation equivalent for חטאת, "purification offering" (cf. *GELS*, 545.3b; BDAG, 789.1g).
61. μακρόβιος, -ον, *long-lived*.
62. Aor. act. inf., ἀφαιρέω, *take away, remove*.
63. Aor. act. inf., δείκνυμι, *show*.
64. Aor. act. inf., πλάσσω, *form*.
65. Aor. act. inf., δικαιόω, *justify*.
66. Adv., *well*; modifies δουλεύοντα.
67. Pres. act. ptc. acc. masc. sg., δουλεύω, *serve*.
68. Fut. act. indic. 3 sg., ἀναφέρω, *bear*.
69. Fut. act. indic. 3 sg., κληρονομέω, *inherit*.
70. ἰσχυρός, -ά, -όν, *strong, mighty*.
71. Fut. act. indic. 3 sg., μερίζω, *divide*.
72. σκῦλον, -ου, τό, *spoils*.
73. The autonomous relative ἀνθ' ὧν (lit., "in return for which things") is used to express cause.

(on which see Goldingay and Payne 2014, 290–94). Most interpreters read כן in verse 14aβ not as the correlative of כאשר in verse 14aα but as introducing a parenthesis. If this is correct, then the apodosis is introduced with כן in verse 15. The Greek translator renders כן in both verse 14aβ and verse 15aα with οὕτως.

52:15. θαυμάσονται. The MT reads יַזֶּה ("he will sprinkle/spatter"). Numerous emendations have been proposed (see Goldingay and Payne 2014, 295). Hermisson argues that the MT's יַזֶּה must be emended since נזה in the hiphil never takes a person as its direct object, and a purification ritual makes little contextual sense (Hermisson 2004, 29n42). Note, though, that both Aquila and Theodotian render יזה with ῥαντίσει.

53:1. κύριε. The vocative is not attested in any Hebrew manuscripts. It is present in both citations of Isa. 53:1 in the NT (John 12:38; Rom. 10:16).

53:2. ἀνέτειλε μέν. The MT has ויעל ("he grew up"). Ziegler's (1983) emendation brings the text in line with the Hebrew but requires one to suppose that the translator confused ἀνατέλλω for ἀναγγέλλω and μέν for the first-person plural ending -μεν. Since all Greek manuscripts, along with the patristic witnesses, read ἀνηγγείλαμεν ("we announced"), the emendation may be unnecessary. Ekblad (1999, 199) proposes that the translator read יעל as יעץ ("advise"), while van der Kooij suggests he took יעל in the sense of עלה על-לב ("come to mind") (Baltzer et al. 2011, 2666).

53:4. οὗτος τὰς ἁμαρτίας ἡμῶν φέρει. The MT reads אכן חלינו הוא נשא ("Surely, he bore our infirmities"). The translator reduces אכן . . . הוא to οὗτος, "this one" (cf. Isa. 33:16; 45:13, 18 LXX; Baltzer et al. 2011, 2667), and uses τὰς ἁμαρτίας ἡμῶν to render the term that was previously translated μαλακία (חלי). Elsewhere in the poem the translator uses ἁμαρτία to render אשם (53:10), עון (53:5, 6, 11), חטא (53:12), and פשע (53:12).

53:6. καὶ κύριος παρέδωκεν αὐτὸν ταῖς ἁμαρτίαις ἡμῶν. The MT reads ויהוה הפגיע בו את עון כלנו ("and the LORD let fall upon him all our iniquities"). As in verse 12, the translator uses παραδίδωμι to render פגע, but the choice of ταῖς ἁμαρτίαις is curious. I suspect the translator read את not as the object marker but as a preposition. Be that as it may, I agree with Kraus (2009, 159) that ταῖς ἁμαρτίαις ἡμῶν is best taken as the consequence to which the servant is handed over—that is, *to mistreatment by human beings* (cf. *NETS*: "the Lord handed him over *to* our sins").

53:9. καὶ δώσω τοὺς πονηροὺς ἀντὶ τῆς ταφῆς αὐτοῦ καὶ τοὺς πλουσίους ἀντὶ τοῦ θανάτου αὐτοῦ. The MT reads ויתן את-רשעים קברו ואת-עשיר במתיו ("and he gave his tomb with criminals and with a rich man in his death"). The OG introduces divine speech with δώσω. The translator reads את as a direct object marker and supplies ἀντί to mark the group for which the object is exchanged. The sense is one of divine retribution: the Lord will punish the wicked and the rich for their mistreatment of his righteous servant.

53:10. καὶ κύριος βούλεται καθαρίσαι αὐτὸν τῆς πληγῆς· ἐὰν δῶτε περὶ ἁμαρτίας. The MT reads ויהוה חפץ דכאו [החלים את-שם] אשם נפשו ("yet the LORD, whose plan it was to crush him, healed the one who made his life the means of wiping out guilt"; emended by Hermisson 2004, 27). The uncertainty of the MT has led to numerous emendations (Goldingay and Payne 2014, 321). For καθαρίσαι, the translator may have read the Aramaic דכה, "to cleanse" (Grelot 1981, 107), as in Targum Isaiah. The translator reads החלי as a noun (cf. 4Q58 [4QIsa[d]]), as also in verse 3, and renders it with the ablatival genitive τῆς πληγῆς. The protasis may be translated, "If you [pl.] give a sin offering [περὶ ἁμαρτίας]." No extant Hebrew manuscript has a plural subject. The translator's *Vorlage* may have had תשימו instead of תשים, or he may have read the former for the latter. The shift from אשם ("reparation offering") to περὶ ἁμαρτίας, the typical translation equivalent for חטאת ("purification offering"), is intriguing, though not without precedent (cf. Gen. 42:21; Lev. 5:7; Num. 18:9; 1 Chron. 21:3; 2 Chron. 28:13). The suggestion seems to be that the congregation (pl. "you") should repent so that they might share in the servant's destiny (Hengel 2004, 129).

53:11. καὶ πλάσαι τῇ συνέσει. The MT reads בדעתו ישבע ("[and] he will find satisfaction in his knowledge"; *waw* in 1QIsa[a] but not 1Q8 [1QIsa[b]]). Some prefer the emendation πλῆσαι (*NETS*). Thus, instead of "to form [him] in understanding," we would read, "to fill him with understanding."

δικαιῶσαι δίκαιον εὖ δουλεύοντα πολλοῖς. The MT reads יצדיק צדיק עבדי לרבם ("the righteous one, my servant [1Q8: עבדו, his servant], will make many righteous"). The translator makes God the subject of יצדיק (read as inf.) and צדיק its object and reads עבדי as a participle with לרבם as its object. Hengel (2004, 128) remarks on the OG, "Here lies the root of the New Testament idea of the resurrection as the justification or vindication of the crucified one (1 Tim. 3:16; John 16:10; cf. also Rom. 4:25)."

1.3

2 Maccabees

Second Maccabees is a second- or first-century BCE epitome of the (now lost) five-volume history of Jason of Cyrene (cf. 2 Macc. 2:23, 26). The narrative centers on the Hasmonean uprising against the Seleucid tyrant Antiochus IV Epiphanes, but with marked differences from 1 Maccabees. In particular, the epitomizer wants to establish the dynamics of the covenant relationship: punishment for sin as divine discipline designed to preserve the Jewish people (cf. 2 Macc. 6:12–16). Here enter the Maccabean martyrs, whose deaths, the epitomizer suggests, are the catalyst for divine redemption, the event that flips the Deuteronomic script, as it were.

The reading passage covers the epitomizer's account of the martyrdom of an unnamed mother and her seven sons, which follows on the heels of the martyrdom of Eleazar (2 Macc. 6:18–31; cf. 4 Macc. 6:1–30, §1.4.1 below). These are some of our earliest examples of a Jewish iteration of the "noble death tradition" (Henten and Avemarie 2002). The martyrs are emboldened to die, as they make abundantly clear to their torturers, because they trust that their God has the power to raise and reconstitute their dismembered bodies (cf. 2 Macc. 7:11, 14, 23, 29, 36).

Text: Hanhart 1959

Recommended Translation: *NETS* (http://ccat.sas.upenn.edu/nets/edition/21-2makk-nets.pdf)

Supplemental Scripture: Deut. 32; 4 Macc. 14:11–16:2; T. Mos. 9

1.3.1

The Martyrdom of a Jewish Mother and Her Seven Sons

2 Maccabees 7

7:1Συνέβη¹ δὲ καὶ ἑπτὰ ἀδελφοὺς μετὰ τῆς μητρὸς συλλημφθέντας² ἀναγκάζεσθαι³ ὑπὸ τοῦ βασιλέως ἀπὸ τῶν ἀθεμίτων⁴ ὑείων⁵ κρεῶν⁶ ἐφάπτεσθαι⁷ μάστιξιν⁸ καὶ νευραῖς⁹ αἰκιζομένους.¹⁰ **²**εἷς δὲ αὐτῶν γενόμενος προήγορος¹¹ οὕτως ἔφη Τί μέλλεις ἐρωτᾶν¹² καὶ μανθάνειν¹³ ἡμῶν; ἕτοιμοι¹⁴ γὰρ ἀποθνῄσκειν ἐσμὲν ἢ παραβαίνειν¹⁵ τοὺς πατρίους¹⁶ νόμους. **³**ἔκθυμος¹⁷ δὲ γενόμενος ὁ βασιλεὺς προσέταξεν¹⁸ τήγανα¹⁹ καὶ λέβητας²⁰ ἐκπυροῦν.²¹ **⁴**τῶν δὲ παραχρῆμα²² ἐκπυρωθέντων²³ τὸν γενόμενον αὐτῶν προήγορον προσέταξεν γλωσσοτομεῖν²⁴ καὶ περισκυθίσαντας²⁵ ἀκρωτηριάζειν²⁶ τῶν λοιπῶν ἀδελφῶν καὶ τῆς μητρὸς

---

1. Aor. act. indic. 3 sg., συμβαίνω, (quasi-impers.) *it happens*; with acc. and inf. (cf. BDF §408; S §1985; *CGCG* §36.4).
2. Aor. pass. ptc. acc. masc. pl., συλλαμβάνω, (pass.) *be seized, arrested*; circ.
3. Pres. pass. inf., ἀναγκάζω, *be compelled*; with inf.
4. ἀθέμιτος, -ον, *unlawful*.
5. ὕειος, -α, -ον, *of/pertaining to pigs*.
6. κρέας, κρέως, τό, *meat*.
7. Pres. mid. inf., ἐφάπτομαι, *partake of*; with (ἀπό) gen.; comp. of ἀναγκάζεσθαι.
8. μάστιξ, -ιγος, ἡ, *whip*; dat. of instrument.
9. νευρά, -ᾶς, ἡ, *sinew, cord of sinew*; dat. of instrument.
10. Pres. pass. ptc. acc. masc. sg., αἰκίζω, (pass.) *be tortured*; circ.
11. προήγορος, -ου, ὁ, *spokesman*.
12. Pres. act. inf., ἐρωτάω, *ask*.
13. Pres. act. inf., μανθάνω, *learn*; with gen. (source).
14. ἕτοιμος, -η, -ον, *ready*. ἕτοιμος . . . ἤ is used "to indicate preference for one of two or more alternatives, which is equivalent to disjunctive expression, 'not A, but B'" (*SSG* §23bdb).
15. Pres. act. inf., παραβαίνω, *transgress*; epex. (cf. BDF §394; S §2002; *CGCG* §51.18).
16. πάτριος, -α, -ον, *ancestral*.
17. ἔκθυμος, -ον, *enraged*.
18. Aor. act. indic. 3 sg., προστάσσω, *command, order*; with acc. and inf.
19. τήγανον, -ου, τό, *frying pan*.
20. λέβης, -ητος, ὁ, *cauldron*.
21. Pres. act. inf., ἐκπυρόω, *heat*. Supply the accusative subject of the infinitive: "He ordered [them] to heat the frying pans and cauldrons."
22. Adv., *immediately*.
23. Aor. pass. ptc. gen. neut. pl., ἐκπυρόω, (pass.) *be heated*; gen. absol.
24. Pres. act. inf., γλωσσοτομέω, *cut out the tongue*.
25. Aor. act. ptc. acc. masc. pl., περισκυθίζω, *scalp*; circ.
26. Pres. act. inf., ἀκρωτηριάζω, *cut off hands and feet*.

συνορώντων.²⁷ ⁵ἄχρηστον²⁸ δὲ αὐτὸν τοῖς ὅλοις²⁹ γενόμενον ἐκέλευσεν³⁰ τῇ πυρᾷ³¹ προσάγειν³² ἔμπνουν³³ καὶ τηγανίζειν.³⁴ τῆς δὲ ἀτμίδος³⁵ ἐφ' ἱκανὸν³⁶ διαδιδούσης³⁷ τοῦ τηγάνου³⁸ ἀλλήλους παρεκάλουν³⁹ σὺν τῇ μητρὶ γενναίως⁴⁰ τελευτᾶν⁴¹ λέγοντες οὕτως ⁶Ὁ κύριος ὁ θεὸς ἐφορᾷ⁴² καὶ ταῖς ἀληθείαις ἐφ' ἡμῖν παρακαλεῖται,⁴³ καθάπερ διὰ τῆς κατὰ πρόσωπον ἀντιμαρτυρούσης⁴⁴ ᾠδῆς διεσάφησεν⁴⁵ Μωυσῆς λέγων Καὶ ἐπὶ τοῖς δούλοις αὐτοῦ παρακληθήσεται.

⁷Μεταλλάξαντος⁴⁶ δὲ τοῦ πρώτου τὸν τρόπον τοῦτον⁴⁷ τὸν δεύτερον ἦγον ἐπὶ τὸν ἐμπαιγμὸν⁴⁸ καὶ τὸ τῆς κεφαλῆς δέρμα⁴⁹ σὺν ταῖς θριξὶν⁵⁰ περισύραν-

τες⁵¹ ἐπηρώτων⁵² Εἰ⁵³ φάγεσαι πρὸ τοῦ τιμωρηθῆναι⁵⁴ τὸ σῶμα κατὰ μέλος;⁵⁵ ⁸ὁ δὲ ἀποκριθεὶς τῇ πατρίῳ φωνῇ⁵⁶ προσεῖπεν⁵⁷ Οὐχί. διόπερ⁵⁸ καὶ οὗτος τὴν ἑξῆς⁵⁹ ἔλαβεν βάσανον⁶⁰ ὡς ὁ πρῶτος. ⁹ἐν ἐσχάτῃ δὲ πνοῇ⁶¹ γενόμενος εἶπεν Σὺ μέν,⁶² ἀλάστωρ,⁶³ ἐκ τοῦ παρόντος⁶⁴ ἡμᾶς ζῆν ἀπολύεις,⁶⁵ ὁ δὲ τοῦ κόσμου βασιλεὺς ἀποθανόντας⁶⁶ ἡμᾶς ὑπὲρ τῶν αὐτοῦ νόμων εἰς αἰώνιον ἀναβίωσιν⁶⁷ ζωῆς ἡμᾶς ἀναστήσει.

¹⁰Μετὰ δὲ τοῦτον ὁ τρίτος ἐνεπαίζετο⁶⁸ καὶ τὴν γλῶσσαν αἰτηθεὶς⁶⁹ ταχέως προέβαλεν⁷⁰ καὶ τὰς χεῖρας εὐθαρσῶς⁷¹ προέτεινεν⁷² ¹¹καὶ γενναίως εἶπεν Ἐξ

27. Pres. act. ptc. gen. masc. pl., συνοράω, *look on*; gen. absol.
28. ἄχρηστος, -ον, *useless*.
29. Dat. of respect; masc., "in all his body parts"; or more likely, neut., "in every way" (Ehorn 2020, 244).
30. Aor. act. indic. 3 sg., κελεύω, *command, order*; with acc. and inf.
31. πυρά, -ᾶς, ἡ, *fire*.
32. Pres. act. inf., προσάγω, *lead*.
33. ἔμπνους, -ουν, *alive*.
34. Pres. act. inf., τηγανίζω, *fry*.
35. ἀτμίς, -ίδος, ἡ, *smoke*.
36. ἐφ' ἱκανόν, *for some time*.
37. Pres. act. ptc. gen. fem. sg., διαδίδωμι, (intrans.) *spread about*; gen. absol.
38. τήγανον, -ου, τό, *frying pan*.
39. Impf. act. indic. 3 pl., παρακαλέω, *encourage, exhort*; with acc. and inf.
40. Adv., *nobly*.
41. Pres. act. inf., τελευτάω, *die*.
42. Pres. act. indic. 3 sg., ἐφοράω, *watch over*.
43. Pres. pass. indic. 3 sg., παρακαλέω, (pass.) *be moved to compassion, swayed* (GELS, 527.6).
44. Pres. act. ptc. gen. fem. sg., ἀντιμαρτυρέω, *bear witness against*; attrib.
45. Aor. act. indic. 3 sg., διασαφέω, *declare*.
46. Aor. act. ptc. gen. masc. sg., μεταλάσσω, (euph.) *die*; gen. absol.
47. Adv. acc. (manner), *in this way* (cf. S §1608; CGCG §30.18).
48. ἐμπαιγμός, -οῦ, ὁ, *mockery*. ἐπὶ τὸν ἐμπαιγμόν is purposive: "for mockery," "to mock [him]" (cf. S §1689.3.d).
49. δέρμα, -ατος, τό, *skin*.
50. θρίξ, τριχός, ἡ, *hair*.

51. Aor. act. ptc. nom. masc. pl., περισύρω, *tear*; circ.
52. Impf. act. indic. 3 pl., ἐπερωτάω, *ask*.
53. One expects εἰ to mark an indirect question (cf. BDF §368; S §2671; CGCG §42.3), but here it marks a direct question: "Will you eat?" Muraoka discusses other similar instances in LXX texts (cf. SSG §88).
54. Aor. pass. inf., τιμωρέω, (pass.) *be punished*. Here, πρὸ τοῦ plus the infinitive expresses preference (cf. MGS, 1741. II.D): "Will you eat rather than have your body punished limb by limb?" (NETS).
55. μέλος, -ους, τό, *part*. κατά is distributive: "limb by limb" (S §1690.2.c).
56. Dat. of respect; i.e., "in Hebrew."
57. Aor. act. indic. 3 sg., προσεῖπον, *speak to, address*.
58. Adv., *on account of which*.
59. Adv., *successively, in turn*; modifies the noun; thus, "He took the next torture" (SSG §24b).
60. βάσανος, -ου, ἡ, *torture*.
61. πνοή, -ῆς, ἡ, *breath*.
62. μέν . . . δέ; point/counterpoint (cf. Runge 2010, 75–83; BDF §447; S §2904; CGCG §59.24).
63. ἀλάστωρ, -ορος, ὁ, a person whose deeds merit vengeance (LSJ, 61.II); here as voc.: "Accursed wretch!"
64. Pres. act. ptc. gen. masc. sg., πάρειμι, *be present*; attrib. modifier of gen. art. inf., which is the obj. of ἐκ. Without the preposition, the noun phrase would be τὸ πάρον ἡμᾶς ζῆν, "our present living."
65. Pres. act. indic. 2 sg., ἀπολύω, *release*.
66. Aor. act. ptc. acc. masc. pl., ἀποθνήσκω, *die*; circ. (causal).
67. ἀναβίωσις, -εως, ἡ, *renewal of life*; εἰς αἰώνιον ἀναβίωσιν expresses the purpose/goal of the verb (cf. S §1686.1.d).
68. Impf. pass. indic. 3 sg., ἐμπαίζω, (pass.) *be mocked*.
69. Aor. pass. ptc. nom. masc. sg., αἰτέω, (pass.) *be asked*; circ.
70. Aor. act. indic. 3 sg., προβάλλω, *put forth*.
71. Adv., *courageously*.
72. Aor. act. indic. 3 sg., προτείνω, *stretch forth*.

οὐρανοῦ ταῦτα κέκτημαι⁷³ καὶ διὰ τοὺς αὐτοῦ νόμους ὑπερορῶ⁷⁴ ταῦτα καὶ παρ' αὐτοῦ ταῦτα πάλιν ἐλπίζω κομίσασθαι·⁷⁵ ¹²ὥστε αὐτὸν τὸν βασιλέα καὶ τοὺς σὺν αὐτῷ ἐκπλήσσεσθαι⁷⁶ τὴν τοῦ νεανίσκου⁷⁷ ψυχήν, ὡς ἐν οὐδενὶ⁷⁸ τὰς ἀλγηδόνας⁷⁹ ἐτίθετο.

¹³Καὶ τούτου δὲ μεταλλάξαντος τὸν τέταρτον ὡσαύτως ἐβασάνιζον αἰκιζόμενοι. ¹⁴καὶ γενόμενος πρὸς τὸ τελευτᾶν⁸⁰ οὕτως ἔφη Αἱρετὸν⁸¹ μεταλλάσσοντας ἀπ' ἀνθρώπων⁸² τὰς ὑπὸ τοῦ θεοῦ προσδοκᾶν⁸³ ἐλπίδας πάλιν ἀναστήσεσθαι⁸⁴ ὑπ' αὐτοῦ· σοὶ μὲν⁸⁵ γὰρ ἀνάστασις⁸⁶ εἰς ζωὴν οὐκ ἔσται.

¹⁵Ἐχομένως⁸⁷ δὲ τὸν πέμπτον προσάγοντες ᾐκίζοντο. ¹⁶ὁ δὲ πρὸς αὐτὸν ἰδὼν εἶπεν Ἐξουσίαν ἐν ἀνθρώποις ἔχων φθαρτὸς⁸⁸ ὢν ὃ θέλεις ποιεῖς· μὴ δόκει⁸⁹ δὲ τὸ γένος⁹⁰ ἡμῶν ὑπὸ τοῦ θεοῦ καταλελεῖφθαι.⁹¹ ¹⁷σὺ δὲ καρτέρει⁹² καὶ θεώρει⁹³ τὸ μεγαλεῖον⁹⁴ αὐτοῦ κράτος,⁹⁵ ὡς σὲ καὶ τὸ σπέρμα σου βασανιεῖ.⁹⁶

¹⁸Μετὰ δὲ τοῦτον ἦγον τὸν ἕκτον, καὶ μέλλων ἀποθνῄσκειν ἔφη Μὴ πλανῶ⁹⁷ μάτην,⁹⁸ ἡμεῖς γὰρ δι' ἑαυτοὺς ταῦτα πάσχομεν⁹⁹ ἁμαρτόντες εἰς τὸν ἑαυτῶν θεόν. ἄξια¹⁰⁰ θαυμασμοῦ¹⁰¹ γέγονεν· ¹⁹σὺ δὲ μὴ νομίσῃς¹⁰² ἀθῷος¹⁰³ ἔσεσθαι θεομαχεῖν¹⁰⁴ ἐπιχειρήσας.¹⁰⁵

²⁰Ὑπεραγόντως¹⁰⁶ δὲ ἡ μήτηρ θαυμαστὴ καὶ μνήμης¹⁰⁷ ἀγαθῆς ἀξία, ἥτις ἀπολλυμένους¹⁰⁸ υἱοὺς ἑπτὰ συνορῶσα μιᾶς ὑπὸ καιρὸν ἡμέρας¹⁰⁹ εὐψύχως¹¹⁰ ἔφερεν διὰ τὰς ἐπὶ κύριον ἐλπίδας. ²¹ἕκαστον δὲ αὐτῶν παρεκάλει τῇ πατρίῳ φωνῇ γενναίῳ πεπληρωμένη¹¹¹

---

73. Pf. mid. indic. 1 sg., κτάομαι, *obtain*, (pf.) *acquired*.
74. Pres. act. indic. 1 sg., ὑπεροράω, *disregard*.
75. Aor. mid. inf., κομίζω, *receive*; comp. of ἐλπίζω (cf. BDF §338; S §1999; CGCG §51.31)..
76. Pres. pass. inf., ἐκπλήσσω, (pass.) *be astonished at*; result clause (cf. BDF §391; S §2269; CGCG §46.6).
77. νεανίσκος, -ου, ἡ, *young man*.
78. ἐν οὐδενί indicates manner: "He regarded his sufferings *as nothing*."
79. ἀλγηδών, -όνος, ἡ, *pain*.
80. The art. inf. is the object of πρός, which, as an adverbial modifier of γενόμενος, should be understood directionally (cf. GELS, 589.IIIa); i.e., "when he had neared death."
81. αἱρετός, -ή, -όν, (quasi-impers.) *it is preferable*; with acc. and inf. (cf. BDF §393; S §1984; CGCG §36.8).
82. Hanhart follows MS A in reading ἀπ' ἀνθρώπων; other MSS read ὑπ' ἀνθρώπων, "at the hands of men."
83. Pres. act. inf., προσδοκάω, *await*.
84. Fut. mid. inf., ἀνίστημι, *rise* (from the dead); epex. (τὰς . . . ἐλπίδας).
85. μέν . . . δέ. Transitional: the μέν-clause buttresses (γάρ) the previous assertion, while the δέ-clause transitions back to the main narrative.
86. ἀνάστασις, -εως, ἡ, *resurrection*.
87. Adv., *next*.
88. φθαρτός, -ή, -όν, *mortal*. I read φθαρτὸς ὢν as concessive: "Since you have authority among men, *even though you are mortal*, you do what you wish" (cf. SSG §31di).
89. Pres. act. impv. 2 sg., δοκέω, *think, presume*.
90. γένος, -ους, τό, *people group, race*.
91. Pf. pass. inf., καταλείπω, (pass.) *be abandoned*; indir. disc. (cf. BDF §397; S §2016; CGCG §51.19).
92. Pres. act. impv. 2 sg., καρτερέω, *be patient, wait*.
93. Pres. act. impv. 2 sg., θεωρέω, *see*. σὺ δὲ καρτέρει καὶ θεώρει, "You just wait" (Schwartz 2008, 306), captures the sense.
94. μεγαλεῖος, -ον, *mighty*.
95. κράτος, -ους, τό, *power*.
96. Fut. act. indic. 3 sg., βασανίζω, *torment, torture*.
97. Pres. mid. impv. 2 sg., πλανάω, (mid.) *deceive* (oneself).
98. Adv., *in futility, in vain*.
99. Pres. act. indic. 1 pl., πάσχω, *suffer*.
100. ἄξιος, -α, -ον, *worthy*; with gen.
101. θαυμασμός, -οῦ, ὁ, *marveling, amazement*. ἄξια θαυμασμοῦ γέγονεν is absent in a few MSS, and scholars are divided as to whether it is original or a marginal gloss.
102. Pres. act. subj. 2 sg., νομίζω, *think, suppose*; prohibitive (cf. BDF §364; S §1800; CGCG §34.7).
103. ἀθῷος, -ον, *not deserving of punishment*.
104. Pres. act. inf., θεομαχέω, *war against a god*; comp. of ἐπιχειρήσας.
105. Aor. act. ptc. nom. masc. sg., ἐπιχειρέω, *attempt*; with inf.; circ. (causal).
106. Adv., *exceedingly*.
107. μνήμη, -ης, ἡ, *memory*.
108. Pres. mid. ptc. acc. masc. pl., ἀπόλλυμι, (mid.) *perish*; supp. (συνορῶσα).
109. μιᾶς ὑπὸ καιρὸν ἡμέρας, "in the space of one day" (cf. SSG §39aa).
110. Adv., *courageously*.
111. Pf. pass. ptc. nom. fem. sg., πληρόω, (pass.) *be filled*; with dat.; circ.

φρονήματι[112] καὶ τὸν θῆλυν[113] λογισμὸν[114] ἄρσενι[115] θυμῷ[116] διεγείρασα[117] λέγουσα πρὸς αὐτούς **22**Οὐκ οἶδ᾽, ὅπως εἰς τὴν ἐμὴν ἐφάνητε[118] κοιλίαν,[119] οὐδὲ ἐγὼ τὸ πνεῦμα καὶ τὴν ζωὴν ὑμῖν ἐχαρισάμην,[120] καὶ τὴν ἑκάστου στοιχείωσιν[121] οὐκ ἐγὼ διερρύθμισα·[122] **23**τοιγαροῦν[123] ὁ τοῦ κόσμου κτίστης[124] ὁ πλάσας[125] ἀνθρώπου γένεσιν[126] καὶ πάντων ἐξευρὼν[127] γένεσιν καὶ τὸ πνεῦμα καὶ τὴν ζωὴν ὑμῖν πάλιν ἀποδίδωσιν[128] μετ᾽ ἐλέους, ὡς νῦν ὑπερορᾶτε ἑαυτοὺς διὰ τοὺς αὐτοῦ νόμους.

24Ὁ δὲ Ἀντίοχος οἰόμενος[129] καταφρονεῖσθαι[130] καὶ τὴν ὀνειδίζουσαν[131] ὑφορώμενος[132] φωνὴν ἔτι τοῦ νεωτέρου περιόντος οὐ μόνον[133] διὰ λόγων ἐποιεῖτο τὴν παράκλησιν, ἀλλὰ καὶ δι᾽ ὅρκων[134] ἐπίστου[135] ἅμα[136] πλουτιεῖν[137] καὶ μακαριστὸν ποιήσειν μεταθέμενον[138] ἀπὸ τῶν πατρίων καὶ φίλον[139] ἕξειν καὶ χρείας ἐμπιστεύσειν.[140] **25**τοῦ δὲ νεανίου μηδαμῶς[141] προσέχοντος[142] προσκαλεσάμενος[143] ὁ βασιλεὺς τὴν μητέρα παρῄνει[144] γενέσθαι τοῦ μειρακίου[145] σύμβουλον[146] ἐπὶ σωτηρίᾳ. **26**πολλὰ δὲ αὐτοῦ παραινέσαντος ἐπεδέξατο[147] πείσειν[148] τὸν υἱόν· **27**προσκύψασα[149] δὲ αὐτῷ χλευάσασα[150] τὸν ὠμὸν[151] τύραννον[152] οὕτως ἔφησεν τῇ πατρίῳ φωνῇ Υἱέ, ἐλέησόν[153] με τὴν ἐν γαστρὶ περιενέγκασάν[154] σε μῆνας[155] ἐννέα καὶ θηλάσασάν[156] σε ἔτη τρία καὶ ἐκθρέψασάν[157] σε καὶ ἀγαγοῦσαν εἰς τὴν ἡλικίαν[158] ταύτην καὶ τροφοφορήσασαν.[159] **28**ἀξιῶ[160] σε, τέκνον, ἀναβλέψαντα εἰς τὸν οὐρανὸν καὶ τὴν γῆν καὶ τὰ ἐν αὐτοῖς πάντα ἰδόντα γνῶναι ὅτι οὐκ ἐξ ὄντων ἐποίησεν αὐτὰ ὁ θεός, καὶ τὸ τῶν ἀνθρώπων γένος οὕτω

---

112. φρόνημα, -ατος, τό, *mind, spirit*.
113. θῆλυς, -εια, -υ, *female*.
114. λογισμός, -οῦ, ὁ, *reasoning*.
115. ἄρσην (ἄρρην), -εν, *male*.
116. θυμός, -οῦ, ὁ, *fervor, spirit, courage*.
117. Aor. act. ptc. nom. fem. sg., διεγείρω, *arouse*.
118. Aor. pass. indic. 2 pl., φαίνω, (pass.) *appear*.
119. κοιλία, -ας, ἡ, *womb*.
120. Aor. mid. indic. 1 sg., χαρίζομαι, *give, gift*.
121. στοιχείωσις, -εως, ἡ, *teaching of fundamentals* (GELS, 637); here "fundamental elements" (cf. Ehorn 2020, 262).
122. Aor. act. indic. 1 sg., διαρρυθμίζω, *arrange in order*.
123. Partic., emphatic consequence (τοιγάρ, οὖν), *therefore, hence* (cf. CGCG §59.38).
124. κτίστης, -ου, ὁ, *creator*.
125. Aor. act. ptc. nom. masc. sg., πλάσσω, *form*; attrib. (subst.).
126. γένεσις, -εως, ἡ, *origin, genesis*.
127. Aor. act. ptc. nom. masc. sg., ἐξευρίσκω, *invent, devise*; attrib. (subst.).
128. Pres. act. indic. 3 sg., ἀποδίδωμι, *give back, repay*.
129. Pres. mid. ptc. nom. masc. sg., οἴομαι, *think, suppose*; circ. (causal).
130. Pres. pass. inf., καταφρονέω, (pass.) *be treated with contempt*; indir. disc. See n. 91.
131. Pres. act. ptc. acc. fem. sg., ὀνειδίζω, *reproach*; attrib.
132. Pres. mid. ptc. nom. masc. sg., ὑφοράω, *suspect, be suspicious of*; circ. (causal).
133. οὐ μόνον . . . ἀλλὰ καί, *not only . . . but also*.
134. ὅρκος, -ου, ὁ, *oath*.
135. Impf. act. indic. 3 sg., πιστόω, *promise*.
136. ἅμα . . . καί, *both . . . and*.

137. Pres. act. inf., πλουτίζω, *enrich*; indir. disc. (see n. 91): "he promised to enrich [him]."
138. Aor. mid. ptc. acc. masc. sg., μετατίθημι, (mid.) *change for oneself, distance oneself*; circ. (conditional).
139. φίλος, -η, -ον, (subst.) *friend*.
140. Fut. act. inf., ἐμπιστεύω, with χρείας, *entrust with an office* or *duties* (cf. BDAG, 1088.4).
141. Adv., *absolutely not, not at all*.
142. Pres. act. ptc. gen. masc. sg., προσέχω, *pay attention, give heed*; gen. absol.
143. Aor. mid. ptc. nom. masc. sg., προσκαλέω, *summon*; circ.
144. Impf. act. indic. 3 sg., παραινέω, *advise, urge, exhort*; with acc. and inf.
145. μειράκιον, -ου, τό, *lad*.
146. σύμβουλος, -ου, ὁ, *adviser, counsellor*; pred. acc.
147. Aor. mid. indic. 3 sg., ἐπιδέχομαι, *accept, admit*.
148. Fut. act. inf., πείθω, *persuade*.
149. Aor. act. ptc. nom. fem. sg., προσκύπτω, *lean toward*; circ.
150. Aor. act. ptc. nom. fem. sg., χλευάζω, *scoff at*; circ.
151. ὠμός, -ή, -όν, *unrefined, uncultured*.
152. τύραννος, -ου, ὁ, *ruler, tyrant*.
153. Aor. act. impv. 2 sg., ἐλεέω, *show mercy*.
154. Aor. act. ptc. acc. fem. sg., περιφέρω, *carry around*; attrib. (subst.).
155. μήν, -νός, ὁ, *month*; acc. of time: "for nine months."
156. Aor. act. ptc. acc. fem. sg., θηλάζω, *nurse*; attrib. (subst.).
157. Aor. act. ptc. acc. fem. sg., ἐκτρέφω, *rear, nurture*; attrib. (subst.).
158. ἡλικία, -ας, ἡ, *age, period of life*.
159. Aor. act. ptc. acc. fem. sg., τροφοφορέω, *sustain by providing food*; attrib. (subst.).
160. Pres. act. indic. 1 sg., ἀξιόω, *request*; with acc. and inf.

γίνεται. ²⁹μὴ φοβηθῇς τὸν δήμιον¹⁶¹ τοῦτον, ἀλλὰ τῶν ἀδελφῶν ἄξιος γενόμενος ἐπίδεξαι τὸν θάνατον, ἵνα ἐν τῷ ἐλέει¹⁶² σὺν τοῖς ἀδελφοῖς σου κομίσωμαί¹⁶³ σε.

³⁰Ἄρτι¹⁶⁴ δὲ ταύτης καταληγούσης¹⁶⁵ ὁ νεανίας εἶπεν Τίνα μένετε;¹⁶⁶ οὐχ ὑπακούω¹⁶⁷ τοῦ προστάγματος¹⁶⁸ τοῦ βασιλέως, τοῦ δὲ προστάγματος ἀκούω τοῦ νόμου τοῦ δοθέντος τοῖς πατράσιν ἡμῶν διὰ Μωυσέως. ³¹σὺ δὲ πάσης κακίας εὑρετὴς¹⁶⁹ γενόμενος εἰς τοὺς Ἑβραίους οὐ μὴ διαφύγῃς¹⁷⁰ τὰς χεῖρας τοῦ θεοῦ. ³²ἡμεῖς γὰρ διὰ τὰς ἑαυτῶν ἁμαρτίας πάσχομεν. ³³εἰ δὲ χάριν¹⁷¹ ἐπιπλήξεως¹⁷² καὶ παιδείας¹⁷³ ὁ ζῶν κύριος ἡμῶν βραχέως¹⁷⁴ ἐπώργισται,¹⁷⁵ καὶ πάλιν καταλλαγήσεται¹⁷⁶ τοῖς ἑαυτοῦ δούλοις. ³⁴σὺ δέ, ὦ ἀνόσιε¹⁷⁷ καὶ πάντων ἀνθρώπων μιαρώτατε,¹⁷⁸ μὴ μάτην μετεωρίζου¹⁷⁹ φρυαττόμενος¹⁸⁰ ἀδήλοις¹⁸¹ ἐλπίσιν ἐπὶ τοὺς οὐρανίους παῖδας¹⁸² ἐπαιρόμενος¹⁸³ χεῖρα· ³⁵οὔπω γὰρ τὴν τοῦ παντοκράτορος¹⁸⁴ ἐπόπτου¹⁸⁵ θεοῦ κρίσιν ἐκπέφευγας. ³⁶οἱ μὲν γὰρ νῦν ἡμέτεροι ἀδελφοὶ βραχὺν ὑπενέγκαντες¹⁸⁶ πόνον ἀενάου¹⁸⁷ ζωῆς ὑπὸ διαθήκην θεοῦ πεπτώκασιν·¹⁸⁸ σὺ δὲ τῇ τοῦ θεοῦ κρίσει δίκαια τὰ πρόστιμα¹⁸⁹ τῆς ὑπερηφανίας¹⁹⁰ ἀποίσῃ.¹⁹¹ ³⁷ἐγὼ δέ, καθάπερ οἱ ἀδελφοί, καὶ σῶμα καὶ ψυχὴν προδίδωμι¹⁹² περὶ τῶν πατρίων νόμων ἐπικαλούμενος τὸν θεὸν ἵλεως¹⁹³ ταχὺ¹⁹⁴ τῷ ἔθνει γενέσθαι καὶ σὲ μετὰ ἐτασμῶν¹⁹⁵ καὶ μαστίγων ἐξομολογήσασθαι¹⁹⁶ διότι μόνος αὐτὸς θεός ἐστιν, ³⁸ἐν ἐμοὶ δὲ καὶ τοῖς ἀδελφοῖς μου στῆσαι¹⁹⁷ τὴν τοῦ παντοκράτορος ὀργὴν τὴν ἐπὶ τὸ σύμπαν¹⁹⁸ ἡμῶν γένος¹⁹⁹ δικαίως ἐπηγμένην.²⁰⁰ ³⁹Ἔκθυμος δὲ γενόμενος ὁ βασιλεὺς τούτῳ παρὰ τοὺς ἄλλους χείριστως²⁰¹ ἀπήντησεν²⁰² πικρῶς²⁰³ φέρων ἐπὶ τῷ μυκτηρισμῷ.²⁰⁴ ⁴⁰καὶ οὗτος οὖν καθαρῶς μετήλλαξεν παντελῶς²⁰⁵ ἐπὶ τῷ κυρίῳ πεποιθώς.

⁴¹Ἐσχάτη δὲ τῶν υἱῶν ἡ μήτηρ ἐτελεύτησεν.

161. δήμιος, -ου, ὁ, *executioner*.
162. ἔλεος, -ους, τό, *mercy*.
163. Aor. mid. subj. 1 sg., κομίζω, *receive*; purpose clause (cf. BDF §369; S §2193; CGCG §45.3).
164. Emendation based on 9:5: ἄρτι δὲ αὐτοῦ καταλήξαντος. Manuscripts read Ἔτι, which as Goldstein notes (1983, 315), is perfectly intelligible.
165. Pres. act. ptc. gen. fem. sg., καταλέγω, *recount*; gen. absol.
166. Pres. act. indic. 2 pl., μένω, *wait for* (something; cf. GELS, 449.4). The shift to a plural subject indicates that the young man now addresses his executioners.
167. Pres. act. indic. 1 sg., ὑπακούω, *obey*.
168. πρόσταγμα, -ατος, τό, *ordinance*.
169. εὑρετής, -οῦ, ὁ, *deviser*.
170. Pres. act. subj. 2 sg., διαφεύγω, *escape*; emphatic neg. οὐ μή with subj. (cf. BDF §365; S §1804; CGCG §34.9).
171. Prep. with gen., *on account of, for the sake of*.
172. ἐπίπληξις, -εως, ἡ, *rebuke*.
173. παιδεία, -ας, ἡ, *discipline, punishment*.
174. Adv., *for a little while*.
175. Pf. mid. indic. 3 sg., ἐποργίζομαι, *be angry*.
176. Fut. pass. indic. 3 sg., καταλάσσω, (pass.) *be reconciled*.
177. Voc., ἀνόσιος, -α, -ον, *impious*.
178. Voc. superl., μιαρός, -ά, -όν, *most abominable, polluted*.
179. Pres. mid. impv. 2 sg., μετεωρίζω, *be elated*.
180. Pres. pass. ptc. nom. masc. sg., φρυάσσω (Att. φρυάττω), (pass.) *be haughty, puffed up*; circ.
181. ἄδηλος, -ον, *uncertain*.
182. παῖς, παιδός, ὁ, *child, servant*.
183. Pres. mid. ptc. nom. masc. sg., ἐπαίρω, *raise*; circ.
184. παντοκράτωρ, -ορος, ὁ, *almighty*.
185. ἐπόπτος, -ου, ὁ, *pertaining to one who oversees* (all things).
186. Aor. act. ptc. nom. masc. pl., ὑποφέρω, *endure*; circ.
187. ἀένάος, -ον, *everlasting*. ἀενάου ζωῆς could modify either βραχὺν πόνον ("brief suffering for everlasting life") or ὑπὸ διαθήκην θεοῦ ("under God's covenant of everlasting life"). The former is preferable (Nicklas 2011, 1395).
188. Pf. act. indic. 3 pl., πίπτω, *fall*.
189. πρόστιμον, -ου, τό, *penalty*.
190. ὑπερηφανία, -ας, ἡ, *arrogance*.
191. Fut. mid. indic. 2 sg., ἀποφέρω, (mid.) *gain, obtain*.
192. Pres. act. indic. 1 sg., προδίδωμι, *give for, on behalf of*.
193. ἵλεως, -ων, *propitious, gracious*.
194. Adv., *swiftly, soon*.
195. ἐτασμός, -οῦ, ὁ, *torment, trial*.
196. Aor. mid. inf., ἐξομολογέομαι, *confess*; comp. of ἐπικαλούμενος: "[calling on God] for you to confess."
197. Aor. act. inf., ἵστημι, (intrans.) *stop, come to an end*.
198. σύμπας, -ασα, -αν, *all, whole, entire*.
199. γένος, -ους, τό, *people group, race*.
200. Pf. pass. ptc. acc. fem. sg., ἐπάγω, (pass.) *brought upon*; attrib.
201. Adv., *in a worse way*; with παρὰ τοὺς ἄλλους, "worse than the others."
202. Aor. act. indic. 3 sg., ἀπαντάω, *deal with*, with dat. pers.
203. Adv., *bitterly*; adv. with φέρων, "carrying bitterness" (cf. SSG §24a).
204. μυκτηρισμός, -οῦ, ὁ, *scorn, mocking*.
205. Adv., *completely, entirely*.

⁴²Τὰ μὲν οὖν²⁰⁶ περὶ τοὺς σπλαγχνισμοὺς²⁰⁷ καὶ τὰς ὑπερβαλλούσας²⁰⁸ αἰκίας²⁰⁹ ἐπὶ τοσοῦτον δεδηλώσθω.²¹⁰

NOTES

7:6. καὶ ταῖς ἀληθείαις ἐφ' ἡμῖν παρακαλεῖται. The brothers begin to exhort (παρεκάλουν) one another that the Lord now relents (παρακαλεῖται) on their account. Goldstein (1983, 304) comments, "Even when confronted by such terrible tortures, the martyrs believed that the prediction at Deut 32:36 is being fulfilled."

διὰ τῆς κατὰ πρόσωπον ἀντιμαρτυρούσης ᾠδῆς διεσάφησεν Μωυσῆς. Cf. Deut. 31:21 LXX.

Καὶ ἐπὶ τοῖς δούλοις αὐτοῦ παρακληθήσεται. This is a citation of Deut. 32:36 LXX (cf. 2 Macc. 7:33 [see note below]; 8:29).

7:8. τῇ πατρίῳ φωνῇ. Cf. 7:21, 27. The decision to answer the pagan tyrant "in the ancestral language" (i.e., in Hebrew) is an act of defiance on the part of the Jewish martyrs.

7:9. ἀλάστωρ. Doran (2012, 156–57) notes that the term "was used by the tragedians of the avenging deity (Aeschylus, *Pers.* 354; Aeschylus, *Ag.* 1501, 1508), and then of the one who suffers from such vengeance (Aeschylus, *Eum.* 236; Sophocles, [*Aj.*] 374)."

---

206. Partic. combination: "a transition to a more-to-the-point, relevant text segment (οὖν) [that] occurs in two stages (μέν . . . δέ)" (*CGCG* §59.73). The μέν-clause concludes the section and points ahead to the δέ-clause of the new section (8:1).
207. σπλαγχνισμός, -οῦ, ὁ, *eating of sacrificial entrails*.
208. Pres. act. ptc. acc. fem. pl., ὑπερβάλλω, *exceed, go beyond*; attrib.
209. αἰκία, -ας, ἡ, *torture*.
210. Pf. pass. impv. 3 sg., δηλόω, (pass.) *be shown*; with ἐπὶ τοσοῦτον (extent); lit., "to so great an extent"; i.e., "sufficient." In other words, "So much then for our discussion of the consumption of sacrificial meat and the excessive tortures."

ἀποθανόντας ἡμᾶς ὑπὲρ τῶν αὐτοῦ νόμων . . . ἡμᾶς ἀναστήσει. The martyrs assert that they will receive the reward of resurrection *because they have died for the law* (see Henten 1997, 173–75). The collocation ἀποθνήσκω ὑπέρ plus the genitive is a common way to designate the reason why a person gives his or her life. On "dying for" language, see Eschner (2010) and Versnel (2012).

7:11. This is the first in a litany of references to resurrection (cf. 7:14, 23, 29, 36). Moss (2012, 42) astutely notes, "In many respects, not just the exercise of power but also mythological accounts of the afterlife are being subverted. Whereas Greek religion maintained that proper burial was a prerequisite for safe passage to Hades and that disfigurement in death imprinted itself on the shade of a warrior, the Maccabean martyrs are confident that their God will be able to restore their bodies to wholeness. Greek might is thwarted by Jewish eschatology."

7:12. ὥστε αὐτὸν τὸν βασιλέα καὶ τοὺς σὺν αὐτῷ ἐκπλήσσεσθαι. An allusion to Isaiah's fourth servant poem: "As many *will be astonished at you* [ἐκστήσονται ἐπὶ σὲ πολλοί] . . . so many nations will marvel at him [οὕτως θαυμάσονται ἔθνη πολλὰ ἐπ' αὐτῷ] and kings will shut their mouths" (Isa. 52:14–15; Nickelsburg 2006b, 131).

7:19. θεομαχεῖν. The verb θεομαχέω, "war against the god," is a central motif of Euripides's *Bacchae* (ll. 45, 325, 1255), wherein the hapless Pentheus struggles in vain with the god Dionysus (see §8.4.1; see also Euripides, *Iph. aul.* 1408; Josephus, *B.J.* 5.378; Epictetus, *Diatr.* 3.24.24; Plutarch, *Mor.* 168c). According to Luke, the rabbi Gamaliel warned his fellow council members that resistance to the Jesus movement might render them θεομάχοι (Acts 5:39).

7:21. τὸν θῆλυν λογισμὸν ἄρσενι θυμῷ διεγείρασα. As Doran (2012, 159) notes, "The androcentric mentality is obvious" (see also Moore and Anderson 1998; Schwartz 2008, 308–9). The Maccabean mother became the prototype for Christian mothers and a model for the passions of Symphorosa and Felicitas (Moss 2012, 44).

7:28. γνῶναι ὅτι οὐκ ἐξ ὄντων ἐποίησεν αὐτὰ ὁ θεός. Christian interpreters since Origen (*Comm. Jo.* 1.17.103; *Princ.* 2.1.5) have read this line as proof of the doctrine *creatio ex nihilo* (see Goldstein 1984).

7:33. χάριν ἐπιπλήξεως καὶ παιδείας. Once again, the epitomizer appears to draw on the language of Isaiah's fourth servant poem (cf. Isa. 53:5 LXX).

καταλλαγήσεται τοῖς ἑαυτοῦ δούλοις. The epitomizer uses the same collocation in 8:29, which echoes the language of Deut. 32:36 (cited in 7:6).

7:34. ἐπὶ τοὺς οὐρανίους παῖδας ἐπαιρόμενος χεῖρα. Cf. 3 Macc. 6:28; Wis. 2:13; 12:6. The language evokes the Song of Moses (cf. Deut. 32:43) and Isaiah's servant poems (Nickelsburg 2006b, 132).

1.4

4 Maccabees

Fourth Maccabees is a philosophical treatise that was composed in the first or second century CE. The writer reworks established Maccabean martyrdom traditions (2 Macc. 6:18–7:24) to argue his thesis: pious reason (ὁ εὐσεβὴς λογισμός) is master over the passions (4 Macc. 1:1). His is a kind of philosophical Judaism in which training in the law (ἡ τοῦ νόμου παιδεία) provides the necessary (or at least the most expedient) path to a life in accordance with nature (cf. 4:35). Thus Eleazar, the famed scribe and priest, cries out, "I will not play false to you, O law that trained me, nor will I renounce you, beloved self-control. I will not put you to shame, philosophical reason, nor will I deny you, honored priesthood and knowledge of our law code" (5:34–35 NETS).

The reading passage is an account of Eleazar's martyrdom. The writer takes up traditional material (cf. 2 Macc. 6:18–31) in fresh and interesting ways. For example, he casts Eleazar's death in an explicitly sacrificial register (4 Macc. 6:29; cf. 17:22), a move that is often compared to early Christian discourse about Jesus's death (Hiebert 2015, 316). Moreover, as Boyarin (1999, 117) notes, "There are important similarities between 4 Maccabees itself and early Christian martyrologies that suggest shared innovation."

Text: Rahlfs and Hanhart 2006
Recommended Translation: NETS (http://ccat.sas.upenn.edu/nets/edition/23-4makk-nets.pdf)
Supplemental Scripture: 2 Macc. 6:18–31; Rom. 3:21–26

1.4.1

The Martyrdom of Eleazar

4 Maccabees 6

6:1Τοῦτον τὸν τρόπον¹ ἀντιρρητορεύσαντα² ταῖς τοῦ τυράννου³ παρηγορίαις⁴ παραστάντες⁵ οἱ δορυφόροι⁶ πικρῶς⁷ ἔσυραν⁸ ἐπὶ τὰ βασανιστήρια⁹ τὸν Ελεαζαρον. **²**καὶ πρῶτον μὲν¹⁰ περιέδυσαν¹¹ τὸν γεραιὸν¹² ἐγκοσμούμενον¹³ τῇ περὶ τὴν εὐσέβειαν¹⁴ εὐσχημοσύνῃ.¹⁵ **³**ἔπειτα περιαγκωνίσαντες¹⁶ ἑκατέρωθεν¹⁷ μάστιξιν¹⁸ κατήκιζον,¹⁹ **⁴**Πείσθητι²⁰ ταῖς τοῦ βασιλέως ἐντολαῖς, ἑτέρωθεν²¹ κήρυκος²² ἐπιβοῶντος.²³ **⁵**ὁ δὲ μεγαλόφρων²⁴ καὶ εὐγενὴς²⁵ ὡς ἀληθῶς Ελεαζαρος ὥσπερ ἐν ὀνείρῳ²⁶ βασανιζόμενος²⁷ κατ' οὐδένα τρόπον μετετρέπετο,²⁸ **⁶**ἀλλὰ ὑψηλοὺς²⁹ ἀνατείνας³⁰ εἰς οὐρανὸν τοὺς ὀφθαλμοὺς ἀπεξαίνετο³¹ ταῖς μάστιξιν τὰς σάρκας ὁ γέρων³² καὶ κατερρεῖτο³³ τῷ αἵματι

---

1. Adv. acc. (manner), *in this way* (cf. S §1608; *CGCG* §30.18).
2. Aor. act. ptc. acc. masc. sg., ἀντιρρητορεύω, *offer a counter speech against*; with dat; circ. Note the separation between the participle and its subject, τὸν Ελεαζαρον (cf. *SSG* §31df).
3. τύραννος, -ου, ὁ, *ruler, tyrant*.
4. παρηγορία, -ας, ἡ, *exhortation*.
5. Aor. act. ptc. nom. masc. pl., παρίστημι, *be present*; circ.
6. δορυφόρος, -ου, ὁ, *bodyguard*.
7. Adv., *harshly, violently*.
8. Aor. act. indic. 3 pl., σύρω, *drag*.
9. βασανιστήριον, -ου, τό, *instrument of torture*.
10. πρῶτον μὲν . . . ἔπειτα, *first . . . next* (cf. S §2904).
11. Aor. act. indic. 3 pl., περιδύω, *strip*.
12. γεραιός, -ά, -όν, (subst.) *old man*.
13. Pres. pass. ptc. acc. masc. sg., ἐγκοσμέω, *adorned*; circ. (concessive).
14. εὐσέβια, -ας ἡ, *piety, godliness*.
15. εὐσχημοσύνη, -ης, ἡ, *gracefulness*.
16. Aor. act. ptc. nom. masc. pl., περιαγκωνίζω, *tie hands behind the back*; circ.
17. Adv., *on either side*.
18. μάστιξ, -γος, ἡ, *whip*; dat. of instrument.
19. Impf. act. indic. 3 pl., καταικίζω, *torture*.
20. Aor. pass. impv. 2 sg., πείθω, (mid.-pass.) *obey*; with dat.
21. Adv., *from the opposite side*.
22. κῆρυξ, -κος, ὁ, *herald*.
23. Pres. act. ptc. gen. masc. sg., ἐπιβοάω, *call out*; gen. absol.
24. μεγαλόφρων, -ον, *high-minded*.
25. εὐγενής, -ές, *noble*.
26. ὄνειρος, -ου, ὁ, *dream*.
27. Pres. pass. ptc. nom. masc. sg., βασανίζω, (pass.) *be tormented/tortured*; circ. (comparison).
28. Impf. mid. indic. 3 sg., μετατρέπω, (mid.) *change course*.
29. ὑψηλός, -ή, -όν, *high, elevated*; adv. *aloft*.
30. Aor. act. ptc. nom. masc. sg., ἀνατείνω, *extend upward*; circ.
31. Impf. pass. indic. 3 sg., ἀποξαίνω, (pass.) *have torn/lacerated*; with acc. of respect.
32. γέρων, -οντος, ὁ, *old man*.
33. Impf. pass. indic. 3 sg., καταρρέω, *run down, drip*; with αἵματι (cf. LSJ, 909.II).

καὶ τὰ πλευρὰ³⁴ κατετιτρώσκετο.³⁵ ⁷καὶ πίπτων εἰς τὸ ἔδαφος³⁶ ἀπὸ τοῦ μὴ φέρειν³⁷ τὸ σῶμα τὰς ἀλγηδόνας³⁸ ὀρθὸν³⁹ εἶχεν καὶ ἀκλινῆ⁴⁰ τὸν λογισμόν.⁴¹ ⁸λάξ⁴² γέ τοι⁴³ τῶν πικρῶν τις δορυφόρων εἰς τοὺς κενεῶνας⁴⁴ ἐναλλόμενος⁴⁵ ἔτυπτεν,⁴⁶ ὅπως ἐξανίσταιτο⁴⁷ πίπτων. ⁹ὁ δὲ ὑπέμενε⁴⁸ τοὺς πόνους⁴⁹ καὶ περιεφρόνει⁵⁰ τῆς ἀνάγκης⁵¹ καὶ διεκαρτέρει⁵² τοὺς αἰκισμούς,⁵³ ¹⁰καὶ καθάπερ γενναῖος⁵⁴ ἀθλητὴς⁵⁵ τυπτόμενος⁵⁶ ἐνίκα⁵⁷ τοὺς βασανίζοντας⁵⁸ ὁ γέρων· ¹¹ἱδρῶν⁵⁹ γέ τοι⁶⁰ τὸ πρόσωπον καὶ ἐπασθμαίνων⁶¹ σφοδρῶς⁶² καὶ ὑπ' αὐτῶν τῶν βασανιζόντων ἐθαυμάζετο⁶³ ἐπὶ τῇ εὐψυχίᾳ.⁶⁴

¹²Ὅθεν⁶⁵ τὰ μὲν⁶⁶ ἐλεῶντες⁶⁷ τὰ τοῦ γήρως⁶⁸ αὐτοῦ, ¹³τὰ δὲ ἐν συμπαθείᾳ⁶⁹ τῆς συνηθείας⁷⁰ ὄντες, τὰ δὲ ἐν θαυμασμῷ⁷¹ τῆς καρτερίας⁷² προσιόντες⁷³ αὐτῷ τινες τοῦ βασιλέως ἔλεγον ¹⁴Τί τοῖς κακοῖς τούτοις σεαυτὸν ἀλογίστως⁷⁴ ἀπόλλεις,⁷⁵ Ελεαζαρ; ¹⁵ἡμεῖς μέν τοι⁷⁶ τῶν ἡψημένων⁷⁷ βρωμάτων⁷⁸ παραθήσομεν,⁷⁹ σὺ δὲ ὑποκρινόμενος⁸⁰ τῶν ὑείων⁸¹ ἀπογεύεσθαι⁸² σώθητι.

¹⁶Καὶ ὁ Ελεαζαρος ὥσπερ πικρότερον⁸³ διὰ τῆς συμβουλίας⁸⁴ αἰκισθεὶς⁸⁵ ἀνεβόησεν⁸⁶ ¹⁷Μὴ οὕτως κακῶς

34. πλευρόν, -οῦ, τό, *side*.
35. Impf. pass. indic. 3 sg., κατατιτρώσκω, (pass.) *be wounded*.
36. ἔδαφος, -ους, τό, *ground*.
37. The collocation ἀπὸ τοῦ with an infinitive expresses cause (cf. *GELS*, 70.4c): "although falling [concessive] to the ground *because* his body could not bear the pain."
38. ἀλγηδών, -όνος, ἡ, *pain, agony*.
39. ὀρθός, -ή, -όν, *straight, upright*; pred. comp.
40. ἀκλινής, -ές, *unswerving*; pred. comp.
41. λογισμός, -οῦ, ὁ, *reason*.
42. Adv., *with the foot*.
43. Partic. combination: concentration/limitation (γέ) brought to the attention of the addressee (τοι) (cf. *CGCG* §59.51, 53). The combination helps the reader connect λάξ with the verb at the end of the clause: "struck him *with his foot*."
44. κενεών, -ῶνος, ὁ, *side* (of the body, between ribs and hip).
45. Pres. mid. ptc. nom. masc. sg., ἐνάλλομαι, *leap on*; circ.
46. Impf. act. indic. 3 sg., τύπτω, *strike*.
47. Pres. mid. opt. 3 sg., ἐξανίστημι, (intrans.) *arise*; oblique opt. for subj. in a purpose clause (cf. BDF §386; S §2196; *CGCG* §45.3).
48. Impf. act. indic. 3 sg., ὑπομένω, *endure*.
49. πόνος, -ου, ὁ, *suffering*.
50. Impf. act. indic. 3 sg., περιφρονέω, *disregard, despise*; with gen.
51. ἀνάγκη, -ης, ἡ, *forceful compulsion*.
52. Impf. act. indic. 3 sg., διακαρτερέω, *persevere, hold out against*.
53. αἰκισμός, -οῦ, ὁ, *torture*.
54. γενναῖος, -α, -ον, *noble*.
55. ἀθλητής, -οῦ, ὁ, *athlete*.
56. Pres. pass. ptc. nom. masc. sg., τύπτω, (pass.) *struck, beaten*; circ. (compar.).
57. Impf. act. indic. 3 sg., νικάω, *conquer*.
58. Pres. act. ptc. acc. masc. sg., βασανίζω, *torture*; attrib. (subst.).
59. Pres. act. ptc. nom. masc. sg., ἱδρόω, *sweat*; circ.
60. Partic. combination: concentration/limitation (γέ) brought to the attention of the addressee (τοι): "*Sweating profusely* from his face, . . . he was admired by these very torturers."

61. Pres. act. ptc. nom. masc. sg., ἐπασθμαίνω, *breathe heavily*; circ.
62. Adv., *exceedingly*.
63. Impf. pass. indic. 3 sg., θαυμάζω, (pass.) *be marveled at*.
64. εὐψυχία, -ας, ἡ, *good courage*. ἐπὶ τῇ εὐψυχίᾳ expresses cause or reason (S §1689.2.c).
65. Adv., *hence*.
66. τὰ μέν . . . τὰ δέ . . . τὰ δέ, *partly . . . partly . . . partly* (cf. BDF §250; S §1102; *CGCG* §28.27).
67. Pres. act. ptc. nom. masc. pl., ἐλεάω, *show mercy*; circ. (causal).
68. γῆρας, -ως, ὁ, *old age*.
69. συμπάθεια, -ας, ἡ, *sympathy*.
70. συνήθεια, -ας, ἡ, *acquaintance*.
71. θαυμασμός, -οῦ, ὁ, *astonishment, amazement*.
72. καρτερία, -ας, ἡ, *persistence*.
73. Pres. act. ptc. nom. masc. pl., πρόσειμι, *approach*; with dat.; circ.
74. Adv., *against reason*.
75. Pres. act. indic. 2 sg., ἀπόλλω, *destroy*.
76. μέν τοι . . . δέ; point/counterpoint set (cf. Runge 2010, 75–83; BDF §447; S §2904; *CGCG* §59.24), in which τοι draws the statement to the addressee's attention: "We (take note) will set before you some cooked meat; save yourself by pretending to taste of the pork."
77. Pf. pass. ptc. gen. neut. pl., ἕψω, *cooked*; attrib.
78. βρῶμα, -ατα, τό, *food*.
79. Fut. act. indic. 1 pl., παρατίθημι, *set before*.
80. Pres. mid. ptc. nom. masc. sg., ὑποκρίνω, *pretend, act*; circ. (means).
81. ὕειος, -α, -ον, *of / pertaining to pigs*.
82. Pres. mid. inf., ἀπογεύω, *taste of*; with gen.
83. Compar. adv., πικρός, *more bitterly*.
84. συμβουλία, -ας, ἡ, *advice, council*.
85. Aor. pass. ptc. nom. masc. pl., αἰκίζω, *tortured*; circ. (compar.).
86. Aor. act. indic. 3 sg., ἀναβοάω, *cry out*.

φρονήσαιμεν⁸⁷ οἱ Ἀβρααμ παῖδες⁸⁸ ὥστε μαλακοψυχήσαντας⁸⁹ ἀπρεπὲς⁹⁰ ἡμῖν δρᾶμα⁹¹ ὑποκρίνασθαι.⁹² ¹⁸καὶ γὰρ⁹³ ἀλόγιστον⁹⁴ εἰ πρὸς ἀλήθειαν ζήσαντες τὸν μέχρι⁹⁵ γήρως βίον καὶ τὴν ἐπ᾽ αὐτῷ δόξαν νομίμως⁹⁶ φυλάσσοντες⁹⁷ νῦν μεταβαλοίμεθα⁹⁸ ¹⁹καὶ αὐτοὶ μὲν⁹⁹ ἡμεῖς γενοίμεθα¹⁰⁰ τοῖς νέοις¹⁰¹ ἀσεβείας¹⁰² τύπος,¹⁰³ ἵνα παράδειγμα¹⁰⁴ γενώμεθα τῆς μιαροφαγίας.¹⁰⁵ ²⁰αἰσχρὸν¹⁰⁶ δὲ εἰ ἐπιβιώσομεν¹⁰⁷ ὀλίγον χρόνον καὶ τοῦτον καταγελώμενοι¹⁰⁸ πρὸς ἁπάντων ἐπὶ δειλίᾳ¹⁰⁹ ²¹καὶ ὑπὸ μὲν τοῦ τυράννου καταφρονηθῶμεν¹¹⁰ ὡς ἄνανδροι,¹¹¹ τὸν δὲ θεῖον¹¹² ἡμῶν νόμον μέχρι θανάτου μὴ προασπίσαιμεν.¹¹³ ²²πρὸς ταῦτα¹¹⁴ ὑμεῖς μέν,¹¹⁵ ὦ Ἀβρααμ παῖδες, εὐγενῶς¹¹⁶ ὑπὲρ τῆς εὐσεβείας τελευτᾶτε.¹¹⁷ ²³οἱ δὲ τοῦ τυράννου δορυφόροι, τί μέλλετε;¹¹⁸

²⁴Πρὸς τὰς ἀνάγκας οὕτως μεγαλοφρονοῦντα¹¹⁹ αὐτὸν ἰδόντες καὶ μηδὲ πρὸς τὸν οἰκτιρμὸν¹²⁰ αὐτῶν μεταβαλλόμενον ἐπὶ τὸ πῦρ αὐτὸν ἀνῆγον.¹²¹ ²⁵ἔνθα¹²² διὰ κακοτέχνων¹²³ ὀργάνων¹²⁴ καταφλέγοντες¹²⁵ αὐτὸν ὑπερρίπτοσαν,¹²⁶ καὶ δυσώδεις¹²⁷ χυλοὺς¹²⁸ εἰς τοὺς μυκτῆρας¹²⁹ αὐτοῦ κατέχεον.¹³⁰ ²⁶ὁ δὲ μέχρι τῶν ὀστέων¹³¹ ἤδη κατακεκαυμένος¹³² καὶ μέλλων λιποθυμεῖν¹³³ ἀνέτεινε¹³⁴ τὰ ὄμματα¹³⁵ πρὸς τὸν θεὸν καὶ εἶπεν ²⁷Σὺ οἶσθα,¹³⁶ θεέ, παρόν¹³⁷ μοι σῴζεσθαι

87. Aor. act. opt. 1 pl., φρονέω, *think*; cupitive (cf. BDF §384; S §1814; CGCG §34.14).
88. παῖς, παιδός, ὁ, *child, servant*.
89. Aor. act. ptc. acc. masc. pl., μαλακοψυχέω, *be cowardly*; circ.
90. ἀπρεπής, -ές, *unbefitting*; with dat.; pred.
91. δρᾶμα, -ατος, τό, *role*.
92. Result clause (cf. BDF §391; S §2269; CGCG §46.6), signposted by οὕτως.
93. Partic. combination: additional information (καί) that has explanatory force (γάρ) (CGCG §59.66).
94. ἀλόγιστος, -α, -ον, (quasi-impers.) *it is contrary to reason*. Here it forms the apodosis. Muraoka (SSG §89a) notes that there are no complete fourth-class conditions in LXX texts.
95. Prep. with gen., *until, up to*.
96. Adv., *according to the law*.
97. Pres. act. ptc. nom. masc. sg., φυλάσσω, *guard*; circ.
98. Aor. mid. opt. 1 pl., μεταβάλλω, *change course*; potential protasis: εἰ with opt. (cf. S §2329; CGCG §49.8).
99. μέν . . . δέ. Transitional: the μέν-clause rounds off the string of conditional clauses, while the δέ-clause introduces the apodosis of the next condition. See n. 76.
100. Aor. mid. opt. 1 pl., γίνομαι, *become*; potential protasis: εἰ with opt. See n. 98.
101. νέος, -α, -ον, *young*.
102. ἀσεβεία, -ας, ἡ, *impiety*.
103. τύπος, -ου, ὁ, *model*; pred. nom.
104. παράδειγμα, -ατος, τό, *example*; pred. nom.
105. μιαροφαγία, -ας, ἡ, *ritually defiled food*.
106. αἰσχρός, -ά, -όν, (quasi-impers.) *it would be shameful*; apodosis. The protasis has the future indicative, subjunctive, and optative so that "no functional opposition can be identified between the future, the subjunctive, and the optative" (SSG §89aaa).
107. Fut. act. indic. 1 pl., ἐπιβιόω, *survive*.
108. Pres. pass. ptc. nom. masc. pl., καταγελάω, (pass.) *be derided, laughed at*; circ.
109. δειλία, -ας, ἡ, *fearfulness*. ἐπὶ δειλίᾳ expresses cause or reason.
110. Aor. pass. subj. 1 pl., καταφρονέω, (pass.) *be despised*.

111. ἄνανδρος, -ον, *unmanly, cowardly*.
112. θεῖος, -α, -ον, *divine*.
113. Aor. act. opt. 1 pl., προασπίζω, *champion*.
114. πρὸς ταῦτα, *in view/consequence of these things* (cf. LSJ, 1498.III.2).
115. μέν . . . δέ; point/counterpoint set. See n. 76.
116. Adv., *nobly*.
117. Aor. act. impv. 2 pl., τελευτάω, *die*.
118. τί μέλλετε;, *What are you waiting for?, Why are you delaying?* (BDAG, 628.4).
119. Pres. act. ptc. acc. masc. sg., μεγαλοφρονέω, *be highminded*; supp. (ἰδόντες).
120. οἰκτιρμός, -οῦ, ὁ, *pity*.
121. Impf. act. indic. 3 pl., ἀνάγω, *lead up*.
122. Demon. adv., *there*.
123. κακότεχνος, -ον, *crafted for malice*.
124. ὄργανον, -ου, τό, *instrument*.
125. Pres. act. ptc. nom. masc. pl., καταφλέγω, *burn*; circ.
126. Aor. act. indic. 3 pl., ὑπορρίπτω, *throw down*.
127. δυσώδης, -ές, *stinking*.
128. χυλός, -οῦ, ὁ, *liquid*.
129. μυκτήρ, -ῆρος, ὁ, *nostril*.
130. Impf. act. indic. 3 pl., καταχέω, *pour*.
131. ὀστέον, -ου, τό, *bone*; μέχρι τῶν ὀστέων, "to the bone."
132. Pf. pass. ptc. nom. masc. sg., κατακαύω, (pass.) *be burned up*; circ.
133. Pres. act. inf., λιποθυμέω, *faint*; comp. of μέλλων.
134. Impf. act. indic. 3 sg., ἀνατείνω, *extend upward*.
135. ὄμμα, -ατος, τό, *eye*.
136. Pf. act. indic. 2 sg., οἶδα, *know*.
137. Pres. act. ptc. acc. neut. sg., πάρειμι, (impers.) *it is possible*; with dat. and inf.; acc. absol. (cf. BDF §424; S §2076; CGCG §52.33); here as a concession: "Even though *it is possible* for me to be delivered."

βασάνοις¹³⁸ καυστικαῖς¹³⁹ ἀποθνῄσκω διὰ τὸν νόμον. ²⁸ἵλεως¹⁴⁰ γενοῦ τῷ ἔθνει σου ἀρκεσθεὶς¹⁴¹ τῇ ἡμετέρᾳ ὑπὲρ αὐτῶν δίκῃ.¹⁴² ²⁹καθάρσιον¹⁴³ αὐτῶν ποίησον τὸ ἐμὸν αἷμα καὶ ἀντίψυχον¹⁴⁴ αὐτῶν λαβὲ τὴν ἐμὴν ψυχήν. ³⁰καὶ ταῦτα εἰπὼν ὁ ἱερὸς¹⁴⁵ ἀνὴρ εὐγενῶς¹⁴⁶ ταῖς βασάνοις ἐναπέθανεν¹⁴⁷ καὶ μέχρι τῶν τοῦ θανάτου βασάνων ἀντέστη¹⁴⁸ τῷ λογισμῷ διὰ τὸν νόμον.

³¹Ὁμολογουμένως¹⁴⁹ οὖν δεσπότης¹⁵⁰ τῶν παθῶν¹⁵¹ ἐστιν ὁ εὐσεβὴς¹⁵² λογισμός. ³²εἰ γὰρ τὰ πάθη τοῦ λογισμοῦ κεκρατήκει,¹⁵³ τούτοις ἂν ἀπέδομεν¹⁵⁴ τὴν τῆς ἐπικρατείας¹⁵⁵ μαρτυρίαν· ³³νυνὶ δὲ τοῦ λογισμοῦ τὰ πάθη νικήσαντος¹⁵⁶ αὐτῷ προσηκόντως¹⁵⁷ τὴν τῆς ἡγεμονίας¹⁵⁸ προσνέμομεν¹⁵⁹ ἐξουσίαν. ³⁴καὶ δίκαιόν ἐστιν ὁμολογεῖν¹⁶⁰ ἡμᾶς τὸ κράτος¹⁶¹ εἶναι τοῦ λογισμοῦ, ὅπου γε καὶ τῶν ἔξωθεν¹⁶² ἀλγηδόνων¹⁶³ ἐπικρατεῖ,¹⁶⁴ ἐπεὶ καὶ γελοῖον.¹⁶⁵ ³⁵καὶ οὐ μόνον¹⁶⁶ τῶν ἀλγηδόνων ἐπιδείκνυμι¹⁶⁷ κεκρατηκέναι¹⁶⁸ τὸν λογισμόν, ἀλλὰ καὶ τῶν ἡδονῶν¹⁶⁹ κρατεῖν καὶ μηδὲν αὐταῖς ὑπείκειν.¹⁷⁰

NOTES

6:5. ὡς ἀληθῶς Ελεαζαρος. The Hebrew name means "God helps." The comparison may suggest that he has demonstrated himself worthy of the name of Israel's second high priest (cf. Num. 20:25–28; Deut. 10:6). Eleazar is compared to Aaron at 4 Macc. 7:11–12 (cf. Num. 16:41–50; Wis. 18:20–25). Thus, this could be translated "like a true Eleazar" or simply mean that God is his helper—thus, "as truly (an) Eleazar." DeSilva (2006, 143) comments in favor of the latter: "He experiences 'truly' what his name means, God helping him to bear the torments."

6:7. Even though Eleazar can no longer keep his body upright, he never wavers in holding reason (τὸν λογισμόν) upright (ὀρθόν). Eventually, his tormenters ask him, "Why do you irrationally [ἀλογίστως] destroy yourself?" (6:14). Yet he maintains that it would be irrational (ἀλόγιστον) to waver in any way from God's law (6:18–20).

6:10. καὶ καθάπερ γενναῖος ἀθλητὴς τυπτόμενος. The writer has a penchant for athletic imagery (cf. 9:8; 11:20–21; 14:5; 15:29; 16:16; 17:12–16; Klauck 2011, 1465), which is also a motif of Christian martyrology (e.g., Ign. *Pol.* 1.3; 2.3; 3.1) and of the noble death tradition more broadly. The athletic contest

138. βάσανος, -ου, ἡ, *torment, torture*.
139. καυστικός, -ή, -όν, *fiery*.
140. ἵλεως, -ων, *propitious, gracious*.
141. Aor. pass. ptc. nom. masc. sg., ἀρκέω, *content, satisfied*; with dat.; circ.
142. δίκη, -ης, ἡ, *punishment*.
143. καθάρσιος, -ον, (subst.) *purification*; pred. comp.
144. ἀντίψυχος, -ον, *a life in exchange for*; pred. comp.
145. ἱερός, -ή, -όν, *priestly*.
146. Adv., *nobly*.
147. Aor. act. indic. 3 sg., ἐναποθνῄσκω, *die*.
148. Aor. act. indic. 3 sg., ἀνθίστημι, *resist*.
149. Adv., lit., *confessedly*; essentially *quod erat demonstrandum* ("which was to be demonstrated," Klauck 2011, 1466).
150. δεσπότης, -ου, ὁ, *master*; pred. nom.
151. πάθος, -ους, τό, (pl.) *the passions*.
152. εὐσεβής, -ές, *pious*.
153. Plpf. act. indic. 3 sg., κρατέω, *overcome*; with gen.; second-class (contrafactual) condition (cf. BDF §360; S §2302; CGCG §49.10).
154. Aor. act. indic. 1 pl., ἀποδίδωμι, *give* (what is due).
155. ἐπικράτεια, -ας, ἡ, *mastery, dominance*.
156. Aor. act. ptc. gen. masc. sg., νικάω, *conquer*; gen. absol. (causal).
157. Adv., *properly*.
158. ἡγεμονία, -ας, ἡ, *act of governing/ruling*.
159. Pres. act. indic. 1 pl., προσνέμω, *assign*.
160. Pres. act. inf., ὁμολογέω, *confess*; comp. of δίκαιόν ἐστιν: "It is right for us *to confess* that such power belongs to reason."
161. κράτος, -ους, τό, *power*.
162. Adv., *externally*.
163. ἀλγηδών, -όνος, ἡ, *agony, pain*.
164. Pres. act. indic. 3 sg., ἐπικρατέω, *have mastery over*.
165. γελοῖος, -α, -ον, *ludicrous*. The meaning of ἐπεὶ καὶ γελοῖον is uncertain; perhaps something like, "since (not to do so) would be ludicrous."
166. οὐ μόνον . . . ἀλλὰ καί, *not only . . . but also*.
167. Pres. act. indic. 1 sg., ἐπιδείκνυμι, *demonstrate*.
168. Pf. act. inf., κρατέω, *overcome*; indir. disc (cf. BDF §397; S §2016; CGCG §51.19).
169. ἡδονή, -ῆς, ἡ, *pleasure*.
170. Pres. act. inf., ὑπείκω, *concede, yield*; indir. disc. See n. 168.

is a moral one in which the athlete wrestles to overcome the passions and win immortality (cf. Wis. 4:2; 10:12; Philo, *Sobr.* 65; Heb. 12:1–4).

6:21. ὡς ἄνανδροι. Concern over "true" masculinity is a commonplace in ancient martyrology. The writer casts his protagonist as "manly" and antagonists as "effeminate" (Moore and Anderson 1998). Later, he expands on the encomium to the mother of seven sons in 2 Maccabees (cf. 2 Macc. 7:20–23): "But pious reason [ὁ εὐσεβὴς λογισμός], empowering her to act like a man [ἀνδρειώσας] in the very midst of her emotions, strengthened her to disregard, for the time, her parental love. . . . O mother of the nation, vindicator of the law and champion of religion, who carried away the prize of the contest in your heart! O more noble than males in steadfastness, and more manly [ἀνδρειοτέρα] than men [ἀνδρῶν] in endurance!" (4 Macc. 15:23, 29–30). That the mother performs "masculinity" in a manner superior to men is a testament to the supreme power of ὁ εὐσεβὴς λογισμός (cf. 14:11–12).

6:29. Cf. 17:21–22: "The tyrant was punished, and the homeland purified [καθαρισθῆναι]—they having become, as it were, a ransom for the sin of our nation [ἀντίψυχον . . . τῆς τοῦ ἔθνους ἁμαρτίας]. And through the blood of those pious ones [διὰ τοῦ αἵματος τῶν εὐσεβῶν ἐκείνων] and their atoning death [τοῦ ἱλαστηρίου τοῦ θανάτου αὐτῶν], divine providence preserved Israel that previously had been mistreated." The passage is often compared to Rom. 3:21–26. For further discussion about the Maccabean martyrs giving their lives in exchange for others, see Henten (1997), Versnel (2012), and Eberhart (2013, 101–3).

PART 2

Reading the Apostolic Fathers

The term "Apostolic Fathers" designates a collection of some of our earliest Christian texts.[1] These writings are essential witnesses to the growth and development of Christianity in the early to mid-second century. For example, they allude to developments in church governance (i.e., the office of the monarchical bishop), discuss matters of pressing theological concern (e.g., the possibility of postbaptismal repentance), and provide the earliest evidence for the reception of New Testament texts (see Gregory and Tuckett 2005). They also bear witness to the diversity of early Christianity—not only to its latent theologies (à la Bauer's [1971] influential thesis) but also to the very social imaginaries that came to undergird what it means to be "Christian."[2]

The Apostolic Fathers are thus an excellent place to begin your journey beyond the New Testament. The five passages in this chapter represent the range of this important collection. They come from 1 Clement, the letters of Ignatius of Antioch, the Martyrdom of Polycarp, the Epistle of Barnabas, and the Epistle to Diognetus.

---

1. J.-B. Cotelier published the first collection of these writings in 1672 and included the Epistle of Barnabas, 1–2 Clement, the Shepherd of Hermas, the letters of Ignatius, the Epistle of Polycarp, and the Martyrdom of Polycarp. Gallandi subsequently expanded the collection in 1765 to include the Epistle to Diognetus, the fragments of Papias, and the fragment of Quadratus. The Didache was the last to be added, after its discovery in 1873.

2. The best place to begin your study of the Apostolic Fathers is with the essays in Pratscher 2010 and Bird and Harrower 2021. For critical editions with English translations, see Ehrman 2003 and Holmes 2007, which is a fresh edition of Lightfoot and Harmer 1891 (which is still useful).

2.1

1 Clement

First Clement is a missive dispatched from the ecclesial authorities in Rome to Christians in Corinth, probably in the last decade of the first century CE. While the letter is anonymous, ancient tradition, along with the majority of manuscripts, designates its author as a certain Clement. Numerous attempts have been made to identify this Clement, but the most we can say is that he was among the leaders of the Roman church. To identify him as the third bishop of Rome, as Irenaeus does (*Haer.* 3.3.3; cf. Eusebius, *Hist. eccl.* 3.4.21), presupposes the existence of an ecclesial structure for which there is scant evidence.

The letter's antiquity, along with its style, rhetoric, and themes, renders it an essential document for the study of ancient Christianity. For example, the writer chastises his audience for the same schismatic tendencies for which Paul chastised the Corinthians a generation earlier (1 Clem. 46–47). First Clement is also an important witness to the reception of New Testament writings (Gregory 2005) and the first to suggest that the Apostle Paul reached "the farthest limits of the west" (5.7; cf. Rom. 15:24–28).

The reading passage appears to take its inspiration from the list of exempla in Hebrews 11. Yet the writer is interested not in "faith" (πίστις) per se but in "obedience" (ὑπακοή). In fact, "faith" must be accompanied by "hospitality," both of which, the writer contends, are the reason Abraham received the promised offspring and Rahab received deliverance.

Text and Translation: Ehrman 2003
Supplemental Scripture: Heb. 11:1–19, 31; James 2:20–26

2.1.1

Exemplars of Faithful Obedience

1 Clement 9.1–12.8

9.1Διὸ ὑπακούσωμεν[1] τῇ μεγαλοπρεπεῖ[2] καὶ ἐνδόξῳ[3] βουλήσει[4] αὐτοῦ, καὶ ἱκέται[5] γενόμενοι τοῦ ἐλέους[6] καὶ τῆς χρηστότητος[7] αὐτοῦ προσπέσωμεν[8] καὶ ἐπιστρέψωμεν[9] ἐπὶ τοὺς οἰκτιρμοὺς[10] αὐτοῦ, ἀπολιπόντες[11] τὴν ματαιοπονίαν[12] τήν τε ἔριν[13] καὶ τὸ εἰς θάνατον ἄγον ζῆλος.[14] **2**ἀτενίσωμεν[15] εἰς τοὺς τελείως[16] λειτουργήσαντας[17] τῇ μεγαλοπρεπεῖ δόξῃ αὐτοῦ. **3**λάβωμεν Ἐνώχ, ὃς ἐν ὑπακοῇ[18] δίκαιος εὑρεθεὶς μετετέθη,[19] καὶ οὐχ εὑρέθη αὐτοῦ θάνατος. **4**Νῶε πιστὸς εὑρεθεὶς διὰ τῆς λειτουργίας[20] αὐτοῦ παλιγγενεσίαν[21] κόσμῳ ἐκήρυξεν,[22] καὶ διέσωσεν[23] δι' αὐτοῦ ὁ δεσπότης[24] τὰ εἰσελθόντα ἐν ὁμονοίᾳ[25] ζῷα[26] εἰς τὴν κιβωτόν.[27]

10.1Ἀβραάμ, ὁ φίλος προσαγορευθείς,[28] πιστὸς εὑρέθη ἐν τῷ αὐτὸν ὑπήκοον γενέσθαι[29] τοῖς ῥήμασιν τοῦ θεοῦ. **2**οὗτος δι' ὑπακοῆς ἐξῆλθεν ἐκ τῆς γῆς αὐτοῦ καὶ ἐκ τῆς συγγενείας[30] αὐτοῦ καὶ ἐκ τοῦ οἴκου τοῦ πατρὸς αὐτοῦ, ὅπως γῆν ὀλίγην[31] καὶ συγγένειαν

---

1. Aor. act. subj. 1 pl., ὑπακούω, *obey*; with dat.; hortatory (cf. BDF §364; S §1797; CGCG §52.42).
2. μεγαλοπρεπής, -ές, *majestic, noble*.
3. ἔνδοξος, -ον, *glorious, honored*.
4. βούλησις, -εως, ἡ, *will*.
5. ἱκέτης, -ου, ὁ, *supplicant*.
6. ἔλεος, -ους, τό, *mercy*.
7. χρηστότης, -ητος, ἡ, *goodness*.
8. Aor. act. subj. 1 pl., προσπίπτω, *fall before*; hortatory. See n. 1.
9. Aor. act. subj. 1 pl., ἐπιστρέφω, *turn back, return*; hortatory. See n. 1.
10. οἰκτιρμός, -οῦ, ὁ, *compassion*.
11. Aor. act. ptc. nom. masc. pl., ἀπολείπω, *leave, desert*; circ.
12. ματαιοπονία, -ας, ἡ, *vain/empty labor*.
13. ἔρις, -ιδος, ἡ, *strife*.
14. ζῆλος, -ους, τό, *jealousy*.
15. Aor. act. subj. 1 pl., ἀτενίζω, *look steadfastly*; hortatory. See n. 1.
16. Adv., *perfectly*.
17. Aor. act. ptc. acc. masc. pl., λειτουργέω, *serve*; with dat.; attrib. (subst.).
18. ὑπακοή, -ῆς, ἡ, *obedience*.
19. Aor. pass. indic. 3 sg., μετατίθημι, (pass.) *be transferred*.
20. λειτουργία, -ας, ἡ, *service*.
21. παλιγγενεσία, -ας, ἡ, *regeneration*.
22. Aor. act. indic. 3 sg., κηρύσσω, *announce, herald*.
23. Aor. act. indic. 3 sg., διασῴζω, *rescue, deliver, save*.
24. δεσπότης, -ου, ὁ, *master*.
25. ὁμόνοια, -ας, ἡ, *harmony, concord*.
26. ζῷον, -ου, τό, *living creature, animal*.
27. κιβωτός, -οῦ, ἡ, *ark*.
28. Aor. pass. ptc. nom. masc. sg., προσαγορεύω, (pass.) *be designated, called*; attrib. (subst.).
29. ἐν τῷ with an infinitive expresses action contemporaneous to the main verb (cf. BDF §404): "He was found faithful *when* he became obedient to the words of God."
30. συγγένεια, -ας, ἡ, *kinship group*.
31. ὀλίγος, -η, -ον, *little, small*.

ἀσθενῆ³² καὶ οἶκον μικρὸν καταλιπὼν³³ κληρονομήσῃ³⁴ τὰς ἐπαγγελίας τοῦ θεοῦ. λέγει γὰρ αὐτῷ· ³ἄπελθε ἐκ τῆς γῆς σου καὶ ἐκ τῆς συγγενείας σου καὶ ἐκ τοῦ οἴκου τοῦ πατρός σου εἰς τὴν γῆν, ἣν ἄν σοι δείξω·³⁵ καὶ ποιήσω σε εἰς ἔθνος μέγα καὶ εὐλογήσω³⁶ σε καὶ μεγαλυνῶ³⁷ τὸ ὄνομά σου, καὶ ἔσῃ εὐλογημένος.³⁸ καὶ εὐλογήσω τοὺς εὐλογοῦντάς σε καὶ καταράσομαι³⁹ τοὺς καταρωμένους σε, καὶ εὐλογηθήσονται ἐν σοὶ πᾶσαι αἱ φυλαὶ⁴⁰ τῆς γῆς. ⁴καὶ πάλιν ἐν τῷ διαχωρισθῆναι⁴¹ αὐτὸν ἀπὸ Λὼτ εἶπεν αὐτῷ ὁ θεός· Ἀναβλέψας⁴² τοῖς ὀφθαλμοῖς σου, ἴδε ἀπὸ τοῦ τόπου οὗ⁴³ νῦν σὺ εἶ, πρὸς βορρᾶν⁴⁴ καὶ λίβα⁴⁵ καὶ ἀνατολὰς⁴⁶ καὶ θάλασσαν,⁴⁷ ὅτι πᾶσαν τὴν γῆν,⁴⁸ ἣν σὺ ὁρᾷς, σοὶ δώσω αὐτὴν καὶ τῷ σπέρματί σου ἕως⁴⁹ αἰῶνος. ⁵καὶ ποιήσω τὸ σπέρμα σου ὡς τὴν ἄμμον⁵⁰ τῆς γῆς· εἰ δύναταί τις ἐξαριθμῆσαι⁵¹ τὴν ἄμμον τῆς γῆς, καὶ⁵² τὸ σπέρμα σου ἐξαριθμηθήσεται. ⁶καὶ πάλιν λέγει· ἐξήγαγεν ὁ θεὸς τὸν Ἀβραὰμ καὶ εἶπεν αὐτῷ· ἀνάβλεψον εἰς τὸν οὐρανὸν καὶ ἀρίθμησον τοὺς ἀστέρας,⁵³ εἰ δυνήσῃ ἐξαριθμῆσαι αὐτούς· οὕτως ἔσται τὸ σπέρμα σου. ἐπίστευσεν δὲ Ἀβραὰμ τῷ θεῷ, καὶ ἐλογίσθη⁵⁴ αὐτῷ εἰς δικαιοσύνην. ⁷διὰ πίστιν καὶ φιλοξενίαν⁵⁵ ἐδόθη αὐτῷ υἱὸς ἐν γήρᾳ,⁵⁶ καὶ δι' ὑπακοῆς προσήνεγκεν⁵⁷ αὐτὸν θυσίαν τῷ θεῷ πρὸς ἓν τῶν ὀρέων⁵⁸ ὧν ἔδειξεν αὐτῷ.

11.1Διὰ φιλοξενίαν καὶ εὐσέβειαν⁵⁹ Λὼτ ἐσώθη ἐκ Σοδόμων, τῆς περιχώρου⁶⁰ πάσης κριθείσης⁶¹ διὰ πυρὸς⁶² καὶ θείου,⁶³ πρόδηλον⁶⁴ ποιήσας ὁ δεσπότης, ὅτι τοὺς ἐλπίζοντας ἐπ' αὐτὸν οὐκ ἐγκαταλείπει,⁶⁵ τοὺς δὲ ἑτεροκλινεῖς⁶⁶ ὑπάρχοντας εἰς κόλασιν⁶⁷ καὶ αἰκισμὸν⁶⁸ τίθησιν. ²συνεξελθούσης⁶⁹ γὰρ αὐτῷ τῆς γυναικὸς ἑτερογνώμονος⁷⁰ ὑπαρχούσης καὶ οὐκ ἐν ὁμονοίᾳ, εἰς τοῦτο σημεῖον⁷¹ ἐτέθη, ὥστε γενέσθαι⁷²

---

32. ἀσθενής, -ές, *weak*.
33. Aor. act. ptc. nom. masc. sg., καταλείπω, *leave behind, abandon*; circ.
34. Aor. act. subj. 3 sg., κληρονομέω, *inherit*; purpose clause (cf. BDF §369; S §2193; CGCG §45.3).
35. Aor. act. subj. 3 sg., δείκνυμι, *show*; conditional relative clause (cf. BDF §380; S §2560; CGCG §50.20).
36. Fut. act. indic. 1 sg., εὐλογέω, *bless*.
37. Fut. act. indic. 1 sg., μεγαλύνω, *enlarge, magnify*.
38. Pf. mid. ptc. nom. masc. sg., εὐλογέω; periphrastic (equivalent of fut.-pf. tense).
39. Fut. mid. indic. 1 sg., καταράομαι, *curse*.
40. φυλή, -ῆς, ἡ, *tribe*.
41. Aor. pass. inf., διαχωρίζω, *depart, separate*; ἐν τῷ with inf. See n. 29.
42. Aor. act. ptc. nom. masc. sg., ἀναβλέπω, *look up*. Broadly speaking, the mood of the participle is relative to that of the main verb (cf. S §2069; CGCG §52.6). Thus, here it has imperatival force. Its discourse function is as a circumstantial frame (cf. Runge 2010, 249–55).
43. Adv., *where*.
44. βορρᾶς, -ᾶ, ὁ, *north*.
45. λίψ, λιβός, ὁ, *south*.
46. ἀνατολή, -ῆς, ἡ, *east*.
47. θάλασσα, -ης, ἡ, *sea*; thus, "west."
48. The citation agrees with Gen. 13:15 LXX, in which the fronted constituent (*casus pendens*) is resumed by a pronoun in the same case (πᾶσαν τὴν γῆν . . . αὐτήν), the result of quantitative representation of the Hebrew syntax (cf. SSG §84b)
49. Prep. with gen., *up to, as far as*; ἕως αἰῶνος, lit., "unto the age."
50. ἄμμος, -ου, ἡ, *sand*.
51. Aor. act. inf., ἐξαριθμέω, *count*.
52. Introduces the apodosis (reflecting apodotic *waw*; cf. SSG §90g; BDF §442).
53. ἀστήρ, -έρας, ὁ, *star*.
54. Aor. pass. indic. 3 sg., λογίζομαι, (impers.) *it was credited*; pass. with εἰς marks pred. comp. (cf. BDAG, 596.1; BDF §145.2).
55. φιλοξενία, -ας, ἡ, *hospitality*.
56. γῆρας, -ως, τό, *old age*.
57. Aor. act. indic. 3 sg., προσφέρω, *offer* (a sacrifice).
58. ὄρος, -εος, τό, *mountain*.
59. εὐσέβεια, -ας, ἡ, *piety*.
60. περίχωρος, -ου, ἡ, *surrounding region*.
61. Aor. pass. ptc. gen. fem. sg., κρίνω, (pass.) *be judged*; gen. absol.
62. πῦρ, πυρός, τό, *fire*.
63. θεῖον, -ου, τό, *sulfur*.
64. πρόδηλος, -ον, *very clear*.
65. Pres. act. indic. 3 sg., ἐγκαταλείπω, *abandon, forsake*.
66. ἑτεροκλινής, -ές, *turning/leaning in the other direction*.
67. κόλασις, -εως, ἡ, *punishment*.
68. αἰκισμός, -οῦ, ὁ, *torture, torment*.
69. Aor. pass. ptc. gen. fem. sg., συνεξέρχομαι, *go out with*; gen. absol.
70. ἑτερογνώμων, -ον, *of a different opinion*.
71. σημεῖον, -ου, τό, *sign*; pred. comp. of pass. constr. (cf. BDF §159; S §1747; CGCG §35.15).
72. Result clause (cf. BDF §391; S §2269; CGCG §46.6), signposted by εἰς τοῦτο.

αὐτὴν στήλην⁷³ ἁλὸς⁷⁴ ἕως τῆς ἡμέρας ταύτης, εἰς τὸ γνωστὸν εἶναι⁷⁵ πᾶσιν, ὅτι οἱ δίψυχοι⁷⁶ καὶ οἱ διστάζοντες⁷⁷ περὶ τῆς τοῦ θεοῦ δυνάμεως εἰς κρίμα καὶ εἰς σημείωσιν⁷⁸ πάσαις ταῖς γενεαῖς γίνονται.

12.1 Διὰ πίστιν καὶ φιλοξενίαν ἐσώθη Ῥαὰβ ἡ πόρνη.⁷⁹ **2** ἐκπεμφθέντων⁸⁰ γὰρ ὑπὸ Ἰησοῦ τοῦ⁸¹ τοῦ Ναυὴ κατασκόπων⁸² εἰς τὴν Ἰεριχώ, ἔγνω ὁ βασιλεὺς τῆς γῆς ὅτι ἥκασιν⁸³ κατασκοπεῦσαι⁸⁴ τὴν χώραν αὐτῶν, καὶ ἐξέπεμψεν ἄνδρας τοὺς συλλημψομένους⁸⁵ αὐτούς, ὅπως συλλημφθέντες θανατωθῶσιν.⁸⁶ **3** ἡ οὖν φιλόξενος⁸⁷ Ῥαὰβ εἰσδεξαμένη⁸⁸ αὐτοὺς ἔκρυψεν⁸⁹ εἰς τὸ ὑπερῷον⁹⁰ ὑπὸ τὴν λινοκαλάμην.⁹¹ **4** ἐπισταθέντων⁹² δὲ τῶν παρὰ τοῦ βασιλέως καὶ λεγόντων· πρὸς σὲ εἰσῆλθον οἱ κατάσκοποι τῆς γῆς ἡμῶν· ἐξάγαγε αὐτούς, ὁ γὰρ βασιλεὺς οὕτως κελεύει,⁹³ ἥδε ἀπεκρίθη· εἰσῆλθον μὲν⁹⁴ οἱ ἄνδρες, οὓς ζητεῖτε, πρός με, ἀλλὰ εὐθέως ἀπῆλθον καὶ πορεύονται τῇ ὁδῷ, ὑποδεικνύουσα⁹⁵ αὐτοῖς ἐναλλάξ.⁹⁶ **5** καὶ εἶπεν πρὸς τοὺς ἄνδρας· γινώσκουσα γινώσκω⁹⁷ ἐγὼ ὅτι κύριος ὁ θεὸς παραδίδωσιν ὑμῖν τὴν γῆν ταύτην· ὁ γὰρ φόβος καὶ ὁ τρόμος⁹⁸ ὑμῶν ἐπέπεσεν τοῖς κατοικοῦσιν⁹⁹ αὐτήν. ὡς ἐὰν οὖν γένηται λαβεῖν αὐτὴν ὑμᾶς, διασώσατέ με καὶ τὸν οἶκον τοῦ πατρός μου. **6** καὶ εἶπαν αὐτῇ· ἔσται οὕτως, ὡς ἐλάλησας ἡμῖν. ὡς ἐὰν οὖν γνῶς παραγινομένους¹⁰⁰ ἡμᾶς, συνάξεις¹⁰¹ πάντας τοὺς σοὺς ὑπὸ τὸ στέγος¹⁰² σου, καὶ διασωθήσονται· ὅσοι γὰρ ἐὰν εὑρεθῶσιν ἔξω τῆς οἰκίας, ἀπολοῦνται.¹⁰³ **7** καὶ προσέθεντο¹⁰⁴ αὐτῇ δοῦναι σημεῖον, ὅπως ἐκκρεμάσῃ¹⁰⁵ ἐκ τοῦ οἴκου αὐτῆς κόκκινον,¹⁰⁶ πρόδηλον ποιοῦντες ὅτι διὰ τοῦ αἵματος τοῦ κυρίου λύτρωσις¹⁰⁷ ἔσται πᾶσιν

---

73. στήλη, -ης, ἡ, *pillar*; pred. acc.
74. ἅλς, ἁλός, ὁ, *salt*.
75. εἰς τό with an infinitive expresses purpose (cf. BDF §391).
76. δίψυχος, -ον, *double-minded*.
77. Pres. act. ptc. nom. masc. pl., διστάζω, *doubt*; attrib. (subst.).
78. σημείωσις, -εως, ἡ, *sign, signal*.
79. πόρνη, -ης, ἡ, *prostitute*. A number of MSS add ἐπιλεγομένη, "called the prostitute."
80. Aor. pass. ptc. gen. masc. pl., ἐκπέμπω, *send out*; gen. absol.
81. An appositive to Ἰησοῦ. The nominative would be Ἰησοῦς ὁ τοῦ Ναυή.
82. κατάσκοπος, -ου, ὁ, *spy*.
83. Pf. act. indic. 3 pl., ἥκω, *come*.
84. Aor. act. inf., κατασκοπεύω, *spy out*; purpose (BDF §390; S §2008; CGCG §51.16).
85. Fut. mid. ptc. acc. masc. pl., συλλαμβάνω, *arrest*; attrib. (subst.) expressing purpose (cf. BDF §351; S §2044; CGCG §52.49).
86. Aor. pass. subj. 3 pl., θανατόω, *be put to death*; purpose clause. See n. 34.
87. φιλόξενος, -ον, *hospitable*.
88. Aor. mid. ptc. nom. fem. sg., εἰσδέχομαι, *welcome in, take in*; circ.
89. Aor. act. indic. 3 sg., κρύπτω, *hide*.
90. ὑπερῷον, -ου, τό, *upstairs room*.
91. λινοκαλάμη, -ης, ἡ, *flax straw*.
92. Aor. pass. ptc. gen. masc. pl., ἐφίστημι, (intrans.) *stand near, be present*; gen. absol.
93. Pres. act. indic. 3 sg., κελεύω, *order, command*.
94. Here μέν *solitarium* is completed by ἀλλά, which indicates that the μέν-clause is no longer relevant (cf. *CGCG* 59.24): "The men whom you seek did indeed come to me; but they left immediately and went on their way."
95. Pres. act. ptc. nom. fem. sg., ὑποδείκνυμι, *point, gesture toward*; circ.
96. Adv., *in the opposite direction*.
97. LXX translators used the collocation of a circumstantial participle plus a finite verb to render the Hebrew collocation of an infinitive absolute plus a finite verb (cf. *SSG* §31db; BDF §422; on the Hebrew construction, see Williams 2007, §205). This construction occurs in the NT only in citations of the Jewish scriptures (e.g., Matt. 13:14; Acts 7:34; Heb. 6:14). Curiously, no Hebrew or Greek manuscript of Joshua supports this reading. Rather, the locution appears to be the writer's creation. Translate as, "I am absolutely convinced."
98. τρόμος, -ου, ὁ, *trembling*.
99. Pres. act. ptc. dat. masc. pl., κατοικέω, *inhabit*; attrib. (subst.).
100. Pres. mid. ptc. acc. masc. pl., παραγίνομαι, *draw near, present*; supp. (γνῷς).
101. Fut. act. indic. 2 sg., συνάγω, *gather*; imperatival (cf. BDF §362; S §1917; *CGCG* §33.44).
102. στέγος, -ους, τό, *roof*.
103. Fut. mid. indic. 3 pl., ἀπόλλυμι, (mid.) *perish*; third-class condition (cf. BDF §373; S §2323; *CGCG* §49.6).
104. Aor. mid. indic. 3 pl., προστίθημι, *add*; with inf.
105. Aor. act subj. 3 sg., ἐκκρεμάννυμι, *hang from*; expresses the command and the purpose in giving it (cf. BDAG, 718.2b; S §2218).
106. κόκκινος, -ον, *scarlet*.
107. λύτρωσις, -εως, ἡ, *ransom, redemption*.

τοῖς πιστεύουσιν καὶ ἐλπίζουσιν ἐπὶ τὸν θεόν. ⁸ὁρᾶτε, ἀγαπητοί, ὅτι οὐ μόνον πίστις, ἀλλὰ καὶ προφητεία ἐν τῇ γυναικὶ γέγονεν.

NOTES

9.1. Διὸ ὑπακούσωμεν τῇ μεγαλοπρεπεῖ καὶ ἐνδόξῳ βουλήσει αὐτοῦ. The exhortation is an inference from the previous section on μετανοία (7:1–8:5) and introduces "obedience to his magnificent and glorious will" as a new discourse topic. In the list of exempla (9:3–12:8), prepositional phrases (ἐν ὑπακοῇ and δι' ὑπακοῆς) establish obedience as the frame of reference by which an actor's behavior is assessed (cf. 9:3; 10:2, 7).

τὸ εἰς θάνατον ἄγον ζῆλος. Cf. Wis. 2:24. The writer is likely reflecting on the narrative of Genesis, in which "jealousy" (ζῆλος) becomes the vehicle of fratricide (cf. 1 Clem. 4.1–7; Gen. 4:3–8). "Jealousy" is explicitly mentioned in LAB 59:4 and T. Benj. 7:2–3.

9.3. εὑρεθείς. The writer's use of the passive of εὑρίσκω (9.3, 4; 10.1) is analogous to Hebrews' use of the passive of μαρτυρέω (Heb. 11:2, 4).

Cf. Gen. 5:24; Sir. 44:16; Wis. 4:10; Heb. 11:5. Genesis does not say that Enoch was found "righteous" (δίκαιος), but other traditions do (cf. Gk. 1 En. 1:2; T. Levi 10:5; T. Jud. 18:1; T. Dan 5:6; T. Benj. 9:1; Lona 1998, 194n3). The writer of Hebrews makes a similar move with Abel (cf. Heb. 11:4).

9.4. Cf. Gen. 6:8–13; 7:1; Sir. 44:17–18; Matt. 24:36–44 parr.; Heb. 11:7; 1 Pet. 3:20; 2 Pet. 2:5.

ἐν ὁμονοίᾳ. The term ὁμόνοια ("concord") occurs fourteen times in the letter and is at the center of its rhetorical aim. See Ehrman (2003, 1:19–20) and Bakke (2001). The purpose of the *homonoia* speech is to call the polis to reflect the harmony that is present in nature (cf. 20:10; Dio Chrysostom, *In contione*; see §7.4.2 below).

10.1–3. Cf. Gen. 12:1–3; Heb. 11:8–9.

ὁ φίλος προσαγορευθείς. Cf. 1 Clem. 17.2; Philo, *Abr.* 273; James 2:23. The designation probably developed from the scriptural designation "beloved of God" (cf. Isa. 41:8; 2 Chron. 20:7; Lona 1998, 196).

10.6. Cf. Gen. 15:5–6; Rom. 4:3; Gal. 3:6; James 2:23.

10.7. διὰ πίστιν καὶ φιλοξενίαν. Cf. 11.1; 12.1. The writer attributes the birth of Isaac (Gen. 21:1–7) to both Abraham's faith (cf. Gen. 15:6; Rom. 4:18–21; Heb. 11:11–12) and his hospitality (cf. Gen. 18:1–15; Philo, *Abr.* 114; T. Ab. A17:7). Hospitality (φιλοξενία) is mentioned as one of the cardinal virtues at the outset of the letter (cf. 1 Clem. 1.2; Jaubert 1971, 117n1).

δι' ὑπακοῆς προσήνεγκεν αὐτὸν θυσίαν τῷ θεῷ. Cf. Gen. 22:1–14; 1 Macc. 2:52; Jdt. 8:25–27; Sir. 44:20; 4 Macc. 16:20; Jub. 17:15–18:19; LAB 32:2–4; Heb. 11:17; James 2:21–24; Barn. 7.3; Josephus, *A.J.* 1.222–236 (§5.2.2). The *inclusio* οὗτος δι' ὑπακοῆς (1 Clem. 10.2) . . . δι' ὑπακοῆς (10:7) frames the list of Abraham's actions and undergirds the claim that "Abraham was found faithful *when he obeyed the words of God*" (10:1; cf. Neh. 9:7–8; Sir. 44:20; 1 Macc. 2:52; Jub. 17:17–18; 19:8–9; 4Q226 7, 1–2).

11.1. Cf. Gen. 19:1–15; Luke 17:28–30; 2 Pet. 2:7–10.

11.2. Cf. Gen. 19:26; Wis. 10:7; Luke 17:32; Philo, *Fug.* 122; Josephus, *A.J.* 1.203.

12.1–7. Cf. Josh. 2; Heb. 11:31; James 2:25.

12.7. κόκκινον. The "scarlet thing" (cf. Josh. 2:18) is a "sign" (σημεῖον) that "ransom/redemption" (λύτρωσις) will be for all "through the blood of the Lord" (διὰ τοῦ αἵματος τοῦ κυρίου) (cf. Rom.

3:24; Eph. 1:7; Heb. 9:12). Blood here functions as a prophylactic against death and destruction in a manner analogous to the function of lamb's blood at the first Passover. Compare with Justin Martyr: "As the blood of the Passover saved those who were in Egypt [ὡς δὲ τοὺς ἐν Αἰγύπτῳ ἔσωσε τὸ αἷμα τοῦ πάσχα], so also the blood of Christ rescues from death the ones who trust [οὕτως καὶ τοὺς πιστεύσαντας ῥύσεται ἐκ θανάτου τὸ αἷμα τοῦ Χριστοῦ]" (*Dial.* 111.3).

2.2

Ignatius of Antioch

Ehrman notes that "the letters of Ignatius have received far more scholarly attention than any of the other writings of the Apostolic Fathers" (2003, 1:203). Of primary interest is the light these letters shed on the emergence of proto-orthodoxy (cf. Ign. *Eph.* 6.2; Ign. *Trall.* 6.1) and the institutionalized role of the monarchical bishop (cf. Ign. *Eph.* 6.1; Ign. *Magn.* 3; Ign. *Trall.* 2.2; 3.1; Ign. *Phld.* 2.1; Ign. *Smyrn.* 8.1). Yet surely the most captivating (and for some, off-putting) feature of these letters is the circumstances surrounding them: the bishop of Antioch anticipates his impending martyrdom "with a vivid, almost macabre eagerness ([Ign.] *Rom.* 4.2; 5.3; 7.2)" (Holmes 2007, 169).[1]

Ignatius pens his letters while en route to his execution in Rome. The date of his martyrdom, and thus of the letters, is uncertain.[2] Polycarp, the bishop of Smyrna and the recipient of Ignatius's final letter, mentions Ignatius's death in passing (Pol. *Phil.* 9). Eusebius suggests that Ignatius's martyrdom occurred during the reign of the emperor Trajan (98–117 CE; Eusebius, *Hist. eccl.* 3.36), a datum that most scholars still accept (Holmes 2007, 170). Others, however, such as Harnack (1878), and more recently Schoedel (1993), argue that the window for dating Ignatius's martyrdom should include the reign of the emperor Hadrian (117–138 CE).

The reading passage is an excerpt from Ignatius's letter *To the Ephesians*. Its resonances with New Testament, specifically Pauline, themes are evident. Yet the bishop adapts his material in fresh and creative ways—for instance, he expands the church-as-temple metaphor so that the cross becomes the "crane" by which individual "stones" (believers) are raised to the heavens.

Text and Translation: Ehrman 2003
Supplemental Scripture: 2 Cor. 6:14–18; Eph. 2:14–21

---

1. Droge (1988, 264), for example, describes Ignatius as having a "pathological craving for martyrdom." For further discussion on martyrdom in the letters of Ignatius, see esp. Moss 2012, 52–57.

2. Ignatius's letters are extant in three recensions: the long recension (thirteen letters, six of which are deemed spurious), the middle recension (seven letters), and the short recension (a Syriac abridgment of three letters). Most scholars recognize the middle recension as preserving the original form of seven authentic letters. For discussion of the issues, see Ehrman 2003, 1:209–13.

2.2.1

Warnings about False Teachers

To the Ephesians 7–9

7.1Εἰώθασιν[1] γάρ τινες δόλῳ[2] πονηρῷ τὸ ὄνομα περιφέρειν,[3] ἄλλα τινὰ πράσσοντες ἀνάξια[4] θεοῦ· οὓς δεῖ ὑμᾶς ὡς θηρία[5] ἐκκλίνειν.[6] εἰσὶν γὰρ κύνες[7] λυσσῶντες,[8] λαθροδῆκται·[9] οὓς δεῖ ὑμᾶς φυλάσσεσθαι[10] ὄντας δυσθεραπεύτους.[11] **2**εἷς ἰατρός[12] ἐστιν, σαρκικὸς[13] τε καὶ πνευματικός,[14] γεννητὸς[15] καὶ ἀγέννητος, ἐν σαρκὶ γενόμενος θεός, ἐν θανάτῳ ζωὴ ἀληθινή, καὶ ἐκ Μαρίας καὶ ἐκ θεοῦ, πρῶτον παθητὸς[16] καὶ τότε ἀπαθής,[17] Ἰησοῦς Χριστὸς ὁ κύριος ἡμῶν.

8.1Μὴ οὖν τις ὑμᾶς ἐξαπατάτω,[18] ὥσπερ οὐδὲ ἐξαπατᾶσθε, ὅλοι ὄντες θεοῦ. ὅταν γὰρ μηδεμία ἔρις[19] ἐνήρεισται[20] ἐν ὑμῖν ἡ δυναμένη ὑμᾶς βασανίσαι,[21] ἄρα[22] κατὰ θεὸν ζῆτε. περίψημα[23] ὑμῶν καὶ ἁγνίζομαι[24] ὑμῶν Ἐφεσίων,[25] ἐκκλησίας τῆς διαβοήτου[26] τοῖς αἰῶσιν. **2**οἱ σαρκικοὶ τὰ πνευματικὰ πράσσειν οὐ δύνανται οὐδὲ οἱ πνευματικοὶ τὰ σαρκικά, ὥσπερ οὐδὲ ἡ πίστις τὰ τῆς ἀπιστίας οὐδὲ ἡ ἀπιστία τὰ τῆς πίστεως. ἃ δὲ καὶ κατὰ σάρκα πράσσετε, ταῦτα πνευματικά ἐστιν, ἐν Ἰησοῦ γὰρ Χριστῷ πάντα πράσσετε.

1. Plpf. act. indic. 3 pl., ἔθω, *be accustomed*; with inf.
2. δόλος, -ου, ὁ, *deceit*; dat. of manner.
3. Pres. act. inf., περιφέρω, *carry around*.
4. ἀνάξιος, -ον, *unworthy*; with gen.
5. θηρίον, -ου, τό, *wild animal, beast*.
6. Pres. act. inf., ἐκκλίνω, *turn away from, avoid*; comp. of δεῖ.
7. κύων, -υνός, ὁ, *dog*.
8. Pres. act. ptc. nom. masc. pl., λυσσάω, *be mad, rabid*; attrib.
9. λαθροδήκτης, -ου, ὁ, lit., "one who bites in secret."
10. Pres. mid. inf., φυλάσσω, *guard against*; comp. of δεῖ.
11. δυσθεράπευτος, -ον, *hard to cure*.
12. ἰατρός, -οῦ, ὁ, *physician*.
13. σαρκικός, -ή, -όν, *of flesh*.
14. πνευματικός, -ή, -όν, *of spirit*.
15. γεννητός, -ή, -όν, *begotten, generated*.
16. παθητός, -ή, -όν, *subject to suffering*.
17. ἀπαθής, -ές, *free of suffering*.

18. Pres. act. impv. 3 sg., ἐξαπατάω, *deceive*.
19. ἔρις, -ιδος, ἡ, *strife*.
20. Pf. pass. indic. 3 sg., ἐνερείδω, (pass.) *be thrust in, become fixed*. "ἔρις ἐνήρεισται (gener. accepted conjecture of Zahn for the impossible ἐνείρισται of the mss.) ἐν ὑμῖν *is firmly rooted among you*" (BDAG, 336).
21. Aor. act. inf., βασανίζω, *torment*.
22. Postpositive partic.: "indicates that the speaker, in view of the preceding context, cannot but make the contribution he/she is making" (*CGCG* §59.42). Here it marks the apodosis as a necessary conclusion.
23. περίψημα, -ατος, τό, *dirt, offscouring*. περίψημα ὑμῶν might have the sense of "your humble/lowly servant" (cf. BDAG, 808). See further discussion in notes.
24. Pres. mid. indic. 1 sg., ἁγνίζω, (mid.) *be consecrated/dedicated*; with (ὑπὲρ) ὑμῶν.
25. Ἐφέσιος, -η, -ον, *Ephesian*.
26. διαβόητος, -ον, *renowned*.

9.1 Ἔγνων δὲ παροδεύσαντάς²⁷ τινας ἐκεῖθεν,²⁸ ἔχοντας κακὴν διδαχήν·²⁹ οὓς οὐκ εἰάσατε³⁰ σπεῖραι³¹ εἰς ὑμᾶς, βύσαντες³² τὰ ὦτα,³³ εἰς τὸ μὴ παραδέξασθαι³⁴ τὰ σπειρόμενα ὑπ' αὐτῶν, ὡς ὄντες³⁵ λίθοι ναοῦ³⁶ πατρός, ἡτοιμασμένοι³⁷ εἰς οἰκοδομὴν³⁸ θεοῦ πατρός, ἀναφερόμενοι³⁹ εἰς τὰ ὕψη⁴⁰ διὰ τῆς μηχανῆς⁴¹ Ἰησοῦ Χριστοῦ, ὅς⁴² ἐστιν σταυρός, σχοινίῳ⁴³ χρώμενοι⁴⁴ τῷ πνεύματι τῷ ἁγίῳ· ἡ δὲ πίστις ὑμῶν ἀναγωγεὺς⁴⁵ ὑμῶν, ἡ δὲ ἀγάπη ὁδὸς ἡ ἀναφέρουσα εἰς θεόν. **²**ἐστὲ οὖν καὶ σύνοδοι⁴⁶ πάντες, θεοφόροι καὶ ναοφόροι, χριστοφόροι, ἁγιοφόροι,⁴⁷ κατὰ πάντα κεκοσμημένοι⁴⁸ ἐν ἐντολαῖς⁴⁹ Ἰησοῦ Χριστοῦ· οἷς καὶ ἀγαλλιώμενος,⁵⁰ ὅτι ἠξιώθην⁵¹ δι' ὧν⁵² γράφω προσομιλῆσαι⁵³ ὑμῖν καὶ συγχαρῆναι,⁵⁴ ὅτι κατ' ἀνθρώπινον⁵⁵ βίον οὐδὲν ἀγαπᾶτε εἰ μὴ μόνον τὸν θεόν.

NOTES

7.1. τὸ ὄνομα περιφέρειν. The false teachers "carry about the name"; that is, they are itinerate preachers (cf. Ign. *Eph.* 9.1; 11.2; Ign. *Magn.* 1.2; Ign. *Trall.* 12.2; Schoedel 1985, 59).

κύνες λυσσῶντες. The metaphor evokes the infectious, and incurable, condition of the false teachers. Josephus remarks that during the famine the insurrectionists were "like rabid dogs" (ὥσπερ λυσσῶντες κύνες), gnawing on and devouring anything they could get their hands on (Josephus, *B.J.* 6.196–197).

λαθροδῆκται. The term taps "a widespread proverb that referred to a fawning behavior masking an intent to do harm" (Schoedel 1985, 59).

7.2. γεννητὸς καὶ ἀγέννητος. The language of "begotten and unbegotten" is different from, though not necessarily incompatible with, later orthodox theology. Ignatius uses these terms to distinguish between the Son's humanity and divinity, while later theologians use them to distinguish between relations within the godhead.

ἐν σαρκὶ γενόμενος θεός. Cf. John 1:14. Ehrman (2003) follows manuscripts G L against patristic quotations, "God in a human being" (ἐν ἀνθρώπῳ θεός).

---

27. Aor. act. ptc. acc. masc. pl., παροδεύω, *pass by*; supp. (Ἔγνων).
28. Adv., *from there* (in the sense of "from elsewhere").
29. διδαχή -ῆς -ἡ, *teaching*.
30. Aor. act. indic. 2 pl., ἐάω, *permit*; with inf.
31. Aor. act. inf., σπείρω, *sow*.
32. Aor. act. ptc. nom. masc. pl., βύω, *plug*; circ. (manner).
33. οὖς, ὠτός, τό, *ear*.
34. Aor. mid. inf., παραδέχομαι, *receive*. εἰς τό with an infinitive expresses purpose (cf. BDF §391).
35. ὡς with a circumstantial participle provides "a 'subjective' reason or motivation, for which responsibility lies with the subject of the matrix verb" (*CGCG* §52.39; cf. BDF §453; S §2086).
36. ναός, -οῦ, ὁ, *sanctuary* (of the temple).
37. Pf. pass. ptc. nom. masc. pl., ἑτοιμάζω, (pass.) *be prepared*.
38. οἰκοδομή, -ῆς, ἡ, *building*.
39. Pres. pass. ptc. nom. masc. pl., ἀναφέρω, (pass.) *be carried upward*.
40. ὕψος, -ους, τό, *height*.
41. μηχανή, -ῆς, ἡ, *crane*.
42. The relative pronoun does not match the gender of its antecedent, τῆς μηχανῆς. This is an instance where sense agreement supersedes the rule of concord, so-called *constructio ad sensum* (cf. BDF §134; S §2502.a; *CGCG* §27.6).
43. σχοινίον, -ου, τό, *rope*; pred. comp.
44. Pres. mid. ptc. nom. masc. pl., χράομαι, *use*; with dat.
45. ἀναγωγεύς, -έως, ὁ, *one who leads upward*.
46. σύνοδος, -ου, ὁ, *traveling companion*.
47. θεοφόρος, -ου, ὁ, *god-bearer*; ναοφόρος, *temple-bearer*; χριστοφόρος, *Christ-bearer*; ἁγιοφόρος, *bearer of what is holy*.
48. Pf. pass. ptc. nom. masc. pl., κοσμέω, (pass.) *be adorned*.
49. ἐντολή, -ῆς, ἡ, *command*.
50. Pres. mid. ptc. nom. masc. sg., ἀγαλλιάω, *exult, rejoice*.
51. Aor. pass. indic. 1 sg., ἀξιόω, (pass.) *be deemed worthy*.
52. The relative pronoun is attracted to the case of its omitted antecedent (cf. BDF §294; S §2531; *CGCG* §50.13).
53. Aor. act. inf., προσομιλέω, *converse with*; with dat.
54. Aor. pass. inf., συγχαίρω, *rejoice with*; with dat.
55. Ehrman's conjecture. Lightfoot (1875) conjectures ἀνθρώπων, Zahn (1873) ὅλον. MSS G L (A) read ἄλλον.

καὶ ἐκ Μαρίας καὶ ἐκ θεοῦ. Cf. Ign. *Eph.* 18.2; Ign. *Trall.* 9.1; Ign. *Rom.* 7.3; Ign. *Smyrn.* 1.1; Rom. 1:3; Gal. 4:4.

πρῶτον παθητὸς καὶ τότε ἀπαθής. The temporal adverb τότε ascribes impassibility to the resurrected Son (cf. Heb. 5:7–10).

8.1. περίψημα ὑμῶν. The phrase is taken in a variety of ways: "I am your lowly scapegoat" (Ehrman 2003), "I am a humble sacrifice" (Holmes 2007), "I am a sacrifice for you" (Grant 1966, 39), and "your lowliest servant" (Lightfoot 1891). The term περίψημα occurs once in the New Testament, where Paul refers to himself as the "refuse of the cosmos" (περικαθάρματα τοῦ κόσμου) and "offscouring of all" (πάντων περίψημα; 1 Cor. 4:13), and can function as a manner of humble self-deprecation (i.e., "your humble servant"; cf. Barn. 4.9; 6.5). To my mind, there is no justification for translating περίψημα as "sacrifice" (*pace* Grant 1966, 39). This should be clear enough from Ignatius's other use of the term: "my spirit is the περίψημα of the cross" (*Eph.* 18:1). This almost certainly does not mean "My spirit is a sacrificial offering bound to the cross" (Ehrman 2003) or "My spirit is a humble sacrifice for the cross" (Holmes 2007). Rather, the context suggests that Ignatius presents his πνεῦμα as a "humble servant" of the cross, and so, like Paul, as the "dregs of all things."

8.2. ἃ δὲ καὶ κατὰ σάρκα πράσσετε, ταῦτα πνευματικά ἐστιν. Given the Pauline overtones (cf. Rom. 8:5; 1 Cor. 2:14–15; Gal. 5:16–26), it is somewhat jarring that Ignatius uses κατὰ σάρκα πράσσω to describe *Christian* behavior. According to Schoedel (1985), "An almost conscious correction of the Pauline antithesis lies before us" (cf. Ign. *Smyrn.* 3.2; Ign. *Pol.* 2.2). Ignatius's basic point, however, is not anti-Pauline.

9:1. ὡς ὄντες λίθοι ναοῦ πατρός. Ignatius may have had in mind a specific tradition (e.g., Eph. 2:20–22), though the community-as-temple metaphor is too widespread to pin down to a single source (cf. Ign. *Eph.* 15.3; Ign. *Magn.* 7.7; Ign. *Phld.* 7.2; 1 Cor. 3:16–17; 6:19; 2 Cor. 6:16; 1 Pet. 2:4–6; Herm. Vis. 3; Herm. Sim. 9; Lookadoo 2018, 148–80).

διὰ τῆς μηχανῆς Ἰησοῦ Χριστοῦ, ὅς ἐστιν σταυρός. The likeliest antecedent of the relative pronoun is τῆς μηχανῆς (see Lookadoo 2018, 163–65). The cross becomes a "crane" that raises up "stones" (individual believers) to the heavens so that they can be incorporated into the building.

9.2. Schoedel (1985, 67) comments, "The list of epithets allows Ignatius to indulge in his love of -φορος compounds ('-bearers'), including one that corresponds to his own second name, Theophorus, 'God-bearer.'" The image is one of the Ephesians as mobile shrines in ritual procession (cf. Plutarch, *Mor.* 325b; Harland 2003).

2.3

Polycarp of Smyrna

According to Irenaeus of Lyons, Polycarp was a direct successor of John the Evangelist, who appointed him bishop of Smyrna (cf. *Haer.* 3.3.4; Eusebius, *Hist. eccl.* 5.20.7). Within the Apostolic Fathers, "there is one text written *to* him (by Ignatius), another written *about* him (the *Martyrdom of Polycarp*), and yet another written by him, a letter sent to the Christians of Philippi" (Ehrman 2003, 1:324). These texts written to, about, and by Polycarp contain a wealth of information, albeit at times tauntingly opaque, about the nature of apostolic succession and the early reception of writings that would be included in the New Testament (e.g., Hartog 2002).

The Martyrdom of Polycarp had a significant impact on the theological imaginations of early Christians. As Gerd Buschmann (2010, 135) notes, "[It] presents us the oldest martyrdom handed down as an independent text from the middle of the second century, which influenced the form of later martyrdom literature and is influenced by Jewish martyrdom texts from the intertestamental period."[1] The inscription of the letter identifies the sender as "the church of God that sojourns at Smyrna" and the recipient as "the church of God that sojourns in Philomelium," a town in the province of Phrygia. The Philomelians had apparently requested an account "in some detail" of what had taken place, and the Smyrnaeans complied by sending the letter "through our brother Marcion" (20.1). The letter thus frames the narrative of Polycarp's martyrdom as a resource for "communal moral formation (17.3–19.2)" (Hartog 2013, 166).

The reading passage is Polycarp's trial before the Roman proconsul (chaps. 9–11). The writer is a participant in a burgeoning discourse about what it means to die a noble death as a Christian. The bishop of Smyrna is cool and collected, always in control of his passions, brave ("manly") in the face of his irrational adversaries, and witty to the very end.

Text and Translation: Ehrman 2003
Supplemental Scripture: 1 Pet. 2:11–17; 4:12–19

---

1. The dating of the Martyrdom of Polycarp is wrapped up in how scholars address several critical issues, but most proposals fall within the range of 155–177 CE (Buschmann 2010, 139–40), though see Moss 2010.

2.3.1

The Trial of Polycarp

Martyrdom of Polycarp 9.1–11.2

9.1Τῷ δὲ Πολυκάρπῳ εἰσιόντι[1] εἰς τὸ στάδιον[2] φωνὴ ἐξ οὐρανοῦ ἐγένετο· ἴσχυε,[3] Πολύκαρπε, καὶ ἀνδρίζου.[4] καὶ τὸν μὲν[5] εἰπόντα οὐδεὶς εἶδεν, τὴν δὲ φωνὴν τῶν ἡμετέρων οἱ παρόντες[6] ἤκουσαν. καὶ λοιπὸν[7] προσαχθέντος[8] αὐτοῦ, θόρυβος[9] ἦν μέγας ἀκουσάντων, ὅτι Πολύκαρπος συνείληπται.[10] **2**προσαχθέντα οὖν αὐτὸν ἀνηρώτα[11] ὁ ἀνθύπατος,[12] εἰ αὐτὸς εἴη[13] Πολύκαρπος· τοῦ δὲ ὁμολογοῦντος,[14] ἔπειθεν[15] ἀρνεῖσθαι[16] λέγων·

αἰδέσθητί[17] σου τὴν ἡλικίαν,[18] καὶ ἕτερα τούτοις ἀκόλουθα,[19] ὧν[20] ἔθος[21] αὐτοῖς λέγειν· ὄμοσον[22] τὴν καίσαρος τύχην,[23] μετανόησον,[24] εἶπον, αἶρε τοὺς ἀθέους.[25] ὁ δὲ Πολύκαρπος ἐμβριθεῖ[26] τῷ προσώπῳ εἰς πάντα τὸν ὄχλον τὸν ἐν τῷ σταδίῳ ἀνόμων ἐθνῶν ἐμβλέψας[27] καὶ ἐπισείσας[28] αὐτοῖς τὴν χεῖρα, στενάξας[29] τε καὶ ἀναβλέψας εἰς τὸν οὐρανὸν εἶπεν· αἶρε τοὺς ἀθέους. **3**ἐγκειμένου[30] δὲ τοῦ ἀνθυπάτου καὶ λέγοντος

1. Pres. act. ptc. dat. masc. sg., εἴσειμι, *enter*; circ.
2. στάδιον, -ου, τό, *stadium*.
3. Pres. act. impv. 2 sg., ἰσχύω, *be strong*.
4. Pres. mid. impv. 2 sg., ἀνδρίζομαι, *act like a man, be brave*.
5. μέν . . . δέ; point/counterpoint set (cf. Runge 2010, 75–83; BDF §447; S §2904; *CGCG* §59.24).
6. Pres. act. ptc. nom. masc. pl., πάρειμι, *be present*; attrib. (subst.).
7. λοιπός, -ή, -όν, as adv., *then*.
8. Aor. pass. ptc. gen. masc. sg., προσάγω, (pass.) *be led forward*; gen. absol.
9. θόρυβος, -ου, ὁ, *uproar*.
10. Pf. pass. indic. 3 sg., συλλαμβάνω, (pass.) *be arrested*.
11. Aor. act. indic. 3 sg., ἀνερωτάω, *ask*.
12. ἀνθύπατος, -ου, ὁ, *proconsul*.
13. Pres. act. opt. 3 sg., εἰμί; oblique opt. in an indir. quest. (cf. BDF §386; S §2677; *CGCG* §42.7).
14. Pres. act. ptc. gen. masc. sg., ὁμολογέω, *confess*; gen. absol.
15. Impf. act. indic. 3 sg., πείθω, *persuade*; with acc. and inf.
16. Pres. mid. inf., ἀρνέομαι, *deny*.

17. Aor. pass. impv. 2 sg., αἰδέομαι, (intrans.) *show respect for* (something).
18. ἡλικία, -ας, ἡ, *age, time of life*; here, "old age."
19. ἀκόλουθος, -ον; with dat.; thus lit., "and other things following these"; i.e., *and so forth* (BDAG, 37).
20. Following MS m (*lectio difficilior*). MS g reads ὡς (cf. BDAG, 277.1).
21. ἔθος, -ους, τό, *custom*; impers. with dat. and inf.: "it is customary for them to say."
22. Aor. act. impv. 2 sg., ὀμνύω, *swear*.
23. τύχη, -ης, ἡ, *genius, numen*; with acc. of swearing, "swear by the genius of Caesar!" (cf. S §1596).
24. Aor. act. impv. 2 sg., μετανοέω, *repent*.
25. ἄθεος, -ον, (subst.) *those who deny the gods*, hence "atheists."
26. ἐμβριθής, -ές, *serious*.
27. Aor. act. ptc. nom. masc. sg., ἐμβλέπω, *look at*; circ.
28. Aor. act. ptc. nom. masc. sg., ἐπισείω, *shake at/against*; circ.
29. Aor. act. ptc. nom. masc. sg., στενάζω, *groan*; circ.
30. Pres. mid. ptc. gen. masc. sg., ἔγκειμαι, *insist, urgently warn*; gen. absol.

ὄμοσον, καὶ ἀπολύω σε, λοιδόρησον³¹ τὸν Χριστόν, ἔφη ὁ Πολύκαρπος· ὀγδοήκοντα καὶ ἓξ ἔτη³² δουλεύω³³ αὐτῷ, καὶ οὐδέν με ἠδίκησεν.³⁴ καὶ πῶς δύναμαι βλασφημῆσαι³⁵ τὸν βασιλέα μου τὸν σώσαντά με;

10.1 Ἐπιμένοντος³⁶ δὲ πάλιν αὐτοῦ καὶ λέγοντος, ὄμοσον τὴν καίσαρος τύχην, ἀπεκρίνατο· εἰ κενοδοξεῖς³⁷ ἵνα ὀμόσω τὴν καίσαρος τύχην, ὡς σὺ λέγεις, προσποιεῖ³⁸ δὲ ἀγνοεῖν³⁹ με, τίς εἰμι, μετὰ παρρησίας⁴⁰ ἄκουε· Χριστιανός εἰμι. εἰ δὲ θέλεις τὸν τοῦ Χριστιανισμοῦ μαθεῖν⁴¹ λόγον, δὸς ἡμέραν καὶ ἄκουσον. **²** ἔφη ὁ ἀνθύπατος· πεῖσον τὸν δῆμον.⁴² ὁ δὲ Πολύκαρπος εἶπεν· σὲ μὲν⁴³ καὶ λόγου ἠξίωκα, δεδιδάγμεθα⁴⁴ γὰρ ἀρχαῖς καὶ ἐξουσίαις ὑπὸ τοῦ θεοῦ τεταγμέναις⁴⁵ τιμὴν κατὰ τὸ προσῆκον⁴⁶ τὴν μὴ βλάπτουσαν⁴⁷ ἡμᾶς ἀπονέμειν·⁴⁸ ἐκείνους δὲ οὐκ ἡγοῦμαι⁴⁹ ἀξίους τοῦ ἀπολογεῖσθαι⁵⁰ αὐτοῖς.

11.1 Ὁ δὲ ἀνθύπατος εἶπεν· θηρία⁵¹ ἔχω, τούτοις σε παραβαλῶ, ἐὰν μὴ μετανοήσῃς.⁵² ὁ δὲ εἶπεν· κάλει, ἀμετάθετος⁵³ γὰρ ἡμῖν ἡ ἀπὸ τῶν κρειττόνων ἐπὶ τὰ χείρω μετάνοια·⁵⁴ καλὸν⁵⁵ δὲ μετατίθεσθαι⁵⁶ ἀπὸ τῶν χαλεπῶν ἐπὶ τὰ δίκαια. **²** ὁ δὲ πάλιν πρὸς αὐτόν· πυρί σε ποιῶ δαπανηθῆναι,⁵⁷ εἰ τῶν θηρίων καταφρονεῖς,⁵⁸ ἐὰν μὴ μετανοήσῃς. ὁ δὲ Πολύκαρπος· πῦρ ἀπειλεῖς⁵⁹ τὸ πρὸς ὥραν καιόμενον⁶⁰ καὶ μετ' ὀλίγον⁶¹ σβεννύμενον·⁶² ἀγνοεῖς γὰρ τὸ τῆς μελλούσης κρίσεως⁶³ καὶ αἰωνίου κολάσεως⁶⁴ τοῖς ἀσεβέσι τηρούμενον⁶⁵ πῦρ. ἀλλὰ τί βραδύνεις;⁶⁶ φέρε, ὃ βούλει.

NOTES

9.1. φωνὴ ἐξ οὐρανοῦ ἐγένετο. Cf. Mark 1:11 parr. "The passage parallels literary traditions of a *bath qol* or *vox de caelis* [i.e., the divine voice that descends from heaven]" (Hartog 2013, 296).

ἀνδρίζου. Early Christian martyrs are often depicted as performing "masculinity" (Cobb 2008; Moss 2012; cf. notes on 2 Macc. 7:21; 4 Macc. 6:21).

31. Aor. act. impv. 2 sg., λοιδορέω, *revile*.
32. Acc. of extent (time), *for eighty-six years*.
33. Pres. act. indic. 1 sg., δουλεύω, *serve*; with dat.
34. Aor. act. indic. 3 sg., ἀδικέω, *do injustice, wrong*; with internal (οὐδέν) and external (με) acc. (cf. BDF §156; S §1619).
35. Aor. act. inf., βλασφημέω, *blaspheme*.
36. Pres. act. ptc. gen. masc. sg., ἐπιμένω, *remain/continue in*; gen. absol.
37. Fut. act. indic. 2 sg., κενοδοκέω, *think vainly*.
38. Pres. mid. indic. 3 sg., προσποιέω, (mid.) *pretend*.
39. Pres. act. inf., ἀγνοέω, *not know, be ignorant of*.
40. παρρησία, -ας, ἡ, *boldness, openness, frankness of speech*.
41. Aor. act. inf., μανθάνω, *learn*.
42. δῆμος, -ου, ὁ, *people*.
43. μέν . . . δέ; point/counterpoint: "You [σέ] I deem worthy, . . . but as for these people [ἐκείνους] . . ." See n. 5.
44. Pf. pass. indic. 1 pl., διδάσκω, (pass.) *be taught*.
45. Pf. pass. ptc. dat. fem. pl., τάσσω, (pass.) *be appointed*; attrib.
46. Pres. act. ptc. acc. neut. sg., προσήκω, *befitting*; κατὰ τὸ προσῆκον, "as is proper."
47. Aor. act. ptc. acc. fem. sg., βλάπτω, *harm*; attrib.
48. Pres. act. inf., ἀπονέμω, *show*; indir. disc. (cf. BDF §397; S §2016; CGCG §51.19).
49. Pres. mid. indic. 1 sg., ἡγέομαι, *think, consider*.
50. Pres. mid. inf., ἀπολογέομαι, *defend oneself*; comp. of ἄξιος (cf. BDF §400; S §2032).

51. θηρίον, -ου, τό, *wild animal, beast*.
52. Aor. act. subj. 2 sg., μετανοέω, *repent*; third-class condition (BDF §373; S §2565; CGCG §49.6).
53. ἀμετάθετος, -ον, *unalterable, unchangeable*.
54. μετάνοια, -ας, ἡ, *repentance*.
55. καλός, -ή, -όν, (quasi-impers.) *it is good*; with acc. and inf. (cf. BDF §393; S §1985; CGCG §36.8).
56. Pres. mid. inf., μετατίθημι, *change*.
57. Aor. pass. inf., δαπανάω, (pass.) *be destroyed*; epex. (cf. S §2004; CGCG §51.18): "I make you *to be destroyed* by fire."
58. Pres. act. indic. 2 sg., καταφρονέω, *despise*; with gen.
59. Pres. act. indic. 2 sg., ἀπειλέω, *threaten*.
60. Pres. pass. ptc. acc. neut. sg., καίω, (pass.) *burn*; attrib.
61. μετ' ὀλίγον, (temp.) *after a little while*.
62. Pres. pass. ptc. acc. neut. sg., σβέννυμι, *be quenched, go out*; attrib.
63. κρίσις, -εως, ἡ, *judgment*.
64. κόλασις, -εως, ἡ, *punishment*.
65. Pres. pass. ptc. acc. neut. sg., τηρέω, (pass.) *be kept*; attrib.
66. Pres. act. indic. 2 sg., βραδύνω, *delay*; ἀλλὰ τί βραδύνεις, "Well then, why do you delay?" (cf. Denniston 1966, 9).

9.2. ὄμοσον τὴν καίσαρος τύχην, μετανόησον, εἶπον, αἶρε τοὺς ἀθέους. Christians refused to swear by the numen or genius of Caesar (cf. *Mart. Apoll.* 3; Tertullian, *Apol.* 32.2; Origen, *Mart.* 7; Origen, *Cels.* 8.65). As a result, "the charge of 'atheism' was frequently levelled against the early Christians, who were often viewed as eccentric, subversive, and even treasonous" (Hartog 2013, 297).

ἐμβλέψας καὶ ἐπισείσας αὐτοῖς τὴν χεῖρα, στενάξας τε καὶ ἀναβλέψας εἰς τὸν οὐρανὸν εἶπεν· αἶρε τοὺς ἀθέους. Note the number of circumstantial participles used to frame the main verb. The intentionality with which Polycarp looks and gestures at the crowd, combined with his groan and gaze to heaven, disambiguates the meaning of his cry, "Away with the atheists!" On the use of double meaning in martyrdom traditions, see Boyarin (1999, 50–51).

10.1. Χριστιανός εἰμι. The designation may have developed as a stigmatizing label (cf. 1 Pet. 4:14; Pliny the Younger, *Ep.* 10.96–7; Horrell 2013, 164–210). The declaration "Χριστιανός εἰμι" features in numerous martyrdom traditions (cf. *Mart. Carp.* A.5; *Mart. Justin* 3–4; *Lyons* 1.10, 19–20; *Acts Scill.* 9–10, 13; *Mart. Apoll.* 2; *Passio* 6.3–4). Boyarin (1999, 95) describes such language as "a ritualized and performative speech act," which "becomes the central action of the martyrology. In rabbinic texts, this is the declaration of the oneness of God via the recitation of the 'Hear O Israel.' For Christians, it is the declaration of the essence of self: 'I am a Christian.' In both, this is the final act of the martyr's life. For Christian texts, this is new with *Martyrium Polycarpi*. For rabbinic Jews, it begins with the stories about Polycarp's contemporary, Rabbi Akiva."

τὸν τοῦ Χριστιανισμοῦ . . . λόγον. The term Χριστιανισμός first appears in the letters of Ignatius (*Magn.* 8.1; 10.1, 3; *Phld.* 6.1), where it is set in opposition to Ἰουδαϊσμός (Lieu 1996, 23–56). Here the concern is different. The "doctrine of Christianity" constitutes the scaffolding and plausibility structure that establishes the bond between martyr and audience; that is to say, the martyr dies for the ideology by which the audience must live.

δὸς ἡμέραν. Cf. 1 Cor. 4:3: "But with me it is a very small thing that I should be judged by you or *by any human court* [ὑπὸ ἀνθρωπίνης ἡμέρας]." The Latin phrase *diem dicere* means "to grant a trial" (Hartog 2013, 300).

2.4

The Epistle of Barnabas

The Epistle of Barnabas is an anonymous second-century text attributed to Paul's travel companion (cf. Acts 13:2; Gal. 2:13). While the date and provenance of the epistle are unknown, most scholars agree on two points. First, "the broad parameters for the date of the book are clear: it mentions the destruction of the Jerusalem (Herodian) Temple (16.3–4), and so must have been written after 70 CE; and it assumes that the Temple was still in ruins, so that it must have been written before Hadrian constructed a new, Roman temple on the site, around 135" (Ehrman 2003, 2:6–7).[1] Second, most think it has an Egyptian provenance, "in view of its numerous affinities in hermeneutical approach and style with Alexandrian Judaism and Christianity and because its earliest witness is Clement of Alexandria (who accorded it the same authority as the Catholic Epistles)" (Holmes 2007, 373; see also Paget 1994, 36–42).

The reading passage is an allegorical interpretation of the Yom Kippur ritual (cf. Lev. 16). The writer likens Jesus to *both* goats of the ritual, the goat for the Lord and the goat for Azazel (i.e., the scapegoat). As the scapegoat, he is crucified—that is, "cursed." As the goat for the Lord, he fulfills "the type that was set forth in Isaac, when he was offered upon the altar" (Barn. 7.3).

Text and Translation: Ehrman 2003
Supplemental Scripture: Lev. 16; Mark 14:53–65 parr.; Heb. 9

---

1. On the dating of Barnabas, see Paget (1994, 9–30), who finds it plausible that the letter was written during the reign of Nerva (96–98 CE).

2.4.1

Lessons from the Day of Atonement
Epistle of Barnabas 7

7.1Οὐκοῦν[1] νοεῖτε,[2] τέκνα εὐφροσύνης,[3] ὅτι πάντα ὁ καλὸς κύριος προεφανέρωσεν[4] ἡμῖν, ἵνα γνῶμεν, ᾧ κατὰ πάντα εὐχαριστοῦντες[5] ὀφείλομεν[6] αἰνεῖν.[7] **2**εἰ οὖν ὁ υἱὸς τοῦ θεοῦ, ὢν κύριος καὶ μέλλων κρίνειν ζῶντας καὶ νεκρούς, ἔπαθεν,[8] ἵνα ἡ πληγὴ[9] αὐτοῦ ζωοποιήσῃ[10] ἡμᾶς, πιστεύσωμεν ὅτι ὁ υἱὸς τοῦ θεοῦ οὐκ ἠδύνατο παθεῖν εἰ μὴ δι' ἡμᾶς. **3**ἀλλὰ καὶ[11] σταυρωθεὶς[12] ἐποτίζετο[13] ὄξει[14] καὶ χολῇ.[15] ἀκούσατε, πῶς περὶ τούτου πεφανέρωκαν[16] οἱ ἱερεῖς[17] τοῦ ναοῦ.[18] γεγραμμένης ἐντολῆς,[19] ὅς ἂν μὴ νηστεύσῃ[20] τὴν νηστείαν,[21] θανάτῳ ἐξολεθρευθήσεται,[22] ἐνετείλατο[23] κύριος ἐπεὶ καὶ αὐτὸς ὑπὲρ τῶν ἡμετέρων ἁμαρτιῶν ἔμελλεν τὸ σκεῦος[24] τοῦ πνεύματος προσφέρειν[25] θυσίαν,[26] ἵνα καὶ ὁ τύπος[27] ὁ γενόμενος ἐπὶ Ἰσαὰκ τοῦ προσενεχθέντος ἐπὶ τὸ θυσιαστήριον[28] τελεσθῇ.[29] **4**τί οὖν λέγει

1. Partic. (οὐκ, οὖν), (inferential) *therefore, then* (cf. *CGCG* §59.33).
2. Pres. act. impv. 2 pl., νοέω, *understand*.
3. εὐφροσύνη, -ης, ἡ, *joy*.
4. Aor. act. indic. 3 sg., προφανερόω, *reveal in advance*.
5. Pres. act. ptc. nom. masc. pl., εὐχαριστέω, *give thanks*; circ.
6. Pres. act. indic. 1 pl., ὀφείλω, *ought to*; with inf.
7. Pres. act. inf., αἰνέω, *praise*; with dat.
8. Aor. act. indic. 3 sg., πάσχω, *suffer*.
9. πληγή, -ῆς, ἡ, *blow, wound*.
10. Aor. act. subj. 3 sg., ζωοποιέω, *make alive*; purpose clause (cf. BDF §369; S §2193; *CGCG* §45.3).
11. As in 9:4 and 10:6, the writer uses ἀλλὰ καί to shift to a new topic that still remains in continuity with the main theme of the section.
12. Aor. pass. ptc. nom. masc. sg., σταυρόω, (pass.) *be crucified*; circ.
13. Impf. pass. indic. 3 sg., ποτίζω, (pass.) *be given to drink*; with dat.
14. ὄξος, -ους, τό, *vinegar, sour wine*.
15. χολή, -ῆς, ἡ, *gall*.
16. Pf. act. indic. 3 pl., φανερόω, *reveal*.
17. ἱερεύς, -έως, ὁ, *priest*.
18. ναός, -οῦ, ὁ, *sanctuary* (of the temple).
19. Gen. absol.; explicates the content περὶ τούτου by introducing the citation of Lev. 23:29.
20. Aor. act. subj. 3 sg., νηστεύω, *fast*; conditional rel. clause (cf. BDF §380; S §2560; *CGCG* §50.20).
21. νηστεία, -ας, ἡ, *fast*; cognate acc. (cf. BDF §153; S §1564; *CGCG* §30.12).
22. Fut. pass. indic. 3 sg., ἐξολεθρεύω, (pass.) *be completely destroyed*.
23. Aor. mid. indic. 3 sg., ἐντέλλω, *command*; anacoluthon (cf. BDF §466; S §3004). Supply the object based on context; i.e., "The Lord commanded *this* [i.e., Lev. 23:29] since he was about to . . ."
24. σκεῦος, -ους, τό, *vessel*.
25. Pres. act. inf., προσφέρω, *offer*; comp. of ἔμελλεν.
26. θυσία, -ας, ἡ, *sacrifice*; pred. comp.
27. τύπος, -ου, ὁ, *type*.
28. θυσιαστήριον, -ου, τό, *altar*.
29. Aor. pass. subj. 3 sg., τελέω, (pass.) *be made complete*; purpose clause. See n. 10.

ἐν τῷ προφήτῃ; καὶ φαγέτωσαν³⁰ ἐκ τοῦ τράγου³¹ τοῦ προσφερομένου τῇ νηστείᾳ ὑπὲρ πασῶν τῶν ἁμαρτιῶν. προσέχετε³² ἀκριβῶς·³³ καὶ φαγέτωσαν οἱ ἱερεῖς μόνοι πάντες τὸ ἔντερον³⁴ ἄπλυτον³⁵ μετὰ ὄξους. ⁵πρὸς τί;³⁶ ἐπειδὴ ἐμὲ ὑπὲρ ἁμαρτιῶν μέλλοντα τοῦ λαοῦ μου τοῦ καινοῦ προσφέρειν τὴν σάρκα μου μέλλετε ποτίζειν³⁷ χολὴν μετὰ ὄξους, φάγετε ὑμεῖς μόνοι, τοῦ λαοῦ νηστεύοντος καὶ κοπτομένου³⁸ ἐπὶ σάκκου³⁹ καὶ σποδοῦ,⁴⁰ ἵνα δείξῃ⁴¹ ὅτι δεῖ αὐτὸν παθεῖν ὑπ' αὐτῶν. ⁶ἃ ἐνετείλατο, προσέχετε· λάβετε δύο τράγους καλοὺς καὶ ὁμοίους⁴² καὶ προσενέγκατε, καὶ λαβέτω ὁ ἱερεὺς τὸν ἕνα εἰς ὁλοκαύτωμα⁴³ ὑπὲρ ἁμαρτιῶν. ⁷τὸν δὲ ἕνα⁴⁴ τί ποιήσουσιν; ἐπικατάρατος,⁴⁵ φησίν, ὁ εἷς. προσέχετε, πῶς ὁ τύπος τοῦ Ἰησοῦ φανεροῦται. ⁸καὶ ἐμπτύσατε⁴⁶ πάντες καὶ κατακεντήσατε⁴⁷ καὶ περίθετε⁴⁸ τὸ ἔριον⁴⁹ τὸ κόκκινον⁵⁰ περὶ τὴν κεφαλὴν αὐτοῦ, καὶ οὕτως εἰς ἔρημον βληθήτω.⁵¹ καὶ ὅταν γένηται οὕτως, ἄγει ὁ βαστάζων⁵² τὸν τράγον εἰς τὴν ἔρημον καὶ ἀφαιρεῖ τὸ ἔριον καὶ ἐπιτίθησιν αὐτὸ ἐπὶ φρύγανον⁵³ τὸ λεγόμενον ῥαχή,⁵⁴ οὗ καὶ τοὺς βλαστοὺς⁵⁵ εἰώθαμεν⁵⁶ τρώγειν⁵⁷ ἐν τῇ χώρᾳ εὑρίσκοντες. οὕτω μόνης τῆς ῥαχῆς οἱ καρποὶ⁵⁸ γλυκεῖς⁵⁹ εἰσίν. ⁹τί οὖν τοῦτό ἐστιν; προσέχετε· τὸν μὲν⁶⁰ ἕνα ἐπὶ τὸ θυσιαστήριον, τὸν δὲ ἕνα ἐπικατάρατον, καὶ ὅτι τὸν ἐπικατάρατον ἐστεφανωμένον.⁶¹ ἐπειδὴ ὄψονται αὐτὸν τότε τῇ ἡμέρᾳ τὸν ποδήρη⁶² ἔχοντα τὸν κόκκινον περὶ τὴν σάρκα καὶ ἐροῦσιν· οὐχ οὗτός ἐστιν, ὅν ποτε ἡμεῖς ἐσταυρώσαμεν καὶ ἐξουθενήσαντες⁶³ καὶ κατακεντήσαντες καὶ ἐμπτύσαντες; ἀληθῶς οὗτος ἦν, ὁ τότε λέγων ἑαυτὸν υἱὸν τοῦ θεοῦ εἶναι. ¹⁰πῶς γὰρ ὅμοιος ἐκείνῳ; εἰς τοῦτο⁶⁴ ὁμοίους τοὺς τράγους, καλούς, ἴσους,⁶⁵ ἵνα ὅταν ἴδωσιν αὐτὸν τότε ἐρχόμενον, ἐκπλαγῶσιν⁶⁶ ἐπὶ τῇ ὁμοιότητι⁶⁷ τοῦ τράγου. οὐκοῦν ἴδε τὸν τύπον τοῦ μέλλοντος πάσχειν Ἰησοῦ. ¹¹τί δέ,⁶⁸ ὅτι τὸ ἔριον εἰς μέσον τῶν ἀκανθῶν⁶⁹ τιθέασιν; τύπος ἐστὶν τοῦ Ἰησοῦ τῇ ἐκκλησίᾳ κείμενος,⁷⁰ ὅτι ὃς ἐὰν θέλῃ τὸ ἔριον ἆραι τὸ κόκκινον, δεῖ αὐτὸν πολλὰ παθεῖν διὰ τὸ εἶναι⁷¹

30. Aor. act. impv. 3 pl., ἐσθίω, *eat*.
31. τράγος, -ου, ὁ, *male goat*.
32. Pres. act. impv. 2 pl., προσέχω, *give heed, pay attention*.
33. Adv., *in a careful/precise manner*.
34. ἔντερον, -ου, τό, *intestine*.
35. ἄπλυτος, -ον, *unwashed*.
36. πρὸς τί, *For what reason? Why?*
37. The verb takes a double accusative: person (ἐμέ) and object (χολήν).
38. Pres. mid. ptc. gen. masc. sg., κόπτω, *mourn*; gen. absol.
39. σάκκος, -ου, ὁ, *sackcloth*.
40. σποδός, -οῦ, ἡ, *ashes*.
41. Aor. act. subj. 3 sg., δείκνυμι, *show*; purpose clause. See n. 10.
42. ὅμοιος, -α, -ον, *like, similar*.
43. ὁλοκαύτωμα, -ατος, τό, *whole burnt offering*. εἰς marks the predicate complement (cf. BDF §145).
44. τὸν ἕνα in the sense of τὸν ἕτερον (cf. BDF §247).
45. ἐπικατάρατος, -ον, *cursed*.
46. Aor. act. impv. 2 pl., ἐμπτύω, *spit*.
47. Aor. act. impv. 2 pl., κατακεντάω, *pierce, stab*.
48. Aor. act. impv. 2 pl., περιτίθημι, *put around*.
49. ἔριον, -ου, τό, *wool*.
50. κόκκινος, -η, -ον, *scarlet*.
51. Aor. pass. impv. 3 sg., βάλλω, (pass.) *be thrown*.
52. Pres. act. ptc. nom. masc. sg., βαστάζω, *bear*; attrib. (subst.).
53. φρύγανον, -ου, τό, *bush, shrub*.
54. ῥαχή (ῥαχία), -ῆς, ἡ, (name of a berry bush) *blackberry* (BDAG, 904).
55. βλαστός, -οῦ, ὁ, *sprout, bud*.
56. Pf. act. indic. 1 pl., ἔθω, *be accustomed*; with inf.
57. Pres. act. inf., τρώγω, *eat*.
58. καρπός, -οῦ, ὁ, *fruit*.
59. γλυκύς, -εῖα, -ύ, *sweet*.
60. τὸν μὲν ἕνα . . . τὸν δὲ ἕνα, *the one . . . the other*.
61. Pf. pass. ptc. acc. masc. sg., στεφανόω, (pass.) *be crowned*.
62. ποδήρης, -ες, (subst.) *robe* (long, reaching to the feet).
63. Aor. act. ptc. nom. masc. pl., ἐξουθενέω, *despise, insult*; circ.
64. εἰς τοῦτο, *for this reason*; cataphoric (points to the ἵνα-clause).
65. ἴσος, -η, -ον, *equal*.
66. Aor. pass. subj. 3 pl., ἐκπλήσσω, *be amazed*; purpose clause. See n. 10.
67. ὁμοιότης, -ητος, ἡ, *similarity*.
68. Marks development to a new question.
69. ἄκανθα, -ας, ἡ, *thorny plant*.
70. Pres. pass. ptc. nom. masc. sg., κεῖμαι, *set forth*.
71. διὰ τό with an infinitive expresses cause (cf. BDF §402; CGCG §51.40).

φοβερὰν τὴν ἄκανθαν, καὶ θλιβέντα⁷² κυριεῦσαι⁷³ αὐτοῦ. οὕτω, φησίν, οἱ θέλοντές με ἰδεῖν καὶ ἅψασθαί⁷⁴ μου τῆς βασιλείας ὀφείλουσιν θλιβέντες καὶ παθόντες λαβεῖν με.

NOTES

7.3. ἀλλὰ καὶ σταυρωθεὶς ἐποτίζετο ὄξει καὶ χολῇ. The parallel of "sour wine" (ὄξος) and "gall" (χολή) is found in Ps. 68:22 LXX, a passage that is applied to Jesus's crucifixion (cf. Matt. 27:34, 48 parr.; Gos. Pet. 16; Melito, *Pascha* 79, 80, 93; Irenaeus, *Epid.* 82).

ὅς ἂν μὴ νηστεύσῃ τὴν νηστείαν, θανάτῳ ἐξολεθρευθήσεται. Cf. Lev. 23:29 LXX. "In the late Second Temple period, νηστεία had become the most common Greek name for Yom Kippur" (Stökl Ben Ezra 2003, 15–16; cf. Acts 27:9; Josephus, *A.J.* 17.165–166; 18.94; Philo, *Spec.* 1.168, 186; 2.41, 193, 194, 197, 200; Philo, *Leg.* 306; Philo, *Mos.* 2.23; Philo, *Decal.* 159).

ἵνα καὶ ὁ τύπος ὁ γενόμενος ἐπὶ Ἰσαὰκ τοῦ προσενεχθέντος ἐπὶ τὸ θυσιαστήριον τελεσθῇ. Cf. Gen. 22:9. The purpose of Christ's sacrifice is to complete the "type" (τύπος) established in Isaac. The writer uses τύπος throughout to move from scriptural figures to their ultimate realities (cf. Barn. 6.11; 7.10, 11; 8.1; 12.5, 6, 10; 13.5; 19.7).

7.4. τί οὖν λέγει ἐν τῷ προφήτῃ. The source of the quotation is unknown. The Jewish scriptures never command the priests to eat of the goat for the Lord on Yom Kippur (Lev. 16:8–9). (For the connection between the priest's consumption of the prebend and the accomplishment of atonement, cf. Lev. 10 and discussion thereof in Gane 2005, 91–105.) Rather, the sacrificial remains are taken to the designated unclean place outside the camp (cf. Lev. 16:27–28). Numbers 29:11 mentions "one male goat for a sin offering, in addition to the sin offering of atonement," whose flesh, a reader might suppose, would be consumed by the priests (NRSV; cf. Philo, *Spec.* 1.190; m. Menah. 11.7; Tertullian, *Marc.* 3.7.8).

7.5. The rhetoric of this passage is highly polemical. "You" (priests) will give "me" (Jesus) "gall" and "sour wine" to drink "when I am about to offer my flesh for the sins of my *new* people." The effect of such language is to distinguish "the identity of *Barnabas*' priestly community, which eats the Eucharist, from that of the fasting people (Jews), which does not" (Stökl Ben Ezra 2003, 152; cf. Tertullian, *Marc.* 3.7.7).

7.6. Leviticus 16 says nothing about the goats being "fine and alike" (cf. Barn. 7.10, which adds ἴσος, "equal"), but see m. Yoma 6.1; Justin Martyr, *Dial.* 40.4; Tertullian, *Marc.* 3.7.7. Prior to the casting of lots, one for the Lord and one for Azazel, Leviticus describes both he-goats as being περὶ ἁμαρτίας (Lev. 16:5 LXX).

7.7. ἐπικατάρατος. The scapegoat is designated as "cursed" (cf. Philo, *Spec.* 1.188), which reflects Jesus's death by crucifixion (cf. Deut. 21:23; 27:26; Gal. 3:10, 13; Justin Martyr, *Dial.* 96.1; Tertullian, *Marc.* 3.7.7).

7.8. The Jewish scriptures say nothing about the mistreatment of the scapegoat, but the idea was well established by the time of Barnabas (cf. m. Yoma 6.4), in part due to the influence of other Mediterranean apotropaic rituals, such as the expulsion of the φαρμακός (see Bremmer 1983). The "prepared man" leads the scapegoat into the wilderness (cf. Lev. 16:21). (Origen would interpret this figure as a type of Christ's descent to hell; cf. *Hom. Lev.* 9.) The scarlet wool that the scapegoat carries into the

---

72. Aor. pass. ptc. acc. masc. sg., θλίβω, (pass.) *be afflicted*; circ. (manner).
73. Pres. act. inf., κυριεύω, *gain possession of*; with gen.; comp. of δεῖ.
74. Aor. mid. inf., ἅπτω, (mid.) *grasp*; with gen.

wilderness has a parallel in m. Yoma 4.2; 6.6 (cf. Tertullian, *Marc.* 3.7.7; Hippolytus, *Fr. Prov.* 75). Rabbi Ishmael is reported to have said, "Had they not another sign also?—a thread of crimson wool was tied to the door of the Sanctuary and when the he-goat reached the wilderness the thread turned white; for it is written, *Though your sins be as scarlet they shall be as white as snow* [Isa. 1:8]" (m. Yoma 6.8, trans. Danby 1933, 170).

7.9. τὸν μὲν ἕνα ἐπὶ τὸ θυσιαστήριον, τὸν δὲ ἕνα ἐπικατάρατον. Cf. Lev. 16:8–10. Christ is *both* the goat for the altar (i.e., for the Lord) and the "cursed" scapegoat (i.e., for Azazel).

καὶ ὅτι τὸν ἐπικατάρατον ἐστεφανωμένον. The writer wants the audience to observe a second and related point: the "cursed" goat is "crowned." Thus he connects the wool of the scapegoat to the "crown" and "scarlet robe" (τὸν ποδήρη τὸν κόκκινον) of Jesus (cf. Matt. 27:28). In the Greek scriptures ποδήρη is used to describe the high priest's robe (cf. Exod. 25:7; 28:4, 31; 29:5; 35:9); note especially Zech. 3:5, where the high priest Joshua (Ἰησοῦς) is crowned and dons the ποδήρη (Stökl Ben Ezra 2003, 194–97). The image, then, is of Jesus as the high priest who is vindicated in the presence of his enemies "on that day"—that is, at his parousia.

2.5

The Epistle to Diognetus

The Epistle to Diognetus is the only Christian apologia, or apologetic treatise, in the Apostolic Fathers (except for the fragment of Quadratus). It has been recognized as, "after Scripture, the finest monument we know of sound Christian feeling, noble courage, and manly eloquence" (Bunsen 1954, 170); "the noblest of early Christian writings" (Lightfoot 1875, 154–55); and "one of the true literary gems of early Christianity" (Ehrman 2003, 2:122). Yet for all its modern acclaim, the epistle is shrouded in mystery. "The author is anonymous, the identity of the recipient is uncertain, the date is unknown, the ending is missing, and, rather surprisingly, no ancient or medieval writer is known to have mentioned it" (Holmes 2007, 688).[1] The most one can say is that the Epistle to Diognetus fits broadly within a second-century milieu and "anticipates later Alexandrian writers" (Holmes 2007, 687).[2]

The name Diognetus means "born of Zeus," an apt designation for a pagan interlocutor (real or imagined). The writer instructs this "most excellent Diognetus" in the way of Christian piety. To distinguish Christian identity from Greek "paganism" and Jewish "superstition," the writer classifies Christians as "this new race" (καινὸν τοῦτο γένος), analogous to the claim that Christians are a *tertium genus*, "third race" (e.g., Tertullian, *Scorp.* 10; see esp. Buell 2005).

The reading passage outlines the writer's case for *Christian* distinctiveness, which despite his rhetorical barbs, is heavily indebted to philosophical discourse (Jewish and pagan) about what it means to be a "citizen of the world."

Text and Translation: Ehrman 2003
Supplemental Scripture: Phil. 4:20; 1 Pet. 1:1–9; 2:11–17

---

1. The Epistle to Diognetus was preserved and later connected with the writings of Justin Martyr, who was long assumed to be the author. "After the authorship of Justin was rejected," however, as Lona (2010, 211) notes, "the suggestions of names of the supposed author piled up. The time and place of origin could be determined to a great extent in connection with the suggested figure of the moment, assuming that the suggestion of the moment was able to persuade. That is sadly not the case." Among the proposed candidates for the unknown author are Aristides, Quadratus, Polycarp, Justin, Hippolytus, Pantaenus, Clement of Alexandria, and many more.

2. For a survey of scholarship, see Jefford (2013, 15–29). He agrees with Harnack (1878) and Marrou (1965) that "the final setting was likely Egyptian Alexandria and the dates for the last recension lay at the end of the 2nd or early in the 3rd century" (29). Yet he holds out the possibility that "the original form of the text whose roots lie behind chs. 1–10" (29) may have an earlier date and alternative provenance.

2.5.1

A Case for Christian Distinctiveness
Epistle to Diognetus 5

5:1Χριστιανοὶ γὰρ οὔτε γῇ οὔτε φωνῇ οὔτε ἔθεσι[1] διακεκριμένοι[2] τῶν λοιπῶν εἰσιν ἀνθρώπων. **2**οὔτε[3] γάρ που[4] πόλεις ἰδίας[5] κατοικοῦσιν[6] οὔτε διαλέκτῳ[7] τινὶ παρηλλαγμένῃ[8] χρῶνται[9] οὔτε βίον παράσημον[10] ἀσκοῦσιν.[11] **3**οὐ μὴν[12] ἐπινοίᾳ[13] τινὶ καὶ φροντίδι[14] πολυπραγμόνων[15] ἀνθρώπων μάθημα[16] τοῦτ' αὐτοῖς ἐστιν εὑρημένον, οὐδὲ δόγματος[17] ἀνθρωπίνου[18] προεστᾶσιν[19] ὥσπερ ἔνιοι.[20] **4**κατοικοῦντες δὲ πόλεις ἑλληνίδας τε καὶ βαρβάρους, ὡς ἕκαστος ἐκληρώθη,[21] καὶ τοῖς ἐγχωρίοις[22] ἔθεσιν ἀκολουθοῦντες[23] ἔν τε ἐσθῆτι[24] καὶ διαίτῃ[25] καὶ τῷ λοιπῷ βίῳ[26] θαυμαστὴν[27] καὶ ὁμολογουμένως[28] παράδοξον[29] ἐνδείκνυν-

1. ἔθος, -ους, τό, *custom* (following Stephanus); dat. of respect.
2. Pf. pass. ptc. nom. masc. pl., διακρίνω, (pass.) *be differentiated from* (gen.); periphrastic (equivalent of pf. pass.).
3. οὔτε . . . οὔτε . . . οὔτε, *neither . . . nor . . . nor*.
4. Adv., *anywhere*; with neg., *nowhere*.
5. ἴδιος, -ία, -ον, *one's own*.
6. Pres. act. indic. 3 pl., κατοικέω, *dwell in, inhabit*.
7. διάλεκτος, -ου, ἡ, *language*.
8. Pf. mid. ptc. dat. fem. sg., παραλλάσσω, *change*; attrib.: in the sense of *strange* or *peculiar* (BDAG, 768).
9. Pres. mid. indic. 3 pl., χράομαι, *use*; with dat.
10. παράσημον, -ον, *peculiar, odd*.
11. Pres. act. indic. 3 pl., ἀσκέω, *practice*.
12. Postpositive partic., *I assure you, really, in fact*: "indicates that the speaker is committed to the truth or relevance of his/her utterance, and anticipates or assumes a possible lack of commitment on the part of the addressee" (*CGCG* §59.49).
13. ἐπινοία, -ας, ἡ, *thought*.
14. φροντίς, -ίδος, ἡ, *reflection, reasoning*.

15. πολυπράγμων, -ον, *inquisitive*, though probably in a pejorative sense, "meddlesome" (Ehrman 2003); pertaining to an "agitated mind" (Marrou 1965, 63).
16. μάθημα, -ατος, τό, *knowledge, teaching*.
17. δόγμα, -ατος, τό, *doctrine, dogma*.
18. ἀνθρώπινος, -η, -ον, *human*.
19. Pf. act. indic. 3 pl., προΐστημι, *show concern for*; with gen.
20. ἔνιοι, -αι, -α, *some*.
21. Aor. pass. indic. 3 pl., κληρόω, (pass.) *be allotted/assigned*.
22. ἐγχώριος, -ον, *local*.
23. Pres. act. ptc. nom. masc. pl., ἀκολουθέω, *follow*; with dat.; circ.
24. ἐσθής, -ῆτος, ἡ, *clothing, attire*.
25. δίαιτη, -ης, ἡ, *food, diet*.
26. βίος, -ου, ὁ, *life*.
27. θαυμαστός, -ή, -όν, *marvelous, wonderful*; pred. adj.
28. Adv., *admittedly, undeniably*; modifies παράδοξον.
29. παράδοξος, -ον, *strange*; pred. adj.

A marginal note reads, ἔνθεν περὶ Χριστιανῶν ἄρχεται, "here begins (the section) *On Christians*" (Marrou 1965, 62).

ται³⁰ τὴν κατάστασιν³¹ τῆς ἑαυτῶν πολιτείας.³² ⁵πατρίδας³³ οἰκοῦσιν ἰδίας, ἀλλ' ὡς πάροικοι·³⁴ μετέχουσι³⁵ πάντων ὡς πολῖται,³⁶ καὶ πάνθ' ὑπομένουσιν³⁷ ὡς ξένοι·³⁸ πᾶσα ξένη πατρίς ἐστιν αὐτῶν, καὶ πᾶσα πατρὶς ξένη. ⁶γαμοῦσιν³⁹ ὡς πάντες, τεκνογονοῦσιν·⁴⁰ ἀλλ' οὐ ῥίπτουσι⁴¹ τὰ γεννώμενα. ⁷τράπεζαν κοινὴν παρατίθενται,⁴² ἀλλ' οὐ κοίτην.⁴³ ⁸ἐν σαρκὶ τυγχάνουσιν,⁴⁴ ἀλλ' οὐ κατὰ σάρκα ζῶσιν. ⁹ἐπὶ γῆς διατρίβουσιν,⁴⁵ ἀλλ' ἐν οὐρανῷ πολιτεύονται.⁴⁶ ¹⁰πείθονται⁴⁷ τοῖς ὡρισμένοις⁴⁸ νόμοις, καὶ τοῖς ἰδίοις βίοις νικῶσι⁴⁹ τοὺς νόμους. ¹¹ἀγαπῶσι πάντας, καὶ ὑπὸ πάντων διώκονται.⁵⁰ ¹²ἀγνοοῦνται,⁵¹ καὶ κατακρίνονται·⁵² θανατοῦνται,⁵³ καὶ ζωοποιοῦνται.⁵⁴ ¹³πτωχεύουσι,⁵⁵ καὶ πλουτίζουσι⁵⁶ πολλούς· πάντων ὑστεροῦνται,⁵⁷ καὶ ἐν πᾶσι περισσεύουσιν.⁵⁸ ¹⁴ἀτιμοῦνται,⁵⁹ καὶ ἐν ταῖς ἀτιμίαις δοξάζονται· βλασφημοῦνται,⁶⁰ καὶ δικαιοῦνται. ¹⁵λοιδοροῦνται,⁶¹ καὶ εὐλογοῦσιν·⁶² ὑβρίζονται,⁶³ καὶ τιμῶσιν.⁶⁴ ¹⁶ἀγαθοποιοῦντες⁶⁵ ὡς κακοὶ κολάζονται·⁶⁶ κολαζόμενοι χαίρουσιν ὡς ζωοποιούμενοι.⁶⁷ ¹⁷ὑπὸ Ἰουδαίων ὡς ἀλλόφυλοι⁶⁸ πολεμοῦνται,⁶⁹ καὶ ὑπὸ Ἑλλήνων διώκονται· καὶ τὴν αἰτίαν⁷⁰ τῆς ἔχθρας εἰπεῖν οἱ μισοῦντες⁷¹ οὐκ ἔχουσιν.

30. Pres. mid. indic. 3 pl., ἐνδείκνυμι, *show forth, exhibit*.
31. κατάστασις, -εως, ἡ, *state of being, character*.
32. πολιτεία, -ας, ἡ, *citizenship*.
33. πατρίς, -ίδος, ἡ, *homeland*.
34. πάροικος, -ον, (subst.) *alien*.
35. Pres. act. indic. 3 pl., μετέχω, *participate in*; with gen.
36. πολίτης, -ου, ὁ, *citizen*.
37. Pres. act. indic. 3 pl., ὑπομένω, *endure*.
38. ξένος, -η, -ον, (subst.) *foreigner*.
39. Pres. act. indic. 3 pl., γαμέω, *marry*.
40. Pres. act. indic. 3 pl., τεκνογονέω, *have children*.
41. Pres. act. indic. 3 pl., ῥίπτω, *expose* (newborns).
42. Pres mid. indic. 3 pl., παρατίθημι, *set, spread*; with τράπεζαν (BDAG, 772.1).
43. κοίτη, -ης, ἡ, *marriage bed*. Emendation: all the witnesses read κοινήν, "common."
44. Pres. act. indic. 3 pl., τυγχάνω, *happen to be*.
45. Pres. act. indic. 3 pl., διατρίβω, *spend time*.
46. Pres. mid. indic. 3 pl., πολιτεύομαι, *live as a citizen*.
47. Pres. mid. indic. 3 pl., πείθω, (mid.) *obey*; with dat.
48. Pf. mid. ptc. dat. masc. pl., ὁρίζω, (pass.) *be ordained, determined*; attrib.
49. Pres. act. indic. 3 pl., νικάω, *outstrip, transcend* (BDAG, 673.3).
50. Pres. pass. indic. 3 pl., διώκω, (pass.) *be persecuted*.
51. Pres. pass. indic. 3 pl., ἀγνοέω, (pass.) *be unknown/unrecognized*.
52. Pres. pass. indic. 3 pl., κατακρίνω, (pass.) *be condemned*.
53. Pres. pass. indic. 3 pl., θανατόω, (pass.) *be killed*.
54. Pres. pass. indic. 3 pl., ζωοποιέω, (pass.) *be made alive*.
55. Pres. act. indic. 3 pl., πτωχεύω, *be poor*.
56. Pres. act. indic. 3 pl., πλουτίζω, *make rich*.
57. Pres. pass. indic. 3 pl., ὑστερέω, *lack*; with gen.

NOTES

5:1. The writer begins his exposition (γάρ) of the distinctly Christian way of life (5:1–6:10). For similar descriptions of the Christian life, cf. Aristides, *Apol.* 15; Justin Martyr, *1 Apol.* 14–17; and further discussion in Marrou (1965, 149–76).

5:3. The writer is keen to rule out certain human means by which Christian "learning" (μάθημα) or "dogma" (δόγμα) is discerned. The term πολυπράγμων probably has a pejorative connotation ("meddlesome") and evokes the insatiable human desire to discover any new idea (cf. Acts 17:21).

5:4. ἐνδείκνυνται τὴν κατάστασιν τῆς ἑαυτῶν πολιτείας. The term πολιτεία ("citizenship") is cen-

58. Pres. act. indic. 3 pl., περισσεύω, *abound*.
59. Pres. pass. indic. 3 pl., ἀτιμάω, (pass.) *be dishonored*.
60. Pres. pass. indic. 3 pl., βλασφημέω, (pass.) *be slandered*.
61. Pres. pass. indic. 3 pl., λοιδορέω, (pass.) *be reviled*.
62. Pres. act. indic. 3 pl., εὐλογέω, *bless*.
63. Pres. pass. indic. 3 pl., ὑβρίζω, (pass.) *be subject to insult*.
64. Pres. act. indic. 3 pl., τιμάω, *give honor*.
65. Pres. act. ptc. nom. masc. pl., ἀγαθοποιέω, *do good*.
66. Pres. pass. indic. 3 pl., κολάζω, (pass.) *be punished*.
67. ὡς with a circumstantial participle gives "the 'subjective' reason, for the responsibility lies with the subject of the matrix verb" (*CGCG* §52.39; cf. BDF §425.3; S §2086). Thus, "They rejoice when they are being punished *as though they are being made alive*."
68. ἀλλόφυλος, -ον, (subst.) *foreigner*.
69. Pres. pass. indic. 3 pl., πολεμέω, (pass.) *be attacked*; agent: ὑπὸ Ἰουδαίων.
70. αἰτία, -ας, ἡ, *reason*.
71. Pres. act. ptc. nom. masc. pl., μισέω, *hate*; attrib. (subst.).

tral to the question of a people's identity (e.g., Plato, *Leg.* 832D; Aristotle, *Pol.* 42.1; 2 Macc. 4:11; 8:17; 3 Macc. 3:21, 23; 4 Macc. 3:20; 8:7; 17:9; Eph. 2:12; Philo, *Spec.* 1.9; 2.25; Josephus, *A.J.* 4.8.2; 12.3.1–2). The writer's discourse about a distinctly *Christian* πολιτεία may have multiple aims. On the one hand, it seems clear enough that his primary objective is to form an identity that is "neither Jew nor Greek." On the other hand, he may also want to assert that a Christian πολιτεία is a legitimate (i.e., licit) way of being in the Roman Empire (cf. Acts 22:28).

5:5. Jefford (2013, 221–22) outlines the two-part A–B / B–C structure as follows: (1) a contrast between *expectations* ("traits expected of all citizens") and *tolerations* ("unfortunate necessities of life within an orderly community," 5:5–11) and (2) a contrast between *tolerations* and *exceptions* ("happily superseded typical expectations," 5:12–15). The general thrust is to lay claim to a "citizenship of the world" (e.g., Philo, *Opif.* 49–50; Epictetus, *Diatr.* 3.24.9–21). Thus, despite the writer's claims to the contrary, the values he espouses "are, ironically, the values already established by Jewish communities in the Diaspora and by Jewish apologetic writings" (Lieu 2016, 195).

5:6. ἀλλ' οὐ ῥίπτουσι τὰ γεννώμενα. The exposure of infants is a common topic among early Christian apologists (cf. Justin Martyr, *1 Apol.* 27; Tertullian, *Apol.* 9.6–8).

5:14–16. Note the lexical and conceptual similarities with 1 Peter: δοξάζω (1 Pet. 2:12; 4:11, 16), βλασφημέω (4:4), λοιδορέω (2:23; λοιδορία, 3:9), εὐλογέω (3:9), τιμάω (2:17), ἀγαθοποιέω (2:15, 20; 3:6, 17).

PART 3

Reading Old Testament Pseudepigrapha

The term "Old Testament Pseudepigrapha" describes a vast and diverse body of Jewish and Christian literature: rewritten scripture, apocalypses, testaments, psalms, poetry, and much more.[1] These works are so designated because many of their authors claim to be prominent figures of the Old Testament (e.g., Enoch, David, Solomon, Ezra, and Baruch). Yet the label is imprecise. For example, some of these works are falsely attributed to figures of the author's own time (e.g., the Letter of Aristeas), while others are attributed to their real authors (e.g., Aristobulus, Artapanus, Ezekiel the Tragedian, and Theodotus).

Old Testament pseudepigrapha are vital resources for the study of the Bible.[2] Yet these texts are not mere "background" literature but evidence of the rich and variegated histories of ancient Judaism and Christianity.[3] In fact, one of the reasons the pseudepigrapha are so fascinating is that they complicate the extent to which one can confidently label a text "Jewish" or "Christian." Moreover, the vast majority of these texts were preserved by Christians and are extant only in translation (or a translation of a translation). In many instances, the line between transmission and reception has been so thoroughly blurred that one cannot simply detect and remove "Christian interpolations."

In this chapter, we focus on Old Testament pseudepigrapha of the Jewish diaspora: the Letter of Aristeas, Joseph and Aseneth, Sibylline Oracles, Pseudo-Phocylides, and fragments of Hellenistic Jewish writers.

---

1. The "canon" of the Old Testament Pseudepigrapha continues to expand. See Bauckham, Davila, and Panayotov (2013), which builds on the legacy of Charles's *APOT* (1913) and Charlesworth's *OTP* (1983, 1985).

2. The best point of departure for your study is *OTP*. These volumes include introductions, translations, notes, and bibliographies produced by an international team of scholars. The critical editions of the Old Testament Pseudepigrapha are not always easily accessible, but many are now available online at https://pseudepigrapha.org/.

3. In his forward to *OTP*, Sandmel remarks, "I do not think it is wrong to say that much of the Christian interest in the Pseudepigrapha in the early nineteenth century was based on the light this literature was deemed to throw on early Christianity. Since the documents in the Pseudepigrapha were not being studied for their own sake, often that roundedness which one should expect from the best of scientific scholarship was absent" (xii).

3.1

The Letter of Aristeas

The Letter of Aristeas tells the story of how the Pentateuch was translated into Greek by a group of seventy-two Jewish scribes who made the trip from Jerusalem to Alexandria. The writer, almost certainly an Alexandrian Jew, identifies himself as Aristeas (cf. 19, 40, 43), a gentile courtier of the Egyptian king Ptolemy II Philadelphus (285–247 BCE) who wishes to pass on this most "remarkable narrative" to his brother, Philocrates (1–8, 322).[1] The work has "two broad and intersecting goals: (1) to construct/reinforce a Jewish identity that would provide a solid justification for elite, educated Jews to participate in the larger Hellenistic world of Alexandria *as Jews* and (2) to offer a myth of origins for the primary basis on which a *Jewish* identity should be built, the Greek version of the Pentateuch, the Septuagint" (Wright 2015, 66, emphasis original).

The reading passages illustrate these two major aims. In the first passage, Pseudo-Aristeas recounts the high priest Eleazar's apologia on the Jewish law—namely, that the central aim of the Torah is to orient all things toward δικαιοσύνη (131, 168–169). In the second passage, the writer narrates the translation of the Torah into Greek. The "agreement" (συμφωνία) among the translators, along with the universal acclaim of their work, solidifies the Greek Pentateuch as sacred scripture.

Text: Pelletier 1962
Recommended Translation: Shutt, *OTP*
Supplemental Scripture: Lev. 11; Barn. 10 (§3.1.1); Deut. 4:2; Prologue to Sir. (§3.1.2)

---

[1]. On the identity of the author and the provenance of the Letter of Aristeas, see Hadas 1951, 5–6; Shutt, *OTP* 2:9; Wright 2015, 16–20.

3.1.1

The Rationale of Jewish Law

Letter of Aristeas 128–143, 170–171

¹²⁸Ἄξιον¹ δὲ ἐπιμνησθῆναι² [διὰ] βραχέων³ τῶν ὑποδειχθέντων⁴ ὑπ' αὐτοῦ πρὸς τὰ δι' ἡμῶν ἐπιζητηθέντα.⁵ Νομίζω⁶ γὰρ τοὺς πολλοὺς περιεργίαν⁷ ἔχειν τινὰ τῶν ἐν τῇ νομοθεσίᾳ⁸ περί τε⁹ τῶν βρωτῶν¹⁰ καὶ ποτῶν¹¹ καὶ τῶν νομιζομένων ἀκαθάρτων¹² εἶναι κνωδάλων.¹³

¹²⁹Πυνθανομένων¹⁴ γὰρ ἡμῶν διὰ τί,¹⁵ μιᾶς καταβολῆς¹⁶ οὔσης, τὰ μὲν¹⁷ ἀκάθαρτα νομίζεται πρὸς βρῶσιν,¹⁸ τὰ δὲ καὶ πρὸς τὴν ἁφὴν¹⁹—δεισιδαιμόνως²⁰ γὰρ τὰ πλεῖστα²¹ τὴν νομοθεσίαν ἔχειν,²² ἐν δὲ τούτοις πάνυ²³ δεισιδαιμόνως—πρὸς ταῦτα²⁴ οὕτως ἐνήρξατο.²⁵ **¹³⁰**Θεωρεῖς, ἔφη, τὰς ἀναστροφὰς²⁶ καὶ

---

1. ἄξιος, -η, -ον, (quasi-impers.) *it is fitting*; with acc. inf. (cf. BDF §393; S §1985; CGCG §36.8).
2. Aor. pass. inf., ἐπιμιμνήσκομαι, *recall*; with gen.
3. διὰ βραχέων, *in a few words, briefly* (cf. LSJ, 389.A.III.c). All MSS and Eusebius read βραχέων. Pelletier (1962, 166) follows Wendland's emendation in reading the prepositional phrase.
4. Aor. pass. ptc. gen. neut. pl., ὑποδείκνυμι, (pass.) *be shown/indicated*; attrib. (subst.). The referent of the agent (ὑπ' αὐτοῦ) is Eleazar.
5. Aor. pass. ptc. acc. neut. pl., ἐπιζητέω, (pass.) *sought, inquired after*. The referent of the agent (δι' ἡμῶν) is Aristeas, who speaks on behalf of the king and his coterie.
6. Pres. act. indic. 1 sg., νομίζω, *consider*.
7. περιεργία, -ας, ἡ, *curiosity*.
8. νομοθεσία, -ας, ἡ, *legislation*.
9. τε . . . καί . . . καί, *X, Y, and Z*.
10. βρωτός, -ή, -όν, (subst.) *food*.
11. ποτός, -ή, -όν, (subst.) *drink*.
12. ἀκάθαρτος, -ον, *unclean*.
13. κνώδαλον, -ου, τό, *animal*. The term encompasses both "wild" (ἄγριος) and "tame" (ἥμερος) animals (cf. Let. Aris. 170).

14. Pres. mid. ptc. gen. masc. pl., πυνθάνομαι, *inquire*; gen. absol.
15. διὰ τί, *why?*
16. καταβολή, -ῆς, ἡ, *foundation, origin* (of the world).
17. τὰ μέν . . . τὰ δέ, *some things . . . other things* (cf. BDF §250; S §1107; CGCG §28.27).
18. βρῶσις, -εως, ἡ, *eating*.
19. ἁφή, -ῆς, ἡ, *touch*; with adv. καί: "others *even* to touch."
20. Adv., *piously, religiously*. The term can have either positive ("in a god-fearing manner") or negative ("in a superstitious manner") connotations (cf. LSJ, 375).
21. Superl., πολύς; τὰ πλεῖστα as adv. acc.: "to a large degree," "in most matters."
22. ἔχω with an adverb used as periphrasis for εἰμί with an adjective (cf. BDF §308; S §1438; CGCG §26.11).
23. Adv., *very, especially*.
24. Anacoluthon (cf. BDF §466; S §1793): πρὸς ταῦτα is anaphoric, οὕτως is cataphoric: "to these things [previous inquiry] he began thus."
25. Aor. mid. indic. 3 sg., ἐνάρχομαι, *begin*.
26. ἀναστροφή, -ῆς, ἡ, *conduct of life*.

τὰς ὁμιλίας,²⁷ οἷον ἐνεργάζονται²⁸ πρᾶγμα,²⁹ διότι³⁰ κακοῖς ὁμιλήσαντες³¹ διαστροφὰς³² ἐπιλαμβάνουσιν ἄνθρωποι, καὶ ταλαίπωροι³³ δι' ὅλου τοῦ ζῆν³⁴ εἰσιν· ἐὰν δὲ σοφοῖς³⁵ καὶ φρονίμοις³⁶ συζῶσιν,³⁷ ἐξ ἀγνοίας³⁸ ἐπανορθώσεως³⁹ εἰς τὸν βίον ἔτυχον.⁴⁰ ¹³¹Διαστειλάμενος⁴¹ οὖν τὰ τῆς εὐσεβείας⁴² καὶ δικαιοσύνης πρῶτον ὁ νομοθέτης⁴³ ἡμῶν, καὶ διδάξας ἕκαστα περὶ τούτων, οὐκ ἀπαγορευτικῶς⁴⁴ μόνον ἀλλ' ἐνδεικτικῶς,⁴⁵ καὶ τὰς βλάβας⁴⁶ προδηλώσας⁴⁷ καὶ τὰς ὑπὸ τοῦ θεοῦ γινομένας ἐπιπομπὰς⁴⁸ τοῖς αἰτίοις⁴⁹—¹³²προϋπέδειξε⁵⁰ γὰρ πάντων πρῶτον ὅτι μόνος ὁ θεός ἐστι, καὶ διὰ πάντων ἡ δύναμις αὐτοῦ φανερὰ⁵¹ γίνεται, πεπληρωμένου⁵² παντὸς τόπου τῆς δυναστείας,⁵³ καὶ οὐθὲν αὐτὸν λανθάνει⁵⁴ τῶν ἐπὶ γῆς γινομένων ὑπ' ἀνθρώπων κρυφίως,⁵⁵ ἀλλ' ὅσα ποιεῖ τις αὐτῷ φανερὰ καθέστηκε,⁵⁶ καὶ τὰ μέλλοντα γίνεσθαι—¹³³ταῦτ' οὖν⁵⁷ ἐξεργαζόμενος⁵⁸ ἀκριβῶς⁵⁹ καὶ πρόδηλα⁶⁰ θεὶς ἔδειξεν ὅτι, κἂν⁶¹ ἐννοηθῇ⁶² τις κακίαν ἐπιτελεῖν,⁶³ οὐκ ἂν λάθοι,⁶⁴ μὴ ὅτι καὶ πράξας,⁶⁵ διὰ πάσης τῆς νομοθεσίας τὸ τοῦ θεοῦ δυνατὸν ἐνδεικνύμενος.⁶⁶

¹³⁴Ποιησάμενος οὖν τὴν καταρχὴν⁶⁷ ταύτην, καὶ δείξας ὅτι πάντες οἱ λοιποὶ παρ'⁶⁸ ἡμᾶς ἄνθρωποι πολλοὺς θεοὺς εἶναι νομίζουσιν, αὐτοὶ δυναμικώτεροι⁶⁹

27. ὁμιλία, -ας, ἡ, *relationship*. The fronting of τὰς ἀναστροφὰς καὶ τὰς ὁμιλίας is an instance of prolepsis, whereby the subject of the subordinate clause is made the object of the main clause (cf. BDF §476; S §2182; *CGCG* §60.37).
28. Pres. mid. indic. 3 pl., ἐνεργάζομαι, *produce*.
29. πρᾶγμα, -ατος, τό, *thing, occurrence*.
30. Expresses either cause or content, but the latter is preferable (Pelletier 1962, 169; contra Wright 2015, 246).
31. Aor. act. ptc. nom. masc. pl., ὁμιλέω, *associate with*; with dat.; circ.
32. διαστροφή, -ῆς, ἡ, (fig.) *corruption, perversion*.
33. ταλαίπωρος, -ον, *miserable, wretched*.
34. The articular infinitive is the object of διά (cf. BDF §398; S §2032.g; *CGCG* §51.39): "through the whole of their life."
35. σοφός, -ή, -όν, *wise*.
36. φρόνιμος, -ον, *prudent*.
37. Pres. act. subj. 3 pl., συζάω, *live with*; with dat.; pres. general condition with a gnomic aor. in the apodosis (cf. BDF §373; S §§2337–38; *CGCG* §49.12).
38. ἄγνοια, -ας, ἡ, *ignorance*.
39. ἐπανόρθωσις, -εως, ἡ, *improvement, advantage*.
40. Aor. act. indic. 3 pl., τυγχάνω, *attain/obtain* (something); with gen.
41. Aor. mid. ptc. nom. masc. sg., διαστέλλω, *distinguish, define*; circ.
42. εὐσεβεία, -ας, ἡ, *piety*.
43. νομοθέτης, -ου, ὁ, *lawgiver*.
44. Adv., *prohibitively*.
45. Adv., *indicatively*; i.e., in the sense of providing the rationale for the legislation.
46. βλάβη, -ης, ἡ, *damage, harm*.
47. Aor. act. ptc. nom. masc. sg., προδηλόω, *show plainly*; circ.
48. ἐπιπομπή, -ῆς, ἡ, *punishment*.
49. αἴτιος, -ία, -ον, (subst.) *the guilty*.
50. Aor. act. indic. 3 sg., προϋποδείκνυμι, *show first*.
51. φανερός, -ά, -όν, *manifest*; pred. adj.

52. Pf. pass. ptc. gen. masc. sg., πληρόω, (pass.) *be full of*; with gen.; gen. absol. (causal).
53. δυναστεία, -ας, ἡ, *sovereignty*.
54. Pres. act. indic. 3 sg., λανθάνω, *escape the notice of* (someone).
55. Adv., *secretly*; modifies τῶν γινομένων.
56. Pf. act. indic. 3 sg., καθίστημι, (intrans.) *be*.
57. The string of circumstantial participles (Διαστειλάμενος ... διδάξας ... προδηλώσας), which was interrupted by a parenthesis (Let. Aris. 132), is resumed by ταῦτ' οὖν (anacoluthon). On the resumptive οὖν, see Denniston 1966, 428.
58. Pres. mid. ptc. nom. masc. sg., ἐξεργάζομαι, *work out*; circ.
59. Adv., *accurately*.
60. πρόδηλος, -ον, *evident, clear*.
61. Crasis: καὶ ἄν, *even if*; concessive clause (cf. BDF §457; S §2369; *CGCG* §49.19).
62. Aor. pass. subj. 3 sg., ἐννοέω, *have in mind, consider*; with inf.
63. Pres. act. inf., ἐπιτελέω, *accomplish*.
64. Aor. act. opt. 3 sg., λανθάνω, *escape the notice* (of someone); potential opt. in the apodosis (cf. S §2326.d).
65. Aor. act. ptc. nom. masc. sg., πράσσω, *do*; circ. (conditional). The clause builds on the structure: ἔδειξεν ὅτι ... μὴ ὅτι καὶ πράξας. The pragmatic effect of the tail may be expressed with the question, If the mere thought of doing evil will not go unpunished, what need is there to speak of what will happen to the person who carries out the act?
66. Pres. mid. ptc. nom. masc. sg., ἐνδείκνυμι, *show forth*; circ.
67. καταρχή, -ῆς, ἡ, *beginning*.
68. Here, παρά plus an accusative marks an exception: "except us."
69. Compar., δυναμικός, -ή, -όν, *more powerful*.

πολλῷ καθεστῶτες[70] ὧν[71] σέβονται[72] ματαίως[73]— [135]ἀγάλματα[74] γὰρ ποιήσαντες ἐκ λίθων[75] καὶ ξύλων,[76] εἰκόνας[77] φασὶν εἶναι τῶν ἐξευρόντων[78] τι πρὸς τὸ ζῆν[79] αὐτοῖς χρήσιμον,[80] οἷς προσκυνοῦσι,[81] παρὰ πόδας[82] ἔχοντες τὴν ἀναισθησίαν.[83] [136]Εἴτε[84] γὰρ κατ᾽ ἐκεῖνό τις θεοῖ,[85] κατὰ τὴν ἐξεύρεσιν, παντελῶς ἀνόητον· τῶν γὰρ ἐν τῇ κτίσει[86] λαβόντες τινὰ συνέθηκαν[87] καὶ προσυπέδειξαν[88] εὔχρηστα,[89] τὴν κατασκευὴν[90] αὐτῶν οὐ ποιήσαντες αὐτοί· διὸ κενὸν[91] καὶ μάταιον[92] τοὺς ὁμοίους[93] ἀποθεοῦν.[94] [137]Καὶ γὰρ[95] ἔτι καὶ νῦν εὐρεματικώτεροι[96] καὶ πολυμαθέστεροι[97] τῶν ἀνθρώπων τῶν[98] πρίν εἰσι πολλοί, καὶ οὐκ ἂν φθάνοιεν[99] αὐτοὺς προσκυνοῦντες. Καὶ νομίζουσιν οἱ ταῦτα διαπλάσαντες[100] καὶ μυθοποιήσαντες[101] τῶν Ἑλλήνων οἱ σοφώτατοι[102] καθεστάναι. [138]Τῶν γὰρ ἄλλων πολυματαίων[103] τί δεῖ καὶ λέγειν, Αἰγυπτίων τε καὶ τῶν παραπλησίων,[104] οἵτινες ἐπὶ θηρία καὶ τῶν ἑρπετῶν τὰ πλεῖστα καὶ κνωδάλων τὴν ἀπέρεισιν[105] πεποίηνται, καὶ ταῦτα προσκυνοῦσι, καὶ θύουσι[106] τούτοις καὶ ζῶσι καὶ τελευτήσασι; [139]Συνθεωρήσας[107] οὖν ἕκαστα σοφὸς ὢν ὁ νομοθέτης, ὑπὸ θεοῦ κατεσκευασμένος[108] εἰς ἐπίγνωσιν τῶν ἁπάντων, πε-

70. Pf. act. ptc. nom. masc. pl., καθίστημι, (intrans.) *be*; circ. (concessive): "they being so much more powerful than those whom they worship in vain."

71. The relative pronoun has been attracted to the case of its suppressed antecedent (cf. BDF §294; S §2531; *CGCG* §50.15).

72. Pres. mid. indic. 3 pl., σέβω, *venerate, honor, worship*.

73. Adv., *in vain*.

74. ἄγαλμα, -ατος, τό, *statue*.

75. λίθος, -ου, ὁ, *stone*.

76. ξύλον, -ου, τό, *wood*.

77. εἰκών, -όνος, ὁ, *image*.

78. Aor. act. ptc. gen. masc. pl., ἐξευρίσκω, *discover, invent*; attrib. (subst.).

79. The articular infinitive is the object of πρός and modifies τι . . . χρήσιμον: "something beneficial to them *with respect to living*."

80. χρήσιμος, -ον, *beneficial*.

81. Pres. act. indic. 3 pl., προσκυνέω, *prostrate before, worship*; with dat.

82. παρὰ πόδας, lit., "near/at the feet." The English equivalent is "close at hand."

83. ἀναισθησία, -ας, ἡ, *without sense perception*.

84. Partic., εἰ with τε, *if*. Most MSS read εἴ τι.

85. Pres. act. indic. 3 sg., θεόω, *be divinized, become divine*. Pelletier follows Tramontano in reading θεοῖ as an indicative, from which the optative θείη would be a corruption. Something like, "And if someone is divinized on that basis [κατ᾽ ἐκεῖνο]—that is, on the basis of their discovery—this would be totally foolish."

86. κτίσις, -εως, ἡ, *creation*. The article is a function marker: τῶν . . . ἐν τῇ κτίσει, "of the things in creation."

87. Aor. act. indic. 3 pl., συντίθημι, *place together, combine*.

88. Aor. act. indic. 3 pl., προσυποδείκνυμι, *show in addition*.

89. εὔχρηστος, -ον, *useful*.

90. κατασκευή, -ῆς, ἡ, *constitution* (as found in creation).

91. κενός, -ή, -όν, (quasi-impers.) *it is empty*; with acc. and inf. See n. 1.

92. μάταιος, -α, -ον, (quasi-impers.) *it is vain*; with acc. and inf. See n. 1.

93. ὁμοῖος, -α, -ον, *like, equal*.

94. Pres. act. inf., ἀποθεόω, *make god, deify*.

95. Partic. combination: additional information (καί) that has explanatory force (γάρ) (cf. *CGCG* §59.66).

96. Compar., εὑρεματικός, -ή, -όν, *more prone to discover, more inventive*.

97. Compar., πολυμαθής, -ές, *more learned*.

98. The article is a function marker: τῶν makes πρίν an adjective, modifying τῶν ἀνθρώπων (gen. compar.).

99. Aor. act. opt. 3 pl., φθάνω, *arrive first, be ready/eager to*; with supp. ptc.; potential opt. (cf. BDF §385; S §1824; *CGCG* §34.13); neg. οὐκ: "They would not be so quick to worship them."

100. Aor. act. ptc. nom. masc. pl., διαπλάσσω, *form*; attrib. (subst.).

101. Aor. act. ptc. nom. masc. pl., μυθοποιέω, *make myths*; attrib. (subst.).

102. Superl., σοφός, -ή, -όν, *wisest*.

103. New theme (cf. *CGCG* §60.33): "Now of the other very vain peoples, what more must we say?" The writer divides this class into two groups: Egyptians (τε) and those like them (καί).

104. παραπλήσιος, -α, -ον, *very similar*.

105. ἀπέρεισις, -εως, ἡ, *leaning*. The whole clause is, "who lean on beasts [ἐπὶ θηρία], most reptiles [τῶν ἑρπετῶν τὰ πλεῖστα], and monsters [κνωδάλων]."

106. Pres. act. indic. 3 pl., θύω, *sacrifice*.

107. Aor. act. ptc. nom. masc. sg., συνθεωρέω, *observe completely*; circ.

108. Pf. pass. ptc. nom. masc. sg., κατασκευάζω, (pass.) *be furnished/fully equipped*; circ.

ριέφραξεν[109] ἡμᾶς ἀδιακόποις[110] χάραξι[111] καὶ σιδηροῖς[112] τείχεσιν,[113] ὅπως μηθενὶ τῶν ἄλλων ἐθνῶν ἐπιμισγώμεθα[114] κατὰ μηδέν, ἁγνοὶ[115] καθεστῶτες κατὰ σῶμα καὶ κατὰ ψυχήν, ἀπολελυμένοι[116] ματαίων δοξῶν,[117] τὸν μόνον θεὸν καὶ δυνατὸν σεβόμενοι παρ' ὅλην τὴν πᾶσαν κτίσιν. **140**Ὅθεν[118] οἱ Αἰγυπτίων καθηγεμόνες[119] ἱερεῖς, ἐγκεκυφότες[120] εἰς πολλὰ καὶ μετεσχηκότες[121] πραγμάτων, ἀνθρώπους θεοῦ προσονομάζουσιν[122] ἡμᾶς· ὃ τοῖς λοιποῖς οὐ πρόσεστιν,[123] εἰ μή τις σέβεται τὸν κατὰ ἀλήθειαν θεόν, ἀλλ' εἰσὶν ἄνθρωποι βρωτῶν καὶ ποτῶν καὶ σκέπης.[124] **141**ἡ γὰρ πᾶσα διάθεσις[125] αὐτῶν ἐπὶ ταῦτα καταφεύγει.[126] Τοῖς δὲ παρ' ἡμῶν ἐν οὐδενὶ ταῦτα λελόγισται,[127] περὶ δὲ τῆς τοῦ θεοῦ δυναστείας[128] δι' ὅλου τοῦ ζῆν ἡ σκέψις[129] αὐτοῖς ἐστιν. **142**Ὅπως οὖν μηθενὶ συναλισγούμενοι[130] μηδ' ὁμιλοῦντες φαύλοις[131] διαστροφὰς[132] λαμβάνωμεν, πάντοθεν ἡμᾶς περιέφραξεν ἁγνείαις[133] καὶ διὰ βρωτῶν καὶ ποτῶν καὶ ἁφῶν καὶ ἀκοῆς[134] καὶ ὁράσεως[135] νομικῶς.[136] **143**Τὸ γὰρ καθόλου[137] πάντα πρὸς τὸν φυσικὸν[138] λόγον ὅμοια[139] καθέστηκεν, ὑπὸ μιᾶς δυνάμεως οἰκονομούμενα,[140] καὶ καθ' ἓν ἕκαστον ἔχει λόγον βαθύν,[141] ἀφ' ὧν[142] ἀπεχόμεθα[143] κατὰ τὴν χρῆσιν,[144] καὶ οἷς συγχρώμεθα.[145] . . .

170Ἐμοὶ μὲν οὖν[146] καλῶς ἐνόμιζε[147] περὶ ἑκάστων ἀπολογεῖσθαι·[148] καὶ γὰρ ἐπὶ τῶν προσφερομένων[149] ἔλεγε μόσχων[150] τε καὶ κριῶν[151] καὶ χιμάρων,[152] ὅτι δεῖ

ἀλίσγομαι, which is attested in MS T and Eusebius). This is the only instance of the verb in the extant literature.
131. φαῦλος, -η, -ον, *bad, evil*.
132. διαστροφή, -ῆς, ἡ, *twisting, distortion*.
133. ἁγνεία, -ας, ἡ, *purity, purification*; dat. of means.
134. ἀκοή, -ῆς, ἡ, *hearing*.
135. ὅρασις, -εως, ἡ, *seeing*.
136. Adv., *lawfully*.
137. Adv., τὸ καθόλου, *in general*.
138. φυσικός, -ή, -όν, *natural*; πρὸς τὸν φυσικὸν λόγον, "in regard to natural reason."
139. ὅμοιος, -α, -ον, *similar*.
140. Pres. pass. ptc. nom. neut. pl., οἰκονομέω, (pass.) *be managed, governed*; circ.
141. βαθύς, -εῖα, -ύ, *deep, profound*.
142. Both relative pronouns, ὧν and οἷς, have a suppressed antecedent: "The things from which [ἀφ' ὧν] we turn and *the things* in which [οἷς] we partake."
143. Pres. mid. indic. 1 pl., ἀπέχω, *stay away, restrain oneself*.
144. χρῆσις, -εως, ἡ, *use*.
145. Pres. mid. indic. 1 pl., συγχράομαι, *make use of*; with dat.
146. Partic. combination: "A transition to a more to-the-point, relevant text segment (οὖν) [that] occurs in two stages (μέν . . . δέ)" (*CGCG* §59.73). μὲν οὖν indicates the summary of the previous discourse, and δέ marks the development to a new section (*Let. Aris.* 172).
147. Impf. act. indic. 3 sg., νομίζω, *be accustomed to do*; with inf.
148. Pres. mid. inf., ἀπολογέομαι, *give an account of* (something).
149. Pres. pass. ptc. gen. neut. pl., προσφέρω, (pass.) *be offered*; attrib. (subst.).
150. μόσχος, -ου, ὁ, *calf, young bull*.
151. κριός, -οῦ, ὁ, *ram*.
152. χίμαρος, -ου, ὁ, *he-goat*.

---

109. Aor. act. indic. 3 sg., περιφράσσω, *surround, enclose*.
110. ἀδιάκοπος, -ον, *uninterrupted*.
111. χάραξ, -ακος, ὁ/ἡ, *pointed stake, palisade*; dat. of instrument.
112. σίδηρος, -ου, ὁ, *made of iron*.
113. τεῖχος, -ους, τό, *wall*; dat. of instrument.
114. Pres. mid. subj. 1 pl., ἐπιμίσγω, *mix, intermingle with*; with dat.; purpose clause (cf. BDF §369; S §2193; *CGCG* §45.3).
115. ἁγνός, -ή, -όν, *pure*.
116. Pf. pass. ptc. nom. masc. pl., ἀπολύω, *set free*; with abl. gen.
117. δόξα, -ᾶς, ἡ, *opinion*.
118. Adv., *whence, for which reason*.
119. καθηγεμών, -όνος, *guide, leader*; adj. of ἱερεῖς, "leading priests."
120. Pf. act. ptc. nom. masc. pl., ἐγκύπτω, *investigate, study*; circ.
121. Pf. act. ptc. nom. masc. pl., μετέχω, *take part in*; with gen.; circ.
122. Pres. act. indic. 3 pl., προσονομάζω, *call, denominate*.
123. Pres. act. indic. 3 sg., πρόσειμι, *belong to*; with dat.
124. σκέπη, -ης, ἡ, *shelter*.
125. διάθεσις, -εως, ἡ, *disposition, state*.
126. Pres. act. indic. 3 sg., καταφεύγω, *take refuge, seek assistance*.
127. Pf. pass. indic. 3 sg., λογίζομαι, (pass.) *be reckoned/regarded*; with ἐν οὐδενί, "of no concern."
128. δυναστεία, -ας, ἡ, *sovereignty*.
129. σκέψις, -εως, ἡ, *reflection*.
130. Pres. pass. ptc. nom. masc. pl., συναλισγέομαι, (pass.) *be contaminated together*; with dat. (MGS, 2022; LSJ lists as συν-

ταῦτα ἐκ βουκολίων¹⁵³ καὶ ποιμνίων¹⁵⁴ λαμβάνοντας ἥμερα¹⁵⁵ θυσιάζειν,¹⁵⁶ καὶ μηθὲν ἄγριον,¹⁵⁷ ὅπως οἱ προσφέροντες τὰς θυσίας μηθὲν ὑπερήφανον¹⁵⁸ ἑαυτοῖς συνιστορῶσι,¹⁵⁹ σημειώσει¹⁶⁰ κεχρημένοι τοῦ διατάξαντος. Τῆς γὰρ ἑαυτοῦ ψυχῆς τοῦ παντὸς τρόπου¹⁶¹ τὴν προσφορὰν¹⁶² ποιεῖται ὁ τὴν θυσίαν προσάγων.
¹⁷¹Καὶ περὶ τούτων οὖν νομίζω τὰ τῆς ὁμιλίας ἄξια λόγου καθεστάναι· διὸ τὴν σεμνότητα¹⁶³ καὶ φυσικὴν διάνοιαν¹⁶⁴ τοῦ νόμου προῆγμαι¹⁶⁵ διασαφῆσαί¹⁶⁶ σοι, Φιλόκρατες,¹⁶⁷ δι' ἣν ἔχεις φιλομάθειαν.¹⁶⁸

NOTES

128. For the Mosaic legislation on pure and impure food, as well as on clean and unclean animals, cf. Lev. 11. The writer presupposes that "most people" (τοὺς πολλούς)—that is, ostensibly, both Jews and gentiles—are interested in the rationale of Mosaic dietary restrictions.

130. ἐὰν δὲ σοφοῖς καὶ φρονίμοις συζῶσιν. The protasis trades on the Aristotelian distinction between σοφία (wisdom of universal truths) and φρόνησις (practical wisdom) (cf. Aristotle, *Eth. nic.* 6.1139a–1145a; Hadas 1951, 153). Wright (2015, 256) notes additional examples of Aristotelian influence in 83–120 (cf. Aristotle, *Pol.* 7) and 121–127 (cf. Aristotle, *Eth. nic.* 1105b–1107a).

131. τὰ τῆς εὐσεβείας καὶ δικαιοσύνης. The notion that Mosaic legislation is principally concerned with εὐσεβεία and δικαιοσύνη is not unique to the Letter of Aristeas (cf. Philo, *Spec.* 2.63; Philo, *Decal.* 110; Philo, *Virt.* 57; Philo, *Abr.* 208; Josephus, *B.J.* 2.139; Josephus, *A.J.* 18.117; Matt. 5:20; 6:1; Allison 2005, 149–65).

134. The referent of παρ' ἡμᾶς raises an interesting question. Does the pronoun refer exclusively to Eleazar and the Jews, as most interpreters conclude, or does it include gentile monotheists, as Wright suggests (2015, 258–59)? The immediate context favors the former (cf. Let. Aris. 139–140). Yet this seems difficult to square with the claim that some gentiles worship the Jewish God by the name Zeus or Jove (cf. Let. Aris. 16; Collins 2000, 192). My own take is that "us" in 134 and 140 has an *inclusive* sense. The writer does not view gentile monotheism as "simply a hypothetical possibility." Rather, "the narrative presents us with real examples of Gentiles who have arrived at this destination without reference to Judaism or its law" (Donaldson 2007, 114).

135–138. The writer's critique of gentile idolatry is twofold. First, he argues that the gods are human beings who have been deified on account of their euergetism (the benefits they bestow on humanity). Second, he concludes, almost in passing, with a critique of Egyptian theriolatry (cf. Wis. 12:23–27; Philo, *Decal.* 76–80). As Honigman notes, "The stance of [the Letter of Aristeas's] author in this case would certainly not be seen as that of a Jewish philosopher targeting 'pagan' views en bloc. His shafts come from within the realm of Greek

---

153. βουκόλιον, -ου, τό, *herd*.
154. ποίμνιον, -ου, τό, *flock*.
155. ἥμερος, -ον, *tame*.
156. Pres. act. inf., θυσιάζω, *sacrifice*; comp. of δεῖ: "It is necessary [for them] to sacrifice these [animals], having taken tame ones from the herds and flocks."
157. ἄγριος, -ον, *wild*.
158. ὑπερήφανος, -ον, *arrogant*.
159. Pres. act. subj. 3 pl., συνιστορέω, *be concious of* (something); purpose clause. See n. 114.
160. σημείωσις, -εως, ἡ, *sign, symbol*.
161. τρόπος, -ου, ὁ, *way of life*; gen. of explanation: "Offering of his soul, *all its dispositions*."
162. προσφορά, -ᾶς, ἡ, *offering*.
163. σεμνότης, -ητος, ἡ, *dignity*.
164. διάνοια, -ας, ἡ, *thought, intention*.
165. Pf. pass. indic. 1 sg., προάγω, (pass.) *be persuaded*; with inf. (cf. LSJ, 1466.4).
166. Aor. act. inf., διασαφέω, *make clear, show plainly*.
167. Philocrates is the fictive addressee (cf. Let. Aris. 1).
168. φιλομάθεια, -ας, ἡ, *love of learning*.

philosophical polemic. . . . The attacks contained in the Apology are aimed at specific aspects of Greek (and Egyptian) philosophy and religion that were widely criticized by Greeks themselves" (2003, 21, 23; cf. Hadas 1951, 62–64).

139. περιέφραξεν ἡμᾶς ἀδιακόποις χάραξι καὶ σιδηροῖς τείχεσιν. The main clause is introduced by two circumstantial frames and an inferential οὖν, which positions the decision to "fence us in with unbroken palisades and with iron walls" as both the necessary response to gentile idolatry and a task for which Moses was uniquely prepared. In 142, the writer associates these "palisades and walls" πάντοθεν ("on all sides") with purification rituals and dietary restrictions. Their purpose is to prevent any "mixing" with the other nations. Yet, as Donaldson notes, "The separation toward which the law is directed is a separation not from Gentiles per se, but from polytheistic worship. . . . The goal . . . is the preservation of monotheism and the nurture of a kind of life appropriate for people who desire to live under the sovereignty of the one true God" (2007, 112–13). According to the Letter of Aristeas, gentiles who share Eleazar's critique of idolatry are enlightened monotheists (cf. 16, 140) and thus allies of the Jewish people.

140. ἀνθρώπους θεοῦ προσονομάζουσιν ἡμᾶς· ὃ τοῖς λοιποῖς οὐ πρόσεστιν, εἰ μή τις σέβεται τὸν κατὰ ἀλήθειαν θεόν, ἀλλ' εἰσὶν ἄνθρωποι βρωτῶν καὶ ποτῶν καὶ σκέπης. The relative clause creates the appearance of a strict dichotomy. This is immediately qualified, however, by the clause of exception (εἰ μή), which suggests that an enlightened monotheist from "the rest" (i.e., gentiles) could be counted among the "people of God." The final clause marks a correction (ἀλλά) that explains why the epithet "people of God" is, in practice, inappropriate for gentiles: the vast majority are not monotheists but are instead concerned primarily with the necessities of daily life.

171. φυσικὴν διάνοιαν τοῦ νόμου. The phrase "likely pertains to the allegorical interpretations and the philosophical quality of the law" (Wright 2015, 308). In 143, Pseudo-Aristeas contends that Mosaic prohibitions are generally oriented "toward natural reason" (πρὸς τὸν φυσικὸν λόγον) and that each specific prohibition has a "deep reason" (λόγον βαθύν) behind it.

3.1.2

The Translation of the Law

Letter of Aristeas 301–316

301Μετὰ δὲ τρεῖς ἡμέρας ὁ Δημήτριος[1] παραλαβὼν αὐτούς, καὶ διελθὼν τὸ τῶν ἑπτὰ σταδίων ἀνάχωμα[2] τῆς θαλάσσης πρὸς τὴν νῆσον,[3] καὶ διαβὰς τὴν γέφυραν,[4] καὶ προσελθὼν ὡς[5] ἐπὶ τὰ βόρεια[6] μέρη,[7] συνέδριον[8] ποιησάμενος εἰς κατεσκευασμένον[9] οἶκον παρὰ τὴν ἠϊόνα,[10] διαπρεπῶς[11] ἔχοντα καὶ πολλῆς ἡσυχίας[12] ἔφεδρον,[13] παρεκάλει[14] τοὺς ἄνδρας τὰ τῆς ἑρμηνείας[15] ἐπιτελεῖν,[16] παρόντων[17] ὅσα πρὸς τὴν χρείαν ἔδει καλῶς. **302**Οἱ δὲ ἐπετέλουν ἕκαστα σύμφωνα[18] ποιοῦντες πρὸς ἑαυτοὺς ταῖς ἀντιβολαῖς·[19] τὸ δὲ ἐκ τῆς συμφωνίας[20] γινόμενον πρεπόντως[21] ἀναγραφῆς[22] οὕτως ἐτύγχανε[23] παρὰ τοῦ Δημητρίου. **303**Καὶ μέχρι[24] μὲν[25] ὥρας ἐνάτης τὰ τῆς συνεδρείας[26] ἐγίνετο· μετὰ δὲ ταῦτα περὶ τὴν τοῦ σώματος θερα-

1. Demetrius of Phalerum had been appointed overseer of the king's library (cf. Let. Aris. 9).
2. ἀνάχωμα, -ατος, τό, *dike, jetty*; with τῶν ἑπτὰ σταδίων, "seven stadia long" (about a mile).
3. νῆσος, -ου, ἡ, *island*.
4. γέφυρα, -ας, ἡ, *bridge*.
5. ὡς with ἐπί indicates direction *to* or *toward* (MGS, 2429.H.C).
6. βόρειος, -α, -ον, *northern*.
7. μέρος, -ους, τό, *part*.
8. συνέδριον, -ου, τό, *council, meeting place*.
9. Pf. pass. ptc. acc. neut. sg., κατασκευάζω, (pass.) *be prepared, made ready*; attrib.
10. ἠϊών, -όνος, ἡ, *beach*.
11. Adv., *magnificently*; ἔχω with adv. (cf. BDF §308; S §1438; CGCG §26.11), "was magnificent."
12. ἡσυχία, -ας, ἡ, *quiet*.
13. ἔφεδρος, -ον, *seated, placed*; with gen.
14. Impf. act. indic. 3 sg., παρακαλέω, *exhort, entreat*; with acc. and inf.
15. ἑρμηνεία, -ας, ἡ, *translation*.
16. Pres. act. inf., ἐπιτελέω, *complete*.
17. Pres. act. ptc. gen. neut. pl., πάρειμι, *be at hand*; gen. absol. (causal). The subject is explicated by the relative clause ὅσα πρὸς τὴν χρείαν ἔδει, "[These things] being at hand, however much was necessary for the task."
18. σύμφωνος, -ον, *harmonious*.
19. ἀντιβολή, -ῆς, ἡ, *comparison*. Full clause: "So they went about completing their several tasks, reaching agreement among themselves on each by comparison."
20. συμφωνία, -ας, ἡ, *harmony, agreement*.
21. Adv., *fittingly, suitably*.
22. ἀναγραφή, -ῆς, ἡ, *copy*.
23. Impf. act. indic. 3 sg., τυγχάνω, *reach, obtain*; with gen.
24. Prep. with gen., *up to* (a point).
25. μέν . . . δέ; point/counterpoint set (cf. Runge 2010, 75–83; BDF §447; S §2904; CGCG §59.24).
26. συνεδρεία, -ας, ἡ, *meeting, session*.

πείαν²⁷ ἀπελύοντο²⁸ γίνεσθαι, χορηγουμένων²⁹ αὐτοῖς δαψιλῶς³⁰ ὧν προηροῦντο³¹ πάντων. ³⁰⁴Ἐκτὸς³² δὲ καὶ καθ' ἡμέραν,³³ ὅσα βασιλεῖ παρεσκευάζετο,³⁴ καὶ τούτοις ὁ Δωρόθεος³⁵ ἐπετέλει· προστεταγμένον³⁶ γὰρ ἦν αὐτῷ διὰ τοῦ βασιλέως. Ἅμα³⁷ δὲ τῇ πρωΐᾳ παρεγίνοντο εἰς τὴν αὐλὴν³⁸ καθ' ἡμέραν, καὶ ποιησάμενοι τὸν ἀσπασμὸν³⁹ τοῦ βασιλέως, ἀπελύοντο πρὸς τὸν ἑαυτῶν τόπον. ³⁰⁵Ὡς δὲ ἔθος⁴⁰ ἐστὶ πᾶσι τοῖς Ἰουδαίοις, ἀπονιψάμενοι⁴¹ τῇ θαλάσσῃ τὰς χεῖρας, ὡς ἂν εὔξωνται⁴² πρὸς τὸν θεόν, ἐτρέποντο⁴³ πρὸς τὴν ἀνάγνωσιν⁴⁴ καὶ τὴν ἑκάστου διασάφησιν.⁴⁵ ³⁰⁶Ἐπηρώτησα δὲ καὶ τοῦτο· Τίνος χάριν⁴⁶ ἀπονιζόμενος τὰς χεῖρας τὸ τηνικαῦτα⁴⁷ εὔχονται; Διεσάφουν⁴⁸ δέ, ὅτι μαρτύριόν ἐστι τοῦ μηδὲν εἰργάσθαι⁴⁹ κακόν· πᾶσα γὰρ ἐνέργεια⁵⁰ διὰ τῶν χειρῶν γίνεται· καλῶς καὶ ὁσίως μεταφέροντες⁵¹ ἐπὶ τὴν δικαιοσύνην καὶ τὴν ἀλήθειαν πάντα. ³⁰⁷Καθὼς δὲ προειρήκαμεν,⁵² οὕτως καθ' ἑκάστην⁵³ εἰς τὸν τόπον, ἔχοντα τερπνότητα⁵⁴ διὰ τὴν ἡσυχίαν⁵⁵ καὶ καταύγειαν,⁵⁶ συναγόμενοι τὸ προκείμενον⁵⁷ ἐπετέλουν. Συνέτυχε δὲ οὕτως, ὥστε ἐν ἡμέραις ἑβδομήκοντα δυσὶ⁵⁸ τελειωθῆναι⁵⁹ τὰ τῆς μεταγραφῆς,⁶⁰ οἱονεὶ⁶¹ κατὰ πρόθεσίν⁶² τινα τοῦ τοιούτου γεγενημένου. ³⁰⁸Τελείωσιν⁶³ δὲ ὅτε ἔλαβε, συναγαγὼν ὁ Δημήτριος τὸ πλῆθος τῶν Ἰουδαίων εἰς τὸν τόπον, οὗ⁶⁴ καὶ τὰ τῆς ἑρμηνείας ἐτελέσθη, παρανέγνω⁶⁵ πᾶσι, παρόντων καὶ τῶν διερμηνευσάντων,⁶⁶ οἵτινες μεγάλης ἀποδοχῆς⁶⁷ καὶ παρὰ τοῦ πλήθους ἔτυχον, ὡς ἂν μεγάλων ἀγαθῶν

---

27. θεραπεία, -ας, ἡ, *attendance, care for*; with gen.
28. Impf. pass. indic. 3 pl., ἀπολύω, *released*; iterative (BDF §325; S §1893; CGCG §33.24).
29. Pres. pass. ptc. gen. neut. pl., χορηγέω, (pass.) *be furnished*; gen. absol.
30. Adv., *abundantly*.
31. Impf. mid. indic. 3 pl., προαιρέω, *choose deliberately, prefer* (i.e., they received everything for which they expressed preference).
32. Adv., *in addition* (LSJ, 523.3).
33. Distributive: "each day."
34. Impf. pass. indic. 3 sg., παρασκευάζω, (pass.) *be prepared, provided*.
35. Dorotheus had been appointed by Nicanor to attend to the guests (cf. Let. Aris. 182).
36. Pf. pass. ptc. nom. neut. sg., προστάσσω, (pass.) *be ordered*; impers. periphrastic as equivalent of plpf. tense, which is used in narrative to provide remote background information (cf. CGCG §33.50).
37. Prep. with dat., *at*; ἅμα τῇ πρωΐᾳ, *in the early morning*.
38. αὐλή, -ῆς, ἡ, *court*.
39. ἀσπασμός, -οῦ, ὁ, *greeting, salutation*.
40. ἔθος, -ους, τό, *custom*; (impers.) ὡς ἔθος ἐστί, with dat., "as is their [dat.] custom."
41. Aor. mid. ptc. nom. masc. pl., ἀπονίζω, *wash* (esp. hands).
42. Pres. mid. subj. 3 sg., εὔχομαι, *pray*; either purpose (cf. BDF §369; S §2201; CGCG §45.4) or general temp. (cf. BDAG, 1106.8c). See notes.
43. Impf. mid. indic. 3 pl., τρέπω, *turn*; iterative. See n. 28.
44. ἀνάγνωσις, -εως, ἡ, *reading*.
45. διασάφησις, -εως, ἡ, *explanation, interpretation*; elsewhere only in Gen. 30:8 LXX (cf. GELS, 158.1). Shutt notes, "Its root meaning is that of clarifying, or making clear, without indicating whether the clarification is a translation or a commentary or both" (OTP 2:33nj3). The verbal form is used in Let. Aris. 306.
46. τίνος χάριν, *For what reason?, Why?*
47. Adv., τὸ τηνικαῦτα, *at that time*.
48. Impf. act. indic. 3 pl., διασαφέω, *explain*.
49. Gen. art. inf. that explicates μαρτύριόν ἐστι (cf. BDF §400; S §2032.e; CGCG §51.46): "It is a testimony *that they have done no evil*."
50. ἐνέργεια, -ας, ἡ, *activity*.
51. Pres. act. ptc. nom. masc. pl., μεταφέρω, *carry over, refer to*; circ.
52. Pf. act. indic. 1 pl., προερέω, *say previously*.
53. καθ' ἑκάστην = καθ' ἑκάστην ἡμέραν.
54. τερπνότης, -ητος, ἡ, *delight*; with ἔχοντα (attrib.), "which was delightful."
55. ἡσυχία, -ας, ἡ, *quietness*.
56. καταύγεια, -ας, ἡ, *brightness*.
57. Pres. pass. ptc. acc. neut. sg., πρόκειμαι; subst., "the task set before [them]."
58. Dat. of time, "in seventy-two days."
59. Aor. pass. inf., τελειόω, *complete*; result clause (cf. BDF §391; S §2269; CGCG §46.6), signposted by οὕτως.
60. μεταγραφή, -ῆς, ἡ, *transcription, translation*.
61. οἱονεί (οἷον, εἰ) with gen. absol., "*as if that which came about*" (cf. S §2085; CGCG §52.39).
62. πρόθεσις, -εως, ἡ, *plan, design*.
63. τελείωσις, -εως, ἡ, *completion*.
64. Adv., *where*.
65. Aor. act. indic. 3 sg., παραναγινώσκω, *read publicly*.
66. Aor. act. ptc. gen. masc. pl., διερμενεύω, *translate*; attrib. (subst.).
67. ἀποδοχή, -ῆς, ἡ, *acceptance, approval*; comp. of ἔτυχον.

παραίτιοι⁶⁸ γεγονότες.⁶⁹ ³⁰⁹ʹΩσαύτως⁷⁰ δὲ καὶ τὸν Δημήτριον ἀποδεξάμενοι παρεκάλεσαν μεταδοῦναι⁷¹ τοῖς ἡγουμένοις⁷² αὐτῶν, μεταγράψαντα⁷³ τὸν πάντα νόμον. ³¹⁰Καθὼς δὲ ἀνεγνώσθη τὰ τεύχη,⁷⁴ στάντες οἱ ἱερεῖς καὶ τῶν ἑρμηνέων οἱ πρεσβύτεροι καὶ τῶν ἀπὸ τοῦ πολιτεύματος⁷⁵ οἵ τε ἡγούμενοι τοῦ πλήθους εἶπον· Ἐπεὶ καλῶς καὶ ὁσίως διηρμήνευται καὶ κατὰ πᾶν ἠκριβωμένως,⁷⁶ καλῶς ἔχον ἐστὶν ἵνα διαμείνῃ⁷⁷ ταῦθ᾽ οὕτως ἔχοντα,⁷⁸ καὶ μὴ γένηται μηδεμία διασκευή.⁷⁹ ³¹¹Πάντων δ᾽ ἐπιφωνησάντων⁸⁰ τοῖς εἰρημένοις, ἐκέλευσαν⁸¹ διαράσασθαι,⁸² καθὼς ἔθος αὐτοῖς ἐστιν, εἴ τις διασκευάσει⁸³ προστιθεὶς⁸⁴ ἢ μεταφέρων τι τὸ σύνολον τῶν γεγραμμένων ἢ ποιούμενος ἀφαίρεσιν,⁸⁵ καλῶς τοῦτο πράσσοντες, ἵνα διὰ παντὸς⁸⁶ ἀέννασ⁸⁷ καὶ μένοντα φυλάσσηται.⁸⁸

³¹²Προσφωνηθέντων⁸⁹ δὲ καὶ τούτων τῷ βασιλεῖ μεγάλως ἐχάρη· τὴν γὰρ πρόθεσιν⁹⁰ ἣν εἶχεν ἀσφαλῶς⁹¹ ἔδοξε τετελειῶσθαι. Παρανεγνώσθη δὲ αὐτῷ καὶ πάντα, καὶ λίαν⁹² ἐξεθαύμασε⁹³ τὴν τοῦ νομοθέτου⁹⁴ διάνοιαν.⁹⁵ Καὶ πρὸς τὸν Δημήτριον εἶπε· Πῶς τηλικούτων⁹⁶ συντετελεσμένων⁹⁷ οὐδεὶς ἐπεβάλετο⁹⁸ τῶν ἱστορικῶν⁹⁹ ἢ ποιητῶν¹⁰⁰ ἐπιμνησθῆναι;¹⁰¹ ³¹³Ἐκεῖνος δὲ ἔφη· Διὰ τὸ σεμνὴν¹⁰² εἶναι¹⁰³ τὴν νομοθεσίαν καὶ διὰ θεοῦ γεγονέναι· καὶ τῶν ἐπιβαλλομένων τινὲς ὑπὸ τοῦ θεοῦ πληγέντες¹⁰⁴ τῆς ἐπιβολῆς ἀπέστησαν.¹⁰⁵ ³¹⁴Καὶ γὰρ¹⁰⁶ ἔφησεν ἀκηκοέναι¹⁰⁷ Θεοπόμπου,¹⁰⁸ διότι μέλλων τινὰ τῶν προηρμηνευμένων¹⁰⁹ ἐπισφαλέστε-

---

68. παραίτιος, -ον, *responsible*.

69. ὡς (ἄν) with a circumstantial participle gives "a 'subjective' reason or motivation, for which responsibility lies with the subject of the matrix verb" (*CGCG* §52.39; cf. S §2996).

70. Adv., *likewise*.

71. Aor. act. inf., μεταδίδωμι, *distribute*.

72. Pres. mid. ptc. dat. masc. pl., ἡγέομαι, *lead*; attrib. (subst.).

73. Aor. act. ptc. acc. masc. sg., μεταγράφω, *copy, transcribe*; circ. (causal).

74. τεῦχος, -εος, τό, *scroll*.

75. πολίτευμα, -ατος, τό, *political community*. See notes.

76. Adv., *exactly*.

77. Aor. act. subj. 3 sg., διαμένω, *remain*; content clause (cf. BDAG, 476.2.c; BDF §394).

78. ἔχω with adv.; οὕτως ἔχοντα, "as they are."

79. διασκευή, -ῆς, ἡ, *new edition/recension* (of a work).

80. Aor. act. ptc. gen. masc. pl., ἐπιφωνέω, *respond*; gen. absol.

81. Aor. act. indic. 3 pl., κελεύω, *order, bid*; with (acc. and) inf.

82. Aor. mid. inf., διαράομαι, *curse*.

83. Fut. act. indic. 3 sg., διασκευάζω, *revise*. εἰ with a future indicative reflects the protasis of the curse (cf. BDF §372): "If someone should make a revision . . . [omitted apodosis: let that one be accursed!]" (cf. S §2352.d).

84. Pres. act. ptc. nom. masc. sg., προστίθημι, *add to*; circ.

85. ἀφαίρεσις, -εως, ἡ, *deletion*.

86. Idiom, "always" (lit., "through all [time]").

87. ἀέννασς, -α, -ον, *eternal*.

88. Pres. pass. subj. 3 sg., φυλάσσω, (pass.) *be guarded/preserved*; the ἵνα-clause explicates the content of τοῦτο.

89. Aor. pass. ptc. gen. neut. pl., προσφωνέω, (pass.) *be announced*; gen. absol.

90. πρόθεσις, -εως, ἡ, *purpose*.

91. Adv., *securely*.

92. Adv., *greatly*.

93. Aor. act. indic. 3 sg., ἐκθαυμάζω, *marvel*.

94. νομοθέτης, -ου, ὁ, *lawgiver*.

95. διάνοια, -ας, ἡ, *intelligence, understanding*.

96. τηλικοῦτος, τηλικαύτη, τηλικοῦτον, *so great*.

97. Pf. pass. ptc. gen. neut. pl., συντελέω, (pass.) *be completed*; gen. absol.

98. Aor. mid. indic. 3 sg., ἐπιβάλλω, (mid.) *attempt, undertake*; with inf.

99. ἱστορικός, -ή, -όν, (subst.) *historian*.

100. ποιητής, -οῦ, ὁ, *poet*.

101. Aor. pass. inf., ἐπιμιμνήσκομαι, *make mention of*; with gen.

102. σεμνός, -ή, -όν, *august, holy*.

103. The verb φημί introduces reported speech and almost always takes the infinitive, as here (εἶναι and γεγονέναι) (cf. BDF §397; S §2017.a; *CGCG* §51.19n1).

104. Aor. pass. ptc. nom. masc. pl., πλήσσω, (pass.) *be stricken/afflicted*; circ.

105. Aor. act. indic. 3 pl., ἀφίστημι, *cease from*; with abl. gen.

106. Partic. combination: additional information (καί) that has explanatory force (γάρ).

107. Pf. act. inf., ἀκούω, *hear*; with gen.; indir. disc. See n. 103.

108. Theopompus was a fourth-century BCE historian from Chios who lived in Egypt during the reign of Ptolemy I.

109. Pres. pass. ptc. gen. neut. pl., προηρμηνεύω, (pass.) *be previously translated*; attrib. (subst.).

ρον¹¹⁰ ἐκ τοῦ νόμου προσιστορεῖν¹¹¹ ταραχὴν¹¹² λάβοι¹¹³ τῆς διανοίας πλεῖον¹¹⁴ ἡμερῶν τριάκοντα· κατὰ δὲ τὴν ἄνεσιν¹¹⁵ ἐξιλάσκεσθαι¹¹⁶ τὸν θεόν σαφὲς¹¹⁷ αὐτῷ γενέσθαι τίνος χάριν τὸ συμβαῖνόν ἐστι. ³¹⁵Δι' ὀνείρου¹¹⁸ δὲ σημανθέντος,¹¹⁹ ὅτι τὰ θεῖα¹²⁰ βούλεται¹²¹ περιεργασάμενος¹²² εἰς κοινοὺς ἀνθρώπους ἐκφέρειν, ἀποσχόμενον¹²³ δὲ οὕτως ἀποκαταστῆναι.¹²⁴ ³¹⁶Καὶ παρὰ Θεοδέκτου¹²⁵ δὲ¹²⁶ τοῦ τῶν τραγῳδιῶν¹²⁷ ποιητοῦ μετέλαβον ἐγὼ διότι παραφέρειν¹²⁸ μέλλοντός τι τῶν ἀναγεγραμμένων ἐν τῇ βίβλῳ πρός τι δρᾶμα¹²⁹ τὰς

ὄψεις ἀπεγλαυκώθη·¹³⁰ καὶ λαβὼν ὑπόνοιαν¹³¹ ὅτι διὰ τοῦτ' αὐτῷ τὸ σύμπτωμα¹³² γέγονεν, ἐξιλασάμενος τὸν θεὸν ἐν πολλαῖς ἡμέραις ἀποκατέστη.

NOTES

110. Compar., ἐπισφαλής -ές, *highly dubious*; adv. προσιστορεῖν.
111. Pres. act. inf., προσιστορέω, *narrate*.
112. ταραχή, -ῆς, ἡ, *disturbance*; with gen.
113. Aor. act. opt. 3 sg., λαμβάνω; oblique opt. in reported speech (cf. S §1862; *CGCG* §41.12). The shift puts the reporter between the original speaker and the addressee (cf. *CGCG* §41.13).
114. Compar., πολύς, πολλή, πολύ, *more*; with gen. compar.; acc. of extent (time).
115. ἄνεσις, -εως, ἡ, *remission, abatement*. The preposition κατά functions as a marker of temporal aspect (cf. BDAG, 512.2): "at its [mental upset] abatement."
116. Pres. mid. inf., ἐξιλάσκομαι, *propitiate*; indir. disc. See n. 103.
117. σαφής, -ές, *clear*; pred. adj., "to make *clear* to him why this happened."
118. ὄνειρος, -ου, ὁ, *dream*.
119. Aor. pass. ptc. gen. masc. sg., σημαίνω, (pass.) *be shown*.
120. θεῖος, -α, -ον, *divine*.
121. Pres. mid. indic. 3 sg., βούλομαι, *desire*; with inf.
122. Aor. mid. ptc. nom. masc. sg., περιεργάζομαι, *meddle, interfere with*; circ. (manner).
123. Aor. mid. ptc. acc. masc. sg., ἀπέχω, (mid.) *cease*. The circumstantial participle is in the accusative case to agree with the subject of indirect discourse (ἔφησεν).
124. Aor. pass. inf., ἀποκαθίστημι, (pass.) *be restored*; indir. disc. See n. 103.
125. Theodektes was "a fourth-century BCE rhetorician and tragic poet. He was a friend of Aristotle. Both he and Theopompus were students of Isocrates" (Wright 2015, 453). For an example of a Jewish dramatist who took license with the biblical text, see Ezekiel the Tragedian (see §3.5.2).
126. Partic. combination, *and furthermore*: "Introduces new, closely related information (καί), which is nevertheless somehow distinct from the preceding context (δέ)" (cf. *CGCG* §59.67).
127. τραγῳδία, -ας, ἡ, *tragedy*.
128. Pres. act. inf., παραφέρω, *bring over to*; comp. of μέλλοντος; gen. absol.
129. δρᾶμα, -ατος, τό, *drama, play*.

301. τὴν νῆσον. Cf. Wright (2015, 435): "Later ancient tradition and most modern scholars identify that island as Pharos, location of the famous lighthouse (see especially Philo, *Mos.* 2.35), and the ancient geographer Strabo (first century BCE) describes a seven stadia long breakwater that reached Pharos from the mainland and that had two openings for ships (17.792)."

305. Pseudo-Aristeas associates handwashing and prayer as being customary of "all the Jews" (cf. Sib. Or. 3:591–593; Mark 7:3). Translators disagree on the relationship between these two actions. Some (e.g., Hadas 1951, 219; Pelletier 1962, 233) translate them as two coordinated actions. Shutt (*OTP* 2:33) takes ὡς ἄν plus the subjunctive temporally: "They wash their hands in the sea in the course of their prayers to God." Wright (2015, 434), by contrast, understands ὡς ἄν plus the subjunctive as expressing purpose: "When they had washed their hands in the sea in order that they might offer prayer to God." He bolsters his interpretation by noting other examples of ritual washing before prayer (440; cf. Jdt. 12:7–8; Sib. Or. 3:591–593).

τὴν ἀνάγνωσιν καὶ τὴν ἑκάστου διασάφησιν. Scholars note similarities between the practice of the Jewish translators and those of the Alexandrian grammarians, who would read Homer aloud (ἀνάγνωσιν) and offer explanation (ἐξήγησις) of various poetic tropes (Hadas 1951, 218; Honigman

130. Aor. pass. indic. 3 sg., ἀπογλαυκόομαι, *be afflicted with glaucoma*; τὰς ὄψεις, "in the eyes."
131. ὑπόνοια, -ας, ἡ, *suspicion, conjecture*.
132. σύμπτωμα, -ατος, τό, (in diseases) *symptom*.

2003, 47). Pseudo-Aristeas may have chosen the uncommon term διασάφησις to distinguish the work of the translators from the kind of ἐξήγησις in which the Alexandrian grammarians were engaged or, at the very least, to make clear that their interpretation depended on inspiration from the Jewish God (Wright 2015, 437).

310. τῶν ἀπὸ τοῦ πολιτεύματος. πολίτευμα "has a range of meanings and represents different sorts of organizational possibilities—from an ethnic political organization in which its officials had jurisdiction over certain judicial and regulatory matters regulated by their ethnic laws (πάτριοι νόμοι) to a voluntary civil organization" (Wright 2015, 448). Scholars debate whether the group Pseudo-Aristeas mentions constitutes an official political body or a voluntary association.

3.2

Joseph and Aseneth

Joseph and Aseneth responds to the Bible's silence on the question of how the daughter of an Egyptian priest, Aseneth (MT: אָסְנַת; LXX: Ἀσεννέθ), became the matriarch of two of the twelve tribes of Israel (Ephraim and Manasseh). The writer, an Egyptian Jew writing sometime between the second century BCE and the second century CE,[1] answers the question in the form of a novella that employs features of the Greek Jewish scriptures and Hellenistic romances.[2] Aseneth's desire for Joseph leads her to recognize the insurmountable chasm between herself and this "son of God"—that is, between worshipers of dead idols (gentiles) and worshipers of the living God (Jews). As a result, she enters a seven-day period of repentance, after which she is invited by an angel to partake of the same heavenly food as Joseph, who now recognizes her as a member of the covenant people and thus as a suitable spouse.

The reading passages encompass two pivotal moments in the narrative. The first recounts Joseph's rejection of Aseneth, followed by his prayer for her conversion. In the second, the archangel Michael invites Aseneth to partake of the heavenly food that is reserved for the covenant people.

Text: Burchard 2003[3]
Recommended Translation: Burchard, OTP
Supplemental Scripture: Gen. 41:45, 50; 46:20; John 6:35–59

---

1. Cf. Burchard, OTP 2:187, "Every competent scholar has since [Batiffol 1889–90] affirmed that Joseph and Aseneth is Jewish, with perhaps some Christian interpolations; none has put the book much after A.D. 200, and some have placed it as early as the second century B.C. As to the place of origin, the majority of scholars look to Egypt. Those in favor of a Semitic origin suggest Palestine; and there is a plea for Syria." The point is slightly overstated since there are highly competent scholars (e.g., Kraemer 1998) who argue, albeit not persuasively, that the author is a Christian.

2. For a comparison between Joseph and Aseneth and Hellenistic romances, see Philonenko 1968, 43–48.

3. Burchard's "longer version" (2003) differs significantly from Philonenko's "shorter version" (1968). I have adopted the style of versification in Burchard's English translation (OTP 2:202–47), which includes the versification in Philonenko's edition in parenthesis. So, for example, 8:5 (4) = 8:5 (Burchard), 8:4 (Philonenko).

3.2.1

Joseph Prays for Aseneth's Conversion

Joseph and Aseneth 8:5–9 (4–11)

8:5 (4)καὶ ὡς προσῆλθεν Ἀσενὲθ φιλῆσαι¹ τὸν Ἰωσὴφ ἐξέτεινεν² Ἰωσὴφ τὴν χεῖρα αὐτοῦ τὴν δεξιὰν καὶ ἔθηκε πρὸς τὸ στῆθος³ αὐτῆς ἀνάμεσον⁴ τῶν δύο μασθῶν⁵ αὐτῆς καὶ ἦσαν οἱ μασθοὶ αὐτῆς ἤδη ἑστῶτες ὥσπερ μῆλα⁶ ὡραῖα.⁷ **(5)**καὶ εἶπεν Ἰωσήφ· "οὐκ ἔστι προσῆκον⁸ ἀνδρὶ θεοσεβεῖ⁹ ὃς εὐλογεῖ¹⁰ τῷ στόματι αὐτοῦ τὸν θεὸν τὸν ζῶντα καὶ ἐσθίει ἄρτον εὐλογημένον ζωῆς καὶ πίνει ποτήριον¹¹ εὐλογημένον ἀθανασίας¹² καὶ χρίεται¹³ χρίσματι¹⁴ εὐλογημένῳ ἀφθαρσίας¹⁵ φιλῆσαι γυναῖκα ἀλλοτρίαν¹⁶ ἥτις εὐλογεῖ τῷ στόματι αὐτῆς εἴδωλα νεκρὰ καὶ κωφὰ¹⁷ καὶ ἐσθίει ἐκ τῆς τραπέζης¹⁸ αὐτῶν ἄρτον ἀγχόνης¹⁹ καὶ πίνει ἐκ τῆς σπονδῆς²⁰ αὐτῶν ποτήριον ἐνέδρας²¹ καὶ χρίεται χρίσματι ἀπωλείας.²² **6(6)**ἀλλ' ἀνὴρ θεοσεβὴς φιλήσει τὴν μητέρα αὐτοῦ καὶ τὴν ἀδελφὴν τὴν ἐκ τῆς μητρὸς αὐτοῦ καὶ τὴν ἀδελφὴν τὴν ἐκ τῆς φυλῆς²³ καὶ τῆς συγγενείας²⁴ αὐτοῦ καὶ τὴν γυναῖκα τὴν σύγκοιτον²⁵ αὐτοῦ αἵτινες εὐλογοῦσι τῷ στόματι αὐτῶν τὸν θεὸν τὸν ζῶντα· **7(7)**ὁμοίως καὶ γυναικὶ θεοσεβεῖ οὐκ ἔστι προσῆκον φιλῆσαι ἄνδρα ἀλλότριον διότι βδέλυγμα²⁶ ἐστι τοῦτο ἐνώπιον κυρίου τοῦ θεοῦ." **8(8)**καὶ ὡς ἤκουσεν Ἀσενὲθ τὰ ῥήματα

---

1. Aor. act. inf., φιλέω, *kiss*; purpose (cf. BDF §390; S §2009; CGCG §51.16).
2. Aor. act. indic. 3 sg., ἐκτείνω, *stretch out*.
3. στῆθος, -εος, τό, *chest*.
4. ἀνάμεσος, -ον, *between*; with gen.
5. μαστός, -οῦ, ὁ, *breast*.
6. μῆλον, -ου, τό, *apple*.
7. ὡραῖος, -α, -ον, (of fruits in season) *ripe*.
8. Pres. act. ptc. nom. neut. sg., προσήκω, quasi-impers. periphrastic, "it is not fitting"; with dat. and inf. (cf. BDF §393; S §1985; CGCG §§ 36.3–4).
9. θεοσεβής, -ές, *pious, God worshiper*.
10. Pres. act. indic. 3 sg., εὐλογέω, *bless*.
11. ποτήριον, -ου, τό, *cup*.
12. ἀθανασία, -ας, ἡ, *immortality*.
13. Pres. pass. indic. 3 sg., χρίω, (pass.) *be anointed*.
14. χρῖσμα, -ατος, τό, *anointing, unction*.
15. ἀφθαρσία, -ας, ἡ, *incorruptibility*.
16. ἀλλότριος, -α, -ον, *strange, foreign*.
17. κωφός, -ή, -όν, *mute*.
18. τράπεζα, -ης, ἡ, *table*.
19. ἀγχόνη, -ης, ἡ, *strangulation, hanging*. MS D reads αἰσχύνης, bread "of shame" (cf. Burchard 2003, 117).
20. σπονδή, -ῆς, ἡ, *libation*.
21. ἐνέδρα, -ας, ἡ, lit., *lying in ambush*, (metaph.) *treachery*.
22. ἀπώλεια, -ας, ἡ, *destruction*.
23. φυλή, -ῆς, ἡ, *tribe, clan*.
24. συγγενεία, -ας, ἡ, *family, kinsfolk*.
25. σύγκοιτος, -ου, ὁ/ἡ, *bedfellow*.
26. βδέλυγμα, -ατος, τό, *abomination*; pred. nom.

ταῦτα Ἰωσὴφ κατενύγη²⁷ ἰσχυρῶς²⁸ καὶ ἐλυπήθη²⁹ σφόδρα³⁰ καὶ ἀνεστέναξε³¹ καὶ ἦν ἀτενίζουσα³² εἰς τὸν Ἰωσὴφ ἀνεῳγμένων³³ τῶν ὀφθαλμῶν αὐτῆς καὶ ἐπλήσθησαν³⁴ δακρύων³⁵ οἱ ὀφθαλμοὶ αὐτῆς. **⁽⁹⁾** καὶ εἶδεν αὐτὴν Ἰωσὴφ καὶ ἠλέησεν³⁶ αὐτὴν σφόδρα καὶ κατενύγη καὶ αὐτὸς διότι ἦν Ἰωσὴφ πραΰς³⁷ καὶ ἐλεήμων³⁸ καὶ φοβούμενος τὸν θεόν. ⁹καὶ ἐπῆρε³⁹ τὴν χεῖρα αὐτοῦ τὴν δεξιὰν καὶ ἔθηκεν ἐπάνω⁴⁰ τῆς κεφαλῆς αὐτῆς καὶ εἶπε·

> **⁽¹⁰⁾**"Κύριε ὁ θεὸς τοῦ πατρός μου Ἰσραὴλ
> ὁ ὕψιστος⁴¹ ὁ δυνατὸς τοῦ Ἰακὼβ
> ὁ ζωοποιήσας⁴² τὰ πάντα
> καὶ καλέσας ἀπὸ τοῦ σκότους εἰς τὸ φῶς
> καὶ ἀπὸ τῆς πλάνης⁴³ εἰς τὴν ἀλήθειαν
> καὶ ἀπὸ τοῦ θανάτου εἰς τὴν ζωήν
> σὺ κύριε εὐλόγησον τὴν παρθένον⁴⁴ ταύτην
> **⁽¹¹⁾**καὶ ἀνακαίνισον⁴⁵ αὐτὴν τῷ πνεύματί σου
> καὶ ἀνάπλασον⁴⁶ αὐτὴν τῇ χειρί σου τῇ
>   [κρυφαίᾳ]⁴⁷
> καὶ ἀναζωοποίησον⁴⁸ αὐτὴν τῇ ζωῇ σου
> καὶ φαγέτω ἄρτον ζωῆς σου
> καὶ πιέτω ποτήριον εὐλογίας σου
> καὶ συγκαταρίθμησον⁴⁹ αὐτὴν τῷ λαῷ σου⁵⁰
> ὃν ἐξελέξω⁵¹ πρὶν γενέσθαι⁵² τὰ πάντα
> καὶ εἰσελθάτω εἰς τὴν κατάπαυσίν⁵³ σου
> ἣν ἡτοίμασας⁵⁴ τοῖς ἐκλεκτοῖς σου.
> καὶ ζησάτω ἐν τῇ αἰωνίῳ ζωῇ σου εἰς τὸν
>   αἰῶνα χρόνον."

NOTES

8:5–7 (4–7). Joseph's response to Aseneth is illustrative of the antithesis between Jews and Egyptians (Philonenko 1968, 49). Hicks-Keeton (2018, 22) notes,

> An important clue in the story suggests that the boundaries the narrative attempts to enact between Hebrew Joseph and Egyptian persons and his host culture are meant to carry relevance not only for the patriarch but also for *Joseph and Aseneth*'s original readers, living centuries after the narrative setting. . . . Nothing in the plotline of *Joseph and Aseneth* demands that Joseph extend his prohibition to a woman. Not only is there no female character considering an exogamous union, but—at this point in the story—there simply is no woman who worships God. What *Joseph and Aseneth* does here is use the character of Joseph to articulate the proper behavior of God-worshippers more broadly, generalizing Joseph's refusal to kiss Aseneth into an example for its readers to follow.

27. Aor. pass. indic. 3 sg., κατανύσσω, (pass.) *be sorely pricked* (to the heart).
28. Adv., *strongly, greatly*.
29. Aor. pass. indic. 3 sg., λυπέω, (pass.) *be grieved*.
30. Adv., *greatly, exceedingly*.
31. Aor. act. indic. 3 sg., ἀναστενάζω, *groan*.
32. Pres. act. ptc. nom. fem. sg., ἀτενίζω, *stare/gaze at*; periphrastic.
33. Pf. pass. ptc. gen. masc. pl., ἀνοίγω, (pass.) *be open*; gen. absol.
34. Aor. pass. indic. 3 pl., πίμπλημι, (pass.) *be full of*; with gen.
35. δάκρυον, -ου, τό, *tears* (usually pl.).
36. Aor. act. indic. 3 sg., ἐλεέω, *have mercy*.
37. πραΰς, -εῖα, -ύ, *meek, gentle*.
38. ἐλεήμων, -ον, *merciful*.
39. Aor. act. indic. 3 sg., ἐπαίρω, *lift*.
40. Prep. with gen., *above*.
41. ὕψιστος, -η, -ον, (divine epithet) *Most High*.
42. Aor. act. ptc. nom. masc. sg., ζωοποιέω, *make alive, give life*; attrib. (subst.).
43. πλάνη, -ης, ἡ, *going astray, wandering* (in error).
44. παρθένος, -ου, ἡ, *virgin, maiden*.
45. Aor. act. impv. 2 sg., ἀνακαινίζω, *renew*.
46. Aor. act. impv. 2 sg., ἀναπλάσσω, *form anew*.
47. κρύφαιος, -α, -ον, *hidden*.
48. Aor. act. impv. 2 sg., ἀναζωοποιέω, *make alive again*.
49. Aor. act. impv. 2 sg., συγκαταριθμέω, *number among*.
50. Philonenko (1968, 158) omits this line. Burchard (2003, 120) cites MSS E G as witnesses that include the line but in a different place (i.e., after the following line).
51. Aor. mid. indic. 2 sg., ἐκλέγω, *choose, elect*.
52. πρὶν (ἤ) with an infinitive expresses action subsequent to the main verb (cf. BDF §395; S §2453; CGCG §47.14).
53. κατάπαυσις, -εως, ἡ, *rest*.
54. Aor. act. indic. 2 sg., ἑτοιμάζω, *prepare*.

8:5 (5). καὶ ἐσθίει ἄρτον εὐλογημένον ζωῆς καὶ πίνει ποτήριον εὐλογημένον ἀθανασίας καὶ χρίεται χρίσματι εὐλογημένῳ ἀφθαρσίας. In Burchard's edition, the triad of bread, cup, and oil appears a total of three times (8:5; 15:5; 16:16; once in Philonenko, 15:4 [Burchard's 15:5]), as does the dyad of bread and cup (8:9; 19:5; 21:21; twice in Philonenko, 8:5, 11 [Burchard's 8:9]). Scholars dispute whether the so-called meal formula envisages some sort of ritual meal or mundane self-maintenance (cf. Burchard, *OTP* 2:211*n*i). For further discussion, see Burchard (1987) and Chesnutt (1995, 20–64, 128–35). On the inclusion of oil in the meal formula, see Chesnutt (2005, 132), who concludes, "Though expressive of the whole Jewish way of life, this language [in the meal formula] grows out of and represents something very concrete in the Jewish community—the effort to maintain a distinctive way of life in precisely those daily realities where susceptibility to gentile impurity was considered greatest, namely, food, drink, and oil contaminated by idolatry."

3.2.2

Aseneth Partakes of the Heavenly Food

Joseph and Aseneth 15:1–10 (1–11); 15:13–16:16 (15:14–16:9)

15:1 (1)Καὶ ἦλθε πρὸς τὸν ἄνθρωπον[1] εἰς τὸν θάλαμον[2] αὐτῆς τὸν πρῶτον καὶ ἔστη ἐνώπιον αὐτοῦ. καὶ εἶπεν αὐτῇ ὁ ἄνθρωπος· "ἀπόστειλον[3] δὴ[4] τὸ θέριστον[5] ἀπὸ τῆς κεφαλῆς σου καὶ ἵνα τί[6] σὺ τοῦτο πεποίηκας; διότι σὺ εἶ παρθένος[7] ἁγνὴ[8] σήμερον[9] καὶ ἡ κεφαλή σοῦ ἐστιν ὡς ἀνδρὸς νεανίσκου." [10] **2 (2)**καὶ ἀπέστειλεν Ἀσενὲθ τὸ θέριστρον ἀπὸ τῆς κεφαλῆς αὐτῆς. καὶ εἶπεν αὐτῇ ὁ ἄνθρωπος· "θάρσει[11] Ἀσενὲθ ἡ παρθένος ἁγνή. ἰδοὺ ἀκήκοα πάντων τῶν ῥημάτων τῆς ἐξομολογήσεώς[12] σου καὶ τῆς προσευχῆς[13] σου. **3**ἰδοὺ ἑώρακα καὶ τὴν ταπείνωσιν[14] καὶ τὴν θλῖψιν[15] τῶν ἑπτὰ ἡμερῶν τῆς ἐνδείας[16] σου. ἰδοὺ ἐκ τῶν δακρύων[17] σου καὶ τῆς τέφρας[18] ταύτης πηλὸς[19] πολὺς γέγονε πρὸ προσώπου σου. **4 (3)**θάρσει Ἀσενὲθ ἡ παρθένος ἁγνή. ἰδοὺ γὰρ ἐγράφη τὸ ὄνομά σου ἐν βίβλῳ τῶν ζώντων ἐν τῷ οὐρανῷ ἐν ἀρχῇ τῆς βίβλου πρῶτον πάντων [ἐγράφη] τὸ ὄνομά σου τῷ δακτύλῳ[20] μου καὶ οὐκ ἐξαλειφθήσεται[21] εἰς τὸν αἰῶνα. **5 (4)**ἰδοὺ δὴ ἀπὸ τῆς σήμερον ἀνακαινισθήσῃ[22] καὶ ἀναπλασθήσῃ[23] καὶ ἀναζωοποιηθήσῃ[24] καὶ φάγεις ἄρτον εὐλογημένον ζωῆς καὶ πιεῖς[25] ποτήριον[26] εὐλογημένον ἀθανασίας[27] καὶ

1. The referent is the man from heaven (cf. 14:2).
2. θάλαμος, -ου, ὁ, *chamber*.
3. Aor. act. impv. 2 sg., ἀποστέλλω, *remove* (clothing).
4. Partic.: "indicates that the speaker considers (and invites the addressee to consider) the text segment or word (group) which it modifies as evident, clear, or precise" (*CGCG* §59.44). δή is the only postpositive particle the writer uses with any frequency (eleven times), which except in 26:1, always underscores an imperative (Philonenko 1968, 30).
5. θέριστον, -ου, τό, *veil*.
6. ἵνα τί, *For what purpose?*, *Why?*
7. παρθένος, -ου, ἡ, *virgin, maiden*.
8. ἁγνός, -ή, -όν, *pure, chaste*.
9. Adv., *today*.
10. νεανίσκος, -ου, ὁ, *young man*.
11. Pres. act. impv. 2 sg., θαρσέω, *be of good courage*.
12. ἐξομολόγησις, -εως, ἡ, *confession*.
13. προσευχή, -ῆς, ἡ, *prayer*.

14. ταπείνωσις, -εως, ἡ, *humiliation*.
15. θλῖψις, -εως, ἡ, *affliction*.
16. ἔνδεια, -ας, ἡ, *lack of* (something). In context, it refers to a lack of food from fasting.
17. δάκρυον, -ου, τό, *tears* (usually pl.).
18. τέφρα, -ας, ἡ, *ashes*.
19. πηλός, -οῦ, ὁ, *mud*.
20. δάκτυλος, -ου, ὁ, *finger*; dat. of instrument.
21. Fut. pass. indic. 3 sg., ἐξαλείφω, (pass.) *be wiped out / erased*.
22. Fut. pass. indic. 2 sg., ἀνακαινίζω, (pass.) *be renewed*.
23. Fut. pass. indic. 2 sg., ἀναπλάσσω, (pass.) *be formed anew*.
24. Fut. pass. indic. 2 sg., ἀναζωοποιέω, (pass.) *be made alive again*.
25. Fut. act. indic. 2 sg., πίνω, *drink*.
26. ποτήριον, -ου, τό, *cup*.
27. ἀθανασία, -ας, ἡ, *immortality*.

χρισθήση²⁸ χρίσματι²⁹ εὐλογημένῳ τῆς ἀφθαρσίας.³⁰ **6 ⁽⁵⁾**θάρσει Ἀσενὲθ ἡ παρθένος ἁγνή. ἰδοὺ δέδωκέν σε σήμερον νύμφην³¹ τῷ Ἰωσὴφ καὶ αὐτὸς ἔσται σου νυμφίος³² εἰς τὸν αἰῶνα χρόνον. **⁷ ⁽⁶⁾**καὶ τὸ ὄνομά σου οὐκέτι κληθήσεται³³ Ἀσενὲθ ἀλλ' ἔσται τὸ ὄνομά σου πόλις καταφυγῆς³⁴ διότι ἐν σοὶ καταφεύξονται³⁵ ἔθνη πολλὰ ἐπὶ κύριον τὸν θεὸν τὸν ὕψιστον³⁶ καὶ ὑπὸ τὰς πτέρυγάς³⁷ σου σκεπασθήσονται³⁸ λαοὶ πολλοὶ πεποιθότες³⁹ ἐπὶ κυρίῳ [τῷ θεῷ] καὶ ἐν τῷ τείχει⁴⁰ σου διαφυλαχθήσονται⁴¹ οἱ προσκείμενοι⁴² τῷ θεῷ τῷ ὑψίστῳ⁴³ [ἐν ὀνόματι τῆς] μετανοίας.⁴⁴ **⁽⁷⁾**διότι ἡ μετάνοιά ἐστι ἐν τοῖς οὐρανοῖς θυγάτηρ ὑψίστου καλὴ καὶ ἀγαθὴ σφόδρα.⁴⁵ καὶ αὐτὴ ἐκλιπαρεῖ⁴⁶ τὸν θεὸν τὸν ὕψιστον ὑπὲρ σοῦ πᾶσαν ὥραν καὶ ὑπὲρ πάντων τῶν μετανοούντων⁴⁷ ἐν ὀνόματι θεοῦ τοῦ ὑψίστου ἐπειδὴ πατήρ ἐστι τῆς μετανοίας. καὶ [αὐτή] ἐστιν ἐπίσκοπος⁴⁸ πάντων τῶν παρθένων καὶ φιλεῖ ὑμᾶς σφόδρα καὶ περὶ ὑμῶν ἐρωτᾷ⁴⁹ πᾶσαν ὥραν τὸν ὕψιστον καὶ πᾶσι τοῖς μετανοοῦσι τόπον ἀναπαύσεως⁵⁰ ἡτοίμασεν⁵¹ ἐν τοῖς οὐρανοῖς καὶ ἀνακαινιεῖ πάντας τοὺς μετανοήσαντας καὶ [αὐτὴ] διακονήσει⁵² αὐτοῖς εἰς τὸν αἰῶνα χρόνον. **⁸ ⁽⁸⁾**καὶ ἔστιν ἡ μετάνοια καλὴ σφόδρα παρθένος καθαρὰ⁵³ καὶ γελῶσα⁵⁴ πάντοτε καὶ ἔστιν ἐπιεικὴς⁵⁵ καὶ πραεῖα.⁵⁶ καὶ διὰ τοῦτο ὁ πατὴρ ὁ ὕψιστος ἀγαπᾷ αὐτὴν καὶ πάντες οἱ ἄγγελοι αἰδοῦνται⁵⁷ αὐτήν. κἀγὼ ἀγαπῶ αὐτὴν σφόδρα διότι ἀδελφή μού ἐστι καὶ αὐτή. καὶ καθότι⁵⁸ ὑμᾶς τὰς παρθένους ἀγαπᾷ κἀγὼ ὑμᾶς ἀγαπῶ. **⁹ ⁽⁹⁾**καὶ ἰδοὺ ἐγὼ ἀπέρχομαι πρὸς Ἰωσὴφ καὶ λαλήσω αὐτῷ περὶ σοῦ πάντα τὰ ῥήματά μου. καὶ ἐλεύσεται πρὸς σὲ Ἰωσὴφ σήμερον καὶ ὄψεταί σε καὶ χαρήσεται ἐπὶ σὲ καὶ ἀγαπήσει σε καὶ ἔσται σου νυμφίος καὶ σὺ ἔσῃ αὐτῷ νύμφη εἰς τὸν αἰῶνα χρόνον. **¹⁰ ⁽¹⁰⁾**καὶ νῦν ἄκουσόν μου Ἀσενὲθ ἡ παρθένος ἁγνὴ καὶ ἔνδυσαι⁵⁹ τὴν στολὴν⁶⁰ γάμου⁶¹ σου τὴν στολὴν τὴν ἀρχαίαν⁶² καὶ πρώτην τὴν ἀποκειμένην⁶³ ἐν τῷ θαλάμῳ σου ἀπ' ἀρχῆς καὶ πάντα τὸν κόσμον⁶⁴ τοῦ γάμου σου περίθου⁶⁵ καὶ κατακόσμησον⁶⁶ σεαυτὴν ὡς νύμφην ἀγαθὴν καὶ πορεύου εἰς συνάντησιν⁶⁷ τῷ Ἰωσήφ. **⁽¹¹⁾**ἰδοὺ γὰρ αὐτὸς παραγίνεται πρὸς σὲ σήμερον καὶ ὄψεταί σε καὶ χαρήσεται." . . .

¹³ ⁽¹⁴⁾Καὶ εἶπεν Ἀσενὲθ "εἰ εὗρον χάριν ἐνώπιόν σου κύριε καὶ γνώσομαι ὅτι ποιήσεις πάντα τὰ ῥήματά σου ὅσα εἶπας πρὸς με λαλησάτω δὴ ἡ παιδίσκη⁶⁸ σου ἐνώπιόν σου." **¹⁴**καὶ εἶπεν αὐτῇ ὁ ἄνθρωπος· "λάλησον." [καὶ] ἐξέτεινε⁶⁹ Ἀσενὲθ τὴν χεῖρα αὐτῆς τὴν δεξιὰν

28. Fut. pass. indic. 2 sg., χρίω, (pass.) *be anointed*.
29. χρῖσμα, -ατος, τό, *anointing, unction*; dat. of instrument.
30. ἀφθαρσία, -ας, ἡ, *incorruptibility*.
31. νύμφη, -ης, ἡ, *bride*; pred. comp.
32. νυμφίος, -ου, ὁ, *bridegroom*.
33. Fut. pass. indic. 3 sg., καλέω, (pass.) *be called*.
34. καταφυγή, -ῆς, ἡ, *refuge*.
35. Fut. mid. indic. 3 pl., καταφεύγω, *flee for refuge*.
36. ὕψιστος, -η, -ον, (divine epithet) *Most High*.
37. πτέρυξ, -γας, ἡ, *wing*.
38. Fut. pass. indic. 3 pl., σκεπάζω, (pass.) *be sheltered*.
39. Pf. act. ptc. nom. masc. pl., πείθω, *trust*; with dat.; circ.
40. τεῖχος, -εος, τό, *wall*.
41. Fut. pass. indic. 3 pl., διαφυλάσσω, (pass.) *be guarded*.
42. Pres. mid. ptc. nom. masc. pl., πρόσκειμαι, *cling to*; with dat.; attrib. (subst.).
43. ὕψιστος, -η, -ον, (divine epithet) *Most High*.
44. μετάνοια, -ας, ἡ, *repentance*.
45. Adv., *greatly, exceedingly*.
46. Pres. act. indic. 3 sg., ἐκλιπαρέω, *entreat*.
47. Pres. act. ptc. gen. masc. pl., μετανοέω, *repent*; attrib. (subst.).
48. ἐπίσκοπος, -ου, ὁ, *overseer*.
49. Pres. act. indic. 3 sg., ἐρωτάω, *ask, entreat*.
50. ἀνάπαυσις, -εως, ἡ, *rest*.
51. Aor. act. indic. 3 sg., ἑτοιμάζω, *prepare*.
52. Fut. act. indic. 3 sg., διακονέω, *minister to*; with dat.
53. καθαρός, -ά, -όν, *pure*.
54. Aor. act. ptc. nom. fem. sg., γελάω, *laugh*; attrib.
55. ἐπιεικής, -ές, *gentle*.
56. πραΰς, -εῖα, -ΰ, *meek*.
57. Pres. mid. indic. 3 pl., αἰδέομαι, *revere*.
58. καθότι . . . κἀγώ, *inasmuch as . . . I also*.
59. Aor. mid. impv. 2 sg., ἐνδύω, *put on, wear*.
60. στολή, -ῆς, ἡ, *robe*.
61. γάμος, -ου, ὁ, *wedding*.
62. ἀρχαῖος, -α, -ον, *from the beginning, ancient*.
63. Pres. pass. ptc. acc. fem. sg., ἀπόκειμαι, (pass.) *be stored up*; attrib.
64. κόσμος, -ου, ὁ, *adornment, ornament*.
65. Pres. mid. impv. 2 sg., περιτίθημι, *put around*.
66. Aor. act. impv. 2 sg., κατακοσμέω, *adorn*.
67. συνάντησις, -εως, ἡ, *meeting*.
68. παιδίσκη, -ης, ἡ, *maidservant*.
69. Aor. act. indic. 3 sg., ἐκτείνω, *stretch out*.

καὶ τέθηκεν ἐπὶ τῶν γονάτων⁷⁰ αὐτοῦ καὶ εἶπε [αὐτῷ]· "δέομαι⁷¹ σου κύριε κάθισον⁷² δὴ μικρὸν⁷³ ἐπὶ τῆς κλίνης⁷⁴ ταύτης διότι ἡ κλίνη αὕτη ἐστὶ καθαρὰ καὶ ἀμίαντος⁷⁵ καὶ ἀνὴρ ἢ γυνὴ οὐκ ἐκάθισεν ἐπ' αὐτὴν πώποτε. καὶ παραθήσω σοι τράπεζαν καὶ εἰσοίσω⁷⁶ σοι ἄρτον καὶ φάγεσαι καὶ οἴσω σοι ἐκ τοῦ ταμιείου⁷⁷ μου οἶνον⁷⁸ παλαιὸν⁷⁹ καὶ καλὸν οὗ ἡ πνοὴ⁸⁰ αὐτοῦ ἐλεύσεται ἕως⁸¹ τοῦ οὐρανοῦ καὶ πίεσαι ἐξ αὐτοῦ. καὶ μετὰ ταῦτα ἀπελεύσῃ τὴν ὁδὸν σου." ¹⁵καὶ εἶπεν αὐτῇ ὁ ἄνθρωπος· "σπεῦσον⁸² καὶ φέρε συντόμως."⁸³ ¹⁶:¹καὶ ἔσπευσεν Ἀσενὲθ καὶ παρέθηκεν αὐτῷ τράπεζαν καινὴν καὶ ἐπορεύετο κομίσαι⁸⁴ αὐτῷ ἄρτον.

(16:1)Καὶ εἶπεν αὐτῇ ὁ ἄνθρωπος φέρε δή μοι καὶ κηρίον⁸⁵ μελίσσης.⁸⁶ ²καὶ ἔστη Ἀσενὲθ καὶ ἐλυπήθη⁸⁷ διότι οὐκ εἶχε κηρίον μελίσσης ἐν τῷ ταμιείῳ αὐτῆς. ³καὶ εἶπεν αὐτῇ ὁ ἄνθρωπος· "τίνος χάριν ἵστασαι;" ⁴ ⁽²⁾καὶ εἶπεν Ἀσενέθ· "πέμψω⁸⁸ δὴ παιδάριον⁸⁹ εἰς τὸ προάστειον⁹⁰ διότι ἐγγὺς⁹¹ ἐστιν ὁ ἀγρὸς⁹² τῆς κλη-ρονομίας⁹³ ἡμῶν καὶ οἴσει σοι ἐκεῖθεν ταχέως⁹⁴ κηρίον μελίσσης καὶ παραθήσω σοι κύριε." ⁵ ⁽³⁾καὶ εἶπεν αὐτῇ ὁ ἄνθρωπος· "βάδιζε⁹⁵ καὶ εἴσελθε εἰς τὸ ταμιεῖόν σου καὶ εὑρήσεις κηρίον μελίσσης ἐπὶ τῆς τραπέζης κείμενον. ἆρον αὐτὸ καὶ κόμισον⁹⁶ ὧδε." ⁶καὶ εἶπεν Ἀσενέθ· "κύριε κηρίον μελίσσης ἐν τῷ ταμιείῳ μου οὐκ ἔστιν." ⁷καὶ εἶπεν ὁ ἄνθρωπος· "βάδιζε καὶ εὑρήσεις." ⁸ ⁽⁴⁾καὶ εἰσῆλθεν Ἀσενὲθ εἰς τὸ ταμιεῖον αὐτῆς καὶ εὗρε κηρίον μελίσσης κείμενον ἐπὶ τῆς τραπέζης. καὶ ἦν τὸ κηρίον μέγα καὶ λευκὸν⁹⁷ ὡσεὶ χιὼν⁹⁸ καὶ πλῆρης⁹⁹ μέλιτος.¹⁰⁰ καὶ ἦν τὸ μέλι ἐκεῖνο ὡς δρόσος¹⁰¹ τοῦ οὐρανοῦ καὶ ἡ πνοὴ αὐτοῦ ὡς πνοὴ ζωῆς. ⁹καὶ ἐθαύμασεν Ἀσενὲθ καὶ εἶπεν ἐν ἑαυτῇ· "ἆρα γε¹⁰² τὸ κηρίον τοῦτο ἐκ τοῦ στόματος τοῦ ἀνθρώπου τούτου ἐξῆλθε διότι ἡ πηνὴ αὐτοῦ ὡς πνοὴ τοῦ στόματος [τοῦ ἀνθρώπου τούτου] ἐστίν." ¹⁰ ⁽⁵⁾καὶ ἔλαβεν Ἀσενὲθ τὸ κηρίον ἐκεῖνο καὶ ἤνεγκε τῷ ἀνθρώπῳ καὶ παρέθηκεν αὐτὸ ἐπὶ τῆς τραπέζης [ἣν ἡτοίμασεν ἐνώπιον αὐτοῦ].

Καὶ εἶπεν αὐτῇ ὁ ἄνθρωπος· "τί ὅτι εἶπας ὅτι οὐκ ἔστι κηρίον μελίσσης ἐν τῷ ταμιείῳ μου; καὶ ἰδοὺ ἐνήνοχας¹⁰³ κηρίον μελίσσης θαυμαστόν." ¹¹ ⁽⁶⁾καὶ ἐφοβήθη Ἀσενὲθ καὶ εἶπεν· "κύριε ἐγὼ οὐκ εἶχον κηρίον μέλιτος ἐν τῷ [ταμιείῳ] μου πώποτε ἀλλὰ σὺ ἐλάλησας καὶ γέγονε. μήτιγε¹⁰⁴ τοῦτο ἐκ τοῦ στόματός σου ἐξῆλθε διότι ἡ πνοὴ αὐτοῦ ὡς πνοὴ [τοῦ στόματος

---

70. γόνυ, -ατος, τό, *knee*.
71. Pres. mid. indic. 1 sg., δέομαι, *beg, beseech*; with gen.
72. Aor. act. impv. 2 sg., καθίζω, *sit*.
73. Acc. of extent (time).
74. κλίνη, -ης, ἡ, *bed*.
75. ἀμίαντος, -ον, *undefiled*.
76. Fut. act. indic. 1 sg., εἰσφέρω, *bring to*.
77. ταμιεῖον, -ου, τό, *storeroom*.
78. οἶνον, -ου, τό, *wine*.
79. παλαιός, -ά, -όν, *old*.
80. πνοή, -ῆς, ἡ, *vapor, exhalation*.
81. Prep. with gen., *as far as*.
82. Aor. act. impv. 2 sg., σπεύδω, *make haste*.
83. Adv., *quickly, immediately*.
84. Aor. act. inf., κομίζω, *prepare*; purpose (cf. BDF §390; S §2009; CGCG §51.16).
85. κηρίον, -ου, τό, *honeycomb*.
86. μέλισσα, -ης, ἡ, *honeybee*. Philonenko reads κηρίον μέλιτος, "comb of honey." Cf. Burchard, *OTP* 2:228*n*b: "The rendering 'honeycomb' may do justice to both variants, as 'bee' perhaps is used in metonymy for 'honey.'"
87. Aor. pass. indic. 3 sg., λυπέω, (pass.) *be grieved*.
88. Fut. act. indic. 1 sg., πέμπω, *send*.
89. παιδάριον, -ου, ὁ, *little boy, young slave*.
90. προάστειος, -ον, *suburban*, (subst.) *suburb*.
91. Adv., *near*.
92. ἀγρός, -οῦ, ὁ, *field*.
93. κληρονομία, -ας, ἡ, *inheritance*.
94. Adv., *quickly*.
95. Pres. act. impv. 2 sg., βαδίζω, *go*.
96. Aor. act. impv., κομίζω, *bring* (to a place).
97. λευκός, -ή, -όν, *white*.
98. χιών, -όνος, ἡ, *snow*.
99. πλήρης, -ες, *full of*; with gen.
100. μέλι, -ιτος, τό, *honey*.
101. δρόσος, -ου, ἡ, *dew*.
102. Burchard reads ἆρα γε as introducing a question but notes, "This could be a statement" (*OTP* 2:228*n*g). The particle ἆρα (or partic. combination ἆρα γε), however, tends to follow interrogatives (cf. Denniston 1966, 39–40). Given its position in the clause, it may be better to take ἆρα γε as marking a declarative statement. Were it marking a question, it would be accented ἆρά γε.
103. Pf. act. indic. 2 sg., φέρω, *carry*.
104. Adv. (μήτι, γε), *not to mention, surely* (cf. BDAG, 649).

σου] ἐστιν;" ¹²καὶ ἐμειδίασεν¹⁰⁵ ὁ ἄνθρωπος ἐπὶ τῇ συνέσει¹⁰⁶ Ἀσενέθ ¹³καὶ ἐκάλεσεν αὐτὴν πρὸς ἑαυτὸν ⁽⁷⁾ καὶ ἐξέτεινε τὴν χεῖρα αὐτοῦ τὴν δεξιὰν καὶ ἐκράτησε τὴν κεφαλὴν αὐτῆς καὶ ἐπέσεισε¹⁰⁷ τῇ χειρὶ αὐτοῦ τῇ δεξιᾷ τὴν κεφαλὴν αὐτῆς. καὶ ἐφοβήθη Ἀσενὲθ τὴν χεῖρα τοῦ ἀνθρώπου διότι σπινθῆρες¹⁰⁸ ἀπεπήδων¹⁰⁹ ἀπὸ τῆς χειρὸς αὐτοῦ ὡς ἀπὸ σιδήρου κοχλάζοντος.¹¹⁰ καὶ ἐπέβλεψεν Ἀσενὲθ ἀτενίζουσα τοῖς ὀφθαλμοῖς αὐτῆς εἰς τὴν χεῖρα τοῦ ἀνθρώρου. ¹⁴[καὶ εἶδεν] ὁ ἄνθρωπος καὶ [ἐμειδίασε] καὶ εἶπεν· "μακαρία εἶ σὺ Ἀσενὲθ διότι ἀπεκαλύφθη σοι τὰ ἀπόρρητα¹¹¹ μυστήρια τοῦ ὑψίστου καὶ μακάριοι πάντες οἱ προσκείμενοι κυρίῳ τῷ θεῷ ἐν μετανοίᾳ ὅτι ἐκ τούτου τοῦ κηρίου φάγονται. ⁽⁸⁾διότι τοῦτο τὸ κηρίον ἐστὶ πνεῦμα ζωῆς. καὶ τοῦτο πεποιήκασιν αἱ μέλισσαι τοῦ παραδείσου¹¹² τῆς τρυφῆς¹¹³ ἐκ τῆς δρόσου τῶν ῥόδων¹¹⁴ τῆς ζωῆς τῶν ὄντων ἐν τῷ παραδείσῳ τοῦ θεοῦ. καὶ πάντες οἱ ἄγγελοι τοῦ θεοῦ ἐξ αὐτοῦ ἐσθίουσι καὶ πάντες οἱ ἐκλεκτοὶ τοῦ θεοῦ καὶ πάντες οἱ υἱοὶ τοῦ ὑψίστου ὅτι κηρίον ζωῆς ἐστι τοῦτο καὶ πᾶς ὃς ἂν φάγῃ ἐξ αὐτοῦ οὐκ ἀποθανεῖται εἰς τὸν αἰῶνα χρόνον."

¹⁵ ⁽⁹⁾Καὶ ἐξέτεινε ὁ ἄνθρωπος τὴν χεῖρα αὐτοῦ τὴν δεξιὰν καὶ ἀπέκλασεν¹¹⁵ ἀπὸ τοῦ κηρίου μέρος μικρὸν καὶ ἔφαγεν <αὐτὸς> καὶ τὸ κατάλοιπον¹¹⁶ ἐνέβαλε τῇ χειρὶ αὐτοῦ εἰς στόμα Ἀσενὲθ καὶ εἶπεν αὐτῇ· "φάγε." καὶ ἔφαγεν. ¹⁶καὶ εἶπεν ὁ <ἄνθρωπος> τῇ Ἀσενέθ· "ἰδοὺ δὴ ἔφαγες ἄρτον ζωῆς καὶ ἔπιες ποτήριον ἀθανασίας καὶ κέχρισαι χρίσματι ἀφθαρσίας. ἰδοὺ δὴ ἀπὸ τῆς σήμερον αἱ σάρκες σου βρύουσιν¹¹⁷ ὡς ἄνθη ζωῆς ἀπὸ τῆς γῆς τοῦ ὑψίστου καὶ τὰ ὀστᾶ¹¹⁸ σου πιανθήσονται¹¹⁹ ὡς αἱ κέδροι¹²⁰ τοῦ παραδείσου τῆς τρυφῆς τοῦ θεοῦ καὶ δυνάμεις ἀκάματοι¹²¹ περισχήσουσί¹²² σε καὶ ἡ νεότης¹²³ σου γῆρας¹²⁴ οὐκ ὄψεται καὶ τὸ κάλλος¹²⁵ σου εἰς τὸν αἰῶνα οὐκ ἐκλείψει.¹²⁶ καὶ ἔσῃ ὡς μητρόπολις¹²⁷ τετειχισμένη¹²⁸ πάντων τῶν καταφευγόντων ἐπὶ τῷ ὀνόματι κυρίου τοῦ θεοῦ <τοῦ βασιλέως τῶν αἰώνων>." ¹⁶ˣκαὶ¹²⁹ ἐξέτεινε τὴν χεῖρα αὐτοῦ <τὴν> δεξιὰν ὁ ἄνθρωπος καὶ ἥψατο¹³⁰ τοῦ κηρίου οὗ¹³¹ ἀπέκλασε καὶ ἀπεκατεστάθη¹³² καὶ ἐπληρώθη καὶ <εὐθὺς> ἐγένετο ὁλόκληρον¹³³ ὡς ἦν ἐν ἀρχῇ.

NOTES

15:1 (1). καὶ ἡ κεφαλή σοῦ ἐστιν ὡς ἀνδρὸς νεανίσκου. Philonenko (1968, 181) takes this to mean that the young man (i.e., the angel Michael) considers Aseneth androgynous. Burchard (*OTP* 2:226*n*b) rightly rejects this interpretation and posits that it may point to the notion of the equality of the sexes before God (cf. 1 Cor. 11:11–12).

105. Aor. act. indic. 3 sg., μειδιάω, *smile*.
106. σύνεσις, -εως, ἡ, *understanding*.
107. Aor. act. indic. 3 sg., ἐπισείω, *shake*.
108. σπινθήρ, -ρος, ὁ, *spark*.
109. Impf. act. indic. 3 pl., ἀποπηδάω, *spring from*.
110. Pres. act. ptc. gen. masc. sg., κοχλάζω, *bubble* (cf. LSJ, 933); attrib.
111. ἀπόρρητος, -ον, *ineffable, secret*.
112. παράδεισος, -ου, ὁ, *enclosed park, garden, paradise* (cf. Gen. 2:15 LXX).
113. τρυφή, -ῆς, ἡ, *delight*. The same term is used to translate the garden of Eden (cf. Gen. 3:23, 24 LXX).
114. ῥόδον, -ου, τό, *rose*.
115. Aor. act. indic. 3 sg., ἀποκλάω, *break off*.
116. κατάλοιπον, -ου, τό, *remainder*.
117. Pres. act. indic. 3 pl., βρύω, *abound, burst forth*, in the sense of "flourish."
118. ὀστέον, -ου, τό, *bone*.
119. Fut. pass. indic. 3 pl., πιαίνω, (intrans.) *grow strong* (cf. "bones" in Isa. 58:11; Sir. 26:13; Prov. 15:32; GELS, 556).
120. κέδρος, -ους, ἡ, *cedar tree*.
121. ἀκάματος, -ον, *untiring*.
122. Fut. act. indic. 3 pl., περιέχω, *enfold, embrace*.
123. νεότης, -ητος, ἡ, *youth*.
124. γῆρας, -ως, τό, *old age*.
125. κάλλος, -ου, τό, *beauty*.
126. Fut. act. indic. 3 sg., ἐκλείπω, *cease*.
127. μητρόπολις, -εως, ἡ, *metropolis, mother-city*.
128. Pf. pass. ptc. nom. fem. sg., τειχίζω, (pass. ptc.) *walled, fortified*; attrib.
129. Burchard follows Riessler's versification and uses the letters *x* and *y* to indicate new material added to the verse (see Burchard, *OTP* 2:200).
130. Aor. mid. indic. 3 sg., ἅπτω, (mid.) *grasp*; with gen.
131. Either adv., *where*, or the relative pronoun ὅν has been attracted to the case of its genitive antecedent.
132. Aor. pass. indic. 3 sg., ἀποκαθίστημι, (pass.) *be restored*.
133. ὁλόκληρος, -ον, *whole*.

15:3 (2). The seven-day repentance cycle echoes the seven days of creation. Thiessen (2014) argues that it also draws on the seven-day processes that culminate on the eighth day in the circumcision of male infants (cf. Gen. 17:12; Lev. 12:3) and the consecration of priests (cf. Lev. 8). Hicks-Keeton (2018, 134) demurs, however, on the grounds that Thiessen's interpretation would require a covenantal paradigm in which "the *telos* of inclusion is 'becoming Jewish.'"

15:4 (3). On the "book of life," cf. Exod. 32:32–33; Ps. 68:29; Isa. 4:3; Dan. 12:1; 1QM 12:1; 1 En. 47:3; 104:1; Jub. 30:22; 36:10; Luke 10:20; Rev. 20:12, 15.

15:7 (6). Aseneth is portrayed as Mother Zion (cf. Isa. 62:4–12; Jer. 50:5; 4 Ezra 9–10; Gal. 4:26). See also 16:16 (9), where the writer describes her "as a walled metropolis for all those who take refuge in the name of the Lord" (cf. Philo, *Conf.* 78; Philo, *Fug.* 94; Philo, *Somn.* 1.41, 181; Philo, *Flacc.* 46; Philo, *Legat.* 203, 281, 294, 305, 334; see also Pearce 2004). The declaration "Many nations [ἔθνη πολλά] will take refuge in you [ἐν σοί]" echoes God's promise to Abraham, "In you [ἐν σοί] all the tribes of the earth shall be blessed" (Gen. 12:3). One might compare this language to Paul's argument in Gal. 3, on which see Hicks-Keeton (2018, 131–35).

16:1 (1). κηρίον μελίσσης. The "honeycomb" symbolizes the manna God rained down from heaven (cf. Exod. 16:31; Josephus, *A.J.* 3.1.6). Both are compared to the dew and said to be white like snow or frost (cf. Exod. 16:13–14; Num. 11:7–9; Jos. Asen. 16:8 (4); Chesnutt 2005, 117n13).

16:14 (8). πάντες οἱ ἄγγελοι τοῦ θεοῦ ἐξ αὐτοῦ ἐσθίουσι. Cf. Ps. 77:24–25a LXX: "He rained on them manna to eat, bread from heaven he gave to them; humans ate the bread of angels [ἄρτον ἀγγέλων ἔφαγεν ἄνθρωπος]" (cf. Wis. 16:20; LAB 19:5). In Joseph and Aseneth not only do the righteous share the same food as angels, but they also become like the angels—that is, "sons and daughters of God" (cf. Jos. Asen. 14:8 (7); 21:4 (3); Collins 2000, 236).

καὶ πᾶς ὃς ἂν φάγῃ ἐξ αὐτοῦ οὐκ ἀποθανεῖται εἰς τὸν αἰῶνα χρόνον. Cf. John 6:50–51.

3.3

Sibylline Oracles

The sibyl, an aged woman known to have uttered ecstatic prophecies, became a fixture of the ancient Mediterranean world (Parke 1988). Her influence spanned across multiple ethnic groups and cultures so that "there were supposed to be multiple sibyls, including Babylonian, Persian, Egyptian, and eventually Hebrew sibyls as well as Greek" (Collins 2000, 83). Jewish writers found her a helpful device "to put the praise of Judaism in the mouth of a pagan prophetess of hoary antiquity and respected authority" (84). Some even constructed their own myth of her origins: she was the daughter, or daughter-in-law, of Noah (cf. Sib. Or. 1:289; 3:827).

The Sibylline Oracles share a set of stylistic and thematic features. First, they are composed in dactylic hexameter, the meter of epic poetry. Second, they tend to focus on predictions of woes and disasters, often in the form of *ex eventu* prophecy, and divide history into distinct periods (Collins, *OTP* 1:318–19). Third, they appear to have been useful as political propaganda. For example, Augustus was said to have destroyed numerous prophecies, including sibylline oracles, because he found them politically subversive (cf. Suetonius, *Aug.* 31.1).

The reading passage is a portion of Sibylline Oracles 3, most of which was composed in the mid-second century BCE in Egypt.[1] I have included the oracle of a deliverer figure (the "king from the sun") followed by the oracles about the final assault on the Jerusalem temple and the salvation of God's elect. For readers who are new to epic poetry, I have included notes on morphology. For a discussion of dactylic hexameter, see §8.1.

Text: Geffcken 1902
Recommended Translation: Collins, *OTP*
Supplemental Scripture: Ps. 2; Isa. 2:1–4; Ezek. 38–39

---

1. Collins 1972, 21–32; *OTP* 1:334–56. For an alternative account, see Buitenwerf 2003, 126–34, who argues that the work is a unified whole written between 80 and 40 BCE in Asia Minor.

3.3.1

A King from the Sun and the Final Assault on the Temple

Sibylline Oracles 3:652–668, 702–723

3:652καὶ τότ' ἀπ' ἠελίοιο[1] θεὸς πέμψει[2] βασιλῆα,[3]
653ὃς πᾶσαν γαῖαν[4] παύσει[5] πολέμοιο[6] κακοῖο,
654οὓς μὲν[7] ἄρα[8] κτείνας,[9] οἷς δ' ὅρκια[10] πιστὰ τελέσσας.[11]

655οὐδέ γε[12] ταῖς ἰδίαις βουλαῖς[13] τάδε πάντα ποιήσει,
656ἀλλὰ θεοῦ μεγάλοιο[14] πιθήσας[15] δόγμασιν[16] ἐσθλοῖς.[17]
657ναὸς[18] δ' αὖ[19] μεγάλοιο θεοῦ περικαλλέι[20] πλούτῳ[21]

---

1. Epic 2nd decl. gen. masc. sg., ἥλιος, -ου, ὁ, *sun* (cf. Benner 2001, 364 [§73]).
2. Fut. act. indic. 3 sg., πέμπω, *send*.
3. The stem is βασιλῆ- (cf. Benner 2001, 366 [§86]). The paradigm of βασιλεύς with which you may be more familiar is the result of quantitative metathesis—i.e., a shift in the length of the vowels: -ῆος to -έως.
4. γαῖα, -ας, ἡ, *earth*; acc. of extent (space).
5. Fut. act. indic. 3 sg., παύω, *make* (acc.), *cease from* (gen.); with gen.
6. πόλεμος, -ου, ὁ, *war*. See n. 1.
7. οὓς μέν ... οἷς δ', *some ... others* (cf. BDF §250; S §1107; CGCG §28.27).
8. Postpositive partic.: "indicates that the speaker, in view of the preceding context, cannot but make the contribution that he/she is making" (CGCG §59.42).
9. Aor. act. ptc. nom. masc. sg., κτείνω, *kill*; circ.
10. ὅρκον, -ου, τό, *oath*; ὅρκια πιστά, "oaths of loyalty" or "treaties."
11. Aor. act. ptc. nom. masc. sg., τελέω, *carry out*; circ.

12. Postpositive partic.: "focuses attention on the word or phrase it follows ... and limits the applicability of the content of the utterance to *at least* or (*more*) *precisely* that specific element" (cf. CGCG §59.53). That is, that the king does *nothing* on his own accord.
13. βουλή, -ῆς, ἡ, *plan, council*.
14. μέγας (μεγάλου), μεγάλη, μέγα, *great*. See n. 1.
15. Aor. act. ptc. nom. masc. sg., πείθω (can shift to πιθ- in fut. and aor.), *obey* or *trust*; with dat; circ.
16. δόγμα, -ατος, τό, *decree, ordinance*.
17. ἐσθλός, -ή, -όν, *noble*.
18. Emendation. MS fam. Φ has λαός; MS fam. Ψ has λαούς. Cf. Buitenwerf 2003, 276: "The word group λαὸς μεγάλοιο θεοῦ does not occur elsewhere in this work; ναὸς μεγάλοιο θεοῦ occurs in lines 274, 565, 575, 657. As regards content, the emendation ναός is obvious."
19. Stronger development than δέ alone (cf. S §2839). Here it marks a shift to a new oracle.
20. περικαλλής, -ές, *very beautiful*.
21. πλοῦτος, -ου, ὁ, *wealth, riches*.

⁶⁵⁸βεβριθώς,²² χρυσῷ²³ τε καὶ ἀργύρῳ²⁴ ἠδέ²⁵ τε κόσμῳ²⁶
⁶⁵⁹πορφυρέῳ·²⁷ καὶ γαῖα τελεσφόρος²⁸ ἠδὲ θάλασσα
⁶⁶⁰τῶν ἀγαθῶν πλήθουσα.²⁹ καὶ ἄρξονται βασιλῆες
⁶⁶¹ἀλλήλοις κοτέειν³⁰ ἐπαμύνοντες³¹ κακὰ θυμῷ·
⁶⁶²ὁ φθόνος³² οὐκ ἀγαθὸν πέλεται³³ δειλοῖσι³⁴ βροτοῖσιν.
⁶⁶³ἀλλὰ πάλιν βασιλῆες ἐθνῶν ἐπὶ τήνδε γε γαῖαν
⁶⁶⁴ἀθρόοι³⁵ ὁρμήσονται³⁶ ἑαυτοῖς κῆρα³⁷ φέροντες·
⁶⁶⁵σηκὸν³⁸ γὰρ μεγάλοιο θεοῦ καὶ φῶτας³⁹ ἀρίστους⁴⁰

⁶⁶⁶πορθεῖν⁴¹ βουλήσονται,⁴² ὁπηνίκα⁴³ γαῖαν ἵκωνται.⁴⁴
⁶⁶⁷θήσουσιν κύκλῳ⁴⁵ πόλεως μιαροὶ⁴⁶ βασιλῆες
⁶⁶⁸τὸν θρόνον αὐτοῦ ἕκαστος ἔχων καὶ λαὸν ἀπειθῆ.⁴⁷
. . . .
⁷⁰²υἱοὶ δ' αὖ⁴⁸ μεγάλοιο θεοῦ περὶ ναὸν⁴⁹ ἅπαντες
⁷⁰³ἡσυχίως⁵⁰ ζήσοντ' εὐφραινόμενοι⁵¹ ἐπὶ τούτοις,
⁷⁰⁴οἷς⁵² δώσει κτίστης⁵³ ὁ δικαιοκρίτης⁵⁴ τε μόναρχος.⁵⁵
⁷⁰⁵αὐτὸς γὰρ σκεπάσειε⁵⁶ μόνος μεγαλωστὶ⁵⁷ παραστάς,⁵⁸
⁷⁰⁶κύκλοθεν ὡσεὶ⁵⁹ τεῖχος⁶⁰ ἔχων πυρὸς αἰθομένοιο.⁶¹

22. Pf. act. ptc. nom. masc. sg., βρίθω, *be laden*; with dat.
23. χρυσός, -οῦ, ὁ, *gold*.
24. ἄργυρος, -ου, ὁ, *silver*.
25. Partic.; coordinates elements within the sentence (cf. S §2867; CGCG §59.22): τε καί . . . ἠδέ τε, *X, Y, and Z*.
26. κόσμος, -ου, ὁ, *ornament*.
27. πορφύρεος, -η, -ον, *purple*.
28. τελεσφόρος, -ον, *fruit-bearing*.
29. Pres. act. ptc. nom. fem. dual, πλήθω, *be full of*; with gen.; attrib.
30. Pres. act. inf., κοτέω (no contraction), *be angry at*; with dat. pers.
31. Pres. act. ptc. nom. masc. pl., ἐπαμύνω, *help, come to the aid of*; with dat. The phrase ἐπαμύνοντες κακὰ θυμῷ is awkward. Ψ solves the issue by reading κακῷ θυμῷ, thus "coming to assist ill-bearing wrath."
32. φθόνος, -ου, ὁ, *envy*.
33. Pres. mid. indic. 3 sg., πέλω, (copula) *be*.
34. δειλός, -ή, -όν, *miserable, wretched*. δειλοὶ βροτοί, "poor mortals," is Homeric.
35. ἀθρόος, -α, -ον, *all together*.
36. Fut. mid. indic. 3 pl., ὁρμάω, *attack*.
37. κήρ, κηρός, ἡ, *goddess of doom or death*; (by extens.) *disaster, death*.
38. σηκός, -οῦ, ὁ, *sacred enclosure, temple*.
39. φώς, φωτός, ὁ, *man, mortal*.
40. Superl., ἀγαθός, -ή, -όν, *best, most excellent*.

41. Pres. act. inf., πορθέω, *destroy*; comp. of βουλήσονται.
42. Fut. mid. indic. 3 pl., βούλομαι, *want, desire*.
43. Adv., *at the time when*.
44. Aor. mid. subj. 3 pl., ἱκνέομαι, *reach, arrive at*; fut. temp. clause (cf. BDF §381; S §§2401–2; CGCG §47.8; sometimes without ἄν in poetry).
45. Dat. of place, *in a circle*; with gen. of place.
46. μιαρός, -ά, -όν, *defiled, polluted*.
47. ἀπειθής, -ές, *disobedient*.
48. Once again δ' αὖ marks the beginning of a new section.
49. ναός, -οῦ, ὁ, *sanctuary*.
50. Adv., *peacefully*.
51. Pres. mid. ptc. nom. masc. pl., εὐφραίνω, *rejoice*; circ.
52. The relative pronoun is attracted to the case of its antecedent (cf. BDF §294; S §2532; CGCG §50.31).
53. κτίστης, -ου, ὁ, *creator*.
54. δικαιοκρίτης, -ου, ὁ, *just judge*.
55. μόναρχος, -ου, ὁ, *only/absolute ruler*.
56. Aor. act. opt. 3 sg., σκεπάζω, *shelter*. Cf. Buitenwerf 2003, 162: "The author of Sib. Or. III frequently uses the optative (without κέν or ἄν) instead of the future indicative. Examples of such use of the *optativus aoristi* can be found in III 259, 501, 521, 646, 705, 761, 818."
57. Adv., *over a great space, far and wide.*.
58. Aor. act. ptc. nom. masc. sg., παρίστημι, *stand by/near*; circ.
59. Adv. (= ὡς εἰ), *as if*.
60. τεῖχος, -εος, τό, *wall*.
61. Pres. pass. ptc. gen. neut. sg., αἴθω, (pass.) *burn, blaze*; attrib. See n. 1.

⁷⁰⁷ἀπτόλεμοι⁶² δ' ἔσσονται⁶³ ἐν ἄστεσιν⁶⁴ ἠδ'
ἐνὶ χώραις.⁶⁵
⁷⁰⁸οὐ χεὶρ γὰρ πολέμοιο κακοῦ, μάλα⁶⁶ δ'
ἔσσεται αὐτοῖς
⁷⁰⁹αὐτὸς ὑπέρμαχος⁶⁷ ἀθάνατος⁶⁸ καὶ χεὶρ
Ἁγίοιο.⁶⁹
⁷¹⁰καὶ τότε δὴ νῆσοι⁷⁰ πᾶσαι πόλιές τ'
ἐρέουσιν,⁷¹
⁷¹¹ὁππόσον⁷² ἀθάνατος⁷³ φιλέει⁷⁴ τοὺς ἄνδρας
ἐκείνους.
⁷¹²πάντα γὰρ αὐτοῖσιν⁷⁵ συναγωνιᾷ⁷⁶ ἠδὲ
βοηθεῖ,⁷⁷
⁷¹³οὐρανὸς ἠέλιός τε θεήλατος⁷⁸ ἠδὲ⁷⁹
σελήνη.⁸⁰
⁷¹⁴[γαῖα δὲ παγγενέτειρα⁸¹ σαλεύσεται⁸²
ἤμασι⁸³ κείνοις.⁸⁴]⁸⁵

⁷¹⁵ἡδὺν⁸⁶ ἀπὸ στομάτων⁸⁷ δὲ λόγον ἄξουσιν
ἐν ὕμνοις.⁸⁸
⁷¹⁶"δεῦτε, πεσόντες ἅπαντες ἐπὶ χθονὶ⁸⁹
λισσώμεσθα⁹⁰
⁷¹⁷ἀθάνατον βασιλῆα, θεὸν μέγαν ἀέναόν⁹¹
τε.⁹²
⁷¹⁸πέμπωμεν⁹³ πρὸς ναόν, ἐπεὶ μόνος ἐστὶ
δυνάστης.⁹⁴
⁷¹⁹καὶ νόμον ὑψίστοιο⁹⁵ θεοῦ φραζώμεθα⁹⁶
πάντες,
⁷²⁰ὅστε⁹⁷ δικαιότατος πέλεται πάντων κατὰ
γαῖαν.
⁷²¹ἡμεῖς δ' ἀθανάτοιο⁹⁸ τρίβου πεπλανημένοι⁹⁹
ἦμεν,
⁷²²ἔργα δὲ χειροποίητα¹⁰⁰ σεβάσμεθα¹⁰¹
ἄφρονι¹⁰² θυμῷ¹⁰³

---

62. ἀπτόλεμος, -ον (poetic for ἀπόλεμος), *without war, peaceful*.
63. Epic fut. mid. indic. 3 pl., εἰμί.
64. ἄστυ, -εος, τό, *town*.
65. χώρα, -ας, ἡ, *country*.
66. Adv. acc., *very much, indeed*.
67. ὑπέρμαχος, -ου, ὁ, *defender*; pred. nom.
68. ἀθάνατος, -ον, *immortal*.
69. ἅγιος, -η, -ον, (epithet) *Holy One*. See n. 1.
70. νῆσος, -ου, ἡ, *island*.
71. Epic fut. act. indic. 3 pl., εἴρω, *say*.
72. Epic adv. acc. (degree), ὁπόσος, -η, -ον, *how much?* Some read it as the beginning of direct speech (e.g., Collins, *OTP* 1:378).
73. ἀθάνατος, -ον, *immortal*.
74. Pres. act. indic. 3 sg., φιλέω (no contraction), *love*.
75. αὐτοῖσιν = αὐτοῖς (cf. S §229).
76. Pres. act. indic. 3 sg., συναγωνιάω, *share in the fight with*; with dat.
77. Pres. act. indic. 3 sg., βοηθέω, *help, assist*; with dat.
78. θεήλατος, -ον, *driven/sent by god*.
79. τε . . . ἠδέ, *X and Y*.
80. σελήνη, -ης, ἡ, *moon*.
81. Epithet for the earth, *all-bearing mother*.
82. Fut. mid. indic. 3 sg., σαλεύω, (intrans.) *be shaken*.
83. ἦμαρ, -ατος, τό, *day*; dat. of time.
84. κείνοις = ἐκείνοις (cf. Benner 2001, 373 [§120]).
85. Geffcken omits 714, which is identical to 675.

86. ἡδύς, -εῖα, -ύ, *sweet, pleasant, delightful*.
87. στόμα, -ατος, τό, *mouth*.
88. ὕμνος, -ου, ὁ, *hymn*.
89. χθών, -ονός, ἡ, *earth, ground*.
90. Pres. mid. subj. 1 pl., λίσσομαι, *entreat* (a god); hortatory (BDF §418; S §2063; *CGCG* §52.42).
91. ἀέναος, -ον, *eternal*.
92. In poetry, τέ "often connects single parallel nouns and pronouns so that the two connected ideas form a whole" (S §2968 N).
93. Pres. act. subj. 1 pl., πέμπω, *send*; hortatory. See n. 90.
94. δυνάστης, -ου, ὁ, *sovereign*.
95. ὕψιστος, -η, -ον, (divine epithet) *Most High*. See n. 1.
96. Pres. mid. subj. 1 pl., φράζω, (mid.) *think upon, consider, ponder*; hortatory. See n. 90.
97. ὅστε, ἥτε, ὅτε, *who, which* (cf. Benner 2001, 374 [§123]). The relative pronoun has two possible antecedents: νόμον or ὑψίστοιο θεοῦ. The former seems preferable (so also Buitenwerf 2003, 282; *pace* Collins, *OTP* 1:379).
98. Either an adjective modifying τρίβου (abl. gen.), "from the *immortal* path," or more likely, an epithet for the deity, "from the path of *the Immortal One*."
99. Pf. pass. ptc. nom. masc. pl., πλανάω, (intrans.) *wander, stray*; periphrastic (equivalent of plpf. tense).
100. χειροποίητος, -ον, *made with hands*.
101. There is an issue with the printed text. Read σεβάσθημεν (MS Ψ): Aor. pass. indic. 1 pl., σεβάζομαι, *revere, worship*.
102. ἄφρων, -ον, *senseless, foolish*.
103. θυμός, -οῦ, ὁ, *mind, spirit*.

⁷²³εἴδωλα ξόανά¹⁰⁴ τε καταφθιμένων¹⁰⁵
ἀνθρώπων."

NOTES

3:652. The identity of the king ἀπ' ἠελίοιο ("from the sun") is the subject of debate. Collins is the leading proponent of the view that the writer envisages a Ptolemaic savior of the Jewish people. He claims, "The closest parallel that we have to the phrase in *Sib. Or.* 3:652 is in fact found in an Egyptian document of the Hellenistic age, the *Potter's Oracle*: 'and then Egypt will increase when the king from the sun, who is benevolent for fifty-five years, becomes present, appointed by the greatest goddess Isis'" (2000, 94). Others take ἀπ' ἠελίοιο ("from the east") as an allusion to the Isaian oracle about Cyrus the Persian (cf. Isa. 41:2, 25; Sib. Or. 3:286), a reference either to the historical figure (Nikiprowetzky 1970, 135–37) or to a future pagan king (Buitenwerf 2003, 273–75). In any case, the sibyl's model of deliverance is that of Deutero-Isaiah; she espies a messiah "in the same sense that Second Isaiah looks for a Persian one" (Collins 2000, 95).

3:663–668. These lines present "the traditional motif of the *Völkersturm*, a last attempt of the peoples of the earth to conquer Judaea and destroy the temple and the people" (Buitenwerf 2003, 277). Cf. Ps. 2:1–2; Ezek. 38–39. The scenario plays out in various Second Temple texts (e.g., 1 En. 56–57; 4 Ezra 13:33; Rev. 16:12–16; 19:19).

3:702. Divine sonship is a common attribute of the people of God and often occurs in contexts that anticipate divine deliverance (cf. Tob. 13:4; Sir. 36:17; Wis. 2:13, 16; 5:5; 4Q174 1:11; 4Q372 1:16–17; Jub. 1:22–25; Pss. Sol. 17:27; T. Mos. 10:3; 4 Ezra 6:58; 2 Bar. 13:9).

3:709. The battle does not belong to the people; rather, "the hand of the Holy One" alone fights for them (cf. Exod. 14:25; Isa. 41:10; 2 Macc. 8:24; Collins, *OTP* 1:378).

3:715–723. This is "the first song to be sung by the non-Jews who will convert to the true religion" (Buitenwerf 2003, 282). At the eschaton, the nations will bring their gifts to the Jerusalem temple (cf. Isa. 18:7; 60:5; Tob. 13:13), where they will worship Israel's God and contemplate his Torah (cf. Isa. 2:2–3; Mic. 4:2).

---

104. ξόανον, -ου, τό, *statue*.
105. Aor. pass. ptc. gen. masc. pl., καταφθίνω, (pass.) *dead*; attrib.

3.4

The Sentences of Pseudo-Phocylides

Phocylides of Miletus, an Ionic poet of the sixth century BCE, was "famous in antiquity as a writer of maxims with useful advice for daily life" (Horst, *OTP* 2:565). The poem written in his name was not recognized as pseudonymous until the end of the sixteenth century.[1] Since the writer betrays at least some knowledge of Septuagint texts, as well as an affinity to Stoic philosophers such as Seneca and Musonius Rufus, most date the poem between 100 BCE and 110 CE (Horst, *OTP* 2:567).[2]

The decision of a Jewish writer to adopt the persona of gentile is by no means unprecedented. Indeed, within Jewish pseudepigrapha, "a veritable who's who of Greek bards—Orpheus, Homer, Hesiod, Aeschylus, Sophocles, Euripides, Menander, and so on—is made to express sentiments amenable to Judaism" (Wilson 2005, 3). Pseudo-Phocylides's poem is "remarkable for its distillation of the ethical message of Judaism and its suppression of the distinctive indicators of Judaism as a religion set apart" (Collins 2000, 174).

The reading covers the writer's view of mercy (esp. charity and hospitality). For readers who are new to epic poetry, I have included notes on morphology. For a discussion of dactylic hexameter, see §8.1.

Text: Young and Diehl 1971[3]
Recommended Translation: Horst, *OTP*
Supplemental Scripture: Prov. 3:27–28; James 2:14–17

---

1. For a detailed history of research, see Horst 1978, 3–54.
2. Scholars favor an Alexandrian provenance, but this is by no means certain. See Horst, *OTP* 2:568; Collins 2000, 168–69; Wilson 2005, 12–13, 143–45.
3. Young uses *iota* adscript (e.g., εἴπηις instead of εἴπῃς). Since you may encounter this feature elsewhere, I have included it for practice.

3.4.1

Admonition to Mercy

Pseudo-Phocylides 22–41

[22]πτωχῶι[1] δ' εὐθὺ[2] δίδου μὴ δ' αὔριον[3] ἐλθέμεν[4] εἴπηις·[5]
[23]πληρώσει[6] σέο[7] χεῖρ'. ἔλεον[8] χρήιζοντι[9] παράσχου.[10]
[24]ἄστεγον[11] εἰς οἶκον δέξαι[12] καὶ τυφλὸν[13] ὁδήγει.[14]

[25]ναυηγοὺς[15] οἴκτιρον,[16] ἐπεὶ πλόος[17] ἐστὶν ἄδηλος.[18]
[26]χεῖρα πεσόντι[19] δίδου, σῶσον δ' ἀπερίστατον[20] ἄνδρα.
[27]Κοινὰ πάθη[21] πάντων· ὁ βίος[22] τροχός·[23] ἄστατος[24] ὄλβος.[25]
[28]πλοῦτον[26] ἔχων σὴν χεῖρα πενητεύουσιν[27] ὄρεξον.[28]
[29]ὧν σοι ἔδωκε θεός, τούτων χρήιζουσι παράσχου.

1. πτωχός, -ή, -όν, *poor*; iota adscript.
2. Adv., *at once, straightaway* (cf. LSJ, 716.B.I.3). MSS M P read εὐθύς.
3. Adv., *tomorrow*.
4. Aor. act. inf., ἔρχομαι, -έμεν = Epic act. inf. (cf. S §469 D); indir. disc. (BDF §396; S §2016; CGCG §51.19).
5. *Iota* adscript; εἴπηις = εἴπῃς; prohibitive (cf. BDF §364; S §1800; CGCG §34.7).
6. Fut. mid. indic. 2 sg., πληρόω, *fill*. The reading is difficult: "You must fill your hand" (Horst, *OTP* 2:575). See further discussion in notes.
7. σέο = σοῦ (cf. S §325 D).
8. ἔλεος, -ου, ὁ, here *alms*; direct obj. of the implied verb δίδου.
9. Pres. act. ptc. dat. masc. pl., χρῄζω, *lack, be in need*; attrib. (subst.).
10. Adv., *immediately*.
11. ἄστεγος, -ον, lit., "without a roof"; thus *homeless*.
12. Aor. mid. impv. 2 sg., δέχομαι, *receive*.
13. τυφλός, -ή, -όν, *blind*.
14. Pres. act. impv. 2 sg., ὁδηγέω, *lead, guide*.

15. ναυηγός, -όν, *shipwrecked*.
16. Aor. act. impv. 2 sg., οἰκτείρω, *pity*.
17. πλόος, -όου, ὁ, *sailing, sea voyage*.
18. ἄδηλος, -ον, *unsure*.
19. Aor. act. ptc. dat. masc. sg., πίπτω, *fall*; attrib. (subst.).
20. ἀπερίστατος, -ον; lit., "not stood around"; thus, *unguarded, helpless*.
21. πάθος, -ους, τό, *suffering*.
22. βίος, -ου, ὁ, *life*.
23. τροχός, -οῦ, ὁ, *wheel*.
24. ἄστατος, -ον, *unstable*.
25. ὄλβος, -ου, ὁ, *prosperity*.
26. πλοῦτος, -ου, ὁ, *wealth*.
27. Pres. act. ptc. dat. masc. pl., πενητεύω, *be poor*; attrib. (subst.).
28. Aor. act. impv. 2 sg., ὀρέγω, *reach out*.

³⁰ἔστω κοινὸς ἅπας ὁ βίος καὶ ὁμόφρονα²⁹ πάντα.
³¹[Αἷμα δὲ μὴ φαγέειν,³⁰ εἰδωλοθύτων³¹ ἀπέχεσθαι.³²]
³²Τὸ ξίφος³³ ἀμφιβαλοῦ³⁴ μὴ πρὸς φόνον,³⁵ ἀλλ' ἐς³⁶ ἄμυναν.³⁷
³³εἴθε δὲ μὴ χρήιζοις³⁸ μήτ' ἔκνομα³⁹ μήτε δικαίως.⁴⁰
³⁴ἢν⁴¹ γὰρ ἀποκτείνῃς⁴² ἐχθρόν, σέο χεῖρα μιαίνεις.⁴³
³⁵Ἀγροῦ⁴⁴ γειτονέοντος⁴⁵ ἀπόσχεο⁴⁶ μὴ δ' ἄρ'⁴⁷ ὑπερβῇις.⁴⁸
³⁶πάντων μέτρον⁴⁹ ἄριστον, ὑπερβασίαι⁵⁰ δ' ἀλεγειναί.⁵¹

³⁷[κτῆσις⁵² ὀνήσιμός⁵³ ἐσθ'⁵⁴ ὁσίων,⁵⁵ ἀδίκων δὲ πονηρά.]
³⁸μηδέ τιν' αὐξόμενον⁵⁶ καρπὸν λωβήσηι⁵⁷ ἀρούρης.⁵⁸
³⁹Ἔστωσαν δ' ὁμότιμοι⁵⁹ ἐπήλυδες⁶⁰ ἐν πολιήταις·⁶¹
⁴⁰πάντες γὰρ πενίης⁶² πειρώμεθα⁶³ τῆς πολυπλάγκτου,⁶⁴
⁴¹χώρης⁶⁵ δ' οὔ τι βέβαιον⁶⁶ ἔχει πέδον⁶⁷ ἀνθρώποισιν.⁶⁸

NOTES

22–26. The opening section of the larger segment (22–41) is framed by the imperative δίδου (22a, 26a). Pseudo-Phocylides's concern is with the destitute: the beggarly poor, the homeless, the shipwrecked, and so on (cf. Seneca, *Clem.* 2.6.2; Wilson 2005, 98).

22. Cf. Prov. 3:27–28 LXX; James 2:15–16. The obligation to care for the poor is a common motif in Wisdom literature (cf. Prov. 14:21, 31; 17:5, 17; 22:9;

29. ὁμόφρονων, -ον, *concordant*.
30. Aor. act. inf., ἐσθίω, *eat*; -έειν = Epic 2nd aor. act. inf.; imperatival (cf. BDF §389; S §2013; CGCG §51.47).
31. εἰδωλόθυτος, -ον, *food sacrificed to idols*.
32. Pres. mid. inf., ἀπέχω, *abstain from*; with gen.; imperatival. See n. 30.
33. ξίφος, -εος, τό, *sword*.
34. Aor. mid. impv. 2 sg., ἀμφιβάλλω, *put around*.
35. φόνος, -ου, ὁ, *murder*.
36. ἐς = εἰς.
37. ἄμυνα, -ης, ἡ, *defense*.
38. Pres. act. opt. 2 sg., χρῄζω, *need*; cupitive with εἴθε (cf. S §1815; CGCG §34.14).
39. Adv., *unlawfully*.
40. Adv., *justly*.
41. ἤν = ἐάν.
42. Pres. act. subj. 2 sg., ἀποκτείνω, *kill*; pres. general condition (cf. BDF §373; S §2337; CGCG §49.13).
43. Pres. act. indic. 2 sg., μιαίνω, *stain*; (moral) *defile, pollute*.
44. ἀγρός, -οῦ, ὁ, *field*.
45. Pres. act. ptc. gen. masc. sg., γειτονέω, (subst.) *neighbor*.
46. Aor. mid. impv. 2 sg., ἀπέχω, *keep off of / away from*.
47. Partic. combination, *and so*; development (δέ) with necessary contribution (ἄρα) (cf. CGCG §59.42).
48. Aor. act. subj. 2 sg., ὑπερβαίνω, *trespass*; iota adscript; prohibitive. See n. 5.
49. μέτρον, -ου, τό, *moderation*.
50. ὑπερβασία, -ας, ἡ, *excess*.
51. ἀλεγεινός, -ή, -όν, *causing pain, grievous*.

52. κτῆσις, -εως, ἡ, *acquisition*; with gen.
53. ὀνήσιμος, -ον, *useful*.
54. Elision: ἐσθ' = ἐστι. Final vowels and diphthongs that are superfluous to the meter are typically elided (cf. Benner 2001, 357 [§40]).
55. ὅσιος, -α, -ον, *lawful*.
56. Pres. pass. ptc. acc. masc. sg., αὐξάνω, (pass.) *be grown*; attrib.
57. Aor. mid. subj. 2 sg., λωβάομαι, *damage*; iota adscript; prohibitive. See n. 45.
58. ἄρουρα, -ης, ἡ, *field*.
59. ὁμότιμος, -ον, *equally valued/honored*.
60. ἔπηλυς, -δος, ὁ/ἡ, *stranger, foreigner*.
61. πολιήτης, -ου, ὁ, *citizen*.
62. πενίη, -ης, ἡ, *poverty*.
63. Pres. mid. indic. 1 pl., πειράω, *experience*; with gen.
64. πολύπλαγκτος, -ον, *much-wandering*.
65. χώρα, -ας, ἡ (Ion. χώρη), *land*.
66. βέβαιος, -ον, *steadfast, durable*.
67. πέδον, -ου, τό, *ground, earth*; head noun of χώρης (hyperbaton; cf. S §3028; CGCG §60.18).
68. Epic 2nd decl. dat. masc. pl., ἀνθρώποισιν = ἀνθρώποις (cf. S §229).

28:27; Sir. 4:1–8; 10:23) as well as in Homeric epic, "where the practice of aiding a πτωχός is taken for granted (*Od.* 6.207–208, 14.57–59, 17.10–12) and failure to give alms to the indigent strangers is characterized as shameful (17.500–504)" (Wilson 2005, 99).

23. πληρώσει σέο χεῖρ'. The reading in manuscripts M B V is difficult. Manuscript P reads πληρώσεις, and manuscript L reads πληρώσας, both of which are preferred by some. As Horst (1978, 129) notes, πληρώσεις might be read as either a *futurum pro imperativo*, "You shall fill his hand" (πληρώσεις ἕο χεῖρ'), or a noun (pl. πληρώσις) with the latter half of verse 22, "Do not say that tomorrow satisfaction will come" (μὴ δ' αὔριον ἐλθέμεν εἴπῃς πληρώσεις). In the end, however, he advocates for the more difficult πληρώσει, which may be taken as fut. act. indic. 3 sg. or, more likely, as fut. mid. indic. 2 sg.: "You should give with full hands [to the poor of v. 22]."

ἔλεον. The term is an equivalent of ἐλεημοσύνη, "almsgiving" (cf. Tob. 1:3; 2:14; 4:7–11; 12:8–9; Sir. 3:30; 7:10; 12:3–7; 16:14; 17:22; 29:8; 31:11; 35:2; 40:17, 24; Matt. 6:2–4; Acts 3:2–3; 9:36; 10:2, 4; 24:17; Did. 1.5; 4.5–8; 15.4; Horst 1978, 129). A theology of charity is rooted in the conviction that people who give gifts to those who cannot reciprocate will be honored by God (see Anderson 2014; Barclay 2015, 39–44).

27. Numerous Greek writers speak of the common fate (τύχη) of all human beings (e.g., Isocrates, *Demon.* 29; Menander, *Mon.* 10; Horst 1978, 132). Likewise, "the wheel served as a cross-cultural symbol for the twists and turns of life: everyone will eventually encounter some difficulty" (Wilson 2005, 101). So, for example, Herodotus observes, "Human fortunes are on a wheel, which in its turning suffers not the same one to prosper forever" (*Hist.* 1.207, as cited in Wilson 2005, 101; cf. Philo, *Somn.* 2.44; Plutarch, *Num.* 14.5).

31. An interpolation. Cf. Acts 15:29.

35–38. Verses 35 and 38 share a common theme (agriculture). Since verse 36 is identical to verse 69b, "either both vv. are to be retained or v. 36 has to be athetized since 3 important mss. (L, P, V) omit it" (Horst 1978, 137). Verse 37 is attested in only one manuscript and "interrupts (with v. 36) the coherence between verses 35 and 38" (138). As a result, many prefer to remove verses 36 and 37.

3.5
Fragments of Hellenistic Jewish Writers

Many fragments of Hellenistic Jewish writers were preserved by the first-century BCE historian Cornelius Alexander of Miletus, surnamed Polyhistor. While his *On the Jews* did not survive the vicissitudes of history, excerpts were preserved by church fathers (esp. Eusebius). Polyhistor appears to have been "primarily a compiler of quotations, a *grammatikos*, as ancient tradition puts it" (Strugnell, *OTP* 2:778). The extant fragments suggest his method of citation was consistent: he reports prose in indirect speech and cites poetry (more or less) verbatim.

Among those whom Polyhistor cites are Jewish poets (Philo the Epic Poet and Theodotus), oracular poets (Orphica), dramatists (Ezekiel the Tragedian), philosophers (Aristobulus), and historians (Demetrius the Chronographer, Aristeas the Exegete, Eupolemus, Cleodemus Malchus, and Artapanus). This section includes readings from Theodotus, Ezekiel the Tragedian, Aristobulus, and Eupolemus.

3.5.1

Theodotus the Poet

Theodotus was an epic poet who flourished in the late third or early second century BCE. Earlier scholarship concluded that he was a Samaritan, due in large measure to the poet's focus on Shechem (e.g., frag. 1, line 16), but it seems equally if not more plausible that he was a Jew.[1] Eight fragments of Theodotus's poem, a total of forty-seven lines of hexameter, are preserved in Eusebius's *Praeparatio evangelica* (9.22). "Because of the presence of the distinctive epic vocabulary and meter within," Fallon notes, "it is clear that Alexander [Polyhistor] has faithfully preserved the wording of the fragments. In addition, he has provided us with the summaries of the omitted parts of the poem or the omitted parts of this section of the poem, if the poem was actually longer than our fragments" (*OTP* 2:785).

The reading passages are fragments 4 and 5, in which the poet positions covenantal circumcision (cf. Gen. 17) as the marker of Jewish identity, an eternal covenant between God and the descendants of Abraham.

Text: *FGH* 3C, no. 732
Recommended Translation: Fallon, *OTP*
Supplemental Scripture: Gen. 17; 34

---

1. For a survey of the evidence, see Holladay 1983–96, 2:158–68, 84–85.

3.5.1.1

Jacob and the Shechemites—Fragment 4

Eusebius, *Praeparatio evangelica* 9.22.4–6

9.22.4ἀπὸ δὲ τοῦ Εὐφράτου¹ φησὶ² τὸν Ἰακὼβ ἐλθεῖν εἰς τὰ Σίκιμα³ πρὸς Ἐμμώρ,⁴ τὸν δὲ ὑποδέξασθαι⁵ αὐτόν, καὶ μέρος⁶ τι τῆς χώρας⁷ δοῦναι· καὶ αὐτὸν μὲν⁸ τὸν Ἰακὼβ γεωμορεῖν,⁹ τοὺς δὲ υἱοὺς αὐτοῦ ἕνδεκα τὸν ἀριθμὸν¹⁰ ὄντας ποιμαίνειν,¹¹ τὴν δὲ θυγατέρα Δείναν¹² καὶ τὰς γυναῖκας ἐριουργεῖν.¹³ καὶ τὴν Δείναν παρθένον¹⁴ οὖσαν εἰς τὰ Σίκιμα ἐλθεῖν πανηγύρεως¹⁵ οὔσης, βουλομένην θεάσασθαι¹⁶ τὴν πόλιν, Συχὲμ¹⁷ δὲ τὸν τοῦ Ἐμμὼρ υἱὸν ἰδόντα ἐρασθῆναι¹⁸ αὐτῆς, καὶ ἁρπάσαντα¹⁹ ὡς ἑαυτὸν διακομίσαι,²⁰ καὶ φθεῖραι²¹ αὐτήν. **⁵**αὖθις²² δὲ σὺν τῷ πατρὶ ἐλθόντα πρὸς τὸν Ἰακὼβ αἰτεῖν²³ αὐτὴν πρὸς γάμου κοινωνίαν· τὸν δὲ οὐ φάναι²⁴ δώσειν, πρὶν ἂν ἢ²⁵ πάντας τοὺς οἰκοῦντας τὰ Σίκιμα περιτεμνομένους²⁶ ἰουδαΐσαι·²⁷ τὸν δὲ Ἐμμὼρ

---

1. Εὐφράτης, -ου, ὁ, *Euphrates*.
2. Polyhistor's report of what Theodotus says; i.e., indir. disc.
3. Σίκιμα, -ων, (place) *Shechem*.
4. Ἐμμώρ (indecl.), ὁ, *Hamor*.
5. Aor. mid. inf., ὑποδέχομαι, *welcome, greet*; indir. disc. (cf. BDF §396; S §2017; CGCG §51.19). τόν (Hamor) is the accusative subject, αὐτόν (Jacob) the object.
6. μέρος, -ους, τό, *portion*.
7. χώρα, -ας, ἡ, *land*.
8. μέν ... δέ ... δέ; point/counterpoints (cf. S §2907).
9. Pres. act. inf., γεωμορέω, *be a farmer*; indir. disc. with αὐτόν as pred. adj. (intensive). See n. 5.
10. ἀριθμός, -οῦ, ὁ, *number*; acc. of respect.
11. Pres. act. inf., ποιμαίνω, *be a shepherd*; indir. disc. See n. 5.
12. Δείνα, -ας, ἡ, *Dinah*.
13. Pres. act. inf., ἐριουργέω, *work in wool*; indir. disc. See n. 5.
14. παρθένος, -ου, ἡ, *maiden, virgin*.
15. πανήγυρις, -εως, ἡ, *festival*; subject of gen. absol.
16. Aor. mid. inf., θεάομαι, *see, behold*; comp. of βουλομένην.
17. Συχέμ (indecl.), (pers.) *Sychem* (Shechem).

18. Aor. pass. inf., ἐράω, (pass.) *fall in love with*; with gen.; indir. disc. See n. 5
19. Aor. act. ptc. acc. masc. sg., ἁρπάζω, *sieze*; circ.
20. Aor. act. inf., διακομίζω, *carry off*; indir. disc. See n. 5.
21. Aor. act. inf., φθείρω; indir. disc. (see n. 5). Given the context, "rape" (Holladay 1983–96, 2:115) would seem an appropriate translation.
22. Adv., *thereafter, then*.
23. Pres. act. inf., αἰτέω, *ask* (someone for something) (cf. BDAG, 30.2).
24. Pres. act. inf., φημί, *say*. οὐ negates the infinitive (δώσειν) in indirect discourse (cf. S §1971; CGCG §51.22).
25. The collocation πρὶν (ἤ) ἄν plus a subjunctive is used after a negative clause to express indefinite time: *until* (cf. BDF §383; S §§2430, 2432; CGCG §47.8). Due to indirect discourse, the subjunctive shifts to the infinitive.
26. Pres. pass. ptc. acc. masc. pl., περιτέμνω, (pass.) *be circumcised*; circ. (means).
27. Aor. act. inf., ἰουδαΐζω, *Judaize*.

φάναι πείσειν²⁸ αὐτούς. ⁶φησὶ δὲ περὶ τοῦ δεῖν²⁹ περιτέμνεσθαι αὐτοὺς ὁ Ἰακώβ

"οὐ γὰρ δὴ³⁰ θεμιτόν³¹ γε³² τόδ' Ἑβραίοισι³³ τέτυκται,³⁴
γαμβροὺς³⁵ ἄλλοθεν εἴς γε νυοὺς³⁶ ἀγέμεν³⁷ ποτὶ³⁸ δῶμα,³⁹
ἀλλ' ὅστις γενεῆς⁴⁰ ἐξεύχεται⁴¹ εἶναι ὁμοίης."⁴²

NOTES

9.22.4. Theodotus's account differs from the biblical one, which says that Jacob purchased a portion of land for "one hundred lambs" (Gen. 33:19 LXX; MT: "one hundred pieces of money").

πανηγύρεως οὔσης. The timing of the festival and Dinah's desire to see the city is another detail not mentioned in the biblical account. Josephus, however, reports something very similar to Theodotus (*A.J.* 1.337). Some suspect that he is dependent on Theodotus, whom he mentions elsewhere (cf. *C. Ap.* 1.216). See Holladay (1983–96, 2:174).

Συχὲμ δὲ τὸν τοῦ Ἐμμὼρ υἱὸν ἰδόντα ἐρασθῆναι αὐτῆς, καὶ ἁρπάσαντα ὡς ἑαυτὸν διακομίσαι, καὶ φθεῖραι αὐτήν. "Theodotus' description of both the attitude and action of Shechem is more negative than the biblical account" (Holladay 1983–96, 2:174–75; cf. Gen. 34:5). Josephus's rendition, once again, is remarkably similar to Theodotus's: "There she was perceived by Sychem, a son of king Emmor, who carried her off and ravished her [φθείρει δι' ἁρπαγῆς] and being enamored of her [διατεθεὶς ἐρωτικῶς] besought his father to procure the damsel for him in marriage [λαβεῖν αὐτῷ πρὸς γάμον τὴν κόρην]" (*A.J.* 1.337, trans. Thackeray 1930a).

9.22.5. Cf. Gen. 34:13–17. The verb ἰουδαΐζω involves the performance of the habits, customs, or patterns of worship distinct to the Jewish people (cf. Esther 8:17 LXX; Gal. 2:14; Josephus, *B.J.* 2.454, 463; Plutarch, *Cic.* 7.4–5; see esp. Cohen 1999, 175–97; Mason 2009, 141–84; Novenson 2014). Metilius's promise "to Judaize *up to the point of circumcision*" (μέχρι περιτομῆς ἰουδαΐσειν, *B.J.* 2.454) suggests a spectrum of Judaizing (Donaldson 2007, 474).

9.22.6. Typically Polyhistor uses φησί to report what Theodotus says. Here, however, the following is a direct citation of the poem. Holladay (1983–96, 2:177) comments, "Polyhistor may have cited the following passage verbatim from Theodotus in order to clarify for his Roman readers the significance of circumcision in Judaism." Cf. Rom. 3:27–4:25.

---

28. Fut. act. inf., πείθω, *persuade*. The action is posterior to φάναι (cf. S §1866; *CGCG* §51.26).

29. Art. inf. as obj. of περί; with acc.-and-inf. construction (cf. BDF §393; S §1985; *CGCG* §36.3).

30. Partic. combination, *for indeed, surely then*. The supportive statement (γάρ) is evident, clear, or precise (δή) (cf. *CGCG* §59.44; Denniston 1966, 243).

31. θεμιτός, -ή, -όν, *in conformity with norms, licit, permissible*; with dat.

32. Postpositive partic.; focus/concentration on θεμιτόν (cf. *CGCG* §59.53).

33. Epic 2nd decl. dat. masc. pl., Ἑβραῖος, -α, -ον, *Hebrew*.

34. Pf. mid. indic. 3 sg., τεύχω, (as copula) *be*.

35. γαμβρός, -οῦ, ὁ, *son-in-law*.

36. νυός, -οῦ, ἡ, *daughter-in-law*.

37. Epic pres. act. inf., εἰσάγω, *lead in* (cf. S §469 D). The preposition is separated from the verb; i.e., tmesis (cf. S §1650).

38. ποτί = πρός.

39. δῶμα, -ατος, τό, *house*.

40. γενεή, -ῆς, ἡ (alt. γενεά), *race, family*.

41. Pres. mid. indic. 3 sg., ἐξεύχομαι, *boast aloud*. Since ἐξεύχομαι does not occur in Homer, some prefer to read ἐξ εὔχεται (e.g., Fallon, *OTP* 2:792nf). The only difference is that one would read the preposition with the preceding genitive, which is marked by the shift in accent—i.e., anastrophe (cf. S §175; *CGCG* §60.14).

42. ὁμοῖος, -α, -ον, *same*.

3.5.1.2

On Circumcision—Fragment 5

Eusebius, *Praeparatio evangelica* 9.22.7

9.22.7 εἶτα ὑποβὰς¹ περὶ τῆς περιτομῆς·

"ὅς² ποθ' ἑῆς³ πάτρης⁴ ἐξήγαγε δῖον⁵ Ἀβραὰμ αὐτὸς
ἀπ' οὐρανόθεν⁶ κάλεσ'⁷ ἀνέρα παντὶ σὺν οἴκῳ σάρκ'
ἀποσυλῆσαι⁸ πόσθης⁹ ἄπο,¹⁰ καί ῥ'¹¹ ἐτέλεσσεν·¹²
ἀστεμφὲς¹³ δὲ τέτυκται,¹⁴ ἐπεὶ θεὸς αὐτὸς ἔειπε."¹⁵

1. Aor. act. ptc. nom. masc. sg., ὑποβαίνω, *a little below* (in the book) (LSJ, 1875.IV.2). The theme remains the same: περὶ τῆς περιτομῆς.
2. The referent is God.
3. Epic ἑός, ἑή, ἑόν, *one's own*. ποθ' ἑῆς is Stephanus's emendation of ποτ' ἐπί (MSS ION). Mras (1954–56) reads ποτ' ἐπεί, which is reflected in Fallon's translation (*OTP* 2:792).
4. πάτρη, -ης, ἡ, *fatherland*.
5. δῖος, -α, -ον, *noble, illustrious*.
6. Adv., *from heaven*; sometimes with ἀπό (cf. Homer *Il.* 8.365; 21.199; *Od.* 11.18; 12.381).
7. Aor. act. indic. 3 sg., καλέω, *summon*; with acc. and inf.; omission of the verbal augment (cf. S §438).
8. Aor. act. inf., ἀποσυλάω, *strip off*.
9. πόσθη, -ης, ἡ, *foreskin*.
10. Anastrophe indicates that the object of the preposition precedes it (cf. S §175; *CGCG* §60.14).
11. ῥα = ἄρα. Partic. combination, *and so*; closely related information (καί) that the speaker cannot help but contribute (ἄρα) (cf. *CGCG* §59.42; Denniston 1966, 43).
12. Aor. act. indic. 3 sg., τελέω (root τελεσ-), *complete* (an act).
13. ἀστεμφής, -ές, *unmoved, unshaken*.
14. Pf. mid. indic. 3 sg., τεύχω, (copula) *be*. The verb is impersonal; its implied subject is the command to circumcise.
15. ἔειπε = εἶπε.

NOTE

9.22.7. Cf. Gen. 17:9–14, 22–17. Polyhistor notes that he is skipping down in the section on circumcision. He continues to cite Theodotus directly with the suggestion that Jacob is still the speaker. The poet's emphasis on the divine origin of circumcision can be explained in multiple ways. On the one hand, some have argued that he is combating the discontinuation of the practice among certain Jews or Samaritans. On the other hand, divine etiology of common practices is a stock feature of epic poetry (Holladay 1983–96, 2:179).

3.5.2

Ezekiel the Tragedian

Ezekiel the Tragedian is known for his *Exagōgē* (ca. first century BCE), which retells the exodus narrative (Exod. 1–15) in the form of a Greek drama.[1] The play unfolds in five acts:

Act I	Scene 1: Moses's monologue
	Scene 2: Moses's dialogue with Sepphorah
Act II	Scene 1: Sepphorah's dialogue with Chus
	Scene 2: Moses's dream and Jethro's interpretation
Act III	Scene 1: Moses's dialogue with God
	Scene 2: Moses's instructions to the people
Act IV	Report of the Egyptian messenger
Act V	Elim and the report of the messengers to Moses

The outline is Robertson's (*OTP*, 2:805).

It is uncertain whether he intended the *Exagōgē* for performance, but there is nothing in the drama (at least, as we have it) that undermines this possibility.

The reading is from act II, scene 2: Moses's dream and Jethro's interpretation. This text has garnered significant attention for Ezekiel's depiction of Moses assuming the cosmic throne—an image that, if taken "literally," would appear to militate against certain constructions of Jewish monotheism (e.g., Bauckham 2008, 166–69). For discussion of the iambic trimeter, the standard conversational meter in Greek drama, see §8.3.

Text: *TrGF*, no. 128
Recommended Translation: Robertson, *OTP*
Supplemental Scripture: Gen. 37:9; Ps. 8; Dan. 7:9–14; Phil. 2:9–11; 1 En. 46

---

1. Cf. Let. Aris. 312–316 (§3.1.2). Pseudo-Aristeas claims that the tragic poet Theodektes was subject to divine punishment for attempting to adapt the law of Moses.

3.5.2.1

Moses on the Heavenly Throne—Fragments 6 and 7

Eusebius, *Praeparatio evangelica* 9.29.5–6

9.29.5 (68) [ΜΩΣΗΣ] Ἔδοξ᾽¹ ὄρους² κατ᾽ ἄκρα³
Σιναίου θρόνον
(69) μέγαν τιν᾽ εἶναι μέχρις⁴ οὐρανοῦ πτυχός,⁵
(70) ἐν τῷ⁶ καθῆσθαι⁷ φῶτα⁸ γενναῖόν⁹ τινα
(71) διάδημ᾽¹⁰ ἔχοντα καὶ μέγα σκῆπτρον¹¹ χερὶ
(72) εὐωνύμῳ¹² μάλιστα.¹³ δεξιᾷ¹⁴ δέ μοι
(73) ἔνευσε,¹⁵ κἀγὼ πρόσθεν¹⁶ ἐστάθην θρόνου.
(74) σκῆπτρον δέ μοι παρέδωκε καὶ εἰς θρόνον
μέγαν
(75) εἶπεν καθῆσθαι· βασιλικὸν¹⁷ δ᾽ ἔδωκέ μοι
(76) διάδημα καὶ αὐτὸς ἐκ θρόνων¹⁸
χωρίζεται.¹⁹
(77) ἐγὼ δ᾽ ἐσεῖδον²⁰ γῆν ἅπασαν ἔγκυκλον²¹
(78) καὶ ἔνερθε²² γαίας καὶ ἐξύπερθεν²³
οὐρανοῦ,
(79) καί μοί τι πλῆθος ἀστέρων²⁴ πρὸς
γούνατα²⁵

1. Aor. act. indic. 3 sg., δοκέω, (impers.) *it seems/appears*; with dat. and acc.-and-inf. construct (cf. BDF §408; S §1985; *CGCG* §36.4): "There appeared [to me] on the summit of Mount Sinai a throne."
2. ὄρος, -ους, τό, *mountain*.
3. ἄκρον, -ου, τό, *highest point, summit*.
4. μέχρις = μέχρι; (prep. with gen.) *as far as, up to*.
5. πτύξ, -χος, ἡ, (of the skies) *fold, cleft* (LSJ, 1549.II).
6. The article is used as a relative pronoun (cf. S §1105).
7. Pres. mid. inf., κάθημαι, *seated*; acc.-and-inf. construct. See n. 1.
8. φῶς, φωτός, ὁ, *man*.
9. γενναῖος, -ον, *noble*.
10. διάδημα, -ατος, τό, *crown*.
11. σκῆπτρον, -ου, τό, *scepter*.
12. εὐώνυμος, -ον, (euph.) *left hand*.
13. Horst (1984, 368) suggests that μάλιστα functions as an attitudinal particle, along the lines of *nota bene*.
14. δεξιά, -ᾶς, ἡ, *right hand*.
15. Aor. act. indic. 3 sg., νεύω, *beckon* (with the hand).
16. Prep. with gen., *before*.
17. βασιλικός, -ή, -όν, *royal*.
18. In poetry, the plural is used for the singular to lend dignity (cf. S §1006).
19. Pres. pass. indic. 3 sg., χωρίζω, (pass.) *leave, depart*.
20. Aor. act. indic. 1 sg., ἐσοράω (εἰσοράω), *look at*.
21. ἔγκυκλος, -ον, *circled*.
22. Prep. with gen., *below*.
23. Prep. with gen., *above*.
24. ἀστήρ, -έρος, ὁ, *star*.
25. γόνυ, -ατος, τό, *knee*.

(80)ἔπιπτ', ἐγὼ δὲ πάντας ἠριθμησάμην,²⁶
(81)κἀμοῦ²⁷ παρῆγεν²⁸ ὡς παρεμβολὴ²⁹ βροτῶν.³⁰
(82)εἶτ' ἐμφοβηθεὶς³¹ ἐξανίσταμ'³² ἐξ ὕπνου.³³
9.29.6 (83)[ΡΑΓΟΥΗΛ] Ὦ ξένε,³⁴ καλόν σοι τοῦτ' ἐσήμηνεν³⁵ θεός·
(84)ζῴην³⁶ δ', ὅταν σοι ταῦτα συμβαί[ν]η³⁷ ποτέ.
(85)ἆρά γε³⁸ μέγαν τιν' ἐξαναστήσεις³⁹ θρόνον
(86)καὶ αὐτὸς βραβεύσεις⁴⁰ καὶ καθηγήσῃ⁴¹ βροτῶν;
(87)τὸ δ' εἰσθεᾶσθαι⁴² γῆν ὅλην τ' οἰκουμένην
(88)καὶ τὰ ὑπένερθε καὶ ὑπὲρ οὐρανὸν θεοῦ·
(89)ὄψει τά τ' ὄντα τά τε πρὸ τοῦ τά θ' ὕστερον.

26. Aor. mid. indic. 1 sg., ἀριθμέω, *count, number*.
27. Crasis: κἀμοῦ = καὶ ἐμοῦ. But the genitive does not work. Stephanus emends to κἀμοί, which is the most elegant solution. Renehan's καὶ ἰδού brings the text into conformity with LXX dream narratives (Holladay 1983–96, 2:364).
28. Aor. act. indic. 3 sg., παράγω, *pass by*.
29. παρεμβολή, -ῆς, ἡ, *company* (of soldiers).
30. βροτός, -όν, (subst.) *mortal men*.
31. Aor. pass. ptc. nom. masc. sg., ἐμφοβέω, (pass.) *be seized with fear*; circ.
32. Pres. mid. indic. 1 sg., ἐξανίστημι, *arise*.
33. ὕπνος, -ου, ὁ, *sleep*.
34. ξένος, -ου, ὁ, *guest-friend* (cf. Robertson, OTP 2:812nd2).
35. Aor. act. indic. 3 sg., σημαίνω, *signify, show*.
36. Pres. act. opt. 1 sg.; cupitive (cf. BDF §384; S §1814; CGCG §34.14); emendation (cf. ζῴην δ' in Aristophanes, *Eq.* 833), something like: "May I live to see the day!"
37. Pres. act. subj. 3 sg., συμβαίνω, *happen, come about*; fut. temp. (cf. BDF §381; S §2401; CGCG §47.8).
38. Partic. combination; interrogative (ἆρα) that receives additional focus (γε): "Will you, in fact . . . ?" Since, however, this is Raguel's interpretation of the dream, we should read ἄρά γε (Horst 1984, 369). Thus the speaker underscores (γε) that he cannot but make the contribution (ἄρα): "So, it seems . . ." (cf. CGCG §59.42).
39. Fut. act. indic. 2 sg., ἐξανίστημι, *raise up, erect, remove, expel, overthrow*. Will Moses cause a mighty throne to rise (his own), or will he overthrow a mighty throne (Pharaoh's)? Both interpretations work, but the emphasis seems to be on the former (Horst 1983, 23; Robertson, OTP 2:812).
40. Fut. act. indic. 2 sg., βραβεύω, *act as a judge*.
41. Fut. mid. indic. 2 sg., καθηγέομαι, *lead, command, exercise authority over*; with gen.
42. Pres. mid. inf., εἰσθεάομαι, *watch, observe, contemplate*. Nom. pendent (cf. CGCG §60.34): "As for this beholding of the whole

NOTES

(68). The text follows Dübner's emendation of κατ' ἄκρας ἵνου to κατ' ἄκρα Σιναίου. Manuscripts read ἐξ ὄρους κατ' ἄκρας ἵνου and variations (see Holladay 1983–96, 2:362). The scene may presuppose traditions that link Moses's installation as king with visionary or heavenly ascent (cf. Philo, *Mos.* 1.158; rabbinic traditions in Ginzberg 2003, 1:504n117). Presumably, the "great throne" is informed by biblical traditions of the heavenly throne (cf. Pss. 10:4; 102:19; Ezek. 1:26; 10:1; Dan. 7:9; Rev. 4:2), though none of these locates the throne on a mountain (though cf. 1 En. 18:8; 24:3; 25:3).

(70). φῶτα γενναῖόν τινα. Interpreters debate the identity of this "certain noble man." On the one hand, some argue that he is a human king, Pharaoh or perhaps Enoch. Others argue that the figure is Israel's God, which I find more persuasive (Holladay 1983–96, 2:442). The depiction of God as a human being has precedent in biblical tradition (cf. Ezek. 1:26; Dan. 7:9) and so is rather unremarkable. What is striking, though not entirely without precedent, is that God *vacates* the divine throne so that Moses can assume it.

(74–76). Moses's assumption of the divine throne may be compared to stories about the elect one ("that son of man") in the Parables of Enoch (cf. 1 En. 45:3; 51:3; 55:4; 61:8), as well as to later Enochic traditions (e.g., 3 En. 10:1; 12:1–5). Biblical traditions suggest that the king shared God's throne (cf. 1 Chron. 29:23), and rabbinic traditions react

---

inhabited world, the things below and above God's heaven: you will see things present, past, and future."

against the notion of a second heavenly power (e.g., b. Hag. 15a).

(80). The activity of numbering the stars belongs to God (cf. Ps. 146:4 LXX; Horst 1984, 368) but is also ascribed to Enoch/Metatron (cf. 3 En. 46:1–2).

(81). Dreams are accompanied by fear (cf. Dan. 2:1; 4:5; 7:28) and the motif of awaking in fear (cf. Gen. 28:16–17; 41:7–8; 1 En. 83:6–7; 4 Ezra 12:3–5; 13:14; Holladay 1983–96, 2:446).

3.5.3

Aristobulus the Philosopher

As the forerunner to Philo of Alexandria and "the first theologian of Hellenistic Judaism" (Collins 2000, 189), Aristobulus was an avant-garde of philosophical Judaism. In light of the fragments of his work, his project seems to have been twofold. First, he wanted to establish the legitimacy of allegorical interpretation of the Greek Pentateuch (especially as a means for dealing with anthropomorphisms). Second, he aimed to position Moses as the font of wisdom and the Mosaic law as commensurate with the law of nature. Thus, when the Greek poets and philosophers grasp the truth and live in harmony with nature, they become de facto disciples of Moses.

The reading is an example of how Aristobulus positioned Mosaic wisdom. Herein he also mentions Greek translations of the Pentateuch prior to the one done by the Jerusalem scribes (cf. Let. Aris. 30, 314).

Text: Holladay 1983–96, vol. 3
Recommended Translation: Yarbro Collins, *OTP*
Supplemental Scripture: 2 Macc. 1:10

3.5.3.1

Moses as the Font of All Wisdom—Fragment 3

Eusebius, *Praeparatio evangelica* 13.12.1–2

[Heading]ὅπως καὶ ὁ πρὸ[1] ὑμῶν ἐξ Ἑβραίων Ἀριστόβουλος ὁ περιπατητικὸς[2] ἐκ τῆς παρ' Ἑβραῖος φιλοσοφίας[3] ὡμολογεῖ[4] τοὺς Ἕλληνας ὥρμησθαι·[5] ἐκ τῶν Ἀριστοβούλου βασιλεῖ Πτολεμαίῳ προσπεφωνημένων·[6] **13.12.1**Φανερὸν[7] ὅτι κατηκολούθησεν[8] ὁ Πλάτων[9] τῇ καθ' ἡμᾶς νομοθεσίᾳ[10] καὶ φανερός ἐστι περιειργασμένος[11] ἕκαστα τῶν ἐν αὐτῇ. διηρμήνευται[12] γὰρ πρὸ Δημητρίου τοῦ Φαληρέως[13] δι' ἑτέρων, πρὸ τῆς Ἀλεξάνδρου καὶ Περσῶν ἐπικρατήσεως,[14] τά τε κατὰ τὴν ἐξαγωγὴν[15] τὴν ἐξ Αἰγύπτου τῶν Ἑβραίων, ἡμετέρων δὲ πολιτῶν,[16] καὶ ἡ τῶν γεγονότων ἁπάντων αὐτοῖς ἐπιφάνεια[17] καὶ κράτησις[18] τῆς χώρας καὶ τῆς ὅλης νομοθεσίας ἐπεξήγησις,[19] ὡς εὔδηλον[20] εἶναι[21]

1. Prep. with gen., (temp.) *before*. The referent of the pronoun is Polyhistor's audience.
2. περιπατητικός, -οῦ, ὁ, *Peripatetic*. Cf. Hengel 1974, 2:106n375: "The name did not necessarily mean membership of the Aristotelean school in Alexandria of the third to first century BC, but also 'a literary historian, a biographer or perhaps even a scientific writer.'"
3. φιλοσοφία, -ας, ἡ, *philosophy*.
4. Impf. act. indic. 3 sg. ὁμολογέω, *agree, consent*.
5. Pf. mid. inf., ὁρμάω, *start*; indir. disc. (cf. BDF §396; S §2017; CGCG §51.19).
6. Pf. pass. ptc. gen. neut. pl., προσφωνέω, (pass.) *be dedicated*; attrib. (subst.): "from the [books] of Aristobulus dedicated to King Ptolemy."
7. φανερός, -ά, -όν, (quasi-impers.) *it is clear*. The impersonal subject is explicated by the ὅτι-clause.
8. Aor. act. indic. 3 sg., κατακολουθέω, *follow after, imitate*; with dat.
9. Πλάτων, -ονος, ὁ, *Plato*.
10. νομοθεσία, -ας, ἡ, *legislation*.
11. Pf. mid. ptc. nom. masc. sg., περιεργάζομαι, *investigate thoroughly*.
12. Pf. pass. indic. 3 sg., διερμηνεύω, (pass.) *be translated*.
13. Demetrius of Phalerum (ca. 350–280 BCE; cf. Let. Aris. 9).
14. ἐπικράτησις, -εως, ἡ, *conquest*; head noun of Ἀλεξάνδρου ("Alexander") and Περσῶν ("the Persians").
15. ἐξαγωγή, -ῆς, ἡ, *exodus*.
16. πολίτης, -ου, ὁ, *citizen*.
17. ἐπιφάνεια, -ας, ἡ, *fame, distinction*.
18. κράτησις, -εως, ἡ, *domination, conquest*.
19. ἐπεξήγησις, -εως, ἡ, *detailed account*.
20. εὔδηλος, -ον, (quasi-impers.) *it is abundantly clear*; with acc. and inf.
21. ὡς with the infinitive marks a result clause (cf. BDF §391; S §2260; CGCG §46.7).

τὸν προειρημένον φιλόσοφον²² εἰληφέναι²³ πολλά· γέγονε γὰρ πολυμαθής,²⁴ καθὼς καὶ Πυθαγόρας²⁵ πολλὰ τῶν παρ' ἡμῖν μετενέγκας²⁶ εἰς τὴν ἑαυτοῦ δογματοποιίαν²⁷ κατεχώρισεν.²⁸

²ἡ δ' ὅλη ἑρμηνεία²⁹ τῶν διὰ τοῦ νόμου πάντων ἐπὶ τοῦ προσαγορευθέντος³⁰ Φιλαδέλφου βασιλέως,³¹ σοῦ δὲ προγόνου,³² προσενεγκαμένου³³ μείζονα φιλοτιμίαν,³⁴ Δημητρίου τοῦ Φαληρέως πραγματευσαμένου³⁵ τὰ περὶ τούτων.

NOTES

Heading. ἐκ τῆς παρ' Ἑβραῖος φιλοσοφίας ὡμολογεῖ τοὺς Ἕλληνας ὡρμῆσθαι. On Moses as the inventor of philosophy, cf. Artapanus, frag. 1; 3.4; Eupolemus, frag. 1 (see §3.5.4.1); Philo, *Mos.* 1.21; Josephus, *C. Ap.* 1.1–5; 2.168; Clement of Alexandria, *Strom.* 1.21.101; 25.165–166; 29.180–182; Eusebius, *Hist. eccl.* 6.13.7; Eusebius, *Praep. ev.* 9–11.

1. διηρμήνευται γὰρ πρὸ Δημητρίου τοῦ Φαληρέως δι' ἑτέρων. Cf. Let. Aris. 30, 314. On whether Let. Aris. 30 refers to earlier Greek translations of the Pentateuch, see Wright (2015, 145–49). Pseudo-Aristeas identifies Demetrius of Phalereum as the keeper of the king's library (9) and as the one who transcribed the Greek translation of the law (301–322; §3.1.2).

πρὸ τῆς Ἀλεξάνδρου καὶ Περσῶν ἐπικρατήσεως. The invasion of Egypt by Alexander the Great occurred in 332 BCE. The earlier invasion of the Persians refers to either the invasion by Artaxerxes (343 BCE) or the invasion by Cambyses (525 BCE). "The latter would render more plausible Aristobulus' claim that Jewish traditions were known to Plato (ca. 429–347 BCE) and Pythagoras (6th cent. BCE)" (Holladay 1983–96, 3:214).

22. φιλόσοφος, -ου, ὁ, *philosopher*. "The aforementioned philosopher" is Plato.
23. Pf. act. inf., λαμβάνω, *take*.
24. πολυμαθής, -ές, *very learned*.
25. Πυθαγόρας, -ου, ὁ, *Pythagoras*.
26. Aor. act. ptc. nom. masc. sg., μεταφέρω, *carry over, transfer*; circ.
27. δογματοποιία, -ας, ἡ, *system of belief*.
28. Aor. act. indic. 3 sg., καταχωρίζω, *assign*.
29. ἑρμηνεία, -ας, ἡ, *translation*.
30. Aor. pass. ptc. gen. masc. sg., προσαγορεύω, (pass.) *be called, surnamed*; attrib.
31. Ptolemy II Philadelphus ruled 285–246 BCE.
32. πρόγονος, -ου, ὁ, *ancestor, forefather*.
33. Aor. mid. ptc. gen. masc. sg., προσφέρω, *bring to, apply*; circ.
34. φιλοτιμία, -ας, ἡ, *love of honor*. The comparand must be supplied from context: something like "applying greater zeal [than his predecessors]."
35. Aor. mid. ptc. gen. masc. sg., πραγματεύομαι, *be engaged with, attend to*; gen. absol.

3.5.4

Eupolemus the Historian

The Jewish historian Eupolemus is "almost certainly the Eupolemus named in 1 Maccabees 8:17–18 who was entrusted with a mission to Rome by Judas Maccabee about 160 BCE" (Collins 2000, 46). His oeuvre, *On the Kings in Judea* (the title is taken from Clement of Alexandria, *Strom.* 1.153.4), of which five fragments were preserved by Polyhistor, is focused on the biblical accounts of the construction of the temple (1 Kings 5–8; 2 Chron. 2–5). That he was focused on not only the dedication of the temple but also the conquests of David and Solomon in Seleucid territory seems a clear indication that Eupolemus was a staunch supporter of the Hasmonean agenda (Hengel 1974, 1:93–94).

The reading passage is short but provides an example of what Collins calls "competitive historiography" (2000, 46). The writer's aim is to show that Moses—not Plato—is "the first wise man" and the true sage responsible for gifting humankind letters and laws.

Text: *FGH*, no. 723
Recommended Translation: Fallon, *OTP*
Supplemental Scripture: 1 Macc. 8:17–18; 2 Macc. 4:11

3.5.4.1

Moses as the First Sage—Fragment 1

Eusebius, *Praeparatio evangelica* 9.25.4–26.1

9.25.4 Τοσαῦτα[1] καὶ περὶ τούτων ὁ Πολύϊστωρ. Καὶ περὶ Μωσέως δὲ[2] ὁ αὐτὸς πάλιν πλεῖστα[3] παρατίθεται,[4] ὧν καὶ αὐτῶν ἐπακοῦσαι[5] ἄξιον.[6] **9.26.1** Εὐπόλεμος δέ φησι[7] τὸν Μωσῆν πρῶτον σοφὸν[8] γενέσθαι καὶ γράμματα[9] παραδοῦναι τοῖς Ἰουδαίοις πρῶτον, παρὰ δὲ Ἰουδαίων Φοίνικας[10] παραλαβεῖν,[11] Ἕλληνας δὲ παρὰ Φοινίκων, νόμους τε πρῶτον γράψαι Μωσῆν τοῖς Ἰουδαίοις.

NOTE

9.26.1. Εὐπόλεμος δέ φησι τὸν Μωσῆν πρῶτον σοφὸν γενέσθαι. On the notion that Moses surpassed the Greek sages, especially Plato, cf. Artapanus, frag. 3.4; Aristobulus, frag. 3 (see §3.5.3.1); Philo, *Mos.* 1.21; Josephus, *C. Ap.* 1.1–5; 2.168; Clement of Alexandria, *Strom.* 1.21.101; 25.165–166; 29.180–182; Eusebius, *Hist. eccl.* 6.13.7; Eusebius, *Praep. ev.* 9–11. Other Jewish writers credited Enoch (cf. Jub. 4:17–20) or Abraham (cf. Ps.-Eup.) with the discovery of writing (Holladay 1983–96, 1:137).

1. The demonstrative pronoun is anaphoric: "*So much* [says] Polyhistor concerning these things."
2. Partic. combination, *and furthermore*: "closely related information (καί), which nevertheless is somehow distinct from the previous context (δέ)" (*CGCG* §59.67).
3. Superl., πολύς, πολλή, πολύ, *very many*.
4. Pres. mid. indic. 3 sg., παρατίθημι, *add*.
5. Aor. act. inf., ἐπακούω, *hear*; with gen.
6. ἄξιος, -α, -ον, (quasi-impers.) *it is worthwhile*; with acc. and inf.
7. Polyhistor begins to report what Eupolemus says; i.e., indir. disc.; acc. and inf. (cf. BDF §396; S §2017; *CGCG* §51.19).
8. σοφός, ή, όν, (subst.) *wise man*.
9. γράμμα, -ατος, τό, (pl.) *letters*; i.e., the "alphabet." Clement has γραμματικήν, *grammar, alphabet, script*.
10. Φοῖνιξ, -ικος, ὁ, *Phoenician*; acc. subject of παραλαβεῖν.
11. Aor. act. inf., παραλαμβάνω, *receive*; indir. disc. See n. 7.

PART 4

Reading Philo

Philo (ca. 20 BCE–50 CE) was born to an affluent Jewish family in Alexandria, Egypt. He was privileged with the finest education—"not inexperienced in philosophy," as Josephus says (*A.J.* 18.259)—and had access to the elite political networks. He was not, however, the most esteemed member of his family. Rather, his older brother, Alexander the Alabarch, is said to have "surpassed all his fellow citizens both in ancestry and in wealth" (Josephus, *A.J.* 20.100). Yet when Alexander ran afoul of Gaius Caligula, it was left to Philo to lead the delegation to Rome (38 CE). Caligula's threats to erect his statue in the Jerusalem temple were quelled by his assassination in 41 CE, and Philo found a more favorable hearing with the new emperor, Claudius.

It would be difficult to overstate Philo's importance to the study of early Judaism and Christianity. Yet he has proven to be something of a polarizing figure: a man celebrated by the church fathers but ignored by the rabbis; the greatest synthesizer of Plato and Moses but the worst capitulator to "Hellenism"; one of our best sources for first-century Judaism but one of the reasons why we cannot speak of "normative" Judaism in the first century; either the key that unlocks the mysteries of Christian origins (Sterling 2003) or the red herring that has led generations of scholars away from the "real" Jewish roots of the New Testament. In short, Philo is both a window into the first century and a mirror that reflects scholars' biases.

This section prepares you to read the vast, and at times unwieldly, Philonic corpus.[1] The readings are arranged according to genre: three passages from the Allegorical Commentary, eight passages from the Exposition of the Law, and two passages from the historical and apologetic writings. (Due to space constraints, I was unable to include readings from the philosophical treatises: *On the Eternity of the World*, *Whether Animals Have Reason*, *That Every Good Person Is Free*, and *On Providence*).

---

1. It may take some time to get acclimated to Philo's writings. The best place to begin is with two reference works: Kamesar 2009b; Seland 2014. You may also wish to consult the volumes in the Brill Philo of Alexandria Commentary Series as well as articles published in the journal *The Studia Philonica Annual*.

4.1

Allegorical Commentary

Philo's Allegorical Commentary includes a series of exegetical commentaries on Genesis.[1] Allegory is the mode of interpretation by which he resolves apparent issues in the LXX Pentateuch, and he discovers therein a higher, spiritual meaning (Kamesar 2009a). At the same time, Philo chastises those extremists who wish to detach the "soul" of the text from its "body" (*Migr.* 89–93). Thus he fashions himself an expert in sound biblical interpretation, neither a crude literalist nor a radical allegorizer. For the former, Moses creates "stumbling blocks" designed to guide the reader to the spiritual telos of the text (cf. Origen, *Princ.* 4.2.9). For the latter, he legislates ancestral customs and traditions that are undergirded by the wisdom of the divine mind.

The next three reading passages are from *Allegorical Interpretation*. In the first two passages, Philo distinguishes between the human formed from the earth (Gen. 2:7) and the human fashioned according to the divine image (Gen. 1:26-27). In the third passage, he offers a brief account of the call of Abraham (Gen. 12:1), which he explores in more detail in *On the Migration of Abraham*.

Text and Translation: Colson and Whitaker 1929

Supplemental Scripture: Gen. 1:26–27; 2:7 (§§4.1.1–2); Gen. 12:1–3 (§4.1.3)

---

1. Royse (2009, 40–44) includes a brief description of the contents of each work. According to the manuscript tradition, Philo did not write a commentary on Gen. 1, though scholars are divided on this issue (see, e.g., Niehoff 2018, 247–50). The only extant account of Philo's treatment of Gen. 1 is *On the Creation of the World*, which does not belong to the Allegorical Commentary but introduces the Exposition of the Law (see §4.2 below).

4.1.1

The Heavenly Human and the Earthly Human, Part 1

Allegorical Interpretation 1.31–32

1.31Καὶ ἔπλασεν¹ ὁ θεὸς τὸν ἄνθρωπον χοῦν² λαβὼν ἀπὸ τῆς γῆς, καὶ ἐνεφύσησεν³ εἰς τὸ πρόσωπον αὐτοῦ πνοὴν⁴ ζωῆς, καὶ ἐγένετο ὁ ἄνθρωπος εἰς⁵ ψυχὴν ζῶσαν" [Gen. 2:7]. διττὰ⁶ ἀνθρώπων γένη.⁷ ὁ μὲν⁸ γάρ ἐστιν οὐράνιος⁹ ἄνθρωπος, ὁ δὲ γήϊνος.¹⁰ ὁ μὲν οὖν¹¹ οὐράνιος ἅτε¹² κατ' εἰκόνα¹³ θεοῦ γεγονὼς φθαρτῆς¹⁴ καὶ συνόλως¹⁵ γεώδους¹⁶ οὐσίας¹⁷ ἀμέτοχος,¹⁸ ὁ δὲ γήϊνος ἐκ σποράδος¹⁹ ὕλης,²⁰ ἣν χοῦν κέκληκεν, ἐπάγη·²¹ διὸ τὸν μὲν²² οὐράνιόν φησιν οὐ πεπλάσθαι,²³ κατ' εἰκόνα δὲ τετυπῶσθαι²⁴ θεοῦ, τὸν δὲ γήϊνον πλάσμα,²⁵ ἀλλ' οὐ γέννημα,²⁶ εἶναι τοῦ τεχνίτου.²⁷ **³²**ἄνθρωπον

1. Aor. act. indic. 3 sg., πλάσσω (Att. πλάττω), *form, mold*.
2. χοῦς, χοός, ὁ, *soil*.
3. Aor. act. indic. 3 sg., ἐμφυσάω, *blow in*.
4. πνοή, -ῆς, ἡ, *breath*.
5. Prep. εἰς marks the pred. comp.; lit., "the human became *for* a living being" (cf. *SSG* §22b; BDF §145).
6. δισσός, -ή, -όν (Att. διττός), *twofold*.
7. γένος, -ους, τό, *type, kind*.
8. ὁ μέν ... ὁ δέ, *the one ... the other* (cf. BDF §250; S §1106; *CGCG* §28.27).
9. οὐράνιος, -ον, *heavenly*.
10. γήϊνος, -ον, *earthly*.
11. Partic. combination: "A transition to a more to-the-point, relevant text segment (οὖν) [that] occurs in two stages (μέν ... δέ)" (*CGCG* §59.73).
12. ἅτε with a circumstantial participle (γεγονώς) expresses reason for the speaker's assertion (cf. S §2085; *CGCG* §52.39).
13. εἰκών, -όνος, ὁ, *image*.
14. φθαρτός, -ή, -όν, *corruptible*.
15. Adv., *entirely*.
16. γεώδης, -ες, *of earth, earthen*.
17. οὐσία, -ας, ἡ, *substance*.
18. ἀμέτοχος, -ον, *not participating in*; pred. adj. with gen.
19. σπορἀς, -άδος, ὁ/ἡ, *scattered*.
20. ὕλη, -ης, ἡ, *matter*.
21. Aor. pass. indic. 3 sg., πήγνυμι, (pass.) *be put together*.
22. Point/counterpoint set (cf. Runge 2010, 75–83; BDF §447; S §2904; *CGCG* §59.24).
23. Pf. pass. inf., πλάσσω, (pass.) *be formed*; indir. disc. (cf. BDF §397; S §2016; *CGCG* §51.19).
24. Pf. pass. inf., τυπόω, (pass.) *be impressed*; indir. disc. See n. 23.
25. πλάσμα, -ατος, τό, *something that is formed/molded*; pred. acc.
26. γέννημα, -ατος, τό, *offspring*.
27. τεχνίτος, -ου, ὁ, *craftsman, artificer*.

δὲ τὸν ἐκ γῆς λογιστέον[28] εἶναι νοῦν εἰσκρινόμενον[29] σώματι, οὔπω δ' εἰσκεκριμένον. ὁ δὲ νοῦς οὗτος γεώδης ἐστὶ τῷ ὄντι[30] καὶ φθαρτός, εἰ μὴ ὁ θεὸς ἐμπνεύσειεν[31] αὐτῷ δύναμιν ἀληθινῆς ζωῆς· τότε γὰρ γίνεται, οὐκέτι πλάττεται, εἰς ψυχήν, οὐκ ἀργὸν[32] καὶ ἀδιατύπωτον,[33] ἀλλ' εἰς νοερὰν[34] καὶ ζῶσαν ὄντως·[35] "εἰς ψυχὴν" γάρ φησι "ζῶσαν ἐγένετο ὁ ἄνθρωπος.

NOTES

1.31. Philo devotes considerable attention to Gen. 2:7 (cf. *Opif.* 134; *Leg.* 1.31; *QG* 1.4-5; and various instances where he incorporates his exegesis of Gen. 2:7 into his discussion of other biblical texts, on which see Tobin 1983, 23-24). Philo's citations of Gen. 2:7 agree with our best LXX manuscripts, except for the participle λαβών, which is present in some Greek manuscripts and manuscript families (Wevers 1974, 84).

διττὰ ἀνθρώπων γένη. The differences are illustrated in the chart.

Heavenly Human οὐράνιος ἄνθρωπος	Earthly Human γήϊνος ἄνθρωπος
made according to the image of God κατ' εἰκόνα θεοῦ γεγονώς	compacted out of the matter scattered here and there, which Moses calls "clay." ἐκ σποράδος ὕλης, ἣν χοῦν κέκληκεν, ἐπάγη
without part or lot in corruptible and terrestrial substance φθαρτῆς καὶ συνόλως γεώδους οὐσίας ἀμέτοχος	
not molded but stamped with the image of God οὐ πεπλάσθαι, κατ' εἰκόνα τετυπῶσθαι θεοῦ	molded work of the artificer, not his offspring πλάσμα, οὐ γέννημα, τοῦ τεχνίτου

The key distinction is between the ἄνθρωπος that receives an impress of the divine image (Gen. 1:26-27) and the ἄνθρωπος that is molded from clay (Gen. 2:7). The former is singular, noetic, incorporeal, and Platonic, while the latter is composite, sense perceptible, corporeal, and Stoic (cf. *Leg.* 1.32; *Opif.* 134-135; Tobin 1983, 87-101). Runia (2001, 324) notes, "In many texts Philo tends to reconcile the two accounts to a large degree: cf. *Spec.* 1.171; *Virt.* 203-205; *Det.* 80-86; *Plant.* 18-20; *Her.* 56. In *Mut.* 223 Philo indicates that theologically he has a preference for the Platonizing image-relation rather than the Stoicizing part-whole relation. But both have a biblical foundation." Wyss (2016, 110) posits a development from *On the Creation of the World* and *Questions and Answers on Genesis* to *Allegorical Interpretation*, whereby Philo shifts from speaking of two human types to speaking of two *minds*. (This would, of course, require that Philo wrote *Allegorical Interpretation* after he wrote *On the Creation of the World*.)

28. Verbal adj. of λογίζω, impers. act. construction with dat. agent (cf. S §2152; *CGCG* §37.3); "It is necessary [for us] to regard the human [made] of the earth as a mind."

29. Pres. pass. ptc. acc. masc. sg., εἰσκρίνω, (pass.) *be admitted into, enter*; with dat. Note the distinction: "We should conclude that the human from the earth is [εἶναι] mind entering [εἰσκρινόμενον] but not yet entered [εἰσκεκριμένον] body."

30. Idiom, *in fact, in reality*.

31. Aor. act. opt. 3 sg. ἐμπνέω, *breathe into*. Mixed conditional: εἰ μή (exception), with the opt. in the protasis, and the indic. as the primary tense in the apodosis (cf. S §2359). Thus, "This mind is [would be], in fact, earthen and corruptible, *were it not* that God breathed into it the power of true life."

32. ἀργός, -όν, *inactive, idle*.

33. ἀδιατύπωτος, -ον, *unformed*. MS L reads ἀδιάπτωτον, "infallible," "faultless."

34. νοερός, -ά, -όν, *endowed with intellect/mind*.

35. Adv., *really, actually*.

4.1.2

The Heavenly Human and the Earthly Human, Part 2

Allegorical Interpretation 1.33–42

1.33ζητήσαι[1] δ' ἄν τις, διὰ τί[2] ἠξίωσεν[3] ὁ θεὸς ὅλως[4] τὸν γηγενῆ[5] καὶ φιλοσώματον[6] νοῦν πνεύματος θείου,[7] ἀλλ' οὐχὶ τὸν κατὰ τὴν ἰδέαν[8] γεγονότα καὶ τὴν εἰκόνα[9] ἑαυτοῦ· δεύτερον δέ, τί ἐστι τὸ "ἐνεφύσησε".[10] τρίτον, διὰ τί εἰς τὸ πρόσωπον ἐμπνεῖται·[11] τέταρτον, διὰ τί πνεύματος ὄνομα εἰδώς, ὅταν λέγῃ "καὶ πνεῦμα θεοῦ ἐπεφέρετο[12] ἐπάνω τοῦ ὕδατος" [Gen. 1:2], πνοῆς[13] νῦν ἀλλ' οὐχὶ πνεύματος μέμνηται.[14] **34**πρὸς μὲν οὖν[15] τὸ πρῶτον λεκτέον[16] ἓν μέν,[17] ὅτι φιλόδωρος[18] ὢν ὁ θεὸς χαρίζεται τὰ ἀγαθὰ πᾶσι καὶ τοῖς μὴ τελείοις,[19] προκαλούμενος[20] αὐτοὺς εἰς μετουσίαν[21] καὶ ζῆλον[22] ἀρετῆς,[23] ἅμα καὶ τὸν περιττὸν[24]

---

1. Aor. act. opt. 3 sg., ζητέω, *inquire*; potential (cf. BDF §385; S §1824; *CGCG* §34.13).
2. διὰ τί, *Why?*; indir. quest.
3. Aor. act. indic. 3 sg., ἀξιόω, *deem* (with acc.) *worthy of* (with gen.).
4. Adv., *wholly, entirely*.
5. γηγενής, -ές, *earthborn*.
6. φιλοσώματος, -ον, *body-loving*.
7. θεῖος, -α, -ον, *divine*.
8. ἰδέα, -ας, ἡ, *form*.
9. εἰκών, -όνος, ὁ, *image*.
10. Aor. act. indic. 3 sg., ἐμφυσάω, *blow*. The article τό is used to introduce quotations (cf. BDF §267).
11. Pres. mid. indic. 3 sg., ἐμπνέω, *breathe into*.
12. Impf. mid. indic. 3 sg., ἐπιφέρω, *move along* (over something) (cf. GELS, 286.3).
13. πνοή, -ῆς, ἡ, *breath*.
14. Pf. mid. indic. 3 sg., μιμνήσκω, *make mention of*; with gen.
15. Partic. combination: "a transition to a more to-the-point, relevant text segment (οὖν) [that] occurs in two stages (μέν . . . δέ)" (*CGCG* §59.73); here a transition to his answer to the first question.
16. Verbal adj. of λέγω (cf. S §2152; *CGCG* §37.3); thus "as to the first [question], one thing is to be said [by us]."
17. The use of two μέν particles in the same clause is "for clearness, as an extra signpost, or, perhaps more often, for emphasis" (Denniston 1966, 385). Here it underscores the point/counterpoint: λεκτέον ἓν μέν . . . **(35)**ἕτερον δὲ λεκτέον.
18. φιλόδωρος, -ον, *bountiful*.
19. τέλειος, -α, -ον, *perfect, complete*.
20. Pres. mid. ptc. nom. masc. sg., προκαλέω, *invite, incite*; circ.
21. μετουσία, -ας, ἡ, *participation*; with gen.
22. ζῆλος, -ου, ὁ, *desire*; with gen.
23. ἀρετή, -ῆς, ἡ, *virtue*.
24. περισσός, -ή, -όν (Att. περιττός), *surpassing, extraordinary*.

πλοῦτον ἐπιδεικνύμενος²⁵ αὐτοῦ,²⁶ ὅτι ἐξαρκεῖ²⁷ καὶ τοῖς μὴ λίαν²⁸ ὠφεληθησομένοις.²⁹ τοῦτο δὲ καὶ ἐπὶ τῶν ἄλλων ἐμφαντικώτατα³⁰ παρίστησιν.³¹ ὅταν γὰρ ὕῃ³² μὲν³³ κατὰ θαλάττης, πηγὰς³⁴ δὲ ἐν τοῖς ἐρημοτάτοις³⁵ ἀνομβρῇ,³⁶ τὴν δὲ λεπτόγεων³⁷ καὶ τραχεῖαν³⁸ καὶ ἄγονον³⁹ γῆν ἄρδῃ⁴⁰ ποταμοὺς ἀναχέων⁴¹ ταῖς πλημμύραις,⁴² τί ἕτερον⁴³ παρίστησιν ἢ τὴν ὑπερβολὴν τοῦ τε πλούτου καὶ τῆς ἀγαθότητος ἑαυτοῦ; ἥδ' ἐστὶν αἰτία⁴⁴ δι' ἣν ἄγονον⁴⁵ οὐδεμίαν ψυχὴν ἐδημιούργησεν⁴⁶ ἀγαθοῦ, κἂν⁴⁷ ἡ χρῆσις⁴⁸ ἀδύνατος ἐνίοις⁴⁹ ᾖ αὐτοῦ.

35ἕτερον δὲ λεκτέον ἐκεῖνο· βούλεται τὰ θέσει⁵⁰ δίκαια εἰσαγαγεῖν.⁵¹ ὁ μὲν οὖν⁵² μὴ ἐμπνευσθεὶς τὴν ἀληθινὴν ζωήν, ἀλλ' ἄπειρος⁵³ ὢν ἀρετῆς, κολαζόμενος⁵⁴ ἐφ' οἷς ἡμάρτανεν εἶπεν ἂν⁵⁵ ὡς ἀδίκως κολάζεται, ἀπειρίᾳ⁵⁶ γὰρ τοῦ ἀγαθοῦ σφάλλεσθαι⁵⁷ περὶ αὐτό, αἴτιον⁵⁸ δὲ εἶναι τὸν μηδεμίαν ἐμπνεύσαντα ἔννοιαν⁵⁹ αὐτοῦ· τάχα⁶⁰ δὲ μηδὲ ἁμαρτάνειν φήσει⁶¹ τὸ παράπαν,⁶² εἴ γε⁶³ τὰ ἀκούσια⁶⁴ καὶ κατὰ ἄγνοιαν⁶⁵ οὐδὲ ἀδικημάτων ἔχειν λόγον⁶⁶ φασί τινες.

25. Pres. mid. ptc. nom. masc. sg., ἐπιδείκνυμι, *demonstrate*; circ. ἅμα with a circumstantial participle indicates contemporaneous action (cf. S §2081; CGCG §52.37): "*while* also [καί] *demonstrating* his extraordinary wealth."
26. Note the breathing mark: αὑτοῦ = ἑαυτοῦ.
27. Pres. act. indic. 3 sg., ἐξαρκέω, (impers.) *it is enough for, it suffices for*; with dat.
28. Adv., *very*.
29. Fut. pass. ptc. dat. masc. pl., ὠφελέω, (pass.) *receive advantage/profit*; attrib. (subst.).
30. Superl. adv., ἐμφαντικός, -ή, -όν, *most revealingly*.
31. Pres. act. indic. 3 sg., παρίστημι, *present, show, demonstrate*.
32. Pres. act. subj. 3 sg., ὕω, *make rain*; general temp. clause (cf. BDF §382; S §2409; CGCG §47.9).
33. μέν . . . δέ . . . δέ; point/counterpoints (cf. S §2905).
34. πηγή, -ῆς, ἡ, *spring, fountain*.
35. Superl., ἔρημος, -ον, (subst.) *most desolate places*.
36. Pres. act. subj. 3 sg., ἀνομβρέω, *pour out, flow out*. See n. 32.
37. λεπτόγεως, -ων [λεπτός, γῆ], *that has thin/poor soil* (MGS, 1228).
38. τραχύς, -εῖα, -ύ, *rough, uneven, rocky*.
39. ἄγονος, -ον, *barren*.
40. Pres. act. subj. 3 sg., ἄρδω, *water, irrigate*. See n. 32.
41. Pres. act. ptc. nom. masc. sg., ἀναχέω, *pour on*.
42. πλήμμυρα, -ας, ἡ, *flood, full flow*.
43. ἕτερον . . . ἤ, lit., "*What else* does he show *other than* . . ."
44. αἰτία, -ας, ἡ, *reason*.
45. ἄγονος, -ον, *sterile, barren*; with gen. (ἀγαθοῦ; hyperbaton; cf. S §3028; CGCG §60.18).
46. Aor. act. indic. 3 sg., δημιουργέω, *create*.
47. Crasis: κἂν = καὶ ἐάν; concessive clause (cf. BDF §374; S §2369; CGCG §49.19).
48. χρῆσις, -εως, ἡ, *use*. The head noun is separated from its genitive modifier, αὐτοῦ (hyperbaton; cf. S §3028; CGCG §60.18).
49. ἔνιος, -α, -ον, *some*.

50. θέσις, -εως, ἡ, *what is set/laid down, determination* (cf. LSJ, 795.IV.3).
51. Aor. act. inf., εἰσάγω, *lead in, introduce*; comp. of βούλεται.
52. See n. 15.
53. ἄπειρος, -ον, *lacking experience in, inexperienced*; with gen.
54. Pres. pass. ptc. nom. masc. sg., κολάζω, (pass.) *be punished*; circ. (conditional).
55. Second-class (contrafactual) condition (cf. S §2302; CGCG §34.16). "So, then, the one into whom real life was not in-breathed, but who was without experience in virtue, if he were being punished [κολαζόμενος] for his sins, *would say* that he is unjustly punished."
56. ἀπειρία, -ας, ἡ, *inexperience*; with gen.; dat. of cause.
57. Pres. mid. inf., σφάλλω, (intrans.) *stumble, suffer failure*; indir. disc. (cf. BDF §397; S §2592; CGCG §41.2).
58. αἴτιος, -α, -ον, *culpable, responsible*; pred. acc.
59. ἔννοια, -ας, ἡ, *notion, conception*.
60. Adv., *perhaps*.
61. Fut. act. indic. 3 sg., φημί, *say*; continues indir. disc. (cf. CGCG §41.16).
62. μηδέ . . . τὸ παράπαν, *not at all, in no way whatsoever* (cf. MGS, 1562); with inf. ἁμαρτάνειν.
63. Postpositive partic.; expresses concentration/limitation on the word or phrase it follows (CGCG §59.53): "if, in fact, what is involuntary and done in ignorance does not count for unrighteousness, as some say."
64. ἀκούσιος, -ον, *involuntary*.
65. ἄγνοια, -ας, ἡ, *ignorance*.
66. ἔχειν λόγον, *count for*; with gen. (MGS, 1252.3A); indir. disc. (φασί τινες). See n. 57.

36τό γε μὴν⁶⁷ "ἐνεφύσησεν"⁶⁸ ἴσον ἐστὶ τῷ ἐνέπνευσεν ἢ ἐψύχωσε⁶⁹ τὰ ἄψυχα· μὴ γὰρ τοσαύτης ἀτοπίας⁷⁰ ἀναπλησθείημεν⁷¹ ὥστε νομίσαι⁷² θεὸν στόματος⁷³ ἢ μυκτήρων⁷⁴ ὀργάνοις⁷⁵ χρῆσθαι⁷⁶ πρὸς τὸ ἐμφυσῆσαι·⁷⁷ ἄποιος⁷⁸ γὰρ ὁ θεός, οὐ μόνον οὐκ ἀνθρωπόμορφος. ἐμφαίνει⁷⁹ δέ τι καὶ φυσικώτερον⁸⁰ ἡ προφορά.⁸¹ **37**τρία γὰρ εἶναι δεῖ, τὸ ἐμπνέον, τὸ δεχόμενον, τὸ ἐμπνεόμενον· τὸ μὲν οὖν ἐμπνέον ἐστὶν ὁ θεός, τὸ δὲ δεχόμενον ὁ νοῦς, τὸ δὲ ἐμπνεόμενον τὸ πνεῦμα. τί οὖν ἐκ τούτων συνάγεται;⁸² ἕνωσις⁸³ γίνεται τῶν τριῶν, τείναντος⁸⁴ τοῦ θεοῦ τὴν ἀφ' ἑαυτοῦ δύναμιν διὰ τοῦ μέσου⁸⁵ πνεύματος ἄχρι τοῦ ὑποκειμένου⁸⁶—τίνος ἕνεκα ἢ⁸⁷ ὅπως ἔννοιαν αὐτοῦ λάβωμεν; **38**ἐπεὶ πῶς ἂν ἐνόησεν⁸⁸ ἡ ψυχὴ θεόν, εἰ μὴ ἐνέπνευσε καὶ ἥψατο⁸⁹ αὐτῆς κατὰ δύναμιν; οὐ γὰρ ἂν ἀπετόλμησε⁹⁰ τοσοῦτον⁹¹ ἀναδραμεῖν⁹² ὁ ἀνθρώπινος νοῦς, ὡς ἀντιλαβέσθαι⁹³ θεοῦ φύσεως, εἰ μὴ αὐτὸς ὁ θεὸς ἀνέσπασεν⁹⁴ αὐτὸν πρὸς ἑαυτόν, ὡς ἐνῆν⁹⁵ ἀνθρώπινον νοῦν ἀνασπασθῆναι, καὶ ἐτύπωσε⁹⁶ κατὰ τὰς ἐφικτὰς⁹⁷ νοηθῆναι⁹⁸ δυνάμεις.

39εἰς δὲ τὸ πρόσωπον ἐμπνεῖ⁹⁹ καὶ φυσικῶς¹⁰⁰ καὶ ἠθικῶς.¹⁰¹ φυσικῶς μέν,¹⁰² ὅτι ἐν προσώπῳ τὰς αἰσθήσεις¹⁰³ ἐδημιούργει·¹⁰⁴ τοῦτο γὰρ μάλιστα τοῦ σώματος τὸ μέρος¹⁰⁵ ἐψύχωται καὶ ἐμπέπνευσται· ἠθικῶς δὲ οὕτως· ὥσπερ¹⁰⁶ σώματος ἡγεμονικόν¹⁰⁷ ἐστι τὸ πρόσωπον, οὕτως ψυχῆς ἡγεμονικόν ἐστιν ὁ νοῦς· τούτῳ μόνῳ ἐμπνεῖ ὁ θεός, τοῖς δ' ἄλλοις μέρεσιν οὐκ ἀξιοῖ, ταῖς τε αἰσθήσεσι καὶ τῷ λόγῳ καὶ τῷ γονίμῳ.¹⁰⁸ δεύτερα γάρ ἐστι τῇ δυνάμει. **40**ὑπὸ τίνος οὖν καὶ ταῦτα

67. Partic. combination: concentration/limitation (γε) with commitment to the veracity of the statement (μήν) (cf. *CGCG* §§59.49; 59.53): "This word [τό γε] 'he breathed into' is *clearly* [μήν] equal to 'he inspired' or 'he ensouled' those things that are without soul."
68. Aor. act. indic. 3 sg., ἐμφυσάω, *blow into*. Here begins his response to a second question: τί ἐστι τὸ "ἐνεφύσησεν;"
69. Aor. act. indic. 3 sg., ψυχόω, *give psychē, animate*.
70. ἀτοπία, -ας, ἡ, *absurdity, wickedness*.
71. Aor. pass. opt. 1 pl., ἀναπίμπλημι, *fill*; with gen.; cupitive (cf. BDF §384; S §1814; *CGCG* §34.14).
72. Aor. act. inf., νομίζω, *consider, reckon*; result clause (cf. BDF §391; S §2269; *CGCG* §46.6), signposted by τοσαύτης.
73. στόμα, -ατος, τό, *mouth*.
74. μυκτήρ, -ῆρος, ὁ, *nostril*.
75. ὄργανον, -ου, τό, *organ*.
76. Pres. mid. inf., χράομαι, *use*; with dat.; indir. disc. See n. 57.
77. πρός τό with an infinitive expresses purpose (cf. BDF §402).
78. ἄποιος, -ον, *without a quality/attribute, not of the sort*.
79. Pres. act. indic. 3 sg., ἐμφαίνω, *exhibit, display, indicate*.
80. Compar., φυσικός, -ή, -όν, *much in accordance with nature*; pred. acc.
81. προφορά, -ᾶς, ἡ, *utterance, expression*.
82. Pres. pass. indic. 3 sg., συνάγω, (pass.) *be concluded/inferred* (LSJ, 1692.II.3).
83. ἕνωσις, -εως, ἡ, *a making into one, union*.
84. Aor. act. ptc. gen. masc. sg., τείνω, *stretch out*; gen. absol.
85. μέσος, -η, -ον, *pertaining to the middle / intervening party*; i.e., πνεῦμα is what mediates the power that emanates from God.
86. Pres. mid. ptc. gen. neut. sg., ὑπόκειμαι, (neut. subst.) *the subject*.
87. τίνος ἕνεκα ἢ, *For what purpose other than . . . ?*
88. Aor. act. indic. 3 sg., νοέω, *perceive, apprehend*. The protasis is the exception clause: "How, then, would the soul have apprehended God [implied: it couldn't], *unless* he breathed into and powerfully took hold of it?"
89. Aor. mid. indic. 3 sg., ἅπτω, (mid.) *grasp, take hold of*; with gen.
90. Aor. act. indic. 3 sg., ἀποτολμάω, *dare*. Same construction as the previous sentence: contrafactual apodosis followed by exception clause.
91. Adv. acc. (extent), *so far*. Signpost of the result clause.
92. Aor. act. inf., ἀνατρέχω, *run up, leap*.
93. Aor. mid. inf., ἀντιλαμβάνω, (mid.) *lay hold of*; with gen.; result clause (cf. S §2260; *CGCG* §46.7).
94. Aor. act. indic. 3 sg., ἀνασπάω, *pull, draw up*.
95. Impf. act. indic. 3 sg., ἔνειμι, (impers.) *it is possible*; with acc. and inf.
96. Aor. act. indic. 3 sg., τυπόω, *impress*.
97. ἐφικτός, -ή, -όν, *accessible, within one's reach*.
98. Aor. pass. inf., νοέω, *perceive, apprehend*; epex. (cf. S §2001; *CGCG* 51.18): "He impressed the powers according to what is within its [the mind's] reach *to know*."
99. The new topic addresses the third question [διὰ τί εἰς τὸ πρόσωπον ἐμπνεῖται;]: "Now the [expression] 'he breathed into the face' is both physically and ethically [to be understood]."
100. Adv., *physically* (according to nature).
101. Adv., *ethically* (according to moral character).
102. μέν . . . δέ; point/counterpoint.
103. αἴσθησις, -εως, ἡ, *sense perception*.
104. Impf. act. indic. 3 sg., δημιουργέω, *create*.
105. μέρος, -ους, τό, *part*.
106. ὥσπερ . . . οὕτως, *as . . . so*.
107. ἡγεμονικός, -ή, -όν, *ruling, governing*.
108. γόνιμος, -ον, *concerning reproduction*.

ἐνεπνεύσθη; ὑπὸ τοῦ νοῦ δηλονότι.[109] οὗ γὰρ μετέσχεν ὁ νοῦς παρὰ θεοῦ, τούτου μεταδίδωσι[110] τῷ ἀλόγῳ μέρει τῆς ψυχῆς, ὥστε τὸν μὲν[111] νοῦν ἐψυχῶσθαι ὑπὸ θεοῦ, τὸ δὲ ἄλογον ὑπὸ τοῦ νοῦ· ὡσανεὶ[112] γὰρ θεός ἐστι τοῦ ἀλόγου ὁ νοῦς, παρὸ[113] καὶ Μωυσῆν οὐκ ὤκνησεν[114] εἰπεῖν "θεὸν τοῦ Φαραώ" [Exod. 7:1]. **41**τῶν γὰρ γινομένων τὰ μὲν[115] καὶ ὑπὸ θεοῦ γίνεται καὶ δι' αὐτοῦ, τὰ δὲ ὑπὸ θεοῦ μέν,[116] οὐ δι' αὐτοῦ δέ· τὰ μὲν οὖν[117] ἄριστα καὶ ὑπὸ θεοῦ γέγονε καὶ δι' αὐτοῦ· προελθὼν γοῦν[118] ἐρεῖ ὅτι "ἐφύτευσεν ὁ θεὸς παράδεισον" [Gen. 2:8]· τούτων καὶ ὁ νοῦς ἐστι· τὸ δὲ ἄλογον ὑπὸ θεοῦ μὲν γέγονεν, οὐ διὰ θεοῦ δέ, ἀλλὰ διὰ τοῦ λογικοῦ[119] τοῦ ἄρχοντός τε καὶ βασιλεύοντος ἐν ψυχῇ.

42"πνοὴν"[120] δέ, ἀλλ' οὐ πνεῦμα, εἴρηκεν, ὡς διαφορᾶς οὔσης·[121] τὸ μὲν[122] γὰρ πνεῦμα νενόηται κατὰ τὴν ἰσχὺν καὶ εὐτονίαν[123] καὶ δύναμιν, ἡ δὲ πνοὴ ὡς ἂν[124] αὔρα[125] τίς ἐστι καὶ ἀναθυμίασις[126] ἠρεμαία[127] καὶ πραεῖα.[128] ὁ μὲν οὖν[129] κατὰ τὴν εἰκόνα γεγονὼς καὶ τὴν ἰδέαν νοῦς πνεύματος ἂν λέγοιτο[130] κεκοινωνηκέναι[131]—ῥώμην[132] γὰρ ἔχει ὁ λογισμὸς[133] αὐτοῦ—ὁ δὲ ἐκ τῆς ὕλης τῆς κούφης[134] καὶ ἐλαφροτέρας[135] αὔρας[136] ὡς ἂν ἀποφορᾶς[137] τινος, ὁποῖαι γίνονται ἀπὸ τῶν ἀρωμάτων·[138] φυλαττομένων[139] γὰρ οὐδὲν ἧττον[140] καὶ μὴ ἐκθυμιωμένων[141] εὐωδία[142] τις γίνεται.

NOTES

1.33. The passage is structured into four questions, which Philo answers in turn: (1) Why does the earthly human, and not the heavenly, receive divine πνεῦμα? (2) What is the significance of the term "he in-breathed" (ἐνεφύσησε)? (3) Why does Moses say that he "breathed into his face" (εἰς τὸ πρόσωπον ἐμπνεῖται; cf. QG 1.5)? (4) Why does Moses use the term "breath" (πνοή) instead of "spirit" (πνεῦμα)?

1.34–35. The answer to question 1 is twofold. First, God gives good gifts to those who are not perfect (τέλειος) so that he might incite them to *imitatio Dei* (cf. Matt. 5:43–48). Second, God gives divine

---

109. Adv., *manifestly, very clearly*.
110. Pres. act. indic. 3 sg., μεταδίδωμι, *distribute*; with gen.
111. μέν . . . δέ; point/counterpoint.
112. Adv. (ὡς ἂν εἰ), *so to speak, as it were*.
113. παρὸ = παρ' ὅ, *for this reason*.
114. Aor. act. indic. 3 sg., ὀκνέω, *shrink from, hesitate*.
115. τὰ μέν . . . τὰ δέ, *some . . . others*.
116. μέν . . . δέ qualifies τὰ δέ (cf. S §2908): this group comes into being ὑπὸ θεοῦ (μέν) but not δι' αὐτοῦ (δέ).
117. See n. 15.
118. Postpositive partic.: "A combination of γε and οὖν, γοῦν modifies an utterance which elaborates (οὖν) upon (part of) the preceding utterance by restricting its applicability (γε) (*at least, at any rate*). It is often used in sentences which provide the 'minimal evidence' or the 'minimal applicability' for a preceding statement" (*CGCG* §59.54).
119. λογικός, -ή, -όν, *reasonable*.
120. Philo's response to his fourth and final question: διὰ τί . . . πνοῆς νῦν ἀλλ' οὐχὶ πνεύματος μέμνηται;
121. ὡς with a circumstantial participle gives "the 'subjective' reason or motivation, for which responsibility lies with the subject of the matrix verb" (*CGCG* §52.39).
122. μέν . . . δέ; point/counterpoint.
123. εὐτονία, -ας, ἡ, *vigor*.
124. ὡς ἄν, *as if, like*.
125. αὔρα, -ας, ἡ, *breeze*.
126. ἀναθυμίασις, -εως, ἡ, *vapor*.
127. ἠρεμαῖος, -α, -ον, *gentle*.
128. πραΰς, -εῖα, -ύ, *soft, gentle*.
129. See n. 15.
130. Pres. pass. opt. 3 sg., λέγω; potential. See n. 1.
131. Pf. mid. inf., κοινωνέω, *partake of, have a share in*; with gen.; indir. disc. See n. 57.
132. ῥώμη, -ης, ἡ, *strength, might, vigor of life*.
133. λογισμός, -οῦ, ὁ, *reasoning*.
134. κοῦφος, -η, -ον, *light, airy, unsubstantial*.
135. Compar., ἐλαφρός, -ά, -όν, *lighter, less substantial*.
136. αὔρα, -ας, ἡ, *breeze, fresh air*.
137. ἀποφορά, -ᾶς, ἡ, *exhalation*.
138. ἄρωμα, -ατος, τό, *aromatic herb/spice*.
139. Pres. pass. ptc. gen. neut. pl., φυλάσσω (Att. φυλάττω), (pass.) *be kept*; gen. absol.
140. Adv. acc. (degree), οὐδὲν ἧττον, *not in the least, in no way*.
141. Pres. pass. ptc. gen. neut. pl., ἐκθυμιάω, (pass.) *be burned as incense*; gen. absol.
142. εὐωδία, -ας, ἡ, *sweet smell*.

πνεῦμα to human beings to establish a just order lest he be rendered culpable for human sin (cf. Rom. 3:5–8).

1.36–38. The answer to the second question begins as a simple negation of an apparent anthropomorphism. Yet Philo also wants to demonstrate that Moses's language is "entirely in accordance with nature" (φυσικώτερον)—namely, that there is (1) an entity that inspires (ὁ θεός), (2) an entity that receives inspiration (νοῦς), and (3) a medium of inspiration (πνεῦμα). On the close connection of πνεῦμα and νοῦς, see Kooten (2008, 64–65, 277–82).

1.39–41. The third answer is twofold and similar to the one Philo gives in *QG* 1.5. From a "scientific perspective" (φυσικῶς; i.e., pertaining to the study of the natural cosmos) the organs of the face are associated with sense perception, and thus one may suppose that the face is the locus of the ψυχή. From an "ethical perspective" (ἠθικῶς; i.e., pertaining to the study of virtues, vices, and the nature of the good) it seems reasonable that God would breathe into only an entity that is worthy of him—namely, the νοῦς, which operates as both a ruler of the ψυχή and the mediator of the πνεῦμα.

1.42. The fourth and final answer rests on the distinction between "gentle breeze" (πνοή) and "strong wind" (πνεῦμα). See Tobin (1983, 128–29) and Kooten (2008, 65). The earthly human can bear only a gentle breeze (πνοή), while the heavenly human receives God's πνεῦμα directly. Wyss (2016, 113) notes that this is the only instance where Philo reads πνοή; "elsewhere he deals with Gen 2:7 as if it read πνεῦμα."

4.1.3

The Call of Abraham

Allegorical Interpretation 3.83–84

3.83τί δὲ εἰργάσατο¹ ἤδη καλὸν ὁ Ἀβράμ, ὅτι κελεύει² αὐτῷ πατρίδος³ καὶ τῆς γενεᾶς⁴ ταύτης ξενοῦσθαι⁵ καὶ γῆν οἰκεῖν, ἣν [ἂν] αὐτὸς δῷ ὁ θεός; [Gen. 12:1] πόλις δέ ἐστιν ἀγαθὴ καὶ πολλὴ καὶ σφόδρα⁶ εὐδαίμων,⁷ τὰ γὰρ δῶρα τοῦ θεοῦ μεγάλα καὶ τίμια.⁸ ἀλλὰ καὶ τοῦτον τὸν τρόπον⁹ ἐγέννησε τύπον¹⁰ ἔχοντα σπουδῆς¹¹ ἄξιον· ἑρμηνεύεται¹² γὰρ Ἀβρὰμ "πατὴρ μετέωρος,"¹³ δι' ἀμφοτέρων τῶν ὀνομάτων ἐπαινετός.¹⁴ **84**ὁ γὰρ νοῦς, ὅταν μὴ δεσπότου τρόπον¹⁵ ἀπειλῇ¹⁶ τῇ ψυχῇ, ἀλλ' ὡς πατὴρ ἄρχῃ,¹⁷ μὴ τὰ ἡδέα¹⁸ χαριζόμενος αὐτῇ, τὰ δὲ συμφέροντα¹⁹ καὶ ἀκούσῃ²⁰ διδούς, καὶ ἐπίπαν²¹ τῶν ταπεινῶν²² καὶ ἀγόντων ἐπὶ τὰ θνητὰ²³ ἀποστὰς²⁴ μετεωροπολῇ²⁵ καὶ συνδιατρίβῃ²⁶ θεωρήμασι²⁷ τοῖς περὶ κόσμου καὶ τῶν μερῶν²⁸ αὐτοῦ καὶ ἔτι μᾶλλον ἐπανιὼν²⁹ ἐρευνᾷ³⁰ τὸ θεῖον³¹ καὶ τὴν τούτου φύσιν³²

1. Aor. mid. indic. 3 sg., ἐργάζομαι, *do*.
2. Pres. act. indic. 3 sg., κελεύω, *bid, command*; with dat. and inf. The subject is ὁ θεός.
3. πατρίς, -ίδος, ἡ, *homeland*.
4. γενεά, -ᾶς, ἡ, *kindred*.
5. Pres. pass. inf., ξενόω, (pass.) *be exiled from*; with gen.
6. Adv., *very, exceedingly*.
7. εὐδαίμων, -ον, *blessed, prosperous*.
8. τίμιος, -α, -ον, *honorable*.
9. τρόπος, -ου, ὁ, (of a pers.) *character*.
10. τύπος, -ου, ὁ, *form, shape*; pred. comp.
11. σπουδή, -ῆς, ἡ, *esteem*; comp. of ἄξιον.
12. Pres. pass. indic. 3 sg., ἑρμηνεύω, (pass.) *be interpreted*.
13. μετέωρος, -ον, *elevated, lofty, celestial*.
14. ἐπαινετός, -ή, -όν, *praiseworthy*.
15. Acc. of manner; with δεσπότου, "as a master."
16. Pres. act. subj. 3 sg., ἀπειλέω, *threaten*; with dat.; general temp. clause (cf. BDF §382; S §2409; CGCG §47.9).
17. Pres. act. subj. 3 sg., ἄρχω, *rule*. See n. 16.
18. ἡδύς, -εῖα, -ύ, *sweet, pleasant*.
19. Pres. act. ptc. nom. neut. pl., συμφέρω, *be beneficial*; attrib. (subst.).
20. ἄκων, -ουσα, -ον, *unwilling*.
21. ἐπίπαν = ἐπὶ πᾶν, *in everything, in all matters*.
22. ταπεινός, -ά, -όν, *lowly, base*.
23. θνητός, -ή, -όν, *mortal*.
24. Aor. act. ptc. nom. masc. sg., ἀφίστημι, *turn away from*; circ.
25. Pres. act. subj. 3 sg., μετεωροπολέω, *soar aloft*; general temp. clause. See n. 16.
26. Pres. act. subj. 3 sg., συνδιατρίβω, *spend time, occupy oneself with*; with dat.; general temp. clause. See n. 16.
27. θεώρημα, -ατος, τό, *contemplation*.
28. μέρος, -ους, τό, *part*.
29. Pres. act. ptc. nom. masc. sg., ἐπάνειμι, *rise, ascend*; circ.
30. Pres. act. indic. 3 sg., ἐρευνάω, *search out, explore*.
31. θεῖος, -α, -ον, *divine*, (neut. subst.) *the divine/deity*.
32. φύσις, -εως, ἡ, *nature*.

δι' ἔρωτα³³ ἐπιστήμης³⁴ ἄλεκτον,³⁵ μένειν ἐπὶ τῶν ἐξ ἀρχῆς δογμάτων³⁶ οὐ δύναται, ἀλλὰ μετοικίαν³⁷ ζητεῖ βελτιούμενος³⁸ ἀμείνω.³⁹

ἑρμηνεύεται γὰρ Ἀβρὰμ "πατὴρ μετέωρος," δι' ἀμφοτέρων τῶν ὀνομάτων ἐπαινετός. The name midrash distinguishes between Abram, "lofty/high-soaring father," and Abraham, "elect father of sound" (cf. Philo, *Cher.* 4, 7; *Mut.* 66, 69; in *Gig.* 62, he parses Abram as "man of heaven," ἄνθρωπος οὐρανοῦ). Abram is "lofty father" in a twofold sense: first, because he is a student of the heavenly bodies, and second, because his name signifies the mind (νοῦς) that migrates from the body to the incorporeal realm.

NOTES

3.83–84. Philo interprets Gen. 12:1 as both the call of the patriarch and an allegory of the flight of the soul (cf. *Abr.* 68). Abraham's "land" signifies his body, his "kindred" sense perception, and his "father's house" speech (*Migr.* 7).

33. ἔρως, -ωτος, ὁ, *love, desire*.
34. ἐπιστήμη, -ης, ἡ, *knowledge*; obj. gen. of ἔρωτα.
35. ἄλεκτος, -ον, *ineffable*.
36. δόγμα, -ατος, τό, *opinions, beliefs,* (philosophical) *principles*.
37. μετοικία, -ας, ἡ, *change of abode, migration*.
38. Pres. mid. ptc. nom. masc. sg., βελτιόω, *better/improve oneself*; circ.
39. Irreg. compar. of ἀγαθός, *better*.

4.2

Exposition of the Law

Distinct from his Allegorical Commentary, Philo's Exposition of the Law "presents the Pentateuch in a broader and more systematic fashion" (Royse 2009, 45). Included therein are *On the Creation of the World* (Gen. 1–3), *On the Life of Abraham*, *On the Life of Joseph*,[1] *On the Decalogue*, *On the Special Laws* 1–4, *On the Virtues*, and *On Rewards and Punishments*. One thus moves from the fundamental premise that "the world is in harmony with the Law, and the Law with the world" (*Opif.* 3), to exempla of the (unwritten) law prior to its Mosaic instantiation (in the accounts on the lives of the patriarchs), to the rationale of the commandments and legislations (*On the Decalogue* and *Spec.* 1–4), to a systematic treatment of the virtues elucidated by Moses (*On the Virtues*), and finally, to the outcomes (rewards and punishments) that await the obedient and the disobedient (*On Rewards and Punishments*).

I have included eight passages from the Exposition of the Law. The first five are from *On the Creation of the World* (one of Philo's most important works): the prologue (*Opif.* 1–6), the creation of the human being after God's image (*Opif.* 69–71), the significance of the expression "let us make" (*Opif.* 72–76), the creation of woman (*Opif.* 151–152), and the account of the fall (*Opif.* 153–156). Of the remaining three passages, one is from *On the Life of Abraham*, in which Philo focuses on the patriarch's πίστις, and two are from *On the Special Laws* 1, in which Philo focuses on the temple and its sacrificial system, respectively.

Text and Translation: Colson and Whitaker 1929 (§§4.2.1–5); Colson 1935 (§4.2.6); Colson 1937 (§§4.2.7–8)

Supplemental Scripture: Gen. 1:1 (§4.2.1); 1:26–27 (§§4.2.2–3); 2–3 (§§4.2.4–5); 15:1–6 (§4.2.6); Acts 7:44–50 and Heb. 8:1–5 (§4.2.7); Lev. 1–7 (§4.2.8)

---

1. The opening of *On the Life of Joseph* suggests that Philo also wrote *On Isaac* and *On Jacob*. Since we find no mention of these works in Eusebius, they were likely lost very early on in transmission (Royse 2009, 48).

4.2.1

Prologue—Moses the Lawgiver

On the Creation of the World 1–6

1τῶν ἄλλων νομοθετῶν,[1] οἱ μὲν[2] ἀκαλλώπιστα[3] καὶ γυμνὰ[4] τὰ νομισθέντα[5] παρ' αὐτοῖς εἶναι δίκαια διετάξαντο,[6] οἱ δὲ πολὺν ὄγκον[7] τοῖς νοήμασι[8] προσπεριβαλόντες[9] ἐξετύφωσαν[10] τὰ πλήθη,[11] μυθικοῖς[12] πλάσμασι[13] τὴν ἀλήθειαν ἐπικρύψαντες.[14] **2**Μωυσῆς δ', ἑκάτερον[15] ὑπερβάς,[16] τὸ μὲν[17] ὡς ἄσκεπτον[18] καὶ ἀταλαίπωρον[19] καὶ ἀφιλόσοφον,[20] τὸ δ' ὡς καταψευσμένον[21] καὶ μεστὸν[22] γοητείας,[23] παγκάλην καὶ σεμνοτάτην[24] ἀρχὴν ἐποιήσατο τῶν νόμων, μήτ'[25] εὐθὺς ἃ χρὴ[26] πράττειν ἢ τοὐναντίον[27] ὑπειπὼν[28] μήτ', ἐπειδὴ προτυπῶσαι[29] τὰς διανοίας[30] τῶν χρησομένων[31]

1. νομοθέτης, -ου, ὁ, *lawgiver, legislator*. The partitive genitive establishes the theme (cf. *CGCG* §60.33).
2. οἱ μέν . . . οἱ δέ, *some . . . others* (cf. BDF §250; S §1107; *CGCG* §28.27).
3. ἀκαλλώπιστος, -ον, *unadorned*; adv. acc. (manner).
4. γυμνός, -ή, -όν, *naked*; adv. acc. (manner).
5. Aor. pass. ptc. acc. neut. pl., νομίζω, (pass.) *be thought/supposed*; attrib. (subst.). The substantive functions as the direct object of διετάξαντο and introduces indirect discourse (cf. BDF §397; S §2016; *CGCG* §51.19).
6. Aor. mid. indic. 3 pl., διατάσσω, *arrange, order*.
7. ὄγκος, -ου, ὁ, *bulk, cumbersome matter*.
8. νόημα, -ατος, τό, *thought*.
9. Aor. mid. ptc. nom. masc. pl., προσπεριβάλλω, *surround/enfold one thing* (dat.) *with another* (acc.); circ.
10. Aor. act. indic. 3 pl., ἐκτυφόω, *deceive*. MSS M A B P have ἐξετύφλωσαν, "they blinded."
11. πλῆθος, -ους, τό, *multitude*.
12. μυθικός, -ή, -όν, *mythic*.
13. πλάσμα, -ατος, τό, *that which is formed/molded*.
14. Aor. act. ptc. nom. masc. pl., ἐπικρύπτω, *hide, conceal*; circ.
15. ἑκάτερος, -α, -ον, *each* (of the aforementioned groups).
16. Aor. act. ptc. nom. masc. sg., ὑπερβαίνω, *go beyond, surpass*; circ.
17. τὸ μέν . . . τὸ δέ, *the one* (group) . . . *the other* (group). See n. 2.
18. ἄσκεπτος, -ον, *unreflecting*.
19. ἀταλαίπωρος, -ον, *lazy, sluggish*.
20. ἀφιλόσοφος, -ον, *unphilosophic*.
21. Pf. pass. ptc. acc. neut. sg., καταψεύδομαι, (pass.) *be falsely reported*; attrib.
22. μεστός, -ή, -όν, *full of*; with gen.
23. γοητεία, -ας, ἡ, *deception, trickery*.
24. Superl., σεμνός, -ή, -όν, *most venerable*.
25. μήτ' . . . μήτ', *neither . . . nor*.
26. Quasi-impers., *it is necessary*; with acc. and inf. (cf. BDF §405; S §1985; *CGCG* §36.3).
27. Crasis: τὸ ἐναντίον, *the opposite*.
28. Aor. act. ptc. nom. masc. sg., ὑπολέγω, *indicate, explain*; circ.
29. Aor. act. inf., προτυπόω, *form first*.
30. διανοία, -ας, ἡ, *mind*.
31. Fut. mid. ptc. gen. masc. pl., χράομαι, *make use of*; with dat.; attrib. (subst.).

τοῖς νόμοις ἀναγκαῖον³² ἦν, μύθους πλασάμενος³³ ἢ συναινέσας³⁴ τοῖς ὑφ' ἑτέρων συντεθεῖσιν.³⁵ **3** ἡ δ' ἀρχή, καθάπερ ἔφην, ἐστὶ θαυμασιωτάτη,³⁶ κοσμοποιίαν³⁷ περιέχουσα,³⁸ ὡς καὶ τοῦ κόσμου τῷ νόμῳ καὶ τοῦ νόμου τῷ κόσμῳ συνᾴδοντος,³⁹ καὶ τοῦ νομίμου⁴⁰ ἀνδρὸς εὐθὺς ὄντος κοσμοπολίτου,⁴¹ πρὸς τὸ βούλημα⁴² τῆς φύσεως⁴³ τὰς πράξεις ἀπευθύνοντος,⁴⁴ καθ' ἣν καὶ ὁ σύμπας κόσμος διοικεῖται.⁴⁵

4 τὸ μὲν οὖν⁴⁶ κάλλος τῶν νοημάτων τῆς κοσμοποιίας οὐδεὶς, οὔτε ποιητής⁴⁷ οὔτε λογογράφος,⁴⁸ ἀξίως ἂν ὑμνῆσαι⁴⁹ δύναιτο.⁵⁰ καὶ γὰρ⁵¹ λόγον καὶ ἀκοὴν ὑπερβάλλει, μείζω καὶ σεμνότερα⁵² ὄντα ἢ ὡς⁵³ θνητοῦ τινος ὀργάνοις⁵⁴ ἐναρμοσθῆναι.⁵⁵ **5** οὐ μὴν⁵⁶ διὰ τοῦθ' ἡσυχαστέον,⁵⁷ ἀλλ' ἕνεκα τοῦ θεοφιλοῦς⁵⁸ καὶ ὑπὲρ δύναμιν ἐπιτολμητέον⁵⁹ λέγειν, οἴκοθεν⁶⁰ μὲν οὐδέν, ὀλίγα δ' ἀντὶ πολλῶν, ἐφ' ἃ τὴν ἀνθρωπίνην⁶¹ διάνοιαν φθάνειν⁶² εἰκὸς⁶³ ἔρωτι⁶⁴ καὶ πόθῳ⁶⁵ σοφίας κατεσχημένην.⁶⁶ **6** ὡς⁶⁷ γὰρ τῶν κολοσσιαίων⁶⁸ μεγεθῶν⁶⁹ τὰς ἐμφάσεις⁷⁰ καὶ ἡ βραχυτάτη σφραγὶς⁷¹ τυπωθεῖσα⁷² δέχεται, οὕτως τάχα που καὶ τὰ τῆς ἀναγραφείσης⁷³ ἐν τοῖς νόμοις κοσμοποιίας⁷⁴ ὑπερβάλλοντα κάλλη, καὶ ταῖς μαρμαρυγαῖς⁷⁵ τὰς τῶν

---

32. ἀναγκαῖος, -α, -ον, (quasi-impers.) *it is necessary*; with (acc. and) inf. (cf. S §1985; *CGCG* §36.8).
33. Aor. mid. ptc. nom. masc. sg., πλάσσω, *form, shape, invent*; circ.
34. Aor. act. ptc. nom. masc. sg., συναινέω, *consent, approve*; with dat.; circ.
35. Aor. pass. ptc. dat. masc. pl., συντίθημι, (pass.) *be gathered*; attrib. (subst.).
36. Superl., θαυμάσιος, -α, -ον, *most marvelous*.
37. κοσμοποιία, -ας, ἡ, *an account of the creation of the cosmos* (cf. Runia 2001, 103).
38. Pres. act. ptc. nom. fem. sg., περιέχω, *contain*; circ.
39. Pres. act. ptc. gen. masc. sg., συνᾴδω, *be in harmony with*; with dat. Note that ὡς with the circumstantial participle gives "the 'subjective' reason or motivation, for which responsibility lies with the subject of the matrix verb" (cf. *CGCG* §52.39).
40. νόμιμος, -η, -ον, *conforming to customs/laws*.
41. κοσμοπολίτης, -ου, ὁ, *citizen of the cosmos*.
42. βούλημα, -ατος, τό, *purpose, intent*.
43. φύσις, -εως, ἡ, *nature*.
44. Pres. act. ptc. gen. masc. sg., ἀπευθύνω, *regulate*; circ.
45. Pres. pass. indic. 3 sg., διοικέω, (pass.) *be administered, governed*.
46. Partic. combination: "The speaker vouches for the correctness or relevance of his/her utterance (μέν with the force of μήν), and indicates that it is presented in more relevant terms (οὖν)" (cf. *CGCG* §59.72). Note that μὲν οὖν anticipates μήν in *Opif.* 5: "Now indeed X . . . nevertheless Y."
47. ποιητής, -οῦ, ὁ, *poet*.
48. λογογράφος, -ου, ὁ, *prose writer*.
49. Aor. act. inf., ὑμνέω, *celebrate in hymn*; comp. of δύναιτο.
50. Pres. act. opt. 3 sg., δύναμαι, *be able*; potential (cf. BDF §385; S §1824; *CGCG* §34.25).
51. Partic. combination: related information (καί) that has explanatory force (γάρ) (cf. *CGCG* §59.66).
52. Compar., σεμνός, -ή, -όν, *more venerable*.
53. Compar., ἤ with ὡς clause, *too . . . to* (cf. *CGCG* §32.13). Thus, "Being too great and venerable to be adjusted to the instruments of any mortal."
54. ὄργανον, -ου, τό, *instrument*.
55. Aor. pass. inf., ἐναρμόζω, (pass.) *be fit, adjusted*; with dat.
56. Postpositive partic.: "indicates a transition to a point which is somehow unexpected" (*CGCG* §59.49; Denniston 1966, 348); anticipated by μέν.
57. Verbal adj. of ἡσυχάζω, impers. (act.) constr. (cf. S §2152; *CGCG* §37.3). Thus, "We must not [οὐ] pass it over in silence" (lit., "It is not a thing [for us] to pass over in silence").
58. θεοφιλής, -ές, *God-loving, God-beloved*. The latter is to be preferred (Runia 2001, 104).
59. Verbal adj. of τολμάω, impers. (act.) constr., "it is necessary [for us] to dare"; with inf. See n. 57.
60. Adv., *from one's own resources*. The statement is elliptical: "[To say] nothing [οὐδέν] from our own resources, but only a few [ὀλίγα] in place of a great many things [ἀντὶ πολλῶν]."
61. ἀνθρώπινος, -η, -ον, *human*.
62. Pres. act. inf., φθάνω, *arrive at, reach*; with ἐπί (or εἰς) designating point of arrival (cf. BDAG, 1053.2); indir. disc. See n. 5.
63. Pf. act. ptc. acc. neut. sg., ἔοικα, (impers.) *it seems*; acc. absol. (cf. BDF §424; S §2076; *CGCG* §52.33).
64. ἔρως, -ωτος, ὁ, *love, sexual desire*.
65. πόθος, -ου, ὁ, *desire*.
66. Pf. pass. ptc. acc. fem. sg., κατέχω, (pass.) *be possessed*; circ.
67. ὡς . . . καί . . . οὕτως τάχα που καί, *as even . . . so perhaps also*.
68. κολοσσιαῖος, -α, -ον, *colossal*.
69. μέγεθος, -ους, τό, *size, dimension*.
70. ἔμφασις, -εως, ἡ, *appearance, image, likeness*.
71. σφραγίς, -ῖδος, ἡ, *seal*.
72. Aor. pass. ptc. nom. fem. sg., τυπόω, (pass.) *be impressed*; circ.
73. Aor. pass. ptc. gen. fem. sg., ἀναγράφω, (pass.) *be written down*; attrib.
74. κοσμοποιία, -ας, ἡ, (here) *making of the cosmos*.
75. μαρμαρυγή, -ῆς, ἡ, *splendor, radiance*.

ἐντυγχανόντων⁷⁶ ψυχὰς ἐπισκιάζοντα,⁷⁷ βραχυτέροις παραδηλωθήσεται⁷⁸ χαρακτῆρσιν,⁷⁹ ἐπειδὰν ἐκεῖνο μηνυθῇ⁸⁰ πρότερον, ὅπερ οὐκ ἄξιον ἀποσιωπῆσαι.⁸¹

NOTES

2. Cf. *Mos.* 2.48–51. Moses outstrips both groups: the former by forming in advance the minds of the worshipers, the latter by avoiding mythological conventions.

3. ἡ δ' ἀρχή. Cf. Gen. 1:1 LXX. Thus the beginning of Mosaic legislation begins *at the beginning*—that is, with "an account of the creation of the cosmos [κοσμοποιία]" (cf. *Opif.* 4, 129, 170).

ὡς καὶ τοῦ κόσμου τῷ νόμῳ καὶ τοῦ νόμου τῷ κόσμῳ συνᾴδοντος. Runia (2001, 107) notes that Philo's "use of the term *nomos* in §3 is deliberately equivocal. He clearly means the Law of Moses, but also wants to exploit the associations with natural or cosmic law. The Law of Moses is not identical with the cosmic or natural law, but a far-reaching harmony exists between them. In terms of their deeper intentions they may be regarded as amounting to the same (or, in a more Platonic perspective, as model and faithful copy), but the Mosaic law has been adapted to the requirements of human society." Hence the man who lives in accordance with the νόμος is a "citizen of the world" (κοσμοπολίτης), someone who orders his actions in accordance with the rational purpose of nature (πρὸς τὸ βούλημα τῆς φύσεως). This is precisely how Philo describes the patriarchs (e.g., *Abr.* 276; *Spec.* 2.40; 2.223).

---

76. Pres. act. ptc. gen. masc. pl., ἐντυγχάνω, *encounter*; attrib. (subst.).
77. Pres. act. ptc. nom. neut. pl., ἐπισκιάζω, *overshadow*; circ. (concessive).
78. Fut. pass. indic. 3 sg., παραδηλόω, (pass.) *be indicated.*
79. χαρακτήρ, -ῆρος, ἡ, *mark, sign.*
80. Aor. pass. subj. 3 sg., μηνύω, (pass.) *be reported.*
81. Aor. act. inf., ἀποσιωπάω, *be silent*; subject of οὐκ ἄξιον: "about which is not proper [for us] to be silent." Thus he must deal with important prolegomena (*Opif.* 7–12) before he can begin his treatment of Genesis.

4.2.2

The Image of God, Part 1

On the Creation of the World 69–71

69Μετὰ δὴ¹ τἆλλα² πάντα, καθάπερ ἐλέχθη, τὸν ἄνθρωπόν φησι³ γεγενῆσθαι, κατ' εἰκόνα⁴ θεοῦ καὶ καθ' ὁμοίωσιν⁵ [Gen. 1:26]· πάνυ⁶ καλῶς, ἐμφερέστερον⁷ γὰρ οὐδὲν γηγενὲς⁸ ἀνθρώπου θεῷ. τὴν δ' ἐμφέρειαν⁹ μηδεὶς εἰκαζέτω¹⁰ σώματος χαρακτῆρι.¹¹ οὔτε γὰρ ἀνθρωπόμορφος¹² ὁ θεός, οὔτε θεοειδὲς¹³ τὸ ἀνθρώπειον¹⁴ σῶμα. ἡ δὲ εἰκὼν λέλεκται κατὰ τὸν τῆς ψυχῆς ἡγεμόνα¹⁵ νοῦν·¹⁶ πρὸς γὰρ ἕνα, τὸν τῶν ὅλων¹⁷ ἐκεῖνον ὡς ἄν¹⁸ ἀρχέτυπον,¹⁹ ὁ ἐν ἑκάστῳ τῶν κατὰ μέρος²⁰ ἀπεικονίσθη,²¹ τρόπον²² τινὰ θεὸς ὢν τοῦ φέροντος καὶ ἀγαλματοφοροῦντος²³ αὐτόν· ὃν γὰρ ἔχει λόγον²⁴ ὁ μέγας ἡγεμὼν²⁵ ἐν ἅπαντι τῷ κόσμῳ, τοῦτον ὡς ἔοικε²⁶ καὶ ὁ ἀνθρώπινος²⁷ νοῦς ἐν

---

1. Postpositive partic., (here connective) *now* (cf. *CGCG* §59.44; Denniston 1966, 236–40).
2. Crasis: τὰ ἄλλα.
3. The subject is Moses; introduces indir. disc. with acc. and inf. (cf. BDF §397; S §2016; *CGCG* §51.19).
4. εἰκών, -όνος, ἡ, *image*.
5. ὁμοίωσις, -εως, ἡ, *likeness*.
6. Adv., *very, exceedingly*; πάνυ καλῶς, "very well [did he say this]." Philo frequently responds to a biblical reference by praising the words of Moses (cf. *Opif.* 76, 148).
7. Compar., ἐμφερής, -ές, *more similar*; with dat. and gen. of compar.
8. γηγενής, -ές, *earthborn*.
9. ἐμφέρεια, -ας, ἡ, *resemblance*.
10. Pres. act. impv. 3 sg., εἰκάζω, *liken, compare*; with acc. to dat.
11. χαρακτήρ, -ῆρος, ὁ, *characteristic*.
12. ἀνθρωπόμορφος, -ον, *shaped like a human, anthropomorphic*.
13. θεοειδής, -ές, *godlike*.
14. ἀνθρώπειος, -α, -ον, *human*.
15. ἡγεμών, -όνος, ὁ, *leader, ruler, sovereign*.
16. νοῦς, -οῦ, ὁ, *mind*.
17. ὅλος, -ου, ὁ, (subst. sg./pl.) *universe*.
18. ὡς ἄν, "as it were," "as though." The full phrase: "[With respect to the one (mind)], that single [mind] of the universe, an archetype, as it were."
19. ἀρχέτυπος, -ον, *exemplary, ideal*, (subst.) *archetype*.
20. κατὰ μέρος, *in turn, successively*.
21. Aor. pass. indic. 3 sg., ἀπεικονίζω, (pass.) *be portrayed, described*.
22. Adv. acc. (manner), with τινά, "in a certain sense."
23. Pres. act. ptc. gen. masc. sg., ἀγαλματοφορέω, *bear an image* (of the god); attrib. (subst.).
24. The antecedent is incorporated into the relative clause (cf. S §2536; *CGCG* §50.15): "*Which position* the great ruler occupies in the whole cosmos, this also, it seems, the human mind occupies in humans."
25. ἡγεμών, -όνος, ὁ, *leader, ruler, sovereign*.
26. Pf. act. indic. 3 sg., ἔοικα, (impers. with ὡς) *it seems*.
27. ἀνθρώπινος, -η, -ον, *human*.

ἀνθρώπῳ· ἀόρατός²⁸ τε γάρ²⁹ ἐστιν, αὐτὸς τὰ πάντα ὁρῶν, καὶ ἄδηλον³⁰ ἔχει τὴν οὐσίαν,³¹ τὰς τῶν ἄλλων καταλαμβάνων·³² καὶ τέχναις καὶ ἐπιστήμαις³³ πολυσχιδεῖς³⁴ ἀνατέμνων³⁵ ὁδούς, λεωφόρους³⁶ ἁπάσας, διὰ γῆς ἔρχεται καὶ θαλάττης, τὰ ἐν ἑκατέρᾳ φύσει³⁷ διερευνώμενος.³⁸ **⁷⁰**καὶ πάλιν πτηνὸς³⁹ ἀρθείς, καὶ τὸν ἀέρα⁴⁰ καὶ τὰ τούτου παθήματα⁴¹ κατασκεψάμενος,⁴² ἀνωτέρω⁴³ φέρεται πρὸς αἰθέρα⁴⁴ καὶ τὰς οὐρανοῦ περιόδους,⁴⁵ πλανήτων⁴⁶ τε καὶ ἀπλανῶν⁴⁷ χορείαις⁴⁸ συμπεριποληθείς⁴⁹ κατὰ τοὺς μουσικῆς⁵⁰ τελείας νόμους, ἑπόμενος⁵¹ ἔρωτι σοφίας ποδηγετοῦντι,⁵² πᾶσαν τὴν αἰσθητὴν⁵³ οὐσίαν ὑπερκύψας,⁵⁴ ἐνταῦθα⁵⁵ ἐφίεται⁵⁶ τῆς νοητῆς.⁵⁷ **⁷¹**καὶ ὧν εἶδεν ἐνταῦθα αἰσθητῶν ἐν ἐκείνῃ τὰ παραδείγματα⁵⁸ καὶ τὰς ἰδέας⁵⁹ θεασάμενος,⁶⁰ ὑπερβάλλοντα κάλλη, μέθη⁶¹ νηφαλίῳ⁶² κατασχεθείς⁶³ ὥσπερ οἱ κορυβαντιῶντες⁶⁴ ἐνθουσιᾷ,⁶⁵ ἑτέρου γεμισθεὶς⁶⁶ ἱμέρου⁶⁷ καὶ πόθου⁶⁸ βελτίονος,⁶⁹ ὑφ' οὗ πρὸς τὴν ἄκραν⁷⁰ ἁψῖδα⁷¹ παραπεμφθεὶς⁷² τῶν νοητῶν ἐπ' αὐτὸν ἰέναι δοκεῖ⁷³ τὸν μέγαν βασιλέα· γλιχομένου⁷⁴ δ' ἰδεῖν, ἀθρόου⁷⁵ φωτὸς

28. ἀόρατος, -ον, *unseen, invisible*.
29. The particle combination τε γάρ is unusual but not unattested (cf. Denniston 1966, 536). In this case, the structure is τε . . . καί, which serves to support (γάρ) the previous point.
30. ἄδηλος, -ον, *unclear, imperceptible*.
31. οὐσία, -ας, ἡ, *substance, nature*.
32. Pres. act. ptc. nom. masc. sg., καταλαμβάνω, *grasp, understand*; circ. (concessive).
33. Dat. of means, τέχναις καὶ ἐπιστήμαις, "by the arts and sciences."
34. πολυσχιδής, -ές, *split/divided into many branches, manifold*.
35. Pres. act. ptc. nom. masc. sg., ἀνατέμνω, *open up*; circ.
36. λεωφόρος, -ον, *busy, main street*, (pl. subst.) *highways*; appositive to ὁδούς.
37. φύσις, -εως, ἡ, *nature*.
38. Pres. mid. ptc. nom. masc. sg., διερευνάω, *examine, investigate*; circ.
39. πτηνός, -ή, -όν, *flying, winged*, (fig.) *on high*.
40. ἀήρ, -έρος, ὁ, *air*.
41. πάθημα, -ατος, τό, (pl.) *phenomena, accidents, changes*.
42. Aor. mid. ptc. nom. masc. sg., κατασκοπέω, *observe*; circ.
43. Compar. adv. of ἄνω, adv., *further upward, yet higher*.
44. αἰθήρ, -έρος, τό, *ether, substance out of which the heavenly bodies are made*.
45. περίοδος, -ου, ἡ, *circuit, orbit, revolution*.
46. πλανητός, -ή, -όν, (subst.) *wandering heavenly bodies* (i.e., planets).
47. ἀπλανής, -ές, (subst.) *fixed heavenly bodies* (i.e., fixed stars).
48. χορεία, -ας, ἡ, *choral dance*.
49. Aor. pass. ptc. nom. masc. sg., συμπεριπολέω, (pass.) *be carried around*; circ.
50. μουσική, -ῆς, ἡ, *music*.
51. Pres. mid. ptc. nom. masc. sg., ἕπω, *follow*; with dat.
52. Pres. act. ptc. dat. masc. sg., ποδηγετέω, *lead, direct*; attrib.
53. αἰσθητός, -ή, -όν, *of what is perceptible to the senses*.
54. Aor. act. ptc. nom. masc. sg., ὑπερκρύπτω, *look beyond*; circ.
55. Rel. adv., *where, there*.
56. Pres. mid. indic. 3 sg., ἐφίημι, (mid.) *aim at, reach for*; with gen.
57. νοητός, -ή, -όν, *intelligible*, (subst.) *intelligible realm*.
58. παράδειγμα, -ατος, τό, *pattern, model*.
59. ἰδέα, -ας, ἡ, *form*.
60. Aor. mid. ptc. nom. masc. sg., θεάομαι, *see, behold*; circ.
61. μέθη, -ης, ἡ, *intoxication*.
62. νηφάλιος, -α, -ον, *sober*.
63. Aor. pass. ptc. nom. masc. sg., κατέχω, (pass.) *be seized*; circ.
64. Pres. act. ptc. nom. masc. pl., κορυβαντιάω, *dance in the style of the Corybants*. The Phrygian priestesses of the god Dionysus were famous for their frenetic dances.
65. ἐνθουσία, -ας, ἡ, *possession* (by a divinity).
66. Aor. pass. ptc. nom. masc. sg., γεμίζω, *be full* of; with gen.; circ.
67. ἵμερος, -ου, ὁ, *desire, longing*.
68. πόθος, -ου, ὁ, *desire*.
69. Compar. of ἀγαθός, *better*.
70. ἄκρος, -α, -ον, *highest*.
71. ἁψίς, -ῖδος, ἡ, *arch, vault* (of the sky).
72. Aor. pass. ptc. nom. masc. sg., παραπέμπω, (pass.) *be sent, dispatched*; circ.
73. Pres. act. indic. 3 sg., δοκέω, *seem, appear*. Either personal ("It thinks that it is heading toward the great king himself") or impersonal ("It seems to be heading toward the great king himself"; cf. *CGCG* §51.30).
74. Pres. mid. ptc. gen. masc. sg., γλίχομαι, *aspire, desire*; gen. absol.
75. ἀθρόος, -ον, *dense*.

ἄκρατοι⁷⁶ καὶ ἀμιγεῖς⁷⁷ αὐγαὶ⁷⁸ χειμάρρου⁷⁹ τρόπον ἐκχέονται,⁸⁰ ὡς ταῖς μαρμαρυγαῖς⁸¹ τὸ τῆς διανοίας⁸² ὄμμα⁸³ σκοτοδινιᾶν.⁸⁴ ἐπεὶ δ' οὐ σύμπασα⁸⁵ εἰκὼν ἐμφερὴς ἀρχετύπῳ παραδείγματι, πολλαὶ δ' εἰσὶν ἀνόμοιοι,⁸⁶ προσεπεσημήνατο⁸⁷ ἐπειπὼν⁸⁸ τῷ κατ' εἰκόνα τὸ καθ' ὁμοίωσιν, εἰς ἔμφασιν⁸⁹ ἀκριβοῦς⁹⁰ ἐκμαγείου⁹¹ τρανὸν⁹² τύπον ἔχοντος.

70. καὶ πάλιν πτηνὸς ἀρθείς. The flight of the soul (cf. Plato, *Phaedr.* 246d–249d).

71. The ascent culminates when the soul advances beyond the intelligible realm to "the Great King himself." Here, however, the mind's eye is overwhelmed and thrown into a state of vertigo as though by dazzling brightness (ὡς ταῖς μαρμαρυγαῖς), the term Plato uses to describe the light that overwhelms the person who leaves the cave (cf. *Resp.* 515c9; 518a8). Thus, "the ascent ends in a kind of failure. The resemblance of the image reaches its limit. If human beings could truly see God, they would no longer be 'after the image' but equal to him" (Runia 2001, 232–33).

NOTES

69. ἡ δὲ εἰκὼν λέλεκται κατὰ τὸν τῆς ψυχῆς ἡγεμόνα νοῦν. Moses applies "image" to the ruler of the soul—that is, mind/reason (cf. Plato, *Leg.* 631d5; 963a8; *Phaedr.* 247c7). The description facilitates the comparison between the νοῦς as the ruler in the ψυχή and God as "the great governor [ὁ μέγας ἡγεμών; cf. Plato, *Phaedr.* 246e4] in the whole cosmos" (Runia 2001, 225, 227).

---

76. ἄκρατος, -ον, *pure*.
77. ἀμιγής, -ές, *unmixed*.
78. αὐγή, -ῆς, ἡ, *splendor, light*.
79. χείμαρρος, -ον, *flooding with water*, (subst.) *torrent*; χειμάρρου τρόπον, "like a torrent."
80. Pres. mid. indic. 3 pl., ἐκχέω, (pass.) *pour out, stream forth*.
81. μαρμαρυγή, -ῆς, ἡ, *gleam, radiance, splendor*.
82. διανοία, -ας, ἡ, *mind, intellect*.
83. ὄμμα, -τος, τό, *eye*.
84. Pres. act. inf., σκοτοδινιάω, *have a dizzy spell, vertigo*; result clause (cf. S §2260; *CGCG* §46.7).
85. σύμπας (σύν, πᾶς), *the whole, sum total*.
86. ἀνόμοιος, -ον, *dissimilar*.
87. Aor. mid. indic. 3 sg., προσεπισημαίνω, *indicate in addition*.
88. Aor. act. ptc. nom. masc. sg., ἐπιλέγω, *add/attribute* (something to something): "Adding the expression 'according to the likeness' [τὸ καθ' ὁμοίωσιν] to the expression 'according to the image' [τῷ κατ' εἰκόνα]."
89. ἔμφασις, -εως, ἡ, *demonstration; emphasis*; with εἰς marking purpose.
90. ἀκριβής, -ές, *exact*.
91. ἐκμαγεῖον, -ου, τό, *imprint*.
92. τρανός, -ή, -όν, *clear, sure*.

4.2.3

The Image of God, Part 2

On the Creation of the World 72–76

⁷²Ἀπορήσειε¹ δ' ἄν τις οὐκ ἀπὸ σκοποῦ,² τί δήποτε³ τὴν ἀνθρώπου μόνου γένεσιν⁴ οὐχ ἑνὶ δημιουργῷ⁵ καθάπερ τἆλλα⁶ ἀνέθηκεν,⁷ ἀλλ' ὡσανεὶ⁸ πλείοσιν· εἰσάγει⁹ γὰρ τὸν πατέρα τῶν ὅλων¹⁰ ταυτὶ¹¹ λέγοντα· "ποιήσωμεν ἄνθρωπον κατ' εἰκόνα¹² ἡμετέραν καὶ καθ' ὁμοίωσιν."¹³ μὴ γὰρ χρεῖος¹⁴ ἐστιν, εἴποιμ'¹⁵ ἄν, οὑτινοσοῦν,¹⁶ ᾧ πάντα ὑπήκοα;¹⁷ ἢ τὸν μὲν¹⁸ οὐρανὸν ἡνίκα¹⁹ ἐποίει καὶ τὴν γῆν καὶ τὴν θάλατταν, οὐδενὸς ἐδεήθη²⁰ τοῦ συνεργήσοντος,²¹ ἄνθρωπον δὲ βραχὺ ζῷον²² οὕτως καὶ ἐπίκηρον²³ οὐχ οἷός τε ἦν²⁴ δίχα²⁵ συμπράξεως²⁶ ἑτέρων αὐτὸς ἀφ' ἑαυτοῦ κατασκευάσασθαι;²⁷ τὴν μὲν οὖν²⁸ ἀληθεστάτην²⁹ αἰτίαν³⁰ θεὸν ἀνάγκη³¹ μόνον

    1. Aor. act. opt. 3 sg., ἀπορέω, (dialogue) *raise a question/difficulty*; potential (cf. BDF §385; S §1824; *CGCG* §34.13).
    2. Idiom, οὐκ ἀπὸ σκοποῦ, "not off the mark."
    3. τί δήποτε, *just why?*
    4. γένεσις, -εως, ἡ, *genesis, creation*.
    5. δημιουργός, -οῦ, ὁ, *creator*.
    6. Crasis: τὰ ἄλλα.
    7. Aor. act. indic. 3 sg., ἀνατίθημι, *attribute*. The subject of the verb is Moses.
    8. Adv. (ὡς ἄν εἰ), *as if, as it were*.
    9. Pres. act. indic. 3 sg., εἰσάγω, *introduce*.
    10. ὅλος, -η, -ον, (neut. pl. subst.) *universe*.
    11. The demonstrative takes the deictic *iota* (cf. S §334.g; *CGCG* §29.36).
    12. εἰκών, -όνος, ἡ, *image*.
    13. ὁμοίωσις, -εως, ἡ, *likeness*.
    14. χρεῖος, -ον, *needing*; with gen.
    15. Aor. act. opt. 1 pl., λέγω; potential. See n. 1.
    16. ὁστισοῦν, ἡτισοῦν, ὁτιοῦν, *whichever, whatever*.
    17. ὑπήκοος, -οον, *subject, obedient*.
    18. μέν ... δέ; point/counterpoint (cf. Runge 2010, 75–83; BDF §447; S §2904; *CGCG* §59.24).
    19. Adv., *when*.
    20. Aor. pass. indic. 3 sg., δέω, *be in need of*; with gen.
    21. Fut. act. ptc. gen. masc. sg., συνεργέω, *work together*, (subst.) *coworker*.
    22. ζῷον, -ου, τό, *animal*.
    23. ἐπίκηρος, -ον, *perishable*.
    24. Idiom, οἷός τε (εἰμι), *be able to, be capable of*; with inf. (cf. S §2497; *CGCG* §51.9).
    25. Prep. with gen., *without, apart from*.
    26. σύμπραξις, -εως, ἡ, *help, assistance*.
    27. Aor. mid. inf., κατασκευάζω, *fashion, furnish*.
    28. Partic. combination: "a transition to a more to-the-point, relevant text segment (οὖν) [that] occurs in two stages (μέν ... δέ), with the relevant new step presented in the δέ-segment" (*CGCG* §59.73).
    29. Superl., ἀληθής, -ές, *truest*.
    30. αἰτία, -ας, ἡ, *reason*.
    31. Quasi-impers. ἀνάγκη (ἐστι), *it is necessary*; with acc. and inf. (cf. S §1985; *CGCG* §36.8).

εἰδέναι, τὴν δ' εἰκότι³² στοχασμῷ³³ πιθανὴν³⁴ καὶ εὔλογον³⁵ εἶναι δοκοῦσαν³⁶ οὐκ ἀποκρυπτέον.³⁷ ἔστι δὲ ἥδε. ⁷³τῶν ὄντων τὰ μὲν³⁸ οὔτ' ἀρετῆς³⁹ οὔτε κακίας μετέχει,⁴⁰ ὥσπερ φυτὰ⁴¹ καὶ ζῷα ἄλογα,⁴² τὰ μὲν⁴³ ὅτι ἄψυχά⁴⁴ τέ ἐστι καὶ ἀφαντάστῳ⁴⁵ φύσει⁴⁶ διοικεῖται,⁴⁷ τὰ δ' ὅτι νοῦν καὶ λόγον ἐκτέτμηται·⁴⁸ κακίας δὲ καὶ ἀρετῆς ὡς ἂν⁴⁹ νοῦς καὶ λόγος, ᾧ πεφύκασιν⁵⁰ ἐνδιαιτᾶσθαι.⁵¹ τὰ δ' αὖ μόνης κεκοινώνηκεν⁵² ἀρετῆς ἀμέτοχα⁵³ πάσης ὄντα κακίας, ὥσπερ οἱ ἀστέρες·⁵⁴ οὗτοι γὰρ ζῷά τε εἶναι λέγονται καὶ ζῷα νοερά,⁵⁵ μᾶλλον δὲ νοῦς⁵⁶ αὐτὸς ἕκαστος, ὅλος δι' ὅλων⁵⁷ σπουδαῖος⁵⁸ καὶ

32. Pf. act. ptc. dat. neut. sg., ἔοικα, *seem* (plausible); attrib.
33. στοχασμός, -οῦ, ὁ, *conjecture*.
34. πιθανός, -ή, -όν, *persuasive*.
35. εὔλογος, -ον, *reasonable*.
36. Pres. act. ptc. acc. fem. sg., δοκέω, *appear*; with inf.; attrib.: τὴν ... δοκοῦσαν, "the [reason] that appears to be reasonable and persuasive, based on likely conjecture."
37. Verbal adj. of ἀποκρύπτω, impers. (act.) constr. (cf. S §2152; CGCG §37.3): "It is necessary [for us] not to conceal."
38. τὰ μέν ... τὰ δ' αὖ ... τὰ δέ, *some* (group 1) ... *others* (group 2) ... *others* (group 3) (cf. BDF §250; S §1107; CGCG §28.17).
39. ἀρετή, -ῆς, ἡ, *virtue*.
40. Pres. act. indic. 3 sg., μετέχω, *partake of*; with gen.
41. φυτόν, -οῦ, τό, *plant*.
42. ζῷον ἄλογον, *irrational creature*; i.e., *animal*.
43. τὰ μέν ... τὰ δέ, *the former* (plants) ... *the latter* (animals); a subdivision within group 1 (cf. S §2908).
44. ἄψυχος, -ον, *without soul*.
45. ἀφάνταστος, -ον, *without imagination*.
46. φύσις, -εως, ἡ, *nature*.
47. Pres. pass. indic. 3 sg., διοικέω, (pass.) *be ruled, regulated*.
48. Pf. pass. indic. 3 sg., ἐκτέμνω, (pass.) *be cut away from*. MSS A B P read οὐ κέκτηται, "do not possess."
49. ὡς ἄν, *as it were, so to speak*.
50. Pf. act. indic. 3 pl., φύω, *be naturally inclined*; with inf. The antecedent of the compound subject is κακίας καὶ ἀρετῆς (prolepsis; cf. S §3045; CGCG §60.37): "And belonging to vice and virtue are, as it were, mind and reason, in which [mind and reason] they [vice and virtue] naturally dwell."
51. Aor. mid. inf., ἐνδιαιτάομαι, *inhabit*.
52. Pf. act. indic. 3 sg., κοινωνέω, *share in, participate in*; with gen.
53. ἀμέτοχος, -ον, *nonparticipating*; with gen.
54. ἀστήρ, -έρος, ὁ, *star*.
55. νοερός, -ά, -όν, *endowed with intelligence*.
56. νοῦς, νόος, ὁ, *mind*.
57. Idiom, ὅλος δι' ὅλων, "through and through," "entirely."
58. σπουδαῖος, -α, -ον, *virtuous*.

παντὸς ἀνεπίδεκτος⁵⁹ κακοῦ· τὰ δὲ τῆς μικτῆς⁶⁰ ἐστι φύσεως, ὥσπερ ἄνθρωπος, ὃς ἐπιδέχεται τἀναντία,⁶¹ φρόνησιν⁶² καὶ ἀφροσύνην,⁶³ σωφροσύνην⁶⁴ καὶ ἀκολασίαν,⁶⁵ ἀνδρείαν⁶⁶ καὶ δειλίαν,⁶⁷ δικαιοσύνην καὶ ἀδικίαν, καὶ συνελόντι φράσαι⁶⁸ ἀγαθὰ καὶ κακά, καλὰ καὶ αἰσχρά, ἀρετὴν καὶ κακίαν. ⁷⁴τῷ δὴ⁶⁹ πάντων πατρὶ θεῷ τὰ μὲν⁷⁰ σπουδαῖα δι' αὐτοῦ μόνου ποιεῖν οἰκειότατον⁷¹ ἦν ἕνεκα⁷² τῆς πρὸς αὐτὸν συγγενείας,⁷³ τὰ δὲ ἀδιάφορα⁷⁴ οὐκ ἀλλότριον,⁷⁵ ἐπειδὴ καὶ ταῦτα τῆς ἐχθρᾶς αὐτῷ κακίας ἀμοιρεῖ,⁷⁶ τὰ δὲ μικτὰ τῇ μὲν⁷⁷ οἰκεῖον τῇ δ' ἀνοίκειον, οἰκεῖον μὲν ἕνεκα τῆς ἀνακεκραμένης⁷⁸ βελτίονος ἰδέας,⁷⁹ ἀνοίκειον δὲ ἕνεκα τῆς ἐναντίας⁸⁰ καὶ χείρονος. ⁷⁵διὰ τοῦτ' ἐπὶ μόνης τῆς ἀνθρώπου γενέσεώς φησιν ὅτι εἶπεν ὁ θεὸς "ποιήσωμεν," ὅπερ ἐμφαίνει⁸¹ συμπαράληψιν⁸² ἑτέρων ὡς

59. ἀνεπίδεκτος, -α, -ον, *unreceptive*; with gen.
60. μικτός, -ά, -όν, *mixed*.
61. Crasis: τὰ ἐναντία, *things of the opposite nature*.
62. φρόνησις, -εως, ἡ, *wisdom, moral reasoning*.
63. ἀφροσύνη, -ης, ἡ, *foolishness, absence of moral reasoning*.
64. σωφροσύνη, -ης, ἡ, *self-control*.
65. ἀκολασία, -ας, ἡ, *lack of restraint*.
66. ἀνδρεία, -ας, ἡ, *courage, manliness*.
67. δειλία, -ας, ἡ, *cowardice*.
68. Idiom, συνελόντι φράσαι, "to summarize," "to put it briefly."
69. Postpositive partic.: "Indicates that the speaker considers (and invites the addressee to consider) the text segment or word (group) which it modifies as evident, clear or precise" (cf. CGCG §59.44).
70. μέν ... δέ ... δέ; point/counterpoints (cf. S §2907).
71. Superl., οἰκεῖος, -α, -ον, *most suitable*; quasi-impers. οἰκειότατον ἦν; with dat. and inf.
72. Prep. with gen., *on account of, for the sake of, because*.
73. συγγενεία, -ας, ἡ, *kinship*.
74. ἀδιάφορος, -ον, *indifferent*.
75. Quasi-impers. οὐκ ἀλλότριον (ἐστί), "it is not foreign"; with dat. and inf.
76. Pres. act. indic. 3 sg., ἀμοιρέω, *have no lot/share in*; with gen.
77. τῇ μέν ... τῇ δέ, *partly* (οἰκεῖον) ... *partly* (ἀνοίκειον).
78. Pf. pass. ptc. gen. fem. sg., ἀνακεράννυμι, (pass.) *be mixed*; attrib.
79. ἰδέα, -ας, ἡ, *form, genus, type*.
80. ἐναντία, -ας, ἡ, *opposite*.
81. Pres. act. indic. 3 sg., ἐμφαίνω, *show, demonstrate*.
82. συμπαράληψις, -εως, ἡ, *an undertaking together*.

ἂν συνεργῶν, ἵνα ταῖς μὲν[83] ἀνεπιλήπτοις[84] βουλαῖς[85] τε καὶ πράξεσιν[86] ἀνθρώπου κατορθοῦντος[87] ἐπιγράφηται[88] θεὸς ὁ πάντων ἡγεμών, ταῖς δ' ἐναντίαις ἕτεροι τῶν ὑπηκόων·[89] ἔδει γὰρ ἀναίτιον[90] εἶναι κακοῦ τὸν πατέρα τοῖς ἐκγόνοις· κακὸν δ' ἡ κακία καὶ αἱ κατὰ κακίαν ἐνέργειαι.[91] **76** πάνυ δὲ καλῶς, τὸ γένος[92] ἄνθρωπον εἰπών, διέκρινε[93] τὰ εἴδη[94] φήσας ἄρρεν[95] τε καὶ θῆλυ[96] δεδημιουργῆσθαι,[97] μήπω[98] τῶν ἐν μέρει[99] μορφὴν[100] λαβόντων, ἐπειδὴ τὰ προσεχέστατα[101] τῶν εἰδῶν ἐνυπάρχει[102] τῷ γένει, καὶ ὥσπερ ἐν κατόπτρῳ[103] διαφαίνεται[104] τοῖς ὀξὺ[105] καθορᾶν[106] δυναμένοις.

83. μέν ... δέ; point/counterpoint. See n. 18.
84. ἀνεπίληπτος, -ον, *irreproachable*.
85. βουλή, -ῆς, ἡ, *decision*.
86. πρᾶξις, -εως, ἡ, *action*.
87. Pres. act. ptc. gen. masc. sg., κατορθόω, *act uprightly*; attrib.
88. Pres. pass. subj. 3 sg., ἐπιγράφω, (pass.) *be credited* (for something); purpose clause (cf. BDF §369; S §2193; CGCG §45.3).
89. ὑπήκοος, -οον, (subst.) *subordinate*.
90. ἀναίτιος, -ον, *blameless, innocent, not responsible for*; with gen.
91. ἐνέργεια, -ας, ἡ, *operative power, activity*.
92. γένος, -ους, τό, *type, kind, species*.
93. Aor. act. indic. 3 sg., διακρίνω, *distinguish, differentiate* (between).
94. εἶδος, -ους, τό, *form*.
95. ἄρρην, -εν, *male*.
96. θῆλυς, -εια, -υ, *female*.
97. Pf. pass. inf., δημιουργέω, (pass.) *be created*; indir. disc. (cf. BDF §397; S §2592; CGCG §41.2).
98. Adv., *not yet*.
99. μέρος, -ους, τό, *part*. The idea is that he identified the γένος as male and female even though it had yet to take shape "in parts" (ἐν μέρει).
100. μορφή, -ῆς, ἡ, *form, shape*.
101. Superl., προσεχής, -ές, *closest, nearest*.
102. Pres. act. indic. 3 sg., ἐνυπάρχω, *exist in, subsist*; with dat.
103. κάτοπτρον, -ου, τό, *mirror*.
104. Pres. pass. indic. 3 sg., διαφαίνω, (pass.) *be evident/clear/manifest*.
105. Adv., ὀξύς, -εῖα, -ύ, *sharply, keenly*.
106. Pres. act. inf., καθοράω, *perceive clearly*; comp. of τοῖς δυναμένοις.

NOTES

72–75. Philo addresses the question implicit in the plural ποιήσωμεν (Gen. 1:26). The answer cannot be that God was incapable of creating human beings (i.e., "a small and perishable creature") by himself. Rather, there are three types of beings (cf. Aristotle, *Metaph.* 981a27–b27): (1) those without reason (i.e., plants and animals), (2) those with reason that partake only of virtue (i.e., heavenly bodies), and (3) those with reason that partake of both virtue and vice (i.e., human beings). It was not fitting, Philo argues, for the creator to fashion those beings of a "mixed nature" by himself, lest the deity be held responsible for the evil of human beings (cf. Plato, *Resp.* 617e5).

76. τὸ γένος ἄνθρωπον. Platonic realism assumes that the genus contains the species (τὰ εἴδη) so that one may thus infer from the idea "human being" a male and a female variety. Yet the ἄνθρωπος is not, properly speaking, part of the noetic world, since according to Philo, God fashioned the intelligible world on day one (cf. *Opif.* 35). The genus is thus an idealization, the human being "identified primarily with his intellect (cf. §69)" (Runia 2001, 243). As an ideal, the ἄνθρωπος is "male and female," which is to say, "neither male nor female" (*Opif.* 134).

4.2.4

The First Humans in the Garden, Part 1

On the Creation of the World 151–152

151Ἐπεὶ δ' οὐδὲν τῶν ἐν γενέσει[1] βέβαιον,[2] τροπὰς[3] δὲ καὶ μεταβολὰς[4] ἀναγκαίως[5] τὰ θνητὰ[6] δέχεται, ἐχρῆν[7] καὶ τὸν πρῶτον ἄνθρωπον ἀπολαῦσαί[8] τινος κακοπραγίας.[9] ἀρχὴ δὲ τῆς ὑπαιτίου[10] ζωῆς αὐτῷ γίνεται γυνή· μέχρι[11] μὲν[12] γὰρ εἷς ἦν, ὡμοιοῦτο[13] κατὰ τὴν μόνωσιν[14] κόσμῳ καὶ θεῷ, καὶ τῆς ἑκατέρου φύσεως[15] ἐναπεμάττετο[16] τῇ ψυχῇ τοὺς χαρακτῆρας,[17] οὐ πάντας ἀλλ' ὅσους χωρῆσαι[18] δυνατὸν[19] θνητὴν σύστασιν·[20] ἐπεὶ δ' ἐπλάσθη[21] καὶ γυνή, θεασάμενος[22] ἀδελφὸν εἶδος[23] καὶ συγγενῆ[24] μορφὴν[25] ἡσμένισε[26] τῇ θέᾳ[27] καὶ προσιὼν[28] ἠσπάζετο.[29] **152**ἡ δ' οὐδὲν ἐκείνου

    1. γένεσις, -εως, ἡ, *genesis, origin*. The article substantivizes the prepositional phrase: "None of the things in genesis [as described in Genesis]."
    2. βέβαιος, -α, -ον, *stable, fixed*.
    3. τροπή, -ῆς, ἡ, *change, transformation*.
    4. μεταβολή, -ῆς, ἡ, *change*.
    5. Adv., *necessarily*.
    6. θνητός, -ή, -όν, *mortal*.
    7. Impf. act. indic. 3 sg. from χρή, (quasi-impers.) *it is necessary*; with acc. and inf. (cf. S §1985; *CGCG* §36.3).
    8. Aor. act. inf., ἀπολαύω, *enjoy*; with gen.
    9. κακοπραγία, -ας, ἡ, *ill fortune*.
    10. ὑπαίτιος, -ον, *guilty, blameworthy*.
    11. Adv., *up to that point*.
    12. μέν . . . δ'; point/counterpoint.
    13. Impf. pass. indic. 3 sg., ὁμοιόω, (pass.) *be made like, be likened to*; with dat.
    14. μόνωσις, -εως, ἡ, *solitariness, singleness*.
    15. φύσις, -εως, ἡ, *nature*.
    16. Impf. mid. indic. 3 sg., ἐναπομάσσω (Att. ἐναπομάττω), (mid.) *receive an impression* (LSJ, 555).
    17. χαρακτήρ, -έρος, ὁ, *impression, mark*.
    18. Aor. act. inf., χωρέω, *accept, receive*.
    19. δυνατός, -ή, -όν, (quasi-impers.) *it is possible*; with acc. and inf.
    20. σύστασις, -εως, ἡ, *composition, constitution*.
    21. Aor. pass. indic. 3 sg., πλάσσω, (pass.) *be formed, molded*.
    22. Aor. mid. ptc. gen. masc. sg., θεάομαι, *see, behold*.
    23. εἶδος, -ους, τό, *form*; ἀδελφὸν εἶδος, "brotherly/sisterly figure."
    24. συγγενής, -ές, *of the same family, kindred*.
    25. μορφή, -ῆς, ἡ, *form*.
    26. Aor. act. indic. 3 sg., ἀσμενίζω, *gladly welcome*; with dat.
    27. θέα, -ας, ἡ, *sight*.
    28. Pres. act. ptc. nom. masc. sg., πρόσειμι, *approach*; circ.
    29. Impf. act. indic. 3 sg., ἀσπάζομαι, *greet*.

προσβλέπουσα³⁰ ζῷον ἐμφερέστερον³¹ ἑαυτῇ γάνυταί³² τε καὶ ἀντιπροσφθέγγεται³³ μετ᾽ αἰδοῦς·³⁴ ἔρως³⁵ δ᾽ ἐπιγενόμενος³⁶ καθάπερ ἑνὸς ζῴου διττὰ³⁷ τμήματα³⁸ διεστηκότα³⁹ συναγαγὼν εἰς ταὐτὸν⁴⁰ ἁρμόττεται,⁴¹ πόθον⁴² ἐνιδρυσάμενος⁴³ ἑκατέρῳ τῆς πρὸς θάτερον⁴⁴ κοινωνίας εἰς τὴν τοῦ ὁμοίου⁴⁵ γένεσιν· ὁ δὲ πόθος οὗτος καὶ τὴν τῶν σωμάτων ἡδονὴν⁴⁶ ἐγέννησεν, ἥτις ἐστὶν ἀδικημάτων⁴⁷ καὶ παρανομημάτων⁴⁸ ἀρχή, δι᾽ ἣν ὑπαλλάττονται⁴⁹ τὸν θνητὸν καὶ κακοδαίμονα⁵⁰ βίον⁵¹ ἀντ᾽⁵² ἀθανάτου⁵³ καὶ εὐδαίμονος.⁵⁴

NOTES

151. οὐδὲν τῶν ἐν γενέσει βέβαιον. The claim follows logically from Philo's cosmology: everything

30. Pres. act. ptc. nom. fem. sg., προσβλέπω, *look at/upon*; circ.
31. Compar., ἐμφερής, -ές, *more similar*; with dat. The fronting of the genitive ἐκείνου is an example of hyperbaton for emphasis: "Seeing no other living creature more like herself than *he*" (cf. *CGCG* §60.18).
32. Pres. mid. indic. 3 sg., γάνυμαι, *be happy*.
33. Pres. mid. indic. 3 sg., ἀντιπροσφθέγγομαι, *respond*.
34. αἰδώς, -οῦς, ἡ, *sense of shame, modesty*.
35. ἔρως, -ωτος, ὁ, *erotic love, desire*.
36. Aor. mid. ptc. nom. masc. sg., ἐπιγίγνομαι, *follow, come after*; circ.
37. δισσός (Att. διττός), -ή, -όν, *double, twofold*.
38. τμῆμα, -ατος, τό, *part cut off, piece*.
39. Pf. act. ptc. acc. neut. pl., διίστημι, (pass.) *divide, separate*; attrib.
40. ταὐτός, -ή, -όν (crasis: τὸ αὐτό), *same*.
41. Pres. mid. indic. 3 sg., ἁρμόζω (Att. ἁρμόττω), *put together, conjoin*.
42. πόθος, -ου, ὁ, *desire*; with obj. gen. τῆς . . . κοινωνίας.
43. Aor. mid. ptc. nom. masc. sg., ἐνιδρύω, *establish*.
44. Alt. form of ἕτερος, -α, -ον, *other* (of two).
45. ὅμοιος, -α, -ον, (subst.) *like kind*.
46. ἡδονή, -ῆς, ἡ, *pleasure*.
47. ἀδίκημα, -ατος, τό, *injustice, wrongdoing*.
48. παρανόμημα, -ατος, τό, *violation of the law, transgression*.
49. Pres. mid. indic. 3 pl., ὑπαλλάσσω (Att. ὑπαλλάττω), *exchange*.
50. κακοδαίμων, -ον, *unfortunate, wretched*.
51. βίος, -ου, ὁ, *life*.
52. Prep. with gen., *for, in place of*.
53. ἀθάνατος, -ον, *immortal*.
54. εὐδαίμων, -ον, *fortunate, happy*.

in the sense-perceptible world has an origin (as described in Genesis) and so is subject to a constant state of flux (cf. *Opif.* 12). Cf. Runia (2001, 356): "Philo does not give the impression of regarding the descent into wickedness as a 'fall from grace,' i.e., a single event which might not have happened, but rather as a structural feature of the world of becoming."

ἀρχὴ δὲ τῆς ὑπαιτίου ζωῆς αὐτῷ γίνεται γυνή. That Philo was a misogynist is not in dispute. His concern here, however, is the loss of the oneness (μόνωσις) whereby the solitary human resembled and participated in the nature of God and the cosmos (cf. Plato, *Tim.* 30c–31b). See Loader (2011, 21–26, 45–55); the foundational study is Sly (1990).

ἐπλάσθη καὶ γυνή. Philo skips over the creation of the woman from the man's "rib" (cf. Gen. 2:21-22; on the term צֵלָע, see Meyers 2013, 74–75). The choice of "the verb ἐπλάσθη (cf. §153 διαπλασθείσης), not used in Gen. 2:21-25, has the effect of relating the creation of woman to the fundamental anthropological text of Gen. 2:7" (Runia 2001, 357).

152. μετ᾽ αἰδοῦς. The manner in which the woman greets the man, as Sly notes, reflects assumptions about propriety, not shame per se (1990, 205–6; cf. Philo, *Spec.* 3.25, 176; Philo, *Contempl.* 33). Cf. Runia (2001, 357): "Philo is importing into the scene what he regards as ideal womanly behavior, and this involves an appropriately modest response to the man's overture."

ἔρως δ᾽ ἐπιγενόμενος καθάπερ ἑνὸς ζῴου διττὰ τμήματα διεστηκότα συναγαγὼν εἰς ταὐτὸν ἁρμόττεται. This line is a clear allusion to the speech of Aristophanes in Plato's *Symposium* (189–193), in which he attributes ἔρως to the incessant search of the divided halves to be reunited.

ὁ δὲ πόθος οὗτος καὶ τὴν τῶν σωμάτων ἡδονὴν ἐγέννησεν, ἥτις ἐστὶν ἀδικημάτων καὶ παρανομημάτων ἀρχή. Philo grants that sexual desire is necessary for procreation. The problem, however, is that desire inevitably begets bodily pleasure, which Philo says is the beginning of transgression. Here, then, is another reason why he identifies woman as the ἀρχή of blameworthy life: without her, pleasure (ἡδονή), which is the ἀρχή of transgression (*Opif.* 151), does not exist.

4.2.5

The First Humans in the Garden, Part 2

On the Creation of the World 153–156

153Ἔτι δὲ τοῦ ἀνδρὸς μονήρη¹ βίον² ζῶντος, μήπω³ διαπλασθείσης⁴ τῆς γυναικός, φυτευθῆναι⁵ λόγος ἔχει παράδεισον⁶ ὑπὸ θεοῦ τοῖς παρ' ἡμῖν οὐδὲν⁷ προσεοικότα⁸ [Gen. 2:8–9]· τῶν μὲν⁹ γάρ ἐστιν ἄψυχος¹⁰ ἡ ὕλη,¹¹ παντοίων¹² δένδρων¹³ κατάπλεως,¹⁴ τῶν μὲν¹⁵ ἀειθαλῶν¹⁶ πρὸς τὴν ὄψεως¹⁷ ἀδιάστατον¹⁸ ἡδονήν,¹⁹ τῶν δὲ ταῖς ἐαρινοῖς²⁰ ὥραις²¹ ἡβώντων²² καὶ βλαστανόντων,²³ καὶ τῶν μὲν ἥμερον καρπὸν ἀνθρώποις φερόντων, οὐ πρὸς ἀναγκαίαν²⁴ μόνον²⁵ χρῆσιν²⁶ τροφῆς²⁷ ἀλλὰ καὶ πρὸς περιττὴν²⁸ ἀπόλαυσιν²⁹ ἁβροδιαίτου³⁰ βίου, τῶν δ' οὐχ ὅμοιον, ὃς ἀναγκαίως θηρίοις³¹ ἀπενεμήθη·³² κατὰ δὲ τὸν θεῖον³³ παράδεισον

1. μονήρη, -ες, *solitary.*
2. βίος, -ου, ὁ, *life.*
3. Adv., *not yet.*
4. Aor. pass. ptc. gen. fem. sg., διαπλάσσω, (pass.) *be molded/formed*; gen. absol.
5. Aor. pass. inf., φυτεύω, *be planted*; indir. disc. (λόγος ἔχει) (cf. BDF §397; S §2016; CGCG §51.19).
6. παράδεισος, -ου, ὁ, *enclosed park, garden of pleasure*; or better, given Philo's aversion to pleasure, "garden of delights" (Runia 2001, 364).
7. Adv. acc., "in no way."
8. Pf. act. ptc. acc. neut. sg., προσέοικα, *be similar, resemble*; with dat.
9. τῶν (παραδείσων) μέν . . . κατὰ δὲ τὸν θεῖον παράδεισον; point/counterpoint (cf. Runge 2010, 75–83; BDF §447; S §2904; CGCG §59.24).
10. ἄψυχος, -ον, *without soul.*
11. ὕλη, -ης, ἡ, *wood.*
12. παντοῖος, -α, -ον, *of all kinds.*
13. δένδρον, -ου, τό, *trees.*
14. κατάπλεως, -ων, *full*; with gen.
15. τῶν μέν . . . τῶν δέ . . . καὶ τῶν μέν . . . τῶν δ', *some . . . others . . . and some . . . others.* Two related point/counterpoint sets further describe the initial μέν-clause (cf. S §2908).

16. ἀειθαλής, -ές, *evergreen, everblooming.*
17. ὄψις, -εως, ἡ, *sight, eyes.*
18. ἀδιάστατος, -ον, *continuous.*
19. ἡδονή, -ῆς, ἡ, *pleasure.*
20. ἐαρινός, -ή, -όν, *of spring.*
21. ὥρα, -ας, ἡ, *season.*
22. Pres. act. ptc. gen. neut. pl., ἡβάω, *be in bloom*; attrib.
23. Pres. act. ptc. gen. neut. pl., βλαστάνω, *sprout*; attrib.
24. ἀναγκαῖος, -α, -ον, *necessary.*
25. οὐ μόνον . . . ἀλλὰ καί, *not only . . . but also.*
26. χρῆσις, -εως, ἡ, *use.*
27. τροφή, -ῆς, ἡ, *nourishment.*
28. περισσός (Att. περιττός), -ή, -όν, *excessive, superfluous.*
29. ἀπόλαυσις, -εως, ἡ, *enjoyment.*
30. ἁβροδίαιτος, -ον, *refined, luxurious.*
31. θηρίον, -ου, τό, *wild beast.*
32. Aor. pass. indic. 3 sg., ἀπονέμω, (pass.) *be assigned*; with dat.
33. θεῖος, -α, -ον, *divine.*

ἔμψυχα³⁴ καὶ λογικὰ³⁵ φυτὰ³⁶ πάντ' εἶναι συμβέβηκε,³⁷ καρπὸν φέροντα τὰς ἀρετὰς³⁸ καὶ προσέτι³⁹ τὴν ἀδιάφθορον⁴⁰ σύνεσιν⁴¹ καὶ ἀγχίνοιαν,⁴² ᾗ γνωρίζεται⁴³ τὰ καλὰ καὶ τὰ αἰσχρά, ζωήν τ' ἄνοσον⁴⁴ καὶ ἀφθαρσίαν⁴⁵ καὶ πᾶν εἴ τι τούτοις ὁμοιότροπον.⁴⁶ ¹⁵⁴ταῦτα δέ μοι δοκεῖ⁴⁷ συμβολικῶς⁴⁸ μᾶλλον ἢ κυρίως⁴⁹ φιλοσοφεῖσθαι·⁵⁰ δένδρα γὰρ ἐπὶ γῆς οὔτε πέφηνέ⁵¹ πω⁵² πρότερον οὔτ' αὖθις⁵³ εἰκὸς⁵⁴ φανεῖσθαι ζωῆς ἢ συνέσεως.⁵⁵ ἀλλ' ὡς ἔοικεν⁵⁶ αἰνίττεται⁵⁷ διὰ μὲν⁵⁸ τοῦ παραδείσου τὸ τῆς ψυχῆς ἡγεμονικόν,⁵⁹ ὅπερ ἐστὶ κατάπλεων οἷα φυτῶν μυρίων⁶⁰ ὅσων δοξῶν,⁶¹ διὰ δὲ τοῦ δένδρου τῆς ζωῆς τὴν μεγίστην⁶² τῶν ἀρετῶν θεοσέβειαν,⁶³ δι' ἧς ἀθανατίζεται⁶⁴ ἡ ψυχή, διὰ δὲ τοῦ καλῶν καὶ πονηρῶν γνωριστικοῦ⁶⁵ φρόνησιν⁶⁶ τὴν μέσην,⁶⁷ ᾗ διακρίνεται⁶⁸ τἀναντία⁶⁹ φύσει. ¹⁵⁵θέμενος δὲ τούτους τοὺς ὅρους⁷⁰ ἐν ψυχῇ καθάπερ δικαστὴς⁷¹ ἐσκόπει,⁷² πρὸς πότερον⁷³ ἐπικλινῶς⁷⁴ ἕξει. ὡς δὲ εἶδε ῥέπουσαν⁷⁵ μὲν ἐπὶ πανουργίαν,⁷⁶ εὐσεβείας⁷⁷ δὲ καὶ ὁσιότητος⁷⁸ ὀλιγωροῦσαν,⁷⁹ ἐξ ὧν ἡ ἀθάνατος ζωὴ περιγίνεται,⁸⁰ προὔβαλετο⁸¹ κατὰ τὸ εἰκὸς⁸² καὶ ἐφυγάδευσεν⁸³ ἐκ τοῦ παραδείσου, μηδ' ἐλπίδα

34. ἔμψυχος, -ον, *endowed with soul.*
35. λογικός, -ή, -όν, *endowed with reason.*
36. φυτόν, -οῦ, τό, *plant.*
37. Pf. act. indic. 3 sg., συμβαίνω, *happen to be*; with acc. and inf. (cf. BDF §408; S §1985; CGCG §36.4).
38. ἀρετή, -ῆς, ἡ, *virtue.*
39. Adv., *further, moreover.*
40. ἀδιάφθορος, -ον, *incorruptible.* MSS A B P¹ read ἀδιάφορος, "neutral."
41. σύνεσις, -εως, ἡ, *understanding.*
42. ἀγχίνοια, -ας, ἡ, *insight.*
43. Pres. pass. indic. 3 sg., γνωρίζω, (pass.) *be made known, revealed.*
44. ἄνοσος, -ον, *without disease.*
45. ἀφθαρσία, -ας, ἡ, *incorruptibility, indestructibility.*
46. ὁμοιότροπος, -ον, *similar*; with dat.
47. Pres. act. indic. 3 sg., δοκέω, (impers.) *it seems/appears*; with dat. and inf.
48. Adv., *symbolically, figuratively.*
49. Adv., *properly, actually*; i.e., "in the literal sense of the words" (cf. Runia 2001, 366).
50. Aor. pass. inf., φιλοσοφέω, (pass.) *discussed, examined philosophically*; indir. disc. See n. 5.
51. Pf. act. indic. 3 sg., φαίνω, *appear.*
52. Adv., *yet* (usually neg.).
53. Adv., *hereafter.*
54. Pf. act. ptc. acc. neut. sg., ἔοικα, (impers.) *it seems*; acc. absol. (cf. BDF §424; S §2076; CGCG §52.33).
55. σύνεσις, -εως, ἡ, *understanding*; separated from head noun, δένδρα (hyperbaton; cf. S §3028; CGCG §60.18).
56. Pf. act. indic. 3 sg., ἔοικα, *seem*; ὡς ἔοικεν, (impers.) "it seems."
57. Pres. mid. indic. 3 sg., αἰνίσσω (Att. αἰνίττω), *speak in riddles, hint, intimate.*
58. διὰ μέν . . . διὰ δέ . . . διὰ δέ, "by paradise . . . by tree of life . . . by [tree] of the knowing of good and evil" (cf. S §2907).
59. ἡγεμονικός, -ή, -όν, (subst.) *dominant part* (of the soul; i.e., reason).

60. μυρίος, -α, -ον, *innumerable, countless.*
61. δόξα, -ης, ἡ, *opinion, belief.*
62. Superl., μέγας, μεγάλη, μέγα, *greatest.*
63. θεοσέβεια, -ας, ἡ, *piety, reverence for God.*
64. Pres. pass. indic. 3 sg., ἀθανατίζω, (pass.) *become immortal.*
65. γνωριστικός, -ή, -όν, *capable of knowing*; with gen.; emendation. Most MSS read γνωστικοῦ, "of/for knowing." M reads ὁριστικοῦ, "of/for defining."
66. φρόνησις, -εως, ἡ, *prudence, wisdom.*
67. μέσος, -η, -ον, *in the middle, intermediate.* The tail specifies that φρόνησις is "in between" since it must be exercised in choices for good or for evil (Runia 2001, 368).
68. Pres. pass. indic. 3 sg., διακρίνω, (pass.) *be discerned, distinguished.*
69. Crasis: τὰ ἐναντία, "the opposite things."
70. ὅρος, -ου, ὁ, *limit, boundary.*
71. δικαστής, -οῦ, ὁ, *judge.*
72. Impf. act. indic. 3 sg., σκοπέω, *look at, watch.*
73. πότερος, -α, -ον, *either of the two* (ways).
74. Adv., *manner of inclination*; adv. with ἔχω (here fut.): "It would incline."
75. Pres. act. ptc. acc. fem. sg., ῥέπω, *incline, bend*; supp. (εἶδε).
76. πανουργία, -ας, ἡ, *cunning, craftiness.*
77. εὐσεβεία, -ας, ἡ, *piety.*
78. ὁσιότης, -ητος, ἡ, *holiness.*
79. Pres. act. ptc. acc. fem. sg., ὀλιγωρέω, *make light of*; supp. (εἶδε).
80. Pres. mid. indic. 3 sg., περιγίνομαι (Att. περιγίγνομαι), *be a result/consequence* (MGS, 1623.E).
81. Aor. mid. indic. 3 sg., προβάλλω, *cast forth.*
82. Idiom, κατὰ τὸ εἰκός, "as seems fitting."
83. Aor. act. indic. 3 sg., φυγαδεύω, *banish, expel.*

τῆς εἰσαῦθις⁸⁴ ἐπανόδου⁸⁵ δυσίατα⁸⁶ καὶ ἀθεράπευτα⁸⁷ πλημμελούσῃ⁸⁸ ψυχῇ παρασχών,⁸⁹ ἐπεὶ καὶ ἡ τῆς ἀπάτης⁹⁰ πρόφασις⁹¹ ἐπίληπτος⁹² ἦν οὐ μετρίως,⁹³ ἣν οὐκ ἄξιον παρασιωπῆσαι.⁹⁴ ¹⁵⁶λέγεται τὸ παλαιὸν τὸ ἰοβόλον⁹⁵ καὶ γηγενὲς⁹⁶ ἑρπετὸν⁹⁷ [ὄφις]⁹⁸ ἀνθρώπου φωνὴν προΐεσθαι,⁹⁹ καί ποτε προσελθὸν¹⁰⁰ τῇ τοῦ πρώτου φύντος¹⁰¹ ἀνδρὸς γυναικὶ τῆς βραδυτῆτος¹⁰² καὶ τῆς ἄγαν¹⁰³ εὐλαβείας¹⁰⁴ ὀνειδίσαι,¹⁰⁵ διότι μέλλει¹⁰⁶ καὶ ὑπερτίθεται¹⁰⁷ πάγκαλον ὀφθῆναι¹⁰⁸ καὶ ἥδιστον¹⁰⁹ ἀπολαυσθῆναι¹¹⁰ καρπὸν δρέπεσθαι,¹¹¹ πρὸς δὲ καὶ ὠφελιμώτατον,¹¹² ᾧ δυνήσεται γνωρίζειν¹¹³ ἀγαθά τε αὖ καὶ κακά· τὴν δὲ ἀνεξετάστως¹¹⁴ ἀπὸ γνώμης¹¹⁵ ἀβεβαίου¹¹⁶ καὶ ἀνιδρύτου¹¹⁷ συναινέσασαν¹¹⁸ ἐμφαγεῖν¹¹⁹ τοῦ καρποῦ καὶ τῷ ἀνδρὶ μεταδοῦναι¹²⁰—καὶ τοῦτ' ἐξαπιναίως¹²¹ ἀμφοτέρους ἐξ ἀκακίας καὶ ἁπλότητος¹²² ἠθῶν¹²³ εἰς πανουργίαν μετέβαλεν¹²⁴—ἐφ' ᾧ τὸν πατέρα χαλεπήναντα¹²⁵—ἡ γὰρ πρᾶξις ὀργῆς ἀξία, ἐπεὶ παρελθόντες τὸ ζωῆς ἀθανάτου φυτόν, τὴν ἀρετῆς παντέλειαν, ὑφ' ἧς μακραίωνα¹²⁶ καὶ εὐδαίμονα¹²⁷ βίον ἐδύναντο καρποῦσθαι,¹²⁸ τὸν ἐφήμερον¹²⁹ καὶ θνητὸν οὐ βίον ἀλλὰ χρόνον κακοδαιμονίας¹³⁰ μεστὸν εἵλοντο¹³¹—κολάσεις¹³² ὁρίσαι¹³³ κατ' αὐτῶν τὰς προσηκούσας.¹³⁴

84. Adv., *again, subsequently*.
85. ἐπανόδος, -ου, ἡ, *return*.
86. δυσίατος, -ον, *difficult to heal, incurable*; internal acc. of πλημμελούσῃ.
87. ἀθεράπευτος, -ον, *incurable*; internal acc. of πλημμελούσῃ.
88. Pres. act. ptc. dat. fem. sg., πλημμελέω, *err*; attrib.
89. Aor. act. ptc. nom. masc. sg., παρέχω, *supply, offer*; circ.
90. ἀπάτη, -ης, ἡ, *deception*.
91. πρόφασις, -εως, ἡ, *reason*.
92. ἐπίληπτος, -ον, *blameworthy*.
93. Adv. with οὐ, "in no small measure."
94. Aor. act. inf., παρασιωπάω, *pass over in silence*; comp. of ἄξιον: "which [reason] it is not right [for us] to pass over in silence." The same expression Philo used at the end of *Opif*. 6.
95. ἰοβόλος, -ον, *poisonous*.
96. γηγενής, -ές, *earthborn*.
97. ἑρπετόν, -οῦ, τό, *reptile*.
98. ὄφις, -εως, ὁ, *serpent*.
99. Pres. mid. inf., προΐημι, *send forth*; indir. disc. (λέγεται). See n. 5.
100. Aor. act. ptc. nom. neut. sg., προσέρχομαι, *approach*; with dat.; circ. (temporal). Most MSS read προσελθών (with ὄφις).
101. Pres. act. ptc. gen. masc. sg., φύω, (intrans.) *be brought forth, born*; attrib.
102. βραδυτής, -ῆτος, ἡ, *slowness*.
103. Adv., *very*.
104. εὐλαβεία, -ας, ἡ, *circumspection*.
105. Aor. act. inf., ὀνειδίζω, *reproach*; with dat. and gen. (cause); indir. disc. (λέγεται). See n. 5.
106. Pres. act. indic. 3 sg., μέλλω, (always be) *going to*; hence, *delay*.
107. Pres. mid. indic. 3 sg., ὑπερτίθημι, *postpone, defer*; with inf.
108. Epex. inf.: "very beautiful *to behold*" (cf. S §2002; *CGCG* §51.18).
109. Superl., ἡδύς, -εῖα, -ύ, *sweetest*.
110. Aor. pass. inf., ἀπολαύω, *enjoy*; epex.: "sweetest *to enjoy*." See n. 108.
111. Pres. mid. inf., δρέπω, (mid.) *gather, pick*.

112. Superl., ὠφελιμός, -όν, *most useful*.
113. Pres. act. inf., γνωρίζω, *know, recognize*.
114. Adv., *without examination*.
115. γνώμη, -ης, ἡ, *faculty of knowing*.
116. ἀβέβαιος, -ον, *insecure*.
117. ἀνίδρυτος, -ον, *unestablished, unstable*.
118. Aor. act. ptc. acc. fem. sg., συναινέω, *consent/agree* (to do something); with inf.; circ.
119. Aor. act. inf., ἐμφάγω (ἐν, φαγεῖν), *eat* (greedily).
120. Aor. act. inf., μεταδίδωμι, *distribute*.
121. Adv., *suddenly*.
122. ἁπλότης, -ητος, ἡ, *simplicity, innocence*.
123. ἦθος, -ους, τό, *usual manner, habit; moral character*.
124. Aor. act. indic. 3 sg., μεταβάλλω, *change*.
125. Aor. act. ptc. acc. masc. sg., χαλεπαίνω, *be angry*; circ.
126. μακραίων, -ον, *enduring, prolonged*.
127. εὐδαίμων, -ον, *happy, fortunate*.
128. Aor. mid. inf., καρπέω, *enjoy the fruits of*.
129. ἐφήμερος, -ον, *ephemeral*.
130. κακοδαιμονία, -ας, ἡ, *misfortune, misery*; comp. of μεστόν.
131. Aor. mid. indic. 3 pl., αἱρέω, (mid.) *choose*.
132. κολάσις, -εως, ἡ, *punishment*.
133. Aor. act. inf., ὁρίζω, *determine, establish*; indir. disc. See n. 5.
134. Pres. act. ptc. acc. fem. pl., προσήκω, *be fitting, appropriate*; attrib. (subst.).

NOTES

154. διὰ . . . τοῦ καλῶν καὶ πονηρῶν γνωριστικοῦ φρόνησιν τὴν μέσην. Philo relies on the Aristotelian tradition that distinguishes between σοφία, theoretical wisdom, and φρόνησις, practical wisdom (cf. Aristotle, *Eth. nic.* 6.7, 1141a8–21). He describes φρόνησις as "intermediate" because it is fallible (Runia 2001, 368).

156. ἀνθρώπου φωνὴν προΐεσθαι. Philo seems to assume that animals could speak at some point in the distant past (cf. Philo, *QG* 1.32; Josephus, *A.J.* 1.41; Jub. 3:28; Kugel 1998, 99). He is more interested, however, in what the serpent signifies: desire oriented toward pleasure (cf. *QG* 1.31; Rom. 7:7–12).

4.2.6

The Faith of Abraham

On the Life of Abraham 262, 268–269, 273–276

262Ἔστι δὲ καὶ ἀνάγραπτος[1] ἔπαινος[2] αὐτῷ χρησμοῖς[3] μαρτυρηθείς,[4] οὓς Μωυσῆς ἐθεσπίσθη,[5] δι' οὗ μηνύεται[6] ὅτι "ἐπίστευσε τῷ θεῷ," ὅπερ λεχθῆναι[7] μὲν[8] βραχύτατόν ἐστιν, ἔργῳ δὲ βεβαιωθῆναι[9] μέγιστον. . . .

268μόνον οὖν ἀψευδὲς[10] καὶ βέβαιον[11] ἀγαθὸν ἡ πρὸς θεὸν πίστις, παρηγόρημα[12] βίου,[13] πλήρωμα[14] χρηστῶν ἐλπίδων, ἀφορία[15] μὲν κακῶν, ἀγαθῶν δὲ φορά,[16] κακοδαιμονίας[17] ἀπόγνωσις,[18] γνῶσις εὐσεβείας,[19] κλῆρος[20] εὐδαιμονίας,[21] ψυχῆς ἐν ἅπασι βελτίωσις[22] ἐπερηρεισμένης[23] καὶ ἐφιδρυμένης[24] τῷ πάντων αἰτίῳ[25] καὶ δυναμένῳ μὲν[26] πάντα, βουλομένῳ δὲ τὰ ἄριστα.[27] **269**καθάπερ[28] γὰρ οἱ μὲν[29] δι' ὀλισθηρᾶς[30] ὁδοῦ βαδίζοντες[31] ὑποσκελίζονται[32] καὶ πίπτουσιν, οἱ

---

1. ἀνάγραπτος, -ον, *recorded.*
2. ἔπαινος, -ου, ὁ, *praise.*
3. χρησμός, -οῦ, ὁ, *prophetic oracle*; dat. of means.
4. Aor. pass. ptc. nom. masc. sg., μαρτυρέω, (pass.) *be attested.*
5. Aor. pass. (as mid.) indic. 3 sg., θεσπίζω, *prophesy.*
6. Pres. pass. indic. 3 sg., μηνύω, (pass.) *be disclosed.*
7. Aor. pass. inf., λέγω; epex.; lit., "littlest thing *to be said*" (cf. S §2002; CGCG §51.18).
8. μέν . . . δέ; point/counterpoint (cf. Runge 2010, 75–83; BDF §447; S §2904; CGCG §59.24).
9. Aor. pass. inf., βεβαιόω, (pass.) *be confirmed/established*; epex.; lit., "greatest *to be established* by action."
10. ἀψευδής, -ές, *without falsehood.*
11. βέβαιος, -ον, *secure, established.*
12. παρηγόρημα, -ατος, τό, *consolation.*
13. βίος, -ου, ὁ, *life.*
14. πλήρωμα, -ατος, τό, *fullness.*
15. ἀφορία, -ας, ἡ, *not bearing*, hence *nonproduction, dearth*; with gen.
16. φορά, -ᾶς, ἡ, *that which is borne, harvest.*
17. κακοδαιμονία, -ας, ἡ, *misfortune, misery.*
18. ἀπόγνωσις, -εως, ἡ, *disavowal, renunciation*; with gen.
19. εὐσεβεία, -ας, ἡ, *piety.*
20. κλῆρος, -ου, ὁ, *lot.*
21. εὐδαιμονία, -ας, ἡ, *happiness, good fortune.*
22. βελτίωσις, -εως, ἡ, *betterment.*
23. Pf. pass. ptc. gen. fem. sg., ἐπερείδω, (intrans.) *be leaned on*; with dat.; attrib.
24. Pf. pass. ptc. gen. fem. sg., ἐφιδρύω, (intrans.) *be set on*; with dat.; attrib.
25. αἴτιον, -ου, τό, *cause.*
26. μέν . . . δέ; point/counterpoint. See n. 8.
27. Superl., ἀγαθός, -ή, -όν, *best.*
28. καθάπερ . . . οὕτως, *(just) as . . . so.*
29. οἱ μέν . . . οἱ δέ, *some . . . others* (cf. BDF §250; S §1107; CGCG §28.17).
30. ὀλισθηρός, -ά, -όν, *slippery.*
31. Pres. act. ptc. nom. masc. pl., βαδίζω, *go.*
32. Pres. pass. indic. 3 pl., ὑποσκελίζω, (intras.) *be tripped up.*

δὲ διὰ ξηρᾶς³³ καὶ λεωφόρου³⁴ ἀπταίστῳ³⁵ χρῶνται³⁶ πορείᾳ,³⁷ οὕτως οἱ διὰ τῶν σωματικῶν μὲν καὶ τῶν ἐκτὸς³⁸ τὴν ψυχὴν ἄγοντες οὐδὲν ἀλλ' ἢ πίπτειν αὐτὴν ἐθίζουσιν³⁹—ὀλισθηρὰ γὰρ ταῦτά γε⁴⁰ καὶ πάντων ἀβεβαιότατα,—οἱ δὲ διὰ τῶν κατὰ τὰς ἀρετὰς⁴¹ θεωρημάτων⁴² ἐπὶ θεὸν σπεύδοντες⁴³ ἀσφαλῆ⁴⁴ καὶ ἀκράδαντον⁴⁵ ὁδὸν εὐθύνουσιν,⁴⁶ ὡς ἀψευδέστατα⁴⁷ φάναι,⁴⁸ ὅτι ὁ μὲν⁴⁹ ἐκείνοις πεπιστευκὼς ἀπιστεῖ θεῷ, ὁ δ' ἀπιστῶν ἐκείνοις πεπίστευκε θεῷ. . . .

²⁷³ὃς⁵⁰ τῆς πρὸς αὐτὸν πίστεως ἀγάμενος⁵¹ τὸν ἄνδρα πίστιν ἀντιδίδωσιν⁵² αὐτῷ, τὴν δι' ὅρκου⁵³ βεβαίωσιν⁵⁴ ὧν ὑπέσχετο⁵⁵ δωρεῶν, οὐκέτι μόνον ὡς ἀνθρώπῳ θεός, ἀλλὰ καὶ ὡς φίλος⁵⁶ γνωρίμῳ⁵⁷ διαλεγόμενος· φησὶ γὰρ "κατ' ἐμαυτοῦ ὤμοσα," παρ' ᾧ ὁ λόγος ὅρκος ἐστίν, ἕνεκα τοῦ τὴν διάνοιαν⁵⁸ ἀκλινῶς⁵⁹ καὶ παγίως⁶⁰ ἔτι μᾶλλον ἢ πρότερον ἐρηρεῖσθαι.⁶¹ ²⁷⁴πρεσβύτερος μὲν οὖν⁶² καὶ πρῶτος ἔστι τε καὶ λεγέσθω ὁ ἀστεῖος,⁶³ νεώτερος δὲ καὶ ἔσχατος πᾶς ἄφρων,⁶⁴ τὰ νεωτεροποιὰ⁶⁵ καὶ ἐν ἐσχατιαῖς ταττόμενα⁶⁶ μετιών.⁶⁷

²⁷⁵Ταῦτα μὲν οὖν⁶⁸ ἐπὶ τοσοῦτον εἰρήσθω.⁶⁹ τῷ δὲ πλήθει⁷⁰ καὶ μεγέθει⁷¹ τῶν ἐπαίνων ἐπιτιθεὶς⁷² ὥσπερ τινὰ κεφαλὴν τοῦ σοφοῦ⁷³ φησιν, ὅτι τὸν θεῖον⁷⁴ νόμον καὶ τὰ θεῖα προστάγματα⁷⁵ πάντα ἐποίησεν ὁ ἀνὴρ οὗτος, οὐ γράμμασιν ἀναδιδαχθείς,⁷⁶ ἀλλ' ἀγράφῳ τῇ φύσει⁷⁷ σπουδάσας⁷⁸ ὑγιαινούσαις⁷⁹ καὶ ἀνόσοις⁸⁰

---

33. ξηρός, -ά, -όν, *dry*.
34. λεωφόρος, -ον, *of a highway*.
35. ἄπταιστος, -ον, *not stumbling*.
36. Pres. mid. indic. 3 pl., χράομαι, *use*; with dat.
37. πορεία, -ας, ἡ, *mode of walking, travel*.
38. Adv., *outside*; substantivized by τῶν, "external things."
39. Pres. act. indic. 3 pl., ἐθίζω, *accustom*; with inf.; lit., "They accustom it [the soul] to nothing except to fall."
40. Postpositive partic.; focuses/limits the discussion to ταῦτα (cf. *CGCG* §59.53): "For *these* [i.e., bodily and external things] are slippery and the most insecure of all."
41. ἀρετή, -ῆς, ἡ, *virtue*.
42. θεώρημα, -ατος, τό, *principle, theory, doctrine*.
43. Pres. act. ptc. nom. masc. pl., σπεύδω, *strive after*; attrib. (subst.).
44. ἀσφαλής, -ές, *secure, sure, safe*.
45. ἀκράδαντος, -ον, *unshaken*.
46. Pres. act. indic. 3 pl., εὐθύνω, *walk straight*.
47. Superl. adv., ἀψευδής, -ές, *most truthfully* (lit., "in the least deceitful way possible").
48. Pres. act. inf., φημί, *say*; result clause (cf. S §2260; *CGCG* §46.7).
49. ὁ μέν . . . ὁ δέ, *the one . . . the other*. See n. 29.
50. The antecedent is θεός.
51. Pres. mid. ptc. nom. masc. sg., ἄγαμαι, *wonder at, admire*; with acc. and gen. of cause; circ.
52. Pres. act. indic. 3 sg., ἀντιδίδωμι, *repay*.
53. ὅρκος, -ου, ὁ, *oath*.
54. βεβαίωσις, -εως, ἡ, *confirmation*; appositive to πίστιν.
55. Aor. mid. indic. 3 sg., ὑπισχνέομαι, *promise*.
56. φίλος, -ου, ὁ, *friend*.
57. γνώριμος, -ον, *familiar, well-known*.

58. διάνοια, -ας, ἡ, *mind*.
59. Adv., *unswervingly*.
60. Adv., *firmly*.
61. Pf. pass. inf., ἐρείδω, (intrans.) *be fixed*; gen. obj. of ἕνεκα (cf. S §2032; *CGCG* §51.46): "for the sake of the mind being fixed still more unswervingly and firmly than before."
62. Partic. combination: indicates "a transition to a more to-the-point, relevant text segment (οὖν); the transition occurs in two stages (μέν . . . δέ)" (*CGCG* 59.73).
63. ἀστεῖος, -α, -ον, *good, noble, honorable*.
64. ἄφρων, -ον, *foolish*.
65. νεωτεροποιός, -όν, *innovating, revolutionary*.
66. Pres. pass. ptc. nom. neut. pl., τάσσω (Att. τάττω), (pass.) *be ordered/assigned to a position*; attrib. (subst.).
67. Pres. act. ptc. nom. masc. sg., μέτειμι, *go after*; circ. (causal).
68. See n. 62.
69. ἐπὶ τοσοῦτον εἰρήσθω, "these things [ταῦτα] must suffice" (lit., "these things must have been said to a great enough extent").
70. πλῆθος, -ους, τό, *multitude*.
71. μέγεθος, -ους, τό, *greatness*.
72. Pres. act. ptc. nom. masc. sg., ἐπιτίθημι, *add to*; with dat.; circ.
73. σοφός, -ή, -όν, (subst.) *wise man* (i.e., Abraham).
74. θεῖος, -α, -ον, *divine*.
75. πρόσταγμα, -ατος, τό, *command, ordinance*.
76. Aor. pass. ptc. nom. masc. sg., ἀναδιδάσκω, (pass.) *be taught, instructed*; circ.
77. φύσις, -εως, ἡ, *nature*.
78. Aor. act. ptc. nom. masc. sg., σπουδάζω, *be eager, endeavor to*; with inf.; circ.
79. Pres. act. ptc. dat. fem. pl., ὑγιαίνω, *be healthy*; attrib.
80. ἄνοσος, -ον, *without sickness*.

ὁρμαῖς[81] ἐπακολουθῆσαι·[82] περὶ δὲ ὧν[83] ὁ θεὸς ὁμολογεῖ,[84] τί προσῆκεν[85] ἀνθρώπους ἢ βεβαιότατα πιστεύειν; [276]τοιοῦτος ὁ βίος τοῦ πρώτου καὶ ἀρχηγέτου[86] τοῦ ἔθνους ἐστίν, ὡς μὲν[87] ἔνιοι[88] φήσουσι, νόμιμος,[89] ὡς δ' ὁ παρ' ἐμοῦ λόγος ἔδειξε,[90] νόμος αὐτὸς ὢν καὶ θεσμὸς[91] ἄγραφος.

NOTES

262. Cf. Neh. 9:7–8; Jdt. 8:25–27; 1 Macc. 2:52; Sir. 44:19–20; Jub. 17:17–18; 19:8–9; 4Q246 frag. 7:1–2; Heb. 11:8–19; James 2:21–22; 1 Clem. 10.1–7; and Kugel (1998, 296–309). Abraham's πίστις, according to Philo, is his firm and unwavering confidence in the invisible αἴτιος of the cosmos (*Abr.* 268; *Leg.* 3.228; *Her.* 90–93; Morgan 2015, 202).

273. The faith pledge that God repays Abraham (πίστιν ἀντιδίδωσιν αὐτῷ) is the oath God swore at the Aqedah: "By myself I have sworn [κατ' ἐμαυτοῦ ὤμοσα], says the Lord: Because you have done this, and have not withheld your son, your only son, I will indeed bless you, and I will make your offspring as numerous as the stars of heaven and as the sand that is on the seashore" (Gen. 22:16–17 LXX). The oath confirms the covenant God made with Abraham in Gen. 15:7–21 (cf. Heb. 6:13–18).

ὡς φίλος. Cf. Isa. 41:8; 2 Chron. 20:7; Wis. 7:27. The writer of Jubilees concludes that Abraham "was found faithful and he was recorded as a friend of the Lord in the heavenly tablets" (19:9). Likewise, James 2:23 follows a citation of Gen. 15:6 with the claim "and he was called 'friend of God' [φίλος θεοῦ]." Both writers interpret the designation "friend of God" as the reward for the faith(fulness) Abraham displays in his life, paradigmatically in Gen. 22. So also 1 Clem. 10.1.

275–276. Cf. Gen. 12:4; 22:18; 26:5; and Hayes (2015, 92–139). Philo's argument rests on the assumption that the Mosaic law is in accord with the law of nature (*Abr.* 1–6; cf. *Opif.* 1–3; *Mos.* 2.46–52). Thus, while some call Abraham νόμιμος, one should rather say, argues Philo, that "he himself *is* a law and an unwritten statute," an exemplum of the life lived in accordance with nature.

---

81. ὁρμή, -ῆς, ἡ, *impulse*.
82. Aor. act. inf., ἐπακολουθέω, *follow*; with dat.; comp. of σπουδάσας.
83. Relative attraction with an omitted antecedent is common after prepositions (cf. S §2531; CGCG §50.13).
84. Pres. act. indic. 3 sg., ὁμολογέω, *promise*.
85. Impf. act. indic. 3 sg., προσήκω, (quasi-impers.) *it befits*; with acc. and inf. (cf. S §1985; CGCC §51.8). ἤ is used with τί to mark a comparison (cf. S 2863.a): "what is fitting for humans [to do] *except* to trust in them most firmly."
86. ἀρχηγέτης, -ου, ὁ, *founder*.
87. μέν . . . δέ; point/counterpoint. See n. 8.
88. ἔνιοι, -αι, -α, *some*.
89. νόμιμος, -η, -ον, *lawful, law-abiding*.
90. Aor. act. indic. 3 sg., δείκνυμι, *show*.
91. θεσμός, -οῦ, ὁ, *law, ordinance*.

4.2.7

The Cosmic Temple and the Jerusalem Temple

On the Special Laws 1.66–70

1.66Τὸ μὲν¹ ἀνωτάτω² καὶ πρὸς ἀλήθειαν ἱερὸν³ θεοῦ νομίζειν⁴ τὸν σύμπαντα χρὴ⁵ κόσμον εἶναι, νεὼ⁶ μὲν⁷ ἔχοντα τὸ ἁγιώτατον τῆς τῶν ὄντων οὐσίας⁸ μέρος,⁹ οὐρανόν, ἀναθήματα¹⁰ δὲ τοὺς ἀστέρας,¹¹ ἱερέας¹² δὲ τοὺς ὑποδιακόνους¹³ αὐτοῦ τῶν δυνάμεων ἀγγέλους, ἀσωμάτους ψυχάς, οὐ κράματα¹⁴ ἐκ λογικῆς¹⁵ καὶ ἀλόγου¹⁶ φύσεως,¹⁷ οἵας τὰς ἡμετέρας εἶναι συμβέβηκεν,¹⁸ ἀλλ᾽ ἐκτετμημένας¹⁹ τὸ ἄλογον,²⁰ ὅλας δι᾽ ὅλων²¹ νοεράς,²² λογισμοὺς²³ ἀκραιφνεῖς,²⁴ μονάδι²⁵ ὁμοιουμένας.²⁶ **67**τὸ δὲ χειρόκμητον·²⁷ ἔδει γὰρ ὁρμὰς²⁸ ἀνθρώπων μὴ ἀνακόψαι²⁹ φοράς³⁰ τὰς εἰς εὐσέβειαν³¹

---

1. μέν . . . δέ; point/counterpoint: cosmic temple (theme 1), temple made with human hands (theme 2, *Spec.* 67; cf. Runge 2010, 75–83; BDF §447; S §2904; *CGCG* §59.24).
2. Superl., ἄνω, *highest* (of all).
3. ἱερόν, -οῦ, τό, *temple*.
4. Pres. act. inf., νομίζω, *consider, believe*.
5. Quasi-impers. χρή, *it is necessary*; with (acc. and) inf. (cf. S §1985; *CGCG* §36.3).
6. νεώς, -ώ, ὁ, *sanctuary*; pred. comp.
7. μέν . . . δέ . . . δέ; point/counterpoints (cf. S §2907) that explicate the *substance*, μέν-clause (cf. S §2908).
8. οὐσία, -ας, ἡ, *substance, essence*.
9. μέρος, -ους, τό, *part, portion*.
10. ἀνάθημα, -ατος, τό, *votive offering*; pred. comp.
11. ἀστήρ, -έρος, ὁ, *star*.
12. ἱερεύς, -έως, ὁ, *priest*; pred. comp.
13. ὑποδιάκονος, -ου, ὁ, *underservant*.
14. κρᾶμα, -ατος, τό, *mixture*.
15. λογικός, -ή, -όν, *rational*.
16. ἄλογος, -ον, *irrational*.
17. φύσις, -εως, ἡ, *nature*.
18. Pf. act. indic. 3 sg., συμβαίνω, (quasi-impers.) *happen to be*; with acc. and inf.
19. Pf. pass. ptc. acc. fem. pl., ἐκτέμνω, (pass.) *be cut away, removed from*; attrib..
20. ἄλογος, -ον, *irrational*.
21. Idiom, ὅλας δι᾽ ὅλων, "through and through."
22. νοερός, -ά, -όν, *noetic, spiritual*.
23. λογισμός, -οῦ, ὁ, *reason, rationality*.
24. ἀκραιφνής, -ές, *unmixed, pure*.
25. μονάς, -άδος, ἡ, *monad*.
26. Pres. pass. ptc. acc. fem. pl., ὁμοιόω, (intrans.) *be like*; attrib.
27. χειρόκμητος, -ον, *made by hand*; new theme.
28. ὁρμή, -ῆς, ἡ, *impulse*.
29. Aor. act. inf., ἀνακόπτω, *restrain, stop, check*.
30. φορά, -ᾶς, ἡ, *tribute, contribution*.
31. εὐσέβεια, -ας, ἡ, *piety*.

συντελούντων³² καὶ θυσίαις³³ βουλομένων ἢ³⁴ ἐπὶ τοῖς συμβαίνουσιν ἀγαθοῖς εὐχαριστεῖν³⁵ ἢ ἐφ' οἷς³⁶ ἂν ἁμαρτάνωσι³⁷ συγγνώμην³⁸ καὶ παραίτησιν³⁹ αἰτεῖσθαι.⁴⁰ προὐνόησε⁴¹ δ' ὡς οὔτε πολλαχόθι⁴² οὔτ' ἐν ταὐτῷ⁴³ πολλὰ κατασκευασθήσεται⁴⁴ ἱερά, δικαιώσας,⁴⁵ ἐπειδὴ εἷς ἐστιν ὁ θεός, καὶ ἱερὸν ἓν εἶναι μόνον. **⁶⁸εἶτα⁴⁶** τοῖς βουλομένοις ἐν ταῖς οἰκίαις αὐτῶν ἱερουργεῖν⁴⁷ οὐκ ἐφίησιν,⁴⁸ ἀλλ' ἀνισταμένους⁴⁹ ἀπὸ περάτων⁵⁰ γῆς εἰς τοῦτ' ἀφικνεῖσθαι⁵¹ κελεύει,⁵² ἅμα καὶ τῶν τρόπων⁵³ ἀναγκαιοτάτην⁵⁴ λαμβάνων⁵⁵ βάσανον.⁵⁶ ὁ γὰρ μὴ μέλλων θύειν εὐαγῶς⁵⁷ οὐκ ἂν ὑπομείναι⁵⁸ ποτὲ πατρίδα⁵⁹ καὶ φίλους⁶⁰ καὶ συγγενεῖς⁶¹ ἀπολιπὼν⁶² ξενιτεύειν,⁶³ ἀλλ' ἔοικεν⁶⁴ ὑπὸ δυνατωτέρας ὁλκῆς⁶⁵ ἀγόμενος τῆς πρὸς εὐσέβειαν ὑπομένειν τῶν συνηθεστάτων⁶⁶ καὶ φιλτάτων⁶⁷ ὥσπερ τινῶν ἡνωμένων⁶⁸ μερῶν ἀπαρτᾶσθαι.⁶⁹

⁶⁹καὶ τοῦδε σαφεστάτη⁷⁰ πίστις⁷¹ τὰ γινόμενα· μυρίοι⁷² γὰρ ἀπὸ μυρίων ὅσων πόλεων, οἱ μὲν διὰ γῆς, οἱ δὲ διὰ θαλάττης, ἐξ ἀνατολῆς⁷³ καὶ δύσεως⁷⁴ καὶ ἄρκτου⁷⁵ καὶ μεσημβρίας⁷⁶ καθ' ἑκάστην ἑορτὴν⁷⁷ εἰς τὸ ἱερὸν καταίρουσιν⁷⁸ οἷά⁷⁹ τινα κοινὸν ὑπόδρομον⁸⁰ καὶ καταγωγὴν⁸¹ ἀσφαλῆ⁸² πολυπράγμονος⁸³ καὶ ταραχωδεστάτου⁸⁴ βίου,⁸⁵ ζητοῦντες εὐδίαν⁸⁶ εὑρεῖν καὶ φροντίδων⁸⁷ ἀνεθέντες,⁸⁸ αἷς ἐκ πρώτης

32. Pres. act. ptc. gen. masc. pl., συντελέω, *contribute* (payment).
33. θυσία, -ας, ἡ, *sacrifice*.
34. ἤ . . . ἤ, *either . . . or*.
35. Pres. act. inf., εὐχαριστέω, *give thanks*.
36. Relative attraction with omission of antecedent is common after prepositions (cf. S §2531; *CGCG* 50.13).
37. Pres. act. subj. 3 pl., ἁμαρτάνω, *sin, err*; conditional rel. clause (cf. S §2567; *CGCG* §50.20).
38. συγγνώμη, -ης, ἡ, *pardon*.
39. παραίτησις, -εως, ἡ, *forgiveness*.
40. Pres. mid. inf., αἰτέω, *ask*.
41. Aor. act. indic. 3 sg., προνοέω, *provide*.
42. Adv., *in many places*.
43. ταὐτός, -ή, -όν (crasis: τὸ αὐτό), *same*; dat. of place, "in the same place."
44. Fut. pass. indic. 3 sg., κατασκευάζω, (pass.) *be prepared/built*; effort clause: ὡς with fut. indic. (cf. S §2209; *CGCG* §44.2).
45. Aor. act. ptc. nom. masc. sg., δικαιόω, *hold/deem right*; circ. (causal).
46. Adv. of consequence, *therefore, accordingly*.
47. Pres. act. inf., ἱερουργέω, *perform sacred rites*; comp. of τοῖς βουλομένοις.
48. Pres. act. indic. 3 sg., ἐφίημι, *permit*; with dat.
49. Aor. act. ptc. acc. masc. pl., ἀνίστημι, *arise*; circ.
50. πέρας, -ατος, τό, *end, limit*.
51. Pres. mid. inf., ἀφικνέομαι, *come to, arrive at*.
52. Pres. act. indic. 3 sg., κελεύω, *bid*; with acc. and inf.
53. τρόπος, -ου, ὁ, *character, way of life*.
54. Superl., ἀναγκαῖος, -α, -ον, *most severe*.
55. Gen. absol.; ἅμα with circ. ptc. expresses action contemporaneous to the main verb (cf. S §2081; *CGCG* §52.37).
56. βάσανος, -ου, ἡ, *test*.
57. Adv., *in a pure/guiltless manner*.
58. Aor. act. opt. 3 sg., ὑπομένω, *endure*. Potential opt. in apodosis (cf. S §2356): "For if someone were not intending to sacrifice in a pure manner, she or he *would not endure . . . to* live in a foreign land."

59. πατρίς, -ίδος, ἡ, *homeland*.
60. φίλος, -ου, ὁ, *friend*.
61. συγγενής, -ές, (subst.) *relative*.
62. Aor. act. ptc. nom. masc. pl., ἀπολείπω, *leave*; circ.
63. Pres. act. inf., ξενιτεύω, *live in a foreign land*; comp. of ὑπομείναι.
64. Pf. act. indic. 3 sg., ἔοικα, (impers.) *it seems*; with inf.
65. ὁλκή, -ῆς, ἡ, *draw, pull*.
66. Superl., συνήθης, -ες, *closest*.
67. Superl., φίλος, -ή, -όν, *dearest*.
68. Pf. pass. ptc. gen. masc. pl., ἑνόω, (pass.) *be united*; attrib.
69. Pres. pass. inf., ἀπαρτάω, (pass.) *be separated from*; with gen.
70. Superl., σαφής, -ές, *clearest*.
71. πίστις, -εως, ἡ, *proof*.
72. μυρίος, -α, -ον, (subst.) *myriads, countless multitudes*.
73. ἀνατολή, -ῆς, ἡ, *east*.
74. δύσις, -εως, ἡ, *west*.
75. ἄρκτος, -ου, ἡ, *north*.
76. μεσημβρία, -ας, ἡ, *south*.
77. ἑορτή, -ῆς, ἡ, *feast, festival*; καθ' ἑκάστην ἑορτήν, "at every feast."
78. Pres. act. indic. 3 pl., καταίρω, (of ships) *put into port*.
79. Adv. acc., *such as*.
80. ὑπόδρομος, -ου, ὁ, *shelter, cover, haven*.
81. καταγωγή, -ῆς, ἡ, *landing, resting place*.
82. ἀσφαλής, -ές, *secure*.
83. πολυπράγμων, -ον, *busy about many things*.
84. Superl., ταραχώδης, -ες, *most disturbing*.
85. βίος, -ου, ὁ, *life*.
86. εὐδία, -ας, ἡ, *calm weather, tranquility*.
87. φροντίς, -ίδος, ἡ, *thought, care, attention*.
88. Aor. pass. ptc. nom. masc. pl., ἀνίημι, *let go, leave behind*; circ.

ἡλικίας⁸⁹ καταζεύγνυνται⁹⁰ καὶ πιέζονται,⁹¹ βραχύν τινα διαπνεύσαντες⁹² χρόνον ἐν ἱλαραῖς⁹³ διάγειν⁹⁴ εὐθυμίαις·⁹⁵ **⁷⁰**ἐλπίδων τε χρηστῶν γεμισθέντες⁹⁶ σχολάζουσι⁹⁷ τὴν ἀναγκαιοτάτην σχολὴν ὁσιότητι⁹⁸ καὶ τιμῇ θεοῦ, φιλίαν⁹⁹ καὶ πρὸς τοὺς τέως¹⁰⁰ ἀγνοουμένους¹⁰¹ συντιθέμενοι¹⁰² καὶ κρᾶσιν¹⁰³ ἠθῶν¹⁰⁴ ἐπὶ θυσιῶν καὶ σπονδῶν¹⁰⁵ εἰς βεβαιοτάτην πίστιν ὁμονοίας¹⁰⁶ ποιούμενοι.

NOTES

1.66. Philo works with a model of *temple as cosmos*, on which see Klawans (2006, 116–23). The notion that the earthly temple symbolizes the celestial temple is implicit in Priestly material (e.g., Gen. 1; Exod. 25–40) and was developed by early Jewish interpreters. Philo associates the inner sanctum with "heaven," or the incorporeal realm of the forms (cf. *Mos.* 2.74; *Ebr.* 132, 134).

1.67. In contrast to certain New Testament passages that (appear to) polemicize against the temple made "with hands" (cf. Mark 14:48; Acts 7:48; Heb. 9:11), Philo does not use τὸ χειρόκμητον in a pejorative sense. On the contrary, it was fitting that the building "made with hands," which symbolizes the cosmic temple, should incorporate the material elements of the cosmos (*Mos.* 2.88).

εἷς ἐστιν ὁ θεός. An allusion to the Shema (Deut. 6:4 LXX): the one God must be worshiped in the one temple (cf. Deut. 12:5-7, 11–14, 17–18; Josephus, *C. Ap.* 2.193; see §5.4.1).

1.69–70. Widespread participation in the festivals provides evidence of the commitment of the Jewish people to the one God. For further discussion, see Leonhardt (2001, 18–52).

---

89. ἡλικία, -ας, ἡ, *age, time of life*.
90. Pres. pass. indic. 3 pl., καταζεύγνυμι, (pass.) *be constrained/confined*.
91. Pres. pass. indic. 3 pl., πιέζω, (pass.) *be weighed down*.
92. Aor. act. ptc. nom. masc. pl., διαπνέω, *catch one's breath*; circ.
93. ἱλαρός, -ά, -όν, *cheerful*.
94. Pres. act. inf., διάγω, *pass* (time); comp. of ζητοῦντες.
95. εὐθυμία, -ας, ἡ, *contentment*.
96. Aor. pass. ptc. nom. masc. pl., γεμίζω, (intrans.) *be full of*; with gen.; circ.
97. Pres. act. indic. 3 pl., σχολάζω, *have leisure for* (something); here with cognate acc.; lit., "they are at leisure with a most necessary leisure in piety and honor of God."
98. ὁσιότης, -ητος, ἡ, *piety, holiness*.
99. φιλία, -ας, ἡ, *affection, friendship*.
100. Adv., *hitherto, up to that time*.
101. Pres. pass. ptc. acc. masc. pl., ἀγνοέω, (pass.) *be unknown*; attrib. (subst.).
102. Pres. mid. ptc. nom. masc. pl., συντίθημι, (mid.) *arrange, establish*; circ.
103. κρᾶσις, -εως, ἡ, *blending, union*.
104. ἦθος, -ους, τό, *habit, custom*.
105. σπονδή, -ῆς, ἡ, *libation*.
106. ὁμόνοια, -ας, ἡ, *concord*.

4.2.8

The Sacrificial System

On the Special Laws 1.194–197

1.194Τοσαῦτα περὶ τούτων διαλεχθεὶς[1] ἄρχεται διαιρεῖν[2] τὰ τῶν θυσιῶν[3] γένη[4] καὶ τέμνων[5] εἰς εἴδη[6] τρία τὰ ἀνωτάτω[7] τὸ μὲν[8] ὁλόκαυτον[9] καλεῖ, τὸ δὲ σωτήριον,[10] τὸ δὲ περὶ ἁμαρτίας·[11] εἶθ᾽[12] ἕκαστον τοῖς ἁρμόττουσιν[13] ἐπικοσμεῖ[14] τοῦ πρέποντος[15] ἅμα καὶ εὐαγοῦς[16] οὐ μετρίως[17] στοχασάμενος.[18] **195**παγκάλη δὲ καὶ προσφυεστάτη[19] τοῖς πράγμασιν[20] ἡ διαίρεσις[21] ἀκολουθίαν[22] ἔχουσα καὶ εἱρμόν·[23] εἰ γὰρ βούλοιτό[24] τις ἐξετάζειν[25] ἀκριβῶς[26] τὰς αἰτίας,[27] ὧν ἕνεκα[28] τοῖς πρώτοις ἔδοξεν[29] ἀνθρώποις ἐπὶ τὰς διὰ θυσιῶν εὐχαριστίας ὁμοῦ[30] καὶ λιτὰς[31] ἐλθεῖν, εὑρήσει δύο τὰς ἀνωτάτω· μίαν μὲν[32] τὴν πρὸς θεὸν τιμήν, τὴν ἄνευ[33] τινὸς ἑτέρου δι᾽ αὐτὸν μόνον γινομένην ὡς ἀναγκαῖον [καὶ] καλόν, ἑτέραν δὲ τὴν τῶν θυόντων[34]

1. Aor. pass. ptc. nom. masc. sg., διαλέγω, (pass.) *be discussed*; circ. The subject is Moses.
2. Pres. act. inf., διαιρέω, *distinguish between*.
3. θυσία, -ας, ἡ, *sacrifice*.
4. γένος, -ους, τό, *kind, type*.
5. Pres. act. ptc. nom. masc. pl., τέμνω, *divide*; circ.
6. εἶδος, -ους, τό, *class, kind*.
7. Superl. of ἄνω substantivized by the article, "the ones of highest importance."
8. μέν . . . δέ . . . δέ; point/counterpoints (cf. S §2907).
9. ὁλόκαυτος, -ον, (subst.) *whole burnt offering*.
10. σωτήριος, -ον, (subst.) *deliverance offering*.
11. τὸ περὶ ἁμαρτίας, *the one for sin*, thus *sin offering*.
12. Adv. (εἶτα), *next, then*.
13. Pres. act. ptc. dat. neut. pl., ἁρμόζω (Att. ἁρμόττω), *fit well, be well suited*; attrib. (subst.).
14. Pres. act. indic. 3 sg., ἐπικοσμέω, *adorn, add ornament to*.
15. Pres. act. ptc. gen. neut. sg., πρέπω, (subst.) *that which is suitable, propriety*.
16. εὐαγής, -ές, (subst.) *purity, reverence*.
17. Adv. with neg. οὐ, "in no small measure."
18. Aor. mid. ptc. nom. masc. sg., στοχάζομαι, *aim at, endeavor after*; with gen.; circ.
19. Superl., προσφυής, -ές, *most natural to*; with dat.
20. πρᾶγμα, -ατος, τό, *thing, concrete reality*.
21. διαίρεσις, -εως, ἡ, *division*.
22. ἀκολουθία, -ας, ἡ, *sequence, succession, order*.
23. εἱρμός, -οῦ, ὁ, *sequence, series*.
24. Mixed condition; εἰ with opt. in the protasis, fut. indic. in the apodosis (cf. S §2361; *CGCG* §49.17).
25. Pres. act. inf., ἐξετάζω, *examine*.
26. Adv., *carefully*.
27. αἰτία, -ας, ἡ, *reason*.
28. Prep. with gen., *on account of*.
29. Aor. act. indic. 3 sg., δοκέω, (impers.) *it seems good*; with dat. and inf. (cf. *CGCG* §51.30).
30. Adv., *together*.
31. λιτή, -ῆς, ἡ, *prayer*.
32. μίαν μέν . . . ἑτέραν δέ, *the one (reason) . . . the other (reason)*.
33. Prep. with gen., *without*.
34. Pres. act. ptc. gen. masc. pl., θύω, *sacrifice*; attrib. (subst.).

προηγουμένην[35] ὠφέλειαν·[36] διττή[37] δ' ἐστίν, ἡ μὲν[38] ἐπὶ μετουσίᾳ[39] ἀγαθῶν, ἡ δὲ ἐπὶ κακῶν ἀπαλλαγῇ.[40] **[196]**τῇ μὲν οὖν[41] κατὰ θεὸν καὶ δι' αὐτὸν μόνον γινομένῃ προσήκουσαν[42] ὁ νόμος ἀπένειμε[43] θυσίαν τὴν ὁλόκαυτον, ὁλοκλήρῳ[44] καὶ παντελεῖ[45] μηδὲν ἐπιφερομένῃ[46] τῆς θνητῆς φιλαυτίας[47] ὁλόκληρον καὶ παντελῆ· τὴν[48] δὲ χάριν[49] ἀνθρώπων, ἐπειδὴ διαίρεσιν ἐπεδέχετο ἡ δόξα,[50] καὶ αὐτὸς διεῖλε,[51] κατὰ μὲν[52] τὴν μετουσίαν τῶν ἀγαθῶν ὁρίσας[53] θυσίαν ἣν ὠνόμασε[54] σωτήριον, τῇ δὲ φυγῇ[55] τῶν κακῶν ἀπονείμας τὴν περὶ ἁμαρτίας. **[197]**ὡς τρεῖς εἶναι[56] δεόντως[57] ἐπὶ τρισί, τὴν μὲν[58] ὁλόκαυτον δι' αὐτὸν μόνον τὸν θεόν, ὃν καλὸν τιμᾶσθαι, μὴ δι' ἕτερον, τὰς δ' ἄλλας δι' ἡμᾶς,

τὴν μὲν[59] σωτήριον ἐπὶ σωτηρίᾳ καὶ βελτιώσει[60] τῶν ἀνθρωπίνων πραγμάτων, τὴν δὲ περὶ ἁμαρτίας ἐπὶ θεραπείᾳ[61] ὧν ἐπλημμέλησεν[62] ἡ ψυχή.

NOTE

1.194. Philo divides the sacrificial system into three categories: the whole burnt offering (Lev. 1:3–17), the salvation offering (Lev. 3:1–17), and the sin offering (Lev. 4). He discusses the grain offering elsewhere (*Somn.* 2.71–74; cf. Lev. 2) and treats the reparation offering as a subcategory of the sin offering (*Spec.* 234; cf. Lev. 5:14–6:7). For further discussion of sacrifice in Philo, see Leonhardt (2001, 241–51); Gilders (2011).

35. Pres. mid. ptc. acc. fem. sg., προηγέομαι, *lead, precede, go before*; attrib.
36. ὠφέλεια, -ας, ἡ, *benefit*.
37. δισσός, -ή, -όν (Att. διττός), *twofold*.
38. ἡ μέν . . . ἡ δέ, *the one . . . the other* (cf. BDF §250; S §1107; CGCG §28.17).
39. μετουσία, -ας, ἡ, *share*; with gen.
40. ἀπαλλαγή, -ῆς, ἡ, *deliverance, release*.
41. Partic. combination: "transition to a more to-the-pint, relevant text segment (οὖν) [that] occurs in two stages (μέν . . . δέ)" (*CGCG* §59.73).
42. Pres. act. ptc. acc. fem. sg., προσήκω, *belong to*; with dat.; attrib.
43. Aor. act. indic. 3 sg., ἀπονέμω, *assign*.
44. ὁλόκληρος, -ον, *complete*.
45. παντελής, -ές, *all-complete, perfect*.
46. Pres. mid. ptc. dat. fem. sg., ἐπιφέρω, *bear*; circ. (causal); lit., "To the one [αἰτία] that is whole and complete, *since it bears no amount of mortal self-interest, the law assigned a sacrifice that is whole and complete*."
47. φιλαυτία, -ας, ἡ, *self-love, self-interest*.
48. τήν = τὴν αἰτίαν.
49. Prep. with gen., *for the sake of*.
50. δόξα, -ας, ἡ, *form, appearance*. The article marks possession: "since *its* appearance accepts a division."
51. Aor. act. indic. 3 sg., διαιρέω, *divide*.
52. μέν . . . δέ; point/counterpoint.
53. Aor. act. ptc. nom. masc. sg., ὁρίζω, *delineate*.
54. Aor. act. indic. 3 sg., ὀνομάζω, *name*.
55. φυγή, -ῆς, ἡ, *flight from, avoidance of*; with gen.
56. Result clause; ὡς with inf. (cf. S §2260; *CGCG* §46.7).
57. Adv., *very suitably*.
58. μέν . . . δέ; point/counterpoint.

59. μέν . . . δέ; point/counterpoint; subdivides the initial δέ-clause (cf. S §2908).
60. βελτίωσις, -εως, ἡ, *betterment*.
61. θεραπεία, -ας, ἡ, *healing*.
62. Aor. act. indic. 3 sg., πλημμελέω, *sin, err*. The object of the verb has been attracted to the case of its antecedent: "for healing *of the sins that* the soul has committed."

4.3

Historical and Apologetic Works

Philo's historical and apologetic works include *On the Life of Moses* 1–2, *Hypothetica* (fragments), *On the Contemplative Life* (fragments), *Against Flaccus*, and *On the Embassy to Gaius*. The Alexandrian Jew fashions himself "as an advocate of Judaism and of the Jewish people in its social and political struggles of the day" (Royse 2009, 50). As Niehoff observes, "Under Philo's pen in Rome Judaism becomes an urban philosophy or religion that is centered in the synagogues and promotes civic virtues" (2018, 65).

The two reading passages are from *Against Flaccus* and *On the Embassy to Gaius*. The former details the first pogrom, acts of violence against Alexandrian Jews that broke out in 38 CE. The latter is an effusive encomium to Augustus, whom Philo positions as the model to which the current emperor, Claudius, should aspire.

Text and Translation: Colson 1941 (§4.3.1); Colson 1962 (§4.3.2)

Supplemental Scripture: Mark 15:16–20 parr. (§4.3.1); Mark 1:1 (§4.3.2)

4.3.1

The Mockery of King Agrippa

Against Flaccus 36–43

36 Ἦν τις μεμηνὼς¹ ὄνομα Καραβᾶς² οὐ τὴν ἀγρίαν³ καὶ θηριώδη⁴ μανίαν⁵—ἄσκηπτος⁶ γὰρ αὕτη γε⁷ καὶ τοῖς ἔχουσι καὶ τοῖς πλησιάζουσιν⁸—, ἀλλὰ τὴν ἀνειμένην⁹ καὶ μαλακωτέραν.¹⁰ οὗτος διημέρευε¹¹ καὶ διενυκτέρευε¹² γυμνὸς¹³ ἐν ταῖς ὁδοῖς οὔτε θάλπος¹⁴ οὔτε κρυμὸν¹⁵ ἐκτρεπόμενος,¹⁶ ἄθυρμα¹⁷ νηπίων¹⁸ καὶ μειρακίων¹⁹ σχολαζόντων.²⁰ **37** συνελάσαντες²¹ τὸν ἄθλιον²² ἄχρι²³ τοῦ γυμνασίου²⁴ καὶ στήσαντες μετέωρον,²⁵ ἵνα καθορῷτο²⁶ πρὸς πάντων, βύβλον²⁷ μὲν²⁸ εὐρύναντες²⁹ ἀντὶ³⁰ διαδήματος ἐπιτιθέασιν

    1. Pf. act. ptc. nom. masc. sg., μαίνομαι, *be mad*; periphrastic (plpf. for backgrounding; *CGCG* §33.50).
    2. Καραβᾶς, -οῦ, ὁ, *Carabas*.
    3. ἄγριος, -α, -ον, *savage, fierce*.
    4. θηριώδης, -ες, *of wild beasts, savage*.
    5. μανία, -ας, ἡ, *madness*; acc. of manner.
    6. ἄσκηπτος, -ον, *that cannot be feigned* (cf. LSJ, 257). The word is otherwise unattested. Colson 1941 suggests ἀσκεπής, "uncovered," and by extension "indefensible" or "dangerous."
    7. Postpositive partic.: "focuses attention on the word or phrase it follows . . . and limits the applicability of the content of the utterance to *at least* or (*more*) *precisely* that specific element" (*CGCG* §59.53).
    8. Pres. act. ptc. dat. masc. pl., πλησιάζω, *draw near*; attrib. (subst.).
    9. Pf. pass. ptc. acc. fem. sg., ἀνίημι, (pass.) *be slackened/relaxed*; attrib.
    10. Compar., μαλακός, -ή, -όν, *softer*.
    11. Impf. act. indic. 3 sg., διημερεύω, *spend the day*.
    12. Impf. act. indic. 3 sg., διανυκτερεύω, *spend the night*.
    13. γυμνός, -ή, -όν, *naked*.
    14. θάλπος, -εος, τό, *warmth*.

    15. κρυμός, -οῦ, ὁ, *cold*.
    16. Pres. mid. ptc. nom. masc. sg., ἐκτρέπω, *turn away from*; circ.
    17. ἄθυρμα, -ατος, τό, *plaything, toy*; appositive to οὗτος.
    18. νήπιον, -ου, τό, *young child*.
    19. μειράκιον, -ου, τό, *youth, young man*.
    20. Pres. act. ptc. gen. neut. pl., σχολάζω, *be unoccupied, have leisure*.
    21. Aor. act. ptc. nom. masc. pl., συνελαύνω, *drive together*. The subject of the participle is the mob mentioned in *Flacc*. 35.
    22. ἄθλιος, -α, -ον, *pitiful, wretched*.
    23. Prep. with gen., *up to*.
    24. γυμνάσιον, -ου, τό, *gymnasium*.
    25. μετέωρος, -ον, *raised from off the ground*.
    26. Pres. mid. opt. 3 sg., καθοράω, *look down from above*; purpose clause; opt. for subj. (cf. S §2196; *CGCG* §45.3).
    27. βύβλος, -ου, ἡ, *biblus* (Egyptian papyrus).
    28. μέν . . . δέ . . . δέ (cf. S §2907).
    29. Aor. act. ptc. nom. masc. pl., εὐρύνω, *widen* (i.e., to flatten out the sheet of papyrus); circ.
    30. Prep. with gen., *in exchange for, in place of*; ἀντὶ διαδήματος, *in place of a diadem*.

αὐτοῦ τῇ κεφαλῇ, χαμαιστρώτῳ[31] δὲ τὸ ἄλλο σῶμα περιβάλλουσιν[32] ἀντὶ χλαμύδος,[33] ἀντὶ δὲ σκήπτρου[34] βραχύ τι παπύρου τμῆμα[35] τῆς ἐγχωρίου[36] καθ' ὁδὸν ἐρριμμένον[37] ἰδών τις ἀναδίδωσιν. **[38]**ἐπεὶ δὲ ὡς ἐν θεατρικοῖς μίμοις[38] τὰ παράσημα[39] τῆς βασιλείας ἀνειλήφει[40] καὶ διεκεκόσμητο[41] εἰς βασιλέα, νεανίαι[42] ῥάβδους[43] ἐπὶ τῶν ὤμων[44] φέροντες ἀντὶ λογχοφόρων[45] ἑκατέρωθεν[46] εἱστήκεσαν μιμούμενοι[47] δορυφόρους.[48] εἶθ' ἕτεροι προσῄεσαν,[49] οἱ μὲν[50] ὡς ἀσπασόμενοι,[51] οἱ δὲ ὡς δικασόμενοι,[52] οἱ δ' ὡς ἐντευξόμενοι[53] περὶ κοινῶν πραγμάτων.[54] **[39]**εἶτ' ἐκ τοῦ περιεστῶτος ἐν κύκλῳ πλήθους ἐξῄχει[55] βοή[56] τις ἄτοπος[57] Μάριν ἀποκαλούντων[58]—οὕτως δέ φασι τὸν κύριον ὀνομάζεσθαι[59] παρὰ Σύροις[60]—· ᾔδεσαν γὰρ Ἀγρίππαν[61] καὶ γένει[62] Σύρον καὶ Συρίας μεγάλην ἀποτομὴν[63] ἔχοντα, ἧς ἐβασίλευε. **[40]**ταῦτα δὲ ἀκούων, μᾶλλον δὲ ὁρῶν ὁ Φλάκκος,[64] δεόντως[65] ἂν καὶ τὸν μεμηνότα συλλαβὼν[66] καὶ καθείρξας,[67] ἵνα μὴ παρέχῃ[68] τοῖς κατακερτομοῦσιν[69] ἀφορμὴν[70] εἰς ὕβριν[71] τῶν βελτιόνων, καὶ τοὺς ἐνσκευάσαντας[72] τιμωρησάμενος,[73] ὅτι γε[74] βασιλέα καὶ φίλον Καίσαρος καὶ ὑπὸ τῆς Ῥωμαίων βουλῆς[75] τετιμημένον[76] στρατηγικαῖς[77] τιμαῖς ἐτόλμησαν[78] καὶ ἔργοις καὶ λόγοις καὶ φανερῶς[79] καὶ πλαγίως[80] ὑβρίζειν,[81] οὐ μόνον οὐκ ἐπέπληξεν,[82]

31. χαμαίστρωτος, -ον, *spread out on the ground*; (subst.) *mat, rug*.
32. Pres. act. indic. 3 pl., περιβάλλω, *put around, clothe*.
33. χλαμύς, -ύδος, ἡ, *mantle* (of a king).
34. σκῆπτρον, -ου, τό, *scepter*.
35. τμῆμα, -ατος, τό, *part cut off, piece*; βραχύ τι παπύρου τμῆμα, "a little piece of papyrus."
36. ἐγχώριος, -ον, *native to the area*.
37. Pf. pass. ptc. acc. neut. sg., ῥίπτω, (pass.) *be thrown*; supp. (ἰδών).
38. μῖμος, -ου, ὁ, *actor, mime*; ὡς ἐν θεατρικοῖς μίμοις, "as in acts of theatrical mimicry."
39. παράσημον, -ου, τό, *distinguished mark*, (pl.) *insignia*.
40. Plpf. act. indic. 3 sg., ἀναλαμβάνω, *receive*.
41. Plpf. pass. indic. 3 sg., διακοσμέω, (pass.) *be adorned throughout*; prep. εἰς marks pred. comp.: "decked out as king."
42. νεανίας, -ου, ὁ, *young man*.
43. ῥάβδος, -ου, ἡ, *rod*.
44. ὦμος, -ου, ὁ, *shoulder*.
45. λογχοφόρος, -ον, *spear bearing*; ἀντὶ λογχοφόρων, "in place of spears."
46. Adv., *on either side*.
47. Pres. mid. ptc. nom. masc. pl., μιμέω, *imitate*; circ.
48. δορυφόρος, -ον, (subst.) *bodyguard* (royal).
49. Impf. act. indic. 3 pl., πρόσειμι, *approach*.
50. οἱ μέν... οἱ δέ... οἱ δέ, *some... others... others* (cf. BDF §250; S §1107; CGCG §28.17).
51. Fut. mid. ptc. nom. masc. pl., ἀσπάζομαι, *greet, salute*; purpose (cf. S §2065; CGCG §52.41).
52. Fut. mid. ptc. nom. masc. pl., δικάζω, (mid.) *take to court*; purpose. See n. 51.
53. Fut. mid. ptc. nom. masc. pl., ἐντυγχάνω, *converse with*; purpose. See n. 51.
54. πρᾶγμα, -ατος, τό, *matter, affair*.
55. Impf. act. indic. 3 sg., ἐξηχέω, *resound*.
56. βοή, -ῆς, ἡ, *shout*.
57. ἄτοπος, -ον, *extraordinary*.
58. Pres. act. ptc. gen. masc. pl., ἀποκαλέω, (pass.) *be called/named*; gen. absol.
59. Pres. pass. inf., ὀνομάζω, *called*; indir. disc. (φασι) (cf. BDF §397; S §2016; CGCG §51.19).
60. Σύρος, -ου, ὁ, *Syrian*.
61. Ἀγρίππας, -ου, ὁ, *Agrippa*.
62. γένος, -ους, τό, *race*; dat. of respect.
63. ἀποτομή, -ῆς, ἡ, *segment*.
64. Φλάκκος, -ου, ὁ, *Flaccus* (prefect of Roman Egypt from 33 to 38 CE).
65. Adv., *as it ought*; with ἄν as expressing a contrafactual (cf. S §2344; CGCG §52.40): "It was his duty [implied: but he didn't do it] to arrest and lock up the madman."
66. Aor. act. ptc. nom. masc. sg., συλλαμβάνω, *seize, apprehend*; circ. (conditional).
67. Aor. act. ptc. nom. masc. sg., κατείργω, *confine*; circ. (conditional).
68. Pres. act. subj. 3 sg., παρέχω, *allow*; purpose clause (cf. BDF §369; S §2193; CGCG §45.3).
69. Pres. act. ptc. dat. masc. pl., κατακερτομέω, *rail violently*; attrib. (subst.).
70. ἀφορμή, -ῆς, ἡ, *occasion*.
71. ὕβρις, -εως, ἡ, *insult*.
72. Aor. act. ptc. acc. masc. pl., ἐνσκευάζω, *dress in*; attrib. (subst.).
73. Aor. mid. ptc. nom. masc. sg., τιμωρέω, *punish*; circ.
74. See n. 7.
75. βουλή, -ῆς, ἡ, (Roman) *senate*.
76. Pf. pass. ptc. acc. masc. sg., τιμάω, (pass.) *be honored*; attrib.
77. στρατηγικός, -ή, -όν, *praetorian*.
78. Aor. act. indic. 3 pl., τολμάω, *dare to*.
79. Adv., *openly*.
80. Adv., *indirectly* (by way of inuendo).
81. Pres. act. inf., ὑβρίζω, *insult*; comp. of ἐτόλμησαν.
82. Aor. act. indic. 3 sg., ἐπιπλήσσω, *punish*.

ἀλλ' οὐδ' ἐπισχεῖν⁸³ ἠξίωσεν⁸⁴ ἄδειαν⁸⁵ καὶ ἐκεχειρίαν⁸⁶ διδοὺς τοῖς ἐθελοκακοῦσι⁸⁷ καὶ ἐθελέχθρως⁸⁸ ἔχουσι, προσποιούμενος⁸⁹ ἅ τε ἑώρα μὴ ὁρᾶν καὶ ὧν ἤκουε μὴ ἀκούειν. **⁴¹**ὅπερ συναισθόμενος⁹⁰ ὁ ὄχλος—οὐχ ὁ καθεστὼς⁹¹ καὶ δημοτικός,⁹² ἀλλ' ὁ πάντα θορύβου⁹³ καὶ ταραχῆς⁹⁴ εἰωθὼς⁹⁵ ἀναπιμπλάναι⁹⁶ διὰ φιλοπραγμοσύνην⁹⁷ καὶ ζῆλον⁹⁸ ἀβιώτου βίου καὶ τὴν ἐξ ἔθους⁹⁹ ἀργίαν¹⁰⁰ καὶ σχολήν,¹⁰¹ πρᾶγμα ἐπίβουλον¹⁰²—συρρυέντες¹⁰³ εἰς τὸ θέατρον ἐξ ἑωθινοῦ¹⁰⁴ Φλάκκον ἤδη τιμῶν¹⁰⁵ ἀθλίων ἐωνημένοι,¹⁰⁶ ἃς ὁ δοξομανὴς¹⁰⁷ καὶ παλίμπρατος¹⁰⁸ ἐλάμβανεν οὐ καθ' αὑτοῦ μόνον ἀλλὰ καὶ τῆς κοινῆς ἀσφαλείας,¹⁰⁹ ἀνεβόησαν¹¹⁰ ἀφ' ἑνὸς συνθήματος¹¹¹ εἰκόνας¹¹² ἐν ταῖς προσευχαῖς¹¹³ ἀνατιθέναι,¹¹⁴ καινότατον¹¹⁵ καὶ μηδέπω πραχθὲν εἰσηγούμενοι¹¹⁶ παρανόμημα.¹¹⁷ **⁴²**καὶ τοῦτ' εἰδότες—ὀξύτατοι¹¹⁸ γὰρ τὴν μοχθηρίαν¹¹⁹ εἰσί—κατασοφίζονται¹²⁰ τὸ Καίσαρος ὄνομα προκάλυμμα¹²¹ ποιησάμενοι, ᾧ προσάπτειν¹²² τι τῶν ἐπαιτίων¹²³ οὐ θεμιτόν.¹²⁴

⁴³τί οὖν ὁ τῆς χώρας ἐπίτροπος;¹²⁵ ἐπιστάμενος,¹²⁶ ὅτι καὶ¹²⁷ ἡ πόλις οἰκήτορας¹²⁸ ἔχει διττούς,¹²⁹ ἡμᾶς τε καὶ τούτους, καὶ πᾶσα Αἴγυπτος, καὶ ὅτι οὐκ ἀποδέουσι¹³⁰ μυριάδων ἑκατὸν οἱ τὴν Ἀλεξάνδρειαν καὶ τὴν χώραν Ἰουδαῖοι κατοικοῦντες ἀπὸ τοῦ πρὸς

---

83. Pres. act. inf., ἐπίσχω, *restrain*; indir. disc. See n. 59.
84. Pres. act. indic. 3 sg., ἀξιόω, *think it necessary*.
85. ἄδεια, -ας, ἡ, *freedom from fear*.
86. ἐκεχειρία, -ας, ἡ, *free license*.
87. Pres. act. ptc. dat. masc. pl., ἐθελοκακέω, *desire to do wrong*; attrib. (subst.).
88. Adv., *with a grudge*; ἔχω with adv. (cf. S §1438; *CGCG* §26.11).
89. Pres. act. ptc. nom. masc. sg., προσποιέω, *pretend*; circ.
90. Aor. mid. ptc. nom. masc. sg., συναισθάνομαι, *perceive together*; circ.
91. Pf. act. ptc. nom. masc. sg., καθίστημι, *be calm*; attrib.
92. δημοτικός, -ή, -όν, *democratic*, (by extens.) *well-disposed*.
93. θόρυβος, -ου, ὁ, *uproar*.
94. ταραχή, -ῆς, ἡ, *upheaval*.
95. Pf. act. ptc. nom. masc. sg., ἔθω, *be accustomed*; with inf.; attrib.
96. Aor. act. inf., ἀναπίμπλημι, *fill up*.
97. φιλοπραγμοσύνη, -ης, ἡ, *love of meddling*.
98. ζῆλος, -ου, ὁ, *zeal*; with obj. gen., ἀβιώτου βίου, "zeal for a life not worth living."
99. ἔθος, -ους, τό, *custom, habit*.
100. ἀργία, -ας, ἡ, *idleness, laziness*.
101. σχολή, -ῆς, ἡ, *leisure*.
102. ἐπίβουλος, -ον, *insidious, treacherous*; the tail πρᾶγμα ἐπίβουλον comes as a final interjection: "an insidious thing."
103. Aor. act. ptc. nom. masc. pl., συρρέω, *stream together*; circ.
104. ἑωθινός, -ή, -όν, *in the morning, early*; adv., "early in the morning."
105. τιμή, -ῆς, ἡ, *price, value*; gen. of price: "[purchased] for a miserable price."
106. Pf. mid. ptc. nom. masc. pl., ὠνέομαι, *purchase*; circ.
107. δοξομανής, -ές, *mad after fame*.
108. παλίμπρατος, -ον, (of an enslaved person who passes from hand to hand) *sold again* (LSJ, 1292).

109. ἀσφαλεία, -ας, ἡ, *assurance, security*.
110. Aor. act. indic. 3 pl., ἀναβοάω, *cry out*.
111. σύνθημα, -ατος, τό, *agreement*; ἀφ' ἑνὸς συνθήματος, "in one accord."
112. εἰκών, -όνος, ὁ, *image*.
113. προσευχή, -ῆς, ἡ, *place of prayer*; equivalent of συναγωγή (cf. BDAG, 878.2).
114. Pres. act. inf., ἀνατίθημι, *set up*; indir. disc. See n. 59.
115. Superl., καινός, -ή, -όν, *newest, entirely novel*.
116. Pres. mid. ptc. nom. masc. pl., εἰσηγέομαι, *lead in, introduce*; circ.
117. παρανόμημα, -ατος, τό, *breach of law*.
118. Superl., ὀξύς, -ύ, *sharpest, keenest*.
119. μοχθηρία, -ας, ἡ, *wickedness, depravity*; acc. of respect.
120. Pres. mid. indic. 3 pl., κατασοφίζομαι, *outwit by sophism*.
121. προκάλυμμα, -ατος, τό, *screen, cloak*; pred. comp.: "using the name of Caesar *as a screen*."
122. Pres. act. inf., προσάπτω, *attach to*.
123. ἐπαίτιος, -ον, *blameworthy, guilty*.
124. θεμιτός, -ή, -όν, (quasi-impers.) *it is permitted*; with acc. and inf.: "to which [the name of Caesar] it is not permissible [for them] to attach anything blameworthy."
125. ἐπίτροπος, -ου, ὁ, *governor*. Supply the verb: "What, then, did the governor of the land *do*?"
126. Aor. mid. ptc. nom. masc. sg., ἐπίσταμαι, *know*; circ. (concessive).
127. καί . . . καί, *both* (the city = Alexandria) . . . *and* (all Egypt).
128. οἰκήτωρ, -ορος, ὁ, *inhabitant*.
129. δισσός, -ή, -όν (Att. διττός), *divided, two* (kinds).
130. Pres. act. indic. 3 pl., ἀποδέω, *be in want of, lack*; often with numbers: "They were not less than a million" (μυριάδων ἑκατόν; lit., "one hundred of ten thousand").

Λιβύην[131] καταβαθμοῦ[132] μέχρι τῶν ὁρίων Αἰθιοπίας,[133] καὶ ὡς ἡ πεῖρα[134] κατὰ πάντων ἐστὶ καὶ ὡς οὐ λυσιτελὲς[135] ἔθη πάτρια κινεῖν,[136] ἀμελήσας[137] ἀπάντων ἐπιτρέπει[138] ποιήσασθαι τὴν ἀνάθεσιν,[139] μυρία καὶ πάντα προνοητικὰ[140] δυνάμενος ἢ ὡς ἄρχων κελεύειν[141] ἢ συμβουλεύειν[142] ὡς φίλος.

NOTES

36. ὄνομα Καραβᾶς. The origin of the name is uncertain. Cohn conjectures Barab(b)as, the name of the insurrectionist whom Pilate released in place of Jesus (cf. Matt. 27:16; Mark 15:6; Luke 23:18; John 18:40; see Horst 2003, 128). Box (1939) derives the name from an unattested Aramaic word for "cabbage." Other suggestions are based on the word κάραβος, which can refer to a "small ship," a kind of "beetle" or "crayfish," or perhaps a person's way of walking. See Horst (2003, 128).

37–39. This section is reminiscent of the mocking of Jesus (cf. Matt. 27:27–31; Mark 15:16–20). See Winter (1974, 147–49).

Μάριν. The title is (close to) a transliteration of the Aramaic "our lord" (cf. 1 Cor. 16:22). Since Greek has no word for Aramaic, ancient writers used "Hebrew" or "Syriac" to designate Aramaic speakers of Syria-Palestine. The Greek-speaking mob may have taken up the Aramaic word "to emphasize the allegation that the Jews' first loyalty was to the Aramaic-speaking ruler of Palestine" (Horst 2003, 131, citing Feldman 1993, 115).

40. βασιλέα καὶ φίλον Καίσαρος. Philo underscores that Agrippa, the target of the crowd's mockery, was both a king and a "friend of Caesar." Cf. John 19:12, where the crowd threatens Pilate: "If you release this man, you are not a friend of Caesar [φίλος τοῦ Καίσαρος]." (For Philo's take on Pilate, cf. *Legat.* 299–305.) If Philo is using the term in its technical sense, he means that Agrippa is an *amicus Caesaris*, a member of a group to which Flaccus belonged (cf. *Flacc.* 2).

41. εἰκόνας ἐν ταῖς προσευχαῖς ἀνατιθέναι. Philo uses the term προσευχή, which was "the main term for the Jewish place of assembly in the Diaspora" (Leonhardt 2001, 76), nineteen times. To erect statues of the emperor would have been an extreme violation (παρανόμημα) of the prohibition against graven images (cf. Exod. 20:4; Deut. 4:16–18; Josephus, *C. Ap.* 2.73; Tacitus, *Hist.* 5.5.4).

43. μυριάδων ἑκατόν. The number is wildly inflated. Alexandria probably had a population of around five hundred thousand. If Jews composed one-fourth of the population, which is plausible since they held two of the five quarters of the city, they would have numbered approximately one hundred thousand (Horst 2003, 136).

---

131. Λιβύη, -ης, ἡ, *Libya*.
132. καταβαθμός, -οῦ, ὁ, *slope* (which separates Egypt from Nubia).
133. Αἰθιοπία, -ας, ἡ, *Ethiopia*.
134. πεῖρα, -ας, ἡ, *an attempt on/against* (someone).
135. λυσιτελής, -ές, (impers.) *it is profitable, advantageous*; with (acc. and) inf.
136. Pres. act. inf., κινέω, *move, alter*.
137. Aor. act. ptc. nom. masc. sg., ἀμελέω, *show no concern for*; with gen.; circ.
138. Pres. act. indic. 3 sg., ἐπιτρέπω, *permit*; with acc. and inf.
139. ἀνάθεσις, -εως, ἡ, *installation*.
140. προνοητικός, -ή, -όν, *cautious, wary*.
141. Pres. act. inf., κελεύω, *order*.
142. Pres. act. inf., συμβουλεύω, *council*.

4.3.2

In Praise of Caesar Augustus

On the Embassy to Gaius 143–150

143Τί δέ;[1] ὁ τὴν ἀνθρωπίνην[2] φύσιν[3] ὑπερβαλὼν[4] ἐν ἁπάσαις ταῖς ἀρεταῖς,[5] ὁ διὰ μέγεθος[6] ἡγεμονίας[7] αὐτοκρατοῦς[8] ὁμοῦ[9] καὶ καλοκαγαθίας[10] πρῶτος ὀνομασθεὶς[11] Σεβαστός,[12] οὐ διαδοχῇ[13] γένους ὥσπερ τι κλήρου μέρος τὴν ἐπωνυμίαν[14] λαβών, ἀλλ' αὐτὸς γενόμενος ἀρχὴ σεβασμοῦ[15] καὶ τοῖς ἔπειτα;[16] ὁ τοῖς μὲν[17] πράγμασι[18] τεταραγμένοις[19] καὶ συγκεχυμένοις[20] ἐπιστάς,[21] ὅτε εὐθὺς παρῆλθεν ἐπὶ τὴν τῶν κοινῶν ἐπιμέλειαν;[22] **144**νῆσοι[23] γὰρ πρὸς ἠπείρους[24] καὶ ἤπειροι πρὸς νήσους περὶ πρωτείων[25] ἀντεφιλονείκουν[26] ἡγεμόνας[27] ἔχουσαι καὶ προαγωνιστὰς[28] Ῥωμαίων τοὺς ἐν τέλει δοκιμωτάτους[29]· καὶ αὖθις[30] τὰ μεγάλα

1. Elliptical τί δέ; functions as a transition: "And what [of this that follows]?" (Denniston 1966, 176).
2. ἀνθρώπινος, -η, -ον, *human*.
3. φύσις, -εως, ἡ, *nature*.
4. Aor. act. ptc. nom. masc. sg., ὑπερβάλλω, *surpass, transcend*; attrib. (subst.). Throughout, Philo uses left dislocation for the purposes of thematic highlighting: "He who . . . he who . . . this is he who . . ."
5. ἀρετή, -ῆς, ἡ, *virtue*.
6. μέγεθος, -ους, τό, *greatness, magnitude*.
7. ἡγεμονία, -ας, ἡ, (Lat.) *imperium*.
8. αὐτοκρατής, -ές, *ruling by oneself, absolute*.
9. Adv. with καί, *as well as*.
10. καλοκαγαθία, -ας, ἡ, *nobility of character, nobleness*.
11. Aor. pass. ptc. nom. masc. sg., ὀνομάζω, (pass.) *be called/named*; attrib. (subst.).
12. σεβαστός, -ή, -όν, *venerable, august*.
13. διαδοχή, -ῆς, ἡ, *succession*; οὐ διαδοχῇ γένους, "not by succession in lineage."
14. ἐπωνυμία, -ας, ἡ, *surname, cognomen*.
15. σεβασμός, -οῦ, ὁ, *reverance, veneration*.
16. The article substantivizes the adverb: "to future generations."

17. μέν *solitarium* (cf. S §2896; *CGCG* §59.24) anticipates ὅτε εὐθύς: "who *indeed* took charge of affairs troubled and chaotic *right when* he entered public office."
18. πρᾶγμα, -ατος, τό, *matter, affair*.
19. Pf. pass. ptc. dat. neut. pl., ταράσσω, (pass.) *be troubled*; attrib.
20. Pf. pass. ptc. dat. neut. pl., συγχέω, (pass.) *be confused*; attrib.
21. Aor. act. ptc. nom. masc. sg., ἐφίστημι, *take charge, be set over*; with dat.; attrib. (subst.).
22. ἐπιμέλεια, -ας, ἡ, *office*.
23. νῆσος, -ου, ἡ, *island*.
24. ἤπειρος, -ου, ἡ, *mainland*.
25. πρωτεῖον, -ου, τό, *first position, preeminence*.
26. Impf. act. indic. 3 pl., ἀντιφιλονεικέω, *contend* (out of envy or rivalry).
27. ἡγεμών, -ονος, ὁ, *ruler*; pred. comp.
28. προαγωνιστής, -οῦ, ὁ, *one who fights for another, champion*; pred. comp.
29. Superl., δόκιμος, -ον (with ἐν τέλει), *most esteemed* (in office; cf. LSJ, 1773.3).
30. Adv., *again*.

τμήματα³¹ τῆς οἰκουμένης,³² Ἀσία πρὸς Εὐρώπην καὶ Εὐρώπη πρὸς Ἀσίαν, ἡμιλλῶντο³³ περὶ κράτους³⁴ ἀρχῆς, τῶν Εὐρωπαίων καὶ Ἀσιανῶν ἐθνῶν ἀπὸ ἐσχάτων γῆς ἀναστάντων καὶ βαρεῖς³⁵ πολέμους³⁶ ἀντεπιφερόντων³⁷ διὰ πάσης γῆς καὶ θαλάττης πεζομαχίαις³⁸ [καὶ ναυμαχίαις³⁹], ὡς μικροῦ⁴⁰ σύμπαν τὸ ἀνθρώπων γένος ἀναλωθὲν⁴¹ ταῖς ἀλληλοκτονίαις⁴² εἰς τὸ παντελὲς ἀφανισθῆναι,⁴³ εἰ μὴ⁴⁴ δι' ἕνα ἄνδρα καὶ ἡγεμόνα, τὸν Σεβαστὸν [οἶκον], ὃν ἄξιον⁴⁵ καλεῖν ἀλεξίκακον.⁴⁶ ¹⁴⁵οὗτός⁴⁷ ἐστιν ὁ Καῖσαρ, ὁ τοὺς καταρράξαντας⁴⁸ πανταχόθι⁴⁹ χειμῶνας⁵⁰ εὐδιάσας,⁵¹ ὁ τὰς κοινὰς νόσους⁵² Ἑλλήνων καὶ βαρβάρων ἰασάμενος,⁵³ αἳ κατέβησαν μὲν⁵⁴ ἀπὸ τῶν μεσημβρινῶν⁵⁵ καὶ ἑῴων,⁵⁶ ἔδραμον δὲ καὶ μέχρι⁵⁷ δύσεως⁵⁸ καὶ πρὸς ἄρκτον,⁵⁹ τὰ μεθόρια⁶⁰ χωρία⁶¹ καὶ πελάγη⁶² κατασπείρασαι⁶³ τῶν ἀβουλήτων·⁶⁴ ¹⁴⁶οὗτός ἐστιν ὁ τὰ δεσμά,⁶⁵ οἷς κατέζευκτο⁶⁶ καὶ ἐπεπίεστο⁶⁷ ἡ οἰκουμένη, παραλύσας,⁶⁸ οὐ μόνον ἀνείς·⁶⁹ οὗτος ὁ καὶ τοὺς φανεροὺς καὶ ἀφανεῖς πολέμους διὰ τὰς ἐκ λῃστῶν⁷⁰ ἐπιθέσεις⁷¹ ἀνελών·⁷² οὗτος ὁ τὴν θάλατταν πειρατικῶν⁷³ μὲν σκαφῶν⁷⁴ κενὴν⁷⁵ ἐργασάμενος φορτίδων⁷⁶ δὲ πληρώσας. ¹⁴⁷οὗτος ὁ τὰς πόλεις ἁπάσας εἰς ἐλευθερίαν ἐξελόμενος,⁷⁷ ὁ τὴν ἀταξίαν εἰς τάξιν⁷⁸ ἀγαγών, ὁ τὰ ἄμικτα⁷⁹ ἔθνη καὶ θηριώδη⁸⁰ πάντα ἡμερώσας⁸¹ καὶ ἁρμοσάμενος,⁸² ὁ τὴν μὲν Ἑλλάδα⁸³

31. τμῆμα, -ατος, τό, *section*.
32. οἰκουμένη, -ης, ἡ, *inhabited world*.
33. Impf. mid. indic. 3 pl., ἁμιλλάομαι, *contend*.
34. κράτος, -ους, τό, *power*.
35. βαρύς, -εῖα, -ύ, *heavy to bear, grievous*.
36. πόλεμος, -ου, ὁ, *war*.
37. Pf. act. ptc. gen. neut. pl., ἀντιφέρω, *set against*; gen. absol.
38. πεζομαχία, -ας, ἡ, *battle on foot*.
39. ναυμαχία, -ας, ἡ, *battle on the sea*.
40. Adv., *almost*; μικροῦ . . . εἰς τὸ παντελές, "almost entirely."
41. Aor. pass. ptc. nom. neut. sg., ἀναλίσκω, (pass.) *perish*; circ.
42. ἀλληλοκτονία, -ας, ἡ, *mutual slaughter*.
43. Aor. pass. inf., ἀφανίζω, (pass.) *be done away with, removed*; result clause: ὡς with inf. (cf. S §2260; *CGCG* §46.7).
44. εἰ μή marks an exception: "*were it not* for that one man and leader."
45. Quasi-impers., "it is right/fitting"; with (acc. and) inf.
46. ἀλεξίκακος, -ου, ὁ, *averter of evil*; pred. comp.
47. The first of a series of clauses that begin with οὗτος: "*This is the Caesar who. . . .*"; anaphora (cf. S §3010).
48. Aor. act. ptc. acc. masc. pl., καταράσσω, (as adj.) *violent, raging*.
49. Adv., *in every place*.
50. χειμών, -ῶνος, ὁ, *storm*.
51. Aor. act. ptc. nom. masc. sg., εὐδιάζω, *calm, still*; attrib. (subst.; apposition).
52. νόσος, -ου, ἡ, *sickness, disease, plague*.
53. Aor. mid. ptc. nom. masc. sg., ἰάομαι, *heal*; attrib. (subst.; apposition).
54. μέν . . . δέ; point/counterpoint (cf. Runge 2010, 75–83; BDF §447; S §2904; *CGCG* §59.24).
55. μεσημβρινός, -ή, -όν, *southern*.
56. ἑῷος, -α, -ον, *eastern*.
57. Prep. with gen., *up to*.
58. δύσις, -εως, ἡ, *west*.
59. ἄρκτος, -ου, ἡ, *north*.
60. μεθόριος, -α, -ον, *between*.
61. χωρίον, -ου, τό, *land*; acc. of extent (space).
62. πέλαγος, -εος, τό, *open sea*; acc. of extent (space).
63. Aor. act. ptc. nom. fem. pl., κατασπείρω, *sow*; circ.
64. ἀβούλητος, -ον, *of what is not desired or willed*.
65. δεσμός, -οῦ, ὁ, (pl.) *bonds*.
66. Plpf. pass. indic. 3 sg., καταζεύγνυμι, (pass.) *be confined*.
67. Plpf. pass. indic. 3 sg., πιέζω, (pass.) *be pressed/weighed down*.
68. Aor. act. ptc. nom. masc. sg., παραλύω, *make an end to*; attrib. (subst.).
69. Aor. act. ptc. nom. masc. sg., ἀνίημι, *release*; circ. The tail underscores the nature of Augustus's beneficence: "This is the man who put an end to the chains by which the inhabited world was confined and pressed down—*he did not merely release [them]*."
70. λῃστής, -οῦ, ὁ, *robber, brigand*.
71. ἐπίθεσις, -εως, ἡ, *attack, raid*.
72. Aor. act. ptc. nom. masc. sg., ἀναιρέω, *destroy*; attrib. (subst.).
73. πειρατικός, -ή, -όν, *for piracy*.
74. σκάφος, -εος, τό, *ship*.
75. κενός, -ή, -όν, *empty*; with gen.; pred. comp.
76. φορτίς, -ίδος, ἡ, *merchant* (ships).
77. Aor. mid. ptc. nom. masc. sg., ἐξαιρέω, (mid.) *set free, deliver*; attrib. (subst.). The collocation ἐξελέσθαι εἰς ἐλευθερίαν is a legal term for manumission (Colson 1962).
78. τάξις, -εως, ἡ, *order*.
79. ἄμικτος, -ον, *not mixing with others, unsociable*.
80. θηριώδης, -ες, *of beasts, savage*.
81. Aor. act. ptc. nom. masc. sg., ἡμερόω, *civilize*; attrib. (subst.).
82. Aor. mid. ptc. nom. masc. sg., ἁρμόζω, *join/fit together, make harmonious*; attrib. (subst.).
83. Ἑλλάς, -άδος, ἡ, *Hellas, Greece*.

Ἑλλάσι πολλαῖς παραυξήσας,⁸⁴ τὴν δὲ βάρβαρον⁸⁵ ἐν τοῖς ἀναγκαιοτάτοις τμήμασιν⁸⁶ ἀφελληνίσας,⁸⁷ ὁ εἰρηνοφύλαξ,⁸⁸ ὁ διανομεὺς⁸⁹ τῶν ἐπιβαλλόντων⁹⁰ ἑκάστοις, ὁ τὰς χάριτας ἀταμιεύτους⁹¹ εἰς μέσον προθείς,⁹² ὁ μηδὲν ἀποκρυψάμενος⁹³ ἀγαθὸν ἢ καλὸν ἐν ἅπαντι τῷ ἑαυτοῦ βίῳ.⁹⁴ **148**τοῦτον οὖν τὸν τοσοῦτον εὐεργέτην⁹⁵ ἐν τρισὶ καὶ τεσσαράκοντα ἐνιαυτοῖς,⁹⁶ οὓς⁹⁷ ἐπεκράτησεν⁹⁸ Αἰγύπτου, παρεκαλύψαντο,⁹⁹ μηδὲν ἐν προσευχαῖς ὑπὲρ αὐτοῦ, μὴ ἄγαλμα,¹⁰⁰ μὴ ξόανον,¹⁰¹ μὴ γραφὴν¹⁰² ἱδρυσάμενοι.¹⁰³ **149**καὶ μὴν¹⁰⁴ εἴ τινι καινὰς καὶ ἐξαιρέτους¹⁰⁵ ἔδει ψηφίζεσθαι¹⁰⁶ τιμάς, ἐκείνῳ προσῆκον¹⁰⁷ ἦν, οὐ μόνον¹⁰⁸ ὅτι τοῦ Σεβαστοῦ γένους ἀρχή τις ἐγένετο καὶ πηγή,¹⁰⁹ οὐδὲ ὅτι πρῶτος καὶ μέγιστος καὶ κοινὸς εὐεργέτης ἀντὶ¹¹⁰ πολυαρχίας¹¹¹ ἑνὶ κυβερνήτῃ¹¹² παραδοὺς τὸ κοινὸν σκάφος¹¹³ οἰακονομεῖν¹¹⁴ ἑαυτῷ,¹¹⁵ θαυμασίῳ¹¹⁶ τὴν ἡγεμονικὴν¹¹⁷ ἐπιστήμην¹¹⁸—τὸ γὰρ "οὐκ ἀγαθὸν πολυκοιρανίη"¹¹⁹ λέλεκται δεόντως, ἐπειδὴ πολυτρόπων αἴτιαι¹²⁰ κακῶν αἱ πολυψηφίαι¹²¹—, ἀλλ' ὅτι καὶ πᾶσα ἡ οἰκουμένη τὰς ἰσολυμπίους¹²² αὐτῷ τιμὰς ἐψηφίσαντο. **150**καὶ μαρτυροῦσι ναοί,¹²³ προπύλαια,¹²⁴ προτεμενίσματα,¹²⁵ στοαί,¹²⁶ ὡς ὅσαι τῶν πόλεων, ἢ νέα ἢ παλαιά, ἔργα φέρουσι μεγαλοπρεπῆ,¹²⁷ τῷ κάλλει¹²⁸ καὶ μεγέθει τῶν Καισαρείων¹²⁹ παρευημερεῖσθαι,¹³⁰ καὶ μάλιστα¹³¹ κατὰ τὴν ἡμετέραν Ἀλεξάνδρειαν.

84. Aor. act. ptc. nom. masc. sg., παραυξάνω, *enlarge*; attrib. (subst.).
85. βάρβαρος, -ον, (subst.) *barbarian world*.
86. τμῆμα, -ατος, τό, *section*; ἐν τοῖς ἀναγκαιοτάτοις τμήμασιν, "in its most important [lit., necessary] regions."
87. Aor. act. ptc. nom. masc. sg., ἀφελληνίζω, *hellenize*; attrib. (subst.).
88. εἰρηνοφύλαξ, -ακος, ὁ, *guardian of peace*.
89. διανομεύς, -έως, ὁ, *distributor*.
90. Pres. act. ptc. gen. neut. pl., ἐπιβάλλω, *belonging to, fall to the share of* (LSJ, 624.6); attrib. (subst.).
91. ἀταμίευτος, -ον, *that cannot be stored*.
92. Aor. act. ptc. nom. masc. sg., προτίθημι; with εἰς μέσον προτίθημι, *set as common possession to all* (LSJ, 1107.2.b); attrib. (subst.).
93. Aor. mid. ptc. nom. masc. sg., ἀποκρύπτω, *hide*; attrib. (subst.).
94. βίος, -ου, ὁ, *life*.
95. εὐεργέτης, -ου, ὁ, *benefactor*. The topic remains in clause-initial position (thus retaining the anaphoric structure of the passage) but now functions as the direct object.
96. ἐνιαυτός, -οῦ, ὁ, *year*; ἐν τρισὶ καὶ τεσσαράκοντα ἐνιαυτοῖς, "for [a period of] forty-three years" (cf. S §1542.c).
97. Acc. of extent (time).
98. Aor. act. indic. 3 sg., ἐπικρατέω, *exercise mastery over*; with gen.
99. Aor. mid. indic. 3 pl., παρακαλύπτω, (mid.) *ignore*.
100. ἄγαλμα, -ατος, τό, *statue*.
101. ξόανον, -ου, τό, *image carved of wood*.
102. γραφή, -ῆς, ἡ, *painting*.
103. Aor. mid. ptc. nom. masc. pl., ἱδρύω, *dedicate* (temples, statues, etc.); circ.
104. Partic. combination, *and yet, but, and in fact*: "The speaker adds information (καί) and indicates that he/she vouches for the correctness or relevance of the addition (μήν)" (CGCG §59.71).
105. ἐξαιρετός, -ή, -όν, *special, remarkable*.
106. Pres. mid. inf., ψηφίζω, (mid.) *vote*.

107. Pres. act. ptc. nom. neut. sg., προσήκω, (quasi-impers.) *it is fitting*; with (acc. and) inf.
108. οὐ μόνον . . . οὐδέ . . . ἀλλά, *not only . . . nor . . . but*.
109. πηγή, -ῆς, ἡ, *font*.
110. Prep. with gen., *in place of, instead of*.
111. πολυαρχία, -ας, ἡ, *rule by many*.
112. κυβερνήτης, -ου, ὁ, *pilot*.
113. σκάφος, -εος, τό, *ship*.
114. Pres. act. inf., οἰακονομέω, *steer*; purpose (BDF §390; S §2008; CGCG §51.16).
115. Appositive to ἑνὶ κυβερνήτῃ.
116. θαυμάσιος, -α, -ον, *wonderful, marvelous*; appositive.
117. ἡγεμονικός, -ή, -όν, *what pertains to ruling*.
118. ἐπιστήμη, -ης, ἡ, *knowledge, science*; acc. of respect.
119. Epic and Ion. form of πολυκοιρανία, -ας, ἡ, *rule of many*; citation of Homer, *Il.* 2.204.
120. αἰτία, -ας, ἡ, *cause*; pred. nom.
121. πολυψηφία, -ας, ἡ, perhaps *plurality of votes*, or *extension of the vote to many* (MGS, 1721). The only other extant use of the term is Thucydides, *Hist. pel.* 3.10.5, where it means "contrast in voting" or "dissension."
122. ἰσολύμπιος, -ον, *like those given to the Olympians*.
123. ναός, -οῦ, ὁ, *sanctuary, shrine*.
124. προπύλαιος, -α, -ον, (subst.) *gateway*.
125. προτεμένισμα, -ατος, τό, *vestibule, outer court*.
126. στοά, -ᾶς, ἡ, *stoa, portico*.
127. μεγαλοπρεπής, -ές, *magnificent*.
128. κάλλος, -εος, τό, *beauty*.
129. Καισάρειος, -α, -ον, *belonging to Caesar*.
130. Pres. pass. inf., παρευημερέω, (pass.) *be surpassed*; indir. disc. (cf. BDF §397; S §2016; CGCG §51.19).
131. Superl. adv. of μάλα, *especially*.

NOTES

143. ὁ τὴν ἀνθρωπίνην φύσιν ὑπερβαλών. On the divinity of the emperor and the potential implications of emperor worship for early Christology, see especially Peppard (2011).

πρῶτος ὀνομασθεὶς Σεβαστός... αὐτὸς γενόμενος ἀρχὴ σεβασμοῦ. Σεβαστός is the equivalent of *Augustus* in Latin. Cf. Dio Cassius, *Hist. rom.* 53.16.4, and my notes thereon (§6.4.1).

144. Philo's portrait of Augustus as savior of the world fits hand in glove with Augustan propaganda. See especially Zanker (1988); Galinsky (1996).

PART 5

Reading Josephus

Josephus (37 CE–ca. 100 CE) was a priest of Hasmonean descent. In his *The Life*, he claims to have spent three years, from age sixteen to nineteen, immersed in philosophical training. First he tested the three major schools of Judaism (Pharisees, Sadducees, and Essenes), and then, when these did not prove rigorous enough, he attached himself to an ascetic teacher named Bannus (*Vita* 7–12). These years, the much-maligned historian assures us, prepared him for public life as a member of the political aristocracy. At the outset of the war against the Romans (66 CE), he was commissioned to lead the Jewish forces in Galilee. The details of his six months of service are hazy (Mason 2003, 41–44), but eventually he was forced to surrender to the Romans—not, he insists, because he was afraid to die but because the Jewish God had selected him to proclaim Roman fortunes to the rest of the world (*B.J.* 3.137–138). After the war, Josephus resided in Vespasian's former residence in Rome, where he penned *Jewish War*, *Jewish Antiquities*, *The Life*, and *Against Apion*.

Josephus is our most important source for the history of first-century Judea. Yet the prospect of reading through his writings (even in translation) is daunting. "The result," as Mason notes, "is that Josephus's works often suffer the same fate as the King James Version of the Bible—a perennial best-seller, much loved, occasionally quoted, but hardly ever read" (2003, 3). Fortunately, we now have excellent resources for those who wish to orient themselves to the man and his work.[1] My aim is to complement these by preparing you to read Josephus in Greek.

The eleven reading passages are arranged in order of composition: five from *Jewish War*, four from *Jewish Antiquities*, one from *The Life*, and one from *Against Apion*.

---

1. Mason 2003 is an ideal primer. For detailed analysis, readers should consult the commentaries in The Brill Josephus Project, edited by Mason and produced by an international team of experts.

5.1

Jewish War

Josephus wrote the bulk of *Jewish War* between 75 and 79 CE and the final volume during the reign of Domitian (81–96 CE; Cohen 2002, 84–90). Mason identifies "a range of coherent major interests" that motivated the historian, all of which "confront the triumphalist view . . . which dominated Josephus's environment, the city of Rome in the 70s" (2003, 68–69). First, Josephus wanted to preserve the dignity and innocence of the Jewish ruling class, of which he was a proud member. Second, he aimed to show that the Jews were not a bellicose people but the unfortunate victims of a few bad apples. Tellingly, he opens his narrative proper with the term στάσις ("sedition," 1.31), which is a theme he deftly weaves into the prologue (1.10, 24, 25, 27) and is one with which his Roman audience would be sympathetic since they, too, had just endured a period of extreme civil unrest (cf. 4.545–548; Mason 2003, 81). Third, he contends that the Romans are, in fact, pawns of the Jewish God (cf. Isa. 45:1–7). And fourth, he writes to counter pro-Roman accounts of the war by highlighting the virtue and fortitude of the Jewish people.

This section includes two passages from the prologue (1.1–30), two passages from the lengthy excursus on the philosophical schools of Judaism (2.119–166), and an account of Jesus son of Ananias, who predicted the destruction of the temple four years before the outbreak of the war (6.300–309).

Text: Thackeray 1927 (§§5.1.1–4); Thackeray 1928 (§5.1.5)

Recommended Translation: Williamson 1981

Supplemental Scripture: Mark 7:1–13; 12:18–27; Acts 23:6–10 (§§5.1.–4); Mark 13 parr. (§5.1.5)

5.1.1

Prologue, Part 1

Jewish War 1.1–6

1.1Ἐπειδὴ[1] τὸν Ἰουδαίων πρὸς Ῥωμαίους πόλεμον[2] συστάντα[3] μέγιστον[4] οὐ μόνον[5] τῶν[6] καθ' ἡμᾶς, σχεδὸν δὲ καὶ ὧν ἀκοῇ[7] παρειλήφαμεν[8] ἢ πόλεων πρὸς πόλεις ἢ ἐθνῶν ἔθνεσι συρραγέντων,[9] οἱ μὲν[10] οὐ παρατυχόντες[11] τοῖς πράγμασιν[12] ἀλλ' ἀκοῇ συλλέγοντες[13] εἰκαῖα[14] καὶ ἀσύμφωνα[15] διηγήματα[16] σοφιστικῶς[17] ἀναγράφουσιν,[18] **2**οἱ παραγενόμενοι[19] δὲ ἢ κολακείᾳ[20] τῇ πρὸς Ῥωμαίους ἢ μίσει[21] τῷ πρὸς Ἰουδαίους καταψεύδονται[22] τῶν πραγμάτων, περιέχει[23] δὲ αὐτοῖς ὅπου μὲν[24] κατηγορίαν[25] ὅπου δὲ ἐγκώμιον[26] τὰ συγγράμματα,[27] τὸ δ' ἀκριβὲς[28] τῆς ἱστορίας[29] οὐδαμοῦ,[30] **3**προυθέμην[31] ἐγὼ τοῖς κατὰ τὴν Ῥωμαίων

1. Introduces a subordinate clause that encompasses 1.1–2.
2. πόλεμος, -ου, ὁ, *war*. The discourse theme is set in left periphery (cf. *CGCG* §60.33). Grammatically πόλεμον is the direct object of the main verb, ἀναγράφουσιν.
3. Aor. act. ptc. acc. masc. sg., συνίστημι, (intrans.) *take shape, exist*; circ.
4. Superl., μέγας, μεγάλη, μέγα, *greatest*.
5. οὐ μόνον . . . σχεδὸν δὲ καί, *not only . . . but also nearly*.
6. Gen. of comparison, "greatest . . . of the [wars] in our time."
7. ἀκοή, -ῆς, ἡ, *report*; dat. of means.
8. Pf. act. indic. 1 pl., παραλαμβάνω, *receive*.
9. Aor. act. ptc. gen. masc. pl., συρρήγνυμι, *break out*; circ.
10. οἱ μέν . . . οἱ δέ, *some . . . others* (cf. BDF §250; S §1107; *CGCG* §28.27). Note, however, that the clauses are not parallel: "some [οἱ μέν] . . . the ones who were there [οἱ παραγενόμενοι]."
11. Aor. act. ptc. nom. masc. pl., παρατυγχάνω, *be present*; with dat.; circ.
12. πρᾶγμα, -ατος, τό, *deed, matter*.
13. Pres. act. ptc. nom. masc. pl., συλλέγω, *gather*; circ.
14. εἰκαῖος, -α, -ον, *taken at random, common, ordinary*.
15. ἀσύμφωνος, -ον, *discordant, contradictory*.
16. διήγημα, -ατος, τό, *narrative account*.

17. Adv., *in a sophistic manner*.
18. Pres. act. indic. 3 pl., ἀναγράφω, *record*.
19. Aor. mid. ptc. nom. masc. pl., παραγίγνομαι, *be present*; attrib. (subst.).
20. κολακεία, -ας, ἡ, *flattery*; dat. of cause.
21. μῖσος, -ους, τό, *hatred*; dat. of cause.
22. Pres. mid. indic. 3 pl., καταψεύδομαι, *give a false account*; with gen.
23. Pres. act. indic. 3 sg., περιέχω, *enfold/surround* (dat. with acc.).
24. ὅπου μέν . . . ὅπου δέ, *in some places . . . in other places* (cf. S §2904).
25. κατηγορία, -ας, ἡ, *accusation, invective*.
26. ἐγκώμιον, -ου, τό, *encomium*.
27. σύγγραμμα, -ατος, τό, *work, composition, book*; subject of the clause: "*Their writings* enfold these [αὐτοῖς = the events of the war], in some places with invective, in others with encomium."
28. ἀκριβής, -ές, *precise, exact, accurate*.
29. ἱστορία, -ας, ἡ, *history*.
30. Adv., *in no way, not at all*.
31. Aor. mid. indic. 1 sg., προτίθημι, (mid.) *propose*; with inf.

ἡγεμονίαν,³² Ἑλλάδι γλώσσῃ μεταβαλὼν³³ ἃ³⁴ τοῖς ἄνω βαρβάροις³⁵ τῇ πατρίῳ³⁶ συντάξας³⁷ ἀνέπεμψα³⁸ πρότερον³⁹ ἀφηγήσασθαι,⁴⁰ Ἰώσηπος Ματθίου παῖς,⁴¹ [γένει Ἑβραῖος,]⁴² ἐξ Ἱεροσολύμων ἱερεύς,⁴³ αὐτός τε Ῥωμαίους πολεμήσας⁴⁴ τὰ πρῶτα⁴⁵ καὶ τοῖς ὕστερον⁴⁶ παρατυχὼν ἐξ ἀνάγκης.⁴⁷

⁴γενομένου γάρ, ὡς ἔφην, μεγίστου τοῦδε τοῦ κινήματος,⁴⁸ ἐν Ῥωμαίοις μὲν⁴⁹ ἐνόσει⁵⁰ τὰ οἰκεῖα,⁵¹ Ἰουδαίων δὲ τὸ νεωτερίζον⁵² τότε τεταραγμένοις⁵³ ἐπανέστη⁵⁴ τοῖς καιροῖς ἀκμάζον⁵⁵ κατά τε χεῖρα⁵⁶ καὶ χρήμασιν,⁵⁷ ὡς δι' ὑπερβολὴν θορύβων⁵⁸ τοῖς μὲν⁵⁹ ἐν ἐλπίδι κτήσεως⁶⁰ τοῖς δ' ἐν ἀφαιρέσεως⁶¹ δέει⁶² γίνεσθαι⁶³ τὰ πρὸς τὴν ἀνατολήν,⁶⁴ ⁵ἐπειδὴ Ἰουδαῖοι μὲν⁶⁵ ἅπαν τὸ ὑπὲρ Εὐφράτην⁶⁶ ὁμόφυλον⁶⁷ συνεπαρθήσεσθαι⁶⁸ σφίσιν⁶⁹ ἤλπισαν, Ῥωμαίους δὲ οἵ τε γείτονες⁷⁰ Γαλάται⁷¹ παρεκίνουν⁷² καὶ τὸ Κελτικὸν⁷³ οὐκ ἠρέμει,⁷⁴ μεστὰ⁷⁵ δ' ἦν πάντα θορύβων μετὰ Νέρωνα,⁷⁶ καὶ πολλοὺς μὲν⁷⁷ βασιλειᾶν⁷⁸ ὁ καιρὸς ἀνέπειθεν,⁷⁹ τὰ στρατιωτικὰ⁸⁰ δὲ ᾖρα μεταβολῆς⁸¹ ἐλπίδι λημμάτων.⁸²

32. ἡγεμονία, -ας, ἡ, (Lat.) *imperium*.
33. Aor. act. ptc. nom. masc. sg., μεταβάλλω, *change*; circ. Here it has the sense of "translate."
34. Antecedent of the relative pronoun is omitted (cf. S §2509; CGCG §50.7).
35. The article substantivizes the prepositional phrase. The identity of "the upper-country barbarians" is expounded in 1.6.
36. πάτριος, -ον, *ancestral*; τῇ πατρίῳ = τῇ πατρίῳ γλώσσῃ.
37. Aor. act. ptc. nom. masc. sg., συντάσσω, *arrange, set down*; circ.
38. Aor. act. indic. 1 sg., ἀναπέμπω, *send*.
39. πρότερος, -α, -ον, (as adv.) *formerly*; modifies ἀνέπεμψα.
40. Aor. mid. inf., ἀφηγέομαι, *relate, expound*; comp. of προυθέμην.
41. παῖς, παιδός, ὁ, *child, son*. The tale characterizes the persona of ἐγώ (cf. CGCG §60.35; Runge 2010, 317–35).
42. MS P and Eusebius omit γένει Ἑβραῖος, "a Hebrew in race."
43. ἱερεύς, -έως, ὁ, *priest*.
44. Aor. act. ptc. nom. masc. sg., πολεμέω, *fight*; circ.
45. Adv. acc. (extent): "in the former parts."
46. Dat. comp. of παρατυχών, "in the latter parts."
47. ἀνάγκη, -ης, ἡ, *force, compulsion* (i.e., as a prisoner).
48. κίνημα, -ατος, τό, *movement, upheaval*. The genitive absolute clause resumes the discourse topic (τὸν Ἰουδαίων πρὸς Ῥωμαίους πόλεμον) by providing support (γάρ) for the initial claim (συστάντα μέγιστον).
49. μέν . . . δέ; point/counterpoint (cf. Runge 2010, 75–83; BDF §447; S §2904; CGCG §59.24).
50. Impf. act. indic. 3 sg., νοσέω, (of the political situation) *be troubled, in crisis, suffer* (MGS, 1407.1).
51. οἰκεῖος, -α, -ον, *pertaining to the family, homeland*.
52. Pres. act. ptc. nom. neut. sg., νεωτερίζω, (subst.) *revolutionary party*.
53. Pf. pass. ptc. dat. neut. pl., ταράσσω, (pass.) *be in a state of chaos*; circ.
54. Aor. act. indic. 3 sg., ἐπανίστημι, (intrans.) *rise up*.
55. Pres. act. ptc. nom. neut. sg., ἀκμάζω, *be at the peak*; circ.
56. χείρ, -ρος, ἡ, *hand*, (by extens.) *number* (of soldiers) (MGS, 2351.5A).

57. χρῆμασις, -εως, ἡ, *fortune*.
58. θόρυβος, -ου, ὁ, *tumult, disturbance*; δι' ὑπερβολὴν θορύβων, "on account of the excess of disturbances."
59. τοῖς μέν . . . τοῖς δέ, *for some . . . for others*. See n. 10.
60. κτῆσις, -εως, ἡ, *acquisition*; obj. gen.: "hope *of gain*."
61. ἀφαίρεσις, -εως, ἡ, *reduction, diminution*; obj. gen., "fear *of loss*."
62. δέος, -ους, τό, *fear*.
63. Result clause, ὡς with inf. (cf. S §2260; CGCG §46.7).
64. ἀνατολή, -ῆς, ἡ, *east*. The substantivized prepositional phrase τὰ πρὸς τὴν ἀνατολήν ("the regions to the east") is the accusative subject of the infinitive clause.
65. μέν . . . δέ . . . δ'; point/counterpoints (cf. S §2097).
66. Εὐφράτης, -ου, ὁ, *Euphrates*.
67. ὁμόφυλος, -ον, *of the same race/descent*.
68. Fut. pass. inf., συνεπαίρω, (intrans.) *rise together with*; with dat.; indir. disc. (cf. BDF §397; S §2016; CGCG §51.19).
69. σφίσιν = αὐτοῖς, 3 pl. pronoun σφεῖς (cf. S §325).
70. γείτων, -ονος, ὁ, *neighbor*.
71. Γαλάτης, -ου, ὁ, (pl.) *Gauls*.
72. Impf. act. indic. 3 pl., παρακινέω, *agitate, disturb*.
73. Κελτικός, -όν, *Celtic*, (subst.) *the Celts*.
74. Pres. act. indic. 3 sg., ἠρεμέω, *be still, at peace*.
75. μεστός, -ή, -όν, *full*; with gen.
76. Νέρων, -ονος, ὁ, *Nero*; μετὰ Νέρωνα (June of 68 CE).
77. μέν . . . δέ; point/counterpoint. See n. 49.
78. Pres. act. inf., βασιλειάω, *desire to rule*.
79. Impf. act. indic. 3 sg., ἀναπείθω, *persuade, convince*; with acc. and inf.
80. στρατιωτικός, -ή, -όν, *pertaining to the military*, (subst.) *troops*.
81. μεταβολή, -ῆς, ἡ, *change*; obj. gen.: "in the hope of *change* that would lead to their profit."
82. λῆμμα, -ατος, τό, *gain, profit*.

⁶ἄτοπον⁸³ ἡγησάμενος⁸⁴ περιιδεῖν⁸⁵ πλαζομένην⁸⁶ ἐπὶ τηλικούτοις⁸⁷ πράγμασι τὴν ἀλήθειαν, καὶ Πάρθους⁸⁸ μὲν⁸⁹ καὶ Βαβυλωνίους⁹⁰ Ἀράβων⁹¹ τε τοὺς πορρωτάτω καὶ τὸ ὑπὲρ Εὐφράτην ὁμόφυλον ἡμῖν Ἀδιαβηνούς⁹² τε γνῶναι διὰ τῆς ἐμῆς ἐπιμελείας⁹³ ἀκριβῶς,⁹⁴ ὅθεν τε ἤρξατο καὶ δι' ὅσων ἐχώρησεν⁹⁵ παθῶν ὁ πόλεμος καὶ ὅπως κατέστρεψεν,⁹⁶ ἀγνοεῖν⁹⁷ δὲ Ἕλληνας ταῦτα καὶ Ῥωμαίων τοὺς μὴ ἐπιστρατευσαμένους,⁹⁸ ἐντυγχάνοντας ἢ κολακείαις⁹⁹ ἢ πλάσμασι.¹⁰⁰

NOTES

1.1. τὸν Ἰουδαίων πρὸς Ῥωμαίους πόλεμον. Josephus is indebted to Thucydides, to whom he pays literary homage: γενομένου γάρ ... μεγίστου τοῦδε τοῦ κινήματος (1.4; cf. Thucydides, *Pel. War* 1.2: κίνησις γὰρ αὕτη μεγίστη); Ἰουδαίων δὲ τὸ νεωτερίζον ... ἀκμάζον (1.4; cf. Thucydides, *Pel. War* 1.1: ἀκμάζοντές τε ἦσαν ἐς αὐτὸν ἀμφότεροι). See further in Mader (2000, 55–103). Josephus appears also to have been significantly influenced by Polybius (Eckstein 1990).

1.2. τῆς ἱστορίας. The term ἱστορία (ἱστορίη) originally meant "inquiry," or the results thereof. Cf. Herodotus, *Hist.* 1.1 (see §6.1.1).

1.3. τοῖς ἄνω βαρβάροις. Cf. 1.6. The Jewish historian positions himself on the "right side" of the Greek-barbarian divide (cf. Herodotus, *Hist.* 1.1; Thucydides, *Pel. War* 1.2). He thus makes his claim to Greek identity through παιδεία (see Hall 2002, 223–26).

1.4. ἐν Ῥωμαίος ... ἐνόσει τὰ οἰκεῖα. Greek and Latin authors often use verbs of disease, such as νοσέω, to describe the deleterious effects of factionalism (cf. Thucydides, *Pel. War* 2.48–59; Plato, *Resp.* 5.470c; Plato, *Soph.* 228a; Sallust, *Bell. Cat.* 36.5; Sallust, *Hist.* 2.77; Tacitus, *Ann.* 1.43.4; Tacitus, *Hist.* 1.26.1; Mason 2009, 65n65, citing Keitel 1984, 320).

83. ἄτοπος, -ον, (quasi-impers.) *disgusting, monstrous, reprehensible*; with (acc. and) inf.
84. Aor. mid. ptc. nom. masc. sg., ἡγέομαι, *think, consider*; circ.
85. Aor. act. inf., περιοράω, *overlook, tolerate*.
86. Pres. pass. ptc. acc. fem. sg., πλάζω, (pass.) *go astray*; supp. (περιιδεῖν).
87. τηλίκος, -η, -ον, *so great*.
88. Πάρθος, -ου, ὁ, *Parthian*.
89. μέν ... τε ... δέ. The τε-clause adds an additional point about their knowledge (indir. questions: [1] how the war began; [2] through what great suffering it advanced; and [3] how it ended); the counterpoint comes with the δέ-clause.
90. Βαβυλωνίος, -ου, ὁ, *Babylonian*.
91. Ἄραβος, -ου, ὁ, *person from Arabia*; Ἀράβων τοὺς πορρωτάτω, "the most remote groups of the Arabians."
92. Ἀδιαβηνός, οῦ, ὁ, *inhabitant of Adiabene*.
93. ἐπιμελεία, -ας, ἡ, *care, diligent attention*.
94. Adv., *accurately*.
95. Aor. act. indic. 3 sg., χωρέω, *proceed, advance*.
96. Aor. act. indic. 3 sg., καταστρέφω, *end*.
97. Pres. act. inf., ἀγνοέω, *be ignorant*; comp. of ἄτοπον (εἶναι).
98. Aor. mid. ptc. acc. masc. pl., ἐπιστρατεύω, *engage in battle*; attrib. (subst.).
99. κολακεία, -ας, ἡ, *flattery*.
100. πλάσμα, -ματος, τό, *invention, contrivance*.

5.1.2

Prologue, Part 2

Jewish War 1.7–16

1.7Καίτοι γε¹ ἱστορίας² αὐτὰς ἐπιγράφειν³ τολμῶσιν,⁴ ἐν αἷς πρὸς τῷ μηδὲν ὑγιὲς⁵ δηλοῦν⁶ καὶ τοῦ σκοποῦ δοκοῦσιν⁷ ἔμοιγε⁸ διαμαρτάνειν.⁹ βούλονται μὲν¹⁰ γὰρ μεγάλους τοὺς Ῥωμαίους ἀποδεικνύειν,¹¹ καταβάλλουσιν¹² δὲ ἀεὶ¹³ τὰ Ἰουδαίων καὶ ταπεινοῦσιν.¹⁴

8οὐχ ὁρῶ δέ, πῶς ἂν εἶναι μεγάλοι δοκοῖεν¹⁵ οἱ μικροὺς νενικηκότες.¹⁶ καὶ οὔτε¹⁷ τὸ μῆκος¹⁸ αἰδοῦνται¹⁹ τοῦ πολέμου²⁰ οὔτε τὸ πλῆθος²¹ τῆς Ῥωμαίων καμούσης²² στρατιᾶς²³ οὔτε τὸ μέγεθος²⁴ τῶν στρατηγῶν,²⁵ οἳ πολλὰ περὶ τοῖς Ἱεροσολύμοις ἱδρώσαντες,²⁶ οἶμαι,²⁷ ταπεινουμένου τοῦ κατορθώματος²⁸ αὐτοῖς ἀδοξοῦσιν.²⁹

1. Partic. combination, *and yet, and that even though*: "invites a reconsideration of what the speaker has just said" (καίτοι) that receives focus/concentration (γε) (*CGCG* §59.23; cf. §59.53).
2. ἱστορία, -ας, ἡ, *history*; pred. comp.
3. Pres. act. inf., ἐπιγράφω, *title*.
4. Pres. act. indic. 3 pl., τολμάω, *dare*; with inf.
5. ὑγιής, -ές, *healthy, sound*.
6. Pres. act. inf., δηλόω, *indicate, show*. The infinitive is the dative object of πρός, "*in addition to showing* nothing sound" (cf. MGS, 1789.II.B.C).
7. Pres. act. indic. 3 pl., δοκέω, *seem, appear*; with dat. and inf.
8. Dat. of reference with γε, *to me at least, as far as I am concerned* (cf. S §2821.a; *CGCG* §59.53n1).
9. Pres. act. inf., διαμαρτάνω (with τοῦ σκοποῦ), *miss the mark entirely*.
10. μέν . . . δέ; a point/counterpoint set that provides explanation/support (γάρ) (cf. Runge 2010, 75–83; BDF §447; S §2904; *CGCG* §59.24).
11. Pres. act. inf., ἀποδείκνυμι, *demonstrate*.
12. Pres. act. indic. 3 pl., καταβάλλω, *cast down*.
13. Adv., *always*.
14. Pres. act. indic. 3 pl., ταπεινόω, *disparage*.

15. Pres. act. opt. 3 pl., δοκέω, *seem, appear*; with inf.; potential (cf. BDF §385; S §1824; *CGCG* §34.13).
16. Pf. act. ptc. nom. masc. pl., νικάω, *conquer*; attrib. (subst.).
17. οὔτε . . . οὔτε . . . οὔτε, *neither . . . nor . . . nor*.
18. μῆκος, -ους, τό, *length*.
19. Pres. mid. indic. 3 pl., αἰδέομαι, *respect*.
20. πόλεμος, -ου, ὁ, *war*.
21. πλῆθος, -ους, τό, *multitude*.
22. Pres. act. ptc. gen. fem. sg., κάμνω, *wearied* (from toil or hardship); attrib.
23. στρατιά, -ᾶς, ἡ, *army*.
24. μέγεθος, -ους, τό, *greatness*.
25. στρατηγός, -οῦ, ὁ, *commander, general*.
26. Aor. act. ptc. nom. masc. pl., ἱδρόω, *sweat*, (by extens.) *labor*; circ.
27. Pres. act. indic. 1 sg., οἴομαι, *think, suppose*.
28. κατόρθωμα, -ατος, τό, *success*; subject of gen. absol. (conditional): "if their success is disparaged by them."
29. Pres. act. indic. 3 pl., ἀδοξέω, *be held in no esteem, dishonored*.

⁹Οὐ μὴν³⁰ ἐγὼ τοῖς ἐπαίρουσι³¹ τὰ Ῥωμαίων ἀντιφιλονεικῶν³² αὔξειν³³ τὰ τῶν ὁμοφύλων³⁴ διέγνων,³⁵ ἀλλὰ τὰ μὲν³⁶ ἔργα μετ' ἀκριβείας³⁷ ἀμφοτέρων διέξειμι,³⁸ τοὺς δ' ἐπὶ τοῖς πράγμασι λόγους ἀνατίθημι³⁹ τῇ διαθέσει,⁴⁰ καὶ τοῖς ἐμαυτοῦ πάθεσι⁴¹ διδοὺς ἐπολοφύρεσθαι⁴² ταῖς τῆς πατρίδος⁴³ συμφοραῖς.⁴⁴ ¹⁰ὅτι γὰρ αὐτὴν στάσις⁴⁵ οἰκεία καθεῖλεν,⁴⁶ καὶ τὰς Ῥωμαίων χεῖρας ἀκούσας⁴⁷ καὶ τὸ πῦρ ἐπὶ τὸν [ἅγιον]⁴⁸ ναὸν⁴⁹ εἵλκυσαν⁵⁰ οἱ Ἰουδαίων τύραννοι,⁵¹ μάρτυς αὐτὸς ὁ πορθήσας⁵² Καῖσαρ Τίτος, ἐν παντὶ τῷ πολέμῳ τὸν μὲν⁵³ δῆμον⁵⁴ ἐλεήσας⁵⁵ ὑπὸ τῶν στασιαστῶν⁵⁶ φρουρούμενον,⁵⁷ πολλάκις δὲ ἑκὼν⁵⁸ τὴν ἅλωσιν⁵⁹ τῆς πόλεως ὑπερτιθέμενος⁶⁰ καὶ διδοὺς τῇ πολιορκίᾳ⁶¹ χρόνον εἰς μετάνοιαν τῶν αἰτίων.⁶² ¹¹εἰ δέ τις ὅσα πρὸς τοὺς τυράννους ἢ τὸ ληστρικὸν⁶³ αὐτῶν κατηγορικῶς⁶⁴ λέγοιμεν⁶⁵ ἢ τοῖς δυστυχήμασι⁶⁶ τῆς πατρίδος ἐπιστένοντες⁶⁷ συκοφαντοίη,⁶⁸ διδότω παρὰ⁶⁹ τὸν τῆς ἱστορίας νόμον συγγνώμην⁷⁰ τῷ πάθει· πόλιν [μὲν] γὰρ δὴ⁷¹ τῶν ὑπὸ Ῥωμαίοις πασῶν τὴν ἡμετέραν ἐπὶ πλεῖστόν τε εὐδαιμονίας⁷² συνέβη⁷³ προελθεῖν⁷⁴

30. Partic., *I assure you, truly, certainly*: "indicates that the speaker is committed to the truth or relevance of his/her utterance, and anticipates or assumes a possible lack of commitment on the part of the addressee" (cf. *CGCG* §59.49). He assures his readers that he has no intention of doing X (οὐ μήν) but rather Y (ἀλλά).
31. Pres. act. ptc. dat. masc. pl., ἐπαίρω, *raise up*; attrib. (subst.).
32. Pres. act. ptc. nom. masc. sg., ἀντιφιλονεικέω, *be in contrast, rival*; with dat.; circ.
33. Aor. act. inf., αὐξάνω, *increase, amplify*.
34. ὁμόφυλος, -ον, *of the same race/descent*.
35. Aor. act. indic. 1 sg., διαγινώσκω, *decide, intend*; with inf.
36. μέν . . . δέ; point/counterpoint. See n. 10.
37. ἀκρίβεια, -ας, ἡ, *accuracy*.
38. Pres. act. indic. 1 sg., διέξειμι, *narrate*.
39. Pres. act. indic. 1 sg., ἀνατίθημι, *set forth, declare*.
40. διάθεσις, -εως, ἡ, *disposition, personal feelings*; dat. of manner.
41. πάθος, -ους, τό, (pl.) *emotions*.
42. Pres. mid. inf., ἐπολοφύρομαι, *groan*; with dat.; obj./purpose (BDF §390; S 2009; *CGCG* §51.16); "giving [occasion] to my emotions *to groan* at the misfortunes that befell my homeland."
43. πατρίς, -ίδος, ἡ, *homeland*.
44. συμφορά, -ᾶς, ἡ, *misfortune*.
45. στάσις, -εως, ἡ, *sedition*; στάσις οἰκεία, "homegrown sedition," "civil conflict."
46. Aor. act. indic. 3 sg., καταιρέω, *destroy*.
47. ἄκων, -ουσα, -ον, *unwillingly*.
48. MSS P and M* omit ἅγιον.
49. ναός, -οῦ, ὁ, *sanctuary* (of the temple).
50. Aor. act. indic. 3 pl., ἕλκω, *drag*.
51. τύραννος, -ου, ὁ, *self-appointed ruler*, (neg.) *tyrant*.
52. Aor. act. ptc. nom. masc. sg., πορθέω, *sack, destroy*; attrib. (subst.).
53. μέν . . . δέ; point/counterpoint. See n. 10.
54. δῆμος, -ου, ὁ, *people*.
55. Aor. act. ptc. nom. masc. sg., ἐλεέω, *pity, have mercy on*; circ.
56. στασιαστής, -οῦ, ὁ, *insurrectionist*; agent of the pass. ptc. φρουρούμενον.
57. Pres. pass. ptc. acc. masc. sg., φρουρέω, (pass.) *be guarded, watched over*; circ.
58. ἑκών, -οῦσα, -όν, *willing*.
59. ἅλωσις, -εως, ἡ, *capture*.
60. Pres. mid. ptc. nom. masc. sg., ὑπερτίθημι, *(of time) postpone, defer* (MGS, 2210.2C).
61. πολιορκία, -ας, ἡ, *siege*.
62. αἴτιος, -ία, -ιον, (subst.) *the culprits*; subjective gen.
63. ληστρικός, -ή, -όν, (neut. subst.) *band of robbers*.
64. Adv., *in an accusatory manner*.
65. Pres. act. opt. 1 pl., λέγω. In conditional relative clauses, the potential optative may be used without ἄν (cf. S §2552; *CGCG* §50.22). "However much [ὅσα] *we may have spoken* in an accusatory fashion about the tyrants or their band of robbers or bewailed the misfortunes of the homeland."
66. δυστύχημα, -ματος, τό, *misfortune*.
67. Pres. act. ptc. nom. masc. pl., ἐπιστένω, *groan, wail*; circ.
68. Pres. act. opt. 3 sg., συκοφαντέω, *criticize in a nitpicky way, quibble about*. As is often the case, we have a mixed condition: εἰ with opt. in the protasis, impv. in the apodosis (cf. S §2364).
69. Prep. with acc., *contrary to*.
70. συγγνώμη, -ης, ἡ, *concession, indulgence*.
71. Partic. combination: "δή may lend a nuance of certainty or obviousness to the explanation/motivation given by γάρ" (*CGCG* §59.62).
72. εὐδαιμονία, -ας, ἡ, *happiness, good fortune*.
73. Aor. act. indic. 3 sg., συμβαίνω, (quasi-impers.) *it happens, befalls*; with acc. and inf. (cf. S §1985; *CGCG* §36.4).
74. Aor. act. inf., προέρχομαι, *advance*; with ἐπὶ πλεῖστον εὐδαιμονίας, "to the highest degree of happiness."

καὶ πρὸς ἔσχατον συμφορῶν⁷⁵ αὖθις⁷⁶ καταπεσεῖν.⁷⁷ **12**τὰ γοῦν⁷⁸ πάντων ἀπ' αἰῶνος ἀτυχήματα⁷⁹ πρὸς τὰ Ἰουδαίων ἡττῆσθαι⁸⁰ δοκῶ κατὰ σύγκρισιν,⁸¹ καὶ τούτων αἴτιος οὐδεὶς ἀλλόφυλος,⁸² ὥστε ἀμήχανον⁸³ ἦν ὀδυρμῶν⁸⁴ ἐπικρατεῖν.⁸⁵ εἰ δέ τις οἴκτου σκληρότερος⁸⁶ εἴη⁸⁷ δικαστής,⁸⁸ τὰ μὲν⁸⁹ πράγματα τῇ ἱστορίᾳ προσκρινέτω,⁹⁰ τὰς δ' ὀλοφύρσεις⁹¹ τῷ γράφοντι.

13Καίτοι γε⁹² ἐπιτιμήσαιμ'⁹³ ἂν αὐτὸς δικαίως τοῖς Ἑλλήνων λογίοις,⁹⁴ οἳ τηλικούτων⁹⁵ κατ' αὐτοὺς πραγμάτων γεγενημένων,⁹⁶ ἃ κατὰ σύγκρισιν ἐλαχίστους ἀποδείκνυσι⁹⁷ τοὺς πάλαι⁹⁸ πολέμους, τούτων μὲν⁹⁹ κάθηνται¹⁰⁰ κριταὶ¹⁰¹ τοῖς φιλοτιμουμένοις¹⁰² ἐπηρεάζοντες,¹⁰³ ὧν εἰ καὶ¹⁰⁴ τῷ λόγῳ πλεονεκτοῦσι,¹⁰⁵ λείπονται¹⁰⁶ τῇ προαιρέσει·¹⁰⁷ αὐτοὶ δὲ τὰ Ἀσσυρίων¹⁰⁸ καὶ Μήδων¹⁰⁹ συγγράφουσιν¹¹⁰ ὥσπερ ἧττον¹¹¹ καλῶς ὑπὸ τῶν ἀρχαίων¹¹² συγγραφέων¹¹³ ἀπηγγελμένα.¹¹⁴ **14**καίτοι τοσούτῳ¹¹⁵ τῆς ἐκείνων ἡττῶνται δυνάμεως¹¹⁶ ἐν τῷ γράφειν, ὅσῳ καὶ τῆς γνώμης.¹¹⁷ τὰ γὰρ κατ' αὐτοὺς ἐσπούδαζον¹¹⁸ ἕκαστοι γράφειν, ὅπου καὶ τὸ παρατυχεῖν¹¹⁹ τοῖς πράγμασιν

75. συμφορά, -ᾶς, ἡ, *misfortune, bad luck, disaster*.
76. Adv., *then, in turn*.
77. Aor. act. inf., καταπίπτω, *fall to*; with πρὸς ἔσχατον συμφορῶν, "to the lowest depths of misfortune."
78. Partic.: "a combination of γε and οὖν, γοῦν modifies an utterance which elaborates (οὖν) upon (part of) the preceding utterance by restricting its applicability (γε) (*at least, at any rate*)" (CGCG §59.54).
79. ἀτύχημα, -ματα, τό, *misfortune*.
80. Pf. pass. inf., ἥσσάομαι (Att. ἡττάομαι), (pass.) *be less, fall short*; indir. disc. (δοκῶ). "It seems to me that the misfortunes of all other people groups from old pale in comparison to [the misfortunes] of the Jews."
81. σύγκρισις, -εως, ἡ, *comparison*; κατὰ σύγκρισιν, "by comparison."
82. ἀλλόφυλος, -ον, *of another ethnic group*.
83. ἀμήχανος, -ον, (quasi-impers.) *it is impossible*; with (acc. and) inf.
84. ὀδυρμός, -οῦ, ὁ, *lamentation*.
85. Pres. act. inf., ἐπικρατέω, *restrain*; with gen.
86. Compar., σκληρός, -ά, -όν, *harsher*; with οἴκτου, "a judge too harsh for mercy."
87. Pres. act. opt. 3 sg., εἰμί. Same structure as above: εἰ with opt. in the protasis, impv. in the apodosis. See n. 68.
88. δικαστής, -οῦ, ὁ, *judge*.
89. μέν . . . δέ; point/counterpoint. See n. 10.
90. Pres. act. impv. 3 sg., προσκρίνω, *adjudicate, attribute*.
91. ὀλόφυρσις, -εως, ἡ, *lamentation*.
92. Partic. combination: as in the opening of 1.7, there is a shift in expectation (καίτοι) that is strengthened by γε. See n. 1.
93. Aor. act. opt. 1 sg., ἐπιτιμάω, *rebuke, censure*; with dat.; potential. See n. 15.
94. λόγιος, -α, -ον, *educated*.
95. τηλικοῦτος, -αύτη, -οῦτο, *so great*.
96. Gen. absol., "when such great deeds have occurred in their time."

97. Pres. act. indic. 3 sg., ἀποδείκνυμι, *show, demonstrate*. The subject of the verb is the relative ἅ: "which prove the wars of old to be by comparison of least significance."
98. Adv., *long ago, of old*.
99. μέν . . . δέ; point/counterpoint. See n. 10.
100. Pres. mid. indic. 3 pl., κάθημαι, *sit*.
101. κριτής, -οῦ, ὁ, *judge*.
102. Pres. mid. ptc. dat. masc. pl., φιλοτιμέομαι, *have as an ambition*; attrib. (subst.): "those who have as their ambition [to study the events of the war]."
103. Pres. act. ptc. nom. masc. pl., ἐπηρεάζω, *revile*; with dat.; circ.
104. Concessive clause (cf. BDF §374; S §2369; CGCG §49.19).
105. Pres. act. indic. 3 pl., πλεονεκτέω, *have the advantage, be superior*; with gen.
106. Pres. pass. indic. 3 pl., λείπω, (pass.) *be lacking*.
107. προαίρεσις, -εως, ἡ, *discernment, mode of action/thought*; dat. of respect.
108. Ἀσσύριος, -α, -ον, *Assyrian*.
109. Μῆδος, -ου, *of Media, Mede*.
110. Pres. act. indic. 3 pl., συγγράφω, *describe, expound*.
111. ἥσσων, -ον (Att. ἥττων), *lesser, inferior*; as adv. with καλῶς, "altogether inferiorly."
112. ἀρχαῖος, -α, -ον, *ancient*.
113. συγγραφεύς, -έως, ὁ, *writer, historian*; agent of the pass. ptc. ἀπηγγελμένα.
114. Pf. pass. ptc. acc. neut. pl., ἀπαγγέλλω, (pass.) *be reported*; circ. (comparison).
115. τοσούτῳ . . . ὅσῳ καί, *as (much as)* . . . *so also* (cf. BDF §304; S §2468; CGCG §32.11).
116. δύναμις, -εως, ἡ, *ability*; gen. of distinction; lit., "They are inferior to them *in ability* with reference to writing."
117. γνώμη, -ης, ἡ, *thought, opinion, judgment*; gen. of distinction.
118. Impf. act. indic. 3 pl., σπουδάζω, *hasten, be eager to*; with inf.
119. Aor. act. inf., παρατυγχάνω, *be present*; with dat.; art. inf. as subject (cf. BDF §399; S §2025; CGCG §51.40).

ἐποίει τὴν ἀπαγγελίαν ἐναργῆ[120] καὶ τὸ ψεύδεσθαι[121] παρ' εἰδόσιν[122] αἰσχρὸν[123] ἦν. **15**τό γε μὴν[124] μνήμῃ[125] τὰ [μὴ] προϊστορηθέντα[126] διδόναι καὶ τὰ τῶν ἰδίων χρόνων τοῖς μετ' αὐτὸν συνιστάνειν[127] ἐπαίνου καὶ μαρτυρίας ἄξιον· φιλόπονος[128] δὲ οὐχ ὁ μεταποιῶν[129] οἰκονομίαν[130] καὶ τάξιν[131] ἀλλοτρίαν,[132] ἀλλ' ὁ μετὰ τοῦ καινὰ λέγειν καὶ τὸ σῶμα τῆς ἱστορίας κατασκευάζων[133] ἴδιον.[134] **16**κἀγὼ μὲν[135] ἀναλώμασι[136] καὶ πόνοις μεγίστοις ἀλλόφυλος ὢν Ἕλλησί τε καὶ Ῥωμαίοις τὴν μνήμην τῶν κατορθωμάτων[137] ἀνατίθημι.[138] τοῖς δὲ γνησίοις[139] πρὸς μὲν[140] τὰ λήμματα[141] καὶ τὰς δίκας[142] κέχηνεν[143] εὐθέως τὸ στόμα καὶ

γλῶσσα λέλυται, πρὸς δὲ τὴν ἱστορίαν, ἔνθα[144] χρὴ[145] τἀληθῆ[146] λέγειν καὶ μετὰ πολλοῦ πόνου τὰ πράγματα συλλέγειν,[147] πεφίμωνται[148] παρέντες[149] τοῖς ἀσθενεστέροις[150] καὶ μηδὲ γινώσκουσι τὰς πράξεις[151] τῶν ἡγεμόνων[152] γράφειν. τιμάσθω[153] δὴ[154] παρ' ἡμῖν τὸ τῆς ἱστορίας ἀληθές, ἐπεὶ παρ' Ἕλλησιν ἠμέληται.[155]

NOTE

1.10. στάσις οἰκεία. The thesis is that "homegrown insurrection" (or "civil war")—not the power of the Romans and their gods or the weakness of the Jews and their God—is responsible for the destruction of the Jerusalem temple. The topic of στάσις becomes a refrain in the prologue (1.24, 25, 27), and στάσις is the first word the audience encounters at the outset of the narrative proper (1.31). Here, too, Josephus appears to be dependent on Thucydides, specifically the latter's treatment of civil strife at Corcyra (*Pel. War* 3.82–84; Rajak 1983, 91–94). Yet Josephus reuses the language of the renowned historian to his own rhetorical ends: "[to connect] the Judean *seditio* . . . with the many *Roman* civil wars, especially the one concluded just before his arrival with Titus in Rome, which was also fresh in the experience of his Roman audience" (Mason 2009, 65).

120. ἐναργής, -ές, *lucid*; pred. comp.
121. Pres. mid. inf., ψεύδομαι, *lie*; art. inf. as subject. See n. 119.
122. Pf. act. ptc. dat. masc. pl., οἶδα; attrib. (subst.): "in the presence of those who knew [what took place]."
123. αἰσχρός, -ά, -όν, *shameful*.
124. Partic. combination: concentration/limitation (γε) with assurance on the part of the speaker (μήν) (cf. *CGCG* §§59.53; 59.49).
125. μνήμη, -ης, ἡ, *memory, remembrance*.
126. Aor. pass. ptc. acc. neut. pl., προϊστορέω, (pass.) *be mentioned first*; attrib. (subst.).
127. Pres. act. inf., συνίστημι, *commend*. The article τό governs διδόναι and συνιστάνειν, both of which take the predicate adjective ἄξιον (ἐστίν).
128. φιλόπονος, -ον, *industrious*; pred. adj.
129. Pres. act. ptc. nom. masc. sg., μεταποιέω, *change, transform*; attrib. (subst.).
130. οἰκονομία, -ας, ἡ, *distribution, disposition* (of themes or material).
131. τάξις, -εως, ἡ, *order, arrangement*.
132. ἀλλότριος, -α, -ον, *belonging to another*.
133. Pres. act. ptc. nom. masc. sg., κατασκευάζω, *prepare*; attrib. (subst.).
134. ἴδιος, -α, -ον, *one's own*.
135. μέν . . . δέ; point/counterpoint. See n. 10.
136. ἀνάλωμα, -ατος, τό, *expense, expenditure*; dat. of means.
137. κατόρθωμα, -ατος, τό, *achievement*.
138. Pres. act. indic. 1 sg., ἀνατίθημι, *present*.
139. γνήσιος, -α, -ον, *belonging to the ethnic group, native*; dat. of respect.
140. μέν . . . δέ; point/counterpoint that explicates the δέ-clause (cf. S §2908).
141. λῆμμα, -ατος, τό, *gain, profit*.
142. δίκη, -ης, ἡ, *penalty, lawsuit*.
143. Pf. act. indic. 3 sg., χάσκω, *be open, gape wide*.

144. Rel. adv., *where*.
145. Quasi-impers., χρή, *it is necessary*; with (acc. and) inf. (cf. BDF §405; S §1985; *CGCG* §36.3).
146. Crasis: τὰ ἀληθῆ.
147. Pres. act. inf., συλλέγω, *gather*.
148. Pf. pass. indic. 3 pl., φιμόω, (pass.) *be muzzled, silenced*.
149. Aor. act. ptc. nom. masc. pl., παρίημι, *leave* (a thing to another); circ.
150. Compar., ἀσθενής, -ές, *weaker, less capable*.
151. πρᾶξις, -εως, ἡ, *deed, action*.
152. ἡγεμών, -όνος, ὁ, *ruler*.
153. Pres. pass. impv. 3 sg., τιμάω, *be honored*.
154. Partic.: "Indicates that the speaker considers (and invites the addressee to consider) the text segment or word (group) which it modifies as evident, clear, or precise" (*CGCG* §59.44).
155. Pf. pass. indic. 3 sg., ἀμελέω, (pass.) *be slighted, overlooked*.

5.1.3
The Philosophical Schools of Judaism, Part 1

Jewish War 2.119–123, 137–142

2.119Τρία γὰρ¹ παρὰ Ἰουδαίοις εἴδη² φιλοσοφεῖται,³ καὶ τοῦ μὲν⁴ αἱρετισταὶ⁵ Φαρισαῖοι, τοῦ δὲ Σαδδουκαῖοι, τρίτον δέ, ὃ δὴ⁶ καὶ δοκεῖ⁷ σεμνότητα⁸ ἀσκεῖν,⁹ Ἐσσηνοὶ¹⁰ καλοῦνται, Ἰουδαῖοι μὲν¹¹ γένος¹² ὄντες, φιλάλληλοι¹³ δὲ καὶ τῶν ἄλλων πλέον.¹⁴ **120**οὗτοι τὰς μὲν¹⁵ ἡδονὰς¹⁶ ὡς κακίαν ἀποστρέφονται,¹⁷ τὴν δὲ ἐγκράτειαν¹⁸ καὶ τὸ μὴ τοῖς πάθεσιν¹⁹ ὑποπίπτειν²⁰ ἀρετὴν²¹ ὑπολαμβάνουσιν.²² καὶ γάμου²³ μὲν²⁴ παρ' αὐτοῖς ὑπεροψία,²⁵ τοὺς δ' ἀλλοτρίους²⁶ παῖδας²⁷

1. This particle introduces a lengthy parenthesis on the schools of Judaism, which is prompted by the statement that Judas the Galilean was "a sophist who founded a sect of his own [ἰδίας αἱρέσεως], having nothing in common with the others [τοῖς ἄλλοις]" (2.118).
2. εἶδος, -ους, τό, *form.*
3. Pres. pass. indic. 3 sg., φιλοσοφέω, (pass.) *be practiced at philosophy.*
4. τοῦ μέν ... τοῦ δέ, *of the one (form) ... of the other (form)* (cf. BDF §250; S §1106; *CGCG* §28.27).
5. αἱρετιστής, -οῦ, ὁ, *follower of a party / philosophical school.*
6. Partic.: "indicates that the speaker considers (and invites the addressee to consider) the text segment or word (group) which it modifies as evident, clear, or precise" (cf. *CGCG* §59.44).
7. Pres. act. indic. 3 sg., δοκέω, *seem, appear;* with inf.
8. σεμνότης, -ητος, ἡ, *dignity, solemnity, piety.*
9. Pres. act. inf., ἀσκέω, *practice.*
10. Ἐσσηνός, -οῦ, ὁ, *Essene.*
11. μέν ... δέ; point/counterpoint (cf. Runge 2010, 75–83; BDF §447; S §2904; *CGCG* §59.24).
12. γένος, -ους, τό, *race.*
13. φιλάλληλος, -ον, *displaying mutual love/affection.*
14. Compar., πολύς, πολλή, πολύ, *greater;* with gen. of compar., τῶν ἄλλων.
15. μέν ... δέ; point/counterpoint. See n. 11.
16. ἡδονή, -ῆς, ἡ, *pleasure.*
17. Pres. mid. indic. 3 pl., ἀποστρέφω, *turn from.*
18. ἐγκράτεια, -ας, ἡ, *self-mastery.*
19. πάθος, -ους, τό, (pl.) *passions.*
20. Pres. act. inf., ὑποπίπτω, *fall;* with dat.; art. inf. as obj. (cf. BDF §399; S §2034; *CGCG* §51.39).
21. ἀρετή, -ῆς, ἡ, *virtue;* pred. comp.
22. Pres. act. indic. 3 pl., ὑπολαμβάνω, *to receive.*
23. γάμος, -ου, ὁ, *marriage;* new topic (cf. *CGCG* §60.27).
24. μέν ... δέ; point/counterpoint. See n. 11.
25. ὑπεροψία, -ας, ἡ, *contempt, disdain;* with obj. gen.
26. ἀλλότριος, -α, -ον, *belonging to another.*
27. παῖς, παιδός, ὁ, *child.*

ἐκλαμβάνοντες²⁸ ἁπαλοὺς²⁹ ἔτι πρὸς τὰ μαθήματα³⁰ συγγενεῖς³¹ ἡγοῦνται³² καὶ τοῖς ἤθεσιν³³ αὐτῶν ἐντυποῦσι,³⁴ ¹²¹τὸν μὲν³⁵ γάμον καὶ τὴν ἐξ αὐτοῦ διαδοχὴν³⁶ οὐκ ἀναιροῦντες,³⁷ τὰς δὲ τῶν γυναικῶν ἀσελγείας³⁸ φυλαττόμενοι³⁹ καὶ μηδεμίαν τηρεῖν⁴⁰ πεπεισμένοι⁴¹ τὴν πρὸς ἕνα πίστιν.

¹²²Καταφρονηταὶ⁴² δὲ πλούτου,⁴³ καὶ θαυμάσιον⁴⁴ [παρ'] αὐτοῖς τὸ κοινωνικόν,⁴⁵ οὐδὲ ἔστιν εὑρεῖν⁴⁶ κτήσει⁴⁷ τινὰ παρ' αὐτοῖς ὑπερέχοντα·⁴⁸ νόμος γὰρ τοὺς εἰς τὴν αἵρεσιν εἰσιόντας⁴⁹ δημεύειν⁵⁰ τῷ τάγματι⁵¹ τὴν οὐσίαν,⁵² ὥστε ἐν ἅπασιν μήτε πενίας⁵³ ταπεινότητα⁵⁴ φαίνεσθαι⁵⁵ μήθ' ὑπεροχὴν⁵⁶ πλούτου, τῶν δ' ἑκάστου κτημάτων ἀναμεμιγμένων⁵⁷ μίαν ὥσπερ ἀδελφοῖς ἅπασιν οὐσίαν εἶναι. ¹²³κηλῖδα⁵⁸ δ' ὑπολαμβάνουσι τοὔλαιον,⁵⁹ κἂν ἀλειφθῇ⁶⁰ τις ἄκων,⁶¹ σμήχεται⁶² τὸ σῶμα· τὸ γὰρ αὐχμεῖν⁶³ ἐν καλῷ τίθενται,⁶⁴ λευχειμονεῖν⁶⁵ τε διαπαντός.⁶⁶ χειροτονητοὶ⁶⁷ δ' οἱ τῶν κοινῶν ἐπιμεληταὶ⁶⁸ καὶ ἀδιαίρετοι⁶⁹ πρὸς ἁπάντων εἰς τὰς χρείας ἕκαστοι. . . .

¹³⁷Τοῖς δὲ ζηλοῦσιν⁷⁰ τὴν αἵρεσιν αὐτῶν οὐκ εὐθὺς ἡ πάροδος,⁷¹ ἀλλ' ἐπὶ ἐνιαυτὸν ἔξω μένοντι τὴν αὐτὴν ὑποτίθενται⁷² δίαιταν,⁷³ ἀξινάριόν⁷⁴ τε καὶ τὸ προειρημένον⁷⁵ περίζωμα⁷⁶ καὶ λευκὴν⁷⁷ ἐσθῆτα⁷⁸ δόντες. ¹³⁸ἐπειδὰν δὲ τούτῳ τῷ χρόνῳ πεῖραν⁷⁹ ἐγκρατείας

28. Pres. act. ptc. nom. masc. pl., ἐκλαμβάνω, *receive*; circ.
29. ἁπαλός, -ή, -όν, *tender, impressionable*.
30. μάθημα, -ατος, τό, *learning, knowledge*.
31. συγγενής, -ές, *kindred*; pred. comp.
32. Pres. mid. indic. 3 pl., ἡγέομαι, *consider*.
33. ἦθος, -ους, τό, *custom, habit, character*.
34. Pres. act. indic. 3 pl., ἐντυπόω, *mold, impress*.
35. μέν . . . δέ; point/counterpoint. See n. 11.
36. διαδοχή, -ῆς, ἡ, *succession, propagation*.
37. Pres. act. ptc. nom. masc. sg., ἀναιρέω, *abolish, abrogate*; circ.
38. ἀσέλγεια, -ας, ἡ, *licentiousness, sensuality*.
39. Pres. mid. ptc. nom. masc. pl., φυλάσσω (Att. φυλάττω), (mid.) *be on guard against*; circ.
40. Pres. act. inf., τηρέω, *keep, guard*; indir. disc. (cf. BDF §397; S §2016; *CGCG* §51.19): "persuaded that no woman [μηδεμίαν] keeps [τηρεῖν] her pledge toward one man [τὴν πρὸς ἕνα πίστιν]."
41. Pf. pass. ptc. nom. masc. sg., πείθω, (pass.) *be persuaded*; circ. (causal).
42. καταφρονητής, -οῦ, ὁ, *despiser*.
43. πλοῦτος, -ου, ὁ, *riches, wealth*.
44. θαυμάσιος, -α, -ον, *remarkable, wonderful*.
45. κοινωνικός, -ή, -όν, *of common ownership*.
46. Aor. act. inf., εὑρίσκω, *find, discover*; subjective comp. of impers. ἔστιν; lit., "It is not that [one] finds any among them surpassing [others] in possessions."
47. κτῆσις, -εως, ἡ, *property, possession*; dat. of respect.
48. Pres. act. ptc. acc. masc. sg., ὑπερέχω, *surpass, exceed*; supp. (εὑρεῖν).
49. Pres. act. ptc. acc. masc. pl., εἴσειμι, *enter*; attrib. (subst.).
50. Pres. act. inf., δημεύω, *confiscate*; comp. of νόμος (cf. *CGCG* §51.9): "It is the law for those entering the school *to hand over* their property to the order."
51. τάγμα, -ατος, τό, *group, order*.
52. οὐσία, -ας, ἡ, *property*.
53. πενία, -ας, ἡ, *poverty*.
54. ταπεινότης, -ητος, ἡ, *lowliness*.

55. Pres. pass. inf., φαίνω, (pass.) *appear*; result clause (cf. BDF §391; S §2269; *CGCG* §46.6).
56. ὑπεροχή, -ῆς, ἡ, *being above, superiority*.
57. Pf. pass. ptc. gen. neut. pl., ἀναμείγνυμι, *mix, mingle*; gen. absol.
58. κηλίς, -ῖδος, ἡ, *stain, defiling stain*; pred. comp.
59. Crasis: τὸ ἔλαιον, *oil*.
60. Aor. pass. subj. 3 sg., ἀλείφω, (pass.) *be anointed/smeared with oil*; concessive clause (cf. BDF §374; S §2369; *CGCG* §49.19).
61. ἄκων, -ουσα, -ον, *unwilling, involuntary*.
62. Pres. mid. indic. 3 sg., σμήχω, *wash*.
63. Pres. act. inf., αὐχμέω, *be dry*; art. inf. as obj. See n. 20.
64. The collocation ἐν καλῷ τίθημι means "consider something good," wherein ἐν with the dative marks the predicate complement.
65. Pres. act. inf., λευχειμονέω, *wear white*; art. inf. as obj. See n. 20.
66. Adv., *always*.
67. χειροτονητός, -ή, -όν, *elected* (by show of hands).
68. ἐπιμελητής, -οῦ, ὁ, *administrator*.
69. ἀδιαίρετος, -ον, *undivided*.
70. Pres. act. ptc. dat. masc. pl., ζηλέω, *be zealous for, desire to join* (the school); attrib. (subst.); new discourse topic.
71. πάροδος, -ου, ἡ, *passage, admission*.
72. Pres. mid. indic. 3 pl., ὑποτίθημι, (mid.) *prescribe, enjoin*.
73. δίαιτα, -ης, ἡ, *lifestyle, standard of living*.
74. ἀξινάριον, -ου, τό, *hatchet*.
75. Pf. pass. ptc. acc. neut. sg., προερέω, (pass.) *be previously discussed*; attrib.
76. περίζωμα, -ατος, τό, *loincloth*.
77. λευκός, -ή, -όν, *white*.
78. ἐσθής, -ῆτος, ἡ, *garment*.
79. πεῖρα, -ας, ἡ, *proof*.

δῷ, πρόσεισιν⁸⁰ μὲν⁸¹ ἔγγιον⁸² τῇ διαίτῃ καὶ καθαρωτέρων⁸³ τῶν πρὸς ἁγνείαν⁸⁴ ὑδάτων μεταλαμβάνει,⁸⁵ παραλαμβάνεται δὲ εἰς τὰς συμβιώσεις⁸⁶ οὐδέπω.⁸⁷ μετὰ γὰρ τὴν τῆς καρτερίας ἐπίδειξιν⁸⁸ δυσὶν ἄλλοις ἔτεσιν τὸ ἦθος δοκιμάζεται⁸⁹ καὶ φανεὶς⁹⁰ ἄξιος οὕτως εἰς τὸν ὅμιλον⁹¹ ἐγκρίνεται.⁹² **139**πρὶν δὲ τῆς κοινῆς ἅψασθαι⁹³ τροφῆς⁹⁴ ὅρκους⁹⁵ αὐτοῖς ὄμνυσι⁹⁶ φρικώδεις,⁹⁷ πρῶτον μὲν⁹⁸ εὐσεβήσειν⁹⁹ τὸ θεῖον,¹⁰⁰ ἔπειτα τὰ πρὸς ἀνθρώπους δίκαια φυλάξειν¹⁰¹ καὶ μήτε κατὰ γνώμην¹⁰² βλάψειν¹⁰³ τινὰ μήτε ἐξ ἐπιτάγματος,¹⁰⁴ μισήσειν¹⁰⁵ δ' ἀεὶ¹⁰⁶ τοὺς ἀδίκους καὶ συναγωνιεῖσθαι¹⁰⁷ τοῖς δικαίοις· **140**τὸ πιστὸν ἀεὶ πᾶσιν παρέξειν,¹⁰⁸ μάλιστα δὲ τοῖς κρατοῦσιν·¹⁰⁹ οὐ γὰρ δίχα¹¹⁰ θεοῦ περιγενέσθαι¹¹¹ τινὶ τὸ ἄρχειν·¹¹² κἂν¹¹³ αὐτὸς ἄρχῃ, μηδέποτε ἐξυβρίσειν¹¹⁴ εἰς τὴν ἐξουσίαν, μηδ' ἐσθῆτί τινι ἢ πλείονι κόσμῳ τοὺς ὑποτεταγμένους¹¹⁵ ὑπερλαμπρύνεσθαι.¹¹⁶ **141**τὴν ἀλήθειαν ἀγαπᾶν ἀεὶ καὶ τοὺς ψευδομένους προβάλλεσθαι·¹¹⁷ χεῖρας κλοπῆς¹¹⁸ καὶ ψυχὴν ἀνοσίου κέρδους¹¹⁹ καθαρὰν φυλάξειν, καὶ μήτε κρύψειν¹²⁰ τι τοὺς αἱρετιστὰς μήθ' ἑτέροις αὐτῶν τι μηνύσειν,¹²¹ κἂν μέχρι¹²² θανάτου τις βιάζηται.¹²³ **142**πρὸς¹²⁴ τούτοις ὄμνυσιν μηδενὶ μὲν¹²⁵ μεταδοῦναι¹²⁶ τῶν δογμάτων ἑτέρως¹²⁷ ἢ ὡς αὐτὸς μετέλαβεν,¹²⁸ ἀφέξεσθαι¹²⁹ δὲ λῃστείας¹³⁰ καὶ συντηρήσειν¹³¹ ὁμοίως

---

80. Pres. act. indic. 3 pl., πρόσειμι, *approach*; with dat.
81. μέν . . . δέ; point/counterpoint. See n. 11.
82. Compar. adv., ἐγγύς, *more closely*.
83. Compar., καθαρός, -ά, -όν, *purer*.
84. ἁγνεία, -ας, ἡ, *purity*; πρὸς ἁγνείαν, "the purer water used for purity (i.e., purification rituals)."
85. Pres. act. indic. 3 sg., μεταλαμβάνω, *partake of*; with gen.
86. συμβίωσις, -εως, ἡ, *living together*.
87. Adv., *not yet*.
88. ἐπίδειξις, -εως, ἡ, *demonstration*.
89. Pres. pass. indic. 3 sg., δοκιμάζω, (pass.) *be tested*.
90. Aor. pass. ptc. nom. masc. sg., φαίνω, *appear*; circ. (conditional).
91. ὅμιλος, -ου, ὁ, *group, society*.
92. Pres. pass. indic. 3 sg., ἐγκρίνω, (pass.) *be selected/admitted*.
93. Aor. mid. inf., ἅπτω, (mid.) *outshine*; with gen.; πρίν with inf. expresses action prior to the main verb (cf. BDF §395; S §2453; *CGCG* §47.14).
94. τροφή, -ῆς, ἡ, *food*.
95. ὅρκος, -ου, ὁ, *oath*.
96. Pres. act. indic. 3 sg., ὄμνυμι, *swear*.
97. φρικώδης, -ες, *of that which strikes terror/horror*.
98. πρῶτον μέν . . . ἔπειτα, *first . . . then* (cf. S §2910).
99. Fut. act. inf., εὐσεβέω, *show piety, reverence*; indir. disc. See n. 40.
100. θεῖος, -α, -ον, *divine*, (subst.) *the deity*.
101. Fut. act. inf., φυλάσσω (Att. φυλάττω), *guard, keep*; indir. disc. See n. 40.
102. γνώμη, -ης, ἡ, *decision*.
103. Fut. act. inf., βλάπτω, *harm, injure*; indir. disc. See n. 40.
104. ἐπίταγμα, -ατος, τό, *order, command*.
105. Fut. act. inf., μισέω, *hate*. See n. 40.
106. Adv., *always*.
107. Fut. mid. inf., συναγωνίζομαι, *contend together with*; with dat.; indir. disc. See n. 40.

108. Fut. act. inf., παρέχω, *offer, present*; indir. disc. See n. 40.
109. Pres. act. ptc. dat. masc. pl., κρατέω, *rule*; attrib. (subst.).
110. Prep with gen., *separately, without*.
111. Aor. mid. inf., περιγίνομαι, *left over, remain*.
112. Pres. act. inf., ἄρχω, *rule*; art. inf. as subject (cf. BDF §399; S §2031; *CGCG* §51.39).
113. Crasis: κἂν = καὶ ἐάν; third-class condition with the fut. inf. for the fut. indic. because of indir. disc. (cf. BDF §373; S §2323; *CGCG* §49.6).
114. Fut. act. inf., ἐξυβρίζω, with εἴς τινα, *abuse someone/something*; indir. disc. See n. 40.
115. Pf. pass. ptc. acc. masc. pl., ὑποτάσσω, (pass.) *be subject/subordinate*; attrib. (subst.).
116. Pres. mid. inf., ὑπερλαμπρύνομαι, *outshine* (someone); indir. disc. See n. 40.
117. Pres. mid. inf., προβάλλω, *cast forward, expose*; indir. disc. See n. 40.
118. κλοπή, -ῆς, ἡ, *theft*; gen. of separation.
119. κέρδος, -ους, τό, *gain, profit*; gen. of separation.
120. Fut. act. inf., κρύπτω, *conceal*; with double acc. (something from someone); indir. disc. See n. 40.
121. Fut. act. inf., μηνύω, *report*; indir. disc. See n. 40.
122. Prep. with gen., *up to*.
123. Pres. mid. subj. 3 sg., βιάζω, *use force/violence*; concessive clause. See n. 60.
124. πρὸς τούτοις, "in addition to these things" (LSJ 1497.B.III).
125. μέν . . . δέ; point/counterpoint. See n. 11.
126. Aor. act. inf., μεταδίδωμι, *impart, transmit*; with gen.; indir. disc. See n. 40.
127. Adv., *differently*; ἑτέρως ἤ, "[do something] in a manner different than."
128. Aor. act. indic. 3 sg., μεταλαμβάνω, *receive*.
129. Fut. mid. inf., ἀπέχω, *keep oneself from*, with abl. gen.; indir. disc. See n. 40.
130. λῃστεία, -ας, ἡ, *robbery*.
131. Fut. act. inf., συντηρέω, *preserve*; indir. disc. See n. 40.

τά τε τῆς αἱρέσεως αὐτῶν βιβλία καὶ τὰ τῶν ἀγγέλων ὀνόματα. τοιούτοις μὲν[132] ὅρκοις τοὺς προσιόντας ἐξασφαλίζονται.[133]

NOTES

2.119. Τρία γὰρ παρὰ Ἰουδαίοις εἴδη φιλοσοφεῖται. B.J. 2.119-166 is Josephus's longest description of the three philosophical schools of Judaism (cf. Josephus, A.J. 13.171-173, 293-300; 18.11-22; on the term αἵρεσις, see Mason 2009, 219n4). The lengthy excursus has a concentric structure (Pharisees and Sadducees—Essenes—Pharisees and Sadducees) and is prompted by Josephus's narrative about Judas the Galilean (B.J. 2.117-118), whom he describes as "a sophist of his own sect [σοφιστὴς ἰδίας αἱρέσεως], having nothing in common with the others." Later, in *Jewish Antiquities*, Josephus describes Judas as the founder of a "fourth philosophy," which "agrees in all other respects with the opinions of the Pharisees, except that they have a passion for liberty that is almost unconquerable, since they are convinced that God alone is their leader and master" (18.23). He is clear, however, that this "intrusive fourth philosophy" (18.9) has no place among the three legitimate "schools" of Judaism (Klawans 2012, 11).

Φαρισαῖοι. Cf. B.J. 1.571; 2.162-163; A.J. 13.171-173, 288-298, 400-432; 15.3; 17.41-45; 18.12-15; *Vita* 10-12, 189-198. On the Pharisees more broadly, see Neusner and Chilton (2007) and Sievers and Levine (2021). On the Pharisees in Josephus, see Mason (1991).

Σαδδουκαῖοι. Cf. B.J. 2.164-165; A.J. 13.171-173, 293, 296-298; 18.17; 20.199; *Vita* 10-12. On the Sadducees, see Le Moyne (1972), Stemberger (1999), and Regev (2009). Josephus's anti-Sadducean bias is shared by the New Testament and rabbinic sources as well as by many modern scholars (Klawans 2012, 23-26).

Ἐσσηνοί. Cf. B.J. 1.78, 213; 2.567; 3.11; 5.145; A.J. 13.171-173, 298, 311; 15.371-378; 17.346; 18.18-22; *Vita* 10-12; Philo, *Prob*. 75-91; Pliny the Elder, *Nat*. 5.68-73. Most scholars identify the Essenes (or a portion thereof) with the Qumran community (e.g., VanderKam 2010, 97-156).

2.121. Other writers also describe the Essenes as celibate (cf. Philo *apud* Eusebius, *Praep. ev*. 8.11; Pliny the Elder, *Nat*. 5.73). Literary and archaeological evidence suggests that some members of the Qumran community married and had children (cf. 1Q28a 1:4; CD 7:6-7; 1QM 7:4-5; 11Q19 45:11-12; for the archaeological evidence, see Magness 2002, 163-87), which aligns with what Josephus says about "a different order of Essenes," in B.J. 2.160-161.

τὰς τῶν γυναικῶν ἀσελγείας. The phrase is characteristic of Josephus (B.J. 1.439; 4.562; A.J. 8.318; 15.98; cf. Philo, *Mos*. 1.305; Dio Chrysostom, *2 Regn*. 56; Mason 2008, 100n757).

μηδεμίαν τηρεῖν πεπεισμένοι τὴν πρὸς ἕνα πίστιν. Cf. A.J. 17.352: "Glaphyra, you certainly confirm the saying that women are faithless [ἄπιστα]" (cf. A.J. 4.219; 13.430-431; *C. Ap*. 2.201; Euripides, *Iph. taur*. 1298; Plutarch, *Lyc*. 15.9; Plutarch, *Mor*. 228b; Mason 2008, 100n758). On women in Josephus more broadly, see Ilan (2016).

2.137-142. Cf. 1QS 6:14-23, which states that the initiates go through a two-year probationary period.

2.139. The oath the initiates swear reflects the notion that Mosaic legislation is principally concerned with εὐσέβεια ("piety") and δικαιοσύνη ("justice") (cf. A.J. 18.117; *Let. Aris*. 131; Philo, *Spec*. 2.63; Philo, *Decal*. 110; Philo, *Virt*. 57; Philo, *Abr*. 208). Mason (2008, 112n886) notes, "Josephus is keenly

---

132. μέν... δέ. Transitional: μέν-clause concludes the report on their oaths; δέ-clause opens a new section (2.143).

133. Pres. mid. indic. 3 pl., ἐξασφαλίζω, *secure the allegiance* (of persons by oaths).

aware that, especially after the revolt, Judeans are widely accused of impiety (ἀσέβεια) or atheism in relation to the Gods and misanthropy with respect to their fellow human beings (e.g., [*C. Ap.*] 2.148, 291). One of his pervasive themes, therefore, from the beginning to the end of his corpus, is that his people cherish *piety* toward God and *justice* (also philanthropy) toward their neighbors—more, indeed, than any other nation."

2.142. τά τε τῆς αἱρέσεως αὐτῶν βιβλία καὶ τὰ τῶν ἀγγέλων ὀνόματα. Angels played a significant role in the liturgy and social *imaginaire* of the Qumran community. See, for example, Chazon (2000), Schäfer (2006), and Wassén (2017).

5.1.4

The Philosophical Schools of Judaism, Part 2

Jewish War 2.150–166

2.150Διῄρηνται¹ δὲ κατὰ χρόνον τῆς ἀσκήσεως² εἰς μοίρας³ τέσσαρας, καὶ τοσοῦτον οἱ μεταγενέστεροι⁴ τῶν προγενεστέρων⁵ ἐλαττοῦνται⁶ ὥστ', εἰ ψαύσειαν⁷ αὐτῶν, ἐκείνους ἀπολούεσθαι⁸ καθάπερ ἀλλοφύλῳ⁹ συμφυρέντας.¹⁰ **¹⁵¹**καὶ μακρόβιοι¹¹ μέν,¹² ὡς τοὺς πολλοὺς ὑπὲρ ἑκατὸν παρατείνειν¹³ ἔτη, διὰ τὴν ἁπλότητα¹⁴ τῆς διαίτης,¹⁵ ἔμοιγε δοκεῖν,¹⁶ καὶ τὴν εὐταξίαν,¹⁷ καταφρονηταὶ¹⁸ δὲ τῶν δεινῶν,¹⁹ καὶ τὰς μὲν²⁰ ἀλγηδόνας²¹ νικῶντες²² τοῖς φρονήμασιν,²³ τὸν

---

1. Pf. pass. indic. 3 pl., διαιρέω, (pass.) *be distinguished/divided*. The subject is still the Essenes.
2. ἄσκησις, -εως, ἡ, *training, practice, discipline*.
3. μοῖρα, -ας, ἡ, *division, grade*.
4. Compar., μεταγενής, -ές, (subst.) *those later in succession*.
5. Compar., προγενής, -ές, (subst.) *those earlier in succession*.
6. Pres. pass. indic. 3 pl., ἐλασσόω (Att. ἐλαττόω), (pass.) *be less than, inferior to*; with gen. of compar.
7. Aor. act. opt. 3 pl., ψαύω, *touch*, with gen. pers. εἰ with the optative marks the protasis of a fourth-class, or potential, condition (cf. BDF §371; S §2339; *CGCG* §49.8). As is often the case, we have a mixed condition: εἰ with the optative in the protasis, and a present infinitive (result clause) in the apodosis (cf. S §2360; *CGCG* §49.17).
8. Pres. mid. inf., ἀπολούω, *wash*; result clause (cf. BDF §391; S §2269; *CGCG* §46.6).
9. ἀλλόφυλος, -ον, *of another tribe, foreign*.
10. Pres. act. ptc. acc. masc. pl., συμφύρω, *mix together*; with dat.; circ. (comparison).
11. μακρόβιος, -ον, *long-lived*.
12. μέν . . . δέ; point/counterpoint (cf. Runge 2010, 75–83; BDF §447; S §2904; *CGCG* §59.24).
13. Pres. act. inf., παρατείνω, *extend, prolong*; result clause (cf. S §2260; *CGCG* §46.7).
14. ἁπλότης, -ητος, ἡ, *simplicity*.
15. δίαιτα, -ης, ἡ, *lifestyle, standard of living*.
16. Pres. act. inf., δοκέω; inf. absol. (cf. BDF §391a; S §2012; *CGCG* §51.49); ἔμοιγε δοκεῖν, "at least, it seems to me."
17. εὐταξία, -ης, ἡ, *good order*.
18. καταφρονητής, -οῦ, ὁ, *despiser*.
19. δεινός, -ή, -όν, *dangerous*.
20. μέν . . . δέ; point/counterpoint. The point/counterpoint set explicates the previous δέ-clause. See n. 12.
21. ἀλγηδών, -όνος, ἡ, *suffering, pain*.
22. Pres. act. ptc. nom. masc. pl., νικάω, *conquer*; circ.
23. φρόνημα, -ατος, τό, *mindset, reasoning*.

δὲ θάνατον, εἰ μετ' εὐκλείας²⁴ προσίοι,²⁵ νομίζοντες²⁶ ἀθανασίας²⁷ ἀμείνονα.²⁸ ¹⁵²διήλεγξεν²⁹ δὲ αὐτῶν ἐν ἅπασιν τὰς ψυχὰς ὁ πρὸς Ῥωμαίους πόλεμος, ἐν ᾧ στρεβλούμενοί³⁰ τε καὶ λυγιζόμενοι,³¹ καιόμενοί³² τε καὶ κλώμενοι³³ καὶ διὰ πάντων ὁδεύοντες³⁴ τῶν βασανιστηρίων³⁵ ὀργάνων,³⁶ ἵν' ἢ βλασφημήσωσιν τὸν νομοθέτην³⁷ ἢ φάγωσίν τι τῶν ἀσυνήθων,³⁸ οὐδέτερον³⁹ ὑπέμειναν⁴⁰ παθεῖν,⁴¹ ἀλλ' οὐδὲ κολακεῦσαί⁴² ποτε τοὺς αἰκιζομένους⁴³ ἢ δακρῦσαι.⁴⁴ ¹⁵³μειδιῶντες⁴⁵ δὲ ἐν ταῖς ἀλγηδόσιν⁴⁶ καὶ κατειρωνευόμενοι⁴⁷ τῶν τὰς βασάνους προσφερόντων εὔθυμοι⁴⁸ τὰς ψυχὰς ἠφίεσαν⁴⁹ ὡς πάλιν κομιούμενοι.⁵⁰

¹⁵⁴Καὶ γὰρ⁵¹ ἔρρωται⁵² παρ' αὐτοῖς ἥδε ἡ δόξα,⁵³ φθαρτὰ⁵⁴ μὲν⁵⁵ εἶναι τὰ σώματα καὶ τὴν ὕλην⁵⁶ οὐ μόνιμον⁵⁷ αὐτῶν, τὰς δὲ ψυχὰς ἀθανάτους⁵⁸ ἀεὶ διαμένειν,⁵⁹ καὶ συμπλέκεσθαι⁶⁰ μὲν⁶¹ ἐκ τοῦ λεπτοτάτου⁶² φοιτώσας⁶³ αἰθέρος⁶⁴ ὥσπερ εἱρκταῖς⁶⁵ τοῖς σώμασιν ἴυγγί⁶⁶ τινι φυσικῇ⁶⁷ κατασπωμένας,⁶⁸ ¹⁵⁵ἐπειδὰν δὲ ἀνεθῶσι⁶⁹ τῶν κατὰ σάρκα δεσμῶν,⁷⁰ οἷα δὴ μακρᾶς δουλείας ἀπηλλαγμένας,⁷¹ τότε χαίρειν καὶ μετεώρους⁷² φέρεσθαι. καὶ ταῖς μὲν⁷³ ἀγαθαῖς,⁷⁴

48. εὔθυμος, -ον, *cheerful*.
49. Aor. act. indic. 3 pl., ἀφίημι, *release*.
50. Fut. mid. ptc. nom. masc. pl., κομίζω, *receive*. ὡς with a circumstantial participle gives "a 'subjective' reason or motivation, for which responsibility lies with the subject of the matrix verb": *thinking that, in the conviction that* (CGCG §52.39; cf. S §2086).
51. Partic. combination: "additional information (καί) that has explanatory force (γάρ)" (CGCG §59.66).
52. Pf. pass. indic. 3 sg., ῥώννυμαι, (pass.) *be fixed*.
53. δόξα, -ας, ἡ, *belief*.
54. φθαρτός, -ή, -όν, *destructible, perishable*.
55. μέν . . . δέ; point/counterpoint. See n. 12.
56. ὕλη, -ης, ἡ, *material of composition*.
57. μόνιμος, -ον, *that which remains*.
58. ἀθάνατος, -ον, *immortal*.
59. Pres. act. inf., διαμένω, *persist, remain*; indir. disc. (cf. BDF §397; S §2016; CGCG §51.19).
60. Pres. pass. inf., συμπλέκω, (pass.) *be interwoven*; with dat.; indir. disc. See n. 59.
61. μέν . . . δέ; point/counterpoint. See n. 12.
62. Superl., λεπτός, -ή, -όν, *thinnest*.
63. Aor. act. ptc. acc. fem. pl., φοιτάω, *come*; circ.
64. αἰθήρ, -έρος, ὁ, *ether*.
65. εἱρκτή, -ῆς, ἡ, *prison, enclosure*.
66. ἴυγξ, ἴυγγος, ἡ, *magic power, enchantment*; dat. of means.
67. φυσικός, -ή, -όν, *natural, according to nature*.
68. Pf. pass. ptc. acc. fem. pl., κατασπάω, (pass.) *be drawn/pulled down*; circ.
69. Aor. pass. subj. 3 pl., ἀνίημι, (pass.) *be released*; fut. temp. clause (cf. BDF §381; S §2401; CGCG §47.8).
70. δεσμός, -οῦ, ὁ, (pl.) *chains*; gen. of separation.
71. Pres. pass. ptc. acc. fem. pl., ἀπαλλάσσω, (pass.) *be delivered*. οἷα (δή) with the participle gives "an 'objective' reason, for which the speaker/narrator takes responsibility": *since, given that* (CGCG §52.39; cf. S §2085).
72. μετέωρος -ον, *high in the air, aloft*.
73. μέν . . . δέ; point/counterpoint. See n. 12.
74. ταῖς ἀγαθαῖς = ταῖς ἀγαθαῖς ψυχαῖς.

24. εὔκλεια, -ας, ἡ, *fame, honor*.
25. Pres. act. opt. 3 sg., πρόσειμι, *come*; remote protasis: εἰ with opt. The subject of the verb is "death," which is fronted (prolepsis; cf. S §2182) for the μέν . . . δέ construction. See n. 7.
26. Pres. act. ptc. nom. masc. pl., νομίζω, *think, consider*; circ.
27. ἀθανασία, -ας, ἡ, *immortality*; gen. of compar.
28. Irreg. compar. of ἀγαθός, -ή, -όν, *better, more virtuous*; pred. comp.
29. Aor. act. indic. 3 sg., διελέγχω, *demonstrate, prove*.
30. Pres. pass. ptc. nom. masc. pl., στρεβλόω, (pass.) *be racked, twisted*; circ.
31. Pres. pass. ptc. nom. masc. pl., λυγίζω, (pass.) *be bent, twisted*; circ.
32. Pres. pass. ptc. nom. masc. pl., καίω, (pass.) *be burned*; circ.
33. Pres. pass. ptc. nom. masc. pl., κλάω, (pass.) *be broken*; circ.
34. Pres. act. ptc. nom. masc. pl., ὁδεύω, *pass through*.
35. βασανιστήριος, -α, -ον, *related to torture*.
36. ὄργανον, -ου, τό, *instrument*.
37. νομοθέτης, -ου, ὁ, *lawgiver*.
38. ἀσυνήθης, -ες, *what is contrary to ancestral customs*.
39. οὐδέτερος, -α, -ον, *neither of the two* (aforementioned demands).
40. Aor. act. indic. 3 pl., ὑπομένω, *endure*; with inf.
41. Aor. act. inf., πάσχω, *suffer*.
42. Aor. act. inf., κολακεύω, *flatter, coax*; comp. of ὑπέμειναν.
43. Pres. mid. ptc. acc. masc. pl., αἰκίζω, *torture*; attrib. (subst.).
44. Aor. act. inf., δακρύω, *weep*; comp. of ὑπέμειναν.
45. Pres. act. ptc. nom. masc. pl., μειδιάω, *smile*; circ.
46. ἀλγηδών, -όνος, ἡ, *suffering, pain*.
47. Pres. mid. ptc. nom. masc. pl., κατειρωνεύομαι, *banter with, deride in jest*; with gen.

ὁμοδοξοῦντες[75] παισὶν[76] Ἑλλήνων, ἀποφαίνονται[77] τὴν ὑπὲρ ὠκεανὸν[78] δίαιταν[79] ἀποκεῖσθαι[80] καὶ χῶρον[81] οὔτε ὄμβροις[82] οὔτε νιφετοῖς[83] οὔτε καύμασι[84] βαρυνόμενον,[85] ἀλλ᾽ ὃν ἐξ ὠκεανοῦ πραῢς[86] ἀεὶ ζέφυρος[87] ἐπιπνέων[88] ἀναψύχει·[89] ταῖς δὲ φαύλαις[90] ζοφώδη[91] καὶ χειμέριον[92] ἀφορίζονται[93] μυχόν,[94] γέμοντα[95] τιμωριῶν[96] ἀδιαλείπτων.[97] **156** δοκοῦσι δέ μοι κατὰ τὴν αὐτὴν ἔννοιαν[98] Ἕλληνες τοῖς τε[99] ἀνδρείοις[100] αὐτῶν, οὓς ἥρωας[101] καὶ ἡμιθέους[102] καλοῦσιν, τὰς μακάρων νήσους[103] ἀνατεθεικέναι,[104] ταῖς δὲ τῶν πονηρῶν ψυχαῖς καθ᾽ ᾅδου[105] τὸν ἀσεβῶν[106] χῶρον, ἔνθα[107] καὶ κολαζομένους[108] τινὰς μυθολογοῦσιν,[109] Σισύφους[110] καὶ Ταντάλους[111] Ἰξίονάς[112] τε καὶ Τιτυούς,[113] πρῶτον μὲν[114] ἀιδίους[115] ὑφιστάμενοι[116] τὰς ψυχάς, ἔπειτα εἰς προτροπὴν[117] ἀρετῆς[118] καὶ κακίας ἀποτροπήν.[119] **157** τούς τε γὰρ[120] ἀγαθοὺς γίνεσθαι κατὰ τὸν βίον[121] ἀμείνους ἐλπίδι τιμῆς καὶ μετὰ τὴν τελευτήν,[122] τῶν τε κακῶν ἐμποδίζεσθαι[123] τὰς ὁρμὰς[124] δέει[125] προσδοκώντων,[126] εἰ καὶ λάθοιεν[127] ἐν τῷ ζῆν, μετὰ τὴν διάλυσιν[128] ἀθάνατον τιμωρίαν ὑφέξειν.[129]

75. Pres. act. ptc. nom. masc. pl., ὁμοδοξέω, *hold the same opinion/view*; with dat.; circ.
76. παῖς, παιδός, ὁ, *son, child*.
77. Pres. mid. indic. 3 pl., ἀποφαίνω, (mid.) *give an opinion* (LSJ, 225.B.II).
78. ὠκεανός, -οῦ, ὁ, *ocean*.
79. δίαιτα, -ης, ἡ, *dwelling, abode*.
80. Pres. pass. inf., ἀπόκειμαι, (pass.) *be stored up*; indir. disc. See n. 59.
81. χῶρος, -ου, ὁ, *place*.
82. ὄμβρος, -ου, ὁ, *rain shower*.
83. νιφετός, -οῦ, ὁ, *snowfall*.
84. καῦμα, -ατος, τό, *heat*.
85. Pres. pass. ptc. acc. masc. sg., βαρύνω, (pass.) *be weighed down / troubled*; attrib.
86. πραΰς, -εῖα, -ΰ, *gentle*; with ἀεί, "always gentle."
87. ζέφυρος, -ου, ὁ, *zephyr, west wind*.
88. Pres. act. ptc. nom. masc. sg., ἐπιπνέω, *blow*; circ.
89. Pres. act. indic. 3 sg., ἀναψύχω, *refresh, revive*.
90. φαῦλος, -η, -ον, *bad, evil*; ταῖς φαύλαις = ταῖς φαύλαις ψυχαῖς.
91. ζοφώδης, -ες, *dark, gloomy*.
92. χειμέριος, -α, -ον, *stormy*.
93. Pres. mid. indic. 3 pl., ἀφορίζω, (mid.) *mark off, assign for* (someone).
94. μυχός, -οῦ, ὁ, *depth, abyss*.
95. Pres. act. ptc. acc. masc. sg., γέμω, *full of*; with gen.; attrib.
96. τιμωρία, -ας, ἡ, *punishment*.
97. ἀδιάλειπτος, -ον, *unceasing*.
98. ἔννοια, -ας, ἡ, *thought, conception*.
99. τε ... δέ serves a similar function to μέν ... δέ, except that τε does not typically generate the expectation of contrast (cf. S §2981).
100. ἀνδρεῖος, -α, -ον, *brave, manly*.
101. ἥρως, -ωος, ὁ, *hero*; pred. comp.
102. ἡμίθεος, -ου, ὁ, *demigod*; pred. comp.
103. νῆσος, -ου, ἡ, *island*; τὰς μακάρων νήσους, "the Islands of the Blessed."
104. Pf. act. inf., ἀνατίθημι, *set forth, assign*; indir. disc. See n. 59.

105. ᾅδης, -ου, ὁ, *Hades*; καθ᾽ ᾅδου, "down in Hades."
106. ἀσεβής, -ές, *impious, wicked*.
107. Rel. adv., *where*.
108. Pres. pass. ptc. acc. masc. pl., κολάζω, *be punished*; supp. (μυθολογοῦσιν).
109. Pres. act. indic. 3 pl., μυθολογέω, *tell stories/myths*.
110. Σίσυφος, -ου, ὁ, *Sisyphus*.
111. Τάνταλος, -ου, ὁ, *Tantalus*.
112. Ἰξίων, -ονος, ὁ, *Ixion*.
113. Τιτυός, -οῦ, ὁ, *Tityus*.
114. πρῶτον μὲν ... ἔπειτα, *first ... then* (cf. S §2910).
115. ἀίδιος, -ον, *everlasting, eternal*; pred. comp.
116. Aor. mid. ptc. nom. masc. pl., ὑφίστημι, *lay down* (a premise), *establish*; circ.
117. προτροπή, -ῆς, ἡ, *exhortation, enticement*.
118. ἀρετή, -ῆς, ἡ, *virtue*.
119. ἀποτροπή, -ῆς, ἡ, *diversion, repudiation*.
120. Partic. combination: the explanation (γάρ) has two co-ordinated points (τε ... τε).
121. βίος, -ου, ὁ, *life*.
122. τελευτή, -ῆς, ἡ, *death*.
123. Pres. pass. inf., ἐμποδίζω, (pass.) *be hindered/restrained*; indir. disc. See n. 59.
124. ὁρμή, -ῆς, ἡ, *impulse, desire*.
125. δέος, -ους, τό, *fear*.
126. Pres. act. ptc. gen. masc. pl., προσδοκάω, *expect*; with fut. inf.; attrib. (subst.).
127. Aor. act. opt. 3 pl., λανθάνω, *escape notice*; remote concessive clause: "even if *they should escape* [punishment] in living" (cf. BDF §374; S §2369; *CGCG* §49.19). On the use of the optative in a protasis, see n. 7.
128. διάλυσις, -εως, ἡ, *dissolution*.
129. Fut. act. inf., ὑπέχω, *undergo, suffer*; indir. disc. The structure of the condition is εἰ and an optative in the protasis with a future infinitive (for indicative) in the apodosis (cf. S §2361). See n. 59.

¹⁵⁸ταῦτα μὲν οὖν¹³⁰ Ἐσσηνοὶ περὶ ψυχῆς θεολογοῦσιν,¹³¹ ἄφυκτον¹³² δέλεαρ¹³³ τοῖς ἅπαξ γευσαμένοις¹³⁴ τῆς σοφίας αὐτῶν καθιέντες.¹³⁵

¹⁵⁹Εἰσὶν δ' ἐν αὐτοῖς οἳ καὶ τὰ μέλλοντα¹³⁶ προγινώσκειν¹³⁷ ὑπισχνοῦνται,¹³⁸ βίβλοις ἱεραῖς¹³⁹ καὶ διαφόροις¹⁴⁰ ἁγνείαις¹⁴¹ καὶ προφητῶν ἀποφθέγμασιν¹⁴² ἐμπαιδοτριβούμενοι·¹⁴³ σπάνιον¹⁴⁴ δ' εἴ ποτε ἐν ταῖς προαγορεύσεσιν¹⁴⁵ ἀστοχοῦσιν.¹⁴⁶

¹⁶⁰Ἔστιν δὲ καὶ ἕτερον Ἐσσηνῶν τάγμα,¹⁴⁷ δίαιταν μὲν¹⁴⁸ καὶ ἔθη καὶ νόμιμα¹⁴⁹ τοῖς ἄλλοις ὁμοφρονοῦν,¹⁵⁰ διεστὼς¹⁵¹ δὲ τῇ κατὰ γάμον¹⁵² δόξῃ· μέγιστον γὰρ ἀποκόπτειν¹⁵³ οἴονται¹⁵⁴ τοῦ βίου μέρος, τὴν διαδοχήν,¹⁵⁵ τοὺς μὴ γαμοῦντας,¹⁵⁶ μᾶλλον δέ, εἰ πάντες τὸ αὐτὸ φρονήσειαν,¹⁵⁷ ἐκλιπεῖν¹⁵⁸ ἂν τὸ γένος τάχιστα.¹⁵⁹ ¹⁶¹δοκιμάζοντες¹⁶⁰ μέντοι¹⁶¹ τριετίᾳ¹⁶² τὰς γαμετάς,¹⁶³ ἐπειδὰν τρὶς καθαρθῶσιν¹⁶⁴ εἰς πεῖραν¹⁶⁵ τοῦ δύνασθαι τίκτειν,¹⁶⁶ οὕτως ἄγονται.¹⁶⁷ Ταῖς δ' ἐγκύμοσιν¹⁶⁸ οὐχ ὁμιλοῦσιν,¹⁶⁹ ἐνδεικνύμενοι¹⁷⁰ τὸ μὴ δι' ἡδονὴν ἀλλὰ τέκνων χρείαν¹⁷¹ γαμεῖν. λουτρὰ¹⁷² δὲ ταῖς γυναιξὶν ἀμπεχομέναις¹⁷³ ἐνδύματα,¹⁷⁴ καθάπερ τοῖς ἀνδράσιν ἐν περιζώματι.¹⁷⁵ Τοιαῦτα μὲν¹⁷⁶ ἔθη τοῦδε τοῦ τάγματος.

---

130. Partic. combination: "a transition to a more to-the-point, relevant text segment (οὖν) [that] occurs in two stages (μέν . . . δέ), with the relevant new step presented in the δέ-segment; the μέν-clause typically presents a summary or rounding-off of the preceding stretch of text" (CGCG §59.73).
131. Pres. act. indic. 3 pl., θεολογέω, *speak of a god, theologize*.
132. ἄφυκτος, -ον, *inescapable*.
133. δέλεαρ, -ατος, τό, *bait*.
134. Aor. mid. ptc. dat. masc. pl., γεύομαι, *taste*; with gen.; attrib. (subst.).
135. Pres. act. ptc. nom. masc. sg., καθίημι, *set down*; circ.
136. Pres. act. ptc. acc. neut. pl., μέλλω, (subst.) *the future, future events*.
137. Pres. act. inf., προγινώσκω, *know in advance*; indir. disc. See n. 59.
138. Pres. mid. indic. 3 pl., ὑπισχνέομαι, *profess, assert*.
139. ἱερός, -ά, -όν, *holy, sacred*.
140. διάφορος, -ον, *various, different*.
141. ἁγνεία, -ας, ἡ, (pl.) *purification rituals*.
142. ἀπόφθεγμα, -ατος, τό, *utterance, saying*.
143. Pres. pass. ptc. nom. masc. pl., ἐμπαιδοτριβέομαι, (pass.) *be instructed in*; with dat.; circ.
144. Adv., *rarely*; with εἴ ποτε, "rarely, if ever."
145. προαγόρευσις, -εως, ἡ, *prediction*.
146. Pres. act. indic. 3 pl., ἀστοχέω, *miss the mark*.
147. τάγμα, -ατος, τό, *group, order*.
148. μέν . . . δέ; point/counterpoint. See n. 12.
149. νόμιμος, -α, -ον, (neut. pl.) *rules, laws*.
150. Pres. act. indic. 3 pl., ὁμοφρονέω, *be of the same mind as, agree with*; with dat.
151. Pf. act. ptc. nom. masc. sg., διίστημι, (intrans.) *be distinct*.
152. γάμος, -ου, ὁ, *marriage*; τῇ κατὰ γάμον δόξῃ, "[differing] in their opinion on marriage."
153. Pres. act. inf., ἀποκόπτω, *cut off*; indir. disc. (οἴομαι) See n. 59.
154. Pres. mid. indic. 3 pl., οἴομαι, *think*.
155. διαδοχή, -ῆς, ἡ, *succession, propagation*; tail/appositive.
156. Pres. act. ptc. acc. masc. pl., γαμέω, *marry*; attrib. (subst., as acc. subject of inf.).
157. Aor. act. opt. 3 pl., φρονέω, *think*; fourth-class, or potential, condition in indir. disc.: εἰ with opt. in the protasis, ἄν with inf. (for opt.) in the apodosis (cf. S §2329; CGCG §49.8).
158. Aor. act. inf., ἐκλείπω, *cease, come to an end*.
159. Superl. adv. of ταχύς, *very quickly*.
160. Pres. act. ptc. nom. masc. pl., δοκιμάζω, *test*; circ.
161. Postpositive partic., *however*: adversative μέντοι "indicates a transition to a text-segment which contradicts or modifies the expectations raised by the preceding context" (CGCG §59.26).
162. τριετία, -ας, ἡ, *three years*; dat. of time.
163. γαμετή, -ῆς, ἡ, *bride*.
164. Aor. pass. subj. 3 pl., καθαίρω, (pass.) *be purified*; fut. temp. clause. See n. 69.
165. πεῖρα, -ας, ἡ, *proof*. εἰς πεῖραν is purposive.
166. Pres. act. inf., τίκτω, *give birth*; comp. of art. inf. τοῦ δύνασθαι.
167. Pres. mid. indic. 3 pl., ἄγω, (mid.) *lead* (someone into marriage).
168. ἐγκύμων, -ον, (subst.) *pregnant women*.
169. Pres. act. indic. 3 pl., ὁμιλέω, *have intercourse*; with dat.
170. Pres. act. ptc. nom. masc. pl., ἐνδείκνυμι, *show*; circ. (result).
171. χρεία, -ας, ἡ, *want, need*; with gen.
172. λουτρόν, -οῦ, τό, *bath*.
173. Pres. mid. ptc. dat. fem. pl., ἀμπέχω, *put on, wear*; circ.
174. ἔνδυμα, -ατα, τό, *dress*.
175. περίζωμα, -ατος, τό, *loincloth*.
176. μέν . . . δέ; transitional. The μέν-clause concludes the section on the Essenes; the δέ-clause opens a section on the Pharisees and Sadducees.

¹⁶²Δύο δὲ τῶν προτέρων Φαρισαῖοι μὲν¹⁷⁷ οἱ μετὰ ἀκριβείας¹⁷⁸ δοκοῦντες ἐξηγεῖσθαι¹⁷⁹ τὰ νόμιμα καὶ τὴν πρώτην ἀπάγοντες¹⁸⁰ αἵρεσιν¹⁸¹ εἱμαρμένῃ¹⁸² τε καὶ θεῷ προσάπτουσι¹⁸³ πάντα, ¹⁶³καὶ τὸ μὲν¹⁸⁴ πράττειν¹⁸⁵ τὰ δίκαια καὶ μὴ κατὰ τὸ πλεῖστον ἐπὶ τοῖς ἀνθρώποις κεῖσθαι,¹⁸⁶ βοηθεῖν¹⁸⁷ δὲ εἰς ἕκαστον καὶ τὴν εἱμαρμένην· ψυχήν τε¹⁸⁸ πᾶσαν μὲν ἄφθαρτον, μεταβαίνειν¹⁸⁹ δὲ εἰς ἕτερον σῶμα τὴν τῶν ἀγαθῶν μόνην, τὰς δὲ τῶν φαύλων ἀιδίῳ τιμωρίᾳ κολάζεσθαι. ¹⁶⁴Σαδδουκαῖοι δέ, τὸ δεύτερον τάγμα, τὴν μὲν¹⁹⁰ εἱμαρμένην παντάπασιν ἀναιροῦσιν¹⁹¹ καὶ τὸν θεὸν ἔξω τοῦ δρᾶν¹⁹² τι κακὸν ἢ ἐφορᾶν τίθενται ¹⁶⁵φασὶν δ᾽ ἐπ᾽ ἀνθρώπων ἐκλογῇ¹⁹³ τό τε καλὸν καὶ τὸ κακὸν προκεῖσθαι¹⁹⁴ καὶ κατὰ γνώμην¹⁹⁵ ἑκάστου τούτων ἑκατέρῳ προσιέναι.¹⁹⁶ ψυχῆς τε τὴν διαμονὴν¹⁹⁷ καὶ τὰς καθ᾽ ᾅδου τιμωρίας καὶ τιμὰς ἀναιροῦσιν. ¹⁶⁶καὶ Φαρισαῖοι μὲν¹⁹⁸ φιλάλληλοί¹⁹⁹ τε καὶ τὴν εἰς τὸ κοινὸν ὁμόνοιαν²⁰⁰ ἀσκοῦντες,²⁰¹ Σαδδουκαίων δὲ καὶ πρὸς ἀλλήλους τὸ ἦθος ἀγριώτερον,²⁰² αἵ τε ἐπιμιξίαι²⁰³ πρὸς τοὺς ὁμοίους²⁰⁴ ἀπηνεῖς²⁰⁵ ὡς πρὸς ἀλλοτρίους. Τοιαῦτα μὲν²⁰⁶ περὶ τῶν ἐν Ἰουδαίοις φιλοσοφούντων εἶχον εἰπεῖν.

NOTES

2.152. One detects numerous points of resonance with Maccabean martyrdom literature. Mason (2008, 112n931) notes, "Of the 5 occurrences of στρεβλός in Josephus, 4 are in the *War* (1.548; 4.329; 7.373), with several of the following word clusters there as here: βάσανος ("torture"), αἰκία or αἰκίζω ("torment"), διαλέγχω ("test, prove, expose"), ὑπομένω ("endure"). These same words are concentrated, along with others graphically depicting endurance under torture, in 4 Maccabees . . . a

177. μέν . . . δέ; point (Pharisees) / counterpoint (Sadducees). See n. 12.
178. ἀκριβεία, -ας, ἡ, *precision.*
179. Pres. mid. inf., ἐξηγέομαι, *interpret.*
180. Pres. act. ptc. nom. masc. pl., ἀπάγω, *lead/take away, lead astray.* The use of the term is odd since it typically has negative associations and would seem to suggest that the Pharisees lead their followers astray. If, however, one emends to ἐπάγοντες ("lead on, influence"), it makes more sense.
181. αἵρεσις, -εως, ἡ, *philosophical school/group.*
182. εἱμαρμένη, -ης, ἡ, *fate.*
183. Pres. act. indic. 3 pl., προσάπτω, *attribute, ascribe.*
184. μέν . . . δέ. The point/counterpoint set explicates the initial μέν-clause (cf. S §2908).
185. Pres. act. inf., πράσσω (Att. πράττω), *do.* The articular infinitive functions as the accusative subject of the indirect discourse: "[They maintain] that to act justly or not [τὸ πράττειν τὰ δίκαια καὶ μή] rests for the most part with human beings."
186. Pres. pass. inf., κεῖμαι, (pass.) *be set before* (someone); indir. disc. See n. 59.
187. Pres. act. inf., βοηθέω, *aid, assist;* with dat.; indir. disc. (see n. 59): "but that in each action fate also assists [humans]."
188. Partic. combination: addition (τε) of a second point/counterpoint (μέν . . . δέ . . . δέ) set within the initial μέν-clause.
189. Pres. act. inf., μεταβαίνω, *pass* (from one state to another); indir. disc. See n. 59.
190. μέν . . . δέ. The point/counterpoint set explicates the δέ-clause. See n. 184.
191. Pres. act. indic. 3 pl., ἀναιρέω, *do away with.*
192. Pres. act. inf., δράω, *do.* Art. inf. as obj. of ἔξω; lit., "They place God *outside of doing* or *overseeing* any evil."
193. ἐκλογή, -ῆς, ἡ, *free choice.*

194. Pres. pass. inf., πρόκειμαι, *lie before;* indir. disc. (φασίν). See n. 59.
195. γνώμη, -ης, ἡ, *will, disposition, inclination.*
196. Pres. act. inf., πρόσειμι, *go toward;* with dat.; indir. disc. (see n. 59): "and that based on each person's will, she or he pursues one of these or the other [i.e., good or evil]."
197. διαμονή, -ῆς, ἡ, *persistence.*
198. μέν . . . δέ; point/counterpoint. See n. 12.
199. φιλάλληλος, -ον, *displaying mutual love/affection.*
200. ὁμόνοια, -ας, ἡ, *concord;* τὴν εἰς τὸ κοινὸν ὁμόνοιαν, "concord with the general public."
201. Pres. act. ptc. nom. masc. pl., ἀσκέω, *practice.*
202. Compar., ἄγριος, -α, -ον, *harsher, more boorish.*
203. ἐπιμιξία, -ας, ἡ, *mixing, intercourse.*
204. ὅμοιος, -α, -ον, *like, similar.* It is not entirely clear whether "those like them" are members of other schools or fellow Judeans more broadly. In any case, the point is that they engage them "as they would foreigners."
205. ἀπηνής, -ές, *harsh.*
206. μέν . . . δέ; transitional. The μέν-clause concludes the lengthy excursus on the philosophical schools (2.119–166), while the δέ-clause returns to the main narrative (2.167).

fact that seems to highlight Josephus' debt to this work." Additional Maccabean parallels are (1) torture by burning (cf. 4 Macc. 6:26–27), (2) the terms βασανιστήριον (cf. 4 Macc. 6:1) and "instruments [ὄργανα] of torture" (cf. 4 Macc. 6:25), (3) compulsion to eat unlawful food (cf. 2 Macc. 7:1; 4 Macc. 5:1–2), and (4) the martyrs' eager release of their souls (cf. 2 Macc. 6:23; 7:11; 4 Macc. 6:27–30).

2.154–158. Josephus presents the Essene view of the afterlife as a variation of Plato's: bodies return to the earth, souls to the ether. A few Dead Sea Scrolls mention resurrection (most notably, 4Q521), but the concept of bodily resurrection does not feature prominently in this corpus. For further discussion, see Klawans (2012, 111–15) and Elledge (2017).

2.158. θεολογοῦσιν. The verb is attested as early as the pre-Socratics but is rare. Josephus wants his readers to appreciate the contrast: the Greeks *myth*ologize (μυθολογοῦσιν, 2.156), while the Essenes (and Jews in general) *theo*logize (θεολογοῦσιν) (Mason 2008, 128n974).

2.165. ψυχῆς τε τὴν διαμονὴν . . . ἀναιροῦσιν. This statement has been taken to mean that the Sadducees have no concept of the afterlife. As Klawans (2012, 93) notes, however, "When a source tells us that a given group denies resurrection, that may or may not mean that the group denies all forms of the afterlife. Even when we are told that a group denies immortality of the soul, other afterlife notions may have been believed nonetheless." It may be that the Sadducees held to the dominant position of the sages before them (e.g., Proverbs, Ecclesiastes, Sirach): "The only immortality one should wish for is to be remembered for good, by plenty of progeny" (Klawans 2012, 106).

5.1.5

Another Jesus Predicts the Destruction of the Temple

Jewish War 6.300–309

6.300τὸ δὲ τούτων φοβερώτερον,¹ Ἰησοῦς γάρ τις υἱὸς Ἀνανίου² τῶν ἰδιωτῶν³ ἄγροικος,⁴ πρὸ τεσσάρων ἐτῶν τοῦ πολέμου⁵ τὰ μάλιστα⁶ τῆς πόλεως εἰρηνευομένης⁷ καὶ εὐθηνούσης,⁸ ἐλθὼν εἰς τὴν ἑορτήν,⁹ ἐν ᾗ σκηνοποιεῖσθαι¹⁰ πάντας ἔθος¹¹ τῷ θεῷ, κατὰ τὸ ἱερὸν¹² ἐξαπίνης¹³ ἀναβοᾶν¹⁴ ἤρξατο "φωνὴ ἀπὸ ἀνατολῆς,¹⁵ **301**φωνὴ ἀπὸ δύσεως,¹⁶ φωνὴ ἀπὸ τῶν τεσσάρων ἀνέμων,¹⁷ φωνὴ ἐπὶ Ἱεροσόλυμα καὶ τὸν ναόν,¹⁸ φωνὴ ἐπὶ νυμφίους¹⁹ καὶ νύμφας,²⁰ φωνὴ ἐπὶ τὸν λαὸν πάντα." τοῦτο μεθ᾽ ἡμέραν καὶ νύκτωρ²¹ κατὰ πάντας τοὺς στενωποὺς²² περιῄει²³ κεκραγώς.²⁴ **302**τῶν δὲ ἐπισήμων²⁵ τινὲς δημοτῶν²⁶ ἀγανακτήσαντες²⁷ πρὸς τὸ κακόφημον²⁸ συλλαμβάνουσι²⁹ τὸν

1. Compar., φοβερός, -ά, -όν, *more terrifying*; τὸ δὲ τούτων φοβερώτερον, "But there was one more terrifying than these [aforementioned portents]."
2. Ἀνάνιος, -ου, ὁ, *Ananias*. Most MSS read Ἀνάνου, "Ananus."
3. ἰδιώτης, -ου, ὁ, *untrained person, commoner*.
4. ἄγροικος, -ον, *of the countryside, rude, boorish*.
5. πόλεμος, -ου, ὁ, *war*.
6. Adv. acc. of μάλα, *in the highest degree*.
7. Pres. mid. ptc. gen. fem. sg., εἰρηνεύω, *live peaceably*; gen. absol.
8. Pres. act. ptc. gen. fem. sg., εὐθηνέω, *thrive*; gen. absol.
9. ἑορτή, -ῆς, ἡ, *festival*.
10. Pres. mid. inf., σκηνοποιέω, *build tabernacles*.
11. ἔθος, -ους, τό, (quasi-impers.) *it is customary*; with acc. and inf. (cf. S §2004; CGCG §51.9).
12. ἱερόν, -οῦ, τό, *temple*.
13. Adv., *suddenly*.
14. Pres. act. inf., ἀναβοάω, *cry out*; comp. of ἤρξατο.

15. ἀνατολή, -ῆς, ἡ, *east*.
16. δύσις, -εως, ἡ, *west*.
17. ἄνεμος, -ου, ὁ, *wind*.
18. ναός, -οῦ, ὁ, *sanctuary* (of the temple complex).
19. νυμφίος, -ου, ὁ, *bridegroom*.
20. νύμφη, -ης, ἡ, *bride*.
21. μεθ᾽ ἡμέραν καὶ νύκτωρ, "by day and by night" (cf. LSJ, 1109.C.II.2).
22. στενωπός, -ον, (subst.) *narrow passage, alley*.
23. Impf. act. indic. 3 sg., περίημι, *go about*; iterative.
24. Pf. act. ptc. nom. masc. sg., κράζω, *cry out*; circ. (manner).
25. ἐπίσημος, -ον, *leading, distinguished*.
26. δημότης, -ου, ὁ, *citizen*.
27. Aor. act. ptc. nom. masc. pl., ἀγανακτέω, *be vexed, angered*; circ.
28. κακόφημος, -ον, *ill-sounding, ominous*.
29. Pres. act. indic. 3 pl., συλλαμβάνω, *seize, arrest*.

ἄνθρωπον καὶ πολλαῖς αἰκίζονται[30] πληγαῖς.[31] ὁ δὲ οὔθ' ὑπὲρ αὑτοῦ[32] φθεγξάμενος[33] οὔτε ἰδίᾳ[34] πρὸς τοὺς παίοντας,[35] ἃς καὶ πρότερον φωνὰς[36] βοῶν[37] διετέλει.[38] **303**νομίσαντες[39] δὲ οἱ ἄρχοντες, ὅπερ ἦν,[40] δαιμονιώτερον[41] τὸ κίνημα[42] τἀνδρὸς[43] ἀνάγουσιν αὐτὸν ἐπὶ τὸν παρὰ Ῥωμαίοις ἔπαρχον.[44] **304**ἔνθα[45] μάστιξι[46] μέχρι ὀστέων[47] ξαινόμενος[48] οὔθ' ἱκέτευσεν[49] οὔτ' ἐδάκρυσεν,[50] ἀλλ' ὡς ἐνῆν[51] μάλιστα τὴν φωνὴν ὀλοφυρτικῶς[52] παρεγκλίνων[53] πρὸς ἑκάστην ἀπεκρίνατο πληγήν "αἰαὶ[54] Ἱεροσολύμοις." **305**τοῦ δ' Ἀλβίνου[55] διερωτῶντος,[56] οὗτος γὰρ ἔπαρχος ἦν, τίς εἴη[57] καὶ πόθεν,[58] καὶ διὰ τί[59] ταῦτα φθέγγοιτο,[60] πρὸς ταῦτα μὲν[61] οὐδ' ὁτιοῦν[62] ἀπεκρίνατο, τὸν δὲ ἐπὶ τῇ πόλει θρῆνον[63] εἴρων[64] οὐ διέλειπεν,[65] μέχρι καταγνοὺς[66] μανίαν[67] ὁ Ἀλβῖνος ἀπέλυσεν αὐτόν. **306**ὁ δὲ τὸν μέχρι τοῦ πολέμου χρόνον οὔτε προσῄει[68] τινὶ τῶν πολιτῶν[69] οὔτε ὤφθη λαλῶν, ἀλλὰ καθ' ἡμέραν ὥσπερ εὐχὴν μεμελετηκὼς[70] "αἰαὶ Ἱεροσολύμοις" ἐθρήνει.[71] **307**οὔτε δέ τινι τῶν τυπτόντων[72] αὐτὸν ὁσημέραι[73] κατηρᾶτο[74] οὔτε τοὺς τροφῆς[75] μεταδιδόντας εὐλόγει,[76] μία δὲ πρὸς πάντας ἦν ἡ σκυθρωπὴ[77] κληδὼν[78] ἀπόκρισις.[79] **308**μάλιστα δ' ἐν ταῖς ἑορταῖς ἐκεκράγει·[80] καὶ τοῦτ' ἐφ' ἑπτὰ ἔτη καὶ μῆνας πέντε[81] εἴρων οὔτ' ἤμβλυνεν[82] τὴν φωνὴν οὔτ' ἔκαμεν,[83] μέχρις οὗ κατὰ τὴν

30. Pres. mid. indic. 3 pl., αἰκίζω, *torture*.
31. πληγή, -ῆς, ἡ, *blow, stroke*; dat. of means.
32. αὑτοῦ = ἑαυτοῦ.
33. Aor. mid. ptc. nom. masc. sg., φθέγγομαι, *make a sound, utter a word*; circ.
34. Adv., *privately*.
35. Pres. act. ptc. acc. masc. pl., παίω, *strike*; attrib. (subst.).
36. The antecedent is incorporated into the relative clause (cf. S §2536; *CGCG* §50.15): "He would continue crying out *the utterances that* he also cried out before."
37. Pres. act. ptc. nom. masc. sg., βοάω, *shout, cry out*; supp. (διατελέω).
38. Impf. act. indic. 3 pl., διατελέω, *continue, persist*.
39. Aor. act. ptc. nom. masc. pl., νομίζω, *think, suppose*; circ.
40. ὅπερ ἦν, "which was, in fact, the case."
41. Compar., δαιμόνιος, -α, -ον, *more miraculous, supernatural*.
42. κίνημα, -ατος, τό, *movement, impulse*.
43. Crasis: τἀνδρός = τοῦ ἀνδρός.
44. ἔπαρχος, -ου, ὁ, *governor*, (Lat.) *procurator*.
45. Demon. adv., *there*.
46. μάστιξ, -ικος, ἡ, *whip*; dat. of instrument.
47. ὀστέον, -ου, τό, *bone*; μέχρι ὀστέων, "to the bone."
48. Pres. pass. ptc. nom. masc. sg., ξαίνω, (pass.) *be lacerated*; circ.
49. Aor. act. indic. 3 sg., ἱκετεύω, *beg, beseech*.
50. Aor. act. indic. 3 sg., δακρύω, *shed tears*.
51. Impf. act. indic. 3 sg., ἔνειμι, *be possible*; ὡς ἐνῆν μάλιστα, "as much as he was able."
52. Adv., *in a manner of lament*.
53. Pres. act. ptc. nom. masc. sg., παρεγκλίνω, *modify, alter slightly*; circ.
54. Interjection, *Woe!*
55. Ἀλβῖνος, -ου, ὁ, *Albinus* (procurator of Judea, 62–64 CE).
56. Pres. act. ptc. gen. masc. sg., διερωτάω, *cross-question*; gen. absol.
57. Pres. act. opt. 3 sg., εἰμί; oblique opt. in indir. quest. (cf. BDF §368; S §2599; *CGCG* §42.7).
58. Adv., *From where?*
59. διὰ τί, *Why?*
60. Pres. mid. opt. 3 sg., φθέγγομαι, *utter*; oblique opt. in indir. quest. See n. 57.
61. μέν . . . δέ; point/counterpoint set (cf. Runge 2010, 75–83; BDF §447; S §2904; *CGCG* §59.24).
62. ὁστισοῦν, ἡτισοῦν, ὁτιοῦν, *whosoever, whatsoever*.
63. θρῆνος, -ου, ὁ, *dirge, lament*.
64. Pres. act. ptc. nom. masc. sg., εἴρω, *speak*; supp. (διαλείπω).
65. Impf. act. indic. 3 sg., διαλείπω, *cease*.
66. Aor. act. ptc. nom. masc. sg., καταγινώσκω, *pronounce judgment*; circ.
67. μανία, -ας, ἡ, *madness, mania*; pred. comp.
68. Impf. act. indic. 3 sg., πρόσειμι, *approach*; with dat.; iterative.
69. πολίτης, -ου, ὁ, *citizen*.
70. Pf. act. ptc. nom. masc. sg., μελετάω, *recite*; circ. (comparison).
71. Impf. act. indic. 3 sg., θρηνέω, *wail in lament, sing a dirge*.
72. Pres. act. ptc. gen. masc. pl., τύπτω, *strike*; attrib. (subst.).
73. Adv., *daily*.
74. Impf. act. indic. 3 sg., καταράομαι, *call down a curse*.
75. τροφή, -ῆς, ἡ, *food*.
76. Pres. act. indic. 3 sg., εὐλογέω, *bless*.
77. σκυθρωπός, -ή, -όν, *melancholy, gloomy*.
78. κληδών, -όνος, ἡ, *portent, omen*.
79. ἀπόκρισις, -εως, ἡ, *response, reply*.
80. Plpf. act. indic. 3 sg., κράζω, *cry out*. The pluperfect is often used in narrative to provide background information (cf. *CGCG* §33.50).
81. Acc. of extent (time): "for seven years and five months."
82. Aor. act. indic. 3 sg., ἀμβλύνω, *dull, dim, take the edge off*.
83. Aor. act. indic. 3 sg., κάμνω, *become tired*.

πολιορκίαν⁸⁴ ἔργα τῆς κληδόνος ἰδὼν ἀνεπαύσατο.⁸⁵ ³⁰⁹περιὼν⁸⁶ γὰρ ἀπὸ τοῦ τείχους⁸⁷ "αἰαὶ πάλιν τῇ πόλει καὶ τῷ λαῷ καὶ τῷ ναῷ" διαπρύσιον⁸⁸ ἐβόα, ὡς δὲ τελευταῖον⁸⁹ προσέθηκεν⁹⁰ "αἰαὶ δὲ κἀμοί," λίθος ἐκ τοῦ πετροβόλου⁹¹ σχασθεὶς⁹² καὶ πλήξας⁹³ αὐτὸν παραχρῆμα⁹⁴ κτείνει,⁹⁵ φθεγγομένην δ' ἔτι τὰς κληδόνας ἐκείνας τὴν ψυχὴν ἀφῆκε.⁹⁶

NOTES

6.300. Like Jesus of Nazareth, who used the Passover, Jesus son of Ananias (Ananus) used a festival (Sukkoth) as an opportunity to portend the destruction of the temple. For additional portents and predictions of the temple's destruction, cf. Tacitus, *Hist.* 5.13; y. Yoma 1.4, 39a; b. Yoma 39b; b. Pesah. 57a; b. Git. 56a.

6.300–301. The language of Jesus's prophecy recalls Jer. 7:34. Cf. Mark 11:17 parr., which cite Jer. 7:7 as the reason for the temple's destruction. That the deity will abandon his defiled temple (cf. *B.J.* 5.19–20, 411–412) is to be expected. "Indeed, it would appear that practically all extant Jewish literature interpreting the catastrophe of 70 CE—Josephan, apocalyptic, and rabbinic—agrees on these few, not insignificant points: the destruction was orchestrated by God, to punish a sinful people, in a way that recalls earlier catastrophes, especially that of 586 BCE" (Klawans 2012, 201).

---

84. πολιορκία, -ας, ἡ, *siege*.
85. Aor. mid. indic. 3 sg., ἀναπαύω, (mid.) *take rest*.
86. Pres. act. ptc. nom. masc. sg., περίειμι, *go around*; circ.
87. τεῖχος, -ους, τό, *wall*.
88. Adv. acc., διαπρύσιος, -α, -ον, *with piercing sounds, shrilly*.
89. Adv. acc., τελευταῖος, -ον, *finally, at last*.
90. Aor. act. indic. 3 sg., προστίθημι, *add* (something).
91. πετρόβολος, -ου, ὁ, *ballista, engine for throwing stones*.
92. Aor. pass. ptc. nom. masc. sg., σχάζω, (pass.) *be launched*; circ.
93. Aor. act. ptc. nom. masc. sg., πλήσσω, *strike*; circ.
94. Adv., *instantly*.
95. Pres. act. indic. 3 sg., κτείνω, *kill*.
96. Aor. act. indic. 3 sg., ἀφίημι, *let go, release*.

5.2

Jewish Antiquities

Josephus completed his twenty-volume magnum opus, *Jewish Antiquities*, and its appendix, *The Life* (on which, see §5.3), a decade or more after *Jewish War*. The work is structured around the theme of the Jerusalem temple: volume 10 concludes with the destruction of the first temple, while volume 20 concludes on the eve of the destruction of the second temple (Mason 2003, 99). The prologue introduces four major themes of the work: "(a) the antiquity of the Jews; (b) their constitution; (c) their philosophy; and (d) Josephus's moralizing evaluation of major figures" (Mason 2003, 103). Throughout Josephus aims to present a favorable, and indeed definitive, account of Jewish history to the Greco-Roman world.

Moreover, as Feldman (1988, 455) states, "Second only perhaps to his significance as a historian is Josephus's importance for our knowledge of the text and interpretation of the Bible in the first century." Numerous studies are devoted to Josephus's sources and narrative techniques (see, e.g., Attridge 1976; Feldman 1988, 1998; Rodgers 2012). He appears to draw on multiple versions of the Old Testament, relays numerous extrabiblical traditions, and as with many of his contemporaries, does not distinguish between translation and commentary.

This section includes four readings from *Jewish Antiquities*: a section of the prologue, in which Josephus outlines the moral lesson of the work; his retelling of the sacrifice of Isaac (Gen. 22); his account of the departure of Moses (Deut. 34); and his narrative of the conversion of King Izates.

Text and Translation: Thackeray 1930a (§§5.2.1–2); Thackeray 1930b (§5.2.3); Feldman 1965 (§5.2.4)

Supplemental Scripture: Gen. 22 (§5.2.2); Deut. 34; Acts 1:6–11 (§5.2.3); Acts 15:1–21; Gal. 2:1–10 (§5.2.4)

5.2.1

The Moral Lesson of *Jewish Antiquities*

Jewish Antiquities 1.14–17

1.14τὸ σύνολον¹ δὲ μάλιστά² τις ἂν ἐκ ταύτης μάθοι³ τῆς ἱστορίας⁴ ἐθελήσας⁵ αὐτὴν διελεῖν,⁶ ὅτι τοῖς μὲν⁷ θεοῦ γνώμῃ⁸ κατακολουθοῦσι⁹ καὶ τὰ καλῶς νομοθετηθέντα¹⁰ μὴ τολμῶσι¹¹ παραβαίνειν¹² πάντα κατορθοῦται¹³ πέρα¹⁴ πίστεως καὶ γέρας¹⁵ εὐδαιμονία¹⁶ πρόκειται¹⁷ παρὰ θεοῦ· καθ' ὅσον¹⁸ δ' ἂν ἀποστῶσι¹⁹ τῆς τούτων ἀκριβοῦς²⁰ ἐπιμελείας,²¹ ἄπορα²² μὲν²³ γίνεται τὰ πόριμα,²⁴ τρέπεται²⁵ δὲ εἰς συμφορὰς²⁶ ἀνηκέστους²⁷ ὅ τι ποτ' ἂν ὡς ἀγαθὸν δρᾶν²⁸ σπουδάσωσιν.²⁹ **15**ἤδη

1. σύνολος, -ον, (used adverbially, with the art.) *on the whole, in general*.
2. Superl. adv. of μάλα, *above all, for the most part*.
3. Aor. act. opt. 3 sg., μανθάνω, *learn*; potential (cf. BDF §385; S §1824; CGCG §34.13).
4. ἱστορία, -ας, ἡ, *history*.
5. Aor. act. ptc. nom. masc. sg., (ἐ)θέλω, *want, wish*; circ. (conditional).
6. Aor. act. inf., διέρχομαι, *go through*; comp. of ἐθελήσας.
7. μέν . . . δέ; point/counterpoint set (cf. Runge 2010, 75–83; BDF §447; S §2904; CGCG §59.24).
8. γνώμη, -ης, ἡ, *intention, purpose*.
9. Pres. act. ptc. dat. masc. pl., κατακολουθέω, *follow*; with dat.; attrib. (subst.).
10. Aor. pass. ptc. acc. neut. pl., νομοθετέω, (pass.) *be legislated*; attrib. (subst.).
11. Pres. act. ptc. dat. masc. pl., τολμάω, *dare*; attrib. (subst.).
12. Pres. act. inf., παραβαίνω, *transgress*; comp. of τολμῶσι.
13. Pres. pass. indic. 3 sg., κατορθόω, (intrans.) *go on to prosper, succeed*.

14. Prep. with gen., *more than, beyond, exceeding*; πέρα πίστεως, "beyond belief."
15. γέρας, -ως, τό, *reward*; pred. comp.
16. εὐδαιμονία, -ας, ἡ, *blessedness, happiness, prosperity*.
17. Pres. pass. indic. 3 sg., πρόκειμαι, *be set before*.
18. Adv. acc. of extent, *insofar as, to the extent that*.
19. Aor. act. subj. 3 pl., ἀφίστημι, *depart from*; conditional rel. clause (cf. BDF §380; S §2560; CGCG §50.20).
20. ἀκριβής, -ές, *exact, careful, precise*.
21. ἐπιμελεία, -ας, ἡ, *attention*; gen. of separation.
22. ἄπορος, -ον, *impracticable, impossible*.
23. μέν . . . δέ; point/counterpoint set explicates δέ-clause (cf. S §2908).
24. πόριμος, -ον, *practicable, possible*.
25. Pres. pass. indic. 3 sg., τρέπω, (pass.) *be turned, changed*. The impersonal subject is explicated in the relative clause; lit., "*It* is turned toward accompanying disaster, *whatever seemingly good thing they strive at any point to do*."
26. συμφορά, -ᾶς, ἡ, *misfortune*.
27. ἀνήκεστος, -ον, *incurable, fatal*.
28. Pres. act. inf., δράω, *do*.
29. Aor. act. subj. 3 sg., σπουδάζω, *be eager to, strive to*; with inf.; conditional rel. clause. See n. 19.

τοίνυν³⁰ τοὺς ἐντευξομένους³¹ τοῖς βιβλίοις παρακαλῶ³² τὴν γνώμην θεῷ προσανέχειν³³ καὶ δοκιμάζειν³⁴ τὸν ἡμέτερον νομοθέτην,³⁵ εἰ τήν τε φύσιν³⁶ ἀξίως αὐτοῦ κατενόησε³⁷ καὶ τῇ δυνάμει πρεπούσας³⁸ ἀεὶ³⁹ τὰς πράξεις⁴⁰ ἀνατέθεικε⁴¹ πάσης καθαρὸν τὸν περὶ αὐτοῦ φυλάξας⁴² λόγον τῆς παρ' ἄλλοις ἀσχήμονος⁴³ μυθολογίας·⁴⁴ ¹⁶καίτοι γε⁴⁵ ὅσον ἐπὶ μήκει⁴⁶ χρόνου καὶ παλαιότητι⁴⁷ πολλὴν εἶχεν ἄδειαν⁴⁸ ψευδῶν⁴⁹ πλασμάτων·⁵⁰ γέγονε γὰρ πρὸ ἐτῶν δισχιλίων, ἐφ' ὅσον πλῆθος⁵¹ αἰῶνος οὐδ' αὐτῶν οἱ ποιηταὶ⁵² τὰς γενέσεις⁵³ τῶν θεῶν, μήτι γε⁵⁴ τὰς τῶν ἀνθρώπων πράξεις ἢ τοὺς νόμους ἀνενεγκεῖν⁵⁵ ἐτόλμησαν. ¹⁷τὰ μὲν οὖν⁵⁶ ἀκριβῆ τῶν ἐν ταῖς ἀναγραφαῖς⁵⁷ προϊὼν⁵⁸ ὁ λόγος κατὰ τὴν οἰκείαν τάξιν⁵⁹ σημανεῖ·⁶⁰ τοῦτο γὰρ διὰ ταύτης ποιήσειν τῆς πραγματείας⁶¹ ἐπηγγειλάμην⁶² οὐδὲν προσθεὶς⁶³ οὐδ' αὖ⁶⁴ παραλιπών.⁶⁵

NOTE

1.14–16. Cf. Philo, *Opif.* 1–6 (see §4.2.1).

30. Partic., *then, so*: "indicates a transition to a newly relevant, to-the-point text segment (νυν), and stresses the importance or relevance for the addressee of that new point (τοι)" (*CGCG* §59.39).
31. Fut. act. ptc. acc. masc. pl., ἐντυγχάνω, (of books) *read*; with dat.; attrib. (subst.).
32. Pres. act. indic. 1 sg., παρακαλέω, *exhort, entreat*; with acc. and inf.
33. Pres. act. inf., προσανέχω, (with τὴν γνώμην) *fix one's thought upon*; with dat.
34. Pres. act. inf., δοκιμάζω, *test, examine*.
35. νομοθέτης, -ου, ὁ, *lawgiver*.
36. φύσις, -εως, ἡ, *nature*.
37. Aor. act. indic. 3 sg., κατανοέω, *understand, apprehend*.
38. Pres. act. ptc. acc. fem. pl., πρέπω, *be fitting, suitable to*; with dat.; attrib.
39. Adv., *always*.
40. πρᾶξις, -εως, ἡ, *action*.
41. Pf. act. indic. 3 sg., ἀνατίθημι, *assign*.
42. Aor. act. ptc. nom. masc. sg., φυλάσσω, *guard, keep from*; circ.
43. ἀσχήμων, -ον, *unseemly, shameful*.
44. μυθολογία, -ας, ἡ, *mythology*; abl. gen. comp. of καθαρόν; "having kept his speech about him [God] pure *from all unseemly mythology* that is among others [other lawgivers]."
45. Partic. combination, *and yet, and that even though*: "invites a reconsideration of what the speaker has just said" (καίτοι), which receives focused concentration (γε) (*CGCG* §59.23; cf. §59.53).
46. μῆκος, -εος, τό, *length*.
47. παλαιότης, -ητος, ἡ, *antiquity*.
48. ἄδεια, -ας, ἡ, *freedom from fear, license*; with gen.
49. ψευδής, -ές, *false*.
50. πλάσμα, -ατος, τό, *something formed/contrived*.
51. πλῆθος, -ους, τό, *length* (of time); acc. of extent.
52. ποιητής, -οῦ, ὁ, *poet*.
53. γένεσις, -εως, ἡ, *genesis, origin*.
54. Partic., *not to mention, much less*; γε concentrates/focuses on μήτι (BDAG, 649).
55. Aor. act. inf., ἀναφέρω, *carry, trace back*; comp. of ἐτόλημσαν.
56. Partic. combination: "a transition to a more to-the-point, relevant text segment (οὖν) [that] occurs in two stages (μέν . . . δέ)" (*CGCG* §59.73). The μέν-clause presents a summary or rounds off the preceding stretch of text, while the δέ-clause introduces a new point (*A.J.* 1.18).
57. ἀναγραφή, -ῆς, ἡ, *record*; topic: τὰ . . . ἀκριβῆ τῶν ἐν ταῖς ἀναγραφαῖς, "as to the precise details of the things in our scriptural records."
58. Pres. act. ptc. nom. masc. sg., πρόειμι, *go forth, advance, proceed*; circ.
59. τάξις, -εως, ἡ, *order*; κατὰ τὴν οἰκείαν τάξιν, "in their proper order."
60. Fut. act. indic. 3 sg., σημαίνω, *signify, declare, explain*.
61. πραγματεία, -ας, ἡ, *treatment* (of a subject).
62. Aor. mid. indic. 1 sg., ἐπαγγέλλω, *promise*.
63. Aor. act. ptc. nom. masc. sg., προστίθημι, *add*; circ.
64. Adv., *in turn, on the other hand*.
65. Aor. act. ptc. nom. masc. sg., παραλείπω, *pass over, omit*; circ.

5.2.2

The Binding of Isaac

Jewish Antiquities 1.222–224, 228–236

1.222ᵛἼσακον¹ δὲ ὁ πατὴρ Ἅβραμος ὑπερηγάπα² μονογενῆ³ ὄντα καὶ ἐπὶ γήρως οὐδῷ⁴ κατὰ δωρεὰν⁵ αὐτῷ τοῦ θεοῦ γενόμενον. προεκαλεῖτο⁶ δὲ εἰς εὔνοιαν⁷ καὶ τὸ φιλεῖσθαι⁸ μᾶλλον ὑπὸ τῶν γονέων⁹ καὶ αὐτὸς ὁ παῖς¹⁰ ἐπιτηδεύων¹¹ πᾶσαν ἀρετὴν¹² καὶ τῆς τε τῶν πατέρων θεραπείας¹³ ἐχόμενος καὶ περὶ τὴν τοῦ θεοῦ θρησκείαν¹⁴ ἐσπουδακώς.¹⁵ **223**ᵛἌβραμος δὲ τὴν ἰδίαν εὐδαιμονίαν¹⁶ ἐν μόνῳ τῷ¹⁷ τὸν υἱὸν ἀπαθῆ¹⁸ καταλιπὼν¹⁹ ἐξελθεῖν τοῦ ζῆν ἐτίθετο. τούτου μέντοι²⁰ κατὰ τὴν τοῦ θεοῦ βούλησιν²¹ ἔτυχεν,²² ὃς διάπειραν²³ αὐτοῦ βουλόμενος λαβεῖν τῆς περὶ αὐτὸν θρησκείας ἐμφανισθεὶς²⁴ αὐτῷ καὶ πάντα ὅσα εἴη²⁵ παρεσχημένος καταριθμησάμενος,²⁶ **224**ὡς πολεμίων²⁷ τε κρείττονα

1. Ἴσακος, -ου, ὁ (Ἴσαακ in LXX); topic (cf. *CGCG* §60.27).
2. Impf. act. indic. 3 sg., ὑπεραγαπάω, *love exceedingly*.
3. μονογενής, -ές, *unique, one of a kind*.
4. οὐδός, -οῦ, ὁ, *threshold*; ἐπὶ γήρως οὐδῷ, "at the threshold of old age" (Homeric).
5. δωρεά, -ᾶς, ἡ, *gift, bounty*.
6. Impf. mid. indic. 3 sg., προκαλέω, *call out, invite, incite* (someone to something).
7. εὔνοια, -ας, ἡ, *good will, favor*.
8. Pres. pass. inf., φιλέω, (pass.) *be loved*; art. inf. as obj.: "He incited affection and *being loved* even more by his parents" (cf. BDF §399; S §2034; *CGCG* §51.39).
9. γονεύς, -έως, ὁ, (pl.) *parents*.
10. παῖς, παιδός, ὁ, *child*.
11. Pres. act. ptc. nom. masc. sg., ἐπιτηδεύω, *pursue, practice*; circ.
12. ἀρετή, -ῆς, ἡ, *virtue*.
13. θεραπεία, -ας, ἡ, *service, devotion, care*; gen. comp. of ἐχόμενος.
14. θρησκεία, -ας, ἡ, *devotion/service to a god*.
15. Pf. act. ptc. nom. masc. sg., σπουδάζω, *be eager, zealously pursue*; circ.

16. εὐδαιμονία, -ας, ἡ, *happiness, blessedness*.
17. The articular infinitive τῷ . . . ἐξελθεῖν is the object of the preposition ἐν. Thus, "Abraham placed his own happiness *in only departing* from life leaving his son free from suffering."
18. ἀπαθής, -ές, *without suffering*; pred. comp.
19. Aor. act. ptc. nom. masc. sg., καταλείπω, *leave*; with gen.; circ.
20. Partic., *certainly, of course, in truth*. Assertive μέντοι "indicates that the speaker is committed to the truth or relevance of his statement, no matter what the addressee might expect (μήν), and brings that commitment home to the addressee (τοι)" (*CGCG* §59.28; cf. S §2918).
21. βούλησις, -εως, ἡ, *purpose, will*.
22. Aor. act. indic. 3 sg., τυγχάνω, *obtain*; with gen.
23. διάπειρα, -ας, ἡ, *test, trial, proof*.
24. Aor. pass. ptc. nom. masc. sg., ἐμφανίζω, (pass.) *be manifest*.
25. Pres. act. opt. 3 sg., εἰμί; periphrastic εἴη παρεσχημένος; iterative opt. in past general rel. clause (cf. S §2568; *CGCG* §50.21): "as much as he has granted him."
26. Aor. mid. ptc. nom. masc. sg., καταριθμέω, *enumerate*; circ.
27. πολέμιος, -α, -ον, (subst.) *enemy*; gen. of comparison.

ποιήσειε²⁸ καὶ τὴν παροῦσαν²⁹ εὐδαιμονίαν ἐκ τῆς αὐτοῦ σπουδῆς³⁰ ἔχοι³¹ καὶ τὸν υἱὸν Ἴσακον, ᾔτει³² τοῦτον αὐτῷ θῦμα³³ καὶ ἱερεῖον³⁴ [αὐτὸν] παρασχεῖν,³⁵ ἐκέλευέ³⁶ τε εἰς τὸ Μώριον ὄρος³⁷ ἀναγαγόντα³⁸ ὁλοκαυτῶσαι³⁹ βωμὸν⁴⁰ ἱδρυσάμενον·⁴¹ οὕτως γὰρ ἐμφανίσειν⁴² τὴν περὶ αὐτὸν θρησκείαν, εἰ καὶ τῆς τοῦ τέκνου σωτηρίας προτιμήσειε⁴³ τὸ τῷ θεῷ κεχαρισμένον.⁴⁴ . . .

228 Ὡς δ' ὁ βωμὸς παρεσκεύαστο⁴⁵ καὶ τὰς σχίζας⁴⁶ ἐπενηνόχει⁴⁷ καὶ ἦν εὐτρεπῆ,⁴⁸ λέγει πρὸς τὸν υἱόν "ὦ παῖ, μυρίαις εὐχαῖς⁴⁹ αἰτησάμενός σε γενέσθαι μοι παρὰ τοῦ θεοῦ, ἐπεὶ παρῆλθες εἰς τὸν βίον, οὐκ ἔστιν ὅ τι μὴ⁵⁰ περὶ τὴν σὴν ἀνατροφὴν⁵¹ ἐφιλοτιμησάμην⁵² οὐδ' ἐφ' ᾧ μᾶλλον εὐδαιμονήσειν⁵³ ᾤμην,⁵⁴ ὡς⁵⁵ εἰ σέ τ' ἴδοιμι⁵⁶ ἠνδρωμένον⁵⁷ καὶ τελευτῶν⁵⁸ διάδοχον⁵⁹ τῆς ἀρχῆς τῆς ἐμαυτοῦ καταλίποιμι.⁶⁰ **229** ἀλλ' ἐπεὶ θεοῦ τε βουλομένου⁶¹ σὸς πατὴρ ἐγενόμην καὶ πάλιν τούτῳ δοκοῦν⁶² ἀποτίθεμαί⁶³ σε, φέρε γενναίως⁶⁴ τὴν καθιέρωσιν·⁶⁵ τῷ θεῷ γάρ σε παραχωρῶ⁶⁶ ταύτης ἀξιώσαντι⁶⁷ παρ' ἡμῶν τῆς τιμῆς, ἀνθ' ὧν εὐμενὴς⁶⁸ γέγονέ μοι παραστάτης⁶⁹ καὶ σύμμαχος,⁷⁰ νῦν ἐπιτυχεῖν.⁷¹ **230** ἐπεὶ δ' ἐγεννήθης * *⁷² ἄπιθι⁷³ νῦν οὐ τὸν κοινὸν ἐκ τοῦ ζῆν τρόπον,⁷⁴ ἀλλ' ὑπὸ πατρὸς ἰδίου θεῷ τῷ

---

28. Aor. act. opt. 3 sg., ποιέω, *make*; oblique opt. in indir. disc. (cf. BDF §386; S §2619; *CGCG* §41.9).
29. Pres. act. ptc. acc. fem. sg., πάρειμι, *present*; attrib.
30. σπουδή, -ῆς, ἡ, *earnestness for / attention to* (someone). The point is that God's σπουδή is the source of Abraham's εὐδαιμονία.
31. Pres. act. opt. 3 sg., ἔχω; oblique (indir. disc.). See n. 28.
32. Impf. act. indic. 3 sg., αἰτέω, *ask, demand*; with acc. and inf.
33. θῦμα, -ατος, τό, *sacrificial victim, sacrifice*; pred. comp.
34. ἱερεῖον, -ου, τό, *sacrificial victim*; pred. comp.
35. Aor. act. inf., παρέχω, *offer*; comp. of ᾔτει: "He demanded him to *offer* this one [τοῦτον] to him [αὐτῷ] as a sacrifice and victim."
36. Impf. act. indic. 3 sg., κελεύω, *bid, order*; with (acc. and) inf.
37. τὸ Μώριον ὄρος, "Mount Morion" (i.e., Mount Moriah).
38. Aor. act. ptc. acc. masc. sg., ἀνάγω, *lead up*; circ.
39. Aor. act. inf., ὁλοκαυτόω, *make a burnt offering*.
40. βωμός, -οῦ, ὁ, *altar*.
41. Aor. mid. ptc. acc. masc. sg., ἱδρύω, *set up, erect*; circ.
42. Fut. act. inf., ἐμφανίζω, *reveal, demonstrate*; indir. disc. (cf. BDF §397; S §2016; *CGCG* §51.19).
43. Aor. act. opt. 3 sg., προτιμάω, *honor above/beyond* (acc. with gen.). Mixed condition in indir. disc.: εἰ with opt. in the protasis, fut. inf. (for indic.) in the apodosis (cf. S §2362; *CGCG* §49.17).
44. Pf. pass. ptc. acc. neut. sg., χαρίζω, (subst. ptc.) *that which is pleasing*.
45. Plpf. pass. indic. 3 sg., παρασκευάζω, (pass.) *be prepared*. The pluperfect tense is often used in narrative to provide background information.
46. σχίζα, -ας, ἡ, *piece of wood*.
47. Plpf. act. indic. 3 sg., ἐπιφέρω, *lay on*.
48. εὐτρεπής, -ές, *ready, prepared*.
49. εὐχή, -ῆς, ἡ, *prayer*; dat. of means.
50. μή is used to negate indicative verbs in indefinite relative clauses (cf. S §2506).
51. ἀνατροφή, -ῆς, ἡ, *upbringing*.
52. Aor. mid. indic. 1 sg., φιλοτιμέομαι, *contend/strive for*; with internal acc. (ὅ τι); lit., "There is not any way in which I did not strive concerning your upbringing."
53. Fut. act. inf., εὐδαιμονέω, *be happy, blessed*; indir. disc. See n. 42.
54. Impf. mid. indic. 1 sg., οἴομαι, *think, consider*.
55. Used for ἤ after compar. (cf. S §2991).
56. Aor. act. opt. 1 sg., ὁράω, *see*; remote protasis: εἰ with opt. See n. 43.
57. Pf. pass. ptc. acc. masc. sg., ἀνδρόω, (pass.) *become a man*; supp.
58. Pres. act. ptc. nom. masc. sg., τελευτάω, *die*; circ.
59. διάδοχος, -ου, ὁ, *successor*; pred. comp.
60. Aor. act. opt. 1 sg., καταλείπω, *leave*; remote protasis: εἰ with opt. See n. 43.
61. Gen. absol. (causal).
62. Pres. act. ptc. acc. neut. sg., δοκέω, (impers.) *it seems good*; with dat.; acc. absol. (causal).
63. Pres. mid. indic. 1 sg., ἀποτίθημι, (mid.) *set aside, resign*.
64. Adv., *nobly*.
65. καθιέρωσις, -εως, ἡ, *dedication*.
66. Pres. act. indic. 1 sg., παραχωρέω, *yield, give up*.
67. Aor. act. ptc. dat. masc. sg., ἀξιόω, *think one has a right to* (something); with inf.; circ.
68. εὐμενής, -ές, *gracious, well-disposed*.
69. παραστάτης, -ου, ὁ, *comrade, supporter*.
70. σύμμαχος, -ου, ὁ, *ally*.
71. Aor. act. inf., ἐπιτυγχάνω, *obtain*; with gen.; comp. of ἀξιώσαντι.
72. Lacuna in MSS; supply "out of the course of nature, so . . ." (Thackeray, 1930a).
73. Pres. act. impv. 2 sg., ἄπειμι, *depart*.
74. Acc. of manner, οὐ τὸν κοινὸν τρόπον, "not in the usual manner."

πάντων πατρὶ νόμῳ θυσίας[75] προπεμπόμενος,[76] ἄξιον οἶμαί σε κρίναντος[77] αὐτοῦ μήτε νόσῳ[78] μήτε πολέμῳ[79] μήτε ἄλλῳ τινὶ τῶν παθῶν,[80] ἃ συμπίπτειν πέφυκεν[81] ἀνθρώποις, ἀπαλλαγῆναι[82] τοῦ βίου, **231**μετ᾽ εὐχῶν δὲ καὶ ἱερουργίας[83] ἐκείνου ψυχὴν τὴν σὴν προσδεξομένου[84] καὶ παρ᾽ αὐτῷ καθέξοντος·[85] ἔσῃ τ᾽ ἐμοὶ εἰς κηδεμόνα[86] καὶ γηροκόμον,[87] διὸ καὶ σὲ μάλιστα ἀνετρεφόμην, τὸν θεὸν ἀντὶ[88] σαυτοῦ παρεσχημένος."

232Ἴσακος δέ, πατρὸς γὰρ ἦν οἵου τετυχηκότα[89] γενναῖον[90] ἔδει τὸ φρόνημα[91] εἶναι, δέχεται πρὸς ἡδονὴν[92] τοὺς λόγους καὶ φήσας, ὡς οὐδὲ γεγονέναι τὴν ἀρχὴν ἦν δίκαιος, εἰ θεοῦ καὶ πατρὸς μέλλει κρίσιν ἀπωθεῖσθαι[93] καὶ μὴ παρέχειν αὐτὸν[94] τοῖς ἀμφοτέρων βουλήμασιν[95] ἑτοίμως,[96] ὅτε καὶ μόνου τοῦ πατρὸς ταῦτα προαιρουμένου[97] μὴ ὑπακούειν ἄδικον[98] ἦν, ὥρμησεν[99] ἐπὶ τὸν βωμὸν καὶ τὴν σφαγήν.[100] **233**κἂν ἐπράχθη[101] τὸ ἔργον μὴ στάντος ἐμποδὼν[102] τοῦ θεοῦ· βοᾷ γὰρ ὀνομαστὶ[103] τὸν Ἄβραμον εἴργων[104] τῆς τοῦ παιδὸς σφαγῆς· οὐ γὰρ ἐπιθυμήσας[105] αἵματος ἀνθρωπίνου τὴν σφαγὴν αὐτῷ προστάξαι[106] τοῦ παιδὸς ἔλεγεν, οὐδὲ οὗ πατέρα ἐποίησεν αὐτὸς ἀφελέσθαι[107] τούτου βουλόμενος μετὰ τοιαύτης ἀσεβείας,[108] ἀλλὰ δοκιμάσαι θέλων αὐτῷ τὴν διάνοιαν,[109] εἰ καὶ τοιαῦτα προστασσόμενος ὑπακούοι.[110] **234**μαθὼν[111] δὲ αὐτοῦ τὸ πρόθυμον[112] καὶ τὴν ὑπερβολὴν[113] τῆς θρησκείας

---

75. θυσία, -ας, ἡ, *sacrifice*.
76. Pres. pass. ptc. nom. masc. sg., προπέμπω, (pass.) *be sent forth*; circ.
77. Aor. act. ptc. gen. masc. sg., κρίνω, *decide, determine*; gen. absol.
78. νόσος, -ου, ὁ, *sickness, disease*; dat. of means.
79. πόλεμος, -ου, ὁ, *war*; dat. of means.
80. πάθος, -ους, τό, *misfortune, calamity*.
81. Pf. act. indic. 3 sg., φύω, *be naturally inclined, disposed to*; with inf.
82. Aor. pass. inf., ἀπαλλάσσω (Att. ἀπαλλάττω), (pass.) *be released*; comp. of ἄξιον (cf. S §2002; *CGCG* §51.18).
83. ἱερουργία, -ας, ἡ, *sacrificial rite*.
84. Fut. mid. ptc. gen. masc. sg., προσδέχομαι, *receive*; gen. absol.
85. Fut. act. ptc. gen. masc. sg., κατέχω, *hold fast*; gen. absol.
86. κηδεμών, -όνος, ὁ, *protector, guardian*. εἰς with the accusative marks the equivalent of a predicate complement (cf. BDF §145).
87. γηροκόμος, -ον, (subst.) *one who cares for / supports the aged*.
88. Prep. with gen. *for, in place of*; τὸν θεὸν ἀντὶ σαυτοῦ παρεσχημένος, "offering me God in place of yourself."
89. Pf. act. ptc. acc. masc. sg., τυγχάνω, *reach, obtain, have by chance*; with gen.; periphrastic (equivalent of plpf. tense, which is used in narrative to provide background information). "For to one who had been born of such a father, it was necessary to be brave in spirit."
90. γενναῖος, -α, -ον, *brave*; pred. comp.
91. φρόνημα, -ατος, τό, *mind, spirit*; acc. of respect.
92. ἡδονή, -ῆς, ἡ, *pleasure*; πρὸς ἡδονήν, "as something to be enjoyed."
93. Pres. mid. inf., ἀπωθέω, (mid.) *reject*; comp. of μέλλει.
94. Reflexive: αὐτόν = ἑαυτόν.
95. βούλημα, -ατος, τό, *will*; τοῖς ἀμφοτέρων βουλήμασιν, "to the will of both" (i.e., both God and Abraham).
96. Adv., *readily*.
97. Pres. mid. ptc. gen. masc. sg., προαιρέω, *determine, purpose*; gen. absol. (conditional).
98. Quasi-impers., with (acc. and) inf. (cf. S §1985; *CGCG* §36.8): "It is unjust [for him] not to obey."
99. Aor. act. indic. 3 sg., ὁρμάω, *rush* (toward something).
100. σφαγή, -ῆς, ἡ, *slaughter*.
101. Aor. pass. indic. 3 sg., πράσσω, (pass.) *be done*; second-class (contrafactual) condition (cf. BDF §370; S §2302; *CGCG* §49.10). The genitive absolute construction μὴ στάντος ἐμποδὼν τοῦ θεοῦ forms the protasis.
102. Adv., *in one's way*.
103. Adv., *by name*.
104. Pres. act. ptc. nom. masc. sg., ἔργω (Epic εἴργω), *hinder, prevent*; with gen.; circ.
105. Aor. act. ptc. nom. masc. sg., ἐπιθυμέω, *desire, long for*; with gen.; circ.
106. Aor. act. inf., προστάσσω, *command*; with dat. pers. indir. disc. See n. 42.
107. Aor. mid. inf., ἀφαίρω, *bereave/deprive* (someone of something); with acc. pers. and gen. of thing; comp. of βουλόμενος.
108. ἀσεβεία, -ας, ἡ, *impiety*.
109. διάνοια, -ας, ἡ, *thought, intention, disposition*.
110. Pres. act. opt. 3 sg., ὑπακούω, *obey*; oblique opt. in an indir. quest. (cf. BDF §386; S §2677; *CGCG* §42.7).
111. Aor. act. ptc. nom. masc. sg., μανθάνω, *learn*; circ.
112. πρόθυμος, -ον, (subst.) *eagerness, readiness*.
113. ὑπερβολή, -ῆς, ἡ, *excess, extravagance*.

ἥδεσθαι¹¹⁴ μὲν¹¹⁵ οἷς αὐτῷ παρέσχεν, οὐχ ὑστερήσειν¹¹⁶ δὲ αὐτὸν ἀεὶ¹¹⁷ πάσης ἐπιμελείας¹¹⁸ καὶ τὸ γένος ἀξιοῦντα,¹¹⁹ ἔσεσθαί τε τὸν υἱὸν αὐτοῦ πολυχρονιώτατον¹²⁰ καὶ βιώσαντα¹²¹ εὐδαιμόνως¹²² παισὶν ἀγαθοῖς καὶ γνησίοις¹²³ παραδώσειν¹²⁴ μεγάλην ἡγεμονίαν.¹²⁵ ²³⁵προεδήλου¹²⁶ τε τὸ γένος τὸ αὐτῶν εἰς ἔθνη πολλὰ καὶ πλοῦτον¹²⁷ ἐπιδώσειν, καὶ μνήμην¹²⁸ αἰώνιον αὐτῶν ἔσεσθαι τοῖς γενάρχαις¹²⁹ τήν τε Χαναναίαν ὅπλοις¹³⁰ κατακτησαμένους¹³¹ ζηλωτοὺς¹³² ἔσεσθαι πᾶσιν ἀνθρώποις. ²³⁶ταῦτα ὁ θεὸς εἰπὼν κριὸν¹³³ ἐκ τάφανοῦς¹³⁴ παρήγαγεν αὐτοῖς εἰς τὴν ἱερουργίαν.

οἱ δὲ παρ'¹³⁵ ἐλπίδας αὐτοὺς κεκομισμένοι¹³⁶ καὶ τοιούτων ἀγαθῶν ἐπαγγελίας ἀκηκοότες ἠσπάζοντό¹³⁷ τε ἀλλήλους καὶ θύσαντες¹³⁸ ἀπενόστησαν¹³⁹ πρὸς τὴν Σάρραν καὶ διῆγον¹⁴⁰ εὐδαιμόνως, ἐφ' ἅπασιν οἷς ἐθελήσειαν τοῦ θεοῦ συλλαμβάνοντος¹⁴¹ αὐτοῖς.

NOTES

1.222. μονογενῆ ὄντα. Cf. Gen. 22:2 (MT: יְחִידְךָ ["your only one"]; OG: ἀγαπητόν); Heb. 11:17 (τὸν μονογενῆ); Philo, *Abr.* 168 (both μόνος and ἀγαπητός).

1.223. εὐδαιμονίαν. The term occurs in its nominal, verbal, and adverbial forms (1.223, 224, 228, 234, and 236) and underscores the tragic irony: the father's only happiness is tethered to the happiness of his only son, whom he must sacrifice. Cf. Euripides, *Iph. aul.* 590–591: ἰώ, ἰώ, μεγάλαι μεγάλων εὐδαιμονίαι ("Oh! Oh! Great happiness of the great!"). In contrast to Agamemnon's pitiful apology (*Iph. aul.* 1255–1257), however, Abraham remains stoic throughout.

1.224. τὸ Μώριον ὄρος. The name Moriah could be understood as the "place where God is *seen*" (cf. Jub. 18:13; also Symmachus, the Vulgate, and the Samaritan Pentateuch on Gen. 22:2), and thus comes to be associated with the site of the temple (1.227; cf. 2 Chron. 3:1; Tg. Onq. Gen. 22:14; Tg. Neof. Gen. 22:14; Kugel 1998, 320–21).

---

114. Pres. mid. inf., ἥδομαι, *delight, take pleasure in*; with dat.; indir. disc. (ἔλεγεν). The subject of the infinitive must be God: "He [God] delighted in those things that he [God] provided to him [Abraham]." See n. 42.

115. μέν . . . δέ; point/counterpoint (cf. Runge 2010, 75–83; BDF §447; S §2904; *CGCG* §59.24).

116. Fut. act. inf., ὑστερέω, *fail in, lack*; with gen. The accusative subject (αὐτόν) of the infinitive must be Abraham.

117. Adv., *always*.

118. ἐπιμελεία, -ας, ἡ, *care bestowed upon* (someone).

119. Pres. act. ptc. acc. masc. sg., ἀξιόω, *ask, request*; circ. The sense of the participle is not entirely clear; perhaps something like, "He would not lack in any divine consideration even when *expecting/asking for* τὸ γένος." Thackeray's translation goes in a different (and to my mind, indefensible) direction: "[He = God] would never fail to regard with the tenderest care both him [Abraham] and his race" (1930a, 115).

120. Superl., πολύχρονος, -ον, *very long-lived*.

121. Aor. act. ptc. acc. masc. sg., βιόω, *live*; circ.

122. Adv., *happily, blessedly*.

123. γνήσιος, -α, -ον, *genuine, legitimate*.

124. Fut. act. inf., παραδίδωμι, *hand over, pass down*; indir. disc. See n. 42.

125. ἡγεμονία, -ας, ἡ, *rule*.

126. Impf. act. indic. 3 sg., προδηλόω, *show in advance, predict*.

127. πλοῦτος, -ου, ὁ, *riches, wealth*.

128. μνήμη, -ης, ἡ, *remembrance*.

129. γενάρχης, -ου, ὁ, *founder, first ancestor of the race, progenitor*.

130. ὅπλον, -ου, τό, *arms*; dat. of means.

131. Aor. mid. ptc. acc. masc. pl., κατακτάομαι, *win, take possession of*; circ.

132. ζηλωτός, -ή, -όν, *enviable*; pred. adj.

133. κριός, -οῦ, ὁ, *ram*.

134. Crasis: ἐκ τάφανοῦς = ἐκ τοῦ ἀφανοῦς, "from out of sight," "from obscurity."

135. Prep. with acc., *past, beyond*; παρ' ἐλπίδας, "beyond all hope."

136. Pf. mid. ptc. nom. masc. pl., κομίζω, (mid.) *recover* (for oneself); circ.

137. Impf. mid. indic. 3 pl., ἀσπάζομαι, *greet*.

138. Aor. act. ptc. nom. masc. pl., θύω, *sacrifice*; circ.

139. Aor. act. indic. 3 pl., ἀπονοστέω, *return home*.

140. Impf. act. indic. 3 pl., διάγω, *pass life*.

141. Pres. act. ptc. gen. masc. sg., συλλαμβάνω (with dat. pers.), *assist*; gen. absol.

1.230–231. Cf. Feldman (2000, 91): "It is particularly dramatic that in his address here to Isaac when the latter is about to be sacrificed, Abraham says that it is most appropriate that since Isaac was born out of the course of nature he should not die in the manner that most people die but amid prayers and sacrificial ceremonies."

1.232. On Isaac's willingness to be sacrificed, cf. Jdt. 8:26–27; 4 Macc. 7:12–14; 13:12; 16:20; LAB 18:5; 32:2–3; 40:2; 1 Clem. 31.2–4; Tg. Ps.-J. Gen. 22:10; Pesiq. Rab. 40.6.

1.233. οὐ γὰρ ἐπιθμήσας αἵματος ἀνθρωπίνου. Josephus wants to make the point abundantly clear, as he does with the sacrifice of Jephthah's daughter (cf. *A.J.* 5.266). The question of whether the gods delight in human sacrifice is a motif of Euripidean tragedy (cf. *Iphigenia at Aulis*; *Iphigenia at Tauris*; *Daughters of Troy*; *Children of Hercules*; *Phoenician Maidens*; *Electra*). On Greek sacrifice more broadly, including portraits of sacrifice in tragedy, see Naiden (2013).

1.236. In contrast to the biblical account, where the ram is caught in a thicket by its horns (Gen. 22:13), Josephus says that God delivered the ram from obscurity. Feldman (2000, 94) notes that "in the third-century Dura synagogue painting and in the sixth-century Beth Alpha synagogue the ram is not caught in the thicket by its horns but stands quietly next to, or is tethered to, a tree, as if it had always been there, perhaps reflecting the rabbinic tradition (*'Abot* 5:6) that it has been created at twilight on the eve of the Sabbath of creation for future use."

5.2.3

The Departure of Moses

Jewish Antiquities 4.323–331

4.323πορευομένῳ¹ δ' ἔνθεν² οὗ³ ἔμελλεν ἀφανισθήσεσθαι⁴ πάντες εἵποντο⁵ δεδακρυμένοι,⁶ καὶ Μωυσῆς τοὺς μὲν⁷ πόρρω⁸ τῇ χειρὶ κατασείων⁹ μένειν ἠρεμοῦντας¹⁰ ἐκέλευε,¹¹ τοὺς δ' ἔγγιον¹² λόγοις παρεκάλει¹³ μὴ ποιεῖν αὐτῷ δακρυτὴν¹⁴ τὴν ἀπαλλαγὴν¹⁵ ἑπομένους. **324**οἱ δὲ καὶ τοῦτ' αὐτῷ χαρίζεσθαι κρίνοντες, τὸ κατὰ βούλησιν ἀπελθεῖν αὐτῷ τὴν ἰδίαν ἐφεῖναι,¹⁶ κατέχουσιν¹⁷ ἑαυτοὺς ἐν ἀλλήλοις δακρύοντες. μόνη δ' ἡ γερουσία¹⁸ προὔπεμψεν¹⁹ αὐτὸν καὶ ὁ ἀρχιερεὺς Ἐλεάζαρος καὶ ὁ στρατηγὸς²⁰ Ἰησοῦς. **325**ὡς δ' ἐπὶ τῷ ὄρει τῷ Ἀβαρεῖ καλουμένῳ²¹ ἐγένετο, τοῦτο δὲ ὑψηλὸν²² Ἱεριχοῦντος ἀντικρὺ²³ κεῖται²⁴ γῆν ἀρίστην τῶν Χαναναίων καὶ πλείστην παρέχον²⁵ τοῖς ἐπ' αὐτοῦ κατοπτεύειν,²⁶ ἀπέπεμπε²⁷ τὴν γερουσίαν. **326**ἀσπα-

---

1. The subject of the participle is Moses.
2. Adv., *from there*.
3. Adv., *where*.
4. Fut. pass. inf., ἀφανίζω, (pass.) *disappear*; comp. of ἔμελλεν.
5. Impf. mid. indic. 3 sg., ἕπομαι, *follow*; with dat. pers.
6. Pf. mid. ptc. nom. masc. pl., δακρύω, *weep, shed tears*; circ.
7. μέν … δέ; point/counterpoint (cf. Runge 2010, 75–83; BDF §447; S §2904; *CGCG* §59.24).
8. Adv., *at a distance*. The article substantivizes the adverb: "those who were far off."
9. Pres. act. ptc. nom. masc. sg., κατασείω, *motion* (with the hand); circ.
10. Pres. act. ptc. acc. masc. pl., ἠρεμέω, *be still, quiet*; circ.
11. Impf. act. indic. 3 sg., κελεύω, *bid, order*; with acc. and inf.
12. Compar. adv., ἐγγύς, *closer*. The article substantivizes the adverb: "those who were closer."
13. Impf. act. indic. 3 sg., παρακαλέω, *exhort*; with acc. and inf.
14. δακρυτός, -ή, -όν, *tearful*; pred. comp.
15. ἀπαλλαγή, -ῆς, ἡ, *departure*.
16. Aor. act. inf., ἐφίημι, *leave, permit, allow*; with dat.; an appositive to τοῦτ' (cf. S §2035): "and they, deciding to grant *this* also to him—that is, *to leave* him to depart according to his own wishes."
17. Pres. act. indic. 3 pl., κατέχω, *hold back, restrain*.
18. γερουσία, -ας, ἡ, *council of elders*.
19. Aor. act. indic. 3 sg., προπέμπω, *escort*.
20. στρατηγός, -οῦ, ὁ, *commander, general*.
21. Pres. pass. ptc. dat. neut. sg., καλέω, (pass.) *be called*: "the mountain called Abaris" (MT: *ʿăbārîm*; cf. Deut. 32:49).
22. ὑψηλός, -ή, -όν, *high, lofty*; pred. adj.
23. Prep. with gen., *over against, opposite*; Ἱεριχοῦντος ἀντικρύ, "over against Jericho."
24. Pres. pass. indic. 3 sg., κεῖμαι, (pass.) *be situated, lie*.
25. Pres. act. ptc. nom. neut. sg., παρέχω, *offer, provide*; circ.
26. Pres. act. inf., κατοπτεύω, *spy out*; purpose (cf. S §2008; *CGCG* §51.16): "providing to those on it [the mountain] *to spy out* the best and the largest part of the land of the Canaanites."
27. Impf. act. indic. 3 sg., ἀποπέμπω, *send away, dismiss*.

ζομένου²⁸ δὲ καὶ τὸν Ἐλεάζαρον αὐτοῦ καὶ τὸν Ἰησοῦν καὶ προσομιλοῦντος²⁹ ἔτι, νέφους³⁰ αἰφνίδιον³¹ ὑπὲρ αὐτὸν στάντος ἀφανίζεται³² κατά τινος φάραγγος.³³ γέγραφε δ' αὐτὸν³⁴ ἐν ταῖς ἱεραῖς βίβλοις τεθνεῶτα,³⁵ δείσας³⁶ μὴ δι' ὑπερβολὴν³⁷ τῆς περὶ αὐτὸν ἀρετῆς³⁸ πρὸς τὸ θεῖον³⁹ αὐτὸν ἀναχωρῆσαι⁴⁰ τολμήσωσιν⁴¹ εἰπεῖν.

327Ἐβίωσε⁴² δὲ τὸν πάντα χρόνον ἐτῶν εἴκοσι καὶ ἑκατόν,⁴³ ὧν ἦρξε⁴⁴ τὸ τρίτον μέρος⁴⁵ ἑνὶ λεῖπον⁴⁶ μηνί. ἐτελεύτησε⁴⁷ δὲ τῷ ὑστάτῳ⁴⁸ μηνὶ τοῦ ἔτους, ὑπὸ μὲν⁴⁹ Μακεδόνων Δύστρου⁵⁰ καλουμένου Ἀδάρου⁵¹ δ' ὑφ' ἡμῶν νουμηνίᾳ,⁵² **328**συνέσει⁵³ τε τοὺς πώποτ'⁵⁴ ἀνθρώπους ὑπερβαλὼν⁵⁵ καὶ χρησάμενος⁵⁶ ἄριστα⁵⁷ τοῖς νοηθεῖσιν,⁵⁸ εἰπεῖν τε καὶ πλήθεσιν ὁμιλῆσαι⁵⁹ κεχαρισμένος⁶⁰ τά τε ἄλλα καὶ τῶν παθῶν αὐτοκράτωρ,⁶¹ **329**ὡς μηδὲ ἐνεῖναι⁶² τούτων τῇ ψυχῇ δοκεῖν⁶³ αὐτοῦ καὶ γινώσκειν μόνον αὐτῶν τὴν προσηγορίαν⁶⁴ ἐκ τοῦ παρ' ἄλλοις αὐτὰ βλέπειν⁶⁵ μᾶλλον ἢ παρ' αὐτῷ. καὶ στρατηγὸς μὲν⁶⁶ ἐν ὀλίγοις,⁶⁷ προφήτης δὲ οἷος οὐκ ἄλλος, ὥσθ' ὅ τι ἂν φθέγξαιτο⁶⁸ δοκεῖν αὐτοῦ λέγοντος ἀκροᾶσθαι⁶⁹ τοῦ θεοῦ. **330**πενθεῖ⁷⁰ μὲν οὖν⁷¹ αὐτὸν ὁ λαὸς ἐφ' ἡμέρας τριάκοντα, λύπη⁷² δὲ οὐκ

---

28. Pres. mid. ptc. gen. masc. sg., ἀσπάζομαι, *bid farewell*; gen. absol.
29. Pres. act. ptc. gen. masc. sg., προσομιλέω, *converse with*; gen. absol.
30. νέφος, -ους, τό, *cloud*; νέφους . . . στάντος; gen. absol.
31. Adv., *suddenly*.
32. Pres. pass. indic. 3 sg., ἀφανίζω, (pass.) *disappear*.
33. φάραγξ, -αγγος, ἡ, *ravine*.
34. αὐτόν = ἑαυτόν.
35. Pf. act. ptc. acc. masc. sg., θνήσκω, *die*; supp. ptc. in indir. disc. indicates that "the action is actually realized or that the propositional content is true" (*CGCG* §52.8). "He has written in the holy books that he died."
36. Aor. act. ptc. nom. masc. sg., δείδω, *fear*; circ. (causal); object clause of a verb of fearing: μή ("that") with aor./pres. subj. (cf. S §§2221, 2225; *CGCG* §43.3).
37. ὑπερβολή, -ῆς, ἡ, *excess*.
38. ἀρετή, -ῆς, ἡ, *virtue*.
39. θεῖος, -α, -ον, (subst.) *the deity*.
40. Aor. act. inf., ἀναχωρέω, *return*; indir. disc. (cf. BDF §397; S §2016; *CGCG* §51.19).
41. Aor. act. subj. 3 pl., τολμάω, *dare to*; fear clause. See n. 36.
42. Aor. act. indic. 3 sg., βιόω, *live*.
43. Lit., "twenty and one hundred of years."
44. Aor. act. indic. 3 sg., ἄρχω, *rule*.
45. μέρος, -ους, τό, *part*; ὧν . . . τὸ τρίτον μέρος, "a third of which" (i.e., forty years).
46. Pres. act. ptc. nom. neut. sg., λείπω, (of math) *subtract/drop*; ἑνὶ λεῖπον μηνί, "[a third] less one month."
47. Aor. act. indic. 3 sg., τελευτάω, *die*.
48. ὕστατος, -η, -ον, *last*.
49. μέν . . . δέ; point/counterpoint. See n. 7.
50. Δύστρος, -ου, ὁ, *Dystrus*
51. Ἄδαρ, -ου, ὁ, *Adar*.
52. νουμηνία, -ας, ἡ, *new moon, first of the month*; dat. of time.
53. σύνεσις, -εως, ἡ, *understanding*; dat. of respect.
54. Adv., *ever yet*.
55. Aor. act. ptc. nom. masc. sg., ὑπερβάλλω, *surpass*; circ.
56. Aor. mid. ptc. nom. masc. sg., χράομαι, *make use of*; with dat.
57. Adv. acc. (manner), *in the best way*.
58. Aor. pass. ptc. dat. neut. pl., νοέω, (pass.) *be apprehended*; attrib. (subst.).
59. Aor. act. inf., ὁμιλέω, *address*. This epexegetical infinitive functions like an accusative of respect (cf. S §2005): "favored *in speech* [εἰπεῖν] and *in address* [ὁμιλῆσαι] to the multitudes."
60. Pf. pass. ptc. nom. masc. sg., χαρίζω, (pass.) *find favor*.
61. αὐτοκράτωρ, -ορος, ὁ, *complete master*; τά τε ἄλλα καὶ τῶν παθῶν αὐτοκράτωρ, "and [favored] in all other things, especially as the complete master over the passions."
62. Pres. act. inf., ἔνειμι, *be in*; with inf. indir. disc. (δοκεῖν). See n. 40.
63. Pres. act. inf., δοκέω, *seem, appear*; result clause: ὡς with inf. (cf. S §2260; *CGCG* §46.7): "so that it appears that none of these [i.e., the passions] existed in his soul."
64. προσηγορία, -ας, ἡ, *appellation, name*.
65. The articular infinitive is the object of ἐκ: "He alone knew their names *from seeing* them in others rather than in himself."
66. μέν . . . δέ; point/counterpoint. See n. 7.
67. ἐν ὀλίγοις, *one among few* (LSJ, 1215.IV.3b).
68. Aor. mid. opt. 3 sg., φθέγγομαι, *speak, utter*; potential opt. in a conditional rel. clause (cf. S §2566; *CGCG* §50.22): "such that it seemed, in whatever words he might utter, one was hearing God himself speaking."
69. Aor. mid. inf., ἀκροάομαι, *hear, listen to*; with gen.
70. Pres. act. indic. 3 sg., πενθέω, *mourn*.
71. Partic. combination: "a transition to a more to-the-point, relevant text segment (οὖν) [that] occurs in two stages (μέν . . . δέ)" (*CGCG* §59.73).
72. λύπη, -ης, ἡ, *grief*.

ἄλλη κατέσχεν Ἑβραίους τοσαύτη⁷³ τὸ μέγεθος, ὅση τότε Μωυσέος ἀποθανόντος. ³³¹ἐπόθουν⁷⁴ δ' αὐτὸν οὐχ⁷⁵ οἱ πειραθέντες⁷⁶ αὐτοῦ μόνον, ἀλλὰ καὶ οἱ τοῖς νόμοις ἐντυγχάνοντες⁷⁷ αὐτοῦ δεινὴν⁷⁸ ἐποιοῦντο τὴν ἐπιζήτησιν,⁷⁹ τὸ περιὸν⁸⁰ αὐτοῦ τῆς ἀρετῆς ἐκ τούτων λογιζόμενοι.⁸¹ καὶ τὸ μὲν⁸² κατὰ Μωυσῆν τέλος τοιοῦτον ἡμῖν δεδηλώσθω.⁸³

NOTE

4.326. Cf. Deut. 34:5–6; 2 Macc. 2:4–8; LAB 19:12; Philo, *Mos.* 2.291; Philo, *Sacr.* 10; and additional sources in Kugel (1998, 860–63). Jesus encounters the heavenly Moses on the Mount of Transfiguration (Mark 9:4–5 parr.).

---

73. Correlative pair: τοσαύτη (τὸ μέγεθος) . . . ὅση, *so great (in magnitude)* . . . *as*.
74. Impf. act. indic. 3 pl., ποθέω, *miss (someone)*.
75. οὐχ . . . μόνον . . . ἀλλὰ καί, *not only . . . but also*.
76. Aor. pass. ptc. nom. masc. pl., πειράω, *know by experience*; with gen.; attrib. (subst.).
77. Pres. act. ptc. nom. masc. pl., ἐντυγχάνω, *(of texts) read*; with dat.; attrib. (subst.).
78. δεινός, -ή, -όν, *incredible, awesome, powerful*; pred. comp.
79. ἐπιζήτησις, -εως, ἡ, *desire, longing*; with gen.
80. Pres. act. ptc. acc. neut. sg., περίειμι, *be superior, surpass, excel*; attrib. (subst.); τὸ περιὸν αὐτοῦ τῆς ἀρετῆς, "the surpassing nature of his virtue."
81. Pres. mid. ptc. nom. masc. pl., λογίζομαι, *conclude by reasoning, infer*.
82. Transitional: the μέν-clause concludes the section and points ahead to the δέ-clause of the new section.
83. Pf. pass. impv. 3 sg., δηλόω, (pass.) *be demonstrated*. "And as to the end of Moses, it must be demonstrated by us to be such [what preceded]."

5.2.4

The Conversion of King Izates

Jewish Antiquities 20.38–48

20.38Πυθόμενος[1] δὲ πάνυ[2] τοῖς Ἰουδαίων ἔθεσιν[3] χαίρειν[4] τὴν μητέρα τὴν ἑαυτοῦ ἔσπευσε[5] καὶ αὐτὸς εἰς ἐκεῖνα μεταθέσθαι,[6] νομίζων[7] τε μὴ ἂν εἶναι βεβαίως[8] Ἰουδαῖος, εἰ μὴ περιτέμοιτο,[9] πράττειν[10] ἦν ἕτοιμος. **39**μαθοῦσα[11] δ' ἡ μήτηρ κωλύειν[12] ἐπειρᾶτο[13] ἐπιφέρειν[14] αὐτῷ κίνδυνον[15] λέγουσα· βασιλέα γὰρ εἶναι, καὶ καταστήσειν[16] εἰς πολλὴν δυσμένειαν[17] τοὺς ὑπηκόους[18] μαθόντας, ὅτι ξένων[19] ἐπιθυμήσειεν[20] καὶ ἀλλοτρίων[21] αὐτοῖς ἐθῶν, οὐκ ἀνέξεσθαί[22] τε βασιλεύοντος αὐτῶν Ἰουδαίου. **40**καὶ ἡ μὲν[23] ταῦτ' ἔλεγεν καὶ παντοίως[24] ἐκώλυεν. ὁ δ' εἰς τὸν Ἀνανίαν[25] τοὺς λόγους ἀνέφερεν.[26] τοῦ δὲ τῇ μητρὶ συμφάσκοντος[27]

1. Aor. mid. ptc. nom. masc. sg., πυνθάνομαι, *learn* (through inquiry). The subject of the participle is Izates (king of Adiabene ca. 1–55 CE).
2. Adv., *very*.
3. ἔθος, -ους, τό, *custom*.
4. Pres. act. inf., χαίρω, *take pleasure in*; with dat.; indir. disc. (cf. BDF §397; S §2016; CGCG §51.19).
5. Aor. act. indic. 3 sg., σπεύδω, *hurry, hasten*; with inf.
6. Aor. mid. inf., μετατίθημι, *change to*; here in the sense of religioethnic conversion.
7. Pres. act. ptc. nom. masc. sg., νομίζω, *think, consider*; circ. (causal).
8. Adv., *assuredly*.
9. Aor. pass. opt. 3 sg., περιτέμνω, (pass.) *be circumcised*; fourth-class condition: εἰ with opt. in the protasis, ἄν with opt. in the apodosis (cf. S §2566; CGCG §49.8). In this instance, the infinitive replaces the optative in the apodosis due to indirect discourse.
10. Pres. act. inf., πράσσω (Att. πράττω), *do*; epex. (cf. S §2002; CGCG §51.18): "He was ready *to do it*."
11. Aor. act. ptc. nom. fem. sg., μανθάνω, *learn*; circ.
12. Pres. act. inf., κωλύω, *forbid, hinder*.
13. Impf. mid. indic. 3 sg., πειράω, (mid.) *try/attempt* (to do something); with inf.
14. Pres. act. inf., ἐπιφέρω, *bring upon*; indir. disc. See n. 4.
15. κίνδυνος, -ου, ὁ, *danger*.

16. Fut. act. inf., καθίστημι (with εἰς with acc.), *bring/place* (someone in a situation); indir. disc.: "that *he would bring* his subjects into a state of great hostility when they learn [μαθόντας] that . . ."
17. δυσμένεια, -ας, ἡ, *hostility, animosity*.
18. ὑπήκοος, -ον, (subst.) *subjects*; acc. subject of καταστήσειν.
19. ξένος, -η, -ον, *foreign*.
20. Aor. act. opt. 3 sg., ἐπιθυμέω, *desire, be devoted to*; with gen.; oblique opt. in indir. disc. (cf. BDF §386; S §2619; CGCG §41.9).
21. ἀλλότριος, -α, -ον, *of another, strange, foreign*.
22. Fut. mid. inf., ἀνέχω, *bear, tolerate*; with gen.; indir. disc. See n. 4.
23. μέν . . . δέ; point/counterpoint (cf. Runge 2010, 75–83; BDF §447; S §2904; CGCG §59.24).
24. Adv., *by all means*. Some MSS read τέως, "for a time"; Lat. reads *omnino* (πάντως?), "entirely."
25. Ἀνανίας, -ου, ὁ, *Ananias* (Jewish merchant advising the king and his mother).
26. Impf. act. indic. 3 sg., ἀναφέρω, *refer* (a matter to another).
27. Pres. act. ptc. gen. masc. sg., συμφάσκω (= σύμφημι), *agree with*; with dat.; gen. absol.

καὶ συναπειλήσαντος[28] ὡς εἰ μὴ πείθοι[29] καταλιπὼν[30] ἄπεισιν.[31] **41**δεδοικέναι[32] γὰρ ἔλεγεν, μὴ τοῦ πράγματος[33] ἐκδήλου[34] πᾶσιν γενομένου κινδυνεύσειε[35] τιμωρίαν[36] ὑποσχεῖν[37] ὡς αὐτὸς αἴτιος[38] τούτων καὶ διδάσκαλος τῷ βασιλεῖ ἀπρεπῶν[39] ἔργων γενόμενος, δυνάμενον δ' αὐτὸν ἔφη καὶ χωρὶς[40] τῆς περιτομῆς[41] τὸ θεῖον[42] σέβειν,[43] εἴγε[44] πάντως κέκρικε[45] ζηλοῦν[46] τὰ πάτρια[47] τῶν Ἰουδαίων· τοῦτ' εἶναι κυριώτερον[48] τοῦ περιτέμνεσθαι.[49] **42**συγγνώμην[50] δ' ἕξειν[51] αὐτῷ καὶ τὸν θεὸν φήσαντος[52] μὴ πράξαντι[53] τὸ ἔργον δι' ἀνάγκην[54] καὶ τὸν ἐκ τῶν ὑπηκόων φόβον, ἐπείσθη[55] μὲν[56] τότε τοῖς λόγοις ὁ βασιλεύς. **43**μετὰ ταῦτα δέ τὴν γὰρ ἐπιθυμίαν[57] οὐκ ἐξεβεβλήκει[58] παντάπασιν,[59] Ἰουδαῖός τις ἕτερος ἐκ τῆς Γαλιλαίας ἀφικόμενος[60] Ἐλεάζαρος ὄνομα πάνυ περὶ τὰ πάτρια δοκῶν[61] ἀκριβὴς[62] εἶναι προετρέψατο[63] πρᾶξαι τοὖργον.[64] **44**ἐπεὶ γὰρ εἰσῆλθεν ἀσπασόμενος[65] αὐτὸν καὶ κατέλαβε[66] τὸν Μωυσέος νόμον ἀναγινώσκοντα,[67] "λανθάνεις,"[68] εἶπεν, "ὦ βασιλεῦ τὰ μέγιστα[69] τοὺς νόμους καὶ δι' αὐτῶν τὸν θεὸν ἀδικῶν·[70] οὐ γὰρ ἀναγινώσκειν σε δεῖ μόνον[71] αὐτούς, ἀλλὰ καὶ πρότερον τὰ προστασσόμενα[72] ποιεῖν ὑπ' αὐτῶν. **45**μέχρι τίνος[73] ἀπερίτμητος[74] μενεῖς; ἀλλ' εἰ μήπω[75] τὸν περὶ τούτου νόμον ἀνέγνως, ἵν' εἰδῇς τίς ἐστιν ἡ ἀσέβεια,[76] νῦν ἀνάγνωθι." **46**ταῦτα ἀκούσας ὁ βασιλεὺς οὐχ ὑπερεβάλετο[77] τὴν πρᾶξιν,[78] μεταστὰς

---

28. Aor. act. ptc. gen. masc. sg., συναπειλέω, *threaten together with*; gen. absol.
29. Pres. act. opt. 3 sg., πείθω, *persuade*; mixed condition: εἰ with opt. in the protasis, pres. indic. in the apodosis (cf. S §2360; CGCG §49.17). "If *he should not persuade* [him], he would abandon [him] and depart."
30. Aor. act. ptc. nom. masc. sg., καταλείπω, *abandon*; circ.
31. Pres. act. indic. 3 sg., ἄπειμι, *depart*.
32. Pf. mid. inf., δείδω, *fear*; indir. disc.; obj. clause of a verb of fearing: μή ("that") with aor./pres. subj. (cf. S §§2221, 2225; CGCG §43.3).
33. πρᾶγμα, -ατος, τό, *matter*.
34. ἔκδηλος, -ον, *obvious, evident*.
35. Aor. act. opt. 3 sg., κινδυνεύω, *be in danger of, run the risk of*; with inf.; oblique opt. for subj. in clause of fearing (cf. S §2225; CGCG §43.3).
36. τιμωρία, -ας, ἡ, *punishment*.
37. Aor. act. inf., ὑπέχω, *undergo*.
38. αἴτιος, -α, -ον, *guilty*.
39. ἀπρεπής, -ές, *inappropriate*.
40. Prep. with gen., *apart from*.
41. περιτομή, -ῆς, ἡ, *circumcision*.
42. θεῖος, -α, -ον, (subst.) *the deity*.
43. Pres. act. inf., σέβω, *worship*; comp. of δυνάμενον.
44. Partic., *if, in fact*. γε adds concentration/limitation to εἰ (cf. CGCG §59.53).
45. Pf. act. indic. 3 sg., κρίνω, *decide, determine*.
46. Pres. act. inf., ζηλόω, *be devoted to*.
47. πάτριος, -α, -ον, (subst.) *ancestral customs*.
48. Compar., κύριος, -α, -ον, *more important*.
49. Pres. pass. inf., περιτέμνω, (pass.) *be circumcised*; art. inf. as gen. of compar. (cf. S §2032.c).
50. συγγνώμη, -ης, ἡ, *pardon*.
51. Fut. act. inf., ἔχω, *have, hold*; indir. disc. See n. 4.
52. Aor. act. ptc. gen. masc. sg., φημί, *say*; gen. absol.
53. Aor. act. ptc. dat. masc. sg., πράσσω, *do*; circ. (conditional).
54. ἀνάγκη, -ης, ἡ, *constraint*.
55. Aor. pass. indic. 3 sg., πείθω, (pass.) *be persuaded*.
56. μέν . . . δέ; point/counterpoint. See n. 23.
57. ἐπιθυμία, -ας, ἡ, *desire*.
58. Plpf. act. indic. 3 sg., ἐκβάλλω, *cast away*.
59. Adv., *altogether, entirely*.
60. Aor. mid. ptc. nom. masc. sg., ἀφικνέομαι, *arrive*; circ.
61. Pres. act. ptc. nom. masc. sg., δοκέω, *appear* (by reputation); circ.
62. ἀκριβής, -ές, *exact, precise, strict*. MS M reads εὐσεβής, *pious*.
63. Aor. mid. indic. 3 sg., προτρέπω, *urge on, encourage*; with acc. and inf.
64. Crasis: τὸ ἔργον.
65. Fut. mid. ptc. nom. masc. sg., ἀσπάζομαι, *greet*; purpose (cf. S §2065; CGCG §52.41).
66. Aor. act. indic. 3 sg., καταλαμβάνω, *find, encounter* (MGS, 1061.1.D). MS E reads καταλαβὼν γὰρ αὐτόν.
67. Pres. act. ptc. acc. masc. sg., ἀναγινώσκω, *read*; supp.
68. Pres. act. indic. 2 sg., λανθάνω, *escape the notice of*; with supp. ptc. (cf. S §2096; CGCG §52.11).
69. Adv. acc., *to the greatest degree*.
70. Pres. act. ptc. nom. masc. sg., ἀδικέω, *violate, offend*.
71. οὐ μόνον . . . ἀλλὰ καὶ πρότερον, *not only . . . but also and above all else*.
72. Pres. pass. ptc. acc. neut. pl., προστάσσω, (pass.) *be commanded*; attrib. (subst.).
73. μέχρι τίνος, *Until what point? How long?*
74. ἀπερίτμητος, -ον, *uncircumcised*.
75. Adv., *not yet*.
76. ἀσέβεια, -ας, ἡ, *impiety*.
77. Aor. mid. indic. 3 sg., ὑπερβάλλω, *put off*.
78. πρᾶξις, -εως, ἡ, *act, deed*.

δ' εἰς ἕτερον οἴκημα⁷⁹ καὶ τὸν ἰατρὸν⁸⁰ εἰσκαλεσάμενος⁸¹ τὸ προσταχθὲν ἐτέλει⁸² καὶ μεταπεμψάμενος⁸³ τήν τε μητέρα καὶ τὸν διδάσκαλον Ἀνανίαν ἐσήμαινεν⁸⁴ αὐτὸν⁸⁵ πεπραχέναι⁸⁶ τοὔργον. **⁴⁷**τοὺς δ' ἔκπληξις⁸⁷ εὐθὺς ἔλαβεν καὶ φόβος οὔτι μέτριος,⁸⁸ μὴ τῆς πράξεως εἰς ἔλεγχον⁸⁹ ἐλθούσης κινδυνεύσειεν⁹⁰ μὲν⁹¹ ὁ βασιλεὺς τὴν ἀρχὴν ἀποβαλεῖν οὐκ ἀνασχομένων⁹² τῶν ὑπηκόων ἄρχειν αὐτῶν ἄνδρα τῶν παρ' ἑτέροις ζηλωτὴν⁹³ ἐθῶν, κινδυνεύσειαν δὲ καὶ αὐτοὶ τῆς αἰτίας⁹⁴ ἐπ' αὐτοῖς ἐνεχθείσης.⁹⁵ **⁴⁸**θεὸς δ' ἦν ὁ κωλύσων ἄρα⁹⁶ τοὺς ἐκείνων φόβους ἐλθεῖν ἐπὶ τέλος· πολλοῖς γὰρ αὐτόν τε τὸν Ἰζάτην περιπεσόντα⁹⁷ κινδύνοις καὶ παῖδας τοὺς ἐκείνου διέσωσεν⁹⁸ ἐξ ἀμηχάνων⁹⁹ πόρον¹⁰⁰ εἰς σωτηρίαν παρασχών,¹⁰¹ ἐπιδεικνὺς¹⁰² ὅτι τοῖς εἰς αὐτὸν ἀποβλέπουσιν¹⁰³ καὶ μόνῳ πεπιστευκόσιν ὁ καρπὸς¹⁰⁴ οὐκ ἀπόλλυται ὁ τῆς εὐσεβείας. ἀλλὰ ταῦτα μὲν¹⁰⁵ ὕστερον¹⁰⁶ ἀπαγγελοῦμεν.

NOTES

20.38. On several occasions Josephus portrays prominent gentile women as worshipers of the Jewish God and as sympathetic to the Jewish way of life (cf. *B.J.* 2.560; *A.J.* 17.11; 18.82; Cohen 1999, 170–71).

20.41. Some Second Temple Jews (e.g., the writer of Jubilees) outright rejected the possibility of proselyte circumcision (see esp. Thiessen 2011). In my view, Ananias is not offering a way of "being Jewish" apart from circumcision but, rather, is encouraging Izates to *remain* a God-fearing gentile. The halakic principle of valuing life (or the well-being of the person) above all else may have informed his decision (cf. m. Ned. 3.11; m. Yevam. 8.1).

20.43. Schwartz (1996) notes similarities between the position of Eleazar and the position of the Christ-following Pharisees in Acts 15. Josephus's description of Eleazar as ἀκριβής toward his ancestral traditions lends support to the theory that he was a Pharisee (cf. *B.J.* 1.110; *A.J.* 17.41).

20.44. The Torah is not an à la carte menu (cf. Gal. 5:3; James 2:10).

---

79. οἴκημα, -ατος, τό, *room*.
80. ἰατρός, -οῦ, ὁ, *physician*.
81. Aor. mid. ptc. nom. masc. sg., εἰσκαλέω, *call on, summon*.
82. Impf. act. indic. 3 sg., τελέω, *complete*.
83. Aor. mid. ptc. nom. masc. sg., μεταπέμπομαι, *send for*; circ.
84. Impf. act. indic. 3 sg., σημαίνω, *indicate, show*.
85. MS E reads αὐτοῖς.
86. Pf. act. inf., πράσσω, *do*; indir. disc. See n. 4.
87. ἔκπληξις, -εως, ἡ, *astonishment, deep disturbance*.
88. μέτριος, -α, -ον, *measured, ordinary*. οὔτι μέτριος, "beyond measure," is uncertain; MS E omits it.
89. ἔλεγχος, -ου, ὁ, *testing, examination*. The genitive absolute clause has conditional force: "if the deed should come under examination."
90. Aor. act. opt. 3 sg., κινδυνεύω, *be in danger*; opt. for subj. in a clause of fearing. See n. 32.
91. μέν . . . δέ; point/counterpoint. See n. 23.
92. Aor. mid. ptc. gen. masc. pl., ἀνέχω, *endure, tolerate*; gen. absol. (causal).
93. ζηλωτής, -οῦ, ὁ, *devotee*.
94. αἰτία, -ας, ἡ, *blame*.
95. Aor. pass. ptc. gen. fem. sg., ἐνέχω, (pass.) *be brought upon*; gen. absol. (causal).
96. Partic., *it seems, then, as it turns out*; "indicates that the speaker, in view of the preceding context, cannot but make the contribution he/she is making" (*CGCG* §59.42).
97. Aor. act. ptc. acc. masc. sg., περιπίπτω, *encounter*; with dat.; circ.
98. Aor. act. indic. 3 sg., διασῴζω, *deliver*.
99. ἀμήχανος, -ον, *without hope, impossible*, (subst.) *hopeless situations*.
100. πόρος, -ου, ὁ, *place for passage*.
101. Aor. act. ptc. nom. masc. sg., παρέχω, *offer*; circ.
102. Pres. act. ptc. nom. masc. sg., ἐπιδείκνυμι, *show, demonstrate*; circ.
103. Pres. act. ptc. dat. masc. pl., ἀποβλέπω, *look steadfastly*; attrib. (subst.).
104. καρπός, -οῦ, ὁ, *fruit*.
105. Transitional: the μέν-clause concludes the section and points ahead to the δέ-clause of the new section (20.49).
106. ὕστερος, -α, -ον; as adv., *later*.

5.3

The Life

The *Life* appears as an addendum to *Jewish Antiquities*. Herein the historian proudly details his ancestry, education, and public service; takes on rumors and reports about his conduct during the war; and chronicles his life after the war, first in Alexandria and Jerusalem and then in Rome. In so doing, he positions himself as the exemplar of Jewish virtue. Mason states, "Although historical precision is cavalierly disregarded in the *Life*, what we find in its place is a consistent attention to the moral lessons of Josephus's career, and also characteristic sensitivity to the Roman reader (e.g., *Vita* 1, 12, 16). Virtually every episode in the *Life* serves to illustrate one or another of the author's virtues" (2003, 124–25).

Our reading focuses on the opening of the work. Why would an ancient writer include a genealogy? What purpose would an account of young adulthood serve? Josephus helps us to answer these questions, particularly as they pertain to Roman tastes and conventions.

Text and Translation: Thackeray 1926
Supplemental Scripture: Matt. 1:1–17 // Luke 3:23–38; Luke 2:41–51

5.3.1

Ancestry and Education

The Life 1–12

1Ἐμοὶ δὲ γένος¹ ἐστὶν οὐκ ἄσημον,² ἀλλ' ἐξ ἱερέων³ ἄνωθεν⁴ καταβεβηκός.⁵ ὥσπερ⁶ δ' ἡ παρ' ἑκάστοις ἄλλη τίς ἐστιν εὐγενείας⁷ ὑπόθεσις,⁸ οὕτως παρ' ἡμῖν ἡ τῆς ἱερωσύνης⁹ μετουσία¹⁰ τεκμήριόν¹¹ ἐστιν γένους λαμπρότητος.¹² **2**ἐμοὶ δ' οὐ μόνον¹³ ἐξ ἱερέων ἐστὶν τὸ γένος, ἀλλὰ καὶ ἐκ τῆς πρώτης ἐφημερίδος¹⁴ τῶν εἰκοσιτεσσάρων, πολλὴ δὲ κἂν¹⁵ τούτῳ διαφορά,¹⁶ καὶ τῶν ἐν ταύτῃ δὲ¹⁷ φυλῶν¹⁸ ἐκ τῆς ἀρίστης.¹⁹ ὑπάρχω δὲ καὶ τοῦ βασιλικοῦ²⁰ γένους ἀπὸ τῆς μητρός· οἱ γὰρ Ἀσαμωναίου²¹ παῖδες, ὧν ἔγγονος²² ἐκείνη, τοῦ ἔθνους ἡμῶν ἐπὶ μήκιστον²³ χρόνον ἠρχιεράτευσαν²⁴ καὶ ἐβασίλευσαν.²⁵ **3**ἐρῶ δὲ τὴν διαδοχήν.²⁶ ὁ πρόπαππος²⁷ ἡμῶν Σίμων²⁸ ὁ Ψελλὸς²⁹ ἐπικαλούμενος.³⁰ οὗτος ἐγένετο καθ' ὃν καιρὸν ἠρχιεράτευσεν

1. γένος, -ους, τό, *ancestry*.
2. ἄσημος, -ον, *undistinguished*.
3. ἱερεύς, -έως, ὁ, *priest*.
4. Adv., *from the beginning*.
5. Pf. act. ptc. nom. neut. sg., καταβαίνω, *descend*; attrib.
6. ὥσπερ... οὕτως, *as... so*.
7. εὐγενεία, -ας, ἡ, *noble birth*; indir. quest., τίς ἐστιν εὐγενείας, "as to who is of noble birth."
8. ὑπόθεσις, -εως, ἡ, *basis, foundation*.
9. ἱερωσύνη, -ης, ἡ, *priesthood*.
10. μετουσία, -ας, ἡ, *membership*; with gen.
11. τεκμήριον, -ου, τό, *proof*.
12. λαμπρότης, -ητος, ἡ, *splendor, brilliance*.
13. οὐ μόνον... ἀλλὰ καί, *not only... but also*.
14. ἐφημερίς, -ίδος, ἡ, *day course*; ἐκ τῆς πρώτης ἐφημερίδος τῶν εἰκοσιτεσσάρων, "from the first course of the twenty-four courses" (i.e., of Jehoiarib; cf. 1 Chron. 24:7).
15. Crasis: καὶ ἐν.
16. διαφορός, -ά, -όν, *difference, distinction*. The clause is parenthetical: "And [there is] also great distinction in this."

17. Partic. combination, *and furthermore, and... as well*: "introduces new, closely related information (καί), which nevertheless is somehow distinct from the preceding context (δέ)" (*CGCG* §59.67).
18. φυλή, -ῆς, ἡ, *tribe, clan*.
19. Superl., ἀγαθός, -ή, -όν, *best*.
20. βασιλικός, -ή, -όν, *royal*.
21. Ἀσαμωναῖος, -ου, ὁ, *Asamonaeus*. οἱ Ἀσαμωναίου παῖδες are the Hasmoneans.
22. ἔγγονος, -ου, ἡ, *descendant*.
23. Superl., μακρός, -ά, -όν; acc. of extent (time).
24. Aor. act. indic. 3 pl., ἀρχιερατεύω, *serve as high priest*.
25. Aor. act. indic. 3 pl., βασιλεύω, *rule as king*.
26. διαδοχή, -ῆς, ἡ, *succession*.
27. πρόπαππος, -ου, ὁ, *great-grandfather, patriarch*.
28. Σίμων, -ωνος, ὁ, *Simon*.
29. ψελλός, -ή, -όν, *faltering in speech, stuttering*; surname Psellus (i.e., "the Stutterer").
30. Pres. pass. ptc. nom. masc. sg., ἐπικαλέω, (pass.) *be called*.

Σίμωνος[31] ἀρχιερέως ὁ παῖς, ὃς πρῶτος ἀρχιερέων Ὑρκανὸς[32] ὠνομάσθη.[33] **4** γίνονται δὲ τῷ Ψελλῷ Σίμωνι παῖδες ἐννέα· τούτων ἐστὶν Ματθίας[34] ὁ Ἠφαίου[35] λεγόμενος. οὗτος ἠγάγετο[36] πρὸς γάμον θυγατέρα Ἰωνάθου[37] ἀρχιερέως, τοῦ πρώτου ἐκ τῶν Ἀσαμωναίου παίδων γένους ἀρχιερατεύσαντος, τοῦ ἀδελφοῦ Σίμωνος τἀρχιερέως,[38] καὶ γίνεται παῖς αὐτῷ Ματθίας ὁ Κυρτὸς[39] ἐπικληθείς, ἄρχοντος Ὑρκανοῦ τὸν πρῶτον ἐνιαυτόν.[40] **5** τούτου γίνεται Ἰώσηπος[41] ἐνάτῳ[42] ἔτει τῆς Ἀλεξάνδρας[43] ἀρχῆς, καὶ Ἰωσήπου Ματθίας βασιλεύοντος Ἀρχελάου[44] τὸ δέκατον, Ματθίᾳ δὲ ἐγὼ τῷ πρώτῳ τῆς Γαΐου Καίσαρος[45] ἡγεμονίας.[46] ἐμοὶ δὲ παῖδές εἰσιν τρεῖς, Ὑρκανὸς μὲν[47] ὁ πρεσβύτατος[48] ἔτει τετάρτῳ τῆς Οὐεσπασιανοῦ[49] Καίσαρος ἡγεμονίας, ἑβδόμῳ[50] δὲ Ἰοῦστος,[51] ἐνάτῳ δὲ Ἀγρίππας.[52] **6** τὴν μὲν[53] τοῦ γένους ἡμῶν διαδοχήν, ὡς ἐν ταῖς δημοσίαις[54] δέλτοις[55] ἀναγεγραμμένην[56] εὗρον, οὕτως παρατίθεμαι,[57] τοῖς διαβάλλειν[58] ἡμᾶς πειρωμένοις[59] χαίρειν φράσας.[60]

7 Ὁ πατὴρ δέ μου Ματθίας οὐ διὰ μόνην τὴν εὐγένειαν[61] ἐπίσημος[62] ἦν, ἀλλὰ πλέον διὰ τὴν δικαιοσύνην ἐπηνεῖτο,[63] γνωριμώτατος[64] ὢν ἐν τῇ μεγίστῃ πόλει τῶν παρ' ἡμῖν τοῖς Ἱεροσολυμίταις. **8** ἐγὼ δὲ συμπαιδευόμενος[65] ἀδελφῷ Ματθίᾳ τοὔνομα,[66] γεγόνει γάρ μοι γνήσιος[67] ἐξ ἀμφοῖν[68] τῶν γονέων, εἰς μεγάλην παιδείας[69] προύκοπτον[70] ἐπίδοσιν,[71] μνήμῃ[72] τε καὶ

---

31. The high priest Simon ruled 143/2–135/4 BCE (cf. 1 Macc. 13:1–16:17).
32. Ὑρκανός, -οῦ, ὁ, *Hyrcanus*. John Hyrcanus I ruled 135/4–104 BCE (cf. 1 Macc. 16:16–24).
33. Aor. pass. indic. 3 sg., ὀνομάζω, (pass.) *be named*.
34. Matthias is an alternative form of Mattathias, the name of the priest who began the Maccabean revolt (cf. 1 Macc. 2:1–70).
35. The meaning of Ἠφαίου is uncertain; it may mean something like "of Ephesus." For further discussion, see Mason 2001, 8n24.
36. Aor. mid. indic. 3 sg., ἄγω (with acc. πρὸς γάμον), *marry*; lit., "lead someone into marriage."
37. Ἰωνάθος, -ου, ὁ, *Jonathan* (first Hasmonean high priest; took office ca. 152 BCE; cf. 1 Macc. 9:28–12:53).
38. Crasis: τε ἀρχιερέως.
39. κυρτός, -ή, -όν, *swelling, bulging*; surname Curtus (i.e., "the Swollen" or "the Humpback").
40. ἐνιαυτός, -οῦ, ὁ, *year*. The first year of Hyrcanus's reign was 135/4 BCE (cf. 1 Macc. 16:14).
41. Ἰώσηπος, -ου, ὁ, *Josephus*. Thus, the historian is named after his paternal grandfather.
42. ἔνατος, -η, -ον, *ninth*.
43. Ἀλεξάνδρα, -ας, ἡ, *Alexandra*. Sixty-eight BCE was the ninth and final year of Alexandra Salome's rule (cf. *A.J.* 13.430).
44. Ἀρχέλαος, -ου, ὁ, *Archelaus*. The tenth year of the reign of the ethnarch and eldest son of Herod the Great (6 CE).
45. Καῖσαρ, -αρος, ὁ, *Caesar*. The first year of Gaius's imperium (37 CE).
46. ἡγεμονία, -ας, ἡ, (Lat.) *imperium*. See Mason 2001, 9n34.
47. μέν . . . δέ . . . δέ (cf. S §2907).
48. Superl. adj., πρέσβυς, -εως, ὁ, *eldest*.
49. Οὐεσπασιανός, -οῦ, ὁ, *Vespasian*. Josephus's sons were born in the fourth, eighth, and ninth years of Vespasian's imperium (69–79 CE).
50. ἕβδομος, -η, -ον, *seventh*.
51. Ἰοῦστος, -ου, ὁ, *Iustus*. The name means "just" or "righteous."
52. Ἀγρίππας, -ου, ὁ, *Agrippa*.
53. μέν . . . δέ. Transitional: the μέν-clause concludes the section and points ahead to the δέ-clause of *Vita* 7.
54. δημόσιος, -α, -ον, *public*.
55. δέλτος, -ου, ἡ, *tablet*.
56. Pf. pass. ptc. acc. fem. sg., ἀναγράφω, (pass.) *be recorded*; supp. (εὗρον).
57. Pres. mid. indic. 1 sg., παρατίθημι, *present*.
58. Pres. act. inf., διαβάλλω, *slander, disregard*.
59. Pres. mid. ptc. dat. masc. pl., πειράω, (mid.) *try, attempt*; with inf.; attrib. (subst.).
60. Aor. act. ptc. nom. masc. sg., φράζω, (with χαίρειν; with dat.) *send greetings, bid farewell*; circ.
61. εὐγένεια, -ας, ἡ, *noble birth*.
62. ἐπίσημος, -ον, *outstanding*.
63. Impf. pass. indic. 3 sg., ἐπαινέω, (pass.) *be praised*.
64. Superl., γνώριμος, -ον, *most noble*; γνωριμώτατος ὢν . . . τῶν . . . τοῖς Ἱεροσολυμίταις, "being most noble of those in Jerusalem."
65. Pres. pass. ptc. nom. masc. sg., συμπαιδεύω, *be educated together with*; circ.
66. Crasis: τε ὄνομα.
67. γνήσιος, -α, -ον, *true, genuine*.
68. Dual gen. masc., ἄμφω, *both* (cf. S §229).
69. παιδεία, -ας, ἡ, *training, education*.
70. Impf. act. indic. 1 sg., προκόπτω, *advance*.
71. ἐπίδοσις, -εως, ἡ, *progress, development*.
72. μνήμη, -ης, ἡ, *memory*; dat. of respect.

συνέσει⁷³ δοκῶν⁷⁴ διαφέρειν.⁷⁵ **⁹**ἔτι δ' ἀντίπαις⁷⁶ ὢν περὶ τεσσαρεσκαιδέκατον⁷⁷ ἔτος διὰ τὸ φιλογράμματον⁷⁸ ὑπὸ πάντων ἐπηνούμην⁷⁹ συνιόντων⁸⁰ ἀεὶ⁸¹ τῶν ἀρχιερέων καὶ τῶν τῆς πόλεως πρώτων ὑπὲρ τοῦ παρ' ἐμοῦ περὶ τῶν νομίμων ἀκριβέστερόν⁸² τι γνῶναι.⁸³ **¹⁰**περὶ ἑκκαίδεκα⁸⁴ δὲ ἔτη γενόμενος ἐβουλήθην τῶν παρ' ἡμῖν αἱρέσεων⁸⁵ ἐμπειρίαν⁸⁶ λαβεῖν· τρεῖς δ' εἰσὶν αὗται, Φαρισαίων μὲν ἡ πρώτη καὶ Σαδδουκαίων ἡ δευτέρα, τρίτη δ' Ἐσσηνῶν, καθὼς πολλάκις εἴπομεν· οὕτως γὰρ ᾤμην⁸⁷ αἱρήσεσθαι⁸⁸ τὴν ἀρίστην, εἰ πάσας καταμάθοιμι.⁸⁹ **¹¹**σκληραγωγήσας⁹⁰ οὖν ἐμαυτὸν καὶ πολλὰ πονηθεὶς⁹¹ τὰς τρεῖς διῆλθον· καὶ μηδὲ τὴν ἐντεῦθεν⁹² ἐμπειρίαν ἱκανὴν⁹³ ἐμαυτῷ νομίσας⁹⁴ εἶναι, πυθόμενός⁹⁵ τινα Βάννουν⁹⁶ ὄνομα κατὰ τὴν ἐρημίαν⁹⁷ διατρίβειν,⁹⁸ ἐσθῆτι⁹⁹ μὲν¹⁰⁰ ἀπὸ δένδρων χρώμενον,¹⁰¹ τροφὴν¹⁰² δὲ τὴν αὐτομάτως φυομένην¹⁰³ προσφερόμενον,¹⁰⁴ ψυχρῷ¹⁰⁵ δὲ ὕδατι τὴν ἡμέραν καὶ τὴν νύκτα¹⁰⁶ πολλάκις λουόμενον¹⁰⁷ πρὸς ἁγνείαν,¹⁰⁸ ζηλωτὴς¹⁰⁹ ἐγενόμην αὐτοῦ. **¹²**καὶ διατρίψας παρ' αὐτῷ ἐνιαυτοὺς τρεῖς καὶ τὴν ἐπιθυμίαν¹¹⁰ τελειώσας¹¹¹ εἰς τὴν πόλιν ὑπέστρεφον.¹¹² ἐννεακαιδέκατον δ' ἔτος ἔχων ἠρξάμην [τε] πολιτεύεσθαι¹¹³ τῇ Φαρισαίων αἱρέσει κατακολουθῶν,¹¹⁴ ἣ παραπλήσιός¹¹⁵ ἐστι τῇ παρ' Ἕλλησιν Στωϊκῇ¹¹⁶ λεγομένῃ.

NOTES

1. Priestly ancestry and nobility are central to Josephus's self-presentation (cf. *B.J.* 1.3, 26; 3.352; *A.J.*

73. σύνεσις, -εως, ἡ, *understanding*; dat. of respect.
74. Pres. act. ptc. nom. masc. sg., δοκέω, *appear* (by reputation); with inf.; circ.
75. Pres. act. inf., διαφέρω, *differ, be distinguished*.
76. ἀντίπαις, -παιδος, ὁ, *a mere boy*.
77. τεσσαρεσκαιδέκατος, -η, -ον, *fourteenth*; περὶ τεσσαρεσκαιδέκατον ἔτος, "around fourteen years old."
78. φιλογράμματος, -ον, *loving letters*.
79. Impf. pass. indic. 1 sg., ἐπαινέω, (pass.) *be praised*.
80. Pres. act. ptc. gen. masc. pl., σύνειμι, *attend, associate with* (a teacher).
81. Adv., *always*.
82. Compar., ἀκριβής, -ές, *more precisely*.
83. Art. inf. as obj. of ὑπέρ (cf. S §2032.g): ὑπὲρ τοῦ . . . γνῶναι, "*for the sake of learning* from me something more precisely about the legal matters."
84. ἑκκαίδεκα (indecl.), *sixteen*; περὶ ἑκκαίδεκα ἔτη, "around sixteen years old."
85. αἵρεσις, -εως, ἡ, *philosophical school*.
86. ἐμπειρία, -ας, ἡ, *experience*.
87. Impf. mid. indic. 1 sg., οἴομαι, *think, suppose*.
88. Fut. mid. inf., αἱρέω, (mid.) *choose*; indir. disc. (cf. BDF §397; S §2016; CGCG §51.19).
89. Aor. act. opt. 1 sg., καταμανθάνω, *learn, examine*; mixed condition: εἰ with opt. in protasis, fut. inf. (for indic.) in the apodosis (cf. S §2361; CGCG §49.17).
90. Aor. act. ptc. nom. masc. sg., σκληραγωγέω, *toughen/harden* (oneself); circ.
91. Aor. pass. ptc. nom. masc. sg., πονέω, *labor, toil*; with πολλά (internal acc.).
92. Adv., *from there*.
93. ἱκανός, -ή, -όν, *sufficient, enough*.
94. Aor. act. ptc. nom. masc. sg., νομίζω, *consider, reckon*; circ.

95. Aor. act. ptc. nom. masc. sg., πυνθάνομαι, *learn* (by inquiry); circ.
96. Βάννους, -ου, ὁ, *Bannus*.
97. ἐρημία, -ας, ἡ, *wilderness, desert*.
98. Pres. act. inf., διατρίβω, *spend time, live*; indir. disc. See n. 88.
99. ἐσθής, -ῆτος, ἡ, *clothing*.
100. μέν . . . δέ . . . δέ, point/counterpoints. See n. 47.
101. Pres. mid. ptc. acc. masc. sg., χράομαι, *use*; with dat.; circ.
102. τροφή, -ῆς, ἡ, *food*.
103. Pres. pass. ptc. acc. fem. sg., φύω, (pass.) *grow*; attrib. (subst.).
104. Pres. mid. ptc. acc. masc. sg., προσφέρω, (mid.) *to accept* (for oneself); circ.
105. ψυχρός, -ή, -όν, *cold, icy*.
106. τὴν ἡμέραν καὶ τὴν νύκτα, "by day and by night."
107. Pres. mid. ptc. acc. masc. sg., λούω, (mid.) *wash* (oneself); circ.
108. ἁγνεία, -ας, ἡ, *purity*.
109. ζηλωτής, -οῦ, ὁ, *devotee*.
110. ἐπιθυμία, -ας, ἡ, *longing, desire*.
111. Aor. act. ptc. nom. masc. sg., τελειόω, *complete*; circ.
112. Impf. act. indic. 3 sg., ὑποστρέφω, *return*.
113. Pres. mid. inf., πολιτεύομαι, *be involved in the affairs of the polis, participate in public life*. At age nineteen (56–57 CE) Josephus began his life of public service.
114. Pres. act. ptc. nom. masc. sg., κατακολουθέω, *follow after*; with dat.
115. παραπλήσιος, -α, -ον, *very similar*; with dat.
116. Στωϊκός, -ή, -όν, *Stoic*.

4.304; 10.151–153; 16.187; 20.224–251; *Vita* 13, 29, 80; *C. Ap.* 1.28–54; 2.184–193; Mason 2001, 4n4), which would have resonated with his Roman audience (cf. Polybius, *Hist.* 6.56; Cicero, *Leg.* 2.12.31; Cicero, *Rep.* 2.12–14; Cicero, *Dom.* 1.1; Beard, North, and Price 1998, 1:186–96).

2. ἐκ τῆς πρώτης ἐφημερίδος τῶν εἰκοσιτεσσάρων. Cf. *A.J.* 7.365–367. The clan of Jehoiarib (Ioarib) is the first of the twenty-four priestly clans designated for service (cf. 1 Chron. 24:1–19) and the one from which the Hasmoneans descended (cf. *A.J.* 12.265; 1 Macc. 2:1). Mason (2001, 5n9) says, "By Josephus' time, a weekly rotation was in place (*A.J.* 7.365). Each priestly course came up to Jerusalem from its home territory to serve from one sabbath to the next. Thus each course served twice per year in addition to the three pilgrimage festivals, when all eligible priests were required." Cf. 4Q320, 4Q321; Luke 1:5–8; m. Sukkah 5.6–8.

3. Σίμων ὁ Ψελλός. Mason (2001, 7n20) notes, "Josephus' mention of an obviously revered ancestor with a name indicating a physical disability intersects remarkably well with the paradox of Roman *cognomina*. On the one hand, these third names originated among the nobility, so that they were *ipso facto* a mark of distinction. On the other hand, nearly half (44%) of them indicate some kind of physical peculiarity—just as most of the names that Josephus gives his ancestors" (so also Ματθίας ὁ Κυρτός, *Vita* 4). "This raises the question," Mason continues, "of whether Josephus is not deliberately Romanizing his ancestry; for, paradoxically, such names 'actually became a mark of noble birth, and were consequently avoided in slaves' nomenclature' (Kajanto 1965:68)."

8. παιδείας. Cf. *C. Ap.* 2.171–183. Mason (2001, 12n56) notes, "There is a happy coincidence between the distinctive themes of Judean education as Josephus presents them (here and in the *Against Apion*) and those of the conservative Roman ideal.... In both worlds education is: a paternal responsibility; grounded in ancient laws and customs ([*C. Ap.*] 2.173–74); suffused with the bucolic virtues of simplicity, frugality, and honor ([*C. Ap.*] 2.284, 294); and calculated to produce an effective public figure (*Vita* 12–13). Above all, both Roman and Judean traditionalists define themselves to a large extent *over against the Greeks*."

9. Cf. Luke 2:41–52; Jub. 11:18–24; Plutarch, *Sol.* 2.1; Plutarch, *Them.* 2.1; Plutarch, *Dion* 4.5–7; Plutarch, *Cic.* 2.2; Plutarch, *Alex.* 5.1–6; and Philostratus, *Vit. Apoll.* 1.7.

10. On the three philosophical schools of Judaism, cf. *B.J.* 2.119–166 (§§5.1.3; 5.1.4); *A.J.* 13.171–173, 293–300; 18.11–22. Exposure to the various philosophies of the day became an ideal of the Roman world (cf. Lucian, *Men.* 4–5; Justin Martyr, *Dial.* 2; Rajak 1983, 34–38).

11. Βάννουν. This is the only mention of the ascetic figure. On the wilderness as the necessary training ground, see especially Philo (discussion in Niehoff 2018, 57–63).

12. τῇ Φαρισαίων αἱρέσει κατακολουθῶν. Many take this to mean that Josephus joined the Pharisaic school. Mason, by contrast, argues that Josephus merely shows deference to the Pharisees on account of their outsized influence (cf. *A.J.* 18.17). For the full argument, see Mason (1991, 325–56).

5.4

Against Apion

Josephus's final work takes its name from the historian's primary target, an Egyptian scholar who had relocated to Rome during the reign of Tiberius.[1] As with most works of apologetics, however, *Against Apion* appears to have been written for a sympathetic audience, a "group of amenable Gentiles in Rome" (Mason 2003, 138). Josephus casts his opponents as representative of *Greek* culture, which the Romans despised as soft, effeminate, and morally suspect. *Against Apion* thus reads as Josephus's "last and best effort for sympathetic Gentiles," perhaps an indication that he had grown more confident in his initial calculation: through Rome, Jewish wisdom would indeed spread to the rest of the world (Mason 2003, 140).

The reading passage is part of a larger discussion about the wisdom and supremacy of the Jewish constitution. Josephus transitions from general observations on the constitution to the specific commandments that govern it.

Text and Translation: Thackeray 1926
Supplemental Scripture: Deut. 6:4–9; 12:1–19; 16:5–6

---

1. The actual title of the work has been lost, perhaps something like *On the Antiquity of the Jews*.

5.4.1

Jewish Virtue

Against Apion 2.190–198

2.190Τίνες οὖν εἰσιν αἱ προρρήσεις¹ καὶ ἀπαγορεύσεις;² ἁπλαῖ³ τε καὶ γνώριμοι.⁴ πρώτη δ' ἡγεῖται⁵ ἡ περὶ θεοῦ λέγουσα ὅτι θεὸς ἔχει τὰ σύμπαντα, παντελὴς⁶ καὶ μακάριος,⁷ αὐτὸς αὑτῷ καὶ πᾶσιν αὐτάρκης,⁸ ἀρχὴ καὶ μέσα καὶ τέλος⁹ οὗτος τῶν πάντων, ἔργοις μὲν¹⁰ καὶ χάρισιν ἐναργὴς¹¹ καὶ παντὸς οὗτινος φανερώτερος,¹² μορφὴν¹³ δὲ καὶ μέγεθος¹⁴ ἡμῖν ἄφατος.¹⁵ **191**πᾶσα μὲν¹⁶ ὕλη¹⁷ πρὸς εἰκόνα¹⁸ τὴν τούτου κἂν¹⁹ ᾖ πολυτελὴς²⁰ ἄτιμος,²¹ πᾶσα δὲ τέχνη²² πρὸς μιμήσεως²³ ἐπίνοιαν²⁴ ἄτεχνος.²⁵ οὐδὲν ὅμοιον²⁶ οὔτ' εἴδομεν οὔτ' ἐπινοοῦμεν²⁷ οὔτ' εἰκάζειν²⁸ ἐστὶν ὅσιον.²⁹ **192**ἔργα βλέπομεν αὐτοῦ φῶς, οὐρανὸν, γῆν, ἥλιον, ὕδατα, ζῴων³⁰ γενέσεις,³¹ καρπῶν ἀναδόσεις.³² ταῦτα θεὸς

---

1. προρρήσις, -εως, ἡ, *proclamation*. In the context of mystery rites (cf. 2.189), the term signifies "a public announcement containing elements of information, instruction, and warning (e.g., on eligibility for the rites)" (Barclay 2007, 276n749).
2. ἀπαγόρευσις, -εως, ἡ, *prohibition*.
3. ἁπλοῦς, -ῆ, -οῦν, *simple*.
4. γνώριμος, -ον, *well-known*.
5. Pres. mid. indic. 3 sg., ἡγέομαι, *precede, lead, be at the head*.
6. παντελής, -ές, *perfect*.
7. μακάριος, -α, -ον, *blessed*.
8. αὐτάρκης, -ες, *self-sufficient*.
9. τέλος, -ους, τό, *end*.
10. μέν ... δέ; point/counterpoint (cf. Runge 2010, 75–83; BDF §447; S §2904; CGCG §59.24).
11. ἐναργής, -ές, *visible*.
12. Compar., φανερός, -ά, -όν, *more manifest*; with gen. of comparison, "more manifest than anything else."
13. μορφή, -ῆς, ἡ, *form*; acc. of respect.
14. μέγεθος, -ους, τό, *greatness, magnitude*; acc. of respect.
15. ἄφατος, -ον, *ineffable*.
16. μέν ... δέ; point/counterpoint. See n. 10.
17. ὕλη, -ης, ἡ, *material*.
18. εἰκών, -όνος, ἡ, *image*.
19. Crasis: κἂν = καὶ ἐάν; concessive clause (cf. BDF §374; S §2369; CGCG §49.19).
20. πολυτελής, -ές, *very expensive*.
21. ἄτιμος, -ον, *unworthy*; pred. adj.
22. τέχνη, -ης, ἡ, *art, skill, craft*.
23. μίμησις, -εως, ἡ, *representation*.
24. ἐπίνοια, -ας, ἡ, *power of thought, ability to conceive*; πρὸς μιμήσεως ἐπίνοιαν, "with respect to the ability to conceive of his representation."
25. ἄτεχνος, -ον, *without art/skill*; pred. adj.
26. ὅμοιος, -α, -ον, *like, similar to*.
27. Pres. act. indic. 1 pl., ἐπινοέω, *think of, conceive of*.
28. Pres. act. inf., εἰκάζω, *guess/conjecture* (about something).
29. ὅσιος, -α, -ον, (quasi-impers.) *it is pious/holy*; with acc. and inf. (cf. S §1985; CGCG §36.8).
30. ζῷον, -ου, τό, *living creature, animal*.
31. γένεσις, -εως, ἡ, *genesis, generation*.
32. ἀνάδοσις, -εως, ἡ, *sprouting* (of plants); καρπῶν ἀναδόσεις, "sprouting of crops."

ἐποίησεν οὐ χερσὶν, οὐ πόνοις,³³ οὔ τινων συνεργασομένων³⁴ ἐπιδεηθείς,³⁵ ἀλλ' αὐτοῦ θελήσαντος καλῶς ἦν εὐθὺς γεγονότα. τοῦτον θεραπευτέον³⁶ ἀσκοῦντας³⁷ ἀρετήν·³⁸ τρόπος³⁹ γὰρ θεοῦ θεραπείας⁴⁰ οὗτος ὁσιώτατος.

193Εἷς ναὸς⁴¹ ἑνὸς θεοῦ, φίλον⁴² γὰρ ἀεὶ παντὶ τὸ ὅμοιον, κοινὸς⁴³ ἁπάντων κοινοῦ θεοῦ ἁπάντων. τοῦτον θεραπεύσουσιν μὲν⁴⁴ διὰ παντὸς⁴⁵ οἱ ἱερεῖς, ἡγήσεται δὲ τούτων ὁ πρῶτος ἀεὶ κατὰ γένος.⁴⁶ **194**οὗτος μετὰ τῶν συνιερέων⁴⁷ θύσει⁴⁸ τῷ θεῷ, φυλάξει⁴⁹ τοὺς νόμους, δικάσει⁵⁰ περὶ τῶν ἀμφισβητουμένων,⁵¹ κολάσει⁵² τοὺς ἐλεγχθέντας.⁵³ ὁ τούτῳ μὴ πειθόμενος⁵⁴ ὑφέξει⁵⁵ δίκην ὡς εἰς θεὸν αὐτὸν ἀσεβῶν.⁵⁶ **195**θύομεν τὰς θυσίας οὐκ εἰς μέθην⁵⁷ ἑαυτοῖς, ἀβούλητον⁵⁸ γὰρ θεῷ τόδε, ἀλλ' εἰς σωφροσύνην.⁵⁹ **196**καὶ ἐπὶ ταῖς θυσίαις χρὴ⁶⁰ πρῶτον ὑπὲρ τῆς κοινῆς εὔχεσθαι⁶¹ σωτηρίας, εἶθ' ὑπὲρ ἑαυτῶν· ἐπὶ γὰρ κοινωνίᾳ⁶² γεγόναμεν, καὶ ταύτην ὁ προτιμῶν⁶³ τοῦ καθ' αὐτὸν ἰδίου μάλιστ'⁶⁴ [ἂν] εἴη⁶⁵ θεῷ κεχαρισμένος.⁶⁶ **197**δέησις⁶⁷ δ' ἔστω πρὸς τὸν θεόν, οὐχ ὅπως δῷ τἀγαθά,⁶⁸ δέδωκεν γὰρ αὐτὸς ἑκὼν⁶⁹ καὶ πᾶσιν εἰς μέσον κατατέθεικεν,⁷⁰ ἀλλ' ὅπως δέχεσθαι δυνώμεθα καὶ λαβόντες φυλάττωμεν. **198**ἁγνείας⁷¹ ἐπὶ ταῖς θυσίαις διείρηκεν⁷² ὁ νόμος ἀπὸ κήδους,⁷³ ἀπὸ λεχοῦς,⁷⁴ ἀπὸ κοινωνίας τῆς πρὸς γυναῖκα καὶ πολλῶν ἄλλων [ἃ μακρὸν ἂν εἴη γράφειν.

---

33. πόνος, -ου, ὁ, *hard labor, toil*; dat. of manner.
34. Fut. mid. ptc. gen. masc. pl., συνεργάζομαι, *work with*, (attrib. [subst.]) *coworkers*.
35. Aor. pass. ptc. nom. masc. sg., ἐπιδέω, (pass.) *be in want or need of*; with gen.; circ.
36. Verbal adj. of θεραπεύω, personal (pass.) constr. (cf. S §2151; *CGCG* §37.2): "This one is *to be worshiped* [by us]."
37. Pres. act. indic. acc. masc. pl., ἀσκέω, *practice*. The participle agrees with the implied agent of the verbal adjective, which is usually dative but here is accusative (cf. S §2152.a; *CGCG* §37.3n1).
38. ἀρετή, -ῆς, ἡ, *virtue*.
39. τρόπος, -ου, ὁ, *manner, guise*.
40. θεραπεία, -ας, ἡ, *service, worship*.
41. ναός, -οῦ, ὁ, *sanctuary, shrine*.
42. φίλος, -η, -ον, *dear*; full clause: "for like is always dear to like" (cf. Homer, *Od.* 17.218; Aristotle, *Eth. nic.* 1165b; Sir. 13:15–20).
43. κοινός, -ή, -όν, *common*; κοινὸς ἁπάντων κοινοῦ θεοῦ ἁπάντων, "[one temple] common to all people of the God who is common to all people."
44. μέν . . . δέ; point/counterpoint. See n. 10.
45. διὰ παντός, *continually*.
46. γένος, -ους, τό, *descent*.
47. συνιερεύς, -έως, ὁ, *fellow priest*.
48. Fut. act. indic. 3 sg., θύω, *sacrifice*.
49. Fut. act. indic. 3 sg., φυλάσσω (Att. φυλάττω), *keep, guard*.
50. Fut. act. indic. 3 sg., δικάζω, *act as judge*.
51. Pres. pass. ptc. gen. masc. pl., ἀμφισβητέω, *be the subject of dispute, be in question*; attrib. (subst.).
52. Fut. act. indic. 3 sg., κολάζω, *punish*.
53. Aor. pass. ptc. acc. masc. pl., ἐλέγχω, (pass.) *be proved guilty*; attrib. (subst.).
54. Pres. mid. ptc. nom. masc. sg., πείθω, (mid.) *obey*; with dat.; attrib. (subst.).
55. Fut. act. indic. 3 sg., ὑπέχω, (in legal contexts) *suffer* (a penalty; δίκην).
56. Pres. act. ptc. nom. masc. sg., ἀσεβέω, *act impiously, commit sacrilege*. ὡς with a circumstantial participle gives "a 'subjective' reason or motivation, for which responsibility lies with the subject of the matrix verb" (*CGCG* §52.39): "on the grounds that he has committed sacrilege against God himself."
57. μέθη, -ης, ἡ, *drunkenness*.
58. ἀβούλητος, -ον, *that which is not willed/desired*.
59. σωφροσύνη, -ης, ἡ, *self-control*.
60. Quasi-impers., χρή, *it is necessary*; with (acc. and) inf. (cf. BDF §405; S §1985; *CGCG* §36.3).
61. Pres. mid. inf., εὔχομαι, *pray*.
62. κοινωνία, -ας, ἡ, *fellowship*; ἐπὶ κοινωνίᾳ (purpose).
63. Pres. act. ptc. nom. masc. sg., προτιμέω, *honor* (acc.) *above* (gen.); attrib. (subst.).
64. Superl. adv. of μάλα, *especially*.
65. Pres. act. opt. 3 sg., εἰμί; potential (cf. BDF §385; S §1824; *CGCG* §34.13).
66. Pf. pass. ptc. nom. masc. sg., χαρίζω, (pass.) *be pleasing/dear to*; with dat.; periphrastic.
67. δέησις, -εως, ἡ, *petition*.
68. Crasis: τἀγαθά = τὰ ἀγαθά.
69. ἑκών, ἑκοῦσα, ἑκόν, *as depends on one's will*.
70. Pf. act. indic. 3 sg., κατατίθημι, *put down, deposit*.
71. ἁγνεία, -ας, ἡ, (pl.) *purifications*.
72. Pf. act. indic. 3 sg., διείρω, *expressly state/prescribe*.
73. κῆδος, -ους, τό, *funeral* (i.e., corpse impurity).
74. Either λεχώ, -οῦς, ἡ, *childbirth*; or λέχος, -ους, τό, *bed* (i.e., sexual intercourse). The former reading is preferable since the latter would overlap with κοινωνίας τῆς πρὸς γυναῖκα.

τοιοῦτος μὲν ὁ περὶ θεοῦ καὶ τῆς ἐκείνου θεραπείας λόγος ἡμῖν ἐστιν, ὁ δ᾽ αὐτὸς ἅμα καὶ νόμος.][75]

NOTES

2.190. ἔργοις . . . καὶ χάρισιν ἐναργής. The notion that the invisible God is rendered "visible" by his works and gracious gifts is widespread (cf. Wis. 13:1–9; Rom. 1:19–20).

2.192. Cf. Gen. 1; Josephus, A.J. 1.27–33.

οὔ τινων συνεργασομένων ἐπιδεηθείς. Josephus rejects Plato's claim that the Demiurge used assistants to create the cosmos (Plato, Tim. 41c; 42e). Philo's response to Plato is more nuanced. While he makes it abundantly clear that the one God has no need of helpers (cf. Philo, Opif. 72), he cannot ignore the plural in "Let *us* make humanity in our image" (Gen. 1:26). Thus he makes a virtue out of an exegetical and theological conundrum: not God but his helpers are the cause of human error (cf. Opif. 72–75; see §4.2.3).

ἀρετήν. Cf. A.J. 1.20. Note his subsequent comment that the disposition of the sacrificer should be σωφροσύνη (2.195).

2.193. Εἷς ναὸς ἑνὸς θεοῦ. Cf. Deut. 12:5. Josephus knew of the temple in Leontopolis (cf. B.J. 7.420–432; A.J. 13.62–70), but the Jerusalem temple is sui generis. There is *one* temple for the *one* God (cf. Philo, Spec. 1.67; §4.2.7). Cf. A.J. 4.201: "In no other city let there be either altar or temple; for God is one and the Hebrew race is one" (Thackeray 1930b).

2.194. ὡς εἰς θεὸν αὐτὸν ἀσεβῶν. Cf. Mark 14:63 parr.; Acts 23:3–5; Barclay (2007, 280n777) states, "The authority of the high priest undergirds the constitution (cf. Hecataeus *apud* Diodorus 40.3.6), and his relationship to God is unique."

2.196. Cf. A.J. 4.243. Josephus also divides the various sacrifices into two categories: individual and corporate (A.J. 3.224, 233).

2.197. God's beneficence flows to all. Cf. C. Ap. 2.166, 190, 193; Philo, Leg. 1.34–35 (§4.1.2); Matt. 6:7–8; 7:7–11; Seneca, Ep. 95.47–50; and discussion in Barclay (2007, 281nn786–87).

2.198. ἁγνείας. Like Philo, Josephus is interested in both the rituals themselves and their virtuous ends. Compare what Barclay (2007, 281n788) says: "The two explanatory frameworks sit side by side, since worship of God can be understood as a matter of both ritual and virtue (2.192)."

ἀπὸ κήδους. Cf. Num. 19:10–22; A.J. 3.262; and rationale in C. Ap. 2.205.

ἀπὸ λεχοῦς. Cf. Lev. 12 and rationale in C. Ap. 2.204.

ἀπὸ κοινωνίας τῆς πρὸς γυναῖκα. Cf. Lev. 15:16–18. Josephus offers the rationale in 2.203: "For the Law regards this act as involving a partition of the soul [part of it going] into another place; for it suffers both when being implanted in bodies, and again when severed from them by death" (Thackeray 1926). The assumption is that "the (male) seed carries the 'soul' (ψυχή), a part of the father's soul, splintered or split off. . . . Cf. Philo's comment on children as 'parts' (μέρη) of their parents (Spec. 1.137)" (Barclay 2007, 286n817).

---

75. The bracketed text is in MS L, the Latin, and Eusebius codex I but is absent from the best Eusebius codices.

PART 6

Reading Historians and Biographers

Lucian of Samosata once quipped that "there is no one who is not writing history" (*Hist. cons.* 2, my trans.). Indeed, the second-century satirist only slightly exaggerates, and so we should not be surprised that Jewish and Christian writers were eager participants in the competitive field of ancient Mediterranean historiography.[1] Thus, the aim of this section is to introduce you to the literary culture that shaped large swaths of the New Testament, especially the Gospels and Acts.[2]

I have grouped the readings into three categories. We begin with the font of the historiographical tradition: Herodotus and Thucydides. Next, we turn to two of the annalists: Diodorus Siculus and Dio Cassius. Finally, we explore some of the most important biographers: Plutarch, Lucian, and Philostratus. Of course, it would be impossible to cover all the important voices. The goal, rather, is to expose you to various dialects and styles so that you have the confidence to read any of the Greek historians.

---

1. See, e.g., Aune 1987; Collins 2000; Sterling 2007; Adams 2020.
2. Since the publication of Burridge's *What Are the Gospels?* (1992; 3rd ed., 2020), there has been a growing consensus that the canonical Gospels are Greco-Roman biography. For an important critique of Burridge's approach to genre, see Shively 2020. On Acts as ancient Hellenistic historiography, see Keener 2012.

# 6.1

Herodotus

Herodotus (ca. 484–431 BCE) is known as the father of history. His work *Histories* centers on the war between the Persians and the Greeks, which Herodotus presents, in Homeric manner and verve, as the clash of Eastern (despotic) and Western (democratic) civilizations. Of course, he was not the first to take interest in the founding of cities, the origin of "barbarian" (non-Hellenic) customs, or the geography of the οἰκουμένη. Rather, "what makes Herodotus unique is the range of his interests and his attempt to unite human and natural phenomena, and in so doing to discover the causal interconnection of widely disparate events" (Marincola 2003, xviii).

The reading passages focus on areas of interest to students of biblical studies.[1] In the first, Herodotus describes the purpose of his ἱστορίη, "inquiry." The second is his dramatic presentation of Cyrus's capture of Babylon, and the third is an account of the origins of circumcision.

Text: Godley 1920
Recommended Translation: Marincola 2003
Supplemental Scripture: 2 Chron. 36:22; Ezra 1:1–4; Isa. 45:1; Dan. 5 (§6.1.2)

---

1. For additional practice reading Herodotus in a format designed for intermediate readers, see Jones et al. 2015a.

6.1.1

The Purpose of the Inquiry

Histories 1.1

1.1 Ἡροδότου¹ Ἁλικαρνησσέος² ἱστορίης³ ἀπόδεξις⁴ ἥδε, ὡς μήτε τὰ γενόμενα ἐξ ἀνθρώπων τῷ χρόνῳ ἐξίτηλα⁵ γένηται,⁶ μήτε ἔργα μεγάλα τε καὶ θωμαστά,⁷ τὰ μὲν⁸ Ἕλλησι⁹ τὰ δὲ βαρβάροισι¹⁰ ἀποδεχθέντα,¹¹ ἀκλεᾶ¹² γένηται, τά τε¹³ ἄλλα καὶ δι' αἰτίην¹⁴ ἐπολέμησαν¹⁵ ἀλλήλοισι.¹⁶

1. Ἡρόδοτος, -ου, ὁ, *Herodotus*.
2. Ἁλικαρνησσεύς, έος, ὁ, *Halicarnassian*.
3. ἱστορία, -ας, ἡ, *inquiry, what is learned by inquiry*; Ion. η for ᾱ.
4. ἀπόδεξις, -εως, ἡ, *setting forth, publication*. "This [here] is the setting forth of the inquiry of Herodotus the Halicarnassian"; thus, essentially the title of the work.
5. ἐξίτηλος, -ον, *going out*; hence *faded, blotted out, forgotten*.
6. Purpose clause: ὡς with subj. (cf. BDF §369; S §2193; CGCG §45.2).
7. θωμαστός, -ή, -όν, *wonderful, marvelous*.
8. τὰ μέν ... τὰ δέ, *some (things) ... other (things)* (cf. BDF §250; S §1107; CGCG §28.27).
9. Ἕλλην, -ηνος, ὁ, (pl.) *Hellenes, Greeks*.
10. Ion. 2nd decl. dat. masc. pl., βάρβαρος, -ον, (subst. pl.) *non-Hellenic peoples, barbarians*.
11. Aor. pass. ptc. nom. neut. pl., ἀποδέχομαι, (pass.) *be accepted/admitted*; attrib. (subst.).
12. ἀκλεής, -ές, *without fame/renown*.
13. The particle tacks on an additional point that is coordinated with a second, stronger point (cf. S §2974): "all the rest [τά ἄλλα, appositive to ἔργα], *especially* the reason they went to war against one another."
14. αἰτία, -ας, ἡ, *reason*; Ion. η for ᾱ.
15. Aor. act. indic. 3 pl., πολεμέω, *war against*; with dat.
16. ἀλλήλοισι = ἀλλήλοις (cf. S §229).

NOTES

1.1. ἱστορίης. Herodotus means "inquiry" or the results thereof. The success of his inquiry plays a leading role in the development of the genre ἱστορίη.

τὰ γενόμενα ἐξ ἀνθρώπων. Herodotus's focus on "human achievements" distinguishes his work from epic poetry, in which the deeds of the gods and humans are intertwined. Nonetheless, he clearly emulates Homer when he expresses his desire to ensure that ἔργα μεγάλα τε καὶ θωμαστά are not ἀκλεᾶ (cf. Homer, *Il.* 9.189; Fornara 1983, 31–32, 96–97).

τὰ μὲν Ἕλλησι τὰ δὲ βαρβάροισι ἀποδεχθέντα. The standard polarity of Greeks versus "barbarians"—that is, non-Greeks (in this case, Persians). Cf. Thucydides, *Hist. pel.* 1.2 (§6.2.1); and discussion in Cartledge (1993). Paul employs the same dichotomy in Romans: Ἕλλησίν τε καὶ βαρβάροις, σοφοῖς τε καὶ ἀνοήτοις ὀφειλέτης εἰμί (Rom. 1:14).

6.1.2

Cyrus Captures Babylon

Histories 1.189–191

1.189 Ἐπείτε¹ δὲ ὁ Κῦρος² πορευόμενος ἐπὶ τὴν Βαβυλῶνα³ ἐγίνετο ἐπὶ Γύνδῃ⁴ ποταμῷ,⁵ τοῦ⁶ αἱ μὲν⁷ πηγαὶ⁸ ἐν Ματιηνοῖσι⁹ ὄρεσι,¹⁰ ῥέει¹¹ δὲ διὰ Δαρδανέων,¹² ἐκδιδοῖ¹³ δὲ ἐς¹⁴ ἕτερον ποταμὸν Τίγρην,¹⁵ ὁ δὲ παρὰ Ὦπιν¹⁶ πόλιν ῥέων ἐς τὴν Ἐρυθρὴν¹⁷ θάλασσαν ἐκδιδοῖ, τοῦτον δὴ¹⁸ τὸν Γύνδην ποταμὸν ὡς διαβαίνειν¹⁹ ἐπειρᾶτο²⁰ ὁ Κῦρος ἐόντα²¹ νηυσιπέρητον,²² ἐνθαῦτά²³ οἱ²⁴ τῶν τις ἱρῶν²⁵ ἵππων²⁶ τῶν λευκῶν²⁷ ὑπὸ ὕβριος²⁸ ἐσβὰς²⁹ ἐς τὸν ποταμὸν διαβαίνειν

1. Adv. (ἐπεί, τε), *when*.
2. Κῦρος, -ου, ὁ, *Cyrus*.
3. Βαβυλών, -ῶνος, ἡ, *Babylon*.
4. Γύνδης, -εω, ἡ, *Gyndes* (modern Diala).
5. ποταμός, -οῦ, ὁ, *river*.
6. τοῦ = οὗ. In Ionic literary prose, the relative pronoun is identical to the article in all cases except the nominative masculine singular and, with respect to accent, the nominative feminine singular and nominative masculine or feminine plural (cf. S §338 D.3; *CGCG* §25.31).
7. μέν...δέ...δέ...δέ, point/counterpoints set (cf. S §2907).
8. πηγή, -ῆς, ἡ, (pl.) *font, source*.
9. Ion. 2nd decl. dat. masc. pl., Ματιηνοί, οἱ, *Matieni, Matieneans* (people group in northern Assyria).
10. ὄρος, -εος, τό, *mountain*.
11. Pres. act. indic. 3 sg., ῥέω, *stream*.
12. Δαρδανεύς, -έως, ὁ, (pl.) *Dardanians* (unknown people group); διὰ Δαρδανέων, "through [the country] of the Dardanians."
13. Pres. act. indic. 3 sg., ἐκδίδωμι, (intrans., of rivers) *empty* (itself).
14. ἐς = εἰς.
15. Τίγρης, -ητος, ὁ, *Tigris*; appositive.
16. Ὦπις, -ιδος, ἡ, *Opis* (Assyrian city).
17. Ἐρυθρός, -ή, -όν, *red*; the Red Sea (= Indian Ocean).
18. Partic.: "indicates that the speaker considers (and invites the addressee to consider) the text segment or word (group) that it modifies as evident, clear, or precise" (*CGCG* §59.44). Here with a connecting function: "*Now*, as to *this* river Gyndes (which we previously mentioned) ..."
19. Pres. act. inf., διαβαίνω, *cross over*.
20. Impf. mid. indic. 3 sg., πειράω, *attempt*; with inf.
21. Pres. act. ptc. acc. masc. sg., εἰμί; circ. (concessive).
22. νηυσιπέρητος, -ον, *able to be crossed by boat* (cf. LSJ, 1162).
23. Demon. adv., *here, there*.
24. οἱ = αὐτῷ; 3 pers. pron. οὗ (cf. S §325; *CGCG* §25.28); dat. of the possessor.
25. ἱρός, -ή, -όν (Ion.), *sacred*.
26. ἵππος, -ου, ὁ, *horse*.
27. λευκός, -ή, -όν, *white*.
28. ὕβρις, -ιος, ἡ, *violence, insolence*; ὑπὸ ὕβριος, "driven by insolence" (cause), or "violently" (manner).
29. Aor. act. ptc. nom. masc. sg., ἐσβαίνω (εἰσβαίνω), *enter*; circ.

ἐπειρᾶτο, ὁ δέ μιν³⁰ συμψήσας³¹ ὑποβρύχιον³² οἰχώκεε³³ φέρων, κάρτα³⁴ τε δὴ ἐχαλέπαινε³⁵ τῷ ποταμῷ ὁ Κῦρος τοῦτο ὑβρίσταντι,³⁶ καί οἱ ἐπηπείλησε³⁷ οὕτω δή μιν ἀσθενέα ποιήσειν³⁸ ὥστε τοῦ λοιποῦ³⁹ καὶ γυναῖκάς μιν εὐπετέως⁴⁰ τὸ γόνυ⁴¹ οὐ βρεχούσας⁴² διαβήσεσθαι.⁴³ μετὰ δὲ τὴν ἀπειλὴν⁴⁴ μετεὶς⁴⁵ τὴν ἐπὶ Βαβυλῶνα στράτευσιν⁴⁶ διαίρεε⁴⁷ τὴν στρατιὴν⁴⁸ δίχα,⁴⁹ διελὼν⁵⁰ δὲ κατέτεινε⁵¹ σχοινοτενέας⁵² ὑποδέξας⁵³ διώρυχας⁵⁴ ὀγδώκοντα καὶ ἑκατὸν⁵⁵ παρ' ἑκάτερον τὸ χεῖλος⁵⁶ τοῦ Γύνδεω τετραμμένας⁵⁷ πάντα τρόπον,⁵⁸ διατάξας⁵⁹ δὲ τὸν στρατὸν⁶⁰ ὀρύσσειν⁶¹ ἐκέλευε.⁶² οἷα δὲ ὁμίλου⁶³ πολλοῦ ἐργαζομένου⁶⁴ ἤνετο⁶⁵ μὲν⁶⁶ τὸ ἔργον, ὅμως μέντοι τὴν θερείην⁶⁷ πᾶσαν αὐτοῦ⁶⁸ ταύτῃ⁶⁹ διέτριψαν⁷⁰ ἐργαζόμενοι.

190 Ὡς δὲ τὸν Γύνδην ποταμὸν ἐτίσατο⁷¹ Κῦρος ἐς τριηκοσίας καὶ ἑξήκοντα⁷² διώρυχάς μιν διαλαβών,⁷³ καὶ τὸ δεύτερον ἔαρ⁷⁴ ὑπέλαμπε,⁷⁵ οὕτω δὴ ἤλαυνε⁷⁶ ἐπὶ τὴν Βαβυλῶνα. οἱ δὲ Βαβυλώνιοι ἐκστρατευσάμενοι⁷⁷ ἔμενον⁷⁸ αὐτόν. ἐπεὶ δὲ ἐγένετο ἐλαύνων ἀγχοῦ⁷⁹ τῆς πόλιος,⁸⁰ συνέβαλόν⁸¹ τε οἱ Βαβυλώνιοι

30. μιν = αὐτόν. Herodotus uses μιν as an accusative singular personal pronoun (cf. S §325 D.3; *CGCG* §29.3).
31. Aor. act. ptc. nom. masc. sg., συμψάω, *sweep away*.
32. ὑποβρύχιος, -ον, *underwater*.
33. Plpf. act. indic. 3 sg., οἴχομαι, *come, go*; no augment or reduplication.
34. Adv., *very*; underscored by δή (on which, see n. 18).
35. Impf. act. indic. 3 sg., χαλεπαίνω, *become angry*.
36. Aor. act. ptc. dat. masc. sg., ὑβρίζω (with τοῦτο), *commit this outrage*; circ. (causal).
37. Aor. act. indic. 3 sg., ἐπαπειλέω, *threaten*; with dat. οἱ (= αὐτῷ).
38. Fut. act. inf., ποιέω; indir. disc. (cf. BDF §397; S §2592; *CGCG* §41.2).
39. τοῦ λοιποῦ (χρόνου), *in the future*.
40. Adv., *easily*.
41. γόνυ, -ατος, τό, *knee*.
42. Aor. act. ptc. acc. fem. pl., βρέχω, *wet*; circ.
43. Fut. mid. inf., διαβαίνω, *cross*; result (cf. BDF §391; S §2269; *CGCG* §46.6): "He would make it so [οὕτω δή] weak that even [καί] women would easily cross it not wetting their knees."
44. ἀπειλή, -ῆς, ἡ, *threat*.
45. Aor. act. ptc. nom. masc. sg., μεθίημι, *give up, abandon*; circ.
46. στράτευσις, -εως, ἡ, *expedition, campaign*.
47. Impf. act. indic. 3 sg., διαιρέω, *divide*.
48. στρατιά, -ᾶς, ἡ, *army*; Ion. η for ᾱ.
49. Adv., *in two*.
50. Aor. act. ptc. nom. masc. sg., διαιρέω, *divide*; circ.
51. Aor. act. indic. 3 sg., κατατείνω, *stretch out*.
52. σχοινοτενής, -ές, *drawing in a straight line*.
53. Aor. act. ptc. nom. masc. sg., ὑποδείκνυμι, *mark out*; circ.
54. διῶρυξ, -υχος, ἡ, *ditch, trench, canal*.
55. ὀγδώκοντα καὶ ἑκατόν, *one hundred and eighty* (lit., "eighty and a hundred").
56. χεῖλος, -ου, τό, *edge*; παρ' ἑκάτερον τὸ χεῖλος, "along each edge."
57. Pf. mid. ptc. acc. fem. pl., τρέπω, *run*; attrib.
58. Adv. acc. (manner), πάντα τρόπον, *in every way*.
59. Aor. act. ptc. nom. masc. sg., διατάσσω, *arrange*; circ.
60. στρατός, -οῦ, ὁ, *army*.
61. Pres. act. inf., ὀρύσσω, *dig*.
62. Impf. act. indic. 3 sg., κελεύω, *order, bid*; with acc. and inf.
63. ὅμιλος, -ου, ὁ, *crowd*.
64. οἷα with a circumstantial participle gives an "'objective' reason or motivation, for which responsibility lies with the subject of the matrix verb" (*CGCG* §52.39; cf. S §2085).
65. Impf. pass. indic. 3 sg., ἄνω, (pass.) *be accomplished, completed*.
66. μέν . . . ὅμως μέντοι; stronger contrast than μέν . . . δέ (cf. S §2919; Denniston 1966, 404): "The work was finished; *and yet* they spent the entire summer there working in this way."
67. θερεία, -ας, ἡ, *summer*; Ion. η for ᾱ.
68. Adv., *there*.
69. Dat. of manner, *in this way*.
70. Aor. act. indic. 3 pl., διατρίβω, *spend time*.
71. Aor. mid. indic. 3 sg., τίνω, (mid.) *make pay, punish*.
72. τριακόσιοι (Ion. τριηκ-) καὶ ἑξήκοντα, *three hundred and sixty*.
73. Aor. act. ptc. nom. masc. sg., διαλαμβάνω, *divide*; circ.
74. ἔαρ, -ρος, τό, *spring*.
75. Impf. act. indic. 3 sg., ὑπολάμπω, *begin to shine*; καὶ τὸ δεύτερον ἔαρ ὑπέλαμπε, "and the next spring appeared" (LSJ, 1887.II).
76. Impf. act. indic. 3 sg., ἐλαύνω, (intrans.) *move forward, proceed*.
77. Aor. mid. ptc. nom. masc. pl., ἐκστρατεύω, *march out*; circ.
78. Impf. act. indic. 3 pl., μένω, *await* (someone); with acc.
79. Prep. with gen., *near to, close to*.
80. You might have expected πόλεως, but the Ionic dialect retains the ι-stem (cf. S §268 D.1).
81. Aor. act. indic. 3 pl., συμβάλλω, *join* (in battle).

καὶ ἑσσωθέντες⁸² τῇ μάχῃ⁸³ κατειλήθησαν⁸⁴ ἐς τὸ ἄστυ.⁸⁵ οἷα δὲ ἐξεπιστάμενοι⁸⁶ ἔτι πρότερον τὸν Κῦρον οὐκ ἀτρεμίζοντα,⁸⁷ ἀλλ᾽ ὁρέοντες⁸⁸ αὐτὸν παντὶ ἔθνει ὁμοίως ἐπιχειρέοντα,⁸⁹ προεσάξαντο⁹⁰ σιτία⁹¹ ἐτέων⁹² κάρτα πολλῶν. ἐνθαῦτα⁹³ οὗτοι μὲν⁹⁴ λόγον εἶχον τῆς πολιορκίης⁹⁵ οὐδένα, Κῦρος δὲ ἀπορίῃσι⁹⁶ ἐνείχετο,⁹⁷ ἅτε χρόνου τε ἐγγινομένου⁹⁸ συχνοῦ⁹⁹ ἀνωτέρω τε οὐδὲν¹⁰⁰ τῶν πρηγμάτων¹⁰¹ προκοπτομένων.¹⁰²

191 Εἴτε¹⁰³ δὴ ὦν ἄλλος οἱ¹⁰⁴ ἀπορέοντι¹⁰⁵ ὑπεθήκατο,¹⁰⁶ εἴτε καὶ αὐτὸς ἔμαθε¹⁰⁷ τὸ ποιητέον¹⁰⁸ οἱ ἦν,

82. Aor. pass. ptc. nom. masc. pl., ἑσσόομαι (Att. ἡσσάομαι), (pass.) *be defeated*; circ.
83. μάχη, -ης, ἡ, *battle*.
84. Aor. pass. indic. 3 pl., κατειλέω, (pass.) *be forced into a narrow space*.
85. ἄστυ, -εος, τό, *city*.
86. Pres. mid. ptc. nom. masc. pl., ἐξεπίσταμαι, *know thoroughly*; οἷα with circ. ptc. See n. 64.
87. Pres. act. ptc. acc. masc. sg., ἀτρεμίζω, *remain quiet*; supp. (ἐξεπιστάμενοι).
88. Pres. act. ptc. nom. masc. pl., ὁράω (Ion. ὁρέω), *see*; circ.
89. Pres. act. ptc. acc. masc. sg., ἐπιχειρέω, *attack*; with dat.; supp. (ὁρέοντες).
90. Aor. mid. indic. 3 pl., προσάσσω, *store in advance*.
91. σίτιον, -ου, τό, *grain, food*.
92. ἔτος, -εος, τό, *year*; gen. of measure (cf. S §1325).
93. Adv., *at that time*.
94. μέν . . . δέ; point/counterpoint set (cf. Runge 2010, 75–83; BDF §447; S §2904; *CGCG* §59.24).
95. πολιορκίη, -ης, ἡ, *siege*.
96. Ion. 1st dat. fem. pl. (S §214 D.9), ἀπορία, -ας, ἡ, *bewilderment*; Ion. η for ᾱ.
97. Impf. pass. indic. 3 sg., ἐνέχω, (pass.) *be held in* (a certain state).
98. Pres. mid. ptc. gen. masc. sg., ἐγγίνομαι, *come in, intervene*; ἅτε with circ. ptc. See n. 64.
99. συχνός, -ή, -όν, (of time) *long, much*.
100. Adv. acc. with ἀνωτέρω, "not at all further."
101. πρᾶγμα, -ατος, τό, (pl.) *state of affairs, conditions*.
102. Pres. mid. ptc. gen. neut. pl., προκόπτω, *advance, progress*. See n. 64.
103. εἴτε . . . εἴτε, *either . . . or*.
104. οἱ = αὐτῷ. See n. 24.
105. Pres. act. ptc. dat. masc. sg., ἀπορέω, *be at a loss, be bewildered*; circ.
106. Aor. mid. indic. 3 sg., ὑποτίθημι, *propose*.
107. Aor. act. indic. 3 sg., μανθάνω, *learn*.
108. Verbal adj. of ποιέω; with dat. (cf. S §2152; *CGCG* §37.3): "what must be done by him [οἱ]."

ἐποίεε δὴ τοιόνδε. τάξας¹⁰⁹ τὴν στρατιὴν ἅπασαν ἐξ ἐμβολῆς¹¹⁰ τοῦ ποταμοῦ, τῇ¹¹¹ ἐς τὴν πόλιν ἐσβάλλει, καὶ ὄπισθε¹¹² αὖτις¹¹³ τῆς πόλιος τάξας ἑτέρους, τῇ ἐξιεῖ¹¹⁴ ἐκ τῆς πόλιος ὁ ποταμός, προεῖπε τῷ στρατῷ, ὅταν διαβατὸν¹¹⁵ τὸ ῥέεθρον¹¹⁶ ἴδωνται¹¹⁷ γενόμενον, ἐσιέναι¹¹⁸ ταύτῃ ἐς τὴν πόλιν. οὕτω τε δὴ τάξας καὶ κατὰ ταῦτα παραινέσας¹¹⁹ ἀπήλαυνε¹²⁰ αὐτὸς σὺν τῷ ἀχρηίῳ¹²¹ τοῦ στρατοῦ. ἀπικόμενος¹²² δὲ ἐπὶ τὴν λίμνην,¹²³ τά περ¹²⁴ ἡ τῶν Βαβυλωνίων βασίλεα¹²⁵ ἐποίησε κατά τε τὸν ποταμὸν καὶ κατὰ τὴν λίμνην, ἐποίεε καὶ ὁ Κῦρος ἕτερα τοιαῦτα. τὸν γὰρ ποταμὸν διώρυχι ἐσαγαγὼν¹²⁶ ἐς τὴν λίμνην ἐοῦσαν ἕλος,¹²⁷ τὸ ἀρχαῖον¹²⁸ ῥέεθρον διαβατὸν εἶναι ἐποίσε, ὑπονοστήσαντος¹²⁹ τοῦ ποταμοῦ. γενομένου δὲ τούτου τοιούτου, οἱ Πέρσαι¹³⁰ οἵ περ ἐτετάχατο ἐπ᾽ αὐτῷ τούτῳ κατὰ τὸ ῥέεθρον τοῦ Εὐφρήτεω ποταμοῦ ὑπονενοστηκότος ἀνδρὶ ὡς

109. Aor. act. ptc. nom. masc. sg., τάσσω, *arrange*; circ.
110. ἐμβολή, -ῆς, ἡ, *entrance*.
111. Dat. of place, *where*.
112. Prep. with gen., *behind*.
113. Adv., *in turn*.
114. Pres. act. indic. 3 sg., ἐξίημι, *let out*.
115. διαβατός, -όν, *passable, fordable*.
116. ῥέεθρον, -ου, τό, *river, stream*.
117. Aor. act. subj. 3 sg., ὁράω; fut. temp. clause (cf. BDF §381; S §2401; *CGCG* §47.8).
118. Pres. act. inf., εἴσειμι, *enter*; indir. disc. (command).
119. Aor. act. ptc. nom. masc. sg., παραινέω, *advise, exhort*; circ.
120. Impf. act. indic. 3 sg., ἀπελαύνω, *depart, march from*.
121. ἀχρήιος, -ον, *useless*. The "useless part of the army" consists of those who were injured and could not fight.
122. Aor. mid. ptc. nom. masc. sg., ἀφικνέομαι, *arrive at*; circ.
123. λίμνη, -ης, ἡ, *lake*.
124. Postpositive partic.: "expresses exclusive limitation" (*CGCG* §59.55). "Precisely those things [τά περ] that the queen did at the river and the lake, these [τοιαῦτα] Cyrus also did in turn [ἕτερα]."
125. βασίλεα, -ας, ἡ, *queen*.
126. Aor. act. ptc. nom. masc. sg., εἰσάγω, *lead, draw off*; circ.
127. ἕλος, -εος, τό, *marsh*.
128. ἀρχαῖος, -α, -ον, *ancient*.
129. Aor. act. ptc. gen. masc. sg., ὑπονοστέω, *go down, sink*; gen. absol.
130. Πέρσης, -ου, ὁ, *Persian*.

ἐς μέσον μηρὸν[131] μάλιστά κῃ,[132] κατὰ τοῦτο ἐσήισαν ἐς τὴν Βαβυλῶνα. εἰ μέν νυν[133] προεπύθοντο[134] ἢ ἔμαθον οἱ Βαβυλώνιοι τὸ ἐκ τοῦ Κύρου ποιεύμενον, οἳ δ᾽ ἄν[135] περιιδόντες[136] τοὺς Πέρσας ἐσελθεῖν ἐς τὴν πόλιν διέφθειραν[137] ἂν κάκιστα·[138] κατακληίσαντες[139] γὰρ ἂν πάσας τὰς ἐς τὸν ποταμὸν πυλίδας[140] ἐχούσας[141] καὶ αὐτοὶ ἐπὶ τὰς αἱμασιὰς[142] ἀναβάντες τὰς παρὰ τὰ χείλεα τοῦ ποταμοῦ ἐληλαμένας,[143] ἔλαβον ἂν σφέας[144] ὡς ἐν κύρτῃ.[145] νῦν δὲ ἐξ ἀπροσδοκήτου[146] σφι[147] παρέστησαν[148] οἱ Πέρσαι. ὑπὸ δὲ μεγάθεος[149] τῆς πόλιος, ὡς λέγεται ὑπὸ τῶν ταύτῃ οἰκημένων,[150] τῶν περὶ τὰ ἔσχατα τῆς πόλιος ἑαλωκότων[151] τοὺς τὸ μέσον οἰκέοντας τῶν Βαβυλωνίων οὐ μανθάνειν[152] ἑαλωκότας, ἀλλὰ τυχεῖν[153] γάρ[154] σφι ἐοῦσαν ὁρτήν, χορεύειν[155] τε τοῦτον τὸν χρόνον καὶ ἐν εὐπαθείῃσι[156] εἶναι, ἐς ὅ[157] δὴ καὶ τὸ κάρτα[158] ἐπύθοντο.

NOTES

1.189. τις ἱρῶν ἵππων τῶν λευκῶν ὑπὸ ὕβριος ἐσβὰς ἐς τὸν ποταμὸν . . . κάρτα τε δὴ ἐχαλέπαινε τῷ ποταμῷ ὁ Κῦρος τοῦτο ὑβρίσταντι. The scene illustrates, somewhat comically, the notion that ὕβρις ("insolence") leads to νέμεσις ("destruction"). The horse is swallowed up by the river because of its ὕβρις, which, in turn, Cyrus interprets as an act of ὕβρις on the part of the river. Since white horses were sacred to the sun, Cyrus "punishes" the hubristic river by dividing it into 360 channels, as many days as there are in a year (How and Wells 1928, 1:53).

1.191. τυχεῖν γάρ σφι ἐοῦσαν ὁρτήν. Herodotus's note that the capture took place while the Babylonians were celebrating a festival (perhaps the *akītu*) dovetails with Dan. 5 (though see Collins 1993, 244).

131. μηρός, -οῦ, ὁ, *thigh*.
132. κῃ = πῃ, *somewhere*; ἀνδρί . . . κῃ, "to about the middle of a man's thigh" (LSJ, 1076.III.5).
133. Partic. combination: "a transition to a more to-the-point, relevant text segment (νυν = οὖν); the transition occurs in two stages (μέν . . . δέ)" (CGCG §59.73; cf. 59.30).
134. Aor. mid. indic. 3 pl., προπυνθάνομαι, *learn in advance* (by inquiry).
135. Calls immediate attention to the contrafactual apodosis (cf. S §1765).
136. Aor. act. ptc. nom. masc. pl., περιοράω, *overlook, allow*; circ.
137. Aor. act. indic. 3 sg., διαφθείρω, *destroy*; second-class (contrafactual) condition (cf. S §2302; CGCG §49.10).
138. Superl. adv., κακός, -ή, -όν, *ruthlessly, completely* (annihilate).
139. Aor. act. ptc. nom. masc. pl., κατακληίω, *shut, close*; circ.
140. πυλίς, -ίδος, ἡ, *gate*.
141. Pres. act. ptc. acc. fem. pl., ἔχω, (intrans., of direction) *lead toward* (cf. LSJ, 750.B.III): "[all the gates] leading to the river."
142. αἱμασιά, -ᾶς, ἡ, *wall*.
143. Pf. mid. ptc. acc. fem. pl., ἐλαύνω, *go on*; attrib.: "the ones [i.e., walls] running alongside the banks of the river."
144. σφέας = αὐτούς (cf. S §325 D.2).
145. κύρτη, -ης, ἡ, *fish trap*.
146. ἀπροσδόκητος, -ον, *unexpected*; ἐξ ἀπροσδοκήτου, "unexpectedly."
147. σφι = αὐτοῖς (cf. S §325 D.2).
148. Aor. act. indic. 3 pl., παρίστημι, *draw near*; with dat.
149. μέγαθος, -εος, τό, *great size*.
150. Pres. mid. ptc. gen. masc. pl., οἰκέω, *dwell*; attrib. (subst.).
151. Pf. act. ptc. gen. masc. pl., ἁλίσκομαι, *be taken/conquered, fall into an enemy's hands*; gen. absol.: "when those around the outer parts of the city were captured."
152. In indirect speech (ὡς λέγεται), the infinitive is negated by οὐ, reflecting the structure of direct speech (cf. S §2722; CGCG §51.22).
153. Aor. act. inf., τυγχάνω, *happen to be*; with supp. ptc.; indir. disc.: "There happened to be [ἐοῦσαν] a festival [ὁρτήν = ἑορτήν]." See n. 38.
154. Partic. combination: correction/elimination (ἀλλά) that has explanatory force (γάρ).
155. Pres. act. inf., χορεύω, *to dance*; indir. disc. See n. 38.
156. Ion. 1st dat. fem. pl., εὐπαθεία, -ας, ἡ, *enjoyment*; ἐν εὐπαθείῃσι εἶναι, "make merry."
157. ἐς ὅ, "until the time."
158. καὶ τὸ κάρτα has an ironic sense (LSJ, 880.3): they learned the news "all too well."

6.1.3

On the Origins of Circumcision

Histories 2.104

2.104Φαίνονται¹ μὲν² γὰρ ἐόντες³ οἱ Κόλχοι⁴ Αἰγύπτιοι,⁵ νοήσας⁶ δὲ πρότερον⁷ αὐτὸς ἢ ἀκούσας ἄλλων λέγω. ὡς δέ μοι ἐν φροντίδι⁸ ἐγένετο, εἰρόμην⁹ ἀμφοτέρους, καὶ μᾶλλον¹⁰ οἱ Κόλχοι ἐμεμνέατο¹¹ τῶν Αἰγυπτίων ἢ οἱ Αἰγύπτιοι τῶν Κόλχων. νομίζειν¹² δ' ἔφασαν οἱ Αἰγύπτιοι τῆς Σεσώστριος¹³ στρατιῆς¹⁴ εἶναι τοὺς Κόλχους. αὐτὸς δὲ εἴκασα¹⁵ τῇδε,¹⁶ καὶ ὅτι μελάγχροες¹⁷ εἰσὶ καὶ οὐλότριχες.¹⁸ καὶ τοῦτο μὲν¹⁹ ἐς οὐδὲν ἀνήκει·²⁰ εἰσὶ γὰρ καὶ ἕτεροι τοιοῦτοι· ἀλλὰ τοῖσιδε καὶ μᾶλλον,²¹ ὅτι μοῦνοι²² πάντων ἀνθρώπων Κόλχοι καὶ Αἰγύπτιοι καὶ Αἰθίοπες²³ περιτάμνονται²⁴ ἀπ' ἀρχῆς τὰ αἰδοῖα.²⁵ Φοίνικες²⁶ δὲ καὶ Σύριοι²⁷ ἐν τῇ Παλαιστίνῃ²⁸ καὶ αὐτοὶ ὁμολογέουσι²⁹ παρ' Αἰγυπτίων μεμαθηκέναι,³⁰ Σύριοι

---

1. Pres. pass. indic. 3 pl., φαίνω, (pass.) *appear*; with supp. ptc. (ἐόντες), "are clearly/evidently" (cf. *CGCG* 52.10).
2. μέν . . . δέ, point/counterpoint set (cf. Runge 2010, 75–83; BDF §447; S §2904; *CGCG* §59.24). This section supports / elaborates on (γάρ) the previous discussion
3. Pres. act. ptc. nom. masc. pl., εἰμί; supp. (φαίνονται).
4. Κόλχος, -ου, ὁ, *Colchian*.
5. Αἴγυπτος, -ου, ὁ, *Egyptian*; pred. nom.
6. Aor. act. ptc. nom. masc. sg., νοέω, *understand*; circ.
7. πρότερον . . . ἤ, *earlier than, before*.
8. φροντίς, -ίδος, ἡ, *thought, reflection*; ὥς μοι ἐν φροντίδι ἐγένετο (τὸ πρῆγμα), "when this matter became the subject of my reflection."
9. Impf. mid. indic. 1 sg., εἴρω, *ask*.
10. μᾶλλον . . . ἤ, *more than*.
11. Plpf. mid. indic. 3 pl., μιμνήσκω, *remember*; with gen.
12. Pres. act. inf., νομίζω, *think, consider*; indir. disc. (cf. BDF §397; S §2592; *CGCG* §41.2).
13. Σέσωστρις, -ιος, ὁ, *Sesostris* (Egyptian king).
14. στρατιά, -ᾶς, ἡ, *army*; Ion. η for ᾱ.
15. Aor. act. indic. 1 sg., εἰκάζω, *infer, conjecture*.
16. Dat. of manner; lit., "in this [here] manner"; i.e., "but I myself conclude thusly [that they are]."
17. μελάγχρως, -οος (μέλας χρώς), *dark in skin tone*.
18. οὐλόθριξ, -τριχος, *wooly haired*.
19. μέν . . . ἀλλά. The point (μέν) generates an expectation that is then corrected (ἀλλά).
20. Pres. act. indic. 3 sg., ἀνήκω, *have come to a point*; τοῦτο . . . ἐς οὐδὲν ἀνήκει, "this amounts to nothing."
21. ἀλλὰ τοῖσιδε καὶ μᾶλλον, "rather even more [the real evidence for the claim] in these respects [τοῖσιδε]."
22. μοῦνοι = μόνοι.
23. Αἰθίοψ, -οπος, ὁ, *Ethiopian*.
24. Pres. mid. indic. 3 pl., περιτέμνω, *circumcise*.
25. αἰδοῖον, -ου, τό, *genital organ*.
26. Φοῖνιξ, -ικος, ὁ, *Phoenician*.
27. Σύριος, -ου, ὁ, *Syrian*.
28. Παλαιστίνη, -ης, ἡ, *Palestine*.
29. Pres. act. indic. 3 pl., ὁμολογέω, *acknowledge, concede*.
30. Pf. act. inf., μανθάνω, *learn* (something from someone); indir. disc. See n. 12.

δὲ οἱ περὶ Θερμώδοντα[31] καὶ Παρθένιον[32] ποταμὸν καὶ Μάκρωνες[33] οἱ τούτοισι ἀστυγείτονες[34] ἐόντες ἀπὸ Κόλχων φασὶ νεωστὶ[35] μεμαθηκέναι. οὗτοι γὰρ εἰσὶ οἱ περιταμνόμενοι ἀνθρώπων μοῦνοι, καὶ οὗτοι Αἰγυπτίοισι[36] φαίνονται ποιεῦντες[37] κατὰ ταὐτά. αὐτῶν δὲ Αἰγυπτίων καὶ Αἰθιόπων οὐκ ἔχω εἰπεῖν ὁκότεροι[38] παρὰ τῶν ἑτέρων ἐξέμαθον· ἀρχαῖον[39] γὰρ δή[40] τι φαίνεται ἐόν.[41] ὡς δὲ ἐπιμισγόμενοι[42] Αἰγύπτῳ ἐξέμαθον, μέγα μοι καὶ τόδε τεκμήριον[43] γίνεται· Φοινίκων ὁκόσοι[44] τῇ Ἑλλάδι[45] ἐπιμίσγονται, οὐκέτι Αἰγυπτίους μιμέονται[46] κατὰ τὰ αἰδοῖα. ἀλλὰ τῶν ἐπιγινομένων[47] οὐ περιτάμνουσι τὰ αἰδοῖα.

NOTE

2.104. Σύριοι ἐν τῇ Παλαιστίνῃ. Cf. *Hist.* 7.89. The term Παλαιστίνη stems from the name of the southern part of the coast inhabited by the Philistines (cf. Isa. 14:29, 31). Josephus argues that "Syrians" must mean "Jews" since of all the inhabitants of the region, the Jews alone practiced circumcision (*A.J.* 8.262). The claim is an exaggeration, but Herodotus's comments would nonetheless apply primarily to Jews (Stern 1974–84, 1:3–4).

31. Θερμώδων, -οντος, ὁ, *Thermodon* (river)
32. Παρθένιος, -ου, ὁ, *Parthenius* (river).
33. Μάκρωνες, οἱ, *Macrones* (people of Pontus).
34. ἀστυγείτων, -ον, (subst.) *neighbors*.
35. Adv., *recently*.
36. Dat. comp. of κατὰ ταὐτά (cf. S §1500): "in the same manner as the Egyptians."
37. ποιεῦντες = ποιοῦντες; supp. (φαίνονται). The sense of φαίνομαι with the supplementary participle is "be clearly, be obviously, prove/turn out to be (doing something)" (*CGCG* §52.10). See n. 1.
38. ὁπότερος, -α, -ον (Ion. ὁκότερος), *which* (of two).
39. ἀρχαῖος, -α, -ον, *ancient*.
40. Partic. combination, *for indeed*: The speaker adds certainty (δή) to the explanation (γάρ) (cf. *CGCG* §59.62).
41. Supp. ptc. of φαίνεται: "For indeed, it is obvious [φαίνεται] that this thing [circumcision] is [ἐόν] ancient." See n. 37.
42. Pres. pass. ptc. nom. masc. pl., ἐπιμείγνυμι, (intrans.) *mingle, join*; with dat.; circ.
43. τεκμήριον, -ου, τό, *proof*.
44. ὁπόσος (Ion. ὁκόσος), *as many*.
45. Ἑλλάς, -άδος, ἡ, *Hellas* (Greece); dat. of place.
46. Pres. mid. indic. 3 pl., μιμέω, *imitate*.
47. Pres. mid. ptc. gen. masc. pl., ἐπιγίνομαι, *come into being after*; attrib. (subst.); separated from head noun τὰ αἰδοῖα (hyperbaton; cf. *CGCG* §60.18).

6.2

Thucydides

Thucydides's (ca. 460–400 BCE) *History of the Peloponnesian War* is an account of the battle between Athens and Sparta (431–404 BCE) and was widely regarded by subsequent generations as the gold standard of historiography. In contrast to Herodotus, whose interests were eclectic and at times antiquarian, Thucydides was laser focused on the moral and political implications of a single war (Cartwright 1997, 4–5). His aim was both simple and ambitious: to provide his readers with "a possession for all time" (*Hist. pel.* 1.22.4).

Reading Thucydides is often a challenge. As M.I. Finley notes, "A surprising proportion of commentaries is given over to sorting out just what Thucydides was trying to say in any particular passage" (Warner 1972, 10). Our focus is on the prologue and Thucydides's description of his method for reporting speeches, two of the most widely discussed passages in the work.[1]

Text: Smith 1919
Recommended Translation: Warner 1972
Supplemental Scripture: Luke 1:1–4 (§6.2.1)

---

1. For additional practice with Thucydides, see Jones et al. 2015b. If your goal is to read through book 1, you may wish to acquire Cameron 2003.

6.2.1

Prologue

History of the Peloponnesian War 1.1–3

1.1Θουκυδίδης[1] Ἀθηναῖος[2] ξυνέγραψε[3] τὸν πόλεμον[4] τῶν Πελοποννησίων[5] καὶ Ἀθηναίων ὡς ἐπολέμησαν[6] πρὸς ἀλλήλους, ἀρξάμενος εὐθὺς καθισταμένου[7] καὶ ἐλπίσας[8] μέγαν τε ἔσεσθαι καὶ ἀξιολογώτατον[9] τῶν προγεγενημένων,[10] τεκμαιρόμενος[11] ὅτι ἀκμάζοντές[12] τε ἦσαν ἐς[13] αὐτὸν ἀμφότεροι παρασκευῇ[14] τῇ πάσῃ καὶ ἄλλο Ἑλληνικὸν[15] ὁρῶν ξυνιστάμενον[16] πρὸς ἑκατέρους, τὸ μὲν[17] εὐθύς, τὸ δὲ καὶ διανοούμενον.[18] **2**κίνησις[19] γὰρ αὕτη μεγίστη δὴ[20] τοῖς Ἕλλησιν ἐγένετο καὶ μέρει[21] τινὶ τῶν βαρβάρων, ὡς δὲ εἰπεῖν[22] καὶ ἐπὶ πλεῖστον[23] ἀνθρώπων. **3**τὰ γὰρ πρὸ αὐτῶν καὶ

1. Θουκυδίδης, -ου, ὁ, *Thucydides*.
2. Ἀθηναῖος, -α, -ον, *Athenian*.
3. Aor. act. indic. 3 sg., συγγράφω, *write, expound*.
4. πόλεμος, -ου, ὁ, *war*.
5. Πελοποννήσιος, -α, -ον, *Peloponnesian*.
6. Aor. act. indic. 3 pl., πολεμέω, *fight, battle, wage war*.
7. Pres. mid. ptc. gen. masc. sg., καθίστημι, (intrans., military) *be arranged, drawn up*; gen. absol. The participle may stand alone when the subject is established or obvious (cf. S §2072; CGCG §52.32 n. 1). The full statement would be εὐθὺς καθισταμένου τοῦ πολέμου (Cameron 2003, 18).
8. Aor. act. ptc. nom. masc. sg., ἐλπίζω, *expect*; circ. Verbs meaning "hope," "expect," "promise," "swear," and so on regularly take a future infinitive form (cf. S §1868; CGCG §51.31).
9. Superl., ἀξιόλογος, -ον, *most worthy of mention*; with gen.
10. Pf. mid. ptc. gen. masc. pl., προγίγνομαι, *exist prior*; attrib. (subst.).
11. Pres. mid. ptc. nom. masc. sg., τεκμαίρω, (mid.) *judge/infer from evidence*; circ. (causal).
12. Pres. act. ptc. nom. masc. pl., ἀκμάζω, *reach/be at the highest point*; periphrastic.
13. ἐς = εἰς. ἐς αὐτόν (πόλεμον), "for it (the war)."
14. παρασκευή, -ῆς, ἡ, *preparedness*; dat. of respect.
15. Ἑλληνικός, -ή, -όν, *Hellenic, Greek*; ἄλλο Ἑλληνικόν, "the rest of the Hellenic people."
16. Pres. mid. ptc. acc. neut. sg., συνίστημι, with πρὸς ἑκατέρους, *form an alliance with one side or the other*; supp. (content of ὁρῶν). "Verbs signifying *to see* . . ., when they denote physical (actual) perception take the participle" (S §2110; cf. CGCG §52.10).
17. τὸ μέν . . . τὸ δέ, *one part . . . the other part* (cf. S §§1106–7; CGCG §28.27).
18. Pres. mid. ptc. acc. neut. sg., διανοέω, *have in mind, think*; circ.: "one part joining a side immediately, the other also deliberating [over which side to join]."
19. κίνησις, -εως, ἡ, *movement, convulsion*.
20. Partic.: "The speaker considers (and invites the addressee to consider) the text segment or word (group) which it modifies as evident, clear, or precise" (CGCG §59.44); underscores μεγίστη.
21. μέρος, -ους, τό, *part*; dat. of place.
22. Inf. absol., "so to speak" (cf. BDF §391a; S §2012; CGCG §51.49).
23. Superl., πολύς, πολλή, πολύ. ἐπὶ πλεῖστον ἀνθρώπων, "of the majority of humankind."

τὰ ἔτι παλαίτερα²⁴ σαφῶς²⁵ μὲν²⁶ εὑρεῖν διὰ χρόνου πλῆθος²⁷ ἀδύνατον²⁸ ἦν, ἐκ δὲ τεκμηρίων²⁹ ὧν³⁰ ἐπὶ μακρότατον σκοποῦντί³¹ μοι πιστεῦσαι ξυμβαίνει,³² οὐ μεγάλα νομίζω³³ γενέσθαι οὔτε κατὰ³⁴ τοὺς πολέμους οὔτε ἐς τὰ ἄλλα.

NOTES

1.1. Θουκυδίδης Ἀθηναῖος ξυνέγραψε τὸν πόλεμον τῶν Πελοποννησίων καὶ Ἀθηναίων. The opening line functions as the title of the work.

Thucydides's standard practice for introducing persons is name plus patronymic. So, for example, in 4.104.4, he introduces himself as Θουκυδίδης Ὀλόρου, "Thucydides son of Olorus." Here, however, he conforms to the tradition established by Hecataeus and Herodotus (cf. §6.1.1; Hornblower 1991, 4).

ὡς ἐπολέμησαν πρὸς ἀλλήλους. Cf. Herodotus's δι' αἰτίην ἐπολέμησαν ἀλλήλοισι (*Hist.* 1.1; cf. §6.1.1).

---

24. Compar., παλαῖος, -ά, -όν, *older, earlier*. Theme set in left periphery (nom. pendent) (cf. *CGCG* §60.34): τά . . . πρὸ αὐτῶν καὶ τὰ ἔτι παλαίτερα.
25. Adv., *clearly*.
26. μέν . . . δέ; point/counterpoint set (cf. Runge 2010, 75–83; BDF §447; S §2904; *CGCG* §59.24).
27. πλῆθος, -ους, τό, *magnitude, size, extent*; διὰ χρόνου πλῆθος, "on account of the length of time."
28. ἀδύνατος, -ον, (quasi-impers.) *it is impossible*; with (acc. and) inf.
29. τεκμήριον, -ου, τό, *evidence*.
30. The relative pronoun is attracted to the case of its genitive antecedent (cf. S §2522; *CGCG* §50.13).
31. Pres. act. ptc. dat. masc. sg., σκοπέω, *observe, examine*; circ.
32. Pres. act. indic. 3 sg., συμβαίνω, (quasi-impers.) *happen, come about*; with acc. and inf.; lit., "which things [ὧν = ἅ], investigating [σκοποῦντι agreeing with μοι] to the greatest extent possible [ἐπὶ μακρότατον], happen to me to trust."
33. Pres. act. indic. 1 sg., νομίζω, *consider*.
34. The prepositions κατά and ἐς have the same sense; i.e., "concerning." Thucydides likes to avoid strict parallelism.

6.2.2

Method for Reporting Speeches

History of the Peloponnesian War 1.22.1–4

1.22.1Καὶ ὅσα μὲν[1] λόγῳ[2] εἶπον ἕκαστοι ἢ μέλλοντες πολεμήσειν[3] ἢ ἐν αὐτῷ[4] ἤδη ὄντες, χαλεπὸν[5] τὴν ἀκρίβειαν[6] αὐτὴν τῶν λεχθέντων διαμνημονεῦσαι[7] ἦν ἐμοί τε ὧν αὐτὸς ἤκουσα καὶ τοῖς ἄλλοθέν ποθεν[8] ἐμοὶ ἀπαγγέλλουσιν.[9] ὡς[10] δ' ἂν ἐδόκουν[11] μοι ἕκαστοι περὶ τῶν αἰεὶ[12] παρόντων[13] τὰ δέοντα[14] μάλιστ'[15] εἰπεῖν,[16] ἐχομένῳ[17] ὅτι[18] ἐγγύτατα τῆς ξυμπάσης[19] γνώμης[20] τῶν ἀληθῶς λεχθέντων, οὕτως εἴρηται.[21] **2**τὰ δ' ἔργα[22] τῶν πραχθέντων ἐν τῷ πολέμῳ οὐκ ἐκ τοῦ παρα-

---

1. μέν . . . δέ; point/counterpoint set (cf. Runge 2010, 75–83; BDF §447; S §2904; *CGCG* §59.24). The contrast is between Thucydides's report of the speeches (μέν) and of the events (δέ).
2. Dat. of respect: "as much as each said *in speech*."
3. Fut. act. inf., πολεμέω, *fight, wage war*.
4. The logical antecedent is in the infinitive πολεμήσειν: "whether when they were about to engage in the war or when they were already in it [the war]."
5. χαλεπός, -ή, -όν, (quasi-impers.) *it is difficult*; with (acc. and) inf. and dat.: "It was difficult for me to remember the precise nature of what was said, both what I myself heard and what was reported to me from various other sources."
6. ἀκρίβεια, -ας, ἡ, *accuracy*.
7. Aor. act. inf., διαμνημονεύω, *remember, mention*.
8. ἄλλοθέν ποθεν, "from various other sources."
9. Pres. act. ptc. dat. masc. pl., ἀπαγγέλλω, *report*; attrib. (subst.).
10. ὡς . . . οὕτως, *as . . . so*.
11. Impf. act. indic. 3 pl., δοκέω, (pers.) *seem, appear*; with inf. and dat.

12. αἰεί = ἀεί, *always*.
13. Pres. act. ptc. gen. neut. pl., πάρειμι, *be present*; attrib. (subst.).
14. Pres. act. ptc. acc. neut. sg., δεῖ, *that which is necessary/suitable/appropriate*; attrib. (subst.).
15. Adv. acc., *especially, for the most part*.
16. The infinitive with ἄν represents a potential optative (cf. S §§1845, 1848; *CGCG* § 51.27): "As it seemed to me [lit., as they seemed to me] that each *would say* what is most appropriate under the current circumstances."
17. Pres. mid. ptc. dat. masc. sg., ἔχω, *maintain*; with gen. (cf. LSJ, 750.C.I.2); circ. (manner).
18. ὅτι with superl., *as . . . as possible* (cf. S §1086l; *CGCG* §32.4); ὅτι ἐγγύτατα, *as closely as possible*.
19. ξυμπᾶς = συμπᾶς, *general, overall*.
20. γνώμη, -ης, ἡ, *intention*.
21. Pf. pass. indic. 3 sg., εἴρω, (pass.) *be said, reported*.
22. The nominative pendent establishes a new theme (cf. *CGCG* §60.34): "as for the events in the war" (in contrast to the speeches). See n. 1.

τυχόντος²³ πυνθανόμενος²⁴ ἠξίωσα²⁵ γράφειν οὐδ᾽ ὡς ἐμοὶ ἐδόκει, ἀλλ᾽ οἷς τε αὐτὸς παρῆν²⁶ καὶ παρὰ τῶν ἄλλων²⁷ ὅσον δυνατὸν ἀκριβείᾳ²⁸ περὶ ἑκάστου ἐπεξελθών.²⁹ ³ἐπιπόνως³⁰ δὲ ηὑρίσκετο, διότι οἱ παρόντες τοῖς ἔργοις ἑκάστοις οὐ ταὐτὰ³¹ περὶ τῶν αὐτῶν ἔλεγον, ἀλλ᾽ ὡς ἑκατέρων τις εὐνοίας³² ἢ μνήμης³³ ἔχοι.³⁴ ⁴καὶ ἐς μὲν³⁵ ἀκρόασιν³⁶ ἴσως³⁷ τὸ μὴ μυθῶδες³⁸ αὐτῶν ἀτερπέστερον³⁹ φανεῖται· ὅσοι δὲ βουλήσονται τῶν τε γενομένων τὸ σαφὲς⁴⁰ σκοπεῖν⁴¹ καὶ τῶν μελλόντων⁴² ποτὲ αὖθις⁴³ κατὰ τὸ ἀνθρώπινον⁴⁴ τοιούτων καὶ παραπλησίων⁴⁵ ἔσεσθαι, ὠφέλιμα⁴⁶ κρίνειν αὐτὰ ἀρκούντως ἕξει.⁴⁷ κτῆμά⁴⁸ τε⁴⁹ ἐς αἰεὶ μᾶλλον ἢ ἀγώνισμα⁵⁰ ἐς τὸ παραχρῆμα ἀκούειν ξύγκειται.⁵¹

NOTES

1.22.1. ὡς δ᾽ ἂν ἐδόκουν μοι ἕκαστοι . . . τὰ δέοντα μάλιστ᾽ εἰπεῖν. Given that "most historians went on making speeches without showing any kind of bad conscience about doing so" (Hornblower 1991, 59), Thucydides's transparency is noteworthy. (For examples of subsequent historians denying that they report the words of speakers verbatim, cf. Polybius, *Hist.* 18.11; Sallust, *Bell. Cat.* 50.5; Livy, *Ab urbe cond.* 37.45.11; Tacitus, *Hist.* 1.15–16; Marincola 2007, 120). Scholars continue to debate the significance of τὰ δέοντα (lit., "the necessary things"), not least because Thucydides goes on to assert οὐδ᾽ ὡς ἐμοὶ ἐδόκει ("*not* as it seemed good to me"). Yet the claims are different. On the one hand, Thucydides acknowledges that he has crafted the speeches on the basis of what he believed the

23. Aor. act. ptc. gen. masc. sg., παρατυγχάνω, *be present*; attrib. (subst.), "from someone who just happened to be nearby [me]."
24. Pres. mid. ptc. nom. masc. sg., πυνθάνομαι, *learn by inquiry*; circ.
25. Aor. act. indic. 1 sg., ἀξιόω, *consider appropriate*; with inf.
26. Impf. act. indic. 1 sg., πάρειμι, *be present at*; with dat.
27. The syntax is elliptical (cf. S §3022): παρὰ τῶν ἄλλων = (ἃ) παρὰ τῶν ἄλλων (ἀπηγγέλθη).
28. ἀκρίβεια, -ας, ἡ, *accuracy*; dat. of manner; with adv. acc., ὅσον δυνατόν, "as accurately as possible."
29. Aor. act. ptc. nom. masc. sg., ἐπεξέρχομαι, *examine in detail, investigate*; circ.
30. Adv., *with difficulty*; ἐπιπόνως . . . ηὑρίσκετο (impers.); lit., "It [the content of the speeches] has been discovered with great effort."
31. Crasis: τὰ αὐτά, "the same things."
32. εὔνοια, -ας, ἡ, *benevolence, inclination, affection*; ἑκατέρων . . . εὐνοίας, "good will for one of the two sides."
33. μνήμη, -ης, ἡ, *memory, recollection*.
34. Pres. act. opt. 3 sg., ἔχω, *to be well off for, abound in* (something); with gen. (LSJ, 705.B.II.2b). Indefinite subordinate clauses in secondary sequence take the iterative optative (cf. S §2568; CGCG §40.13).
35. μέν . . . δέ; point/counterpoint. See n. 1.
36. ἀκρόασις, -εως, ἡ, *hearing*.
37. Adv., *probably, perhaps*.
38. μυθώδης, -ες, *of storytelling*. The substantivized adjective is negated by a generic μή (cf. S §2735; CGCG §50.19) and followed by a partitive genitive: "whatever in these pages is not romantic."
39. Compar., ἀτερπής, -ές, *less pleasing*; pred. comp.
40. σαφής, -ές, *clear*; τῶν γενομένων τὸ σαφές, "the *clear truth* of what happened" (cf. LSJ, 1586).
41. Pres. act. inf., σκοπέω, *look into, consider, examine*.

42. The substantival participle takes a future infinitive: "things that are going to be [τῶν μελλόντων . . . ἔσεσθαι] at some point again, in accordance with human nature, like these that happened [τοιούτων = τῶν γενομένων], or very close to them [παραπλησίων]."
43. Adv., *again*; ποτὲ αὖθις, "at some point again."
44. ἀνθρώπινος, -η, -ον, *human*; κατὰ τὸ ἀνθρώπινον, "in accordance with human nature."
45. παραπλήσιος, -α, -ον, *nearly resembling*.
46. ὠφέλιμος, -ον, *beneficial*; pred. comp.
47. ἀρκούντως ἕξει, (idiom) "It will be enough" (cf. S §1438; CGCG §26.11). The implied accusative subject is found in the previous clause: ὅσοι . . . βουλήσονται, "However many desire . . . it is enough [for them] to judge these things [what I write] beneficial."
48. κτῆμα, -ατος, τό, *possession*.
49. Thucydides frequently uses τε to introduce "a clinching or summing up of what precedes" (Denniston 1966, 500).
50. ἀγώνισμα, -ατος, τό, *prize, feat*.
51. Pres. pass. indic. 3 sg., σύγκειμαι, (pass.) (of written works) *be composed*.

historical figures were likely to have said so that "elements both of fidelity and invention are present" (Marincola 2007, 121; cf. Cartwright 1997, 24). On the other hand, he assures his readers that he has not reconstructed the events of the war on the basis of his own whims.

1.22.2. τὰ δ' ἔργα τῶν πραχθέντων. Thucydides's account of the events of the war is based on both his own eyewitness testimony (something Herodotus could not claim) and *careful* (ἀκριβείᾳ) investigation of the reports he has received from others. Cf. Luke 1:2–3.

1.22.4. κτῆμά τε ἐς αἰεὶ μᾶλλον ἢ ἀγώνισμα ἐς τὸ παραχρῆμα ἀκούειν. Thucydides wants his work to be "an everlasting possession" rather than a "showpiece" or "prize composition," which tickles the ears momentarily but then is soon forgotten (cf. Cartwright 1997, 24).

6.3

Diodorus Siculus

Diodorus Siculus ("of Sicily") flourished during the first century BCE (ca. 80–20 BCE). Of his massive forty-volume *Library of History*, only select portions have survived (books 1–5 and 11–20; fragments of the other books are preserved in Eusebius and Byzantine compilers). His stated aim is to compose a universal history, αἱ κοιναὶ ἱστορίαι (1.4.6; 5.1.4), from the mythical period to the present day (59 BCE). While he is often disparaged as a slavish annalist, the absence of Diodorus's artistry may be to our benefit—or as Oldfather puts it, "When he errs in fact the fault is not so much his as that of his sources" (Oldfather 1933, xxiii).

The *Library of History* covers events and traditions that will be of interest to students of early Judaism and Christianity (e.g., Stern 1974–84, 1:167–89). We focus on two of these: Diodorus's report of the various Egyptian lawgivers, among whom he includes Moses, and his account of Antiochus Sidetes's invasion of Judea (ca. 134 BCE).

Text and Translation: Oldfather 1933 (§6.3.1); Walton 1967 (§6.3.2)

Supplemental Scripture: Exod. 3:13–15; 20:1–2 (§6.3.1); 1 Macc. 1:29–62; 15:1–41 (§6.3.2)

6.3.1

Lawgivers from Egypt

Library of History 1.94.1–2

1.94.1Ῥητέον[1] δ' ἡμῖν καὶ περὶ τῶν γενομένων νομοθετῶν[2] κατ' Αἴγυπτον[3] τῶν οὕτως ἐξηλλαγμένα[4] καὶ παράδοξα[5] νόμιμα[6] καταδειξάντων.[7] μετὰ γὰρ τὴν παλαιὰν[8] τοῦ κατ' Αἴγυπτον βίου[9] κατάστασιν,[10] τὴν μυθολογουμένην[11] γεγονέναι ἐπί τε τῶν θεῶν καὶ τῶν ἡρώων,[12] πεῖσαί[13] φασι πρῶτον ἐγγράπτοις[14] νόμοις χρήσασθαι[15] τὰ πλήθη[16] τὸν Μνεύην,[17] ἄνδρα καὶ τῇ ψυχῇ μέγαν καὶ τῷ βίῳ κοινότατον[18] τῶν μνημονευομένων.[19] προσποιηθῆναι[20] δ' αὐτῷ τὸν Ἑρμῆν[21] δεδωκέναι τούτους, ὡς μεγάλων ἀγαθῶν αἰτίους[22] ἐσομένους,[23] καθάπερ παρ' Ἕλλησι ποιῆσαί φασιν ἐν μὲν[24] τῇ Κρήτῃ[25] Μίνωα,[26] παρὰ δὲ Λακεδαιμονί-

---

1. Verbal adj. from εἴρω; with dat. agent (cf. S §2152; *CGCG* §37.3): "It must be said by us."
2. νομοθέτης, -ου, ὁ, *lawgiver*.
3. Αἴγυπτος, -ου, ἡ, *Egypt*; κατ' Αἴγυπτον (spatial), "in Egypt."
4. Pf. pass. ptc. acc. neut. pl., ἐξαλλάσσω, (pass. as adj.) *strange* (cf. LSJ, 583.2.b).
5. παράδοξος, -ον, *paradoxical*.
6. νόμιμος, -η, -ον, (subst.) *customs*.
7. Aor. mid. ptc. gen. masc. pl., καταδείκνυμι, *invent and teach, introduce*; attrib.
8. παλαιός, -ή, -όν, *ancient*.
9. βίος, -ου, ὁ, *manner of life*.
10. κατάστασις, -εως, ἡ, *establishment*.
11. Pres. pass. ptc. acc. fem. sg., μυθολογέω, (pass.) *told as a legend/myth*; attrib.
12. ἥρως, -ωος, ὁ, *hero*.
13. Aor. act. inf., πείθω, *persuade*; with acc. and inf.; indir. disc. (φασι) (cf. BDF §396; S §2016; *CGCG* §51.19).
14. ἔγγραπτος, -ον, *written*.
15. Aor. mid. inf., χράομαι, *use*; with dat.
16. πλῆθος, -ους, τό, *multitude*.
17. Μνεύης, -ου, ὁ, *Mneves* (= Menes, a legendary king who unified Upper and Lower Egypt).
18. Superl., κοινός, -ή, -όν, *most oriented to public affairs*; with τῷ βίῳ (dat. of respect), "most publicly oriented in manner of life."
19. Pres. pass. ptc. gen. masc. pl., μνημονεύω, (pass.) *be remembered*; partitive gen.
20. Aor. pass. inf., προσποιέω, (pass.) *attach to oneself, lay claim to*; with inf.; indir. disc. See n. 13.
21. Ἑρμῆς, -οῦ, ὁ, *Hermes* (Gk. equivalent of Thoth, who was also a lawgiver); indir. disc.: "He claimed for himself that Hermes had given [δεδωκέναι] these customs [τούτους] to him [αὐτῷ]."
22. αἴτιος, -α, -ον, *responsible for, cause of*; with gen.; pred. acc.
23. A future participle (often with ὡς) expresses purpose (cf. S §2086; *CGCG* §52.41).
24. μέν . . . δέ; point/counterpoint (cf. Runge 2010, 75–83; BDF §447; S §2904; *CGCG* §59.24).
25. Κρήτη, -ης, ἡ, *Crete*.
26. Μίνως, -ωος, ὁ, *Minos* (mythological king of Crete).

οις²⁷ Λυκοῦργον,²⁸ τὸν μὲν²⁹ παρὰ Διός,³⁰ τὸν δὲ παρ' Ἀπόλλωνος³¹ φήσαντα τούτους παρειληφέναι.³² ²καὶ παρ' ἑτέροις δὲ πλείοσιν ἔθνεσι παραδέδοται τοῦτο τὸ γένος³³ τῆς ἐπινοίας³⁴ ὑπάρξαι καὶ πολλῶν ἀγαθῶν αἴτιον γενέσθαι τοῖς πεισθεῖσι·³⁵ παρὰ μὲν³⁶ γὰρ τοῖς Ἀριανοῖς³⁷ Ζαθραύστην³⁸ ἱστοροῦσι³⁹ τὸν ἀγαθὸν δαίμονα⁴⁰ προσποιήσασθαι τοὺς νόμους αὐτῷ διδόναι, παρὰ δὲ τοῖς ὀνομαζομένοις⁴¹ Γέταις⁴² τοῖς ἀπαθανατίζουσι⁴³ Ζάλμοξιν⁴⁴ ὡσαύτως⁴⁵ τὴν κοινὴν Ἑστίαν,⁴⁶ παρὰ δὲ τοῖς Ἰουδαίοις Μωυσῆν⁴⁷ τὸν Ἰαὼ ἐπικαλούμενον θεόν, εἴτε⁴⁸ θαυμαστὴν⁴⁹ καὶ θείαν⁵⁰ ὅλως⁵¹ ἔννοιαν⁵² εἶναι κρίναντας⁵³ τὴν μέλλουσαν ὠφελήσειν⁵⁴ ἀνθρώπων πλῆθος, εἴτε καὶ πρὸς τὴν ὑπεροχὴν⁵⁵ καὶ δύναμιν τῶν εὑρεῖν λεγομένων τοὺς νόμους ἀποβλέψαντα⁵⁶ τὸν ὄχλον μᾶλλον ὑπακούσεσθαι⁵⁷ διαλαβόντας.⁵⁸

NOTES

1.94.1. περὶ τῶν γενομένων νομοθετῶν κατ' Αἴγυπτον. Greek writers frequently trace the origins of Jewish practices (e.g., circumcision) to Egypt (e.g., Herodotus, *Hist.* 2.104.1–3; discussed by Josephus in *A.J.* 8.262 and *C. Ap.* 1.168–171). The two people groups were also often grouped together by the Romans (e.g., Suetonius, *Tib.* 26; Tacitus, *Ann.* 2.85.4).

προσποιηθῆναι δ' αὐτῷ τὸν Ἑρμῆν δεδωκέναι τούτους. Artapanus attributes the achievements of the Egyptian heroes to Moses (cf. frag. 3.4–6). For example, he claims, "On account of these things Moses was loved by the masses, and was deemed worthy of godlike honor by the priests and *called Hermes*, on account of the interpretation of the sacred letters" (Collins, *OTP* 2:899, emphasis added).

27. Λακεδαιμόνιος, -ου, ὁ, *Lacedemonian* (i.e., Spartan).
28. Λυκοῦργος, -ου, ὁ, *Lycurgus* (legendary lawgiver of Sparta).
29. τὸν μέν . . . τὸν δέ, *the one (former) . . . the other (latter)*.
30. Ζεύς, Διός, ὁ, *Zeus*.
31. Ἀπόλλων, -ωνος, ὁ, *Apollo*.
32. Pf. act. inf., παραλαμβάνω, *receive*; indir. disc. See n. 13.
33. γένος, -ους, τό, *type, kind*; acc. subject of indir. disc. (παραδέδοται): "It was handed down [tradition says] that this type of device existed [ὑπάρξαι] and became [γενέσθαι] the cause of great good to those who followed it."
34. ἐπινοία, -ας, ἡ, *invention, device*.
35. Aor. pass. ptc. dat. masc. pl., πείθω, (mid.) *obey*; attrib. (subst.).
36. μέν . . . δέ . . . δέ (cf. S §2907). The sequence supports/explains (γάρ) the previous claim.
37. Ἀριανός, -οῦ, ὁ, *Arian* (= Iranian).
38. Ζαθραύστης, -ου, ὁ, *Zathraustes* (Iranian prophet); acc. subject of indir. disc.: "Zathraustes claimed that the good spirit gave the laws to him." See n. 13.
39. Pres. act. indic. 3 pl., ἱστορέω, *record*.
40. δαίμων, -ονος, ὁ, *spirit*.
41. Pres. pass. ptc. dat. masc. pl., ὀνομάζω, (pass.) *be called*; attrib.
42. Γέται, -ων, οἱ, *Getae, Gets*.
43. Pres. act. ptc. dat. masc. pl., ἀπαθανατίζω, *aim at immortality*; attrib.
44. Ζάλμοξις, -ιδος, ὁ, *Zalmoxis* (legendary priest and king of the Getae and the Dacians).
45. Adv., *likewise*. The statement is elliptical: ὡσαύτως τὴν κοινὴν Ἑστίαν = (ἱστοροῦσι) Ζαθραύστην τὴν κοινὴν Ἑστίαν προσποιήσασθαι τοὺς νόμους αὐτῷ διδόναι.
46. Ἑστία, -ας, ἡ, *Hestia* (goddess of the hearth and home).
47. Acc. subject; "Moses [likewise claimed that] the god called Iao [gave the laws to him]."
48. εἴτε . . . εἴτε, *either . . . or*. The subordinate clause introduces a shift from report to evaluative judgment (anacoluthon). The reader must supply a main clause from context: "They did this . . . either thinking [κρίναντας] X . . . or determining Y."
49. θαυμαστός, -ή, -όν, *marvelous*.
50. θεῖος, -α, -ον, *divine*.
51. Adv., *wholly*.
52. ἔννοια, -ας, ἡ, *conception*.
53. Aor. act. ptc. acc. masc. pl., κρίνω, *discern*; circ. (causal). The plural referent is the class of lawgivers.
54. Fut. act. inf., ὠφελέω, *benefit*; comp. of τὴν μέλλουσαν.
55. ὑπεροχή, -ῆς, ἡ, *superiority*.
56. Aor. act. ptc. acc. masc. sg., ἀποβλέπω, *look intently, gaze at*; circ. (conditional): "[τὸν ὄχλον] gazing upon the superiority and power of those who are said to have discovered the laws [τῶν εὑρεῖν λεγομένων τοὺς νόμους]."
57. Fut. mid. inf., ὑπακούω, *obey*; indir. disc. See n. 13.
58. Aor. act. ptc. acc. masc. pl., διαλαμβάνω, *distinguish, determine*; circ. (causal).

The similarities between Diodorus and Artapanus are noteworthy (cf. *Bib. hist.* 1.54.3; 1.56.2; 1.94.4; 1.96.4) and suggest that they may both be dependent on Hecateaus of Abdera (see Stern 1974–84, 1:20–44), Diodorus's primary source for information on Jewish origins.

1.94.2. Ζαθραύστην. The spelling is based on the Old Iranian "Zarathustra." The spelling "Zoroaster," which is more commonly known, is the result of the Greek transliteration Ζωρόαστρης. Diodorus's claim that Zathraustes received the law from "the good spirit" (τὸν ἀγαθὸν δαίμονα) reflects the notion, common among Greek writers of the period, that Zoroastrianism represents the archetypal form of dualism.

τὸν Ἰαὼ ἐπικαλούμενον θεόν. The Greek term is based on an Aramaic version of the divine name (יהו), as attested in the Elephantine papyri (Cowley 1923; Stern 1974–84, 1:172). Also from the first century BCE, 4QLXX Lev[b] (Wevers MS 802) has ΙΑΩ for the divine name at 3:12 and 4:27. The other sources that mention Ἰαώ are Varro (*apud* Lydus, *De Mensibus* 4.53, §75 in Stern 1974–84) and Labeo (*apud* Macrobius 1.18, §445 in Stern 1974–84). For additional Greek transcriptions of the tetragrammaton, see Deissmann (1901, 321–36).

6.3.2

Anti-Jewish Propaganda

Library of History 34.1.1–5

34.1.1 Ὡς Ἀντίοχος¹ ὁ βασιλεύς, φησίν,² ἐπολιόρκει³ τὰ Ἱεροσόλυμα, οἱ δὲ Ἰουδαῖοι μέχρι⁴ μέν⁵ τινος ἀντέσχον,⁶ ἐξαναλωθέντων⁷ δὲ τῶν ἐπιτηδείων⁸ ἁπάντων ἠναγκάσθησαν⁹ περὶ διαλύσεως¹⁰ διαπρεσβεύσασθαι.¹¹ οἱ δὲ πλείους αὐτῷ τῶν φίλων¹² συνεβούλευον¹³ κατὰ κράτος¹⁴ αἱρήσειν¹⁵ τὴν πόλιν καὶ τὸ γένος¹⁶ ἄρδην¹⁷ ἀνελεῖν¹⁸ τῶν Ἰουδαίων· μόνους γὰρ ἁπάντων ἐθνῶν ἀκοινωνήτους¹⁹ εἶναι τῆς πρὸς ἄλλο ἔθνος ἐπιμιξίας²⁰ καὶ πολεμίους²¹ ὑπολαμβάνειν²² πάντας. ἀπεδείκνυον²³ δὲ καὶ τοὺς προγόνους²⁴ αὐτῶν ὡς ἀσεβεῖς²⁵ καὶ μισουμένους²⁶ ὑπὸ τῶν θεῶν ἐξ ἁπάσης τῆς Αἰγύπτου πεφυγαδευμένους.²⁷ **²**τοὺς γὰρ ἀλφοὺς²⁸ ἢ λέπρας²⁹ ἔχοντας

---

1. Ἀντίοχος, -ου, ὁ, *Antiochus* (i.e., Antiochus VII Sidetes).
2. Photius reports what Diodorus says.
3. Impf. act. indic. 3 sg., πολιορκέω, *lay siege*.
4. Prep. with gen., *until, up to*; μέχρι τινος, "to a certain point."
5. μέν . . . δέ; point/counterpoint (cf. Runge 2010, 75–83; BDF §447; S §2904; *CGCG* §59.24).
6. Aor. act. indic. 3 pl., ἀντέχω, *hold out against, withstand*.
7. Aor. pass. ptc. gen. neut. pl., ἐξαναλίσκω, (pass.) *be exhausted, entirely spent*; gen. absol.
8. ἐπιτήδειος, -α, -ον, (pl. subst.) *provisions*.
9. Aor. pass. indic. 3 pl., ἀναγκάζω, (pass.) *be compelled*; with inf.
10. διάλυσις, -εως, ἡ, *cessation*.
11. Aor. mid. inf., διαπρεσβεύομαι, *send embassies*.
12. φίλος, -η, -ον, (subst.) *friend*.
13. Impf. act. indic. 3 pl., συμβουλεύω, *advise*; with dat. and inf.
14. κράτος, -ους, τό, *strength, might*; κατὰ κράτος, (manner) "by force."
15. Fut. act. inf., αἱρέω, *seize*.
16. γένος, -ους, τό, *race*.
17. Adv., *utterly, entirely*.
18. Fut. act. inf., ἀναιρέω, *destroy, wipe out*.
19. ἀκοινώνητος, -ον, *to have no part in*; with gen.; pred. acc. in indir. disc. (cf. BDF §396; S §2016; *CGCG* §51.19).
20. ἐπιμειξία, -ας, ἡ, *mixing with* (others), *dealings*.
21. πολέμιος, -α, -ον, *of a hostile/enemy*; pred. comp.
22. Pres. act. inf., ὑπολαμβάνω, *take, suppose*; indir. disc. See n. 19.
23. Impf. act. indic. 3 pl., ἀποδείκνυμι, *point out, make known*.
24. πρόγονος, -ον, (subst.) *forefather, ancestor*.
25. ἀσεβής, -ές, *impious*.
26. Pres. pass. ptc. acc. masc. pl., μισέω, (pass.) *be hated*; ὡς with the circumstantial participle provides "a 'subjective' reason or motivation, for which responsibility lies with the subject of the matrix verb" (*CGCG* §52.39; cf. S §2086).
27. Pf. pass. ptc. acc. masc. pl., φυγαδεύω, (pass.) *be banished*; supp. (indir. disc.).
28. ἀλφός, -οῦ, ὁ, *dull white* (of leprosy).
29. λέπρα, -ας, ἡ, *leprosy*.

ἐν τοῖς σώμασι καθαρμοῦ χάριν³⁰ ὡς ἐναγεῖς³¹ συναθροισθέντας³² ὑπερορίους³³ ἐκβεβλῆσθαι·³⁴ τοὺς δὲ ἐξορισθέντας³⁵ καταλαβέσθαι μὲν³⁶ τοὺς περὶ τὰ Ἱεροσόλυμα τόπους, συστησαμένους³⁷ δὲ τὸ τῶν Ἰουδαίων ἔθνος παραδόσιμον³⁸ ποιῆσαι τὸ μῖσος³⁹ τὸ πρὸς τοὺς ἀνθρώπους· διὰ τοῦτο δὲ καὶ νόμιμα παντελῶς ἐξηλλαγμένα⁴⁰ καταδεῖξαι,⁴¹ τὸ μηδενὶ ἄλλῳ ἔθνει τραπέζης κοινωνεῖν⁴² μηδ' εὐνοεῖν⁴³ τὸ παράπαν.⁴⁴ ³ὑπέμνησαν⁴⁵ δὲ αὐτὸν καὶ περὶ τοῦ προγενομένου μίσους τοῖς προγόνοις πρὸς τοῦτο τὸ ἔθνος. Ἀντίοχος γὰρ ὁ προσαγορευθεὶς⁴⁶ Ἐπιφανὴς⁴⁷ καταπολεμήσας⁴⁸ τοὺς Ἰουδαίους εἰσῆλθεν εἰς τὸν ἄδυτον⁴⁹ τοῦ θεοῦ σηκόν,⁵⁰ οἷ⁵¹ νόμιμον⁵² εἰσιέναι⁵³ μόνον τὸν ἱερέα·⁵⁴ εὑρὼν δὲ ἐν αὐτῷ λίθινον⁵⁵ ἄγαλμα⁵⁶ ἀνδρὸς βαθυπώγωνος⁵⁷ καθήμενον ἐπ' ὄνου,⁵⁸ μετὰ χεῖρας ἔχον βιβλίον,⁵⁹ τοῦτο μὲν⁶⁰ ὑπέλαβε Μωυσέως εἶναι τοῦ κτίσαντος⁶¹ τὰ Ἱεροσόλυμα καὶ συστησαμένου τὸ ἔθνος, πρὸς δὲ τούτοις⁶² νομοθετήσαντος⁶³ τὰ μισάνθρωπα⁶⁴ καὶ παράνομα⁶⁵ ἔθη⁶⁶ τοῖς Ἰουδαίοις· αὐτὸς δὲ στυγήσας⁶⁷ τὴν μισανθρωπίαν πάντων ἐθνῶν ἐφιλοτιμήθη⁶⁸ καταλῦσαι τὰ νόμιμα. ⁴διὸ τῷ ἀγάλματι τοῦ κτίστου⁶⁹ καὶ τῷ ὑπαίθρῳ⁷⁰ βωμῷ⁷¹ τοῦ θεοῦ μεγάλην ὗν⁷² θύσας,⁷³ τό τε αἷμα προσέχεεν⁷⁴ αὐτοῖς, καὶ τὰ κρέα⁷⁵ σκευάσας⁷⁶ προσέταξε⁷⁷ τῷ

---

30. Prep. gen., *for the sake of*; καθαρμοῦ χάριν, "to purge [the land]."
31. ἐναγής, -ές, *under a curse*.
32. Aor. pass. ptc. acc. masc. pl., συναθροίζω, (pass.) *be gathered, assembled*; circ.
33. ὑπερόριος, -ον, *over the borders, abroad*.
34. Pf. pass. inf., ἐκβάλλω, (pass.) *be cast out*; indir. disc. See n. 19.
35. Aor. pass. ptc. acc. masc. pl., ἐξορίζω, (pass.) *be banished*; attrib. (subst.).
36. μέν . . . δέ; point/counterpoint. See n. 5.
37. Aor. mid. ptc. acc. masc. pl., συνίστημι, *organize*; circ.
38. παραδόσιμος, -ον, *what is handed down by tradition*; pred. comp.: "They made their hatred toward [other] people *a tradition*."
39. μῖσος, -εος, τό, *hatred*.
40. Pf. pass. ptc. acc. neut. pl., ἐξαλλάσσω, (pass. ptc. as adj.) *strange* (cf. LSJ, 583.2.b).
41. Aor. act. inf., καταδείκνυμι, *invent and teach, introduce*; indir. disc. See n. 19.
42. Pres. act. inf., κοινωνέω, *have a share* (in something); with gen. The articular infinitives τὸ κοινωνεῖν μηδ' εὐνοεῖν are appositives to νόμιμα παντελῶς ἐξηλλαγμένα (cf. S §§1987, 2035): "entirely strange laws: not to share table fellowship with any other ethnic group nor to act favorably toward them at all."
43. Pres. act. inf., εὐνοέω, *be favorable toward*; with dat.
44. Adv. (sometimes with art., as here), (neg.) *not at all*.
45. Aor. act. indic. 3 pl., ὑπομιμνήσκω, *remind*.
46. Aor. pass. ptc. nom. masc. sg., προσαγορεύω, (pass.) *be called/surnamed*; attrib.
47. ἐπιφανής, -ές, (of gods) *manifest*.
48. Aor. act. ptc. nom. masc. sg., καταπολεμέω, *defeat in warfare*; circ.
49. ἄδυτος, -ον, *innermost part* (of the sanctuary).
50. σηκός, -οῦ, ὁ, *sanctuary, shrine*.
51. Adv., *where*.
52. νόμιμος, -α, -ον, (quasi-impers.) *it is lawful*; with acc. and inf.
53. Pres. act. inf., εἴσειμι, *enter*.
54. ἱερεύς, -έως, ὁ, *priest*.
55. λίθινος, -η, -ον, *made of stone*.
56. ἄγαλμα, -ατος, τό, *image, statue*.
57. βαθυπώγων, -ον, *with thick beard*.
58. ὄνος, -ου, ὁ, *donkey*.
59. βιβλίος, -ου, ὁ, *book*.
60. μέν . . . δέ; point/counterpoint. See n. 5.
61. Aor. act. ptc. gen. masc. sg., κτίζω, *found*; attrib. (subst.; apposition.
62. πρὸς τούτοις, "in addition to these things"; hence "moreover."
63. Aor. act. ptc. gen. masc. sg., νομοθετέω, *legislate, ordain*; attrib. (subst.; apposition).
64. μισάνθρωπος, -ον, *misanthropic*.
65. παράνομος, -ον, *lawless*.
66. ἔθος, -ους, τό, *custom*.
67. Aor. act. ptc. nom. masc. sg., στυγέω, *abhor, detest*; circ. (causal).
68. Aor. pass. indic. 3 sg., φιλοτιμέομαι, *strive eagerly, endeavor to*; with inf.
69. κτίστης, -ου, ὁ, *founder*.
70. ὑπαίθριος, -ον, *open-air*.
71. βωμός, -οῦ, ὁ, *altar*.
72. ὗς, ὑός, ἡ, *pig*.
73. Aor. act. ptc. nom. masc. sg., θύω, *sacrifice*; circ.
74. Impf. act. indic. 3 sg., προσχέω, *pour to/on*.
75. κρέας, -ων, τό, (pl.) *flesh*.
76. Aor. act. ptc. nom. masc. sg., σκευάζω, *prepare*; circ.
77. Aor. act. indic. 3 sg., προστάσσω, *order, command*; with acc. and inf.

μὲν⁷⁸ ἀπὸ τούτων ζωμῷ⁷⁹ τὰς ἱερὰς⁸⁰ αὐτῶν βίβλους καὶ περιεχούσας⁸¹ τὰ μισόξενα νόμιμα καταρρᾶναι,⁸² τὸν δὲ ἀθάνατον λεγόμενον παρ' αὐτοῖς λύχνον⁸³ καὶ καιόμενον ἀδιαλείπτως⁸⁴ ἐν τῷ ναῷ κατασβέσαι,⁸⁵ τῶν τε κρεῶν ἀναγκάσαι προσενέγκασθαι⁸⁶ τὸν ἀρχιερέα καὶ τοὺς ἄλλους Ἰουδαίους. Ταῦτα δὴ⁸⁷ διεξιόντες⁸⁸ οἱ φίλοι τὸν Ἀντίοχον παρεκάλουν μάλιστα μὲν⁸⁹ ἄρδην ἀνελεῖν τὸ ἔθνος, εἰ δὲ μή, καταλῦσαι τὰ νόμιμα καὶ συναναγκάσαι⁹⁰ τὰς ἀγωγὰς⁹¹ μεταθέσθαι.⁹² ⁵ὁ δὲ βασιλεὺς μεγαλόψυχος⁹³ ὢν καὶ τὸ ἦθος ἥμερος,⁹⁴ λαβὼν ὁμήρους⁹⁵ ἀπέλυσε τῶν ἐγκλημάτων⁹⁶ τοὺς Ἰουδαίους, φόρους τε τοὺς ὀφειλομένους πραξάμενος⁹⁷ καὶ τὰ τείχη⁹⁸ περιελὼν⁹⁹ τῶν Ἱεροσολύμων.

78. μέν ... δέ; point/counterpoint. See n. 5.
79. ζωμός, -οῦ, ὁ, *soup*; dat. of instrument.
80. ἱερός, -ά, -όν, *sacred, holy*.
81. Pres. act. ptc. acc. fem. pl., περιέχω, (of writings) *contain*; attrib.
82. Aor. act. inf., καταραίνω, *sprinkle*.
83. λύχνος, -ου, ὁ, *lamp*.
84. Adv., *ceaselessly*.
85. Aor. act. inf., κατασβέννυμι, *extinguish*; comp. of προσέταξε.
86. Aor. mid. inf., προσφέρω, *partake* (of food); comp. of ἀναγκάσαι.
87. Postpositive partic., *then, so, well*: "indicates that the speaker considers (and invites the addressee to consider) the text segment or word (group) which it modifies as evident, clear, or precise" (*CGCG* §59.44); marks a transition to a summary statement.
88. Pres. act. ptc. nom. masc. pl., διέξειμι, *go through, recount*; circ.
89. μέν ... δέ; point/counterpoint. See n. 5.
90. Aor. act. inf., συναναγκάζω, *join in compelling*.
91. ἀγωγή, -ῆς, ἡ, *way* (of life), *conduct*.
92. Aor. mid. inf., μετατίθημι, *change, alter*; comp. of συναναγκάσαι.
93. μεγαλόψυχος, -ον, *magnanimous*.
94. ἥμερος, -α, -ον, *gentle, civilized*.
95. ὅμηρος, -ου, ὁ, *hostage*.
96. ἔγκλημα, -ατος, τό, *charge, accusation*.
97. Aor. mid. ptc. nom. masc. sg., πράσσω (with φόρους), *exact tributary payment*.
98. τεῖχος, -ους, τό, *wall*.
99. Aor. act. ptc. nom. masc. sg., περιαιρέω, *take away something that surrounds*; circ.

NOTES

34.1.1. Ἀντίοχος. Unlike Antiochus IV Epiphanes, Antiochus VII was known for his intense religious devotion and was thus surnamed Εὐσεβής, "Pious" (Josephus, *A.J.* 13.244).

34.1.2. Diodorus is dependent on Hecateaus (cf. *Bib. hist.* 43.3). Note Josephus's response to Manetho's *Aegyptica*: "But at this point, under the pretext of recording fables and current reports about the Jews, he took the liberty of introducing some incredible tales, wishing to represent us as mixed up with a crowd of Egyptian lepers and others, who for various maladies were condemned, as he asserts, to banish us from the country" (*C. Ap.* 1.229; Thackeray 1926)

34.1.3. εὑρὼν δὲ ἐν αὐτῷ λίθινον ἄγαλμα ἀνδρὸς βαθυπώγωνος καθήμενον ἐπ' ὄνου. Cf. Josephus, *C. Ap.* 2.80: "Within this sanctuary Apion has the effrontery to assert that the Jews kept an ass's head, worshiping that animal and deeming it worthy of the deepest reverence; the fact disclosed, he maintains, on the occasion of the spoliation of the temple by Antiochus Epiphanes, when the head, made of gold and worth a high price, was discovered" (Thackeray 1926; cf. Tacitus, *Hist.* 5.3–4).

34.1.4. The events of Antiochus's desecration of the sanctuary are variously narrated (cf. Dan. 9:27; 11:31; 12:11; 1 Macc. 1:54; Josephus, *A.J.* 12.253).

6.4

Dio Cassius

Lucius Cassius Dio (ca. 150–235 CE) was a Roman statesman, historian, and relative of the famous orator Dio Chrysostom (on whom, see §7.4). His massive, eighty-volume *Roman History*, about a third of which is extant, spans nearly a thousand years, from the arrival of Aeneas in Lavinium to the year of Dio's second consulship (229 CE). Dio made thorough use of the Roman annals and other sources available to him and fashioned himself as a historian in the mold of Thucydides (Cary 1914, xvii). Roman history is told through the lens of an elite politician and champion of monarchy (apologies to Tacitus and his ilk).

The reading passage (from book 53) offers a window into the political calculations Octavian made when he assumed the role of princeps.[1] Dio notes that he assumed the honorific Αὔγουστος because he wanted to avoid any suspicion of a return to monarchy.

Text and Translation: Cary 1917
Supplemental Scripture: Luke 2:1–7

---

1. On the rise of Augustan culture, see esp. Galinsky 1996, as well as the outstanding collection of essays in Galinsky 2005.

6.4.1

How Octavian Received the Honorific *Augustus*

Roman History 53.16.4–8

53.16.4 Ὁ δ' οὖν[1] Καῖσαρ[2] πολλὰ μὲν[3] καὶ πρότερον, ὅτε τὰ περὶ τῆς ἐξωμοσίας[4] τῆς μοναρχίας καὶ τὰ περὶ τῆς τῶν ἐθνῶν διανομῆς[5] διελέχθη,[6] ἔλαβε· καὶ γὰρ[7] τό τε τὰς δάφνας[8] πρὸ τῶν βασιλείων[9] αὐτοῦ προτίθεσθαι,[10] καὶ τὸ τὸν στέφανον[11] τὸν δρύινον[12] ὑπὲρ αὐτῶν ἀρτᾶσθαι,[13] τότε οἱ[14] ὡς καὶ ἀεὶ[15] τούς τε πολεμίους[16] νικῶντι[17] καὶ τοὺς πολίτας[18] σῴζοντι ἐψηφίσθη.[19] **5**(καλεῖται δὲ τὰ βασίλεια παλάτιον,[20] οὐχ

---

1. Partic. combination: "The preceding information is abandoned (δέ, indicating a shift) in favor of a point which is considered more relevant (οὖν) at the particular juncture" (*CGCG* §59.64).
2. Καῖσαρ, -αρος, ὁ, *Caesar* (Octavian).
3. μέν … δέ; point/counterpoint (cf. Runge 2010, 75–83; BDF §447; S §2904; *CGCG* §59.24). The δέ-clause begins midway through 53.16.6: πολλὰ μὲν καὶ πρότερον … ἐπεὶ δὲ καὶ τῷ ἔργῳ αὐτὰ ἐπετέλεσεν.
4. ἐξωμοσία, -ας, ἡ, *declining an office*.
5. διανομή, -ῆς, ἡ, *distribution*.
6. Aor. pass. indic. 3 sg., διαλέγω, (pass.) *be discussed*.
7. Partic. combination: additional information (καί) that has explanatory force (γάρ) (cf. *CGCG* §59.66).
8. δάφνη, -ης, ἡ, *laurel-tree* (symbol of military victory).
9. βασίλειον, -ου, τό, (pl.) *royal residence, palace*.
10. Pres. mid. inf., προτίθημι, *set before*. The articular infinitive τό … προτίθεσθαι functions as the subject of ἐψηφίσθη (cf. BDF §399; S §2031; *CGCG* §51.39).
11. στέφανος, -ου, ὁ, *crown*.
12. δρύινος, -ον, *of oak*. The *corona civica* was given to a soldier who saved the life of his fellow citizen.
13. Pres. mid. inf., ἀρτάω, *hang*; art. inf. as subject. See n. 10.
14. οἱ = αὐτῷ; dat. masc. sg. 3rd pers. pronoun of οὗ (cf. S §325).
15. Adv., *always*.
16. πολέμιος, -η, -ον, (subst.) *enemy*.
17. Pres. act. ptc. dat. masc. sg., νικάω, *defeat*. ὡς with a circumstantial participle gives "a 'subjective' reason or motivation, for which responsibility lies with the subject of the matrix verb" (*CGCG* §52.39; cf. S §2086); thus: "on the grounds that he always defeats his enemies and delivers the citizens."
18. πολίτης, -ου, ὁ, *citizen*.
19. Aor. pass. indic. 3 sg., ψηφίζω, (pass.) *be voted* (to someone).
20. παλάτιον, -ου, τό, (Lat.) *Palatium* (name for both the royal palace and the Palatine hill).

ὅτι καὶ ἔδοξέ²¹ ποτε οὕτως αὐτὰ ὀνομάζεσθαι,²² ἀλλ' ὅτι ἔν τε τῷ Παλατίῳ ὁ Καῖσαρ ᾤκει²³ καὶ ἐκεῖ τὸ στρατήγιον²⁴ εἶχε, καί τινα καὶ πρὸς τὴν τοῦ Ῥωμύλου²⁵ προενοίκησιν²⁶ φήμην²⁷ ἡ οἰκία αὐτοῦ ἀπὸ τοῦ παντὸς ὄρους²⁸ ἔλαβε· ⁶καὶ διὰ τοῦτο κἂν²⁹ ἄλλοθί που³⁰ ὁ αὐτοκράτωρ³¹ καταλύῃ,³² τὴν τοῦ παλατίου ἐπίκλησιν³³ ἡ καταγωγὴ³⁴ αὐτοῦ ἴσχει.³⁵ ἐπεὶ δὲ καὶ τῷ ἔργῳ αὐτὰ ἐπετέλεσεν,³⁶ οὕτω δὴ³⁷ καὶ τὸ τοῦ Αὐγούστου ὄνομα καὶ παρὰ τῆς βουλῆς³⁸ καὶ παρὰ τοῦ δήμου³⁹ ἐπέθετο. ⁷βουληθέντων γὰρ σφῶν⁴⁰ ἰδίως⁴¹ πως αὐτὸν προσειπεῖν, καὶ τῶν μὲν⁴² τὸ τῶν δὲ τὸ καὶ ἐσηγουμένων⁴³ καὶ αἱρουμένων,⁴⁴ ὁ Καῖσαρ ἐπεθύμει⁴⁵ μὲν⁴⁶ ἰσχυρῶς⁴⁷ Ῥωμύλος ὀνομασθῆναι, αἰσθόμενος⁴⁸ δὲ ὅτι ὑποπτεύεται⁴⁹ ἐκ τούτου τῆς βασιλείας ἐπιθυμεῖν, ⁸οὐκέτ' αὐτοῦ ἀντεποιήσατο,⁵⁰ ἀλλὰ Αὔγουστος ὡς καὶ πλεῖόν τι ἢ κατὰ ἀνθρώπους ὤν⁵¹ ἐπεκλήθη· πάντα γὰρ τὰ ἐντιμότατα⁵² καὶ τὰ ἱερώτατα⁵³ αὔγουστα προσαγορεύεται.⁵⁴ ἐξ οὗπερ καὶ σεβαστὸν⁵⁵ αὐτὸν καὶ ἑλληνίζοντές⁵⁶ πως, ὥσπερ τινὰ σεπτόν,⁵⁷ ἀπὸ τοῦ σεβάζεσθαι,⁵⁸ προσεῖπον.

NOTES

53.16.4. τῆς μοναρχίας. Dio was no fool. He clearly saw through Octavian's attempts to present himself as the savior of the res publica: "In this way the power of both people and senate passed entirely into the hands of Augustus, and from his time there was, strictly speaking, a monarchy [ἀρκριβὴς μοναρχία]; for monarchy would be the truest name for it, no matter if two or three did later hold the power at the same time" (53.17.1, trans. Cary 1917; cf. 51.1.1; 52.1.1). Yet in contrast to Tacitus (*Ann.*

21. Aor. act. indic. 3 sg., δοκέω, (impers.) *it seems/appears good*; with inf.
22. Pres. pass. inf., ὀνομάζω, (pass.) *be named*.
23. Impf. act. indic. 3 sg., οἰκέω, *dwell, inhabit*.
24. στρατήγιον, -ου, τό, *military headquarters*.
25. Ῥωμύλος, -ου, ὁ, *Romulus* (mythical founder of Rome).
26. προενοίκησις, -εως, ἡ, *dwelling in* (a place) *before*.
27. φήμη, -ης, ἡ, *good report, reputation*.
28. ὄρος, -ους, τό, *mountain, hill*.
29. κἂν = καὶ ἐάν; concessive clause (cf. BDF §374; S §2369; CGCG §49.19).
30. που adds indefiniteness to ἄλλοθι: "to somewhere [anywhere] else."
31. αὐτοκράτωρ, -ορος, ὁ, *absolute ruler*, (Lat.) *imperator, emperor*.
32. Pres. act. subj. 3 sg., καταλύω, (intrans.) *take up one's quarters, lodge*. See n. 29.
33. ἐπίκλησις, -εως, ἡ, *surname, designation*.
34. καταγωγή, -ῆς, ἡ, *dwelling, residence*.
35. Pres. act. indic. 3 sg., ἴσχω, *keep, maintain*.
36. Aor. act. indic. 3 sg., ἐπιτελέω, *complete*.
37. Postpositive partic., *so, thus, indeed*: "indicates that the speaker considers (and invites the addressee to consider) the text segment or word (group) which it modifies as evident, clear, or precise" (CGCG §59.44); underscores οὕτω. "And when he in fact carried out these things, *so* also was the name Augustus bestowed [upon him] by both the Senate and the people."
38. βουλή, -ῆς, ἡ, (Lat.) *senatus* (senate).
39. δῆμος, -ου, ὁ, (Lat.) *populus* (people).
40. σφων = αὐτῶν (cf. S §325).
41. Adv., with πως, "in some distinct manner."
42. τῶν μέν ... τῶν δέ, "*Some* were introducing and selecting τό [= τὸ ὄνομα, one title] ... *others* were introducing and selecting τό [another]."

43. Pres. mid. ptc. gen. masc. pl., εἰσηγέομαι, *introduce, propose*; gen. absol.
44. Pres. mid. ptc. gen. masc. pl., αἱρέω, (mid.) *choose*.
45. Impf. act. indic. 3 sg., ἐπιθυμέω, *set one's heart upon* (a thing), *desire*; with inf.
46. μέν ... δέ; point/counterpoint. See n. 3.
47. Adv., *strongly*.
48. Pres. mid. ptc. nom. masc. sg., αἰσθάνομαι, *perceive*; circ. (causal).
49. Pres. pass. indic. 3 sg., ὑποπτεύω, (pass.) *be suspected* (of).
50. Aor. mid. indic. 3 sg., ἀντιποιέω, (mid.) *exert oneself about a thing*; with gen.
51. ὡς with circ. ptc.: "in the conviction that he is something more than human." See n. 17.
52. Superl., ἔντιμος, -ον, *most honored*.
53. Superl., ἱερός, -ή, -όν, *most sacred*.
54. Pres. pass. indic. 3 sg., προσαγορεύω, (pass.) *be called*.
55. σεβαστός, -ή, -όν, *venerable/august*; pred. comp.
56. Pres. act. ptc. nom. masc. pl., ἑλληνίζω, *speak Greek*; circ.
57. σεπτός, -ή, -όν, *august*.
58. Pres. pass. inf., σεβάζω, (pass.) *be venerated/honored*; inf. obj. of prep. ἀπό.

1.9–10), Dio was perfectly happy with a monarchy (cf. *Hist. rom.* 44.2; 53.19.1; 54.2.1).

ὡς καὶ ἀεὶ τούς τε πολεμίους νικῶντι καὶ τοὺς πολίτας σώζοντι. Cf. Augustus, *RG* 34:

> In my sixth and seventh consulships [28–27 BCE], after I had put an end to civil wars, although by everyone's agreement I had power over everything, I transferred the state from my power into the control of the Roman senate and people. For this service, I was named Augustus by senatorial decree [*senatus consulto Augustus appellatus sum*], and the doorposts of my house were publicly clothed with laurels, and a civic crown was fastened above my doorway, and a golden shield was set up in the Julian senate house; through an inscription on this shield the fact was declared that the Roman senate and people were giving it to me because of my valor, clemency, justice, and piety. After this time I excelled everyone in influence [*auctoritas*], but I had no more power [*potestas*] than the others who were my colleagues in each magistracy. (Cooley 2009, 98)

Octavian enlarged his *auctoritas* (a kind of unofficial power and influence that emanates from the person) through a series of military victories that culminated in the battle of Actium (31 BCE). See Zanker (1988, 79–100), Galinsky (1996, 10–41), and Cooley (2009, 116–17).

53.16.6–8. Cf. Suetonius, *Aug.* 7.2. For a discussion of the connections between Romulus and Augustus, see Beard, North, and Price (1998, 1:182–84). On the name Augustus, see Galinsky (1996, 315–18, and sources therein). The Greek equivalent σεβαστός is widely attested. See, for example, the heading of the Greek translation of *RG*: "Translated and inscribed below are the achievements and gifts of the god *Sebastos* [Σεβαστοῦ θεοῦ], which he left engraved at Rome upon two bronze tablets" (Cooley 2009, 59 alt.). Cf. also the famous Priene Inscription (*OGIS*, no. 458). On the divinity of the emperor and its relevance for early Christianity, see Peppard (2011).

6.5

Plutarch

Plutarch was a renowned philosopher and biographer who flourished from the mid-first century CE to the beginning of Hadrian's reign (ca. 45–120 CE). All his writings are didactic in nature. The *Moralia*, which we turn to in §7.5, is a collection of treatises on a host of issues, such as education, oratory, philosophy, friendship, and marriage. Here we examine his *Lives* (βίοι, *vitae*)—a collection of biographies about famous Greeks and Romans whom he treats in pairs. He does this (1) to demonstrate that Greek and Roman history are complementary and (2) to inculcate virtue and discourage vice (see esp. Duff 1999).

Both reading passages are from Plutarch's *Alexander*. The first is often used to illustrate the distinction between ἱστορία and βίος (though see the note on *Alex.* 1.2 below). The second is an amusing account of Alexander's encounter with the priest of Ammon (Amun), who mistakenly greets him as "son of Zeus," a slip of the tongue with which the plucky Macedonian is quite pleased.

Text and Translation: Perrin 1919
Supplemental Scripture: Matt. 1:18–25; Luke 1:26–38 (§6.5.1); Mark 3:11; 5:7 (§6.5.2)

6.5.1

The Biographer's Aim

Alexander 1.1–2.4

1.1Τὸν Ἀλεξάνδρου[1] τοῦ βασιλέως βίον[2] καὶ τοῦ Καίσαρος,[3] ὑφ' οὗ κατελύθη[4] Πομπήϊος,[5] ἐν τούτῳ τῷ βιβλίῳ[6] γράφοντες, διὰ τὸ πλῆθος τῶν ὑποκειμένων[7] πράξεων[8] οὐδὲν ἄλλο προεροῦμεν[9] ἢ παραιτησόμεθα[10] τοὺς ἀναγινώσκοντας,[11] ἐὰν μὴ πάντα μηδὲ καθ' ἕκαστον[12] ἐξειργασμένως[13] τι τῶν περιβοήτων[14] ἀπαγγέλλωμεν,[15] ἀλλὰ ἐπιτέμνοντες[16] τὰ πλεῖστα,[17] μὴ συκοφαντεῖν.[18] **2**οὔτε[19] γὰρ ἱστορίας[20] γράφομεν, ἀλλὰ βίους, οὔτε ταῖς ἐπιφανεστάταις[21] πράξεσι πάντως ἔνεστι[22] δήλωσις[23] ἀρετῆς[24] ἢ κακίας, ἀλλὰ πρᾶγμα[25] βραχὺ[26] πολλάκις[27] καὶ ῥῆμα[28] καὶ παιδιά[29] τις ἔμφασιν[30] ἤθους[31] ἐποίησε μᾶλλον ἢ μάχαι[32] μυριόνεκροι[33]

1. Ἀλέξανδρος, -ου, ὁ, *Alexander*.
2. βίος, -ου, ὁ, *life, biography*.
3. Καῖσαρ, -αρος, ὁ, *Caesar*.
4. Aor. pass. indic. 3 sg., καταλύω, (pass.) *be overthrown*.
5. Πομπήϊος, -ου, ὁ, *Pompey*.
6. βιβλίον, -ου, τό, *book*.
7. Pres. pass. ptc. gen. fem. pl., ὑπόκειμαι, (pass.) *be presented*; attrib.; διὰ τὸ πλῆθος τῶν ὑποκειμένων πράξεων, "on account of the multitude of deeds being treated."
8. πρᾶξις, -εως, ἡ, *action, deed*.
9. Fut. act. indic. 1 pl., προερέω, *speak in advance, preface*; with internal acc. (οὐδέν): "I will make *no preface* other than [ἄλλο ... ἤ] I will entreat my readers."
10. Fut. mid. indic. 1 pl., παραιτέω, *entreat*.
11. Pres. act. ptc. acc. masc. sg., ἀναγινώσκω, *read*; attrib. (subst.).
12. καθ' ἕκαστον (distributive), "in each instance."
13. Adv., *exhaustively*.
14. περιβόητος, -ον, *renowned*.
15. Pres. act. subj. 1 pl., ἀπαγγέλλω, *report*; third-class condition (cf. BDF §373; S §2326; CGCG §49.6).
16. Pres. act. ptc. nom. masc. pl., ἐπιτέμνω, *cut short, abbreviate*; circ.
17. Adv. acc. (extent), *for the most part*.
18. Pres. act. inf., συκοφαντέω, *slander, accuse falsely*; imperatival (cf. BDF §389; S §2013; CGCG §51.47).
19. οὔτε ... οὔτε, *neither ... nor*.
20. ἱστορία, -ας, ἡ, *history*.
21. Superl., ἐπιφανής, -ές, *most notable*.
22. Pres. act. indic. 3 sg., ἔνειμι, *be in*; with dat.
23. δήλωσις, -εως, ἡ, *manifestation, demonstration*.
24. ἀρετή, -ῆς, ἡ, *virtue*.
25. πρᾶγμα, -ατος, τό, *thing, matter*.
26. βραχύς, -εῖα, -ύ, *little, small*.
27. Adv., *many times, often*.
28. ῥῆμα, -ατος, τό, *word, saying*.
29. παιδιά, -ᾶς, ἡ, *joke*.
30. ἔμφασις, -εως, ἡ, *appearance, impression*.
31. ἦθος, -ους, τό, *character*.
32. μάχη, -ης, ἡ, *battle*.
33. μυριόνεκρος, -ον, *of myriad corpses*.

καὶ παρατάξεις³⁴ αἱ μέγισται καὶ πολιορκίαι³⁵ πόλεων. **3** ὥσπερ³⁶ οὖν οἱ ζωγράφοι³⁷ τὰς ὁμοιότητας³⁸ ἀπὸ τοῦ προσώπου καὶ τῶν περὶ τὴν ὄψιν³⁹ εἰδῶν,⁴⁰ οἷς ἐμφαίνεται⁴¹ τὸ ἦθος, ἀναλαμβάνουσιν,⁴² ἐλάχιστα⁴³ τῶν λοιπῶν μερῶν⁴⁴ φροντίζοντες,⁴⁵ οὕτως ἡμῖν δοτέον⁴⁶ εἰς τὰ τῆς ψυχῆς σημεῖα μᾶλλον ἐνδύεσθαι⁴⁷ καὶ διὰ τούτων εἰδοποιεῖν⁴⁸ τὸν ἑκάστου βίον, ἐάσαντας⁴⁹ ἑτέροις τὰ μεγέθη⁵⁰ καὶ τοὺς ἀγῶνας.⁵¹

2.1 Ἀλέξανδρος⁵² ὅτι τῷ γένει⁵³ πρὸς πατρὸς μὲν⁵⁴ ἦν Ἡρακλείδης⁵⁵ ἀπὸ Καράνου,⁵⁶ πρὸς δὲ μητρὸς Αἰακίδης⁵⁷ ἀπὸ Νεοπτολέμου,⁵⁸ τῶν πάνυ πεπιστευμένων ἐστί.⁵⁹ λέγεται δὲ Φίλιππος ἐν Σαμοθρᾴκῃ⁶⁰ τῇ Ὀλυμπιάδι⁶¹ συμμυηθεὶς⁶² αὐτός τε μειράκιον⁶³ ὢν ἔτι κἀκείνης⁶⁴ παιδὸς⁶⁵ ὀρφανῆς⁶⁶ γονέων ἐρασθῆναι⁶⁷ καὶ τὸν γάμον οὕτως ἁρμόσαι,⁶⁸ πείσας⁶⁹ τὸν ἀδελφὸν αὐτῆς Ἀρύμβαν.⁷⁰ **2** ἡ μὲν οὖν⁷¹ νύμφη,⁷² πρὸ τῆς νυκτὸς ᾗ συνείρχθησαν⁷³ εἰς τὸν θάλαμον,⁷⁴ ἔδοξε⁷⁵ βροντῆς⁷⁶ γενομένης ἐμπεσεῖν⁷⁷ αὐτῆς τῇ γαστρὶ⁷⁸ κεραυνόν,⁷⁹ ἐκ δὲ τῆς πληγῆς⁸⁰ πολὺ πῦρ ἀναφθέν,⁸¹ εἶτα ῥηγνύμενον⁸² εἰς φλόγας⁸³ πάντῃ⁸⁴ φερομένας διαλυθῆναι.⁸⁵ ὁ δὲ Φίλιππος ὑστέρῳ χρόνῳ μετὰ τὸν γάμον εἶδεν ὄναρ⁸⁶ αὐτὸν⁸⁷ ἐπιβάλλοντα σφραγῖδα⁸⁸

34. παράταξις, -εως, ἡ, *arrangement in battle*.
35. πολιορκία, -ας, ἡ, *siege*.
36. ὥσπερ ... οὕτως, *as . . . so*.
37. ζωγράφος, -ου, ὁ, *painter*.
38. ὁμοιότης, -ητος, ἡ, *likeness*.
39. ὄψις, -εως, ἡ, (sg. in collective sense) *eyes*.
40. εἶδος, -ους, τό, *form, shape*.
41. Pres. pass. indic. 3 sg., ἐμφαίνω, (pass.) *be manifest, become visible*.
42. Pres. act. indic. 3 pl., ἀναλαμβάνω, *take, receive*.
43. Adv. acc. (extent), *very little, almost not at all*.
44. μέρος, -ους, τό, (body) *part*.
45. Pres. act. ptc. nom. masc. pl., φροντίζω, *consider, regard*; with gen.
46. Verbal adj. from δίδωμι; impers. (act.) constr.; with dat. agent (cf. S §2152; *CGCG* §37.3): "It is necessary for us to grant."
47. Pres. mid. inf., ἐνδύω, *undertake*; obj./purpose (cf. S §2009).
48. Pres. act. inf., εἰδοποιέω, *endow with form, portray*; obj./purpose. See n. 47.
49. Aor. act. ptc. acc. masc. pl., ἐάω, *concede, leave*; circ.
50. μέγεθος, -ους, τό, *greatness, magnitude*.
51. ἀγών, -ῶνος, ὁ, *contest, struggle*.
52. The nominative pendent (or absol.) establishes the new theme (*CGCG* §60.34).
53. γένος, -ους, τό, *family lineage*; dat. of respect.
54. μέν ... δέ; point/counterpoint (cf. Runge 2010, 75–83; BDF §447; S §2904; *CGCG* §59.24).
55. Ἡρακλείδης, -ου, ὁ, *descendant of Heracles* (divine hero and son of Zeus). For patronymic suffixes, cf. S §845.
56. Κάρανος, -ου, ὁ, *Caranus*.
57. Αἰακίδης, -ου, ὁ, *descendant of Aeacus* (mythological king of Aegina).
58. Νεοπτόλεμος, -ου, ὁ, *Neoptolemus*.
59. Quasi-impers., τῶν πάνυ πεπιστευμένων ἐστί, "it is of the [reports] that are entirely trustworthy." The subject is explicated by the ὅτι-clause of content.
60. Σαμοθρᾴκη, -ης, ἡ, *Samothrace*.
61. Ὀλυμπιάς, -αδος, ἡ, *Olympias*.
62. Aor. pass. ptc. nom. masc. sg., συμμυέω, *be initiated into the mysteries with*; with dat.
63. μειράκιον, -ου, τό, *youth, lad*.
64. Crasis: κἀκείνης = καὶ ἐκείνης.
65. παῖς, παιδός, ἡ, *child*.
66. ὀρφανός, -ή, -όν, *bereft of*; with gen.
67. Aor. pass. inf., ἔραμαι, *fall in love with*; with gen. pers.; indir. disc. (cf. BDF §396; S §2016; *CGCG* §51.19).
68. Aor. act. inf., ἁρμόζω, with τὸν γάμον, *betroth*; indir. disc. See n. 67.
69. Aor. act. ptc. nom. masc. sg., πείθω, *persuade*; circ.
70. Ἀρύμβας, -ου, ὁ, *Arymbas*. Arymbas was her uncle; hence the emendations: πατράδελφον (anonymous); ἀδελφὸν τοῦ πατρὸς αὐτῆς (Xylander) (Hamilton 1969, 3).
71. Partic. combination: "a transition to a more to-the-point, relevant text segment (οὖν) [that] occurs in two stages (μέν ... δέ)" (*CGCG* §59.73).
72. νύμφη, -ης, ἡ, *bride*.
73. Aor. pass. indic. 3 pl., συνέργω, (pass.) *be joined together*.
74. θάλαμος, -ου, ὁ, *bedroom, bridal chamber*.
75. Aor. act. indic. 3 sg., δοκέω, (impers.) *it seems*; with acc. and inf.
76. βροντή, -ῆς, ἡ, *thunder*. βροντῆς γενομένης is a genitive absolute.
77. Aor. act. inf., ἐμπίπτω, *fall upon*; with dat.; indir. disc. See n. 67.
78. γαστήρ, -έρος, ἡ, *womb*.
79. κεραυνός, -οῦ, ὁ, *thunderbolt*.
80. πληγή, -ῆς, ἡ, *strike*.
81. Aor. pass. ptc. nom. neut. sg., ἀνάπτω, (pass.) *be kindled*; circ.
82. Pres. pass. ptc. nom. neut. sg., ῥήγνυμι, *break out*; circ.
83. φλόξ, φλογός, ἡ, *flame*.
84. Adv., *every way, all about*.
85. Aor. pass. inf., διαλύω, (pass.) *be put to an end, put out*; indir. disc. (ἔδοξε). See n. 67.
86. ὄναρ, ὄνειρος, τό, *dream*.
87. αὑτόν = ἑαυτόν.
88. σφραγίς, -ῖδος, ἡ, *seal*.

τῇ γαστρὶ τῆς γυναικός· ἡ δὲ γλυφὴ[89] τῆς σφραγῖδος, ὡς ᾤετο,[90] λέοντος[91] εἶχεν εἰκόνα.[92] **3**τῶν δὲ ἄλλων μάντεων[93] ὑφορωμένων[94] τὴν ὄψιν,[95] ὡς ἀκριβεστέρας[96] φυλακῆς[97] δεομένων[98] τῷ Φιλίππῳ τῶν περὶ τὸν γάμον, Ἀρίστανδρος[99] ὁ Τελμησσεὺς[100] κύειν[101] ἔφη τὴν ἄνθρωπον, οὐθὲν γὰρ ἀποσφραγίζεσθαι[102] τῶν κενῶν,[103] καὶ κύειν παῖδα θυμοειδῆ[104] καὶ λεοντώδη[105] τὴν φύσιν.[106] **4**ὤφθη δε ποτε καὶ δράκων[107] κοιμωμένης[108] τῆς Ὀλυμπιάδος παρεκτεταμένος[109] τῷ σώματι· καὶ τοῦτο μάλιστα[110] τοῦ Φιλίππου τὸν ἔρωτα[111] καὶ τὰς φιλοφροσύνας[112] ἀμαυρῶσαι[113] λέγουσιν, ὡς μηδὲ φοιτᾶν[114] ἔτι πολλάκις παρ' αὐτὴν ἀναπαυσόμενον,[115] εἴτε δείσαντά[116] τινας μαγείας[117] ἐπ' αὐτῷ καὶ φάρμακα[118] τῆς γυναικός, εἴτε τὴν ὁμιλίαν[119] ὡς κρείττονι συνούσης[120] ἀφοσιούμενον.[121]

---

89. γλυφή, -ῆς, ἡ, *emblem, device*.
90. Impf. mid. indic. 3 sg., οἴομαι, *think, suppose*.
91. λέων, -οντος, ὁ, *lion*.
92. εἰκών, -όνος, ἡ, *image*.
93. μάντις, -εως, ὁ, *seer, diviner*.
94. Pres. pass. ptc. gen. masc. pl., ὑφοράω, *view with suspicion*; gen. absol.
95. ὄψις, -εως, ἡ, *vision*.
96. Compar., ἀκριβής, -ές, *stricter*.
97. φυλακή, -ῆς, ἡ, *watch, guard*.
98. Pres. mid. ptc. gen. masc. pl., δέομαι, *be in need of*; with gen. ὡς with a circumstantial participle gives "a 'subjective' reason or motivation, for which responsibility lies with the subject of the matrix verb" (*CGCG* §52.39).
99. Ἀρίστανδρος, -ου, ὁ, *Aristander*.
100. Τελμησσεύς, -έως, ὁ, *of Telmessos*.
101. Pres. act. inf., κύω, *be pregnant*; indir. disc. (ἔφη). See n. 67.
102. Pres. pass. inf., ἀποσφραγίζω, (pass.) *be sealed up*.
103. κενός, -ή, -όν, *empty*.
104. θυμοειδής, -ές, *bold*.
105. λεοντώδης, -ες, *lionlike*.
106. φύσις, -εως, ἡ, *nature*; acc. of respect.
107. δράκων, -οντος, ὁ, *serpent*.
108. Pres. mid. ptc. gen. fem. sg., κοιμάω, *sleep*; gen. absol.
109. Pf. mid. ptc. nom. masc. sg., παρεκτείνω, *be stretched out*; supp. (ὤφθη).
110. Superl. adv. of μάλα, *especially*.
111. ἔρως, -ωτος, ὁ, *desire*.
112. φιλοφροσύνη, -ης, ἡ, (pl.) *signs of affection*.
113. Aor. act. inf., ἀμαυρόω, *dim, dull*; indir. disc. (λέγουσιν). See n. 67.
114. Pres. act. inf., φοιτάω, *come*; result clause: ὡς with inf. (cf. S §2260; *CGCG* §46.7).
115. Fut. mid. ptc. acc. masc. sg., ἀναπαύω, *rest*; circ.

NOTES

1.2. Cf. Duff (1999, 17):

> The prologue to *Alexander-Caesar*, with its stress on the selection of revealing details rather than the narration of political and military events, has been very influential in determining modern approaches to the *Lives*. It is often elevated into a general statement about the generic differences between history and biography in ancient thought. This is mistaken. The terms which Plutarch uses, while revealing in themselves, should not be taken as implying a widely accepted definition of any distinction between history and biography. The boundaries between history, political biography, and related forms of writing such as *enkomion* and the so-called historiographical monograph, were never clearly drawn; rather, generic differences were open to construction by individual authors in order to distinguish their work from those of rivals.

Duff (1999, 18n14) cites numerous instances where Plutarch refers to his work as ἱστορία. The distinction, then, seems to lie not in a qualitative difference between "history" and "biography" but in a polarity between "little things" and "big things" (Pelling 2002, 260).

---

116. Aor. act. ptc. acc. masc. sg., δείδω, *fear*; circ.
117. μαγεία, -ας, ἡ, *magic, sorcery*.
118. φάρμακον, -ου, τό, *spell, charm*.
119. ὁμιλία, -ας, ἡ, *intercourse*.
120. Pres. act. ptc. gen. fem. sg., σύνειμι, *be with*; with dat.; ὡς with circ. ptc. (see n. 98): "thinking that she had been with a superior being."
121. Pres. mid. ptc. acc. masc. sg., ἀφοσιόω, *eschew on religious grounds*; circ.

2.1. On Alexander's genealogy, cf. Arrian, *Anab.* 1.2.8; Diodorus Siculus, *Bib. hist.* 17.1.5; Livy, *Ab urbe cond.* 45.9. Caranus, a descendant of Heracles, is first mentioned by Theopompus, "evidently an artistic creation designed to link the Macedonian and Argive dynasties" (Hamilton 1969, 2). Neoptolemus I, also called Pyrrhus ("Red," on account of his hair), the son of Achilles and Deidamia, founded the dynasty of the Molossians in Epirus.

2.2. The legend suggests that the maiden Olympias was impregnated by Zeus. Cf. Herodotus's account of the dream of the mother of Pericles (*Hist.* 6.131; cf. Plutarch, *Per.* 3.3). "It may be significant that Alexander's ancestors, Heracles and Achilles, were called 'lion-hearted'; cf., e.g., Homer, *Il.* 5.639, *Od.* 2.267 (Heracles); Hesiod, *Theog.* 1007 (Achilles)" (Hamilton 1969, 3).

2.4. The god Dionysus, in whose rites Olympias is said to have been involved (2.7–9), was known to take the shape of a snake (cf. Euripides, *Bacch.* 1017–1018). Plutarch later reports that Alexander incurred the wrath of Dionysus for his treatment of Thebes (*Alex.* 13.3–5), and he narrates Alexander's downfall (self-destruction) as one of Dionysiac tragedy (Pelling 2002, 203).

6.5.2

Alexander and the Prophet of Ammon

Alexander 27.3–6

27.3'Ἐπεὶ δὲ διεξελθὼν[1] τὴν ἔρημον[2] ἧκεν[3] εἰς τὸν τόπον, ὁ μὲν[4] προφήτης αὐτὸν ὁ Ἄμμωνος[5] ἀπὸ τοῦ θεοῦ χαίρειν, ὡς ἀπὸ πατρός, προσεῖπεν· ὁ δὲ ἐπήρετο[6] μή τις αὐτὸν εἴη[7] διαπεφευγὼς[8] τῶν τοῦ πατρὸς φονέων.[9] **4**εὐφημεῖν[10] δὲ τοῦ προφήτου κελεύσαντος,[11] οὐ γὰρ εἶναι πατέρα θνητὸν[12] αὐτῷ, μεταβαλὼν[13] ἐπυνθάνετο,[14] τοὺς Φιλίππου φονεῖς εἰ πάντας εἴη τετιμωρημένος.[15] εἶτα περὶ τῆς ἀρχῆς, εἰ πάντων αὐτῷ δίδωσιν ἀνθρώπων κυρίῳ γενέσθαι. χρήσαντος[16] δὲ τοῦ θεοῦ καὶ τοῦτο διδόναι καὶ Φίλιππον ἀπέχειν[17] ἔκπλεω[18] τὴν δίκην,[19] ἐδωρεῖτο[20] τὸν θεὸν ἀναθήμασι[21] λαμπροῖς[22] καὶ χρήμασι[23] τοὺς ἀνθρώπους.

5Ταῦτα περὶ τῶν χρησμῶν[24] οἱ πλεῖστοι γράφουσιν· αὐτὸς δὲ Ἀλέξανδρος ἐν ἐπιστολῇ πρὸς τὴν μητέρα φησὶ γεγονέναι τινὰς αὐτῷ μαντείας[25] ἀπορρήτους,[26] ἃς αὐτὸς ἐπανελθὼν[27] φράσει[28] πρὸς μόνην ἐκείνην.

---

1. Aor. act. ptc. nom. masc. sg., διεξέρχομαι, *pass through*; circ.
2. ἔρημος, -ου, ἡ, *desert*.
3. Pf. act. indic. 3 sg., ἥκω, *reach, arrive at*.
4. μέν . . . δέ; point/counterpoint (cf. Runge 2010, 75–83; BDF §447; S §2904; *CGCG* §59.24).
5. Ἄμμων, -ονος, ὁ, *Ammon* (Egyptian god Amun-Re).
6. Impf. mid. indic. 3 sg., ἐπαίρω, *ask*.
7. Pres. act. opt. 3 sg., εἰμί; oblique opt. in an indir. quest. (cf. BDF §386; S §2677; *CGCG* §42.7).
8. Pf. act. ptc. nom. masc. sg., διαφεύγω, *escape*; periphrastic (equivalent of pf. tense).
9. φονεύς, -έως, ὁ, *murderer*.
10. Pres. act. inf., εὐφημέω, *keep a religious silence*.
11. Aor. act. ptc. gen. masc. sg., κελεύω, *bid*; with acc. and inf.; gen. absol.
12. θνητός, -ή, -όν, *mortal*; pred. adj. in indir. disc. (cf. BDF §396; S §2016; *CGCG* §51.19): "For [he said that] his father is not mortal."
13. Aor. act. ptc. nom. masc. sg., μεταβάλλω, *change*; circ.
14. Impf. mid. indic. 3 sg., πυνθάνομαι, *inquire*.
15. Pf. mid. ptc. nom. masc. sg., τιμωρέω, *punish*; periphrastic; oblique opt. in an indir. quest. See n. 7.
16. Aor. act. ptc. gen. masc. sg., χράω, *proclaim*; gen. absol.
17. Pres. act. inf., ἀπέχω, *receive*; indir. disc. See n. 12.
18. ἔκπλεος, -ον (Att. -εως), *complete, abundant*.
19. δίκη, -ης, ἡ, *vengeance*.
20. Impf. mid. indic. 3 sg., δωρέω, *present/gift* (someone with something).
21. ἀνάθημα, -ατος, τό, *sacrificial offering*.
22. λαμπρός, -ά, -όν, *splendid*.
23. χρῆμα, -ατος, τό, *money*.
24. χρησμός, -οῦ, ὁ, *oracle, oracular response*.
25. μαντεία, -ας, ἡ, *prophecy, oracle*.
26. ἀπόρρητος, -ον, *unspeakable, secret*.
27. Aor. act. ptc. nom. masc. sg., ἐπανέρχομαι, *return*; circ.
28. Fut. act. indic. 3 sg., φράζω, *tell*.

ἔνιοι²⁹ δέ φασι τὸν μὲν³⁰ προφήτην Ἑλληνιστὶ³¹ βουλόμενον προσειπεῖν μετά τινος φιλοφροσύνης³² "Ὦ παιδίον,"³³ ἐν τῷ τελευταίῳ³⁴ τῶν φθόγγων³⁵ ὑπὸ βαρβαρισμοῦ³⁶ πρὸς τὸ σίγμα ἐξενεχθῆναι³⁷ καὶ εἰπεῖν "Ὦ παιδίος,"³⁸ ἀντὶ³⁹ τοῦ νῦ τῷ σίγμα χρησάμενον, ἀσμένῳ⁴⁰ δὲ τῷ Ἀλεξάνδρῳ τὸ σφάλμα⁴¹ τῆς φωνῆς γενέσθαι καὶ διαδοθῆναι⁴² λόγον ὡς παῖδα Διὸς⁴³ αὐτὸν τοῦ θεοῦ προσειπόντος. ⁶λέγεται δὲ καὶ Ψάμμωνος⁴⁴ ἐν Αἰγύπτῳ τοῦ φιλοσόφου διακούσας⁴⁵ ἀποδέξασθαι⁴⁶ μάλιστα τῶν λεχθέντων, ὅτι πάντες οἱ ἄνθρωποι βασιλεύονται ὑπὸ θεοῦ· τὸ γὰρ ἄρχον ἐν ἑκάστῳ καὶ κρατοῦν⁴⁷ θεῖόν⁴⁸ ἐστιν· ἔτι δὲ μᾶλλον αὐτὸς περὶ τούτων φιλοσοφώτερον⁴⁹ δοξάζειν καὶ λέγειν, ὡς πάντων μὲν⁵⁰ ὄντα κοινὸν ἀνθρώπων πατέρα τὸν θεόν, ἰδίους δὲ ποιούμενον ἑαυτοῦ τοὺς ἀρίστους.

NOTE

27.5. ἔνιοι δέ φασι. Some scholars conclude that the tradition is meant to be disparaging. Given "the enormous importance of such *lapsus linguae* as omens throughout antiquity," however, it seems more likely to have been the invention of a partisan (Hamilton 1969, 73). Plutarch makes his own position abundantly clear: "From what has been said, then, it is clear that Alexander himself was not foolishly affected or puffed up by the belief in his divinity, but used it for the subjugation of others" (28.3, trans. Perrin 1919; cf. *Mor.* 65d; 330f–331a).

29. ἔνιος, -α, -ον, *some*.
30. μέν . . . δέ; point/counterpoint. See n. 4.
31. Adv., *in Greek*.
32. φιλοφροσύνη, -ης, ἡ, *kind disposition, friendliness*.
33. παιδίον, -ου, τό, *child*.
34. τελευταῖος, -α, -ον, *last*.
35. φθόγγος, -ου, ὁ, *articulated sound*.
36. βαρβαρισμός, -οῦ, ὁ, *barbarism*.
37. Aor. pass. inf., ἐκφέρω, (pass.) *be carried away*; indir. disc. (φασι). See n. 12.
38. Ὦ παιδίος (παῖ Διός), "O son of Zeus."
39. Prep. with gen., *in place of*.
40. ἄσμενος, -η, -ον, *glad*.
41. σφάλμα, -ατος, τό, *trip, false step, error*.
42. Aor. pass. inf., διαδίδωμι, (pass.) (of rumor or news) *be propagated, spread*. See n. 12.
43. Ζεύς, Διός, *Zeus*.
44. Ψάμμων, -ωνος, ὁ, *Psammon*.
45. Aor. act. ptc. nom. masc. sg., διακούω, *listen to*; with gen.
46. Aor. mid. inf., ἀποδέχομαι, *accept, receive*; indir. disc. See n. 12.
47. Pres. act. ptc. nom. neut. sg., κρατέω, *rule*; attrib. (subst.).
48. θεῖος, -α, -ον, *divine*.
49. Compar., φιλόσοφος, -η, -ον, *more philosophical*.
50. μέν . . . δέ; point/counterpoint. See n. 4.

6.6

Lucian

Lucian of Samosata (ca. 120–180 CE), a native of Syria, was a prolific rhetorician and satirist. Throughout the eighty-two writings credited to him (around ten of which must be deemed spurious) he mocks common conventions, ridicules esteemed figures of the past, and blurs categorical distinctions. The audience is always entertained—Lucian would have it no other way—but the treatises are often penetrating as well. After all, good comedy tends to be rooted in uncomfortable truths and told by those who, like Lucian, inhabit hybrid identities.[1]

The reading passages are from Lucian's *Demonax*, another example of Greco-Roman biography (βίος, *vita*). The first passage entails the stated aim of the biography, the second is Lucian's appraisal of the philosopher's lifestyle, and the third consists of examples of aphorisms and witty ripostes.

Text and Translation: Harmon 1913
Supplemental Scripture: Mark 2:1–12 parr.; 2:15–17 parr. (§6.6.2)

---

1. For discussion of Lucian's identity, see esp. Whitmarsh 2001, 248–53.

6.6.1

The Purpose of Biography

Demonax 2

²περὶ δὲ Δημώνακτος¹ ἤδη δίκαιον² λέγειν ἀμφοῖν³ ἕνεκα, ὡς ἐκεῖνός τε διὰ μνήμης⁴ εἴη⁵ τοῖς ἀρίστοις⁶ τό γε⁷ κατ' ἐμὲ καὶ οἱ γενναιότατοι⁸ τῶν νέων⁹ καὶ πρὸς φιλοσοφίαν ὁρμῶντες¹⁰ ἔχοιεν¹¹ μὴ πρὸς τὰ ἀρχαῖα¹² μόνα τῶν παραδειγμάτων¹³ σφᾶς¹⁴ αὐτοὺς ῥυθμίζειν,¹⁵ ἀλλὰ κἀκ¹⁶ τοῦ ἡμετέρου βίου¹⁷ κανόνα¹⁸ προτίθεσαι¹⁹ καὶ ζηλοῦν²⁰ ἐκεῖνον ἄριστον ὧν²¹ οἶδα ἐγὼ φιλοσόφων γενόμενον.

NOTE

1. Δημῶναξ, -ακτος, ὁ, *Demonax*. περὶ Δημώνακτος designates the theme (cf. *CGCG* §60.33).
2. δίκαιος, -α, -ον, (quasi-impers.) *it is right*; with acc. and inf.
3. Dual gen. neut. of ἄμφω, *both* (cf. S §229); gen. obj. of prep. ἕνεκα, "for two reasons."
4. μνήμη, -ης, ἡ, *memory*.
5. Pres. act. opt. 3 sg., εἰμί; oblique opt. in purpose clause (cf. S §§2195–96; *CGCG* §45.3). It rarely occurs after a primary tense "except when that tense implies a reference to the past as well as to the present" (cf. S §2200). Lucian (and other members of the Second Sophistic) are often criticized for using the optative incorrectly. Here one might explain the shift to the optative as an "epistolary" use, in which "the writer . . . may put himself in the position of the reader or beholder who views actions as past" (S §1942).
6. Superl., ἀγαθός, -ή, -όν, *best*.
7. Postpositive partic. that "expresses concentration/limitation" (cf. *CGCG* §59.53); τό γε κατ' ἐμὲ, "*at least*, as far as I am able."
8. Superl., γενναῖος, -α, -ον, *most noble-minded*.
9. νέος, -ή, -όν, *young*; partitive gen.
10. Pres. act. ptc. nom. masc. pl., ὁρμάω, (intrans.) *be driven, inclined*; attrib. (subst.).
11. Pres. act. opt. 3 pl., ἔχω, *be able*; with inf.; purpose clause. See n. 5.

2. περὶ δὲ Δημώνακτος. The thematic transition περὶ δὲ Δημώνακτος (cf. *CGCG* §60.33) establishes Demonax as the subject of the biography. The function of biography, according to Lucian, is to hold forth a subject who is worthy of emulation.

12. ἀρχαῖος, -α, -ον, *ancient*.
13. παράδειγμα, -ατος, τό, *model, pattern*.
14. σφᾶς = αὐτούς, 3rd pers. pron. (cf. S §325); here with αὐτούς (intensive adj.) to underscore a direct reflexive relationship (cf. *CGCG* §29.17): "they might be able to shape *themselves*."
15. Pres. act. inf., ῥυθμίζω, *educate, train*.
16. Crasis: κἀκ = καὶ ἐκ.
17. βίος, -ου, ὁ, *life*.
18. κανών, -όνος, ὁ, *rule, standard*.
19. Read as προτίθεσθαι; pres. act. inf., προτίθημι, (mid.) *set before* (oneself).
20. Pres. act. inf., ζηλόω, *emulate*.
21. The relative pronoun is attracted to the case of its antecedent (cf. BDF §294; S §2522; *CGCG* §50.13); φιλοσόφων (partitive gen.), "the best of the philosophers *whom* I know."

6.6.2

The Lifestyle of Demonax

Demonax 5–7

⁵Φιλοσοφίας δὲ εἶδος[1] οὐχ ἓν ἀποτεμόμενος,[2] ἀλλὰ πολλὰς ἐς[3] ταὐτὸ καταμίξας[4] οὐ πάνυ[5] τι ἐξέφαινε[6] τίνι[7] αὐτῶν ἔχαιρεν· ἐῴκει[8] δὲ τῷ Σωκράτει[9] μᾶλλον ᾠκειῶσθαι,[10] εἰ καὶ τῷ σχήματι[11] καὶ τῇ τοῦ βίου[12] ῥαστώνῃ[13] τὸν Σινωπέα[14] ζηλοῦν[15] ἔδοξεν,[16] οὐ παραχαράττων[17] τὰ εἰς τὴν δίαιταν,[18] ὡς θαυμάζοιτο[19] καὶ ἀποβλέποιτο[20] ὑπὸ τῶν ἐντυγχανόντων,[21] ἀλλ' ὁμοδίαιτος[22] ἅπασι καὶ πεζὸς[23] ὢν καὶ οὐδ' ἐπ' ὀλίγον[24] τύφῳ[25] κάτοχος[26] συνῆν[27] καὶ συνεπολιτεύετο,[28] τὴν μὲν[29] τοῦ Σωκράτους εἰρωνείαν[30] οὐ προσιέμενος,[31] ⁶χάριτος

1. εἶδος, -ους, τό, *form.*
2. Aor. mid. ptc. nom. masc. sg., ἀποτέμνω, (mid.) *cut off* (for oneself); circ.
3. ἐς = εἰς; ἐς ταὐτό (crasis: τὸ αὐτό), "into the same [one]."
4. Aor. act. ptc. nom. masc. sg., καταμίγνυμι, *mix up*; circ.
5. Adv., οὐ πάνυ τι, "not very much."
6. Impf. act. indic. 3 sg., ἐκφαίνω, *reveal.*
7. Indir. quest., "which of these [forms of philosophy] he favored."
8. Plpf. act. indic. 3 sg., ἔοικα, *seem, appear*; with inf.
9. Σωκράτης, -ους, ὁ, *Socrates.*
10. Pf. pass. inf., οἰκειόω, (intrans.) *be favorable, well-disposed to*; with dat.
11. σχῆμα, -ατος, τό, *appearance, dress.*
12. βίος, -ου, ὁ, *lifestyle.*
13. ῥαστώνη, -ης, ἡ, *easiness* (of something).
14. Σινωπεύς, -έως, ὁ, *inhabitant of Sinope*. The "man of Sinope" is Diogenes, one of the founders of the Cynic way of life.
15. Pres. act. inf., ζηλόω, *emulate.*
16. Aor. act. indic. 3 sg., δοκέω, *appear, seem*; with inf.
17. Pres. act. ptc. nom. masc. sg., παραχαράσσω (Att. παραχαράττω), *alter, modify*; circ.
18. δίαιτα, -ας, ἡ, *lifestyle.*
19. Pres. pass. opt. 3 sg., θαυμάζω, (pass.) *be marveled at*; oblique opt. in purpose clause (cf. S §§2195–96; *CGCG* §45.3).
20. Pres. pass. opt. 3 sg., ἀποβλέπω, (pass.) *be gazed at steadfastly*; oblique (purpose). See n. 19.
21. Pres. mid. ptc. gen. masc. pl., ἐντυγχάνω, *happen upon*; attrib. (subst.), agent of pass. verbs.
22. ὁμοδίαιτος, -ον, *of the same life*; with dat.
23. πεζός, -ή, -όν, *ordinary, simple*; lit., "by foot."
24. Adv. acc. (extent), οὐδ' ἐπ' ὀλίγον, "not in the least."
25. τῦφος, -ου, ὁ, *vanity, arrogance.*
26. κάτοχος, -ον, *held down.*
27. Impf. act. indic. 3 sg., σύνειμι, *have to do with, be associated with*; with dat.
28. Impf. mid. indic. 3 sg., συμπολιτεύω, *live and act as a member of the state.*
29. μέν . . . δέ; point/counterpoint set (cf. Runge 2010, 75–83; BDF §447; S §2904; *CGCG* §59.24).
30. εἰρωνεία, -ας, ἡ, *irony.*
31. Pres. mid. ptc. nom. masc. sg., προσίημι, *undertake*; circ.

δὲ Ἀττικῆς μεστὰς³² ἀποφαίνων³³ τὰς συνουσίας,³⁴ ὡς τοὺς προσομιλήσαντας³⁵ ἀπιέναι³⁶ μήτε³⁷ καταφρονήσαντας³⁸ ὡς ἀγεννοῦς³⁹ μήτε τὸ σκυθρωπὸν⁴⁰ τῶν ἐπιτιμήσεων⁴¹ ἀποφεύγοντας,⁴² παντοίους⁴³ δὲ ὑπ' εὐφροσύνης⁴⁴ γενομένους καὶ κοσμιωτέρους⁴⁵ παρὰ πολὺ καὶ φαιδροτέρους⁴⁶ καὶ πρὸς τὸ μέλλον εὐέλπιδας.⁴⁷ ⁷οὐδεπώποτε⁴⁸ γοῦν⁴⁹ ὤφθη κεκραγὼς⁵⁰ ἢ ὑπερδιατεινόμενος⁵¹ ἢ ἀγανακτῶν,⁵² οὐδ' εἰ ἐπιτιμᾶν⁵³ τῳ⁵⁴ δέοι,⁵⁵ ἀλλὰ τῶν μὲν⁵⁶ ἁμαρτημάτων⁵⁷ καθήπτετο,⁵⁸ τοῖς δὲ ἁμαρτάνουσι συνεγίνωσκεν,⁵⁹ καὶ τὸ παράδειγμα⁶⁰ παρὰ τῶν ἰατρῶν⁶¹ ἠξίου⁶² λαμβάνειν τὰ μὲν⁶³ νοσήματα⁶⁴ ἰωμένων,⁶⁵ ὀργῇ δὲ πρὸς τοὺς νοσοῦντας οὐ χρωμένων·⁶⁶ ἡγεῖτο⁶⁷ γὰρ ἀνθρώπου μὲν εἶναι τὸ ἁμαρτάνειν, θεοῦ δὲ ἢ ἀνδρὸς ἰσοθέου⁶⁸ τὰ πταισθέντα⁶⁹ ἐπανορθοῦν.⁷⁰

NOTES

32. μεστός, -ή, -όν, *full of*; with gen.; χάριτος Ἀττικῆς μεστάς, "full of Attic charm."
33. Pres. act. ptc. nom. masc. sg., ἀποφαίνω, *render, make (so and so)*; circ.
34. συνουσία, -ας, ἡ, *conversation, intercourse*.
35. Aor. act. ptc. acc. masc. pl., προσομιλέω, *converse with*; attrib. (subst.).
36. Pres. act. inf., ἄπειμι, *go away, depart*; result clause: ὡς with inf. (cf. BDF §391; S §2260; *CGCG* §46.7).
37. μήτε . . . μήτε, *neither . . . nor*.
38. Aor. act. ptc. nom. masc. pl., καταφρονέω, *despise, have contempt for*; circ.
39. ἀγεννής, -ές, *lowborn*; ὡς ἀγεννοῦς, "as if he were of ignoble birth."
40. σκυθρωπός, -ή, -όν, *of a sad/angry countenance*; acc. of manner.
41. ἐπιτίμησις, -εως, ἡ, *censure, criticism*.
42. Pres. act. ptc. acc. masc. pl., ἀποφεύγω, *flee from*; circ.
43. παντοῖος, -α, -ον, *of all sorts/kinds*; παντοίους ὑπ' εὐφροσύνης γενομένους, "completely disarrayed with joy" (MGS, 1539).
44. εὐφροσύνη, -ης, ἡ, *happiness*.
45. Compar., κόσμιος, -α, -ον, *more well-ordered*; with παρὰ πολύ, "by far."
46. Compar., φαιδρός, -ά, -όν, *brighter, more cheerful*.
47. εὔελπις, -ιδος, ἡ, *full of hope*; with πρὸς τὸ μέλλον, "full of hope regarding what is to come [i.e., the future]."
48. Adv., *not yet at any time*.
49. Postpositive partic.: "a combination of γε and οὖν, γοῦν modifies an utterance which elaborates (οὖν) upon (part of) the preceding utterance by restricting its applicability (γε) (*at least, at any rate*). It is often used in sentences which provide the 'minimal evidence' or 'minimal applicability' for a preceding statement" (*CGCG* §59.54).
50. Pf. act. ptc. nom. masc. sg., κράζω, *cry out, scream*; supp. (ὤφθη).
51. Pres. mid. ptc. nom. masc. sg., ὑπερδιατείνομαι, (mid. pass.) *busy oneself, strive very much* (MGS, 2201); supp. (ὤφθη).
52. Pres. act. ptc. nom. masc. sg., ἀγανακτέω, *become angry*; supp. (ὤφθη).
53. Pres. act. inf., ἐπιτιμάω, *rebuke*; with dat.

5. Φιλοσοφίας δὲ εἶδος. Cf. Josephus, *B.J.* 2.119; §5.1.3. Demonax's philosophy was apparently eclectic, though he is said to have emulated the Cynic Diogenes of Sinope in dress and lifestyle (cf. Diogenes Laertius, *Vit. phil.* 6; §7.6.1). For various ancient portraits of the Cynic, cf. Epictetus, *Diatr.* 3.22; Maximus of Tyre, *Disc.* 36; Julian, *Or.* 6.200c–202c. For further discussion, see Branham and Goulet-Cazé (1996). Lucian portrays Demonax as an irenic, "mild" Cynic (Malherbe 1989, 14–15, 20–23). Indeed, he says, "he was everyone's friend" (*Demon.* 9).

54. Enclitic dat. masc. sg. form of τις (cf. S §334).
55. Pres. act. opt. 3 sg., δεῖ, (quasi-impers.) *it is necessary*; with acc. inf.; neg. concessive clause (cf. S §2381): "not even if it were necessary [for him] to rebuke someone."
56. μέν . . . δέ; point/counterpoint set. See n. 29.
57. ἁμάρτημα, -ατος, τό, *fault, sinful action*.
58. Impf. mid. indic. 3 sg., καθάπτω, (mid.) *assail*; with gen.
59. Impf. act. indic. 3 sg., συγγινώσκω, *pardon*; with dat.
60. παράδειγμα, -ατος, τό, *model, pattern*.
61. ἰατρός, -οῦ, ὁ, *physician*.
62. Impf. act. indic. 3 sg., ἀξιόω, *think proper*.
63. μέν . . . δέ; point/counterpoint set. See n. 29.
64. νόσημα, -ατος, τό, *disease*.
65. Pres. mid. ptc. gen. masc. pl., ἰάομαι, *heal*; circ.
66. Pres. mid. ptc. gen. masc. pl., χράομαι, with ὀργῇ, *feel anger*; circ.
67. Impf. mid. indic. 3 sg., ἡγέομαι, *think, consider*.
68. ἰσόθεος, -ον, *equal to the gods, godlike*.
69. Aor. pass. ptc. acc. neut. pl., πταίω, *make a mistake/error*; attrib. (subst.).
70. Pres. act. inf., ἐπανορθόω, *set straight, correct*; subjective.

7. ἀλλὰ τῶν μὲν ἁμαρτημάτων καθήπτετο, τοῖς δὲ ἁμαρτάνουσι συνεγίνωσκεν. An ancient version of "hate the sin, love the sinner."

καὶ τὸ παράδειγμα παρὰ τῶν ἰατρῶν ἠξίου λαμβάνειν. Ancient philosophers frequently liken themselves to physicians and their addressees to sick patients in need of care (see note on Dio Chrysostom, *Avar.* 2 [§7.4.1]). The connection between sickness and sin is also apparent in the Gospel accounts (e.g., Mark 2:1–12 parr.). Both passages present the work of remission as belonging to a divinity (θεοῦ) or divine man (ἀνδρὸς ἰσοθέου) (cf. Mark 2:7; Boring, Berger, and Colpe 1995, §66). For the various terms applied to the divine man, see Betz (1961, 102–3).

6.6.3

Sayings of Demonax

Demonax 25, 40, 50

²⁵Ὁ δ' αὐτὸς¹ υἱὸν πενθοῦντι² καὶ ἐν σκότῳ³ ἑαυτὸν καθείρξαντι⁴ προσελθὼν ἔλεγεν μάγος⁵ τε εἶναι καὶ δύνασθαι αὐτῷ ἀναγαγεῖν⁶ τοῦ παιδὸς⁷ τὸ εἴδωλον,⁸ εἰ μόνον αὐτῷ τρεῖς τινας ἀνθρώπους ὀνομάσειε⁹ μηδένα πώποτε¹⁰ πεπενθηκότας· ἐπὶ πολὺ¹¹ δὲ ἐκείνου ἐνδοιάσαντος¹² καὶ ἀποροῦντος¹³—οὐ γὰρ εἶχεν τινα, οἶμαι,¹⁴ εἰπεῖν τοιοῦτον—Εἶτ', ἔφη, ὦ γελοῖε,¹⁵ μόνος ἀφόρητα¹⁶ πάσχειν¹⁷ νομίζεις¹⁸ μηδένα ὁρῶν¹⁹ πένθους²⁰ ἄμοιρον;²¹ . . .

⁴⁰Πολυβίου²² δέ τινος, κομιδῇ²³ ἀπαιδεύτου²⁴ ἀνθρώπου καὶ σολοίκου,²⁵ εἰπόντος,²⁶ Ὁ βασιλεύς με τῇ Ῥωμαίων πολιτείᾳ²⁷ τετίμηκεν·²⁸ Εἴθε²⁹ σε, ἔφη, Ἕλληνα μᾶλλον ἢ Ῥωμαῖον πεποιήκει. . . .

1. ὁ αὐτός, "this same man" (= Demonax).
2. Pres. act. ptc. dat. masc. sg., πενθέω, *mourn*; attrib. (subst.).
3. σκότος, -ου, ὁ, *darkness*.
4. Aor. act. ptc. dat. masc. sg., κατείργω, *shut in*; attrib. (subst.).
5. μάγος, -ου, ὁ, *enchanter, sorcerer*; pred. nom.
6. Aor. act. inf., ἀνάγω, *raise*; comp. of δύνασθαι.
7. παῖς, παιδός, ὁ, *child*.
8. εἴδωλον, -ου, τό, *phantom, specter*.
9. Aor. act. opt. 3 sg., ὀνομάζω, *name*; oblique opt. in indir. disc. (cf. S §2615; *CGCG* §41.9).
10. Adv., *ever yet*.
11. Adv. acc. (extent): "for some time."
12. Aor. act. ptc. gen. masc. sg., ἐνδοιάζω, *be at a loss, waver*; gen. absol.
13. Pres. act. ptc. gen. masc. sg., ἀπορέω, *be at a loss, be puzzled*; gen. absol.
14. Pres. mid. indic. 1 sg., οἴομαι, *think, suppose*: "For he was not able, I suppose, to say any such person."
15. γελοῖος, -α, -ον, *ridiculous, absurd*; voc.
16. ἀφόρητος, -ον, *unbearable, unendurable*.
17. Pres. act. inf., πάσχω, *suffer*; indir. disc. (cf. BDF §396; S §2016; *CGCG* §51.19).
18. Pres. act. indic. 2 sg., νομίζω, *think, suppose*.
19. Pres. act. ptc. nom. masc. sg., ὁράω; circ. (causal).
20. πένθος, -ους, τό, *grief, sorrow*.
21. ἄμοιρος, -ον, *without lot/share in*; with gen.; pred. acc.
22. Πολύβιος, -ου, ὁ, *Polybius* (the name means "well to do").
23. Adv., *entirely, altogether*.
24. ἀπαίδευτος, -ον, *uneducated*.
25. σόλοικος, -ον, *speaking incorrectly, using broken Greek*.
26. Aor. act. ptc. gen. masc. sg., λέγω; gen. absol.
27. πολιτεία, -ας, ἡ, *citizenship*; dat. of means.
28. Pf. act. indic. 3 sg., τιμάω, *honor*.
29. Unrealizable wishes are marked by εἴθε (or εἰ γάρ) and a modal (secondary) indicative (aor., impf., or plpf.) (cf. S §1780; *CGCG* §38.39). "Would that he made you a Greek rather than a Roman!"

⁵⁰Ἀστεῖον³⁰ δὲ κἀκεῖνο³¹ αὐτοῦ καὶ δηκτικὸν³² ἅμα τὸ πρὸς τὸν ἀνθύπατον³³ εἰρημένον· ἦν μὲν³⁴ γὰρ τῶν πιττουμένων³⁵ τὰ σκέλη³⁶ καὶ τὸ σῶμα ὅλον· Κυνικοῦ³⁷ δέ τινος ἐπὶ λίθον ἀναβάντος³⁸ καὶ αὐτὸ τοῦτο κατηγοροῦντος³⁹ αὐτοῦ καὶ εἰς κιναιδίαν διαβάλλοντος,⁴⁰ ἀγανακτήσας⁴¹ καὶ κατασπασθῆναι⁴² τὸν Κυνικὸν κελεύσας⁴³ ἔμελλεν ἢ ξύλοις⁴⁴ συντρίψειν⁴⁵ ἢ καὶ φυγῇ ζημιώσειν·⁴⁶ ἀλλ' ὅ γε⁴⁷ Δημῶναξ παρατυχὼν⁴⁸ παρῃτεῖτο⁴⁹ συγγνώμην⁵⁰ ἔχειν αὐτῷ κατά τινα πάτριον⁵¹ τοῖς Κυνικοῖς παρρησίαν⁵² θρασυνομένῳ.⁵³ εἰπόντος δὲ τοῦ ἀνθυπάτου, Νῦν μέν⁵⁴ σοι ἀφίημι⁵⁵ αὐτόν, ἂν⁵⁶ δὲ ὕστερον⁵⁷ τοιοῦτόν τι τολμήσῃ,⁵⁸ τί παθεῖν ἄξιός ἐστιν; καὶ Δημῶναξ, Δρωπακισθῆναι⁵⁹ τότε αὐτὸν κέλευσον.

NOTES

25. Here Demonax feigns that he is a magician able to raise the dead. In other contexts, however, charges of sorcery could be very serious (cf. Mark 3:22; Philostratus, *Vit. Apoll.*).

50. παρρησίαν. Cynics were known for their παρρησία, "frank speech" (see Betz 1961, 210n4; Malherbe 1989, 15). Such boldness of speech, however, could cause problems, and many orators discuss the need for moderation. See note on Plutarch, *Mor.* 74d (§7.5.1).

30. ἀστεῖος, -α, -ον, *witty*.
31. Crasis: καὶ ἐκεῖνο.
32. δηκτικός, -ή, -όν, *biting*.
33. ἀνθύπατος, -ου, ὁ, *proconsul*.
34. μέν . . . δέ. The point/counterpoint set provides background information (γάρ) (cf. Runge 2010, 75–83; BDF §447; S §2904; CGCG §59.24).
35. Pres. mid. ptc. gen. masc. pl., πισσόω (Att. πιττόω), (mid.) *remove hair* (from the body) *by means of a pitch-plaster*; circ. (subst.); partitive gen.
36. σκέλος, -ους, τό, *leg*.
37. κυνικός, -οῦ, ὁ, *Cynic*.
38. Aor. act. ptc. gen. masc. sg., ἀναβαίνω, *go up, mount*; gen. absol.
39. Pres. act. ptc. gen. masc. sg., κατηγορέω (with acc. and gen.), *bring a charge against someone*; gen. absol.
40. Pres. act. ptc. gen. masc. sg., διαβάλλω (with εἰς κιναιδίαν), *accuse someone of effeminacy*; gen. absol.
41. Aor. act. ptc. nom. masc. sg., ἀγανακτέω, *become angry*; circ.
42. Aor. pass. inf., κατασπάω, (pass.) *be pulled down*.
43. Aor. atc. ptc. nom. masc. sg., κελεύω, *order, bid*; with acc. and inf.; circ.
44. ξύλον, -ου, τό, *stocks* (in which the feet were confined).
45. Fut. act. inf., συντρίβω, *crush, wear out* (someone's spirit).
46. Fut. act. inf., ζημιόω, *punish*; with dat. of means φυγῇ, "with exile."
47. Postpositive partic.: "expresses concentration/limitation" (cf. CGCG §59.53). Lucian cuts off the explanation (ἀλλ') and focuses attention on Demonax.
48. Aor. act. ptc. nom. masc. sg., παρατυγχάνω, *happen upon, encounter*; circ.
49. Impf. mid. indic. 3 sg., παραιτέομαι, *beg, petition*; with acc. and inf. "Demonax begged [the proconsul] to have lenience with him [αὐτῷ = the Cynic]."
50. συγγνώμη, -ης, ἡ, *forbearance, lenience*.
51. πάτριος, -α, -ον, *ancestral, traditional*; with dat.; "in a manner traditional to the Cynics."
52. παρρησία, -ας, ἡ, *frankness/boldness of speech*.
53. Pres. pass. ptc. dat. masc. sg., θρασύνω, (in a bad sense) *be overly bold/confident*; circ.: "being overly bold in frank speech according to the traditional Cynic way."
54. μέν . . . δέ; point/counterpoint set. See n. 34.
55. Pres. act. indic. 1 sg., ἀφίημι, *release*.
56. ἄν = ἐάν.
57. Adv. acc., ὕστερος, -α, -ον, *later*.
58. Aor. act. subj. 3 sg., τολμάω, *dare*; protasis of a third-class condition (cf. BDF §373; S §2565; CGCG §49.6): "But if later he dares [to do] such a thing, what should be his punishment [lit., what thing is he worthy to suffer]?"
59. Aor. pass. inf., δρωπακίζω, (pass.) *be depilated, have hair removed* (from body parts). "Order him then [at that time] to be depilated!"

6.7

Philostratus

Philostratus (ca. 170–247 CE) was a renowned Sophist who coined the term "Second Sophistic" to describe a group of philosophers and rhetoricians who flourished from the mid-first to the mid-second century CE (*Vit. soph.*).[1] His most famous work, *Life of Apollonius*, is by far the longest biography (βίος, *vita*) to come down from antiquity. Apollonius was a first-century CE philosopher, wonder-worker, and prophet whose lifestyle and teachings Philostratus endeavored to defend from slander and misunderstanding—sound familiar?

The reading passages share similar features with traditions in the Gospels and Acts. In the first passage, Philostratus narrates Apollonius's birth, including the lingering suspicion that he is the product of divine filiation. The second and third passages are accounts of Apollonius exorcising a demon and raising the dead.

Text and Translation: Jones 2005
Supplemental Scripture: Matt. 1:18–25; Luke 1:28–2:20 (§6.7.1); Mark 5:1–20; Acts 8:4–24 (§6.7.2); Mark 5:35–43 parr.; Luke 7:11–17; Acts 9:36–43 (§6.7.3)

---

1. For an outstanding treatment of the authors of this period, see Whitmarsh 2001.

6.7.1

The Birth of Apollonius

Life of Apollonius 1.4–5

[1.4]Ἀπολλωνίῳ τοίνυν[1] πατρὶς[2] μὲν[3] ἦν Τύανα, πόλις Ἑλλὰς ἐν τῷ Καππαδοκῶν[4] ἔθνει, πατὴρ δὲ ὁμώνυμος,[5] γένος[6] ἀρχαῖον[7] καὶ τῶν οἰκιστῶν[8] ἀνημμένον,[9] πλοῦτος[10] ὑπὲρ τοὺς ἐκεῖ, τὸ δὲ ἔθνος βαθύ.[11] κυούσῃ[12] δὲ αὐτὸν τῇ μητρὶ φάσμα[13] ἦλθεν Αἰγυπτίου[14] δαίμονος[15] ὁ Πρωτεὺς,[16] ὁ παρὰ τῷ Ὁμήρῳ[17] ἐξαλλάττων·[18] ἡ δὲ οὐδὲν δείσασα[19] ἤρετο αὐτόν, τί ἀποκυήσοι·[20] ὁ δὲ "ἐμέ" εἶπε. "σὺ δὲ τίς;" εἰπούσης[21] "Πρωτεὺς" ἔφη "ὁ Αἰγύπτιος θεός." ὅστις μὲν δὴ[22] τὴν σοφίαν[23] ὁ Πρωτεὺς ἐγένετο, τί ἂν ἐξηγοίμην[24] τοῖς γε[25] ἀκού-

1. Partic.: "indicates a transition to a newly relevant, to-the-point text segment (νυν), and stresses the importance or relevance for the addressee of that new point (τοι)" (*CGCG* §59.39). Here it marks a transition from the prooemium to an account of origins: "*Well, then,* as for Apollonius . . ."

2. πατρίς, -ίδος, ἡ, *fatherland.*

3. μέν . . . δέ; point/counterpoint (cf. Runge 2010, 75–83; BDF §447; S §2904; *CGCG* §59.24).

4. Καππαδόκαι, -ων, οἱ, *Cappadocians.*

5. ὁμώνυμος, -ον, *having the same name.*

6. γένος, -ους, τό, *family line.*

7. ἀρχαῖος, -ον, *ancient.*

8. οἰκιστής, -οῦ, ὁ, *founder of a city.*

9. Pf. pass. ptc. nom. neut. sg., ἀνάπτω, (pass.) *be attached to;* with gen.; attrib.

10. πλοῦτος, -ου, ὁ, *wealth, riches.*

11. βαθύς, -ύ, *deep, abundant.* The second δέ-clause increases the significance of the first: "The wealth [of Apollonius's family] surpassed the [other families] there, and this people is deep [in riches]."

12. Pres. act. ptc. dat. fem. sg., κύω, *be pregnant;* circ.

13. φάσμα, -ατος, τό, *apparition.*

14. Αἰγύπτιος, -α, -ον, *Egyptian.*

15. δαίμων, -ονος, ὁ, *god.*

16. Πρωτεύς, -έως, ὁ, *Proteus.* An appositive to φάσμα (cf. S §991; *CGCG* §27.14).

17. Ὅμηρος, -ου, ὁ, *Homer* (epic poet).

18. Pres. act. ptc. nom. masc. sg., ἐξαλλάσσω, *change entirely;* attrib. (subst.): "the shape-shifter."

19. Aor. act. ptc. nom. fem. sg., δείδω, *fear;* circ.

20. Fut. act. opt. 3 sg., ἀποκυέω, *give birth;* indir. quest.: opt. for fut. indic. (cf. S §2677; *CGCG* §41.9).

21. Aor. act. ptc. gen. fem. sg., εἶπον, *say;* gen. absol.

22. μὲν δή . . . τε . . . τε. The two coordinated statements (τε . . . τε) explicate the μέν-clause (cf. S §2913; *CGCG* §59.24), which the speaker considers evident, clear, or precise (δή) (cf. *CGCG* §59.44): "Now as to who [ὅστις] Proteus was in wisdom . . ." (indir. quest.).

23. σοφία, -ας, ἡ, *wisdom;* acc. of respect.

24. Pres. mid. opt. 1 sg., ἐξηγέομαι, *explain;* potential (cf. BDF §385; S §1824; *CGCG* §34.13).

25. Postpositive partic.: "expresses concentration/limitation—γε focuses attention on the word or phrase it follows . . . and limits the applicability of the content of the utterance to *at least* or (*more*) *precisely* that specific element" (*CGCG* §59.53).

ουσι τῶν ποιητῶν,²⁶ ὡς ποικίλος²⁷ τε ἦν καὶ ἄλλοτε ἄλλος²⁸ καὶ κρείττων τοῦ ἁλῶναι,²⁹ γιγνώσκειν τε ὡς ἐδόκει³⁰ καὶ προγιγνώσκειν πάντα; καὶ μεμνῆσθαι³¹ χρὴ³² τοῦ Πρωτέως, μάλιστα³³ ἐπειδὰν προϊὼν³⁴ ὁ λόγος δεικνύῃ³⁵ τὸν ἄνδρα πλείω μὲν³⁶ ἢ ὁ Πρωτεὺς προγνόντα,³⁷ πολλῶν δὲ ἀπόρων³⁸ τε καὶ ἀμηχάνων³⁹ κρείττω γενόμενον ἐν αὐτῷ μάλιστα τῷ ἀπειλῆφθαι.⁴⁰

⁵Τεχθῆναι⁴¹ δὲ ἐν λειμῶνι⁴² λέγεται, πρὸς ᾧ νῦν τὸ ἱερὸν⁴³ αὐτῷ ἐκπεπόνηται.⁴⁴ καὶ μηδὲ ὁ τρόπος⁴⁵ ἀγνοείσθω,⁴⁶ ὃν ἀπετέχθη.⁴⁷ ἀγούσῃ γὰρ τῇ μητρὶ τόκου⁴⁸ ὥραν ὄναρ⁴⁹ ἐγένετο βαδίσαι⁵⁰ ἐς⁵¹ τὸν λειμῶνα καὶ ἄνθη⁵² κεῖραι.⁵³ καὶ δῆτα⁵⁴ ἀφικομένη⁵⁵ αἱ μὲν⁵⁶ δμωαὶ⁵⁷ προσεῖχον⁵⁸ τοῖς ἄνθεσιν ἐσκεδασμέναι⁵⁹ κατὰ τὸν λειμῶνα, αὐτὴ δὲ ἐς ὕπνον⁶⁰ ἀπήχθη⁶¹ κλιθεῖσα⁶² ἐν τῇ πόᾳ.⁶³ κύκνοι⁶⁴ τοίνυν,⁶⁵ οὓς ὁ λειμὼν ἔβοσκε,⁶⁶ χορὸν⁶⁷ ἐστήσαντο περὶ αὐτὴν καθεύδουσαν,⁶⁸ καὶ τὰς πτέρυγας,⁶⁹ ὥσπερ εἰώθασιν,⁷⁰ ἄραντες⁷¹ ἀθρόον⁷² ἤχησαν,⁷³ καὶ γάρ⁷⁴ τι καὶ ζεφύρου⁷⁵ ἦν ἐν τῷ λειμῶνι, ἡ δὲ ἐξέθορέ⁷⁶ τε ὑπὸ τῆς ᾠδῆς⁷⁷ καὶ ἀπέτεκεν, ἱκανὴ⁷⁸

26. ποιητής, -οῦ, ὁ, *poet*.
27. ποικίλος, -η, -ον, *manifold*.
28. ἄλλοτε ἄλλος, "[how he was] different at different times."
29. Aor. act. inf., ἁλίσκομαι, *be caught, seized*. The articular infinitive modifies the comparative adjective: "too great to be caught" (cf. S §§1431, 2032.c).
30. Impf. act. indic. 3 sg., δοκέω, *appear, seem*; with inf.
31. Pf. mid. inf., μιμνήσκω, *remember, hold in mind*; with gen.
32. Quasi-impers., χρή, *it is necessary*; with (acc. and) inf. (cf. BDF §405; S §1985; CGCG §36.3).
33. Adv. acc., *especially*.
34. Pres. act. ptc. nom. masc. sg., πρόειμι, *go forward, advance*; circ.
35. Pres. act. subj. 3 sg., δείκνυμι, (with supp. ptc.) *make evident*; fut. temp. clause (cf. BDF §382; S §2399; CGCG §40.9).
36. μέν . . . δέ; point/counterpoint. See n. 3.
37. Aor. act. ptc. acc. masc. sg., προγιγνώσκω, *know in advance*; supp. (δεικνύῃ): "especially when my narrative [ὁ λόγος] will go on to make clear that the man *had foreknowledge* greater than [πλείω ἤ] Proteus."
38. ἄπορος, -ον, *impassible, difficult*; gen. of compar.
39. ἀμήχανος, -ον, *without means/resources*; gen. of compar.
40. Pf. pass. inf., ἀπολαμβάνω, (pass.) *be cut off, intercepted, cornered*. The articular infinitive functions as the object of ἐν with αὐτῷ in the predicate position: "just when he was cornered" (cf. BDF §404; S §2033).
41. Aor. pass. inf., τίκτω, *be born*; indir. report (λέγεται) (cf. BDF §397; S §2592; CGCG §41.2).
42. λειμών, -ῶνος, ὁ, *meadow*.
43. ἱερόν, -οῦ, τό, *temple*.
44. Pf. pass. indic. 3 sg., ἐκπονέω, (pass.) *be brought to completion, established*.
45. τρόπος, -ου, ὁ, *way, manner*; τρόπος . . . ὅν, *manner in which*.
46. Pres. pass. impv. 3 sg., ἀγνοέω, *be unknown*.
47. Aor. pass. indic. 3 sg., ἀποτίκτω, *be delivered, birthed*.
48. τόκος, -ου, ὁ, *childbirth*; ἀγούσῃ τῇ μητρὶ τόκου ὥραν, "when she was approaching the time to give birth."

49. ὄναρ, ὄνειρος, τό, *dream*.
50. Aor. act. inf., βαδίζω, *go*; indir. disc. (command).
51. ἐς = εἰς.
52. ἄνθος, -ους, τό, *flower*.
53. Aor. act. inf., κείρω, *cut*; indir. disc. (command).
54. Postpositive partic.: a strengthened form of δή (CGCG §59.45); καὶ δῆτα marks a transition to a closely related, obviously relevant, text segment: "*And now* when she reached the meadow . . ."
55. Aor. mid. ptc. nom. fem. sg., ἀφικνέομαι, *reach, arrive at*; circ.; anacoluthon (cf. S §3004): the participle is left hanging as the subject shifts to the handmaids.
56. μέν . . . δέ; point/counterpoint. See n. 3.
57. δμωή, -ῆς, ἡ, *female servant*.
58. Impf. act. indic. 3 pl., προσέχω, *be devoted to* (something); with dat.
59. Pf. pass. ptc. nom. fem. pl., σκεδάννυμι, (pass.) *be scattered, dispersed*; circ.
60. ὕπνος, -ου, ὁ, *sleep*.
61. Aor. pass. indic. 3 sg., ἀπάγω, (pass.) *be carried off*.
62. Aor. pass. ptc. nom. fem. sg., κλίνω, (pass.) *lie down*; circ.
63. πόα, -ας, ἡ, *grass*.
64. κύκνος, -ου, ὁ, *swan*.
65. Partic.: "indicates a transition to a newly relevant, to-the-point text segment (νυν), and stresses the importance or relevance for the addressee of that new point (τοι)" (CGCG §59.39).
66. Impf. act. indic. 3 sg., βόσκω, *feed*.
67. χορός, -οῦ, ὁ, *choir*.
68. Pres. act. ptc. acc. fem. sg., καθεύδω, *sleep*; circ.
69. πτέρυξ, -υγας, ἡ, *wing*.
70. Pf. act. indic. 3 pl., ἔθω, *be accustomed*.
71. Aor. act. ptc. nom. masc. pl., αἴρω, *lift*; circ.
72. ἀθρόος, -α, -ον (adv.), *all at once*.
73. Aor. act. indic. 3 pl., ἠχέω, *make a noise*.
74. Partic. combination: closely related information (καί) that has explanatory force (γάρ) (CGCG §59.66).
75. ζέφυρος, -ου, ὁ, *western wind*.
76. Aor. act. indic. 3 sg., ἐκθρῴσκω, *leap up*.
77. ᾠδή, -ῆς, ἡ, *song*.
78. ἱκανός, -ή, -όν, *sufficient, enough*.

δὲ πᾶσα ἔκπληξις⁷⁹ μαιεύσασθαι⁸⁰ καὶ πρὸ τῆς ὥρας. οἱ δὲ ἐγχώριοί⁸¹ φασιν ὡς ὁμοῦ⁸² τε τίκτοιτο⁸³ καὶ σκηπτὸς⁸⁴ ἐν τῇ γῇ πεσεῖσθαι⁸⁵ δοκῶν⁸⁶ ἐμμετεωρισθείη⁸⁷ τῷ αἰθέρι,⁸⁸ καὶ ἀφανισθείη⁸⁹ ἄνω, τό, οἶμαι,⁹⁰ ἐκφανὲς⁹¹ καὶ ὑπὲρ πάντα τὰ ἐν τῇ γῇ καὶ τὸ ἀγχοῦ⁹² θεῶν καὶ ὁπόσα⁹³ ὅδε ὁ ἀνὴρ ἐγένετο, φαίνοντες οἱ θεοὶ καὶ προσημαίνοντες.⁹⁴

NOTES

1.4. ὁ Πρωτεύς. Cf. Homer, *Od.* 4.431–461. The Egyptian god was associated with the "shifty" Sophists (e.g., Plato, *Euthyphr.* 15d; Whitmarsh 2001, 228n184), but the comparison is not intended to be pejorative (cf. *Vit. Apoll.* 1.2). Perhaps Philostratus thought the comparison apt because Apollonius eventually assumes the features of various gods and heroes. So, for example, Anderson (1986, 235): "Apollonius performs the labors of Herakles, the voyages of Odysseus, the conquests of Alexander, the trial of Socrates, and the transmigration of Pythagoras, all in one. To these modest beginnings are added casual glimpses of Jesus Christ and Herodes Atticus. Not for nothing is Apollonius son of Proteus." This, however, is but one suggestion. For further discussion, see Gyselinck and Demoen (2009, 104–8).

1.5. For a comparison with the birth narratives in Matthew and Luke, see Koskenniemi (1994, 190–93), who concludes, rightly to my mind, that direct dependence is unlikely.

---

79. ἔκπληξις, -εως, ἡ, *disturbance, alarm.*
80. Aor. mid. inf., μαιεύομαι, *cause delivery to take place*; comp. of ἱκανή (cf. S §2002).
81. ἐγχώριος, -ον, (subst.) *inhabitants.*
82. Adv., *together, at once.*
83. Pres. pass. opt. 3 sg., τίκτω, (pass.) *be born.* The choice of the oblique optative "signals that the reporter presents everything from his own, temporal perspective: he puts himself between the original speaker and the addressee, emphasizing his role as mediator" (*CGCG* §41.13; S §2627).
84. σκηπτός, -οῦ, ὁ, *thunderbolt.*
85. Fut. mid. inf., πίπτω, *fall.*
86. Pres. act. ptc. nom. masc. sg., δοκέω, *seem*; with inf.; circ.
87. Aor. pass. opt. 3 sg., ἐμμετεωρίζομαι, *be aloft*; oblique. See n. 83.
88. αἰθήρ, -έρος, ὁ, *ether* (upper air).
89. Aor. pass. opt. 3 sg., ἀφανίζω, (pass.) *disappear*; oblique. See n. 83.
90. Pres. mid. indic. 1 sg., οἴομαι, *think, suppose.*
91. ἐκφανής, -ές, (subst.) *manifestation, brilliance*; τό . . . ἐκφανὲς καὶ ὑπὲρ πάντα τὰ ἐν τῇ γῇ, "his brilliance over everything on earth."
92. Adv., *near*; with gen.; τὸ ἀγχοῦ θεῶν, "proximity to the gods."
93. Rel. pron., ὁπόσος, -η, -ον, (adv.) *as much as*; ὁπόσα ὅδε ὁ ἀνὴρ ἐγένετο, "all that this man would become."
94. Pres. act. ptc. nom. masc. pl., προσημαίνω, *provide a sign in advance*; circ. The entire clause τό, οἶμαι, . . . is extremely convoluted and ungrammatical (anacoluthon). It seems that οἱ θεοί is felt as an appositive to σκηπτός (metonymy), in which case the gods were "revealing" and "signifying in advance" X (τὸ ἐκφανὲς καὶ ὑπὲρ πάντα τὰ ἐν τῇ γῇ), Y (τὸ ἀγχοῦ θεῶν), and Z (ὁπόσα ὅδε ὁ ἀνὴρ ἐγένετο).

6.7.2

Apollonius the Exorcist

Life of Apollonius 4.20.1–3

4.20.1Διαλεγομένου[1] δὲ αὐτοῦ περὶ τοῦ σπένδειν,[2] παρέτυχε[3] μὲν[4] τῷ λόγῳ μειράκιον[5] τῶν ἁβρῶν[6] οὕτως ἀσελγὲς[7] νομιζόμενον,[8] ὡς γενέσθαι[9] ποτὲ καὶ ἁμαξῶν ᾆσμα,[10] πατρὶς[11] δὲ αὐτῷ Κέρκυρα[12] ἦν καὶ ἐς[13] Ἀλκίνουν[14] ἀνέφερε[15] τὸν ξένον[16] τοῦ Ὀδυσσέως τὸν Φαίακα, καὶ διῄει[17] μὲν[18] ὁ Ἀπολλώνιος περὶ τοῦ σπένδειν, ἐκέλευε[19] δὲ μὴ πίνειν τοῦ ποτηρίου[20] τούτου, φυλάττειν[21] δὲ αὐτὸ τοῖς θεοῖς ἄχραντόν[22] τε καὶ ἄποτον.[23] ἐπεὶ δὲ καὶ ὦτα[24] ἐκέλευσε τῷ ποτηρίῳ ποιεῖσθαι καὶ σπένδειν κατὰ τὸ οὖς, ἀφ' οὗ μέρους[25] ἥκιστα[26] πίνουσιν ἄνθρωποι, τὸ μειράκιον κατεσκέδασε[27] τοῦ λόγου πλατύν[28] τε καὶ ἀσελγῆ γέλωτα.[29] ὁ

1. Pres. mid. ptc. gen. masc. sg., διαλέγω, (mid.) *give a lecture*; gen. absol.
2. Pres. act. inf., σπένδω, *pour libations*; art. inf. as obj. of περί (cf. BDF §403; S §2032.g).
3. Aor. act. indic. 3 sg., παρατυγχάνω, *be present at*; with dat.
4. μέν … δέ; point/counterpoint set (cf. Runge 2010, 75–83; BDF §447; S §2904; *CGCG* §59.24).
5. μειράκιον, -ου, τό, *young man*.
6. ἁβρός, -ά, -όν, (subst.) *fancy attire* (i.e., of the delicate things that make one soft or effeminate).
7. ἀσελγής, -ές, *licentious, wanton*.
8. Pres. pass. ptc. nom. neut. sg., νομίζω, (pass.) *be considered*; attrib.
9. Result clause: ὡς with inf. (cf. BDF §391; S §2260; *CGCG* §46.7), signposted by οὕτως.
10. ᾆσμα, -ατος, τό, *song*; ἁμαξῶν ᾆσμα, lit., "song of wagons." Cf. Jones 2005, 361: "Carts were used at the Eleusinian mysteries as a place for bawdy repartee."
11. πατρίς, -ίδος, ἡ, *fatherland*.
12. Κέρκυρα, -ας, ἡ, *Corcyra* (Greek island in the Ionian Sea).
13. ἐς = εἰς.
14. Ἀλκίνουν, -ου, ὁ, *Alcinous* (king of the Phaeacians; cf. Homer, *Od.* 6.12).
15. Impf. act. indic. 3 sg., ἀναφέρω, *carry back*.
16. ξένος, -ου, ὁ, *guest-friend*.
17. Impf. act. indic. 3 sg., δίειμι, *go through* (a subject; περὶ τοῦ σπένδειν).
18. μέν … δέ … δέ; point/counterpoints set (cf. S §2907). The contrast comes with ἐπεὶ δὲ καὶ ὦτα ἐκέλευσε.
19. Impf. act. indic. 3 sg., κελεύω, *order, bid*; with acc. and inf.
20. ποτήριον, -ου, τό, *cup*.
21. Pres. act. inf., φυλάσσω (Att. φυλάττω), *keep*.
22. ἄχραντος, -ον, *undefiled*; pred. comp.
23. ἄποτος, -ον, *not drunk from*; pred. comp.
24. οὖς, ὠτός, τό, *handle* (by way of resemblance to an ear).
25. μέρος, ους, τό, *part*.
26. ἥκιστος, -η, -ον, as adv. ἥκιστα, *least*.
27. Aor. act. indic. 3 sg., κατασκεδάννυμι, *pour out*; with acc. over gen.
28. πλατύς, -εῖα, -ύ, *broad, widespread*.
29. γέλως, -ωτος, ὁ, *laugh*.

δὲ ἀναβλέψας ἐς αὐτὸ "οὐ σὺ" ἔφη "ταῦτα ὑβρίζεις,[30] ἀλλὰ ὁ δαίμων,[31] ὃς ἐλαύνει[32] σε οὐκ εἰδότα."[33]

2 Ἐλελήθει[34] δὲ ἄρα[35] δαιμονῶν[36] τὸ μειράκιον· ἐγέλα[37] τε γὰρ[38] ἐφ' οἷς οὐδεὶς ἕτερος καὶ μετέβαλλεν[39] ἐς τὸ κλάειν[40] αἰτίαν[41] οὐκ ἔχον, διελέγετο τε πρὸς ἑαυτὸν καὶ ᾖδε.[42] καὶ οἱ μὲν[43] πολλοὶ τὴν νεότητα[44] σκιρτῶσαν[45] ᾤοντο[46] ἐκφέρειν[47] αὐτὸ ἐς ταῦτα, ὁ δ' ὑπεκρίνετο[48] ἄρα τῷ δαίμονι, καὶ ἐδόκει παροινεῖν[49] ἃ ἐπαρῴνειτο. ὁρῶντός τε ἐς αὐτὸ τοῦ Ἀπολλωνίου, δεδοικότως[50] τε καὶ ὀργίλως[51] φωνὰς ἡφίει[52] τὸ εἴδωλον,[53] ὁπόσαι[54] καομένων[55] τε καὶ στρεβλουμένων[56] εἰσίν, ἀφέξεσθαί[57] τε τοῦ μειρακίου ὤμνυ[58] καὶ μηδενὶ ἀνθρώπων ἐμπεσεῖσθαι.[59] τοῦ δὲ οἷον[60] δεσπότου[61] πρὸς ἀνδράποδον[62] ποικίλον[63] πανοῦργόν[64] τε καὶ ἀναιδὲς[65] καὶ τὰ τοιαῦτα[66] ξὺν[67] ὀργῇ λέγοντος, καὶ κελεύοντος αὐτῷ ξὺν τεκμηρίῳ[68] ἀπαλλάττεσθαι,[69] "τὸν δεῖνα[70]" ἔφη "καταβαλῶ ἀνδριάντα[71]" δείξας τινὰ τῶν περὶ τὴν βασίλειον στοάν,[72] πρὸς ᾗ ταῦτα ἐπράττετο.[73]

3 Ἐπεὶ δὲ ὁ ἀνδριὰς ὑπεκινήθη[74] πρῶτον, εἶτα ἔπεσε, τὸν μὲν[75] θόρυβον[76] τὸν ἐπὶ τούτῳ, καὶ ὡς ἐκρότησαν[77] ὑπὸ θαύμαστος,[78] τί ἄν τις γράφοι;[79] τὸ δὲ μειράκιον ὥσπερ ἀφυπνίσαν[80] τούς τε ὀφθαλ-

30. Pres. act. indic. 2 sg., ὑβρίζω *insult*; with ταῦτα (internal acc.), "commit these outrages."
31. δαίμων, -ονος, ὁ, *demon*.
32. Pres. act. indic. 3 sg., ἐλαύνω, *drive*.
33. Pf. act. ptc. acc. masc. sg., οἶδα, *know*; circ. (concessive).
34. Plpf. act. indic. 3 sg., λανθάνω, *escape one's notice*.
35. Postpositive partic., *as it turns out*: "indicates that the speaker, in view of the preceding context, cannot but make the contribution he/she is making" (CGCG §59.42).
36. Pres. act. ptc. nom. masc. sg., δαιμονάω, *be under the power of a demon*; supp. (ἐλελήθει).
37. Impf. act. indic. 3 sg., γελάω, *laugh*. Iterative: the string of imperfect tense verbs describes habitual activity.
38. The explanation (γάρ) has two coordinated points (τε…τε).
39. Impf. act. indic. 3 sg., μεταβάλλω, *change over*.
40. Pres. act. inf., κλαίω, *weep*; art. inf. as obj. of ἐς (= εἰς).
41. αἰτία, -ας, ἡ, *reason*.
42. Impf. act. indic. 3 sg., ἀείδω, *sing*.
43. μέν … δέ; point/counterpoint set. See n. 4.
44. νεότης, -ητος, ἡ, *youthful spirit, youthful folly*.
45. Pres. act. ptc. acc. fem. sg., σκιρτάω, *spring, leap*; circ.
46. Impf. mid. indic. 3 pl., οἴομαι, *think, suppose*.
47. Pres. act. inf., ἐκφέρω, *bring forth*; indir. disc. (cf. BDF §397; S §2592; CGCG §41.2).
48. Impf. pass. indic. 3 sg., ὑποκρίνω, (pass.) *be played*; with dat. agent.
49. Pres. act. inf., παροινέω, *play drunken tricks*; comp. of ἐδόκει: "He appeared to be playing the tricks that were being played on him."
50. Adv., *fearfully*; pf. ptc. of δείδω.
51. Adv., *irascibly*.
52. Impf. act. indic. 3 sg., ἀφίημι, *send forth*.
53. εἴδωλον, -ου, τό, *phantom, spirit*.
54. ὁπόσος, -η, -ον, *as great as*.
55. Pres. pass. ptc. gen. masc. pl., καίω, (pass.) *be burned*; attrib. (subst.).
56. Pres. pass. ptc. gen. masc. pl., στρεβλόω, (pass.) *be twisted/racked, tortured*; attrib. (subst.).

57. Fut. mid. inf., ἀπέχω, *keep away* (from someone); with gen.; indir. disc. See n. 47.
58. Impf. act. indic. 3 sg., ὄμνυμι, *swear*.
59. Fut. mid. inf., ἐμπίπτω, *fall upon*; with dat.; indir. disc. See n. 47.
60. οἷος, -α, -ον, (adv. acc.) *like, as for example*. The adverb modifies the genitive absolute τοῦ οἷον δεσπότου: "but when he spoke [to it] angrily *like* a master does to a slave who is wily, full of tricks, shameless, and so on."
61. δεσπότης, -ου, ὁ, *master*.
62. ἀνδράποδον, -ου, τό, *slave*.
63. ποικίλος, -η, -ον, *artful, wily*.
64. πανοῦργος, -ον, *full of tricks, crafty*.
65. ἀναιδής, -ές, *shameless*.
66. τὰ τοιαῦτα; i.e., "and the like."
67. ξύν = σύν.
68. τεκμήριον, -ου, τό, *a sure sign, proof*.
69. Pres. mid. inf., ἀπαλλάσσω (Att. ἀπαλλάττω), (mid.) *depart*; comp. of κελεύοντος: "Bid it to depart with proof."
70. Indecl. pron. (with art.), *such a one* (S §336); here as demon.: "I will cast down *that* statue."
71. ἀνδριάς, -άντος, ὁ, *statue*.
72. στοά, -ᾶς, ἡ, *stoa, colonnade*. The colonnade was in the northwest corner of the Athenian agora.
73. Impf. pass. indic. 3 sg., πράσσω (Att. πράττω), (pass.) *take place*.
74. Aor. pass. indic. 3 sg., ὑποκινέω, (intrans.) *move a little, stir*.
75. μέν … δέ; point/counterpoint. See n. 4.
76. θόρυβος, -ου, ὁ, *uproar, clamor*.
77. Aor. act. indic. 3 pl., κροτέω, *clap*.
78. θαῦμα, -ατος, τό, *amazement*.
79. Pres. act. opt. 3 sg., γράφω, *write*; potential (cf. BDF §385; S §1824; CGCG §34.13). "As to the uproar that resulted over this, how [the people] clapped in amazement—who could describe it?"
80. Aor. act. ptc. nom. neut. sg., ἀφυπνίζω, *wake up from sleep*; circ. (compar.).

μοὺς ἔτριψε,⁸¹ καὶ πρὸς τὰς αὐγὰς⁸² τοῦ ἡλίου εἶδεν, αἰδῶ⁸³ τε ἐπεσπάσατο⁸⁴ πάντων ἐς αὐτὸ ἐστραμμένων,⁸⁵ ἀσελγές τε οὐκέτι ἐφαίνετο, οὐδὲ ἄτακτον⁸⁶ βλέπον, ἀλλ' ἐπανῆλθεν⁸⁷ ἐς τὴν ἑαυτοῦ φύσιν⁸⁸ μεῖον⁸⁹ οὐδὲν ἢ εἰ φαρμακοποσίᾳ⁹⁰ ἐκέχρητο,⁹¹ μεταβαλόν τε τῶν χλανιδίων⁹² καὶ ληδίων⁹³ καὶ τῆς ἄλλης συβάριδος,⁹⁴ ἐς ἔρωτα⁹⁵ ἦλθεν αὐχμοῦ⁹⁶ καὶ τρίβωνος⁹⁷ καὶ ἐς τὰ τοῦ Ἀπολλωνίου ἤθη⁹⁸ ἀπεδύσατο.⁹⁹

information on the demon-possessed men, shifts in perspective (movement between narration and commentary), dramatic contests between the exorcist and the demon, responses of amazement and aporia on the part of the crowds, and so forth. As the formerly naked and uncontrollable demoniac comes to Jesus clothed and of his right mind, so the formerly "soft" and unstable demoniac wishes to take up the "hard" and austere life of the philosopher.

NOTE

4.20. The passage shares similar narrative techniques with Mark 5:1–17: extensive background

---

81. Aor. act. indic. 3 sg., τρίβω, *rub*.
82. αὐγή, -ῆς, ἡ, (pl.) *rays, beams*.
83. αἰδώς, -οῦς, ἡ, *respect*.
84. Aor. mid. indic. 3 sg., ἐπισπάω, (mid.) *attract, gain, win*.
85. Pf. mid. ptc. gen. masc. pl., στρέφω, *turn*; attrib. (subst.).
86. ἄτακτος, -ον, *undisciplined, disorderly*.
87. Aor. act. indic. 3 sg., ἐπανέρχομαι, *return*.
88. φύσις, -εως, ἡ, *nature*.
89. μείων, -ον, *worse*; μεῖον οὐδὲν ἤ, "worse in no way than . . ."
90. φαρμακοποσία, -ας, ἡ, *medicinal elixir, potion*.
91. Plpf. mid. indic. 3 sg., χράομαι, *use*; with dat.
92. χλανίδιον, -ου, τό, *woman's mantle*.
93. λήδιον, -ου, τό, *light garment*.
94. σύβαρις, -ιδος, ἡ, *luxury* (from the place Sybaris).
95. ἔρως, -ωτος, ὁ, *love, desire*.
96. αὐχμός, -οῦ, ὁ, *deprivation*.
97. τρίβων, -ωνος, ὁ, *worn garment* (donned by philosophers).
98. ἦθος, -ους, τό, *custom*.
99. Aor. mid. indic. 3 sg., ἀποδύω, (mid.) *strip oneself, take off*; with gen.

6.7.3

Apollonius Raises the Dead

Life of Apollonius 4.45.1–2

4.45.1Κἀκεῖνο Ἀπολλωνίου θαῦμα·[1] κόρη[2] ἐν ὥρᾳ γάμου[3] τεθνάναι[4] ἐδόκει[5] καὶ ὁ νυμφίος[6] ἠκολούθει[7] τῇ κλίνῃ[8] βοῶν[9] ὁπόσα[10] ἐπ' ἀτελεῖ[11] γάμῳ, ξυνωλοφύρετο[12] δὲ καὶ ἡ Ῥώμη, καὶ γὰρ[13] ἐτύγχανεν[14] οἰκίας ἡ κόρη τελούσης[15] ἐς ὑπάτους.[16] παρατυχὼν[17] οὖν ὁ Ἀπολλώνιος τῷ πάθει[18] "κατάθεσθε"[19] ἔφη "τὴν κλίνην, ἐγὼ γὰρ ὑμᾶς τῶν ἐπὶ τῇ κόρῃ δακρύων[20] παύσω."[21] Καὶ ἅμα[22] ἤρετο, ὅ τι ὄνομα αὐτῇ εἴη.[23] οἱ μὲν[24] δὴ πολλοὶ ᾤοντο[25] λόγον ἀγορεύσειν[26] αὐτόν, οἷοι τῶν λόγων οἱ ἐπικήδειοί[27] τε καὶ τὰς ὀλοφύρσεις[28] ἐγείροντες, ὁ δὲ οὐδὲν ἀλλ' ἢ προσαψάμενος[29] αὐτῆς καί τι ἀφανῶς[30] ἐπειπὼν ἀφύπνισε[31] τὴν κόρην τοῦ

1. θαῦμα, -ατος, τό, *wonder*.
2. κόρη, -ης, ἡ, *girl, maiden*.
3. γάμος, -ου, ὁ, *wedding*.
4. Pf. act. inf., θνῄσκω, *die*.
5. Impf. act. indic. 3 sg., δοκέω, *seem, appear*; with inf.
6. νυμφίος, -ου, ὁ, *bridegroom*.
7. Impf. act. indic. 3 sg., ἀκολουθέω, *follow*; with dat.
8. κλίνη, -ης, ἡ, *funeral bier*.
9. Pres. act. ptc. nom. masc. sg., βοάω, *cry out*; circ. (manner).
10. ὁπόσος, -η, -ον, (adv. acc.) *greatly*.
11. ἀτελής, -ές, *incomplete, unfinished*; ἐπ' ἀτελεῖ γάμῳ, "on account of an unconsummated marriage."
12. Impf. mid. indic. 3 sg., συνολοφύρομαι, *mourn/lament with*; with dat.
13. Partic. combination: related information (καί) that has explanatory force (γάρ) (cf. *CGCG* §59.66).
14. Impf. act. indic. 3 sg., τυγχάνω, *happen to be*.
15. Pres. act. ptc. gen. fem. sg., τελέω (with ἐς ὑπάτους), *belong to* (consuls); attrib.
16. ὕπατος, -η, -ον, (subst.; Lat.) *consul*.
17. Aor. act. ptc. nom. masc. sg., παρατυγχάνω, *happen upon*; with dat.
18. πάθος, -ους, τό, *grief, sorrow*.
19. Aor. mid. impv. 2 pl., κατατίθημι, *put down*.
20. δάκρυον, -ου, τό, *tear*.
21. Fut. act. indic. 1 sg., παύω, *cause to cease from*; with acc. and gen.
22. Adv., *at once, at the same time*.
23. Pres. act. opt. 3 sg., εἰμί, *be*; oblique opt. in indir. quest. (cf. BDF §386; S §2677; *CGCG* §42.7).
24. μὲν δή . . . δέ; point/counterpoint (cf. Runge 2010, 75–83; BDF §447; S §2904; *CGCG* §59.24). The speaker considers the μέν-clause to be evident, clear, or precise (δή) (*CGCG* §59.44): "Many *no doubt* thought that he was going to make a speech . . . but he [said] nothing."
25. Impf. mid. indic. 3 pl., οἴομαι, *think, suppose*.
26. Fut. act. inf., ἀγορεύω, *speak publicly, give a speech*; indir. disc. (cf. BDF §397; S §2592; *CGCG* §41.2).
27. ἐπικήδειος, -ον, *of a funeral*.
28. ὀλόφυρσις, -εως, ἡ, *lamentation*.
29. Aor. mid. ptc. nom. masc. sg., προσάπτω, (mid.) *touch, take hold of*; with gen.; circ.
30. Adv., *secretly*.
31. Aor. act. indic. 3 sg., ἀφυπνίζω, *awaken*.

δοκοῦντος θανάτου, καὶ φωνήν τε ἡ παῖς ἀφῆκεν,³² ἐπανῆλθέ³³ τε ἐς τὴν οἰκίαν τοῦ πατρὸς ὥσπερ ἡ Ἄλκηστις³⁴ ὑπὸ τοῦ Ἡρακλέος³⁵ ἀναβιωθεῖσα.³⁶

²Δωρουμένων³⁷ δὲ αὐτῷ τῶν ξυγγενῶν³⁸ τῆς κόρης μυριάδας δεκαπέντε,³⁹ φερνὴν⁴⁰ ἔφη ἐπιδιδόναι αὐτὰς τῇ παιδί. καὶ εἴτε⁴¹ σπινθῆρα⁴² τῆς ψυχῆς εὗρεν ἐν αὐτῇ, ὃς ἐλελήθει⁴³ τοὺς θεραπεύοντας⁴⁴ (λέγεται γὰρ ὡς ψεκάζοι⁴⁵ μὲν ὁ Ζεύς,⁴⁶ ἡ δὲ ἀτμίζοι⁴⁷ ἀπὸ τοῦ προσώπου), εἴτ' ἀπεσβηκυῖαν⁴⁸ τὴν ψυχὴν ἀνέθαλψέ⁴⁹ τε καὶ ἀνέλαβεν,⁵⁰ ἄρρητος⁵¹ ἡ κατάληψις⁵² τούτου γέγονεν οὐκ ἐμοὶ μόνῳ, ἀλλὰ καὶ τοῖς παρατυχοῦσιν.

NOTE

4.45. There are striking similarities with the Gospel accounts of Jesus raising the dead (e.g., Mark 5:22–24, 35–43 parr.; Luke 7:11–17). For an evaluation of the evidence, see Koskenniemi (1994, 193–98).

32. Aor. act. indic. 3 sg., ἀφίημι, *send forth*; with φωνήν.
33. Aor. act. indic. 3 sg., ἐπανέρχομαι, *return*.
34. Ἄλκηστις, -ιδος, ἡ, *Alcestis*.
35. Ἡρακλῆς, -έος, ὁ, *Heracles*.
36. Aor. pass. ptc. nom. fem. sg., ἀναβιόω, (pass.) *be brought back to life*; circ. (compar.).
37. Pres. mid. ptc. gen. masc. pl., δωρέω, *present* (something to someone); gen. absol.
38. συγγενής, -ές, (subst.) *kinsman*.
39. μυριάδας δεκαπέντε = "150,000 [drachmas]."
40. φερνή, -ῆς, ἡ, *dowry*; pred. comp.
41. εἴτε … εἴτ', *either … or*.
42. σπινθήρ, -ῆρος, ὁ, *spark*.
43. Plpf. act. indic. 3 sg., λανθάνω, *escape the notice of*.
44. Pres. act. ptc. acc. masc. pl., θεραπεύω, *treat medically*; attrib. (subst.).
45. Pres. act. opt. 3 sg., ψεκάζω, *rain in small drops, drizzle*. The choice of an oblique optative "signals that the reporter presents everything from his own, temporal perspective: he puts himself between the original speaker and the addressee, emphasizing his role as mediator" (*CGCG* §41.13; cf. S §2627).
46. Metonymy: the name of the deity for the *sky*.
47. Pres. act. opt. 3 sg., ἀτμίζω, *emit steam*; oblique (λέγεται). See n. 45.
48. Pf. act. ptc. acc. fem. sg., ἀναθάλπω, *extinguish*; circ.
49. Aor. act. indic. 3 sg., θάλπω, *warm up*.
50. Aor. act. indic. 3 sg., ἀναλαμβάνω, *restore, revive*.
51. ἄρρητος, -ον, lit., *that cannot be spoken*; hence *ineffable*.
52. κατάληψις, -εως, ἡ, *apprehension*.

PART 7

Reading Philosophers and Rhetoricians

The modern concept of religion did not exist in ancient Mediterranean cultures. Rather, discourses about the gods, the cosmos, and human flourishing were matters of philosophy. In fact, the practitioners of Hellenistic philosophy, much like the practitioners of religion today,

> conceived of philosophy as a way of addressing the most painful problems of human life. They saw the philosopher as a compassionate physician whose arts could heal many pervasive types of human suffering. They practiced philosophy not as a detached intellectual technique dedicated to the display of cleverness but as an immersed and worldly art of grappling with human misery. They focused their attention, in consequence, on issues of daily and urgent human significance—the fear of death, love and sexuality, anger and aggression—issues that are sometimes avoided as embarrassingly messy and personal by the more detached varieties of philosophy. They confronted these issues as they arose in ordinary human lives, with keen attention to the vicissitudes of those lives, and to what would be necessary and sufficient to make them better. (Nussbaum 1994, 3–4)

These philosophers were also trained rhetoricians, masters of the forms of speech designed to move their audiences. There was, of course, always the danger that the speaker might major in "making the weaker arguments the stronger," as Socrates warned (Plato, *Apol.* 23d), but the stakes were simply too high to surrender rhetoric to the Sophists. Persuasion was not an art one could afford to neglect.

This section introduces you to important Greek philosophers and rhetoricians. We begin with the two most influential: Plato and Aristotle. Next, we turn to prominent members of the so-called Second Sophistic: Epictetus, Dio Chrysostom, and Plutarch. Lastly, we read passages from the great compiler of Greek philosophy, Diogenes Laertius. The primary purpose of these readings is to prepare you to read Attic and Atticizing philosophers.

7.1

Plato

Plato (ca. 427–347 BCE) hardly requires an introduction. In 387 BCE, twelve years after the execution of Socrates, he founded the Academy (located in the sacred grove dedicated to the hero Academus). There he trained youth in political thought through lessons in philosophy, logic, and mathematics. His writings are categorized into three phases: early, middle, and late dialogues (see Kraut 1992, 46n57). The dialogues function as dialectic exercises in which the central character (usually Socrates) presses his interlocutors in the pursuit of truth (e.g., *Euthyphr.* 5c–d; *Theaet.* 149a–152e).[1]

I have included two passages from the *Apology of Socrates*, one from *Timaeus*, and one from *Laws*.

One hears echoes of the *Apology* at several points in Acts (and perhaps in Paul's self-defense in Galatians), while *Timaeus* undergirds the cosmology of numerous ancient writers.[2] *Laws*, a work that reflects Plato's mature political philosophy, distinguishes between divine law (the ideal) and human law (a necessary but imperfect approximation of the former).[3]

Text and Translation: Emlyn-Jones and Preddy 2017 (§§7.1.1–2); Bury 1929 (§7.1.3); Bury 1926 (§7.1.4)

Supplemental Scripture: Acts 5:27–32; 17:22–34 (§§7.1.1–2); Gen. 1:1–4 (§7.1.3); Gal. 3:19–22 (§7.1.4)

---

1. Cf. Kraut 1992, 33: "The exceptions are the *Apology* and the *Letters*, but there is considerable disagreement among scholars about whether the latter were actually written by Plato."

2. Plato's writings are referenced according to the page numbers in Stephanus's (1578) edition. Thus, for example, *Apol.* 17a1 references *Apology*, Stephanus page 17, section a, line 1.

3. For additional practice reading Plato, in a format designed for intermediate readers, see Pratt 2011; Jones et al. 2015b.

7.1.1

Socrates's Prologue to His Defense

Apology of Socrates 17a–18a

17a Ὅ τι μὲν ὑμεῖς, ὦ ἄνδρες Ἀθηναῖοι, πεπόνθατε¹ ὑπὸ τῶν ἐμῶν κατηγόρων,² οὐκ οἶδα· ἐγὼ δ᾽ οὖν³ καὶ αὐτὸς ὑπ᾽ αὐτῶν ὀλίγου⁴ ἐμαυτοῦ ἐπελαθόμην·⁵ οὕτω πιθανῶς⁶ ἔλεγον. Καίτοι⁷ ἀληθές γε,⁸ ὡς ἔπος εἰπεῖν,⁹ οὐδὲν εἰρήκασιν. Μάλιστα δὲ αὐτῶν ἓν ἐθαύμασα¹⁰ τῶν πολλῶν ὧν ἐψεύσαντο, τοῦτο, ἐν ᾧ ἔλεγον ὡς χρὴ¹¹ ὑμᾶς εὐλαβεῖσθαι,¹² μὴ ὑπ᾽ ἐμοῦ ἐξαπατηθῆτε,¹³ **17b** ὡς δεινοῦ¹⁴ ὄντος¹⁵ λέγειν. Τὸ γὰρ μὴ αἰσχυνθῆναι,¹⁶ ὅτι αὐτίκα¹⁷ ὑπ᾽ ἐμοῦ ἐξελεγχθήσονται¹⁸ ἔργῳ, ἐπειδὰν μηδ᾽ ὁπωστιοῦν¹⁹ φαίνωμαι δεινὸς λέγειν, τοῦτό μοι

1. Pf. act. indic. 2 pl., πάσχω, *experience*.
2. κατήγορος, -ου, ὁ, *accuser*; ὑπό with gen. of pers., "at the hands of my accusers."
3. Partic. combination, *be that as it may, but at any rate*: "The preceding information is abandoned (δέ) in favor of a point which is considered more relevant (οὖν) at the particular junction" (*CGCG* §59.64). In other words, "What I said (in the μέν-clause) is impertinent, the real issue is . . ."
4. Adv., *almost*. The full construction would be ὀλίγου δεῖν, "needs a little" (cf. S §1399).
5. Aor. mid. indic. 1 sg., ἐπιλανθάνομαι, *forget*; with gen.
6. Adv., *persuasively*.
7. Partic., *and yet, even though, although*: "indicates a transition to a text segment which adds information (καί) which is worthy of note (τοι) in light of the preceding context—καίτοι invites a reconsideration of what the speaker has just said" (*CGCG* §59.23).
8. Postpositive partic.: "focuses attention on the word or phrase it follows . . . and limits the applicability of the content of the utterance to *at least* or (*more*) *precisely* that specific element" (*CGCG* §59.53).
9. The idiom ὡς ἔπος εἰπεῖν ("so to speak") qualifies what could be deemed an exaggeration (cf. S §2012; *CGCG* §51.49).
10. Aor. act. indic. 1 sg., θαυμάζω, *be astonished*; with αὐτῶν ἕν (cf. S §1388): "But I was especially astonished at one of their many lies that they told."
11. Quasi-impers., χρή, *it is necessary*; with acc. and inf. (cf. BDF §405; S §1985; *CGCG* §36.3).
12. Pres. mid. inf., εὐλαβέομαι, *be cautious*.
13. Aor. pass. subj. 2 pl., ἐξαπατέω, (pass.) *be deceived, led astray*; purpose clause (cf. BDF §369; S §2193; *CGCG* §45.3).
14. δεινός, -ή, -όν, *clever, skillful*.
15. ὡς with a circumstantial participle gives "a 'subjective' reason or motivation, for which responsibility lies with the subject of the matrix verb" (*CGCG* §52.39; cf. S §2121). The infinitive λέγειν functions like an accusative of respect (cf. S §2005): "on the grounds that I am clever *in speaking*."
16. Aor. pass. inf., αἰσχύνομαι, (pass.) *be ashamed*.
17. Adv., *immediately, in the very moment*.
18. Fut. pass. indic. 3 pl., ἐξελέγχω, (pass.) *be convicted, examined critically*.
19. Adv. acc. with μηδέ, *in no way whatsoever*.

ἔδοξεν[20] αὐτῶν ἀναισχυντότατον[21] εἶναι, εἰ μὴ ἄρα[22] δεινὸν καλοῦσιν οὗτοι λέγειν τὸν τἀληθῆ λέγοντα· εἰ μὲν[23] γὰρ τοῦτο λέγουσιν, ὁμολογοίην[24] ἂν ἔγωγε[25] οὐ κατὰ τούτους εἶναι ῥήτωρ.[26] Οὗτοι μὲν οὖν,[27] ὥσπερ ἐγὼ λέγω, ἤ τι ἢ οὐδὲν[28] ἀληθὲς εἰρήκασιν· ὑμεῖς δ' ἐμοῦ ἀκούσεσθε πᾶσαν τὴν ἀλήθειαν. Οὐ μέντοι[29] μὰ Δία,[30] ὦ ἄνδρες Ἀθηναῖοι, κεκαλλιεπημένους[31] γε λόγους, ὥσπερ οἱ **17c**τούτων, ῥήμασί τε καὶ ὀνόμασιν,[32] οὐδὲ κεκοσμημένους,[33] ἀλλὰ ἀκούσεσθε εἰκῇ[34]

λεγόμενα τοῖς ἐπιτυχοῦσιν[35] ὀνόμασιν· πιστεύω γὰρ δίκαια εἶναι ἃ λέγω, καὶ μηδεὶς ὑμῶν προσδοκησάτω[36] ἄλλως· οὐδὲ γὰρ ἂν δήπου[37] πρέποι,[38] ὦ ἄνδρες, τῇδε τῇ ἡλικίᾳ[39] ὥσπερ μειρακίῳ[40] πλάττοντι[41] λόγους εἰς ὑμᾶς εἰσιέναι.[42] Καὶ μέντοι[43] καὶ πάνυ, ὦ ἄνδρες Ἀθηναῖοι, τοῦτο ὑμῶν δέομαι[44] καὶ παρίεμαι·[45] ἐὰν διὰ τῶν αὐτῶν λόγων ἀκούητέ μου ἀπολογουμένου,[46] δι' ὧνπερ εἴωθα[47] λέγειν καὶ ἐν ἀγορᾷ[48] ἐπὶ τῶν τραπεζῶν,[49] ἵνα[50] ὑμῶν πολλοὶ ἀκηκόασι, καὶ ἄλλοθι,[51] μήτε **17d**θαυμάζειν[52] μήτε θορυβεῖν[53] τούτου ἕνεκα.[54]

20. Aor. act. indic. 3 sg., δοκέω, *seem, appear*; with inf. The demonstrative τοῦτο picks up the articular infinitive: "For their not being ashamed [τὸ γὰρ μὴ αἰσχυνθῆναι] . . . *this*, it seems to me, is the most shameless part of their conduct."

21. Superl., ἀναίσχυντος, -ον, *most shameless*.

22. Partic., *unless it turns out, after all*: "indicates that the speaker, in view of the preceding context, cannot but make the contribution he/she is making" (CGCG §59.42; cf. Denniston 1966, 37).

23. μέν solitarium (cf. S §2896; CGCG §59.24). Socrates interrupts himself (οὗτοι μὲν οὖν) before he reaches the δέ-clause.

24. Pres. act. opt. 1 sg., ὁμολογέω, *confess*. Mixed condition: pres. indic. in the protasis, potential opt. in the apodosis (cf. S §2360).

25. Postpositive particle γε is added to ἐγώ: *I at least*.

26. ῥήτωρ, -ορος, ὁ, *public speaker, orator*; pred. nom. The concession is qualified by οὐ κατὰ τούτους, "not an orator after their style" (cf. S §1690.1c).

27. Partic. combination: "a transition to a more to-the-point, relevant text segment (οὖν) [that] occurs in two stages (μέν . . . δέ), with the relevant new step presented in the δέ-segment; the μέν-clause typically presents a summary or rounding-off of the preceding stretch of text" (CGCG §59.73).

28. Idiom: ἤ τι ἢ οὐδέν, "little or nothing."

29. Postpositive partic., *nevertheless, however, mind you*. The adversative μέντοι "indicates a transition to a text-segment which contradicts or modifies the expectations raised by the preceding context" (CGCG §59.27).

30. Ζεύς, Διός, ὁ, *Zeus*. The particle (οὐ) μά takes the accusative of the god by which one swears (cf. S §2894); lit., "by Zeus," though often better translated with a marker of assurance; e.g., "Truly, I assure you."

31. Pf. pass. ptc. acc. masc. pl., καλλιεπέω, (pass.) *be spoken elegantly*; attrib.

32. The collocation ῥήμασί τε καὶ ὀνόμασιν should be rendered "words and phrases."

33. Pf. pass. ptc. acc. masc. pl., κοσμέω, (pass.) *be adorned*; attrib.

34. Adv., *at random*; here something like "not in [proper rhetorical] order."

35. Aor. act. ptc. dat. masc. pl., ἐπιτυγχάνω, *occur*; attrib.

36. Pres. act. impv. 3 sg., προσδοκάω, *expect* (someone will do something).

37. Postpositive partic.: "combines the 'evidential' force of δή with the uncertainty of που—δήπου tentatively suggests that something ought to be as clear or obvious to the addressee as it is to the speaker" (CGCG §59.47).

38. Pres. act. opt. 3 sg., πρέπω, (impers.) *it is fitting*; with dat. and inf.; potential (cf. BDF §385; S §1824; CGCG §34.13).

39. τῇδε τῇ ἡλικίᾳ; lit., "at this age"; assumes an implied μοι, which is the dat. comp. of πρέποι.

40. μειράκιον, -ου, τό, *adolescent*.

41. Pres. act. ptc. dat. masc. sg., πλάσσω (Att. πλάττω) (with λόγους), *invent lies, tell fictions*; circ. (comparison).

42. Pres. act. inf., εἴσειμι (with εἰς with acc.), *appear* (before someone), *go before* (the court) (MGS, 614.B).

43. Partic. combination, *well then, now*: "The speaker adds information (καί), and 'indicates that he/she vouches for the correctness or relevance of the addition, even if the addressee may not expect it (μέντοι)'" (CGCG §59.28; cf. S §2880).

44. Pres. mid. indic. 1 sg., δέομαι (with acc. and gen.), *ask* (something of someone).

45. Pres. mid. indic. 1 sg., παρίημι, (mid.) *entreat, beseech*.

46. Pres. mid. ptc. gen. masc. sg., ἀπολογέω, *make a defense*; supp. (ἀκούητε, with gen.).

47. Pf. act. indic. 1 sg., ἔθω, *be accustomed*; with inf.

48. ἀγορά, -ᾶς, ἡ, *marketplace*.

49. τράπεζα, -ας, ἡ, *table* (of a money changer).

50. Adv., *where*.

51. Adv., *elsewhere*.

52. Pres. act. inf., θαυμάζω, *be amazed*. The infinitives explicate that which (τοῦτο) Socrates begs and beseeches—essentially, an indirect command (cf. S §2013).

53. Pres. act. inf., θορυβέω, *cause an uproar*.

54. Prep. with gen., *because of*.

ἔχει γὰρ οὑτωσί.⁵⁵ Νῦν ἐγὼ πρῶτον ἐπὶ δικαστήριον⁵⁶ ἀναβέβηκα, ἔτη⁵⁷ γεγονὼς ἑβδομήκοντα· ἀτεχνῶς⁵⁸ οὖν ξένως ἔχω⁵⁹ τῆς ἐνθάδε λέξεως.⁶⁰ ὥσπερ οὖν ἄν,⁶¹ εἰ τῷ ὄντι⁶² ξένος ἐτύγχανον⁶³ ὤν, ξυνεγιγνώσκετε⁶⁴ δήπου⁶⁵ ἄν μοι, εἰ ἐν ἐκείνῃ τῇ φωνῇ τε καὶ τῷ τρόπῳ⁶⁶ **18a**ἔλεγον, ἐν οἷσπερ ἐτεθράμμην,⁶⁷ καὶ δὴ καὶ⁶⁸ νῦν τοῦτο ὑμῶν δέομαι δίκαιον, ὥς γέ⁶⁹ μοι δοκῶ, τὸν μὲν⁷⁰ τρόπον τῆς λέξεως ἐᾶν·⁷¹ ἴσως⁷² μὲν⁷³ γὰρ χείρων, ἴσως δὲ βελτίων ἂν εἴη· αὐτὸ δὲ τοῦτο σκοπεῖν⁷⁴ καὶ τούτῳ τὸν νοῦν προσέχειν,⁷⁵ εἰ δίκαια λέγω ἢ μή· δικαστοῦ⁷⁶ μὲν⁷⁷ γὰρ αὕτη ἀρετή,⁷⁸ ῥήτορος δὲ τἀληθῆ λέγειν.

NOTES

17a1. ὦ ἄνδρες Ἀθηναῖοι. This is the standard address for the body politic and is thus an appropriate way to approach the jury (Denyer 2019, 156). Cf. Acts 17:22: ἄνδρες Ἀθηναῖοι. For the similarities between Plato's Socrates and Luke's Paul, see Alexander (1993); Sandnes (1993); MacDonald (2006); Cowan (2021). For similarities between the trial and death of Socrates in Plato and the trial and death of Jesus in Luke-Acts, see Sterling (2001).

17a2. ἐμαυτοῦ ἐπελαθόμην. Cf. *Phaedr.* 223a5. Socrates's near loss of self-knowledge evokes the famous inscription at the temple in Delphi, ΓΝΩΘΙ ΣΕΑΥΤΟΝ, "Know thyself!" (cf. Plato, *Prot.* 343b; Aristophanes, *Nub.* 841–842).

17c4. μειρακίῳ. The term "is an indirect dig at the prosecutor Meletus, who was conspicuously young" (Denyer 2019, 58; cf. Plato, *Apol.* 25d8–9; Plato, *Euthyphr.* 2b; Plato, *Resp.* 466b; Plato, *Gorg.* 499b).

17c8–9. Cf. Acts 17:17.

18a6. τἀληθῆ λέγειν. The expression "comes emphatically at the end of the προοίμον after being led up to at 17b4. . . . It is a clear statement of the Socratic doctrine that the true end of rhetoric is τὸ ἀληθές and not τὸ πιθανόν" (Burnet 1924, 73).

---

55. "The deictic suffix -ῑ may be added to demonstratives for emphasis" (S §333.g). Thus the idiom ἔχει γὰρ οὑτωσί expresses a strong assertion: "For the truth is simply this . . ."
56. δικαστήριον, -ου, τό, *court*.
57. ἔτος, -ους, τό, *year*; acc. of extent (time).
58. Adv., *simply, truly, absolutely*.
59. ἔχω with adv. as a periphrasis for εἰμί with adj., "I am a foreigner."
60. λέξις, -εως, ἡ, *way of speaking*; comp. of ξένως (cf. S §1441).
61. The particle anticipates ἄν in the apodosis (cf. S §1765).
62. Idiom: τῷ ὄντι, "in reality," "in fact."
63. Impf. act. indic. 1 sg., τυγχάνω, *happen*; with supp. ptc.
64. Impf. act. indic. 2 pl., συγγιγνώσκω, *pardon*; with dat.; contrafactual (cf. S §2302; CGCG §49.10).
65. Postpositive partic.: "combines the 'evidential' force of δή with the uncertainty of που—δήπου tentatively suggests that something ought to be as clear or obvious to the addressee as it is to the speaker" (*CGCG* §59.47).
66. Denyer 2019, 60: "Here φωνή seems to be accent in particular . . . while τρόπος seems to cover other features that make a dialect alien."
67. Plpf. pass. indic. 1 sg., τρέφω, (pass.) *be nourished, raised*.
68. Partic. combination, *and in particular, and above all*: "adds an extra piece of information (καί . . . καί), and singles out the addition (δή)" (*CGCG* §59.69).
69. Concentration/limitation: "*at least*, as it seems to me." See n. 8.
70. μέν . . . δέ; point/counterpoint set (cf. Runge 2010, 75–83; BDF §447; S §2904; *CGCG* §59.24).
71. Pres. act. inf., ἐάω, *allow, permit*; appositive to τοῦτο.
72. Adv., *perhaps*; ἴσως μὲν γὰρ χείρων, ἴσως δὲ βελτίων ἂν εἴη, "For perhaps it may be worse, perhaps it may be better"; potential opt. See n. 38.
73. μέν . . . δέ. The point/counterpoint set qualifies the μέν-clause (cf. S §2908).
74. Pres. act. inf., σκοπέω, *observe*; appositive to τοῦτο.
75. Pres. act. inf., προσέχω (with τὸν νοῦν), *pay attention*.
76. δικαστής, -οῦ, ὁ, *judge*.
77. μέν . . . δέ; point/counterpoint. See n. 70.
78. ἀρετή, -ῆς, ἡ, *virtue*.

7.1.2

Socrates's Resolution in the Face of Death

Apology of Socrates 29b–30c

29bκαὶ τοῦτο πῶς οὐκ ἀμαθία[1] ἐστὶν αὕτη ἡ ἐπονείδιστος,[2] ἡ τοῦ οἴεσθαι[3] εἰδέναι ἃ οὐκ οἶδεν; ἐγὼ δ', ὦ ἄνδρες, τούτῳ καὶ ἐνταῦθα[4] ἴσως[5] διαφέρω[6] τῶν πολλῶν ἀνθρώπων, καὶ εἰ δή[7] τῳ[8] σοφώτερός[9] του[10] φαίην[11] εἶναι, τούτῳ ἄν, ὅτι οὐκ εἰδὼς ἱκανῶς[12] περὶ τῶν ἐν Ἅιδου[13] οὕτω καὶ οἴομαι οὐκ εἰδέναι· τὸ δὲ ἀδικεῖν καὶ ἀπειθεῖν[14] τῷ βελτίονι,[15] καὶ θεῷ καὶ ἀνθρώπῳ, ὅτι κακὸν καὶ αἰσχρόν ἐστιν οἶδα. πρὸ[16] οὖν τῶν κακῶν, ὧν[17] οἶδα ὅτι κακά ἐστιν, ἃ μὴ[18] οἶδα εἰ ἀγαθὰ ὄντα τυγχάνει[19] οὐδέποτε φοβήσομαι οὐδὲ φεύξομαι· **29c**ὥστε οὐδ' εἴ με νῦν ὑμεῖς ἀφίετε[20] Ἀνύτῳ[21] ἀπιστήσαντες,[22] ὅς ἔφη ἢ[23] τὴν ἀρχὴν[24] οὐ δεῖν[25] ἐμὲ δεῦρο εἰσελθεῖν ἤ, ἐπειδὴ εἰσῆλθον, οὐχ οἷόν τ' εἶναι[26] τὸ μὴ ἀποκτεῖναί με, λέγων πρὸς ὑμᾶς

---

1. ἀμαθία, -ας, ἡ, *ignorance*.
2. ἐπονείδιστος, -ον, *shameful, disgraceful*.
3. Pres. mid. inf., οἴομαι, *suppose*; art. inf. as epex. gen. (cf. S §2032): "the [ignorance] that *presumes* to know what it does not know."
4. Adv., *herein, in this position*.
5. Adv., *perhaps, may*.
6. Pres. act. indic. 1 sg., διαφέρω, *be different from*; with gen. of compar. with dat. of manner (τούτῳ).
7. Postpositive partic., *actually, indeed, in fact*: "indicates that the speaker considers (and invites the addressee to consider) the text segment or word (group) which it modifies as evident, clear, or precise" (*CGCG* §59.44).
8. τῳ (enclitic) = τινί; dat. of manner: τῳ ... τούτῳ (cf. S §334).
9. Compar., σοφός, -ή, -όν, *wiser*.
10. τοῦ = τινός. See n. 8.
11. Aor. act. opt. 1 sg., φημί, *say*; fourth-class, or potential, condition (cf. S §2329; *CGCG* §49.8): "And if I were to say that I am in any way wiser than anyone, it would be in this [τούτῳ ἄν]."
12. Adv., *sufficiently, enough*.
13. περὶ τῶν ἐν (δόμῳ) Ἅιδου, *about the things in the house of Hades*.
14. Pres. act. inf., ἀπειθέω, *disobey*; with dat.; acc. art. inf. as contrastive topic (cf. S §2034; *CGCG* §51.39): "But as for *doing injustice* and *disobeying* my better, . . . I know that it is evil and shameful."
15. Compar., ἀγαθός, -ή, -όν, *better*.
16. Prep. with gen., *instead of, rather than*.
17. The relative pronoun, which has been attracted to the case of its antecedent, is proleptic (cf. S §2182; *CGCG* §60.37).
18. The conditional relative clause is negated by μή (cf. S §2560; *CGCG* §50.19): "Those things which I do not know whether they happen to be good I will never fear nor flee."
19. Pres. act. indic. 3 sg., τυγχάνω, *happen*; with supp. ptc.
20. Pres. act. indic. 2 pl., ἀφίημι, *release*.
21. Ἄνυτος, -ου, ὁ, *Anytus* (one of the prosecutors).
22. Aor. act. ptc. nom. masc. pl., ἀπιστέω, *distrust, disbelieve*; with dat.; circ. (causal).
23. ἤ . . . ἤ, *either . . . or*.
24. Acc. of respect, "in the first place."
25. Quasi-impers., δεῖ, *it is necessary*; with acc. and inf. The indirect discourse retains οὐ from the corresponding statement in direct discourse.
26. Idiom: (quasi-impers.) οἷόν τέ ἐστι, *it is possible*; with acc. and inf. (cf. S §1985; *CGCG* §36.8); indir. disc. (cf. BDF §397; S §2592; *CGCG* §41.2).

ὡς, εἰ διαφευξοίμην,²⁷ ἤδη ἂν ὑμῶν οἱ υἱεῖς²⁸ ἐπιτηδεύοντες²⁹ ἃ Σωκράτης διδάσκει πάντες παντάπασι³⁰ διαφθαρήσονται,³¹ —εἴ μοι πρὸς ταῦτα εἴποιτε·³² ὦ Σώκρατες, νῦν μὲν³³ Ἀνύτῳ οὐ πεισόμεθα, ἀλλ' ἀφίεμέν σε, ἐπὶ τούτῳ μέντοι, ἐφ' ᾧτε³⁴ μηκέτι ἐν ταύτῃ τῇ ζητήσει³⁵ διατρίβειν μηδὲ φιλοσοφεῖν· ²⁹ᵈἐὰν δὲ ἁλῷς³⁶ ἔτι τοῦτο πράττων, ἀποθανεῖ· εἰ οὖν με, ὅπερ εἶπον, ἐπὶ τούτοις ἀφίοιτε,³⁷ εἴποιμ' ἂν ὑμῖν ὅτι ἐγὼ ὑμᾶς, ἄνδρες Ἀθηναῖοι, ἀσπάζομαι³⁸ μὲν καὶ φιλῶ,³⁹ πείσομαι δὲ μᾶλλον τῷ θεῷ ἢ ὑμῖν, καὶ ἕωσπερ⁴⁰ ἂν ἐμπνέω⁴¹ καὶ οἷός⁴² τε ὦ, οὐ μὴ παύσωμαι⁴³ φιλοσοφῶν καὶ ὑμῖν παρακελευόμενός⁴⁴ τε καὶ ἐνδεικνύμενος⁴⁵ ὅτῳ⁴⁶ ἂν ἀεὶ ἐντυγχάνω ὑμῶν, λέγων οἷάπερ εἴωθα,⁴⁷ ὅτι, ὦ ἄριστε ἀνδρῶν, Ἀθηναῖος⁴⁸ ὤν, πόλεως τῆς μεγίστης καὶ εὐδοκιμωτάτης⁴⁹ εἰς σοφίαν καὶ ἰσχύν, χρημάτων⁵⁰ μὲν⁵¹ οὐκ αἰσχύνει⁵² ἐπιμελούμενος,⁵³ ὅπως⁵⁴ σοι ἔσται ὡς πλεῖστα, ²⁹ᵉκαὶ δόξης καὶ τιμῆς, φρονήσεως⁵⁵ δὲ καὶ ἀληθείας καὶ τῆς ψυχῆς, ὅπως ὡς βελτίστη ἔσται,⁵⁶ οὐκ ἐπιμελεῖ οὐδὲ φροντίζεις;⁵⁷ καὶ ἐάν τις ὑμῶν ἀμφισβητῇ⁵⁸ καὶ φῇ⁵⁹ ἐπιμελεῖσθαι, οὐκ εὐθὺς ἀφήσω αὐτὸν οὐδ' ἄπειμι,⁶⁰ ἀλλ' ἐρήσομαι αὐτὸν καὶ ἐξετάσω⁶¹ καὶ ἐλέγξω,⁶² ³⁰ᵃκαὶ ἐάν μοι

---

27. Fut. mid. opt. 1 sg., διαφεύγω, *escape* (the charges; i.e., be acquitted); oblique opt. for fut. indic. in indir. disc. (cf. S §2629; *CGCG* §49.27).

28. υἱεῖς = υἱοί.

29. Pres. act. ptc. nom. masc. pl., ἐπιτηδεύω, *pursue*; circ.

30. Adv., *in every way, entirely*.

31. Fut. pass. indic. 3 pl., διαφθείρω, *be corrupted*. It is highly unusual to have ἄν with a future indicative; it may be taken as an anacoluthon (cf. S §1793).

32. Aor. act. opt. 2 pl., λέγω, *say*. The clause εἴ μοι πρὸς ταῦτα εἴποιτε resumes εἴ με νῦν ὑμεῖς ἀφίετε (anacoluthon). Note that the condition has become more remote.

33. μέν . . . μέντοι; stronger contrast than μέν . . . δέ (cf. S §2919).

34. ἐφ' ᾧτε, *on the condition that*; with inf.; may be introduced by ἐπὶ τούτῳ (cf. S §2279; *CGCG* §49.26).

35. ζήτησις, -εως, ἡ, *search, inquiry, investigation*.

36. Aor. act. subj. 2 sg., ἁλίσκομαι, *be caught*; third-class condition (cf. S §2323; *CGCG* §49.6).

37. Pres. act. opt. 2 pl., ἀφίημι; fourth-class condition (see n. 11). The protasis resumes the interruption: εἴ με νῦν ὑμεῖς ἀφίετε . . . εἴ μοι πρὸς ταῦτα εἴποιτε . . . εἰ οὖν με, ὅπερ εἶπον, ἐπὶ τούτοις ἀφίοιτε, εἴποιμ' ἂν ὑμῖν, "If you release me now . . . if you *should say* these things [the following] to me . . . if, therefore, *you should release* me for these reasons, based on what I have said, then *I would say* to you . . ."

38. Pres. mid. indic. 1 sg., ἀσπάζομαι, *respect*.

39. Pres. act. indic. 1 sg., φιλέω, *love*.

40. Adv., *as long as*.

41. Pres. act. subj. 1 sg., ἐμπνέω, *have breath, live*; general temp. clause (cf. BDF §383; S §2409; *CGCG* §47.9).

42. Idiom, οἷός τέ ἐστι, *be able*.

43. Pres. mid. subj. 1 sg., παύω, *cease*; with supp. ptc.; emphatic neg.: οὐ μή with subj. (BDF §365; S §1804; *CGCG* §34.9).

44. Pres. mid. ptc. nom. masc. sg., παρακελεύομαι, *exhort*; with dat.; supp. (παύσωμαι).

45. Pres. mid. ptc. nom. masc. sg., ἐπιδείκνυμι, *demonstrate, show*; supp. (παύσωμαι).

46. ὅτῳ = ᾧτινι (see n. 8); thus, "demonstrating [this truth] *to whomever* of you I should happen upon."

47. Pf. act. indic. 1 sg., ἔθω, *be accustomed*; λέγων οἷάπερ εἴωθα, "saying what sort of things I am accustomed [to say]."

48. Read Ἀθηναῖος as if it were Ἀθηνῶν, "belonging to Athens," and take πόλεως as an appositive (cf. S §978).

49. Superl., εὐδόκιμος, -ον, *most renowned*; εἰς σοφίαν καὶ ἰσχύν, "renowned for wisdom and power."

50. χρῆμα, -ατος, τό, *wealth, money*.

51. μέν . . . δέ; point/counterpoint.

52. αἰσχύνει = αἰσχύνῃ; pres. pass. indic. 2 sg., αἰσχύνω, (pass.) *be ashamed*.

53. Pres. mid. ptc. nom. masc. sg., ἐπιμελέω, *care for*; with gen.; circ.

54. The participle ἐπιμελούμενος takes an object clause of effort: ὅπως with a future indicative (cf. S §2210; *CGCG* §44.2). "*that* they [wealth, glory, and honor] *are* yours as much as possible [ὡς πλεῖστα]."

55. φρόνησις, -εως, ἡ, *wisdom, prudence*.

56. Effort clause (see n. 54). Translation: "[You do not care] that they [wisdom, truth, and the soul] are as good as possible [ὡς βελτίστη]."

57. Pres. act. indic. 2 sg., φροντίζω, *take thought for, regard* (something); with gen.

58. Pres. act. subj. 3 sg., ἀμφισβητέω, *dispute*; third-class condition. See n. 36.

59. Pres. act. subj. 3 sg., φημί, *say*. See n. 36.

60. Pres. (as fut.) act. indic. 1 sg., ἄπειμι, *depart*.

61. Fut. act. indic. 1 sg., ἐξετάζω, *examine*.

62. Fut. act. indic. 1 sg., ἐλέγχω, *cross-examine*.

μὴ δοκῇ⁶³ κεκτῆσθαι⁶⁴ ἀρετήν, φάναι⁶⁵ δέ, ὀνειδιῶ,⁶⁶ ὅτι τὰ πλείστου ἄξια περὶ ἐλαχίστου⁶⁷ ποιεῖται, τὰ δὲ φαυλότερα περὶ πλείνος.⁶⁸ Ταῦτα καὶ νεωτέρῳ καὶ πρεσβυτέρῳ, ὅτῳ⁶⁹ ἂν ἐντυγχάνω, ποιήσω, καὶ ξένῳ⁷⁰ καὶ ἀστῷ,⁷¹ μᾶλλον δὲ τοῖς ἀστοῖς, ὅσῳ μου ἐγγυτέρῳ⁷² ἐστὲ γένει.⁷³ Ταῦτα γὰρ κελεύει⁷⁴ ὁ θεός, εὖ ἴστε,⁷⁵ καὶ ἐγὼ οἴομαι οὐδέν πω⁷⁶ ὑμῖν μεῖζον ἀγαθὸν γενέσθαι ἐν τῇ πόλει ἢ τὴν ἐμὴν τῷ θεῷ ὑπηρεσίαν.⁷⁷ Οὐδὲν γὰρ ἄλλο πράττων ἐγὼ περιέρχομαι ἢ πείθων⁷⁸ ὑμῶν καὶ νεωτέρους καὶ πρεσβυτέρους **30b**μήτε σωμάτων ἐπιμελεῖσθαι μήτε χρημάτων πρότερον⁷⁹ μηδὲ οὕτω σφόδρα ὡς τῆς ψυχῆς, ὅπως⁸⁰ ὡς ἀρίστη ἔσται, λέγων, ὅτι οὐκ ἐκ χρημάτων ἀρετὴ γίγνεται, ἀλλ' ἐξ ἀρετῆς χρήματα καὶ τὰ ἄλλα ἀγαθὰ τοῖς ἀνθρώποις ἅπαντα καὶ ἰδίᾳ καὶ δημοσίᾳ.⁸¹ Εἰ μὲν οὖν⁸² ταῦτα λέγων διαφθείρω⁸³ τοὺς νέους, ταῦτ' ἂν εἴη βλαβερά.⁸⁴ εἰ δε τίς με φησιν ἄλλα λέγειν ἢ ταῦτα, οὐδέν λέγει.⁸⁵ πρὸς ταῦτα,⁸⁶ φαίην ἄν, ὦ Ἀθηναῖοι, ἢ πείθεσθε Ἀνύτῳ ἢ μή, καὶ ἢ ἀφίετε ἢ μὴ ἀφίετε, **30c**ὡς ἐμοῦ οὐκ ἂν ποιήσοντος⁸⁷ ἄλλα, οὐδ' εἰ μέλλω πολλάκις τεθνάναι.⁸⁸

NOTES

29d3–4. πείσομαι δὲ μᾶλλον τῷ θεῷ ἢ ὑμῖν. The statement is not an attack on the laws but a response to "the imaginary and procedurally quite improper offer from the jury" (Denyer 2019, 94). Compare Acts 5:29: Ἀποκριθεὶς δὲ Πέτρος καὶ οἱ ἀπόστολοι εἶπαν πειθαρχεῖν δεῖ θεῷ μᾶλλον ἢ ἀνθρώποις.

30b1–2. σωμάτων ... χρημάτων ... τῆς ψυχῆς. Note the climatic position of τῆς ψυχῆς. Plato frequently argues that care for the soul should be our greatest concern (cf. *Leg.* 697b; 726a; *Phaedr.* 241c; *Alc. maj.* 130e–131b).

---

63. Pres. act. subj. 3 sg., δοκέω, *seem, appear*; with inf. and dat.; third-class condition. See n. 36.
64. Pf. mid. inf., κτάομαι, *acquire*, (pf.) *possess*; indir. disc. See n. 26.
65. Addition to the protasis (indir. disc.; see n. 26): "But he says [he does possess virtue]."
66. Fut. act. indic. 1 sg., ὀνειδίζω, *reproach*.
67. περὶ ἐλαχίστου, *of least value*; gen. of value.
68. περὶ πλείνος, *of greater value*; gen. of value.
69. ὅτῳ = ᾧτινι (cf. S §339).
70. ξένος, -ου, ὁ, *foreigner*.
71. ἀστός, -οῦ, ὁ, *citizen*.
72. Compar. adv. from ἐγγύς, -ύ, *closer*; with gen. and with dat. of measure of difference (ὅσῳ).
73. γένος, -ους, τό, *family group, descent*; dat. of respect.
74. Pres. act. indic. 3 sg., κελεύω, *bid, order*; with acc. and inf.
75. Pf. act. impv. 2 pl., οἶδα; εὖ ἴστε, *know well!*
76. Partic., *up to this point, ever*.
77. ὑπηρεσία, -ας, ἡ, *service*.
78. Pres. act. ptc. nom. masc. sg., πείθω, *persuade*; with acc. and inf.; conative (S §1878.a; *CGCG* §33.17): "*trying to persuade* yours, both young and old, not to care for bodies or possessions."
79. μήτε ... πρότερον μηδὲ οὕτω σφόδρα ὡς, "neither first ... nor even as much as ..."
80. Clause of effort: "that it [the soul] will be as noble as possible." See n. 54.
81. καὶ ἰδίᾳ καὶ δημοσίᾳ, "both individually and publicly."
82. Partic. combination: "a transition to a more to-the-point, relevant text segment (οὖν) [that] occurs in two stages (μέν ... δέ)" (*CGCG* §59.73).

83. Pres. act. indic. 1 sg., διαφθείρω, *corrupt*.
84. βλαβερός, -ά, -όν, *harmful, injurious*; mixed condition: εἰ with pres. indic., ἄν with pres. opt. (cf. S §2356). "If, then, by saying these things I corrupt the youth, then these things would be harmful."
85. Idiom, οὐδέν λέγει, "he speaks nonsense."
86. πρὸς ταῦτα, *therefore*; "marking the transition from a defiant statement to an imperative" (Denyer 2019, 97 and sources therein).
87. ὡς with circ. ptc.: "thinking that I would not do anything else." The genitive absolute represents ἂν ποιήσω ἄλλα, "There is no prospect of me doing otherwise" (Denyer 2019, 97). Due to the paucity of ἄν with the future indicative, many emend to οὐκ ἂν ποιήσαντος, representing οὐκ ἂν ποιήσαιμι (Burnet 1924, 125), so that the participle represents a potential optative (cf. S §1848; *CGCG* §52.7).
88. Pf. act. inf., θνήσκω, *die*.

7.1.3

The Act of Creation

Timaeus 29d–30c

29dΣΩΚΡΑΤΗΣ. Ἄριστα,¹ ὦ Τίμαιε, παντάπασί² τε ὡς κελεύεις³ ἀποδεκτέον.⁴ τὸ μὲν οὖν⁵ προοίμιον⁶ θαυμασίως⁷ ἀπεδεξάμεθά σου, τὸν δὲ δὴ νόμον⁸ ἡμῖν ἐφεξῆς⁹ πέραινε.¹⁰

ΤΙΜΑΙΟΣ. Λέγωμεν δὴ¹¹ δι᾽ ἥν τινα αἰτίαν¹² γένεσιν¹³ καὶ τὸ πᾶν¹⁴ τόδε ὁ ξυνιστὰς¹⁵ ξυνέστησεν. **29e**ἀγαθὸς ἦν, ἀγαθῷ δὲ οὐδεὶς περὶ οὐδενὸς οὐδέποτε ἐγγίγνεται¹⁶ φθόνος.¹⁷ τούτου δ᾽ ἐκτὸς¹⁸ ὢν πάντα ὅ τι μάλιστα¹⁹ γενέσθαι ἐβουλήθη παραπλήσια²⁰ ἑαυτῷ. Ταύτην δὲ γενέσεως καὶ κόσμου μάλιστ᾽ ἄν²¹ τις

1. Adv. acc., superl. of ἀγαθός, -ή, -όν, (in affirmative responses) *Excellent!*
2. Adv., *by all means.*
3. Pres. act. indic. 2 sg., κελεύω, *bid, urge*; with acc. and inf.
4. Verbal adj. from ἀποδέχομαι, impers. (act.) constr.: "It is necessary [for us] to accept" (cf. S §2152; *CGCG* §37.3).
5. Partic. combination: "a transition to a more to-the-point, relevant text segment (οὖν) [that] occurs in two stages (μέν ... δέ), with the relevant new step presented in the δέ-segment" (*CGCG* §59.73).
6. προοίμιον, -ου, τό, (Lat.) *prooemium, preface, prelude.*
7. Adv., *exceedingly.*
8. The term νόμος (melody) works with the term προοίμιον, which is the prelude or overture of a piece of music. Socrates thus bids Timaeus, "Carry on your song." Or in rhetorical terms, continue on with the λόγος.
9. Adv., *successively.*
10. Pres. act. impv. 2 sg., περαίνω, *complete, finish, recite in entirety.*

11. Postpositive partic.: "indicates that the speaker considers (and invites the addressee to consider) the text segment or word (group) which it modifies as evident, clear, or precise" (*CGCG* §59.44). As a response to the previous line: τὸν δὲ δὴ νόμον ἡμῖν ἐφεξῆς πέραινε.... Λέγωμεν δή, "so *now* proceed straight on to the main theme.... Let us *now* state ..."
12. αἰτία, -ας, ἡ, *cause.*
13. γένεσις, -εως, ἡ, *becoming.*
14. τὸ πᾶν, *the universe.*
15. Aor. act. ptc. nom. masc. sg., συνίστημι, *put together, construct*; attrib. (subst.).
16. Pres. mid. indic. 3 sg., ἐγγίγνομαι, *spring up, appear in*; with dat.
17. φθόνος, -ου, ὁ, *envy*; οὐδεὶς ... φθόνος, "In him who is good, no envy concerning anything ever arises."
18. Prep. with gen., *without, outside*; τούτου δ᾽ ἐκτὸς ὢν (causal): "and being without this [i.e., envy]."
19. ὅ τι μάλιστα, "as much as possible" (cf. S §1086; *CGCG* §32.4).
20. παραπλήσιος, -α, -ον, *resembling, like*; with dat.
21. Anticipates ἄν at the end of the sentence (cf. S §1765).

ἀρχὴν κυριωτάτην²² παρ' ἀνδρῶν φρονίμων²³ ἀποδεχόμενος²⁴ ὀρθότατα²⁵ ἀποδέχοιτ'²⁶ ἄν. **30a**βουληθεὶς γὰρ ὁ θεὸς ἀγαθὰ μὲν²⁷ πάντα, φλαῦρον²⁸ δὲ μηδὲν εἶναι κατὰ δύναμιν,²⁹ οὕτω δὴ πᾶν ὅσον ἦν ὁρατὸν³⁰ παραλαβὼν οὐχ ἡσυχίαν³¹ ἄγον ἀλλὰ κινούμενον³² πλημμελῶς³³ καὶ ἀτάκτως,³⁴ εἰς τάξιν³⁵ αὐτὸ ἤγαγεν ἐκ τῆς ἀταξίας,³⁶ ἡγησάμενος³⁷ ἐκεῖνο τούτου πάντως ἄμεινον. θέμις³⁸ δὲ οὔτ' ἦν οὔτ' ἔστι τῷ ἀρίστῳ δρᾶν³⁹ ἄλλο πλὴν⁴⁰ τὸ κάλλιστον· λογισάμενος⁴¹ οὖν εὕρισκεν ἐκ τῶν κατὰ **30b**φύσιν⁴² ὁρατῶν οὐδὲν ἀνόητον⁴³ τοῦ νοῦν⁴⁴ ἔχοντος ὅλον ὅλου⁴⁵ κάλλιον⁴⁶ ἔσεσθαί⁴⁷ ποτ'⁴⁸ ἔργον, νοῦν δ' αὖ⁴⁹ χωρὶς⁵⁰ ψυχῆς ἀδύνατον⁵¹ παραγενέσθαι τῳ.⁵² διὰ δὴ τὸν λογισμὸν⁵³ τόνδε νοῦν μὲν⁵⁴ ἐν ψυχῇ, ψυχὴν δὲ ἐν σώματι ξυνιστὰς τὸ πᾶν ξυνετεκταίνετο,⁵⁵ ὅπως ὅ τι κάλλιστον⁵⁶ εἴη⁵⁷ κατὰ φύσιν ἄριστόν τε ἔργον ἀπειργασμένος.⁵⁸ οὕτως οὖν δὴ⁵⁹ κατὰ λόγον τὸν εἰκότα⁶⁰ δεῖ λέγειν τόνδε τὸν κόσμον ζῷον⁶¹ ἔμψυχον⁶² ἔννουν⁶³ **30c**τε τῇ ἀληθείᾳ διὰ τὴν τοῦ θεοῦ γενέσθαι πρόνοιαν.⁶⁴

22. Superl., κύριος, -α, -ον, *most important, supreme*.
23. φρόνιμος, -ον, *wise*.
24. Pres. mid. ptc. nom. masc. sg., ἀποδέχομαι, *receive*; circ. (conditional): "In receiving this [ταύτην] from wise men as the supreme originating principle [ἀρχὴν κυριωτάτην] of becoming and the cosmos, one would be wholly correct [lit., would receive it entirely correctly]."
25. Adv. acc., superl. of ὀρθός, -ή, -όν, *entirely correct*.
26. Pres. mid. opt. 3 sg., ἀποδέχομαι; potential opt. in apodosis (cf. BDF §385; S §2353; CGCG §49.8).
27. μέν . . . δέ; point/counterpoint (cf. Runge 2010, 75–83; BDF §447; S §2904; CGCG §59.59).
28. φλαῦρος, -α, -ον, *bad, wicked*.
29. κατὰ δύναμιν, "to the extent possible."
30. ὁρατός, -ή, -όν, *visible*.
31. Idiom, ἡσυχίαν ἄγω, *be at rest*.
32. Pres. mid. ptc. nom. neut. sg., κινέω, (intrans.) *be in motion*.
33. Adv., *in a faulty manner, erroneously*.
34. Adv., *disorderly*.
35. τάξις, -εως, ἡ, *order*.
36. ἀταξία, -ας, ἡ, *disorder*.
37. Aor. mid. ptc. nom. masc. sg., ἡγέομαι, *consider*; circ. (causal): "Considering that the former [ἐκεῖνο = being at rest] is in all ways better than the latter [τούτου = faulty and disorderly motion] . . ."
38. Quasi-impers., θέμις (ἐστίν), *it is right, proper*; with dat. and inf.
39. Pres. act. inf., δράω, *perform, accomplish*.
40. Much like ἤ, πλήν works with ἄλλος to form a comparison: "For he who is the best [the creator], it neither was nor is permissible to do *anything other than* [ἄλλο πλήν] what is most beautiful."
41. Aor. mid. ptc. nom. masc. sg., λογίζομαι, *consider*; circ.
42. φύσις, -εως, ἡ, *nature*; ἐκ τῶν κατὰ φύσιν ὁρατῶν, "out of the things that are visible by nature."
43. ἀνόητος, -ον, *irrational*.
44. νοῦς, νοῦ, ὁ, *mind, intellect*, (perhaps better) *reason* (so Menn 1995).
45. ὅλον, ὅλου, lit., "whole [compared to] whole," in which ὅλον agrees with the acc. subject and ὅλου agrees with the gen. comparand.
46. Compar., καλός, -ή, -όν, *finer, more beautiful, more noble*.
47. Fut. mid. inf., εἰμί; indir. disc. (cf. BDF §397; S §2592; CGCG §41.2).
48. Adv., *at some time*.
49. Stronger development than δέ alone (cf. S §2839).
50. Prep. with gen., *apart from*.
51. ἀδύνατος, -α, -ον, (quasi-impers.) *it is impossible*; with (acc. and) inf.
52. τῳ = τινί (cf. S §334).
53. λογισμός, -οῦ, ὁ, *reasoning*.
54. μέν . . . δέ; point/counterpoint. See n. 27.
55. Impf. mid. indic. 3 sg., συντεκταίνομαι, *construct with*; acc. and dat.
56. ὅ τι with superl., ὅ τι κάλλιστον, "as beautiful as possible" (cf. S §1086).
57. Opt. for subj. in purpose clause (cf. S §2196; CGCG §45.3).
58. Pf. mid. ptc. nom. masc. sg., ἀπεργάζομαι, *complete*; periphrastic (with εἴη). This is the standard form for the perfect optative (cf. S §407).
59. Partic. combination: "transition to more to-the-point, crucial or relevant information" (οὖν) that "the speaker considers (and invites the addressee to consider) . . . as evident, clear, or precise" (δή) (CGCG §§59.34; 59.44).
60. Pf. act. ptc. acc. neut. sg., ἔοικα, (ptc.) *likely, probably*; κατὰ λόγον τὸν εἰκότα, "in accordance with the likely account."
61. Pres. act. ptc. acc. masc. sg., ζάω, *live*; attrib.
62. ἔμψυχος, -ον, *ensouled*.
63. ἔννους, -ουν, *intelligent*.
64. πρόνοια, -ας, ἡ, *providence*.

NOTES

29d7. γένεσιν. Timaeus has already established that the cosmos has an origin: "Now the whole heaven or cosmos, or if there is any other name which it specially prefers, by that let us call it . . . whether it has always existed [ἦν ἀεί], having no beginning of generation [γενέσεως ἀρχήν], or whether it has come into existence [γέγονεν], having begun from some beginning [ἀπ' ἀρχῆς τινὸς ἀρξάμενος]. It has come into existence [γέγονεν]" (*Tim.* 28b; cf. *Leg.* 715e–716a). Cf. Gen. 1:1 LXX; 2 Macc. 7:23; Heb. 11:3. The Platonic concept that the sensible world is based on the intelligible world has potential resonance with the Jewish concept that God formed the world through Wisdom (cf. Prov. 8:22–27; Wis. 9:9; Philo, *Opif.* 29; Philo, *Leg.* 1.1; Frg. Tg. Gen. 1:1; Tg. Neof. Gen. 1:1).

29e1. ἀγαθὸς ἦν. Plato reacts against concepts of divine vengeance and nemesis in Greek mythology. The creator's goodness is his singular motivation, not envy (φθόνος) of any kind (cf. *Phaedr.* 247a7).

30a1–6. Desiring to make all things good and, as much as possible, to eliminate evil, the artificer sets out to create order out of disorder (εἰς τάξιν αὐτὸ ἤγαγεν ἐκ τῆς ἀταξίας). Note in particular the line οὐχ ἡσυχίαν ἄγον ἀλλὰ κινούμενον πλημμελῶς καὶ ἀτάκτως, which seems to suggest some kind of precosmic chaos. For a metaphorical reading of precosmic chaos, see Dillon (1997). Alternatively, one might see "the creation as an on-going process in time. . . . The disorder that used to characterize the world seems not simply to be a fact about the past. It is also the state of affairs that generally does or would characterize the world whenever god absents himself from it" (Johansen 2004, 90).

30b8. τόνδε τὸν κόσμον ζῷον. Plato maintains that the cosmos is a "living being" endowed with soul (ἔμψυχον) and reason (ἔννουν) (cf. Plato, *Tim.* 32d1–34a6, 92c6; Plato, *Pol.* 269d; so too the Stoics: cf. Cicero, *Nat. d.* 2.23–30; *SVF* 1.100, 2.633–34).

7.1.4

Human Law as the Second-Best Option

Laws 874e–875d

874eπρορρητέον[1] δή[2] τι περὶ πάντων τῶν τοιούτων τοιόνδε, ὡς ἄρα[3] νόμους ἀνθρώποις ἀναγκαῖον[4] τίθεσθαι καὶ ζῆν κατὰ νόμους, ἢ μηδὲν[5] διαφέρειν[6] τῶν πάντῃ ἀγριωτάτων[7] θηρίων.[8] **875a**ἡ δὲ αἰτία[9] τούτων ἥδε, ὅτι φύσις[10] ἀνθρώπων οὐδενὸς ἱκανὴ[11] φύεται[12] ὥστε γνῶναί[13] τε τὰ συμφέροντα[14] ἀνθρώποις εἰς πολιτείαν[15] καὶ γνοῦσα τὸ βέλτιστον[16] ἀεὶ[17] δύνασθαί[18] τε καὶ ἐθέλειν[19] πράττειν.[20] γνῶναι μὲν[21] γὰρ πρῶτον χαλεπὸν[22] ὅτι πολιτικῇ[23] καὶ ἀληθεῖ τέχνῃ[24] οὐ τὸ ἴδιον ἀλλὰ τὸ κοινὸν ἀνάγκη[25] μέλειν[26]—τὸ

1. Verbal adj. from προείρω, impers. (act.) constr., "a certain thing *to be stated* [by us]" (S §2152; *CGCG* §37.3). When the text has consecutive *rho*s, the editor may elect to add a smooth and a rough breathing mark. This convention, however, is less common today.
2. Postpositive partic., (as marking a transition) *now*: "indicates that the speaker considers (and invites the addressee to consider) the text segment or word (group) which it modifies as evident, clear, or precise" (*CGCG* §59.44).
3. Postpositive partic., *then, it seems*: "indicates that the speaker, in view of the preceding context, cannot but make the contribution he/she is making" (*CGCG* §59.42).
4. ἀναγκαῖος, -α, -ον, (quasi-impers.) *it is necessary*; with acc. and inf.
5. Adv. acc., *in no way*; with πάντῃ, "in no way whatsoever."
6. Pres. act. inf., διαφέρω, (intrans.) *differ from*; with gen.
7. Superl., ἄγριος, -α, -ον, *wildest*.
8. θηρίον, -ου, τό, *beast*.
9. αἰτία, -ας, ἡ, *reason*.
10. φύσις, -εως, ἡ, *nature*.
11. ἱκανός, -ή, -όν, *sufficient, able*; with gen.
12. Pres. mid. indic. 3 sg., φύω, *be by nature*.
13. Aor. act. inf., γινώσκω; result clause (cf. BDF §391; S §2269; *CGCG* §46.6).
14. Pres. act. ptc. acc. neut. pl., συμφέρω, (intrans.) *be beneficial, profitable*; with dat.; attrib. (subst.).
15. πολιτεία, -ας, ἡ, *civil polity*.
16. Superl., ἀγαθός, -ή, -όν, *best, most excellent*.
17. Adv., *always*.
18. Pres. mid. inf., δύναμαι; result clause.
19. Pres. act. inf., ἐθέλω, *will, desire*; result clause.
20. Pres. act. inf., πράσσω (Att. πράττω), *do*.
21. μέν . . . πρῶτον (first) . . . δεύτερον δέ (second); point/counterpoint set (cf. Runge 2010, 75–83; BDF §447; S §2904; *CGCG* §59.69), which provides support/explanation (γάρ) for the two points that were raised in the result clause.
22. χαλεπός, -ή, -όν, (quasi-impers.) *it is difficult*; with (acc. and) inf.
23. πολιτικός, -ή, -όν, *of / relating to civic life*.
24. τέχνη, -ης, ἡ, *art*.
25. Quasi-impers., ἀνάγκη, *it is necessary*; with acc. and inf.: "It is necessary not for the private but for the public to be concerned with the true, civic art."
26. Pres. act. inf., μέλω, *care for, be concerned with*; with dat.

μὲν²⁷ γὰρ κοινὸν ξυνδεῖ,²⁸ τὸ δὲ ἴδιον διασπᾷ²⁹ τὰς πόλεις—καὶ ὅτι ξυμφέρει³⁰ τῷ κοινῷ τε καὶ ἰδίῳ, τοῖν ἀμφοῖν,³¹ ἤν³² τὸ κοινὸν τιθῆται καλῶς μᾶλλον ἢ τὸ ἴδιον· **875b**δεύτερον δέ, ἐὰν ἄρα³³ καὶ³⁴ τὸ γνῶναί τις ὅτι ταῦτα οὕτω πέφυκε³⁵ λάβῃ ἱκανῶς³⁶ ἐν τέχνῃ, μετὰ δὲ τοῦτο ἀνυπεύθυνός³⁷ τε καὶ αὐτοκράτωρ³⁸ ἄρξῃ³⁹ πόλεως, οὐκ ἄν ποτε⁴⁰ δύναιτο⁴¹ ἐμμεῖναι⁴² τούτῳ τῷ δόγματι⁴³ καὶ διαβιῶναι⁴⁴ τὸ μὲν⁴⁵ κοινὸν ἡγούμενον⁴⁶ τρέφων⁴⁷ ἐν τῇ πόλει, τὸ δὲ ἴδιον ἑπόμενον⁴⁸ τῷ κοινῷ, ἀλλ' ἐπὶ πλεονεξίαν⁴⁹ καὶ ἰδιοπραγίαν⁵⁰ ἡ θνητή⁵¹ φύσις αὐτὸν ὁρμήσει⁵² ἀεί, φεύγουσα⁵³ μὲν⁵⁴ ἀλόγως⁵⁵ τὴν λύπην,⁵⁶ **875c**διώκουσα⁵⁷ δὲ τὴν ἡδονήν,⁵⁸ τοῦ δὲ δικαιοτέρου τε καὶ ἀμείνονος ἐπίπροσθεν⁵⁹ ἄμφω τούτω⁶⁰ προστήσεται,⁶¹ καὶ σκότος ἀπεργαζομένη⁶² ἐν αὐτῇ⁶³ πάντων κακῶν ἐμπλήσει⁶⁴ πρὸς τὸ τέλος⁶⁵ αὐτήν τε καὶ τὴν πόλιν ὅλην· ἐπεὶ ταῦτα⁶⁶ εἴ ποτέ τις ἀνθρώπων φύσει ἱκανός, θείᾳ μοίρᾳ⁶⁷ γεννηθείς, παραλαβεῖν δυνατὸς εἴη, νόμων οὐδὲν ἂν δέοιτο⁶⁸ τῶν ἀρξόντων⁶⁹ ἑαυτοῦ· ἐπιστήμης⁷⁰ γὰρ οὔτε νόμος οὔτε τάξις οὐδεμία κρείττων, οὐδὲ θέμις ἐστὶ νοῦν οὐδενὸς ὑπήκοον⁷¹ οὐδὲ δοῦλον ἀλλὰ πάντων ἄρχοντα εἶναι, **875d**ἐάνπερ⁷² ἀληθινὸς ἐλεύθερός τε

27. μέν ... δέ; point/counterpoint in the μέν-clause (cf. S §2908).
28. Pres. act. indic. 3 sg., συνδέω, *bind together*.
29. Pres. act. indic. 3 sg., διασπάω, *tear apart*.
30. Pres. act. indic. 3 sg., συμφέρω, (impers.) *it benefits*; with dat.
31. Dat. neut. dual form of ἄμφω (cf. S §§229, 332), "*both* [public and private interests] alike."
32. ἤν = ἐάν; pres. general condition: ἐάν with subj. in the protasis, pres. indic. in the apodosis (cf. S §2337).
33. Postpositive partic., *then, it seems*: "indicates that the speaker, in view of the preceding context, cannot but make the contribution he/she is making" (CGCG §59.42).
34. ἐάν ... καί is concessive: "even if" (cf. S §2369; CGCG §49.19).
35. Pf. act. indic. 3 sg., φύω, *be by nature*; the cognitive content (τὸ γνῶναι = obj. inf.) that τις should grasp: "that these things are so by nature."
36. Adv., *sufficiently*.
37. ἀνυπεύθυνος, -ον, *unaccountable*.
38. αὐτοκράτωρ, -ορος, ὁ, *autocrat, absolute ruler*.
39. Aor. act. subj. 3 sg., ἄρχω, *rule over*; with gen.; additional element of the protasis of a third-class (mixed) condition: ἐάν with subj. in the protasis, potential opt. and fut. indic. in the apodosis (cf. S §2326; CGCG §49.6). The optative is used for the remote possibility (what will not happen), while the future is used to complete the third-class condition.
40. Adv., *at any time*.
41. Pres. mid. opt. 3 sg., δύναμαι; potential opt. in apodosis. See n. 39.
42. Aor. act. inf., ἐμμένω, *remain in*; with dat.
43. δόγμα, -ατος, τό, *opinion, belief*.
44. Aor. act. inf., διαβιόω, *continue*.
45. μέν ... δέ; point/counterpoint. See n. 21.
46. Pres. mid. ptc. acc. neut. sg., ἡγέομαι, (of logical priority) *be antecedent/primary* (as the leading principle); attrib. (pred. comp.).
47. Pres. act. ptc. nom. masc. sg., τρέφω, *nourish, foster, cherish*; supp. (διαβιῶναι).
48. Pres. mid. ptc. acc. neut. sg., ἕπομαι, *follow, be secondary to*; with dat.; attrib. (pred. comp.).

49. πλεονεξία, -ας, ἡ, *greediness*.
50. ἰδιοπραγία, -ας, ἡ, *pursuit of private interest*.
51. θνητός, -ή, -όν, *mortal*.
52. Fut. act. indic. 3 sg., ὁρμάω, *set in motion, urge on*. See n. 39.
53. Pres. act. ptc. nom. fem. sg., φεύγω, *flee from*; circ.
54. μέν ... δέ; point/counterpoint. See n. 21.
55. Adv., *irrationally, unreasonably*.
56. λύπη, -ης, ἡ, *pain*.
57. Pres. act. ptc. nom. fem. sg., διώκω, *pursue*; circ.
58. ἡδονή, -ῆς, ἡ, *pleasure*.
59. Adv. with gen., "prefer one *before* another."
60. The dual form is used because the adjective is modifying ἄμφω (cf. S §333).
61. Fut. mid. indic. 3 sg., προστίθημι, *prefer, value above* (another).
62. Pres. mid. ptc. nom. fem. sg., ἀπεργάζομαι, *finish, complete*; circ. The participle takes σκότος as its object.
63. ἐν αὐτῇ = ἐν ἑαυτῇ, "in itself."
64. Fut. act. indic. 3 sg., ἐμπίμπλημι, *fill* (acc.) *with* (gen.).
65. πρὸς τὸ τέλος, "to the utmost" (i.e., to the point of being completely full).
66. Proleptic: "and yet as to *these things*, if ever there should be a human able and capable by nature to receive *them*."
67. μοῖρα, -ας, ἡ, *lot, destiny*.
68. Pres. mid. opt. 3 sg., δέομαι, *be in need of*; with gen.; fourth-class, or potential, condition (cf. S §2329; CGCG §49.8).
69. Fut. act. ptc. gen. masc. pl., ἄρχω, *rule over*; with gen.; purpose (cf. S §2086; CGCG §52.41).
70. ἐπιστήμη, -ης, ἡ, *knowledge*; gen. of comparison.
71. ὑπήκοος, -ον, *obedient, subservient*. The full clause is "Nor is it permissible [θέμις ἐστί] for reason [νοῦν] to be subservient or slave to anything, but rather to be ruler of all."
72. Postpositive partic.: "expresses exclusive limitation—limits the applicability of an utterance's content to exactly and

ὄντως ἦ κατὰ φύσιν. νῦν δε—οὐ γάρ ἐστιν οὐδαμοῦ[73] οὐδαμῶς,[74] ἀλλ' ἢ[75] κατὰ βραχύ.[76] διὸ δὴ τὸ δεύτερον αἱρετέον,[77] τάξιν τε καὶ νόμον, ἃ δὴ τὸ μὲν[78] ὡς ἐπὶ τὸ πολὺ[79] ὁρᾷ καὶ βλέπει, τὸ δ' ἐπὶ πᾶν ἀδυνατεῖ.[80]

NOTES

875a2. φύσις ἀνθρώπων οὐδενὸς ἱκανὴ φύεται. Herein lies the fundamental problem and thus the reason why laws are necessary: human nature is *by nature* incapable of both knowing and doing what is beneficial. The laws are a necessary measure (lest humans devolve into wild beasts) because of the loss of the age of Cronos (Plato, *Leg.* 713a–714a). Yet their very presence represents the failure of human beings (Laks 2000, 266). Moreover, Plato was skeptical, as were many of the ancients, that human laws could ever perfectly legislate the contingencies of life (*Pol.* 294a10–b6).

875b7–9. Mortal nature drives a person (especially someone in a position of power) to self-interest and greed (πλεονεξία; cf. Rom. 1:29; Eph. 4:19; Col. 3:15).

875c5–8. ἐπεὶ ταῦτα εἴ ποτέ τις ἀνθρώπων φύσει ἱκανός, θείᾳ μοίρᾳ γεννηθείς, παραλαβεῖν δυνατὸς εἴη, νόμων οὐδὲν ἂν δέοιτο τῶν ἀρξόντων ἑαυτοῦ. The "future less vivid" condition suggests he thinks the possibility an unlikely one. Nonetheless, the ideal is clearly expressed: were human beings to have the divine law "written on their hearts," as it were—that is, to be living laws themselves—there would be no need for human laws to regulate their lives (Plato, *Pol.* 297a; Hayes 2015, 67).

---

only the word (group) it follows" (*CGCG* §59.55). Translation: "if, of course, [νοῦς] is true and truly free by nature."

73. Adv., *nowhere*.
74. Adv., *not at all*.
75. ἀλλ' ἤ marks an exception (cf. S §2778): "For no such nature exists anywhere at all, *except* in small degree."
76. κατὰ βραχύ, "in small degree."
77. Verbal adj. from αἱρέω, impers. (act.) constr. "It is necessary [for us] to choose the second-best option." See n. 1.
78. τὸ μέν ... τὸ δέ, *on the one hand ... on the other hand* (cf. S §1111; *CGCG* §28.27): "which things [ἅ = τάξιν τε καὶ νόμον], on the one hand, mostly see and perceive but, on the other hand, are unable to do so completely."
79. ὡς ἐπὶ τὸ πολύ ... ἐπὶ πᾶν, *for the most part ... completely* (cf. LSJ, 2038.Ab.III.e).
80. Pres. act. indic. 3 sg., ἀδυνατέω, *be unable*.

7.2

Aristotle

Like Plato, Aristotle (384–322 BCE) is one of the giants of philosophy. In 367 BCE, the Macedonian left his home in the township of Stagira for Athens and Plato's Academy, where he would remain until the death of his teacher (347 BCE). When Aristotle eventually returned to Athens in 335 BCE, however, he did not rejoin the Academy but instead founded his own school (Peripatetic), which met in the Lyceum.

To call Aristotle a prolific writer would be a massive understatement. Diogenes Laertius credits him with writing more than 150 works (*Vit. phil.* 5.22–27), of which only some thirty have survived (Barnes 1995, 9). His writings combine rigorous empiricism, logical deduction, and the categorical insistence that the sciences be kept separate from each other (a departure from Plato). Yet one does not find in Aristotle's oeuvre—perhaps more akin to lecture notes than polished literature—a "systematic construction." Voltaire (1733) famously quipped that Aristotle "has been explained a thousand ways, because he is unintelligible." Thus, we typically encounter him betwixt and between aporia and confidence so that, we might say, "there was a system *in posse* but not *in esse*; a virtual but not an actual system" (Barnes 1995, 24).

The reading passages fall under the rubric of the practical (ethics and politics) and productive (poetics and rhetoric) sciences.[1] In the first, Aristotle probes the telos of the human function (ἔργον). In the second, he writes about household management, an important discussion for the interpretation of New Testament household codes. In the third, he provides a summary of the forms of rhetoric and the ends they serve.[2]

Text and Translation: Rackham 1926 (§7.2.1); Rackham 1932 (§7.2.2); Freese 1926 (§7.2.3)

Supplemental Scripture: Eph. 5:21–6:9; Col. 3:18–4:1; 1 Pet. 2:18–3:7 (§7.2.2)

---

1. For a full list of the four categories of science (i.e., organon, theoretical sciences, practical sciences, and productive sciences), see Shields 2012, 12–13.

2. Aristotle's writings are referenced according to the page numbers in Bekker's edition (1831–70). Thus, for example, 1097a26 corresponds to page 1097, first column (column a), line 26 in Bekker.

7.2.1

On the Telos of the Human Function

Nicomachean Ethics 1097a26–1098a20

1097a26 ἐπεὶ δὴ¹ πλείω² φαίνεται τὰ τέλη,³ τούτων δ' αἱρούμεθά⁴ τινα δι' ἕτερα, οἷον⁵ πλοῦτον,⁶ αὐλοὺς⁷ καὶ ὅλως⁸ τὰ ὄργανα,⁹ δῆλον¹⁰ ὡς οὐκ ἔστι πάντα τέλεια·¹¹ τὸ δ' ἄριστον¹² τέλειόν τι φαίνεται. ὥστ' εἰ μέν¹³ ἐστιν ἕν τι μόνον τέλειον, τοῦτ' ἂν εἴη¹⁴ τὸ ζητούμενον,¹⁵ εἰ δὲ πλείω,¹⁶ τὸ τελειότατον¹⁷ τούτων. τελειότερον δὲ λέγομεν τὸ καθ' αὑτὸ διωκτὸν¹⁸ τοῦ δι' ἕτερον καὶ μηδέποτε¹⁹ δι' ἄλλο αἱρετὸν²⁰ τῶν καὶ καθ' αὑτὰ καὶ διὰ τοῦθ' αἱρετῶν, καὶ ἁπλῶς²¹ δὴ τέλειον τὸ καθ' αὑτὸ αἱρετὸν ἀεὶ²² καὶ μηδέποτε δι' ἄλλο[.]²³ τοιοῦτον δ' ἡ εὐδαιμονία²⁴ μάλιστ'²⁵ εἶναι δοκεῖ·²⁶ ταύτην γὰρ αἱρούμεθα ἀεὶ δι' αὐτὴν καὶ οὐδέποτε δι' ἄλλο, τιμὴν²⁷ δὲ καὶ

---

1. Postpositive partic., *now, then*: "indicates that the speaker considers (and invites the addressee to consider) the text segment or word (group) which it modifies as evident, clear, or precise" (*CGCG* §59.44).
2. Compar., πολύς, -ή, -ύ, *several, manifold*. The form is the result of Attic contraction (cf. S §293).
3. τέλος, -ους, τό, *end* (goal).
4. Pres. mid. indic. 1 pl., αἱρέω, *choose*.
5. Adv. acc., *as for instance, for example*.
6. πλοῦτος, -ου, ὁ, *wealth*.
7. αὐλός, -οῦ, ὁ, *flute*.
8. Adv., *generally*.
9. ὄργανον, -ου, τό, *instrument*.
10. δῆλος, -ον, (quasi-impers.) *it is clear*; with ὡς clause of content.
11. τέλειος, -α, -ον, *final, complete, self-sufficient*.
12. Superl., ἀγαθός, -ή, -όν, *best, supreme*.
13. μέν . . . δέ; point/counterpoint (cf. Runge 2010, 75–83; BDF §447; S §2904; *CGCG* §59.24).
14. Pres. act. opt. 3 sg., εἰμί; mixed condition: pres. indic. in the protasis, ἄν with opt. in apodosis (cf. S §2356).
15. Pres. pass. ptc. nom. neut. sg., ζητέω, (pass.) *be sought*; attrib. (subst.).

16. The condition is elliptical: "But if [the ends] are several, then the most final of these [would be that which ought to be sought by us]."
17. Superl., τέλειος, -α, -ον, *most final*; with gen. of comparison.
18. διωκτός, -ή, -όν, *pursued*.
19. Adv., *at no time, never*.
20. αἱρετός, -ή, -όν, *chosen*. The καί carries the structure and thought of the previous clause: "And that which is never chosen as the means to another [is more final] than the things that are chosen both as ends to themselves and as means to another."
21. Adv., *simply, absolutely*; underscored by the particle δή. See n. 1.
22. Adv., *always*.
23. This punctuation is not in Rackham (1926), but it seems necessary to make sense of the text.
24. εὐδαιμονία, -ας, ἡ, *happiness, blessedness*.
25. Adv. acc., *above all else*.
26. Pres. act. indic. 3 sg., δοκέω, *seem, appear*; with inf.
27. τιμή, -ῆς, ἡ, *honor*.

ἡδονὴν²⁸ καὶ νοῦν²⁹ καὶ πᾶσαν ἀρετὴν³⁰ **1097b1**αἱρούμεθα μὲν³¹ καὶ δι' αὐτὰ (μηθενὸς³² γὰρ ἀποβαίνοντος³³ ἑλοίμεθ'³⁴ ἂν ἕκαστον αὐτῶν), αἱρούμεθα δὲ καὶ τῆς εὐδαιμονίας χάριν,³⁵ διὰ τούτων ὑπολαμβάνοντες³⁶ εὐδαιμονήσειν·³⁷ τὴν δ' εὐδαιμονίαν οὐδεὶς αἱρεῖται τούτων³⁸ χάριν, οὐδ' ὅλως δι' ἄλλο.

Φαίνεται δὲ καὶ ἐκ τῆς αὐταρκείας³⁹ τὸ αὐτὸ συμβαίνειν.⁴⁰ τὸ γὰρ τέλειον ἀγαθὸν αὔταρκες⁴¹ εἶναι δοκεῖ. τὸ δ' αὔταρκες λέγομεν οὐκ αὐτῷ μόνῳ, τῷ ζῶντι βίον⁴² μονώτην,⁴³ ἀλλὰ καὶ γονεῦσι⁴⁴ καὶ τέκνοις καὶ γυναικὶ καὶ ὅλως τοῖς φίλοις⁴⁵ καὶ πολίταις,⁴⁶ ἐπειδὴ φύσει⁴⁷ πολιτικὸν⁴⁸ ὁ ἄνθρωπος. τούτων δὲ ληπτέος⁴⁹ ὅρος⁵⁰ τις· ἐπεκτείνοντι⁵¹ γὰρ ἐπὶ τοὺς γονεῖς καὶ τοὺς ἀπογόνους⁵² καὶ τῶν φίλων τοὺς φίλους εἰς ἄπειρον⁵³ πρόεισιν.⁵⁴ ἀλλὰ τοῦτο μὲν⁵⁵ εἰσαῦθις⁵⁶ ἐπισκεπτέον,⁵⁷ τὸ δ' αὔταρκες τίθεμεν ὃ μονούμενον⁵⁸ αἱρετὸν ποιεῖ τὸν βίον καὶ μηδενὸς ἐνδεᾶ·⁵⁹ τοιοῦτον δὲ τὴν εὐδαιμονίαν οἰόμεθα⁶⁰ εἶναι. ἔτι δὲ⁶¹ πάντων αἱρετωτάτην⁶² μὴ συναριθμουμένην⁶³—συναριθμουμένην⁶⁴ γὰρ δῆλον ὡς αἱρετωτέραν μετὰ τοῦ ἐλαχίστου τῶν ἀγαθῶν, ὑπεροχὴ⁶⁵ γὰρ ἀγαθῶν γίνεται τὸ προστιθέμενον,⁶⁶ ἀγαθῶν δὲ τὸ μεῖζον αἱρετώτερον ἀεί. τέλειον δή⁶⁷ τι φαίνεται καὶ αὔταρκες ἡ εὐδαιμονία, τῶν πρακτῶν⁶⁸ οὖσα τέλος.

---

28. ἡδονή, -ῆς, ἡ, *pleasure*.
29. νοῦς, νοῦ, ὁ, *intelligence*.
30. ἀρετή, -ῆς, ἡ, *virtue*.
31. μέν . . . δέ. The point/counterpoint set explicates the δέ-clause (cf. S §2908).
32. μηθενός = μηδενός.
33. Pres. act. ptc. gen. neut. sg., ἀποβαίνω, *come up, result*; gen. absol. (concessive): "Even though nothing [extraneous] comes about, we would choose each of them."
34. Aor. mid. opt. 1 pl., αἱρέω, *choose*; potential (cf. BDF §385; S §1824; CGCG §34.13).
35. Prep. with gen., *for the sake of*.
36. Pres. act. ptc. nom. masc. pl., ὑπολαμβάνω, *assume, suppose*; circ.
37. Fut. act. inf., εὐδαιμονέω, *be happy, blessed*; indir. disc. (cf. BDF §397; S §2592; CGCG §41.2).
38. τούτων = ἡδονὴν καὶ νοῦν καὶ πᾶσαν ἀρετήν.
39. αὐτάρκεια, -ας, ἡ, *self-sufficiency*.
40. Pres. act. inf., συμβαίνω, *happen, come to pass*; comp. of φαίνεται: "The same also appears *to follow* from a consideration of self-sufficiency." See n. 37.
41. αὐτάρκης, -ες, *self-sufficient*; pred. adj.
42. βίος, -ου, ὁ, *life*.
43. μονώτης, -ου, ὁ, *isolated, solitary*.
44. γονεύς, -έως, ὁ, (pl.) *parents*.
45. φίλος, -ου, ὁ, *friend, kin*.
46. πολίτης, -ου, ὁ, *citizen*.
47. φύσις, -εως, ἡ, *nature*; dat. of respect.
48. Thus "a political thing." Lᵇ reads πολιτικός. Aristotle, *Pol.* 1253a2 adds ζῷον, "a political animal."
49. Verbal adj. from λαμβάνω, personal (pass.) constr. (cf. S §2151; CGCG §37.2), "a certain limit *to be assumed* [by us]."
50. ὅρος, -ου, ὁ, *limit, boundary*.
51. Pres. act. ptc. dat. masc. sg., ἐπεκτείνω, *extend*; circ. (conditional; cf. S §1497): "For if we extend [the term "self-sufficient"] to parents, ancestors, and friends of friends, it will continue on ad infinitum."
52. ἀπόγονος, -ου, ὁ, *descendant*.
53. ἄπειρος, -ον, *boundless, infinite*.
54. Pres. (as fut.) act. indic. 3 sg., πρόειμι, *advance, go on*.
55. ἀλλά . . . μέν . . . δ'; point/counterpoint. ἀλλά indicates that the μέν-clause is correcting an assumption (i.e., that the previous point will be further developed), while the δέ-clause picks up the main argument.
56. Adv., *subsequently*.
57. Verbal adj. from ἐπισκοπέω, impers. (act.) constr. (cf. S §2152; CGCG §37.3): "This is *to be observed* [by us]."
58. Pres. mid. ptc. nom. neut. sg., μονόω, *be alone, solitary, isolated*; circ.
59. ἐνδεής, -ές, *wanting, lacking*.
60. Pres. mid. indic. 1 pl., οἴομαι, *consider*.
61. ἔτι δ', *moreover*.
62. Superl., αἱρετός, -ή, -όν, *most desirable*; pred. acc. (τὴν εὐδαιμονίαν).
63. Pres. pass. ptc. acc. fem. sg., συναριθμέω, (pass.) *be numbered with, counted among*; circ. (concessive).
64. The circumstantial participle has conditional force: "If it were so numbered [among the rest of the good things], it would be clear that it is more desirable when accompanied by the least of the good things."
65. ὑπεροχή, -ῆς, ἡ, *excess* (of a sum).
66. Pres. pass. ptc. nom. neut. sg., προστίθημι, (pass.) *be added*; attrib. (subst.).
67. Postpositive partic., *now, then*: "indicates that the speaker considers (and invites the addressee to consider) the text segment or word (group) which it modifies as evident, clear, or precise" (CGCG §59.44).
68. πρακτός, -ή, -όν, *concerned with action*. Cf. Rackham 1926, 30: "'Practice' for Aristotle denotes purposeful conduct, of which only rational beings are capable."

Ἀλλ' ἴσως⁶⁹ τὴν μὲν⁷⁰ εὐδαιμονίαν τὸ ἄριστον λέγειν ὁμολογούμενόν⁷¹ τι φαίνεται, ποθεῖται⁷² δ' ἐναργέστερον⁷³ τί ἐστιν ἔτι λεχθῆναι.⁷⁴ τάχα⁷⁵ δὴ γένοιτ'⁷⁶ ἂν τοῦτ', εἰ ληφθείη⁷⁷ τὸ ἔργον τοῦ ἀνθρώπου. ὥσπερ⁷⁸ γὰρ αὐλητῇ⁷⁹ καὶ ἀγαλματοποιῷ⁸⁰ καὶ παντὶ τεχνίτῃ,⁸¹ καὶ ὅλως ὧν ἐστὶν ἔργον τι καὶ πρᾶξις, ἐν τῷ ἔργῳ δοκεῖ τἀγαθὸν⁸² εἶναι καὶ τὸ εὖ,⁸³ οὕτω δόξειεν⁸⁴ ἂν καὶ ἀνθρώπῳ, εἴπερ⁸⁵ ἔστι τι ἔργον αὐτοῦ. πότερον⁸⁶ οὖν τέκτονος⁸⁷ μὲν καὶ σκυτέως⁸⁸ ἐστὶν ἔργα τινὰ καὶ πράξεις, ἀνθρώπου δ' οὐδέν ἐστιν, ἀλλ' ἀργὸν⁸⁹ πέφυκεν; ἢ καθάπερ⁹⁰ ὀφθαλμοῦ καὶ χειρὸς καὶ ποδὸς καὶ ὅλως ἑκάστου τῶν μορίων φαίνεταί τι ἔργον, οὕτω καὶ ἀνθρώπου παρὰ πάντα ταῦτα⁹¹ θείη⁹² τις ἂν ἔργον τι; τί οὖν δὴ⁹³ τοῦτ' ἂν εἴη ποτέ; τὸ μὲν γὰρ ζῆν κοινὸν εἶναι φαίνεται καὶ τοῖς φυτοῖς,⁹⁴ ζητεῖται δὲ τὸ ἴδιον.⁹⁵ ἀφοριστέον⁹⁶ ἄρα⁹⁷ τὴν **1098a1**θρεπτικὴν⁹⁸ καὶ αὐξητικὴν⁹⁹ ζωήν. ἑπομένη¹⁰⁰ δὲ αἰσθητική¹⁰¹ τις ἂν εἴη· φαίνεται δὲ καὶ αὐτὴ κοινὴ καὶ ἵππῳ¹⁰² καὶ βοῒ¹⁰³ καὶ παντὶ ζῴῳ.¹⁰⁴ λείπεται¹⁰⁵ δὴ πρακτική τις τοῦ λόγον ἔχοντος (τούτου δὲ τὸ μὲν¹⁰⁶ ὡς ἐπιπειθὲς¹⁰⁷ λόγῳ, τὸ δ' ὡς ἔχον καὶ διανοούμενον¹⁰⁸)· διττῶς¹⁰⁹ δὲ καὶ ταύτης λεγομένης τὴν κατ' ἐνέργειαν¹¹⁰ θετέον.¹¹¹ κυριώτερον¹¹² γὰρ αὕτη δοκεῖ λέγεσθαι. εἰ δὴ ἐστὶν

69. Adv., *probably, perhaps*.
70. ἀλλὰ . . . μὲν . . . δ'; point/counterpoint. ἀλλά indicates that the μέν-clause is correcting an assumption (i.e., that what was just established is the end of his argument), while the δέ-clause provides the new step.
71. Pres. pass. ptc. nom. neut. sg., ὁμολογέω, (pass.) *be granted, conceded*; supp. (φαίνεται) (cf. S §2143; CGCG §52.10): "Now perhaps to say that happiness is the highest good turns out to be granted [i.e., we are stating the obvious]."
72. Pres. pass. indic. 3 sg., ποθέω, (pass.) *be desired*.
73. Compar., ἐναργής, -ές, *clearer, more distinct*; as adv.
74. Subjective inf. (S §1984; CGCG §51.10): "It is desired still *to be said* [by us] more clearly what it [happiness] is."
75. Adv., *perhaps*; underscored by the particle δή. See n. 1.
76. Pres. mid. opt. 3 sg., γίγνομαι, *be*; fourth-class, or potential, condition (cf. S §2329; CGCG §49.8).
77. Aor. pass. opt. 3 sg., λαμβάνω, (pass.) *be taken hold of, grasped*.
78. ὥσπερ . . . οὕτω . . . καί, *as . . . so also*.
79. αὐλητής, -οῦ, ὁ, *flute player*.
80. ἀγαλματοποιός, -οῦ, ὁ, *sculptor*.
81. τεχνίτης, -ου, ὁ, *craftsman*.
82. Crasis: τἀγαθὸν = τὸ ἀγαθόν, "goodness."
83. The article substantivizes εὖ: *wellness, happiness*.
84. Aor. act. opt. 3 sg., δοκέω, *seem, appear*; potential. See n. 34.
85. Postpositive partic.: "expresses exclusive limitation—περ limits the applicability of an utterance's content to exactly and only the word (group) it follows" (CGCG §59.55).
86. Adv. used at the beginning of a question that contains two alternative propositions, the latter of which is marked by ἤ.
87. τέκτων, -ονος, ὁ, *carpenter*.
88. σκυτεύς, -έως, ὁ, *shoemaker*.
89. ἀργός, -ή, -όν, *idle, lazy*; i.e., without ἔργον or πρᾶξις.
90. καθάπερ . . . οὕτω καί, *just as . . . so too*.
91. παρὰ πάντα ταῦτα, (compar.) "over and above all these [body members]" (cf. S §1692.3.c).
92. Aor. act. opt. 3 sg., τίθημι, *assign*; potential. See n. 34.
93. Partic. combination, *What precisely, then?*: "transition to more to-the-point, crucial or relevant information" (οὖν) that "the speaker considers (and invites the addressee to consider) . . . as evident, clear, or precise" (δή) (CGCG §§59.34; 59.44).
94. φυτόν, -οῦ, τό, *plant*.
95. τὸ ἴδιον = τὸ ἴδιον ἔργον, "the particular function [of human beings]."
96. Verbal adj. from ἀφορίζω, impers. (act.) constr. (see n. 57). "It is necessary [for us] to set aside life that concerns nourishment and growth."
97. Postpositive partic., *it seems, then, so*: "indicates that the speaker, in view of the preceding context, cannot but make the contribution he/she is making" (CGCG §59.42).
98. θρεπτικός, -ή, -όν, *of nourishment*.
99. αὐξητικός, -ή, -όν, *of growth*.
100. Pres. mid. ptc. nom. fem. sg., ἕπτομαι, (in sequence) *follow*; periphrastic.
101. αἰσθητικός, -ή, -όν, *sense-perceptible*.
102. ἵππος, -ου, ὁ, *horse*.
103. βοῦς, βοῦ, ὁ, *ox*.
104. ζῷον, -ου, τό, *animal*.
105. Pres. pass. indic. 3 sg., λείπω, (pass.) *be left, remain*.
106. τὸ μέν . . . τὸ δέ, *the one part . . . the other part*.
107. ἐπιπειθής, -ές, *obedient*.
108. Pres. mid. ptc. nom. neut. sg., διανοέω, (mid. with λόγῳ) *exercise reason*; circ. (cf. S §2086; CGCG §52.39).
109. Adv., *in a twofold manner*.
110. ἐνέργεια, -ας, ἡ, *activity, actuality* (in contrast to potentiality).
111. Verbal adj. of τίθημι, impers. (act.) construction (see n. 57): "Since this [i.e., rational life] of which we are speaking [ταύτης λεγομένης; gen. absol.] is twofold, it is necessary [for us] to postulate that we are speaking about the one that concerns active exercise of the rational faculty."
112. Compar. adv., κύριος, -η, -ον, *more authoritative, gloss*.

ἔργον ἀνθρώπου ψυχῆς ἐνέργεια κατὰ λόγον ἢ μὴ ἄνευ[113] λόγου, τὸ δ' αὐτό φαμεν ἔργον εἶναι τῷ γένει[114] τοῦδε καὶ τοῦδε σπουδαίου[115] (ὥσπερ κιθαριστοῦ[116] καὶ σπουδαίου κιθαριστοῦ, καὶ ἁπλῶς[117] δὴ τοῦτ' ἐπὶ πάντων) προστιθεμένης[118] τῆς κατ' ἀρετὴν ὑπεροχῆς πρὸς τὸ ἔργον (κιθαριστοῦ μὲν γὰρ τὸ κιθαρίζειν,[119] σπουδαίου δὲ τὸ[120] εὖ)· εἰ δὴ οὕτως, ἀνθρώπου[121] δὲ τίθεμεν ἔργον ζωήν τινα, ταύτην δὲ ψυχῆς ἐνέργειαν καὶ πράξεις μετὰ λόγου, σπουδαίου δ' ἀνδρὸς εὖ ταῦτα καὶ καλῶς, ἕκαστον δ' εὖ κατὰ οἰκείαν[122] ἀρετὴν ἀποτελεῖται.[123] εἰ δὴ οὕτω,[124] τὸ ἀνθρώπινον[125] ἀγαθὸν ψυχῆς ἐνέργεια γίνεται κατ' ἀρετήν, εἰ δὲ πλείους αἱ ἀρεταί, κατὰ τὴν ἀρίστην καὶ τελειοτάτην. ἔτι δ' ἐν βίῳ τελείῳ· μία γὰρ χελιδὼν[126] ἔαρ[127] οὐ ποιεῖ, οὐδὲ μία ἡμέρα· οὕτω δὲ οὐδὲ μακάριον[128] καὶ εὐδαίμονα[129] μία ἡμέρα οὐδ' ὀλίγος χρόνος.

113. Prep. with gen., *without, apart from*.
114. γένος, -ους, τό, *class, kind*.
115. σπουδαῖος, -α, -ον, *good, excellent*.
116. κιθαριστής, -οῦ, ὁ, *cithara player*.
117. Adv., *generally*; underscored by the particle δή. See n. 1.
118. Gen. absol.: προστιθεμένης τῆς κατ' ἀρετὴν ὑπεροχῆς, "the surplus in virtue [of the latter = τοῦδε σπουδαίου] being added to the function [πρὸς τὸ ἔργον]."
119. Pres. act. inf., κιθαρίζω, *play the cithara*; art. inf. as subject (cf. S §2031; CGCG §51.39).
120. τό = τὸ κιθαρίζειν.
121. Hyperbaton for emphasis (cf. CGCG 60.18): "And if we assign a certain form of life as the function of *human beings*..."
122. οἰκεῖος, -α, -ον, *proper* (to a thing).
123. Pres. mid. indic. 3 sg., ἀποτελέω, *bring to completion*.
124. Anaphora: the protasis is repeated for emphasis and to underscore the apodosis (cf. S §3010). "*If* this is so . . . *if* this is so, then the good of humankind is the active exercise of the soul in accordance with virtue."
125. ἀνθρώπινος, -η, -ον, *human*.
126. χελιδών, -όνος, ὁ, *swallow*.
127. ἔαρ, ἔαρος, τό, *spring*.
128. μακάριος, -α, -ον, *happy, blessed*. The term is derived from μάκαρ, an adjective that (in Greek mythology) is applied to the gods and to those humans who are admitted to the Isles of the Blessed.
129. εὐδαίμων, -ον, *happy, blessed*.

NOTES

1097b1. ἡ εὐδαιμονία. The term is most often rendered "happiness," though some prefer alternative translations (e.g., "success"; Hutchinson 1995, 200) or transliteration (Reeve 2014). According to Aristotle, εὐδαιμονία is both the "final" end (τέλειος; that is, that which is chosen for its own sake and never for the sake of anything else) and "self-sufficient" (αὔταρκες; that is, that which lacks nothing in addition). Thus it is *the* end (τέλος)—the τέλος of the τέλος, as it were—at which all actions aim (*Eth. nic.* 1097b20), neither the maximization of pleasure (1095b16–17) nor the accumulation of honor (1095b22–23) but the life of contemplation (1095b19); that is, the state in which the gods exist (1178b8–23; cf. Aristotle, *Metaph.* 1072b26–28). Aristotle distinguishes, however, between theoretical wisdom, which is the virtue of νοῦς and associated with εὐδαιμονία, and practical wisdom, which is the virtue of the human compound of body and soul and is associated with "the second-best kind of *eudaimonia*" (Reeve 2014, 32). In fact, it is this second-best kind of εὐδαιμονία that governs most of human life.

1097b25. τὸ ἔργον τοῦ ἀνθρώπου. The "human function" must reside in an action that is distinct to human beings. It cannot be "nutritional" life (θρεπτική), since even plants are nourished and grow. Nor can it be "perceptual" life (αἰσθητική), since animals also share in sense-perception. It must therefore be "practical" life (πρακτική), which is marked by an active exercising (ἐνέργεια) of the ψυχή in accordance with reason (1098a7).

1098a18. ἐν βίῳ τελείῳ. The exercise of reason toward virtuous ends requires ongoing practice. Cf. *Eth. nic.* 1103a34–103b2: "We learn an art or craft by doing the things that we shall have to do when we have learnt it: for instance, men become builders by building houses, harpers by playing on the harp. Similarly we become just by doing just acts, temperate by doing temperate acts, brave by doing brave acts" (Rackham 1926, 73).

7.2.2

On Household Management

Politics 1253b1–32, 1254a9–24, 1254b3–24, 1260a8–33

1253b1Ἐπεὶ δὲ φανερὸν¹ ἐξ ὧν μορίων² ἡ πόλις συνέστηκεν,³ ἀναγκαῖον⁴ πρῶτον περὶ οἰκονομίας⁵ εἰπεῖν· πᾶσα γὰρ σύγκειται⁶ πόλις ἐξ οἰκιῶν. οἰκονομίας δὲ μέρη⁷ ἐξ ὧν πάλιν⁸ οἰκία συνέστηκεν· οἰκία δὲ τέλειος⁹ ἐκ δούλων καὶ ἐλευθέρων.¹⁰ ἐπεὶ δ' ἐν τοῖς ἐλαχίστοις πρῶτον ἕκαστον ζητητέον,¹¹ πρῶτα δὲ καὶ ἐλάχιστα μέρη οἰκίας δεσπότης¹² καὶ δοῦλος, καὶ πόσις¹³ καὶ ἄλοχος,¹⁴ καὶ πατὴρ καὶ τέκνα, περὶ τριῶν ἂν τούτων σκεπτέον¹⁵ εἴη τί ἕκαστον καὶ ποῖον δεῖ εἶναι, ταῦτα δ' ἐστὶ δεσποτικὴ¹⁶ καὶ γαμικὴ¹⁷ (ἀνώνυμον¹⁸ γὰρ ἡ γυναικὸς καὶ ἀνδὸς σύζευξις¹⁹) καὶ τρίτον τεκνοποιητική²⁰ (καὶ γὰρ αὕτη οὐκ ὠνόμασται²¹ ἰδίῳ ὀνόματι)· ἔστωσαν δὴ²² αὗται τρεῖς ἃς εἴπομεν. ἔστι δὲ τι μέρος²³ ὃ δοκεῖ²⁴ τοῖς μὲν²⁵ εἶναι οἰκονομία τοῖς δὲ μέγιστον

---

1. φανερός, -ά, -όν, *clear, evident.*
2. μόριον, -ου, τό, *part.* The noun has been incorporated into the relative clause (cf. S §2536; *CGCG* §50.15): "Since *the parts*, of which the city is composed, are clear."
3. Aor. act. indic. 3 sg., συνίστημι (with ἔκ τινος), *be made up of something.*
4. ἀναγκαῖος, -α, -ον, (quasi-impers.) *it is necessary*; with acc. and inf.
5. οἰκονομία, -ας, ἡ, *household management.*
6. Pres. mid. indic. 3 sg., σύγκειμαι (with ἔκ τινος), *be made up of, composed of.*
7. μέρος, -ους, τό, *part.*
8. Adv., *in turn.*
9. τέλειος, -α, -ον, *perfect, complete.*
10. ἐλεύθερος, -α, -ον, (subst.) *free person.*
11. Verbal adj. from ζητέω, impers. (act.) constr. (cf. S §2152; *CGCG* §37.3): "Each thing is first *to be investigated* [by us] in its smallest parts [ἐν τοῖς ἐλαχίστοις]," or "We must investigate each thing in its smallest parts."
12. δεσπότης, -ου, ὁ, *master.*
13. πόσις, -ιος, ὁ, *husband.*
14. ἄλοχος, -ου, ἡ, *wife.*
15. Verbal adj. from σκέπτομαι; impers. (act.) constr. (with potential opt.): "And concerning these three *we ought to investigate* what each is [τί ἕκαστον] and what sort it ought to be [ποῖον δεῖ εἶναι]."
16. δεσποτικός, -ή, -όν, (with an implied τεχνή) *art of mastery.*
17. γαμικός, -ή, -όν, (with an implied τεχνή) *art of marriage.*
18. ἀνώνυμος, -ον, *without a name, unspecified.* That is, he applies γαμική, which properly concerns the marriage ceremony, to the marital relationship.
19. σύζευξις, -εως, ἡ, *joining together, union.*
20. τεκνοποιητικός, -ή, -όν, (with an implied τεχνή) *art of child-rearing.*
21. Pf. pass. indic. 3 sg., ὀνομάζω, (pass.) *be named, designated.*
22. Postpositive partic., *now, then*: "indicates that the speaker considers (and invites the addressee to consider) the text segment or word (group) which it modifies as evident, clear, or precise" (*CGCG* §59.44).
23. μέρος, -ους, τό, *part.*
24. Pres. act. indic. 3 sg., δοκέω, *seem*; with dat. and inf.
25. τοῖς μέν ... τοῖς δέ, *to some ... to others.*

μέρος αὐτῆς, ὅπως²⁶ δ' ἔχει, θεωρητέον.²⁷ λέγω δὲ περὶ τῆς καλουμένης χρηματιστικῆς.²⁸

Πρῶτον δὲ περὶ δεσπότου καὶ δούλου εἴπωμεν, ἵνα τά τε πρὸς τὴν ἀναγκαίαν χρείαν²⁹ ἴδωμεν, κἂν³⁰ εἴ τι πρὸς τὸ εἰδέναι περὶ αὐτῶν δυναίμεθα³¹ λαβεῖν βέλτιον τῶν νῦν ὑπολαμβανομένων.³² τοῖς μὲν³³ γὰρ δοκεῖ ἐπιστήμη³⁴ τέ τις εἶναι ἡ δεσποτεία,³⁵ καὶ ἡ αὐτὴ οἰκονομία καὶ δεσποτεία καὶ πολιτικὴ³⁶ καὶ βασιλική,³⁷ καθάπερ εἴπομεν ἀρχόμενοι·³⁸ τοῖς δὲ παρὰ φύσιν³⁹ τὸ δεσπόζειν,⁴⁰ νόμῳ γὰρ τὸν μὲν δοῦλον εἶναι τὸν δ' ἐλεύθερον, φύσει δ' οὐθὲν διαφέρειν,⁴¹ διόπερ οὐδὲ δίκαιον,⁴² βίαιον⁴³ γάρ.

Ἐπεὶ οὖν ἡ κτῆσις⁴⁴ μέρος τῆς οἰκίας ἐστὶ καὶ ἡ κτητικὴ⁴⁵ μέρος τῆς οἰκονομίας (ἄνευ⁴⁶ γὰρ τῶν ἀναγκαίων ἀδύνατον καὶ ζῆν καὶ εὖ⁴⁷ ζῆν), ὥσπερ⁴⁸ δὲ ταῖς ὡρισμέναις τέχναις⁴⁹ ἀναγκαῖον ἂν εἴη⁵⁰ ὑπάρχειν τὰ οἰκεῖα⁵¹ ὄργανα⁵² εἰ μέλλει ἀποτελεσθήσεσθαι⁵³ τὸ ἔργον, οὕτω καὶ τῷ οἰκονομικῷ,⁵⁴ τῶν δ' ὀργάνων τὰ μὲν⁵⁵ ἄψυχα τὰ δ' ἔμψυχα (οἷον⁵⁶ τῷ κυβερνήτῃ⁵⁷ ὁ μὲν οἴαξ⁵⁸ ἄψυχον ὁ δὲ πρωρεὺς⁵⁹ ἔμψυχον, ὁ γὰρ ὑπηρέτης⁶⁰ ἐν ὀργάνου εἴδει⁶¹ ταῖς τέχναις ἐστίν), οὕτω καὶ τὸ κτῆμα⁶² ὄργανον πρὸς ζωήν ἐστι, καὶ ἡ κτῆσις πλῆθος⁶³ ὀργάνων ἐστί, ¹²⁵³ᵇ³²καὶ ὁ δοῦλος κτῆμά τι ἔμψυχον....

¹²⁵⁴ᵃ⁹Τὸ δὲ κτῆμα λέγεται ὥσπερ καὶ τὸ μόριον· τὸ γὰρ μόριον οὐ μόνον⁶⁴ ἄλλου ἐστὶ μόριον, ἀλλὰ καὶ ἁπλῶς⁶⁵ ἄλλου, ὁμοίως δὲ καὶ τὸ κτῆμα. διὸ ὁ μὲν δεσπότης τοῦ δούλου δεσπότης μόνον, ἐκείνου δ' οὐκ

26. Indir. quest.: "and how that is."
27. Verbal adj. from θεωρέω, impers. (act.) constr., "It is necessary [for us] to observe." See n. 11.
28. χρηματιστικός, -ή, -όν, (with an implied τεχνή) *art of making money.*
29. χρεία, -ας, ἡ, *use, utility.*
30. "κἂν εἰ is often used for the simple καὶ εἰ (2372) and without regard to the mood of the following verbs; sometimes there is no verb in the apodosis to which the ἄν may be referred" (S §1766.b).
31. Pres. mid. opt. 1 pl., δύναμαι. The apodosis is omitted (except for ἄν) but is easily supplied from context (cf. S §2351): "And [implied apodosis = we may do so; i.e., speak about the relation of master and slave] in the hope that, with respect to the knowledge of these [πρὸς τὸ εἰδέναι περὶ αὐτῶν], we might receive something better than our present considerations." Here εἰ is used to set forth the motive (i.e., "in the hope that") for the implied action of the apodosis (cf. S §2354; *CGCG* §49.25).
32. Pres. pass. ptc. gen. neut. pl., ὑπολαμβάνω, (pass.) *be considered*; gen. of compar.
33. τοῖς μέν... τοῖς δέ, *to some... to others.*
34. ἐπιστήμη, -ης, ἡ, *knowledge, science.*
35. δεσποτεία, -ας, ἡ, *mastership.*
36. πολιτικός, -ή, -όν, (with an implied τεχνή) *statemanship.*
37. βασιλικός, -ή, -όν, (with an implied τεχνή) *monarchy.*
38. Pres. mid. ptc. nom. masc. pl., ἄρχω, (mid.) *begin*; circ.
39. φύσις, -εως, ἡ, *nature*; παρὰ φύσιν, "contrary to nature."
40. Pres. act. inf., δεσπόζω, *act as master* (of another); art. inf. as subject (cf. BDF §399; S §2031; *CGCG* §51.39).
41. Pres. act. inf., διαφέρω, *differ.*
42. δίκαιος, -α, -ον, (quasi-impers. with οὐδέ) *it is unjust.*
43. βίαιος, -α, -ον, (quasi-impers.) *it is based on force.*

44. κτῆσις, -εως, ἡ, *property.*
45. κτητικός, -ή, -όν, (with an implied τεχνή) *art of acquiring property.*
46. Prep. with gen., *without, apart from.*
47. Adv., *well.*
48. ὥσπερ... οὕτω καί, *just as... so also.*
49. τέχνη, -ης, ἡ, *art, craft*; ταῖς ὡρισμέναις τέχναις, "for the defined arts."
50. Mixed condition: μέλλω + fut. indic. in protasis, ἄν with opt. in the apodosis (cf. S §2356). "And just as for the defined arts it would be necessary for the suitable instruments to exist if their work is to be accomplished..."
51. οἰκεῖος, -α, -ον, *proper, suitable.*
52. ὄργανον, -ου, τό, *instrument, tool.*
53. Fut. pass. inf., ἀποτελέω, *be brought to completion.*
54. οἰκονομικός, -ή, -όν, (subst.) *manager of the household.*
55. τὰ μὲν ἄψυχα τὰ δ' ἔμψυχα, *some are without soul, others are ensouled.* The μέν... δέ construction explicates the new theme (τῶν ὀργάνων).
56. Adv. acc., *for example.*
57. κυβερνήτης, -ου, ὁ, *helmsman, pilot.*
58. οἴαξ, -ακος, ὁ, *rudder.*
59. πρωρεύς, -έως, ὁ, *officer of the prow* (copilot).
60. ὑπηρέτης, -ου, ὁ, *assistant.*
61. εἶδος, -ους, τό, *class, kind*; ἐν ὀργάνου εἴδει, "in the class of tools."
62. κτῆμα, -ατος, τό, *property.*
63. πλῆθος, -ους, τό, *sum.*
64. οὐ μόνον... ἀλλὰ καί, *not only... but also.*
65. Adv., *simply, absolutely.*

ἐστιν· ὁ δὲ δοῦλος οὐ μόνον δεσπότου δοῦλός ἐστιν, ἀλλὰ καὶ ὅλως⁶⁶ ἐκείνου.

Τίς μὲν οὖν⁶⁷ ἡ φύσις τοῦ δούλου καὶ τίς ἡ δύναμις, ἐκ τούτων δῆλον.⁶⁸ ὁ γὰρ μὴ αὑτοῦ⁶⁹ φύσει ἀλλ' ἄλλου ἄνθρωπος ὤν, οὗτος φύσει δοῦλός ἐστιν, ἄλλου δ' ἐστὶν ἄνθρωπος ὃς ἂν κτῆμα ᾖ⁷⁰ ἄνθρωπος ὤν, κτῆμα δὲ ὄργανον πρακτικὸν⁷¹ καὶ χωριστόν.⁷² πότερον⁷³ δ' ἐστί τις φύσει τοιοῦτος ἢ οὔ, καὶ πότερον βέλτιον καὶ δίκαιόν τινι δουλεύειν ἢ οὔ, ἀλλὰ πᾶσα δουλεία παρὰ φύσιν ἐστί, μετὰ ταῦτα σκεπτέον.⁷⁴ οὐ χαλεπὸν⁷⁵ δὲ καὶ τῷ λόγῳ θεωρῆσαι⁷⁶ καὶ ἐκ τῶν γινομένων καταμαθεῖν.⁷⁷ τὸ γὰρ ἄρχειν καὶ ἄρχεσθαι οὐ μόνον τῶν ἀναγκαίων ἀλλὰ καὶ τῶν συμφερόντων⁷⁸ ἐστί, καὶ εὐθὺς ἐκ γενετῆς⁷⁹ ἔνια⁸⁰ διέστηκε⁸¹ τὰ μὲν⁸² **1254a24**ἐπὶ τὸ ἄρχεσθαι τὰ δ' ἐπὶ τὸ ἄρχειν. . . .

1254b3ἔστι δ' οὖν,⁸³ ὥσπερ λέγομεν, πρῶτον ἐν ζῴῳ θεωρῆσαι καὶ δεσποτικὴν ἀρχὴν καὶ πολιτικήν· ἡ μὲν⁸⁴ γὰρ ψυχὴ τοῦ σώματος ἄρχει δεσποτικὴν ἀρχήν,⁸⁵ ὁ δὲ νοῦς τῆς ὀρέξεως⁸⁶ πολιτικὴν καὶ βασιλικήν· ἐν οἷς φανερόν ἐστιν ὅτι κατὰ φύσιν καὶ συμφερον τὸ ἄρχεσθαι τῷ σώματι ὑπὸ τῆς ψυχῆς καὶ παθητικῷ⁸⁷ μορίῳ ὑπὸ τοῦ νοῦ καὶ τοῦ μορίου τοῦ λόγον ἔχοντος, τὸ δ' ἐξ ἴσου ἢ ἀνάπαλιν⁸⁸ βλαβερὸν⁸⁹ πᾶσιν. πάλιν ἐν ἀνθρώπῳ καὶ τοῖς ἄλλοις ζῳοις ὡσαύτως· τὰ μὲν γὰρ ἥμερα⁹⁰ τῶν ἀγρίων⁹¹ βελτίω τὴν φύσιν,⁹² τούτοις δὲ πᾶσι βέλτιον ἄρχεσθαι ὑπ' ἀνθρώπου, τυγχάνει⁹³ γὰρ σωτηρίας οὕτως. ἔτι δὲ⁹⁴ τὸ ἄρρεν⁹⁵ πρὸς τὸ θῆλυ⁹⁶ φύσει τὸ μὲν κρεῖττον τὸ δὲ χεῖρον, τὸ μὲν ἄρχον τὸ δ' ἀρχόμενον. τὸν αὐτὸν δὲ τρόπον⁹⁷ ἀναγκαῖον εἶναι

66. Adv., *wholly, entirely*.
67. Partic. combination: "a transition to a more to-the-point, relevant text segment (οὖν) [that] occurs in two stages (μέν . . . δέ), with the relevant new step presented in the segment" (*CGCG* §59.73).
68. δῆλος, -η, -ον, (quasi-impers.) *it is evident*. The subject consists of the preceding indirect questions: "As to what constitutes the nature of the slave [Τίς . . . ἡ φύσις τοῦ δούλου], and as to what constitutes his faculty [τίς ἡ δύναμις], it is clear from these considerations."
69. αὑτοῦ = ἑαυτοῦ.
70. Pres. subj. of εἰμί in a conditional rel. clause (cf. BDF §380; S §2565; *CGCG* §50.20): "If being a human, he is an article of property."
71. πρακτικός, -ή, -όν, *fit/suitable for action*.
72. χωριστός, -ή, -όν, *separable*.
73. Indir. alt. quest.: πότερον . . . ἤ, *whether X . . . or Y*: "whether someone is by nature of this sort, or not, and whether it is better and just for anyone to be enslaved, or not." The conjuction ἀλλά introduces a correction: "[or whether] by contrast all slavery is contrary to nature."
74. Verbal adj. from σκέπτομαι, impers. (act.) constr. (see n. 11): "It is necessary [for us] to consider [these questions] next [μετὰ ταῦτα, lit., "after these"]."
75. χαλεπός, -ή, -όν, (quasi-impers.) *it is difficult*; with (acc. and) inf.
76. Aor. act. inf., θεωρέω, *observe*; with τῷ λόγῳ, "discern by logical inference" (i.e., deduction).
77. Aor. act. inf., καταμανθάνω, *learn, inquire knowledge of*; with ἐκ τῶν γινομένων, "learn from what has occurred" (i.e., induction).
78. Compar., σύμφορος, -ον, *more useful*.

79. γενετή, -ῆς, ἡ, *birth*; ἐκ γενετῆς, "from the hour of birth."
80. ἔνιος, -α, -ον, *some*.
81. Aor. act. indic. 3 sg., διίστημι, (intrans.) *be set apart, marked out*.
82. τὰ μέν . . . τὰ δέ, *some things . . . other things*.
83. Partic. combination, *anyhow, but to resume*: "The preceding information is abandoned (δέ) in favor of a point which is considered more relevant (οὖν) at the particular juncture" (*CGCG* §59.64).
84. μέν . . . δέ; point/counterpoint.
85. Cognate acc.: "For the soul rules the body *despotically*."
86. Gen. comp. of an implied ἄρχει: "But the mind rules desire politically [πολιτικήν = πολιτικὴν ἀρχήν] and monarchically [βασιλικήν = βασιλικὴν ἀρχήν]."
87. παθητικός, -ή, -όν, *emotional*; dat. comp. of συμφέρον (ἐστιν): "It is beneficial *for the emotional part* to be ruled by the mind, the part that possesses reason."
88. Adv., *contrariwise*; noun phrase τὸ δ' ἐξ ἴσου ἢ ἀνάπαλιν: "But being on equal footing or in the contrary positions is harmful in all circumstances."
89. βλαβερός, -ά, -όν, *harmful*.
90. ἥμερος, -α, -ον, *domesticated*.
91. ἄγριος, -α, -ον, *wild*; gen. of compar.
92. Acc. of respect.
93. Pres. act. indic. 3 sg., τυγχάνω, *reach, attain*; with gen.
94. ἔτι δέ, *moreover*.
95. ἄρρην, -εν, *male*.
96. θῆλυς, -εῖα, -υ, *female*.
97. Acc. of manner, "in the same way."

καὶ ἐπὶ πάντων ἀνθρώπων· ὅσοι μὲν οὖν[98] τοσοῦτον[99] διεστᾶσιν ὅσον ψυχὴ σώματος καὶ ἄνθρωπος θηρίου (διάκεινται[100] δὲ τοῦτον τὸν τρόπον ὅσων ἐστὶν ἔργον ἡ τοῦ σώματος χρῆσις[101] καὶ τοῦτ᾽ ἔστ᾽ ἀπ᾽ αὐτῶν βέλτιστον), οὗτοι μέν εἰσι φύσει δοῦλοι, οἷς βέλτιόν ἐστιν ἄρχεσθαι ταύτην τὴν ἀρχήν, εἴπερ[102] καὶ τοῖς εἰρημένοις. ἔστι γὰρ φύσει δοῦλος ὁ δυνάμενος ἄλλου εἶναι (διὸ καὶ ἄλλου ἐστίν) καὶ ὁ κοινωνῶν[103] λόγου τοσοῦτον ὅσον αἰσθάνεσθαι[104] ἀλλὰ μὴ ἔχειν· τὰ γὰρ ἄλλα ζῷα **1254b24**οὐ λόγῳ αἰσθανόμενα ἀλλὰ παθήμασιν[105] ὑπηρετεῖ.[106] . . .

1260a8ὥστε φύσει πλείω τὰ ἄρχοντα καὶ ἀρχόμενα. ἄλλον γὰρ τρόπον τὸ ἐλεύθερον τοῦ δούλου ἄρχει καὶ τὸ ἄρρεν τοῦ θήλεος καὶ ἀνὴρ παιδός. καὶ πᾶσιν ἐνυπάρχει[107] μὲν τὰ μόρια τῆς ψυχῆς, ἀλλ᾽ ἐνυπάρχει διαφερόντως·[108] ὁ μὲν[109] γὰρ δοῦλος ὅλως οὐκ ἔχει τὸ βουλευτικόν,[110] τὸ δὲ θῆλυ ἔχει μέν,[111] ἀλλ᾽ ἄκυρον,[112] ὁ δὲ παῖς ἔχει μέν, ἀλλ᾽ ἀτελές.[113] διὸ τὸν μὲν[114] ἄρχοντα τελέαν ἔχειν δεῖ τὴν διανοητικὴν[115] ἀρετὴν (τὸ γὰρ ἔργον ἐστὶν ἁπλῶς τοῦ ἀρχιτέκτονος,[116] ὁ δὲ λόγος ἀρχιτέκτων), τῶν δ᾽ ἄλλων ἕκαστον ὅσον ἐπιβάλλει[117] αὐτοῖς. ὁμοίως τοίνυν[118] ἀναγκαίως ἔχειν καὶ περὶ τὰς ἠθικὰς[119] ἀρετὰς ὑποληπτέον,[120] δεῖν μὲν[121] μετέχειν πάντας, ἀλλ᾽ οὐ τὸν αὐτὸν τρόπον, ἀλλ᾽ ὅσον ἑκάστῳ πρὸς τὸ αὑτοῦ ἔργον. ὥστε φανερὸν ὅτι ἐστὶν ἠθικὴ ἀρετὴ τῶν εἰρημένων πάντων, καὶ οὐκ ἡ αὐτὴ σωφροσύνη[122] γυναικὸς καὶ ἀνδρὸς οὐδ᾽ ἀνδρεία[123] καὶ δικαιοσύνη, καθάπερ ᾤετ᾽[124] Σωκράτης,[125] ἀλλ᾽ ἡ μὲν ἀρχικὴ[126] ἀνδρεία, ἡ δ᾽ ὑπηρετική,[127] ὁμοίως δ᾽ ἔχει καὶ περὶ τὰς ἄλλας. δῆλον δὲ τοῦτο καὶ κατὰ μέρος[128] μᾶλλον ἐπισκοποῦσιν·[129] καθόλου[130] γὰρ οἱ λέγοντες ἐξαπατῶσιν[131] ἑαυτοὺς ὅτι τὸ εὖ ἔχειν τὴν

---

98. The μέν-clause is resumed with οὗτοι μέν (cf. Denniston 1966, 384): "*However many* therefore differ to so great an extent as the soul does from the body and the human being from the animal . . . *these* are by nature slaves."

99. τοσοῦτον . . . ὅσον, *as much as*.

100. Pres. mid. indic. 3 pl., διάκειμαι, *exist in a certain state*. "And they exist in this manner, however many whose function is the use of the body and from whom this is the best that comes forth."

101. χρῆσις, -εως, ἡ, *use*.

102. Postpositive partic.: "limits the applicability of an utterance's content to exactly and only the word (group) it follows" (*CGCG* §59.55); with adv. καί, "indeed precisely insofar as [it is better] for the things we have previously mentioned."

103. Pres. act. ptc. nom. masc. sg., κοινωνόω, *participate in*; with gen.; attrib.

104. Pres. mid. inf., αἰσθάνομαι, *perceive*; comp. of ὅσον (cf. S §2003): "insofar as to perceive [reason] but not possess it."

105. πάθημα, -ατος, τό, (pl.) *emotions, feelings*.

106. Pres. act. indic. 3 sg., ὑστερέω, *be subservient to*; with dat.

107. Pres. act. indic. 3 sg., ἐνυπάρχω, *exist in*; with dat.

108. Adv., *differently*.

109. μέν . . . δέ . . . δέ (cf. S §2907).

110. βουλευτικός, -ή, -όν, *deliberative*.

111. μέν . . . ἀλλά. The contrast is in the δέ-clause (cf. S §§2903, 2908), the force of which is to suggest that the point registered in the μέν-clause is basically irrelevant.

112. ἄκυρος, -ον, *lacking authority/importance*.

113. ἀτελής, -ές, *incomplete*.

114. μέν . . . δέ; point/counterpoint.

115. διανοητικός, -ή, -όν, *pertaining to intellect*.

116. ἀρχιτέκτων, -ονος, ὁ, *master craftsman*.

117. Pres. act. indic. 3 sg., ἐπιβάλλω, *belong to, fall to the share of*; with dat.

118. Postpositive partic.: "indicates a transition to a newly relevant, to-the-point text segment (νυν), and stresses the importance or relevance for the addressee of that new point (τοι)" (*CGCG* §59.39); with ὁμοίως, "so likewise."

119. ἠθικός, -ή, -όν, *moral*.

120. Verbal adj. of ὑπολαμβάνω, impers. (act.) constr.: "It is necessary [for us] to assume that the same holds true [ἀναγκαίως ἔχειν] as also concerns the moral virtues." See n. 11.

121. μέν . . . ἀλλά. The truth of the μέν-clause is granted, but the relevant point is that they do not all participate in the moral virtues in the same way—only insofar as is proper to their function.

122. σωφροσύνη, -ης, ἡ, *temperance*.

123. ἀνδρεία, -ας, ἡ, *courage, manliness*.

124. Impf. mid. indic. 3 sg., οἴομαι, *think, suppose*.

125. Σωκράτης, -ου, ὁ, *Socrates*.

126. ἀρχικός, -ή, -όν, *of/for rule*.

127. ὑπηρετικός, -ή, -όν, *subordinate*.

128. Distrib., μέρος, -ους, τό, "part by part"; i.e., in its details.

129. Pres. act. ptc. dat. masc. pl., ἐπισκοπέω, *inspect, observe*; circ. (cf. S §1497).

130. Adv., *on the whole, in general*.

131. Pres. act. indic. 3 pl., ἐξαπατάω, *mislead, deceive*.

ψυχὴν ἀρετὴ ἢ τὸ ὀρθοπραγεῖν[132] ἤ τι τῶν τοιούτων· πολὺ γὰρ ἄμεινον[133] λέγουσιν οἱ ἐξαριθμοῦντες[134] τὰς ἀρετάς, ὥσπερ Γοργίας,[135] τῶν οὕτως ὁριζομένων.[136] διὸ δεῖ, ὥσπερ ὁ ποιητὴς[137] εἴρηκε περὶ γυναικός, οὕτω νομίζειν[138] ἔχειν περὶ πάντων·

γυναικὶ κόσμον[139] ἡ σιγὴ[140] φέρει

ἀλλ' ἀνδρὶ οὐκέτι τοῦτο. ἐπεὶ δ' ὁ παῖς ἀτελής, δῆλον ὅτι τούτου μὲν[141] καὶ ἡ ἀρετὴ οὐκ αὐτοῦ πρὸς αὐτόν ἐστιν, ἀλλὰ πρὸς τὸν τέλειον καὶ τὸν ἡγούμενον. ὁμοίως δὲ καὶ δούλου πρὸς δεσπότην.

NOTES

1253b3. πᾶσα γὰρ σύγκειται πόλις ἐξ οἰκιῶν. Because humans are political animals, the οἶκος arises naturally (κατὰ φύσιν) and becomes the seed of the πόλις, a supra-οἶκος, as it were. The πόλις is "a partnership of families and of clans living well [ἡ τοῦ εὖ ζῆν κοινωνία καὶ ταῖς οἰκίαις καὶ τοῖς γένεσι], and its object is a full [τελείας] and independent [αὐτάρκους] life" (1280b33–34; Rackham 1932, 217). Since, moreover, the part (οἶκος) must share in the qualities of the whole (πόλις), the οἶκος is fundamentally a "moral institution," even the "moral basis" of the πόλις (Nagle 2006, 155; cf. Aristotle, *Eth. eud.* 1242a40–1242b1).

1253b7–8. πρῶτα δὲ καὶ ἐλάχιστα μέρη οἰκίας δεσπότης καὶ δοῦλος, καὶ πόσις καὶ ἄλοχος, καὶ πατὴρ καὶ τέκνα. In *Laws*, Plato lists seven pairs of asymmetrical relationships that concern "ruling and being ruled" (ἄρχειν καὶ ἄρχεσθαι) (690a–d; see 771e–824c for his discussion of household management). Aristotle focuses on three pairs: master and slave, husband and wife, and father and children. His tripartite division of the household becomes axiomatic for subsequent discussion and debate on household management (e.g., Josephus, *C. Ap.* 1.22; Philo, *Decal.* 165–167; Seneca, *Ep.* 94.1–2). Balch (1981, 34) Aristotle's treatment of the household "the most important parallel to the NT codes."

1253b15. Πρῶτον δὲ περὶ δεσπότου καὶ δούλου εἴπωμεν. Aristotle's discussion of slavery is both morally repulsive and logically convoluted. For example, if slaves are so κατὰ φύσιν, why use emancipation as a reward (1330a32–33)? Would this not run παρὰ φύσιν, and so to the detriment of all parties involved? In fact, "it would seem that even Aristotle was ultimately uneasy with his own theory, for he provided in his will that his own slaves be freed" (Smith 1991, 144). Be that as it may, the result of this unholy merger of "natural" slavery with Aristotelian teleology is a vast hierarchy of ontology within the human genus. Davis (1996, 23) says it well:

> The strong teleology that cuts across the classes seems to have been purchased at the price of the classes that it cuts across. It was needed to justify natural slavery, but in doing so it severs the species connection between natural slaves and their masters. The slave is a tool for a use set by the being who uses him. But this relation now serves

---

132. Pres. act. inf., ὀρθοπραγέω, *act rightly*; art. inf. as subject. See n. 40.
133. Irreg. compar. of ἀγαθός, -ή, -όν, as adv. with πολύ (degree), *much better*.
134. Pres. act. ptc. nom. masc. pl., ἐξαριθμέω, *enumerate*; attrib. (subst.).
135. Γοργίας, -ου, ὁ, *Gorgias* (famous Sophist).
136. Pres. mid. ptc. gen. masc. pl., ὁρίζω, *delineate, define*; attrib. (subst.); gen. of compar.
137. ποιητής, -οῦ, ὁ, *poet* (Sophocles; cf. *Aj.* 293).
138. Pres. act. inf., νομίζω, *think*; comp. of δεῖ, which introduces indir. disc.: "Therefore it is necessary [for us], as the poet spoke of woman, so to maintain [νομίζειν] concerning all these persons that they have [them = their respective virtues]."
139. κόσμος, -ου, ὁ, *honor, glory, credit*.
140. σιγή, -ῆς, ἡ, *silence*.
141. μέν . . . ἀλλά. The more relevant point is that the child's virtue (as long as the child remains unformed) is contingent on the virtue of the fully formed person, the ruler of the household. Likewise, Aristotle says, the enslaved person's virtue is πρὸς δεσπότην, "relative to the virtue of the master."

as a paradigm for all relations between lower and higher beings. What first emerged as an hierarchical principle within the whole, useful for defining the relations between classes, has now been used within a class, man, in such a way as to generate two new classes.

1254b13–14. ἔτι δὲ τὸ ἄρρεν πρὸς τὸ θῆλυ φύσει τὸ μὲν κρεῖττον τὸ δὲ χεῖρον, τὸ μὲν ἄρχον τὸ δ' ἀρχόμενον. A common assumption among the elite male authors of antiquity, to be sure. Cf. *Eth. nic.* 1160b32–34: "The relation of the husband to the wife seems to be in the nature of an aristocracy [ἀριστοκρατική]: the husband rules in virtue of fitness [κατ' ἀξίαν], and in matters that belong to a man's sphere; matters suited to a woman he hands over to his wife" (Rackham 1926, 493). His logic appears to be twofold. He maintains that first, since men are more rational than women, their rule is κατ' ἀξίαν. Second, however, since household management is divided into male and female functions, the husband is not to micromanage everything. To do so would be to rule "in violation of fitness" (παρὰ τὴν ἀξίαν; 1160b37). See further discussion in Nagle (2006, 165–67).

1260a31. γυναικὶ κόσμον ἡ σιγὴ φέρει. A citation of Sophocles, *Aj.* 293. Cf. 1 Cor. 14:34–36; 1 Tim. 2:11–12; Plutarch, *Conj. praec.* 32; Livy, *Hist.* 34.2.8–11. For an overview of the silencing of women in Greco-Roman antiquity, see Beard (2017).

7.2.3

On the Three Forms of Rhetoric

Rhetoric 1358a36–1358b32

1358a36Ἔστι δὲ τῆς ῥητορικῆς[1] εἴδη[2] τρία τὸν ἀριθμόν·[3] τοσοῦτοι γὰρ καὶ οἱ ἀκροαταὶ[4] τῶν λόγων ὑπάρχουσιν ὄντες. σύγκειται[5] μὲν[6] γὰρ ἐκ τριῶν ὁ λόγος, ἔκ τε[7] τοῦ λέγοντος καὶ περὶ οὗ λέγει καὶ πρὸς ὅν, **1358b1**καὶ τὸ τέλος[8] πρὸς τοῦτόν ἐστι, λέγω δὲ τὸν ἀκροατήν. ἀνάγκη[9] δὲ τὸν ἀκροατὴν ἢ θεωρὸν[10] εἶναι ἢ κριτήν,[11] κριτὴν δὲ ἢ τῶν γεγενημένων ἢ τῶν μελλόντων. ἔστι δ' ὁ μὲν[12] περὶ τῶν μελλόντων κρίνων οἷον[13] ἐκκλησιαστής,[14] ὁ δὲ περὶ τῶν γεγενημένων οἷον ὁ δικαστής,[15] ὁ δὲ περὶ τῆς δυνάμεως ὁ θεωρός·[16] ὥστ' ἐξ ἀνάγκης[17] ἂν εἴη[18] τρία γένη[19] τῶν λόγων τῶν ῥητορικῶν,[20] συμβουλευτικόν,[21] δικανικόν,[22] ἐπιδεικτικόν.[23]

Συμβουλῆς[24] δὲ τὸ μὲν[25] προτροπὴ[26] τὸ δὲ ἀποτροπή·[27] ἀεὶ[28] γὰρ καὶ οἱ ἰδίᾳ[29] συμβουλεύοντες[30] καὶ οἱ κοινῇ[31] δημηγοροῦντες[32] τούτων θάτερον[33]

1. ῥητορική, -ῆς, ἡ, *rhetoric*.
2. εἶδος, -ους, τό, *form*.
3. ἀριθμός, -οῦ, ὁ, *number*; acc. of respect.
4. ἀκροατής, -οῦ, ὁ, *hearer*.
5. Pres. pass. indic. 3 sg., σύγκειμαι, (pass.) *be composed of*.
6. μέν . . . δέ . . . δέ (cf. S §2907). The μέν-clause explains the previous assertion (γάρ), while the first δέ-clause explicates τὸν ἀκροατήν, and the second κριτήν.
7. The sequence explicates ἐκ τριῶν: τε (1) τοῦ λέγοντος (the speaker), καί (2) περὶ οὗ λέγει (the subject about which he speaks), καί (3) πρὸς ὅν (= τὸν ἀκροατήν, the hearer to whom he speaks).
8. τέλος, -ους, τό, *end* (goal).
9. Quasi-impers., ἀνάγκη, *it is necessary*; with acc. and inf.
10. θεωρός, -οῦ, ὁ, *spectator*.
11. κριτή, -οῦ, ὁ, *judge*.
12. ὁ μέν . . . ὁ δέ [κρίνων] . . . ὁ δέ [κρίνων]. See n. 6.
13. Adv. acc., *for example*.
14. ἐκκλησιαστής, -οῦ, ὁ, *member of the general assembly*.
15. δικαστής, -οῦ, ὁ, *dicast* (juror).
16. θεωρός, -οῦ, ὁ, *spectator*.
17. Idiom, ἐξ ἀνάγκης, *necessarily* (lit., "from necessity").
18. Pres. act. opt. 3 sg., εἰμί; potential (cf. BDF §385; S §1824; CGCG §34.13).
19. γένος, -ους, τό, *kind, type*.
20. ῥητορικός, -ή, -όν, *rhetorical*.
21. συμβουλευτικός, -ή, -όν, *deliberative*.
22. δικανικός, -ή, -όν, *forensic*.
23. ἐπιδεικτικός, -ή, -όν, *epideictic*.
24. συμβουλή, -ῆς, ἡ, *deliberation*.
25. τὸ μέν . . . τὸ δέ, *partly . . . partly* (cf. S §1111; CGCG §28.27).
26. προτροπή, -ῆς, ἡ, *exhortation*.
27. ἀποτροπή, -ῆς, ἡ, *dissuasion*.
28. Adv., *always*.
29. Adv., *privately*.
30. Pres. act. ptc. nom. masc. pl., συμβουλεύω, *give counsel*; attrib. (subst.).
31. Adv., *publicly*.
32. Pres. act. ptc. nom. masc. pl., δημηγορέω, *speak in the assembly*; attrib. (subst.).
33. Alt. form of ἕτερον; τούτων θάτερον, "one of these [συμβουλή or προτροπή] or the other."

ποιοῦσιν. δίκης³⁴ δὲ τὸ μὲν κατηγορία³⁵ τὸ δ᾽ ἀπολογία·³⁶ τούτων γὰρ ὁποτερονοῦν³⁷ ποιεῖν ἀνάγκη τοὺς ἀμφισβητοῦντας.³⁸ ἐπιδεικτικοῦ δὲ τὸ μὲν ἔπαινος³⁹ τὸ δὲ ψόγος.⁴⁰

Χρόνοι δὲ ἑκάστου τούτων εἰσὶ τῷ μὲν⁴¹ συμβουλεύοντι⁴² ὁ μέλλων⁴³ (περὶ γὰρ τῶν ἐσομένων συμβουλεύει ἢ προτρέπων⁴⁴ ἢ ἀποτρέπων⁴⁵), τῷ δὲ δικαζομένῳ⁴⁶ ὁ γενόμενος⁴⁷ (περὶ γὰρ τῶν πεπραγμένων⁴⁸ ἀεὶ ὁ μὲν⁴⁹ κατηγορεῖ⁵⁰ ὁ δὲ ἀπολογεῖται⁵¹), τῷ δ᾽ ἐπιδεικτικῷ κυριώτατος⁵² μὲν⁵³ ὁ παρών·⁵⁴ κατὰ γὰρ τὰ ὑπάρχοντα ἐπαινοῦσιν⁵⁵ ἢ ψέγουσι⁵⁶ πάντες,

προσχρῶνται⁵⁷ δὲ πολλάκις⁵⁸ καὶ τὰ γενόμενα ἀναμιμνήσκοντες⁵⁹ καὶ τὰ μέλλοντα προεικάζοντες.⁶⁰

Τέλος δὲ ἑκάστοις τούτων ἕτερόν ἐστι, καὶ τρισὶν οὖσι τρία,⁶¹ τῷ μὲν⁶² συμβουλεύοντι τὸ συμφέρον⁶³ καὶ βλαβερόν·⁶⁴ ὁ μὲν⁶⁵ γὰρ προτρέπων⁶⁶ ὡς βέλτιον συμβουλεύει, ὁ δὲ ἀποτρέπων⁶⁷ ὡς χεῖρον ἀποτρέπει, τὰ δ᾽ ἄλλα πρὸς τοῦτο συμπαραλαμβάνει,⁶⁸ ἢ δίκαιον ἢ ἄδικον, ἢ καλὸν ἢ αἰσχρόν· τοῖς δὲ δικαζομένοις τὸ δίκαιον καὶ τὸ ἄδικον, τὰ δ᾽ ἄλλα καὶ οὗτοι συμπαραλαμβάνουσι πρὸς ταῦτα· τοῖς δ᾽ ἐπαινοῦσι καὶ ψέγουσι τὸ καλὸν καὶ τὸ αἰσχρόν, τὰ δ᾽ ἄλλα καὶ οὗτοι πρὸς ταῦτα ἐπαναφέρουσιν.⁶⁹

NOTES

34. δίκη, -ης, ἡ, *forensic argumentation*.
35. κατηγορία, -ας, ἡ, *accusation*.
36. ἀπολογία, -ας, ἡ, *defense*.
37. ὁπότερος, -α, -ον, *either* (of the two).
38. Pres. act. ptc. acc. masc. pl., ἀμφισβητέω, *dispute back and forth*; attrib. (subst.); comp. of ἀνάγκη: "It is necessary *for litigants* [lit., "those who argue back and forth"] to do one of these or the other."
39. ἔπαινος, -ου, ὁ, *praise*.
40. ψόγος, -ου, ὁ, *blame*.
41. μέν … δέ … δέ; point/counterpoints. See n. 6.
42. Pres. act. ptc. dat. masc. sg., συμβουλεύω, *advise, counsel*; attrib. (subst.).
43. Subst.: "the future."
44. Pres. act. ptc. nom. masc. sg., προτρέπω, *exhort*; circ.
45. Pres. act. ptc. nom. masc. sg., ἀποτρέπω, *dissuade*; circ.
46. Pres. mid. ptc. dat. masc. sg., δικάζω, (mid.) *argue a case in the court, speak forensically*.
47. Subst.: "the past."
48. Pf. pass. ptc. gen. neut. pl., πράσσω (Att. πράττω), (pass.) *be done*; attrib. (subst.).
49. ὁ μέν … ὁ δέ, *the one … the other*.
50. Pres. act. indic. 3 sg., κατηγορέω, *accuse*.
51. Pres. mid. indic. 3 sg., ἀπολογέομαι, *defend*.
52. Superl., κύριος, -α, -ον, *most appropriate*.
53. μέν … δέ; point/counterpoint set explicates the second δέ-clause (cf. S §2908).
54. Pres. act. ptc. nom. masc. sg., πάρειμι, (subst.) "the present."
55. Pres. act. indic. 3 pl., ἐπαινέω, *praise*.
56. Pres. act. indic. 3 pl., ψέγω, *blame*.

1358a36. Ἔστι δὲ τῆς ῥητορικῆς εἴδη τρία τὸν ἀριθμόν. Aristotle's analytic description of rhetoric is, in part, a response to Socrates's argument in *Gorgias* that rhetoric cannot be considered an art (τέχνη) because it does not require a specific body of knowledge (Kennedy 1994, 53, 57). For

57. Pres. mid. indic. 3 pl., προσχράομαι, *use* (something else) *in addition*.
58. Adv., *often*.
59. Pres. act. ptc. nom. masc. pl., ἀναμιμνήσκω, *recall*; circ.
60. Pres. act. ptc. nom. masc. pl., προεικάζω, *conjecture beforehand*; circ.
61. The clause καὶ τρισὶν οὖσι τρία is compressed: "And for the three [kinds of rhetoric] that exist [τρισὶν οὖσι] there are three [ends; τρία = τρία τέλη]."
62. μέν … δέ … δέ; point/counterpoints. See n. 6.
63. Pres. act. ptc. nom. neut. sg., συμφέρω, *be beneficial*; attrib. (subst.).
64. βλαβερός, -ή, -όν, *harmful*.
65. μέν … δέ … δέ; point/counterpoints set in the μέν-clause (cf. S §2908).
66. Pres. act. ptc. nom. masc. sg., προτρέπω, *exhort*; attrib. (subst.).
67. Pres. act. ptc. nom. masc. sg., ἀποτρέπω, *dissuade*; attrib. (subst.).
68. Pres. act. indic. 3 sg., συμπαραλαμβάνω, *take along with, include as accessory*; thus: "He includes the rest—justice and injustice, honor and shame—as accessory to this end."
69. Pres. act. indic. 3 pl., ἐπαναφέρω, *refer*.

subsequent discussion of the various forms of rhetoric, see, for example, Quintilian, *Inst.* 3.4.

1358b 8–29. The three forms of rhetoric are subdivided and correspond to three different times, as the table below shows (adapted from Grimaldi 1980, 82).

In its developed form, classical rhetorical education was divided into five parts: invention (identification of the question or issue), arrangement (organization of the speech into parts), style (diction and composition), memory (memorization of the speech for oral performance), and delivery (voice modulation and bodily gestures) (Kennedy 1994, 4–6).

Kind (γένος)	Formality	Time (χρόνος)	Proximate τέλος	Ultimate τέλος
Deliberative (συμβουλευτικόν)	Exhortation and dissuasion	Future (ὁ μέλλων)	What is advantageous and harmful	The audience
Forensic (δικανικόν)	Accusation and defense	Past (ὁ γενόμενος)	Justice and injustice	The audience
Epideictic (ἐπιδεικτικόν)	Praise and blame	Present (ὁ παρών)	What is honorable and dishonorable	The audience

7.3

Epictetus

Epictetus (ca. 55–135 CE) is arguably the most important philosopher of the Hellenistic period. He was born to an enslaved woman in Hierapolis, Phrygia, and was himself enslaved to Epaphroditus, the administrative secretary of Nero. During the period of his enslavement, he began to study under the renowned Stoic philosopher Musonius Rufus. When Domitian banished the philosophers from Rome, Epictetus settled in Nicopolis, where he established a school. His student Flavius Arrian recorded and published his teachings in eight books of *Diatribai* (*Discourses*), four of which survive, and in the compendium *Encheiridion* (*Handbook*).

Epictetus's teachings have long been compared to the apostle Paul's. As Eastman notes, "No other Hellenistic philosopher has so frequently been associated with Paul himself. This association has a long lineage; there are three extant adaptations of Epictetus's *Encheiridion* for use by Christian monks, dating back to at least the tenth century. In one instance, a Christian adaptation of the *Encheiridion* substitutes the name Paul for that of Socrates" (2017, 32). Modern scholars, too, have found in Epictetus (and the Stoics more generally) a framework of thought that is remarkably compatible with the apostle's (esp., Engberg-Pedersen 2000; 2010). Moreover, the dialogical style of the *Diatribai* has been an essential resource for understanding Paul's use of the diatribe, especially in Romans (Stowers 1981; 1994).

The reading passages are the discourses (or portions thereof) that Epictetus used with his students to reinforce important points. Be on alert for various devices of the diatribe: the construction of fictive interlocutors (προσωποποιία), apostrophe (the direct address of fictive interlocutors), rhetorical questions (e.g., τί οὖν;), the presentation of false opinions (e.g., "someone will say . . ."), and the summary rejection thereof (e.g., μὴ γένοιτο).

Text and Translation: Oldfather 1925–28
Supplemental Scripture: Eph. 6:5–9 (§7.3.1); Rom. 14:1–15:7; James 2:1–6 (§7.3.2); Rom. 2:17–29; James 2:14–26 (§7.3.3); Rom. 7:13–24 (§§7.3.4–5)

7.3.1

How May Each Several Thing Be Done Acceptably to the Gods?

Discourses 1.13.1–5

1.13.1Πυθομένου¹ δέ τινος, πῶς ἔστιν² ἐσθίειν ἀρεστῶς³ θεοῖς, Εἰ δικαίως ἔστιν, ἔφη,⁴ καὶ εὐγνωμόνως⁵ καὶ ἴσως⁶ καὶ ἐγκρατῶς⁷ καὶ κοσμίως,⁸ οὐκ ἔστι καὶ ἀρεστῶς τοῖς θεοῖς; ²ὅταν δὲ θερμὸν⁹ αἰτήσαντός σου μὴ ὑπακούσῃ¹⁰ ὁ παῖς¹¹ ἢ ὑπακούσας χλιαρώτερον¹² ἐνέγκῃ ἢ μηδ' εὑρεθῇ ἐν τῇ οἰκίᾳ, τὸ μὴ χαλεπαίνειν¹³ μηδὲ ῥήγνυσθαι¹⁴ οὐκ ἔστιν ἀρεστὸν τοῖς θεοῖς; ³—Πῶς οὖν τις ἀνάσχηται¹⁵ τῶν τοιούτων;—Ἀνδράποδον,¹⁶ οὐκ ἀνέξῃ τοῦ ἀδελφοῦ τοῦ σαυτοῦ,¹⁷ ὃς ἔχει τὸν Δία¹⁸ πρόγονον,¹⁹ ὥσπερ υἱὸς ἐκ τῶν αὐτῶν σπερμάτων γέγονεν καὶ τῆς αὐτῆς ἄνωθεν καταβολῆς,²⁰ ⁴ἀλλ' εἰ ἐν τινι τοιαύτῃ χώρᾳ²¹ κατετάγης²² ὑπερεχούσῃ,²³ εὐθὺς τύραννον²⁴ καταστήσεις²⁵ σεαυτόν; οὐ μεμνήσῃ²⁶ τί εἶ καὶ τίνων ἄρχεις; ὅτι συγγενῶν,²⁷ ὅτι ἀδελφῶν φύσει,²⁸

1. Aor. mid. ptc. gen. masc. sg., πυνθάνομαι, *inquire*; gen. absol.
2. Impers. (recessive accent) *it is possible*; with inf. (cf. S §1985; *CGCG* §26.10).
3. Adv., *acceptably*.
4. Introduces Epictetus's response.
5. Adv., *gratefully, kindly, courteously*.
6. Adv., *fairly*.
7. Adv., *self-restrainedly*.
8. Adv., *orderly, decently*.
9. θερμός, -ή, -όν, *warm* (water).
10. Aor. act. subj. 3 sg., ὑπακούω, *obey*; general temp. clause (cf. BDF §382; S §2409; *CGCG* §47.9).
11. παῖς, παιδός, ὁ, *slave*.
12. Compar., χλιαρός, -ά, -όν, *lukewarm*.
13. Pres. act. inf., χαλεπαίνω, *become angry*; art. inf. as subject (cf. BDF §399; S §2031; *CGCG* §51.39).
14. Pres. pass. inf., ῥήγνυμι, *burst out*. See n. 13.
15. Aor. mid. subj. 3 sg., ἀνέχω, *bear with, endure*; deliberative (cf. BDF §368; S §1805; *CGCG* §34.8). Epictetus has answered the interlocutor's first question (πῶς ἔστιν), which now leads to a second (πῶς οὖν): "How, then, can anyone endure such things?"
16. Voc., ἀνδράποδον, -ου, τό, *slave*.
17. σαυτοῦ = σεαυτοῦ.
18. Ζεύς, Διός, ὁ, *Zeus*.
19. πρόγονος, -ου, ὁ, *progenitor*; pred. comp.
20. καταβολή, -ῆς, ἡ, *sowing*.
21. χώρα, -ας, ἡ, *place*.
22. Aor. pass. indic. 2 sg., κατατάσσω, (pass.) *be stationed*.
23. Pres. act. ptc. dat. fem. sg., ὑπερέχω, (pass.) *be more prominent*; attrib.
24. τύραννος, -ου, ὁ, (neg.) *tyrant*.
25. Fut. act. indic. 2 sg., καθίστημι, *set up, position*.
26. Fut. pf. mid. indic. 2 sg., μιμνήσκω, *remember*.
27. συγγενής, -ές, *of the same race/family, kin*.
28. φύσις, -εως, ἡ, *nature*; dat. of respect.

ὅτι τοῦ Διὸς ἀπογόνων;[29] 5—'Ἀλλ' ὠνὴν[30] αὐτῶν ἔχω, ἐκεῖνοι δ' ἐμοῦ οὐκ ἔχουσιν.—'Ὁρᾷς ποῦ[31] βλέπεις; ὅτι εἰς τὴν γῆν, ὅτι εἰς τὸ βάραθρον,[32] ὅτι εἰς τοὺς ταλαιπώρους[33] τούτους νόμους τοὺς τῶν νεκρῶν, εἰς δὲ τοὺς τῶν θεῶν οὐ βλέπεις;

NOTES

1.13.1. πῶς ἔστιν ἐσθίειν ἀρεστῶς θεοῖς. Cf. Rom. 14:6; 1 Cor. 10:23–33.

1.13.3. οὐκ ἀνέξῃ τοῦ ἀδελφοῦ τοῦ σαυτοῦ . . . ; Epictetus assumes that humans always have the freedom to exercise "volition" (προαίρεσις) in their responses (e.g., Diatr. 1.17.21; Long 2002, 207). Here, the argument is that we must bear with (ἀνέχω) fellow human beings because we are all "children of god" (cf. esp. Diatr. 1.3.1; ἀνέχω ἀλλήλων at Eph. 4:2; Col. 3:13). Indeed, divine filiation ought to be the perspective through which we view others and, most importantly, ourselves so that it relativizes our "earthly" stations (cf. Epictetus, Ench. 17; 2 Cor. 5:16; Eph. 4:6; 5:21–6:9). Thus it is no irony that Epictetus responds to his interlocutor—a persona in the guise of the master—"Slave!" (cf. Diatr. 4.1.40).

29. ἀπόγονος, -ου, ὁ, *offspring*.
30. ὠνή, -ῆς, ἡ, *deed of sale*. The interlocutor tries to correct the premise that he and the slave are by nature the same.
31. Adv., *to where*. "Do you see to where [the direction to which] you direct your sight?"
32. βάραθρον, -ου, τό, *deep pit, abyss*.
33. ταλαίπωρος, -ον, *miserable, wretched*.

7.3.2

On Preconceptions

Discourses 1.22.1–4

1.22.1Προλήψεις[1] κοιναὶ πᾶσιν ἀνθρώποις εἰσίν· καὶ πρόληψις προλήψει οὐ μάχεται.[2] τίς γὰρ ἡμῶν οὐ τίθησιν,[3] ὅτι τὸ ἀγαθὸν συμφέρον[4] ἐστὶ καὶ αἱρετὸν[5] καὶ ἐκ πάσης αὐτὸ περιστάσεως[6] δεῖ μετιέναι[7] καὶ διώκειν;[8] τίς δ' ἡμῶν οὐ τίθησιν, ὅτι τὸ δίκαιον καλὸν ἐστι καὶ πρέπον;[9] **2**πότ'[10] οὖν ἡ μάχη[11] γίνεται; περὶ τὴν ἐφαρμογὴν[12] τῶν προλήψεων ταῖς ἐπὶ μέρους οὐσίαις,[13] **3**ὅταν ὁ μὲν[14] εἴπῃ "καλῶς ἐποίησεν, ἀνδρεῖός[15] ἐστιν." "οὔ, ἀλλ' ἀπονενοημένος."[16] ἔνθεν[17] ἡ μάχη γίνεται τοῖς ἀνθρώποις πρὸς ἀλλήλους. **4**αὕτη ἐστὶν ἡ Ἰουδαίων καὶ Σύρων[18] καὶ Αἰγυπτίων[19] καὶ Ῥωμαίων μάχη, οὐ περὶ τοῦ ὅτι τὸ ὅσιον[20] πάντων προτιμητέον[21] καὶ ἐν παντὶ μεταδιωκτέον,[22] ἀλλὰ πότερον[23] ἐστιν ὅσιον τοῦτο τὸ χοιρείου[24] φαγεῖν ἢ ἀνόσιον.

---

1. πρόληψις, -εως, ἡ, *preconception, prolepsis*.
2. Pres. mid. indic. 3 sg., μάχομαι, *oppose, stand in contrast*; with dat.
3. This use of τίθημι concerns the mental act of "establishing" or "setting down" a premise, the content of which is explicated by the ὅτι-clause; thus, *assume, hold, regard*.
4. Pres. act. ptc. nom. neut. sg., συμφέρω, (intrans.) *be beneficial*; attrib. (pred. adj.).
5. αἱρετός, -ή, -όν, *to be chosen/desirable*.
6. περιστάσις, -εως, ἡ, *circumstance*.
7. Pres. act. inf., μέτειμι, *go after*; comp. of quasi-impers. δεῖ: "It is necessary [for us] *to go after and pursue* it [αὐτό = τὸ ἀγαθόν]."
8. Pres. act. inf., διώκω, *pursue*.
9. Pres. act. ptc. nom. neut. sg., πρέπω, *be suitable*; attrib. (pred. adj.).
10. Adv., *ever, at any time*.
11. μάχη, -ης, ἡ, *conflict, contradiction*.
12. ἐφαρμογή, -ῆς, ἡ, *adaptation*.
13. οὐσία, -ας, ἡ, *essence, substance*; with ἐπὶ μέρους, "in particular instances."
14. μέν . . . ἀλλά. The assertion of the μέν-clause is corrected by the counter-assertion of the ἀλλά-clause: "One person says, 'He did well, he is brave.' [Another] says, 'No, rather, he is crazy.'"
15. ἀνδρεῖος, -α, -ον, *brave, manly*.
16. Pf. mid. ptc. nom. masc. sg., ἀπονοέομαι, *be out of one's mind*.
17. Adv., *from here, hence*.
18. Σύρος, -ου, ὁ, *Syrian*.
19. Αἰγύπτιος, -α, -ον, *Egyptian*.
20. ὅσιος, -α, -ον, (subst.) *holiness*.
21. Verbal adj. from προτιμέω, impers. (act.) construction (cf. S §2152; *CGCG* §37.3): "It is necessary [for us] to honor holiness before all things [πάντων]."
22. Verbal adj. from μεταδιώκω, impers. (act.) construction (see n. 21): "It is necessary [for us] to pursue it [holiness] in every circumstance [ἐν παντί]."
23. Adv. used as the beginning of a question that contains two alt. propositions, the second of which is introduced by ἤ.
24. χοίρειος, -α, -ον, *of swine*; comp. of the nom. inf. τὸ φαγεῖν.

NOTES

1.22.2. πότ' οὖν ἡ μάχη γίνεται; The "objective" basis of Stoic ethics is the order of nature (Long 1971). The issue, however, as Epictetus observes, is that humans do not apply their preconceptions in the same way. Hence arises the exigency of education (*Diatr.* 1.22.9).

1.22.4. πότερόν ἐστιν ὅσιον τοῦτο τὸ χοιρείου φαγεῖν ἢ ἀνόσιον. Roman authors mocked Jews for abstaining from pork (cf. Seneca, *Ep.* 108.22; Plutarch, *Cic.* 7.4–5; Juvenal, *Sat.* 14.96–106), but that is not Epictetus's aim. Rather, he wishes to show that the conflict—whether or not to eat pork—concerns a failure to apply preconceptions correctly.

7.3.3

That Although We Are Unable to Fulfill the Profession of a Human, We Adopt That of a Philosopher

Discourses 2.9.13–22

2.9.13Διὰ τοῦτο παραγγέλλουσιν[1] οἱ φιλόσοφοι[2] μὴ ἀρκεῖσθαι[3] μόνῳ τῷ μαθεῖν,[4] ἀλλὰ καὶ μελέτην[5] προσλαμβάνειν,[6] εἶτα ἄσκησιν.[7] **14**πολλῷ γὰρ χρόνῳ τὰ ἐναντία[8] ποιεῖν εἰθίσμεθα[9] καὶ τὰς ὑπολήψεις[10] τὰς ἐναντίας ταῖς ὀρθαῖς[11] χρηστικὰς[12] ἔχομεν. ἂν[13] οὖν μὴ καὶ τὰς ὀρθὰς χρηστικὰς ποιήσωμεν, οὐδὲν ἄλλο ἢ ἐξηγηταὶ[14] ἐσόμεθα ἀλλοτρίων[15] δογμάτων.[16] **15**ἄρτι[17] γὰρ τίς ἡμῶν οὐ δύναται τεχνολογῆσαι[18] περὶ ἀγαθῶν καὶ κακῶν; ὅτι τῶν ὄντων τὰ μὲν[19] ἀγαθά, τὰ δὲ κακά, τὰ δ' ἀδιάφορα·[20] ἀγαθὰ μὲν οὖν[21] ἀρεταὶ[22] καὶ τὰ μετέχοντα[23] τῶν ἀρετῶν· κακὰ τὰ δ' ἐναντία· ἀδιάφορα

1. Pres. act. indic. 3 pl., παραγγέλλω, *admonish*; with acc. and inf.
2. φιλόσοφος, -ου, ὁ, *philosopher*.
3. Pres. pass. inf., ἀρκέω, *be content/satisfied with*; with dat.
4. Aor. act. inf., μανθάνω, *learn*; art. inf. as dat. comp. of ἀρκεῖσθαι.
5. μελέτη, -ης, ἡ, *practice*.
6. Pres. act. inf., προσλαμβάνω, *take in addition*.
7. ἄσκησις, -εως, ἡ, *training*.
8. ἐναντίον, -ου, τό, *opposite*.
9. Plpf. pass. indic. 1 pl., ἐθίζω, *be/become accustomed*.
10. ὑπόληψις, -εως, ἡ, *conception, opinion*.
11. ὀρθός, -ή, -όν, *upright, correct*; dat. comp. of τὰς ἐναντίας: "We have in use conceptions that are opposite to the correct ones [conceptions]."
12. χρηστικός, -ή, -όν, *in use, current*.
13. ἄν = ἐάν; third-class condition (cf. BDF §373; S §2323; *CGCG* §49.6); protasis: "If, then, we do not make correct conceptions [τὰς ὀρθάς] our in use conceptions [χρηστικάς] . . ."
14. ἐξηγητής, -οῦ, ὁ, *interpreter*.
15. ἀλλότριος, -α, -ον, *of that which belongs to another*.
16. δόγμα, -ατος, τό, *teaching, judgment*.
17. Adv., *even now*.
18. Aor. act. inf., τεχνολογέω, *give a philosophical discourse*; comp. of δύναται.
19. τὰ μέν . . . τὰ δέ . . . τὰ δέ, *other things . . . other things*.
20. ἀδιάφορος, -ον, *indifferent*.
21. Partic. combination: "a transition to a more to-the-point, relevant text segment (οὖν) [that] occurs in two stages (μέν . . . δέ . . . δέ)" (*CGCG* §59.73).
22. ἀρετή, -ῆς, ἡ, *virtue*.
23. Pres. act. ptc. nom. neut. pl., μετέχω, *participate in*; with gen.; attrib. (subst.).

δὲ πλοῦτος,²⁴ ὑγεία,²⁵ δόξα.²⁶ ¹⁶εἶτ' ἄν²⁷ μεταξὺ²⁸ λεγόντων ἡμῶν ψόφος²⁹ μείζων γένηται ἢ τῶν παρόντων³⁰ τις καταγελάσῃ³¹ ἡμῶν, ἐξεπλάγημεν.³² ¹⁷ποῦ³³ ἐστιν, φιλόσοφε, ἐκεῖνα ἃ ἔλεγες; πόθεν³⁴ αὐτὰ προφερόμενος³⁵ ἔλεγες; ἀπὸ τῶν χειλῶν³⁶ αὐτόθεν.³⁷ τί οὖν ἀλλότρια βοηθήματα³⁸ μολύνεις;³⁹ τί κυβεύεις⁴⁰ περὶ τὰ μέγιστα; ¹⁸ἄλλο γὰρ ἐστιν⁴¹ ὡς εἰς ταμιεῖον⁴² ἀποθέσθαι⁴³ ἄρτους καὶ οἶνον, ἄλλο ἐστὶ φαγεῖν. τὸ βρωθὲν⁴⁴ ἐπέφθη,⁴⁵ ἀνεδόθη,⁴⁶ νεῦρα⁴⁷ ἐγένετο, σάρκες, ὀστέα,⁴⁸ αἷμα, εὔχροια,⁴⁹ εὔπνοια.⁵⁰ τὰ ἀποκείμενα⁵¹ ὅταν μὲν⁵² θελήσῃς ἐκ προχείρου⁵³ λαβὼν δεῖξαι δύνασαι, ἀπ' αὐτῶν δέ σοι ὄφελος⁵⁴ οὐδὲν εἰ μέχρι⁵⁵ τοῦ δοκεῖν⁵⁶ ὅτι ἔχεις. ¹⁹τί γὰρ διαφέρει⁵⁷ ταῦτα ἐξηγεῖσθαι⁵⁸ ἢ τὰ τῶν ἑτεροδόξων;⁵⁹ τεχνολόγει νῦν καθίσας τὰ Ἐπικούρου⁶⁰ καὶ τάχα⁶¹ ἐκείνου χρηστικώτερον⁶² τεχνολογήσεις. τί οὖν Στωικὸν⁶³ λέγεις σεαυτόν, τί ἐξαπατᾷς⁶⁴ τοὺς πολλούς, τί ὑποκρίνῃ⁶⁵ Ἰουδαῖον ὢν Ἕλλην;⁶⁶ ²⁰οὐχ ὁρᾷς, πῶς ἕκαστος λέγεται Ἰουδαῖος, πῶς Σύρος,⁶⁷ πῶς Αἰγύπτιος;⁶⁸ καὶ ὅταν τινὰ ἐπαμφοτερίζοντα⁶⁹ ἴδωμεν, εἰώθαμεν⁷⁰ λέγειν "οὐκ ἔστιν Ἰουδαῖος, ἀλλ' ὑποκρίνεται." ὅταν δ' ἀναλάβῃ⁷¹ τὸ πάθος⁷² τὸ τοῦ βεβαμμένου⁷³ καὶ ᾑρημένου,⁷⁴ τότε καὶ ἔστι τῷ ὄντι⁷⁵ καὶ καλεῖται Ἰουδαῖος. ²¹οὕτως καὶ ἡμεῖς παραβαπτισταί,⁷⁶ λόγῳ μὲν⁷⁷ Ἰουδαῖος, ἔργῳ δ' ἄλλο τι, ἀσυμπαθεῖς⁷⁸ πρὸς τὸν

24. πλοῦτος, -ου, ὁ, *wealth*.
25. ὑγεία, -ας, ἡ, *health*.
26. δόξα, -ας, ἡ, *reputation*.
27. ἄν = ἐάν. See n. 13.
28. Adv., *in the middle of*.
29. ψόφος, -ου, ὁ, *sound*.
30. Pres. act. ptc. gen. masc. pl., πάρειμι, *be present*; attrib. (subst.); partitive gen.
31. Aor. act. subj. 3 sg., καταγελάω, *mock, laugh at*; with gen.
32. Aor. pass. indic. 1 pl., ἐκπλάσσω, (pass.) *be upset*.
33. Interrogative adv., *To where?*
34. Interrogative adv., *From where?*
35. Pres. mid. ptc. nom. masc. sg., προφέρω, *bring forward*.
36. χεῖλος, -εος, τό, (pl.) *lips*.
37. Adv., *merely, only*.
38. βοηθήμα, -ατος, τό, *helpful principles*.
39. Pres. act. indic. 2 sg., μολύνω, *defile, pollute*.
40. Pres. act. indic. 2 sg., κυβεύω, *play dice, gamble*.
41. ἄλλο ἐστίν . . . ἄλλο ἐστί, *it is one thing . . . it is another thing*.
42. ταμιεῖον, -ου, τό, *storehouse*.
43. Aor. mid. inf., ἀποτίθημι, *put away, store away*.
44. Aor. pass. ptc. nom. neut. sg., βιβρώσκω, (pass.) *be eaten*; attrib. (subst.).
45. Aor. pass. indic. 3 sg., πέσσω, (pass.) *be digested*.
46. Aor. pass. indic. 3 sg., ἀναδίδωμι, (pass.) *be distributed*.
47. νεῦρον, -ου, τό, *sinew, tendon*.
48. ὀστέον, -ου, τό, *bone*.
49. εὔχροια, -ας, ἡ, *well colored, healthy* (appearance).
50. εὔπνοια, -ας, ἡ, *ease in breathing*.
51. Pres. pass. ptc. nom. neut. pl., ἀπόκειμαι, (pass.) *be set aside, stored away*; attrib. (subst.). Prolepsis is used to treat the dislocated constituent τὰ ἀποκείμενα as the given topic (cf. *CGCG* §60.37).
52. μέν . . . δέ; point/counterpoint (cf. Runge 2010, 75–83; BDF §447; S §2904; *CGCG* §59.24).
53. πρόχειρος, -ον, *at hand, readily*.

54. ὄφελος, -ου, τό, *benefit, advantage*.
55. Prep. with gen., *up to, as far as*.
56. Pres. act. inf., δοκέω, (impers.) *it seems*; art. inf. as obj. of μέχρι (cf. BDF §403; S 2032.g): "insofar as it seems that you have it [τὰ ἀποκείμενα]."
57. Pres. act. indic. 3 sg., διαφέρω, (impers.) *it is better*; with inf.: "For how much [τί] better is it to set forth these principles than [ἤ] those of another school of thought?"
58. Pres. mid. inf., ἐξηγέομαι, *recount in detail*.
59. ἑτερόδοξος, -ον, *differing in opinion*.
60. Ἐπίκουρος, -ου, ὁ, *Epicurus*.
61. Adv., *perhaps*.
62. Compar. as adv., χρηστικός, -ή, -όν, *more effectively*.
63. Στωικός, -ή, -όν, *Stoic*; pred. comp.
64. Pres. act. indic. 2 sg., ἐξαπατάω, *deceive, mislead*.
65. Pres. mid. indic. 2 sg., ὑποκρίνω, *act/play the part*.
66. Emendation; MS reads ιουδαῖος ὢν ἕλληνας, "Being a Jew [why do you play] the part of Greeks?"
67. Σύρος, -ου, ὁ, *Syrian*.
68. Αἰγύπτιος, -α, -ον, *Egyptian*.
69. Pres. act. ptc. acc. masc. sg., ἐπαμφοτερίζω, *be in between two sides*; supp. (ἴδωμεν).
70. Pf. act. indic. 1 pl., ἐθίζω, *be accustomed*; with inf.
71. Aor. act. subj. 3 sg., ἀναλαμβάνω, *take upon oneself, assume*.
72. πάθος, -ους, τό, *state, condition*.
73. Pf. pass. ptc. gen. masc. sg., βάπτω, (pass.) *be immersed, baptized*; attrib. (subst.).
74. Pf. mid. ptc. gen. masc. sg., αἱρέω, *choose*; attrib. (subst.).
75. Idiom, τῷ ὄντι, *in reality, in fact*.
76. παραβαπτιστής, -οῦ, ὁ, *counterfeit/illegitimate baptist*; pred. nom.
77. μέν . . . δέ; point/counterpoint. See n. 52.
78. ἀσυμπαθής, -ές (with πρός and acc.), *without sympathy toward* (someone or something); ἀσυμπαθεῖς πρὸς τὸν λόγον, "without sympathy toward reason."

λόγον, μακρὰν ἀπὸ τοῦ χρῆσθαι⁷⁹ τούτοις ἃ λέγομεν, ἐφ' οἷς ὡς εἰδότες⁸⁰ αὐτὰ ἐπαιρόμεθα.⁸¹ ²²οὕτως οὐδὲ τὴν τοῦ ἀνθρώπου ἐπαγγελίαν⁸² πληρῶσαι δυνάμενοι προσλαμβάνομεν⁸³ τὴν τοῦ φιλοσόφου, τηλικοῦτο φορτίον,⁸⁴ οἷον⁸⁵ εἴ δέκα λίτρας⁸⁶ ἆραι μὴ δυνάμενος τὸν τοῦ Αἴαντος⁸⁷ λίθον βαστάζειν⁸⁸ ἤθελεν.

NOTES

2.9.13. μὴ ἀρκεῖσθαι μόνῳ τῷ μαθεῖν, ἀλλὰ καὶ μελέτην προσλαμβάνειν, εἶτα ἄσκησιν. The end of philosophical pedagogy is not mere learning (μαθεῖν) but "practice" or "training" (ἄσκησις). Throughout his discourses Epictetus makes the point that pseudophilosophers are recognized by the ways their words are contradicted by their actions (cf. *Diatr.* 1.29.35, 55–57; 3.24.10; 4.8.8–12; Johnson 2009, 70).

2.9.17. ποῦ ἐστιν, φιλόσοφε, ἐκεῖνα ἃ ἔλεγες; The creation of a fictive interlocutor (προσωποποιία) is a common feature of the diatribe. Epictetus's apostrophe to the pseudophilosopher (*Diatr.* 2.9.17–21) may be compared to Paul's apostrophes to the self-righteous judge (Rom. 2:1–5) and the so-called Jew (Rom. 2:17–29) as well as to James's apostrophe to the empty person (James 2:20–26).

2.9.18. ὄφελος. Cf. James 2:14, 18: Τί τὸ ὄφελος … τί τὸ ὄφελος;

2.9.19–20. τί ὑποκρίνῃ Ἰουδαῖον ὢν Ἕλλην; Oldfather (1925–28, 1:266n40) concludes, "It would appear (especially from the expression 'counterfeit baptists' below) that Epictetus is here speaking really of the Christians, who were in his time not infrequently confused with the Jews." This may be so, though there is ample evidence to suggest that Jewish teachers had made inroads in Rome (cf. Josephus, *A.J.* 18.81–82; Plutarch, *Cic.* 7.4–5; Horace, *Sat.* 1.4.139–143; Seneca, *apud* Augustine, *Civ.* 6.11; Valerius Maximus 1.3.3; Tacitus, *Hist.* 5.5.1–2). And one should not assume that immersion without circumcision necessarily makes the ritual "Christian" (Donaldson 2007, 391). In any case, the observation that "the Jew" is put on the positive side of the Roman ledger, over and against "the Greek" (the profligate from a Roman perspective), is noteworthy. So too is the charge of hypocrisy one faces when caught "waffling in-between" (ἐπαμφοτερίζοντα): "He is not a Jew; he is only playing the part [ὑποκρίνεται]!" (Epictetus, *Diatr.* 2.9.20). Cf. Rom. 2:17–29 (Stowers 1994, 144–58; Thiessen 2016, 54–71); Gal. 2:11–14 (Novenson 2014).

2.9.21. λόγῳ μὲν Ἰουδαῖος, ἔργῳ δ' ἄλλο τι. Cf. Lev. 12:3; 26:41; Jer. 4:4; 9:26; Jub. 1:23; 15:11–33; Matt. 3:9 parr.; Luke 3:8; Rom. 2:28–29; James 2:18–26.

2.9.22. τὴν τοῦ ἀνθρώπου ἐπαγγελίαν. Epictetus uses the term ἐπαγγελία throughout to delineate what is expected of human beings (i.e., the human task/vocation), which is to exercise their reason (cf. Aristotle, *Eth. nic.* 1097a26–1098a; Engberg-Pedersen 2000, 48–53; and now the important

---

79. Pres. mid. inf., χράομαι, *use*; with dat.; art. inf. as obj. of ἀπό. See n. 56.
80. ὡς with a circumstantial participle provides "a 'subjective' reason or motivation, for which responsibility lies with the subject of the matrix verb": *thinking that, on the grounds that* (*CGCG* §52.39).
81. Pres. pass. indic. 1 pl., ἐπαίρω, (pass.) *be exalted at* (something); with dat.
82. The term designates "what a person or thing promises or is expected to perform" (Oldfather 1925–28, 1:260n37)—thus, "profession" or "vocation."
83. Pres. act. indic. 1 pl., προσλαμβάνω, *take in addition*.
84. φορτίον, -ου, τό, *burden*; an appositive to τὴν [ἐπαγγελίαν] τοῦ φιλοσόφου.
85. τηλικοῦτο … οἷον, *so great … as*.
86. λίτρα, -ας, ἡ, *pound*.
87. Αἴας, -αντος, ὁ, *Ajax*.
88. Pres. act. inf., βαστάζω, *bear, carry*; comp. of ἤθελεν.

monograph by Dürr 2021). The problem, however, is that human beings are also mortal creatures (ζῷον θνητόν; Epictetus, *Diatr.* 2.9.1) that frequently act contrary to reason and thus devolve to beastly behavior (2.9.2–12). And these are the creatures who, caught in their contradictions, want to take on τὴν τοῦ φιλοσόφου ἐπαγγελίαν—so huge a burden (τηλικοῦτο φορτίον) indeed! One detects a similar line of thought in Paul's argument in Romans (Stowers 1994, 273–84).

7.3.4

How Ought We Adjust Our Preconceptions to Individual Instances?

Discourses 2.17.14–22

2.17.14Καὶ τί μοι¹ νῦν πρὸς ἀλλήλους μάχην² παραφέρειν³ καὶ ταύτης μεμνῆσθαι;⁴ σὺ αὐτὸς⁵ εἰ ἐφαρμόζεις⁶ καλῶς τὰς προλήψεις,⁷ διὰ τί⁸ δυσροεῖς,⁹ διὰ τί ἐμποδίζῃ;¹⁰ **15**ἀφῶμεν¹¹ ἄρτι¹² τὸν δεύτερον τόπον¹³ τὸν περὶ τὰς ὁρμὰς¹⁴ καὶ τὴν κατὰ ταύτας περὶ τὸ καθῆκον¹⁵ φιλοτεχνίαν.¹⁶ ἀφῶμεν καὶ τὸν τρίτον τὸν περὶ τὰς συγκαταθέσεις.¹⁷ **16**χαρίζομαί σοι ταῦτα πάντα. στῶμεν ἐπὶ τοῦ πρώτου καὶ σχεδὸν¹⁸ αἰσθητὴν¹⁹ παρέχοντος²⁰ τὴν ἀπόδειξιν²¹ **17**τοῦ μὴ ἐφαρμόζειν²² καλῶς τὰς προλήψεις. νῦν σὺ θέλεις τὰ δυνατὰ καὶ τὰ σοὶ δυνατά; τί οὖν ἐμποδίζῃ; διὰ τί δυσροεῖς; νῦν οὐ φεύγεις τὰ ἀναγκαῖα;²³ διὰ τί οὖν περιπίπτεις²⁴ τινί, διὰ τί δυστυχεῖς; διὰ τί θέλοντός σού τι οὐ γίνεται καὶ μὴ θέλοντος γίνεται; **18**ἀπόδειξις γὰρ αὕτη μεγίστη

1. Dat. of interest (cf. S §1479): "And what need is there for me [lit., what is it to me] now to bring forward conflict against one another and to make mention of that [conflict]?"
2. μάχη, -ης, ἡ, *strife, conflict.*
3. Pres. act. inf., παραφέρω, *bring forward, present.*
4. Pf. mid. inf., μιμνήσκω, *remember, recall*; with gen.
5. Nom. pendent (cf. CGCG §60.34): "*You yourself* [intensive use of αὐτός], if you adjust your prolepsis correctly . . ."
6. Pres. act. indic. 2 sg., ἐφαρμόζω, *fit, adjust, accommodate, apply.*
7. πρόληψις, -εως, ἡ, *preconception, prolepsis.*
8. διὰ τί, *Why?*
9. Pres. act. indic. 2 sg., δυσροέω, *have unfavorable flow*; opposite of εὐροέω, "which is a metaphor derived from the even flow of quiet waters" (Oldfather 1925–28, 1:332n73).
10. Pres. pass. indic. 2 sg., ἐμποδίζω, (pass.) *be fettered.*
11. Aor. act. subj. 1 pl., ἀφίημι, *let go of*; hortatory (cf. BDF §364; S §1797; CGCG §34.6).
12. Adv., *now.*
13. τόπος, -ου, ὁ, *topic* (of study).
14. ὁρμή, -ῆς, ἡ, *choice.*
15. Pres. act. ptc. acc. neut. sg., καθήκω, (subst. ptc.) *duty, one's concern to do.*
16. φιλοτεχνία, -ας, ἡ, *philosophical discourse*; τὴν κατὰ ταύτας περὶ τὸ καθῆκον φιλοτεχνίαν, "discourse around what we ought to do in regard to these things [κατὰ ταύτας = τὰς ὁρμάς]."
17. συγκατάθεσις, -εως, ἡ, *assent.*
18. Adv., *nearly, almost.*
19. αἰσθητός, -ή, -όν, *perceptible.*
20. Pres. act. ptc. gen. masc. sg., παρέχω, *present*; attrib.
21. ἀπόδειξις, -εως, ἡ, *proof.*
22. The articular infinitive modifies the head noun τὴν ἀπόδειξιν (cf. BDF §400; S §2032; CGCG §51.39): "proof *that you are not applying* your preconceptions rightly."
23. ἀναγκαῖος, -α, -ον, *necessary, inevitable.*
24. Pres. act. indic. 2 sg., περιπίπτω, *fall into* (trouble); with dat.

δυσροίας²⁵ καὶ κακοδαιμονίας.²⁶ θέλω τι καὶ οὐ γίνεται· καὶ τί ἐστιν ἀθλιώτερον²⁷ ἐμοῦ; οὐ θέλω τι καὶ γίνεται· καὶ τί ἐστιν ἀθλιώτερον ἐμοῦ;

¹⁹Τοῦτο καὶ ἡ Μήδεια²⁸ οὐχ ὑπομείνασα²⁹ ἦλθεν ἐπὶ τὸ ἀποκτεῖναι τὰ τέκνα. μεγαλοφυῶς³⁰ κατά γε³¹ τοῦτο. εἶχε γὰρ ἣν δεῖ φαντασίαν,³² οἷόν ἐστι τὸ ἅ θέλει τινὶ μὴ **²⁰**προχωρεῖν.³³ "εἶτα οὕτως τιμωρήσομαι³⁴ τὸν ἀδικήσαντά³⁵ με καὶ ὑβρίσαντα.³⁶ καὶ τί ὄφελος³⁷ τοῦ κακῶς οὕτως διακειμένου;³⁸ πῶς οὖν γένηται; ἀποκτείνω μὲν³⁹ τὰ τέκνα. **²¹**ἀλλὰ καὶ ἐμαυτὴν τιμωρήσομαι. καὶ τί μοι μέλει;"⁴⁰ τοῦτ' ἐστιν ἔκπτωσις⁴¹ ψυχῆς μεγάλα νεῦρα⁴² ἐχούσης. οὐ γὰρ ᾔδει, ποῦ⁴³ κεῖται⁴⁴ τὸ ποιεῖν ἃ θέλομεν, ὅτι τοῦτο οὐκ ἔξωθεν⁴⁵ δεῖ λαμβάνειν οὐδὲ τὰ πράγματα⁴⁶ μετατιθέντα⁴⁷ καὶ μεθαρμοζόμενον.⁴⁸ μὴ θέλε τὸν ἄνδρα, καὶ οὐδὲν ὧν θέλεις οὐ γίνεται. μὴ θέλε αὐτὸν ἐξ ἅπαντός⁴⁹ σοι συνοικεῖν,⁵⁰ μὴ θέλε μένειν ἐν Κορίνθῳ⁵¹ καὶ ἁπλῶς⁵² μηδὲν ἄλλο θέλε ἢ ἃ ὁ θεὸς θέλει. καὶ τίς σε κωλύσει,⁵³ τίς ἀναγκάσει;⁵⁴ οὐ μᾶλλον ἢ τὸν Δία.⁵⁵

NOTE

2.17.18–22. Cf. Rom. 7:18–24; Epictetus, *Diatr.* 1.3.5, wherein the multitudes complain, "'τί γὰρ εἰμί; ταλαίπωρον ἀνθωπάριον' καὶ 'τὰ δύστηνά μου σαρκίδα.'" The starting point of the tradition, as Stowers notes (1994, 260–64), is Euripides's *Medea* 1077–1080: "I know well what pain I am about to undergo, but my wrath overbears my deliberate purpose, wrath that brings mortal men their gravest hurt" (Kovacs 1994, 383 alt.; cf. Euripides, *Hipp.* 377–83; Plato, *Prot.* 352d; Galen, *Hippoc. et Plat.* 4.274.15–22; Ovid, *Metam.* 7.17–21). Note, in particular, Seneca's *Medea* (990): "What, wretched woman, have I done?" (Quid, misera, feci?).

25. δυσροία, -ας, ἡ, *unfavorable flow,* (metaph.) *bad luck.*
26. κακοδαιμονία, -ας, ἡ, *misfortune.*
27. Compar., ἄλιος, -α, -ον, *more miserable/wretched.*
28. Μήδεια, -ας, ἡ, *Medea.* The discourse topic (τοῦτο) of the previous paragraph is carried to its exemplar. "For example, Medea, since she was unable to endure *this,* came to the point of killing her children."
29. Aor. act. ptc. nom. fem. sg., ὑπομένω, *endure*; circ. (causal).
30. Adv., *magnanimously, nobly.*
31. Postpositive partic.: "focuses attention on the word or phrase it follows . . . and limits the applicability of the content of the utterance to *at least* or (*more*) precisely that specific element" (CGCG §59.53). "*At least* in this respect she acted nobly."
32. φαντασία, -ας, ἡ, *mental representation, conception.* The antecedent is incorporated into the relative clause (cf. S §2536; CGCG §50.15): "She had *the conception that* she ought [to have]."
33. Pres. act. inf., προχωρέω, *proceed, advance*; with dat.; art. inf. as subject (cf. BDF §399; S §2031; CGCG §51.39): "What sort of thing it is when that which one wills [ἃ θέλει] does not come about for him/her."
34. Fut. mid. indic. 1 sg., τιμωρέω, *punish.*
35. Aor. act. ptc. acc. masc. sg., ἀδικέω, *wrong, treat unjustly*; attrib. (subst.). The referent is Medea's husband, Jason.
36. Aor. act. ptc. acc. masc. sg., ὑβρίζω, *insult*; attrib. (subst.).
37. ὄφελος, -ου, τό, *benefit, advantage*; with gen.: "What benefit is [to me] out of his remaining in such a bad state?"
38. Pres. mid. ptc. gen. masc. sg., διάκειμαι, *remain*; attrib. (subst.).
39. μέν . . . ἀλλά. The supposition of the μέν-clause (i.e., that killing her children will be of some benefit to her) is canceled by the ἀλλά-clause.
40. Pres. act. indic. 3 sg., μέλω, (impers.) *it concerns*; with dat.
41. ἔκπτωσις, -εως, ἡ, *emission, outburst*; pred. nom.
42. νεῦρον, -ου, τό, (fig.) *vigor, force.*
43. Adv., *where.*
44. Pres. pass. indic. 3 sg., κεῖμαι, *lie.*
45. Adv., *from outside.*
46. πρᾶγμα, -ατος, τό, (pl.) *matters, affairs.*
47. Pres. act. ptc. acc. masc. sg., μετατίθημι, *change, alter*; circ. (agreeing with the acc. subject of λαμβάνειν).
48. Pres. mid. ptc. acc. masc. sg., μεθαρμόζω, *rearrange*; circ. (agreeing with the acc. subject of λαμβάνειν).
49. ἐξ ἅπαντος, "by any means necessary."
50. Pres. act. inf., συνοικέω, *dwell with*; with dat.
51. Κόρινθος, -ου, ὁ, *Corinth.*
52. Adv., *generally.*
53. Fut. act. indic. 3 sg., κωλύω, *hinder, prevent.*
54. Fut. act. indic. 3 sg., ἀναγκάζω, *compel.*
55. Ζεύς, Διός, ὁ, *Zeus*; οὐ μᾶλλον ἢ τὸν Δία, "There is not [anyone who will hinder or compel you] anymore than [there is someone who would hinder or compel] Zeus."

7.3.5

What Is the Distinctive Characteristic of Error?

Discourses 2.26.1–5

2.26.1Πᾶν ἁμάρτημα¹ μάχην² περιέχει.³ ἐπεὶ γὰρ ὁ ἁμαρτάνων οὐ θέλει ἁμαρτάνειν, ἀλλὰ κατορθῶσαι,⁴ δῆλον⁵ ὅτι ὃ μὲν⁶ θέλει οὐ ποιεῖ. ²τί γὰρ ὁ κλέπτης⁷ θέλει πρᾶξαι;⁸ τὸ αὐτῷ συμφέρον.⁹ οὐκ οὖν, εἰ ἀσύμφορόν¹⁰ ἐστιν αὐτῷ τὸ κλέπτειν,¹¹ ὃ μὲν θέλει ποιεῖ. ³πᾶσα δὲ ψυχὴ λογικὴ¹² φύσει¹³ διαβέβληται¹⁴ πρὸς μάχην· καὶ μέχρι¹⁵ μὲν¹⁶ ἂν μὴ παρακολουθῇ¹⁷ τούτῳ, ὅτι ἐν μάχῃ ἐστίν, οὐδὲν κωλύεται¹⁸ τὰ μαχόμενα¹⁹ ποιεῖν· παρακολουθήσαντα²⁰ δὲ πολλὴ ἀνάγκη ἀποστῆναι²¹

1. ἁμάρτημα, -ατος, τό, *error, sin*.
2. μάχη, -ης, ἡ, *conflict, contradiction*.
3. Pres. act. indic. 3 sg., περιέχω, *encompass*.
4. Aor. act. inf., κατορθόω, *act uprightly*; comp. of θέλει.
5. δῆλος, -ον, (quasi-impers.) *it is clear*; with ὅτι-clause of content.
6. μέν ... δέ; point/counterpoint (cf. Runge 2010, 75–83; BDF §447; S §2904; *CGCG* §59.24). The resumption of the μέν-clause is emphatic, as the example underscores the principle: to err is to do what one does *not* desire; cf. Denniston 1966, 384.
7. κλέπτης, -ου, ὁ, *thief*.
8. Aor. act. inf., πράσσω, *accomplish, achieve*; comp. of θέλει.
9. Pres. act. ptc. acc. neut. sg., συμφέρω, *be beneficial*; attrib. (subst.).
10. ἀσύμφορος, -ον, *not beneficial, against one's interests*.
11. Pres. act. inf., κλέπτω, *steal*; art. inf. as subject (cf. BDF §399; S §2031; *CGCG* §51.39).

12. λογικός, -ή, -όν, *rational*.
13. φύσις, -εως, ἡ, *nature*.
14. Pf. pass. indic. 3 sg., διαβάλλω, (pass.) *be averse (to something)*.
15. Adv., *as long as*.
16. μέν ... δέ; point/counterpoint. See n. 6.
17. Pres. act. subj. 3 sg., παρακολουθέω, *be aware/conscious of* (the fact that); with dat. (MGS, 1555.C); general temp. clause (cf. BDF §383; S §2409; *CGCG* §47.9).
18. Pres. pass. indic. 3 sg., κωλύω, (pass.) *be hindered, prevented*; with inf.: "It [the soul] is in no way hindered from doing contradictory things."
19. Pres. mid. ptc. acc. neut. pl., μάχομαι, *be in conflict, contradiction*; attrib. (subst.).
20. The participle is accusative because ἀνάγκη ("it is necessary") takes the accusative and infinitive, but note that the gender has shifted from feminine (ψυχή) to masculine (generic person): "When he does understand [that he exists in contradiction], it is entirely necessary for [him] to abandon the contradiction and flee from it."
21. Aor. act. inf., ἀφίστημι, *abandon*; with gen.

τῆς μάχης καὶ φυγεῖν οὕτως ὡς καὶ²² ἀπὸ τοῦ ψεύδους²³ ἀνανεῦσαι²⁴ πικρὰ²⁵ ἀνάγκη τῷ αἰσθανομένῳ,²⁶ ὅτι ψεῦδός ἐστιν· μέχρι δὲ τοῦτο μὴ φαντάζηται,²⁷ ὡς ἀληθεῖ²⁸ ἐπινεύει²⁹ αὐτῷ.

⁴Δεινὸς³⁰ οὖν ἐν λόγῳ, ὁ δ' αὐτὸς καὶ προτρεπτικὸς³¹ καὶ ἐλεγκτικὸς³² οὗτος ὁ δυνάμενος ἑκάστῳ παραδεῖξαι³³ τὴν μάχην, καθ' ἣν ἁμαρτάνει, καὶ σαφῶς³⁴ παραστῆσαι,³⁵ πῶς ὃ θέλει οὐ ποιεῖ καὶ ὃ μὴ θέλει ποιεῖ. ⁵ἂν³⁶ γὰρ τοῦτο δείξῃ³⁷ τις, αὐτὸς ἀφ' αὑτοῦ³⁸ ἀναποχωρήσει.³⁹ μέχρι δὲ μὴ δεικνύῃς, μὴ θαύμαζε,⁴⁰ εἰ ἐπιμένει· κατορθώματος⁴¹ γὰρ φαντασίαν⁴² λαμβάνων ποιεῖ αὐτό.

NOTE

2.26.4. Cf. Seneca, *Ep.* 94, wherein he addresses objections to the stated value of the philosopher's exposing error. On the locution πῶς ὃ θέλει οὐ ποιεῖ καὶ ὃ μὴ θέλει ποιεῖ, cf. Rom. 7:14–25. Paul here exposes the inherent contradiction of the (gentile) interlocutor who seeks to take on the law as an instrument of moral therapy.

22. οὕτως ὡς καί, *just as also*.
23. ψεῦδος, -ους, τό, *falsehood*.
24. Aor. act. inf., ἀνανεύω, *shrink* (from something).
25. πικρός, -ά, -όν, *bitter*.
26. Pres. mid. ptc. dat. masc. sg., αἰσθάνομαι, *perceive*; attrib. (subst.); dat. comp. of ἀνάγκη.
27. Pres. pass. subj. 3 sg., φαντάζω, (pass.) *be shown, appear*; general temp. clause. See n. 17.
28. ἀληθής, -ές, *true*; ὡς ἀληθεῖ, "as though it [falsehood] were true."
29. Pres. act. indic. 3 sg., ἐπινεύω, *assent, agree with*; with dat.
30. δεινός, -ή, -όν, *extraordinary, strong*; ἐν λόγῳ (dat. of respect), "in argument."
31. προτρεπτικός, -ή, -όν, *able to exhort*.
32. ἐλεγκτικός, -ή, -όν, *able to reprove*.
33. Aor. act. inf., παραδείκνυμι, *show, demonstrate*; comp. of δυνάμενος.
34. Adv., *clearly, obviously*.
35. Aor. act. inf., παρίστημι, *present*.
36. ἄν = ἐάν.
37. Aor. act. subj. 3 sg., δείκνυμι, *show*; third-class condition (cf. BDF §373; S §2323; CGCG §49.6).
38. ἀφ' αὑτοῦ, *of his own accord*.
39. Fut. act. indic. 3 sg., ἀναποχωρέω, *leave, abandon*.
40. Pres. act. impv. 2 sg., θαυμάζω, *be amazed*.
41. κατόρθωμα, -ατος, τό, *that which is done uprightly/virtuously*.
42. φαντασία, -ας, ἡ, *impression*.

7.4

Dio Chrysostom

Dio Cocceianus (ca. 40–120 CE), surnamed Chrysostom ("Golden-Mouthed"), was a native of Prusa, in Bithynia. As one might expect of a Chrysostom, he was an accomplished rhetorician—though he was not initially taken by philosophy. In fact, when he first arrived in Rome, he was critical of the philosophers in general and of Musonius Rufus in particular. But eventually Epictetus's teacher won him over, and Dio joined the ranks of the Stoics. In 82 CE, he was exiled by the emperor Domitian and no longer welcome in either Italy or his native Bithynia. As a result, Dio was forced to assume the austere lifestyle of a Cynic. Eventually he was restored by the emperor Nerva (96–98 CE) and lived out the rest of his life in Prusa. What remains of Dio's oeuvre are eighty discourses, two of which (the thirty-seventh and the sixty-fourth) are now attributed to his student Favorinus.

The reading passages are from Dio's seventeenth and forty-eighth discourses. In the former, *On Covetousness*, he makes the case that instruction for moral formation requires persistent repetition. In the latter, *A Political Address in the Assembly* (Πολιτικὸς ἐν ἐκκλησίᾳ), he takes up the theme of concord. As with the readings in Epictetus (§7.3), these passages are diatribal in nature: rhetorical questions (e.g., τί οὖν;), the presentation of false opinions (e.g., "Is it not the case that . . . ?"), stock locutions (e.g., νὴ Δία), and so forth.

Text and Translation: Cohoon 1939 (§7.4.1); Crosby 1946 (§7.4.2)

Supplemental Scripture: 2 Tim. 3:1–8 (§7.4.1); Eph. 4:1–16; 1 Clem. 20 (§7.4.2)

7.4.1

On the Need for Repetition

On Covetousness 1–6

¹Οἱ μὲν¹ πολλοὶ τῶν ἀνθρώπων ὑπὲρ τούτων οἴονται² δεῖν³ λέγειν ὑπὲρ ὧν ἕκαστος οὐκ ἔχει τὴν ἀληθῆ⁴ δόξαν,⁵ ὅπως ἀκούσαντες ὑπὲρ ὧν ἀγνοοῦσιν⁶ μάθωσι·⁷ περὶ δὲ τῶν γνωρίμων⁸ καὶ πᾶσιν ὁμοίως φαινομένων⁹ περιττὸν¹⁰ εἶναι διδάσκειν. ἐγὼ δὲ εἰ μὲν¹¹ ἑώρων ἡμᾶς οἷς¹² νομίζομεν¹³ ὀρθῶς ἔχειν ἐμμένοντας¹⁴ καὶ μηδὲν ἔξωθεν¹⁵ πράττοντας¹⁶ τῆς ὑπαρχούσης ὑπολήψεως,¹⁷ οὐδ᾽ ἂν αὐτὸς ᾤμην¹⁸ ἀναγκαῖον¹⁹ εἶναι διατείνασθαι²⁰ περὶ τῶν προδήλων.²¹ ²ἐπεὶ δὲ οὐχὶ τὴν ἄγνοιαν²² ἡμᾶς τῶν ἀγαθῶν καὶ τῶν κακῶν το-

---

1. Οἱ μὲν πολλοί . . . δέ . . . ἐγὼ δέ . . . μέν . . . δέ. The primary contrast is between οἱ πολλοί and ἐγώ, but the actions of each are also divided into μέν . . . δέ constructions (cf. Runge 2010, 75–83; BDF §447; S §2904; *CGCG* §59.24).
2. Pres. mid. indic. 3 pl., οἴομαι, *think, suppose*.
3. Quasi-impers., δεῖ, *it is necessary*; with acc. and inf.; indir. disc. (cf. BDF §396; S §2016; *CGCG* §51.19).
4. ἀληθής, -ές, *true*.
5. δόξα, -ας, ἡ, *belief, opinion*.
6. Pres. act. indic. 3 pl., ἀγνοέω, *be ignorant*.
7. Aor. act. subj. 3 pl., μανθάνω, *learn*; purpose clause (cf. BDF §369; S §2193; *CGCG* §45.2).
8. γνώριμος, -ον, *well-known*.
9. Pres. pass. ptc. gen. neut. pl., φαίνω, (pass.) *be made clear*; attrib. (subst.).
10. περισσός, -ή, -όν (Att. περιττός); quasi-impers. (περιττὸν εἶναι) in indir. disc. (οἴονται): "They suppose that *it is superfluous* [περιττὸν εἶναι] to teach on matters that are well known and clear to all alike." See n. 3.
11. μέν . . . δέ. The point/counterpoint explicates the δέ-clause (S §2908).

12. The relative pronoun is attracted to the case of an omitted antecedent, the object of ἐμμένοντας (cf. BDF §294; S §2522; *CGCG* §50.13): "if I saw that we are remaining *in those beliefs that* we believe are correct."
13. Pres. act. indic. 1 pl., νομίζω, *consider*. The complementary infinitive ἔχειν with an adverb is equivalent to εἶναι with an adjective.
14. Pres. act. ptc. acc. masc. pl., ἐμμένω, *remain in*; with dat.; supp. (ἑώρων).
15. Adv., *from without/outside*.
16. Pres. act. ptc. acc. masc. pl., πράσσω (Att. πράττω), *do*; supp. (ἑώρων).
17. ὑπόληψις, -εως, ἡ, *assumption, notion*.
18. Impf. act. indic. 1 sg., οἴομαι, *think, suppose*; second-class (contrafactual) condition (cf. BDF §360; S §2303; *CGCG* §49.10). Note the intensifying αὐτός: "*I myself* would not think it necessary."
19. ἀναγκαῖος, -α, -ον, (quasi-impers.) *it is necessary*; with inf. in indir. disc. (ᾤμην). See n. 3.
20. Pres. mid. inf., διατείνω, (mid.) *stretch/exert oneself*.
21. πρόδηλος, -ον, *clear, evident*.
22. ἄγνοια, -ας, ἡ, *ignorance*.

σοῦτον²³ ὁρῶ λυποῦσαν²⁴ ὅσον τὸ μὴ πείθεσθαι²⁵ τοῖς ὑπὲρ τούτων διαλογισμοῖς²⁶ μηδὲ ἀκολουθεῖν²⁷ αἷς ἔχομεν αὐτοὶ δόξαις,²⁸ μεγάλην ὠφέλειαν²⁹ ἡγοῦμαι³⁰ τὸ συνεχῶς³¹ ἀναμιμνῄσκειν³² καὶ διὰ τοῦ λόγου παρακαλεῖν³³ πρὸς τὸ πείθεσθαι καὶ φυλάττειν³⁴ ἔργῳ τὸ προσῆκον.³⁵

Ὥσπερ³⁶ γὰρ, οἶμαι, καὶ τοὺς ἰατροὺς³⁷ καὶ τοὺς κυβερνήτας³⁸ ὁρῶμεν πολλάκις³⁹ τὰ αὐτὰ προστάττοντας,⁴⁰ καίτοι⁴¹ τὸ πρῶτον ἀκηκοότων οἷς ἂν κελεύωσιν,⁴² ἀλλ᾽ ἐπειδὰν ἀμελοῦντας⁴³ αὐτοὺς καὶ μὴ προσέχοντας⁴⁴ βλέπωσιν, οὕτως καὶ κατὰ τὸν βίον⁴⁵ χρήσιμόν⁴⁶ ἐστι γίγνεσθαι πολλάκις περὶ τῶν αὐτῶν τοὺς λόγους, ὅταν εἰδῶσι μὲν⁴⁷ οἱ πολλοὶ τὸ δέον,⁴⁸ μὴ μέντοι πράττωσιν. ³οὐ γάρ ἐστι τέλος⁴⁹ οὔτε⁵⁰ τοῖς κάμνουσι⁵¹ τὸ γνῶναι τὸ συμφέρον⁵² αὐτοῖς, ἀλλ᾽, οἶμαι, τὸ χρήσασθαι·⁵³ τοῦτο γὰρ αὐτοῖς παρέξει τὴν ὑγίειαν·⁵⁴ οὔτε τοῖς ἄλλοις τὸ μαθεῖν τά τε ὠφελοῦντα⁵⁵ καὶ βλάπτοντα⁵⁶ πρὸς τὸν βίον, ἀλλὰ τὸ μὴ διαμαρτάνειν⁵⁷ τῇ τούτων αἱρέσει.⁵⁸ καθάπερ⁵⁹ γὰρ ἔστιν ἰδεῖν τοὺς ὀφθαλμιῶντας⁶⁰ ἐπισταμένους⁶¹

23. Acc. of extent, τοσοῦτον ... ὅσον, *as much as.*
24. Pres. act. ptc. acc. fem. sg., λυπέω, *grieve, vex*; supp. (ὁρῶ, "see that"; cf. *CGCG* §52.10).
25. Pres. mid. inf., πείθω, (mid.) *obey*; with dat. The articular infinitive is the comparand of τὴν ἄγνοιαν (cf. BDF §399; S §2034; *CGCG* §51.39).
26. διαλογισμός, -οῦ, ὁ, *consideration.*
27. Pres. act. inf., ἀκολουθέω, *follow*; with dat.; another comparand of τὴν ἄγνοιαν. See n. 25.
28. The antecedent has been incorporated into the relative clause (cf. S §2536; *CGCG* §50.15): "[I see that] we ourselves [intensive αὐτοί] are not following the *beliefs that* we have."
29. ὠφέλεια, -ας, ἡ, *benefit*; pred. acc.
30. Pres. mid. indic. 1 sg., ἡγέομαι, *consider.*
31. Adv., *without ceasing, continually.*
32. Pres. act. inf., ἀναμιμνῄσκω, *remind, recall*; art. inf. as acc. subject of indir. disc. See nn. 3, 25.
33. Pres. act. inf., παρακαλέω, *exhort*; art. inf. as acc. subject of indir. disc. See nn. 3, 25.
34. Pres. act. inf., φυλάσσω (Att. φυλάττω), *keep, guard.* πρός with the infinitive indicates purpose (BDF §402; S §2034.b). "Exhorting [us] through reason [διὰ τοῦ λόγου] *to obey and guard* what is proper by action [ἔργῳ]."
35. Pres. act. ptc. acc. neut. sg., προσήκω, (attrib.) *that which is suitable/fitting*; attrib. (subst.).
36. ὥσπερ ... οὕτως καί, *just as ... so also.*
37. ἰατρός, -οῦ, ὁ, *physician.*
38. κυβερνήτης, -ου, ὁ, *steersman, pilot.*
39. Adv., *often.*
40. Pres. act. ptc. acc. masc. pl., προστάσσω, *command, issue an order*; supp. (ὁρῶμεν; indir. disc.).
41. Partic., *although*: "indicates a transition to a text segment which adds information (καί) which is worthy of note (τοι) in light of the preceding context—καίτοι invites a reconsideration of what the speaker has just said" (*CGCG* §59.23).

42. Pres. act. subj. 3 pl., κελεύω, *command*; with dat.; conditional rel. clause (cf. BDF §380; S §2560; *CGCG* §50.20): "though at first [τὸ πρῶτον] those whom they ordered [οἷς ἂν κελεύωσιν] obeyed [ἀκηκοότων = gen. absol.]." That is, the relative clause is the subject of the genitive absolute construction.
43. Pres. act. ptc. acc. masc. pl., ἀμελέω, *be neglectful*; supp. (βλέπωσιν); general temp. clause (cf. BDF §382; S §2409; *CGCG* §47.9).
44. Pres. act. ptc. acc. masc. pl., προσέχω, *hold fast to*; supp. (βλέπωσιν). See n. 43.
45. βίος, -ου, ὁ, *life.*
46. χρήσιμος, -η, -ον, (quasi-impers.) *it is useful*; with acc. and inf.
47. μέν ... μέντοι; stronger contrast than μέν ... δέ (cf. S §2919; *CGCG* §59.27).
48. Pres. act. ptc. acc. neut. sg., δεῖ, (subst.) *what is necessary.*
49. τέλος, -ους, τό, *end* (goal).
50. οὔτε ... οὔτε, *neither* (the sick) ... *nor* (the rest).
51. Pres. act. ptc. dat. masc. pl., κάμνω, *to be sick*; attrib. (subst.).
52. Pres. act. ptc. acc. neut. sg., συμφέρω, *be beneficial*; attib. (subst.).
53. Pres. mid. inf., χράομαι, *make use of*; art. inf. as subject of impers.: "It is not the goal for the sick to know what is beneficial for them, but, I think, *to do it.*"
54. ὑγίεια, -ας, ἡ, *health.*
55. Pres. act. ptc. acc. neut. pl., ὠφελέω, *be of use, beneficial*; attrib. (subst.).
56. Pres. act. ptc. acc. neut. pl., βλάπτω, *harm*; attrib. (subst.).
57. Pres. act. inf., διαμαρτάνω, *miss the mark entirely, err severely*; art. inf. as subject of impers. ἐστι τέλος.
58. αἵρεσις, -εως, ἡ, *choice.*
59. καθάπερ ... παραπλησίως καί, *just as ... likewise also.*
60. Pres. act. ptc. acc. masc. pl., ὀφθαλμιάω, *suffer from ophthalmia* (inflammation of the eye); attrib. (subst.).
61. Pres. mid. ptc. acc. masc. pl., ἐπίσταμαι, *know*; supp. (ἰδεῖν).

μὲν⁶² ὅτι λυπεῖ⁶³ τὸ προσάγειν⁶⁴ τοῖς ὀφθαλμοῖς τὰς χεῖρας, ὅμως⁶⁵ δὲ οὐκ ἐθέλοντας ἀπέχεσθαι,⁶⁶ παραπλησίως καὶ περὶ τὰ ἄλλα πράγματα⁶⁷ οἱ πολλοὶ καὶ λίαν εἰδότες⁶⁸ ὡς οὐ λυσιτελεῖ⁶⁹ τι ποιεῖν, οὐδὲν ἧττον⁷⁰ ἐμπίπτουσιν⁷¹ εἰς αὐτό. ⁴τίς γοῦν⁷² οὐκ οἶδε τὴν ἀκρασίαν⁷³ ὡς μέγα ἐστὶ κακὸν τοῖς ἔχουσιν; ἀλλ' ὅμως μυρίους ἄν τις ἀκρατεῖς⁷⁴ εὕροι.⁷⁵ καὶ νὴ⁷⁶ Δία γε τὴν ἀργίαν⁷⁷ ἅπαντες ἴσασιν⁷⁸ ὡς οὐ μόνον⁷⁹ οὐχ οἷά τε⁸⁰ πορίζειν⁸¹ τὰ δέοντα⁸² πρὸς τὸ ζῆν, ἀλλ' ἔτι καὶ τὰ ὄντα ἀπόλλυσι.⁸³ καίτοι⁸⁴ τῷ ὄντι⁸⁵ πλείους ἔστιν εὑρεῖν τοὺς ἀργοὺς τῶν ἐθελόντων τι πράττειν. ⁵ὅθεν,⁸⁶ οἶμαι, προσήκει⁸⁷ τοὺς ἄμεινον φρονοῦντας⁸⁸ ἀεὶ⁸⁹ συνεχῶς ὑπὲρ τούτων λέγειν, ἐάν πως γένηται δυνατὸν ἐπιστρέψαι⁹⁰ καὶ βιάσασθαι⁹¹ πρὸς τὸ κρεῖττον. ὥσπερ⁹² γὰρ ἐν τοῖς μυστηρίοις⁹³ ὁ ἱεροφάντης⁹⁴ οὐχ ἅπαξ προαγορεύει⁹⁵ τοῖς μυουμένοις⁹⁶ ἕκαστον ὧν χρή,⁹⁷ τὸν αὐτὸν τρόπον καὶ τοὺς ὑπὲρ τῶν συμφερόντων λόγους ὥσπερ τινὰ πρόρρησιν⁹⁸ ἱερὰν λυσιτελεῖ πολλάκις, μᾶλλον δὲ ἀεὶ λέγεσθαι. ⁶τὰ γοῦν⁹⁹ φλεγμαίνοντα¹⁰⁰ τῶν σωμάτων οὐκ εὐθὺς ἐνέδωκε¹⁰¹ πρὸς τὴν πρώτην καταιόνησιν,¹⁰² ἀλλ'

62. μέν . . . δέ; point/counterpoint. See n. 1.
63. Pres. act. indic. 3 sg., λυπέω, *cause pain*.
64. Pres. act. inf., προσάγω, *lead toward*; art. inf. as subject: "*leading* the hands *to* the eyes."
65. Adv., *nevertheless*.
66. Pres. mid. inf., ἀπέχω, *hold* (one's hands) *away from*; comp. of ἐθέλοντας.
67. πρᾶγμα, -ατος, τό, (pl.) *matters, affairs*; περὶ τὰ ἄλλα πράγματα marks the new theme (cf. *CGCG* §60.33).
68. Concessive force (καί; cf. S §2083): καὶ λίαν εἰδότες, "even though they know well."
69. Pres. act. indic. 3 sg., λυσιτελέω, (impers.) *it profits*; with dat. of pers.
70. Idiom, οὐδὲν ἧττον, "nonetheless."
71. Pres. act. indic. 3 pl., ἐμπίπτω, *fall on*; with εἰς αὐτό.
72. Postpositive partic., *at least, at any rate*: "a combination of γε and οὖν, γοῦν modifies an utterance which elaborates (οὖν) upon (part of) the preceding utterance by restricting its applicability (γε). It is often used in sentences which provide 'minimal evidence' or the 'minimal applicability' for the preceding statement" (*CGCG* §59.54).
73. ἀκρασία, -ας, ἡ, *intemperance* (opposite of σωφροσύνη). Prolepsis: the subject of the dependent clause is made the object of the main clause (cf. BDF §476; S §2182; *CGCG* §60.37).
74. ἀκρατής, -ές, *intemperate, without command over one's passions*; pred. comp.
75. Aor. act. opt. 3 sg., εὑρίσκω, *find*; potential (cf. BDF §385; S §1824; *CGCG* §34.13).
76. Partic. of strong affirmation with acc. of oath (underscored by γε), "Yes, indeed, by Zeus!" or simply, "Yes, indeed!" (cf. S §§1596, 2922).
77. ἀργία, -ας, ἡ, *idleness*; prolepsis. See n. 73.
78. ἴσασιν = οἴδασιν.
79. οὐ μόνον . . . ἀλλ' ἔτι καί, *not only . . . but still also*.
80. Idiom, οἷός τε (εἰμί), *capable*; with inf. (cf. S §2497; *CGCG* §51.9).
81. Pres. act. inf., πορίζω, *provide, furnish*.
82. Pres. act. ptc. acc. neut. pl., δεῖ, (subst.) *that which is necessary*.

83. Pres. act. indic. 3 sg., ἀπόλλυμι, *destroy*.
84. Partic., *although*: "indicates a transition to a text segment which adds information (καί) which is worthy of note (τοι) in light of the preceding context—καίτοι invites a reconsideration of what the speaker has just said" (*CGCG* §59.23).
85. Idiom, *in reality, in fact*.
86. Adv., *whence, therefore*.
87. Pres. act. indic. 3 sg., προσήκω, (impers.) *it is fitting*; with acc. and inf.
88. Pres. act. ptc. acc. masc. pl., φρονέω (with ἄμεινον), *be superior in thinking*; attrib. (subst.).
89. Adv., *always*.
90. Aor. act. inf., ἐπιστρέφω, *turn, change course*; comp. of quasi-impers. γένηται δυνατόν: "It might be possible to turn and force them to the better course."
91. Aor. mid. inf., βιάζω, *force*.
92. ὥσπερ . . . τὸν αὐτὸν τρόπον καί, "just as . . . in the same manner also."
93. μυστήριον, -ου, τό, (pl.) *the mysteries*.
94. ἱεροφάντης, -ου, ὁ, *hierophant, initiating priest*.
95. Pres. act. indic. 3 sg., προαγορεύω, *explain beforehand*.
96. Pres. pass. ptc. dat. masc. pl., μυέω, (pass.) *be initiated into the mysteries*; attrib. (subst.).
97. Quasi-impers., χρή, *it is necessary*; with acc. and inf.; ἕκαστον ὧν χρή, "each of the things that are necessary [for them to do]." The relative pronoun ὧν has been attracted to the case of its omitted antecedent.
98. πρόρρησις, -εως, ἡ, *instruction, warning*; ὥσπερ τινὰ πρόρρησιν ἱεράν, "like a sacred admonition."
99. Postpositive partic.: "A combination of γε and οὖν, γοῦν modifies an utterance which elaborates (οὖν) upon (part of) the preceding utterance by restricting its applicability (γε)" (*CGCG* §59.54).
100. Pres. act. ptc. nom. neut. pl., φλεγμαίνω, *be inflamed*.
101. Aor. act. indic. 3 sg., ἐνδίδωμι, *give over, surrender*.
102. καταιόνησις, -εως, ἡ, *fomentation*.

ἄν[103] συνεχῶς τοῦτο ποιῇ τις, ἐμαλάχθη[104] καὶ ῥᾷον[105] ἔσχεν· οὐκοῦν[106] ὁμοίως καὶ τὴν ἐν τῇ ψυχῇ τῶν πολλῶν φλεγμονὴν[107] ἀγαπητὸν[108] εἴ τις δύναιτο[109] πραΰναι[110] διηνεκῶς[111] τῷ λόγῳ χρώμενος.

NOTES

1. The need for repetition arises from the marked dissonance between belief and practice (cf. Dio Chrysostom, *Exil.* 13; James 1:22–25; Epictetus, *Diatr.* 2.9; Seneca, *Ep.* 94.32–35).

2. καὶ διὰ τοῦ λόγου παρακαλεῖν πρὸς τὸ πείθεσθαι καὶ φυλάττειν ἔργῳ τὸ προσῆκον. Note the dative of means ἔργῳ. *Action* is the only way to hold fast to proper belief (cf. James 2:18–26).

3. ὥσπερ γάρ, οἶμαι, καὶ τοὺς ἰατρούς. The philosopher qua physician is a common motif of ancient Mediterranean rhetoric (cf. Mark 2:17 parr.; Luke 4:23; Ign. *Eph.* 7.2; Diogn. 9.6; Musonius Rufus, *Frag.* 2; Plutarch, *Mor.* 74d; Seneca, *Ep.* 75). Indeed, a number of philosophers were physicians, so many that Galen could title his work, *That the Best Physician Is Also a Philosopher*. For further discussion, see Malherbe (1989, 128–30).

4. τὴν ἀκρασίαν. "Intemperance" is the opposite of "self-mastery" (ἐγκράτεια; cf. Aristotle, *Eth. nic.* 1150b6–7). Aristotle opens book 7 of *Nicomachean Ethics* with the question of whether proper knowledge is sufficient to subdue ἀκρασία.

---

103. ἄν = ἐάν.
104. Aor. pass. indic. 3 sg., μαλάσσω, (pass.) *be softened*.
105. Compar., ῥᾴδιος, -α, -ον, adv. with ἔχω, (of a sick person) *get better*.
106. Partic.: essentially the equivalent of οὖν (cf. *CGCG* §59.33).
107. φλεγμονή, -ῆς, ἡ, *inflammation*. Prolepsis designates the topic: "So in like manner also *as it pertains to the inflammation in the souls of the many*, we must be content if one is able to soothe *them*, making unceasing use of reasoned speech."
108. ἀγαπητός, -ή, -όν, (quasi-impers.) *it is something with which one must be content*; apodosis.
109. Pres. mid. opt. 3 sg., δύναμαι; potential protasis of a mixed condition (cf. S §2360).
110. Aor. act. inf., πραΰνω, *soothe*.
111. Adv., *unceasingly*.

7.4.2

On Concord

A Political Address in the Assembly 14–16

14'Ἐμοὶ μέλει[1] μὲν[2] καὶ τοῦ καθ' ὑμᾶς, μέλει δὲ καὶ τοῦ κατ' ἐμαυτόν. εἰ γὰρ φιλόσοφος[3] πολιτείας[4] ἁψάμενος[5] οὐκ ἐδυνήθη παρέχειν[6] ὁμονοοῦσαν[7] πόλιν,[8] τοῦτο δεινὸν[9] ἤδη καὶ ἄφυκτον,[10] ὥσπερ εἰ ναυπηγὸς[11] ἐν νηὶ[12] πλέων[13] μὴ παρέχοι[14] τὴν ναῦν πλέουσαν, καὶ εἰ κυβερνήτης[15] φάσκων[16] εἶναι πρὸς αὐτὸ τὸ κῦμα[17] ἀποκλίνοι,[18] ἢ λαβὼν οἰκίαν οἰκοδόμος,[19] ὁρῶν πίπτουσαν,[20] ὁ δὲ τούτου μὲν[21] ἀμελῶν,[22] κονιῶν[23] δὲ καὶ χρίων[24] οἴοιτό[25] τι ποιεῖν.

Εἴ μοι προέκειτο[26] νῦν ὑπὲρ ὁμονοίας[27] λέγειν, εἶπον ἄν[28] πολλὰ καὶ περὶ τῶν ἀνθρωπίνων[29] καὶ περὶ τῶν οὐρανίων[30] παθημάτων,[31] ὅτι τὰ θεῖα[32] ταῦτα καὶ

---

1. Pres. act. indic. 3 sg., μέλω; μέλει μοί τινος, *I care / am concerned for something* (cf. S §1567; CGCG §36.15).
2. μέν . . . δέ; point/counterpoint (cf. Runge 2010, 75–83; BDF §447; S §2904; CGCG §59.24).
3. φιλόσοφος, -ου, ὁ, *philosopher*.
4. πολιτεία, -ας, ἡ, *government*.
5. Aor. mid. ptc. nom. masc. sg., ἅπτω, (mid.) *take hold of*; with gen.; circ.
6. Pres. act. inf., παρέχω, *produce*; comp. of ἐδυνήθη.
7. Pres. act. ptc. acc. fem. sg., ὁμονοέω, *be of one mind, united*; attrib.
8. πόλις, -εως, ἡ, *city*.
9. δεινός, -ή, -όν, *fearful, terrible, dangerous*.
10. ἄφυκτος, -ον, *unescapable*.
11. ναυπηγός, -οῦ, ὁ, *shipbuilder*.
12. ναῦς, νᾶος (Epic νηῦς, νηός), ἡ, *ship*.
13. Pres. act. ptc. nom. masc. sg., πλέω, *sail*; circ.
14. Pres. act. opt. 3 sg., παρέχω, *yield, produce*. Comparative conditional clauses often take the optative, as here (cf. S §2478; CGCG §49.22).
15. κυβερνήτης, -ου, ὁ, *pilot*; pred. nom.
16. Pres. act. ptc. nom. masc. sg., φάσκω, *claim*; circ.
17. κῦμα, -ατα, τό, *wave*; with intensive αὐτό.
18. Pres. act. opt. 3 sg., ἀποκλίνω, *turn aside, swerve*; compar. conditional clause. See n. 14.
19. οἰκοδόμος, -ου, ὁ, *builder*.
20. Pres. act. ptc. acc. fem. sg., πίπτω, *fall (into decay)*; supp. (ὁρῶν).
21. μέν . . . δέ; point/counterpoint. See n. 2.
22. Pres. act. ptc. nom. masc. sg., ἀμελέω, *show no concern for*; with gen.
23. Pres. act. ptc. nom. masc. sg., κονιάω, *plaster with stucco*; circ.
24. Pres. act. ptc. nom. masc. sg., χρίω, *wash with color*; circ.
25. Pres. mid. opt. 3 sg., οἴομαι, *consider, presume*; compar. conditional clause. See n. 14.
26. Impf. pass. indic. 3 sg., πρόκειμαι, (impers.) *it lies before (someone)*. The subject is explicated by ὑπὲρ ὁμονοίας λέγειν.
27. ὁμονοία, -ας, ἡ, *harmony, concord*.
28. Second-class (contrafactual) condition (cf. BDF §360; S §2303; CGCG §49.10).
29. ἀνθρώπινος, -η, -ον, *human*.
30. οὐράνιος, -α, -ον, *heavenly*.
31. πάθημα, -ατος, τό, (pl.) *incidents, occurrences*.
32. θεῖος, -α, -ον, *divine*.

μεγάλα ὁμονοίας τυγχάνει³³ δεόμενα³⁴ καὶ φιλίας·³⁵ εἰ δὲ μή, κίνδυνος³⁶ ἀπολέσθαι³⁷ καὶ φθαρῆναι³⁸ τῷ καλῷ τούτῳ δημιουργήματι³⁹ τῷ κόσμῳ. **¹⁵**ἀλλ' ἴσως⁴⁰ μακρολογῶ,⁴¹ δέον⁴² βαδίζειν⁴³ καὶ παρακαλεῖν⁴⁴ τὸν ἡγεμόνα.⁴⁵ τοσοῦτον δὴ⁴⁶ μόνον ἐρῶ· οὐκ αἰσχρόν⁴⁷ ἐστιν, εἰ μέλιτται⁴⁸ μὲν ὁμονοοῦσι, καὶ οὐδεὶς οὐδέποτε⁴⁹ ἑώρακεν ἐσμὸν⁵⁰ στασιάζοντα⁵¹ καὶ μαχόμενον⁵² αὐτῷ·⁵³ συνεργάζονται⁵⁴ δὲ καὶ ζῶσιν ἅμα, καὶ παρέχουσαι τὴν τροφὴν⁵⁵ αὐταῖς καὶ χρώμεναι; τί οὖν;⁵⁶ οὐχὶ κἀκεῖ⁵⁷ γίγνονται κηφῆνές⁵⁸ τινες λεγόμενοι χαλεποὶ⁵⁹ καὶ κατεσθίοντες⁶⁰ τὸ μέλι;⁶¹ νὴ Δία,⁶² γίγνονται μέν·⁶³ ὅμως⁶⁴ δὲ καὶ τούτους πολλάκις ἐῶσιν⁶⁵ οἱ γεωργοί,⁶⁶ μὴ βουλόμενοι ταράττειν⁶⁷ τὸν ἐσμόν, καὶ βέλτιον⁶⁸ νομίζουσι⁶⁹ παραναλίσκειν⁷⁰ τοῦ μέλιτος ἢ πάσας θορυβῆσαι⁷¹ τὰς μελίττας. **¹⁶**οὐ μέντοι παρ' ἡμῖν τυχὸν⁷² οὐδείς ἐστι κηφὴν ἀργός,⁷³ βομβῶν⁷⁴ σαθρόν,⁷⁵ γευόμενος⁷⁶ τοῦ μέλιτος. καὶ μέντοι⁷⁷ καὶ μύρμηκας⁷⁸ πάνυ ἡδέως ἰδεῖν ἔστιν,⁷⁹ ὅπως μὲν⁸⁰ οἰκοῦσι μετ'

33. Pres. act. indic. 3 sg., τυγχάνω, *happen to be*; with supp. ptc.
34. Pres. mid. ptc. nom. neut. pl., δέω, (mid.) *need, be in want of*; with gen.; supp. (τυγχάνει).
35. φιλία, -ας, ἡ, *friendship*.
36. κίνδυνος, -ου, ὁ, *danger*.
37. Aor. mid. inf., ἀπόλλυμι, (mid.) *perish*; epex. (κίνδυνος; cf. S §2001; *CGCG* §51.18): "Then there is danger *of perishing and being ruined* for this good creation, the cosmos."
38. Aor. pass. inf., φθείρω, (pass.) *be ruined*; epex. See n. 37.
39. δημιούργημα, -ατος, τό, *creation*.
40. Adv., *perhaps*.
41. Pres. act. indic. 1 sg., μακρολογέω, *speak at length*.
42. Pres. act. ptc. acc. neut. sg., δεῖ, *be necessary*; with acc. and inf.; acc. absol. (cf. BDF §424; S §2076; *CGCG* §52.33).
43. Pres. act. inf., βαδίζω, *go*.
44. Pres. act. inf., παρακαλέω, *summon*.
45. ἡγεμών, -όνος, ὁ, (here) *proconsul* (i.e., the provincial governor).
46. Postpositive partic.: "indicates that the speaker considers (and invites the addressee to consider) the text segment or word (group) which it modifies as evident, clear, or precise" (*CGCG* §59.44); underscores τοσοῦτον: "*This much* alone I will say."
47. αἰσχρός, -ά, -όν, (quasi-impers.) *it is shameful*; apodosis: "Is it not shameful . . . ?" (Answer: yes!) The content of οὐκ αἰσχρόν ἐστιν, while implicit, is filled out at the end of the paragraph: οὔκουν αἰσχρόν . . .
48. μέλισσα, -ας, ἡ (Att. μέλιττα), *bee*.
49. Adv., *never, not at any time*.
50. ἐσμός, -οῦ, ὁ, *swarm*.
51. Pres. act. ptc. acc. masc. sg., στασιάζω, *be factious*; supp. (ἑώρακεν).
52. Pres. mid. ptc. acc. masc. sg., μάχομαι, *fight*; supp.
53. αὑτῷ = ἑαυτῷ.
54. Pres. mid. indic. 3 sg., συνεργάζομαι, *work together*.
55. τροφή, -ῆς, ἡ, *nourishment, food*.
56. τί οὖν; is common in the diatribe. Here it marks a *false conclusion*: "What, then? Is it not also the case there [i.e., in the example I just gave] that some bees are called drones, irksome creatures that devour honey?"

57. Crasis: κἀκεῖ = καὶ ἐκεῖ.
58. κηφήν, -ῆνος, ὁ, *drone* (used of things in nature that are drone-like).
59. χαλεπός, -ή, -όν, *hard to deal with, irksome*.
60. Pres. act. ptc. nom. masc. pl., κατεσθίω, *devour*.
61. μέλι, -ιτος, τό, *honey*.
62. Partic. of strong affirmation with acc. of oath, "Yes, by Zeus!" or "Yes, of course!" (cf. S §§1596, 2922).
63. μέν . . . δέ . . . μέντοι. The μέν-clause is his concession ("Yes, of course there are."); the δέ-clause is his counter with a concession, while the μέντοι-clause challenges the premise altogether.
64. Adv., *nevertheless*.
65. Pres. act. indic. 3 pl., ἐάω, *permit, tolerate*.
66. γεωργός, -οῦ, ὁ, *farmer*.
67. Pres. act. inf., ταράσσω (Att. ταράττω), *trouble, disturb*; comp. of βουλόμενοι.
68. Compar. of ἀγαθός, -ή, -όν, *better*; quasi-impers. with acc. and inf.; indir. disc. (cf. BDF §396; S §2016; *CGCG* §51.19).
69. Pres. act. indic. 3 pl., νομίζω, *think, consider*.
70. Pres. act. inf., παραναλίσκω, *squander, waste*; comp. of βέλτιον, with partitive gen.: "It is better to waste *some of* the honey."
71. Aor. act. inf., θορυβέω, *throw into confusion*.
72. Aor. act. ptc. acc. neut. sg., τυγχάνω, (as acc. absol.) "by chance." See n. 42.
73. ἀργός, -όν, *idle, lazy*.
74. Pres. act. ptc. nom. masc. sg., βομβέω, *make a buzzing noise*.
75. σαθρός, -ά, -όν, (adv. acc.) *impotently*.
76. Pres. mid. ptc. nom. masc. sg., γεύω, *taste, eat of*; with gen.
77. Partic. combination: additional closely related information (καί) that "contradicts or modifies the expectations raised by the preceding context (μέντοι)" (*CGCG* §59.26)—thus he provides an additional example that renders the false conclusion irrelevant.
78. μύρμηξ, -ηκος, ὁ, *ant*.
79. Impers. (recessive accent) with καί . . . πάνυ ἡδέως, "it is also most delightful."
80. μέν . . . δέ . . . δέ . . . δέ; sequence (cf. S §2907).

ἀλλήλων εὐκόλως,⁸¹ ὅπως δὲ ἐξίασιν,⁸² ὅπως δὲ τὰ βάρη⁸³ μεταλαμβάνουσι,⁸⁴ ὅπως δὲ παραχωροῦσιν⁸⁵ ἀλλήλοις τῶν ὁδῶν. οὔκουν⁸⁶ αἰσχρὸν ἀνθρώπους ὄντας ἀφρονεστέρους⁸⁷ εἶναι θηρίων⁸⁸ οὕτω σμικρῶν⁸⁹ καὶ ἀφρόνων;

NOTES

14. ὑπὲρ ὁμονοίας λέγειν. Speeches on ὁμόνοια/*concordia* were common in the ancient Mediterranean world (cf. Isocrates, *Panegyricus*; Plato, *Ep.* 7; Xenophon, *Mem.* 4.4.15–16; Cicero, *Rhet. Her.* 4.19; Plutarch, *Mor.* 144b–c; Pseudo-Sallust, *Ep.* 2; Aristides, *Or.* 23–24; 1 Clem. 20; Ign. *Eph.* 4.1–2). On ὁμόνοια speeches in Dio Chrysostom, cf. *Or.* 1–4; 38–41; and Lau (2010, 157–207).

15–16. τί οὖν. Crosby (1946) suggests the rhetorical question comes from an interlocutor: "'What!' someone objects, 'do we not find there too bees that are called drones, annoying creatures which devour the honey?'" Yet it seems more likely that Dio Chrysostom introduces the rhetorical objection himself. In any case, the sequence is as follows: (1) objection (τί οὖν), (2) concession (νὴ Δία, γίγνονται μέν), (3) qualified rejoinder (ὅμως δὲ καί), (4) further rejoinder that nullifies the objection (μέντοι), and (5) another rejoinder that nullifies the objection (καὶ μέντοι καί).

---

81. Adv., *contentedly*.
82. Pres. act. indic. 3 pl., ἐξίημι, *go out*.
83. βάρος, -ους, τό, *burden*.
84. Pres. act. indic. 3 pl., μεταλαμβάνω, *have a share in*.
85. Pres. act. indic. 3 pl., παραχωρέω, *step aside out of the way* (for another); with dat. of pers. and gen. of thing.
86. Partic.: "introduces yes/no questions; the negative has its usual force of indicating that a positive answer is expected, and οὖν serves its regular function of 'getting to the point' (*isn't it the case, then?*)" (CGCG §59.33).
87. Compar., ἄφρων, -ον, *more senseless, more foolish*.
88. θηρίον, -ου, τό, *beast*; gen. of compar.
89. σμικρός, -ά, -όν, *tiny*.

7.5

Plutarch

In part 6.5, we met Plutarch (45–120 CE) the biographer. Here, we engage his *Moralia*, an expansive collection of dialogues, letters, and lectures.[1] Plutarch is the preeminent representative of Middle Platonism, a movement that combines traditional Platonic doctrine with the insights of other philosophical schools (see Dillon 1977). His interests were aimed at the moral therapy of the "everyday" person and have long been recognized as vital resources for the study of the New Testament (Betz 1978). "Especially to Christians," Babbitt notes, "Plutarch has always made a strong appeal, since his writings have much in common with the New Testament, being derived in some cases from the same sources" (Babbitt 1927, xvii).

The readings entail excerpts from three treatises: *How to Tell a Flatterer from a Friend*, *Advice to Bride and Groom*, and *On Superstition*. The first is used to introduce the rhetorical practice of adaptation and modulation. The second provides close linguistic (and perhaps conceptual) parallels to Paul's instructions to husbands and wives. The third is Plutarch's critique of "popular" religion, or superstition, in which he targets, among other things, the Jewish practice of keeping the Sabbath.

Text and Translation: Babbitt 1927 (§7.5.1); Babbitt 1928 (§§7.5.2–3)

Supplemental Scripture: Luke 5:27–31 (§7.5.1); Eph. 5:21–33 (§7.5.2); John 7:19–24 (§7.5.3)

---

1. Plutarch's *Moralia* is referenced according to the page numbers in Stephanus's (1572) edition. Thus, for example, *Mor.* 74d references *Moralia*, Stephanus page 74, section d.

7.5.1

On Balancing Rhetoric

How to Tell a Flatterer from a Friend 37 (Mor. 74d–e)

37'Ἐπεὶ τοίνυν,[1] ὥσπερ εἴρηται, πολλάκις[2] ἡ παρρησία[3] τῷ θεραπευομένῳ[4] λυπηρὰ[5] πέφυκε,[6] δεῖ μιμεῖσθαι[7] τοὺς ἰατρούς·[8] οὔτε[9] γὰρ ἐκεῖνοι τέμνοντες[10] ἐν τῷ πονεῖν[11] καὶ ἀλγεῖν[12] καταλείπουσι[13] τὸ πεπονθός,[14] ἀλλ' ἐνέβρεξαν[15] προσηνῶς[16] καὶ κατῄόνησαν,[17] οὔθ' οἱ νουθετοῦντες[18] ἀστείως[19] τὸ πικρὸν[20] καὶ δηκτικὸν[21] προσβαλόντες[22] ἀποτρέχουσιν,[23] ἀλλ' ὁμιλίαις[24] ἑτέραις καὶ λόγοις ἐπιεικέσιν[25] ἐκπραΰνουσι[26] καὶ διαχέουσιν,[27] ὥσπερ οἱ λιθοξόοι[28] τὰ πληγέντα[29] καὶ περικοπέντα[30] τῶν ἀγαλμάτων[31] ἐπιλεαίνοντες[32]

1. Partic.: "Indicates a transition to a newly relevant, to-the-point text segment (νυν), and stresses the importance or relevance for the addressee of that new point (τοι)" (*CGCG* §59.39). Ἐπεὶ τοίνυν ("since, then, ...") introduces the final major point in the treatise: how to balance "frankness" (παρρησία) with a gentle touch.
2. Adv., *often*.
3. παρρησία, -ας, ἡ, *frankness*.
4. Pres. pass. ptc. dat. masc. sg., θεραπεύω, (pass.) *be attended to, treated*; attrib. (subst.).
5. λυπηρός, -ά, -όν, *painful*.
6. Pf. act. indic. 3 sg., φύω, *be so by nature*.
7. Pres. mid. inf., μιμέομαι, *imitate*; comp. of δεῖ.
8. ἰατρός, -οῦ, ὁ, *physician*.
9. οὔτε ... οὔθ', *neither ... nor*.
10. Pres. act. ptc. nom. masc. pl., τέμνω, *cut* (a body part [in an operation]); circ.
11. Pres. act. inf., πονέω, *suffer*. The articular infinitive functions as the object of ἐν, whereby the preposition designates the circumstance in which the part would be abandoned (cf. BDF §404; S §2033.b).
12. Pres. act. inf., ἀλγέω, *be in pain*. See n. 11.
13. Pres. act. indic. 3 pl., καταλείπω, *leave, abandon*.
14. Pf. act. ptc. neut. acc. sg., πάσχω, (pass.) *be affected*; attrib. (subst.).

15. Aor. act. indic. 3 pl., ἐμβρέχω, *douse, inundate*.
16. Adv., *gently*.
17. Aor. act. indic. 3 pl., καταιονάω, *foment*.
18. Pres. act. ptc. nom. masc. pl., νουθετέω, *admonish*; attrib. (subst.).
19. Adv., *elegantly, brilliantly*.
20. πικρός, -ή, -όν, (subst.) *bitterness*.
21. δηκτικός, -ή, -όν, (subst.) *bite, sting*.
22. Aor. act. ptc. nom. masc. pl., προσβάλλω, *apply*; circ.
23. Pres. act. indic. 3 pl., ἀποτρέχω, *run away*.
24. ὁμιλία, -ας, ἡ, *conversation*; dat. of means.
25. ἐπιεικής, -ές, *suitable*, (by extens.) *moderate, lenient*.
26. Pres. act. indic. 3 pl., ἐκπραΰνω, *soften, mollify*.
27. Pres. act. indic. 3 pl., διαχέω, *relax*.
28. λιθοξόος, -ου, ὁ, *stonecutter*.
29. Aor. pass. ptc. acc. neut. pl., πλήσσω, (pass.) *be struck*; attrib. (subst.).
30. Aor. pass. ptc. acc. neut. pl., περικόπτω, (pass.) *be cut around*.
31. ἄγαλμα, -ατος, τό, *statue*.
32. Pres. act. ptc. nom. masc. pl., ἐπιλεαίνω, *smooth over*; circ. (compar.).

καὶ γανοῦντες.³³ ὁ δὲ πληγεὶς μὲν³⁴ τῇ παρρησίᾳ καὶ χαραχθείς,³⁵ ἀφεθεὶς³⁶ δὲ τραχὺς³⁷ καὶ οἰδῶν³⁸ καὶ ἀνώμαλος³⁹ ὑπ' ὀργῆς δυσανάκλητος⁴⁰ αὖθις⁴¹ ἐστι καὶ δυσπαρηγόρητος.⁴² διὸ καὶ τοῦτο δεῖ παραφυλάττειν⁴³ ἐν τοῖς μάλιστα⁴⁴ τοὺς νουθετοῦντας καὶ μὴ προαπολείπειν,⁴⁵ μηδὲ ποιεῖσθαι πέρας⁴⁶ ὁμιλίας καὶ συνουσίας⁴⁷ τὸ λυποῦν⁴⁸ καὶ παροξῦνον⁴⁹ τοὺς συνήθεις.⁵⁰

παρρησία could have negative repercussions (cf. 2 Cor. 1:23–2:4).

δεῖ μιμεῖσθαι τοὺς ἰατρούς. Cf. *Mor.* 465d; 523e–524a. See note on Dio Chrysostom, *Avar.* 2 (§7.4.1).

NOTES

ἡ παρρησία. Philosophers and orators recognized the importance of "frank speech" (παρρησία) but held that it needed to be timely—that is, "in season" (cf. Philo, *Somn.* 2.78–92; Dio Cassius, *Hist. rom.* 65.12.1; Malherbe 1989, 139 and references therein). Moreover, as Plutarch stresses in the passage, παρρησία must be properly modulated (cf. Dio Chrysostom, *1 Regn.* 5), since excessive

33. Pres. act. ptc. nom. masc. pl., γανόω, *polish*; circ. (compar.).
34. μέν . . . δέ; point/counterpoint set (cf. Runge 2010, 75–83; BDF §447; S §2904; CGCG §59.24).
35. Aor. pass. ptc. nom. masc. sg., χαράσσω, (pass.) *be scratched, scored*.
36. Aor. pass. ptc. nom. masc. sg., ἀφίημι, (pass.) *be left*; circ.
37. τραχύς, -εῖς, -ύ, *rough*.
38. Pres. act. ptc. nom. masc. sg., οἰδέω, *be swollen*; attrib.
39. ἀνώμαλος, -ον, *uneven*.
40. δυσανάκλητος, -ον, *hard to call back/restore*; with ὑπ' ὀργῆς (cause).
41. Adv., *again, next time*.
42. δυσπαρηγόρητος, -ον, *inconsolable*.
43. Pres. act. inf., παραφυλάσσω (Att. παραφυλάττω), *guard carefully*; comp. of δεῖ with acc. subject τοὺς νουθετοῦντας.
44. Adv. acc., *especially*; ἐν τοῖς μάλιστα, "in these respects especially."
45. Pres. act. inf., προαπολείπω, *leave beforehand*; comp. of δεῖ.
46. πέρας, -ατος, τό, *end*; with gen.; pred. comp.
47. συνουσία, -ας, ἡ, *social intercourse*.
48. Pres. act. ptc. acc. neut. sg., λυπέω, *grieve, cause pain*; attrib. (subst.).
49. Pres. act. ptc. acc. neut. sg., παροξύνω, *provoke, irritate*; attrib. (subst.).
50. συνήθης, -ες, (pl. subst.) *acquaintances*; obj. of τὸ λυποῦν καὶ παροξῦνον.

7.5.2

Advice to Bride and Groom

Advice to Bride and Groom 33–34 (*Mor.* 142e–f)

33Οἱ πλούσιοι¹ καὶ οἱ βασιλεῖς τιμῶντες² τοὺς φιλοσόφους³ αὑτούς⁴ τε κοσμοῦσι⁵ κἀκείνους,⁶ οἱ δὲ φιλόσοφοι τοὺς πλουσίους θεραπεύοντες⁷ οὐκ ἐκείνους ποιοῦσιν ἐνδόξους⁸ ἀλλ' αὑτοὺς ἀδοξοτέρους.⁹ τοῦτο συμβαίνει¹⁰ καὶ περὶ τὰς γυναῖκας. ὑποτάττουσαι¹¹ μὲν¹² γὰρ ἑαυτὰς τοῖς ἀνδράσιν ἐπαινοῦνται,¹³ κρατεῖν¹⁴ δὲ βουλόμεναι μᾶλλον τῶν κρατουμένων ἀσχημονοῦσι.¹⁵

κρατεῖν δὲ δεῖ τὸν ἄνδρα τῆς γυναικὸς οὐχ ὡς δεσπότην¹⁶ κτήματος¹⁷ ἀλλ' ὡς ψυχὴν σώματος, συμπαθοῦντα¹⁸ καὶ συμπεφυκότα¹⁹ τῇ εὐνοίᾳ.²⁰ ὥσπερ²¹ οὖν σώματος ἔστι²² κήδεσθαι²³ μὴ δουλεύοντα²⁴ ταῖς ἡδοναῖς²⁵ αὐτοῦ καὶ ταῖς ἐπιθυμίαις,²⁶ οὕτω γυναικὸς ἄρχειν εὐφραίνοντα²⁷ καὶ χαριζόμενον.²⁸

1. πλούσιος, -α, -ον, *rich*.
2. Pres. act. ptc. nom. masc. pl., τιμάω, *honor*; circ.
3. φιλόσοφος, -ου, ὁ, *philosopher*.
4. αὑτούς = ἑαυτούς.
5. Pres. act. indic. 3 pl., κοσμέω, *adorn*.
6. Crasis: καὶ ἐκείνους.
7. Pres. act. ptc. nom. masc. pl., θεραπεύω, *pay court to, flatter*; circ.
8. ἔνδοξος, -ον, *held in esteem/honor*; pred. comp.
9. Compar., ἄδοξος, -ον, *more disreputable*; pred. comp.
10. Pres. act. indic. 3 sg., συμβαίνω, *happens, turns out to be*.
11. Pres. act. ptc. nom. fem. pl., ὑποτάσσω (Att. ὑποτάττω), *subordinate*; circ. (conditional).
12. μέν . . . δέ; point/counterpoint provides support/explanation (γάρ) (cf. Runge 2010, 75–83; BDF §447; S §2904; *CGCG* §59.24).
13. Pres. pass. indic. 3 pl., ἐπαινέω, (pass.) *be praised*.
14. Pres. act. inf., κρατέω, *exercise control over, be master of*; with gen.; comp. of βουλόμεναι.
15. Pres. act. indic. 3 pl., ἀσχημονέω, *behave unseemly, be disgraced*.
16. δεσπότης, -ου, ὁ, *master*.
17. κτῆμα, -ατος, τό, *property*.
18. Pres. act. ptc. acc. masc. sg., συμπαθέω, *share the pathos of another*.
19. Pf. act. ptc. acc. masc. sg., συμφύω, *be joined/united together*.
20. εὔνοια, -ας, ἡ, *goodwill*.
21. ὥσπερ . . . οὕτω, *as . . . so*.
22. Impers. (recessive accent), *it is possible*; with inf. (cf. S §1985; *CGCG* §26.10).
23. Pres. mid. inf., κήδω, (mid.) *care for*; with gen.
24. Pres. act. ptc. acc. masc. pl., δουλεύω, *be a slave*; with dat.; circ.
25. ἡδονή, -ῆς, ἡ, *pleasure*.
26. ἐπιθυμία, -ας, ἡ, *desire*.
27. Pres. act. ptc. acc. masc. sg., εὐφραίνω, *cheer, gladden, delight*; circ.
28. Pres. mid. ptc. acc. masc. sg., χαρίζω, *gratify*; circ.

³⁴Τῶν σωμάτων οἱ φιλόσοφοι τὰ μὲν²⁹ ἐκ διεστώτων³⁰ λέγουσιν εἶναι καθάπερ στόλον³¹ καὶ στρατόπεδον,³² τὰ δ' ἐκ συναπτομένων³³ ὡς οἰκίαν καὶ ναῦν,³⁴ τὰ δ' ἡνωμένα³⁵ καὶ συμφυῆ³⁶ καθάπερ ἐστι τῶν ζῴων³⁷ ἕκαστον. σχεδὸν³⁸ οὖν καὶ γάμος³⁹ ὁ μὲν⁴⁰ τῶν ἐρώντων⁴¹ ἡνωμένος καὶ συμφυής ἐστι, ὁ δὲ τῶν διὰ προῖκας⁴² ἢ τέκνα γαμούντων⁴³ ἐκ διεστώτων, ὁ δὲ τῶν συγκαθευδόντων⁴⁴ ἐκ διεστώτων, οὓς συνοικεῖν⁴⁵ ἄν τις ἀλλήλοις οὐ συμβιοῦν⁴⁶ νομίσειε.⁴⁷ δεῖ δέ, ὥσπερ οἱ φυσικοὶ⁴⁸ τῶν ὑγρῶν⁴⁹ λέγουσι δι' ὅλων⁵⁰ γενέσθαι τὴν κρᾶσιν,⁵¹ οὕτω τῶν γαμούντων καὶ σώματα καὶ χρήματα καὶ φίλους καὶ οἰκείους ἀναμειχθῆναι⁵² δι' ἀλλήλων. καὶ γὰρ⁵³ ὁ Ῥωμαῖος νομοθέτης⁵⁴ ἐκώλυσε⁵⁵ δῶρα διδόναι καὶ λαμβάνειν παρ' ἀλλήλων τοὺς γεγαμηκότας, οὐχ ἵνα μηδενὸς μεταλαμβάνωσιν,⁵⁶ ἀλλ' ἵνα πάντα κοινὰ νομίζωσιν.

NOTES

29. τὰ μέν . . . τὰ δέ . . . τὰ δέ, *some* (*bodies*) . . . *other* (*bodies*) . . . *other* (*bodies*) (cf. BDF §250; S §1107; CGCG §28.27); explicates the theme (τῶν σωμάτων).
30. Pf. act. ptc. gen. neut. pl., διΐστημι, *be separate*; attrib. (subst.).
31. στόλος, -ου, ὁ, *army, fleet*.
32. στρατόπεδον, -ου, τό, *encampment, army, squadron*.
33. Pres. pass. ptc. gen. neut. pl., συνάπτω, *be joined together*; attrib. (subst.).
34. ναῦς, νᾶος, ἡ, *ship*.
35. Pf. pass. ptc. gen. neut. pl., ἑνόω, (pass.) *be made one*; attrib.
36. συμφυής, -ές, *naturally united*.
37. ζῷον, -ου, τό, *living creature, animal*.
38. Adv., *more or less*.
39. γάμος, -ου, ὁ, *marriage*; nom. pendent designates the new topic: "So, too, is more or less the case with marriage."
40. ὁ μέν . . . ὁ δέ . . . ὁ δέ, *the one* (*kind of marriage*) . . . *the other* (*kind of marriage*) . . . *the other* (*kind of marriage*). See n. 29.
41. Pres. act. ptc. gen. masc. pl., ἐράω, *be in love*; attrib. (subst.).
42. προίξ, -ικός, ἡ, *gift, dowry*.
43. Pres. act. ptc. gen. masc. pl., γαμέω, *marry*; attrib. (subst.): "The other [kind of marriage] is of separate persons who marry for dowry or children."
44. Pres. act. ptc. gen. masc. pl., συγκαθεύδω, *sleep together*: "The other [kind of marriage] is of separate parts who sleep together."
45. Pres. act. inf., συνοικέω, *cohabitate*; indir. disc. (cf. BDF §396; S §2016; CGCG §51.19) : "one may conclude that they dwell [συνοικεῖν]—not live [συμβιοῦν]—with one another."
46. Pres. act. inf., συμβιόω, *live together*; indir. disc. See n. 45.
47. Aor. act. opt. 3 sg., νομίζω, *consider, regard*; potential (cf. BDF §385; S §1824; CGCG §34.13).
48. φυσικός, -ή, -όν, (subst.) *one who studies the natural world, scientist*.
49. ὑγρός, -ά, -όν, *liquid*; separated from the head noun, τὴν κρᾶσιν (hyperbaton; cf. S §3028; CGCG §60.18).
50. Idiom, δι' ὅλων, *completely, entirely*; lit., "throughout the whole."

33 (*Mor.* 142e). ὑποτάττουσαι μέν . . . κρατεῖν δὲ βουλόμεναι. Cf. Eph. 5:21–22: ὑποτασσόμενοι ἀλλήλοις ἐν φόβῳ Χριστοῦ, αἱ γυναῖκες τοῖς ἰδίοις ἀνδράσιν ὡς τῷ κυρίῳ. And Col. 3:18: αἱ γυναῖκες, ὑποτάσσεσθε τοῖς ἀνδράσιν ὡς ἀνῆκεν ἐν κυρίῳ. Paul does not, however, address the concern of wives "ruling over" their husbands (though cf. 1 Tim. 2:12), nor does he instruct couples that "a virtuous household is carried on by both parties in agreement, but discloses the husband's leadership and preferences" (Plutarch, *Conj. praec.* 11 [*Mor.* 139d], trans. Babbitt 1928). Unfortunately, the construct of a "biblical" marriage has often had more to do with Plutarch (and Aristotle) than Paul.

ὡς ψυχὴν σώματος. Platonic dualism distinguishes between body and soul, in which the former is coded as female and the latter is coded as male (cf. Plato, *Tim.* 21c; Aristotle, *Pol.* 1254b12–13; Philo, *Fug.* 51; Philo, *Opif.* 165; Philo, *QG* 1.37; Gos. Thom. 114).

51. κρᾶσις, -εως, ἡ, *mixing*.
52. Aor. pass. inf., ἀναμείγνυμι, (pass.) *be mixed*; comp. of δεῖ. See n. 45.
53. Partic. combination, *in fact*: "additional information (καί) which has explanatory force (γάρ)" (CGCG §59.66).
54. νομοθέτης, -ου, ὁ, *lawgiver*.
55. Aor. act. indic. 3 sg., κωλύω, *prevent*; with acc. and inf.
56. Pres. act. subj. 3 pl., μεταλαμβάνω, *share in*; with gen.; purpose clause (cf. BDF §369; S §2193; CGCG §45.3).

7.5.3

Attacking Barbarian Superstition

On Superstition 3, 8 (*Mor.* 165d–166a, 169c)

³Φόβων δὲ πάντων ἀπρακτότατος¹ καὶ ἀπορώτατος² ὁ τῆς δεισιδαιμονίας.³ οὐ φοβεῖται θάλατταν⁴ ὁ μὴ πλέων⁵ οὐδὲ πόλεμον⁶ ὁ μὴ στρατευόμενος,⁷ οὐδὲ λῃστὰς⁸ ὁ οἰκουρῶν⁹ οὐδὲ συκοφάντην¹⁰ ὁ πένης¹¹ οὐδὲ φθόνον¹² ὁ ἰδιώτης,¹³ οὐδὲ σεισμὸν¹⁴ ὁ ἐν Γαλάταις¹⁵ οὐδὲ κεραυνὸν¹⁶ ὁ ἐν Αἰθίοψιν.¹⁷ ὁ δὲ θεοὺς δεδιὼς¹⁸ πάντα δέδιε, γῆν θάλατταν ἀέρα οὐρανὸν σκότος φῶς κληδόνα¹⁹ σιωπὴν²⁰ ὄνειρον.²¹ οἱ δοῦλοι τῶν δεσποτῶν²² ἐπιλανθάνονται²³ καθεύδοντες,²⁴ τοῖς πεδήταις²⁵ ἐπελαφρύνει²⁶ τὸν δεσμὸν²⁷ ὁ ὕπνος,²⁸

1. Superl., ἄπρακτος, -ον, *most unprofitable, most impotent*; with partitive gen. (φόβων πάντων).
2. Superl., ἄπορος, -ον, *most intractable, most helpless*; with partitive gen. (φόβων πάντων).
3. δεισιδαιμονία, -ας, ἡ, *superstition*. The term can have positive connotations (cf. Let. Aris. 129), but Plutarch clearly uses it in a pejorative sense.
4. θάλασσα (Att. θάλαττα), -ας, ἡ, *sea*.
5. Pres. act. ptc. nom. masc. sg., πλέω, *go by sea, sail*; attrib. (subst.).
6. πόλεμος, -ου, ὁ, *war*.
7. Pres. mid. ptc. nom. masc. sg., στρατεύω, (mid.) *serve in the army*; attrib. (subst.).
8. λῃστής, -οῦ, ὁ, *robber*.
9. Pres. act. ptc. nom. masc. sg., οἰκουρέω, *stay at home*; attrib. (subst.).
10. συκοφάντης, -ου, ὁ, *swindler*.
11. πένης, -ητος, ὁ, *poor man*.
12. φθόνος, -ου, ὁ, *envy*.
13. ἰδιώτης, -ου, ὁ, *someone without professional training/office*.
14. σεισμός, -οῦ, ὁ, *earthquake*.
15. Γαλάται, -ῶν, οἱ, *Gauls*.
16. κεραυνόν, -οῦ, ὁ, *thunderbolt*.
17. Αἰθίοψ, -οπος, ὁ, *Ethiopia*.
18. Pf. act. ptc. nom. masc. sg., δείδω, *fear*; attrib. (subst.).
19. κληδών, -όνος, ὁ, *shouting*.
20. σιωπή, -ῆς, ἡ, *silence*.
21. ὄνειρον, -ου, τό, *dream*.
22. δεσπότης, -ου, ὁ, *master*.
23. Pres. mid. indic. 3 pl., ἐπιλανθάνομαι, *forget*; with gen.
24. Pres. act. ptc. nom. masc. pl., καθεύδω, *sleep*; circ.
25. πεδήτης, -ου, ὁ, *prisoner*.
26. Pres. act. indic. 3 sg., ἐπελαφρύνω, *lighten*.
27. δεσμός, -οῦ, ὁ, *chains*.
28. ὕπνος, -ου, ὁ, *sleep*.

φλεγμοναὶ²⁹ περὶ τραύματα³⁰ καὶ νομαὶ³¹ σαρκὸς θηριώδεις³² καὶ περιωδυνίαι³³ κοιμωμένων³⁴ ἀφίστανται³⁵

ὦ³⁶ φίλον ὕπνου θέλγητoρον³⁷ ἐπίκουρον³⁸ νόσου,³⁹
ὡς ἡδύ⁴⁰ μοι προῆλθες ἐν δέοντί⁴¹ γε.⁴²

τοῦτ᾽ οὐ δίδωσιν εἰπεῖν⁴³ ἡ δεισιδαιμονία (μόνη γὰρ οὐ σπένδεται⁴⁴ πρὸς τὸν ὕπνον, οὐδὲ τῇ ψυχῇ ποτε γοῦν⁴⁵ δίδωσιν ἀναπνεῦσαι⁴⁶ καὶ ἀναθαρρῆσαι⁴⁷ τὰς πικρὰς⁴⁸ καὶ βαρείας⁴⁹ περὶ τοῦ θεοῦ δόξας⁵⁰ ἀπωσαμένη⁵¹), ἀλλ᾽ ὥσπερ ἐν ἀσεβῶν χώρῳ⁵² τῷ ὕπνῳ τῶν δεισιδαιμόνων εἴδωλα⁵³ φρικώδη⁵⁴ καὶ τεράστια⁵⁵ φάσματα⁵⁶ καὶ ποινάς⁵⁷ τινας ἐγείρουσα⁵⁸ καὶ στροβοῦσα⁵⁹ τὴν ἀθλίαν⁶⁰ ψυχὴν ἐκδιώκει⁶¹ τοῖς ὀνείροις⁶² ἐκ τῶν ὕπνων, μαστιζομένην⁶³ καὶ κολαζομένην⁶⁴ αὐτὴν ὑφ᾽ αὑτῆς ὡς ὑφ᾽ ἑτέρου, καὶ δεινὰ⁶⁵ προστάγματα⁶⁶ καὶ ἀλλόκοτα⁶⁷ λαμβάνουσαν. εἶτ᾽ ἐξαναστάντες⁶⁸ οὐ κατεφρόνησαν⁶⁹ οὐδὲ κατεγέλασαν,⁷⁰ οὐδ᾽ ᾔσθοντο⁷¹ ὅτι τῶν ταραξάντων⁷² οὐδὲν ἦν ἀληθινόν, ἀλλὰ σκιὰν⁷³ φεύγοντες ἀπάτης⁷⁴ οὐδὲν κακὸν ἐχούσης ὕπαρ⁷⁵ ἐξαπατῶσαν⁷⁶ ἑαυτοὺς καὶ δαπανῶσι⁷⁷ καὶ ταράττουσιν, εἰς ἀγύρτας⁷⁸ καὶ γόητας⁷⁹ ἐμπεσόντες⁸⁰ λέγοντας⁸¹

---

29. φλεγμονή, -ῆς, ἡ, *inflammation*.
30. τραῦμα, -ατος, τό, *wound*.
31. νομή, -ῆς, ἡ, *spreading* (of sores).
32. θηριώδης, -ες, (medical; of ulcers) *malignant*.
33. περιωδυνία, -ας, ἡ, *extreme pain*.
34. Pres. mid. ptc. gen. masc. pl., κοιμάω, *sleep*; attrib. (subst.); ablative gen.
35. Pres. pass. indic. 3 pl., ἀφίστημι, (intrans.) *be away from* (someone).
36. Citation of Euripides, *Orest.* 211–212.
37. θέλγητρον, -ου, τό, *charm*; ὦ φίλον ὕπνου θέλγητρον, "O dear charm of sleep."
38. ἐπίκουρος, -ου, ὁ, *helper*.
39. νόσος, -ου, ὁ, *illness, sickness, disease*.
40. ἡδύς, -εῖα, -ύ, *sweet*; with ὡς, "How sweet!"
41. Pres. act. ptc. dat. masc. sg., δέω, *be in need*; attrib.; "ἐν δέοντι (sc. καιρῷ) in *good time*" (LSJ, 379).
42. Postpositive partic.: "expresses concentration/limitation—γε focuses attention on the word or phrase it follows . . . and limits the applicability of the content of the utterance to at least or (more) precisely that specific element" (*CGCG* §59.53).
43. Obj./purpose (cf. BDF §390; S §2008; *CGCG* §51.16); lit., "Superstition does not grant [us] *to say* this."
44. Pres. mid. indic. 3 sg., σπένδω, (mid.) *make a treaty with*.
45. Postpositive partic., *at least, at any rate*: "modifies an utterance which elaborates (οὖν) upon (part of) the preceding utterance by restricting its applicability (γε) . . . often used in sentences which provide 'minimum evidence' or the 'minimal applicability' for a preceding statement" (*CGCG* §59.54).
46. Aor. act. inf., ἀναπνέω, *recover breath*; purpose. See n. 43.
47. Aor. act. inf., ἀναθαρσέω, *regain courage*; purpose. See n. 43.
48. πικρός, -ά, -όν, *bitter*.
49. βαρύς, -εῖα, -ύ, *grievous, burdensome*.
50. δόξα, -ας, ἡ, *beliefs, opinions*.
51. Aor. mid. ptc. dat. fem. sg., ἀπωθέω, *push/drive away*; circ.
52. χῶρος, -ου, ὁ, *place*; ὥσπερ ἐν ἀσεβῶν χώρῳ, "as though it [the soul] were in the place of the impious."
53. εἴδωλον, -ου, τό, *phantom, image*.
54. φρικώδης, -ες, *causing one to shudder*; hence, *terrible, horrifying*.
55. τεράστιος, -ον, *monstrous*.
56. φάσμα, -ατος, τό, *apparition, phantom*.
57. ποινή, -ῆς, ἡ, *punishment*.
58. Pres. act. ptc. nom. fem. sg., ἐγείρω, *raise up*; circ. The subject of the participle is ἡ δεισιδαιμονία.
59. Pres. act. ptc. nom. fem. sg., στροβέω, *distract, distress*; circ.
60. ἄθλιος, -α, -ον, *miserable, wretched*.
61. Pres. act. indic. 3 sg., ἐκδιώκω, *chase out of*.
62. ὄνειρος, -ου, ὁ, *dream*; dat. of means.
63. Pres. pass. ptc. acc. fem. sg., μαστίζω, (pass.) *be whipped, flogged*; circ.
64. Pres. pass. ptc. acc. fem. sg., κολάζω, (pass.) *be punished*; circ.
65. δεινός, -ή, -όν, *dreadful*.
66. πρόσταγμα, -ατος, τό, *command, ordinance*.
67. ἀλλόκοτος, -ον, *of an unusual nature*.
68. Aor. act. ptc. nom. masc. pl., ἐξανίστημι, *arise*. The participle marks a shift from the feminine singular (soul of the superstitious) to the masculine plural (the superstitious).
69. Aor. act. indic. 3 pl., καταφρονέω, *contempt, look down on*.
70. Aor. act. indic. 3 pl., καταγελάω, *mock, deride*.
71. Aor. mid. indic. 3 pl., αἰσθάνομαι, *perceive*.
72. Aor. act. ptc. gen. neut. pl., ταράσσω (Att. ταράττω), *trouble*; attrib. (subst.).
73. σκιά, -ᾶς, ἡ, *shadow*.
74. ἀπάτη, -ης, ἡ, *deception, delusion*.
75. Adv., *in a waking state, awake*.
76. Pres. act. indic. 3 pl., ἐξαπατάω, *deceive, mislead*.
77. Pres. act. indic. 3 pl., δαπανάω, *spend, waste*.
78. ἀγύρτης, -ου, ὁ, *mendicant, wandering soothsayer*.
79. γόης, -ητος, ὁ, *sorcerer*.
80. Aor. act. ptc. nom. masc. pl., ἐμπίπτω, *fall to/upon*.
81. The citation (of an unknown author) functions as the protasis.

ἀλλ' εἴτ' ἔνυπνον⁸² φάντασμα⁸³ φοβῇ,
χθονίας θ' Ἑκάτης⁸⁴ κῶμον⁸⁵ ἐδέξω,⁸⁶

τὴν περιμάκτριαν⁸⁷ κάλει γραῦν⁸⁸ καὶ βάπτισον⁸⁹ σεαυτὸν εἰς θάλατταν καὶ καθίσας⁹⁰ ἐν τῇ γῇ διημέρευσον.⁹¹

ὦ⁹² βάρβαρ'⁹³ ἐξευρόντες⁹⁴ Ἕλληνες κακὰ

τῇ δεισιδαιμονίᾳ, πηλώσεις⁹⁵ καταβορβορώσεις⁹⁶ βαπτισμούς,⁹⁷ ῥίψεις⁹⁸ ἐπὶ πρόσωπον, αἰσχρὰς⁹⁹ προκαθίσεις,¹⁰⁰ ἀλλοκότους προσκυνήσεις.¹⁰¹ ...

8 ὁ Ἡσίοδος¹⁰² κελεύει¹⁰³ πρὸ ἀρότου¹⁰⁴ καὶ σπόρου¹⁰⁵ τὸν γεωργὸν¹⁰⁶

εὔχεσθαί¹⁰⁷ τ'¹⁰⁸ Διί¹⁰⁹ χθονίῳ Δημήτερί¹¹⁰ θ' ἁγνῇ

τῆς ἐχέτλης¹¹¹ ἐχόμενον, Ὅμηρος¹¹² δὲ τὸν Αἴαντα¹¹³ φησι τῷ Ἕκτορι μέλλοντα μονομαχεῖν¹¹⁴ εὔχεσθαι κελεύειν¹¹⁵ τοὺς Ἕλληνας ὑπὲρ αὐτοῦ τοῖς θεοῖς, εἶτ' εὐχομένων ἐκείνων ὁπλίζεσθαι.¹¹⁶ καὶ ὁ Ἀγαμέμνων¹¹⁷ ὅτε τοῖς μαχομένοις¹¹⁸ προσέταξεν¹¹⁹

εὖ¹²⁰ μέν τις δόρυ¹²¹ θηξάσθω,¹²² εὖ δ' ἀσπίδα¹²³ θέσθω,

τότε παρὰ τοῦ Διὸς αἰτεῖ
   δός με κατὰ πρηνὲς βαλέειν¹²⁴ Πριάμοιο
      μέλαθρον·

ἀρετῆς¹²⁵ γὰρ ἐλπὶς ὁ θεός ἐστιν, οὐ δειλίας¹²⁶ πρόφασις.¹²⁷ ἀλλ' Ἰουδαῖοι σαββάτων ὄντων ἐν ἀγνάμπτοις¹²⁸ καθεζόμενοι, τῶν πολεμίων κλίμακας¹²⁹ προστιθέντων¹³⁰ καὶ τὰ τείχη¹³¹ καταλαμβανόντων,

---

82. ἔνυπνος, -ον, *in sleep*.
83. φάντασμα, -ατος, τό, *apparition, phantom*.
84. Ἑκάτη, -ης, ἡ, *Hecate*; χθονία Ἑκάτη, *chthonic Hecate* (i.e., Hecate of the underworld).
85. κῶμος, -ου, ὁ, *band of revelers*.
86. Aor. mid. indic. 2 sg., δέχομαι, *welcome*; general condition (cf. S §2342).
87. περιμάκτρια, -ας, ἡ, *one who purifies by magic*.
88. γραῦς, γραός, ἡ, *old woman*.
89. Aor. act. impv. 2 sg., βαπτίζω, *immerse*.
90. Aor. act. ptc. nom. masc. sg., καθίζω, *sit*.
91. Aor. act. impv. 2 sg., διημερεύω, *spend the day*.
92. The quotation is from Euripides, *Tro*. 764.
93. βάρβαρος, -ον, *barbarian*; neut. pl. adj. agreeing with κακά.
94. Aor. act. ptc. nom. masc. pl., ἐξευρίσκω, *find out, discover*.
95. πήλωσις, -εως, ἡ, *smearing with mud*.
96. καταβορβόρωσις, -εως, ἡ, *wallowing in mud*.
97. βαπτισμός, -οῦ, ὁ, *immersion*. Bentley's emendation; MSS read σαββατισμούς, "Sabbaths."
98. ῥῖψις, -εως, ἡ, *throwing, hurling*.
99. αἰσχρός, -ά, -όν, *shameful*.
100. προκάθισις, -εως, ἡ, *sitting in public*.
101. προσκύνησις, -εως, ἡ, *obedience*.
102. Ἡσίοδος, -ου, ὁ, *Hesiod*; cf. Hesiod, *Op*. 465.
103. Pres. act. indic. 3 sg., κελεύω, *bid, advise*; with acc. and inf.
104. ἄροτος, -ου, ὁ, *plowing*.
105. σπόρος, -ου, ὁ, *sowing*.
106. γεωρός, -οῦ, ὁ, *farmer*.
107. Pres. mid. inf., εὔχομαι, *pray*.
108. τέ ... τέ, *X and Y*.
109. Ζεύς, Διός, ὁ, *Zeus*; Ζεὺς χθόνιος, *chthonic Zeus*.
110. Δημήτηρ, -ερος, ἡ, *Demeter*.

111. ἐχέτλη, -ης, ἡ, *plow handle*; obj. of ἐχόμενον, "while holding the handle of the plow."
112. Ὅμηρος, -ου, ὁ, *Homer*; cf. Homer, *Il*. 7.193–195.
113. Αἴας, -αντος, ὁ, *Ajax*.
114. Pres. act. inf., μονομαχέω, *engage in single combat*; comp. of μέλλοντα.
115. Main verb of indir. disc. (cf. BDF §396; S §2016; *CGCG* §51.19): "Homer says that Ajax, as he was about to engage Hector in single combat, bid the Greeks to pray to the gods on his behalf."
116. Pres. mid. inf., ὁπλίζω, *equip, arm oneself*; indir. disc.: "Next, he [Homer] says that he [Ajax] armed himself while they [the Greeks] were praying."
117. Ἀγαμέμνων, -ονος, ὁ, *Agamemnon*.
118. Pres. mid. ptc. dat. masc. pl., μάχομαι, *fight*; attrib. (subst.).
119. Aor. act. indic. 3 sg., προστάσσω, *enjoin*; with dat. The following lines are adapted from Homer, *Il*. 2.413–414.
120. Adv., *well*.
121. δόρυ, δόρατος, τό, *spear*.
122. Aor. pass. impv. 3 sg., θήγω, (pass.) *be sharpened*.
123. ἀσπίς, -ίδος, ἡ, *shield*.
124. Epic aor. act. inf., βαλέειν = βαλεῖν; obj./purpose (see n. 43): "Grant me *to throw* the roof of Priam [Πριάμοιο μέλαθρον] to the ground [κατὰ πρηνές]" (adaptation of Homer, *Il*. 2.414).
125. ἀρετή, -ῆς, ἡ, *virtue, valor*.
126. δειλία, -ας, ἡ, *cowardice*.
127. πρόφασις, -εως, ἡ, *pretense, excuse*.
128. ἄγναμπτος, -ον, *inflexible, inexorable*; dat. of manner.
129. κλῖμαξ, -ακος, ἡ, *ladder*.
130. Pres. act. ptc. gen. masc. pl., προστίθημι, *add*; gen. absol.
131. τεῖχος, -ους, τό, *wall*.

οὐκ ἀνέστησαν ἀλλ' ἔμειναν ὥσπερ ἐν σαγήνῃ[132] μιᾷ τῇ δεισιδαιμονίᾳ συνδεδεμένοι.[133]

NOTES

3 (*Mor.* 165d). ὁ τῆς δεισιδαιμονίας. Superstitious fear, according to Plutarch, is all encompassing and thus a major threat to true piety (cf. *Mor.* 351c–384c). For another example of the philosopher's critique of δεισιδαιμονία, see Diogenes Laertius, *Vit. phil.* 6.37–38 (§7.6.1).

3 (*Mor.* 166a). ὦ βάρβαρ' ἐξευρόντες Ἕλληνες κακά. A citation of Euripides, *Tro.* 764. Its function is to insinuate that the "purity" of Greek religion and culture is under the threat of "barbarian superstition," in which Plutarch includes σαββατισμούς, "Sabbaths" (βαπτισμούς is an emendation; cf. Donaldson 2007, 385n37). Cf. Horace, *Sat.* 1.4.139–143 (Fairclough 1926): "This is one of those lesser frailties I spoke of, and if you should make no allowance for it, then would a big band of poets come to my aid—for we are the big majority—and we, like the Jews, will compel you to make one of our throng." And also Seneca, *apud* Augustine, *Civ.* 6.11: "Meanwhile the customs of this accursed race have gained such influence that they are now received throughout the world. The vanquished have given laws to the victors" (Green 1963).

8 (*Mor.* 169c). ἀλλ' Ἰουδαῖοι. . . . The event Plutarch references is unclear (cf. 1 Macc. 2:29–38; Josephus, *A.J.* 7.274; Josephus, *C. Ap.* 1.205–211; Dio Cassius, *Hist. rom.* 37.16; for pagan comments on the Sabbath, cf. Plutarch, *Quaest. conv.* 669c–672b; Horace, *Sat.* 1.9.63–72; Ovid, *Ars* 1.75–76, 413–416; Juvenal, *Sat.* 14.96–106). The sources suggest that Sabbath observance would have been appealing to at least some segment of the Roman population.

---

132. σαγήνη, -ης, ἡ, *large dragnet* (for fishing).
133. Pf. pass. ptc. nom. masc. pl., συνδέω, (pass.) *be bound together*; circ.

7.6

Diogenes Laertius

Diogenes Laertius (probably third century CE) is a fitting author with whom to conclude this section—though not because he was an established philosopher or literary genius. Rather, "Diogenes has acquired an importance out of all proportion to his merits because the loss of many primary sources and of the earlier secondary compilations has accidentally left him the chief continuous source for the history of Greek philosophy" (Long, preface to Hicks 1925, 1:xix). His ten-volume *Lives of Eminent Philosophers* is not a work of philosophy but a compendium of anecdotes, aphorisms, summaries, and catalogs, the value of which depends on the reliability of his sources.

The reading passages are designed to introduce you to important philosophical schools and movements. The first passage is from the life of Diogenes of Sinope (ca. 412–323 BCE), one of the founders of the Cynic way of life. The second and third passages are from the life of Zeno of Citium (ca. 335–262 BCE), who founded the school that met in the stoa (portico) in the agora of Athens (hence the name "Stoics"). The final passage is from the life of Epicurus (the founder of Epicureanism), whose school met in a garden just outside Athens.

Text and Translation: Hicks 1925
Supplemental Scripture: Matt. 8:20 parr.; Acts 17:27–28 (§7.6.1; §7.6.4); 17:16–34 (§7.6.2); 2 Pet. 3:8–13 (§7.6.3)

7.6.1

The Lifestyle of the Cynic

Lives of Eminent Philosophers 6.37–38

6.37 Θεασάμενός[1] ποτε παιδίον[2] ταῖς χερσὶ πῖνον[3] ἐξέρ-ριψε[4] τῆς πήρας[5] τὴν κοτύλην,[6] εἰπών, "παιδίον με νενίκηκεν[7] εὐτελείᾳ."[8] ἐξέβαλε δὲ καὶ τὸ τρυβλίον,[9] ὁμοίως παιδίον θεασάμενος, ἐπειδὴ κατέαξε[10] τὸ σκεῦος,[11] τῷ κοίλῳ[12] τοῦ ψωμίου[13] τὴν φακῆν[14] ὑπο-δεχόμενον.[15] συνελογίζετο[16] δὲ καὶ οὕτως· τῶν θεῶν ἐστι πάντα· φίλοι[17] δὲ οἱ σοφοὶ[18] τοῖς θεοῖς· κοινὰ[19] δὲ τὰ τῶν φίλων. πάντ' ἄρα[20] ἐστὶ τῶν σοφῶν. θεα-σάμενός ποτε γυναῖκα ἀσχημονέστερον[21] τοῖς θεοῖς προσπίπτουσαν,[22] βουλόμενος αὐτῆς περιελεῖν[23] τὴν δεισιδαιμονίαν,[24] καθά[25] φησι Ζωίλος ὁ Περγαῖος,[26] προσελθὼν εἶπεν, "οὐκ εὐλαβῇ,[27] ὦ γύναι, μή ποτε θεοῦ ὄπισθεν[28] ἑστῶτος—πάντα γάρ ἐστιν αὐτοῦ πλήρη[29]—ἀσχημονήσῃς;"[30] **38** τῷ Ἀσκληπιῷ[31] ἀνέθηκε[32]

1. Aor. mid. ptc. nom. masc. sg., θεάομαι, *watch, observe*; circ. (temp. ποτέ, "once").
2. παιδίον, -ου, τό, *child*.
3. Pres. act. ptc. acc. neut. sg., πίνω, *drink*; supp. (θεασάμενος); with dat. of instrument (ταῖς χερσί).
4. Aor. act. indic. 3 sg., ἐκρίπτω, *cast off*.
5. πήρα, -ας, ἡ, *leather pouch*.
6. κοτύλη, -ης, ἡ, *small vessel, cup*.
7. Pf. act. indic. 3 sg., νικάω, *conquer, outstrip, surpass*.
8. εὐτέλεια, -ας, ἡ, *plain living*; dat. of respect.
9. τρυβλίον, -ου, τό, *bowl*.
10. Aor. act. indic. 3 sg., κατάγνυμι, *break*.
11. σκεῦος, -εος, τό, *vessel, implement of any kind*.
12. κοῖλος, -η, -ον, *hollow*; dat. of means.
13. ψωμίον, -ου, τό, *small piece, mouthful*.
14. φακῆ, -ῆς, ἡ, *(dish of) lentils*.
15. Pres. mid. ptc. acc. neut. sg., ὑποδέχομαι, *take up*; supp. (θεασάμενος).
16. Impf. mid. indic. 3 sg., συλλογίζομαι, *infer*.
17. φίλος, -η, -ον, (subst.) *friend*; pred. nom.
18. σοφός, -ή, -όν, *wise*.
19. κοινός, -ή, -όν, *common, shared*; with gen.

20. Partic., *so, then, it seems*: "indicates that the speaker, in view of the preceding context, cannot but make the contribution he/she is making" (CGCG §59.42).
21. Compar. adv., ἀσχήμων, -ον, *in a most indecorous manner*.
22. Pres. act. ptc. acc. fem. sg., προσπίπτω, *fall before*; supp. (θεασάμενος).
23. Aor. act. inf., περιαιρέω, *take away*; comp. of βουλόμενος.
24. δεισιδαιμονία, -ας, ἡ, *superstition*.
25. Adv. (καθ' ἅ), *in the way in which, according as*.
26. Zoïlos of Perga (fourth-century Cynic philosopher).
27. Pres. mid. indic. 2 sg., εὐλαβέομαι, *be cautious, beware*.
28. Adv., *behind*; modifies gen. absol. θεοῦ ἑστῶτος.
29. πλήρης, -ες, *full of*; with gen.
30. Pres. act. subj. 2 sg., ἀσχημονέω, *behave unseemly, disgrace oneself*; fear clause: μή with subj. (cf. S §2224.a; CGCG §43.4).
31. Ἀσκληπιός, -οῦ, ὁ, *Asclepius*.
32. Aor. act. indic. 3 sg., ἀνατίθημι, *dedicate*.

πλήκτην,³³ ὃς τοὺς ἐπὶ στόμα πίπτοντας ἐπιτρέχων³⁴ συνέτριβεν.³⁵

Εἰώθει³⁶ δὲ λέγειν τὰς τραγικὰς³⁷ ἀρὰς³⁸ αὐτῷ συνηντηκέναι·³⁹ εἶναι γοῦν⁴⁰

    ἄπολις,⁴¹ ἄοικος,⁴² πατρίδος⁴³ ἐστερημένος,⁴⁴ πτωχός,⁴⁵ πλανήτης,⁴⁶ βίον⁴⁷ ἔχων τοὐφ'⁴⁸ ἡμέραν.

ἔφασκε⁴⁹ δ' ἀντιτιθέναι⁵⁰ τύχῃ⁵¹ μὲν⁵² θάρσος,⁵³ νόμῳ δὲ φύσιν,⁵⁴ πάθει⁵⁵ δὲ λόγον.

NOTES

6.37. Cynics were known for their austere and itinerant lifestyles. Malherbe (1989, 12) notes, "What made a Cynic was his dress and conduct, self-sufficiency, harsh behavior toward what appeared as excesses, and a practical ethical idealism, but not a detailed arrangement of a system resting on Socratic-Antisthenic principles." For various ancient portraits of the Cynic, cf. Epictetus, *Diatr.* 3.22; Lucian, *Demonax*; Maximus of Tyre, *Disc.* 36; Julian, *Or.* 6.200c–202c; for further discussion, see Branham and Goulet-Cazé (1996).

τῶν θεῶν ἐστι πάντα· φίλοι δὲ οἱ σοφοὶ τοῖς θεοῖς· κοινὰ δὲ τὰ τῶν φίλων. πάντ' ἄρα ἐστὶ τῶν σοφῶν. Were we to change τῶν θεῶν to τοῦ θεοῦ, the claim would seem at home in a Pauline epistle (with the caveat, of course, that σοφός must be reconfigured by the cross; cf. 1 Cor. 1:18–31). Begging is not shameful to the Cynic since he or she has chosen a lifestyle of poverty; that is, he or she has hosen to be *free*. Moreover, as Branham shows, the account is supposed to be humorous: "The form of the syllogism allows Diogenes to invoke the authority of reason even as he parodies its procedures in a single gesture" (Branham and Goulet-Cazé 1996, 93). Cf. *Vit. phil.* 6.60: "Alexander once came and stood opposite him and said, 'I am Alexander the great king.' 'And I,' said he, 'am Diogenes the Cynic [ὁ κύων].' Being asked what he had done to be called a dog [κύων], he said, 'I wag my tail at those who give me anything, I bark at those who do not, and I set my teeth in rascals'" (Hicks 1925 alt.). Cf. *Vit. phil.* 6.46, 49, 56, 59.

    33. πλήκτης, -ου, ὁ, *brawler*.
    34. Pres. act. ptc. nom. masc. sg., ἐπιτρέχω, *run up to* (someone); circ.
    35. Aor. act. indic. 3 sg., συντρίβω, *beat to a pulp*.
    36. Pf. act. indic. 3 sg., ἔθω, *be accustomed*; with inf.
    37. τραγικός, -ή, -όν, *of tragedy*.
    38. ἀρά, -ᾶς, ἡ, *curse*.
    39. Pf. act. inf., συναντάω, *happen to, befall*; with dat.; indir. disc. (cf. BDF §397; S §2016; *CGCG* §51.19).
    40. Partic.: "a combination of γε and οὖν, γοῦν modifies an utterance which elaborates (οὖν) upon (part of) the preceding utterance by restricting its applicability (γε)" (*CGCG* §59.45).
    41. ἄπολις, -ιδος, ὁ, *without city*.
    42. ἄοικος, -ου, ὁ, *without home*.
    43. πατρίς, -ίδος, ἡ, *homeland*.
    44. Pf. pass. ptc. nom. masc. sg., στερέω, (pass.) *be deprived of*; with gen.; attrib.
    45. πτωχός, -ή, -όν, *poor*.
    46. πλανήτης, -ου, ὁ, *wanderer*.
    47. βίος, -ου, ὁ, *means of life, sustenance*.
    48. Crasis: τοὐφ' = τὸ ἐπί; τοὐφ' ἡμέραν, "each day."
    49. Impf. act. indic. 3 sg., φάσκω, *claim*.
    50. Pres. act. inf., ἀντιτίθημι, *oppose* (one thing to another); indir. disc. See n. 39.
    51. τυχή, -ῆς, ἡ, *luck, fortune*.
    52. μέν … δέ … δέ; point/counterpoints (cf. S §2907).
    53. θάρσος, -εος, τό, *courage*.
    54. φύσις, -εως, ἡ, *nature*.
    55. πάθος, -ους, τό, *passion, emotion*.

7.6.2

Stoic Theology

Lives of Eminent Philosophers 7.148–149

7.148Οὐσίαν[1] δὲ θεοῦ Ζήνων[2] μέν[3] φησι τὸν ὅλον[4] κόσμον καὶ τὸν οὐρανόν, ὁμοίως δὲ καὶ Χρύσιππος[5] ἐν τῷ πρώτῳ[6] Περὶ θεῶν καὶ Ποσειδώνιος[7] ἐν πρώτῳ Περὶ θεῶν. καὶ Ἀντίπατρος[8] ἐν ἑβδόμῳ[9] Περὶ κόσμου ἀεροειδῆ[10] φησιν αὐτοῦ τὴν οὐσίαν· Βόηθος[11] δὲ ἐν τῇ Περὶ φύσεως[12] οὐσίαν θεοῦ τὴν τῶν ἀπλανῶν[13] σφαῖραν.[14] φύσιν δὲ ποτὲ μὲν[15] ἀποφαίνονται[16] τὴν συνέχουσαν[17] τὸν κόσμον, ποτὲ δὲ τὴν φύουσαν[18] τὰ ἐπὶ γῆς. ἔστι δὲ φύσις ἕξις[19] ἐξ αὑτῆς κινουμένη[20] κατὰ σπερματικοὺς[21] λόγους ἀποτελοῦσά[22] τε καὶ συνέχουσα τὰ ἐξ αὑτῆς ἐν ὡρισμένοις[23] χρόνοις καὶ τοιαῦτα δρῶσα[24] ἀφ' οἵων ἀπεκρίθη.[25] **149**ταύτην δὲ

1. οὐσία, -ας, ἡ, *substance*; theme: οὐσίαν θεοῦ; acc. subject of indir. disc. (cf. BDF §397; S §2016; CGCG §51.19): "Now, as it pertains to the substance of God, Zeno says that it is [implied εἶναι] the entire cosmos and heaven."
2. Ζήνων, -ονος, ὁ, *Zeno*.
3. Ζήνων μέν … Βόηθος δέ; point/counterpoint (cf. Runge 2010, 75–83; BDF §447; S §2904; CGCG §59.24).
4. ὅλος, -η, -ον, *whole*.
5. Χρύσιππος, -ου, ὁ, *Chrysippus*.
6. τῷ πρώτῳ = τῷ πρώτῳ βιβλίῳ. The title of the book is Περὶ θεῶν, *On the Gods*.
7. Ποσειδώνιος, -ου, ὁ, *Posidonius*.
8. Ἀντίπατρος, -ου, ὁ, *Antipater*.
9. ἕβδομος, -η, -ον, *seventh*.
10. ἀεροειδής, -ές, *like the air*; pred. acc.
11. Βόηθος, -ου, ὁ, *Boethus*.
12. φύσις, -εως, ἡ, *nature*. The title of the writing (ἐν τῇ = ἐν τῇ γραφῇ) is Περὶ φύσεως, *On Nature*.
13. ἀπλανής, -ές, (of stars) *fixed* (as opposed to the stars that wander; i.e., planets).
14. σφαῖρα, -ας, ἡ, *sphere*; pred. acc. in indir. disc. See n. 1.
15. ποτὲ μέν … ποτὲ δέ, *sometimes … sometimes*.
16. Pres. mid. indic. 3 pl., ἀποφαίνω, (mid.) *set forth (an opinion), propound*.
17. Pres. act. ptc. acc. fem. sg., συνέχω, *hold together*; attrib. (subst.).
18. Pres. act. ptc. acc. fem. sg., φύω, *make grown*; attrib. (subst.).
19. ἕξις, -εως, ἡ, *state/condition*.
20. Pres. pass. ptc. nom. fem. sg., κινέω, (pass.) *be put in motion*; attrib.
21. σπερματικός, -ή, -όν, *seminal*; κατὰ σπερματικοὺς λόγους, "in accordance with seminal principles."
22. Pres. act. ptc. nom. fem. sg., ἀποτελέω, *produce*; attrib.
23. Pf. pass. ptc. dat. masc. pl., ὁρίζω, (pass.) *defined, determined*; attrib.
24. Pres. act. ptc. nom. fem. sg., δράω, *accomplish*; attrib.
25. Aor. pass. indic. 3 sg., ἀποκρίνω, (pass.) *be distinctly formed*.

καὶ τοῦ συμφέροντος²⁶ στοχάζεσθαι²⁷ καὶ ἡδονῆς,²⁸ ὡς δῆλον²⁹ ἐκ τῆς τοῦ ἀνθρώπου δημιουργίας.³⁰ καθ' εἱμαρμένης³¹ δέ φασι τὰ πάντα γίγνεσθαι Χρύσιππος ἐν τοῖς Περὶ εἱμαρμένης καὶ Ποσειδώνιος ἐν δευτέρῳ Περὶ εἱμαρμένης καὶ Ζήνων, Βόηθος δ' ἐν τῷ πρώτῳ Περὶ εἱμαρμένης. ἔστι δ' εἱμαρμένη αἰτία³² τῶν ὄντων εἰρομένη³³ ἢ λόγος καθ' ὃν ὁ κόσμος διεξάγεται.³⁴ καὶ μὴν³⁵ καὶ μαντικὴν³⁶ ὑφεστάναι³⁷ πᾶσάν φασιν, εἰ καὶ πρόνοιαν³⁸ εἶναι· καὶ αὐτὴν καὶ τέχνην³⁹ ἀποφαίνουσι διά τινας ἐκβάσεις,⁴⁰ ὥς φησι Ζήνων τε καὶ Χρύσιππος ἐν τῷ δευτέρῳ Περὶ μαντικῆς⁴¹ καὶ Ἀθηνόδωρος⁴² καὶ Ποσειδώνιος ἐν τῷ δευτέρῳ τοῦ Φυσικοῦ⁴³ λόγου καὶ ἐν τῷ πέμπτῳ Περὶ μαντικῆς. ὁ μὲν⁴⁴ γὰρ Παναίτιος⁴⁵ ἀνυπόστατον⁴⁶ αὐτήν φησιν.

NOTES

7.148. For the Stoics, study of the natural world (i.e., physics) undergirds "life in agreement with nature" (τὸ ὁμολογουμένως τῇ φύσει ζῆν; i.e., ethics; 7.87). "Physics therefore provides us with the understanding of who we are and of how we fit into the general workings of the world. Since the world is the 'substance' of god, and god is the 'nature which sustains the world and makes things grow' [Vit. phil. 7.148], physics, in final analysis, is theology" (Long and Sedley 1987, 1:267).

7.149. ἔστι δ' εἱμαρμένη αἰτία τῶν ὄντων εἰρομένη ἢ λόγος καθ' ὃν ὁ κόσμος διεξάγεται. On causation and fate in the Stoics, see Long and Sedley 1987, 1:333–43. Determinism does not, however, exempt moral responsibility. Cf. Diogenes Laertius, Vit. phil. 7.23: "We are told that when he was once chastising a slave for stealing, and when the latter pleaded that it was his fate to steal, 'Yes, and to be beaten too,' said Zeno" (Hicks 1925; cf. Cicero, Fat. 39–43; Epictetus, Diatr. 1.1.7–12; and Long and Sedley 1987, 1:392–94).

26. Pres. act. ptc. gen. neut. sg., συμφέρω, *confer benefit, be useful*; attrib. (subst.).
27. Pres. mid. inf., στοχάζομαι, *aim at, endeavor after*; with gen.; indir. disc. See n. 1.
28. ἡδονή, -ῆς, ἡ, *pleasure*.
29. Quasi-impers., ὡς δῆλον, "as is clear/evident."
30. δημιουργία, -ας, ἡ, *creation*.
31. εἱμαρμένη, -ης, ἡ, *fate*. The title of Chrysippus's treatise is Περὶ εἱμαρμένης, *On Fate*, in which he claims (indir. disc.; see n. 1)—as do Posidonius, Zeno, and Boethus—that all things happen in accordance with fate (καθ' εἱμαρμένης).
32. αἰτία, -ας, ἡ, *cause*.
33. Pres. pass. ptc. nom. fem. sg., εἴρω, *be called*; periphrastic.
34. Pres. pass. indic. 3 sg., διεξάγω, (pass.) *be directed/administered*.
35. Partic. combination, (as a new step in the argument) *and in fact*: "The speaker adds information (καί), and indicates that he/she vouches for the correctness or relevance of the addition, even if the addressee may not expect it (μήν)" (CGCG §59.71).
36. μαντικός, -ή, -όν, (subst.) ἡ μαντική (τέχνη), *divination*.
37. Pf. act. inf., ὑφίστημι, *exist*; indir. disc. See n. 1.
38. πρόνοια, -ας, ἡ, *providence*; εἰ καὶ πρόνοιαν εἶναι, "if, in fact, providence exists" (cf. S §2375).
39. τέχνη, -ης, ἡ, *art, science*; pred. acc.
40. ἔκβασις, -εως, ἡ, *fulfillment* (of divination).
41. The title of the work is Περὶ μαντικῆς, *On Divination*.
42. Ἀθηνόδωρος, -ου, ὁ, *Athenodorus*.
43. φυσικός, -ή, -όν, *concerning nature / the natural world*. The title of the work is τοῦ Φυσικοῦ λόγου (*Physical Discourse*).

44. μέν . . . δέ. The μέν-clause concludes the section with elaboration (γάρ—unlike the aforementioned Stoics, Panaetius denies that divination has any bearing on reality), while the δέ-clause (7.150) begins a new discourse topic.
45. Παναίτιος, -ου, ὁ, *Panaetius*.
46. ἀνυπόστατος, -ον, *nonexistent*.

7.6.3

Stoic Cosmology

Lives of Eminent Philosophers 7.156

7.156Δοκεῖ[1] δ' αὐτοῖς τὴν μὲν[2] φύσιν[3] εἶναι πῦρ τεχνικόν,[4] ὁδῷ βαδίζον[5] εἰς γένεσιν,[6] ὅπερ ἐστὶ πνεῦμα πυροειδὲς[7] καὶ τεχνοειδές·[8] τὴν δὲ ψυχὴν αἰσθητικὴν[9] φύσιν. ταύτην δ' εἶναι τὸ συμφυὲς[10] ἡμῖν πνεῦμα· διὸ καὶ σῶμα εἶναι καὶ μετὰ τὸν θάνατον ἐπιμένειν.[11] φθαρτὴν[12] δ' ὑπάρχειν, τὴν[13] δὲ τῶν ὅλων ἄφθαρτον,[14] ἧς μέρη[15] εἶναι τὰς[16] ἐν τοῖς ζῴοις.[17] Ζήνων[18] δ' ὁ Κιτιεὺς[19] καὶ Ἀντίπατρος[20] ἐν τοῖς[21] Περὶ ψυχῆς καὶ Ποσειδώνιος[22] πνεῦμα ἔνθερμον[23] εἶναι τὴν ψυχήν· τούτῳ γὰρ ἡμᾶς εἶναι ἔμπνους[24] καὶ ὑπὸ τούτου κινεῖσθαι.[25] Κλεάνθης[26] μὲν οὖν[27] πάσας[28] ἐπιδιαμέ-

1. Pres. act. indic. 3 sg., δοκέω, (impers.) *it seems*; with dat. and acc. and inf. (cf. BDF §397; S §2018; *CGCG* §51.19): "It seems to them that nature is [εἶναι] an artistic fire . . . while the soul [is] a nature capable of perception."
2. μέν . . . δέ; point/counterpoint (cf. Runge 2010, 75–83; BDF §447; S §2904; *CGCG* §59.24). The subsequent clauses build on the δέ-clause (concerning the ψυχή).
3. φύσις, -εως, ἡ, *nature*.
4. τεκνικός, -ή, -όν, *artistic, skillful*.
5. Pres. act. ptc. acc. neut. sg., βαδίζω, *go*; attrib.
6. γένεσις, -εως, ἡ, *genesis, generation*; εἰς γένεσιν (purpose).
7. πυροειδής, -ές, *like fire*.
8. τεχνοειδής, -ές, *artistic, like that which is crafted*.
9. αἰσθητικός, -ή, -όν, *capable of perception*.
10. συμφυής, -ές, *inborn, congenital, natural*. (indir. disc.; see n. 1)
11. Pres. act. inf., ἐπιμένω, *remain*; indir. disc. (see n. 1): "Therefore [it seems] both that [it = τὴν ψυχήν] is a body and that it persists after death."
12. φθαρτός, -ή, -όν, *perishable*; φθαρτὴν δ' ὑπάρχειν (indir. disc.; see n. 1), "yet [it = τὴν ψυχήν] is perishable."
13. τὴν τῶν ὅλων = τὴν ψυχὴν τῶν ὅλων, "the soul of the universe."

14. ἄφθαρτος, -η, -ον, *imperishable*.
15. μέρος, -ους, τό, *part*; pred. acc.
16. τάς = τὰς ψυχάς.
17. ζῷον, -ου, τό, *living creature, animal*.
18. Ζήνων, -ονος, ὁ, *Zeno*.
19. Κιτιεύς, -έως, ὁ, *of Citium*.
20. Ἀντίπατρος, -ου, ὁ, *Antipater*.
21. ἐν τοῖς = ἐν τοῖς λόγοις Περὶ ψυχῆς, "in their treatises *On Soul*."
22. Ποσειδώνιος, -ου, ὁ, *Posidonius*.
23. ἔνθερμος, -ον, *hot*.
24. ἔμπνους, -ουν, *animate*.
25. Pres. pass. inf., κινέω, (pass.) *be put into motion*; indir. disc. See n. 1.
26. Κλεάνθης, -ου, ὁ, *Cleanthes*.
27. Partic. combination: "a transition to a more to-the-point, relevant text segment (οὖν) [that] occurs in two stages (μέν . . . δέ), with the new step presented in the δέ-segment; the μέν-clause typically presents a summary or rounding-off of the preceding stretch of text" (*CGCG* §59.73).
28. πάσας = πάσας ψυχάς.

νειν²⁹ μέχρι³⁰ τῆς ἐκπυρώσεως,³¹ Χρύσιππος δὲ τὰς τῶν σοφῶν³² μόνον.

NOTES

7.156. φύσιν εἶναι πῦρ τεχνικόν, ὁδῷ βαδίζον εἰς γένεσιν, ὅπερ ἐστὶ πνεῦμα πυροειδὲς καὶ τεχνοειδές. Cf. Aetius 1.7.33: "The Stoics made god out to be intelligent, a designing fire which methodically proceeds towards creation of the world [πῦρ τεχνικόν ὁδῷ βαδίζον ἐπὶ γενέσει κόσμου], and encompasses all the seminal principles according to which everything comes about according to fate, and a breath [πνεῦμα] pervading the whole world, which takes on different names owing to the alternations of the matter through which it passes" (Long and Sedley 1987, 1:274–75).

μέχρι τῆς ἐκπυρώσεως. Cf. 2 Pet. 3:12; Philo, *Aet.* 76–77, 90; Seneca, *Ep.* 9.16; Plutarch, *Mor.* 1053b, 1067a, 1075d; Aristocles, *apud* Eusebius, *Praep. ev.* 15.14.2; Origen, *Cels.* 4.14; Alexander Lycopolis 19.2–4 (Long and Sedley 1987, 1:276–77).

29. Pres. act. inf., ἐπιδιαμένω, *continue, persist*; indir. disc. See n. 1.
30. Prep. with gen., *up to*.
31. ἐκπύρωσις, -εως, ἡ, *conflagration*.
32. σοφός, -ή, -όν, *wise*.

7.6.4

An Epicurean Perspective on Death

Lives of Eminent Philosophers 10.124–127

10.124"Συνέθιζε¹ δὲ ἐν τῷ νομίζειν² μηδὲν πρὸς ἡμᾶς εἶναι τὸν θάνατον· ἐπεὶ πᾶν ἀγαθὸν καὶ κακὸν ἐν αἰσθήσει·³ στέρησις⁴ δὲ ἐστιν αἰσθήσεως ὁ θάνατος. ὅθεν⁵ γνῶσις ὀρθὴ⁶ τοῦ⁷ μηθὲν εἶναι πρὸς ἡμᾶς τὸν θάνατον ἀπολαυστὸν⁸ ποιεῖ τὸ τῆς ζωῆς θνητόν,⁹ οὐκ ἄπειρον¹⁰ προστιθεῖσα¹¹ χρόνον ἀλλὰ τὸν τῆς ἀθανασίας¹² ἀφελομένη¹³ πόθον.¹⁴ **125**οὐθὲν γάρ ἐστιν ἐν τῷ ζῆν δεινὸν¹⁵ τῷ κατειληφότι¹⁶ γνησίως¹⁷ τὸ μηθὲν ὑπάρχειν ἐν τῷ μὴ ζῆν δεινόν. ὥστε μάταιος¹⁸ ὁ λέγων δεδιέναι¹⁹ τὸν θάνατον οὐχ ὅτι λυπήσει²⁰ παρών,²¹ ἀλλ' ὅτι λυπεῖ μέλλων.²² ὃ γὰρ παρὸν οὐκ ἐνοχλεῖ,²³ προσδοκώμενον²⁴ κενῶς²⁵ λυπεῖ. τὸ φρικωδέστατον²⁶ οὖν τῶν κακῶν ὁ θάνατος οὐθὲν πρὸς ἡμᾶς, ἐπειδή περ²⁷

1. Pres. act. impv. 2 sg., συνέθιζω, *become accustomed*.
2. Pres. act. inf., νομίζω, *think*; art. inf. as obj. of ἐν (cf. S §2033; BDF §404); introduces indir. disc. (cf. BDF §397; S §2016; CGCG §51.19).
3. αἴσθησις, -εως, ἡ, *sense perception*.
4. στέρησις, -εως, ἡ, *negation, privation*.
5. Adv., *whence, therefore*.
6. ὀρθός, -ή, -όν, *right*.
7. The genitive of explanation (cf. S §1322) governs μηθὲν εἶναι πρὸς ἡμᾶς τὸν θάνατον; thus, "Hence right knowing, *that death is nothing to us*."
8. ἀπολαυστός, -όν, *enjoyable*; pred. comp.
9. θνητός, -ή, -όν, (subst.) *mortality*.
10. ἄπειρος, -ον, *boundless, infinite*.
11. Pres. act. ptc. nom. fem. sg., προστίθημι, *add to* (something); circ.
12. ἀθανασία, -ας, ἡ, *immortality*.
13. Aor. mid. ptc. nom. fem. sg., ἀφαιρέω, *remove*; circ.
14. πόθος, -ου, ὁ, *desire, yearning*; with gen.

15. δεινός, -ή, -όν, *terrible, terrifying*.
16. Pf. act. ptc. dat. masc. sg., καταλαμβάνω, *comprehend*; attrib. (subst.); introduces indir. disc. (see n. 2): "For there is nothing dreadful in living to the person who genuinely comprehends that there is nothing dreadful in not living."
17. Adv., *genuinely*.
18. μάταιος, -α, -ον, *vain, empty*.
19. Pf. act. inf., δείδω, *fear*; indir. disc. See n. 2.
20. Fut. act. indic. 3 sg., λυπέω, *pain, grieve*.
21. Fut. act. ptc. nom. masc. sg., πάρειμι, *be present, at hand*; circ.
22. In other words, the issue is not that human beings will experience pain (fut.) when they approach death (pres.) but that they are pained (pres.) about the prospect of their approaching death (fut.).
23. Pres. act. indic. 3 sg., ἐνοχλέω, *trouble, annoy*.
24. Pres. pass. ptc. nom. neut. sg., προσδοκέω, (pass.) *be expected/anticipated*. The contrast is between παρόν ("being present") and προσδοκώμενον ("being anticipated").
25. Adv., *in a vain/empty manner*.
26. Superl., φρικώδης, -ες, *most awful*.
27. Partic.: "expresses exclusive limitation—περ limits the applicability of an utterance's content to exactly and only the word (group) it follows" (*CGCG* §59.55).

ὅταν μὲν²⁸ ἡμεῖς ὦμεν, ὁ θάνατος οὐ πάρεστιν· ὅταν δ' ὁ θάνατος παρῇ, τόθ' ἡμεῖς οὐκ ἐσμέν. οὔτε οὖν πρὸς τοὺς ζῶντάς ἐστιν οὔτε πρὸς τοὺς τετελευτηκότας,²⁹ ἐπειδήπερ περὶ οὓς μὲν³⁰ οὐκ ἔστιν, οἱ δ' οὐκέτι εἰσίν. ἀλλ' οἱ πολλοὶ τὸν θάνατον³¹ ὁτὲ μὲν³² ὡς μέγιστον τῶν κακῶν φεύγουσιν,³³ ὁτὲ δὲ ὡς ἀνάπαυσιν³⁴ τῶν ἐν τῷ ζῆν κακῶν αἱροῦνται.³⁵ ¹²⁶ὁ δὲ σοφὸς³⁶ οὔτε παραιτεῖται³⁷ τὸ ζῆν οὔτε φοβεῖται³⁸ τὸ μὴ ζῆν· οὔτε γὰρ αὐτῷ προσίσταται³⁹ τὸ ζῆν οὔτε δοξάζεται⁴⁰ κακὸν εἶναι τὸ μὴ ζῆν. ὥσπερ⁴¹ δὲ τὸ σιτίον⁴² οὐ τὸ πλεῖον πάντως⁴³ ἀλλὰ τὸ ἥδιστον⁴⁴ αἱρεῖται, οὕτω καὶ χρόνον οὐ τὸν μήκιστον⁴⁵ ἀλλὰ τὸν ἥδιστον καρπίζεται.⁴⁶ ὁ δὲ παραγγέλλων⁴⁷ τὸν μὲν νέον⁴⁸ καλῶς ζῆν, τὸν δὲ γέροντα⁴⁹ καλῶς καταστρέφειν⁵⁰ εὐήθης⁵¹ ἐστὶν οὐ μόνον⁵² διὰ τὸ τῆς ζωῆς ἀσπαστόν,⁵³ ἀλλὰ καὶ διὰ τὸ τὴν αὐτὴν εἶναι⁵⁴ μελέτην⁵⁵ τοῦ καλῶς ζῆν καὶ τοῦ καλῶς ἀποθνῄσκειν. Πολὺ δὲ χεῖρον⁵⁶ καὶ ὁ λέγων, καλὸν μὲν μὴ φῦναι,⁵⁷

φύντα δ' ὅπως ὤκιστα⁵⁸ πύλας⁵⁹ Ἀΐδαο⁶⁰ περῆσαι.⁶¹

¹²⁷εἰ μὲν γὰρ πεποιθὼς⁶² τοῦτό φησι, πῶς οὐκ ἀπέρχεται τοῦ ζῆν; ἐν ἑτοίμῳ⁶³ γὰρ αὐτῷ τοῦτ' ἔστιν, εἴπερ⁶⁴ ἦν βεβουλευμένον⁶⁵ αὐτῷ βεβαίως.⁶⁶ εἰ δὲ μωκώμενος,⁶⁷ μάταιος ἐν τοῖς οὐκ ἐπιδεχομένοις.⁶⁸

---

28. μέν ... δέ; point/counterpoint (cf. Runge 2010, 75–83; BDF §447; S §2904; *CGCG* §59.24).
29. Pf. act. ptc. acc. masc. pl., τελευτέω, *die*; attrib. (subst.).
30. περὶ οὓς μέν ... οἱ δ', *in the case of the former ... the latter*. See n. 28.
31. The phrase οἱ πολλοὶ τὸν θάνατον is proleptic: "Yet as to how the vast majority approach death ..."
32. ὁτὲ μέν ... ὁτὲ δέ, *at one time ... at another time*.
33. Pres. act. indic. 3 pl., φεύγω, *flee*.
34. ἀνάπαυσις, -εως, ἡ, *rest*; with τῶν ἐν τῷ ζῆν κακῶν, "rest from the evils of life."
35. Pres. mid. indic. 3 pl., αἱρέω, *choose*.
36. σοφός, -ή, -όν, *wise*.
37. Pres. mid. indic. 3 pl., παραιτέομαι, *depreciate*.
38. Pres. mid. indic. 3 pl., φοβέω, (mid.) *be afraid of* (something).
39. Pres. pass. indic. 3 sg., προσίστημι, (intrans.) *give offense*; with dat.
40. Pres. pass. indic. 3 sg., δοξάζω, (pass.) *be thought of, held as a matter of opinion*.
41. ὥσπερ ... οὕτω καί, *as* (with food) ... *so also* (with time).
42. σιτίον, -ου, τό, *food*.
43. οὐ πάντως, *by no means*.
44. Superl., ἡδύς, -εῖα, -ύ, *sweetest*. The contrast is between the sweetest portion (τὸ ἥδιστον) and the larger portion (τὸ πλεῖον).
45. Superl., μακρός, -ά, -όν, (of time) *longest*.
46. Pres. mid. indic. 3 sg., καρπίζω, *enjoy the fruits of*. The subject is ὁ σοφός.
47. Pres. act. ptc. nom. masc. sg., παραγγέλλω, *exhort, admonish*; with acc. and inf.
48. νέος, -α, -ον, *young*.
49. γέρων, -οντος, ὁ, *old man*.
50. Pres. act. inf., καταστρέφω, *make an end*.
51. εὐήθης, -ες, *simpleminded, silly*; pred. adj. (ὁ παραγγέλλων).
52. οὐ μόνον ... ἀλλὰ καί, *not only ... but also*.
53. ἀσπαστός, -ή, -όν, *of a thing to be welcomed*.
54. διὰ τό with inf. expresses cause (cf. BDF §402; *CGCG* §51.46): "Because the same exercise [acc. subject] is applied to [lit., is of] living well and dying well."
55. μελετή, -ῆς, ἡ, *exercise*.
56. Compar., κακός, -ή, -όν, *worse*; with adv. acc. "much worse."
57. Aor. act. inf., φύω, (intrans.) *be born*; comp. of quasi-impers. καλόν: "[Who says] that it is good not to be born."
58. Superl. adv., ὠκύς, -εῖα, -ύ, *most swiftly*.
59. πύλη, -ης, ἡ, *gate*.
60. Ἅιδης, -αο, ὁ, *Hades*.
61. Aor. act. inf., περάω, *pass through*; comp. of καλόν (εἶναι).
62. Pf. act. ptc. nom. masc. sg., πείθω, (intrans.) *be persuaded, convinced*; circ.
63. ἕτοιμος, -ον, (of the future) *easy to be done*.
64. Partic., *if and only if*: "expresses exclusive limitation—περ limits the applicability of an utterance's content to exactly and only the word (group) it follows" (*CGCG* §59.55).
65. Pf. pass. ptc. nom. neut. sg., βουλεύω, (pass.) *be determined*; periphrastic (equivalent of plpf. tense).
66. Adv., *securely, firmly*.
67. Pres. mid. ptc. nom. masc. sg., μωκάομαι, *mock*; circ.
68. Pres. mid. ptc. dat. masc. pl., ἐπιδέχομαι, *accept, admit*; attrib. (subst.): "on account of the ones who do not accept [his word]."

NOTES

10.124–127. The passage is a citation of Epicurus, *Men.* 124–127. Cf. Lucretius 3.830–911, 966–1023, 1087–1094. "That death is complete extinction is the message forcefully driven home by the Epicurean analysis of the soul as a temporary amalgam of atomic particles. . . . The moral corollary, that you should not let the fear of death ruin your life, is a cardinal tenet of Epicurean ethics" (Long and Sedley 1987, 1:153).

PART 8

Reading Poets and Playwrights

Every writer you encounter in this reader—from Plato and Aristotle to Philo and Josephus—negotiated the cosmos that the epic poets Homer and Hesiod constructed and that the tragic playwrights Sophocles and Euripides interrogated. The ubiquity of these authors in ancient texts (note the number of citations in this reader alone) corresponds to their representation in the holdings of ancient libraries (Koester 1995, 99). Thus to study these writers is to engage the very source and center of Greek παιδεία (education and culture).

This section is merely an introduction to ancient Greek poetry and drama. My decision to restrict the scope to Homer, Hesiod, Sophocles, and Euripides is strategic, but it means that we must leave aside a host of noteworthy poets (e.g., Pindar and Sappho) and playwrights (e.g., Aeschylus and Aristophanes).[1] In my introductions to Homer and Sophocles, I provide basic instruction on dactylic hexameter and iambic trimeter.[2] The notes after each reading include scansions of select lines for practice.

---

1. For an introductory reader of lyric, elegiac, and iambic poetry, see Campbell 2014.
2. The standard work on meter is West 1984 (more succinctly, West 1987).

8.1

Homer

The most influential works of Greek literature are the epics of Homer: the *Iliad* and the *Odyssey*. So claims the grammarian Heraclitus: "From the very earliest infancy young children are nursed in their learning by Homer, and swaddled in his verses we water our souls with them as though they were nourishing milk. He stands beside each of us as we start out and gradually grow into men, he blossoms as we do, and until old age we never grow tired of him, for as soon as we set him aside we thirst for him again; it may be said that the same limit is set to both Homer and life" (*Homeric Problems* 1.5–7, quoted in Hunter 2004, 235).

Epic poetry is composed in dactylic hexameter. The meter is represented as follows:

$$- \smile\smile \mid - \smile\smile \mid - \smile\smile \mid - \smile\smile \mid \smile \smile \mid - \text{x}$$

Each line consists of six feet, and each foot consists of a dactyl, which is one long (—) and two short (⌣) syllables, for which a spondee—that is, two long syllables (— —)—may be substituted. The sixth foot always scans the same (— x), either two long syllables or one long (the first) and one short (the second). A syllable is long either by nature (i.e., long vowel or diphthong) or by position (i.e., short vowel followed by two or more consonants or by ζ, ξ, ψ). So, for example: νοῦσον ἀνὰ στρατὸν ὦρσε κακήν,

ὀλέκοντο δὲ λαοί, in which the ultima of ἀνά and the penult of ὀλέκοντο are long by position.

The two reading passages are taken from the *Iliad*, the epic poem of the war between Achaeans (Greeks) and Trojans. The first passage describes the wrath of Achilles, the primary catalyst of the poem. The second passage is the scene in which Achilles slays Hector, the preeminent Trojan warrior who had previously killed Achilles's dear friend, Patroclus.[1]

Text: Murray 1924–25

Recommended Translation: Lattimore 1961[2]

---

1. One detects allusions to Homer and the use of Homeric motifs in the New Testament, but there are no citations of the poet. MacDonald (2000; 2015) has argued that whole books of the New Testament are based on Homer, but his case is greatly overstated. Nonetheless, I would recommend his work as a point of departure for further research. I suspect that there is much value in reading Homer alongside the New Testament, so long as we temper our temptation to "parallelomania."

For additional practice reading Homer, see Benner 2001, which includes substantial passages from the *Iliad* along with notes and a short Homeric grammar. (It's an open-access resource and is available at https://archive.org/details/selectionsfromh-01brengoog/page/10/mode/2up.) Cunliffe's lexicon (1963) is also quite useful. For details on Homeric scansion, see West 1984; 1987.

2. Lattimore at times opts for obscure vocabulary, but his translation is fairly wooden and is thus a helpful resource with which to compare the Greek.

8.1.1

The Wrath of Achilles

Iliad 1.1–21

[1]Μῆνιν[1] ἄειδε,[2] θεά,[3] Πηληϊάδεω[4] Ἀχιλῆος[5]
οὐλομένην,[6] ἣ μυρί'[7] Ἀχαιοῖς[8] ἄλγε'[9] ἔθηκε,
πολλὰς δ' ἰφθίμους[10] ψυχὰς Ἄϊδι[11] προΐαψεν[12]

ἡρώων,[13] αὐτοὺς δὲ ἑλώρια[14] τεῦχε[15]
κύνεσσιν[16]
[5]οἰωνοῖσί[17] τε πᾶσι, Διὸς[18] δ' ἐτελείετο[19]
βουλή,[20]

1. μῆνις, -ιος, ἡ, *wrath*.
2. Pres. act. impv. 2 sg., ἀείδω, *sing*.
3. The goddess addressed here is the Muse (cf. Homer, *Od.* 1.1; Hesiod, *Theog.* 1; Hesiod, *Op.* 1).
4. Πηλεύς, -ῆος, ὁ, with masc. patronymic suffix -ιάδης (cf. S §§845–46) and the masc. gen. ending -εω (cf. S §214 D.5); thus, "of the son of Peleus."
5. Ἀχι(λ)λεύς, -ῆος, ὁ, *Achilles*.
6. οὐλομένος (Att. ὀλόμενος), -η, -ον, *baneful, wretched*.
7. μυρίος, -α, -ον, *countless*. The ᾱ for the neuter plural ending has elided (cf. Benner 2001, 357 [§40]; BDF §17; S §§70–75).
8. Ἀχαιός, -ά, -όν, (pl.) *Achaeans*.
9. ἄλγος, -εος, τό, (pl.) *sufferings*. The ᾱ for the neuter plural ending has elided. See n. 7.
10. ἴφθιμος, -ον, *strong, mighty, brave*.
11. Epic Ἄϊδης, -αο, ὁ, *Hades*.
12. Aor. act. indic. 3 sg., προιάπτω, *send forth* (to the netherworld).
13. ἥρως, -ωος, ὁ, *hero, warrior*; partitive gen.
14. ἑλώρια, τά, *booty, spoils*; pred. comp.
15. Impf. act. indic. 3 sg., τεύχω, *make*; with acc. pers. "In Homer and the lyric poets either the syllabic or the temporal augment is often absent" (S §438.c; cf. Benner 2001, 375 [§125]).
16. Epic 3rd decl. masc. pl. dat., κύων, -ονος, ὁ, *dog* (cf. Benner 2001, 365 [§78]; S §210).
17. οἰωνός, -οῦ, ὁ, *bird*.
18. Ζεύς, Διός, ὁ, *Zeus*.
19. Impf. pass. indic. 3 sg., τελέω, (pass.) *be brought to completion*.
20. βουλή, -ῆς, ἡ, *counsel, purpose, will*.

ἐξ οὗ²¹ δὴ²² τὰ πρῶτα²³ διαστήτην²⁴ ἐρίσαντε²⁵
Ἀτρεΐδης²⁶ τε ἄναξ²⁷ ἀνδρῶν καὶ δῖος²⁸
Ἀχιλλεύς.
Τίς τ' ἄρ²⁹ σφωε³⁰ θεῶν ἔριδι³¹ ξυνέηκε³²
μάχεσθαι;³³
Λητοῦς³⁴ καὶ Διὸς υἱός· ὃ³⁵ γὰρ βασιλῆϊ³⁶
χολωθεὶς³⁷

¹⁰νοῦσον³⁸ ἀνὰ³⁹ στρατὸν⁴⁰ ὄρσε⁴¹ κακήν, ὀλέ-
κοντο⁴² δὲ λαοί,
οὕνεκα⁴³ τὸν Χρύσην⁴⁴ ἠτίμασεν⁴⁵ ἀρητῆρα⁴⁶
Ἀτρεΐδης· ὃ γὰρ ἦλθε θοὰς⁴⁷ ἐπὶ νῆας⁴⁸
Ἀχαιῶν
λυσόμενός⁴⁹ τε θύγατρα⁵⁰ φέρων τ' ἀπερείσι'⁵¹
ἄποινα,⁵²
στέμματ'⁵³ ἔχων ἐν χερσὶν ἑκηβόλου⁵⁴
Ἀπόλλωνος
¹⁵χρυσέῳ⁵⁵ ἀνὰ σκήπτρῳ,⁵⁶ καὶ λίσσετο⁵⁷ πάντας Ἀχαιούς,
Ἀτρεΐδα⁵⁸ δὲ μάλιστα δύω, κοσμήτορε⁵⁹ λαῶν·

---

21. ἐξ οὗ, either "from the time when" (providing the starting point of Zeus's plan) or "from the point at which" (depending on "Sing, Muse,...") (Kirk 1985, 53).

22. Postpositive partic.: "indicates that the speaker considers (and invites the addressee to consider) the text segment or word (group) which it modifies as evident, clear, or precise" (CGCG §59.44).

23. Adv. acc. of πρῶτος, -η, -ον, *first, at the beginning*.

24. διαστήτην = διεστήτην; aor. (no aug.; see n. 15) act. indic. dual, διίστημι, *stand apart* (cf. Benner 2001, 377 [§134]). The dual is used because the subject of the verb is the two men, Agamemnon and Achilles.

25. Aor. act. ptc. nom. masc. dual, ἐρίζω, *rival, vie with*; circ. (manner).

26. Ἀτρεύς with patronymic suffix -ιάδης, "son of Atreus." See n. 4.

27. ἄναξ, -ακτος, ὁ, *king*. "King of men" is an epithet for Agamemnon.

28. δῖος, -ον, *noble, illustrious, goodly*.

29. Partic., *then*: "indicates that the speaker, in view of the preceding context, cannot but make the contribution that he/she is making" (CGCG §59.42). The particle combination τ' ἄρα is frequently used to introduce questions in Homer (cf. Denniston 1966, 43).

30. 3rd pers. pron. acc. dual *these two* (cf. S §325). For the forms of the personal pronouns in Homer, cf. S §325 D; Benner 2001, 371 (§110).

31. ἔρις, -ιδος, ἡ, *contention, rivalry*.

32. Aor. act. indic. 3 sg., συνίημι, *bring together*.

33. Pres. mid. inf., μάχομαι, *fight, contend*; purpose/result (cf. S §2008, §2011; CGCG §51.6); cf. Benner 2001, 397 (§212): "The infinitive sometimes expresses result, although it is often impossible to dissociate the idea of purpose, too."

34. Λητώ, -οῦς, ἡ, *Leto*. The son of Leto and Zeus is Apollo.

35. Masc. sg. demon. pron. (cf. Benner 2001, 372 [§118]; S §338 D.1). Here ὅ is more or less equivalent to the personal pronoun αὐτός.

36. βασιλεύς, -ῆος, ὁ, *king* (cf. Benner 2001, 366 [§86]; S §274 D).

37. Aor. pass. ptc. nom. masc. sg., χολόω, (pass.) *be angered, provoked to anger*; with dat. pers.

38. νοῦσος, -ου, ἡ, *sickness, pestilence*.

39. Prep. with acc., *throughout*.

40. στρατός, -οῦ, ὁ, *army*.

41. Aor. (no aug.; see n. 15) act. indic. 3 sg., ὄρνυμι, *arouse, incite*.

42. Impf. (no aug.; see n. 15) pass. indic. 3 pl., ὀλέκω, (pass.) *perish, die*.

43. Crasis: οὕνεκα = τοῦ ἕνεκα, "because."

44. Χρύσης, -ου, ὁ, *Chryses*.

45. Aor. act. indic. 3 sg., ἀτιμάζω, *dishonor*.

46. ἀρητήρ, -ρος, ὁ, *priest*.

47. θοός, -ή, -όν, *swift, quick*.

48. Epic νηῦς, -ός, ἡ, *ship*.

49. Fut. mid. ptc. nom. masc. sg., λύω, (mid.) *ransom*; purpose (cf. S §2065; CGCG §52.41).

50. θύγατρα = θυγατέρα; θυγάτηρ, -ρος, ἡ, *daughter*.

51. ἀπερείσιος, -ον, *boundless*. The ᾱ for the neuter plural ending has elided. See n. 7.

52. ἄποινα, τά, *ransom*.

53. στέμμα, -ατος, τό, *wreath, garland* (esp. of the priest's laurel wreath). Line 15 "reveals that the στέμματα must be fillets (probably of wool) tied to his priestly staff or sceptre—it is *that which he holds*—as a sign of holiness" (Kirk 1985, 55).

54. ἑκηβόλος, -ον, *attaining his aim*; later understood as *far shooting*. The epithet stems from Apollo being the archer god whose pestilence always hits its target.

55. χρυσέῳ = χρυσῷ; χρυσός, -οῦ, ὁ, (as adj.) *golden*.

56. σκῆπτρον, -ου, τό, *staff*. The fillets of Apollo are wound around a golden staff (χρυσέῳ ἀνὰ σκήπτρῳ).

57. Impf. (no aug.; see n. 15) mid. indic. 3 sg., λίσσομαι, *beseech, entreat*.

58. Acc. masc. dual (cf. S §212; Benner 2001, 363 [§65]); Ἀτρεΐδα δὲ μάλιστα δύω, "but most of all [he was beseeching] the two [δύω = δύο] sons of Atreus."

59. Dual acc. masc., κοσμήτωρ, -ορος, ὁ, *marshaler*.

"Ἀτρεΐδαι τε καὶ ἄλλοι ἐϋκνήμιδες[60] Ἀχαιοί,
ὑμῖν μὲν[61] θεοὶ δοῖεν[62] Ὀλύμπια δώματ'[63] ἔχοντες
ἐκπέρσαι[64] Πριάμοιο[65] πόλιν, εὖ δ' οἴκαδ' ἱκέσθαι·[66]
[20] παῖδα δ' ἐμοὶ λύσαιτε[67] φίλην,[68] τὰ δ' ἄποινα δέχεσθαι,[69]
ἁζόμενοι[70] Διὸς υἱὸν ἑκηβόλον Ἀπόλλωνα.

$$- \breve{\,} \breve{\,} \mid - \mid - \mid - \breve{\,} \breve{\,} - \breve{\,} \breve{\,} \mid - x$$
πολλὰς δ' ἰφθίμους ψυχὰς Ἄϊδι προΐαψεν

$$- \mid - \mid - \breve{\,} \breve{\,} \mid - \breve{\,} \breve{\,} - \breve{\,} \breve{\,} \mid - x$$
ἡρώων, αὐτοὺς δὲ ἑλώρια τεῦχε κύνεσσιν

$$- \mid - \breve{\,} \breve{\,} \mid - \breve{\,} \breve{\,} \mid - \breve{\,} \breve{\,} - \breve{\,} \breve{\,} \mid - x$$
οἰωνοῖσί τε πᾶσι, Διὸς δ' ἐτελείετο βουλή,

$$- \mid - \mid - \mid - \mid - \breve{\,} \breve{\,} \mid - x$$
ἐξ οὗ δὴ τὰ πρῶτα διαστήτην ἐρίσαντε

$$- \breve{\,} \breve{\,} \mid - \mid - \mid - \mid - \breve{\,} \breve{\,} \mid - x$$
Ἀτρεΐδης τε ἄναξ ἀνδρῶν καὶ δῖος Ἀχιλλεύς.

NOTES

Scansion for *Il.* 1.1-7:

$$- \breve{\,} \breve{\,} \mid - \mid - \mid - \breve{\,} \breve{\,} \mid - \breve{\,} \breve{\,} \mid - x$$
Μῆνιν ἄειδε, θεά, Πηληϊάδεω[71] Ἀχιλῆος

$$- \breve{\,} \breve{\,} \mid - \mid - \breve{\,} \breve{\,} \mid - - \mid - \breve{\,} \breve{\,} \mid - x$$
οὐλομένην, ἣ μυρί' Ἀχαιοῖς ἄλγε' ἔθηκε,

60. ἐϋκνήμιδες (κνημίς), (epithet) *well-greaved* (armor that protects the lower leg).

61. μέν … δέ; point/counterpoint (cf. Runge 2010, 75–83; BDF §447; S §2904; *CGCG* §59.24).

62. Aor. act. opt. 3 pl., δίδωμι, *give, grant*; cupitive (cf. S §1814; *CGCG* §34.14; Benner 2001, 395 [§201]).

63. δῶμα, -ατος, τό, *house*.

64. Aor. act. inf., ἐκπέρθω, *sack*; obj./purpose (cf. Benner 2001, 397 [§211]; S §2009).

65. Epic 2nd decl. gen. masc. sg., Πρίαμος, -οιο, ὁ, *Priam* (cf. Benner 2001, 364 [§73]; S §229).

66. Aor. mid. inf., ἱκνέομαι, *come, go*; with adv. εὖ οἴκαδ', "return home safely"; obj./purpose. See n. 64.

67. Aor. act. opt. 2 pl., λύω, *release*. The cupitive optative may be used to express a cautious command (cf. Benner 2001, 395 [§204]; S §1820).

68. φίλος, -η, -ον, *dear* (also often in Homer with the force of *own*).

69. Imperatival (wish) inf. (cf. Benner 2001, 397 [§213]; BDF §389; S §2014; *CGCG* §51.47).

70. Pres. mid. ptc. nom. masc. pl., ἅζομαι, *stand in awe of*; circ. (causal).

71. The vowels εω are pronounced as one syllable (synthesis); cf. Benner 2001, 358 (§43).

8.1.2

Achilles Slays Hector

Iliad 22.289–336

Ἦ[1] ῥα,[2] καὶ ἀμπεπαλών[3] προΐει[4] δολιχόσκιον[5] ἔγχος,[6]
²⁹⁰καὶ βάλε[7] Πηλεΐδαο[8] μέσον σάκος[9] οὐδ᾽
ἀφάμαρτε·[10]
τῆλε[11] δ᾽ ἀπεπλάγχθη[12] σάκεος δόρυ.[13] Χώσατο[14] δ᾽ Ἕκτωρ

ὅττι[15] ῥά οἱ[16] βέλος[17] ὠκὺ[18] ἐτώσιον[19] ἔκφυγε
χειρός,
στῆ[20] δὲ κατηφήσας,[21] οὐδ᾽ ἄλλ᾽ ἔχε μείλινον[22]
ἔγχος.
Δηΐφοβον[23] δ᾽ ἐκάλει λευκάσπιδα[24] μακρὸν[25]
ἀΰσας.[26]
²⁹⁵ᾔτεέ[27] μιν[28] δόρυ μακρόν· ὁ δ᾽ οὔ τί οἱ ἐγγύθεν[29] ἦεν.[30]

1. ἦ = ἔφη.
2. ῥα = ἄρα; postpositive partic.: "indicates that the speaker, in view of the preceding context, cannot but make the contribution that he/she is making" (*CGCG* §59.42).
3. Aor. act. ptc. nom. masc. sg., ἀναπάλλω, *swing to and fro*; circ.
4. Impf. act. indic. 3 sg., προΐημι, *hurl*.
5. δολιχόσκιος, -ον, (epithet) *casting a long shadow*.
6. ἔγχος, -εος, τό, *spear*.
7. Aor. (no aug.) act. indic. 3 sg., βάλλω, *strike, hit*. "In Homer and the lyric poets either the syllabic or the temporal augment is often absent" (S §438.c; cf. Benner 2001, 375 [§125]).
8. Πηλεύς, -ῆος, ὁ, with masc. patronymic suffix -ιάδης (cf. S §§845–46) and first decl. masc. gen. ending -αο (cf. S §214 D.5; Benner 2001, 363 [§65]); thus, "of the son of Peleus."
9. σάκος, -εος, τό, *shield*.
10. Aor. act. indic. 3 sg., ἀφαμαρτάνω, *miss the mark*.
11. Adv., *far from*; with gen.
12. Aor. pass. indic. 3 sg., ἀποπλάζω, (pass.) *spring back, rebound*.
13. δόρυ, -ατος, τό, *spear*.
14. Aor. (no aug.) mid. indic. 3 sg., χώομαι, *become angry*. See n. 7.

15. ὅττι = ὅτι.
16. οἱ = αὐτῷ; dat. masc. sg. 3 pers. pron., οὗ (cf. S §325; Benner 2001, 371 [§110]); dat. of disadvantage (cf. S §1481).
17. βέλος, -εος, τό, *missile*.
18. ὠκύς, -εῖα, -ύ, *swift*.
19. ἐτώσιος, -ον, (as adv.) *in vain*.
20. Aor. act. indic. 3 sg., ἵστημι, *stand*.
21. Aor. act. ptc. nom. masc. sg., κατηφέω, *be downcast*; circ.
22. μείλινος, -η, -ον, *of ash*.
23. Δηΐφοβος, -ον, ὁ, *Deïphobos* (Hector's brother).
24. λεύκασπις, -ιδος, ὁ, (epithet) *white-shielded*.
25. Adv., (with verbs of shouting) *loudly*.
26. Aor. act. ptc. nom. masc. sg., αὔω, *cry out, call aloud*; circ.
27. Impf. act. indic. 3 sg., αἰτέω, *ask*; with double acc.: "He asked *him* [μιν] for a *long spear* [δόρυ μακρόν]."
28. μιν = αὐτόν.
29. Adv., *nearby*; with dat; οὔ τί οἱ ἐγγύθεν, "not at all near to him."
30. ἦεν = ἦν.

Ἕκτωρ δ' ἔγνω ᾗσιν³¹ ἐνὶ φρεσὶ³² φώνησέν τε·
"ὢ πόποι,³³ ἦ μάλα δή³⁴ με θεοὶ θανατόνδε³⁵ κάλεσσαν.³⁶
Δηΐφοβον γὰρ ἐγώ γ'³⁷ ἐφάμην³⁸ ἥρωα³⁹ παρεῖναι·⁴⁰
ἀλλ' ὁ μὲν⁴¹ ἐν τείχει,⁴² ἐμὲ δ' ἐξαπάτησεν⁴³ Ἀθήνη.⁴⁴
³⁰⁰Νῦν δὲ δὴ ἐγγύθι⁴⁵ μοι θάνατος κακός, οὐδ' ἔτ' ἄνευθεν,⁴⁶
οὐδ' ἀλέη·⁴⁷ ἦ γάρ ῥα⁴⁸ πάλαι⁴⁹ τό γε φίλτερον⁵⁰ ἦεν

Ζηνί τε καὶ Διὸς υἷι ἑκηβόλῳ,⁵¹ οἵ με πάρος⁵² γε
πρόφρονες⁵³ εἰρύατο·⁵⁴ νῦν αὖτέ⁵⁵ με μοῖρα⁵⁶ κιχάνει.⁵⁷
Μὴ μὰν⁵⁸ ἀσπουδί⁵⁹ γε καὶ ἀκλειῶς⁶⁰ ἀπολοίμην⁶¹
³⁰⁵ἀλλὰ μέγα ῥέξας⁶² τι καὶ ἐσσομένοισι⁶³ πυθέσθαι.⁶⁴"
Ὣς ἄρα⁶⁵ φωνήσας εἰρύσσατο⁶⁶ φάσγανον⁶⁷ ὀξύ,⁶⁸
τό⁶⁹ οἱ⁷⁰ ὑπὸ λαπάρην⁷¹ τέτατο⁷² μέγα τε στιβαρόν⁷³ τε,

31. Dat. fem. pl. of ἑός, ἑή, ἑόν, *one's own* (cf. S §§332 D, 1100; Benner 2001, 372 [§115]).
32. φρήν, φρενός, ἡ, (often in pl.) *heart*.
33. Exclamation, (ὤ) πόποι, *Impossible! Incredible!*
34. Postpositive partic., (with ἦ μάλα) *very clearly indeed*: "indicates that the speaker considers (and invites the addressee to consider) the text segment or word (group) which it modifies as evident, clear, or precise" (CGCG §59.44).
35. Adv., *to death, deathward*.
36. Aor. (no aug.) act. indic. 3 pl., καλέω, *call, summon*. See n. 7.
37. Postpositive partic.: "focuses attention on the word or phrase it follows (or sometimes the clause as a whole), and limits the applicability of the content of the utterance to *at least* or (more) *precisely* that specific element" (CGCG §59.53).
38. Impf. mid. indic. 1 sg., φημί, *say/think* (the two ideas are not always easily distinguishable).
39. ἥρως, -ωος, ὁ, *hero, warrior*.
40. Pres. act. inf., πάρειμι, *be at hand*; indir. disc. (cf. BDF §397; S §2016; CGCG §51.19).
41. μέν . . . δέ; point/counterpoint (cf. Runge 2010, 75–83; BDF §447; S §2904; CGCG §59.24).
42. τεῖχος, -εος, τό, *wall*.
43. Aor. act. indic. 3 sg., ἐξαπατάω, *deceive/beguile*.
44. Ἀθήνη, -ης, ἡ, *Athena*.
45. Adv., *near*; with dat.
46. Adv., *far away*.
47. ἀλέη, -ης, ἡ, *avoiding, escape*.
48. Partic. combination; based on the preceding context, the speaker must make (ῥα) the supporting point (γάρ).
49. Adv., *of old*.
50. Compar., φίλος, -η, -ον, *more pleasing*; underscored by γε, "*This* is most pleasing to Zeus and to the son of Zeus [i.e., Apollo], the one who always hits his mark." The comparative φίλτερον means this doom of Hector rather than any other fate was the pleasure of Zeus (Benner 2001, 339n301).

51. ἑκηβόλος, -ον, *attaining his aim*; later understood as *far-shooting*.
52. Adv., (temp.) *before*; qualified by γε (see n. 37), "Formerly, they were eager and willing to succor me."
53. πρόφρων, -ον, *gracious, willing*.
54. Plpf. mid. indic. 3 pl., ἐρύω, *protect, guard*.
55. Adv., *on the other hand, however*; νῦν αὖτε, "now, however . . ."
56. μοῖρα, -ης, ἡ, *lot, portion, fate*.
57. Pres. act. indic. 3 sg., κιχάνω, *reach, come upon*.
58. μάν = μήν, *truly, certainly*; postpositive partic.: "indicates that the speaker is committed to the truth or relevance of his/her utterance" (CGCG §59.49).
59. Adv., *without effort/struggle*; qualified by γε (see n. 37), "at least not without struggle."
60. Adv., *ingloriously*.
61. Aor. mid. opt. 1 sg., ἀπόλλυμι, (mid.) *perish*; cupitive (cf. S §1814; CGCG §34.14).
62. Aor. act. ptc. nom. masc. sg., ῥέζω, *do, accomplish*; circ. (manner).
63. Fut. mid. ptc. dat. masc. pl., εἰμί; attrib. (subst.).
64. Aor. mid. inf., πυνθάνομαι, *hear/learn a thing*; epex. (cf. Benner 2001, 397 [§211]; S §2001; CGCG §51.18): "a great thing and [one] *to be heard of* by future generations."
65. Postpositive partic., *then*: "indicates that the speaker, in view of the preceding context, cannot but make the contribution that he/she is making" (CGCG §59.42).
66. Aor. mid. indic. 3 sg., ἐρύω, *draw* (a weapon).
67. φάσγανον, -ου, τό, *sword*.
68. ὀξύς, -εῖα, -ύ, *sharp*.
69. τό = ὅ; art. as rel. pron. (cf. S §1105).
70. οἱ = αὐτῷ; dat. of advantage. See n. 16.
71. λαπάρη, -ης, ἡ, (part of the body between the ribs and hip) *flank*.
72. Plpf. pass. indic. 3 sg., τείνω, (pass.) *be suspended*.
73. στιβαρός, -ή, -όν, *strong*.

οἴμησεν⁷⁴ δὲ ἀλεὶς⁷⁵ ὥς τ' αἰετὸς⁷⁶ ὑψιπετήεις,⁷⁷
ὅς τ' εἶσιν⁷⁸ πεδίονδε⁷⁹ διὰ νεφέων⁸⁰ ἐρεβεννῶν⁸¹
³¹⁰ἁρπάξων⁸² ἢ ἄρν'⁸³ ἀμαλὴν⁸⁴ ἢ πτῶκα⁸⁵ λαγωόν⁸⁶·
ὣς Ἕκτωρ οἴμησε τινάσσων⁸⁷ φάσγανον ὀξύ.
ὁρμήθη⁸⁸ δ' Ἀχιλεύς, μένεος⁸⁹ δ' ἐμπλήσατο⁹⁰ θυμὸν⁹¹
ἀγρίου,⁹² πρόσθεν δὲ σάκος στέρνοιο⁹³ κάλυψε⁹⁴
καλὸν δαιδάλεον,⁹⁵ κόρυθι⁹⁶ δ' ἐπένευε⁹⁷ φαεινῇ⁹⁸

³¹⁵τετραφάλῳ⁹⁹· καλαὶ δὲ περισσείοντο¹⁰⁰ ἔθειραι¹⁰¹
χρύσεαι, ἃς Ἥφαιστος¹⁰² ἵει¹⁰³ λόφον¹⁰⁴ ἀμφὶ θαμειάς.¹⁰⁵
Οἷος δ' ἀστὴρ¹⁰⁶ εἶσι μετ' ἀστράσι νυκτὸς ἀμολγῷ¹⁰⁷
ἕσπερος,¹⁰⁸ ὃς κάλλιστος ἐν οὐρανῷ ἵσταται ἀστήρ,
ὣς αἰχμῆς¹⁰⁹ ἀπέλαμπ'¹¹⁰ εὐήκεος,¹¹¹ ἣν ἄρ' Ἀχιλλεὺς
³²⁰πάλλεν¹¹² δεξιτερῇ¹¹³ φρονέων¹¹⁴ κακὸν Ἕκτορι δίῳ,¹¹⁵
εἰσορόων¹¹⁶ χρόα¹¹⁷ καλόν, ὅπῃ¹¹⁸ εἴξειε¹¹⁹ μάλιστα.

74. Aor. act. indic. 3 sg., οἰμάω, *swoop*.
75. Aor. pass. ptc. nom. masc. sg., εἴλω, (pass.) *gather one's self together*; circ.
76. αἰετός, -οῦ, ὁ, *eagle*.
77. ὑψιπετήεις, -εσσα, -εν, *high-soaring*.
78. Pres. act. indic. 3 sg., εἶμι, *go* (cf. S §1880).
79. Adv., *to the plain*.
80. νέφος, -εος, τό, *cloud*.
81. ἐρεβεννός, -ή, -όν, *dark*.
82. Fut. act. ptc. nom. masc. sg., ἁρπάζω, *seize*; purpose (cf. S §2065; CGCG §52.41).
83. ἀρήν, ἀρνός, ὁ, *lamb*.
84. ἀμαλός, -ή, -όν, *soft, weak, tender*.
85. πτώξ, -ωκός, *cowering*.
86. λαγωός, -οῦ, ὁ, *hare*.
87. Pres. act. ptc. nom. masc. sg., τινάσσω, *brandish, shake*.
88. Aor. (no aug.) pass. indic. 3 sg., ὁρμάω, (intrans.) *rush*.
89. μῆνις, -εος, ἡ, *wrath*.
90. Aor. (no aug.) mid. indic. 3 sg., ἐμπίπλημι, *fill* (acc. with gen.).
91. θυμός, -οῦ, ὁ, *heart, spirit*.
92. ἄγριος, -α, -ον, *wild, fierce*.
93. Epic gen. masc. sg., στέρνον, τό, *breast* (cf. Benner 2001, 364 [§73]; S §229); gen. obj. of prep. πρόσθεν, "in front of his chest."
94. Aor. (no aug.) act. indic. 3 sg., καλύπτω, *put over as a covering*. See n. 7.
95. δαιδάλεος, -α, -ον, *cunningly wrought*.
96. κόρυς, -υθος, ἡ, *helmet*; instrumental dat.
97. Impf. act. indic. 3 sg., ἐπινεύω, *nod*.
98. φαεινός, -ή, -όν, *bright, radiant*.

99. τετράφαλος, -ον, *four-horned*.
100. Impf. (no aug.) pass. indic. 3 pl., περισσείομαι, (pass.) *be shaken around, waved around*.
101. ἔθειρα, -ας, ἡ, (pl.) *plumes* (made of horsehair).
102. Ἥφαιστος, -ου, ὁ, *Hephaestus* (god of fire and craftsman in metal).
103. Impf. act. indic. 3 sg., ἵημι, *set*.
104. λόφος, -ου, ὁ, *crest* (of the helmet); acc. obj. of ἀμφί, "around the crest."
105. θαμέες, -εῖαι, -εν, (pl.) *thick*; pred. comp.
106. ἀστήρ, -έρος, ὁ, *star*.
107. ἀμολγός, -οῦ, ὁ, *darkness*.
108. ἕσπερος, -ον, *of the evening*.
109. αἰχμή, -ῆς, ἡ, *tip of the spear*; gen. of source.
110. Impf. act. indic. 3 sg., ἀπολάμπω, *shine/beam from*; impers.: "Like a star goes . . . so *it was shining brightly*."
111. εὐήκης, -ες, *well-pointed*.
112. Impf. (no aug.) act. indic. 3 sg., πάλλω, *brandish*. See n. 7.
113. δεξιτερῇ = δεξιτερῇ χερί; dat. of instrument, "with his right hand."
114. Pres. act. ptc. nom. masc. sg., φρονέω, *purpose, devise*.
115. δῖος, -ον, *noble, illustrious, goodly*.
116. Pres. act. ptc. nom. masc. sg., εἰσοράω, *look on*.
117. χρώς, -οός, ὁ, *skin/flesh*.
118. Adv., (indirect interrogative) *where*.
119. Aor. act. opt. 3 sg., εἴκω, *yield, give way*; oblique opt. in an indir. quest. (cf. S §2677; CGCG §42.7): "where it would be most susceptible [to his spear]"; or impers., "where there was the best opportunity [to strike]."

Τοῦ[120] δὲ καὶ ἄλλο τόσον[121] μὲν[122] ἔχε χρόα χάλ-
κεα τεύχεα,[123]
καλά, τὰ[124] Πατρόκλοιο[125] βίην[126] ἐνάριξε[127]
κατακτάς.[128]
φαίνετο[129] δ' ᾗ[130] κληῖδες[131] ἀπ' ὤμων[132] αὐχέν'[133]
ἔχουσι,
325 λαυκανίην,[134] ἵνα[135] τε ψυχῆς ὤκιστος[136]
ὄλεθρος·[137]
τῇ[138] ῥ' ἐπὶ οἷ μεμαῶτ'[139] ἔλασ'[140] ἔγχεϊ δῖος
Ἀχιλλεύς,
ἀντικρὺ[141] δ' ἁπαλοῖο[142] δι' αὐχένος ἤλυθ'
ἀκωκή.[143]
Οὐδ' ἄρ' ἀπ' ἀσφάραγον[144] μελίη[145] τάμε[146]
χαλκοβάρεια,[147]

ὄφρα τί μιν προτιείποι[148] ἀμειβόμενος[149]
ἐπέεσσιν.[150]
330 ἤριπε[151] δ' ἐν κονίης·[152] ὁ δ' ἐπεύξατο[153] δῖος
Ἀχιλλεύς·
"Ἕκτορ,[154] ἀτάρ[155] που[156] ἔφης Πατροκλῆ'
ἐξεναρίζων[157]
σῶς[158] ἔσσεσθ',[159] ἐμὲ δ' οὐδὲν ὀπίζεο[160] νό-
σφιν[161] ἐόντα,
νήπιε·[162] τοῖο[163] δ' ἄνευθεν ἀοσσητὴρ[164] μέγ'
ἀμείνων[165]
νηυσὶν[166] ἔπι γλαφυρῇσιν[167] ἐγὼ μετόπισθε[168]
λελείμμην,[169]

120. Art. as demon. pron. See n. 31.
121. The grammar is convoluted (see, e.g., Benner 2001, 339n322). Translate ἄλλο τόσον as "all the rest."
122. μέν … δέ; point/counterpoint. See n. 41.
123. τεῦχος, -εος, τό, (pl.) *armor*.
124. Art. as rel. pron. See n. 69.
125. Epic gen. masc. sg., Πάτροκλος, -οιο, ὁ, *Patroclus*. See n. 93.
126. Adv., *forcefully*.
127. Aor. act. indic. 3 sg., ἐναρίζω, *strip* (of a slain foe).
128. Aor. act. ptc. nom. masc. sg., κατακτείνω, *slay*; circ.
129. Pres. pass. indic. 3 sg., φαίνω, (pass.) *be revealed, exposed*.
130. Rel. pron. as adv., *whereat*.
131. κληίς, -ῖδος, ἡ, *collarbone*.
132. ὦμος, -ου, ὁ, *shoulder*.
133. αὐχήν, -ένος, ὁ, *neck*.
134. λαυκανίη, -ης, ἡ, *throat*; an appositive to αὐχέν.
135. Adv., *where*.
136. Superl., ὠκύς, -εῖα, -ύ, *most swift*.
137. ὄλεθρος, -ου, ὁ, *ruin, destruction, death*.
138. Adv., *here, there*.
139. Pf. act. ptc. acc. masc. sg., (always in pf.) μέμαα, *press on* (cf. Cunliffe 1963, 257); circ. The subject is Hector: "So there noble Achilles struck him [Hector] with the spear *as he* [Hector] *was rushing* [μεμαῶτ'] upon him [ἐπὶ οἷ]."
140. Aor. act. indic. 3 sg., ἐλαύνω, *drive* (with the spear).
141. Adv., *straight through*.
142. Epic gen. masc. sg., ἁπαλός, *tender*. See n. 93.
143. ἀκωκή, -ῆς, ἡ, *point*.
144. ἀσφάραγος, -ου, ὁ, *throat*.
145. Epic μελίη, -ης, ἡ, *ashen spear*.
146. Aor. (no aug.) act. indic. 3 sg., τέμνω, *cut, slice*; with adv. ἀπ'. See n. 7.
147. χαλκοβαρής, -βάρεια, -ές, *bronze-bearing*.

148. Aor. act. opt. 3 sg., προσεῖπον, *address*; with internal acc. (τι) and external acc. (μιν); oblique opt. in purpose clause, marked by ὄφρα (cf. S §2193.a).
149. Pres. mid. ptc. nom. masc. sg., ἀμείβω, (mid.) *answer, respond*; circ.
150. Epic 3rd decl. dat. neut. pl., ἔπος, -εος, τό, *word*.
151. Aor. act. indic. 3 sg., ἐρείπω, *fall down*.
152. Epic and Ion. dat. fem. pl., κονίη, -ης, ἡ, *dust*.
153. Aor. mid. indic. 3 sg., ἐπεύχομαι, *exalt over*.
154. Voc.
155. Partic.: "similar in function to δέ, although the 'break' suggested by ἀτάρ is often a bit stronger than by δέ. It is usually found in contexts where δέ cannot be used, e.g. together with vocatives (often at the beginning of a new speaking turn)" (CGCG §59.18).
156. Postpositive partic., *I think, I suppose*: hedging device (cf. CGCG §59.50).
157. Pres. act. ptc. nom. masc. sg., ἐξεναρίζω, *spoil* (a foe slain in a fight).
158. Adj., σῶς, *safe*.
159. Fut. mid. inf., εἰμί; indir. disc. See n. 40.
160. Impf. (no aug.) mid. indic. 2 sg., ὀπίζομαι, *regard* (with awe and dread); with internal acc. (οὐδέν) and external acc. (ἐμέ).
161. Adv., *far away*.
162. νήπιος, -η, -ον, *childish, foolish*; as voc., "Fool!"
163. τοῖο = τοῦ; art. as demon. pron. (see n. 31); gen. obj. of ἄνευθεν, "far from him [Patroclus]."
164. ἀοσσητήρ, -ῆρος, ὁ, *avenger*.
165. ἀμείνων, -ον, *greater*; with adv. acc. μέγ', "by far greater [than you]."
166. Dat. pl., νηῦς, -ός, ἡ, *ship*; obj. of ἔπι. Note the shift in accent (anastrophe; cf. S §175; CGCG §60.14).
167. γλαφυρός, -ά, -όν, *hollow, hollowed*.
168. Adv., (place) *back*.
169. Plpf. pass. indic. 1 sg., λείπω, (pass.) *be left behind*.

³³⁵ὅς τοι¹⁷⁰ γούνατ'¹⁷¹ ἔλυσα. Σὲ μὲν¹⁷² κύνες¹⁷³ ἠδ' οἰωνοὶ¹⁷⁴ ἑλκήσουσ'¹⁷⁵ ἀϊκῶς,¹⁷⁶ τὸν δὲ κτεριοῦσιν¹⁷⁷ Ἀχαιοί."¹⁷⁸

NOTES

Scansion for *Il.* 22.289–293:

Ἦ ῥα, καὶ¹⁷⁹ ἀμπεπαλὼν προΐει δολιχόσκιον ἔγχος,

Καὶ βάλε Πηληϊάδαο¹⁸⁰ μέσον σάκος οὐδ' ἀφάμαρτε·

τῆλε δ' ἀπεπλάγχθη σάκεος δόρυ Χώσατο δ' Ἕκτωρ

ὅττι ῥά οἱ βέλος ὠκὺ ἐτώσιον ἔκφυγε χειρός,

στῆ δὲ κατηφήσας, οὐδ' ἄλλ' ἔχε μείλινον ἔγχος.

170. Postpositive partic., *mark you, note*: "serves to bring an utterance to the specific attention of the addressee" (*CGCG* §59.51).
171. γόνυ (Epic γούνατος), τό, *knee*.
172. μέν ... δέ; point/counterpoint. See n. 41.
173. κύων, -ονος, ὁ, *dog*.
174. οἰωνός, -οῦ, ὁ, *bird*.
175. Fut. act. indic. 3 pl., ἑλκέω, *drag about, tear asunder*.
176. Adv. *in an unseemly manner*.
177. Fut. act. indic. 3 pl., κτερίζω, *bury* (with honor).
178. Ἀχαιός, -ά, -όν, (pl.) *Achaeans*.
179. The diphthong -αι is shortened (Epic correction); cf. Benner 2001, 355 (§28).
180. The α is naturally long in gen. ending -αο; cf. Benner 2001, 363 (§65).

8.2

Hesiod

Hesiod was the only figure whom the ancients dared to put in the same breath as Homer (cf. Herodotus, *Hist.* 2.53). The great achievement of the archaic poet was to explain the nature of the cosmos that Homer presupposed. As Jenny Strauss Clay notes, "Taken together the *Theogony* and the *Works and Days* offer perhaps the earliest sustained and systematic reflections in the Greek sphere on the perennial and fundamental issues which haunt us still: what is the relationship between human beings and those powerful beings called gods? Is the world in which we find ourselves friendly, hostile, or indifferent to human life? And how should human beings live in the world as it is constituted?" (2003, 2).

Both passages are from the *Theogony*, Hesiod's account of the genesis of the cosmos and of the gods who rule over it. The first passage is an etiology of sacrifice, the second an etiology of woman.

Text and Translation: Most 2018
Supplemental Scripture: Gen. 2–3 (§8.2.2)

8.2.1

An Etiology of Sacrifice

Theogony 535–560

⁵³⁵καὶ γὰρ¹ ὅτ' ἐκρίνοντο² θεοὶ θνητοί³ τ' ἄνθρωποι
Μηκώνη,⁴ τότ' ἔπειτα μέγαν βοῦν⁵ πρόφρονι⁶ θυμῷ⁷
δασσάμενος⁸ προέθηκε,⁹ Διὸς¹⁰ νόον¹¹ ἐξαπαφίσκων.¹²

τῷ¹³ μὲν¹⁴ γὰρ σάρκας τε καὶ ἔγκατα¹⁵ πίονα¹⁶ δημῷ¹⁷
ἐν ῥινῷ¹⁸ κατέθηκε, καλύψας¹⁹ γαστρὶ²⁰ βοείη,²¹
⁵⁴⁰τῷ²² δ' αὖτ'²³ ὀστέα²³ λευκὰ²⁴ βοὸς δολίῃ²⁵ ἐπὶ τέχνῃ²⁶

1. Partic. combination: introduces additional information (καί) that has explanatory force (γάρ) (*CGCG* §59.66).
2. Impf. mid. indic. 3 pl., κρίνω, *decide, determine*. Cf. Most (2018, 45n27): "The precise meaning of the verb Hesiod uses is obscure; it seems to indicate that gods and men were now being separated definitively from one another, presumably after a time when they had been together."
3. θνητός, -ή, -όν, *mortal*.
4. Μηκώνη, -ης, ἡ, *Mecone* (later identified as Sicyon).
5. βοῦς, -οος, ὁ, *ox*.
6. πρόφρων, -ον, *eager, willing*.
7. θυμός, -οῦ, ὁ, *spirit*.
8. Aor. mid. ptc. nom. masc. sg., δατέομαι, *divide*. The subject of the participle is Prometheus.
9. Aor. act. indic. 3 sg., προτίθημι, *set before*.
10. Ζεύς, Διός, ὁ, *Zeus*.
11. νοῦς, νόος, ὁ, *mind*.
12. Pres. act. ptc. nom. masc. sg., ἐξαπατάω (Epic ἐξαπαφίσκω), *deceive*; "*trying* to deceive the mind of Zeus." The present participle with the iterative suffix -σκ lends itself to a conative *Aktionsart*.

13. Art. as demon. pron. (cf. S §1100; *CGCG* §28.26). Thus, "He [Prometheus] set down on the skin *before him* [Zeus] the innards, rich in fat."
14. μέν ... δ' αὖτ'; stronger contrast than μέν ... δέ, which has explanatory force (γάρ) (cf. *CGCG* §59.13).
15. ἔγκατα, -ων, τά, *entrails*.
16. πίων, πῖον, (of animals) *fat, rich*.
17. δημός, -οῦ, ὁ, *fat*; dat. of respect.
18. ῥινός, -οῦ, ἡ, (of dead animals) *hide*.
19. Aor. act. ptc. nom. masc. sg., καλύπτω, *hide, conceal*; circ.
20. γαστήρ, -έρος, ἡ, *stomach*.
21. βόειος, -η, -ον, *of an ox*.
22. West (1966, 319) emends to τοῖς, but cf. Most 2018, 47n28: "This passage has been much misunderstood and often emended. But the transmitted text makes excellent sense, so long as we recall that in Epic usage, μέν and δέ can distinguish not only two persons but also two actions directed toward the same person. ... Prometheus sets both portions before Zeus and lets him choose freely between them."
23. ὀστέον, -ου, τό, *bone*.
24. λευκός, -ή, -όν, *white*.
25. δόλιος, -η, -ον, *deceitful*.
26. τέχνη, -ης, ἡ, *craft*; δολίῃ ἐπὶ τέχνῃ (means), "with deceptive craft."

εὐθετίσας²⁷ κατέθηκε, καλύψας ἀργέτι²⁸ δημῷ.
δὴ²⁹ τότε μιν³⁰ προσέειπε³¹ πατὴρ ἀνδρῶν τε θεῶν τε
"'Ιαπετιονίδη,³² πάντων ἀριδείκετ'³³ ἀνάκτων,³⁴
ὦ πέπον,³⁵ ὡς ἑτεροζήλως³⁶ διεδάσσαο³⁷ μοίρας."³⁸
⁵⁴⁵ὣς φάτο³⁹ κερτομέων⁴⁰ Ζεὺς ἄφθιτα⁴¹ μήδεα⁴² εἰδώς.
τὸν⁴³ δ' αὖτε⁴⁴ προσέειπε Προμηθεὺς ἀγκυλομήτης⁴⁵
ἦκ'⁴⁶ ἐπιμειδήσας,⁴⁷ δολίης δ' οὐ λήθετο⁴⁸ τέχνης

"Ζεῦ κύδιστε⁴⁹ μέγιστε θεῶν αἰειγενετάων,⁵⁰
τῶν⁵¹ δ' ἕλευ⁵² ὁπποτέρην⁵³ σε ἐνὶ⁵⁴ φρεσὶ⁵⁵ θυμὸς ἀνώγει."⁵⁶
⁵⁵⁰φῆ ῥα⁵⁷ δολοφρονέων·⁵⁸ Ζεὺς δ' ἄφθιτα μήδεα εἰδὼς
γνῶ⁵⁹ ῥ' οὐδ' ἠγνοίησε⁶⁰ δόλον⁶¹ κακὰ δ' ὄσσετο⁶² θυμῷ
θνητοῖς ἀνθρώποισι,⁶³ τὰ καὶ τελέεσθαι⁶⁴ ἔμελλεν.
χερσὶ δ' ὅ γ'⁶⁵ ἀμφοτέρῃσιν⁶⁶ ἀνείλετο⁶⁷ λευκὸν ἄλειφαρ.⁶⁸

27. Aor. act. ptc. nom. masc. sg., εὐθετίζω, *arrange*.
28. ἀργής, -ῆτος, ὁ, (used as adj. of fat) *shining*.
29. Postpositive (except in poets) partic.: "indicates that the speaker considers (and invites the addressee to consider) the text segment or word (group) which it modifies as evident, clear or precise" (*CGCG* §59.44).
30. μιν = αὐτόν (cf. S §325 D; *CGCG* §7.2).
31. Aor. act. indic. 3 sg., προσεῖπον, *address*; always uncontracted in Homer and Hesiod.
32. Voc., Ἰαπετιονίδης, -ου, ὁ, *son of Iapetos* (a titan). For patronymic suffixes, cf. S §845.
33. ἀριδείκετος, -ον, *famous, eminent*. The vocative ending -ε has elided (cf. Benner 2001, 357 [§40]; BDF §17; S §§70–75).
34. ἄναξ, -ακτος, ὁ, *ruler*.
35. πέπων, -ον, a form of address in Homer and Hesiod, along the lines of "O kind sir!"
36. Adv., *unfairly*.
37. Aor. mid. indic. 2 sg., διαδατέομαι, *divide up*.
38. μοῖρα, -ας, ἡ, *portion*.
39. Epic aor. (no aug.) act. indic. 3 sg., φημί, *say, speak*. "In Homer and the lyric poets either the syllabic or the temporal augment is often absent" (S §438.c; cf. Benner 2001, 375 [§125]).
40. Pres. act. ptc. nom. masc. sg., κερτομέω, *insult, taunt*; circ.
41. ἄφθιτος, -ον, *eternal*.
42. μῆδος, -εος, τό, (only in pl.) *counsels, plans*.
43. Art. as demon. pron. See n. 13.
44. Marks stronger opposition than δέ alone, *on the other hand, in turn* (cf. S §2839).
45. ἀγκυλομήτης, -ου, ὁ, (epithet) *crooked of counsel*.
46. Adv. (ἦκα), *slightly*. See n. 33.
47. Aor. act. ptc. nom. masc. sg., ἐπιμειδάω, *smile at*; circ.
48. Impf. (no aug.) act. indic. 3 sg., λανθάνω, *forget*; with gen. (see n. 39). The point is that he will not give up his deceptive ways.

49. Superl., κυδρός, -ή, -όν, *most honored*.
50. αἰειγενέτης, -ου, ὁ, (epithet of the gods) *everlasting*.
51. Art. as demon. pron. (see n. 13); partitive gen.
52. Aor. mid. impv. 2 sg., αἱρέω, (mid.) *choose*.
53. ὁπότερος, -α, -ον (Epic ὁππότερος), *whichever*.
54. ἐνί = ἐν.
55. φρήν, -ενός, ἡ, *heart*.
56. Pf. act. indic. 3 sg., ἄνωγα (pf. with pres. sense), *command, bid*.
57. ῥα = ἄρα. Partic., *so, then, it seems*: "indicates that the speaker, in view of the preceding context, cannot but make the contribution he/she is making (often surprisingly) from the preceding context" (*CGCG* §59.42).
58. Pres. act. ptc. nom. masc. sg., δολοφρονέω, *plan deceit*; circ.
59. γνῶ = ἔγνω. See n. 39.
60. Aor. act. indic. 3 sg., ἀγνοέω (Epic ἀγνοι-), *not recognize*.
61. δόλος, -ου, ὁ, *deceit, deception*.
62. Impf. (no aug.) act. indic. 3 sg., ὄσσομαι, *envision*. See n. 39.
63. ἀνθρώποισι = ἀνθρώποις (cf. S §234).
64. Pres. pass. inf., τελέω, (pass.) *be fulfilled*; comp. of ἔμελλεν.
65. Postpositive partic.: "expresses concentration/limitation—focuses attention on the word or phrase it follows . . . and limits the applicability of the content of the utterance to *at least* or (*more*) *precisely* that specific element" (*CGCG* §59.53).
66. Epic 1st decl. dat. pl., ἀμφότεραι, "with both hands."
67. Aor. mid. indic. 3 sg., ἀναιρέ, (mid.) *pick up*.
68. ἄλειφαρ, -ατος, τό, *fat*.

χώσατο⁶⁹ δὲ φρένας ἀμφί,⁷⁰ χόλος⁷¹ δέ μιν
  ἵκετο⁷² θυμόν,⁷³
⁵⁵⁵ὡς ἴδεν⁷⁴ ὀστέα λευκὰ βοὸς δολίῃ ἐπὶ
  τέχνῃ.
ἐκ τοῦ⁷⁵ δ' ἀθανάτοισιν⁷⁶ ἐπὶ χθονὶ⁷⁷ φῦλ'⁷⁸
  ἀνθρώπων
καίουσ'⁷⁹ ὀστέα λευκὰ θυηέντων⁸⁰ ἐπὶ
  βωμῶν.⁸¹
  τὸν δὲ μέγ' ὀχθήσας⁸² προσέφη νεφεληγε-
    ρέτα⁸³ Ζεύς
"Ἰαπετιονίδη, πάντων πέρι⁸⁴ μήδεα εἰδώς,
⁵⁶⁰ὦ πέπον, οὐκ ἄρα πω⁸⁵ δολίης ἐπιλήθεο⁸⁶
  τέχνης.

$$\bar{\ } \ \breve{\ } \breve{\ } \mid \bar{\ } \mid \bar{\ } \breve{\ } \breve{\ } \mid \bar{\ } \mid \bar{\ } \breve{\ } \breve{\ } \mid \bar{\ } \ x$$
Μηκώνῃ, τότ' ἔπειτα μέγαν βοῦν πρόφρονι θυμῷ

$$\bar{\ } \breve{\ } \breve{\ } \mid \bar{\ } \breve{\ } \breve{\ } \mid \bar{\ } \breve{\ } \breve{\ } \mid \bar{\ } \breve{\ } \breve{\ } \mid \bar{\ } \ x$$
δασσάμενος προέθηκε, Διὸς νόον ἐξαπαφίσκων.

$$\bar{\ } \mid \bar{\ } \mid \bar{\ } \mid \bar{\ } \breve{\ } \breve{\ } \mid \bar{\ } \breve{\ } \breve{\ } \mid \bar{\ } \ x$$
τῷ μὲν γὰρ σάρκας τε καὶ⁸⁷ ἔγκατα πίονα δημῷ

$$\bar{\ } \mid \bar{\ } \breve{\ } \breve{\ } \mid \bar{\ } \breve{\ } \breve{\ } \mid \bar{\ } \mid \bar{\ } \breve{\ } \breve{\ } \mid \bar{\ } \ x$$
ἐν ῥινῷ κατέθηκε, καλύψας γαστρὶ βοείῃ

The Prometheus myth is an etiology of sacrifice and the creation of woman (cf. Hesiod, *Op.* 42–105, which truncates the former and expands on the latter). On the importance of the myth for Greek sacrifice, see Vernant (1989). On Greek sacrifice more broadly, see especially Naiden (2013). West (1966, 321) notes, "It has long been recognized that in the original story Zeus did not see through the trick, but was thoroughly deceived" (cf. Hyginus, *Astr.* 2.15; Lucian, *Prom.* 3; Lucian, *Dial. d.* 1.1).

NOTES

Scansion for *Theog.* 535–539:

$$\bar{\ } \breve{\ } \breve{\ } \mid \bar{\ } \mid \bar{\ } \breve{\ } \breve{\ } \mid \bar{\ } \mid \bar{\ } \mid \bar{\ } \ x$$
καὶ γὰρ ὅτ' ἐκρίνοντο θεοὶ θνητοί τ' ἄνθρωποι

69. Aor. mid. indic. 3 sg., χώομαι, *become angry*.
70. Prep. with acc., *around, about*; no anastrophe (cf. Benner 2001, 388 [§168]).
71. χόλος, -ου, ὁ, *anger, wrath*.
72. Aor. mid. indic. 3 sg., ἱκνέομαι, *arrive at, reach*.
73. Acc. of respect; lit., "Wrath came upon him *in his spirit*."
74. ἴδεν = εἶδεν. See n. 39.
75. ἐκ τοῦ = ἐκ τούτου (χρόνου), *from that time*. See n. 13.
76. ἀθανάτοισιν = ἀθανάτοις, "for the immortals." See n. 63.
77. χθών, -ονός, ἡ, *earth*.
78. φυλή, -ῆς, ἡ, *tribe*.
79. Pres. act. ptc. nom. fem. pl., καίω, *burn*. The ending -αι has elided. See n. 33.
80. θυήεις, -εσσα, -εν, *smoking with incense*.
81. βωμός, -οῦ, ὁ, *altar*.
82. Aor. act. ptc. nom. masc. sg., ὀχθέω, *be sorely angered*; circ.
83. γεφεληγερέτα, -αο (νεφέλη ἀργείω), *gatherer of rain clouds*.
84. The anastrophe (cf. S §175; CGCG §60.14) indicates that the object precedes the preposition; πέρι πάντων, "*beyond* all others."
85. Partic., (neg.) *at all*.
86. Impf. (no aug.) mid. indic. 2 sg., ἐπιλανθάνομαι, *forget*; with gen.
87. The diphthong -αι is shortened (Epic correction); cf. Benner 2001, 355 (§28).

8.2.2

An Etiology of Woman

Theogony 561–616

⁵⁶¹ὣς φάτο¹ χωόμενος² Ζεὺς³ ἄφθιτα⁴ μήδεα⁵ εἰδώς
ἐκ τούτου⁶ δὴ⁷ ἔπειτα δόλου⁸ μεμνημένος⁹ αἰεὶ¹⁰
οὐκ ἐδίδου μελίῃσι¹¹ πυρὸς μένος¹² ἀκαμάτοιο¹³
θνητοῖς¹⁴ ἀνθρώποις, οἳ ἐπὶ χθονὶ¹⁵ ναιετάουσιν.¹⁶

⁵⁶⁵ἀλλά μιν¹⁷ ἐξαπάτησεν¹⁸ ἐὺς¹⁹ πάις²⁰ Ἰαπετοῖο²¹
κλέψας²² ἀκαμάτοιο²³ πυρὸς τηλέσκοπον²⁴ αὐγὴν²⁵
ἐν κοίλῳ²⁶ νάρθηκι·²⁷ δάκεν²⁸ δ' ἄρα²⁹ νειόθι³⁰ θυμόν³¹

1. Aor. (no aug.) act. indic. 3 sg., φημί, *say, speak*. "In Homer and the lyric poets either the syllabic or the temporal augment is often absent" (S §438.c).
2. Pres. mid. ptc. nom. masc. sg., χώομαι, *be enraged*; circ.
3. Ζεύς, Διός, ὁ, *Zeus*.
4. ἄφιτος, -ον, *unceasing, unchanging*.
5. μῆδος, -εος, τό, (only in pl.) *counsels, plans*.
6. Temp., "from then."
7. Postpositive partic.: "indicates that the speaker considers (and invites the addressee to consider) the text segment or word (group) which it modifies as evident, clear, or precise" (*CGCG* §59.44).
8. δόλος, -ου, *deceit*.
9. Pf. mid. ptc. nom. masc. sg., μιμνήσκω, *remember, be mindful of*; with gen.
10. Adv., *always*.
11. Epic dat. fem. pl., μελία (Epic μελίη), -ας, ἡ, *ash tree*.
12. μένος, -εος, τό, *strength*.
13. Epic 2nd decl. gen. masc. sg., ἀκάματος, -ον, *tireless* (cf. S §230 D.1).
14. θνητός, -ή, -όν, *mortal*.
15. χθών, -ονός, ἡ, *earth*.
16. Pres. act. indic. 3 pl., ναιετάω, *dwell*.

17. μιν = αὐτόν (cf. S §325 D.3; *CGCG* §7.2)
18. Aor. act. indic. 3 sg., ἐξαπατάω, *deceive*.
19. ἐύς, -ύ, *good, noble, brave*.
20. παῖς (Epic πάϊς), παιδός, ὁ, *child, son*.
21. Epic gen. masc. sg., Ἰαπετός, -οῦ, ὁ, *Iapetos* (titan father of Prometheus). See n. 13.
22. Aor. act. ptc. nom. masc. sg., κλέπτω, *steal*; circ.
23. Epic 2nd decl. gen. masc. sg., ἀκάματος, -ον, *tireless*. See n. 13.
24. τηλέσκοπος, -ον, *far-seen, conspicuous*.
25. αὐγή, -ῆς, ἡ, *bright light*.
26. κοῖλος, -η, -ον, *hollow*.
27. νάρθηξ, -ηκος, ὁ, *giant fennel*.
28. Aor. act. indic. 3 sg., δάκνω, *bite, sting*. The impersonal subject of the verb is explicated in the subsequent ὡς-clause: "*It stung him to his heart's core . . . when he saw a conspicuous gleam of fire among human beings.*"
29. Partic. combination: development to a new text segment (δέ) that "indicates that the speaker, in view of the preceding context, cannot but make the contribution he/she is making (often surprisingly) from the preceding context (ἄρα)" (*CGCG* §59.42). δ' ἄρα is common in epic poetry (Denniston 1966, 33–35).
30. Adv., *at the bottom*; with δάκεν θυμόν, "It stung Zeus *to his* heart's *core*" (LSJ, 1165).
31. θυμός, -οῦ, ὁ, *spirit, heart*; acc. of respect.

Ζῆν᾽,³² ὑψιβρεμέτην,³³ ἐχόλωσε³⁴ δέ μιν φίλον³⁵ ἦτορ,³⁶
ὡς ἴδ᾽ ἐν ἀνθρώποισι³⁷ πυρὸς τηλέσκοπον αὐγήν.
⁵⁷⁰αὐτίκα³⁸ δ᾽ ἀντὶ³⁹ πυρὸς τεῦξεν⁴⁰ κακὸν ἀνθρώποισι·
γαίης⁴¹ γὰρ σύμπλασσε⁴² περικλυτὸς⁴³ Ἀμφιγυήεις⁴⁴
παρθένῳ⁴⁵ αἰδοίῃ⁴⁶ ἴκελον⁴⁷ Κρονίδεω⁴⁸ διὰ βουλάς·⁴⁹
ζῶσε⁵⁰ δὲ καὶ κόσμησε⁵¹ θεὰ γλαυκῶπις⁵² Ἀθήνη⁵³
ἀργυφέῃ⁵⁴ ἐσθῆτι·⁵⁵ κατὰ κρῆθεν⁵⁶ δὲ καλύπτρην⁵⁷

⁵⁷⁵δαιδαλέην⁵⁸ χείρεσσι⁵⁹ κατέσχεθε,⁶⁰ θαῦμα⁶¹ ἰδέσθαι·⁶²
ἀμφὶ⁶³ δὲ οἱ⁶⁴ στεφάνους⁶⁵ νεοθηλέας,⁶⁶ ἄνθεα⁶⁷ ποίης,⁶⁸
ἱμερτοὺς⁶⁹ περίθηκε καρήατι⁷⁰ Παλλὰς⁷¹ Ἀθήνη.
ἀμφὶ δέ οἱ στεφάνην χρυσέην⁷² κεφαλῆφιν⁷³ ἔθηκε,
τὴν⁷⁴ αὐτὸς ποίησε περικλυτὸς Ἀμφιγυήεις
⁵⁸⁰ἀσκήσας⁷⁵ παλάμῃσι,⁷⁶ χαριζόμενος⁷⁷ Διὶ⁷⁸ πατρί.

32. Acc. masc. sg., Ζεύς, Ζηνός, ὁ, Zeus.
33. ὑψιβρεμέτης, -ου, ὁ, high-thundering.
34. Aor. act. indic. 3 sg., χολόω, (impers.) anger/provoke (someone); with acc. pers.
35. φίλος, -η, -ον, one's own.
36. ἦτορ, -ορος, τό, heart; acc. of respect.
37. ἀνθρώποισι = ἀνθρώποις (cf. S §234).
38. Adv., at once, immediately.
39. Prep. with gen., in exchange for.
40. Aor. act. indic. 3 sg., τεύχω, prepare, devise.
41. γαῖα, -ας, ἡ (Epic γαίη), earth; gen. of source.
42. Aor. (no aug.) act. indic. 3 sg., συμπλάσσω, fashion together. See n. 1.
43. περικλυτός, -όν, much renowned.
44. Ἀμφιγυήεις, ὁ, (epithet) lame one (of the god Hephaestus).
45. παρθένος, -ου, ἡ, maiden.
46. αἰδοῖος, -α, -ον, having a claim to regard, reverenced.
47. ἴκελον, -η, -ον, resembling; with dat.
48. Epic 1st decl. gen. masc. sg., Κρονίδης, -ου, ὁ, son of Kronos (i.e., Zeus). For patronymic suffixes, cf. S §845; on gen. -εω, cf. S §214 D.5; Benner 2001, 363 (§65).
49. βουλή, -ῆς, ἡ, (pl.) counsels, plans.
50. Aor. (no aug.)act. indic. 3 sg., ζώννυμι, gird. See n. 1.
51. Aor. (no aug.) act. indic. 3 sg., κοσμέω, adorn. See n. 1.
52. γλαυκῶπις, ἡ, (epithet) bright-eyed.
53. Ἀθήνη, -ης, ἡ, Athena.
54. ἀργύφεος, -η, -ον, silver-shining.
55. ἐσθής, -ῆτος, ἡ, clothes; dat. of instrument.
56. Adv., κατὰ κρῆθεν, down from the head.
57. καλύπτρα, -ης, ἡ, veil.

58. δαιδάλεος, -α, -ον, cunningly wrought.
59. Dat. fem. pl., χείρ, hand (cf. S §250 D.2); dat. of instrument.
60. Aor. act. indic. 3 sg., (poetic 2nd aor. of) κατέχω, cover, spread out.
61. θαῦμα, -ατος, τό, wonder; tail (an appositive to ἴκελον; cf. CGCG §60.35): "The much renowned Lame One fashioned the resemblance of a reverenced maiden . . . a wonder to behold."
62. Aor. mid. inf., ὁράω, see, behold; epex. (cf. BDF §394; S §2004; CGCG §51.18).
63. Adv., around.
64. 3rd pers. dat. sg. pron., οὗ (cf. S §325); dat. of advantage (cf. S §1481).
65. στέφανος, -ου, ὁ, garland.
66. νεοθηλής, -ές, freshly budding.
67. ἄνθος, -εος, τό, (pl.) flowers.
68. ποίη, -ης, ἡ, grass, meadow.
69. ἱμερτός, -ή, -όν, desired, lovely.
70. κάρα (Epic κάρη), -ατος, τό, head.
71. Παλλάς, -άδος, ἡ, Pallas (epithet for Athena).
72. χρυσέος, -α, -ον, golden.
73. In epic poetry, forms ending in -φι (properly instrumental) indicate dative (true dative, locative, instrumental) or genitive (ablative) ideas (cf. Benner 2001, 385 [§155]; Cunliffe 1963, 225). Here the dative κεφαλῆφιν goes with ἀμφί: "set a golden crown around her head."
74. Art. as rel. pron. (cf. S §1105; Benner 2001, 372 [§118]).
75. Aor. act. ptc. nom. masc. sg., ἀσκέω, work (raw materials); circ.
76. παλάμη, -ης, ἡ, (pl.) hands (used in works of art), skilled hands (cf. S §214 D.9).
77. Pres. mid. ptc. nom. masc. sg., χαρίζω, do a favor for; with dat.
78. Ζεύς, Διός, ὁ, Zeus.

τῇ[79] δ' ἔνι[80] δαίδαλα πολλὰ τετεύχατο,
  θαῦμα ἰδέσθαι,
κνώδαλ'[81] ὅσ'[82] ἤπειρος[82] πολλὰ[83] τρέφει[84]
  ἠδὲ[85] θάλασσα,
τῶν ὅ γε[86] πόλλ' ἐνέθηκε, χάρις[87] δ' ἐπὶ
  πᾶσιν ἄητο,[88]
θαυμάσια,[89] ζῴοισιν[90] ἐοικότα[91]
  φωνήεσσιν.[92]
585 αὐτὰρ[93] ἐπεὶ δὴ[94] τεῦξε καλὸν κακὸν
  ἀντ' ἀγαθοῖο.[95]
ἐξάγαγ'[96] ἔνθά[97] περ ἄλλοι ἔσαν θεοὶ ἠδ'
  ἄνθρωποι,

κόσμῳ[98] ἀγαλλομένην[99] γλαυκώπιδος
  Ὀβριμοπάτρης.[100]
θαῦμα δ' ἔχ' ἀθανάτους[101] τε θεοὺς θνητούς τ'
  ἀνθρώπους,
ὡς εἶδον δόλον αἰπύν,[102] ἀμήχανον[103]
  ἀνθρώποισιν.
590 ἐκ τῆς[104] γὰρ γένος[105] ἐστὶ γυναικῶν
  θηλυτεράων,[106]
τῆς γὰρ ὀλώιόν[107] ἐστι γένος καὶ φῦλα
  γυναικῶν,
πῆμα[108] μέγα θνητοῖσι, μετ' ἀνδράσι
  ναιετάουσαι,[109]
οὐλομένης[110] πενίης[111] οὐ σύμφοροι,[112] ἀλλὰ
  κόροιο.[113]
ὡς δ' ὁπότ'[114] ἐν σμήνεσσι[115] κατηρεφέεσσι[116]
  μέλισσαι[117]

79. Art. as demon. pron. (cf. S §1100; *CGCG* §28.26; Benner 2001, 372 [§118]).
80. The anastrophe (cf. S §175; *CGCG* §60.14) indicates that the object precedes the preposition: τῇ . . . ἔνι, *on this*.
81. κνώδαλον, -ου, τό, *wild creature, monster*. The ᾱ for the neuter plural ending has elided (cf. Benner 2001, 357 [§40]; BDF §17; S §§70–75).
82. ἤπειρος, -ου, ἡ, *land*.
83. ὅσ' . . . πολλά, "all that."
84. Pres. act. indic. 3 sg., τρέφω, *nourish*.
85. Epic conjunction, *and*.
86. Postpositive partic.: "expresses concentration/limitation—focuses attention on the word or phrase it follows . . . and limits the applicability of the content of the utterance to *at least* or (more) *precisely* that specific element" (*CGCG* §59.53). "Of which he [Zeus] put many on . . ."
87. χάρις, -ιτος, ἡ, *charm*.
88. Impf. pass. indic. 3 sg., ἄημι, (pass.) *be breathed*.
89. θαυμάσιος, -α, -ον, *wondrous*; tail (an appositive to κνώδαλ'). See n. 61.
90. ζῷον, -ου, τό, *living creature, animal* (cf. S §234).
91. Pf. act. ptc. acc. neut. pl., ἔοικα, *be similar to*; with dat.; attrib.
92. φωνήεις, -εσσα, -εν, *endowed with speech*.
93. Partic.: "very similar to δέ, although the 'break' suggested by ἀτάρ [or αὐτάρ] is often a bit stronger than by δέ" (*CGCG* §59.18).
94. Postpositive partic.: "indicates that the speaker considers (and invites the addressee to consider) the text segment or word (group) which it modifies as evident, clear or precise" (*CGCG* §59.44).
95. That "good thing" for which the "beautiful evil" is given in exchange is the fire that Prometheus stole from the gods.
96. Aor. act. indic. 3 sg., ἐξάγω, *lead out*.
97. Rel. adv., *where*; with περ (cf. *CGCG* §59.55): "He led her out *to the place where* the rest of the gods and humans were."

98. κόσμος, -ου, ὁ, *adornment*.
99. Pres. pass. ptc. acc. fem. sg., ἀγάλλω, *glory/exult in* (something); with dat.; circ.
100. Ὀβριμοπάτρα, -ας (ὄβριμος, πατήρ), *daughter of a powerful father* (epithet of Athena).
101. ἀθάνατος, -ον, *immortal*.
102. αἰπύς, -εῖα, -ύ, *steep*.
103. ἀμήχανος, -ον, *against whom nothing can be done, irresistible*.
104. Art. as demon. pron., "from her [that woman]." See n. 79.
105. γένος, -εος, τό, *race*.
106. Compar., θῆλυς, -εια, -υ, *female*. From an English perspective, the use of the comparative seems odd. The use in Greek suggests a comparison between male and female, not between some women who are more female than others.
107. Compar., ὀλοός, -ή, -όν, *more deadly*.
108. πῆμα, -ατος, τό, *misery, calamity*.
109. Pres. act. indic. 3 pl., ναιετάω, *dwell*. Alternative readings are as follows: πῆμα μέγ' αἴ θνητοῖσι μετ' ἀνδράσι ναιετάουσιν or πῆμα μέγα θνητοῖσι, σὺν ἀνδράσι ναιετάουσαι.
110. οὐλομένος, -η, -ον, *accursed, wretched*.
111. πενίη, -ης, ἡ, *poverty*.
112. σύμφορος, -ον, (pl. subst.) *companions*; with gen.
113. Epic 2nd decl. gen. masc. sg., κόρος, -ου, ὁ, *satiety* (implies wealth, often with the sense of wealth that leads to one's downfall).
114. ὡς δ' ὁπότ' . . . ὣς δ' αὔτως, *as when(ever) . . . in just the same manner*.
115. σμῆνος, -εος, τό, *beehive*.
116. κατηρεφής, -ές, *vaulted, overhanging*.
117. μέλισσα, -ας, ἡ, *bee*.

⁵⁹⁵κηφῆνας¹¹⁸ βόσκωσι,¹¹⁹ κακῶν ξυνήονας¹²⁰
  ἔργων·
αἳ μέν¹²¹ τε πρόπαν ἦμαρ¹²² ἐς¹²³ ἠέλιον
  καταδύντα¹²⁴
ἠμάτιαι¹²⁵ σπεύδουσι¹²⁶ τιθεῖσί τε κηρία¹²⁷ λευκά,
οἳ δ' ἔντοσθε¹²⁸ μένοντες ἐπηρεφέας¹²⁹ κατὰ
  σίμβλους¹³⁰
ἀλλότριον¹³¹ κάματον¹³² σφετέρην¹³³ ἐς γαστέρ'
  ἀμῶνται.¹³⁴
⁶⁰⁰ὣς δ' αὔτως ἀνδρέσσι¹³⁵ κακὸν θνητοῖσι
  γυναῖκας
Ζεὺς ὑψιβρεμέτης θῆκεν, ξυνήονας ἔργων
ἀργαλέων.¹³⁶ ἕτερον δὲ πόρεν¹³⁷ κακὸν ἀντ'
  ἀγαθοῖο,
ὅς κε¹³⁸ γάμον¹³⁹ φεύγων¹⁴⁰ καὶ μέρμερα¹⁴¹ ἔργα
  γυναικῶν

μὴ γῆμαι¹⁴² ἐθέλῃ, ὀλοὸν δ' ἐπὶ γῆρας¹⁴³
  ἵκηται¹⁴⁴
⁶⁰⁵χήτεϊ¹⁴⁵ γηροκόμοιο·¹⁴⁶ ὅ δ'¹⁴⁷ οὐ βιότου¹⁴⁸ γ'
  ἐπιδευής¹⁴⁹
ζώει,¹⁵⁰ ἀποφθιμένου¹⁵¹ δὲ διὰ ζωὴν¹⁵²
  δατέονται¹⁵³
χηρωσταί.¹⁵⁴ ᾧ δ' αὖτε¹⁵⁵ γάμου μετὰ μοῖρα¹⁵⁶
  γένηται,¹⁵⁷
κεδνὴν¹⁵⁸ δ' ἔσχεν ἄκοιτιν,¹⁵⁹ ἀρηρυῖαν¹⁶⁰
  πραπίδεσσι,¹⁶¹

118. κηφήν, -ῆνος, ὁ, drone.
119. Pres. act. subj. 3 pl., βόσκω, feed, nourish; general temp. clause (cf. BDF §382; S §2409; CGCG §47.9).
120. ξυνήων, -ονος, ὁ/ἡ, partner in (a thing); with gen.
121. μέν... δέ; point (bees) / counterpoint (drones) (cf. Runge 2010, 75–83; BDF §447; S §2904; CGCG §59.24).
122. ἦμαρ, -ατος, τό, day; with πρόπαν, "all day."
123. ἐς = εἰς.
124. Aor. act. ptc. acc. masc. sg., καταδύω, (of the sun) set.
125. ἡμάτιος, -η, -ον, by day, during the day.
126. Pres. act. indic. 3 pl., σπεύδω, (intrans.) hasten.
127. κηρίον, -ου, τό, honeycomb.
128. Adv., from within.
129. ἐπηρεφής, -ές, overhanging.
130. σίμβλος, -ου, ὁ, beehive.
131. ἀλλότριος, -α, -ον, of another.
132. κάματος, -ου, ὁ, toil, labor.
133. σφέτερος, -α, -ον, their.
134. Pres. mid. indic. 3 pl., ἀμάω, gather.
135. Epic 3rd decl. dat. masc. pl. of ἀνήρ (cf. Benner 2001, 365 [§78]; S §210).
136. ἀργαλέος, -α, -ον, painful, distressful.
137. Aor. act. indic. 3 sg., πόρω, furnish, give.
138. κε = ἄν (cf. S §1761); conditional rel. clause (cf. BDF §380; S §2560; CGCG §50.21).
139. γάμος, -ου, ὁ, marriage.
140. Pres. act. ptc. nom. masc. sg., φεύγω, flee; circ.
141. μέρμερος, -ον, baneful, dire.

142. Aor. act. inf., γαμέω, marry; comp. of ἐθέλῃ.
143. γῆρας, -αος, τό, old age; ὀλοὸν... ἐπὶ γῆρας, "[arrives] at deadly old age."
144. Aor. mid. subj. 3 sg., ἱκνέομαι, arrive; conditional rel. clause. See n. 138.
145. χῆτος, -εος, τό, want, lack; with gen.
146. γηροκόμος, -ον, tending old age.
147. Apodotic δέ (cf. CGCG §59.17; S §2837): "Whoever escapes marriage... [then] when he is alive, he does not lack the means of sustenance, but when he has died, his distant relatives divide up his substance."
148. βίοτος, -ου, ὁ, sustenance.
149. ἐπιδευής, -ές, in need, in want of; with gen.
150. Pres. act. indic. 3 sg., ζάω, live.
151. Aor. mid. ptc. gen. masc. sg., ἀποφθίνω, perish; gen. absol.
152. ζωή, -ῆς, ἡ, property.
153. Pres. mid. indic. 3 pl., δατέομαι, divide.
154. χηρωσταί, -ῶν, οἱ, distant relatives.
155. Partic., often with δέ, on the other hand: "indicates a shift to a different topic—αὖ(τε) signals that the speaker is moving on to another, related discourse topic" (CGCG §59.13).
156. μοῖρα, -ας, ἡ, lot, portion, share.
157. The use of the verb is based on the collocation μέτεστί μοί τινος, "I have a share in something," but in this case, there is a personal subject (μοῖρα). A good idiomatic translation would be, "to whom the fate of marriage falls."
158. κεδνός, -ή, -όν, cherished.
159. ἄκοιτις, -ιος, ἡ, spouse, wife.
160. Pf. act. ptc. acc. fem. sg., ἀραρίσκω, (intrans.) be well fitted; attrib.
161. Epic 3rd decl. dat. pl., πραπίς, -ίδος, ἡ, thoughts; dat. of respect.

τῷ¹⁶² δέ τ' ἀπ' αἰῶνος¹⁶³ κακὸν ἐσθλῷ¹⁶⁴
ἀντιφερίζει¹⁶⁵
⁶¹⁰ἐμμενές·¹⁶⁶ ὃς δέ κε¹⁶⁷ τέτμῃ¹⁶⁸ ἀταρτηροῖο¹⁶⁹
γενέθλης,¹⁷⁰
ζώει ἐνὶ στήθεσσιν¹⁷¹ ἔχων ἀλίαστον¹⁷²
ἀνίην¹⁷³
θυμῷ καὶ κραδίῃ, καὶ ἀνήκεστον¹⁷⁴ κακόν
ἐστιν.
ὣς οὐκ ἔστι¹⁷⁵ Διὸς κλέψαι νόον οὐδὲ
παρελθεῖν.
οὐδὲ γὰρ Ἰαπετιονίδης¹⁷⁶ ἀκάκητα¹⁷⁷
Προμηθεὺς
⁶¹⁵τοῖό¹⁷⁸ γ' ὑπεξήλυξε¹⁷⁹ βαρὺν¹⁸⁰ χόλον, ἀλλ'
ὑπ' ἀνάγκης¹⁸¹
καὶ πολύιδριν¹⁸² ἐόντα¹⁸³ μέγας κατὰ¹⁸⁴
δεσμὸς¹⁸⁵ ἐρύκει.¹⁸⁶

162. Art. as demon. pron. See n. 79.
163. ἀπ' αἰῶνος, "all one's long life."
164. ἐσθλός, -ή, -όν, good.
165. Pres. act. indic. 3 sg., ἀντιφερίζω, (intrans.) *be balanced with*; with dat.
166. ἐμμενής, -ές, (as adv.) *continually*.
167. κε = ἄν. See n. 138.
168. Epic aor. act. subj. 3 sg., τέτμον (cf. LSJ, 1779) *meet*; with gen.; conditional rel. clause. See n. 138.
169. ἀταρτηρός, -όν, *baneful*.
170. γενέθλη, -ης, ἡ, *race, species*.
171. Epic 3rd decl. of στῆθος, -εος, τό, *breast*. See n. 135.
172. ἀλίαστος, -ον, *unabated, incessant*.
173. ἀνίη, -ης, ἡ, *grief, sorrow, distress*.
174. ἀνήκεστος, -ον, *incurable*.
175. Impers. (recessive accent), *it is possible*; with inf.
176. Ἰαπετιονίδης, -ου, ὁ, *son of Iapetos* (a titan); for patronymic suffixes, cf. S §845.
177. ἀκάκητα, ὁ, *innocent, guileless* (epithet for Hermes and Prometheus).
178. τοῖο = τοῦ; art. as demon. pron. See n. 79.
179. Aor. act. indic. 3 sg., ὑπεξαλύσκω, *escape*.
180. βαρύς, -εῖα, -ύ, *heavy*.
181. ὑπ' ἀνάγκης, "by necessity."
182. πολύιδρις (πολύς, ἴδρις), *that knows many things, shrewd*.
183. ἐόντα = ὄντα; circ. (concessive).
184. Adv., *down*.
185. δεσμός, -οῦ, ὁ, *chains*.
186. Pres. act. indic. 3 sg., ἐρύκω, *restrain*.

NOTES

Scansion for *Theog*. 561–565:

– ⏑ ⏑ | – ⏑ ⏑ | – – | – ⏑ ⏑ | – ⏑ ⏑ | – x
ὣς φάτο χωόμενος Ζεὺς ἄφθιτα μήδεα εἰδώς

– – | – ⏑ ⏑ | – – | – – | – ⏑ ⏑ | – x
ἐκ τούτου δὴ¹⁸⁷ ἔπειτα δόλου μεμνημένος αἰεὶ

– – | – ⏑ ⏑ | – ⏑ ⏑ | – ⏑ ⏑ | – ⏑ ⏑ | – x
οὐκ ἐδίδου μελίῃσι πυρὸς μένος ἀκαμάτοιο

– – | – ⏑ ⏑ | – – | – ⏑ ⏑ | – ⏑ ⏑ | – x
θνητοῖς ἀνθρώποις, οἳ¹⁸⁸ ἐπὶ χθονὶ ναιετάουσιν.

– ⏑ ⏑ | – ⏑ ⏑ | – – | – – | – ⏑ ⏑ | – x
ἀλλά μιν ἐξαπάτησεν ἐὺς πάις Ἰαπετοῖο

The fashioning (συμπλάσσω) of the woman, Pandora, out of the earth (γαίη) resonates with the Genesis account in which the human is fashioned (πλάσσω) out of the dust of the earth (χοῦς ἀπὸ τῆς γῆς; Gen. 2:7 LXX; cf. Philo, *Opif.* 151, which applies πλάσσω to the creation of the woman). This is but one of the many instances where the *Theogony* betrays dependence on ancient Near Eastern mythology (West 1966, 28). On the more favorable account of the creation of woman in Genesis, see Meyers 2013. The Hesiodic alliteration καλὸν κακόν captures well the angst of the elite male writers of antiquity.

187. The long vowel η is shortened (Epic correption); cf. Benner 2001, 355 (§28).
188. The diphthong -οι is shortened (Epic correption).

8.3

Sophocles

Sophocles (ca. 496–406 BCE) is the most decorated of the Greek dramatists. He is the author of more than 120 works, seven of which have survived in their complete form: *Ajax, Antigone, Women of Trachis, Oedipus the King, Elektra, Philoctetes,* and *Oedipus at Colonus*. The most famous of these, *Oedipus the King*, was treated as the paragon of the Greek tragedy (so, e.g., Aristotle, *Poetica*).

The conversational meter of Greek drama is iambic trimeter, which is as follows:

x — ⏑ — | x — ⏑ — | x — ⏑ x

Each metron consists of an anceps (x) that can be either long or short, a long syllable (—), a short syllable (⏑), and a long syllable (—). A syllable is long either by nature (i.e., long vowel or diphthong) or by position (i.e., short vowel followed by two or more consonants, or by ζ, ξ, ψ). Note that the second and fourth elements of the metron may be divided into two short syllables (except for the last metron). This is called *resolution*:

ὦ πάντα νωμῶν Τειρεσία, διδακτά τε

The reading passages are two iconic scenes from two iconic plays: *Oedipus the King* and *Antigone*.[1] The first passage includes excerpts from the conversation between Oedipus (the king blinded to the reality that he has murdered his father and married his mother) and Teiresias (the blind seer who perceives all too well the tragedy that has taken place). The second passage is Antigone's defiant response (she must honor the unwritten laws over the laws of men) to her father, King Creon.

Text and Translation: Lloyd-Jones 1994a (§8.3.1); Lloyd-Jones 1994b (§8.3.2)

Supplemental Scripture: Mark 10:46–52 (§8.3.1); Phil 1:18b–26 (§8.3.2)

---

1. For additional practice reading Sophocles (*Oedipus the King*), in a format designed for second-year Greek students, see Jones et al. 2015a.

8.3.1

Oedipus and Teiresias

Oedipus the King 300–315, 447–462

³⁰⁰ΟΙΔΙΠΟΥΣ. ὦ πάντα νωμῶν¹ Τειρεσία,²
  διδακτά³ τε
ἄρρητά⁴ τ', οὐράνια⁵ τε καὶ χθονοστιβῆ,⁶
πόλιν⁷ μέν,⁸ εἰ καὶ⁹ μὴ βλέπεις, φρονεῖς¹⁰ δ'
  ὅμως¹¹
οἵᾳ νόσῳ¹² σύνεστιν· ἧς σὲ προστάτην¹³

σωτῆρά¹⁴ τ', ὦναξ,¹⁵ μοῦνον¹⁶ ἐξευρίσκομεν.¹⁷
³⁰⁵Φοῖβος¹⁸ γάρ, εἴ καὶ μὴ¹⁹ κλύεις²⁰ τῶν
  ἀγγέλων,
πέμψασιν²¹ ἡμῖν ἀντέπεμψεν,²² ἔκλυσιν²³
μόνην ἂν ἐλθεῖν²⁴ τοῦδε τοῦ νοσήματος,²⁵
εἰ τοὺς κτανόντας²⁶ Λάϊον²⁷ μαθόντες²⁸ εὖ²⁹

1. Pres. act. ptc. voc. masc. sg., νωμάω, *ponder, grasp, comprehend*; attrib.
2. Τειρεσίας, -ου, ὁ, *Teiresias*. The blind seer has just entered the stage, led by a boy.
3. διδακτός, -ή, -όν, *that which may be explained*.
4. ἄρρητος, -ον, *that which may not be spoken, secret*.
5. οὐράνιος, -α, -ον, *heavenly, in heaven*.
6. χθονοστιβής, -ές, *earthly*.
7. Prolepsis: The subject of the dependent clause is made the object of the verb of the principle clause (cf. S §2182; *CGCG* §60.37): "As to our *city*, . . . you know in what sort of plague *it* exists."
8. μέν . . . δέ; point/counterpoint (cf. Runge 2010, 75–83; BDF §447; S §2904; *CGCG* §59.24). The line combines two different constructions: βλέπεις μὲν οὔ, φρονεῖς δ' and εἰ μὴ βλέπεις, ὅμως φρονεῖς.
9. Concessive clause (cf. BDF §374; S §2370; *CGCG* §49.19): "*Although / granting that* you do not see, you nonetheless know well."
10. Pres. act. indic. 2 sg., φρονέω, *be well aware, know well*.
11. Conj., often after a concessive clause, *nevertheless* (cf. S §2370).
12. νόσος, -ου, ὁ, *sickness, disease, plague*; indir. quest.
13. προστάτης, -ου, ὁ, *protector*.

14. σωτήρ, -ῆρος, ὁ, *savior*.
15. Crasis: ὦναξ = ὦ ἄναξ, "O lord!"
16. μοῦνον = μόνον.
17. Pres. act. indic. 1 pl., ἐξευρίσκω, *seek out*.
18. Φοῖβος, -ου, ὁ, *Phoibos* (epithet for Apollo, god of the plague).
19. Concessive clause (see n. 9): "On the chance that you have not heard the messengers."
20. Pres. act. indic. 2 sg., κλύω, *have heard* (from); with gen.
21. Aor. act. ptc. dat. masc. pl., πέμπω, *send*; circ. "Phoebus . . . *when we sent* [to him], responded to us."
22. Aor. act. indic. 3 sg., ἀντιπέμπω, *send back an answer*.
23. ἔκλυσις, -εως, ἡ, *release*.
24. Reported speech as fourth-class condition: εἰ with opt. in the protasis, ἄν with inf. (for opt.) in the apodosis (S §§1848, 2329; *CGCG* §§49.8; 51.27).
25. νόσημα, -ατος, τό, *plague, disease*.
26. Aor. act. ptc. acc. masc. pl., κτείνω, *kill*; attrib. (subst.).
27. Λάϊος, -ου, ὁ, *Laios* (father of Oedipus and king of Thebes).
28. Aor. act. ptc. nom. masc. pl., μανθάνω, *learn*; circ.
29. Adv., *well*; modifies μαθόντες.

κτείναιμεν³⁰ ἢ γῆς φυγάδας³¹ ἐκπεμψαίμεθα.³²
³¹⁰σύ νυν³³ φθονήσας³⁴ μήτ'³⁵ ἀπ' οἰωνῶν³⁶
    φάτιν³⁷
μήτ' εἴ τιν' ἄλλην μαντικῆς³⁸ ἔχεις ὁδόν,
ῥῦσαι³⁹ σεαυτὸν καὶ πόλιν, ῥῦσαι δ' ἐμέ,
ῥῦσαι δὲ πᾶν μίασμα⁴⁰ τοῦ τεθνηκότος.
ἐν σοὶ γὰρ ἐσμέν· ἄνδρα δ' ὠφελεῖν⁴¹ ἀφ' ὧν
³¹⁵ἔχοι⁴² τε καὶ δύναιτο,⁴³ κάλλιστος⁴⁴
    πόνων.⁴⁵

. . . .

ΤΕΙΡΕΣΙΑΣ. εἰπὼν ἄπειμ'⁴⁶ ὧν⁴⁷ οὕνεκ'⁴⁸
    ἦλθον, οὐ τὸ σὸν

δείσας⁴⁹ πρόσωπον· οὐ γὰρ ἔσθ'⁵⁰ ὅπου μ'
    ὀλεῖς.⁵¹
λέγω δε σοι· τὸν ἄνδρα τοῦτον,⁵² ὃν πάλαι⁵³
⁴⁵⁰ζητεῖς ἀπειλῶν⁵⁴ κἀνακηρύσσων⁵⁵ φόνον⁵⁶
τὸν Λαΐειον,⁵⁷ οὗτός ἐστιν ἐνθάδε,⁵⁸
ξένος⁵⁹ λόγῳ⁶⁰ μέτοικος·⁶¹ εἶτα⁶² δ' ἐγγενὴς⁶³
φανήσεται⁶⁴ Θηβαῖος,⁶⁵ οὐδ' ἡσθήσεται⁶⁶
τῇ ξυμφορᾷ·⁶⁷ τυφλὸς⁶⁸ γὰρ ἐκ δεδορκότος⁶⁹
⁴⁵⁵καὶ πτωχὸς⁷⁰ ἀντὶ⁷¹ πλουσίου⁷² ξένην ἔπι⁷³
σκήπτρῳ⁷⁴ προδεικνὺς⁷⁵ γαῖαν ἐμπορεύσεται.⁷⁶
φανήσεται δὲ παισὶ⁷⁷ τοῖς αὐτοῦ ξυνῶν⁷⁸

30. Aor. act. opt. 1 pl., κτείνω, *kill*. See n. 24.
31. φυγάς, -άδος, ὁ, *runaway, exile*.
32. Aor. mid. opt. 1 pl., ἐκπέμπω, *expel*; with acc. and gen. of separation. See n. 24.
33. Partic.: "a transition to a new text segment which proceeds from the preceding text segment . . . indicates that the directive flows naturally from the preceding context (*then, so*)" (*CGCG* §59.29).
34. Aor. act. ptc. nom. masc. sg., φθονέω, *begrudge, refuse to grant* (a thing); circ.
35. μήτ' . . . μήτ', *neither . . . nor*.
36. οἰωνός, -οῦ, ὁ, *bird of omen*.
37. φάτις, -εως, ἡ, *oracle*.
38. μαντική, -ῆς, ἡ, *divination, prophecy*; τιν' ἄλλην μαντικῆς . . . ὁδόν, "any other way of prophecy."
39. Aor. mid. impv. 2 sg., ῥύομαι, *save, protect*. Sophocles uses ῥύομαι in a double sense: "*Rescue* yourself and the city, and *rescue* me, and *rescue* [us] *from* all the pollution."
40. μίασμα, -ατος, τό, *pollution*; with τοῦ τεθνηκότος, "pollution *arising from* the dead man."
41. Pres. act. inf., ὠφελέω, *help, assist*; subjective (cf. S §1984; *CGCG* §51.9); with ἄνδρα as the acc. subject.
42. Pres. act. opt. 3 sg., ἔχω, *have*; opt. for ἄν + subj., which is rare in primary sequence (cf. Kühner §1252): "from whatever resources and ability he has."
43. Pres. mid. opt. 3 sg., δύναμαι, *be able*. See n. 42.
44. Superl., καλός, -ή, -όν, *best*.
45. πόνος, -ου, ὁ, *task, labor, trouble*; partitive gen.
46. Pres. (as fut.) act. indic. 1 sg., ἄπειμι, *go, depart*.
47. The omitted antecedent (ταῦτα) has been attracted to the case of the relative pronoun (cf. S §2529; *CGCG* §50.13).
48. Prep. with gen., *on account of*. ὧν οὕνεκ' ἦλθον, "for which reason I came," is ironic since Teiresias came intending to say nothing (cf. *Oed. tyr.* 17–22).

49. Aor. act. ptc. nom. masc. pl., δείδω, *fear*; circ. (causal).
50. Elision: ἔσθ' = ἔστι (recessive accent); with ὅπου, *there is no case/moment in which* (MGS, 1475.1C).
51. Fut. act. indic. 2 sg., ὄλλυμι, *make an end of, do evil/harm to*.
52. Inverse relative attraction: τὸν ἄνδρα τοῦτον is attracted to ὅν (cf. S §2533; *CGCG* §50.14).
53. Adv., *all this time, long*.
54. Pres. act. ptc. nom. masc. sg., ἀπειλέω, *threaten*; with dat.; circ. (manner).
55. Crasis: κἀνακηρύσσων = καὶ ἀνακηρύσσων, "and making public proclamations."
56. φόνος, -ου, ὁ, *murder*.
57. Λαΐειος, -α, -ον, *of Laïus*.
58. Adv., *here*.
59. ξένος, -ου, ὁ, *foreigner*.
60. Dat. of respect.
61. μέτοικος, -ου, ὁ, *immigrant*; in apposition to ξένος.
62. Adv., *soon, presently*.
63. ἐγγενής, -ές, *native*.
64. Fut. pass. indic. 3 sg., φαίνω, (pass.) *be revealed*.
65. Θηβαῖος, -α, -ον, *of Thebes, Theban*.
66. Fut. pass. indic. 3 sg., ἥδομαι, (pass.) *be glad, delight*; with dat.
67. συμφορά, -ᾶς, ἡ, *event, circumstance, happening*.
68. τυφλός, -ή, -όν, *blind*.
69. Pf. act. ptc. gen. masc. sg., δέρκομαι, *see*; attrib. (subst.): "a blind man from [in the sense of "instead of"] a man who sees."
70. πτωχός, -ή, -όν, *poor*.
71. Prep. with gen., *for, instead of*.
72. πλούσιος, -α, -ον, *rich, wealthy*.
73. The preposition follows its object, which is marked by anastrophe (cf. S §175; *CGCG* §60.14): ξένην ἔπι . . . γαῖαν, "to a strange/foreign land."
74. σκῆπτρον, -ου, τό, *staff*; dat. of instrument.
75. Pres. act. ptc. nom. masc. sg., προδείκνυμι, *point* (with the scepter) *before oneself*.
76. Fut. mid. indic. 3 sg., ἐμπορεύομαι, *travel*.
77. παῖς, παιδός, ὁ, *child*.
78. Pres. act. ptc. nom. masc. sg., σύνειμι, *live with*; with dat.; supp. (φανήσεται).

ἀδελφὸς αὐτὸς[79] καὶ πατήρ, κἀξ[80] ἧς ἔφυ[81]
γυναικὸς[82] υἱὸς καὶ πόσις,[83] καὶ τοῦ πατρὸς
460ὁμόσπορός[84] τε καὶ φονεύς.[85] καὶ ταῦτ' ἰὼν[86]
εἴσω[87] λογίζου.[88] κἂν λάβῃς ἐψευσμένον,[89]
φάσκειν[90] ἔμ' ἤδη μαντικῇ[91] μηδὲν φρονεῖν.[92]

οἵᾳ νόσῳ σύνεστιν· ἧς σὲ προστάτην

σωτῆρά τ', ὦναξ, μοῦνον ἐξευρίσκομεν.

Sophocles deploys the classic type of the blind seer (cf. Mark 10:46 parr.) in a tragedy that is all about (in)sight, or the lack thereof. (In a sense the play navigates the epistemological predicament of the human condition.) The concept of μίασμα (on which see Parker 1983) is similar to the concept of pollution in the Hebrew Bible (on which see Milgrom 1976; 1993; Klawans 2000). One might compare the μίασμα brought about by Laïus's murder to the discussion of the pollution of the land in Num. 35:33–34.

NOTES

Scansion for *Oed. tyr.* 300–305:

ὦ πάντα νωμῶν Τειρεσία,[93] διδακτά τε

ἄρρητά τ', οὐράνιά[94] τε καὶ χθονοστιβῆ,

πόλιν μέν, εἰ καὶ μὴ βλέπεις, φρονεῖς δ' ὅμως

79. αὐτός = ὁ αὐτός; lit., "*the same man* brother and father"; or better, "at the same time brother and father."
80. Crasis: κἀξ = καὶ ἐξ.
81. Aor. act. indic. 3 sg., φύω, *beget, engender*.
82. The antecedent is incorporated into the relative clause (cf. S §2536; *CGCG* §50.15).
83. πόσις, -εως, ὁ, *husband*; pred. nom.
84. ὁμόσπορος, -ον, *sharing the same bed with*; with gen.
85. φονεύς, -έως, ἡ, *murderer*.
86. Pres. act. ptc. nom. masc. sg., εἶμι, *go*.
87. Adv., *inside*.
88. Pres. mid. impv. 2 sg., λογίζομαι, *consider*.
89. Pf. mid. ptc. acc. masc. sg., ψεύδω, *speak falsely*; supp.: "If you find out [λάβῃς] that I have spoken falsely."
90. Pres. act. inf., φάσκω, *say, declare*; imperatival (cf. BDF §389; S §2013; *CGCG* §51.47).
91. μαντικός, -ή, -όν; by itself, the feminine stands for τέχνη μαντική, "faculty *of divination/prophecy*" (cf. LSJ, 1080).
92. Pres. act. inf., φρονέω, *have understanding, wisdom*; indir. disc. (cf. BDF §397; S §2016; *CGCG* §51.19). The accusative subject is ἔμ': "Declare already that *I have no wisdom* [μηδέν as internal acc.] in my prophecies."
93. Resolution.
94. Resolution.

8.3.2

Antigone Defies Creon

Antigone 450–470

⁴⁵⁰οὐ γάρ¹ τί μοι² Ζεὺς ἦν ὁ κηρύξας³ τάδε,
οὐδ' ἡ ξύνοικος⁴ τῶν κάτω⁵ θεῶν Δίκη⁶
τοιούσδ'⁷ ἐν ἀνθρώποισιν⁸ ὥρισεν⁹ νόμους·
οὐδὲ σθένειν¹⁰ τοσοῦτον ᾠόμην¹¹ τὰ σὰ
κηρύγμαθ',¹² ὥστ' ἄγραπτα¹³ κἀσφαλῆ¹⁴ θεῶν

⁴⁵⁵νόμιμα¹⁵ δύνασθαι θνητὸν¹⁶ ὄνθ'
ὑπερδραμεῖν.¹⁷
οὐ γάρ τι νῦν γε¹⁸ κἀχθές,¹⁹ ἀλλ' ἀεί²⁰ ποτε
ζῇ ταῦτα, κοὐδεὶς οἶδεν ἐξ ὅτου²¹ 'φάνη.²²
τούτων ἐγὼ οὐκ ἔμελλον, ἀνδρὸς οὐδενὸς
φρόνημα²³ δείσασ',²⁴ ἐν θεοῖσι²⁵ τὴν δίκην

1. "In dialogue, γάρ can be used by one speaker to connect his/her utterance to that of another (especially in answers to questions: the answer 'yes' or 'no' is often implicit in the use of γάρ, which then provides an explanation for that answer) (*yes/no, for*)" (*CGCG* §59.14; cf. Denniston 1966, 73–74). In this case, Creon has just asked her, "And yet you were so bold to transgress the laws?" To which she replies, "*Yes, for* it was not Zeus who declared this order."
2. Indir. obj. of κηρύξας.
3. Aor. act. ptc. nom. masc. sg., κηρύσσω, *proclaim*; attrib. (subst.).
4. σύνοικος, -ον, *dwelling with*.
5. Adv., *below*.
6. Δίκη, -ης, ἡ, *Justice*.
7. τοιόσδε, τοιάδε, τοιόνδε, *of such a kind*.
8. ἀνθρώποισιν = ἀνθρώποις.
9. Aor. act. indic. 3 sg., ὁρίζω, *mark out, define*.
10. Pres. act. inf., σθένω, *have strength/power* (to do); indir. disc. (cf. BDF §397; S §2016; *CGCG* §51.19).
11. Impf. mid. indic. 1 sg., οἴομαι, *think, suppose*.
12. κήρυγμα, -ατος, τό, *that which is proclaimed, mandate*.
13. ἄγραπτος, -ον, *unwritten*.
14. Crasis: κἀσφαλῆ = καὶ ἀσφαλῆ; ἀσφαλής, -ές, *immovable*.

15. νόμιμος, -η, -ον, (neut. pl.) *customs, laws*.
16. θνητός, -ή, -όν, *mortal*; pred. to circ. ptc. ὄντα (causal), "since you are mortal." The implied accusative subject (σε) may be inferenced from τὰ σὰ κηρύγμαθ'.
17. Aor. act. inf., ὑπερτρέχω, *run over, prevail against*; comp. of δύνασθαι; result clause (cf. BDF §391; S §2260; *CGCG* §46.7); signposted by τοσοῦτον (acc. of extent).
18. Postpositive partic.: "focuses attention on the word or phrase it follows . . . and limits the applicability of the content of the utterance to *at least* or (*more*) *precisely* that specific element" (*CGCG* §59.53); underscores both temporal adverbs to mark the contrast with ἀλλ' ἀεί.
19. Adv., *yesterday*.
20. Adv., with ποτε, *from all time*.
21. ὅτου = οὗτινος (cf. S §339.b); ἐξ ὅτου, *from which time*.
22. Aor. pass. indic. 3 sg., φαίνω, (pass.) *appear*. In poetry, an ε at the beginning of a word may elide when preceded by a word ending in a long vowel or diphthong. The term for this is "aphaeresis," or inverse elision (cf. S §76).
23. φρόνημα, -ατος, τό, *thought, purpose*.
24. Aor. act. ptc. nom. fem. sg., δείδω, *fear*; circ.
25. θεοῖσι = θεοῖς (cf. S §230 D.3)

⁴⁶⁰δώσειν·²⁶ θανουμένη²⁷ γὰρ ἐξῄδη,²⁸ τί δ' οὔ;²⁹
κεἰ³⁰ μὴ σὺ προυκήρυξας·³¹ εἰ δὲ τοῦ χρόνου
πρόσθεν³² θανοῦμαι,³³ κέρδος³⁴ αὔτ'³⁵ ἐγὼ
λέγω.
ὅστις γὰρ ἐν πολλοῖσιν ὡς ἐγὼ κακοῖς
ζῇ, πῶς ὅδ' οὐχὶ κατθανών³⁶ κέρδος φέρει;
⁴⁶⁵οὕτως ἔμοιγε³⁷ τοῦδε τοῦ μόρου³⁸ τυχεῖν³⁹
παρ' οὐδὲν⁴⁰ ἄλγος·⁴¹ ἀλλ' ἄν,⁴² εἰ τὸν ἐξ ἐμῆς
μητρὸς θανόντ'⁴³ ἄθαπτον⁴⁴ ἠνσχόμην⁴⁵
νέκυν,⁴⁶
κείνοις⁴⁷ ἂν ἤλγουν·⁴⁸ τοῖσδε δ' οὐκ
ἀλγύνομαι.

26. Fut. act. inf., δίδωμι; comp. of ἔμελλον: "I was not about . . . to give the gods a reason for retribution."
27. Fut. mid. ptc. nom. fem. sg., θνῄσκω, *die*; supp. (ἐξῄδη).
28. Plpf. act. indic. 1 sg., ἔξοιδα, *know well*.
29. τί δ' οὔ, "How could I not?" (cf. Denniston 1966, 175).
30. Crasis: κεἰ = καὶ εἰ; concessive clause (cf. BDF §374; S §2369; CGCG §49.19).
31. Aor. act. indic. 2 sg., προκηρύσσω, *proclaim publicly*.
32. Prep. with gen., *before*.
33. "Emotional future" condition: εἰ with fut. indic. in the protasis (cf. S §2328). Note, however, that "the value of the indicative is really no different than in other neutral conditions, although its value lends itself well for contexts of skepticism, threat, etc." (CGCG §49.5).
34. κέρδος, -εος, τό, *gain, profit*.
35. Adv., *then, in turn*.
36. Aor. act. ptc. nom. masc. sg., καταθνῄσκω, *die*; circ.
37. The particle of scope combines with the personal pronoun and the accent recedes, *(at least) to me*.
38. μόρος, -ου, ὁ, *fate, destiny*.
39. Aor. act. inf., τυγχάνω, *encounter*; with gen; subjective (cf. S §1984; CGCG §51.9).
40. παρ' οὐδέν, "to count/consider *as nothing*" (cf. MGS, 1542. II.C.B).
41. ἄλγος, -εος, τό, *grief*.
42. Anticipates κείνοις ἂν ἤλγουν (cf. S §1765); second-class (contrafactual) condition (cf. BDF §360; S §2302; CGCG §49.10).
43. Attrib. (subst.): τὸν ἐξ ἐμῆς μητρὸς θανόντ', "the dead one from my mother" (i.e., my dead brother).
44. ἄθαπτος, -ον, *unburied*.
45. Aor. mid. indic. 1 sg., ἀνέχω, *suffer, endure*.
46. νέκυς, -υος, ὁ, *corpse*.
47. κείνοις = ἐκείνοις.
48. Impf. act. indic. 1 sg., ἀλγέω, *be pained at* (something); with dat.

σοὶ δ' εἰ δοκῶ⁴⁹ νῦν μῶρα⁵⁰ δρῶσα⁵¹ τυγχάνειν,
⁴⁷⁰σχεδόν⁵² τι μώρῳ μωρίαν ὀφλισκάνω.⁵³

NOTES

Scansion for *Ant.* 450–455:

‒ ‒ | ‒ ̆ ̆ | ‒ ‒ | ‒ ̆ ̆ | ‒ ‒ | ‒ x
οὐ γάρ τί μοι Ζεὺς ἦν ὁ κηρύξας τάδε,

‒ ‒ | ‒ ̆ ̆ | ‒ ‒ | ‒ ‒ | ‒ ‒ | ‒ x
οὐδ' ἡ ξύνοικος τῶν κάτω θεῶν Δίκη

‒ ‒ | ̆ ̆ ‒ | ‒ ̆ ̆ | ‒ ̆ | ‒ ̆ ̆ | ‒ x
τοιούσδ' ἐν ἀνθρώποισιν ὥρισεν νόμους·

‒ ‒ | ̆ ̆ ‒ | ‒ ̆ ̆ | ‒ ‒ | ‒ ̆ ̆ | ‒ x
οὐδὲ σθένειν τοσοῦτον ᾠόμην τὰ σὰ

‒ ‒ | ‒ ̆ ̆ | ‒ ‒ | ‒ ̆ ̆ | ‒ ̆ ̆ | ‒ x
κηρύγμαθ', ὥστ' ἄγραπτα κἀσφαλῆ θεῶν

That the dead must be properly buried was one of the unwritten laws of ancient Mediterranean cultures (cf. Tob. 1:17–18; 2:7; 4:3; 12:12–13; Sir. 38:6; Philo, *Hypoth.* 7.7; Josephus, *C. Ap.* 2.211; Euripides, *Suppl.* 524–541; Pausanias, *Descr.* 1.32.5). Compare Antigone's statement that she would count premature death as "gain" (κέρδος) to Paul's claim: Ἐμοὶ γὰρ τὸ ζῆν Χριστὸς καὶ τὸ ἀποθανεῖν κέρδος (Phil. 1:21; Boring, Berger, and Colpe 1995, §792).

49. Pres. act. indic. 1 sg., δοκέω, *seem, appear*; with dat. and inf.
50. μῶρος, -α, -ον, *foolish*.
51. Pres. act. ptc. nom. fem. sg., δράω, *do*; supp. (τυγχάνειν). "And if it seems to you [lit., I seem to you] that *I happen to be acting* [δρῶσα τυγχάνειν] foolish . . ."
52. Adv., σχεδόν τι, "perhaps."
53. Pres. act. indic. 1 sg., ὀφλισκάνω, *incur a charge*; apodosis: "Then perhaps I incur the charge of folly [μωρίαν] by a fool [μώρῳ]."

8.4

Euripides

Euripides (ca. 485–406 BCE) is another of the great tragedians. One of the hallmarks of Euripidean tragedy is its exploration of the most vexing anthropological and sociological tensions. Such may explain why eighteen of his plays have survived in full (compared to only seven of Sophocles's): *Alcestis, Medea, Hippolytus, Hecuba, Andromache, Children of Hercules, Electra, Supplicant Women, Hercules, Daughters of Troy, Helen, Iphigenia at Tauris, Ion, Phoenician Women, Orestes, Iphigenia at Aulis, Bacchae,* and *Cyclops.* Of these, the *Bacchae* is the most important to the study of ancient Judaism and Christianity (see esp. Friesen 2015).

The reading passages are taken from the *Bacchae* and *Iphigenia at Aulis*.[1] The first is the extended exchange between a disguised Dionysus and Pentheus, who is the king of Thebes and the antagonist of the foreign deity (θεόμαχος). The second passage is the report to King Agamemnon of the sacrifice of his daughter Iphigenia.

Text: Kovacs 2002

Supplemental Scripture: John 18:1–11, 28–38 (§8.4.1); Gen. 22:1–19; Judg. 11:34–40 (§8.4.2)

---

1. For additional practice reading Euripides (*Medea*) in a format designed for second-year Greek students, see Jones et al. 2015b.

8.4.1

Pentheus Interrogates Dionysus

Bacchae 434–518

ΘΕΡΑΠΩΝ.[1] Πενθεῦ,[2] πάρεσμεν[3] τήνδ'
 ἄγραν[4] ἠγρευκότες[5]
435ἐφ' ἣν ἔπεμψας, οὐδ' ἄκρανθ'[6]
 ὡρμήσαμεν.[7]
ὁ θὴρ[8] δ' ὅδ' ἡμῖν[9] πρᾷος[10] οὐδ' ὑπέσπασεν[11]
φυγῇ πόδ', ἀλλ' ἔδωκεν οὐκ ἄκων[12] χέρας,[13]
οὐκ ὠχρός,[14] οὐδ' ἤλλαξεν[15] οἰνωπὸν[16]
 γένυν,[17]

γελῶν[18] δὲ καὶ δεῖν κἀπάγειν ἐφίετο[19]
440ἔμενέ[20] τε, τοὐμὸν[21] εὐτρεπὲς[22]
 ποιούμενος.
κἀγὼ δι' αἰδοῦς[23] εἶπον· Ὦ ξέν',[24] οὐχ ἑκὼν[25]
ἄγω σε, Πενθέως δ' ὅς μ' ἔπεμψ' ἐπιστολαῖς.[26]
ἃς δ' αὖ[27] σὺ βάκχας[28] εἷρξας,[29] ἃς
 συνήρπασας[30]
κᾄδησας[31] ἐν δεσμοῖσι πανδήμου[32] στέγης,[33]

---

1. θεράπων, -ονος, ὁ, *attendant, servant*.
2. Voc., Πενθεύς, -έως, ὁ, *Pentheus*. The name derives from the word πένθος, "sorrow," which suits his fate in the play (cf. 508, below).
3. Pres. act. indic. 1 pl., πάρειμι, *be present, at hand*.
4. ἄγρα, -ας, ἡ, *prey*.
5. Pf. act. ptc. nom. masc. pl., ἀγρεύω, *take by hunting/catching*; circ.
6. ἄκραντος, -ον, *fruitless, in vain*.
7. Aor. act. indic. 1 pl., ὁρμάω, (intrans.) *be set in motion*.
8. θήρ, -ηρός, ὁ, *beast*.
9. Ethical dat. (cf. S §1486; *CGCG* §30.53).
10. πρᾷος, -ον, *gentle, meek, tame*.
11. Aor. act. indic. 3 sg,. ὑποσπάω, *draw away*; with φυγῇ πόδ': lit., "He did not carry away his foot in flight."
12. ἄκων, -ουσα, -ον, *unwillingly*.
13. χέρας = χεῖρας.
14. ὠχρός, -ά, -όν, (of complexion) *pale*. The emendation for οὐδ' ὠχρός, "not *even* turning pale," may be unnecessary (see Dodds 1960, 131).
15. Aor. act. indic. 3 sg., ἀλλάσσω, *change/alter*.
16. οἰνωπόν, -ή, -όν, *ruddy* (lit., "wine-colored") *complexion*.
17. γένυς, -υος, ἡ, *cheek*.

18. Pres. act. ptc. nom. masc. sg., γελάω, *laugh*; circ. (manner).
19. Pres. mid. indic. 3 sg., ἐφίημι, *bid*; with acc. and inf.: "He bid [us] to bind and lead [him] away."
20. Impf. act. indic. 3 sg., μένω (with acc. and inf.), *wait for*; i.e., "He was waiting [on us to do it]."
21. Crasis: τοὐμόν = τὸ ἐμόν (ἔργον), "my (task)."
22. εὐτρεπής, -ές, *ready/easy*; pred. comp.
23. αἰδώς, -οῦς, ἡ, *shame*.
24. Voc., ξένος, -ου, ὁ, *stranger*.
25. ἑκών, -οῦσα, -όν, *willingly*.
26. ἐπιστολή, -ῆς, ἡ, *order, commission*; dat. of cause.
27. δ' αὖ marks a transition from the servant's report of his arrest of the stranger to the news that the bacchants whom Pentheus had imprisoned have (miraculously) been set free.
28. Βάκχη, -ης, ἡ, *bacchant*. The antecedent has been incorporated into the relative clause: "Now, then, as for *the bacchants whom* you shut up . . ."
29. Aor. act. indic. 2 sg., ἔργω, *shut up, restrain*.
30. Aor act. indic. 2 sg., συναρπάζω, *seize*.
31. Crasis: κᾄδησας = καὶ ἐδήσας; with ἐν δεσμοῖσι (instrument).
32. πάνδημος, -ον, *public*.
33. στέγη, -ης, ἡ, *(any) roofed place*; here, the prison.

⁴⁴⁵φροῦδαί³⁴ γ'³⁵ ἐκεῖναι λελυμέναι πρὸς
    ὀργάδας³⁶
σκιρτῶσι³⁷ Βρόμιον³⁸ ἀνακαλούμεναι³⁹ θεόν·
αὐτόματα⁴⁰ δ' αὐταῖς δεσμὰ διελύθη ποδῶν
κλῇδές⁴¹ τ' ἀνῆκαν⁴² θύρετρ'⁴³ ἄνευ⁴⁴ θνητῆς⁴⁵
    χειρός.
πολλῶν δ' ὅδ' ἀνὴρ θαυμάτων⁴⁶ ἥκει⁴⁷
    πλέως⁴⁸
⁴⁵⁰ἐς⁴⁹ τάσδε Θήβας.⁵⁰ σοὶ δὲ τἄλλα χρὴ⁵¹
    μέλειν.⁵²
ΠΕΝΘΕΥΣ. μέθεσθε⁵³ χειρῶν τοῦδ'· ἐν ἄρκυ-
    σιν⁵⁴ γὰρ ὢν
οὐκ ἔστι οὕτως ὠκὺς⁵⁵ ὥστε μ' ἐκφυγεῖν.⁵⁶

ἀτὰρ⁵⁷ τὸ μὲν⁵⁸ σῶμ' οὐκ ἄμορφος⁵⁹ εἶ, ξένε,
ὡς ἐς γυναῖκας, ἐφ' ὅπερ⁶⁰ ἐς Θήβας πάρει·
⁴⁵⁵πλόκαμός⁶¹ τε γάρ σου ταναὸς⁶² οὐ
    πάλης⁶³ ὕπο,
γένυν παρ' αὐτὴν κεχυμένος,⁶⁴ πόθου⁶⁵
    πλέως·
λευκὴν⁶⁶ δὲ χροιὰν ἐκ παρασκευῆς⁶⁷ ἔχεις,
οὐχ ἡλίου βολαῖσιν⁶⁸ ἀλλ' ὑπὸ σκιᾶς
τὴν Ἀφροδίτην⁶⁹ καλλονῇ⁷⁰ θηρώμενος.⁷¹
    ⁴⁶⁰πρῶτον μὲν οὖν⁷² μοι λέξον⁷³ ὅστις⁷⁴ εἶ
    γένος.
ΔΙΟΝΥΣΟΣ. οὐκ ὄκνος⁷⁵ οὐδείς· ῥᾴδιον⁷⁶ δ'
    εἰπεῖν τόδε.

34. φροῦδος, -η, -ον, *gone*.
35. Postpositive partic.: "focuses attention on the word or phrase it follows . . . and limits the applicability of the content of the utterance to *at least* or (*more*) *precisely* that specific element" (*CGCG* §59.53).
36. ὀργάς, -άδος, ἡ, *meadowland*.
37. Pres. act. indic. 3 pl., σκιρτάω, *spring, leap, bound*.
38. Βρόμιος, -ου, ὁ, *Bromios* (epithet for Dionysus).
39. Pres. mid. ptc. nom. fem. pl., ἀνακαλέω, *call on*; circ.
40. αὐτόματος, -η, -ον, *of one's own accord, spontaneous*.
41. κλῇς, -ῃδός, ἡ, *lock/latch*.
42. Aor. act. indic. 3 pl., ἀνίημι, *loosen, unfasten*; hence, *open*.
43. θύρετρα, -ων, τά, *doors*.
44. Prep. with gen., *without*.
45. θνητός, -ή, -όν, *mortal*.
46. θαῦμα, -ατος, τό, *wonder, marvel*.
47. Pres. act. indic. 3 sg., ἥκω, *have come, arrived*.
48. πλέως, -έα, -έων, *full of*; with gen.
49. ἐς = εἰς.
50. Θῆβαι, -ῶν, αἱ, *Thebes*.
51. Quasi-impers. χρή, *it is necessary*; with acc. and inf. (cf. BDF §405; S §1985; *CGCG* §36.3).
52. Pres. act. inf., μέλω, *concerns* (cf. S §1360); with dat.; comp. of χρή: "The rest [what follows] must be your concern."
53. Pres. mid. impv. 2 pl., μεθίημι, *release*; with gen.
54. ἄρκυς, -υος, ἡ, *net*.
55. ὠκύς, -εῖα, -ύ, *swift*.
56. Pres. act. inf., ἐκφύγω, *escape*; result clause (cf. BDF §391; S §2269; *CGCG* §46.6), signposted by οὕτως. At this point the actors playing the servants would take the shackles of Dionysus.

57. Partic.: "similar in function to δέ, although the 'break' suggested by ἀτάρ is often a bit stronger than by δέ. It is usually found in contexts where δέ cannot be used, e.g. together with vocatives (often at the beginning of a new speaking turn)" (*CGCG* §59.18); thus, "Well!"
58. μέν . . . τε; γάρ . . . δέ; point / additional supporting point / counterpoint (cf. S §2913).
59. ἄμορφος, -ον, *unsightly*; οὐκ ἄμορφος . . . ὡς ἐς γυναῖκας, "not unattractive . . . to a woman's tastes."
60. ἐφ' ὅπερ, "for which reason."
61. πλόκαμος, -ου, ὁ, *lock* (of hair).
62. ταναός, -ή, -όν, (of locks) *long, flowing*.
63. πάλη, -ης, ἡ, *wrestling*; obj. of ὕπο (anastrophe) ; lit., "by not wrestling"; i.e., "proving you no wrestler."
64. Pf. mid. ptc. nom. masc. sg., χύω, *flow*; γένυν παρ' αὐτὴν κεχυμένος, "flowing down to by your cheek."
65. πόθος, -ου, ὁ, *desire*; gen. comp. of πλέως, "full of desire."
66. λευκός, -ή, -όν, *fair*; pred. comp.
67. παρασκευή, -ῆς, ἡ, *preparation*; ἐκ παρασκευῆς, "by deliberate contrivance" (Dodds 1960, 134).
68. βολή, -ῆς, ἡ, (pl.) *rays* (of the sun).
69. Ἀφροδίτη, -ης, ἡ: the name of the goddess is used as an appellative for *sexual love*.
70. καλλονή, -ῆς, ἡ, *beauty*; dat. of means.
71. Pres. mid. ptc. nom. masc. sg., θηράω, *hunt*; circ.
72. Partic. combination: "a transition to a more to-the-point, relevant text segment (οὖν) [that] occurs in two stages (μέν . . . δέ)" (*CGCG* §59.73). The μέν-clause concludes Pentheus's speech, while the δέ-clause begins Dionysus's response.
73. Aor. act. impv. 2 sg., λέγω, *say, speak*.
74. The indefinite relative pronoun introduces an indirect question (cf. BDF §300; S §1263): "Tell me what race you are."
75. Conjecture for οὐ κόμπος, which is problematic (Dodd 1960, 135); lit., "There is no hesitation."
76. ῥᾴδιος, -ον, *easy*, (quasi-impers.) *it is easy*; with acc. and inf.

τὸν ἀνθεμώδη⁷⁷ Τμῶλον⁷⁸ οἶσθά⁷⁹ που⁸⁰ κλύων.⁸¹
ΠΕΝΘΕΥΣ. οἶδ', ὃς τὸ Σάρδεων⁸² ἄστυ⁸³ περιβάλλει⁸⁴ κύκλῳ.⁸⁵
ΔΙΟΝΥΣΟΣ. ἐντεῦθέν⁸⁶ εἰμι, Λυδία δέ μοι πατρίς.⁸⁷
⁴⁶⁵ΠΕΝΘΕΥΣ. πόθεν⁸⁸ δὲ τελετὰς⁸⁹ τάσδ' ἄγεις ἐς Ἑλλάδα;
ΔΙΟΝΥΣΟΣ. Διόνυσος αὐτός μ' εἰσέβησ',⁹⁰ ὁ τοῦ Διός.⁹¹
ΠΕΝΘΕΥΣ. Ζεὺς δ' ἔστ' ἐκεῖ τις, ὃς νέους τίκτει⁹² θεούς;
ΔΙΟΝΥΣΟΣ. οὔκ, ἀλλ' ὁ Σεμέλην⁹³ ἐνθάδε⁹⁴ ζεύξας⁹⁵ γάμοις.
ΠΕΝΘΕΥΣ. πότερα⁹⁶ δὲ νύκτωρ⁹⁷ σ' ἢ κατ' ὄμμ'⁹⁸ ἠνάγκασεν;⁹⁹
⁴⁷⁰ΔΙΟΝΥΣΟΣ. ὁρῶν ὁρῶντα,¹⁰⁰ καὶ δίδωσιν ὄργια.¹⁰¹

ΠΕΝΘΕΥΣ. τὰ δ' ὄργι' ἐστὶ τίν' ἰδέαν¹⁰² ἔχοντά σοι;
ΔΙΟΝΥΣΟΣ. ἄρρητ'¹⁰³ ἀβακχεύτοισιν¹⁰⁴ εἰδέναι βροτῶν.¹⁰⁵
ΠΕΝΘΕΥΣ. ἔχει δ' ὄνησιν¹⁰⁶ τοῖσι θύουσιν¹⁰⁷ τίνα;
ΔΙΟΝΥΣΟΣ. οὐ θέμις¹⁰⁸ ἀκοῦσαί σ', ἔστι δ' ἄξι'¹⁰⁹ εἰδέναι.
⁴⁷⁵ΠΕΝΘΕΥΣ. εὖ τοῦτ' ἐκιβδήλευσας,¹¹⁰ ἵν' ἀκοῦσαι θέλω.
ΔΙΟΝΥΣΟΣ. ἀσέβειαν¹¹¹ ἀσκοῦντ'¹¹² ὄργι' ἐχθαίρει¹¹³ θεοῦ.
ΠΕΝΘΕΥΣ. ὁ θεός, ὁρᾶν γὰρ¹¹⁴ φῂς σαφῶς, ποῖός τις¹¹⁵ ἦν;
ΔΙΟΝΥΣΟΣ. ὁποῖος¹¹⁶ ἤθελ'· οὐκ ἐγὼ 'τασσον¹¹⁷ τόδε.

77. ἀνθεμώδης, -ες, *flowery*.
78. Τμῶλος, -ου, ὁ, (Mount) *Tmolus*.
79. Pf. act. indic. 2 sg., οἶδα, *know*.
80. Partic., *perhaps, possibly, I suppose* (a hedging device; cf. *CGCG* §59.50).
81. Pres. act. ptc. nom. masc. sg., κλύω, *hear* (of a thing); circ.
82. Σάρδεις, -εων, αἱ, *Sardis* (capital of Lydia).
83. ἄστυ, -εος, τό, *city*.
84. Pres. act. indic. 3 sg., περιβάλλω, *surround*.
85. Dat. of manner, "in a circle."
86. Adv., *from there*.
87. πατρίς, -ίδος, ἡ, *homeland*.
88. Interrogative adv., *From where?*
89. τελετή, -ῆς, ἡ, *rite* (esp. of initiation in the mysteries).
90. Aor. act. indic. 3 sg., εἰσβαίνω, *initiate*.
91. Ζεύς, Διός, ὁ, *Zeus*; ὁ τοῦ Διός, "the son of Zeus."
92. Pres. act. indic. 3 sg., τίκτω, *beget, father*.
93. Σεμέλη, -ης, ἡ, *Semele* (daughter of Cadmus and mother of Dionysus by Zeus; cf. 2-3).
94. Adv., *here*.
95. Aor. act. ptc. nom. masc. sg., ζεύγνυμι, *yoke*; with acc. in wedlock (γάμοις); attrib. (subst.).
96. πότερα . . . ἤ, *whether . . . or*.
97. Adv., *by night*; i.e., in a dream.
98. ὄμμα, -ατος, τό, *eye*; κατ' ὄμμ', "in your [waking] sight."
99. Aor. act. indic. 3 sg., ἀνάγκω, *compel, conscript*.
100. In context, ὁρῶν ὁρῶντα must mean "he, seeing [me] seeing [him]."
101. ὄργια, -ίων, τά, *secret rites*.

102. ἰδέα, -ας, ἡ, *form*; with interrogative adj. τίνα: "As to these rites of yours [σοι as dat. of interest]—*of what kind/appearance are they?*" Note that τὰ ὄργι' is a nominative pendant. Cf. Dodds (1960, 137): "P[entheus] picks up D[ionysus]'s word ὄργια, which is consequently put in the emphatic position at the expense of postponing the interrogative."
103. ἄρρητος, -ον, *that which must not be spoken*.
104. ἀβάκχευτος, -ον, *uninitiated in the Bacchic rites*.
105. βροτός, -οῦ, ὁ, *mortal man*.
106. ὄνησις, -εως, ἡ, *benefit, advantage*; with interrogative adj. τίνα.
107. Pres. act. ptc. dat. masc. pl., θύω, *sacrifice*; attrib. (subst.).
108. Quasi-impers. θέμις, *it is not permitted*; with acc. and inf.
109. ἄξιος, -α , -ον, (quasi-impers.) *it is worthwhile*; with epex. inf. εἰδέναι.
110. Aor. act. indic. 2 sg., κιβδηλεύω, *counterfeit*; εὖ τοῦτ' ἐκιβδήλευσας, "You faked that answer cleverly" (Dodds 1960, 137).
111. ἀσέβεια, -ας, ἡ, *impiety*.
112. Pres. act. ptc. acc. masc. sg., ἀσκέω, *practice*; attrib. (subst.). "The rites of the god scorn *the one who practices* impiety."
113. Pres. act. indic. 3 sg., ἐχθαίρω, *hate, detest*.
114. Provides the reason for the question: "As for the god [nom. pendent]—for you claim to have seen him clearly—what was his appearance?"
115. The indefinite pronoun emphasizes the indefiniteness of the interrogative ποῖος (cf. LSJ, 1431.4).
116. ὁποῖος, -α, -ον, *of what sort/quality*.
117. Impf. act. indic. 1 sg., τάσσω, *order, prescribe*. "I had no say in this matter" (Kovacs 2002) captures the sense.

ΠΕΝΘΕΥΣ. τοῦτ' αὖ[118] παρωχέτευσας[119] εὖ γ'[120] οὐδὲν λέγων.
[480]ΔΙΟΝΥΣΟΣ. δόξει[121] τις ἀμαθεῖ[122] σοφὰ λέγων οὐκ εὖ φρονεῖν.
ΠΕΝΘΕΥΣ. ἦλθες δὲ πρῶτα δεῦρ'[123] ἄγων τὸν δαίμονα;[124]
ΔΙΟΝΥΣΟΣ. πᾶς ἀναχορεύει[125] βαρβάρων[126] τάδ' ὄργια.
ΠΕΝΘΕΥΣ. φρονοῦσι γὰρ κάκιον[127] Ἑλλήνων πολύ.
ΔΙΟΝΥΣΟΣ. τάδ' εὖ γε μᾶλλον·[128] οἱ νόμοι δὲ διάφοροι.[129]
[485]ΠΕΝΘΕΥΣ. τὰ δ' ἱερὰ νύκτωρ ἢ μεθ' ἡμέραν[130] τελεῖς;[131]
ΔΙΟΝΥΣΟΣ. νύκτωρ τὰ πολλά·[132] σεμνότητ'[133] ἔχει σκότος.[134]

ΠΕΝΘΕΥΣ. τοῦτ' ἐς[135] γυναῖκας δόλιόν[136] ἐστι καὶ σαθρόν.[137]
ΔΙΟΝΥΣΟΣ. κἂν[138] ἡμέρᾳ τό γ' αἰσχρὸν ἐξεύροι[139] τις ἄν.
ΠΕΝΘΕΥΣ. δίκην σε δοῦναι δεῖ σοφισμάτων[140] κακῶν.
[490]ΔΙΟΝΥΣΟΣ. σὲ δ' ἀμαθίας[141] γε κἀσεβοῦντ'[142] ἐς τὸν θεόν.
ΠΕΝΘΕΥΣ. ὡς θρασὺς[143] ὁ βάκχος[144] κοὐκ ἀγύμναστος[145] λόγων.
ΔΙΟΝΥΣΟΣ. εἴφ'[146] ὅ τι παθεῖν δεῖ· τί με τὸ δεινὸν[147] ἐργάσῃ;
ΠΕΝΘΕΥΣ. πρῶτον μὲν[148] ἁβρὸν[149] βόστρυχον[150] τεμῶ[151] σέθεν.[152]

118. Adv., *again*.
119. Aor. act. indic. 2 sg., παρωχετεύω, *divert*.
120. Postpositive partic. (see n. 35), focuses attention on the adv. εὖ: "very cleverly speaking nonsense."
121. Fut. act. indic. 3 sg., δοκέω, *seem, appear*; with inf.; full line, lit.: "Someone saying wise things will seem to a fool not to be of sound mind." More dynamically, "Speak wisdom to a fool and he will think you foolish" (Kovacs 2002).
122. ἀμαθής, -ές, *ignorant, stupid*.
123. Adv., (with verbs of motion) *to here*.
124. δαίμων, -ονος, ὁ, *god*.
125. Pres. act. indic. 3 sg., ἀναχορεύω, *dance*.
126. Cf. Dodds 1960, 138: "πᾶς . . . βαρβάρων, 'every one of the foreigners,' is more emphatic than πάντες βάρβαροι."
127. Compar. adv. of κάκος (with πολύ), *much worse*. Pentheus's response, "since barbarians are far less reasonable than Greeks," stylizes the ruler as "the typical arrogant Greek" (Dodds 1960, 138).
128. The adverb μᾶλλον should be understood as marking a correction. Supply φρονοῦσιν: "They, rather [than you think], have these things figured out well."
129. διάφορος, -α, -ον, *different*.
130. μεθ' ἡμέραν, "by day."
131. Pres. act. indic. 2 sg., τελέω, *perform* (sacred rites; τὰ ἱερά).
132. Adv. acc., *mostly*.
133. σεμνότης, -ητος, ἡ, *solemnity*.
134. σκότος, -ου, ὁ, *darkness*.

135. ἐς = εἰς.
136. δόλιος, -α, -ον, *deceitful*.
137. σαθρός, -ά, -όν, *unsound, immoral*.
138. Crasis: κἂν = καὶ ἐάν; concessive clause (cf. BDF §374; S §2369; *CGCG* §49.19): "though even by day someone might seek out what is shameful."
139. Aor. act. opt. 3 sg., ἐξευρίσκω, *discover, seek out*; potential opt. in apodosis (cf. S §2356).
140. σόφισμα, -ατος, τό, (with κακῶν) *sly trick, artifice* (cf. LSJ, 1622.II.2). The genitive expresses the crime for which a δίκη must be paid (cf. S §1375). Thus, "It is necessary for you to pay the penalty for your sly trickery."
141. ἀμαθία, -ας, ἡ, *ignorance, stupidity*; gen. of cause (crime). The line relies on the structure of the previous line: "And [it is necessary] for you [to pay the penalty] for your ignorance and as one acting impiously toward the god."
142. Pres. act. ptc. acc. masc. sg., ἀσεβέω (with with acc. pers.), *sin against*; circ. (causal).
143. θρασύς, -εῖα, -ύ, *overbold, rash*; with ὡς marking an exclamation: "How rash [is] this bacchant!"
144. The bacchant, not the god.
145. ἀγύμναστος, -ον, *untrained*.
146. Elided form of εἶπον, *say, tell*; aor. act. impv. 2 sg.
147. δεινός, -ή, -όν, *terrible, dreadful*. Here the verb ἐργάζομαι takes a double accusative: "*What terrible thing* will you do to *me*?"
148. πρῶτον μέν . . . ἔπειτα, *first . . . next*.
149. ἁβρός, -ά, -όν, *delicate*.
150. βόστρυχος, -ον, *lock* (of hair); sg. in a collective sense.
151. Fut. act. indic. 1 sg., τέμνω, *cut*.
152. σέθεν = σοῦ.

ΔΙΟΝΥΣΟΣ. ἱερὸς ὁ πλόκαμος· τῷ θεῷ δ' αὐτὸν τρέφω.[153]
495 ΠΕΝΘΕΥΣ. ἔπειτα θύρσον[154] τόνδε παράδος[155] ἐκ χεροῖν.[156]
ΔΙΟΝΥΣΟΣ. αὐτός μ' ἀφαιροῦ·[157] τόνδε Διονύσῳ φορῶ.[158]
ΠΕΝΘΕΥΣ. εἱρκταῖσί[159] τ' ἔνδον[160] σῶμα σὸν φυλάξομεν.
ΔΙΟΝΥΣΟΣ. λύσει μ' ὁ δαίμων αὐτός, ὅταν ἐγὼ θέλω.
ΠΕΝΘΕΥΣ. ὅταν γε καλέσῃς αὐτὸν ἐν βάκχαις σταθείς.
500 ΔΙΟΝΥΣΟΣ. καὶ νῦν ἃ πάσχω πλησίον[161] παρὼν ὁρᾷ.
ΠΕΝΘΕΥΣ. καὶ ποῦ 'στιν;[162] οὐ γὰρ φανερὸς ὄμμασίν γ' ἐμοῖς.
ΔΙΟΝΥΣΟΣ. παρ' ἐμοί·[163] σὺ δ' ἀσεβὴς αὐτὸς ὢν οὐκ εἰσορᾷς.
ΠΕΝΘΕΥΣ. λάζυσθε·[164] καταφρονεῖ[165] με καὶ Θήβας ὅδε.

ΔΙΟΝΥΣΟΣ. αὐδῶ[166] με μὴ δεῖν σωφρονῶν[167] οὐ σώφροσιν.[168]
505 ΠΕΝΘΕΥΣ. ἐγὼ δὲ δεῖν γε, κυριώτερος σέθεν.
ΔΙΟΝΥΣΟΣ. οὐκ οἶσθ' ὅ τι ζῇς, οὐδ' ὃ δρᾷς, οὐδ' ὅστις εἶ.[169]
ΠΕΝΘΕΥΣ. Πενθεύς, Ἀγαυῆς[170] παῖς, πατρὸς δ' Ἐχίονος.[171]
ΔΙΟΝΥΣΟΣ. ἐνδυστυχῆσαι[172] τοὔνομ'[173] ἐπιτήδειος[174] εἶ.
ΠΕΝΘΕΥΣ. χώρει·[175] καθείρξατ'[176] αὐτὸν ἱππικαῖς[177] πέλας[178]
510 φάτναισιν,[179] ὡς ἂν σκότιον εἰσορᾷ[180] κνέφας.[181]
ἐκεῖ χόρευε· τάσδε[182] δ' ἃς ἄγων πάρει κακῶν συνεργοὺς ἢ διεμπολήσομεν[183]

153. Pres. act. indic. 1 sg., τρέφω, *grow*. At this point, Pentheus cuts off the stranger's hair on stage.
154. θύρσος, -ου, ὁ, *thyrsus* (an ivy-covered wand carried by the bacchants).
155. Aor. act. impv. 2 sg., παραδίδωμι, *hand over*.
156. Dual 3rd decl. gen. fem., χείρ, *hand* (cf. S §210).
157. Pres. mid. impv. 2 sg., ἀφαιρέω, (mid.) *take away for oneself*; with intensive αὐτός: "Come take it from me yourself!" At this point, Pentheus takes the thyrsus.
158. Pres. act. indic. 1 sg., φορέω, *bear*.
159. εἱρκτή, -ῆς, ἡ, (sg. and pl.) *prison*.
160. Adv., *within*.
161. Adv., *nearby*.
162. Aphaeresis (cf. S §76). Dodds 1960, 139: "And where *is* he, eh?" On καί in questions of contempt, see Denniston 1966, 309–10.
163. To maintain the irony of the statement, we should translate the phrase as "where I am" (Dodds 1960, 139).
164. Pres. mid. impv. 2 pl., λάζυμαι, *seize, arrest*.
165. Pres. act. indic. 3 sg., καταφρονέω, *despise*.

166. Pres. act. indic. 1 sg., αὐδάω, *order*; with acc. and inf.: "I order [you] not to bind me."
167. Pres. act. ptc. nom. masc. sg., σωφρονέω, *be of sound mind*; circ.
168. σώφρων, -ον, *of sound mind*.
169. Three indirect questions explicate the content of the verb οἶσθα. In the first, ὅ τι must be taken as an internal accusative: "You do not recognize your status as a mere mortal" (Dodds 1960, 140). The third, ὅστις εἶ, means "what your position is [in relation to me]" (140).
170. Ἀγαυή, -ῆς, ἡ, *Agave*.
171. Ἐχίων, -ονος, ὁ, *Echion*.
172. Aor. act. inf., ἐνδυστυχέω, *be unfortunate in*; epex. (ἐπιτήδειος).
173. Crasis: τοὔνομ' = τὸ ὄνομα.
174. ἐπιτήδειος, -α, -ον, *made for, fit for*.
175. Pres. act. impv. 2 sg., χωρέω, *go*; along the lines of, "Off with you!"
176. Aor. act. impv. 2 pl., κατείργω, *shut/lock up*.
177. ἱππικός, -ή, -όν, *of horses*.
178. Adv., *nearby*; with dat.
179. φάτνη, -ης, ἡ, *manger*.
180. Purpose clause: ὡς ἄν with subj. (cf. BDF §369; S §§2193, 2201.b; CGCG §45.4)
181. κνέφας, -ους/-ατος, τό, *darkness*; modified by σκότιον: lit., "dark darkness."
182. Prolepsis: "*As for these women* whom you have brought with you as partners in wrongdoing . . ."
183. Fut. act. indic. 1 pl., διεμπολάω, *sell off*.

ἢ χεῖρα δούπου[184] τοῦδε καὶ βύρσης[185]
  κτύπου[186]
παύσας[187] ἐφ' ἱστοῖς[188] δμωίδας[189]
  κεκτήσομαι.[190]
[515]ΔΙΟΝΥΣΟΣ. στείχοιμ'[191] ἄν· ὅ τι γὰρ μὴ
  χρεών[192] οὔτοι χρεών
παθεῖν. ἀτάρ τοι[193] τῶνδ' ἄποιν'[194]
  ὑβρισμάτων
μέτεισι[195] Διόνυσός σ', ὃν οὐκ εἶναι λέγεις·
ἡμᾶς γὰρ ἀδικῶν κεῖνον[196] ἐς δεσμοὺς ἄγεις.

ἐφ' ἣν ἔπεμψας, οὐδ' ἄκρανθ'[198] ὡρμήσαμεν.

ὁ θὴρ δ' ὅδ' ἡμῖν πρᾶος οὐδ' ὑπέσπασεν

φυγῇ πόδ', ἀλλ' ἔδωκεν οὐκ ἄκων χέρας,

οὐκ ὠχρός, οὐδ' ἤλλαξεν οἰνωπὸν γένυν,

γελῶν δὲ καὶ δεῖν κἀπάγειν ἐφίετο

ἔμενέ[199] τε, τοὐμὸν εὐτρεπὲς ποιούμενος.

NOTES

Scansion for *Bacch.* 434–440:

Πενθεῦ, πάρεσμεν τήνδ' ἄγραν[197] ἠγρευκότες

184. δοῦπος, -ου, ὁ, *heavy sound*.
185. βύρσα, -ης, ἡ, *drum*.
186. κτύπος, -ου, ὁ, *beating* (of drums). βύρσης κτύπου is an appositive to δούπου τοῦδε.
187. Aor. act. ptc. nom. masc. sg., παύω (with acc. and abl. gen.), *make* (someone) *cease from*.
188. ἱστός, -οῦ, ὁ, *loom*.
189. δμωή, -ίδος, ἡ, *female slave*; pred. comp.
190. Fut. pf. mid. indic. 1 sg., κτάομαι, *acquire*, (pf.) *possess*.
191. Pres. act. opt. 1 sg., στείχω, *go, depart*; potential opt. to express consent: "I am ready to go."
192. χρεών = χρή, *what must be*; with acc. and inf.; lit., "For whatever must not be, must not be [for me] to suffer." In other words, he will *only* suffer what he must.
193. Partic. combination. The break (ἀτάρ) is brought to the attention of the addressee (τοι): "But I'll have you know, Dionysus will punish you for this high-handedness." Since Pentheus would have departed with the previous line, the address is probably to the audience (Dodds 1960, 142).
194. ἄποινα, τά, *penalty*; internal acc. of μέτεισι.
195. Pres. act. indic. 3 sg., μέτειμι, (with ἄποινα as internal acc.) *punish*. The genitive ὑβρισμάτων ("outrageous behavior") expresses the crime being punished.
196. κεῖνον = ἐκεῖνον; i.e., Dionysus. "For in treating us unjustly you are leading him [Dionysus] off to prison."
197. One expects ε, ο, and a short α to lengthen when followed by two or more consonants. If, however, the following consonants are a combination of a mute (π, τ, κ, φ, θ, χ, β, δ, γ) followed by a liquid (λ, μ, ν, ρ), the vowel remains short. This is called "Attic correption."

The interrogation of the stranger (i.e., Dionysus in disguise) explores sociocultural and political (so also "religious") tensions. Pentheus, the king of Thebes, is a tragic figure because he resists the incursion of the foreign deity. He suffers the consequences of a θεομάχος—that is, someone who wars against the god (cf. Acts 5:39). The scene includes many motifs that are found in the New Testament—for example, *deus incognito*, solidarity of the god with his worshipers (cf. *Bacch.* 518; Acts 9:4), miraculous release from prison (cf. Acts 5:17–42; 12:6–19; 16:16–40), and so forth. One that I find particularly striking is the showdown between the *deus incognito* and the civic ruler. Compare, for example, the conversation between Dionysus and Pentheus to the one between Jesus and Pilate (John 18:33–38). For additional study, I highly recommend Friesen 2015. Also note that Seaford 1996 includes Pseudo-Gregory's *Christus Patiens* (*The Suffering Christ*), which incorporates material from the *Bacchae*.

198. Attic correption.
199. Resolution.

8.4.2

The Sacrifice of Iphigenia

Iphigenia at Aulis 1540–1562

¹⁵⁴⁰ΑΓΓΕΛΟΣ Β.¹ ἀλλ',² ὦ φίλη³ δέσποινα,⁴
πᾶν πεύσῃ⁵ σαφῶς.⁶
λέξω⁷ δ' ἀπ' ἀρχῆς, ἤν⁸ τι μὴ σφαλεῖσά⁹
που¹⁰
γνώμῃ¹¹ ταράξῃ¹² γλῶσσαν ἐν λόγοις ἐμήν.
ἐπεὶ γὰρ ἱκόμεσθα¹³ τῆς Διὸς κόρης¹⁴

Ἀρτέμιδος¹⁵ ἄλσος¹⁶ λείμακάς¹⁷ τ'
ἀνθεσφόρους,¹⁸
¹⁵⁴⁵ἵν'¹⁹ ἦν Ἀχαιῶν²⁰ σύλλογος²¹
στρατεύματος,²²
σὴν παῖδ' ἄγοντες, εὐθὺς Ἀργείων²³ ὄχλος
ἠθροίζεθ'.²⁴ ὡς δ' ἐσεῖδεν Ἀγαμέμνων ἄναξ²⁵
ἐπὶ σφαγὰς στείχουσαν²⁶ εἰς ἄλσος κόρην,
ἀνεστέναξε²⁷ κἄμπαλιν²⁸ στρέψας κάρα²⁹

1. Voc.; the second messenger.
2. Partic., *all right, of course*: "in dialogue, also frequent in answers, suggesting that no more attention needs to be paid to (an element of) the context eliciting the answer" (*CGCG* §59.11).
3. φίλος, -η, -ον, *dear*.
4. δέσποινα, -ας, ἡ, *lady of the house*; here Clytemnestra (Iphigenia's mother).
5. Fut. mid. indic. 2 sg., πυνθάνομαι, *hear*.
6. Adv., *clearly, plainly*.
7. Fut. act. indic. 1 sg., λέγω, *speak*.
8. ἤν = ἐάν.
9. Aor. act. ptc. nom. fem. sg., σφάλλω, *cause to fall, trip up*; circ.
10. Partic., *perhaps*; a hedging device (cf. *CGCG* §59.50).
11. γνώμη, -ης, ἡ, *mind*.
12. Aor. act. subj. 3 sg., ταράσσω, *trouble, throw into disorder or confusion*; third-class condition (cf. S §2323; *CGCG* §49.6).
13. Aor. mid. indic. 1. pl., ἱκνέομαι, *arrive*.
14. κόρη, -ης, ἡ, *girl*; here, "daughter."

15. Ἄρτεμις, -ιδος, ἡ, *Artemis*.
16. ἄλσος, -εος, τό, *grove*.
17. λεῖμαξ, -ακος, ἡ, *meadow*.
18. ἀνθεσφόρος, -ον, *flower bearing*.
19. Adv., *in which place, where*.
20. Ἀχαιός, -ά, -όν, (pl.) *Achaeans*.
21. σύλλογος, -ου, ὁ, *assembly*.
22. στράτευμα, -ατος, τό, *army*.
23. Ἀργεῖος, -α, -ον, (pl.) *Argives* (term for the Greeks).
24. Impf. pass. indic. 3 sg., ἀθροίζω, (pass.) *be gathered*.
25. ἄναξ -ακτος ὁ, *king*.
26. Pres. act. ptc. acc. fem. sg., στείχω, *approach*; supp.: "When King Agamemnon saw the girl *entering* the grove for the slaughter . . ."
27. Aor. act. indic. 3 sg., ἀναστενάζω, *groan aloud*.
28. Crasis: κἄμπαλιν = καὶ ἔμπαλιν, "and backwards."
29. The Epic κάρα is poetic for κεφαλή.

¹⁵⁵⁰δάκρυα προῆκεν,³⁰ ὀμμάτων πέπλον
προθείς.³¹
ἡ δὲ σταθεῖσα τῷ τεκόντι³² πλησίον³³
ἔλεξε³⁴ τοιάδ᾽· Ὦ πάτερ, πάρειμί³⁵ σοι·
τοὐμὸν³⁶ δὲ σῶμα τῆς ἐμῆς ὑπὲρ πάτρας³⁷
καὶ τῆς ἁπάσης Ἑλλάδος γαίας ὕπερ³⁸
¹⁵⁵⁵θῦσαι³⁹ δίδωμ᾽ ἑκοῦσα⁴⁰ πρὸς βωμὸν⁴¹
θεᾶς
ἄγοντας,⁴² εἴπερ⁴³ ἐστὶ θέσφατον⁴⁴ τόδε.
Καὶ τοὐπ᾽⁴⁵ ἔμ᾽ εὐτυχοῖτε⁴⁶ καὶ νικηφόρου⁴⁷
δορὸς⁴⁸ τύχοιτε⁴⁹ πατρίδα τ᾽ ἐξίκοισθε⁵⁰ γῆν.
πρὸς ταῦτα μὴ ψαύσῃ⁵¹ τις Ἀργείων ἐμοῦ·

30. Aor. act. indic. 3 sg., προίημι, *send forth* (tears, δάκρυα).
31. Aor. act. ptc. nom. masc. sg., προτίθημι, *put before/over*; thus, "covering his eyes with his garment [πέπλον]."
32. Aor. act. ptc. dat. masc. sg., τίκτω, *beget*; attrib. (subst.).
33. Adv., *nearby*; with dat.
34. ἔλεξε = εἶπεν. ἔλεξε τοιάδ᾽, "she said thus [the following]," begins the report of Iphigenia's speech. The conclusion of the report is marked by τοσαῦτ᾽ ἔλεξε, "those were her words" (1559).
35. Pres. act. indic. 1 sg., πάρειμι, *be near to*; with dat. Essentially, she is saying, "I come before you."
36. Crasis: τοὐμὸν = τὸ ἐμόν.
37. πάτρα, -ας, ἡ, *fatherland*.
38. Anastrophe (cf. S §175; CGCG §60.14) indicates that the object precedes the preposition.
39. Aor. act. inf., θύω, *sacrifice*; purpose (cf. BDF §390; S §2008; CGCG §51.6).
40. ἑκών, -οῦσα, -όν, *willingly*.
41. βωμός, -οῦ, ὁ, *altar*.
42. The subject of the participle is the implied recipient of "my body" (τοὐμὸν . . . σῶμα): "I willingly grant [them], having led [me] to the altar of the goddess, to sacrifice my body."
43. Postpositive partic., *precisely if*; "expresses exclusive limitation—περ limits the applicability of an utterance's content to exactly and only the word (group) it follows" (CGCG §59.55).
44. θέσφατος, -ον, *decreed by God, ordained*.
45. Crasis: τοὐπ᾽ = τὸ ἐπί; τοὐπ᾽ ἔμ᾽, "as far as it depends on me."
46. Pres. act. opt. 2 pl., εὐτυχέω, *prosper*; cupitive (cf. BDF §384; S §1814; CGCG §34.14).
47. νικηφόρος, -ον, *victory-bearing, victorious*.
48. δορύ, -ατος, τό, *spear*, (metaph.) *war*; irregular gen. in Att. poetry.
49. Aor. act. opt. 2 pl., τυγχάνω, *obtain*; with gen.; cupitive. See n. 46.
50. Aor. act. opt. 2 pl., ἐξικνέομαι, *arrive at*; cupitive. See n. 46.
51. Aor. act. subj. 3 sg., ψαύω, *lay hands on*; with gen.; prohibitive (cf. BDF §364; S §1800; CGCG §34.7).

¹⁵⁶⁰σφαγῇ παρέξω⁵² γὰρ δέρην⁵³ εὐκαρδίως.⁵⁴
τοσαῦτ᾽ ἔλεξε· πᾶς ἐθάμβησεν⁵⁵ κλυὼν⁵⁶
εὐψυχίαν⁵⁷ τε κἀρετὴν⁵⁸ τῆς παρθένου.⁵⁹

NOTES

Scansion for *Iph. aul.* 1540–1545:

ἀλλ᾽, ὦ φίλη δέσποινα, πᾶν πεύσῃ σαφῶς.

λέξω δ᾽ ἀπ᾽ ἀρχῆς, ἤν τι μὴ σφαλεῖσά που

γνώμη ταράξῃ γλῶσσαν ἐν λόγοις ἐμήν.

ἐπεὶ γὰρ ἱκόμεσθα τῆς Διὸς κόρης

Ἀρτέμιδος⁶⁰ ἄλσος λείμακάς τ᾽ ἀνθεσφόρους,

The report of Iphegenia's sacrifice may be compared to the sacrifices of Isaac and of Jephthah's daughter. Like the former, an animal is a miraculous substitute for a person; like the latter, the young woman loses her life due to her father's rash decision (cf. Josephus, *A.J.* 1.222–236; §5.2.2). Euripidean tragedy includes numerous characters who die *for* (on behalf of) others, a motif that is central to Christian soteriology (see esp. Eschner 2010; Versnel 2012).

52. Fut. act. indic. 1 sg., παρέχω, *present, offer*.
53. δέρη, -ης, ἡ, *neck, throat*.
54. Adv., *bravely*.
55. Aor. act. indic. 3 sg., θαμβέω, *be astounded at*.
56. Pres. act. ptc. nom. masc. sg., κλύω, *hear*; circ.
57. εὐψυχία, -ας, ἡ, *bravery*.
58. Crasis: καὶ ἀρετή, *virtue*.
59. παρθένος, -ου, ἡ, *maiden*.
60. Resolution.

Works Cited

Primary Texts and Compendia

Babbitt, Frank Cole, trans. 1927. *Plutarch: Moralia, Volume 1*. LCL. Cambridge, MA: Harvard University Press.

———. 1928. *Plutarch: Moralia, Volume 2*. LCL. Cambridge, MA: Harvard University Press.

Bauckham, Richard, James R. Davila, and Alexander Panayotov, eds. 2013. *Old Testament Pseudepigrapha: More Noncanonical Scriptures*. Vol. 1. Grand Rapids: Eerdmans.

Bekker, Immanual. 1831–70. *Aristotelis Opera edidit Academia Regia Borussica*. 5 vols. Berlin: Georigium Reimerum.

Box, Herbert, ed. and trans. 1939. *Philonis Alexandrini in Flaccum*. London: Oxford University Press.

Burchard, Christoph, ed. 2003. *Joseph und Aseneth kritisch herausgegeben*. Pseudepigrapha Veteris Testamenti Graece 5. Leiden: Brill.

Burnet, John, ed. 1924. *Plato's Euthyphro, Apology of Socrates, and Crito*. Oxford: Clarendon.

Bury, R. G., trans. 1926. *Plato: Laws*. 2 vols. LCL. Cambridge, MA: Harvard University Press.

———. 1929. *Plato: Timaeus. Critias. Sleitophon. Menexenus. Epistles*. LCL. Cambridge, MA: Harvard University Press.

Campbell, David A. 2014. *Greek Lyric Poetry: A Selection of Early Greek Lyric, Elegiac, and Iambic Poetry*. New York: Macmillan.

Cary, Earnest, trans. 1914. *Dio Cassius: Roman History, Volume 1*. LCL. Cambridge, MA: Harvard University Press.

———. 1917. *Dio Cassius: Roman History, Volume 4*. LCL. Cambridge, MA: Harvard University Press.

Cohoon, J. W., trans. 1939. *Dio Chrysostom: Discourses 12–30*. LCL. Cambridge, MA: Harvard University Press.

Colson, F. H., trans. 1935. *Philo: On Abraham. On Joseph. On Moses*. LCL. Cambridge, MA: Harvard University Press.

———. 1937. *Philo: On the Decalogue. On the Special Laws, Books 1–3*. LCL. Cambridge, MA: Harvard University Press.

———. 1941. *Philo: Every Good Man Is Free. On the Contemplative Life. On the Eternity of the World. Against Flaccus. Apology for the Jews. On Providence*. LCL. Cambridge, MA: Harvard University Press.

———. 1962. *Philo: On the Embassy to Gaius. General Indexes*. LCL. Cambridge, MA: Harvard University Press.

Colson, F. H., and G. H. Whitaker, trans. 1929. *Philo: On the Creation. Allegorical Interpretation of Genesis 2 and 3*. LCL. Cambridge, MA: Harvard University Press.

Cooley, Alison E. 2009. *Res Gestae Divi Augusti: Text, Translation and Commentary*. Cambridge: Cambridge University Press.

Cowley, Arthur Ernest. 1923. *Aramaic Papyri of the Fifth Century*. Oxford: Clarendon.

Crosby, H. Lamar, trans. 1946. *Dio Chrysostom: Discourses 37–60*. LCL. Cambridge, MA: Harvard University Press.

Danby, Herbert, trans. 1933. *The Mishnah*. Oxford: Oxford University Press.

Denyer, Nicholas, ed. 2019. *Plato: The Apology of Socrates and Xenophon; The Apology of Socrates*. Cambridge: Cambridge University Press.

Dodds, E. R., ed. 1960. *Euripides Bacchae*. 2nd ed. Oxford: Clarendon.

Dogniez, Cécile, and Marguerite Harl. 1992. *Le Deutéronome*. Vol. 5, *La Bible d'Alexandrie*. Paris: Cerf.

Ehrman, Bart D., trans. 2003. *The Apostolic Fathers*. 2 vols. LCL. Cambridge, MA: Harvard University Press.

Emlyn-Jones, Christopher, and William Preddy, trans. 2017. *Plato: Euthyphro. Apology. Crito. Phaedo*. LCL. Cambridge, MA: Harvard University Press.

Fairclough, H. Rushton, trans. 1926. *Horace: Satires. Epistles. The Art of Poetry*. LCL. Cambridge, MA: Harvard University Press.

Feldman, Louis H., trans. 1965. *Josephus: Jewish Antiquities, Volume 9*. LCL. Cambridge, MA: Harvard University Press.

Freese, J. H., trans. 1926. *Aristotle: Art of Rhetoric*. LCL. Cambridge, MA: Harvard University Press.

Geffcken, Johannes, ed. 1902. *Die Oracula Sibyllina*. Die griechischen christlichen Schriftsteller der ersten [drei] Jahrhunderte 8. Leipzig: Heinrichs.

Ginzberg, Louis. 2003. *Legends of the Jews*. Translated by Henrietta Szold and Paul Radin. 2 vols. Philadelphia: Jewish Publication Society.

Godley, A. D., trans. 1920. *Herodotus: The Persian Wars, Volume 1*. LCL. Cambridge, MA: Harvard University Press.

Grant, Robert M. 1966. *The Apostolic Fathers: A New Translation and Commentary*. Vol. 4, *Ignatius of Antioch*. Nashville: Thomas Nelson and Sons.

Green, William M. 1963. *Augustine: City of God*. Vol. 2. Cambridge, MA: Harvard University Press.

Hanhart, Robert, ed. 1959. *Maccabaeorum Liber II*. Septuaginta. Vetus Testamentum Graecum 9/2. Göttingen: Vandenhoeck & Ruprecht.

Harmon, A. M., trans. 1913. *Lucian: Phalaris. Hippias or the Bath. Dionysus. Heracles. Amber or the Swans. The Fly. Nigrinus. Demonax. The Hall. My Native Land. Octogenarians. A True Story. Slander. The Consonants at Law. The Carousal (Symposium) or the Lapiths*. LCL. Cambridge, MA: Harvard University Press.

Hicks, R. D., trans. 1925. *Diogenes Laertius: Lives of Eminent Philosophers*. 2 vols. LCL. Cambridge, MA: Harvard University Press.

Holladay, Carl R. 1983–96. *Fragments from Hellenistic Jewish Authors*. 4 vols. Atlanta: Scholars Press.

Holmes, Michael W., trans. 2007. *The Apostolic Fathers: Greek Texts and English Translations*. 3rd ed. Grand Rapids: Baker Academic.

Horst, Pieter van der, ed. 1978. *The Sentences of Pseudo-Phocylides: With Introduction and Commentary*. SVTP 4. Leiden: Brill.

Jacoby, Felix, ed. 1954–64. *Die Fragmente der griechischen Historiker*. 3 vols. Leiden: Brill.

Jaubert, Annie, ed. 1971. *Épître aux Corinthiens: Texte, Traduction, Notes et Index*. SC 167. Paris: Cerf.

Jones, Christopher P., trans. 2005. *Philostratus: Apollonius of Tyana, Volume 1*. LCL. Cambridge, MA: Harvard University Press.

Kovacs, David, trans. 1994. *Euripides: Bacchae. Iphigenia at Aulis. Rhesus*. LCL. Cambridge, MA: Harvard University Press.

Lattimore, Richmond. 1961. *The Iliad of Homer*. Chicago: University of Chicago Press.

Lightfoot, J. B., and J. R. Harmer, eds. 1891. *The Apostolic Fathers: Revised Greek Texts with Introductions and English Translations*. London: Macmillan.

Lloyd-Jones, Hugh. 1994a. *Sophocles: Ajax. Electra. Oedipus Tyrannus*. LCL. Cambridge, MA: Harvard University Press.

———. 1994b. *Sophocles: Antigone. The Women of Trachis. Philoctetes. Oedipus at Colonus*. LCL. Cambridge, MA: Harvard University Press.

Long, A. A., and D. N. Sedley. 1987. *The Hellenistic Philosophers*. 2 vols. Cambridge: Cambridge University Press.

Marincola, John, trans. 2003. *Herodotus: The Histories*. Rev. ed. New York: Penguin.

Marrou, Henri, ed. 1965. *Á Diognète: Introduction, édition critique et commentaire*. 2nd ed. SC 33. Paris: Cerf.

Most, Glenn W., trans. 2018. *Hesiod: Theogony. Works and Days. Testimonia*. LCL. Cambridge, MA: Harvard University Press.

Mras, Karl, ed. 1954–56. *Eusebius Werke*. Vol. 8, *Die Praeparatio Evangelica*. Die griechischen christlichen Schriftsteller der ersten Jahrhunderte 43.1. Berlin: Akademie.

Murray, A. T., trans. 1924–25. *Homer: The Iliad*. 2 vols. LCL. Cambridge, MA: Harvard University Press.

Nikiprowetzky, Valentin. 1970. *La Troisième Sibylle*. Etudes Juives 9. Paris: Mouton.

Oldfather, W. A., trans. 1925–28. *Epictetus*. 2 vols. LCL. Cambridge, MA: Harvard University Press.

———. 1933. *Diodorus Siculus: Library of History, Volume 1*. LCL. Cambridge, MA: Harvard University Press.

Pelletier, André, ed. 1962. *Lettre d'Aristée a Philocrate: Introduction, Texte Critique, Traduction et Notes, Index Complet des Mots Grecs*. SC 89. Paris: Cerf.

Perrin, Bernadotte, trans. 1919. *Plutarch: Lives, Volume 7*. LCL. Cambridge, MA: Harvard University Press.

Philonenko, Marc. 1968. *Joseph et Aséneth: Introduction, texte critique, traduction et notes*. Studia Post-Biblica. Leiden: Brill.

Rackham, H., trans. 1926. *Aristotle: Nicomachean Ethics*. LCL. Cambridge, MA: Harvard University Press.

———. 1932. *Aristotle: Politics*. LCL. Cambridge, MA: Harvard University Press.

Rahlfs, Alfred, and Robert Hanhart, ed. 2006. *Septuaginta. Id est Vetus Testamentum graece iuxta LXX interpretes*. Stuttgart: Deutsche Bibelgesellschaft.

Seaford, Richard, trans. 1996. *Euripides: Bacchae*. Aris and Phillips Classical Texts. Liverpool: Liverpool University Press.

Smith, C. F., trans. 1919. *Thucydides: History of the Peloponnesian War, Volume 1*. LCL. Cambridge, MA: Harvard University Press.

Stephanus, Henricus, ed. 1572. *Plutarchi Chaeronensis opuscula varis: quae magna ex parte sunt philosophica; vulgo autem Moralia opuscula nimis angusta appellatione vocantur*. 13 vols. Paris: Thomam Guarinum.

———, ed. 1578. *Platonis opera quae extant omnia*. 3 vols. Genevae.

Stern, Menahem. 1974–84. *Greek and Latin Authors on Jews and Judaism*. 3 vols. Jerusalem: The Israel Academy of Sciences and Humanities.

Thackeray, H. St. J., trans. 1926. *Josephus: The Life. Against Apion*. LCL. Cambridge, MA: Harvard University Press.

———. 1927. *Josephus: The Jewish War, Volume 1*. LCL. Cambridge, MA: Harvard University Press.

———. 1928. *Josephus: The Jewish War, Volume 3*. LCL. Cambridge, MA: Harvard University Press.

———. 1930a. *Josephus: Jewish Antiquities, Volume 1*. LCL. Cambridge, MA: Harvard University Press.

———. 1930b. *Josephus: Jewish Antiquities, Volume 2*. LCL. Cambridge, MA: Harvard University Press.

Walton, Francis R., trans. 1967. *Diodorus Siculus: Library of History, Volume 12*. LCL. Cambridge, MA: Harvard University Press.

Warner, Rex, trans. 1972. *Thucydides: History of the Peloponnesian War*. Introduction and Notes by M. I. Finley. New York: Penguin.

West, M. L., ed. 1966. *Hesiod: Theogony*. Oxford: Clarendon.

Wevers, John William, ed. 1974. *Genesis*. Septuaginta 1. Göttingen: Vandenhoeck & Ruprecht.

———. 1977. *Deuteronomium*. Septuaginta. Vetus Testamentum Graecum 3/2. Göttingen: Vandenhoeck & Ruprecht.

Williamson, G. A., trans. 1981. *Josephus: The Jewish War*. Revised by E. Mary Smallwood. New York: Penguin.

Young, Douglas, and Ernst Diehl, eds. 1971. *Theognis: Ps-Pythagoras, Ps-Phocylides, Chares, Anonymi Aulodia, fragmentum teleiambicum*. 2nd ed. Leipzig: Teubner.

Ziegler, Joseph, ed. 1983. *Isaias*. Septuaginta. 3rd ed. Vetus Testamentum Graecum 14. Göttingen: Vandenhoeck & Ruprecht.

Other Works

Adams, Sean. 2020. *Greek Genres and Jewish Authors: Negotiating Literary Culture in the Greco-Roman Era*. Waco: Baylor University Press.

Aejmelaeus, Anneli. 1982. *Parataxis in the LXX: A Study of the Renderings of the Hebrew Coordinate Clauses in the Greek Pentateuch*. Annales Academiae Scientiarum Fennicae 31. Helsinki: Suomalainen Tiedeakatemia.

Aitken, James K., ed. 2015. *The T&T Clark Companion to the Septuagint*. London: Bloomsbury T&T Clark.

Alexander, Loveday. 1993. "Acts and Ancient Intellectual Biography." Pages 31–64 in *The Book of Acts in Its Ancient Literary Setting*, edited by Bruce Winter and Andrew D. Clark. Grand Rapids: Eerdmans.

Allison, Dale. 2005. *Resurrecting Jesus: The Earliest Christian Tradition and Its Interpreters*. London: T&T Clark.

Anderson, Gary A. 2014. *Charity: The Place of the Poor in the Biblical Tradition*. New Haven: Yale University Press.

Anderson, Graham. 1986. *Philostratus: Biography and Belles Lettres in the Third Century A.D.* London: Croom Helm.

Attridge, Harold W. 1976. *The Interpretation of Biblical History in the* Antiquitates Judaicae *of Flavius Josephus*. Harvard Dissertations in Religion 7. Missoula: Scholars Press.

Aune, David E. 1987. *The New Testament in Its Literary Environment*. Louisville: Westminster John Knox.

Bakke, O. M. 2001. *"'Concord and Peace': A Rhetorical Analysis of the First Letter of Clement with an Emphasis on the Language of Unity and Sedition*. WUNT 2/143. Tübingen: Mohr Siebeck.

Balch, David L. 1981. *Let Wives Be Submissive: The Domestic Code in 1 Peter*. SBLDS 26. Chico, CA: Scholars Press.

Baltzer, Klaus, Jürgen Kabiersch, Klaus Koenen, Arie van der Kooij, and Florian Wilk. 2011. "Esaias: Isaias / Das Buch Jesaja." Pages 2484–690 in *Septuaginta Deutsch: Erläuterungen und Kommentare*, Vol. 2, *Psalmen bis Daniel*. Stuttgart: Deutsche Bibelgesellschaft.

Barclay, John M. G. 1996. *Jews in the Mediterranean Diaspora from Alexander to Trajan (323 BCE–117 CE)*. Edinburgh: T&T Clark.

———. 2007. *Against Apion: Translation and Commentary*. BJP 10. Leiden: Brill.

———. 2015. *Paul and the Gift*. Grand Rapids: Eerdmans.

Barnes, Jonathan. 1995. "Life and Work." Pages 1–26 in *The Cambridge Companion to Aristotle*, edited by Jonathan Barnes. Cambridge: Cambridge University Press.

Batiffol, Pierre. 1889–90. *Studia patristica: Études d'ancienne-littérature chrétienne*. 2 vols. Paris: Leroux.

Bauckham, Richard. 2008. *Jesus and the God of Israel: God Crucified and Other Studies on the New Testament's Christology of Divine Identity*. Grand Rapids: Eerdmans.

Bauer, Walter. 1971. *Orthodoxy and Heresy in Earliest Christianity*. Edited by Robert A. Kraft and Gerhard Krodel. Philadelphia: Fortress.

Beard, Mary. 2017. *Women & Power: A Manifesto*. New York: Liveright.

Beard, Mary, John North, and Simon Price. 1998. *Religions of Rome*. 2 vols. Cambridge: Cambridge University Press.

Benner, Allen Rogers. 2001. *Selections from Homer's Iliad*. Norman: University of Oklahoma Press.

Betz, Hans Dieter. 1961. *Lukian von Samosata und das Neue Testament: Religionsgeschichtliche und paränetische Parallelen; ein Beitrag zum Corpus Hellenisticum Novi Testamenti*. Texte und Untersuchungen zur Geschichte der altchristlichen Literatur 76. Berlin: Akademie.

———, ed. 1978. *Plutarch's Ethical Writings and Early Christian Literature*. Studia ad Corpus Hellenisticum Novi Testamenti 4. Leiden: Brill.

Bird, Michael F., and Scott Harrower, eds. 2021. *The Cambridge Companion to the Apostolic Fathers*. Cambridge: Cambridge University Press.

Borgen, Peder. 1993. "Heavenly Ascent in Philo: An Examination of Selected Passages." Pages 246–68 in *The Pseudepigrapha and Early Biblical Interpretation*, edited by J. H. Charlesworth and C. A. Evans. JSPSup 14. Sheffield: Sheffield University Press.

———. 1997. *Philo of Alexandria: An Exegete for His Time*. NovTSup 86. Leiden: Brill.

Boring, M. Eugene, Klaus Berger, and Carsten Colpe, eds. 1995. *Hellenistic Commentary to the New Testament*. Nashville: Abingdon.

Boyarin, Daniel. 1999. *Dying for God: Martyrdom and the Making of Christianity and Judaism*. Figurae: Reading Medieval Culture. Stanford: Stanford University Press.

Branham, R. Bracht, and Marie-Odile Goulet-Cazé, eds. 1996. *The Cynics: The Cynic Movement in Antiquity and Its Legacy*. Berkeley: University of California Press.

Bremmer, Jan. 1983. "Scapegoat Rituals in Ancient Greece." *Harvard Studies in Classical Philology* 87:299–320.

Buell, Denise Kimber. 2005. *Why This New Race: Ethnic Reasoning in Early Christianity*. New York: Columbia University Press.

Buitenwerf, Rieuwerd. 2003. *Book III of the Sibylline Oracles and Its Social Setting: With an Introduction, Translation, and Commentary*. SVTP 17. Leiden: Brill.

Bunsen, C. K. J. von. 1954. *Hippolytus and His Age*. London: Longman, Brown, Green, and Longmans.

Burchard, Christoph. 1987. "The Importance of Joseph and Aseneth for the Study of the New Testament: A General Survey and a Fresh Look at the Lord's Supper." *NTS* 33:109–17.

Burridge, Richard A. 2020. *What Are the Gospels? A Comparison with Greco-Roman Biography*. 3rd ed. Waco: Baylor University Press.

Buschmann, Gerd. 2010. "The Martyrdom of Polycarp." Pages 135–57 in *The Apostolic Fathers: An Introduction*, edited by Wilhelm Pratscher. Waco: Baylor University Press.

Cameron, H. D. 2003. *Thucydides Book I: A Students' Grammatical Commentary*. Ann Arbor: University of Michigan Press.

Cartledge, Paul. 1993. *The Greeks: A Portrait of Self and Others*. Oxford: Oxford University Press.

Cartwright, David. 1997. *A Historical Commentary on Thucydides: A Companion to Rex Warner's Penguin Translation*. Ann Arbor: University of Michigan Press.

Chazon, Esther G. 2000. "Liturgical Communion with the Angels at Qumran." Pages 95–110 in *Sapiential, Liturgical, and Poetical Texts from Qumran: Proceedings of the Third Meeting of the International Organization for Qumran Studies, Oslo 1998, Published in Memory of Maurice Baillet*, edited by Daniel K. Falk, Florentino García Martínez, and Eileen M. Schuller. Studies on the Texts of the Desert of Judah 35. Leiden: Brill.

Chesnutt, Randall D. 1995. *From Death to Life: Conversion in Joseph and Aseneth*. JSPSup 16. Sheffield: Sheffield Academic.

———. 2005. "Perceptions of Oil in Early Judaism and the Meal Formula in Joseph and Aseneth." *JSP* 14:113–32.

Clay, Jenny Strauss. 2003. *Hesiod's Cosmos*. Cambridge: Cambridge University Press.

Cobb, L. S. 2008. *Play the Man: Gender and Language in Early Christian Martyr Texts*. New York: Columbia University Press.

Cohen, Shaye J. D. 1999. *The Beginnings of Jewishness: Boundaries, Varieties, Uncertainties*. Berkeley: University of California Press.

———. 2002. *Josephus in Galilee and Rome: His Vita and His Development as a Historian*. 2nd ed. Leiden: Brill.

Collins, John J. 1972. *The Sibylline Oracles of Egyptian Judaism*. SBLDS 13. Missoula: Scholars Press.

———. 1993. *Daniel: A Commentary on the Book of Daniel*. Hermeneia. Minneapolis: Fortress.

———. 2000. *Between Athens and Jerusalem: Jewish Identity in the Hellenistic Diaspora*. 2nd ed. The Biblical Resource Series. Grand Rapids: Eerdmans.

Cowan, J. Andrew. 2021. "Paul and Socrates in Dialogue: Points of Contact between the Areopagus Speech and the Apology." *NTS* 67:121–33.

Cunliffe, Richard John. 1963. *A Lexicon of the Homeric Dialect*. Norman: University of Oklahoma Press.

Davis, Michael. 1996. *The Politics of Philosophy: A Commentary on Aristotle's Politics*. Lanham, MD: Rowan & Littlefield.

Decker, Rodney J. 2007. *Koine Greek Reader: Selections from the New Testament, Septuagint, and Early Christian Writers*. Grand Rapids: Kregel.

Deissmann, Adolf. 1901. *Bible Studies*. Translated by Alexander Grieve. Peabody, MA: Hendrickson.

Denniston, J. D. 1966. *The Greek Particles*. 2nd ed. Oxford: Clarendon.

deSilva, David. 2006. *4 Maccabees: Introduction and Commentary on the Greek Text in Codex Sinaiticus*. SCS. Leiden: Brill.

Dillon, John. 1977. *The Middle Platonists*. Ithaca, NY: Cornell University Press.

———. 1997. "The Riddle of the Timaeus: Is Plato Sowing Clues?" Pages 25–42 in *Studies in Plato and the Platonic Tradition: Essays Presented to John Whittaker*, edited by Mark Joyal. Burlington, VT: Ashgate.

Donaldson, Terence L. 2007. *Judaism and the Gentiles: Jewish Patterns of Universalism (to 135 CE)*. Waco: Baylor University Press.

Doran, Robert. 2012. *2 Maccabees: A Critical Commentary*. Hermeneia. Minneapolis: Fortress.

Droge, Arthur J. 1988. "*Mori Lucrum*: Paul and Ancient Theories of Suicide." *Novum Testamentum* 30:263–86.

Duff, Timothy E. 1999. *Plutarch's Lives: Exploring Virtue and Vice*. New York: Oxford University Press.

Dürr, Simon. 2021. *Paul on the Human Vocation: Reason Language in Romans and Ancient Philosophical Tradition*. BZNW 226. Berlin: de Gruyter.

Eastman, Susan Grove. 2017. *Paul and the Person: Reframing Paul's Anthropology*. Grand Rapids: Eerdmans.

Eberhart, Christian A. 2013. *Kultmetaphorik und Christologie: Opfer- und Sühneterminologie im Neueun Testament*. WUNT 306. Tübingen: Mohr Siebeck.

Eckstein, A. M. 1990. "Josephus and Polybius: A Reconsideration." *Classical Antiquity* 9:175–208.

Ehorn, Seth M. 2020. *2 Maccabees 1–7: A Handbook on the Greek Text*. Baylor Handbook on the Septuagint. Waco: Baylor University Press.

Ekblad, Eugene Robert, Jr. 1999. *Isaiah's Servant Poems according to the Septuagint: An Exegetical and Theological Study*. Contributions to Biblical Exegesis and Theology 23. Leuven: Peeters.

Elledge, C. D. 2017. *Resurrection of the Dead in Early Judaism, 200 BCE–200 CE*. New York: Oxford University Press.

Engberg-Pedersen, Troels. 2000. *Paul and the Stoics*. Louisville: Westminster John Knox.

———. 2010. *Cosmology and Self in the Apostle Paul: The Material Spirit*. New York: Oxford University Press.

Eschner, Christina. 2010. *Gestorben und hingegeben "für" die Sünder: Die griechische Konzeption des Unheil abwendenden Sterbens und deren paulinische Aufnahme für die Deutung des Todes Jesu Christi*. 2 vols. Wissenschaftliche Monographien zum Alten und Neuen Testament 122. Neukirchen-Vluyn: Neukirchener.

Feldman, Louis H. 1988. "Use, Authority and Exegesis of Mikra in the Writings of Josephus." Pages 455–518 in *Mikra: Text, Translation, Reading and Interpretation of the Hebrew Bible in Ancient Judaism and Early Christianity*, edited by Martin Jan Mulder. Compendia Rerum Iudaicarum ad Novum Testamentum 2.1. Minneapolis: Fortress.

———. 1993. *Jew and Gentile in the Ancient World*. Princeton: Princeton University Press.

———. 1998. *Studies in Josephus' Rewritten Bible*. JSJSup 58. Leiden: Brill.

———. 2000. *Judean Antiquities 1–4: Translation and Commentary*. BJP 3. Leiden: Brill.

Fornara, Charles W. 1983. *The Nature of History in Ancient Greece and Rome*. Berkeley: University of California Press.

Friesen, Courtney J. P. 2015. *Reading Dionysus: Euripides' Bacchae and the Cultural Contestations of Greeks, Jews, Romans, and Christians*. Studien und Texte zu Antike und Christentum 95. Tübingen: Mohr Siebeck.

Galinsky, Karl. 1996. *Augustan Culture: An Interpretive Introduction*. Princeton: Princeton University Press.

———, ed. 2005. *The Cambridge Companion to the Age of Augustus*. Cambridge: Cambridge University Press.

Gane, Roy E. 2005. *Cult Character: Purification Offerings, Day of Atonement, and Theodicy*. Winona Lake, IN: Eisenbrauns.

Gignac, Francis T. 1976–81. *A Grammar of the Greek Papyri of the Roman and Byzantine Periods*. 2 vols. Rome: Istituto editoriale cisalpino-La goliardica.

Gilders, William K. 2011. "Jewish Sacrifice: Its Nature and Function (according to Philo)." Pages 94–105 in *Ancient Mediterranean Sacrifice*, edited by Jennifer Wright Knust and Zsuzsana Várhelyi. New York: Oxford University Press.

Goldingay, John, and David Payne. 2014. *Isaiah 40–55: A Critical and Exegetical Commentary*. 2 vols. London: Bloomsbury T&T Clark.

Goldstein, Jonah A. 1983. *II Maccabees: A New Translation with Introduction and Commentary*. Anchor Bible 41A. Garden City, NY: Doubleday.

———. 1984. "The Origins of the Doctrine of Creation Ex Nihilo." *Journal of Jewish Studies* 35:127–35.

Gregory, Andrew F. 2005. "*1 Clement* and the Writings That Later Formed the New Testament." Pages 129–57 in *The Reception of the New Testament in the Apostolic Fathers*, edited by Andrew F. Gregory and Christopher M. Tuckett. Vol. 1 of *The New Testament and the Apostolic Fathers*. Oxford: Oxford University Press.

Gregory, Andrew F., and Christopher M. Tuckett, eds. 2005. *The Reception of the New Testament in the Apostolic Fathers*. Vol. 1 of *The New Testament and the Apostolic Fathers*. Oxford: Oxford University Press.

Grelot, Pierre. 1981. *Les poèmes du Serviteur: De la lecture critique à l'herméneutique*. Lectio divina 103. Paris: Cerf.

Grimaldi, William M. A. 1980. *Aristotle, Rhetoric I: A Commentary*. New York: Fordham University Press.

Gyselinck, Wannes, and Kristoffel Demoen. 2009. "Author and Narrator: Fiction and Metafiction in Philostratus' *Vita Apollonii*." Pages 95–127 in *Theios Sophistes: Essays on Flavius Philostratus' Vita Apollonii*, edited by Kristoffel Demoen and Danny Praet. Mnemosyne Supplements 305. Leiden: Brill.

Hadas, Moses. 1951. *Aristeas to Philocrates (Letter of Aristeas)*. New York: Harper & Brothers.

Hall, Jonathan M. 2002. *Hellenicity: Between Ethnicity and Culture*. Chicago: University of Chicago Press.

Halperin, David J. 1980. *The Merkabah in Rabbinic Literature*. American Oriental Series 62. New Haven: American Oriental Society.

Hamilton, J. R. 1969. *Plutarch: Alexander; A Commentary*. Oxford: Clarendon.

Harland, Philip. 2003. "Christ-Bearers and Fellow-Initiates: Local Cultural Life and Christian Identity in Ignatius' Letter." *Journal of Early Christian Studies* 11:481–99.

Harnack, Adolf von. 1878. *Die Zeit des Ignatius und die Chronologie der antiochenischen Bischöfe bis Tyrannus nach Julius Africanus und den späteren Historikern*. Leipzig: Hinrichs.

Hartog, Paul. 2002. *Polycarp and the New Testament: The Occasion, Rhetoric, Theme, and Unity of the Epistle to the Philippians and Its Allusions to New Testament Literature*. WUNT 2/134. Tübingen: Mohr Siebeck.

———. 2013. *Polycarp's* Epistle to the Philippians *and the* Martyrdom of Polycarp: *Introduction, Text, and Commentary*. Oxford Apostolic Fathers. Oxford: Oxford University Press.

Hayes, Christine. 2015. *What's Divine about Divine Law? Early Perspectives*. Princeton: Princeton University Press.

Hengel, Martin. 1974. *Judaism and Hellenism*. Translated by John Bowden. 2 vols. Philadelphia: Fortress.

———. 2004. "The Effective History of Isaiah 53 in the Pre-Christian Period." Pages 75–146 in *The Suffering Servant: Isaiah 53 in Jewish and Christian Sources*, edited by Bernd Janowski and Peter Stuhlmacher. Translated by Daniel P. Bailey. Grand Rapids: Eerdmans.

Henten, Jan Willem van. 1997. *The Maccabean Martyrs as Saviours of the Jewish People: A Study of 2 and 4 Maccabees*. JSJSup 57. Leiden: Brill.

Henten, Jan Willem van, and Friedrich Avemarie. 2002. *Martyrdom and Noble Death: Select Texts from Graeco-Roman, Jewish and Christian Antiquity*. London: Routledge.

Hermisson, Hans-Jürgen. 2004. "The Fourth Servant Song in the Context of Isaiah." Pages 16–47 in *The Suffering Servant: Isaiah 53 in Jewish and Christian Sources*, edited by Bernd Janowski and Peter Stuhlmacher. Translated by Daniel P. Bailey. Grand Rapids: Eerdmans.

Hicks-Keeton, Jill. 2018. *Arguing with Aseneth: Gentile Access to Israel's Living God in Jewish Antiquity*. New York: Oxford University Press.

Hiebert, Robert J. V. 2015. "4 Maccabees." Pages 306–19 in *The T&T Clark Companion to the Septuagint*, edited by James K. Aitken. London: Bloomsbury T&T Clark.

Honigman, Sylvie. 2003. *The Septuagint and Homeric Scholarship in Alexandria: A Study in the Narrative of 'Letter of Aristeas.'* London: Routledge.

Hornblower, Simon. 1991. *A Commentary on Thucydides*. Vol. 1, *Books I–III*. Oxford: Clarendon.

Horrell, David G. 2013. "The Label Χριστιανός (1 Pet 4.16): Suffering, Conflict, and the Making of Christian Identity." Pages 164–210 in *Becoming Christian: Essays on 1 Peter and the Making of Christian Identity*. Library of New Testament Studies 394. London: Bloomsbury T&T Clark.

Horst, Pieter Willem van der. 1983. "Moses' Throne Vision in Ezekiel the Dramatist." *JSJ* 34:21–29.

———. 1984. "Some Notes on the *Exagoge* of Ezekiel." *Mnemosyne* 37:354–75.

———. 1988. "Pseudo-Phocylides Revisited." *JSP* 3:3–30.

———. 2003. *Philo's* Flaccus: *The First Pogrom; Introduction, Translation and Commentary*. PACS 2. Leiden: Brill.

How, Walter W., and Joseph Wells. 1928. *A Commentary on Herodotus*. 2 vols. Rev. ed. Oxford: Clarendon.

Hunter, Richard. 2004. "Homer and Greek Literature." Pages 235–53 in *The Cambridge Companion to Homer*, edited by Robert Fowler. Cambridge: Cambridge University Press.

Hutchinson, D. S. 1995. "Ethics." Pages 195–232 in *The Cambridge Companion to Aristotle*, edited by Jonathan Barnes. Cambridge: Cambridge University Press.

Ilan, Tal. 2016. "Josephus on Women." Pages 210–21 in *A Companion to Josephus*, edited by Honora Howell Chapman and Zuleika Rodgers. Malden, MA: Blackwell.

Jefford, Clayton N. 2013. *The Epistle to Diognetus (with the Fragment of Quadratus)*. Oxford Apostolic Fathers. Oxford: Oxford University Press.

Jobes, Karen H., and Moisés Silva. *Invitation to the Septuagint*. 2015. 2nd ed. Grand Rapids: Baker Academic.

Johansen, T. K. 2004. *Plato's Natural Philosophy: A Study of the Timaeus-Critias*. Cambridge: Cambridge University Press.

Johnson, Luke Timothy. 2009. *Among the Gentiles: Greco-Roman Religion and Christianity*. AYBRL. New Haven: Yale University Press.

Jones, Peter, Keith C. Sidwell, and Frances E. Corrie, eds. 2015a. *A World of Heroes: Selections from Homer, Herodotus and Sophocles*. 2nd ed. Revised by Anthony Verity, James Neville, Alan Griffiths, and Keith Maclennan. Cambridge: Cambridge University Press.

———. 2015b. *The Intellectual Revolution: Selections from Euripides, Thucydides and Plato*. 2nd ed. Revised by Keith Maclennan and Peter Jones. Cambridge: Cambridge University Press.

Kajanto, Iiro. 1965. *The Latin Cognomina*. Societas Scientiarum Fennica: Commentationes Humanarun Litterarum 36.2. Helsinki, Finland: Keskuskirjapaino.

Kamesar, Adam. 2009a. "Biblical Interpretation in Philo." Pages 65–91 in *The Cambridge Companion to Philo*, edited by Adam Kamesar. Cambridge: Cambridge University Press.

———, ed. 2009b. *The Cambridge Companion to Philo*. Cambridge: Cambridge University Press.

Keener, Craig S. 2012. *Acts: An Exegetical Commentary*. Vol. 1, *Introduction and 1:1–2:47*. Grand Rapids: Baker Academic.

Keitel, Elizabeth. 1984. "Principate and Civil War in the Annals of Tacitus." *American Journal of Philology* 105:306–25.

Kennedy, George A. 1994. *A New History of Classical Rhetoric*. Princeton: Princeton University Press.

Kirk, G. S. 1985. *The Iliad: A Commentary*. Vol. 1, *Books 1–4*. Cambridge: Cambridge University Press.

Klauck, Hans-Josef. 2011. "Makkabaion IV: Das vierte Buch der Makkabäer." Pages 1445–75 in *Genesis bis Makkabäer*, edited by Martin Karrer and Wolfgang Kraus. Vol. 1 of *Septuaginta Deutsch: Erläuterungen und Kommentare*. Stuttgart: Deutsche Bibelgesellschaft.

Klawans, Jonathan. 2000. *Impurity and Sin in Ancient Judaism*. New York: Oxford University Press.

———. 2006. *Purity, Sacrifice, and the Temple: Symbolism and Supersessionism in the Study of Ancient Judaism*. New York: Oxford University Press.

———. 2012. *Josephus and the Theologies of Ancient Judaism*. New York: Oxford University Press.

Koester, Helmut. 1995. *Introduction to the New Testament*. Vol. 1, *History, Culture, and Religion of the Hellenistic Age*. 2nd ed. Berlin: de Gruyter.

Kooij, Arie van der. 2019. "Esaias/Isaias/Isaiah." Pages 515–27 in *Introduction to the LXX*, edited by Siegfried Kreuzer. Translated by David A. Brenner and Peter Altmann. Waco: Baylor University Press.

Kooten, George H. van. 2008. *Paul's Anthropology in Context: The Image of God, Assimilation to God, and the Tripartite Man in Ancient Judaism, Ancient Philosophy and Early Christianity*. WUNT 232. Tübingen: Mohr Siebeck.

Koskenniemi, Erkki. 1994. *Apollonios von Tyana in der neutestamentlichen Exegese: Forschungsbericht und Weiterführung der Diskussion*. WUNT 2/61. Tübingen: Mohr Siebeck.

Kraemer, Ross S. 1998. *When Aseneth Met Joseph: A Late Antique Tale of the Biblical Patriarch and His Egyptian Wife, Reconsidered*. New York: Oxford University Press.

Kraft, Robert A. 1965. *The Apostolic Fathers: A Translation and Commentary*. Vol. 3, *The Didache and Barnabas*. Nashville: Thomas Nelson.

Kraus, Wolfgang. 2009. "Jesaja 53 LXX im frühen Christentum—eine Überprüfung." Pages 149–82 in

Beiträge zur urchristlichen Theologiegeschichte, edited by Wolfgang Kraus. BZNW 163. Berlin: de Gruyter.

Kraut, Richard. 1992. "Introduction to the Study of Plato." Pages 1–50 in *The Cambridge Companion to Plato*, edited by Richard Kraut. Cambridge: Cambridge University Press.

Kreuzer, Siegfried, ed. 2019. *Introduction to the Septuagint*. Translated by David A. Brenner and Peter Altmann. Waco: Baylor University Press.

Kugel, James L. 1998. *Traditions of the Bible: A Guide to the Bible as It Was at the Start of the Common Era*. Cambridge, MA: Harvard University Press.

Kühner, Raphael. 1890–1904. *Ausführliche Grammatik der griechischen Sprache*. Edited by Bernhard Gerth and Friedrich Blass. 4 vols. Hanover: Hahnsche Buchhandlung.

Laks, André. 2000. "The Laws." Pages 258–92 in *The Cambridge History of Greek and Roman Political Thought*, edited by Christopher Rowe and Malcom Schofield. Cambridge: Cambridge University Press.

Lau, Te-Li. 2010. *The Politics of Peace: Ephesians, Dio Chrysostom, and the Confucian* Four Books. NovTSup 133. Leiden: Brill.

Le Moyne, Jean. 1972. *Les Sadducéens*. Etudes bibliques. Paris: Librairie Lecoffre.

Leonhardt, Jutta. 2001. *Jewish Worship in Philo of Alexandria*. Texte und Studien zum antiken Judentum 84. Tübingen: Mohr Siebeck.

Lieu, Judith M. 1996. *Image and Reality: The Jews in the World of Christians*. Edinburgh: T&T Clark.

———. 2016. *Neither Jew nor Greek? Constructing Early Christian Identity*. 2nd ed. London: Bloomsbury T&T Clark.

Lightfoot, J. B. 1875. *Saint Paul's Epistle to the Colossians and Philemon*. London: Macmillan.

Lincicum, David. 2010. *Paul and the Early Jewish Encounter with Deuteronomy*. WUNT 2/284. Tübingen: Mohr Siebeck.

Lindemann, Andreas. 2010. "The First Epistle of Clement." Pages 47–69 in *The Apostolic Fathers: An Introduction*, edited by Wilhelm Pratscher. Waco: Baylor University Press.

Loader, William. 2011. *Philo, Josephus, and the Testaments on Sexuality: Attitude towards Sexuality in the Writings of Philo and Josephus and in the Testaments of the Twelve Patriarchs*. Grand Rapids: Eerdmans.

Lona, Horacio E. 1998. *Der erste Clemensbrief: Übersetzt und Erklärt*. Kommentar zu den Apostolischen Vätern 2. Göttingen: Vandenhoeck & Ruprecht.

———. 2010. "Diognetus." Pages 197–213 in *The Apostolic Fathers: An Introduction*, edited by Wilhelm Pratscher. Waco: Baylor University Press.

Long, A. A. 1971. "The Logical Basis of Stoic Ethics." *Proceedings of the Aristotelian Society* 71:85–104.

———. 2002. *Epictetus: A Stoic and Socratic Guide to Life*. Oxford: Clarendon.

Lookadoo, Jonathon. 2018. *The High Priest and the Temple: Metaphorical Depictions of Jesus in the Letters of Ignatius of Antioch*. WUNT 2/473. Tübingen: Mohr Siebeck.

Lyons, Michael A., and Jacob Stromberg, eds. 2021. *Isaiah's Servants in Early Judaism and Christianity: The Isaian Servant and the Exegetical Formation of Community Identity*. WUNT 2/554. Tübingen: Mohr Siebeck.

MacDonald, Dennis R. 2000. *The Homeric Epics and the Gospel of Mark*. New Haven: Yale University Press.

———. 2006. "A Categorization of Antetextuality in the Gospels and Acts: A Case for Luke's Imitation of Plato and Xenophon to Depict Paul as a Christian Socrates." Pages 211–22 in *The Intertextuality of the Epistles: Explorations of Theory and Practice*, edited by T. L. Brodie, Dennis R. MacDonald, and Stanley Porter. Sheffield: Sheffield University Press.

———. 2015. *The Gospels and Homer: Imitations of Greek Epic in Mark and Luke-Acts*. Vol. 1 of *The New Testament and Greek Literature*. New York: Rowman & Littlefield.

Mader, Gottfried. 2000. *Josephus and the Politics of Historiography: Apologetic and Impression Management in the* Bellum Judaicum. Leiden: Brill.

Magness, Jodi. 2002. *The Archaeology of Qumran and the Dead Sea Scrolls*. Grand Rapids: Eerdmans.

Malherbe, Abraham J. 1986. *Moral Exhortation: A Greco-Roman Sourcebook*. Louisville: Westminster John Knox.

———. 1989. *Paul and the Popular Philosophers*. Minneapolis: Fortress.

Marincola, John. 2007. "Speeches in Classical Historiography." Pages 118–32 in *A Companion to Greek and Roman Historiography*, edited by John Marincola. Malden: Blackwell.

Mason, Steve. 1991. *Flavius Josephus on the Pharisees*. Studia Post-Biblica 39. Leiden: Brill.

———. 2001. *Life of Josephus: Translation and Commentary*. BJP 9. Leiden Brill.

———. 2003. *Josephus and the New Testament*. 2nd ed. Peabody, MA: Hendrickson.

———. 2008. *Judean War 2: Translation and Commentary*. BJP 1b. Leiden: Brill.

———. 2009. *Josephus, Judea, and Christian Origins: Methods and Categories*. Peabody, MA: Hendrickson.

Mayser, Edwin. 1934. *Grammatik der griechischen Papyri aus der Ptolemäerzeit mit Einschluss der gleichzeitigen Ostraka und der Ägypten verfassten Inschriften*. Vol. 2. Berlin: de Gruyter.

Meyers, Carol. 2013. *Rediscovering Eve: Ancient Israelite Women in Context*. Oxford: Oxford University Press.

McLay, R. Timothy. 2003. *The Use of the Septuagint in New Testament Research*. Grand Rapids: Eerdmans.

McLean, B. H. 2014. *Hellenistic and Biblical Greek: A Graduated Reader*. Cambridge: Cambridge University Press.

Meeks, Wayne. 1968. "Moses as God and King." Pages 354–59 in *Religions in Antiquity: Essays in Memory of E. R. Goodenough*, edited by Jacob Neusner. Leiden: Brill.

Menn, Stephen. 1995. *Plato on God and Nous*. Carbondale: Southern Illinois University Press.

Milgrom, Jacob. 1976. "Israel's Sanctuary: The Priestly 'Picture of Dorian Gray.'" *Revue biblique* 83:390–99.

———. 1993. "The Rationale for Biblical Impurity." *Journal of the Ancient Near Eastern Society of Columbia University* 22:107–11.

Moore, Stephen D., and Janice Capel Anderson. 1998. "Taking It Like a Man: Masculinity in 4 Maccabees." *Journal of Biblical Literature* 177:249–73.

Morgan, Teresa. 2015. *Roman Faith and Christian Faith:* Pistis *and* Fides *in the Early Roman Empire and Early Churches*. Oxford: Oxford University Press.

Moss, Candida R. 2010. "On the Dating of Polycarp: Rethinking the Place of *Martyrdom of Polycarp* in the History of Christianity." *Early Christianity* 1:539–74.

———. 2012. *Ancient Christian Martyrdom: Diverse Practices, Theologies, and Traditions*. AYBRL. New Haven: Yale University Press.

Muraoka, Takamitsu. 2016. *A Syntax of Septuagint Greek*. Leuven: Peeters.

Nagle, D. Brendan. 2006. *The Household as the Foundation of the Polis*. Cambridge: Cambridge University Press.

Naiden, F. S. 2013. *Smoke Signals for the Gods: Ancient Greek Sacrifice from the Archaic through Roman Periods*. New York: Oxford University Press.

Neusner, Jacob, and Bruce D. Chilton, eds. 2007. *In Quest of the Historical Pharisees*. Waco: Baylor University Press.

Ngunga, Abi T., and Joachim Schaper. 2015. "Isaiah." Pages 456–68 in *The T&T Clark Companion to the Septuagint*, edited by James K. Aitken. London: Bloomsbury T&T Clark.

Nickelsburg, George W. E. 2006a. "Torah and the Deuteronomic Scheme in Apocrypha and Pseudepigrapha: Variations on a Theme and Some Noteworthy Examples of Its Absence." Pages 222–35 in *Das Gesetz im frühen Judentum und im Neuen Testament: Festschrift für Christoph Burchard*, edited by Dieter Sänger and Matthias Konradt. Studien zur Umwelt des Neuen Testaments 57. Göttingen: Vandenhoeck & Ruprecht.

———. 2006b. *Resurrection, Immortality, and Eternal Life in Intertestamental Judaism and Early Christianity*. Exp. ed. Harvard Theological Studies 56. Cambridge, MA: Harvard University Press.

Nicklas, Tobias. 2011. "Makkabaion II: Das zweite Buch der Makkabäer." Pages 1376–1416 in *Genesis bis Makkabäer*, edited by Martin Karrer and Wolfgang Kraus. Vol. 1 of *Septuaginta Deutsch: Erläuterungen und Kommentare*. Stuttgart: Deutsche Bibelgesellschaft.

Niehoff, Maren R. 2018. *Philo of Alexandria: An Intellectual Biography*. AYBRL. New Haven: Yale University Press.

Nikiprowetzky, Valentin. 1977. *Le commentaire de l'Écriture chez Philon d'Alexandrie*. Arbeiten zur Literatur und Geschichte des hellenistischen Judentums 11. Leiden: Brill.

Novenson, Matthew V. 2014. "Paul's Former Occupation in *Iudaismos*." Pages 24–39 in *Galatians and Christian Theology: Justification, the Gospel, and Ethics in Paul's Letter*, edited by Mark W. Elliott, Scott J. Hafemann, N. T. Wright, and John Frederick. Grand Rapids: Baker Academic.

Nussbaum, Martha C. 1994. *The Therapy of Desire: Theory and Practice in Hellenistic Ethics*. Princeton: Princeton University Press.

Olofsson, Staffan. 1990. *God Is My Rock: A Study of Translation Technique and Theological Exegesis in the Septuagint*. Coniectanea Biblica: Old Testament Series 31. Stockholm: Almqvist & Wiksell International.

Paget, James Carleton. 1994. *The Epistle of Barnabas: Outlook and Background*. WUNT 2/64. Tübingen: Mohr Siebeck.

Palmer, Leonard R. 1946. *A Grammar of the Post-Ptolemaic Papyri*. Vol. 1, *Accidence and Word-Formation*. London: Oxford University Press.

Parke, H. W. 1988. *Sibyls and Sibylline Prophecy in Classical Antiquity*. London: Routledge.

Parker, Robert. 1983. *Miasma: Pollution and Purification in Early Greek Religion*. Oxford: Clarendon.

Pearce, Sarah. 2004. "Jerusalem as 'Mother-City' in the Writings of Philo of Alexandria." Pages 19–36 in *Negotiating Diaspora: Jewish Strategies in the Roman Empire*, edited by John M. G. Barclay. JSPSup 45. London: T&T Clark.

Pelling, Christopher. 2002. *Plutarch and History: Eighteen Studies*. London: Classical Press of Wales and Duckworth.

Peppard, Michael. 2011. *The Son of God in the Roman World: Divine Sonship in Its Social and Political Context*. New York: Oxford University Press.

Peters, Melvin K. H. 2012. "Revisiting the Rock: Tsur as a Translation of Elohim in Deuteronomy and Beyond." Pages 37–51 in *Text-Critical and Hermeneutical Studies in the Septuagint*, edited by Johann Cook and Hermann-Josef Stripp. Supplements to Vetus Testamentum 157. Leiden: Brill.

———. 2019. "Deuteronomion/Deuteronomium/Deuteronomy." Pages 129–41 in *Introduction to the LXX*, edited by Siegfried Kreuzer. Translated by David A. Brenner and Peter Altmann. Waco: Baylor University Press.

Pratscher, Wilhelm, ed. 2010. *The Apostolic Fathers: An Introduction*. Waco: Baylor University Press.

Pratt, Louise. 2011. *Eros at the Banquet: Reviewing Greek with Plato's Symposium*. Norman: University of Oklahoma Press.

Rajak, Tessa. 1983. *Josephus: The Historian and His Society*. London: Duckworth.

Reeve, C. D. C. 2014. "Beginning and Ending with Eudaimonia." Pages 14–33 in *The Cambridge Companion to Aristotle's Nicomachean Ethics*, edited by Ronald Polansky. Cambridge: Cambridge University Press.

Regev, Eyal. 2009. "Sadducees." Pages 32–36 in vol. 5 of *New Interpreters Bible Dictionary*, edited by Katharine Doob Sakenfeld. Nashville: Abingdon.

Rodgers, Zuleika. 2012. "Josephus's Biblical Interpretation." Pages 436–64 in *A Companion to Biblical Interpretation in Early Judaism*, edited by Matthias Henze. Grand Rapids: Eerdmans.

Ross, William A., and Edward Glenny, eds. 2021. *The T&T Clark Handbook of Septuagint Research*. London: Bloomsbury T&T Clark.

Royse, James R. 2009. "The Works of Philo." Pages 32–64 in *The Cambridge Companion to Philo*, edited by Adam Kamesar. Cambridge: Cambridge University Press.

Runge, Steven E. 2010. *Discourse Grammar of the Greek New Testament: A Practical Introduction for Teaching and Exegesis*. Peabody, MA: Hendrickson.

Runia, David T. 1986. *Philo of Alexandria and the Timaeus of Plato*. Philosophia Antiqua 44. Leiden: Brill.

———. 2001. *On the Creation of the Cosmos according to Moses: Introduction, Translation and Commentary*. PACS 1. Leiden: Brill.

Salvesen, Alison G., and Timothy Michael Law, eds. 2021. *The Oxford Handbook of the Septuagint*. New York: Oxford University Press.

Sandnes, Karl O. 1993. "Paul and Socrates: The Aim of Paul's Areopagus Speech." *Journal for the Study of the New Testament* 50:13–26.

Schäfer, Peter. 2006. "Communion with the Angels: Qumran and the Origins of Jewish Mysticism." Pages 37–66 in *Wege mystischer Gotteserfahrung: Judentum, Christentum und Islam*, edited by Peter Schäfer. Munich: Oldenbourg.

Schoedel, William R. 1985. *Ignatius of Antioch: A Commentary on the Letters of Ignatius*. Hermeneia. Philadelphia: Fortress.

———. 1993. "Polycarp of Smyrna and Ignatius of Antioch." *ANRW* 2.27.1: 347–58.

Schwartz, Daniel R. 1996. "God, Gentiles, and Jewish Law: On Acts 15 and Josephus' Adiabene Narrative." Pages 263–82 in vol. 1 of *Geschichte—Tradition—Reflexion: Festschrift für Martin Hengel zum 70 Geburtstag*, edited by Peter Schäfer. Tübingen: Mohr Siebeck.

———. 2008. *2 Maccabees*. CEJL. Berlin: de Gruyter.

Schwyzer, Eduard. 1939. *Griechische Grammatik: Auf der Grundlage von Karl Brugmanns Griechischer Grammatik*. 4 vols. München: Beck.

Seland, Torrey, ed. 2014. *Reading Philo: A Handbook to Philo of Alexandria*. Grand Rapids: Eerdmans.

Shields, Christopher. 2012. "Aristotle's Philosophical Life and Writings." Pages 3–16 in *The Oxford Handbook of Aristotle*, edited by Christopher Shields. Oxford: Oxford University Press.

Shively, Elizabeth E. 2020. "A Critique of Richard Burridge's Genre Theory: Shifting from a One-Dimensional to a Multi-Dimensional Approach to Gospel Genre." Pages 97–112 in *Modern and Ancient Literary Criticism of the Gospels: A Continuing Debate on Gospel Genre(s)*, edited by Robert Matthew Calhoun, David P. Moessner, and Tobias Nicklas. WUNT 451. Tübingen: Mohr Siebeck.

Sievers, Joseph, and Amy Jill Levine, eds. 2021. *The Pharisees*. Grand Rapids: Eerdmans.

Sly, Dorothy. 1990. *Philo's Perception of Women*. Brown Judaic Studies 209. Atlanta: Scholars Press.

Smith, Nicholas D. 1991. "Aristotle's Theory of Natural Slavery." Pages 142–55 in *A Companion to Aristotle's Politics*, edited by David Keyt and Fred D. Miller Jr. Oxford: Blackwell.

Snyder, Graydon F. 1968. "The Text and Syntax of Ignatius ΠΡΟΣ ΕΦΕΣΙΟΥΣ." *Vigiliae Christianae* 22:8–13.

Stemberger, Günter. 1999. "The Sadducees—Their History and Doctrines." Pages 428–43 in *The Early Roman Period*, edited by William Horbury, W. D. Davies, and John Sturdy. Vol. 3 of *The Cambridge History of Judaism*. Cambridge: Cambridge University Press.

Sterling, Gregory. 2001. "Mors Philosophi: The Death of Jesus in Luke." *Harvard Theological Review* 94:383–402.

———. 2003. "Philo Has Not Been Used Half Enough: The Significance of Philo of Alexandria in the Study of the New Testament." *Perspectives in Religious Studies* 30:251–69.

———. 2007. "'The Most Ancient and Reliable Record of the Past': The Jewish Appropriation of Hellenistic Historiography." Pages 231–43 in *A Companion to Greek and Roman Historiography*, edited by John Marincola. Oxford: Blackwell.

Stökl Ben Ezra, Daniel. 2003. *The Impact of Yom Kippur on Early Christianity: The Day of Atonement from Second Temple Judaism to the Fifth Century*. WUNT 163. Tübingen: Mohr Siebeck.

Stowers, Stanley Kent. 1981. *The Diatribe and Paul's Letter to the Romans*. SBLDS 57. Atlanta: Scholars Press.

———. 1994. *A Rereading of Romans: Justice, Jews and Gentiles*. New Haven: Yale University Press.

Thiessen, Matthew. 2011. *Contesting Conversion: Genealogy, Circumcision, and Identity in Ancient Judaism and Christianity*. New York: Oxford University Press.

———. 2014. "Aseneth's Eight-Day Transformation as Scriptural Justification for Conversion." *JSJ* 45:229–49.

———. 2016. *Paul and the Gentile Problem*. New York: Oxford University Press.

Tobin, Thomas H. 1983. *The Creation of Man: Philo and the History of Interpretation*. Catholic Biblical Quarterly Monograph Series 14. Washington, DC: Catholic Association of America.

VanderKam, James C. 2010. *The Dead Sea Scrolls Today*. 2nd ed. Grand Rapids: Eerdmans.

Vernant, Jean-Pierre. 1989. "At Man's Table: Hesiod's Foundation Myth of Sacrifice." Pages 21–86 in *The Cuisine of Sacrifice among the Greeks*, edited by Marcel Detienne and Jean-Pierre Vernant. Translated by Paula Wissing. Chicago: University of Chicago Press.

Versnel, Henk S. 2012. "Making Sense of Jesus' Death: The Pagan Contribution." Pages 213–94 in *Deutungen des Todes Jesu im Neuen Testament*, edited by Jörg Frey and Jens Schröter. 2nd ed. UTB 2953. Tübingen: Mohr Siebeck.

Voltaire. 1733. *Letters on England*, edited by Henry Morley. England: Cassell. https://www.gutenberg.org/files/2445/2445-h/2445-h.htm.

von Siebenthal, Heinrich. 2019. *Ancient Greek Grammar for the Study of the New Testament*. New York: Lang.

Wallace, Daniel B. 1996. *Greek Grammar beyond the Basics: An Exegetical Syntax of the New Testament*. Grand Rapids: Zondervan.

Wagner, J. Ross. 2013. *Reading the Sealed Book: Old Greek Isaiah and the Problem of Septuagint Hermeneutics*. Forschungen zum Alten Testament 88. Tübingen: Mohr Siebeck.

Wassén, Cecilia. 2017. "Good and Bad Angels in the Construction of Identity in the Qumran Movement." Pages 71–97 in *Gottesdienst und Engel im antiken Judentum und frühen Christentum*, edited by Jörg Frey and Michael R. Jost. WUNT 2/446. Tübingen: Mohr Siebeck.

West, M. L. 1984. *Greek Metre*. Oxford: Oxford University Press.

———. 1987. *Introduction to Greek Metre*. Oxford: Clarendon.

Wevers, John William. 1978. *Text History of the Greek Deuteronomy*. Göttingen: Vandenhoeck & Ruprecht.

———. 1995. *Notes on the Greek Text of Deuteronomy*. SCS 39. Atlanta: Scholars Press.

Whitmarsh, Tim. 2001. *Greek Literature and the Roman Empire: The Politics of Imitation*. New York: Oxford University Press.

Williams, Ronald J. 2007. *Williams' Hebrew Syntax*. 3rd ed. Revised and expanded by John C. Beckman. Toronto: University of Toronto Press.

Wilson, Walter T. 2005. *The Sentences of Pseudo-Phocylides*. CEJL. Berlin: de Gruyter.

Winston, David. 2001. *The Ancestral Philosophy: Hellenistic Philosophy in Second Temple Judaism*. Providence: Brown Judaic Studies.

Winter, Paul. 1974. *On the Trial of Jesus*. Studia Judaica. Berlin: de Gruyter.

Wright, Benjamin G., III. 2015. *The Letter of Aristeas: 'Aristeas to Philocrates' or 'On the Translation of the Law of the Jews.'* CEJL. Berlin: De Gruyter.

Wyss, Beatrice. 2016. "From Cosmogony to Psychology: Philo's Interpretation of Gen 2:7 in *De opificio mundi*, *Quaestiones et solutions in Genesin* and *Legum allegoriae*." Pages 99–116 in *Dust of the Ground and Breath of Life (Gen. 2:7): The Problem of a Dualistic Anthropology in Early Judaism and Christianity*, edited by Jacques T. A. G. M. van Ruiten and George H. van Kooten. Themes in Biblical Narrative 20. Leiden: Brill.

Zahn, Theodor. 1873. *Ignatius von Antiochen*. Gotha: Perthes.

Zanker, Paul. 1988. *The Power of Images in the Age of Augustus*. Translated by Alan Shapiro. Ann Arbor: University of Michigan Press.

www.ingramcontent.com/pod-product-compliance
Lightning Source LLC
Chambersburg PA
CBHW081823230426
43668CB00017B/2356